James F. Fitzpatrick
Solicitor
j.fitzpatrick@james-f-fitzpatrick.com
Tel: 028 9024 6741
Mob: 07855 381857

Bingham and Berrymans'
Personal Injury and Motor Claims Cases

Bingham and Berrymans' Personal Injury and Motor Claims Cases

Twelfth Edition

Michael Pether BA

Partner, Berrymans Lace Mawer

Gavin Beardsell LLB

Partner, Berrymans Lace Mawer

David Brown LLB

Partner, Berrymans Lace Mawer

Christopher Newton LLB

Partner, Berrymans Lace Mawer

Sheila Russell

Partner, Berrymans Lace Mawer

Ian Walker LLB

Solicitor, Berrymans Lace Mawer

LexisNexis®
Butterworths

Members of the LexisNexis Group worldwide

United Kingdom	LexisNexis Butterworths, a Division of Reed Elsevier (UK) Ltd, Halsbury House, 35 Chancery Lane, LONDON WC2A 1EL, and RSH, 1–3 Baxter's Place, Leith Walk, EDINBURGH EH1 3AF
Argentina	LexisNexis Argentina, BUENOS AIRES
Australia	LexisNexis Butterworths, CHATSWOOD, New South Wales
Austria	LexisNexis Verlag ARD Orac GmbH & Co KG, VIENNA
Benelux	LexisNexis Benelux, AMSTERDAM
Canada	LexisNexis Canada, MARKHAM, Ontario
Chile	LexisNexis Chile Ltda, SANTIAGO
China	LexisNexis China, BEIJING and SHANGHAI
France	LexisNexis SA, PARIS
Germany	LexisNexis Deutschland GmbH, MUNSTER
Hong Kong	LexisNexis Hong Kong, HONG KONG
India	LexisNexis India, NEW DELHI
Italy	Giuffrè Editore, MILAN
Japan	LexisNexis Japan, TOKYO
Malaysia	Malayan Law Journal Sdn Bhd, KUALA LUMPUR
Mexico	LexisNexis Mexico, MEXICO
New Zealand	LexisNexis NZ Ltd, WELLINGTON
Poland	Wydawnictwo Prawnicze LexisNexis Sp, WARSAW
Singapore	LexisNexis Singapore, SINGAPORE
South Africa	LexisNexis Butterworths, DURBAN
USA	LexisNexis, DAYTON, Ohio

First published 1946 as Bingham and Berrymans' Motor Claims Cases
© Reed Elsevier (UK) Ltd 2006
Published by LexisNexis Butterworths

A CIP Catalogue record for this book is available from the British Library.

ISBN for this volume
ISBN 10: 1 4057 1233 3
ISBN 13: 978 1 4057 1233 0

Typeset by Columns Design Ltd, Reading, England
Printed and bound in Great Britain by William Clowes Limited, Beccles, Suffolk
Visit LexisNexis Butterworths at www.lexisnexis.co.uk

Preface

This, the 12th Edition, brings the law up-to-date to May 2006 and includes most of the cases from the last supplement published in 2002.

Those eagle-eyed subscribers to this book will notice the subtle change of title. This reflects the fact that whilst the book retains its detailed and comprehensive collection of motor liability cases and motor insurance law it is, fundamentally, a personal injury practitioner's handling guide. Most of this edition (and this has been the case for the last two editions) is concerned with the handling of personal injury claims generally with many chapters devoted to procedure, quantum and costs as well as providing the reader with guidance on the general principles of liability including highways and animals.

The format of the book remains the same as the 11th Edition, being divided into four sections: insurance, liability, practice and procedure, quantum and costs. The only change is that costs have moved from the procedure section to quantum to reflect the fact that the legal costs of litigation have become a significant proportion of the overall compensation expense.

There were many and varied reasons for this edition but primarily it was an overwhelming need to reflect and record the very significant developments that have taken place within the area of motor and personal injury claims over the last six years.

Many chapters have been completely re-written, not least those covering the areas of procedure. The 11th Edition was produced just after the introduction of the CPR and those rules were very new. Therefore, the best the 11th Edition could do was set out the rules without any illuminating cases to illustrate how they worked. We now have six years of 'bedding down' on the CPR and a great deal of guidance. Therefore, the practice and procedure section includes not only the latest version of the Civil Procedure Rules, but also the many important cases decided since the introduction of those rules. In particular, the development and amplification of Part 36 continues apace with a number of Court of Appeal decisions.

The quantum chapters have been restructured and updated. Two significant developments, the cost of care (both gratuitous and professional) and periodical payments, are addressed in Chapter 36.

Readers will not recognise the costs chapter from that in the 11th Edition for the good reason that the law relating to the recoverability of costs is unrecognisable from what it was in 2000. The introduction of a new procedural code and the recoverability of additional liabilities has given rise to a substantial increase in technical challenges and a significant body of new case law, which we have included in this 12th Edition.

There have been many important developments in the area of motor insurance since the last edition, such as the Fourth Motor Insurance Directive, implemented by the European Communities (Rights against Insurers) Regulations 2002 and a new MIB agreement. All this, and much more, is included within the first three chapters dealing with motor insurance and MIB claims.

That is not all. Practitioners requiring case law and guidance on highways claims, cases involving animals on the highway, vicarious liability and so on, will find plenty of up-to-date case law and legislation.

As ever, we would like to thank all those who have provided advice, encouragement and assistance in producing this new edition. The editors have been admirably assisted by a team of volunteers who we feel it is only right to name. So, our thanks to Michelle Scott, Tom Pangbourne, Philippa Burnett, Susan Griffiths, Jonathan Harley, Paul Maxwell, Mark Robinson, Lisa Cable, Hannah Davey, Wendy Badsey-Ellis, Zoe Mills, Amy Richardson, Joy Branigan, Helen Cafferata (and the rest of the Information Services team), Sue Bayer and Emma Collings.

Michael Pether
Gavin Beardsell
David Brown
Christopher Newton
Sheila Russell
Ian Walker
November 2006

Table of Contents

Part 2   Liability

Part 3   Procedure

CHAPTER 24 Summary Judgment

CHAPTER 25 Additional Claims

CHAPTER 28   Witnesses

CHAPTER 29   Evidence and Admissibility

Part 4   Quantum and Costs

CHAPTER 37   Damages in Fatal Cases

Table of Statutes

Paragraph references printed in **bold** type indicate where the Statute is set out in part or in full.

Other Jurisdictions

MALAYSIA

Table of Statutory Instruments

Paragraph references printed in **bold** type indicate where the Statutory Instrument is set out in part or in full.

Table of Statutory Instruments

Table of Statutory Instruments

Table of European Legislation

Paragraph references printed in **bold** type indicate where the Legislation is set out in part or in full.

Primary Legislation

CONVENTIONS

Secondary Legislation

DIRECTIVES

Table of Cases

Table of Cases

Table of Cases

C

Table of Cases

F

H

K

M

N

O

Table of Cases

Q

R

S

Table of Cases

Table of Cases

INSURANCE

CHAPTER I

Insurance Principles

1. INTRODUCTION

[1.1]   Since 1930 it has been compulsory for any person having control of a motor vehicle to insure against liability for personal injury to a third party arising out of the use of the vehicle. The obligation to insure was extended to cover passengers in 1971, and the legislation consolidated in the Road Traffic Act 1972 is now contained in the Road Traffic Act 1988, as amended.

An obligation is also imposed on insurers to meet a judgment against their insured, subject to a right of recovery against him personally. In addition, there is a remedy against an uninsured or untraceable driver by virtue of the agreements between the Motor Insurers' Bureau and the Department of Transport (see Chapter 3 generally).

As a result of the 4th Motor Insurance Directive (No 2000/26/EC) insurers must now have a presence in each country where they do business, making it easier for injured parties to bring claims. It is now also possible to commence proceedings directly against the insurer as a result of the European Communities (Rights against Insurers) Regulations 2002, SI 2002/3061 which implement the relevant provisions of the 4th Directive, so avoiding the need to obtain a judgment against the insured party before being able to pursue the insurer.

2. STATUTORY PROVISIONS

Road Traffic Act 1988, s 143, as amended by the *Motor Vehicles* (*Compulsory Insurance*) *Regulations 2000, SI 2000/726*, and *s 144*, as amended (amendments shown in square brackets).

[1.2]

143   Users of motor vehicles to be insured or secured against third-party risks

(1)   Subject to the provisions of this part of this Act—

    (a)   a person must not use a motor vehicle on a road [or other public place] unless there is in force in relation to the use of the vehicle by that person such a policy of insurance or such a security in respect of third party risks as complies with the requirements of this Part of this Act, and

    (b)   a person must not cause or permit any other person to use a motor vehicle on a road [or other public place] unless there is in force in relation to the use of the vehicle by that other person such a policy of insurance or such a security in respect of third party risks as complies with the requirements of this Part of this Act.

(2)   If a person acts in contravention of subsection (1) above he is guilty of an offence.

(3)   A person charged with using a motor vehicle in contravention of this section shall not be convicted if he proves—

    (a)   that the vehicle did not belong to him and was not in his possession under a contract of hiring or of loan,

    (b)   that he was using the vehicle in the course of his employment, and

    (c)   that he neither knew nor had reason to believe that there was not in force in relation to the vehicle such a policy of insurance or security as is mentioned in subsection (1) above.

(4)   This Part of this Act does not apply to invalid carriages.

SUBSECTION (1)(A): 'ROAD OR ANY OTHER PUBLIC PLACE'

[1.3]   Clarke v Kato

[1998] 4 All ER 417, [1998] 1 WLR 1647, [1999] PIQR P1, [1999] RTR 153, (1999) 163 JP 502, (1998) 148 NLJ 1640, [1998] NPC 142, (1998) 95(43) LSG 31, (1998) 142 SJLB 278

The claimant was injured whilst sat in a vehicle which was stationary in a car park. The issue to be decided was whether the car park constituted a road for the purposes of s 145(3)(a) of the Road Traffic Act 1988.

HELD: As a matter of ordinary usage a car park did not constitute a road within the meaning of the Act.

[1.4]   Charlton v Fisher

[2001] EWCA Civ 112

[2002] QB 578, [2001] 3 WLR 1435, [2001] 1 All ER (Comm) 769, [2001] RTR 33, [2001] Lloyd's Rep 387, [2001] PIQR P23, (2001) 98(10) LSG 45

C sustained injuries following an accident in which F had deliberately reversed his car into a stationary parked car and had pleaded guilty to criminal damage. F's insurers, CI, denied that the incident was an accident under the terms of the insurance policy as it had occurred in a car park and not on the road. In addition CI argued there was no statutory obligation to indemnify F.

HELD: Allowing appeal, that as the incident had not happened on the road, C had no rights against CI through the MIB or under the Road Traffic Act 1988, s 151 and CI was not directly liable to her.

[1.5]   Evans v Clarke (t/a FBI Volkswagen Services) and NIG Insurance plc

(2006) unreported

The defendant operated a business repairing camper vans from a workshop on an industrial estate. The claimant had parked his car near a ramp at the defendant's premises. The claimant was injured when a camper van ran back down the ramp striking him as he walked between the camper van and his vehicle. The claimant served a letter of claim alleging negligence. The defendant denied liability asserting that the claimant was the master of his own misfortune.

Proceedings were issued and the defendant's insurers refused to indemnify on the basis that:

(1)   the accident did not occur on a road as defined by the Road Traffic Act 1988; and

(2)   late notification.

In Part 20 proceedings the defendant insurers argued that the policy did not apply because the road alongside the defendant's unit was a private road and not one to which the public had access.

HELD: The road was a road as defined by the 1988 Act as the industrial unit where the defendant's premises was based had a number of units to which the various occupiers desired members of the public to come and do business without making an appointment. The public entered the site without having to obtain access by overcoming physical obstructions or in defiance of a prohibition. Therefore the court held that the public in general had access to the site and not just a selective class. Therefore the 'road' fell within the definition as contained in the 1988 Act and the Part 20 defendant had to meet the claim as it was also found that the late notification was not sufficiently serious to allow the Part 20 defendant to refuse indemnity.

[1.6]   Lloyd-Woolper v Moore

[2004] EWCA Civ 766

[2004] 3 All ER 741, [2004] 1 WLR 2350, [2004] RTR 30, [2004] Lloyd's Rep 730, (2004) 148 SJLB 791

Moore senior insured his vehicle with insurers, N. His son Moore junior was insured to drive on the basis that Moore Junior was over 17 years old, held a full driving licence and would not be permitted to drive a vehicle whose engine capacity was over 1600cc.

Moore junior, who was sixteen years of age at the time, had sat his driving test before he was old enough to do so and was driving a vehicle with an engine capacity of 1760cc, was involved in an accident with L-W. L-W commenced proceedings against Moore junior and N.

N commenced Part 20 proceedings against Moore senior seeking an indemnity from him. Moore senior appealed unsuccessfully.

HELD: Moore senior was liable to indemnify N as he had given Moore junior permission to use the vehicle in the terms of the Road Traffic Act 1988, s 143(1) and s 151(8).

[1.7]

144   Exceptions from requirement of third-party insurance or security

(1)   Section 143 of this Act does not apply to a vehicle owned by a person who has deposited and keeps deposited with the Accountant General of the Supreme Court the sum of [£500,000], at a time when the vehicle is being driven under the owner's control.

(1A) The Secretary of State may by order made by statutory instrument substitute a greater sum for the sum for the time being specified in subsection (1) above.

(1B)   No order shall be made under subsection (1A) above unless a draft of it has been laid before and approved by resolution of each House of Parliament.]

Subsection (2) of s 144, as amended, lists the individuals, organisations and vehicles which are exempt from the requirements of s 143 of the Road Traffic Act 1988.

3.   REQUIREMENTS OF THE POLICY

Road Traffic Act 1988, s 145, as amended.

[1.8]

145   Exceptions from requirement of third-party insurance or security

(1)   In order to comply with the requirements of this Part of this Act, a policy of insurance must satisfy the following conditions.

(2)   The policy must be issued by an authorised insurer.

(3)   Subject to subsection (4) below, the policy—

(a)   must insure such person, persons or classes of persons as may be specified in the policy in respect of any liability which may be incurred by him or them in respect of the death of or bodily injury to any person or damage to property caused by, or arising out of, the use of the vehicle on a road in Great Britain, and [(aa)] must, in the case of a vehicle normally based in the territory of another member State, insure him or them in respect of any civil liability which may be incurred by him or them as a result of an event related to the use of the vehicle in Great Britain if,-

(i)   according to the law of that territory, he or they would be required to be insured in respect of a civil liability which would arise under that law as a result of the event if the place where the vehicle was used when the event occurred were in that territory, and

(ii)   the cover required by that law would be higher than that required by paragraph (a) above, and]

(b)   must [, in the case of a vehicle normally based in Great Britain,] insure him in respect of any liability which may be incurred by him or them in respect of the use of the vehicle and of any trailer, whether or not coupled, in the territory other than Great Britain and Gibraltar of each of the member States of the Communities according to—

(i)   the law on compulsory insurance against civil liability in respect of the use of vehicles of the State in whose territory the event giving rise to the liability occurred; or

(ii)   if it would give higher cove, the law which would be applicable under this Part of this Act if the place where the vehicle was used when that event occurred were in Great Britain; and]

(c)   must also insure him or them in respect of any liability which may be incurred by him or them under the provisions of this Part of this Act relating to payment for emergency treatment.

(4)   The policy shall not, by virtue of subsection (3)(a) above, be required—

(a)   In the case of a person—

(i)   carried in or upon a vehicle, or

(ii)   entering or getting onto, or alighting from, a vehicle,

the provisions of paragraph (a) of subsection (4) above do not apply unless cover in respect of the liability referred to in that paragraph is in fact provided pursuant to a requirement of the Employers' Liability (Compulsory Insurance) Act 1969.]

(5)   'Authorised Insurer' has the same meaning as in section 95.]

(6)   If any person or body of persons ceases to be a member of the Motor Insurers' Bureau, that person or body shall not by virtue of that cease to be treated as an authorised insurer for the purposes of this Part of this Act [or the Road Traffic (NHS Charges) Act 1999]—

(a) in relation to any policy issued by the insurer before ceasing to be such a member, or

(b) in relation to any obligation (whether arising before or after the insurer ceased to be such a member) which the insurer may be called upon to meet under or in consequence of any such policy or under section 157 of this Act [or section 1 of the Act of 1999] by virtue of making a payment in pursuance of such an obligation.

SUBSECTION (3)(A): 'ANY PERSON'

[1.9] **Cooper v Motor Insurers' Bureau**

[1985] QB 575, [1985] 1 All ER 449, [1985] 2 WLR 248, 129 Sol Jo 32, CA

Killacky bought an old motor cycle and took it to Cooper, who he knew had expert knowledge of motor cycles, to try it out. Cooper mounted the machine and rode off. On approaching a major road he applied the brakes and they failed to operate. He collided with a car and was seriously injured. He sued Killacky in negligence for failing to warn him that the brakes were defective and obtained judgment for £214,207. Killacky was not insured and unable to satisfy the judgment. Cooper sued the Motor Insurers' Bureau, claiming that Killacky's liability was a 'relevant liability' within the definition in cl 1 of the Motor Insurers' Bureau Uninsured Driver's Agreement 'a liability in respect of which a policy of insurance must insure a person in order to comply with Part VI of the Road Traffic Act 1972'. It was argued on his behalf that 'any person' in s 145(3)(a) of the 1972 Act included the plaintiff even though he was driving. For the Bureau it was argued that s 143 was vital and that it was the use of the vehicle causing damage to others which was the only liability to be covered. The judge held the Motor Insurers' Bureau not liable. Section 143 spoke first of a person using and second of one who caused or permitted the use; the section was not intended to insure against personal injury to the person actually using the vehicle.

HELD, ON APPEAL: The judge was right. Section 145(3)(a) was not the end of the story. Consideration had to be given to s 143(1). The obligation imposed by that subsection is an obligation to abstain from using, or from causing or permitting any other person to use, a motor vehicle on the road unless there is in force in relation to the use of the vehicle by that person or that other person a policy of insurance complying with the requirements of Part VI of the 1972 Act. A policy covering him 'in respect of third-party risks' clearly does not include the actual driver of the vehicle at the time of the use of the vehicle that gives rise to the damage. The scope of the phrase 'any person' in s 145(3)(a) is limited by s 143(1) so as to exclude the driver of the vehicle.

SUBSECTION (3)(A): 'ARISING OUT OF THE USE OF'

[1.10] **Dunthorne v Bentley and Cornhill**

[1996] RTR 428, CA

A Mrs Faulker stopped her car to assist a friend of hers, Mrs Bentley, who was stationary by the side of the road having run out of petrol. Whilst running across the carriageway to join her, Mrs Bentley was killed by the plaintiff's car. The plaintiff's insurers sought to argue that any claim did not fall within the terms of the motor policy of insurance they had issued as the accident was not caused by or arose out of the use of the vehicle on a road. Laws J found that Mrs Bentley's death was 'closely and causally connected' to the use of the vehicle and therefore within the meaning of s 145(3) of the Road Traffic Act 1988.

SUBSECTION(4)(A): 'ARISING OUT OF AND IN THE COURSE OF'

[1.11]   St Helens Colliery Co v Hewitson
[1924] AC 59, 93 LJKB 177, 130 LT 291, 40 TLR 125, 68 Sol Jo 163, 16 BWCC 230, HL

A workman employed at a colliery travelled by a special train provided by an agreement between his employers and a railway company. The employers paid the railway company and the workman agreed to a deduction from his wages of half the fare paid by his employers and to waive all claims against the railway company.

HELD: The workman was under no obligation or duty to be there, he was not doing something in discharge or performance of a duty to his employers directly or indirectly imposed upon him by or arising out of his contract of service. There was only a right and not an obligation. The use of the vehicle was not 'arising out of and in the course of his employment'.

Note—Hewitson's case was distinguished (except by Viscount Maugham who considered it indistinguishable) in the following case.

[1.12]   Craw v Forrest
1931 SC 634, 24 BWCC Supp 67, Ct of Sess

A girl accepted employment as a weeder and picker on a fruit farm on condition that the employer conveyed her a distance of eight miles each day to her work. The time occupied in this conveyance was not paid for as working time. The worker was neither expressly bound by her contract, nor ordered by her employer or by anyone on his behalf, to use the means of conveyance provided, which was a motor lorry belonging to the employer and under the control of his son. The lorry was the only practicable means by which the worker could get to her work in time to start at the prescribed hours, and but for the offer of the conveyance to her work the worker would not have accepted the employment.

HELD: The worker was neither bound by her contract of service nor ordered by her employer to use the means of transport provided. The use of the vehicle was not 'arising out of and in the course of' her employment.

[1.13]   Allen v Siddons
(1932) 25 BWCC 350

A foreman was employed at a fixed weekly wage of £3 and his hours of work were from 7 am–5 pm. On one job he had to be at work at 7.30 am. He left home at 7 am on his motorcycle and met with an accident on his way to work. The employer argued that he was not concerned with what the man did before 7.30 am. The county court judge held the accident arose out of and in the course of the employment. The Court of Appeal said that although the employer might have had the right to give orders to the workman at any time after 7 am he did not on this occasion exercise that right, and the workman's employment in fact began at 7.30 am. The accident having happened merely when the workman was going to work, did not arise out of and in the course of the employment.

[1.14]   **Black v Aitkenhead**

(1938) 31 BWCC Supp 73, Ct of Sess

A labourer, while engaged on work at a distance from his home, was conveyed over part of the distance on a motor lorry which was provided by his employers. There was no express contract between the workman and his employers for the use of this conveyance; but, before accepting the job, the workman knew that the lorry would be provided free of cost, and he would not have accepted the offer of employment if it had not been available. This free conveyance was entirely optional, but it was used by employees who resided at a distance from the work. There was no direct transport connection between the workman's home and place of work, and travel by the ordinary route would have materially increased both the cost and the time of the journey. While being conveyed to his work, the workman fell from the lorry and was killed.

HELD: As the workman was not under any contractual obligation to use the lorry, his death while he was proceeding to his work on that conveyance was not the result of an accident arising in the course of his employment within the Workmen's Compensation Act 1925, s 1(1).

[1.15]   **Alderman v Great Western Rly Co**

[1938] AC 454, [1937] 2 All ER 408, 30 BWCC 64, HL

A travelling ticket collector signed on for duty at Oxford in the morning, travelled by train to Paddington and there joined a train to Swansea where he signed off duty for the night. The next morning he had to sign on at Swansea and return via Paddington to Oxford where his duties ended. Whilst spending the night at Swansea, he was under an obligation to lodge within a reasonable distance of the station and to leave his address in case of emergency. He was injured on his way from his lodgings to sign on for duty at Swansea station. The House of Lords held that the accident did not arise out of and in the course of the employment.

[1.16]   **Netherton v Coles**

[1945] 1 All ER 227, 37 BWCC 165, CA

A workman was employed at a job 11 miles from his home. He had travelling allowances and free travelling facilities by voucher or otherwise. He left the place of work on a motorcycle and met with an accident on the public road.

HELD: Not 'out of'; the workman outside working hours was at liberty to choose his own time and method of transport.

[1.17]   **Vandyke v Fender**

[1970] 2 QB 292, [1970] 2 All ER 335, [1970] 2 WLR 929, 134 JP 487, 114 Sol Jo 205, CA

Vandyke and Fender were moulders employed by the second defendants at a foundry 30 miles from their homes. The second defendants arranged with Fender to lend him a car in which he could drive to work, bringing Vandyke and two other employees. Although the arrangements for providing the car and paying him an allowance for petrol was part of Fender's contract of service neither he nor Vandyke was obliged to use the car if they did not wish to do so. It was not a term of their contract of service that they must use it. When riding as a passenger in the car on the way to work Vandyke was injured in an accident for which Fender was held to blame.

HELD: Vandyke was in the vehicle 'by reason of ... a contract of employment' but not 'in the course of' his employment. The test whether Vandyke was in the car 'in the course of' his employment was the same as in the leading cases under the Workmen's Compensation Acts, namely, whether he was under an obligation as a term of his employment to travel in the car, and he was not. The words injury 'arising out of and in the course of his employment' were used in the old Workmen's Compensation Acts from 1897 to 1945. The selfsame words have been used in the Road Traffic Acts 1930 and 1960. They have also been used in employers' liability policies. The author's opinion is that they should receive the same interpretation in all three places, for they are all so closely connected that they ought, as matter of common sense, to receive the same interpretation in each. The words were construed and applied in thousands of cases under the Workmen's Compensation Acts: and it is the author's opinion that these cases should be followed. The two leading cases, most apposite for present purposes are *St Helens Colliery Co Ltd v Hewitson* (at para [1.11]) and *Weaver v Tredegar Iron and Coal Co Ltd* [1940] AC 955. They show, quite conclusively that when a man is going to or coming from work, along a public road, as a passenger in a vehicle provided by his employer, he is not then in the course of his employment – unless he is obliged by the terms of his employment to travel in that vehicle. It is not enough that he should have the right to travel in the vehicle, or be permitted to travel in it. He must have an obligation to travel in it, else he is not in the course of his employment. That distinction must be maintained; for otherwise there would be no certainty in this branch of the law: per Lord Denning.

[1.18]   Blee v London and North Eastern Rly Co

[1938] AC 126, [1937] 4 All ER 270, 107 LJKB 62, 158 LT 185, 54 TLR 71, 81 Sol Jo 941, 30 BWCC 364, HL

A platelayer was liable to be called on at any time for emergency work for which he received overtime commencing from the time he left his home. At 10.30 pm after retiring to bed, he was called up on an emergency. On his way from his home to the railway siding, he met with an accident. The House of Lords held that the employment commenced at the time he left home and the accident arose out of and in the course of his employment.

[1.19]   Weaver v Tredegar Iron and Coal Co Ltd

[1940] AC 955, [1940] 3 All ER 157, 109 LJKB 621, 164 LT 231, 56 TLR 813, 84 Sol Jo 584, HL

A railway line passed through the premises of a colliery company. There was a halt station used only by the colliery workmen. The access to the station was the property of the railway company. Workmen obtained tickets from the colliery company, who arranged with the railway company for the trains. The workmen were not compelled to use the trains, but practically all did so. A workman was injured on the platform.

HELD: The employment continued whilst the workman was using facilities provided by his employer and which he was only entitled to use by reason of his status of a workman. The accident arose out of and in the course of the employment.

[1.20]   Dunn v AG Lockwood & Co

[1947] 1 All ER 446, 40 BWCC 60, CA

A workman who lived at Whitstable was employed as a plasterer by a firm of builders at Margate. Work began each day at 8 am but the workman was permitted to catch the 7.40 am train from Whitstable arriving at Margate at 8.15 am and was paid from 8 am. He was permitted to take the train on condition that he started work as soon as possible after he arrived at Margate station. On his way from the station to his work he met with an accident. The Court of Appeal held that the permission to the workman to take a train which caused him to be late for work placed upon him the contractual duty to go from the station to his place of work as quickly as possible. It was in performing this duty to his employers that the accident happened and it accordingly arose out of and in the course of his employment.

[1.21]   Paterson v Costain and Press (Overseas) Ltd
(1979) 123 Sol Jo 142, [1979] 2 Lloyd's Rep 204, CA

The defendants were carrying out constructional work at Bid Boland 170 km from Abadan in Persia. They provided transport in their own vehicles for their employees, of whom the plaintiff was one, from Abadan to Bid Boland where the plaintiff both worked and was housed. The only other way of making the journey was by taxi, very rarely done because it was expensive. After a short holiday in Kuwait, the plaintiff returned to Abadan to make the remainder of the journey by road to Bid Boland; the defendants had arranged for a Land Rover to be available. On the journey to Bid Boland he was injured in an accident. If the accident arose 'in the course of' his employment the defendants would be indemnified by their employers' liability insurers; if not, then by their public liability insurers.

HELD: Applying *St Helens Colliery Co Ltd v Hewitson* (at para [1.11]), the accident arose 'in the course of' the employment. There had to be on the part of the plaintiff an obligation and not merely a right to use the transport provided, but on the facts there was an obligation. It was not a case of a man going from his home to his place of work. It was part of the sphere of his employment to travel on the employer's vehicle from Abadan to the site of his work and his home 170 km away at Bid Boland: [1978] 1 Lloyd's Rep 86 (Talbot J).

An appeal was dismissed. The accident had occurred in Iran; the contract showed that virtually from the time of getting off the aircraft at Abadan the plaintiff was in the defendants' employment. It was clearly distinguishable from the English cases.

[1.22]   Smith v Stages
[1989] AC 928, [1989] 1 All ER 833, [1989] 2 WLR 529, HL

An employee who is paid for travelling from his residence to the site at work is not taken outside the course of his employment simply by reason of his having discretion as to mode of travel.

Comment: The attitude of the judiciary appears to have changed over the years and the courts appear less keen to find that a journey to or from work forms part of the claimant's employment.

4.   BREACH OF STATUTORY DUTY TO INSURE

[1.23]   *Note*—In the case of *Monk v Warbey* at para [1.24]) it was held that s 143 of the Road Traffic Act 1988 imposes a statutory duty similar to that recognised in the case of unfenced machinery in the decision of *Groves v Lord Wimborne* [1898] 2 QB 402, 67 LJQB 862, 79 LT 284, 14 TLR 493, 34 Dig 218. *Monk v Warbey* was followed in *Richards v Port of Manchester* (1934) 152 LT 413, 50 Ll L Rep 132, CA. If, therefore, the owner of a car insured owner-driver only, permits another person to drive his car, and that person being so uninsured has not the means to meet a third-party claim the owner is liable for damages for personal injury sustained by a third party.

[1.24]   Monk v Warbey

[1935] 1 KB 75, 104 LJKB 153, 152 LT 194, 51 TLR 77, 78 Sol Jo 783, 50 LI L Rep 33, CA

The owner of a motor car who, in contravention of the Road Traffic Act 1930, s 35(1) (now replaced by s 143 of the 1988 Act), permits his car to be used by a person who is not insured against third-party risks is liable in damages to a third party who has been injured by the negligent driving of the uninsured person. In such a case the object and purview of the 1930 Act show that the penalties prescribed by s 35(2) were not intended to be the sole remedy for the breach of the owner's statutory duty. Where a person uninsured against third-party risks is permitted by the owner to use a car, and injury is caused by his negligent driving to a third party, the latter may, where the uninsured person is without means, sue the owner of the car directly for damages for breach of statutory duty and need not first sue the uninsured person.

[1.25]   Gregory v Ford

[1951] 1 All ER 121   Byrne J

A lorry owned by the first defendant was driven by their servant, the second defendant, and injured the plaintiff, a motorcyclist. The plaintiff obtained judgment against both defendants. The lorry at the time was uninsured. The first defendant claimed indemnity from the second defendant on the ground of his negligence. The second defendant claimed indemnity from the first defendant on the ground that it was an implied term of the employment that the servant should not be required to do an unlawful act.

The judge referred to the observation of Singleton J in *Blows v Chapman* [1947] 2 All ER 576, 112 JP 8, 63 TLR 575, 46 LGR 13 Div Ct: 'It is not, I think, the duty of a workman to ask his employer each day, is this vehicle insured.'

HELD: The second defendant was entitled to indemnity from the first defendant on this ground. The first defendant was not entitled to indemnity from the second defendant because, although the servant was negligent, it was owing to the breach of statutory duty of the first defendant that the damages fell upon him.

[1.26]   Lister v Romford Ice and Cold Storage Co Ltd

[1957] AC 555, [1957] 1 All ER 125, [1957] 2 WLR 158, 121 JP 98, 101 Sol Jo 106, [1956] 2 Lloyd's Rep 505, HL

Per Lord Morton of Henryton, speaking of *Gregory v Ford* (at para [1.25]): I agree that it was an implied term of the employment that the servant should not be required to do an unlawful act but there is no implied term that the driver is entitled to be personally indemnified by a policy.

(A)   IMPLIED INDEMNITY

[1.27]   Road Transport and General Insurance Co v Adams

[1955] Crim LR 377

The defendant had hired a car from the third party and had asked whether it was insured, to which the third party answered in the affirmative. In fact the car was not covered if the defendant drove it. After a collision, he was convicted of driving uninsured. In the present action the plaintiffs obtained judgment against both the defendant and the third party for the amount expended by the insurers in settling claims arising from the accident. The defendant claimed indemnity from the third party who pleaded that as the damages the defendant had had to pay arose out of a crime the court should not grant relief.

HELD: The defendant was entitled to be indemnified by the third party, as he had been led by him to believe in the existence of a fact, which, if it had been true, would have been an answer to any imputation of illegality (applying *Burrows v Rhodes* [1899] 1 QB 816, 68 LJQB 545, 80 LT 591, 63 JP 532, 48 WR 13, 15 TLR 286).

(B) POLICY AVOIDED

[1.28]   Goodbarne v Buck

[1940] 1 KB 771, [1940] 1 All ER 613, 109 LJKB 837, 162 LT 259, 56 TLR 433, 84 Sol Jo 380, CA

The fact that a policy is avoided by insurers does not bring into operation the principle of *Monk v Warbey* (at para [1.24]).

(C) MOTOR INSURERS' BUREAU NOT A DEFENCE

[1.29]   Corfield v Groves

[1950] 1 All ER 488, [1950] WN 116, 66 (pt 1) TLR 627, 94 Sol Jo 225   Hilbery J

A third party was fatally injured by an uninsured car. The driver was not the servant or agent of the owner. The administratrix, who was the widow and the only dependant, sued the driver for negligence and the owner for breach of statutory duty under *Monk v Warbey* (at para [1.24]), alleging that the driver was without means to satisfy any judgment against him. A witness from the Motor Insurers' Bureau expressed the opinion that under the Motor Insurers' Bureau Agreement the Bureau would satisfy any judgment against the driver. The owner pleaded that as the Bureau would pay the damages, the plaintiff would suffer no loss by reason of the lack of means of the driver or her breach of statutory duty. The driver was found guilty of negligence.

HELD: The breach of statutory duty was a continuing breach operative at the time of the accident (the time of the tortious act), and the cause of action arose at the moment of the tortious act. On the death the widow's right of action under the Fatal Accidents Acts immediately accrued and an enforceable claim against the owner for any damages which she then sustained by reason of the breach of statutory duty which existed at the time of the tortious act. The damage accrued because at the time the driver was uninsured and financially nothing was obtainable from him even by bankruptcy proceedings. Greer LJ in *Monk v Warbey* pointed out that it does not matter, even if it were the fact, that at the time of the tort her damages could not be quantified. In theory, of course, her damages are quantified as on the day of the accruing of her complete cause of action. If the judgment was satisfied by the Bureau, no difficulty arises, because the damages cannot be taken twice by the plaintiff. Judgment was given against both defendants.

Note—Apparently the point dealt with in *Fleming v McGillivray* (at para [1.30]), was not taken.

[1.30]   Fleming v McGillivray

1945 SLT 301   Lord Mackintosh

An action under *Monk v Warbey* (at para [1.24]) is not competent against the owner of the car until it is known that the wrongdoer cannot pay and there is no effective policy. It must be established:
(1)   that the driver could not pay; and
(2)   that the insurers could not be made to pay.

(D)   DAMAGE NOT RESULT OF BREACH

[1.31]   Daniels v Vaux

[1938] 2 KB 203, [1938] 2 All ER 271, 107 LJKB 494, 159 LT 459, 54 TLR 621, 82 Sol Jo 335   Humphreys J

The defendant bought a car and allowed her son to use it, though not insured. About 21 June 1934, the plaintiff was injured. On 29 December 1936, the son died. No action had then been commenced. The son had substantial means.

HELD: (1) The son was not servant or agent.
(2)   The defendant was guilty of breach of statutory duty.
(3)   No legal damage from breach. The damage was due to the delay in commencing the action and not to the defendant's breach of her duty to insure.

Note—The limitation in the Law Reform (Miscellaneous Provisions) Act 1934, that an action is not maintainable unless the cause of action arose not earlier than six months before the death was repealed by the Law Reform (Limitation of Actions) Act 1954, s 4.

5.   CERTIFICATE OF INSURANCE

Road Traffic Act 1988, s 147

From 15 May 1989 the Road Traffic Act 1972, s 147 has been replaced by the Road Traffic Act 1988, s 147 which reads as follows:

[1.32]
147   Issue and surrender of certificates of insurance and of security
    (1)   A policy of insurance shall be of no effect for the purposes of this Part of this Act unless and until there is delivered by the insurer to the person by whom the policy is effected a certificate (in this Part of this Act referred to as a 'certificate of insurance') in the prescribed form and containing such particulars of any conditions subject to which the policy is issued and of any other matters as may be prescribed.
    (2)   A security shall be of no effect for the purposes of this Part of this Act unless and until there is delivered by the person giving the security to the person to whom it is given a certificate (in this Part of this Act referred to as a 'certificate of

security') in the prescribed form and containing such particulars of any conditions subject to which the security is issued and of any other matters as may be prescribed.

(3) Different forms and different particulars may be prescribed for the purposes of subsection (1) or (2) above in relation to different cases or circumstances.

(4) Where a certificate has been delivered under this section and the policy or security to which it relates is cancelled by mutual consent or by virtue of any provision in the policy or security, the person to whom the certificate was delivered must, within seven days from the taking effect of the cancellation—

    (a) surrender the certificate to the person by whom the policy was issued or the security was given, or

    (b) if the certificate has been lost or destroyed, make a statutory declaration to that effect.

(5) A person who fails to comply with subsection (4) above is guilty of an offence.

[1.33]   Starkey v Hall

[1936] 2 All ER 18, 80 Sol Jo 347, 55 Ll L Rep 24, Div Ct

A policy is not in force until delivery of the certificate to the assured and delivery of the certificate to a hire purchase company is not delivery to the assured and the assured is liable for an offence under s 35(1).

Note—Section 35, ie of the Road Traffic Act 1930. See s 143 of the 1988 Act.

[1.34]   Egan v Bower

(1939) 63 Ll L Rep 266, Div Ct

A certificate contained limitation of use to the policyholder's business under a C licence not covering carrying passengers for hire or reward. The policyholder was carrying his wife and children not on business. The insurers wrote to the police that they would indemnify for private pleasure purposes.

HELD: The policy did not cover the risk and the policyholder had committed an offence under s 35(1) of the Road Traffic Act 1930.

[1.35]   Carnill v Rowland

[1953] 1 All ER 486, [1953] 1 WLR 380, 117 JP 127, 97 Sol Jo 134, 51 LGR 180, [1953] 1 Lloyd's Rep 99, Div Ct

A proposal form for motorcycle insurance restricted the cover to use when a sidecar or box carrier was permanently attached. A cover note with a temporary certificate was issued restricted to use of the motorcycle to which a sidecar was permanently attached. The permanent certificate would have contained the words 'use of the cycle is only permitted when a sidecar or box carrier is attached'. The insured removed the sidecar body and drove with only the sidecar chassis and the wheel, and was summoned for driving uninsured. The insurers gave evidence that for the purposes of the policy they regarded what was attached as a sidecar and would have held covered.

HELD: The meaning of the cover note may be a question of doubt. The construction put on it by the insurers was not impossible and the justices were entitled to accept the insurers' construction.

A decision by justices or on appeal of a Divisional Court does not bind the insurer or the insured and the fact that justices have to decide a question of insurance law in the absence of the insurers, who are the parties most interested, makes it desirable to make use of an arrangement that has been entered into with the approval of the appropriate authorities for consultation between the police and insurance companies whether insurers hold covered. If a respectable insurance company consider themselves at risk, the mischief aimed at by the Act does not arise.

Note—The existence of such an 'arrangement' is a matter of doubt. See *Boss v Kingston* [1963] 1 All ER 177, [1963] 1 WLR 99, 106 Sol Jo 1053, 61 LGR 109 (at para [2.170]).

(A)   COVER NOTE

[1.36]   Roberts v Warne
[1973] RTR 217, Div Ct

Roberts (R), a hire-car driver, made an agreement with Davies (D), who ran a hire-car booking office, that he would drive D's car when required on bookings provided by D, who would ensure that R was covered by D's insurance. As the car, when the agreement was made, was insured only for named drivers of whom R was not one, R and D went to the insurance brokers through whom D's insurance was placed, where D in R's presence asked the brokers that the policy should be varied to cover any driver. The brokers telephoned the insurers who specifically authorised them to give insurance cover for any driver of the car. The brokers thereupon issued a 60-day cover note to D providing for such cover. The insurers later decided not to provide 'any driver' cover but their letters to the brokers on the subject were delayed by a postal strike and did not reach them. More than 60 days after the issue of the cover-note R was stopped and charged with driving when uninsured.

HELD, ON APPEAL by case stated: R was rightly convicted. The Road Traffic Act 1960, s 201, requires that there shall be a policy of insurance in force in relation to the persons using the vehicle. The cover note was in itself a policy of insurance (though an insurance certificate is not) albeit a temporary one and there was a certificate printed on it; but the policy had not been amended when the cover note expired and did not cover R. The telephone conversation between brokers and insurers did not amount to an oral variation of the existing written policy. The fact that the insurers might in the circumstances have been stopped as against R from denying that he was entitled to be indemnified did not make up for the lack of a policy on the relevant date so far as s 201 was concerned, since a policy is something which has to be in writing and requires stamping, and no amendment to include R expressly had been done when the cover note expired.

Note—Section 201 of 1960 Act now s 143 of Road Traffic Act 1988.

[1.37]   Cartwright v MacCormack
[1963] 1 All ER 11, [1963] 1 WLR 18, 106 Sol Jo 957, [1962] 2 Lloyd's Rep 328, CA

The defendant claimed to be indemnified by the third party, an insurance company, against damages awarded to the plaintiff for injuries sustained in a road accident. The cover note was on the third party's printed form with some entries in handwriting. It contained the words 'This cover note is only valid for 15 days from the commencement date of risk'. The 'effective time and date of commencement of risk' was entered at '11.45 am' and '2.12.59'. The accident giving rise to the claim occurred at 5.45 pm on 17 December 1959. The third party claimed that the cover note had expired before the accident happened.

HELD: 'Time' and 'date' were used on the cover note as separate terms and the duration of the insurance company's liability was expressed as 15 days from the commencement date. The commencement date was 2 December and the policy therefore expired 15 days from 2 December. On the ordinary rules of construction these words excluded the first date and began at midnight on that date: the defendant was still insured when the accident happened.

Note—A cover note cannot be ante-dated or the certificate is false in a material particular. At the Huddersfield Police Court on 23 March 1939 the Prudential Assurance Co were fined £30 and £10 10s 0d costs for issuing, and the agent Sam Whitehead £3 for aiding and abetting, a cover note which was ante-dated ((1939) Times, 24 March).

[1.38] **London and Scottish Assurance Corpn Ltd v Ridd**

(1940) 65 Ll L Rep 46, Div Ct

The issue of cover notes, even though £3 is paid on account of a premium of £37, does not require insurers to issue a certificate for 12 months, and they cannot be convicted of failing to issue a certificate of insurance under the Motor Vehicle (TP Risks) Regulations 1933.

[1.39] **Neil v South East Lancashire Insurance Co**

1932 SLT 29

'Subject to the usual terms of the company's policy' referred only to the general conditions and did not incorporate the warranty contained in the proposal form.

[1.40] **Broad v Waland**

(1942) 73 Ll L Rep 263   Atkinson J

If the cover note is granted on the faith of a statement in the proposal form, which is a material misrepresentation or non-disclosure, the policy contained in the cover note can be set aside in a declaration action.

(B)   TEMPORARY COVER NOTE

[1.41] **Taylor v Allon**

[1966] 1 QB 304, [1965] 1 All ER 557, [1965] 2 WLR 598, 109 Sol Jo 78, [1965] 1 Lloyd's Rep 155, Div Ct

The defendant's car was insured under a policy which expired on 6 April. The insurance company had sent him the usual renewal notice on the back of which was printed a 'temporary cover note' giving third-party cover for 15 days from the date of expiry. This was expressed to be for the purpose of protecting the policyholder on renewal until his new certificate arrived. In fact the plaintiff had no intention of renewing the policy as he proposed to change his insurance to another company. He did not become insured by the new company until 16 April though he used his car on the 15 April. He was charged with using his car on that day when not insured, contrary the Road Traffic Act 1960, s 201. He produced the temporary cover note sent him by the old company, whose representative gave evidence that they considered themselves liable and in the case of an accident would have paid.

HELD: (1) In the definitions in s 216 of the 1960 Act 'insurance' means insurance pursuant to an enforceable contract and therefore 'covering note' must mean a cover-note enforceable as a contract.

(2)   The evidence of the insurance company's representative could not help the court when the issue was whether there was an enforceable contract.

(3)   If there was any contract embodied in the temporary cover note it could arise only by offer and acceptance. As there was no provision in the policy for an extension of the cover the temporary cover note must be an offer to insure for the future that could be accepted by paying the renewal premium. Even if the policyholder did not communicate his acceptance in this way there might be an implied acceptance from conduct if he took his car out in reliance on the temporary cover, and there would then be liability on him to pay the renewal premium or a premium for the period of cover. But this was not the position in the present case. The defendant had no intention of renewing the policy and had not given evidence that he was relying on the temporary cover note at the time of the offence. The magistrates were right in convicting him.

Note—For section numbers see note following *Biddle v Johnston* (at para [1.47]).

(C)   INEFFECTIVE RESTRICTIONS IN POLICY

Road Traffic Act 1988, s 148

[1.42]
148 (1)   Where a certificate of insurance or certificate of security has been delivered under section 147 of this Act to the person by whom a policy has been effected or to whom a security has been given, so much of the policy or security as purports to restrict—
(a)   the insurance of the persons insured by the policy, or
(b)   the operating of the security,
(as the case may be) by reference to any of the matters mentioned in subsection (2) below shall, as respects such liabilities, as are required to be covered by a policy under section 145 of this Act, be of no effect.
(2)   Those matters are—
(a)   the age or physical or mental condition of persons driving the vehicle,
(b)   the condition of the vehicle,
(c)   the number of persons that the vehicle carries,
(d)   the weight or physical characteristics of the goods that the vehicle carries,
(e)   the time at which or the areas within which the vehicle is used,
(f)   the horsepower or cylinder capacity or value of the vehicle,
(g)   the carrying on the vehicle of any particular apparatus, or
(h)   the carrying on the vehicle of any particular means of identification other than any means of identification required to be carried by or under [the Vehicle Excise and Registration Act 1994].
(3)   Nothing in subsection (1) above requires an insurer or the giver of a security to pay any sum in respect of the liability of any person otherwise than in or towards the discharge of that liability.
(4)   Any sum paid by an insurer or the giver of a security in or towards the discharge of any liability of any person which is covered by the policy or security by virtue only of subsection (1) above is recoverable by the insurer or giver of the security from that person.

P ASSENGERS

[1.43]   *Note*—Under s 149 of the Road Traffic Act 1988 any agreement between a passenger and driver made before liability arises, and which purports to negative or restrict the driver's liability, is of no effect. However it is uncertain whether, where the assured is himself being carried as a passenger by another driver, the protection of compulsory insurance extends to him. Public policy may prevent a passenger from recovering in circumstances where he would otherwise recover.

(D) CERTIFICATE DOES NOT ENLARGE POLICY

[1.44] *Note*—A question which was for some time unsettled was whether a certificate of insurance which contains terms which are different from the terms of the policy has any legal effect at all as regards third parties, or between the insurer and the assured, or whether the conditions of the policy are the only test. It has now been settled in *Spraggon v Dominion Insurance Co Ltd* (1940) 67 Ll L Rep 529 (Stable J); on appeal (1941) 69 Ll L Rep 1, CA (at para [1.46]).

In *Gray v Blackmore* [1934] 1 KB 95, 103 LJKB 145, 150 LT 99, 50 TLR 23, 47 Ll L Rep 69 a policy excluded use for any purpose in connection with the motor trade, and the certificate contained a similar limitation. The argument for the insurers was that there was no estoppel by the certificate because it stated on its face the limitations to which it was subject.

Per Branson J: It is obvious from s 36(5) [of the Road Traffic Act 1930] relating to the certificate of insurance that the policy may contain conditions the nature of which is left completely open. So it clearly contemplates conditions, and unless they are to be conditions limiting the liability of the underwriter, what possible reason can there be for their inclusion in the certificate, the object of which is to make clear to whom it may concern the conditions, if any, subject to which the policy has been issued.

[1.45] McCormick v National Motor Accident Insurance
(1934) 50 TLR 528, 78 Sol Jo 633, 40 Com Cas 76, 49 Ll L Rep 361, CA

Insurers discovered just before the trial of an action brought by a third party against their assured that they were entitled to avoid the policy for false statement in the proposal form. It was contended for the third party that the issue of the certificate prevented insurers from asserting that the policy was avoided.

Per Greer LJ: The effect and need of the certificate is this, that it enables the assured to say: 'Here is my certificate of insurance, and I am not liable as long as I have got an insurance.' It is not a document which is supposed to be addressed to all the world, including people who have never seen it and may never have heard—and a great many people never have heard—either of the Act of Parliament or of the certificate. It is only issued for the purpose of enabling the assured to produce that document when he is on the road, which will show that he has complied with the Act to the extent of getting a policy of insurance; but it is not intended to be a representation that the policy which he has got will in any event become a policy on which he will be entitled in the event of an accident happening and damages resulting.

Per Slesser LJ: The certificate is merely giving the means of enabling a man to drive a motor car. It has no greater effect than that.

Note—For s 36(5), see now s 147 of the Road Traffic Act 1988.

[1.46] Spraggon v Dominion Insurance Co Ltd
(1940) 67 Ll L Rep 529, Stable J; on appeal (1941) 69 Ll L Rep 1, CA

Tomrley hired a car from Warnes. Insurers had issued a policy to Warnes providing indemnity to drivers hiring cars unless within the category of excluded drivers. Excluded drivers included any who had not:

(1)   satisfied the insured (Warnes) by an actual driving test;
(2)   completed a proposal form;
(3)   a current driving licence for 12 months free from endorsements;
(4)   forwarded the proposal form immediately after the driving test to insurers by registered post.

Insurers had issued a certificate to Warnes insuring any driver who held a licence and was not disqualified. Tomrley held a licence and was not disqualified. He was therefore within the wording of the certificate. He had a provisional licence from 25 November 1937 to 22 February 1938, and thereafter an annual licence, which was indorsed with a conviction for speed on 24 March 1938. He did not post the proposal form he signed to insurers. He never had a driving test.

He was therefore not within the wording of the policy. Warnes assured Tomrley that he was covered. An action was brought by a third party against the insurers.

HELD: Insurers were not liable, because it is only where there is a policy of insurance in respect of which the certificate has been issued that the third party had a cause of action against insurers. The accident was not covered by the policy, and the certificate was therefore of no effect: per Stable J.

HELD, ON APPEAL: Tomrley was not insured by the policy; the Court of Appeal made no reference to the certificate.

Note—It follows that the opinion previously widely held by insurers that the insurer is bound by the wording of the certificate as distinct from the policy is without foundation. It is now made perfectly plain that the policy is the only document which creates any liability on insurers, and the certificate is (in this respect) merely a piece of paper to produce to the police to show that there is a policy in existence, without affecting in any way the limitation contained in the policy.

Some policies expressly incorporate the certificate in the policy, and in that case different consideration may arise as between insurers and the assured.

[1.47]   Biddle v Johnston

(1965) 109 Sol Jo 395, [1965] 2 Lloyd's Rep 121, Div Ct

A policy of insurance insured C Ltd and four other named associated companies in respect of the use of a motor vehicle owned by C Ltd, but did not insure R Ltd, a company some of whose shareholders were directors of C Ltd. There had been some co-operation between C Ltd and R Ltd until a receiver of C Ltd was appointed when it largely ceased. The certificate issued under the policy was expressed to cover use by C Ltd 'and/or associated companies', without naming them, in connection with the policyholder's business. The appellant, a director of R Ltd, caused an employee of R Ltd, to drive the vehicle on an occasion after the appointment of the receiver of C Ltd. He was charged with causing him to use the vehicle when uninsured contrary to the Road Traffic Act 1960, s 201 (now s 143 of the 1988 Act). He contended that R Ltd was 'an associated company' covered by the certificate. The justices convicted on the ground that since the appointment of the receiver, who had control of C Ltd, R Ltd and C Ltd were no longer associated companies.

HELD: On a case stated, there was evidence to support the justices' finding. Apart from this, under s 201 of the 1960 Act there must be an enforceable contract of insurance; a cover note referred to in s 216(1) was such a contract, but a certificate, which was not in itself a contract at all, could not comply with the requirements of the 1960 Act. By virtue of s 205(1) a policy of insurance was of no effect unless and until a certificate was delivered, but that did not affect the position. The difficulty here was that the policy and certificates did not agree with each other.

CHAPTER 2

Coverage

1. ISSUE OF THE POLICY – GENERAL PRINCIPLES

(A) THE PROPOSAL FORM

[2.1] *Note*—The legal principles and remedies discussed throughout this chapter should be considered when dealing with policyholders in their private capacity in the light of the Statement of General Insurance Practice issued by the Association of British Insurers.

(I) DUTY TO DISCLOSE MATERIAL FACTS

[2.2] A contract of insurance is a contract *uberrima fides*, that is one of the utmost good faith. This means that the proposer is obliged to disclose to the insurer of all the material information affecting the risk the insurer is taking on. The duty of utmost good faith is mutual.

The principle is long established. Lord Mansfield's judgment in *Carter v Boehm* (1766) 3 Burr 1905 (at 1909) is the classic exposition. He stated:

> 'The special facts, upon which the contingent chance is to be computed, lie more commonly in the knowledge of the insured only; the underwriter trusts to his representation and proceeds upon confidence that he does not keep back any circumstance in his knowledge, to mislead the underwriter into a belief that the circumstance does not exist, to induce him to estimate the risque as if it did not exist. Keeping back such a circumstance is a fraud, and, therefore the policy is void.'

The duty of utmost good faith is not an implied contractual term. *In Bank of Nova Scotia v Hellenic Mutual War Risks Association (Bermuda); The Good Luck* [1989] 3 All ER 628 it was held that the obligation of utmost good faith in a contract of insurance arises by operation of law and not from any implied contractual term and was incapable of supporting a claim to damages.

For a recent decision affirming the principle that a contract of insurance is a contract of utmost good faith see *HIH Casualty & General Insurance Ltd v Chase Manhattan Bank* [2003] UKHL 6, [2003] 1 All ER (Comm) 349, [2003] 2 Lloyd's Rep 61, [2003] 1 CLC 358, [2003] Lloyd's Rep IR 230, (2003) 147 SJLB 264.

(II) DEFINITION OF MATERIALITY

[2.3] The meaning of materiality was considered by the House of Lords in *Pan Atlantic Insurance Co Ltd v Pine Top Insurance Co Ltd* [1994] 3 All ER 581. The case concerned the meaning of s 18 of the Marine Insurance Act 1906. Section 18(1) of that Act provides that 'every material circumstance' must be disclosed. Section 18(2) reads 'every circumstance is material' which would affect the judgment of a prudent insurer in fixing the premium or determining whether he will take the risk.

HELD: (1) The test of materiality of disclosure was, on the natural and ordinary meaning of s 18(2), whether the relevant circumstance would have had an effect on the mind of a prudent insurer in weighing up the risk, not whether had it been fully and accurately disclosed it would have had a decisive effect on the prudent underwriter's decision whether to accept the risk and if so, at what premium. That test accorded with the duty of the assured to disclose all matters which would be taken into account by the underwriter when assessing the risk which he was consenting to assume.

(2)   For an insurer to be entitled to avoid a policy for misrepresentation or non-disclosure, not only does the misrepresentation or non-disclosure have to be material but in addition it has to have induced the making of the policy on the relevant terms. Accordingly, an underwriter who was not induced by the misrepresentation or non-disclosure of a material fact to make the contract cannot rely on the misrepresentation or non-disclosure to avoid the contract.

In *St Paul Fire and Marine Insurance Co (UK) Ltd v McConnell Dowell Constructors Ltd* [1996] 1 All ER 96, [1995] 2 Lloyd's Rep 116 the court accepted that a presumption of inducement could be relied upon to discharge the insurer's duty of proving inducement if the actual underwriter is not called, although the inference that the underwriter was induced is only a *prima facie* one and may be rebutted by counter evidence.

Note—The insured's duty is not limited to answering truthfully questions put to him but extends to disclosing additional facts that are material to the risk.

(III)   EXAMPLES OF MATERIALITY

[2.4]   Dawson Ltd v Bonnin

[1922] 2 AC 413, 91 LJPC 210, 218 LT 1, 38 TLR 836, 11 Ll L Rep 57, 12 Ll L Rep 237, HL

A firm of contractors in Glasgow insured a motor lorry at Lloyds against damage by fire and third-party risks. The policy recited that the proposal should be the basis of the contract and be held as incorporated in the policy, and it was expressed to be granted subject to the conditions at the back thereof. The fourth condition stated 'material mis-statement or concealment of any circumstances by the insured material to assessing the premium herein, or in connection with any claim, shall render the policy void'. In reply to a question in the proposal form, 'State full address at which the vehicle will usually be garaged', the answer given was 'Above address', meaning thereby the firm's ordinary place of business in Glasgow. This was not true, as the lorry was usually garaged at a farm on the outskirts of Glasgow. The inaccurate answer in the proposal was given by inadvertence. The lorry having been destroyed by fire at the garage, the insured claimed payment under the policy.

HELD: (1) This mis-statement in the proposal was not material within the meaning of condition 4.

(2)   The recital in the policy that the proposal should be the basis of the contract made the truth of the statements contained in the proposal, apart from the question of materiality, a condition of the liability for the

insurers; the effect of this recital was not cut down by the special conditions on the back of the policy; and the claim failed.

[2.5]   Mackay v London General Insurance Co Ltd
(1935) 51 LI L Rep 201

The plaintiff answered 'no' to questions as to whether he had ever had to pay an increased premium or been convicted. The answers were made the basis of the contract. In fact some three years earlier the plaintiff had had to take on an excess of £2 10 s to insure his motorbike. This was the insurer's standard practice for minors. He had also been fined 10 s some considerable time earlier for having a loose nut on the brake of his motorbike. The judge held that both these matters were quite immaterial. He expressed sympathy for the plaintiff but said that nonetheless the answers formed the basis of the contract and the insurers were therefore entitled to avoid.

[2.6]   Kelsall v Allstate Insurance Co
(1987) Times 20 March

A warranty in a proposal form of 'no known adverse facts' only requires a policyholder to disclose facts that the reasonable man would recognise as adverse and not to disclose facts not so recognised but which subsequently turn out to be adverse.

[2.7]   Holt's Motors Ltd v South East Lancashire Insurance Co Ltd
[1930] 36 LI L Rep 17; on appeal 35 Com Cas 281, 37 LI L Rep 1   Horridge J, CA

An intimation by a previous insurer that it would not invite renewal is a material fact which should be disclosed by a proposer.

[2.8]   Cornhill Insurance Co Ltd v Assenheim
(1937) 58 LI L Rep 27

The insurer sought a declaration that it was entitled to avoid on grounds of material non-disclosure of the fact that previous underwriters had refused to renew. A proposal had been signed on the 3 April 1935 with the answer 'no' to the question whether any underwriter had refused to renew. Subsequently, in September other insurers declined to renew in respect of other vehicles. At later dates various additions and substitutions were made to the vehicles covered by the policy. The defendant signed proposals in relation to these various alterations which included a declaration that that proposal and the proposal signed on the 3 April 1935 formed the basis of the contract.

HELD: The failure to disclose the letter received in September 1935 from other insurers refusing to renew was a material non-disclosure.

Age of driver/proposer

[2.9]   Merchants' and Manufacturers' Insurance Co Ltd v Hunt
[1940] 4 All ER 205, 57 TLR 32, 84 Sol Jo 670

A proposal form which had the usual declaration and warranty contained the following questions: 'Q. Have you or any person who to your knowledge will drive the car ever been convicted of an offence in connection with a motor vehicle or motor cycle, or is any prosecution pending? A. No.' The proposer knew that his son was likely to drive the car, and the son had been convicted of three motoring offences.

HELD: The representation of fact is material. The answer of an unqualified negative is an assertion:
  (1)   that the proposer has the knowledge which he purports to impart, and
  (2)   that that knowledge is what he is imparting. The answer does not mean 'No, to the best of my knowledge and belief.'

  'Q. Will the car be driven by any person under twenty-one? A. No.'

  The proposer knew that the car would be driven quite frequently by his son, who was 17. The question of age is 'material'. Although each representation was innocent, the information was in fact false.

Note—In the Court of Appeal the case was decided on a different point but Scott LJ agreed with the construction of the questions and answers in the proposal form.

[2.10]   Broad v Waland
(1942) 73 Ll L Rep 263

A cover note was issued on the faith of proposal that the proposer was 21 years of age. The broker had a clear and definite instruction not to issue a cover note to any person under 21. The proposer was 19 years 6 months and 2 weeks.

HELD: In an action for a declaration:
  (1)   the misrepresentation was material;
  (2)   the policy had been 'obtained' by the misrepresentation. The declaration was granted.

Occupation of proposer

[2.11]   Holmes v Cornhill Insurance Co Ltd
(1949) 82 Ll L Rep 575

The proposer orally asked an insurance company for insurance of a motor car for use in his business as a commission agent. The company told him it did not insure bookmakers. The proposer stated he was not a bookmaker but was a commission agent dealing in furniture. He had had a furniture shop for a short time three or four years before but for two years had no shop, warehouse or business premises in connection with furniture dealing and kept no books or records of any such dealing. His main occupation was that of a bookmaker and not that of a dealer. He signed a proposal form stating his occupation as dealer. The proposal form contained the usual declaration and warranty.
  The arbitrator made his award in the form of a special case. His findings were:
  (1)   The description of dealer was untrue.
  (2)   The failure to disclose that he was a bookmaker was material.
  (3)   That (1) and (2) each constituted a breach of the warranty which was made the basis of the policy.
  (4)   The policy was induced by the false representation that he was not a bookmaker.
  The arbitrator found the company not liable. The finding was upheld.

[2.12]   McNealy v The Pennine Insurance Co

(1978) 122 Sol Jo 229, [1978] 2 Lloyd's Rep 18, [1978] RTR 285, CA

Note—See para [2.251].

Owner not proposer

[2.13]   Guardian Assurance Co Ltd v Sutherland

[1939] 2 All ER 246, 55 TLR 576, 83 Sol Jo 398, 63 Ll L Rep 220

On 17 March 1938, Sutherland signed a proposal form for a Mercedes Benz BXD 1 and the plaintiff issued cover notes until the policy was issued on 26 May 1938. On 20 May 1938, Sutherland telegraphed to the plaintiff to transfer to a Lancia car, confirmed on 10 June by an application form signed by Sutherland for substitution, and the policy was endorsed accordingly. On 17 June 1938, at the request of Sutherland an employee of Green Park Motors Ltd telegraphed to the insurer 'Please cover me on Mercedes EYT 114 as well as Lancia, and the insurer issued a cover note. On 20 June 1938, Sutherland signed a form that EYT 114 should be substituted for the Lancia and stating Sutherland was the owner of EYT 114 and that it was registered in his name. On 20 June 1938, before the form signed on 20 June by Sutherland had reached the insurer, car EYT 114 driven by one Sidebotham was involved in an accident causing personal injuries to third parties. EYT 114 was the property of Green Park Motors. Sidebotham introduced one Chang, a Chinese, as purchaser, and on 17 June Chang agreed to purchase. Chang, owning to his foreign nationality, could not get cover without delay. Sidebotham had a policy from 15 August 1937, to 15 August 1938, but he had not revealed in his proposal form a number of convictions for dangerous driving and driving without due care, and some of his previous accidents, and had mis-stated his age as over 21 when in fact it was nineteen and a half and his policy was avoided in October 1938. Sutherland had no interest in EYT 114.

HELD: It was all one contract and was obtained by mis-statement and concealment. If the cover note for EYT 114 was a new contract it was obtained by material misrepresentation. The telegram represented that EYT 114 was Sutherland's property. It was material for the insurer to know that Sutherland had nothing to do with the car, but that it was sold to Chang and about to be driven by Sidebotham with his bad record of offences and accidents. A policy obtained by misrepresentation insures no one and is not a policy within s 36(4) of the Road Traffic Act 1930:

(1)   the opening words of the subsection were inserted to get rid of the difficulty created by the Life Assurance Act 1774;

(2)   the function of the subsection was to get over the difficulty that nobody who was not a party to a contract could sue upon it (compare *Vanderpitte v Preferred Accident Insurance Corpn of New York* [1933] AC 70, 102 LJ PC 21, 148 LT 169, 49 TLR 90).

Sidebotham was not driving EYT 114 on the assured's order or with his permission. Sutherland had no interest whatever in EYT 114 and had no right to give or refuse permission.

Application for declaration granted.

Note—For a recent view of the application of s 2 of the Life Assurance Act 1774, see *Mark Rowlands Ltd v Berni Inns* [1985] 3 All ER 473. Section 148(7) of the Road Traffic Act 1988 has replaced s 36(4) of the 1930 Act.

[2.14] **Zurich General Accident and Liability Insurance Co Ltd v Buck**
(1939) 64 Ll L Rep 115

A, a greengrocer carrying on business at No 56 Brewery Road on 1 September 1936, took out a policy, and two subsequent policies, with the X Co, each of which policies lapsed for the non-payment of a premium. On 4 October 1937, A took out a policy with the plaintiff subject to termination if the hire-purchase agreement terminated except if due to purchase by A. On 9 December 1938, A was fined for speeding. On 15 March 1938, the hire-purchase agreement terminated and the policy was cancelled. Judgment was obtained against A by the motor trader and was unsatisfied.

On 15 March 1938, B, the brother of A, who had a butcher's business next door to A, bought a motor van and lent it to A for use in A's business. It was registered in B's name. The plaintiff's agent received proposal forms and issued cover notes. A informed the agent that the van belonged to A but he wished it to be insured in the name of B, but A would use it in his business and it would be driven by A only. The proposal stated that the proposer was B; that B's business was at No 56 and was a greengrocery business; that no person who would drive had been convicted of a motoring offence; that the proposer had been insured with the co-operative; that no company had cancelled his policy. A had been insured for employers' liability and the plaintiff.

HELD: A policy that is cancelled or refused renewal, does not mean it is allowed to lapse by reason of non-payment. The conviction and some of the mis-statements taken by themselves were not very material, but the proposal as a whole quite obviously did not in the least represent a true state of the facts, and some of the mis-statements would have led an underwriter to consider whether to accept the proposal or at least to make further inquiries. B had nothing to do with A's use of the van, and a third party could have no possible claim against B and B had no insurable interest and the policy was valueless.

Application for declaration granted.

The third party in the previous case afterwards sued B on the principle of *Monk v Warbey* (at para [1.24]).

[2.15] **Goodbarne v Buck**
[1940] 1 KB 771, [1940] 1 All ER 613, 109 LJKB 837, 162 LT 259, 56 TLR 433, 84 Sol Jo 380, CA

HELD: B was never the owner of the van and could not prevent A, who was the owner, from driving it. The policy was voidable, not void; it was valid and subsisting unless and until the insurer elected to avoid it. This did not mean that for all purposes of s 35 of the Road Traffic Act 1930 the policy must be regarded as never having been in existence at all. There was a policy in force at the time which satisfied the section and the fact that it was subsequently avoided did not prevent there having been a policy in force at the material time.

Accident record

[2.16] **Dent v Blackmore**
(1927) 29 Ll L Rep 9

The insurers avoided a policy on the grounds of material non-disclosure. On the proposal was the question 'what accidents have occurred in connection with your motor car during the past two years, including costs?' – the plaintiff replied: damaged wings. In fact the plaintiff had had six accidents with his car all resulting in damage to wings. The judge held that the answer conveyed a clear impression that the plaintiff had suffered one accident only and that the plaintiff was guilty of a material non-disclosure entitling the insurers to avoid the policy.

[2.17]   Dunn v Ocean Accident

(1933) 47 LI L Rep 129, CA

The plaintiff completed a proposal form using her maiden name, although she was in fact married. Her husband was killed whilst driving the car. The facts are unusual in that they had married secretly and lived apart. The husband had bought the car on hire-purchase and 'gave' it to the plaintiff as a present. The husband had use of the vehicle during week days and the plaintiff used it at weekends. The husband was prone to driving at great speed and had had several accidents to the plaintiff's knowledge and had been refused insurance cover. The plaintiff completed a proposal form and answered 'no' to the following questions:

(1)   Have you or your driver during the past five years been convicted of any offence in connection with the driving of a motor vehicle?

(2)   Has a company or underwriter declined your proposal or required you to carry the first portion of any loss?

HELD: The plaintiff's failure to disclose her marital status and the material fact that her husband had been involved in accidents amounted to a material non-disclosure entitling the insurers to avoid the policy. The judge considered it to be of significance that the husband had filled in parts of the proposal form himself.

[2.18]   Trustees of GH Mundy (a bankrupt) v Blackmore

(1928) 32 LI L Rep 150

Mundy took out motor insurance. The insurer asserted that by a proposal incorporated into the contract, Mundy had warranted:

(1)   that during the past two years with eight cars insured, the only accidents were minor accidents; also, he was ran off the road in France owing to tyre bursting; and

(2)   that he had not previously been refused insurance.

In fact the insured's Bugatti had been involved in an accident costing between £130 and £140 to repair. It was a head-on collision and the car had both axles bent, and its gear box thrown out of line. It was argued that if an insurance company accepts a disclosure of a minor accident it cannot afterwards say that I do not think this was a minor accident and you should have mentioned it specifically. The judge found that no reasonably fair-minded man could have called the accident minor and so the insurers were entitled to repudiate notwithstanding the failure to inquire further. It was also held that the failure to disclose the previous refusal was material.

Where vehicle garaged/standard of garage

[2.19]   Dawsons Ltd v Bonnin

[1922] 2 AC 413, 91 LJPC 210, 128 LTI, 38 TLR 836, 11 LI L Rep 57, 12 LI L Rep 237, HL

Note—See para [2.4].

Purchase price – part exchange

[2.20]   **Brewtnall v Cornhill Insurance Co Ltd**
(1931) 40 Ll L Rep 166

An insured car was destroyed by fire. A claim was made, the defence being that there had been a concealment of a material fact in the proposal form. The question was: 'Q. Cost price to proposer. A. £145.'

There was evidence that the proposer gave £45 and another car (agreed price £100) in part exchange – should exchange of the car have been disclosed?

HELD: The defence of concealment failed.
Judgment for assured.

Driving 12 months regularly; provisional licence

[2.21]   **Zurich General Accident and Liability Insurance Co Ltd v Morrison**
[1942] 2 KB 53, [1942] 1 All ER 529, 111 LJKB 601, 167 LT 183, 58 TLR 217, 86 Sol Jo 267, 72 Ll L Rep 167, CA

A question in a proposal form for motor insurance asked 'Have you driven cars regularly and continuously in the UK during the past 12 months?'

HELD: The question was most embarrassing and if taken literally no one could answer it other than in the negative. If the insurer want to know how long a man has driven on the road or for how long he had held a licence, it should ask the questions in plain terms. The proposer had done some driving on a provisional licence and some on works roads during the 12 months preceding the proposal and it could not be said his answer to the question, 'Yes', was untrue. The failure to reveal that he had only a provisional licence to drive and had failed one driving test was not a material non-disclosure since there was no evidence that the insurer would not have issued a policy on the same terms had those matters been disclosed. In a case of this kind the insurer must establish two propositions in order to avoid the policy:
(1)   that the matter relied on was 'material' in the sense that the mind of a prudent insurer would be affected by it, and
(2)   that in fact the underwriter's mind was so affected and the policy thereby obtained. The insurers had not established these propositions.

Note—Followed by Atkinson J in *Broad v Waland* (1942) 73 Ll L Rep 263 at 628 and 679.

Previous convictions – motor offences

[2.22]   **Jester-Barnes v Licenses and General Insurance Co**
(1934) 49 Ll L Rep 231

Per MacKinnon J: If they had asked him the question 'have you or your driver during the past 5 years been convicted of any offence' and he had said 'no' and that was true, I should have come without hesitation to the conclusion that they were not entitled after asking that question and receiving that answer to take it to mean that he had failed to disclose that he had been convicted eight years ago and that it was a material fact.

[2.23]   Mackay v London General Insurance Co
(1935) 51 Ll L Rep 201   Swift J

Note—See para [2.5].

[2.24]   Bond v Commercial Assurance Co
(1930) 35 Com Cas 171, 36 Ll L Rep 107

The appellant took out with the respondent a motor car policy of insurance in respect of a car of which he was the owner. The appellant employed more than one driver in the course of his business and at the time when the insurance was effected the agent of the respondent told him that if he paid an extra premium the policy would protect him whoever might be driving the car, and the appellant paid the extra premium accordingly. During the currency of the policy, the car while being driven by a son of the appellant came into collision with a cyclist. The cyclist brought an action against the appellant for damages, and the appellant referred the claim to the respondent, who repudiated liability on the ground that at the time when the policy was taken out the appellant had failed to disclose a material fact. It appeared that before the insurance was effected, the appellant's son had been convicted several times of motoring offences, chiefly in relation to a motorcycle, and the respondent contended that this was a material fact which ought to have been disclosed by the appellant. Before the policy was issued the appellant had received a proposal form from the respondent and had answered all the questions in that form fully and truthfully and he did not know that any further information was required. At that time he had not his son in mind. The appellant's claim against the respondent was referred to arbitration as required by the policy and the arbitrator awarded in favour of respondent on the ground that a material fact had not been disclosed. The appellant now appealed to the Divisional Court to have the award set aside.

HELD: The arbitrator had decided rightly and the award must be confirmed.

[2.25]   Butcher v Dowlen
(1980) 124 Sol Jo 883, [1981] RTR 24, [1981] 1 Lloyd's Rep 310, CA

The plaintiff claimed money due under a policy of motor insurance issued by the defendant to her husband who had been killed in an accident. The defendant served a defence denying liability under the policy on the ground that her husband had failed to disclose criminal charges and a conviction in the proposal form. The plaintiff, who said she had no knowledge of any conviction, obtained an order for further and better particulars specifying the alleged offences and charges with dates and other details. The defendant was unable to say more in reply than that the deceased had 'been convicted of offences on several occasions' without any details. The plaintiff applied to strike out the defence for failure to supply the particulars ordered.

HELD, dismissing an appeal from a judge: The defence should be struck out. It was not good enough for the defendant to say the action should go to trial so that a police officer could produce evidence from the Criminal Records Office which at present the defendant did not have. The burden of proof was on the defendant and there was not enough to justify the allegations made in the defence going to trial.

Note—But see the contrasting decision in below at para [2.26].

[2.26]   Revell v London General Insurance Co Ltd
(1934) 152 LT 258, 50 Ll L Rep 114   MacKinnon J

A proposal form contained the following question: 'Q. Have you or any of your drivers ever been convicted of any offence in connection with the driving of any motor vehicle? A. No.'
  The driver in fact waspreviously convicted:
  (1)   of unlawfully driving a car without a suitable reflecting mirror;
  (2)   of unlawfully using a car without having in force an insurance policy covering third party risks.

HELD: The question might reasonably mean carefulness of driver and the answer was not untrue.

Previous convictions – non-motor/moral hazard

[2.27]   *Note*—The following cases must be considered in conjunction with the meaning of materiality as defined in *Pan Atlantic Insurance Co Ltd v Pine Top Insurance Co Ltd* [1994] 3 All ER 581.

[2.28]   Locker & Woolf Ltd v Western Australian Insurance Co Ltd
[1936] 1 KB 408, 105 LJKB 444, 154 LT 667, 52 TLR 293, 80 Sol Jo 185, CA

Per Slesser LJ: It is elementary that one of the matters to be considered by an insurance company in entering into contractual relations with a proposed insured is the question of the moral integrity of the proposer – what has been called the moral hazard.

[2.29]   Cleland v London General Insurance Co Ltd
(1935) 51 Ll L Rep 156, CA

The defendant repudiated liability on the ground of the non-disclosure of material facts on the proposal form. It relied upon the following statement in the proposal form: 'I have withheld no information which would tend to increase the risk or influence the acceptance of this proposal'. It was said that the insured had answered 'No' to the question on the proposal form: 'Have you or your driver ever been convicted or had a motor licence indorsed?' when in fact there were convictions against him as follows:
  (1)   10 January 1922: Breaking and entering a garage and stealing a motorcycle and sidecar. Released on recognisances.
  (2)   17 July 1922: Forging a cheque. Five months' imprisonment.
  (3)   26 September 1922: Breach of recognisances. Nine months' imprisonment.
  (4)   19 July 1926: Breaking and entering shop and stealing parcels and other articles. Eighteen months' imprisonment with hard labour. Stealing a fur stole and other articles to the value of £1,000. Three years' penal servitude.
It was submitted that the insured had accurately and truthfully answered the question on the proposal form, because the convictions had no relation to motor car offences. Counsel also contended the insured was under no common law

liability to disclose to the London General his past bad character except so far as that character was material to the subject matter of the policy.

HELD, in the Court of Appeal (affirming Horridge J): A person entering into such a contract was bound to disclose the fact that he had been convicted although those convictions had nothing at all to do with motor offences, and therefore the insurance company were entitled to repudiate liability.

[2.30]   Taylor v Eagle Star Insurance Co Ltd

(1940) 67 Ll L Rep 136   MacNaghten J

A question in a proposal form was as follows: 'Q. Have you or has your driver been convicted of any offence in connection with the driving of any motor vehicle? A. No'.

An accident occurred on 20 April 1937. The assured had been convicted of the following offences.

(1)   7 June 1927: Drunk and disorderly; fined £2. Assaulting the police; one months' imprisonment. Throwing a glass bottle to the public danger; fined £2.

(2)   23 October 1931: Permitting use of uninsured car; fined £2.

(3)   27 March 1933: Driving car without road fund licence; fined 10s.

(4)   13 June 1933: Drunk on licensed premises; fined 10s.

(5)   7 December 1935: Drinking during prohibited hours; fined 15s.

Following *Revell v London General Insurance Co Ltd* (noted at para [2.26]), the answer in respect of the motoring offences was not untrue, but the other convictions were facts material to be known to insurers and not having been disclosed, insurers were not liable on the ground of non-disclosure.

(B)   NON-DISCLOSURE – VOID OR VOIDABLE

[2.31]   The effect of misrepresentation/material non-disclosure is to allow the aggrieved party to elect either to carry on with the contract or not. If that party does not choose to continue the contract then it becomes void *ab initio* by operation of law.

[2.32]   Durrant v Maclaren

[1956] 2 Lloyd's Rep 70, Div Ct

The defendant obtained insurance to drive a hired car by giving replies in a proposal form which were untrue and which would have entitled the insurer to avoid the policy *ab initio*.

He was prosecuted for driving an uninsured car, the argument being put that if the policy can be avoided *ab initio* then it is not a policy in force.

HELD: The argument could not succeed. The Road Traffic Act 1934, s 10 (now ss 151 and 152 of the Road Traffic Act 1988) provides that the insurer must pay if judgment is obtained in respect of an accident unless proceedings are taken under subsection (2). No such proceedings having been taken the insurance was in force at the time when the alleged offence occurred.

[2.33]   Adams v Dunne

[1978] RTR 281, [1978] Crim LR 365, Div Ct

The defendant obtained a cover note from the insurer by concealing the fact that he was disqualified from driving. He was prosecuted for driving uninsured; on the relevant date the insurer had not taken any steps to avoid the contract although it would not have given cover had it known he was disqualified. The prosecution conceded that if the contract was merely voidable the case would be covered by *Durrant v Maclaren* (at para [2.32]) but argued that as the contract was void *ab initio* the case was different; a contract of insurance purporting to insure a disqualified driver was an illegal contract.

HELD: The insurer had been misled and had not, with open eyes, entered into a contract to insure a disqualified driver. Until the insurer took steps to avoid it the contract remained a contract of insurance for the purposes of the Road Traffic Act 1972, s 143 (now the Road Traffic Act 1988, s 143).

Note—See also *Evans v Lewis* (at para [2.150]).

(C) WAIVER OF MATERIALITY

[2.34] Insurers may expressly elect to waive a breach and the contract will continue. They may also be deemed to have waived a breach by conducting themselves in a manner inconsistent with the continuance of their right to rely on the breach.

Note—See also *Greenwood v Martins Bank* (at para [4.54]).

[2.35] **McCormick v National Motor and Accident Insurance Union Ltd**
(1934) 50 TLR 528, 78 Sol Jo 633, 40 Com Cas 76, 49 Ll L Rep 361, CA

During the course of the trial of an action between a third party and the assured, it came out in evidence that the assured had been previously convicted for dangerous driving. He had stated on the proposal form that he had not been convicted. The insurer continued to defend the action, and five days later repudiated liability under the policy.

HELD: This did not amount to waiver. The insurer was entitled to continue to defend the action.

Per Scrutton LJ: Whether you treat it as an election or whether you treat it as a ratification or whether you treat it as a decision simply to act on the knowledge you have acquired, the duty to take action does not arise (1) unless you know all the facts – being put on inquiry is not sufficient; you must know the facts – and (2) unless you have a reasonable time to make up your mind. You are not bound the moment the statement is made to you to make up your mind at once; you are entitled to a reasonable time to consider – to a reasonable time to make inquiries.

Per Slesser LJ: There must be an irresistible inference that the parties intended to adopt one of two courses open to them and to discard or waive the other and in such a manner as to represent to other persons definitely and unequivocally that he has taken that view whereby it may act to their detriment.

[2.36] **Stone v Licenses and General Insurance Co Ltd**
(1942) 71 Ll L Rep 256   Birkett J

16 May, 4am: accident involving lorry carrying load in breach of policy condition. 8am: driver telephoned assured who informed insurers. 6.30pm: branch manager of insurers visited accident and saw the unauthorised load. 17 May: driver made full disclosure at the insurer's office. The insurer then had full knowledge of all material

facts. 23 May: Branch manager gave instructions to remove debris and sell it for £1. The assured was not consulted. 7 June: the insurers wrote repudiating liability under policy and sent its own cheque for £1 to to assured who refused to accept the cheque.

HELD: The breach of condition had been waived.

[2.37]   Lickiss v Milestone Motor Policies at Lloyd's

[1966] 2 All ER 972, [1966] 1 WLR 1334, 110 Sol Jo 600, [1966] 2 Lloyd's Rep 1

Davies and Lickiss were involved in a motor accident. Davies sought to recover the cost of repairing damage to his vehicle from Lickiss. It was a condition precedent of Lickiss's insurance policy that full particulars would be given to the insurer of any accident and that any notice of intended prosecution, writ etc would be sent immediately to the insurer. The accident occurred on 17 May 1964 and Lickiss advised the insurer on 25 May. By that time the insurer had already been made aware of the accident by Davies's solicitors. The insurer sent Lickiss a claim form for completion. The insured subsequently received notice of intended prosecution and a summons but did not forward these to the insurer. The insurer learned of these proceedings from the police before the return date of the summons. The insurer subsequently repudiated liability stating that its position had been prejudiced.

HELD: The insured was in breach of the condition precedent but by writing to the insured enclosing a claim form that breach had been waived.

[2.38]   Baghbadrani v Commercial Union Assurance plc

[2000] Lloyd's Rep IR 94

A school, owned by the claimant and run by her son (K) was badly damaged by fire. The claimant made claims under two policies of insurance with the defendant. Initially the defendant intimated that liability was in dispute but when threatened with proceedings indicated that liability was not in issue. Loss adjusters were appointed and the claim investigated.

It then became apparent that K had made material non-disclosures during the course of the investigation of the claims and the insurer sought to avoid liability.

The claimant commenced proceedings for summary judgment contending that the insurer had waived its rights to avoid the policy by its earlier correspondence and actions.

HELD: (1) The claimant owed a continuing duty of good faith during the claims process.

(2)   By reason of the fraudulent misrepresentations made by K before and during the claims process, the insurer was not in a position to make an informed decision and had not waived its rights under the policy.

(D)   MUTUAL MISTAKE

[2.39]   Magee v Pennine Insurance Co Ltd

[1969] 2 QB 507, [1969] 2 All ER 891, [1969] 2 WLR 1278, 113 Sol Jo 303, [1969] 2 Lloyd's Rep 378, CA

The plaintiff took out a motor insurance policy with the defendant in 1961. There were serious misstatements of fact in the proposal that would entitle the defendant to repudiate liability under the policy or declare it void. In 1964 the car was damaged in an accident. After an inspection by an engineer the defendant wrote to the plaintiff saying it was damaged beyond repair, that its value according to the engineer was (after salvage) £385 and offering him that amount 'in settlement of your claim'. The plaintiff accepted but the insurer then discovered the inaccuracy of the statements in the proposal form and refused to pay. The county court judge found that the plaintiff had not been fraudulent and that the defendant's letter was a binding offer which had been accepted.

HELD: There had been a common mistake of fact, namely, that there was a valid policy of insurance. Accepting that the agreement to pay £385 was a separate contract the defendant was entitled to avoid it on the ground of mutual mistake in a fundamental and vital matter.

Note—The facts of this case must be contrasted with situations where there has been a mistake of law rather than of fact. In those circumstances moneys paid will be irrecoverable.

(E)   POLICY INTERPRETATION

(I)   CONTRA PREFERENS

[2.40]   Thomson v Weems
(1884) 9 App Cas 671   Lord Watson, HL

The question must be interpreted according to the ordinary and natural meaning of the words used, if their meaning be plain and unequivocal, and there is nothing in the context to qualify it. On the other hand, if the words used are ambiguous, they must be construed *contra preferens*, and in favour of the assured.

[2.41]   Cornish v Accident Insurance Co
(1889) 23 QBD 453, 58 LJQB 591, 54 JP 262, 38 WR 139, 5 TLR 733   Lindley LJ

In a case of real doubt, the policy ought to be construed most strongly against the insurers; they frame the policy and insert the exceptions. But this principle ought only to be applied for the purpose of removing doubt, not for the purpose of creating a doubt or magnifying an ambiguity when the circumstances of the case raise no real difficulty.

See also *Dodson v Peter H Dodson Insurance Services* (at para [2.253]) where the court held that 'insureds were entitled to clear wordings and to the benefit of any ambiguity'.

(II)   EJUSDEM GENERIS

[2.42]   Sun Fire Office v Hart
(1889) 14 App Cas 98, 58 LJPC 69, 60 LT 337, 53 JP 548, 37 WR 561, 5 TLR 289, PC

Per Lord Watson: It is well-known canon of construction, that when a particular enumeration is followed by such words as 'or other', the latter expression ought, if not enlarged by the context, to be limited to matters *ejusdem generis* with those specially enumerated. The canon is attended with no difficulty, except in its application. Whether it applies at all, and if so, what effect should be given to it, must in every case depend upon the clause under construction.

Note—The phrase is chiefly used in cases where general words have a meaning attributed to them less comprehensive than they would otherwise bear, by reason of particular words preceding them.

One line of authority is to give all the words their common meaning unless it is reasonably plain on the face of the document itself that they are not used with that meaning.

The other line of authority is that the general words which follow particular and specific words of the same nature as themselves take their meaning from them and are presumed to be restricted to the same genus as those words.

The phrase was considered by Devlin J in the following case (at para [2.43]) citing *Scrutton on Charterparties* (15th edn) p 239:

'It must be remembered that the question is whether a particular thing is within the genus that comprises the specified things. It is not a question (though the point is often so put in argument), whether the particular thing is like one or other of the specified things.'

[2.43]   Chandris v Isbrandtsen-Moller Co Inc

[1951] 1 KB 240, [1950] 1 All ER 768, 66 (pt 1) TLR 971, 94 Sol Jo 303, 83 Lloyd's Rep 385   Devlin J

Per Devlin J: The rule is merely, as I think, an aid to ascertaining the intentions of the parties.

If there is something to show that the literal meaning of the words is too wide, then they will be given such other meaning as seems best to consort with the intention of the parties. In some cases it may be that they will seem to indicate a genus; in others that they perform the simpler office of expanding the meaning of each enumerated item. If a genus cannot be found, doubtless that is one factor indicating that the parties do not intend to restrict the meaning of the words. But I do not take it to be universally true that whenever a genus cannot be found the words must have been intended to have their literal meaning, whatever other indications there may be to the contrary. I see no reason why, if it accords with the apparent intention of the parties, the words should not be treated, as suggested by Lord MacNaghten in *Thames and Mersey Marine Insurance Co Ltd v Hamilton Fraser & Co* ((1887) 12 App Cas 484 at 501), as being 'inserted in order to prevent disputes founded on nice distinctions' and 'to cover in terms whatever may be within the spirit of the cases previously enumerated'.

(III)   CONTINUING WARRANTY

[2.44]   *Note*—The theory that answers in a proposal form, import a warranty which continues during the insurance, did not receive any support in the case of *Woolfall and Rimmer Ltd v Moyle* (at para [2.45]).

[2.45]   Woolfall and Rimmer Ltd v Moyle

[1942] 1 KB 66, [1942] 3 All ER 304, 111 LJKB 122, 166 LT 49, 58 TLR 28, 86 Sol Jo 63, CA

A proposal form for employers' liability contained the question: 'Are your machinery, plant and ways properly fenced and guarded and otherwise in good order and condition?' The answer was 'Yes.' It was contended by the insurer that the question was not limited to the date of the proposal form but continued during the currency of the policy. The Court of Appeal said that it was to enable insurers to find out the character of the risk. There was not a particle of justification for reading into it any element of futurity whatsoever.

[2.46]   Sweeney v Kennedy

(1948) 82 Ll L Rep 294, Eire Div Ct

A proposal dated 4 March 1946, for insurance of a motor lorry contained the question: 'Are any of your drivers under 21 years of age or with less than 12 months' driving experience?' and was answered 'No.'

The policy was issued on 18 March 1946. At that date the answer was true and the assured had no intention of employing a driver under 21. A son of the assured was first employed as a driver on 17 June 1946, and occasionally employed as driver until 2 February 1947, after which date he was regularly so employed. On 7 October 1947, an accident occurred when the son, who was under 21, was driving.

The declaration in the proposal form was stated to be 'promissory and so form the basis of the contract'.

HELD: (1) No such alteration of risk as to avoid policy.
   (2)   No continuing warranty that no driver under 21 would be employed.
   (3)   'Promissory' read with the following words, did not refer to the future.
          It signified a positive declaration: 'I promise you that it is so.'
Underwriters held liable.

[2.47]   Kirkbride v Donner

[1974] 1 Lloyd's Rep 549, Mayor's and City of London Court

Miss Kirkbride filled in a proposal form for insurance of her car. In answer to the question 'Will the car to your knowledge be driven by any person under 25 years of age?' she put merely 'Yes, self.' She signed the usual declaration at the end of the form containing the words 'this declaration signed by me is promissory'. The policy when issued provided that the underwriters would not be liable in respect of loss whilst the car was 'being driven by or in charge for the purpose of any person in whose record there is to the knowledge of the policyholder a prejudice existing such as would amount to material information to be known to the underwriters'. On an occasion when she intended to visit a theatre club she allowed her younger brother to drive there in her car on an arrangement that she would use it to drive him back at the end of the visit. Her brother drove the car there, parked it and handed her the keys. During the evening the car was stolen and not recovered. The underwriters refused to meet the loss.

HELD: They were not entitled to decline liability under the policy, because:
   (1)   on the facts Miss Kirkbride's brother was not in charge of the car when it was stolen, since the purpose for which he had driven the car had come to an end and Miss Kirkbride was herself at the club;
   (2)   the use of the word 'promissory' in the declaration did not mean that she was warranting that the situation implied or expressed in the proposal form would continue into the future: all it meant was, 'At the time of signing the form those are my intentions'. When she signed the

proposal form Miss Kirkbride did not intend that the car would be driven by anyone under the age of 25 other than herself.

(IV)   ASSURED AS A THIRD PARTY

[2.48]   *Note*—There was formerly a difference of opinion on the question whether an assured of a policy could claim against insurers under the policy for personal injury caused to him whilst a passenger in his own car driven by his own servant, or other person driving on his order or with his permission.

The point was the subject of an award by Lord Robertson in an arbitration under the Scottish procedure. The policyholder was injured whilst a passenger in her own car driven by a person with permission. It was admitted the driver was entitled to indemnity if there was a liability to 'third parties', but denied that the policyholder was a third party. The section in the policy was headed 'Liability to Third Parties'. Lord Robertson held that the policyholder was not a third party within the meaning of the policy and there was no liability under it (reported at 73 Lloyd's Rep 189). The same question came before the courts in *Digby v General Accident Fire and Life Assurance Corpn* (at para [2.49]) where in the House of Lords, a conclusion was reached to the contrary.

[2.49]   Digby v General Accident Fire and Life Assurance Corpn

[1943] AC 121, [1942] 2 All ER 319, 111 LJKB 628, 167 LT 222, 58 TLR 375, 87 Sol Jo 29, 73 Ll L Rep 175, HL

The policyholder was a passenger in her own car driven by her servant, owing to his negligent driving she was injured and awarded damages against him (*Thompson v Bundy* (1938) Times, 5 May). He then brought an action against her insurer, claiming indemnity. The judge (Atkinson J) held that the driver was entitled to be indemnified ([1940] 1 All ER 514, 66 Ll L Rep 89). In the Court of Appeal his decision was reversed ([1940] 2 KB 226, [1940] 3 All ER 190, 109 LJKB 740, 163 LT 366).

HELD, ON APPEAL to the House of Lords (Lord Atkin, Lord Wright and Lord Porter, Viscount Simon LC and Viscount Maugham dissenting): The insurer was liable to indemnify the driver against the claim of the assured.

The policy contained six sections of which section 2 (described in the margin as dealing with 'Third-party liability') gave the assured indemnity against '(1) all sums which the policyholder shall become legally liable to pay in respect of any claim by any person (including passengers in the automobile) for loss of life or accidental bodily injury ... caused by, through, or in connexion with such automobile ...'. The same section further provided '(3) The insurance under this section shall also extend to indemnify in like manner any person whilst driving [the car] on the order or with the permission of the policyholder, provided ... that such person shall as though he were the policy-holder observe, fulfil and be subject to the terms, exceptions and conditions of this policy in so far as they can apply'.

Per Lord Atkin: There was no justification for transferring the words from the margin to the body of the document and saying that 'any claim by any person' must be read as 'any claim by any third party'. 'Any person' means any member of the public. In section 2(1) 'any person' cannot include the policyholder because he cannot be liable to pay himself, but in section 2(3) which begins anew with a fresh promise of indemnity the driver is to be indemnified 'in like manner', and on this occasion the policyholder is plainly 'any person'.

Per Lord Wright: By section 2(3) the insurers undertake in favour of the driver a separate insurance against third-party liability so that he becomes the assured whilst the policyholder becomes *pro hac vice* the third party. There is no warrant for extending the meaning of 'any person' in section 2(1) to 'any person other than the policyholder' when the words are brought over into section 2(3).

Per Lord Porter: 'Third-party' is merely a useful description of a particular type of insurance and does not mean that 'any claim by any person' must be confined to a third person who is not a party to the contract. In a policy such as this there is not one contract of insurance only; there is one with the policyholder and one also with each person driving on her order and with her permission. For the purposes of a claim made by her against him, he is the assured, the company are the insurers and she is the third party.

(V)   GOODS IN TRUST

[2.50]   Engel v Lancashire and General Assurance Co Ltd
(1925) 41 TLR 408, 69 Sol Jo 447, 30 Com Cas 202, 21 Ll L Rep 327

The applicants insured the claimant, who was a furrier, against burglary. The policy covered not only goods belonging to the claimant, but goods which were on his premises and were in his possession on trust or on commission and for which he was 'responsible'. A burglary took place, and the claimant lost both goods of his own and goods which were in his custody as a bailee. The laimant had not been guilty of any negligence as a bailer, and so was not liable to the owners of the bailed goods for their loss.

HELD: 'Responsibility' in such a connection meant legal liability only, and therefore, the claimant could not recover on the policy in respect of the bailed goods.

[2.51]   John Rigby (Haulage) Ltd v Reliance Marine Insurance Co Ltd
[1956] 2 QB 468, [1956] 3 All ER 1, [1956] 3 WLR 407, 100 Sol Jo 528, [1956] 2 Lloyd's Rep 10, CA

The plaintiff, a road transport contractor, conducted business through subcontractors. It agreed with a customer to carry goods lying at a Liverpool dock to Birmingham. A man driving a lorry called on the plaintiff and stated he was employed by and the lorry belonged to sub-contractors on the plaintiff's list. He was given a collection order for the goods. He was not a servant of the sub-contractors and the lorry did not belong to them. Neither he nor the goods were ever heard of again. The plaintiff's insurance policy covered 'goods belonging to the assured or held by the assured in trust for which the assured are themselves responsible'.

HELD: The words 'in trust' were not used in a policy in a strict technical sense, and should be construed according to their ordinary meaning. The collection order was as between the plaintiff and the man wholly invalid, but as between the plaintiff and the owner of the goods it was an offer to undertake the carriage of its goods if it would deliver them to the person holding the collection order. The plaintiff was entrusted with the goods, and liable for their loss, and was entitled to indemnity under their policy.

[2.52]   Hepburn v A Tomlinson (Hauliers) Ltd

[1966] AC 451, [1966] All ER 418, [1966] 2 WLR 453, 110 Sol Jo 86, [1966] 1 Lloyd's Rep 309, HL

The plaintiff was a road haulier who regularly carried cigarettes for the Imperial Tobacco Co. The goods carried were insured by the plaintiff under a policy binding the underwriters 'to pay or make good to the assured … or to indemnify them against … all risks of loss or damage however arising'. The goods covered included 'Tobacco … the property of the Imperial Tobacco Co'. The goods were stolen whilst in the plaintiff's lorry, though in circumstances which did not make the plaintiff liable to the owner for the loss. The plaintiff claimed against the underwriters under the policy for the value of the goods lost. The underwriters refused to pay on the grounds that the policy was a contract of indemnity and the plaintiff had suffered no loss.

HELD: The plaintiff was entitled to succeed. A bailee has an insurable interest beyond his own personal loss if the goods are destroyed. This has never been regarded as in any way inconsistent with the overriding principle that insurance of goods is a contract of indemnity. The question is whether the bailee has insured his whole insurable interest – a goods policy – or whether he has only insured against personal loss –a personal liability policy. The policy wording in this case was appropriate to a goods policy and the underwriters must pay the full value of the goods to the plaintiff, who must account to the owner for the money so recovered. The intention of the assured at the time of entering into the policy is irrelevant.

Per Lord Reid: The principle preventing *jus quaesitum tertio* has been firmly established for at least half a century, but I do not think we are bound to be astute to extend it on a logical basis so as to cut down an exception, if it be an exception, which has stood unchallenged since the decision of *Waters'* case more than a century ago.

[2.53]   Ramco (UK) Ltd v International Insurance Co of Hanover

[2004] EWCA Civ 675

[2004] 2 All ER (Comm) 866, [2004] 2 Lloyd's Rep 595, [2004] 1 CIC 1013, [2004] Lloyd's Rep IR 606, (2004) 148 SJLB 695

R took out insurance with the defendant, the policy extending cover to goods 'held by the insured in trust for which they are responsible". In a fire at R's premises goods owned by a third party but bailed to R were damaged. R sought to argue that the words 'for which they are responsible' covered the damaged goods. The insurer contended that this argument represented an unnecessary departure from the principle established in *North British and Mercantile Insurance Co v Moffat* (1871).

HELD: The Court of Appeal accepted the insurer's argument, finding that although the true meaning of the words in question was in some doubt it would not be proper to depart from an interpretation which had stood as accepted for over a century.

Non-compliance with condition

[2.54]   Walker v Pennine Insurance Co Ltd

[1979] 2 Lloyd's Rep 139, Sheen J; affd [1980] 2 Lloyd's Rep 156, CA

On 5 August 1970 Miss W, a passenger in the plaintiff's car, was seriously injured in an accident. The plaintiff was insured under a policy issued by the defendant indemnifying him against liability at law for damages in respect of bodily injury to any person. The policy contained a condition. 'If the company shall disclaim liability to the insured for any claim hereunder and if within 12 calendar months from the date of such disclaimer legal proceedings have not been instituted ... in respect thereof by the insured ... then the claim shall for all purposes be deemed to have been abandoned ...'. In November 1970 Miss W's solicitors wrote to the plaintiff claiming damages for her but he did not reply nor tell the defendant. The solicitors then wrote notifying the claim to the defendant who on making investigations decided not to indemnify the plaintiff because, it maintained, he was in breach of a policy condition as to the roadworthiness of the car at the time of the accident. It notified him through the brokers on 3 February 1971 that it would not meet the claim. On 17 February 1971 the plaintiff's solicitors wrote to the defendant denying the alleged breach of condition and saying the plaintiff expected to be indemnified. The defendant replied on 22 March 1971 maintaining its refusal. It nominated solicitors to accept service of proceedings against itself but the plaintiff took no further step to enforce indemnity for nearly four years. Meanwhile Miss W took proceedings against the plaintiff who did nothing about them until she had obtained judgment in default of appearance and in 1975 was about to have damages assessed. In July 1975 the plaintiff's solicitors wrote to the defendant seeking to revive the claim for indemnity. The defendant denied liability on the ground that he had not instituted proceedings against it within one year of its refusal to indemnify.

HELD: (1) The defendant's letter of 22 March 1971 quite clearly disclaimed liability under the policy and no proceedings had been started against it within a year thereafter. It was not a breach of the contract. The refusal to indemnify was on the terms of the contract.

(2)   It was not necessary that the amount of the claim should be known before it constituted a claim under the policy. The defendant was not liable. An appeal was dismissed. 'I would be content in this case wholly to adopt the judgment of the Learned Judge upon which ... I could not hope to improve' (per Roskill LJ).

(VI)   FALSE REPRESENTATION

[2.55]   Brown, Jenkinson & Co Ltd v Percy Dalton (London) Ltd
[1957] 2 QB 621, [1957] 2 All ER 844, [1957] 3 WLR 403, 101 Sol Jo 610, [1957] 2 Lloyd's Rep 1, CA

The ship owners, at the request of owners of goods shipped on their vessel and on a promise by owners to indemnify, issued bills of lading stating the goods were shipped in apparently good order and condition. Both parties knew that statement was false. The ship owners had to pay a loss to consignees and sued the owners for indemnity.

HELD, by Morris and Pearce LJJ, Lord Evershed MR dissenting: Although ship owners did not desire or intend that anyone should be defrauded, they had made a representation of fact which they knew to be false with intent that it should be acted on, and had committed the tort of deceit, and the indemnity was unenforceable.

(VII)   ADMISSION IN BREACH OF POLICY CONDITION

[2.56]   Terry v Trafalgar Insurance Co

[1970] I Lloyd's Rep 524, Mayor's and City of London Court

The defendant issued to the plaintiff a policy of motor insurance containing the condition 'No liability shall be admitted nor any offer, promise or payment made to third parties without the company's written consent'. After a collision between his car and another he wrote to the other driver later on the same day. 'As damage to your vehicle was not severe I will pay for the making good. Technically the blame for the accident falls on me …'. Afterwards, the third party's damage proving more severe than he had thought, the plaintiff claimed indemnity from the defendant, who refused cover on the ground that there had been a breach of the condition.

HELD: The letter was an admission of liability; judgment for the defendant.

(VIII)   WRITTEN WORDS IN PRINTED DOCUMENT

[2.57]   *Note*—Where an instrument is in a printed form with written additions or alterations, the written words (subject always to be governed in point of construction by the language and terms with which they are accompanied) are entitled, in case of reasonable doubt as to the meaning of the whole, to have a greater effect attributed to them than the printed words: *Halsbury's Laws of England* (2nd edn) vol 10, p 279. Cited in *Addis v Burrows* [1948] 1 KB 444, [1948] 1 All ER 177, [1948] LJR 1033, 64 TLR 169, 92 Sol Jo 124, CA.

(F)   WORDS AND PHRASES COMMONLY FOUND IN POLICIES

Age of insured

[2.58]   Lloyds Bank Ltd v Eagle Star Insurance Co Ltd

[1951] I All ER 914, [1951] I TLR 803, [1951] I Lloyd's Rep 385   Jones J

A proviso in a policy allowed a company to avoid liability if 'under the age of 16 years or over the age of 65 years'.

HELD: The proviso means a person who has reached his 65th birthday and applies to anyone who has lived beyond the attainment of the 65th birthday.

Meaning of 'garage'

[2.59]   Barnett and Block v National Parcels Insurance Co

[1942] I All ER 221, 166 LT 147, 58 TLR 144, 86 Sol Jo 140, Atkinson J; affd [1942] I All ER 55n, 58 TLR 270, 86 Sol Jo 233, 73 Ll L Rep 17, CA

The policy insured against theft from van 'whilst left in a garage'. It was in a yard at the back of a private hotel; there were two gates to the yard, both fastened by bolts on the inner side; it was completely enclosed, partly by buildings and partly by a wall over 12ft high, but there was no roof.

HELD: Applying the test of plaintiff's counsel 'a garage is a place where one can get reasonable protection and shelter for a car' the yard was not a garage. 'Garage' means a building with a roof and is not applicable to an unroofed yard.

Affirmed in Court of Appeal.

Per Goddard LJ (in the Court of Appeal): It is a pure question of fact. If the arbitrator had found the other way, I do not think we should have interfered with his finding.

Civil commotion – riot

[2.60]   **Levy v Assicurazioni Generali**
[1940] AC 791, [1940] 3 All ER 427, 56 TLR 851, 84 Sol Jo 633, 67 Ll L Rep 174, PC

The court approved the definition of 'Civil commotion' in *Welford & Otter v Barry's Fire Insurance* – as follows:

This phrase is used to indicate a state between a riot and civil war. It has been defined to mean an insurrection of the people for general purposes, though not amounting to rebellion; but it is probably not capable of any very precise definition. The element of turbulence or tumult is essential; an organised conspiracy to commit criminal acts, where there is no tumult or disturbance until after the acts, does not amount to civil commotion. It is not, however, necessary to show the existence of any outside organisation at whose instigation the acts were done.

Influence of intoxicating liquor

[2.61]   **Louden v British Merchants Insurance Co Ltd**
[1961] 1 All ER 705, [1961] 1 WLR 798, 105 Sol Jo 209, [1961] 1 Lloyd's Rep 154   Lawton J

A private motor car policy issued by the defendant provided that it would pay compensation for injury or death caused to the policyholder whilst travelling in a motor car not belonging to him, subject to the provisos that the defendant should not be liable for injury sustained by him 'whilst under the influence of drugs or intoxicating liquor'. The plaintiff's husband, the holder of the policy, was killed whilst travelling in a car owned and driven by someone else. The alcohol content of his blood was found to be such as would cause some degree of uncoordination of movement and a tendency to stagger.

HELD: (1) Following the test in *Mair v Railway Passengers Assurance Co Ltd* (1877) 37 LT 356 the words 'under the influence of intoxicating liquor' meant such influence as would disturb 'the quiet, calm, intelligent exercise of his faculties' and, on the facts, the defendant had proved such influence.
   (2)   The word 'whilst' had a temporal, not a causative, meaning. The exemption clause did not call for any causal connection between the bodily injury sustained and the influence of intoxicating liquor. The defendant was not liable under the policy.

[2.62]   **Kennedy v Smith**
1976 SLT 110

After drinking a pint and a half of lager with friends the defendant gave them a lift in his car. On a straight section of a dual carriageway road the car crossed the central intersection and collided with a sign. The two passengers were killed. The defendant's motor policy contained a condition exempting the insurer from liability for any claim arising when the insured was driving and was under the influence of intoxicating liquor. The defendant had signed a declaration when proposing for insurance that he was a total abstainer from birth and would notify the insurers if this ceased to apply.

HELD, ON APPEAL: (1) The phrase 'under the influence of intoxicating liquor' meant under such influence as to disturb the balance of the mind; on the evidence this was not the case here.

    (2)   The declaration of abstinence was not an undertaking by the defendant as to future conduct and the insurer was not excepted from liability by a breach of the declaration.

[2.63]   **Ruiz Bernáldez, Criminal proceedings against**

Case C-129/94: [1996] All ER (EC) 741, ECJ (Fifth Chamber)
28 March 1996

Bernaldez caused a road accident when driving whilst intoxicated in Spain. He sought to be indemnified by his insurers but the Spanish courts held that the insurer was not liable due to a 1986 law that exempted liability insurers in circumstances where the driver is intoxicated. The European Court of Justice held that the Spanish law was incompatible with EC law and that the First Directive (84/5/EEC) precluded an insurer from being able to rely on statutory provision or contractual clauses to refuse to compensate third party victims of an accident caused by an insured vehicle.

'Loss or damage' unauthorised driver

[2.64]   **Greenleaf Associated Ltd v Monksfield**
[1972] RTR 451, [1972] 2 Lloyd's Rep 79

A policy issued by the defendant underwriter to the plaintiff indemnified against 'loss of or damage to the insured car'. A general exception excluded liability in respect of 'any accident, injury, loss, damage or liability … caused sustained or incurred while (the car) is being driven by any person' not specified in the statutory certificate 'which is deemed to be incorporated herein'. The only persons specified in the certificate were Mr and Mrs B. The car was damaged when being driven by a mechanic who had taken it on a joy ride without the insured's consent.

HELD: The plaintiff was not entitled to indemnity for the damage to the car. It had been argued that if the car was being driven without the insured's consent the exception did not apply because the words 'with the consent of the insured' ought to be read into it; but there was no reason for inserting in the policy words that were not there. There was no ambiguity in regard to 'loss' while the vehicle was being driven by an unauthorised person even though the policy covered theft, since there could be no 'loss' by theft in the way of damage to the vehicle because the theft occurred at the moment of taking: 'loss' meant physical not financial loss.

LORRY – INCLUDES REMOVED ENGINE

[2.65] **Seaton v London General Insurance Co Ltd**

(1932) 48 TLR 574, 76 Sol Jo 527, 43 Ll L Rep 398   du Parcq J

The assured removed the engine of his motor lorry to his carpenter's shop 150 yards away for repair, and while there it was destroyed by fire. The proposal form stated the lorry would be garaged on the assured's own premises.

HELD: Insurer was liable. The engine and the rest of the lorry together were still the lorry insured.

Motor car

[2.66] **Laurence v Davies**

[1972] 2 Lloyd's Rep 231   Dunn J

The defendant was insured for use of his motor car by a policy which extended cover to him additionally against third-party claims arising from accidents caused by or in connection with 'the driving by the insured of any motor car ... not belonging to him ...'. He was driving a Ford Transit van not belonging to him when there was an accident in which the plaintiff was injured. The defendant's insurer refused to indemnify him on the ground that the van was not a 'motor car'. The defendant relied on the definition in the Road Traffic Act 1960, s 253(2) (now s 185(1) of the 1988 Act): 'motor car' means a mechanically propelled vehicle, not being a motor cycle or invalid carriage, which is constructed itself to carry a load or passengers and the weight of which unladen ... does not exceed three tons'.

HELD: The van was a motor car. The words had to be considered in the context of motor insurance. If motor insurers wished to put some meaning on words like 'motor car' other than those contained in the Road Traffic Act they should make it abundantly clear in the policy; if they failed to do so the words would be deemed to have the statutory meanings.

Personal luggage

[2.67] **Buckland v R**

[1933] I KB 329, 49 TLR 39, 76 Sol Jo 850, McCardie J; affd [1933] I KB 767, 102 LJKB 404, 148 LT 557, 49 TLR 244, CA

There is no distinction between 'ordinary luggage' and 'passenger luggage' and 'personal luggage'.

The court called attention to various decisions which are difficult to reconcile as follows:

HELD, to be personal luggage: All articles of apparel, whether for use or ornament, the gun case or fishing apparatus of the sportsman, the easel of the artist on a sketching tour, the books of the student, officer's revolver and binoculars.

HELD, not to be personal luggage: Title deeds carried by a solicitor; trunk containing six pairs of sheets, six pairs of blankets, and six quilts; violin-cello carried for professional purposes; the pencil sketches of an artist; hamper containing professional costumes and property of a comedian; sewing machine; invalid chair, bicycle.

The definition adopted by the court was 'articles intended for the traveller's personal use and convenience as distinct from merchandise carried for purposes of business'.

2.   LIMITS OF COVER

(A)   DEFINITION OF DRIVER

Servant driving

[2.68]   Sutch v Burns
[1943] 2 All ER 441, 60 TLR 1, 87 Sol Jo 406, 76 Ll L Rep 203   Atkinson J

A lorry driver delivered goods to a customer. The customer asked the driver to carry some goods of the customer across the road to another branch of the customer's works. The driver agreed. The customer's goods were loaded on to the lorry, and the customer's workmen got on the lorry. The driver turned to the left where the road was wide enough to turn. In turning, some goods were dislodged and knocked one of the workmen off the lorry, and he was killed. The widow brought proceedings against the lorry owner and the driver and obtained judgment against the driver but not the owner. The widow sued the insurer under s 10 of the Road Traffic Act 1934 (now the Road Traffic Act 1988, ss 151 and 152).

The insurer conceded that the policy was to be treated as one which complied with s 35(1) of the 1930 Act. It was admitted that deceased was a passenger by reason of or in pursuance of a contract of service with the customer. The insurer contended that the legal obligation of the section only arose where there was liability of the policyholder, and that the driver was only indemnified where his employer was liable. The third party contended that the policy must cover any permitted driver and that there was no limitation on the use of the vehicle.

HELD: The section did not limit use by a permitted driver to the authority given by the employer. The policy must insure against any liability incurred by the driver to third parties. A person giving permission must insure against all claims of third parties arising out of the user on a road. A policy which purported to insure the employer or the driver to a less extent did not comply with the Act.

Note—In the Court of Appeal the judgment was set aside on the ground that a decision had been sought on a hypothetical policy and a court had no jurisdiction to do this.

The Divisional Court disagreed with the decision of Atkinson J in the following case (at para [2.69].

[2.69]   John T Ellis Ltd v Hinds
[1947] KB 475, [1947] 1 All ER 337, [1947] LJR 488, 176 LT 424, 63 TLR 181, 91 Sol Jo 68, 45 LGR 118, 80 Ll L Rep 231, Div Ct

A company owned a motor vehicle which was driven by a lad of 17 years of age, who was not himself entitled to be treated as insured under the policy. The facts are set out at para [2.91].

HELD: The company was not in breach of the legislation.

If the car is being driven by a servant on the employer's business so that the owner is liable to a third person, and the liability of the owner is covered by insurance, there is in force in relation to the use of the vehicle, whether by the owner or driver, a policy of insurance.

The author does not agree with the decision of *Sutch v Burns* (at para [2.68]). An owner is bound to take out a policy which covers the use of the vehicle by his servant but only whilst on his business. If a servant is driving without authority, his master has not caused or permitted the use of the vehicle. The owner of a car is not bound to cover the liability of his chauffeur on a 'joy ride', or in circumstances that absolve the master from liability. There was no obligation on the facts in *Sutch v Burns* for the employer of the driver to have a policy which would cover the driver when he was not driving on the employer's business.

Note—In *Sutch v Burns* in the Court of Appeal the case was argued on its merits, and the court took time to consider its verdict. Meanwhile the case of *Sun Life Assurance of Canada v Jervis* [1944] AC 111 had been decided in the House of Lords, and in consequence of that decision, it became unnecessary to deal with the arguments.

It was pointed out in argument that if, eg an owner of a motor car insured for pleasure purposes but not for carriage of goods lent his car to a friend for pleasure use, and the friend used it for the carriage of goods, this could not mean that insurers were liable under the policy, nor that the owner was liable on the principle of *Monk v Warbey* (at para [1.24]).

The point has now been settled by *John T Ellis Ltd v Hinds*.

[2.70]   Lees v Motor Insurers' Bureau

[1952] 2 All ER 511, [1952] WN 409, [1952] 2 TLR 356, 96 Sol Jo 548, [1952] Lloyd's Rep 210   Lord Goddard CJ

The owner of a motor lorry had a policy which indemnified him but did not indemnify the driver personally. The policy excluded liability where the accident to the third party arose out of and in the course of his employment by the owner. On 5 May 1948, a servant of the owner was killed by the negligence of the driver in an accident which arose out of and in the course of the employment of the deceased by the owner. The widow sued the driver and obtained a judgment by default against him. She then sued the Motor Insurers' Bureau contending that the judgment was in respect of a liability required to be covered by s 35(1) and s 36(1)(b) of the Road Traffic Act 1930 (now s 143 of the 1988 Act), being a liability incurred by the driver caused by the use by the driver of a vehicle on a road: that the 1930 Act required the policy to cover the driver personally and that the Bureau had incurred a liability to satisfy the judgment under the terms of the agreement.

HELD: On a special case stated by an arbitrator, the contention that the policy was required to insure the driver personally is exactly what was held in *Sutch v* (at para [2.68]) which was overruled in *John T Ellis Ltd v Hinds* (at para [2.69]). Section 35(1) of the Road Traffic Act 1930 required a person to insure because he is the owner, the person who uses or permits the use. What has to be covered is the use of the vehicle not the person using the vehicle. *John T Ellis Ltd v Hinds* and *Marsh v Moores* (at paras [2.69] and [2.71]). In *Richards v Cox* [1943] 1 KB 139, [1942] 2 All ER 624, 112 LJKB 135, 168 LT 313, 59 TLR 123, 87 Sol Jo 92, CA following *Digby v General Accident Fire and Life Assurance Corpn* (at para [2.49]) there were in effect two policies in one document, a policy insuring the owner and a policy insuring the driver. There was no such term in this policy. The policy complied with the Road Traffic Act 1934 and covered all the persons whom the Act required to be covered. It excluded employees of the insured in cases arising out of and in the course of the employment, and underwriters are entitled to exclude that liability under the Act. A policy had been taken out by the owner to cover the use of the vehicle and therefore the vehicle was an insured vehicle and the liability which was incurred was not one which was required to be covered by insurance. The respondent was under no liability to the claimant.

Note—The accident occurred before the abolition of common employment on 5 July 1948. After that date a third party would presumably sue the employers without reference to a motor policy or to the Bureau.

Driver retaining control when teaching

[2.71] Marsh v Moores
[1949] 2 KB 208, [1949] 2 All ER 27, [1949] LJR 1313, 113 JP 346, 65 TLR 318, 93 Sol Jo 450, 47 LGR 418, Div Ct

A policy was issued to a limited company covered the company against third-party risks for social, domestic and business purposes. There was an exception from liability if the car with the company's consent was being driven by a person who to the knowledge of the company was a disqualified person or had never been licensed. A servant of the company who was the son of the managing director on the latter's instructions was making a journey in the car. As a servant of the company he was entrusted by the company with the control, driving and management of the vehicle. He had as passenger his cousin, a girl of 17 who to the son's knowledge had not and never had had a licence. The son allowed the cousin to take over the wheel, whilst he himself retained control of the hand-brake.

HELD: There was an effective policy. The test whether the car was being used uninsured was not whether the son or cousin was insured in respect of his or her personal liability, but whether the company would have been liable to a third party. The son still remained the driver; in allowing his cousin to take the wheel he was still acting within the scope of his employment although in an unauthorised and improper way, and the company would have been liable to a third party. The only person driving with the general consent of the company was the son, who held a licence; the cousin was not driving with the company's consent or knowledge. The policy complied with the requirements of s 35(1) of the Road Traffic Act 1930 (s 143 of the 1988 Act), which does not require a policy covering the driver's personal liability. *John T Ellis Ltd v Hinds* (at para [2.69]) followed.

[2.72] Langman v Valentine
[1952] 2 All ER 803, 116 JP 576, [1952] WN 475, [1952] 2 TLR 731, 96 Sol Jo 712, 50 LGR 685, Div Ct

The owner of a motor car had a policy which covered him and also any person driving with his permission who had or had held and was not disqualified from holding a licence. The owner was teaching a passenger to drive on a road. The passenger had not and had never had a licence. The passenger was sitting in the driver's seat and was steering the car under the guidance of the owner and using the accelerator and the footbrake. The owner was in the passenger's seat with his left hand on the steering wheel and his right hand on the handbrake. He was able to steer the car, stop it and start it, the ignition switch being within his reach and the hand-brake under his control. The passenger was summoned for using a motor car uninsured and for driving without a licence. The owner was summonsed for permitting the former and abetting the latter. The justices held the owner was the driver and dismissed the summonses.

HELD, ON APPEAL, per Lord Goddard CJ and Finnemore J: (1) The passenger was a driver and should have been convicted for driving without a licence.

(2)   There was no evidence that the owner knew the passenger did not have a licence.

(3)   Though not 'the driver', the owner was 'a driver' and an injured person could have brought an action against him and he would have been liable as a driver and there was therefore an effective policy. There could be two drivers at the same time.

Per McNair J dissenting: The passenger was a user of the car and there was no effective policy in relation to her.

John T Ellis Ltd v Hinds (at para [2.69]) and *Marsh v Moores* (at para [2.71]) followed.

Note—The case of *Rubie v Faulkner* [1940] 1 KB 571, [1940] 1 All ER 285, 109 LJKB 241, 163 LT 212, 104JP 161, 56 TLR 303, 84 Sol Jo 257 is not mentioned in the reports.

[2.73]   Evans v Walkden

[1956] 3 All ER 64, [1956] 1 WLR 1019, 120 JP 495, 100 Sol Jo 587, 54 LGR 467, Div Ct

A son who was 15 years old and therefore unlicensed was in the driving seat and his father was seated with him. The car was being driven in bottom gear at not more than 4 or 5mph for a total distance of about 200 yards. The father was in a position to control the driving of the son and was doing so and could have stopped the car immediately. The steering wheel was within the father's reach and also the brake and clutch pedals, the ignition key and the gear handle on the steering wheel. The handbrake was on the right-hand side of the driver and was not accessible to the father. The father's policy excluded liability whilst driven by an unlicensed driver. The justices found that the father was at the same time a driver of the car and dismissed summonses against the son and father for driving without insurance and for permitting respectively.

HELD: There was no evidence to support the finding that the father was in control of the car or that he was a driver of the car. The insurance policy permitted use for tuition provided – 'There shall be present in the insured car as a tutor a person under whose supervision the holder of a provisional licence would be entitled to drive.' This did not affect the exclusion of liability if driven by an unlicensed driver. *Langman v Valentine* [1952] 2 All ER 803, 116 JP 576, [1952] WN 475, [1952] 2 TLR 731, 96 Sol Jo 712, 50 LGR 685 (at para [2.72]) distinguished. Case remitted to justices to convict.

[2.74]   Tyler v Whatmore

[1976] RTR 83, [1976] Crim LR 315, Div Ct

The defendant was charged with 'actually driving a motor vehicle' when in such a position that she could not have proper control. She was sitting beside a man who was in the driving seat operating the pedals. She had both hands on the steering wheel; he made no attempt to steer and his hands were not on the wheel.

HELD: Following *Langman v Valentine* (at para [2.72]) she was 'driving'. It was a question of fact. Both were driving, since he was able to control the propulsion and she was controlling the steering.

Note—See also *R v Wilkins* (at para [2.95]).

Paid driver

[2.75]   Bryan v Forrow

[1950] 1 All ER 294, 114 JP 158, 48 LGR 347, sub nom *Forrow v Bryan* [1950] WN 91, 94 Sol Jo 194, Div Ct

The owner of a motor lorry was insured by a cover note, under which the person or persons allowed to drive were:
  (1)   the above-named proposer only;
  (2)   the above-named proposer or his paid driver;
  (3)   the above-named proposer or his paid employee or any friend or relative of the proposer driving with his unremunerated permission provided such person holds a licence to drive such motor vehicle or had held and is not disqualified by order of a court of law from holding or obtaining such licence.

  The lorry owner contracted with a customer to transport goods of the customer. The lorry owner was ill and arranged for the lorry to be driven by a driver in the regular employ of the customer.
  The owner was prosecuted for permitting the use of the lorry without an effective policy of insurance. It was contended that the customer's driver was not the paid driver of the owner.

HELD: The contrast was between the professional and the non-professional driver – the paid driver and the paid employee. The words 'paid driver' are capable of two constructions:
  (1)   the driver paid by the owner;
  (2)   a driver driving for the owner who is a paid driver. The latter construction is right and the cover note was effective to cover third-party risks and insurers would be liable under it.

Disqualified driver

[2.76]   Saycell v Bool

[1948] 2 All ER 83, 112 JP 341, 64 TLR 421, 92 Sol Jo 311, 46 LGR 447, Div Ct

The respondent was the owner of a motor van and was disqualified from holding a licence. The van was standing in a road outside his premises which was on an incline. His garage was 100 yards lower down. He pushed the van down the incline and when in motion, got into the driving seat and steered it towards the garage. There was no petrol in the tank and the engine was not running.

HELD: The respondent was 'driving' the van, and being disqualified there was no third party insurance in force.

Note—And see *Floyd v Bush* [1953] 1 All ER 265, [1953] 1 WLR 242, 117 JP 88, 97 Sol Jo 80, 51 LGR 162, [1953] 1 Lloyd's Rep 64. See also *R v MacDonagh* (at para [2.96]) and *Blayney v Knight* (at para [2.101]).

Driver not in employ

[2.77]   Lyons v May
[1948] 2 All ER 1062, 113 JP 42, [1948] WN 483, 65 TLR 51, 93 Sol Jo 59, Div Ct

A garage proprietor who had repaired a motor lorry drove it at the owner's request to the owner's premises. The owner's policy covered only the owner or 'any duly authorised person in his employ'. The policy of the garage proprietor did not cover the risk. The justices held the garage proprietor was temporarily in the owner's employ for the purpose of delivering the lorry.

HELD: (1) The garage proprietor was not in the owner's employment. (*Burton v Road Transport and General Insurance Co Ltd* (at para [2.81]) is not mentioned in the report.)
  (2)   The owner had given 'permission'. He had not asked the garage proprietor if he had an effective policy.

[2.78]   Ballance v Brown
[1955] Crim LR 384, [1955] CLY 2451, Div Ct

A policy provided that the company would 'treat as though he were the insured any person in the insured's employ who is driving such a vehicle on the insured's order or with his permission for the purpose of the business of the insured'. The insured, who from time to time bought scrap from the defendant, instructed him to take the insured's car to the defendant's house and to pick him up the next morning to go on a business trip; he also told him to do any business he could.

HELD: The car was insured while being driven by the defendant. *Lyons v May* (at para [2.77]) distinguished.

[2.79]   Tapsell v Maslen
(1966) 110 Sol Jo 853, [1967] Crim LR 53, Div Ct

The respondent allowed Williams to use his motor scooter when there was no policy of insurance in force. When he lent the scooter to Williams he honestly believed Williams had an insurance certificate. The justices dismissed a charge of permitting the use of the scooter when there was no policy in force.

HELD, ON APPEAL: The justices must convict. Section 201 of the Road Traffic Act 1960 (s 143 of the 1988 Act) was expressed in terms whereby all the prosecution had to do was to show first that permission to use had been given and next that there was no insurance cover. *Lyons v May* (at para [2.77]) and *Morris v Williams* (at para [2.166]) were binding authorities for this.

Named driver

[2.80]   Goodwin v Leckey
[1946] NI 40, (1946) LR Dig 118   MacDermott J

A taxi was insured under a policy which indemnified only when driven by the insured or two named drivers. A driver not named was driving with the permission of and in the course of the employment of the insured.

HELD: The policy was inoperative. A policy complies with the Northern Ireland Act although it does not cover any driver with permission. *Sutch v Burns* (at para [2.68]) not followed.

Driver in 'insured's employ'

[2.81] Burton v Road Transport and General Insurance Co Ltd

(1939) 63 Ll L Rep 253   Branson J

Cross, a motor dealer, was insured under a Motor Traders' policy which covered, as if he were the insured, 'any person in the insured's employ'. Cross had a car to sell; in pursuance of a pre-existing arrangement between them, Westwood told Cross of a possible purchaser, Goulding. Cross then commissioned Westwood to take Goulding on a demonstration run. Westwood would be, and was, paid £1 by Cross for doing the demonstration for him, whether or not he succeeded in selling the car. During the run there was a collision in which the plaintiff, a motorcyclist, was injured. Cross's insurer refused to pay damages awarded against Westwood on the ground that he was not in Cross's employment.

HELD: It was not necessary in order to give a business effect to the policy, to restrict the meaning of 'employment' to employment under a contract of service. Cross was using Westwood to try to sell the car to someone introduced by him: in so doing he was 'employing' him. The insurer was liable under s 10 of the Road Traffic Act 1934 (now the 1988 Act, ss 151 and 152).

(B)   DEFINITION OF DRIVING

Driving 'with consent'

[2.82] Paget v Poland

(1947) 80 Ll L Rep 283   Lewis J

The daughter of the owner of a car working for the Ministry of Information had to drive a van of the Ministry from St Albans to Cambridge and obtained the loan of her mother's car to enable her to return. This required that a driver should take the car to Cambridge. The daughter suggested a friend Miss P, but the mother refused to allow her car to be driven by Miss P, and the mother suggested Miss M, a friend of the mother. Miss M started as driver and on the way changed places with Miss P. An accident occurred while Miss P was driving and Miss M was injured.

Miss M recovered judgment against the daughter and Miss P. Presumably the daughter was liable because Miss P was treated as her agent.

Section 1 of the policy on the mother's car read: The underwriters will indemnify under this section any licensed driver personally driving with the insured's consent any motor vehicle hereby insured.

HELD: In an action against the underwriters, Miss P was not personally driving with the consent of the insured, and underwriters were not liable on the policy.

[2.83]   **Herbert v Railway Passengers Assurance Co**

[1938] 1 All ER 650, 158 LT 417, 60 Ll L Rep 143   Porter J

The insured, with a friend in the sidecar, fell ill, and allowed the friend to drive.

HELD: The insurance company was not liable.

[2.84]   **Bankers and Traders Insurance Co Ltd v National Insurance Co Ltd**

[1985] 1 WLR 734, 129 Sol Jo 381, [1985] 2 Lloyd's Rep 195   PC

In 1969, two pedestrians were knocked down and injured on a road in Malaysia by a car owned by Mr Kwang, which was being driven with his consent by Mr Ko. Kwang was insured by Bankers and Traders Insurance Co Ltd under a policy which provided indemnity cover to any driver authorised by the owner, provided that the driver was not indemnified under another policy. Ko was insured by National Insurance Co Ltd under a policy which provided that he would be indemnified while driving a private car which did not belong to him. The question arose as to which insurance company was on risk under the Malaysian Road Traffic Ordinance of 1958, s 80.

HELD, ON APPEAL to the Privy Council: It was clear that Ko was the authorised driver and entitled to an indemnity under his own policy. Kwang's insurer was not on risk. It was not a case of double insurance. Ko's insurer was therefore responsible for indemnifying him against his liability to the pedestrians.

Note—See also *Singh v Rathour, Northern Star Insurance Co (Third Party)* (at para [2.109]).

Driving 'with permission'

[2.85]   **Kelly v Cornhill Insurance Co Ltd**

[1964] 1 All ER 321, [1964] 1 WLR 158, 108 Sol Jo 94, [1964] 1 Lloyd's Rep 1, HL (Sc)

On 11 April 1958 Michael Kelly proposed for insurance to the Cornhill Insurance Co Ltd in respect of his own car. In the proposal form he said the car would be driven by his son, Kevin Kelly, and that he himself had no licence to drive and did not intend having one. Insurance was granted on 26 April 1958 and was renewed for a further year on 26 April 1959. On 2 June 1959 Michael Kelly died. Neither his executrix nor anyone else told the insurers of his death until after 4 February 1960, on which date damage was caused to the car and other property in an accident whilst Kevin Kelly was driving. The latter claimed indemnity under the policy as a person 'driving the insured car ... with the permission of the insured'. It was admitted that whilst Michael Kelly was alive Kevin had permission from him to drive the car without limitation.

HELD: The question for decision was simply whether Kevin Kelly was driving on 4 February 1960 with the permission of his father who had died on 2 June 1959: did a permission to use the car which could at any time be revoked lapse on the death of the person giving it? It had been argued for the respondent that permission necessarily involved a continuing power of control but it could not be said that continuing opportunity or ability to control was necessary, because prolonged absence or illness might negative that. In the absence of any express provision in the policy, there was no reason to hold as a matter of law that a permission should automatically lapse on death of the permittor. The son was entitled to the benefit of the policy on 4 February 1960.

[2.86]   McMinn v McMinn and Aioi Insurance

(2006) unreported

The claimant was a passenger in a van driven by his brother, the first defendant, insured by the second defendant and owned by MEL Ltd. The policy provided cover for the vehicle when it was being driven by someone:
(1)   over the age of 25;
(2)   who held a driving licence;
(3)   who had been permitted by MEL to drive it.
    MEL permitted its employee, Baird, to drive the vehicle. He in turn permitted the first defendant, who was only 17, to drive the vehicle.

HELD: Baird knew that only he had permission to drive the vehicle and was not authorised to give permission to the first defendant to drive it. In the circumstances MEL Ltd was not liable to indemnify the first defendant.

[2.87]   General Accident Assurance Corpn v Shuttleworth

(1938) 60 Ll L Rep 301   Humphreys J

The condition in a policy that the assured shall not be disqualified or the company will not be liable is a limitation of the insurance cover and is outside the purview of the policy or certificate. The insured signed a proposal on 10 June 1936, and declared he had not been convicted of a motoring offence. On 5 August 1936, the assured was convicted of driving a motorcycle without an insurance certificate and disqualified for 12 months. On 11 August 1936, the assured applied to transfer the insurance to another car and signed a declaration that he had not been convicted of a motoring offence. On 5 September 1936, the company issued a cover note and insurance certificate for 14 days, instead of a certificate for 12 months as a means of obtaining payment of the additional premium of £4, in terms of the company's usual form of policy. On 16 September 1936, a third party was injured.

HELD: The risk was outside policy.
    Semble:
(1)   a motor car covers a motor cycle;
(2)   the false declaration invalidated the cover note.

[2.88]   Edwards v Griffiths

[1953] 2 All ER 874, [1953] 1 WLR 1199, 117 JP 514, 97 Sol Jo 595, 51 LGR 549, [1953] 2 Lloyd's Rep 269, Div Ct

The respondent had passed a driving test and obtained a driving licence for motorcycles and tractors in October 1951. In 1952 he was informed by the licensing authority that as he was under supervision under the Mental Deficiency Act 1938, he must not drive a motorcycle. The respondent's application for renewal of the driving licence was refused. His employer's certificate of insurance provided for use by any person driving with permission, provided such person held a licence or had held and was not disqualified from holding or obtaining a licence.

HELD: 'Disqualified' in the certificate meant disqualified by an order of the court and not prohibited from obtaining a licence by mental or physical disability.

[2.89]   Mumford v Hardy

[1956] 1 All ER 337, [1956] 1 WLR 163, 100 Sol Jo 132, 54 LGR 150, [1956] 1 Lloyd's Rep 173, Div Ct

A youth born on 7 June 1939 (i e under 16) obtained a provisional licence to drive a car on 13 April 1955, expiring on 12 July 1955, by falsely stating that he was born on 22 January 1938. His father permitted him to drive a car which was insured to indemnify any driver with consent holding a licence to drive such a car. The son was charged with driving uninsured on 23 April 1955, and 1 June 1955. The father was charged with permitting on 1 June 1955.

The insurers told the justices they would have considered themselves liable by reason of *Edwards v Griffiths* (at para [2.88]). The justices accordingly dismissed the informations.

By the Road Traffic Act 1930, s 9(2) a person under 17 years of age is prohibited from driving a car; by s 9(5) such a person shall be deemed disqualified for holding or obtaining such a licence; s 7(4) provides that a licence obtained by a disqualified person shall be of no effect.

HELD: An offence was proved on each of the three informations.

Note—Destination Table:

Road Traffic Act 1930	Road Traffic Act 1972	Road Traffic Act 1988
s 9(2)	s 4(1) repealed 1976	–
s 9(5)	s 96	s 101
s 7(4)	s 98(2)	s 103(2)

Unaccompanied provisional licence holder

[2.90]   Rendlesham v Dunne

[1964] 1 Lloyd's Rep 192, CC   Herbert J

Dunne, who held only a provisional licence to drive, was driving Griffin's car with his permission. He was unaccompanied and the car was without 'L' plates. Griffin's insurance policy was expressed to indemnify any person driving with his permission provided that 'such person holds a licence to drive' the car. An accident having occurred, the insurer refused to indemnify Dunne.

HELD: The insurer was bound to indemnify him.
  (1)   It was impossible to construe the policy so as to restrict the meaning of the word 'licence' to that of a full licence. The Road Traffic Act 1960 uses the word 'licence' to include both types of licence. It cannot be said that a man has not got a licence to drive a car on the road merely because he has failed to comply with a condition upon which he has been granted a licence.
  (2)   A condition of the policy requiring the insured to take all reasonable steps to safeguard the car from loss and damage was not broken by allowing Dunne to drive. That condition was concerned with the physical condition of the car and did not cover damage caused by negligent driving or driving by somebody in contravention of the terms of his licence.

Unqualified employee of limited company

[2.91]   John T Ellis Ltd v Hinds

[1947] KB 475, [1947] 1 All ER 337, [1947] LJR 488, 176 LT 424, 63 TLR 181, 91 Sol Jo 68, 45 LGR 118, 80 Ll L Rep 231, Div Ct

A company owned a motor vehicle that was driven by a lad under 17 years of age who did not hold and never had held a driving licence and by reason of his age was not qualified to obtain one. The company had no express knowledge of these facts. The driver told the company that he held a licence and that he had already driven for several firms including one that he named. A request to the driver to produce his licence and an investigation would have disclosed the facts and the company recklessly omitted to make these inquiries.

The policy was exempted from liability if a person driving with consent, did not to the knowledge of the insured or his representative who gave consent, hold a licence unless he had held and was not disqualified from obtaining one.

HELD: If a man deliberately shuts his eyes to the obvious, he had as much knowledge as if he were expressly told the facts to which he had closed his eyes, but it is quite another thing to say that because a man has means of knowledge of which he does not avail himself, therefore he has knowledge. If he does not know of something which it is his duty to know, and which, therefore, ought to have known, he cannot plead lack of knowledge, but knowledge and means of knowledge are not the same thing. This is an exception clause which is construed strictly. It would be for insurers to prove that the company knew the driver was unlicensed. It does not impose a duty to make inquiries. In the circumstances the policy was effective.

Note—Contrast this case with *Lester Bros (Coal Merchants) Ltd v Avon Insurance Co Ltd* (at para [2.92]).

[2.92]   Lester Bros (Coal Merchants) Ltd v Avon Insurance Co Ltd

(1942) 72 Ll L Rep 109   Atkinson J

The plaintiffs took out a commercial motor vehicle policy. An employee had an accident whilst driving one of the plaintiff's lorries. The employee had, to the plaintiff's knowledge, applied for a driving licence. The licence had not been received at the time of the accident. The arbitrator was not satisfied that the plaintiff knew that the licence hadn't been obtained but held that they could easily have ascertained this by enquiry of the driver. The policy excluded liability if the vehicle was:

'(b) being driven by the insured unless he (i) holds a licence to drive such vehicle or (ii) has held and is not disqualified from holding or obtaining such a licence;

(c) being driven with the general consent of the insured or his representative by any person who to the knowledge of the insured or such representative does not hold a licence to drive such a vehicle unless such a person has held and is not disqualified from holding or obtaining such a licence.'

The court held that 'being driven by the insured' in this context meant 'being driven by or on behalf of the insured'. The court also rejected the suggestion that the driver would be covered under (c) above unless the plaintiffs knew as a fact that their driver did not hold a licence. Atkinson J stated: 'The result of that from a commercial point of view would be rather startling – they have only to take good care not to make enquiry as to the driver of their lorries, and if an accident happens and it turns out the driver is not licensed, they can say: "I am very sorry, but it did not occur to me that a man would come to drive a lorry who had not got a licence and never had one; at any rate I did not know that he never had one".'

Repairer driving

[2.93]   Samuelson v National Insurance and Guarantee Corpn Ltd
[1984] 3 All ER 107, QBD

The motor policy issued by the defendant to the plaintiff gave indemnity against theft. The 'limitations as to use' were 'social, domestic and pleasure' only, though by general exception 1(a)(i) 'the exclusion of use for any purpose in connection with the Motor Trade' was not to prejudice the indemnity whilst the car was 'in the custody or control of a member of the Motor Trade' for repair. General exception 1(c) excluded indemnity when the car was 'being driven by or for the purpose of being driven' in charge of any person other than the authorised driver. By reference to the certificate of insurance the only authorised driver was 'the policyholder'. A repairer who had the car for some necessary work on it drove it to the manufacturers' agents for some spare parts. He needed to take the car to the agents to ensure that the parts did fit. He parked it nearby but whilst he was away for a few minutes getting the parts the car was stolen and was never recovered. The plaintiff claimed under the policy for the loss.

The judge held that he was not entitled to indemnity. Paragraph 1(a)(i) simply declared that the limitation of use was not breached by delivering it into the custody or control of a member of the motor trade for repair. The exception 1(c) related to driving and was not affected by this. At the time of the theft the car was, for the purpose of being driven, in the charge of a person other than the authorised driver.

HELD, ON APPEAL: The judge was right in saying that clause 1(c) was not cut down by 1(a). But on the facts of this case, namely, that the repairer needed to take the car to the agents to ensure that the new parts would fit, it was, at the moment it was stolen, in the repairer's charge for the purpose of repair and not for the purpose of driving, and the indemnity was restored by general exception 1(a)(i).

Appeal allowed.

Note—See also *Browning v Phoenix* (at para [2.107]).

Definition of driver/more than one driver

[2.94]   By s 192(1) of the Road Traffic Act 1988 it is possible for more than one person to be the 'driver' of a vehicle. If one of such drivers holds a licence to drive, the exceptions clause in the insurance policy providing that the insurers shall not be liable if the insured vehicle is driven by a person not holding a driving licence does not apply, then the vehicle remains insured under the policy.

[2.95]   R v Wilkins
(1951) 115 JP 443, [1951] CLY 9109, Berkshire Quarter Sessions

Section 121(1) of the Road Traffic Act 1930 provided:

'"Driver", where a separate person acts as steersman of a motor vehicle, includes that person as well as any other person engaged in the driving of the vehicle and the expression "drive" shall be construed accordingly.'

There may, therefore, be more than one driver of a vehicle. If one of such drivers holds a licence to drive, the exceptions clause in the insurance policy providing that the insurer shall not be liable if the insured vehicle is driven by a person not holding a driving licence, does not apply, and the vehicle remains insured under the policy.

The appellants, brother and sister, were on a public road on a tractor. The sister, who had no driving licence, was seated in the driving seat. The brother, who had a licence, was standing behind her. Both were charged and convicted of driving a vehicle which was uninsured by reason of the fact that it was being driven by a person who did not hold a driving licence.

HELD: There were two drivers, and since one held a licence, the exceptions clause did not apply and the vehicle was insured.

Note—The definition of 'driver' is now contained in s 192(1) of the Road Traffic Act 1988 but is similar to the definition in s 121(1) of the 1930 Act.

[2.96]   R v MacDonagh
[1974] QB 448, [1974] 2 All ER 257, [1974] 2 WLR 529, 118 Sol Jo 222, CA

A motorist pushing his car with his shoulder against the door pillar and both feet on the road, controlling movement by his hand on the steering wheel, is not 'driving' within the meaning of the Road Traffic Act 1972.

[2.97]   McQuaid v Anderton
[1980] 3 All ER 540, [1981] 1 WLR 154, 144 JP 456, 125 Sol Jo 101, [1980] RTR 371, Div Ct

A motor vehicle was being towed by another vehicle by means of a tow rope. The appellant was sitting in the driver's seat of the towed vehicle steering by means of the steering wheel and able to operate the brakes.

HELD: He was 'driving' the vehicle within the meaning of the Road Traffic Act 1972, s 99.

Note—Section 103(1) of the 1988 Act has replaced s 99 of the 1972 Act.

[2.98]   Caise v Wright, Fox v Wright
[1981] RTR 49, QBD

Caise was driving a car which was towing another car of which Fox was in the driver's seat able to slow, stop and steer it to a limited extent.

HELD, following *McQuaid v Anderton* (at para [2.97]): Fox was 'driving' the towed car.

[2.99]   Burgoyne v Phillips
(1983) 147 JP 375, [1983] RTR 49, [1983] Crim LR 265, QBD

The defendant was sitting at the wheel of his car after dropping a friend off. Assuming the ignition key was still in the ignition lock he released the handbrake and let the car roll forward preparatory to driving away. He then realised he had no keys. The steering was locked and the engine not running. He hastily applied the brakes but the car collided with a vehicle in front, having rolled forward about 30ft.

HELD: He was 'driving' the car. The essence of driving is the use of the driver's control to direct the movement of the car however produced. An important factor was that he had himself deliberately set the vehicle in motion.

[2.100]   Jones v Pratt

[1983] RTR 54, QBD

A front seat passenger, seeing a small animal run across the road, grabbed the steering wheel causing the car to go off the road and crash.

HELD: He was not 'driving' the car.

[2.101]   Blayney v Knight

(1975) 60 Cr App Rep 269, [1975] RTR 279, [1975] Crim LR 237, Div Ct

A taxi driver drove his car to a club to pick up a fare. He got out of the car leaving the engine running and the driver's door open; the automatic transmission lever was in 'drive' but the handbrake was on. He went to the door of the club to speak to his fare and, on turning round, saw the defendant sitting in the driver's seat talking to two men who had got into the rear seat. He went to the car and tried to pull the defendant out of the driver's seat. There was a struggle and the car moved forward along the road. The driver fell off on to the road and the rear wheel passed over his legs. The defendant was charged with various offences including careless driving and driving when not insured. The justices accepted the defendant's evidence that he had not intended to drive and that his foot must accidentally have pressed the accelerator.

HELD, ON APPEAL: He was not 'driving'. Following the test applied in *R v MacDonagh* (at para [2.96]) an activity was not 'driving' if it was not driving in any ordinary sense of the word. It was not a case where a person was consciously seeking the movement of the car in some way and it was thus not 'driving'.

(C)   USING A MOTOR VEHICLE

[2.102]   *Note*—There is nothing in the compulsory insurance sections of the Road Traffic Act 1988 to make an insurer liable when the vehicle is being used outside the limits of the policy. But the insurer may be 'the insurer concerned' for the purposes of the Motor Insurers' Bureau Agreements (see Chapter 3).

Sale of business to new company

[2.103]   Levinger v Licenses and General Insurance Co Ltd

(1936) 54 Ll L Rep 68   Eve J

The proposer insured her car to cover use in her business of milliner. Her business was taken over by a limited company of which she was chief shareholder.

HELD: Car at time of accident was on the business of the company, which had no interest in the policy. The company was not insured, nor its business.

Description of use clause

[2.104] Pailor v Co-operative Insurance Society Ltd
(1930) 38 Ll L Rep 237, CA

A car was driven by an employee of the insured's friend on friend's business – 'The Society will also similarly indemnify any relations or friend of the insured ... whilst driving ... with the insured's knowledge and consent.' 'The Society shall not be liable while the car is being used for other than private pleasure or professional purposes or for driving to and from the insured's place of business or for making personal business calls (excluding commercial travelling) or personal visits to the scene of his business operations.'

CONSTRUCTION: Arbitrator's finding of fact that employee was a friend of the insured.

HELD: That a 'general knowledge and consent' was sufficient to bring the friend within the ambit of the policy, but that the friend's use of the car on his own employer's business did not come within the exception to the exception clause, and that the company were therefore not liable.

Appeal and cross-appeal dismissed.

[2.105] Passmore v Vulcan Boiler and General Insurance Co Ltd
(1935) 154 LT 258, 52 TLR 193, 64 Ll L Rep 92, 80 Sol Jo 167   du Parcq J

A policy covered the assured whilst using her car for the purpose of her business. An exception within the policy stated that the insurer was not liable if the car was used otherwise than in 'description of use' clause, ie business of assured of representative and no other. The assured and another representative both employed by the same company were using the car on employer's business. The car was not being used for the business of the assured alone, but also for the business of the other employee.

HELD: The policy covered the business use of the assured only, and the insurer was not liable when used for business of any other person whether also used for the business of the assured or not. The business of the other person might have been of a different kind and the insurer was entitled to know exactly what business risk it was covering and the extent of the risk it was undertaking.

If the policyholder extended a courtesy to a friend or acquaintance or stranger who was carrying on some business and was assisted in carrying on that business by the use of the car, and the assured gave a lift as a matter of kindness, courtesy or charity, the proper view would be that the car was being used for a social purpose.

Note—See also *DHR Moody (Chemists) Ltd v Iron Trades Mutual Insurance Co Ltd* (1970) 115 Sol Jo 16, 69 LGR 232, [1971] 1 Lloyd's Rep 386, [1971] RTR 120. In *Seddon v Binions* (at para [2.108]) the passage in du Parcq J's judgment summarised in the second paragraph above was considered and explained by all three members of the court. Roskill LJ said that nothing in his judgment in *Seddon's* case was intended to cast any doubt upon the applicability of that passage to a case to which it is appropriate.

[2.106] Jones v Welsh Insurance Corpn Ltd
[1937] 4 All ER 149, 157 LT 483, 54 TLR 22, 81 Sol Jo 886, 59 Ll L Rep 13   Goddard J

The assured was a motor mechanic who earned £2 14s per week. He ceased work at 5pm. He bought five sheep and rented two acres to keep them. He had a private car policy excepting liability if used otherwise than in accordance with the 'description of use' clause, ie 'private purposes and use by assured in person in connection with his business ... of motor engineer and no other ... excluding use for carriage of goods in connection with any trade or business'. The assured's brother took the car and brought two sheep and two lambs to the father's house.

HELD: The assured was not keeping sheep for pleasure or for food for himself and family, but was a sheep farmer in a small way as a sideline, and it was a business, and the car was being used for carriage of goods in connection with business of sheep farming. It was not a case of physical characteristics of the goods but the use of the car for business purposes and carriage of goods in connection with a business.

[2.107] Browning v Phoenix Assurance Co Ltd

[1960] 2 Lloyd's Rep 360 Pilcher J

The owner of a car asked the plaintiff, a garage foreman, to take his car for a long run to get the back axle oil well warmed so that it could be drained and changed: he said that if the plaintiff cared to do this on a Sunday and take his wife and family with him, he had no objection. The owner's insurance policy covered any other person who drove with his permission provided that such person should be subject to the exceptions and conditions of the policy as if he were the insured. A general exception excluded liability of the insurer while the vehicle was being used otherwise than in accordance with the 'description of use'. The latter was set out in a schedule and excluded 'use for any purpose in connection with the Motor Trade'. After the oil had been changed in the back axle the plaintiff took the car out with his brother and brother-in-law as passengers partly, as he alleged, for the pleasure of the ride and partly to check the car for any defects. Whilst on this run there was a collision with another vehicle due to his admitted negligence. The defendant company refused to indemnify him.

HELD: On the facts the plaintiff was not driving with the owner's permission since the long run which the owner asked him to make was for the purpose of draining the oil from the back axle, and that had already been done. But even if the plaintiff had been driving with the owner's permission the policy would not have covered him: he was driving for two purposes:
(1)   the permitted purpose of taking his family for a ride;
(2)   a second purpose which would have been a purpose in connection with the motor trade. The plaintiff's use would thus have been for a permitted purpose and a specifically excluded purpose.
    In these circumstances, following *Passmore v Vulcan Boiler and General Insurance Co Ltd* (at para [2.105]) the plaintiff would not be entitled to recover from the defendant.

[2.108] Seddon v Binions

(1977) 122 Sol Jo 34, [1978] 1 Lloyd's Rep 381, [1978] RTR 163, CA

The defendants were father and son. The son carried on the business of carpet layer. The father helped the son in the business but was not his employee. The son had an employee named Hale. When the son was working on a job some miles from home the father brought Hale in the son's van. Hale claimed he had toothache and wanted to go home at lunchtime. It was the son's normal practice to take Hale to and from jobs. The father intended going home for lunch so it was arranged that he would take Hale in the son's Triumph car. On the journey there was a collision with another vehicle in which the plaintiff was injured. The father had a policy on a car of his own covering him when driving other cars, restricted to use for social, domestic and pleasure purposes or in connection with his own business.

HELD: He was not covered by his policy at the time of the accident. He was driving his son's car for two purposes – his own social and domestic purposes and, in driving Hale home, for purposes of his son's business. An alternative test to apply was to look for the primary purpose, or essential character, of the journey; and in the present case it was to take the son's employee home and was not social, domestic or pleasure.

Per Megaw LJ: If there be such a primary purpose, or essential character, then the courts should not be meticulous to find some possible secondary purpose, or some in essential character, the result of which could be suggested to be that the use of the car fell outside the proper use for the purposes of which cover was given by the insurance company. If, however, there are cases in which there are, in the proper sense of the word, two 'purposes', as was the case in *Passmore v Vulcan Boiler and General Insurance Co Ltd* (1935) 154 LT 258, 52 TLR 193, 64 Ll L Rep 92, 80 Sol Jo 167 [at para [2.105] on the finding of the arbitrator, then I have no reason to disagree in any way with the conclusion in that case as to the results that would follow.

[2.109]   Singh v Rathour, Northern Star Insurance Co Ltd (third party)
[1988] 2 All ER 16, [1988] 1 WLR 422

The defendant borrowed a minibus from an association of which he was a member. The association's representative who gave permission believed the defendant wanted to use it for the purposes of the association. In fact the defendant used it to drive a party of friends to a wedding. The plaintiff, a passenger, was killed in a crash. The defendant's insurance covered him for any car provided he had the consent of the owner. The insurer sought to repudiate on the grounds that he didn't have the consent of the owner of the minibus. The trial judge's finding that the user was outside the consent given was upheld and the insurer was entitled to refuse indemnity.

[2.110]   Farr v Motor Traders' Mutual Insurance Society
[1920] 3 KB 669, 90 LJKB 215, 123 LT 765, 36 TLR 711, CA

The plaintiff was the owner of two taxicabs which he insured with the defendant in February 1918, for one year against damage caused to either of them by accidental external means. In the proposal for the policy, the plaintiff in answer to a question stated that each cab was to be driven in one shift per 24 hours. At the foot of the proposal form the plaintiff stated that the above statement was true, and the policy provided that the statements in the proposal were to be the basis of the contract, and to be considered as incorporated therein. In August 1918, while one of the cabs was undergoing repair, the other cab was driven in two shifts per 24 hours for a very short time, and from that time until the accident hereinafter mentioned happened, the two cabs were driven in one shift only. In November 1918, the cab which had been driven in two shifts in August was damaged by an accident. It was at that time being driven in one shift only. In an action on the policy to recover in respect of the damage so caused, defendants contended that the statement in the proposal that the cab was to be driven in one shift per 24 hours was a warranty, and upon breach thereof the insurance came to an end.

HELD: The statement was not a warranty, but was merely descriptive of the risk, indicating that the cab, whilst being driven in more than one shift per 24 hours, would cease to be covered by the policy, but would be covered whilst being driven in one shift; and defendant was liable.

[2.111]   Roberts v Anglo-Saxon Insurance Association

(1927) 27 Ll L Rep 313, CA

The policy contained the following words: 'Warranted used only for the following purposes – commercial travelling'.

Per Banks LJ: It does not follow at all that because it is not used on one occasion, or on more than one occasion, for other than the described use, the policy is avoided. If the proper construction, on its language, is a description of the limitation of the liability, then the effect would be that the vehicle would be off cover during the period during which it was not being used for the warranted purpose but would come again on the cover when the vehicle was again used for the warranted purpose.

A fire broke out in the car when it was not being used for commercial purposes. The judge held that he did not attach undue importance to the word 'warranted' but when used in conjunction with 'only' then there was a condition that the vehicle should only be used for that purpose and therefore insurers were entitled to refuse indemnity.

Note—Contrast this case with *Provincial Insurance Co Ltd v Morgan* (at para [2.112]).

[2.112]   Provincial Insurance Co Ltd v Morgan

[1933] AC 240, 102 LJKB 164, 49 TLR 179, 44 Ll L Rep 275, 38 Com Cas 92, Sub nom *Morgan v Provincial Insurance Co Ltd* (1932) 148 LT 385 HL

A proposal form contained the following questions and answers. 'Q. State the nature of the goods to be carried. A. (a) The delivery of coal; (b) coal.' The vehicle was used for carrying a load of timber and 5 cwt of coal.

HELD: The questions and answers were intended to ascertain the intentions of the assured with regard to the user of the lorry and the goods to be carried therein and the answers were true, correct and complete, and there was no breach of warranty or of any condition precedent to liability.

[2.113]   Piddington v Co-operative Insurance Society Ltd

[1934] 2 KB 236, 103 LJKB 370, 151 LT 399, 50 TLR 311, 78 Sol Jo
278   Lawrence J

The insurance of a private car excluded liability when used for other than private pleasure: or for conveying goods other than personal luggage. The insured was a designer for a firm of brassworkers, and drove home from work at noon with two laths, 12 or 14ft long, fastened lengthwise on top of the car, intended for the repair of some trellis work in his garden. The same afternoon, without removing the laths, he went on a pleasure run, and met with an accident causing fatal injuries to a pedestrian. The insurer declined liability under the policy, contending that the use was otherwise than 'solely for private purposes' as set out in the proposal form, and was 'conveying goods other than personal luggage'.

HELD: The word 'pleasure' was in contradistinction to 'business' and 'personal luggage' to 'merchandise' and the insured's garden was his pleasure and not his business, and the laths were personal luggage and not merchandise.

[2.114]   Lee v Poole

[1954] Crim LR 942, [1954] CLY 2948, Div Ct

The insured carried some furniture for a friend without payment.

HELD: The case fell within the policy cover.

Note—These cases also illustrate the principle that if a car is being used for two purposes neither of which is predominant and one use is excluded, then the insurer will be able to repudiate liability but the contract will not be void *ab initio* unless the insured warranted that it would only be put to one use (see *Provincial Insurance Co Ltd v Morgan* (at para [2.112])).

Use for hire or reward

[2.115]   Wyatt v Guildhall Insurance Co Ltd

[1937] 1 KB 653, [1937] 1 All ER 792, 106 LJKB 421, 156 LT 292, 53 TLR 389, 81 Sol Jo 358, 57 Ll L Rep 90   Branson J

A motor policy described the permitted use as 'for social, domestic and pleasure purposes' and excluded use for 'hiring'. The plaintiff and another were passengers in a car belonging to Wilcox. All three were going to London on the same business, the passengers had arranged to travel by train but agreed they would travel up in Wilcox's car and each pay a sum equivalent to the train fare. It was accepted that this was an isolated incident and that Wilcox was not in the habit of using his car in this way. An accident occurred and Wyatt was injured.

HELD: The car was being used for hiring and outside the permitted use.

[2.116]   McCarthy v British Oak Insurance Co Ltd

[1938] 3 All ER 1, 159 LT 215, 82 Sol Jo 568, 61 Ll L Rep 194   Atkinson J

The assured, a garage proprietor, without receiving any payment, lent a car for the evening to a driver (who had at times driven a coach for him and done odd jobs for him as a mechanic) for private purposes excluding use for hire. The driver paid the assured 10 s or 12 s for the petrol and oil but nothing more, and the driver took two friends as passengers, and the passengers paid the driver what he had paid for the petrol and oil, and for two quarts of beer which was for the use of the driver and passengers.

HELD: Hire meant a genuine business contract for a stipulated reward. In *Wyatt v Guildhall Insurance Co Ltd* (at para [2.115]) the passenger agreed to pay for conveyance and the money was clear profit for the assured. Here the driver did not make anything for himself and there was nothing to constitute a legal contract for hire, and the insurers were liable.

Note—See now s 150(1) and (2) of the Road Traffic Act 1988.

[2.117]   Bonham v Zurich General Accident and Liability Insurance Co Ltd

[1945] KB 292, [1945] 1 All ER 427, 114 LJKB 273, 172 LT 201, 61 TLR 271, 78 Ll L Rep 245

A proposal form contained the question 'Will passengers be carried for hire or reward?' and the answer was 'No'. The answers in the proposal were made the basis of the contract. The policy excluded use for hiring.

The assured habitually and regularly carried three passengers who worked at the same place. Two passengers paid 1s 2d or 1s 3d per return journey calculated on the cost of railway fares. The other never did pay.

The assured never asked the passengers for payment but the two passengers voluntarily offered him the money. He would have carried them if they had not paid anything. The assured paid for petrol, oil, tyres, insurance and other expenses of the car. The assured would have made the journeys if there were no passengers. An accident occurred and one of the passengers was killed.

HELD, ON APPEAL, per du Parcq LJ and Uthwatt J (MacKinnon LJ dissenting): The insurers was not liable. A distinction is to be drawn between 'hire' and 'reward' or the words 'or reward' would not be necessary. The assured intended to accept from the passengers a payment which he expected to be tendered and which they intended to tender. He took from them each day a sum which they never failed to pay and which he expected to receive. This was carrying passengers for reward.

The reward need not be payable under an agreement enforceable at law. 'Hire' imports an obligation to pay. 'Reward' included cases where there is no obligation to pay. All the judges in the Court of Appeal agreed the car was not being used for hire.

Note—See now s 150(1) and (2) of the Road Traffic Act 1988.

Since 1975 the insurance industry has as a matter of practice regarded contributions to petrol costs alone as not falling within the scope of the 'hire or reward' exclusion. Following consultations with the Government who sought to facilitate car sharing within the terms of the Transport Act 1980, motor insurers agreed, in 1978 to widen the previous interpretation and issued an undertaking in the following terms:

> 'The receipt of contributions as part of a car sharing arrangement for social or other similar purposes in respect of the carriage of passengers on a journey in a vehicle insured under a private car policy will not be regarded as constituting the carriage of passengers for hire or reward (or the use of the vehicle for hiring) provided that:
>
> (a) the vehicle is not constructed or adapted to carry more than seven passengers (excluding the driver);
> (b) the passengers are not being carried in the course of a business of carrying passengers;
> (c) the total contributions received for the journey concerned do not involve an element of profit.'

Private hire

[2.118] **Lyons v Denscombe**
[1949] 1 All ER 977, 113 JP 305, [1949] WN 257, 93 Sol Jo 389, 47 LGR 412, Div Ct

A mineworker drove his car to the colliery each morning and in the evening drove home four fellow workmen under an agreement or contract with one of them to pay 8s per week (2s each) whether they used the car or not. The car was licensed for private hire and hackney purposes. The insurance policy did not cover use for hire or reward other than private hire; which was defined as the 'letting of the vehicle supplied direct from the policyholder's garage'. He was prosecuted for:

(1)   not being insured,
(2)   not holding a licence for an express carriage, and
(3)   not holding a road service licence.

The justices found there was one contract for one fare of 8s paid weekly and not four contracts for 2s each.

HELD: The car was not used as an express carriage under s 61(1) of the Road Traffic Act 1930 and did not require a public service vehicle licence under s 67(1) or a road service licence under s 72(1).

Per Lord Goddard CJ: It is said that the letting of the vehicle was not direct from the policyholder's garage because it was driven to the colliery in the morning and the four men only travelled in the evening. Private hire is distinct, in my opinion, from plying for trade, that is to say, using the car as a taxicab ... if I wanted a car to meet me at a railway station, it has to come to the station from the garage where it is kept. If it does so it is supplied direct from the garage. It is not plying for hire. Can it make any difference for the purpose of insurance that the car is driven to the place where the hirers are going to get into it some hours before they do get into it? Admittedly, if the car came straight out of the garage to the colliery and picked up the men there, it would be letting direct from the garage. Why does it cease to be a letting direct from the garage if it gets to the colliery five minutes before the men get into it? If not, does it cease to be such a letting after half an hour or an hour elapses? Obviously not. For these reasons I think the policy was in force.

Note—The sections referred to above are all now repealed.

Social, domestic and pleasure purposes

[2.119]   Wood v General Accident Fire and Life Assurance Corpn Ltd
[1948] WN 430, 65 TLR 53, 92 Sol Jo 720, 82 Ll L Rep 77   Morris J

A Daimler car was insured for 'social, domestic and pleasure purposes'. The insured, a garage proprietor, used the car for a journey to interview a firm with the object of negotiating a contract in connection with his garage business. He was 67 years old and it was more convenient to travel in his own Daimler which was immediately available than a hired car.

The arbitrator found it was a more comfortable, pleasurable and restful way of making the journey than in a hired car, but held it was not covered by the policy.

On appeal by special case stated, the insured argued that the test was the reason for the use of the journey and not what might happen at the end, and the reason was use in a comfortable and pleasurable way.

HELD: The words were well known and well used, and in their natural, ordinary, normal and reasonable meaning, did not cover the journey.

Appeal dismissed.

[2.120]   Orr v Trafalgar Insurance Co Ltd
(1948) 82 Ll L Rep 1, CA

The insurance policy on a motor car indemnified whilst being used solely for the purposes in the schedule – the schedule stated 'Private purposes only'. The policy defined 'Private purposes' as social, domestic and pleasure purposes and use by the insured in person travelling to and from his permanent place of business. The policy excluded liability if being used for private or public hire.

The insured was in the house of one Gallagher who carried on a private hire business when Gallagher received a telephone request for a hire. Gallagher asked the insured to do the job for him. Whilst doing so the insured's car met with an accident. The insured telephoned Gallagher who went in his car and finished the journey. The passenger asked what the charge would be and Gallagher did not make a charge because the accident caused the passenger to miss his train.

Pritchard J held that he should draw the inference that there was an implied obligation on the passenger to pay; that the use was private hire and insurers were not liable.

Upheld in Court of Appeal.

[2.121–122]   Whitehead v Unwins (Yorks)

(1962) Times, 1 March, [1962] Crim LR 323

A vehicle was used for carrying food for consumption by cows. The policy covered use for 'social and domestic' purposes. The justices dismissed a charge under the Road Traffic Act 1960, s 201, of using the vehicle when not covered by insurance.

HELD: On a case stated, there must be a conviction. The argument that as cows are domestic animals the carrying of food for cows is a domestic use is a complete fallacy. The fact that the vehicle was lent did not itself make the use social.

Note—See also *Seddon v Binions* (at para [2.108]).

[2.123]   DHR Moody (Chemists) Ltd v Iron Trades Mutual Insurance Co Ltd

(1970) 115 Sol Jo 16, 69 LGR 232, [1971] 1 Lloyd's Rep 386, [1971] RTR
120   Wrangham J

The defendant insured the plaintiff's vehicles, the description of use under the policy being 'for social, domestic and pleasure purposes and use for the business of the insured including carriage of goods'. One of the plaintiff's employees was the Chairman of the Town Twinning Committee of Clacton Urban District Council and had borrowed a car from his employer, with its permission, to drive a delegation from a French town back to London airport. The insurer denied liability on the grounds that the vehicle was not being used for a social purpose but rather in connection with duties to the council, ie for 'business purposes'. The judge found that the French visitors were not in England on commercial or industrial business but rather to promote the twinning of their town with Clacton the object being that their respective towns inhabitants would get to know one another and compete against each other in games or sport. The judge considered that to be a social activity. He did not accept the contention that no activities of a local authority could be termed social. He stated: 'It seems to me that just as the activities of an individual can be divided into those which he pursues because he must in order to earn a living, which we call business, and those which he pursues of his own free will, such as social, domestic or pleasure activities, so the activities of a local authority can be either the official duties which they are by statute or convention compelled to carry out, or voluntary activities which may be, and often will be of a social character.'

HELD: In the circumstances the insurer was found liable to indemnify the plaintiff.

[2.124]   Brown v Roberts

[1965] I QB I, [1963] 2 All ER 263, [1963] 3 WLR 75, 107 Sol Jo 666, [1963]
I Lloyd's Rep 314   Megaw J

A van owned and driven by the defendant was drawing up at the kerb when the
passenger, to whom he was giving a lift, opened the nearside door. It struck and
injured the plaintiff who was on the pavement. She claimed damages against the
defendant on the grounds that the passenger was 'using' the vehicle within the
meaning of the Road Traffic Act 1930, s 35(1) (which was in similar terms to s 143
of the 1988 Act) and that, as the defendant's policy did not cover negligence of a
passenger, he was in breach of the statutory duty as in *Monk v Warbey* (at para
[1.24]).

HELD: The passenger thought negligent was not 'using' the vehicle within the
meaning of the section and the defendant was not under a duty to provide
insurance against that negligence. Although there may be more than one person
'using' a vehicle at any given time and though the element of driving the vehicle is
not an essential element of 'using' (*Elliott v Grey* (at para [2.133])) a person, does
not 'use a motor vehicle on the road' for the purposes of s 35(1) of the 1930 Act
unless there is present in the person alleged to be the user an element of
controlling, managing or operating the vehicle at the relevant time. The mere
relationship of a passenger to a motor vehicle or to a particular part of a motor
vehicle is not 'use' for the purposes of the 1930 Act.

Note—See also *Thomas v Hooper* (1985) Times, 25 October.

[2.125]   Leathley v Tatton

[1980] RTR 21, Div Ct

The defendant went to an address with two friends intending to look at a car with
a view to buying it. The owner did not turn up. One of the friends had a key which
fitted the car. The car would not start so one of the friends got into the driving
seat and the defendant pushed the car: when it started he jumped into the
passenger seat. He took no part in the driving of the car. He was charged with
using the car when uninsured contrary to s 143 of the Road Traffic Act 1972.

HELD: There was a case to answer. It was a clear situation in which the defendant
and his friend were acting in concert, a joint enterprise for the purpose of setting
the car in motion and to see how the car functioned. The defendant was 'using' it,
and the fact that someone else was driving it was irrelevant.

Note—*Brown v Roberts* (at para [2.124]) was cited but distinguished on the ground that
it was a case which concerned civil liability and did not reflect on the meaning of 'use' in
the present case.

[2.126]   B v Knight

[1981] RTR 136, QBD

O'Nion took a van without the owner's consent. He drove it to a place where he
met the defendant, B, a minor. B got into the van and O'Nion drove off. During the
journey, but not before, B learned that O'Nion had taken the van without the
owner's consent. He did not ask to be allowed to get out as he 'did not fancy the
idea of walking home'. He was convicted of using the van uninsured contrary to
s 143 of the Road Traffic Act 1972.

HELD, allowing his appeal: He was not 'using' the vehicle. A passenger merely letting himself be driven where there is no element of joint enterprise does not 'use' the vehicle. B was simply getting a lift from O'Nion in the course of O'Nion's 'use'.

[2.127] Cobb v Williams
[1973] RTR 113, [1973] Crim LR 243, Div Ct

The defendant was being brought home from work in his own car driven by a woman who was not his servant when an accident occurred. Neither of them was insured. The defendant was charged with 'using' his car when not insured, contrary to the Road Traffic Act 1960, s 201 (now s 143 of the 1988 Act). The magistrates dismissed the charge on the ground that the meaning of 'use' should not be extended beyond driving and that the charge should have been one of 'permitting'.

HELD: This was not right. The word 'use' is wider than 'drive'. The defendant was using his own car for his own purposes and in person in being driven home, though the driver was somebody else.

[2.128] Bennett v Richardson
[1980] RTR 358, QBD

The defendant, a registered blind person, was charged with, *inter alia*, using a motor vehicle without insurance in force contrary to the Road Traffic Act 1972, s 143. At the time in question he was a passenger sitting in the back of an ice cream van driven by his partner. The van was hired, the two partners being equally liable under the hire terms. The defendant's job in the business was cleaning the van and helping to serve ice cream. It was being used on partnership business. The justices applied Lord Parker's principle in *Windle v Dunning & Son Ltd* (at para [2.172]) and dismissed the charge.

HELD, on the prosecutor's appeal: The justices' decision was right.

Per Lord Widgery: I would be anxious to see that [the] principle was adhered to and not easily jettisoned for some alternative. The principle to which I refer is this. A man cannot be convicted for using a motor vehicle which he is not personally driving unless he is the employer of the driver. If the owner is driving the vehicle then, good enough, he can be charged with using it. If the owner's employee, in the strict sense of the master-servant relationship, is driving the vehicle, again the employer can be regarded as vicariously being responsible ... But if the relationship between driver and would-be defendant is any other than those on which I have referred, then it is not possible to convict the person not driving of these offences ... The fact that [the defendant] was blind was quite irrelevant ... the fact that the driver and the defendant were partners is also irrelevant because there is authority which shows that the mere relationship of partnership between driver and the would-be driver or passenger is not enough.
Cobb v Williams (at para [2.127]) distinguished.

[2.129] Garrett v Hooper
[1973] RTR 1, [1973] Crim LR 61, Div Ct

A co-partner does not 'use' a vehicle merely because it is driven by his partner on partnership business.

[2.130]   Passmoor v Gibbons

[1979] RTR 53, [1978] Crim LR 498, QBD

On the other hand, a partner who did not take part in the day-to-day running of the company nonetheless 'uses' a vehicle when it is being driven by an employee in the course of his business on behalf of the company.

Servant driving

[2.131]   Mickleborough v BRS (Contracts) Ltd

[1977] RTR 389, [1977] Crim LR 568

The defendant was the owner of a vehicle hired out with a driver for five years to a hirer who alone decided what journeys to do and what loads to carry. Having found the vehicle overloaded a traffic examiner prosecuted the defendant for 'using' the vehicle when overloaded. The loading had been done by the hirers. The justices held the defendant was not 'using' the vehicle since the hirers had control of the vehicle.

HELD: This was not right. Citing Lord Parker, in *Windle v Dunning & Son Ltd* (at para [2.172]) where there is an alternative of 'causing or permitting' then 'using' has a restricted meaning. It is not to be extended to cover persons other than the owner and the driver, provided the driver is his servant and engaged at the material time on his employer's business. The driver was driving on his employer's, the defendant, business of hiring out motor lorries and therefore the defendant was 'using' the vehicle at the material time.

[2.132]   Richardson v Baker

[1976] RTR 56, [1976] Crim LR 76

An employee of the defendant without the defendant's knowledge and without his express or implied authority took a tractor unit on to a road to convey a load for the purposes of the defendant's business as a haulage contractor.

HELD: The defendant was guilty of 'using' the vehicle in contravention of the Vehicles (Excise) Act 1971. Even if 'using' was limited to the narrow meaning given when there was an alternative of 'causing or permitting' then *prima facie* a vehicle was being used by a master when it was on a road driven by his servant about his master's business. Absence of any authority from him for such use made no difference.

Vehicle not being driven

[2.133]   Elliott v Grey

[1960] 1 QB 367, [1959] 3 All ER 733, [1959] 3 WLR 956, 124 JP 58, 103 Sol Jo 921, 57 LGR 357

The defendant's car broke down on 20 December 1958, and the defendant placed it outside his house in the road. Before 7 February 1959 he had jacked up the wheels, removed the battery and terminated his insurance cover. On 7 February 1959 he had unjacked the wheels, cleaned the car, and sent its battery to be recharged, but the car could not be mechanically propelled because the engine would not work. He had no intention of driving it on 7 February 1959, or of removing it from its position in the road. He was convicted of using the car whilst uninsured contrary to the Road Traffic Act 1930, s 35(1). The defendant appealed.

HELD: The words 'to use' meant 'to have the use of a motor vehicle on a road' and, as the car could be moved on 7 February 1959, even though it could not be driven, the appellant had the use of it on a road, within the meaning of s 35(1) of the 1930 Act.

Appeal dismissed.

Note—The Road Traffic Act 1930, s 35(1) was in similar terms to s 143 of the 1972 Act.

[2.134]   Napthen v Place
[1970] RTR 248, Div Ct

A motor car was bought at an auction and subsequently stood on the roadway outside the defendant's premises for several weeks untaxed and uninsured. He was charged with using a vehicle on a road uninsured and unlicensed. The prosecution sought to prove that he was the owner but justices did not accept that he was and dismissed the charges.

HELD: On a case stated, it is not essential for either of the charges that the person charged should have been the owner or proved to be the owner of the vehicle in question.

[2.135]   Gosling v Howard
[1975] RTR 429, Div Ct

The defendant's car was parked on a grass verge of a rural road well off the carriageway and had not been moved for three months. The justices dismissed summonses against him for 'using' a vehicle on a road uninsured and without a test certificate.

HELD, on the prosecutor's appeal: This was wrong. There was no evidence that the car was not in running order and as in *Elliott v Grey* (at para [2.133]) the defendant had the use of the vehicle.

[2.136]   Williams v Jones
[1975] RTR 433, Div Ct

The defendant used his employer's trade plates to bring a vehicle back to his premises to do it up for sale. On the way it broke down and the defendant left it on a part of the highway that was no longer used because of road improvements. He removed the trade plates and abandoned the vehicle. He was charged with using the vehicle on a road uninsured, his employer's policy being effective only when the trade plates were on. The justices dismissed the charge, holding there had been no use of the vehicle after removal of the trade plates.

HELD: Following *Elliott v Grey* (at para [2.133]) that notwithstanding that the vehicle was abandoned and the trade plates removed, the defendant was thereafter 'using' the vehicle within the meaning of the Road Traffic Act 1960, s 201 (now the Road Traffic Act 1988, s 143).

[2.137]   Eden v Mitchell

[1975] RTR 425, [1975] Crim LR 467, Div Ct

The defendant was charged with using his car on a road with tyres that did not comply with the Motor Vehicles (Construction and Use) Regulations 1966. It was parked outside his house but he had not driven it for some time and had no intention of doing so having been ill. The justices accepted that his sickness and intention not to drive was as sufficient as if the vehicle itself had been immobilised and dismissed the charge.

HELD, on the prosecutor's appeal: This was the wrong test. The intention of the defendant was immaterial. The true test was whether or not such steps had been taken as to make it impossible for anyone to use the vehicle.

Local authority – s 144(2)(a)

[2.138]   R v Urmston Urban District Council and Jones

(1953) Times, 29 July

An urban district council was summoned for permitting the use of an uninsured motor lorry and the driver for using the uninsured lorry. The lorry was drawing a trailer and the certificate of insurance did not cover the use of the lorry with a trailer. The Manchester county magistrates dismissed the summonses. Local authorities need not insure their motor vehicles when they were being driven by council employees in the course of their employment. The insurance of their vehicles by a local authority was quite voluntary.

Disabled vehicle

[2.139]   Police v Turton

(1953) Post Magazine, 2 May, 488

A haulage contractor towed a lorry belonging to a friend to a garage. The towed lorry had had the engine removed and the tow was for a new engine to be fitted. The policy did not cover the drawing of a trailer other than a disabled mechanically propelled vehicle. He was prosecuted for having no effective insurance. The police relied on *Lawrence v Howlett* [1952] 2 All ER 74, 116 JP 391, [1952] WN 308, [1952] 1 TLR 1476, 96 Sol Jo 397, 50 LGR 531, [1952] 1 Lloyd's Rep 483. The insurer gave evidence that it would regard the towed vehicle as being mechanically disabled and it would have accepted liability for an accident.

The magistrates (Holmfirth) convicted.

Note—See also *Elliott v Grey* (at para [2.133]).

Trailers attached

[2.140] **Leggate v Brown**

[1950] 2 All ER 564, 114 JP 454, [1950] WN 379, 66 (pt 2) TLR 281, 94 Sol Jo 567, 49 LGR 27, 84 Ll L Rep 395, Div Ct

The defendant's motor policy covered a tractor with an endorsement that enabled the tractor to be used with two trailers. The defendant used the tractor on a road towing two laden trailers. The Road Traffic Act 1930, s 18(1) made it an offence for a tractor to draw two laden trailers. The defendant was prosecuted for driving uninsured, and the prosecution contended that as the defendant was using the tractor in an illegal manner, the policy was void because an indemnity against the consequences of an illegal act was void as being against public policy. The magistrates convicted the defendant.

HELD, ON APPEAL: The policy insured the defendant, as the 1930 Act required, against the consequences of the negligent driving of the tractor. It said nothing about laden trailers. It simply allowed the vehicle to be used with two trailers. If the policy had insured the defendant against using the tractor illegally, to that extent it would have been ineffective, but that had nothing to do with injury to third persons. The policy was an insurance against the consequences of negligent driving of the vehicle, because a third party can only claim if there has been negligent driving. If there has been negligent driving, it does not matter whether there were two trailers or none. If the tractor was driven negligently, an injured person has a right to compensation, and this policy indemnified against negligent driving.

Conviction quashed.

[2.141] **Kerridge v Rush**

[1952] 2 Lloyd's Rep 305, Div Ct

The policy of insurance on an agricultural motor tractor excluded indemnity when the vehicle was drawing a greater number of trailers in all than permitted by law. The Road Traffic Act 1930, s 18(1) provided that a motor tractor shall not draw on the highway more than one laden trailer or two if unladen. The tractor was drawing a four-wheel laden trailer and a tumbril, constructed and intended to be drawn by a horse, laden with a horse-hoe frame.

HELD: The tumbril was a trailer. The tractor was drawing a greater number of trailers than was permitted by law and was not insured.

Towing/drawing a trailer

[2.142] **JRM (Plant) Ltd v Hodgson**

[1960] 1 Lloyd's Rep 538

A motor lorry was engaged in carting rubble from a contractor's site. The contractor's foreman asked the driver as a favour to tow a cement mixer a short distance to another site along a public road. The policy had a provision excluding cover when the lorry was used for drawing a trailer 'except the towing of any one disabled mechanically propelled vehicle or any farm implement or machine not constructed or adapted for the conveyance of goods'.

HELD: 'Farm implement or machine' meant 'farm implement or farm machine' and since the cement mixer was neither the policy did not cover the use of the lorry when towing the mixer.

No heavy goods vehicle licence

[2.143]   Police v Hepper
[1978] CLY 2591, Knightsbridge Crown Ct

The defendant was charged with driving a heavy goods vehicle when not insured. There was a policy in force allowing any person to drive who 'holds a licence to drive the vehicle or has held and is not disqualified from holding or obtaining such a licence'. The defendant had held and was not disqualified from holding an ordinary driving licence but had never held a heavy goods vehicle licence.

HELD: The policy did not cover him.

Hired vehicle

[2.144]   Sands v O'Connell
[1981] RTR 42, QBD

The defendant was aged 20. Anticipating difficulty in hiring a car to drive whilst under 21 she induced a friend aged 23 to hire a car for her. He did so by a contract of hire which stipulated 'Drivers must be aged between 21 and 70 years'. He also completed a 'supplementary proposal form' for insurance declaring 'I am not under 21 or over 70 years of age', and that 'the above declaration applies also in respect of all persons who will drive'. The insurance policy covering the vehicle was issued to the company hiring out the vehicle and extended to indemnify any person driving the vehicle 'on the order or with the permission of the policyholder'. The friend lent the vehicle during the hire period to the defendant who drove it for herself. She was charged with driving whilst uninsured.

HELD: (1) The contract of hire by referring to 'drivers' authorised the friend to permit other persons to drive limited to those between 21 and 70.
   (2)   The defendant was not driving on the order or with the permission of the policyholder since she had no direct permission from them and the friend's authority was limited to drivers between 21 and 70.
   (3)   Though by an unusual indorsement the policy extended to treat a person driving the vehicle as if he or she was in the employment of the policyholder under a contract of service, the defendant did not receive authority from the friend within the scope of his employment and such decisions as *Marsh v Moores* (at para [2.71]) were not applicable.
Her appeal against conviction was dismissed.

Crown servant – private use

[2.145] Salt v MacKnight

1947 JC 99, 1947 SLT 327, High Ct of Justiciary

The Road Traffic Act 1930, s 121(2) (which provides that Parts I and III of the Act shall apply to the Crown) is no warrant for the suggestion that Part III of the Act (in which falls s 35) does not apply to servants of the Crown irrespective of what they are doing nor to Crown vehicles irrespective of the purpose for which they are being used. Consequently, a departmental official who is using a Crown vehicle for his own business is not immune from prosecution under s 35 (which requires a third-party insurance to be in force).

Note—The equivalent provisions to s 121(2) of the 1930 Act is s 183(1) of the 1988 Act which reads:

183 Application to the Crown
(1)   Subject to the provisions of this section—
    (a)   Part I of this Act,
    (b)   Part II of this Act, except ss 68 to 74 and 77,
    (c)   Part III of this Act, except s 103(3)
    (d)   Part IV of this Act and,
    (e)   in this part, ss 163, 164, 168, 169, 170(1) to (4), 177, 178, 181 and 182,
apply to vehicles and persons in the public service of the Crown.

Vehicle sold

[2.146] Rogerson v Scottish Automobile and General Insurance Co Ltd

[1931] All ER Rep 606, (1931) 146 LT 26, 48 TLR 17, 75 Sol Jo 724, 41 Ll L Rep 1, HL

The appellant effected motor insurance on a Lancia car. Shortly afterwards he exchanged the car for another of a similar type. He had an accident in the new car and sought an indemnity. The contract included the following clause: 'This insurance shall cover legal liability as aforesaid of the assured in respect of the use by the insured of any motor car, provided that such car is at the time of the accident being used instead of 'the insured car'.'

Per Lord Buckmaster: To me this policy depends upon the hypothesis that there is, in fact, an insured car. When once the car which is the subject of the policy is sold, the owner's rights in respect of it ceases as the policy so far as the car is concerned is at an end.

[2.147] Tattersall v Drysdale

[1935] 2 KB 174, 104 LJKB 511, 153 LT 75, 51 TLR 405, 79 Sol Jo 418, 52 Ll L Rep 21   Goddard J

A policy (third party) contained the following clause: 'Subject to the terms and conditions of this policy, this section is extended to cover: The insured whilst personally driving for private purposes any other private motor car not belonging to the insured in respect of which no indemnity is afforded the insured by any other insurances applying to such car, provided always that the car or cars hereby insured shall not be in use at the same time.'

The insured sold the car referred to in the policy, and after the sale had an accident whilst driving a car lent to him.

HELD: The policy was in respect of the ownership and use of a particular car, and the clause was expressly stated to be an extension clause; the insured had ceased to be interested in the subject matter of the insurance and the extension fell with the rest of the policy.

[2.148] Wilkinson v General Accident Fire and Life Assurance Corpn Ltd
[1967] 2 Lloyd's Rep 182, Manchester Assizes

Middleton, a motor dealer, acted as agent of the defendant to procure insurance business. He had authority to issue cover notes; insurance certificates and policies would be issued by the defendants themselves. The plaintiff had a car insured under a policy issued by the defendants through Middleton's agency. The policy had the usual extension to cover the holder when driving a car not owned by him. In October 1961 he sold the car and Middleton witnessed the hire purchase agreement. In December 1961 Middleton told the plaintiff that his policy would expire if a further premium was not paid. Thereupon the plaintiff paid a year's premium and received in due course a new certificate, which referred to the car which he had sold in October. He did not buy another car but occasionally used his brother-in-law's car. In September 1962 he had an accident whilst doing so. He claimed indemnity under the policy. In this action his counsel conceded that in the ordinary way where an insured parts with the car insured the policy ceases to have effect (*Tattersall v Drysdale* (at para [2.147])), but he contended that as Middleton, the defendant's agent, had known of the sale of the car and yet had invited renewal some weeks later the defendant was estopped from denying that the plaintiff was covered.

HELD: This was not correct. Middleton had obtained knowledge of the sale of the car in his capacity as a motor dealer, not insurance agent, and his knowledge so obtained was not to be imputed to the defendants. Once the car was sold the policy was void: the plaintiff knew Middleton's authority was limited to issuing cover notes and receiving premiums. It would not be possible for such an agent to effect so fundamental a change in the policy as to give general cover to the plaintiff when driving cars belonging to others after he had disposed of his own.

Car hirers' policy

[2.149] Haworth v Dawson
(1946) 80 Ll L Rep 19   Lewis J

The insurer issued a policy to G & K Hire, indemnifying it and any person hiring a car who completed a proposal form which was the basis of the contract and who was not an excluded hirer. A hirer was excluded unless:
(1) he was a person whom G & K Hire had satisfied itself by an actual driving test was a qualified, careful and competent driver;
(2) he had completed a proposal form;
(3) he held a current driving licence which was continuous for at least 12 months and free from any endorsements.

The proposal form required that the hirer should never have been prosecuted under the Motor Car or Road Traffic Acts for any offence thereunder; had never had a licence endorsed or suspended; had not been involved in any motor accidents of any kind whatever during the prior 12 months; and had never been refused insurance nor the renewal of any policy issued. The proposal form required G & K Hire to warrant that:

(1)   it had tested the hirer and satisfied itself of his capability to drive by causing him to drive the car on the highway in their presence;

(2)   to examine the hirer's driving licence and warrant it had been issued for more than twelve months and was free from endorsements; and

(3)   that the car was in sound condition and working order.

Dawson hired a car from G & K Hire, and injured a third party, who sued Dawson and G & K Hire. Judgment was given against Dawson and the action was adjourned to join the insurer as a defendant. It was admitted Dawson was a man of straw, and G & K Hire admitted it was liable under *Monk v Warbey* (at para [1.24]). Dawson's licence was endorsed for speeding in 1937 and again in 1938; he had had two accidents; G & K Hire did not give him any test.

The insurers denied that Dawson or G & K Hire was covered by the policy and that s 10 of the Road Traffic Act 1934 did not apply.

HELD: Dawson was an excluded hirer and the insurer was not liable.

On the question of costs, G & K Hire contended that the insurer had been wrongly joined, as there could have been no cause of action against it at the date of the writ, and the plaintiff ought to have issued a fresh writ, but the court held it had been party to the proceedings without raising any objection, and made an order in the Sanderson form that G & K Hire pay the costs of the insurer.

Note—Section 10 of the 1934 Act is now effectively replaced by ss 151 and 152 of the 1988 Act.

[2.150]   Evans v Lewis

(1964) 108 Sol Jo 259, [1964] 1 Lloyd's Rep 258, Div Ct

The defendant was charged with using a motor vehicle on a road without there being in force a policy of insurance in respect of third party risks contrary to the Road Traffic Act 1960, s 201 (now s 143 of the 1988 Act). At the time of the offence he was driving a car hired from a car-hire garage. There was a policy in force issued by insurer to the garage to cover its vehicles when out on hire. It included the words 'This policy is only to cover any vehicle ... subject ... to the following conditions (a) that the insured shall verify ... that the hirer is not among the excluded persons enumerated below ... (b) publicans ... (c) the Company's form of proposal for hirer driving insurance shall be completed and signed by each hirer'. The defendant was a publican but declared in the proposal form that he was a printer. Relying on *Durrant v Maclaren* (at para [2.32]) he claimed that he was insured by virtue of s 207 of the 1960 Act (ss 151 and 152 of the 1988 Act) until proceedings had been taken under the section by the insurer and this had not been done.

HELD, ON APPEAL from a dismissal of the charge: This case was not the same as *Durrant's*. Here there was no contract of insurance between the defendant and the insurance company and the document he completed was wrongly called a proposal form. The defendant was never covered by the insurance policy, for it specifically excluded publicans: in such circumstances s 207 did not apply.

[2.151]   Boss v Kingston

[1963] 1 All ER 177, [1963] 1 WLR 99, 106 Sol Jo 1053, 61 LGR 109, Div Ct, QBD

Boss was driving Hansford's motorcycle with Hansford on the pillion. Hansford's insurance was effective only when Hansford was driving. Boss had a policy in respect of a Triumph motorcycle which he had sold a fortnight before. This policy afforded cover to Boss when riding 'any motor cycle described in the schedule' and also whilst riding any other motor cycle 'not belonging to him … as though such motor cycle were a motor cycle described in the schedule'. The schedule contained particulars of the Triumph motorcycle only. They were charged with using a motorcycle on a road when there was not in force a policy of insurance in relation to the user of that vehicle contrary to the Road Traffic Act 1960, s 201 (now s 143 of the 1988 Act). The justices convicted on the ground that Boss's policy lapsed when he sold the Triumph because he then ceased to have an insurable interest in the vehicle to which the policy related.

HELD: On a case stated:
  (1)   As Boss's policy, unlike those considered in *Rogerson v Scottish Automobile and General Insurance Co Ltd* (at para [2.146]) and *Tattersall v Drysdale* (at para [2.147]), was in respect of third-party risks only there was no need for him to have an insurable interest in the vehicle and the justices' reasoning was wrong.
  (2)   The decisive question was whether the policy provided two wholly independent indemnities, ie one when riding the Triumph and the other when riding another motorcycle, or whether the second was dependent on the first and lapsed with it. For three reasons the policy could not be construed as providing two separate indemnities:
   (a)   the premium was fixed by reference to the named vehicle;
   (b)   the natural interpretation of the second indemnity was to effect temporary cover whilst the named vehicle was out of use;
   (c)   condition 5 of the policy requiring the insured to keep the Triumph in efficient condition was a condition precedent to liability.
  (3)   Section 201 of the 1960 Act requires the driver of a motor vehicle to have a legally binding policy of insurance in force. It was no defence to bring evidence, as was done in this case, that the insurer would have met any claim.
The conviction was right though for the wrong reasons.

[2.152]   Peters v General Accident Fire and Life Assurance Corpn Ltd

[1938] 2 All ER 267, 158 LT 476, 54 TLR 663, 82 Sol Jo 294, 36 LGR 583, 60 Ll L Rep 311, CA

A sold his van to B and handed over the insurance policy which covered any person driving with the assured's consent or permission. The plaintiff obtained judgment against B and took proceedings against the insurers under s 10 of the Road Traffic Act 1934. Part of the purchase price remained owing on sale.

HELD: (1) The purchaser was not driving with consent or permission of the assured, as the van was the purchaser's own property.
  (2)   The assured was not entitled to assign the policy. It is a contract of personal indemnity and insurers cannot be compelled to accept responsibility of a person who may be quite unknown to them. The

policy was one in which there was inherent a personal element of such a character as to make it quite impossible to say that it was assignable at the volition of the assured.

The risk that A is going to incur liability by driving his motor car, or persons authorised by A, is one thing. The risk that B will incur or persons authorised by B may be a totally different thing. The insurers made inquiries as to the driving record of proposer. A good record may be accepted. A bad record may be refused, or a higher premium required.

[2.153]   Smith v Ralph

[1963] 2 Lloyd's Rep 439, Div Ct

On 15 March 1963 the respondent bought a car from Davies, who handed him a certificate of insurance issued by the motor insurer to Davies valid from 25 February 1963 to 24 February 1964. The respondent was charged with using the car on 13 April 1963 when uninsured. He produced the certificate issued to Davies which was expressed to cover not only the policyholder but any other person who was driving on the policyholder's order or with his permission.

HELD: Any permission or authority given by the policyholder, Davies, could not extend beyond the time of the sale when he ceased to be a policyholder in the sense of having any insurable interest. The respondent was not covered and there must be a conviction.

Vehicle bought on approval

[2.154]   Bullock v Bellamy

(1940) 67 Ll L Rep 392   Cassels J

The plaintiff had obtained judgment against a Mr Borrett in an action arising from a collision caused by Mr Borrett's negligent driving. The plaintiff sought to recover the judgment sum against Borrett's insurer. Borrett had insurance in respect of a Morris and his insurance extended to any vehicle personally belonging to him. The policy also covered him whilst personally driving for pleasure purposes any other motor car not belonging to him and not hired to him under any hire-purchase agreement. At the time of the accident he was driving a Chrysler. Borrett maintained that he was driving this car on approval and that he had paid the seller £10 by way of security. The seller said that the purchase had been completed and the £10 was a deposit. The judge accepted that at the time of the accident Borrett had not purchased the vehicle and therefore the vehicle was covered by the 'any other car' provision.

[2.155]   Simpson v Dan Parkins Ltd

(1995) Lloyd's List, 2 May

It was held that a seller owed a duty of care to a buyer to describe a vehicle correctly for insurance purposes although on the facts of the case the loss suffered did not directly arise from the description of the vehicle given by the seller.

Causing or permitting

[2.156]   *Note*—For s 35(1) of the 1930 Act, see now the Road Traffic Act 1988, s 143 (at para [1.2]).

[2.157]   Goldsmith v Deakin

(1933) 150 LT 157, 98 JP 4, [1933] WN 255, 50 TLR 73, 31 LGR 420, 30 Cox CC 32.

The dictionary definition of 'to permit' is to give lead to; allow; to afford means. The offence of 'permitting use' arises where, to quote the words of Lawrence J: 'Although the respondent may not have known affirmatively the way in which the vehicle was being used, if in fact he allowed it to be used, and did not care whether it was being used in contravention of the statute or not, he did, in my view, permit its use under Road Traffic Act 1930.'

[2.158]   Sidcup Building Estates Ltd v Sidery

(1936) 24 Ry & Can Tr Cas 164

The defendant had threatened drivers with instant dismissal if they worked more than the legal number of hours. It did not dismiss a driver who disobeyed.

HELD: Guilty of 'permitting'.

Note—And see *Cox & Son Ltd v Sidery* (1935) 24 Ry & Can Tr Cas 69.

[2.159]   Clydebank Co-op Society v Binnie

1937 JC 17

A business firm kept cars for hire. A customer hired a car for 13s and arranged with five friends to pay 2s 6d each. The defendant's manager knew other passengers were to be carried, but did not know of the separate payments. The passengers were joining together to make frequent journeys, picked up at different places. The defendant was put on its guard and had a duty to inquire.

HELD: The defendant was guilty of 'permitting'.

[2.160]   Evans v Dell

[1937] 1 All ER 349, 156 LT 240, 101 JP 149, 53 TLR 310, 81 Sol Jo 100, 35 LGR 105, Div Ct

A vehicle was hired by the organisers of a dance to take persons attending the dance from A to C. This intention had been advertised in a newspaper without the respondent's knowledge. At the dance it was announced that passengers must take tickets and contribute not less than sixpence. A number bought tickets which were collected in the coach. Neither the respondent nor his driver knew of the payments.

HELD: That as the respondent had no knowledge of the advertisement or the payments, and had not deliberately shut his eyes to what was being done, he had not 'permitted'.

Per Goddard J: Mens rea is an essential ingredient in offences under the Road Traffic Acts.

[2.161]   Churchill v Norris
(1938) 158 LT 255, 82 Sol Jo 114, 31 Cox CC 1

The defendant told his driver not to drive with too heavy a load, put instructions in the cabin of his vehicle, and instructed the driver if in doubt to weigh the laden vehicle. The efendant knew the weight of timber was by custom measured in a rough and ready way by size, which might be erroneous. He had not ordered his servants specifically never to start a journey without weighing. Having knowledge of the prevailing method, he had connived at conduct which might well lead to commission of the offence, and had therefore 'permitted'. 'Permit' may mean no more than a failure to take proper steps to prevent.

[2.162]   McLeod v Buchanan
[1940] 2 All ER 179, 84 Sol Jo 452, 1940 SC (HL) 17, 1940 SN 20, 1940 SLT 232

A solicitor owned a poultry farm which was managed by his brother. A private car owned by the solicitor was registered and insured in the name of the brother for private and business use of the brother. The solicitor knew that his brother used the car for his private purposes. This car was replaced by a van which was registered and insured in the name of the solicitor for commercial use only. The certificate was sent from the solicitor's office to the brother without any comment, and the brother did not notice that it was limited to commercial use. The solicitor never gave the brother any permission to use the van for private purposes and did not know of this use, nor did he tell the brother that the insurance was restricted or make any conditions as to the use of the van. The brother used it for private purposes.

HELD: The solicitor had permitted the brother to use an uninsured vehicle and was liable on the principle of *Monk v Warbey* (at para [1.24]).

Per Lord Wright: To 'cause' involves some express or positive mandate, or some authority. To 'permit' is a looser and vaguer term. It may denote an express permission, general or particular, as distinguished from a mandate. The other person is not told to use the vehicle in the particular way, but he is told that he may do so if he desires. It includes cases where permission is merely inferred. If the other person is given control of the vehicle, permission may be inferred if the vehicle is left at the other person's disposal in such circumstances as to carry with it a reasonable implication of a discretion or liberty to use it in the manner in which it was used.

   In order to prove permission, it is not necessary to show knowledge of similar use in the past, or actual notice that the vehicle might be, or was likely to be, so used, or that the accused was guilty of a reckless disregard of the probabilities of the case, or a wilful closing of his eyes. He may not have thought of his duties under the section. The sending of the insurance certificate without any further intimation was not sufficient notice to his brother of the change. ... In my opinion the necessary permission is established.

[2.163]   Watkins v O'Shaughnessy
[1939] 1 All ER 385, 161 LT 144, 83 Sol Jo 215, CA

At a public auction held by the second defendant, the first defendant bought a motor car. He drove it away, although, to the knowledge of the servants of the second defendant, the car was uninsured and unlicensed. In fact, the servants of the second defendant lent the first defendant the company's trade number plates for the purpose, and supplied him with a slip, referring to a different car, but altered by them to appear to refer to the car in question, and assured him that such a proceeding was quite in order. The plaintiff was injured by the alleged negligent driving of the first defendant, but, as a judgment against him would be useless, the plaintiff did not ask for judgment against him, but did ask for judgment against the second defendant, alleging that it had caused or permitted the first defendant to use a motor vehicle in respect of which there was not in existence a policy of insurance in accordance with the Road Traffic Act 1930, s 35.

HELD: As the sale had been completed before the driving of the car by the first defendant, the second defendant had no control over him, and could not, therefore, be said to have 'caused or permitted' him to drive, and, in any event, the acts of the servants of the second defendant were quite unauthorised by them.

For A to permit B to do anything, the relation between A and B must be such that it is not open for B lawfully to do the thing in question without such permission. It must be open for A to withhold that permission without which B cannot lawfully do the thing in question. Permission to do that thing must be necessary for the thing's performance.

[2.164] Goodbarne v Buck

[1940] 1 KB 771, [1940] 1 All ER 613, 109 LJKB 837, 162 LT 259, 56 TLR 433, 84 Sol Jo 380, CA

Cause or permit are two different verbs. To make a person liable for 'permitting' another person to use, he must be in a position to forbid the other person to use the vehicle, ie where he is the owner of the car. The fact that one person assisted another to get a worthless piece of paper in place of an effective policy, did not 'cause' him to use the vehicle on the road without an effective policy.

Note—See also *Thompson v Lodwick* [1983] RTR 76.

[2.165] Lloyd v Singleton

[1953] 1 QB 357, [1953] 1 All ER 291, [1953] 2 WLR 278, 117 JP 97, 97 Sol Jo 98, 51 LGR 165, Div Ct

A company owned a motor car which was insured in the name of the managing director of the company and covered who had his permission to drive. The respondent, the assistant general manager of the company, had full discretion himself to use the vehicle for his work or to allow other employees of the company to use it in the course of the company's business. The respondent permitted his brother, who was not an employee of the company, to drive, and was charged with permitting the use without insurance. The justices dismissed the charge on the dictum of MacKinnon LJ in *Goodbarne v Buck* (at para [2.164]).

HELD: The part of that judgment which stated that the person permitting must be in a position to forbid the other person to use, followed. The court was unable to agree with the further statement that the only person who could forbid was the owner, which must have been *per incuriam*.

[2.166] Morris v Williams

(1951) 50 LGR 308, Div Ct

A company owned four vehicles, one of which was a van which was uninsured. The manager of the company instructed an employee to go by car. The employee used the van. The manager was summonsed for permitting a vehicle to be used when uninsured. The magistrates convicted.

HELD, ON APPEAL: The employee was permitted by the manager to use the van. There was implied, if not express, authorisation.

Conviction upheld.

Note—See also *Kelly v Cornhill Insurance Co Ltd* (at para [2.85]).

[2.167]   Shave v Rosner

[1954] 2 QB 113, [1954] 2 All ER 280, [1954] 2 WLR 1057, 18 JP 364, 98 Sol Jo 355, Div Ct

A motor car repairer reshoed the brakes of a motor van and drove it to the owner, who drove the repairer back to his garage, testing the brakes himself. A little later the same day the owner was driving the van when a wheel came off and injured a pedestrian. The wheel came off because the repairer's servants had not properly fastened the hub nuts. The repairer was prosecuted for 'using or causing or permitting to be used' a vehicle 'causing or likely to cause danger to any person'.

HELD: In one sense it might be said the repairer 'caused' the van to be used by delivering it in a dangerous condition and the owner unwittingly using it. He did not 'use' it himself; he did not 'permit' because he could not give permission to the owner to use his own car. When 'causes or permits' are found in contrast, 'permits' means giving leave and licence to somebody to use the car, and 'causes' means ordering or directing someone to use it. The repairer had ceased to have control or dominion over the van, and had not caused its use, and was not criminally liable under the Regulations.

Note—70 LQR 453 points out that the words 'cause' and 'causation' have various meanings depending on the circumstances and that it is clear in a civil action for injuries to the passer-by the defendant would have been liable on the ground that he had caused the accident as it was his negligence which had caused the wheel to break off from the car.

[2.168]   James & Son v Smee

[1955] 1 QB 78, [1954] 3 All ER 273, [1954] 3 WLR 631, 118 JP 536, 98 Sol Jo 771, 52 LGR 545, Div Ct

A motor lorry and trailer left the owner's premises with the brakes complying with the regulations. At the premises of third parties, the driver with a boy assistant, uncoupled the trailer to enable loading. After loading, the driver left the boy to couple the trailer to the lorry. The boy failed to connect the brakes of the trailer properly and the driver took no steps to check the connections. The owner was prosecuted for 'permitting'.

HELD: It had not permitted; conviction quashed. The question should be: 'Has the permitter authorised the very thing which happened?' If so, or if he had more than a very shrewd idea of what would happen, then he should be found guilty. If not, no case has been proved against him. A permission to use it is not, unless more is proved, a permission to use in contravention.

[2.169]   LF Dove Ltd v Tarvin

(1964) 108 Sol Jo 404, Div Ct

A firm of motor engineers lent one of their cars to a customer to use whilst they were repairing his own. He drove it to London and as a result a charge was brought against the motor engineers that they did unlawfully use the car all the tyres of which were not maintained in safe condition contrary to the Motor Vehicles (Construction and Use) Regulations 1955, reg 78. The defendants contended that as they had parted with possession and control of the car to the customer for his use, they were not using it at the time of the offence.

HELD: The point was a good one. The defendants had not been charged with causing or permitting the use of the car. The word 'use' was found in many regulations and there was a clear distinction between 'use' for oneself by oneself or a servant or agent and causing or permitting someone not a servant or agent to use. Here the defendants had not used the car at the time of the offence.

[2.170]   Fransman v Sexton

[1965] Crim LR 556, Div Ct, QBD

The defendant, who operated a self-drive car hire service, was held not guilty of 'permitting' the use of a car with an inadequate braking system where one of the rear brakes was defective and did not work but where new parts had been provided about a year before and the defendant did not know the brake was inoperative. Knowledge is an essential element in 'permitting' something. It is not to be imputed by mere negligence, but by something more, such as recklessly sending out a car not caring what would happen.

[2.171]   Grays Haulage Co Ltd v Arnold

[1966] 1 All ER 896, [1966] 1 WLR 534, 130 JP 196, 110 Sol Jo 122, Div Ct

The defendant was convicted by magistrates of 'permitting' its driver to drive for continuous periods amounting in the aggregate to more than 11 hours contrary to the Road Traffic Act 1960, s 73. He had driven the vehicle from Carlisle to London from 10 am to 10.30 pm with only one hour's rest. The defendant had failed to take steps which would or might have prevented the driver doing as he did such as providing a recorder on the vehicle or making arrangements for the driver to telephone them during the journey by reversing the charges.

HELD, ON APPEAL to the Divisional Court: This was not 'permitting'. In *James & Son Ltd v Smee* (at para [2.168]) it had been pointed out that knowledge is of two kinds, actual knowledge, and knowledge which consists of shutting one's eyes to the obvious, that is, failing to do something or doing something not caring whether contravention takes place or not. Here there was no question of actual knowledge nor was it a case of shutting one's eyes to the obvious. There was no evidence that the defendant had any knowledge of circumstances which it had allowed to go on without caring whether an offence had been committed or not. Knowledge is not imputed by mere negligence.
    Conviction quashed.

[2.172]   Windle v Dunning & Son Ltd

[1968] 2 All ER 46, [1968] 1 WLR 552, 132 JP 264, 112 Sol Jo 196, 66 LGR 516, Div Ct

Lorries hired to the respondent but loaded by it were found by an inspector of weights and measures to be overloaded. The respondent was convicted of 'using' the lorries on a road carrying loads exceeding that allowed by the Construction and Use Regulations 1966, contrary to the Road Traffic Act 1960, s 64(2) (now ss 68–73 of the 1988 Act). The drivers were not the respondent's servants but were hired with the lorries.

HELD, ON APPEAL: The respondent was not 'using' the lorries.

Per Lord Parker: 'Using' when used in connection with causing and permitting has a restricted meaning. It certainly covers the driver; it may also cover the driver's employer if he, the driver, is about his master's business, but beyond that I find it very difficult to conceive that any other person could be said to be using the vehicle as opposed to causing it to be used.

[2.173]   Newbury v Davis
[1974] RTR 367, (1974) 118 Sol Jo 222, Div Ct

The defendant gave permission to Jarvis to borrow his car and use it provided he insured it. Jarvis failed to insure it and was convicted of using the car without insurance. The defendant was charged with 'permitting' Jarvis to use the car uninsured.

HELD: He was not guilty. Permission given subject to a condition which is unfulfilled is no permission at all.

[2.174]   Swan (William) & Co Ltd v MacNab
[1977] JC 57, High Ct of Justiciary

A vehicle driven by an employee was found to have a defective braking system. His employer was charged with 'using' the vehicle when it did not comply with the Road Traffic Act 1972, s 40(5). It contended that it could not be convicted of 'using' but only of 'causing or permitting' the use of the vehicle.

HELD: The offence of 'using' a vehicle could be committed both by the driver of the vehicle and by the company on behalf of whom the vehicle was being driven.

Note—See also *Carmichael & Sons Ltd v Cottle* (1971) 114 Sol Jo 867, [1971] RTR 11 and *Crawford v Haughton* [1972] 1 All ER 535, [1972] 1 WLR 572, 116 Sol Jo 125, [1972] RTR 125. Also *Balfour Beatty v Grindey* [1975] RTR 156 and *Howard v G T Jones & Co Ltd* [1975] RTR 150.

[2.175]   Baugh v Crago
[1975] RTR 453, [1976] 1 Lloyd's Rep 563, Div Ct

The policy of insurance covering the defendant's vehicle was effective only when the driver held a driving licence. He allowed a man to drive who had no licence, though he thought he had.

HELD: The defendant was guilty of a breach of the Road Traffic Act 1972, s 143. It was not the same as in *Newbury v Davis* (at para [2.173]). A distinction must be drawn between a case where the owner of a car grants permission to another to drive believing that the other is covered by insurance when he is not and a case where a person allows another to drive making it a condition that he shall not drive unless and until he is covered by insurance.

[2.176]   DPP v Fisher
[1991] Crim LR 787, Div Ct

The defendant lent his car to A on condition that he find someone to drive it who was insured. A asked B to drive, both A and B assuming that B was properly insured to drive. In fact B was not properly insured. The defendant submitted, relying on *Newbury v Davis* (at para [2.173]) that as he had imposed a condition on the loan, he had discharged his responsibilities and taken all reasonable precautions. The justices dismissed the information and the prosecutor appealed by way of case stated.

HELD, allowing the appeal and remitting the case with a direction to convict: That the principle in *Newbury v Davis* was to be very strictly limited to exceptional cases. Here the defendant had no idea who A would ask to drive, and there was no communication at all between the defendant and B.

3.   BREACH OF CONDITION

(A)   ONUS OF PROOF

[2.177]   *Note*—The burden of proving that a condition has been broken lies on the insurers and will only be shifted to the insured if clear words are used.

[2.178]   Bond Air Services Ltd v Hill
[1955] 2 QB 417, [1955] 2 All ER 476, [1955] 2 WLR 1194, 99 Sol Jo 370, [1955] 1 Lloyd's Rep 488   Lord Goddard CJ

An aircraft insurance policy contained the following general conditions:
    General Condition 8: The observance and performance by the insured of the conditions of this policy as far as they contain anything to be observed or performed by the insured are of the essence of the contract and are conditions precedent to the insured's right to recover hereunder.
    Condition 7: The insured and all persons in his employment or for whom he is responsible shall duly observe the statutory orders, regulations and directions relating to air navigation for the time being in force.
    An aeroplane insured under the policy crashed and the insurer contended that as the policy provides that the observance of the conditions is a condition precedent to the insured's right to recover it is for the insured to prove observance so that the onus is shifted.
    Per Lord Goddard CJ: I do not think it can be doubted that, ordinarily, it is for the underwriter to prove a breach of condition, at least where he is not contending that the policy is void on the ground that there has been a breach of a condition precedent to the formation of the policy. So, too, it is for him to prove an exception. The difference between a condition and an exception is that the former places some duty or responsibility on the assured, while the latter restricts the scope of the policy.
    As to the insurer's contention he deemed this decided by the decision in *Stebbing v Liverpool and London Globe Insurance Co Ltd* [1917] 2 KB 433. In that case there was also a provision that compliance with the conditions should be a condition precedent to any liability on the part of the insurer and the court decided that the burden of proving the falsity of an answer which amounted to a breach of warranty was on the insurer.
    Per Lord Goddard CJ: The parties to a policy can use words which will relieve insurers of the onus and cast it on the assured, as they may with regard to any other matter affecting an insurer's liability. But, in my opinion, much clearer words than are used here would be necessary to change what I think, certainly for a century and probably for much longer, has always been regarded as a fundamental principle of insurance law,

(B) BREACH

(I) CONDITION OF VEHICLE

Damaged or unsafe condition/efficient condition/safeguarding from loss or damage

[2.179] **Jones and James v Provincial Insurance Co Ltd**
(1929) 46 TLR 71, 35 Ll L Rep 135   Rowlatt J

The policy contained a condition that 'the assured shall take all reasonable steps to maintain such vehicle in efficient condition', and it provided that the observance of the conditions should be a condition precedent to the liability of the insurers. The claimants removed the foot-brake from the vehicle, leaving only a hand-brake, and in this state of affairs the vehicle caused damage, and was itself damaged, in an accident, but the exact cause of the accident could not be ascertained.

HELD: The condition was a condition precedent and as it had been broken, the insurer was not liable on the policy.

[2.180] **Barrett v London General Insurance Co**
[1935] 1 KB 238, 104 LJKB 15, 152 LT 256, 51 TLR 97, 78 Sol Jo 898, 50 Ll L Rep 99   Goddard J

By a policy of motor car insurance the defendant agreed to indemnify the assured against third party risks, 'liability in respect of any accident while driving the car in an unsafe or unroadworthy condition' being excluded.

HELD: Applying the principle of marine insurance that there is an implied warranty that a ship is seaworthy at the time of sailing, but no warranty that she shall continue seaworthy throughout the voyage, the policy must be taken to mean that, for the assured to be covered by it, the car must be roadworthy when it set out on its journey but need not continue to be roadworthy throughout the journey. An assignee of the assured was, therefore, entitled to recover in an action against the defendant on the policy where the defendant (on whom lay the onus of proving unroadworthiness) failed to prove that the car was unroadworthy when it began its journey and only showed that, by reason of a defective brake, it was unroadworthy at the time of the accident.

Note—But the reasoning of Goddard J was disapproved in *Trickett v Queensland Insurance Co Ltd* (at para [2.181]).

[2.181] **Trickett v Queensland Insurance Co Ltd**
[1936] AC 159, 105 LJPC 38, 154 LT 228, 52 TLR 164, 80 Sol Jo 74, 53 Ll L Rep 255, PC

A general exceptions clause in a private motor vehicle insurance policy provided that: 'No liability shall attach to the company under this policy in respect of ... any personal accident to the insured occurring: (1) While any motor vehicle in connection with which indemnity is granted under this policy is: (c) Being driven in a damaged or unsafe condition.'
  The insured, while driving at night a motor car covered by the policy, was involved in a collision with another motor car and was killed. At and about the time of the accident the lights of his motor car were not shining. On a claim under the

policy by the insured's daughter as assignee of the rights under the policy from the legal personal representative of the insured:

HELD: At the time of the accident the motor car driven by the insured was in a damaged or unsafe condition within the meaning of the exceptions clause, and that the insurance company was accordingly relieved from liability under the policy irrespective of whether or not the insured was aware at the time of the accident of the damaged or unsafe condition of the car. The terms of the exceptions clauses were unambiguous and plain, and there was no justification for supplementing them by adding 'to the knowledge of the driver', or for reforming the contract into which the insured had entered.

The position of a motor car on land cannot be assimilated to that of a ship at sea and the same code of law rigidly applied to both cases so as to make the exceptions clause to the policy only applicable where the motor vehicle was in a damaged or unsafe condition at the beginning of its journey. Such an argument based on the identity of the conditions which govern the seaworthiness of a ship at sea and the roadworthiness of a motor car on land is unsound.

Reasoning of Goddard J to the contrary in *Barrett v London General Insurance Co Ltd* [1935] 1 KB 238 disapproved. Judgment of the Court of Appeal of New Zealand (1932) NZLR 1727 affirmed.

[2.182] Brown v Zurich Accident and Liability Insurance Co

[1954] 2 Lloyd's Rep 243   Sellers J

The claimant was the owner of a Fordson van insured with the respondent under a comprehensive motor car policy. The van was involved in a collision in December 1950. The tyres of both front wheels were completely devoid of tread though not worn down to the canvas at any point. The collision was due to the van going into an uncontrollable skid on an icy road. The tyres were inspected by the police after the accident but no proceedings were taken by the police under reg 71 of the 1947 regulations. The skid might have occurred even if the front tyres had adequate treads. The respondent contended that the claimant was in breach of the condition requiring him to maintain the vehicle in an efficient condition and was therefore not entitled to recover. Fulfilment of the policy condition was a condition precedent to liability. The arbitrator held that the policy requirement was to take all reasonable steps to safeguard from loss or damage and maintain the vehicle in efficient condition; that the smooth state of the front tyres made the vehicle inefficient and the claimant had failed to take reasonable steps to maintain in efficient condition.

HELD: 'Efficient condition' meant 'roadworthy'. The finding of fact by the arbitrator that the tyres were dangerous and made the vehicle unsafe and inefficient in condition, could not be disturbed by the court. 'Vehicle' includes tyres. *Woolfall and Rimmer Ltd v Moyle* (at para [2.193]) not applicable.

Award for respondents upheld.

[2.183] Clarke v National Insurance and Guarantee Corpn Ltd

[1964] 1 QB 199, [1963] 3 All ER 375, [1963] 3 WLR 710, 107 Sol Jo 573, [1963] 2 Lloyd's Rep 35, CA

The plaintiff was the owner of a Ford Anglia four-seater car for which a motor policy was issued to him by the defendant, an insurance company. A term of the policy excluded liability whilst the car was 'being driven in an unsafe or unroadworthy condition'. The plaintiff was driving the car with eight adult passengers in it when it collided with another car whilst descending a steep hill. The judge found that by reason of the overloading the steering, braking and control of the car were seriously impaired. The defendant refused to meet claims arising from the accident.

HELD, ON APPEAL: The defendant was not liable under the policy. Maritime cases dealing with the warranty of seaworthiness, though by no means governing the matter, are of some assistance; in such cases it has been held that overloading or bad stowage can render a vessel unseaworthy. At the time of the accident the vehicle was unroadworthy through being overloaded and the exception clause applied.

Per Harman LJ: I think that one must regard the car as it was as it proceeded along the road, not look at it empty before it was loaded up and say: This was a safe and mechanically sound car. The words which are important for this purpose are 'being driven' and, when it was being driven it was, by reason of overloading, just as in the ship cases, rendered unsafe and unroadworthy.

[2.184]   Liverpool Corpn v T and H R Roberts

[1964] 3 All ER 56, [1965] 1 WLR 938, 109 Sol Jo 510, [1964] 2 Lloyd's Rep 219   Cumming-Bruce J

The defendant firm, who were motor coach proprietors and operators, were insured against third-party risks under a policy containing the following condition: 'The insured shall take all due and reasonable precautions to safeguard the property insured and to keep it in a good state of repair. The underwriters shall not be liable for damage or injury caused through driving the motor vehicle in an unsafe condition either before or after the accident.' An accident occurred due to the brakes of the defendants' motor coach failing to stop the vehicle within a reasonable distance. A motor engineer inspected the vehicle and found the brake linings worn and the servo mechanism defective due to neglect over a period of months. The firm's business was managed by T Roberts who relied on a qualified mechanic G Roberts to deal with maintenance. The firm had no system of written reports on maintenance and no instructions were given for periodical inspection or overhaul of braking systems.

HELD: (1) The two sentences of the condition were not separate obligations so as to create an absolute obligation by the second sentence to keep the vehicle in safe condition. The second sentence was merely an expression of the consequences of a failure to fulfil the duty imposed by the first sentence. The wording of the condition in *Trickett v Queensland Insurance Co Ltd* (at para [2.181]) was quite different. In the present case the fact that the vehicle was objectively in an unsafe condition irrespective of knowledge or want of precautions on the part of the insured would not be enough to constitute a breach.

(2)   Applying *Woolfall and Rimmer Ltd v Moyle* (at para [2.193]) the duty under the policy to keep the vehicle in a good state of repair was personal to the defendants and a casual act of neglect by an employee would not amount to a breach of it: but on the facts the defective condition of the vehicle was due to the failure of T Roberts to impose or exercise any system for periodical inspection and the condition had been broken.

[2.185]   **Conn v Westminster Insurance Association Ltd**

[1966] 1 Lloyd's Rep 407, CA

The plaintiff was driver and owner of a taxicab for the use of which the defendant issued an insurance policy covering third-party claims and damage. Condition 5 of the policy said 'The Policyholder shall take all reasonable steps to safeguard from loss or damage and maintain in efficient condition the vehicle' insured. Condition 1 made the due observance and fulfilment of the conditions of the policy a condition precedent to the insurer's liability under the policy. The plaintiff was driving the cab when it veered off the roadway into some railings and was damaged beyond repair. After the accident the police found both front tyres were bare of tread and one brake shoe was worn down to the metal. The defendant refused to meet claims under the policy, relying on condition 5. The cause of the accident was not established but there was no evidence that it was due to the condition of the brakes or tyres.

HELD: (1) The words 'efficient condition' in the context of condition 5 meant 'roadworthy condition'.
  (2)   On the plaintiff's evidence that he noticed no symptoms of wear in the brakes, and bearing in mind that the actual state of the brakes could not be ascertained without dismantling them, the defendant had not shown a failure on the part of the plaintiff to take all reasonable steps to maintain his brakes.
  (3)   Unlike the brakes the state of the tyres was plain for anyone to see: having no tread they were unroadworthy and the plaintiff was in breach of condition 5.
  (4)   It was irrelevant whether any breach of condition 5 caused the accident. The only question was whether there was a breach of the condition. There was a breach and the plaintiff could not succeed.

[2.186]   **New India Assurance Co Ltd v Yeo Beng Chow**

[1972] 3 All ER 293, [1972] 1 WLR 786, 116 Sol Jo 373, [1972] 1 Lloyd's Rep 479, [1972] RTR 356, PC

The insurers issued a motor policy to the respondent insured. It was in the form of a comprehensive policy, but cover was restricted to third party liability only by deleting section 1 of the policy which indemnified against loss of or damage to the insured vehicle. The remaining section indemnified against liability in respect of personal injury to any person or damage to property of third parties. The policy contained conditions of which condition 3 required the insured to 'take all reasonable steps to safeguard the vehicle from loss or damage and to maintain the vehicle in efficient condition …'. After a collision in which a motorcyclist was killed, the insured's vehicle was found by a vehicle examiner not to have been kept in an efficient and roadworthy condition. The insurer, in conformity with the compulsory insurance legislation, paid the damages and costs awarded against the insured for the death of the motorcyclist and then claimed these sums from the insured for breach of condition 3. It was argued on his behalf, and accepted by the Federal Court of Malaysia, that, section 1 of the policy having been deleted, condition 3 could not survive unaffected; that as loss or damage was not covered by the policy, so much of the condition as required the insured to safeguard the vehicle from loss or damage could have no application and that the condition had been 'mutilated'.

HELD: This was not right. It did not follow from a limitation of the cover provided by the policy that any alteration was to be implied in the conditions precedent contained in the policy. Insurance companies can insert such conditions as they choose and if the conditions inserted are accepted by the insured, they are binding on him. There is no obligation on an insurance company to relate the conditions to particular aspects of the policy.

[2.187]   Amey Properties Ltd v Cornhill Insurance plc
[1996] LRLR 259

A tractor used in the construction of a runway collided with an aircraft due to defects in the tractor's clutch and handbrake caused by lack of maintenance. It was held that a condition requiring a vehicle to be kept in an 'efficient and roadworthy condition' was to be construed so that insurer need only prove negligence rather than recklessness and was therefore to be distinguished from the construction of reasonable care clauses in cases such as *Sofi v Prudential Assurance Co Ltd* (at para [2.198]).

The company appealed on the first point. Appeal dismissed.

Per Somervill LJ: It would need the plainest possible words if it were desired to exclude the insurance cover by reason of the fact that there was at the back one passenger more than the seating accommodation. I hope any company will print their definition in red ink when the policy is inapplicable when an extra passenger is carried.

Per Denning LJ: If the clause had the meaning contended for, I would regard it was almost a trap.

Per Romer LJ: If this provision is applied to a private motor car, I have not the least idea what it means.

(C)   DUTY TO NOTIFY INSURERS

(I)   'DETAILED PARTICULARS'

[2.188]   Cox v Orion Insurance Co Ltd
[1982] RTR 1, CA

The plaintiff was issued with a motor insurance policy by the defendant whereby it was a condition precedent to its liability that he should give notice and deliver detailed particulars of any accident, loss and damage. Whilst the plaintiff was driving the car it collided with another vehicle and was damaged. He claimed under the policy but declared that someone else was driving the car at the time of the collision. Later he made a claim for theft in respect of the same incident. The defendant repudiated liability under the policy. The plaintiff had been convicted of various road traffic offences as being the driver at the time of the collision.

HELD: The defendant was not entitled to repudiate. The plaintiff was in breach of the condition precedent in that it had not been given detailed particulars of the collision. *Lickiss v Milestone Motor Policies at Lloyd's* (at para [2.37]) distinguished.

(II)   'AS SOON AS POSSIBLE'

[2.189]   Verelst's Administratrix Motor Union Insurance Co Ltd
[1925] 2 KB 137, 94 LJKB 659, 133 LT 364, 41 TLR 343, 69 Sol Jo 412   Roche J

A policy of insurance covering (*inter alia*) the death of the insured by accident, contained the following condition: 'In the case of any accident, injury, damage or loss ... the insured or the insured's representative for the time being shall give notice ... in writing to the head office of the company of such accident, injury, damage or loss as soon as possible after it has come to the knowledge of the insured or of the insured's representative for the time being.'

During the currency of the policy namely, on 14 January 1923, the insured was killed in a motor accident in India. Knowledge of her death reached her personal representative in England within a month, but the personal representative did not know of the existence of the policy of insurance until January 1924. Notice was given to the insurance company as soon as possible thereafter. The insurance company repudiated liability on the ground that notice was not given 'as soon as possible' within the meaning of the condition.

HELD: In considering whether notice was given 'as soon as possible' within the meaning of the condition, all existing circumstances must be taken into account, including the available means of knowledge of the insured's personal representative of the existence of the policy and the identity of the insurance company; and the arbitrator, to whom the dispute had been submitted, was entitled to find that notice had been given 'as soon as possible'.

[2.190]   Allen v Robles

[1969] 3 All ER 154, [1969] I WLR 1193, 113 Sol Jo 484, [1969] 2 Lloyd's Rep 61, CA

The defendant took out an insurance policy with the third party, a French insurance company, for the use of his motor car. On 9 April he collided with the plaintiff's house, causing damage. The policy contained a condition which relieved the company of liability to the insured if he failed to give notice within five days of having knowledge of a claim. The defendant received a letter from the plaintiff on 18 April claiming damages, but he did not report the claim to the company until some date in August. The company's solicitors wrote to the defendant's solicitors on 10 August, saying their clients reserved their position under the policy. Shortly afterwards they wrote to the plaintiff's solicitors that the company was not indemnifying the defendant but did not write to the defendant's solicitors to this effect until 29 November.

HELD: There was a breach of condition and the insurer had not lost its right to rely on it merely by their delay in notifying the defendant. The position was that when the insurer discovered in August:
(1)   that there was a claim; and
(2)   that the defendant was in breach of his condition,
it was in a position then either to elect whether to repudiate or accept liability or it was open to it to delay its decision, particularly in view of the letter of 10 August. Mere lapse of time would only operate against it if the insured was thereby prejudiced or if rights of third parties intervened or the delay was so long as to be evidence that it had accepted liability. None of these possibilities arose in the present case.

Note—See also *Pioneer Concrete (UK) Ltd v National Employers Mutual Insurance Association Ltd* [1985] 2 All ER 395.

Condition will also bind a driver who is not the policyholder.

[2.191]   **Alfred McAlpine plc v Bai (Run Off) Ltd**

(5 May 1998, unreported)   Colman J, QBD (CAOMM)

O'Malley was an employee of Moss, a sub-contractor to RC Construction Ltd (RCCL) who in turn were subcontracted to the claimant. In proceedings by O'Malley against the claimant a payment into court was accepted. The claimant then sought to recover a contribution from RCCL who by this stage had gone into liquidation. The defendant, who was the insurer of RCCL sought to avoid liability on the grounds that RCCL had not complied with the terms of its policy which required that it give notice 'as soon as possible' of any claim or occurrence. In the alternative the defendant argued that the failure to give notice was a repudiatory breach of the agreement and that it had been prejudiced by the delay.

HELD, ON APPEAL: The defendant could not establish any failure on the part of RCCL to act in good faith.

Per Waller LJ: Failure to supply details of a claim cannot constitute a breach of the obligation of good faith. Dishonesty would have to be established.

(III)   IMPOSSIBILITY OF COMPLIANCE

[2.192]   **Re Coleman's Depositories Ltd and Life and Health Assurance Association**

[1907] 2 KB 798, 76 LJKB 865, 97 LT 420, 23 TLR 638, CA

On 28 December 1904, the assured signed a proposal form for an employer's liability policy and a cover note was issued which did not contain any conditions. On 3 January 1905 a policy was issued and delivered to the assured on 9 January 1905, in force from 1 January. The policy contained a condition requiring immediate notice of accident which was of the essence of the contract. On 2 January 1905, an accident occurred to a workman which was believed slight, and no notice given. Dangerous symptoms supervened. Notice was given on 14 March, and the workman died on 15 March.

HELD: The assured did not know and had no opportunity of knowing of the existence of the condition at the date of the accident, the condition was one with which it was impossible to comply, and the policy did not impose a condition on the assured in respect of this accident, and the assured was entitled to indemnity.

Note—It is now common practice for the cover note to contain a statement that it is issued subject to the conditions of the policy.

(D)   REPUGNANCY OF CONDITIONS

[2.193]   **Woolfall and Rimmer Ltd v Moyle**

[1942] 1 KB 66, [1941] 3 All ER 304, 111 LJKB 122, 166 LT 49, 58 TLR 28, 86 Sol Jo 63, CA

An employer's liability policy issued to a limited company contained the condition: 'The assured shall take reasonable precautions to prevent accidents and to comply with all statutory obligations.'

The purchase and supply of timber for scaffolding was left entirely to the foreman, who was competent and skilled. Scaffolding was erected and a ledger broke, injuring workmen. The foreman admitted he had no suitable timber available.

HELD, in the Court of Appeal: The assured had taken reasonable precautions by employing a competent foreman. Insurers could not say, I will insure you against negligence on condition that you are not negligent. They could not grant an indemnity with one hand and take it away with the other, but could say the assured should not carry on business in a reckless manner. The contention that the condition applied to the negligence of the foreman was a complete misconception. The condition was not a warranty that everybody employed by the assured, or in fact anybody except the assured, would take reasonable precautions. In appointing the foreman the assured ws not delegating its duty under the condition, but performing it.

[2.194]   Maltby (TF) Ltd v Pelton Steamship Co Ltd

[1951] 2 All ER 954n, [1951] WN 531, 95 Sol Jo 834, [1951] 2 Lloyd's Rep 332   Devlin J

Ship owners indemnified stevedores against claims by workmen arising from use of gear, provided they took reasonable precautions to prevent accidents and to comply with statutory requirements, and that their gear was regularly and properly tested, and did not use improper or inadequate gear. On a claim by stevedores for an indemnity under the contract, the court found the foreman of the stevedores was negligent.

HELD: The decision in *Woolfall and Rimmer Ltd v Moyle* (at para [2.193]) made it impossible to contend that the negligence of the foreman brought them within the first part of the stipulations.

   With regard to the gear, the words must be construed as meaning 'You the owner of the business shall not use improper or inadequate gear.' It did not mean 'You through your foreman, shall not use improper or inadequate gear.' The claim for indemnity succeeded.

[2.195]   Fraser v BN Furman (Productions) Ltd

[1967] 3 All ER 57, [1967] 1 WLR 898, 111 Sol Jo 471, [1967] 2 Lloyd's Rep 1, CA

The defendant was found liable in damages to the plaintiff, its employee, for negligence and breach of statutory duty in failing to guard a welding machine in which she sustained injury. It had originally had a guard but the defendant had removed it. It sued insurance brokers in third-party proceedings for an indemnity against these damages for breach of contract in having failed to insure it against the plaintiff's claim. The policy which it had been intended to obtain for the defendant, was an Eagle Star employers' liability policy which contained the condition 'The insured shall take reasonable precautions to prevent accidents'. The brokers denied liability on the ground that if the policy had been issued the insurer would have been entitled to repudiate liability under it for breach of the condition.

HELD: (1) Following *Woolfall and Rimmer Ltd v Moyle* (at para [2.193]) the obligation to take precautions is on the insured personally: failure by an employee to do so would not be a breach of the condition.
   (2)   'Reasonable precautions' means reasonable as between insurer and insured, without being repugnant to the commercial purpose of the contract. By this test what is reasonable is that the insured must not deliberately court a danger by taking measures which he knows are inadequate to avert it. It is not enough that his omission to take some precaution is negligent: it must be reckless, not caring, though aware of

the danger, whether it is averted or not. The purpose of the condition is to ensure that the insured will not refrain from taking precautions simply because he is covered. That was not the case here: the defendant had not appreciated the risk to which it was exposing the plaintiff.

(3)   It was not a defence to show merely that the insurer would have been entitled to repudiate. It must be shown that it would in fact have done so. The good repute of the company in question and the absence of any evidence that it would have sought to rely on the alleged breach of condition made it impossible to hold that it would have done so.

The brokers were liable to indemnify the defendant.

[2.196]   W and J Lane v Spratt

[1970] 2 QB 480, [1970] 1 All ER 162, [1969] 3 WLR 950, 113 Sol Jo 920, [1969] 2 Lloyd's Rep 229   Roskill J

The plaintiffs, haulage contractors, were insured under a goods in transit policy issued by the defendant, an underwriter at Lloyd's. It contained the condition 'the Insured shall take all reasonable precautions for the protection and safeguarding of the goods ...'. The plaintiffs engaged a driver after interviewing him and after making one abortive attempt to follow up a reference by telephone. On his first day at work he drove off with a lorry load of merchandise and was not seen again. The defendant refused to indemnify the plaintiffs on the ground that there had been a breach of condition.

HELD: In failing to take up references the plaintiffs had failed to take the elementary precautions which were usual in the trade and if the only duty was to take reasonable care they had failed in that duty. But that did not put them in breach of the condition. Following *Fraser v BN Furman (Productions) Ltd* (at para [2.195]) it is not enough that the omission to take a particular precaution should be negligent, it must be at least reckless, not caring whether the danger was averted or not. That was not true of these plaintiffs and they were entitled to indemnity.

[2.197]   Devco Holder Ltd v Legal and General Assurance Society Ltd

[1993] 2 Ll L Rep 567, CA

A Ferrari motor car was stolen from a station car park. The insured's driver had left the car unlocked with the key in the ignition. The car was stolen whilst he was in his office on a road opposite the station.

The insurance policy included the following condition: 'You may take all reasonable steps to protect your car against loss or damage and to maintain it in a safe and efficient condition.'

The court found that the keys had been left in the car deliberately and not inadvertently.

Per Slade LJ: (Counsel on behalf of the insurers) submitted that the judge in applying what I may call the 'deliberate courting the danger' test, adopted too high a test of negligence for the relevant purpose. He pointed out that, as Diplock LJ himself had made clear in *Fraser v B N Furman (Productions) Ltd* [1967] 3 All ER 57, [1967] 1 WLR 898, 111 Sol Jo 471, [1967] 2 Lloyd's Rep 1, CA [at para [2.195]] a condition, such as general condition 2, has to be construed in the context of the particular policy in which it appears, and in the context of the commercial purpose of that policy. He submitted that, where a claim is asserted under the theft provisions of a policy of motor insurance rather than under a policy of employers liability insurance (such as that dealt with by Diplock LJ in *Fraser*) a condition obliging the insured to take all reasonable steps to protect his car is not limited in its effect to precluding a deliberate courting of recognised risks by the insured, but extends to ordinary negligence. He submits that to give it a broader ambit in this way would not involve any repugnancy with the operative provisions of the policy giving insurance cover. Beyond saying that I see some force in those submissions, I do not find it necessary to deal with them.

[2.198]   Sofi v Prudential Assurance Co Ltd
[1993] 2 Lloyd's Rep 559

An insurance policy contained a term requiring the insured to take 'all reasonable steps to safeguard any property insured and to avoid accidents which may lead to damage or injury …'. The insured set out for a holiday in France but parked in a car park near Dover Castle leaving jewellery valued at £42,000 locked in the car glove compartment. On his return about half an hour later the valuables had been stolen. The judge held that the recklessness test defined in *Fraser v B N Furman (Productions) Ltd* (at para [2.195]) was equally applicable in both property and liability insurance. On the facts of the case the judge did not regard the decision to leave the valuables locked in the glove compartment as reckless.

[2.199]   Bushell v General Accident
[1992] CLY 2614

A motorist whose car was stolen was in breach of a requirement to take reasonable care in circumstances where he left the key in the ignition but locked the car door. The insured admitted that he had been leaving the key in the ignition for up to two years due to a faulty ignition barrel and that he had taken no steps during that period to rectify the position.

4.   AVOIDANCE OF LIABILITY

(A)   DUTY OF INSURERS TO SATISFY JUDGMENTS

Road Traffic Act 1988, s 151

[2.200]
151   Duty of insurers or persons giving security to satisfy judgment against persons insured or secured against third-party risks
  (1)   This section applies where, after a certificate of insurance or certificate of security has been delivered under section 147 of this Act to the person by whom a policy has been effected or to whom a security has been given, a judgment to which this subsection applies is obtained.
  (2)   Subsection (1) above applies to judgments relating to a liability with respect to any matter where liability with respect to that matter is required to be covered by a policy of insurance under section 145 of this Act and either—
    (a)   it is a liability covered by the terms of the policy or security to which the certificate relates, and the judgment is obtained against any person who is insured by the policy or whose liability is covered by the security, as the case may be, or
    (b)   it is a liability, other than an excluded liability, which would be so covered if the policy insured all persons or, as the case may be, the security covered the liability of all persons, and the judgment is obtained against any person other than one who is insured by the policy or, as the case may be, whose liability is covered by the security.

(3)   In deciding for the purposes of subsection (2) above whether a liability is or would be covered by the terms of a policy or security, so much of the policy or security as purports to restrict, as the case may be, the insurance of the persons insured by the policy or the operation of the security by reference to the holding by the driver of the vehicle of a licence authorising him to drive it shall be treated as of no effect.

(4)   In subsection (2)(b) above 'excluded liability' means a liability in respect of the death of, or bodily injury to, or damage to the property of, any person who, at the time of the use which gave rise to the liability, was allowing himself to be carried in or upon the vehicle and knew or had reason to believe that the vehicle had been stolen or unlawfully taken, not being a person who—

(a)   did not know and had no reason to believe that the vehicle had been stolen or unlawfully taken until after the commencement of his journey, and

(b)   could not reasonably have been expected to have alighted from the vehicle.

In this subsection the reference to a person being carried in or upon a vehicle includes a reference to a person entering or getting on to, or alighting from, the vehicle.

(5)   Notwithstanding that the insurer may be entitled to avoid or cancel, or may have avoided or cancelled, the policy or security, he must, subject to the provisions of this section, pay to the persons entitled to the benefit of the judgment—

(a)   as regards liability in respect of death or bodily injury, any sum payable under the judgment in respect of the liability, together with any sum which, by virtue of any enactment relating to interest on judgments, is payable in respect of interest on that sum,

(b)   as regards liability in respect of damage to property, any sum required to be paid under subsection (6) below, and

(c)   any amount payable in respect of costs.

(6)   This subsection requires—

(a)   where the total of any amounts paid, payable or likely to be payable under the policy or security in respect of damage to property caused by, or arising out of, the accident in question does not exceed £250,000, the payment of any sum payable under the judgment in respect of the liability, together with any sum which, by virtue of any enactment relating to interest on judgments, is payable in respect of interest on that sum,

(b)   where that total exceeds £250,000, the payment of either—

(i)   such proportion of any sum payable under the judgment in respect of the liability as £250,000 bears to that total, together with the same proportion of any sum which, by virtue of any enactment relating to interest on judgments, is payable in respect of interest on that sum, or

(ii)   the difference between the total of any amounts already paid under the policy or security in respect of such damage and £250,000, together with such proportion of any sum which, by virtue of any enactment relating to interest on judgments, is payable in respect of interest on any sum payable under the judgment in respect of the liability as the difference bears to that sum,

whichever is the less, unless not less than £250,000 has already been paid under the policy or security in respect of such damage (in which case nothing is payable).

(7)   Where an insurer becomes liable under this section to pay an amount in respect of a liability of a person who is insured by a policy or whose liability is covered by a security, he is entitled to recover from that person—

(a)   that amount, in a case where he became liable to pay it by virtue only of subsection (3) above, or

(b)   in a case where that amount exceeds the amount for which he would, apart from the provisions of this section, be liable under the policy or security in respect of that liability, the excess.

(8)   Where an insurer becomes liable under this section to pay an amount in respect of a liability of a person who is not insured by a policy or whose liability is not covered by a security, he is entitled to recover the amount from that person or from any person who—

    (a)   is insured by the policy, or whose liability is covered by the security, by the terms of which the liability would be covered if the policy insured all persons or, as the case may be, the security covered the liability of all persons, and

    (b)   caused or permitted the use of the vehicle which gave rise to the liability.

(9)   In this section—

    (a)   'insurer' includes a person giving a security,

    (b)   repealed by the Road Traffic Act 1991, s 38, Sch 8, and

    (c)   'liability covered by the terms of the policy or security' means a liability which is covered by the policy or security or which would be so covered but for the fact that the insurer is entitled to avoid or cancel, or has avoided or cancelled, the policy or security.

(10)   In the application of this section to Scotland, the words 'by virtue of any enactment relating to interest on judgments' in subsections (5) and (6) (in each place where they appear) shall be omitted.

[2.201]   Charlton v Fisher

[2001] EWCA Civ 112

[2002] QB 578, [2001] 1 All ER (Comm) 769, [2001] 3 WLR 1435, [2001] RTR 33, [2001] Lloyd's Rep IR 387, [2001] PIQR P23, (2001) 98(10) LSG 45

C sustained injuries following an accident in which F had deliberately reversed his car into a stationary parked car and had pleaded guilty to criminal damage. F's insurer, CI, denied that the incident was an accident under the terms of the insurance policy as it had occurred in a car park and not on the road. In addition CI argued there was no statutory obligation to indemnify F.

HELD: Allowing the appeal that as the incident had not happened on the road, C had no rights against CI through the Motor Insurers' Bureau nor under the Road Traffic Act 1988, s 151, and CI was not directly liable to her.

[2.202]   Lloyd-Woolper v Moore

[2004] EWCA Civ 766

[2004] 3 All ER 741, [2004] 1 WLR 2350, [2004] RTR 30, [2004] Lloyd's Rep IR 730, (2004) 148 SJLB 791

Moore senior insured his vehicle with insurer, N. His son Moore junior was insured to drive on the basis that Moore junior was over 17 years old, held a full driving licence and would not be permitted to drive a vehicle whose engine capacity was over 1600cc.

Moore junior, who was sixteen years of age at the time, had sat his driving test before he was old enough to do so and was driving a vehicle with an engine capacity of 1760 cc was involved in an accident with L-W. L-W commenced proceedings against Moore junior and N.

N commenced Part 20 proceedings against Moore senior seeking an indemnity from him. Moore senior appealed unsuccessfully.

HELD: Moore senior was liable to indemnify N as he had given Moore junior permission to use the vehicle in the terms of the Road Traffic Act 1988, s 143(1) and s 151(8).

Road Traffic Act 1988, s 152

[2.203]

152 Exceptions to section 151

(1)   No sum is payable by an insurer under section 151 of this Act—

    (a)   in respect of any judgment unless, before or within seven days after the commencement of the proceedings in which the judgment was given, the insurer had notice of the bringing of the proceedings, or

    (b)   in respect of any judgment so long as execution on the judgment is stayed pending an appeal, or

    (c)   in connection with any liability if, before the happening of the event which was the cause of the death or bodily injury or damage to property giving rise to the liability, the policy or security was cancelled by mutual consent or by virtue of any provision contained in it, and also—

        (i)   before the happening of that event the certificate was surrendered to the insurer, or the person to whom the certificate was delivered made a statutory declaration stating that the certificate had been lost or destroyed, or

        (ii)   after the happening of that event, but before the expiration of a period of fourteen days from the taking effect of the cancellation of the policy or security, the certificate was surrendered to the insurer, or the person to whom it was delivered made a statutory declaration stating that the certificate had been lost or destroyed, or

        (iii)   either before or after the happening of that event, but within that period of fourteen days, the insurer has commenced proceedings under this Act in respect of the failure to surrender the certificate.

(2)   Subject to subsection (3) below, no sum is payable by an insurer under section 151 of this Act if, in an action commenced before or within three months after, the commencement of the proceedings in which the judgment was given, he has obtained a declaration—

    (a)   that, apart from any provision contained in the policy of security, he is entitled to avoid it on the ground that it was obtained—

        (i)   by the non-disclosure of a material fact, or

        (ii)   by a representation of fact which was false in some material particular, or

    (b)   if he has avoided the policy or security on that ground, that he was entitled so to do apart from any provision contained in it [and for the purposes of this section, 'material' means of such a nature as to influence the judgment of a prudent insurer in determining whether he will take the risk, and, if so, at what premium and on what conditions] [amended by the Road Traffic Act 1991, s 48, Sch 4, para 66].

(3)   An insurer who has obtained such a declaration as is mentioned in subsection (2) above in an action does not by reason of that become entitled to the benefit of that subsection as respects any judgment obtained in proceedings commenced before the commencement of that action unless before, or within seven days after, the commencement of that action he has given notice of it to the person who is the plaintiff (or in Scotland pursuer) in those proceedings specifying the non-disclosure or false representation on which he proposes to rely.

(4)   A person to whom notice of such an action is so given is entitled, if he thinks fit, to be made a party to it.

(B)   NOTICE TO INSURERS

[2.204]   *Note*—Pursuant to subsection (1)(a) of s 152 of the Road Traffic Act 1988, a claimant's solicitor should give formal notice to the insurer of the commencement of proceedings. The subsection speaks of commencement of proceedings, not the service of the claim form. Presumably it is intended to protect the insurers where an insured fails to send on the writ to insurers and judgment is signed in default, rendering the insurers liable without having had the opportunity to defend.

Similar notice is required to achieve for the plaintiff the protection of the Motor Insurers' Bureau Uninsured Drivers Agreement:

[2.205]   **Herbert v Railway Passengers Assurance Co**

[1938] 1 All ER 650, 158 LT 417, 60 Ll L Rep 143   Porter J

Notice under s 152(1)(a) of the Road Traffic Act 1988 must be something more formal than a casual mention of the proceedings in a conversation. There must be something which indicates that notice is being given.

[2.206]   **Weldrick v Essex and Suffolk Equitable Insurance Society**

(1949) 83 Ll L Rep 91, erratum p 477   Birkett J

On 11 July 1947 solicitors acting for a passenger wrote to the insurer of the car as follows: 'We have been consulted by Mrs Eva Weldrick of 42a High Street, King's Lynn, who is a partner in the business of a drapery peddling carried on by Mr Jan Mahomed, who, we are advised, sustained injuries as a result of an accident which occurred as long ago as 11 March 1947 as a result of Mahomed's car, in which she was travelling in connection with the said business, coming into collision with a stationary lorry. We understand your Society has repudiated liability, and we shall be grateful to have your confirmation thereof in writing, because you will appreciate, we shall have to take proceedings as against Mahomed, and as against the owner of the other vehicle, and at the same time give notice to the Motor Insurers' Bureau of your repudiation of liability.'

The insurer replied on 18 July as follows: 'We are in receipt of your letter of the 11th inst, and in reply have to confirm that we have repudiated liability in respect of the unfortunate accident.'

HELD: The insurer had notice that proceedings would almost inevitably be brought but that was not sufficient to satisfy the requirements of s 10(2)(a) of the 1934 Act (now s 152 of the 1988 Act). Adopting Porter J in *Herbert v Railway Passengers Assurance Co* (at para [2.205]), formality was necessary for such a notice and a statutory requirement of this kind must be pretty strictly fulfilled. There was no evidence that the defendant had notice of the proceedings either before or within seven days after they had been brought. What it did have was an intimation that in certain circumstances proceedings might be brought, but not necessarily that they would be brought. The requirements of s 10 (now s 152 of the 1988 Act) had not been fulfilled. The insurer did not have notice of the bringing of the action.

Judgment for insurer.

[2.207]   **Ceylon Motor Insurance Association v Thambugala**

[1953] AC 584, [1953] 2 All ER 870, [1953] 1 Lloyd's Rep 289, PC

The Motor Car Ordinance of Ceylon contains provisions in the same terms as s 152 of the Road Traffic Act 1988.

On 21 May 1946 the claimant's solicitors wrote to the insurer that they were instructed to file an action on behalf of T of (address) for the recovery of damages against K of (address) caused by car No X 4851 on 1 September 1945; that the claim was Rs 15,000; that they understood the car was insured with the insurer, and that unless the claim was settled on or before the 31st, they were instructed to file action against the owner of the car.

HELD: The notice was sufficient. The name of the court was not required, and the words 'unless the claim is settled' did not affect the notice. *Weldrick v Essex and Suffolk Equitable Insurance Society* (at para [2.206]) not relevant.

Note—For a further illustration of this point, see *Harrington v Link Motor Policies at Lloyd's* [1989] 2 Lloyd's Rep 310, CA.

[2.208]   Wake v Wylie
[2001] RTR 20, [2001] PIQR P13

The claimant purported to give the defendant insurer notice pursuant to s 152(1)(a) of the Road Traffic Act 1988 in a letter containing a great deal of other information and sent 17 months prior to the issue of proceedings. The defendant successfully argued that this constituted insufficient notice.

HELD, ON APPEAL: That the letter did not constitute adequate notice.

[2.209]   Nawaz v Crowe Insurance Group
[2003] EWCA Civ 316

[2003] CP Rep 41, [2003] RTR 29, [2003] Lloyd's Rep IR 471, [2003] PIQR 27

The claimant brought proceedings against Crowe arising out of an accident involving its insured. He obtained a default judgment which Crowe had set aside on the grounds that N had failed to give notice to Crowe. Crowe had told the claimant's solicitors to serve on its insured direct.

The claimant's solicitors telephoned Crowe's solicitors and spoke to an experienced legal secretary, asking for the insured's address as proceedings were about to be issued. The secretary failed to pass on the message.

HELD, ON APPEAL: It had been sufficient to give notice to an experienced secretary. Although the purpose of the call had been to obtain the insured's address it had been made very clear that proceedings were to be issued.

Counterclaim: notice

[2.210]   Cross v British Oak Insurance Co Ltd
[1938] 2 KB 167, [1938] 1 All ER 383, 107 LJKB 577, 159 LT 286, 60 Ll L Rep 46   du Parcq J

Fowler, insured by the defendant, was driving a motor vehicle on 7 January 1936, and injured Cross and Baker. In March 1936, Baker commenced an action against Fowler in the county court. Fowler brought in Cross on a third-party notice. Cross filed a counterclaim in the county court against Fowler. Cross recovered £90 damages and £28 9s 9d costs against Fowler. The company was served with notice of the third-party proceedings but not of the counterclaim.

HELD: The counterclaim was the commencement of separate proceedings, and notice of those proceedings, not having been given within seven days the company was not liable on the certificate. Proceedings means the proceedings begun by a person who may for this purpose be regarded as a plaintiff, which results in the judgment upon which reliance is placed as against the insurer.

No notice must be pleaded

[2.211]   Baker v Provident Accident and White Cross Insurance Co Ltd
[1939] 2 All ER 690, 83 Sol Jo 565, 64 Ll L Rep 14   Cassels J

Absence of notice, if relied on, should be pleaded by insurers.

Setting aside default judgment

[2.212]   **Windsor v Chalcraft**

[1939] 1 KB 279, [1938] 2 All ER 751, 107 LJKB 609, 159 LT 104, 54 TLR 834, 82 Sol Jo 432, 61 Ll L Rep 69, CA

A third party issued a writ against the assured and gave notice to the insurer under s 10 of the Road Traffic Act 1934 (now s 152 of the 1988 Act). The writ was served and the assured did not inform the insurer and allowed judgment to go by default. Damages were assessed by a master. The third party sued the insurer on the certificate. No notice was given by the third party to the insurer that the writ was served or that the case was set down.

HELD: (Slesser LJ dissenting): The insurer was entitled under RSC Ord XXVII, r 15 (now Ord 13, r 9), which empowers the court to set aside a judgment by default on terms, to have the judgment set aside on the ground that it had an actual interest by reason of the liability imposed by statute and was injuriously affected by it. (*Jacques v Harrison* (1884) 12 QBD 136 followed.)

(C)   DECLARATION PROCEEDINGS

[2.213]   *Note*—An action under s 152 of the 1988 Act for a declaration is still essential for an insurer in cases where liability arises under s 151 and where it is sought to make the insurers of a potential co-defendant who is only fractionally to blame entirely liable for the judgment by operation of the provisions of the Motor Insurers' Bureau Domestic Agreement.

[2.214]   **Zurich General Accident and Liability Insurance Co v Livingston**

1938 SC 582, 1938 SLT 441, Scot

The insurer brought proceedings for a declaration and third parties, who had not commenced proceedings against the assured before the commencement of the action for a declaration, applied for leave to be joined as defendants.

HELD: That the third parties were entitled to be added as defendants, in respect that while they had not a statutory title by virtue of the proviso to s 10(3) of the Road Traffic Act 1934, they had at common law a title to defend an action which might deprive them of the statutory right conferred upon them by s 10(1).

Note—For s 10(1) and s 10(3) of the 1934 Act, see now the Road Traffic Act 1988 s 152 (at para [2.203]).

Rights limited to notice

[2.215]   **Contigency Insurance Co v Lyons**

(1939) 65 Ll L Rep 53, CA

The insurer issued a writ for declaration and served notice on the third party on the ground that the car, insured for private pleasure, was being used for hiring. In the Statement of Claim it added grounds, not mentioned in the notice, of non-disclosure of material facts in the proposal form. The third party applied to strike out the additional grounds from the Statement of Claim.

The Court of Appeal declined to strike out and held the questions should be dealt with at the trial.

SEMBLE (per MacKinnon LJ): It is doubtful if grounds not stated in the notice are open to the insurer.

Note—This point was afterwards decided in the following case (at para [2.216]).

[2.216]   Zurich General Accident and Liability Insurance Co v Morrison
[1942] 2 KB 53, [1942] 1 All ER 529, 111 LJKB 601, 167 LT 183, 58 TLR 217, CA

A declaration cannot be made against a third party on grounds not stated in the notice. The court cannot vary the section of the Act.
  Per MacKinnon LJ: The grounds are limited to those specified in the notice.

Delay in declaration action

[2.217]   Trafalgar Insurance Co Ltd v McGregor
[1942] 1 KB 275, 111 LJKB 193, 166 LT 213, 71 Ll L Rep 107, CA

The insurer on 4 October 1939 issued a writ for a declaration for non-disclosure of all motoring convictions. On 11 March 1940 the third party wrote for particulars. On 15 March 1940, on motion by the insurer for judgment in default against the assured, Charles J adjourned the motion until trial and ordered the particulars. The assured disappeared and the insurer was unable to obtain the information required for the particulars. After 18 months the third party applied for dismissal of the action for non-compliance with the order for particulars.
  ORDERED: That the insurer be precluded at the trial from giving evidence in support of certain parts of the Statement of Claim. The judge at the trial has discretion to admit evidence on terms.

Declaration action: position of MIB

[2.218]   *Note*—See *Fire Auto and Marine Insurance Co Ltd v Greene* [1964] 2 QB 687, [1964] 2 All ER 761, [1964] 3 WLR 319, 108 Sol Jo 603, [1964] 2 Lloyd's Rep 72 (at para [3.44]).

Discovery of documents

[2.219]   Merchants' and Manufacturers' Insurance Co v Davies
[1938] 1 KB 196, [1937] 2 All ER 767, 106 LJKB 423, 156 LT 524, 53 TLR 717, 81 Sol Jo 457, 58 Ll L Rep 61, CA

In a declaration action by a motor insurer to avoid a policy for non-disclosure of convictions the defendant applied for discovery of documents against the insurer to show cases where non-disclosure of convictions had not been relied on as a ground for refusing cover. The application was refused.

Liability covered by the terms of the policy

[2.220]   Lockerbie v Eagle Star Insurance Co
(20 March 1936, unreported)   Lord Jamieson

The pursuer was a passenger (not within the category of passengers required to be covered) in a motor car belonging to one Lee and was injured in an accident to the car. She obtained a judgment for damages against Lee and then sued Lee's insurer under s 10(1) of the Road Traffic Act 1934 (now s 152 of the 1988 Act).

The words 'being a liability covered by the terms of the policy' did not apply. That would bring within the scope of the section any liability covered by the policy whether required to be covered or not. That is clearly not the meaning of the section. It is limited to cases in which liability is required to be covered. The words quoted are necessary to protect insurers who are not liable unless the liability is in fact covered by the policy.

[2.221]   WR Chown & Co Ltd v Herbert
(1950) 100 LJo 597   Judge Hodgson, Wandsworth Cty Ct

The Trafalgar insured the defendant under a motor policy containing the condition 'the insured shall repay to the company all sums paid by the company in discharge satisfaction or settlement of the liability' required by the Road Traffic Act to be covered by insurance 'incurred to a third party by the insured ... which the company would not have been liable to pay but for the provisions of the Act'. After a collision between the insured's car and a cab the Trafalgar refused indemnity because of a mis-statement in the proposal form but settled the cab driver's claim for damages for personal injury at £75 and also paid the hospital charges of £15. The plaintiffs sued the defendant for damage to the cab; the defendant joined the Trafalgar as third parties in the action, claiming indemnity and the Trafalgar counterclaimed for the £90 it had paid to the cab driver. The judge held that the Trafalgar was entitled to refuse indemnity because of the mis-statement, but on the counterclaim:

HELD: The Trafalgar could not recover the £75 paid to the cab driver from the defendant. The liability to pay the cab driver under the Road Traffic Act 1934, s 10 (now s 152 of the 1988 Act) did not arise until there was a judgment and there had been no judgment. The condition in the policy covered an existing liability only, not a contingent one. The payment of hospital charges was a statutory liability, however, and the Trafalgar was entitled to be repaid the £15 by the defendant under the terms of the condition.

[2.222]   Campbell v McFarland and Armagh Urban District Council
[1972] NI 31

In a collision between McFarland's car and a refuse lorry a dustman was injured. He sued McFarland and his own employer, the owner of the lorry, and obtained judgment for £12,500 against both. The judgment allocated 25% blame to McFarland and gave a right to contribution as between the defendants. McFarland's insurer had refused to indemnify him under their policy on the ground of misrepresentation and took no part in the action. The plaintiff demanded that his employer should satisfy the whole of the judgment and it did so. The employer then applied to the court to order direct reimbursement to it from McFarland's insurer of one-quarter of the damages by virtue of the Motor Vehicles and Road

Traffic Act (Northern Ireland) 1934, s 18 (which was similar in effect to s 207 of the Road Traffic Act 1960 (now s 152 of the Road Traffic Act 1988)).

HELD: The application failed. The question was whether a policy issued for the purposes of that part of the 1934 Act requiring compulsory insurance against third-party risks is required to cover liability under an order for contribution. There were two distinct liabilities facing McFarland:

(1)   his liability at common law to the plaintiff for which he was obliged to have compulsory insurance, and

(2)   his liability under the Law Reform (Miscellaneous Provisions) Act (Northern Ireland) 1937, s 16 (which was to the same effect as the Law Reform (Married Women and Tortfeasors) Act 1935, s 6).

The first was a liability to meet in full a judgment obtained against him by the plaintiff, and he was bound by statute to insure against it; but the second was a separate liability created by the Law Reform Act. Though the policy did give cover against the liability to contribute it was not a liability the policy was required to cover by the compulsory insurance provisions of the Road Traffic Act. Following *Lockerbie v Eagle Star Insurance Co* (at para [2.220]) a liability which was covered by the policy but which was not required to be covered, did not come within the scope of s 18 of the 1934 Act.

5.   DOUBLE INSURANCE

[2.223]   *Note*—The right of contribution in a case of double insurance is a part of the equity of contribution, which is most prominent in the law of guaranty. The right of contribution does not depend on contract but on principles of equity and natural justice (see *Godin v London Assurance Co* (1758) 1 Burr 489).

[2.224]   Austin v Zurich General Accident and Liability Insurance Co Ltd

[1945] KB 250, [1945] 1 All ER 316, 114 LJKB 340, 172 LT 174, 61 TLR 214, 78 Ll L Rep 185, CA

The plaintiff, Austin, was insured with the Bell Assurance Association, and was driving a car belonging to Aldridge, who was insured with the Zurich Insurance Co. Aldridge and one Nicholson were passengers in the car which met with an accident. Aldridge was killed and Nicholson injured. The accident occurred on 23 May 1938. By two informations dated 22 June 1938, Austin was charged with dangerous driving and careless driving. The summonses were returnable on 20 July. Austin gave no notice to the Zurich Co of these impending prosecutions.

The Bell settled a claim by Aldridge's executors for £4,000 and costs and a claim by Nicholson for £305 and costs. The Bell in the name of Austin as plaintiff sued the Zurich for these sums, claiming in right of subrogation.

The Zurich policy provided indemnity to any person driving the vehicle with the insured's (ie Aldridge's) permission subject to the terms of the policy. It was a condition of the policy that notice should be given to the insurers as soon as possible after an accident or of an impending prosecution.

HELD: (1) There was a right to sue in subrogation, apart from the right of one insurer to claim in contribution from another.

(2)   Austin was entitled to sue the Zurich though not named in its policy. Subsection (4) of s 36 of the Road Traffic Act 1930 applied. This subsection did not include the words 'in respect of a liability required

to be covered by a policy issued under this section', which appear in s 10 of the 1934 Act, and is not confined to a liability required to be covered by s 36.

(3) Each insurer was liable for 50%.

(4) The Zurich cover was subject to the fulfilment of the policy conditions by Austin, and one condition required notice in writing immediately if the insured shall have knowledge of any impending prosecution. Austin could have obtained information of the provisions of the Zurich policy, and he had not fulfilled the condition. On this ground only, judgment was for the Zurich with one-third of the costs: [1944] 2 All ER 243, 77 Ll L Rep 409 (Tucker J).

ON APPEAL: As to subrogation and double insurance: the plaintiff having been completely indemnified by one insurer, was not entitled to claim on the principle of subrogation. The claim would be by and in the name of that insurer against the other insurer for contribution on the principle of double insurance.

As to s 36(4): the subsection gave Austin a right to sue the Zurich company but in so doing he was claiming a benefit under a document to which he was not a party. A person who claims the benefit of a document in that way is bound to take it as he finds it. He cannot claim the benefit of anything which the document gives him without complying with its terms.

Note—Section 36(4) of the 1930 Act is now s 148(7) of the Road Traffic Act 1988; s 10 of the 1934 Act is ss 151 and 152 of the 1988 Act; and s 36 is now s 145 of the 1988 Act.

(A)   PRO-RATA CONTRIBUTION CLAUSE

[2.225]   *Note*—If at the time of loss or damage happening to any property insured by this policy, there be any other subsisting insurance or insurances, whether effected by the insured, or by any other person, covering the same property or any part thereof, this policy shall not be liable to pay or contribute in respect of such loss or damage more than its rateable proportion of the aggregate liability under all the insurances covering such property.

[2.226]   Drake Insurance plc (in provisional liquidation) v Provident Insurance plc

[2003] EWCA Civ 1834

[2004] QB 601, [2004] 2 All ER (Comm) 65, [2004] 2 WLR 530, [2004] 1 Lloyd's Rep 268, [2004] 1 CLC 574, [2004] RTR 19, [2004] Lloyd's Rep IR 277

Drake insured a car belonging to Mrs Kaur. The policy also covered her whilst driving other vehicles with the owner's permission. Provident insured a vehicle belonging to her husband Dr Singh. Mrs Kaur was a named driver on that policy. Whilst driving Dr Singh's car, Mrs Kaur had an accident and made a claim to Drake who paid the claim in full and sought a contribution from Provident. Provident purportedly avoided Dr Singh's policy for non-disclosure and defended the proceedings by Drake on the grounds that:

(1) it had avoided the policy;

(2) a 'rateable proportion' clause in Drake's policy limited its liability to 50% and by paying in full Drake was a volunteer and could not recover from Provident.

In arbitration proceedings between Dr Singh and Provident the arbitrator found that Provident had validly avoided the policy.

In the proceedings between Drake and Provident the Court of Appeal held that:

(1) Provident had not validly avoided the policy.

(2)   A rateable proportion clause did not of itself exclude the equitable rule of contribution.

(B)   NON-CONTRIBUTION CLAUSE

[2.227]   *Note*—This insurance does not cover any loss or damage which at the time of the happening of such loss or damage is insured by or would, but for the existence of this policy, be insured by any other existing policy or policies except in respect of any excess beyond the amount which would have been payable under such other policy or policies had this insurance not been effected.

[2.228]   Gale v Motor Union Insurance Co Ltd
Loyst v General Accident Fire and Life Assurance Corpn Ltd
[1928] 1 KB 359, 96 LJKB 199, 38 LT 712, 43 TLR 15, 70 Sol Jo 1140, 26 Ll L Rep 65   Roche J

G took with the M Co a motor car insurance policy covering himself and any friend driving with G's consent and providing as follows: 'Condition 6. The extension of the indemnity to friends or relatives of the insured is conditional upon such friend or relative being a licensed and competent driver and not being insured under any other policy. Condition 10. If at the happening of any accident, injury, damage or loss covered by this policy there shall be subsisting any other insurance or indemnity of any nature whatever covering same, whether effected by insured or by any other person, then the company shall not be liable to pay or contribute towards any such damages or loss more than a rateable proportion of any sum payable in respect thereof for compensation.' L, G's brother-in-law, took out with the G Co a similar policy, providing that 'insured will also be indemnified hereunder while personally driving a car not belonging to him provided that there is no other insurance in respect of such other car whereby insured may be indemnified', and that 'if at the time of the occurrence of any accident, loss or damage, there shall be any other indemnity or insurance subsisting, whether effected by insured or by any other person, the corporation shall not be liable to pay or contribute more than a rateable proportion of any sums payable in respect of such accident, loss or damage'. While L was driving G's car with G's consent it had a collision and L had to pay damages. G, as trustee for L, claimed against the M Co and L, on his own behalf, claimed against the G Co.

HELD: In each policy the provision as to rateable contribution qualified the preceding clause, and each company was liable to pay claimants half the amount claimed.

[2.229]   Portavon Cinema Co v Price and Century Insurance Co Ltd
[1939] 4 All ER 601, 161 LT 417, 84 Sol Jo 152, 65 Ll L Rep 161   Branson J

This clause (non-contribution) should be applied only to cases which are strictly cases of double insurance.

[2.230]   Weddell v Road Transport and General Insurance Co Ltd
[1932] 2 KB 563, 101 LJKB 620, 146 LT 162, 48 TLR 59, 75 Sol Jo 852, 41 Ll L Rep 69   Rowlatt J

A motor car accident policy issued by the respondent company to JRW extended the insurance to a relative driving the car provided that the latter was not entitled to indemnity for the same risk under another policy. LWW, a relative of JRW, while driving the car, injured a third party, who claimed damages. LWW was himself insured with the C insurance company against claims for injuries caused by him while driving a car not belonging to him, provided that he was not entitled to an indemnity in respect thereof from another company. The respondent denied liability on the ground of the proviso in its policy exempting it where the claimant was entitled to indemnity under another policy.

HELD: On the proper construction of the policies, the insurance clause in each policy expressed to be cancelled by the co-existence of a similar clause in the other policy should be excluded from the category of co-existing cover, and that therefore the respondent, not being protected by their proviso, was liable.

Note—Weddell v Road Transport and General Insurance Co Ltd (at para [2.230]) and *Gale v Motor Union Insurance Co Ltd* (at para [2.228]) were approved in *Steelclad Ltd v Iron Trades Mutual Insurance Co Ltd* 1984 SLT 304.

[2.231]   National Employers Mutual General Insurance Association Ltd v Hayden

[1979] 2 Lloyd's Rep 235 (Lloyd J); revsd [1980] 2 Lloyd's Rep 149, CA

A firm of solicitors were covered, in respect of a claim against them for professional negligence, by two policies of insurance. The first, issued by the plaintiff company, contained a clause: 'This policy does not indemnify the insured in respect of any claim made against him for which the insured is or would but for the existence of this policy be entitled to indemnity under any other policy except in respect of any excess beyond the amount payable by such other policy.' The second had a provision: 'This insurance shall not indemnify the assured in respect of any loss arising out of any claim in respect of any circumstance or occurrence which has been notified under any other insurance.'

HELD: There was dual insurance. Both clauses were exceptions clauses even though one was narrower than the other, but even if they were not exclusion clauses in the strict sense but clauses restricting cover, it would still be impossible to distinguish between them. By giving effect to both clauses neither policy would pay. In those circumstances the principle in *Weddell v Road Transport and General Insurance Co Ltd* (at para [2.230]) should be applied: if each policy would cover but for the existence of the other then the exclusions are treated as cancelling each other out. The plaintiff was entitled to contribution.

Note—The defendant appealed and the appeal was allowed. The principle of *Weddell's* case, said the court, was not in doubt but it could only apply where an insured is covered by both policies, were it not for the excluding clauses. On the construction of the policies in the present case, however, there was no co-existing cover. The two policies were not concurrent but consecutive. The NEM were alone liable ([1980] 2 Lloyd's Rep 149, CA).

See also the decision of Tucker J on this point in *Austin v Zurich General Accident and Liability Insurance Co Ltd* (at para [2.224]).

A case in practice arose where the assured had failed to give notice of the loss to one insurer and that insurer was in consequence not liable to the assured. The question was whether that insurer was nevertheless liable on the principle of dual insurance.

The case went to arbitration. The arbitrator held there does not appear to be any direct authority and considered the question to be 'Is the right of contribution an independent right arising as between insurers or merely a benefit accruing to the insurer who pays by subrogation?' The principle does not seem to have been dealt with since *Newby v Reed* (1763) 1 Wm BL 416, and *Rogers v Davis* (1777) 2 Park Marine Insces 8th edn, 601. He considered that the principle of natural justice as between co-insurers was the principle to be applied and not subrogation, and that the right of contribution is an independent right of the insurers against his co-insurer which arises as a contingent right when the loss occurs though not enforceable until payment is made. This view is supported by the Marine Insurance Act 1906, s 80. Being an independent right, the failure of the assured to comply with a policy condition cannot take away that right. On the basis of apportionment, he referred to *American Surety Co of New York v Wrighton* (1910) 103 LT 663, 27 TLR 91, 16 Com Cas 37. But see the following case (at para [2.232]).

(C) BREACH OF CONDITION OF THE POLICY

[2.232]   **Monksfield v Vehicle and General Insurance Co Ltd**
[1971] 1 Lloyd's Rep 139, Mayor's and City of London Court

P was involved in an accident when driving a car belonging to W. He was insured under a policy issued to himself by the plaintiff, a member of Lloyds, who dealt with and paid the third party claim. W had a policy issued by the defendant which extended to cover P but neither P nor W reported the claim to it nor claimed indemnity under that policy. Each policy had a term excluding cover if the driver was entitled to indemnity under any other policy, so that, other considerations apart, there was dual insurance as in *Weddell v Road Transport and General Insurance Co Ltd* (at para [2.230]). A condition in W's policy required the insured to give notice in writing to the company as soon as possible after the occurrence of any accident, but the defendant did not hear of the accident until eight months later.

HELD: The fact that there had been a breach of condition of its policy by failing to report the accident relieved the defendant of the liability to make contribution. It would clearly have been in a position to repudiate a claim by W; it could not be an equitable result that the insurer who had no notice of the accident and had no say in the handling of the claim should be called upon to make a contribution when it would have been entitled to repudiate if the claim had been brought under the terms of its own policy.

[2.233]   **Legal and General v Drake Insurance**
[1992] QB 887, [1992] 1 All ER 283

On facts very similar to those in *Monksfield v Vehicle and General Insurance Co Ltd* (at para [2.232]), the Court of Appeal decided that *Monksfield* had been wrongly decided.

Per Lloyd J: The fact that a co-obligor has 'no say' in the handling of the claim has never been an answer to a contribution, whether in the field of insurance or in any other field in which the equitable doctrine prevails. As to the right to repudiate, this would, as I have said, have been a good defence to a claim for contribution if the assured had been in breach of condition prior to the loss and a breach of condition subsequent to the loss by failing to give notice in time vitiates, if I may respectfully say so, the learned judge's conclusion. So I would hold that *Monksfield's* case was wrongly decided.

6. THE 4TH MOTOR INSURANCE DIRECTIVE AND THIRD PARTIES (RIGHTS AGAINST INSURERS) ACT 1930

[2.234]   As far as motor claims are concerned the Third Parties (Rights against Insurers) Act 1930 has been rendered largely redundant by EU Directive No 2000/26/EC, commonly called the 4th Motor Insurance Directive, which came into force on 20 January 2003 and applies to accidents occurring after that date. The Directive was implemented by the European Communities (Rights against Insurers) Regulations 2002, SI 2002/3061 and enables claimants to commence proceedings directly against the other driver's insurers, so obviating the need to obtain a judgment against the driver before being able to enforce it against the Insurer.

Clause 3 of the 2002 Regulations provides:

'Right of Action

3 – (1) Paragraph (2) of this regulation applies where an entitled party has a cause of action against an insured person in tort or (as the case may be) delict, and that cause of action arises out of an accident.

(2)   Where this paragraph applies, the entitled party may, without prejudice to his right to issue proceedings against the insured person, issue proceedings against the insurer which issued the policy of insurance relating to the insured vehicle, and that insurer shall be directly liable to the entitled party to the extent that he is liable to the insured person."

7.   EXCESS CLAUSE

[2.235]   **Beacon Insurance Co Ltd v Langdale**

[1939] 4 All ER 204, 83 Sol Jo 908, 65 Ll L Rep 57, CA

A motor policy covering third party risks contained a condition that the company should be entitled, if it so desired, to take over and conduct in the name of the assured the defence or settlement of any claim and should have full discretion in the settlement of any claim. The policy was subject to a £5 excess.

The company settled a third-party claim by a cyclist without the express sanction of the assured and also against his view of the rights of the matter, as he wished to claim against the third party. The company made what it believed to be, in his interest and theirs, an advantageous settlement, and it was at pains to show that the settlement should be made with a denial of liability, so that no one could say that they had admitted any culpability whatever on his behalf. The assured contended that the company was not entitled to settle the claim without notice to him and that it had not acted reasonably in the exercise of its authority.

HELD (distinguishing *Groom v Crocker* [1939] 1 KB 194, [1938] 2 All ER 394, 108 LJKB 296, 158 LT 477, 54 TLR 861, 82 Sol Jo 374, 60 Ll L Rep 393, CA): The policy gave the company power to settle the claim without consulting the assured, and the assured was liable to pay the company the £5 excess.

8.   KNOCK-FOR-KNOCK AGREEMENT

[2.236]   *Comment*: In recent years the 'knock-for-knock' agreement has fallen into disuse with more and more insurers withdrawing from the agreement. In its place, most insurers now subscribe to the 'Memorandum of Understanding' ('MoU'). In cases where the operation of the MoU is confirmed, insurers' outlay is excluded from litigation and the insurers agree to settle their respective claims in line with the outcome on liability in the proceedings. To further reduce costs between subscribing insurers the 'RIPE

(Reduction in Paperwork Exchange) Agreement' provides that where payment of outlay by one insurer to another is to be made there is no requirement to provide documentary evidence in support of that outlay.

[2.237]   Morley v Moore

[1936] 2 KB 359, [1936] 2 All ER 79, 105 LJKB 421, 154 LT 646, 52 TLR 510, 80 Sol Jo 424, 55 Ll L Rep 10, CA

The plaintiff was insured for damage to his car bearing a £5 excess. The car damage was £33 2s 8d, and his insurers paid the £28 2s 8d. The plaintiff sued for £33 2s 8d. The defendant pleaded the 'knock-for-knock' agreement and pleaded that that the plaintiff was only entitled to receive £5.

HELD: The plaintiff was entitled to recover £33 2s 8d, but he would hold £28 2s 8d as trustee for his insurer, it being subrogated in his rights. The 'knock-for-knock' agreement does not prevent a plaintiff who has been paid for damage to his car by his own insurer from suing the negligent party for such damage in spite of a direction from his own insurer that it does not want him to claim it. The insurer is entitled to be subrogated but had no right to forbid the assured from exercising his common law right against the wrongdoer.

[2.238]   Bourne v Stanbridge

[1965] 1 All ER 241, [1965] 1 WLR 189, 108 Sol Jo 991, CA

In an action in the county court the plaintiff claimed £230 being the cost of repairs to his car, damaged in a collision with the defendant's car. His driver being found two-thirds to blame he recovered only £76 being one-third of the amount claimed. When the judge was considering costs, counsel for the defendant revealed that, as the plaintiff knew before proceedings, there was a knock-for-knock agreement between the plaintiff's and defendant's insurers and that the only sum in respect of repairs for which the plaintiff was liable was his excess of £10. The judge then awarded the plaintiff his costs only on Scale 2 and not on Scale 3.

HELD: Though the judge had a discretion under CCR Ord 47, r 1, he had not exercised it on a right principle. The plaintiff was quite entitled to bring an action for the whole amount of the damage as *Morley v Moore* (at para [2.237]) shows; the knock-for-knock agreement between the insurers was not a matter which he should have considered as of any relevance in respect of the award of costs.

Note—But see next case (at para [2.239]).

[2.239]   Hobbs v Marlowe

[1978] AC 16, [1977] 2 All ER 241, [1977] 2 WLR 777, 121 Sol Jo 272, [1977] RTR 253, HL

The plaintiff's car was damaged in a collision for which the defendant was wholly to blame. The cost of repairs at £237.59 (less the excess) was paid by the plaintiff's insurer, who was party to a knock-for-knock agreement with the defendant's insurer. The plaintiff's uninsured loss amounted to £73.53 which was not enough under the County Court Rules to entitle him to an award of costs (except the court fee) in an action against the defendant. His solicitors, solely to obtain an award of their costs, sued on his behalf for the whole of the cost of the repairs and uninsured losses, ie £301.12. On payment of a judgment for the whole amount the defendant's insurer were entitled under the knock-for-knock agreement to payment of £227.59 from the plaintiff's insurer who would then recover that sum from the plaintiff. In county court proceedings the defendant (by his insurer) admitted liability and paid into court £73.53. The judge, following *Morley v Moore* (at para [2.237]) gave judgment for the whole amount claimed but in awarding costs held that the inflation of the claim solely for costs was an abuse of the process of the court and awarded only the costs appropriate to an award of £73.53, i e the court fee of £7.50.

HELD, ON APPEAL to the House of Lords: (1) *Morley v Moore* was rightly decided and the plaintiff was not precluded from suing for the full amount of the damages by reason of the fact that he had already received a large part of that sum from his insurers.

(2)   The judge's exercise of his discretion on the award of costs was a proper one and there were no grounds for an appellate court to interfere with it. *Bourne v Stanbridge* (at para [2.238]) should be regarded as wrongly decided.

Note—If a policy indemnity is limited to a named figure, and litigation is begun, and the damages are likely to exceed the indemnity, the business plan is to pay over the limit, otherwise the costs of litigation must also be paid.

9.   MOTOR REPAIRS AND REPAIRERS

[2.240]   Godfrey Davis Ltd v Culling and Hecht
(1962) 106 Sol Jo 918, [1962] 2 Lloyd's Rep 349, CA

The defendants, insured by the Brandaris Insurance Company, sustained damage to their car. They delivered the car to the plaintiff, a motor repairer, who sent them an estimate for repairs costing £160 and invited instructions from them or their insurers. The defendants sent the estimate to the Brandaris who instructed assessors to inspect the damage. The assessors wrote to the plaintiff saying they would make an examination 'on behalf of [the defendants'] insurers' and after inspection wrote to the plaintiffs confirming that it would be in order for it to proceed with the repairs to the Brandaris. When the repairs were done the defendants collected the car from the plaintiff who charged them only the £10 excess under the policy and an agreed payment for a new tyre. The Brandaris went into liquidation and the plaintiff received no payment from that company for the work done. It then sought in this action to make the defendants liable for the whole cost of the repairs.

HELD: An insurer is not by necessary implication an agent of the insured to arranging for repairs to be done. On the letters which passed in this case, it was clear that the insurers had themselves made a contract with the plaintiff to do the repairs. There was no holding out and no circumstances from which an agency could be implied. There is no general rule of law that when an insured person surrenders or subrogates to the insurer all his rights and liabilities over a particular accident giving rise to a claim that what the insurer thereafter does he does as agent of the insured person: that depends entirely on the terms of the policy or some express or ostensible authority. The defendants were not liable.

[2.241]   Cooter and Green Ltd v Tyrrell
[1962] 2 Lloyd's Rep 377, CA

The defendant's car was damaged in an accident. His father asked the plaintiffs, who were motor repairers, for an estimate of the cost of the repairs. The plaintiffs sent a provisional estimate which was sent on to the defendant's insurer. The plaintiffs knew the estimate was required for the insurer, who instructed assessors to inspect the car. As a result and at the request of the assessors, a revised estimate was prepared and sent to them by the plaintiffs. The assessors wrote in reply confirming their inspection on behalf of the insurer, approving the estimate, and confirming that repairs might proceed accordingly. The letter asked the insurer to collect the excess of £15 from the defendant and said the insurer's net liability would be £241: they asked for a satisfaction note and account to be forwarded to them. The repairs were shortly afterwards completed: they had been started before the assessors' letter was received because the plaintiffs knew the defendant and his father personally and the defendant had frequently telephoned asking them to expedite the work. He eventually signed the satisfaction note after trying the car. The insurer shortly afterwards became insolvent and failed to pay the plaintiffs' account for the repairs. The plaintiffs then sued the defendant for the whole cost of the repairs. The policy contained a provision: 'The company may at its own option repair ... such motor car ... or may pay in cash the amount of loss or damage ...'.

HELD: The defendant was not liable. The letter from the assessors was an offer that was accepted by the conduct of the plaintiffs in completing the repairs and complying with the request for the satisfaction note and account to be sent to the assessors. There was a binding contract between the plaintiffs and the insurer and no one else. The insurer had exercised its choice under the policy by electing to place its own contract for the repairs. The father's request for an estimate was not the same as an order for the work: the final estimate was not discussed with the defendant at all and his telephone calls gave rise to no inference which could affect the contract.

[2.242] Brown and Davis Ltd v Galbraith

[1972] 3 All ER 31, [1972] 1 WLR 997, 116 Sol Jo 545, [1972] 2 Lloyd's Rep 1, [1972] RTR 523, CA

The owner of a car damaged in an accident took it to repairers telling them it was comprehensively insured and asking for an estimate of the cost of repair. The estimate was sent to him a few days later. He also notified his insurer who sent its assessor to see the repairers. Agreement was reached between the assessor and the insurer on the cost of repairs and a printed form was filled in by the assessor which *inter alia* notified the repairers of the need for them to collect the £25 excess from the owner. The repairs were then carried out and an invoice sent by the repairers to the insurer, though without a signed satisfaction note from the owner, as he was not satisfied with the work done. He had some work done to the car elsewhere (the cost of which he deducted from the excess) and then took the signed satisfaction note to the repairers. By that time the insurer had gone into liquidation and the repairers were not paid. They sued the owner for the whole cost of the repairs.

HELD: There were two contracts involved, one between the repairers and the insurer whereby the insurer undertook to pay for the repairs and one between the owner and repairers (to be implied from his having taken the vehicle to them for repair) by which the repairers undertook to carry out the work expeditiously (as in *Charnock v Liverpool Corpn* (at para [2.246])). But there was nothing from which in the contract between the owner and repairers a term could be implied that the owner had a liability to pay for the repairs beyond the amount of the excess. The facts of the case were clearly parallel with those in *Godfrey Davis Ltd v Culling and*

Hecht (at para [2.240]) and *Cooter and Green Ltd v Tyrrell* at para [2.241]) and there was nothing in the judgments in *Charnock's* case to controvert the principles applied in either of those cases.

Indemnity or insurance

[2.243]   **Dane v Mortgage Insurance Corpn Ltd**
[1894] 1 QB 54, 63 LJQB 144, 70 LT 83, 10 TLR 86

The principle operates when there is a contract of indemnity but does not apply to insurances which are not contracts of indemnity.

[2.244]   **Kirkland's Garage (Kinrose) Ltd v Clark**
1967 SLT (Sh Ct) 60

The pursuers carried out repairs to the defendant's car on the instructions of insurance assessors after the defendant had filled in a claim form from his insurer. He signed a satisfaction note and collected the car. The insurer did not pay for the repairs and subsequently went into liquidation. The pursuers claimed that as the defendant's name appeared on documents passing between them, the assessors and the insurer, it proved that the insurer was acting as the defendant's agents in ordering the repairs.

HELD: So far as the documents went, the defendant's name appeared only as a reference; the insurer appeared to be acting as principal and made no disclosure that it was to be treated as agent of the defendant. That being so the pursuers could not succeed unless there was a general rule of law that insurers are always acting as agents for the insured in instructing repairs. *Godfrey Davis Ltd v Culling and Hecht* (at para [2.240]) and *Cooter and Green Ltd v Tyrrell* (at para [2.241]) show that there is no such rule.

A contrary decision

[2.245]   **Martin v Stannard**
[1964] CLY 585   Judge Dow, Cty Ct

The plaintiff carried out repairs to the defendant's motor vehicle at the defendant's request after his insurance company had sent an assessor to inspect the damage and had intimated by telephone through the defendant's insurance brokers, that the work could proceed on the plaintiff's estimate of £138. After carrying out the work the plaintiff released the vehicle to the defendant on receiving an assurance over the telephone from the insurance brokers that if the defendant signed a satisfaction note the insurance company would pay. On the insurers becoming insolvent without paying, the plaintiff claimed the £138 from the defendant.

HELD: The contract for the repairs was between the plaintiff and the defendant (who had received the benefit of them), the insurance company being merely in the position of a guarantor. The plaintiff was entitled to recover the £138 from the defendant.

[2.246]   **Charnock v Liverpool Corpn**

[1968] 3 All ER 473, [1968] 1 WLR 1498, 112 Sol Jo 781, [1968] 2 Lloyd's Rep 113, CA

The plaintiff's car was damaged in an accident by negligence of the first defendant's servant. He took the car to a garage where he wanted the repairs done and by arrangement met his insurer's assessor there. The repairers prepared an estimate and eventually the insurer wrote to them: 'We confirm it is in order to proceed with the repairs as per your estimate ... Please forward your final account to this office on completion, together with a signed satisfaction note.' A reasonable period for doing the repairs was five weeks but the repairers took eight. The plaintiff hired a car for the whole of the eight weeks and sued the first defendant and the repairers for the costs. The first defendant was admittedly liable for five weeks' hire charges: the judge held the repairers liable for the other three on the grounds that they had impliedly contracted with the plaintiff to do the repairs within a reasonable time and were in breach of that contract.

HELD, ON APPEAL by the repairers: The judge was right. The decisions in *Cooter and Green Ltd v Tyrrell* (at para [2.241]) and *Godfrey Davis Ltd v Culling and Hecht* (at para [2.240]) did not decide that there was no contract of any sort between the owner and repairer. In those cases the question was whether the contract to pay for the repairs was made between the insurer and the repairers or between the owner and repairers. In the present case there was a clear contract to be inferred from the facts between the repairers and the plaintiff that in consideration of his leaving his car with them for repair they would carry out the repairs with reasonable expedition and care and that they would be paid by the insurance company. The repairers were in breach of this contract.

[2.247]   **Davidson v Guardian Royal Exchange Assurance**

[1979] 1 Lloyd's Rep 406, Ct of Sess

The insurer issued a comprehensive motor policy covering 'loss of or damage to the vehicle' and containing a provision in the case of damage: 'The company may at its own option repair the vehicle.' There was an exemption from liability to pay for 'loss of use'. The insured's car was damaged by fire; the insurer elected to repair it and sent it away for this purpose. It was not returned repaired until 40 weeks had elapsed. A reasonable time for repair would have been eight weeks. The insured claimed damages for loss of use of the car.

HELD: (1) Having undertaken to repair the car the insurer was bound to do so within a reasonable time. There was a breach of this implied term for the period beyond the eighth week.
    (2)   If there was any ambiguity in the policy the construction had to be *contra proferentum*.
    (3)   The insured's claim in this action was based on breach of contract; the policy was not concerned with breach of contract and the exemption clause did not apply.

10.   BROKERS AND AGENTS

Broker's negligence

[2.248]   Osman v J Ralph Moss Ltd
[1970] 1 Lloyd's Rep 313, CA

The plaintiff, a Turk having only a limited knowledge of English asked the defendant, an insurance broker, to provide him with motor insurance. It recommended a policy underwritten by a company which it knew was of doubtful stability. The plaintiff accepted its recommendation and paid a year's premium. Shortly afterwards the insurer went into liquidation and the plaintiff was uninsured. He did not realise this. A letter the defendant sent him was misleading and inadequate to warn him. A few weeks later he had an accident as a result of which he was prosecuted for having no insurance, fined £25 and incurred 30 guineas costs. In addition, he was sued by the other party in the accident and judgment was given against him for £207 and £37 costs which, being uninsured, he had to meet himself.

HELD: The defendant was liable for negligence in failing properly to acquaint him that he was uninsured. He was entitled to be repaid the amount of the premium and:
(1)   the damages he had to pay plus £5 of the costs,
(2)   the amount of the fine and the costs in the magistrate's court.
It was foreseeable that by reason of the defendant's breach of duty and negligence he might incur liability for damages but he should have mitigated the loss of costs by submitting to judgment when the claim was made. It was not against public policy that he should be indemnified against the fine because there had been no mens rea and no personal negligence.

[2.249]   Bromley London Borough Council v Ellis
(1970) 114 Sol Jo 906, [1971] 1 Lloyd's Rep 97, CA

In July Mrs D sold a car to E and agreed to have insurance transferred to him. E asked her broker to do this and it agreed. It filled up a proposal form, which he signed, but failed to send it off until November. The insurer wrote asking a question which the broker did not answer. The insurer wrote in December saying that in the absence of a reply within seven days the insurance would be cancelled. The broker did nothing and did not tell E. The insurer cancelled the policy. In February E collided with the plaintiff's car and was found liable for £805 damage and loss. Only after the accident did he discover he was not insured. He claimed indemnity from the broker.

HELD: The broker, though agent for the insurance company and not for E, was under a duty of care to look after his interests. It had failed to use reasonable care and was liable to indemnify him.

[2.250]   Warren v Henry Sutton & Co Ltd
[1976] 2 Lloyd's Rep 276, CA

The plaintiff, about to go abroad with his car, telephoned his insurer and asked for his insurance to be extended to cover a friend whom he knew to have a bad driving record. He gave his insurer the name of his broker; the insurer telephoned the broker for details and was told by him that the plaintiff's friend had 'no accidents, no conviction and no disabilities'. A bad accident occurred whilst the friend was driving and on discovering his bad record the insurer refused indemnity to the plaintiff, who then sued the broker.

HELD: It was the duty of the broker when obtaining extension of the cover to make such inquiries about the friend's record as would enable him to make a truthful statement to the insurers. His recklessness in making the statement he did was the cause of the insurer's repudiation and he was liable to the plaintiff in damages.

[2.251]   McNealy v Pennine Insurance Co Ltd
[1978] 2 Lloyd's Rep 18, [1978] RTR 285, (1978) 122 Sol Jo 229, CA

The plaintiff's main occupation was the repair of property, but he was also an expert guitarist and sometimes played in a band. Before going abroad with a band he went to a broker to get insurance for his car. The policy suggested by the broker excluded cover for part-time musicians and it knew this. It asked the plaintiff what his occupation was and he said 'property repairer'. A policy was issued. When an accident occurred the insurer refused indemnity; it was conceded it was entitled so to do. The plaintiff sued the broker.

HELD: The plaintiff was entitled to succeed. It was the duty of the broker to use all reasonable care to see that the assured was properly covered. It should have gone through the list of excluded categories and asked the plaintiff if he was or had been a part-time musician. It was its duty to ensure as far as possible that he came within the list of categories acceptable to the insurance company. It was in breach of its duty of care.

[2.252]   T O'Donoghue Ltd v Harding and Hamilton & Carter Ltd
[1988] 2 Lloyd's Rep 281, QBD

The plaintiffs were jewellers who employed Mr Collins as a travelling salesman. Following the usual practice of the trade, he carried a valuable stock case of jewellery with him which he kept under close attention. On 6 November 1984 the stock case, containing jewellery worth £145,000, was stolen whilst he was paying for petrol at a garage. The plaintiffs claimed against the insurer, the first defendants, who denied liability by relying on an exclusion clause in the policy which provided that cover would not be available in respect of thefts from unattended road vehicles. The plaintiffs also claimed against their broker, the second defendant, who had stated orally in January 1984 that the policy would cover loss in the specific circumstances mentioned above.

HELD: Mr Collins had behaved in a perfectly responsible manner and, according to the evidence, had kept the car and the case under observation as much as possible. The crime had probably been committed by a skilled gang of thieves. Accordingly, there was no negligence on the part of the plaintiffs and the insurer could not claim the benefit of the exclusion clause. *Per curiam*: if the circumstances of the theft had been different, and the court had found on the evidence that the car had not been attended, the advice of the broker could have rendered it liable in negligence to the plaintiffs.

[2.253]   Dodson v Peter H Dodson Insurance Services

[2001] 3 All ER 75, [2001] 1 All ER (Comm) 300, [2001] 1 WLR 1012, [2001] 1 Lloyd's M Rep 520, [2001] RTR 13, [2001] Lloyd's Rep IR 278, (2001) 98(4) LSG 49

The claimant, son of the principal of the defendant broker took out a motor insurance policy with Eagle Star, through the broker. The policy contained a provision permitting the claimant to drive any other vehicle with the owner's permission. Six months after taking out the policy the claimant sold the insured vehicle. He was advised by the defendant that the policy would continue to cover him when driving other vehicles with the owner's permission. Whilst driving his mother's vehicle the claimant was involved in a serious accident. Eagle Star refused to indemnify on the grounds that the policy became void when the claimant sold his own vehicle. The claimant sued the defendants in negligence.

HELD on appeal to the Court of Appeal: The defendant was not negligent in advising that the policy continued to provide cover to the claimant when driving other vehicles with the permission of the owner. The insurer was taken to have accepted the risk that the claimant may dispose of his vehicle and not immediately obtain another.

Broker not liable to insured

[2.254]   O'Connor v BDB Kirby & Co

[1972] 1 QB 90, [1971] 2 All ER 1415, [1971] 2 WLR 1233, 115 Sol Jo 267, [1971] 1 Lloyd's Rep 454, [1971] RTR 440, CA

The plaintiff having bought a car went to the defendant, an insurance broker, to take out an insurance policy. The broker filled in a proposal form for him, for the T company. He told the plaintiff the premium would be higher if he did not have a garage for the car, and he also told the plaintiff to check the proposal form to see if it was correct before signing it. On the form the broker had shown incorrectly that the car would be kept in a private garage. The plaintiff signed the form and in due course a policy was issued. Subsequently, the insurer on finding that the car was parked in the street refused to indemnify the plaintiff against a loss he sustained. The plaintiff claimed damages against the broker alleging breach of a contractual duty to fill in the form properly.

HELD: It was the duty of a proposer for insurance to see and make sure that the information in the proposal form was accurate and he cannot be heard to say that he did not read it properly or was not fully appraised of its contents. The plaintiff should have read the form: he signed it and if he was so careless as not to read it properly he had only himself to blame.
   Judgment for the defendant.

[2.255]   Harvest Trucking Co Ltd v Davis

[1991] 2 Lloyd's Rep 638, 135 Sol Jo 443

The duty of care on an insurance intermediary was similar to that on a broker and included the duty to ensure that the assured was made aware of any new and onerous or unusual terms which were a condition precedent to recovery.

Agent is agent of proposer

[2.256] Newsholme Bros v Road Transport and General Insurance Co Ltd

[1929] 2 KB 356, 98 LJKB 751, 141 LT 570, 45 TLR 573, 73 Sol Jo 465, CA

With regard to mis-statements in a proposal form the insurance agent is the agent of the assured and not of the insurer. A proposal form for the insurance of a motor-bus was signed by the person wishing to effect the insurance, but the answers to the questions therein, which were warranted to be true and to form the basis of the contract, were filled in by the insurance company's agent, who, although told the true facts, wrote, for some unexplained reason, answers which were untrue in a material respect. The agent was not authorised by the insurance company to fill in proposal forms and it did not appear that the company knew that he had in fact done so. His duties were to procure persons to effect insurance and to see, so far as he could, that proposal forms were correctly filled up; he was not authorised to give a cover note or to enter into a policy of insurance. A policy was issued to the person who had signed the proposal form and during its currency he made a claim under it, but the insurance company repudiated liability on the ground of the untrue statements in the proposal form.

HELD: The agent of the insurance company in filling in the proposal form was merely the *amanuensis* of the proposer, that the knowledge of the true facts by the agent could not be imputed to the insurance company, and, therefore, that the insurance company was entitled to repudiate liability on the ground of the untrue statements in the proposal form.

[2.257] Facer v Vehicle and General Insurance Co Ltd

[1965] 1 Lloyd's Rep 113   Marshall J

The plaintiff signed a proposal form which was filled in for him by a Mr Bonham, a sub-agent or servant of Mr Braun, who was an agent of the defendant. The answer 'No' was written on the proposal form to the question 'Do you suffer from any defective vision or hearing or from any physical infirmity?' though the plaintiff had disclosed to Bonham that he had only one eye. The proposal form ended 'I agree that this proposal and declaration shall be the basis of the contract between the company and myself, and also said 'If this proposal is written by another it shall be deemed he shall be my agent and not an agent of the company.'

HELD: The vital question was whether Bonham, when he inaccurately answered the question about defective vision by putting in the word 'No' was the agent of the plaintiff in filling in the form or the agent of the defendants. The case was governed by *Newsholme Bros v Road Transport & General Insurance Co Ltd* (at para [2.256]) with this further strengthening factor that in the present case there was an express declaration in the proposal that the person filling in the form was to be deemed the agent of the proposer and not of the company. The defendant was not entitled to avoid the policy.

Note—But contrast with *Stone v Reliance Mutual Insurance Society Ltd* (at para [2.258]).

[2.258] Stone v Reliance Mutual Insurance Society Ltd

[1972] 1 Lloyd's Rep 469, CA

In 1966 the plaintiff insured his house with the defendant under a fire and theft policy. In 1967 there was a fire and the defendant paid him £280. The policy then lapsed. In 1968 the defendant's district inspector called with a view to getting the plaintiff to take out a new policy. He called only on people who had previously held policies and it was the company's practice that for the proposal form he should put the question orally and write down the answers himself. He filled in a proposal form without asking any questions and plaintiff's wife signed it without reading it. The form contained a declaration by the proposer that the person writing down the answers did so as the proposer's agent. Two of the answers filled in by the inspector were to the effect that the plaintiff had not previously held a policy with the defendant and that he had not previously made any claims in respect of the risks proposed. Later a burglary took place for which the plaintiff claimed, disclosing on the claim form the earlier fire claim. The defendant refused to indemnify on the ground of non-disclosure of the fire claim in the proposal form.

HELD: Though the proposal form was expressed to be filled in by the inspector as the plaintiff's agent his express evidence had been that it was company practice that he should put the questions and write down the answers. The proper inference was that it was his duty, owed to his employer, to take proper care. It was quite different from *Newsholme Bros v Road Transport and General Insurance Co Ltd* (at para [2.256]) and was far more like *Bawden v London Edinburgh & Glasgow Assurance Co* (at para [2.260]). The inspector knew of the earlier policy and of the fire claim: it was his mistake and not the proposer's. The company could not rely on it to avoid the policy.

Note—An insured will not generally be responsible for the agent's failure to pass on relevant information. Knowledge of such information is to be imputed to insurers. The insured may still be liable in contract.

[2.259]   Magee v Pennine Insurance Co Ltd

[1969] 2 QB 507, [1969] 2 All ER 891, [1969] 2 WLR 1278, 113 Sol Jo 303, [1969] 2 Lloyd's Rep 378, CA

Note—See further para [2.39].

[2.260]   Bawden v London Edinburgh & Glasgow Assurance Co

[1892] 2 QB 534, 57 JP 116, CA

Bawden was an illiterate man and had lost the sight of one eye. Quinn, the insurer's local agent, was aware of this. Quinn prepared a proposal form for accident insurance and completed this to Bawden's dictation. The answers included a statement that Bawden was in good health, free from disease, not ruptured and had no physical infirmity. Quinn did not inform the company that Bawden had only one eye. An accident occurred and Bawden claimed on the policy. The insurer refused to indemnify.

HELD: Quinn was an agent of the company to negotiate the terms of the proposal and to induce a person who wished to insure to make the proposal.

Per Lord Esher MR: He was not merely the agent to take the piece of paper containing the proposal to the company. The company could not alter the proposal. He must accept it or decline it. Quinn, then, having authority to negotiate and settle the terms of a proposal, what happened? He went to a man who had one eye, and persuaded him to make a proposal to the company, which the company might either accept or reject. He saw that the man only had one eye. The proposal must be construed as having been negotiated and settled by the agent with a one eyed man. In that sense the knowledge of the agent was the knowledge of the company.

[2.261]   **Holdsworth v Lancashire and Yorkshire Insurance Co**
(1907) 23 TLR 521

The plaintiff was a joiner and builder. He effected insurance in respect of his liability to his workmen under the Workmen's Compensation Act 1897. The insurer's agent knew that the plaintiff was a joiner and builder. The agent filled in a proposal form which was stated to be the basis of the contract in which the plaintiff was described as a joiner. When the plaintiff got the policy he objected to being so described and the agent got sanction from the insurer's branch office to insert the words 'and builder', no communication of this was made to Head Office. A workman was injured and the insurer sought to avoid liability.

HELD: (1) By receiving premiums the insurer was precluded from denying the agent's authority to contract and in those circumstances the knowledge of the agent was the knowledge of the company;
(2)   Even if the policy hadn't been altered, the company would have been liable because the contract must be treated as having been negotiated by the agent with a joiner and builder, and the knowledge of the agent must be treated as the knowledge of the company.

The broker's implied authority to bind insurers

[2.262]   **Stockton v Mason**
[1978] 2 Lloyd's Rep 430, CA

The policyholder had a policy covering a Ford Anglia car. He exchanged the car for an MG. His wife telephoned the broker on 8 April and told them; she asked that the MG be substituted for the Anglia as the car insured under the policy. The broker said 'Yes, that will be all right. We will see to that.' On 18 April at 3.30 pm the plaintiff was seriously injured when travelling as a passenger in the MG driven by the policyholder's son. The policy covered driving by any authorised driver. At 5.15 pm on the 18th the policyholder received a letter from the broker written on the 17th saying cover for the MG was limited to himself only. The judge held that the broker's remark was merely a statement that it would seek to negotiate a contract of insurance on the MG; the insurer was not liable and the broker was liable in negligence to the policyholder's son for failing to notify the policyholder of its failure to get insurance on the desired terms.

HELD, ON APPEAL: There was a valid contract of interim insurance. A broker had implied authority to issue on behalf of the insurer or enter into as agent for the insurer contracts of interim insurance normally recorded in cover notes. In making the remark quoted the broker was acting as agent for the insurer and not for the person wishing to be insured. Such an interim contract of insurance can be made orally and in informal colloquial language. The insurer was liable.

CHAPTER 3

Motor Insurers' Bureau

1.   BACKGROUND

(A)   COMPENSATION FOR THE VICTIMS OF UNINSURED DRIVERS

[3.1]   Since its invention in the late nineteenth century, the horseless carriage has been an effective means of causing damage to people and their property. By the 1920s the number of cars on Britain's roads had risen to a level where road traffic accidents were becoming very common. This led to the passing of the Road Traffic Act 1930, which for the first time made motor insurance compulsory for car drivers. However, there remained significant gaps in the protection afforded to the innocent victim of an accident. Where, despite the 1930 Act, the negligent driver had not taken out a policy of insurance, unless the driver possessed the means to pay damages the victim could go uncompensated. The same could happen where, even though a policy of insurance was in existence, the insurer was entitled to avoid the policy for some technical reason such as a material non-disclosure. In other cases, the victim may simply have been unable to identify the driver who made a hasty get-away after causing an accident.

The need to fill some of these gaps was recognised by a committee chaired by Sir Felix Cassel KC. In its report of July 1937, the Cassel Committee concluded that there should be a central fund to compensate third party victims of road traffic accidents where insurance cover did not exist or where such cover as existed was ineffective to provide compensation to the victim. The Committee decided that the fund should not extend to providing compensation for the victims of untraced drivers.

The Second World War having intervened, it was not until the end of 1945 that measures were put in place for the creation of a body that would hold and administer a fund designed to implement some of the recommendations of the Cassel Committee. The body now known as the Motor Insurers' Bureau (MIB) was set up by the motor insurance market, its precise legal status being a company limited by guarantee. It is not itself an insurance company but has been aptly described as 'a novel piece of extra statutory machinery'. Most motor insurers and Lloyd's motor syndicates became members of MIB at the outset and the fund has since its inception been provided by the members themselves.

Liability under the original MIB agreement commenced on 1 July 1946. The 1946 Agreement survived until 1 February 1971 and, since then, new agreements have been entered into on 22 November 1972, 21 December 1988 and 13 August 1999. Since 1974 all authorised insurers as defined in the Road Traffic Act 1972, s 145 (Road Traffic Act 1988, s 145) have been required to be members of the Bureau.

The 1946 Agreement still left uncompensated the victim of a 'hit-and-run' driver, ie a driver whose identity was unknown, except that by Note 6 to the Agreement the Bureau undertook to give 'sympathetic consideration to the making of an ex gratia payment to the victim'. This loose arrangement was replaced in 1969 by an Untraced Drivers Agreement establishing a detailed procedure by which to deal with such cases. Subsequent Untraced Drivers Agreements have been effective from 22 November 1972, 14 June 1996 and 14 February 2003. The latest agreement covers accidents in England, Scotland and Wales and is set out below (at para [3.78]). There are also agreements dealing with untraced motor accidents on the islands of Alderney, Jersey,

Guernsey, Sark, the Isle of Man and Gibraltar. These agreements are, for reasons of space, not set out in this chapter but all can be accessed via the MIB's website at: www.mib.org.uk.

The Bureau deals also with claims against foreign motorists visiting Britain in its capacity as the Green Card Bureau (see paras [3.62]), where, although the user of the vehicle may be insured, it acts as guarantor for the payment of damages and handles the claims where the insurer has not appointed a representative or has become insolvent.

For the purposes of the Fourth Directive (2000/26/EC), the Bureau has further been appointed as the Compensation Body and its subsidiary company, Motor Insurers' Information Centre (MIIC) as the Information Centre.

The importance of the role of MIB today in handling the claims of road accident victims can scarcely be overstated. It is thought that on the roads of Britain there are as many as 1.25 million uninsured vehicles, some 5% of the total number of vehicles. The cost of claims brought against drivers with no or no effective insurance is estimated at £500 million, of which MIB deals with £300 million worth directly.

(B)   THE OTHER MAJOR SAFETY NET FOR VICTIMS: SECTIONS 151 AND 152 OF THE ROAD TRAFFIC ACT 1988

[3.2]   It is very important that the practitioner is aware of the other important mechanism for compensating victims of uninsured drivers, so that time and money are not wasted involving MIB where it is not necessary to do so. Of most importance are the compulsory indemnity provisions at ss 151 and 152 of the Road Traffic Act 1988. The effect of these provisions is, in certain cases, to compel the insurer to compensate the third party victim notwithstanding that he, the insurer, may be able to refuse to indemnify his insured under the policy. In these cases the insurer is known as the 'Road Traffic Act insurer'. The Road Traffic Act insurer is not to be confused with what used to be called the 'Domestic Regulations insurer', who is now referred to as the 'Article 75 insurer'. A full explanation of the latter two terms is provided below (at paras [3.61] and [3.62] below).

(C)   FUTURE DEVELOPMENTS

[3.3]   It is possible that an amendment to the Pre-Action Protocol for Personal Injury Claims will be made to bring claims against MIB within its provisions. This is consistent with MIB's desire to be put as far as possible in the position of a defendant and thus able to take advantage of the more positive aspects of the revision of the civil procedure rules. Pending this possible change, it is fair to say that MIB seeks to operate within the Personal Injury Protocol in cases under the Uninsured Drivers Agreement.

A new Untraced Drivers Agreement came into force on 14 February 2003 and this extends the benefits available to victims to include:
- damage to property where the vehicle can be identified but the driver cannot;
- a right to a public oral hearing on appeal;
- interest on awards; and
- a revised scale of contribution to the cost of legal advice for successful applicants.

From 20 January 2003, the Motor Insurance Database (MID), operated by MIIC, became fully effective, enabling the insurer of any vehicle to be identified from its registration number. Whilst access to the database is restricted to MIB, the police and insurers, information can be obtained by victims, subject to the Data Protection Act 1998, either via their own motor insurers, or if the victim is not a motorist by applying direct to MIIC. Efforts are now being made by the MIB to ensure the police have easier access to the system in practice and to encourage those who fail to register details of those vehicles forming part of a fleet to do so.

2.   THE UNINSURED DRIVERS AGREEMENTS

(A)   GENERALLY

[3.4]   The current agreement and its two predecessors are reproduced in full below (at paras [3.5], [3.12] and [3.19]). They apply as follows:
- for accidents occurring between 1 December 1972 and 30 December 1988, the 1972 Agreement applies;
- for accidents occurring between 31 December 1988 and 30 September 1999 the 1988 Agreement applies;
- thereafter the 1999 Agreement applies.

Since 1972 there have also been changes to primary road traffic legislation. The Road Traffic Act 1972 came into force on 1 July 1972. In order to comply with the Second Council Directive 84/5/EEC (dealing with compulsory insurance cover for liability for property damage) it was amended by the Motor Vehicles (Compulsory Insurance) Regulations 1987, SI 1987/2171 with effect from 31 December 1988. The 1972 Act was then replaced in its entirety by the Road Traffic Act 1988, which came into force on 15 May 1989.

Since then, there have been several important amendments to Part VI of the 1988 Act (dealing with insurance against third party liabilities) and it is very important that the agreements are interpreted and applied by reference to the correct 'version' of the Act for the date of the accident in question.

Each Agreement and its Notes are an official publication and are Crown copyright. They are reproduced by permission of the Controller of HM Stationery Office, from which copies can be bought.

The parties to the Agreement dated 22 November 1972 are MIB and the Secretary of State for the Environment. The parties to the 1988 Agreement are the Secretary of State for Transport and the Motor Insurers' Bureau, and for the 1999 Agreement the Secretary of State for the Environment, Transport and the Regions and MIB. There is therefore no privity of contract between the Bureau and a claimant, nor between the Bureau and the uninsured driver. Nevertheless, the Bureau allows itself to be sued if a breach of the terms of the agreement is alleged. The whole of the Bureau's duties and liabilities in respect of a claim against an uninsured driver arise from the agreement. Thus the first essential for anyone conducting such a claim is to read the relevant Agreement and the Notes appended to it. This is especially important in the case of the 1999 Agreement where the Notes to the Agreement have undergone some recent revisions, as from 15 April 2002, which can be seen on MIB's website at: www.mib.org.uk and the Agreement reproduced (at para [3.19] below).

(B)   TEXT OF AGREEMENT DATED 22 NOVEMBER 1972

[3.5]   Text of an Agreement dated 22 November 1972 between the Secretary of State for the Environment and the Motor Insurers' Bureau together with some notes on its scope and purpose.

In accordance with the Agreement made on 31 December 1945 between the Minister of War Transport and insurers transacting compulsory motor vehicle insurance business in Great Britain (published by the Stationery Office under the title 'Motor Vehicle Insurance Fund') a corporation called the 'Motor Insurers' Bureau' entered into an agreement on 17 June 1946 with the Minister of Transport to give effect from 1 July 1946 to the principle recommended in July 1937 by the Departmental Committee under Sir Felix Cassel (Cmd 5528), to secure compensation to third party victims of road accidents in cases where, notwithstanding the provisions of the Road Traffic Acts relating to compulsory insurance, the victim is deprived of compensation by the absence of insurance, or of effective insurance. That Agreement was replaced by an Agreement which operated in respect of accidents occurring on or after 1 March 1971. The Agreement of 1971 has now been replaced by a new Agreement which operates in respect of accidents occurring on or after 1 December 1972.

The text of the new Agreement is as follows—

MEMORANDUM OF AGREEMENT made the 22nd day of November 1972 between the Secretary of State for the Environment and the Motor Insurers' Bureau, whose registered office is at [Linford Wood House, 6–12 Capital Drive, Linford Wood, Milton Keynes MK14 6XT (DX 142620 MILTON KEYNES 10] (hereinafter referred to as 'MIB') SUPPLEMENTAL to an Agreement (hereinafter called 'the Principal Agreement') made the 31st day of December 1945 between the Minister of War Transport and the insurers transacting compulsory motor vehicle insurance business in Great Britain by or on behalf of whom the said Agreement was signed in pursuance of paragraph 1 of which MIB was incorporated.

(I)   DEFINITIONS

IT IS HEREBY AGREED AS FOLLOWS—

Definitions
1   In this Agreement—
   'contract of insurance' means a policy of insurance of a security;
   'insurer' includes the giver of a security;
   'relevant liability' means a liability in respect of which a policy of insurance must insure a person in order to comply with Part VI of the Road Traffic Act 1972.

(II)   SATISFACTION OF CLAIMS BY MIB
2   If judgment in respect of any relevant liability is obtained against any person or persons in any court in Great Britain whether or not such a person or persons be in fact covered by a contract of insurance and any such judgment is not satisfied in full within seven days from the date upon which the person or persons in whose favour the judgment was given became entitled to enforce it then MIB will, subject to the provisions of Clauses 4, 5 and 6 hereof, pay or satisfy or cause to be paid or satisfied to or to the satisfaction of the person or persons in whose favour the judgment was given any sum payable or remaining payable there under in respect of the relevant liability including any sum awarded by the Court in respect of interest on that sum and any taxed costs or any costs awarded by the Court without taxation (or such proportion thereof as is attributable to the relevant liability) whatever may be the cause of the failure of the judgment debtor to satisfy the judgment.

(III) PERIOD OF AGREEMENT

3   This Agreement shall be determinable by the Secretary of State at any time or by MIB on twelve months' notice without prejudice to the continued operation of the Agreement in respect of accidents occurring before the date of termination.

(IV) RECOVERIES

4   Nothing in this Agreement shall prevent insurers from providing by conditions in their contracts of insurance that all sums paid by them or by MIB by virtue of the Principal Agreement or this Agreement in or towards the discharge of the liability of their assured shall be recoverable by them or by MIB from the assured or from any other person.

(V) CONDITIONS PRECEDENT TO MIB

5 (1)   MIB shall not incur any liability under Clause 2 of this Agreement unless—

NOTICE OF PROCEEDINGS

(a)   Notice of the bringing of the proceedings is given before or within seven days after the commencement of the proceedings—
  (i)   to MIB in the case of proceedings in respect of a relevant liability which is either not covered by a contract of insurance or covered by a contract of insurance with an insurer whose identity cannot be ascertained, or
  (ii)   to the insurer in the case of proceedings in respect of a relevant liability which is covered by a contract of insurance with an insurer whose identity can be ascertained.

SUPPLY OF INFORMATION

(b)   Such information relating to the proceedings as MIB may reasonably require is supplied to MIB by the person bringing the proceedings.

JUDGMENT AGAINST PERSONS LIABLE

(c)   If so required by MIB and subject to full indemnity from MIB as to costs the person bringing the proceedings has taken all reasonable steps to obtain judgment against all the persons liable in respect of the injury or death of the third party and, in the event of such a person being a servant or agent, against his principal.

ASSIGNMENT OF JUDGMENT

(d)   the judgment referred to in Clause 2 of this Agreement and any judgment referred to in paragraph (c) of this Clause which has been obtained (whether or not either judgment includes an amount in respect of a liability other than a relevant liability) and any order for costs are assigned to MIB or their nominee.

(2)   In the event of any dispute as to the reasonableness of a requirement by MIB for the supply of information or that any particular step should be taken to obtain judgment against other persons it may be referred to the Secretary of State whose decision shall be final.

(3)   Where a judgment which includes an amount in respect of a liability other than a relevant liability has been assigned to MIB or their nominee in pursuance of para (1)(d) of this Clause MIB shall apportion any moneys received in pursuance of the judgment according to the proportion which the damages in respect of the relevant liability bear to the damages in respect of the other liabilities and shall account to the person in whose favour the judgment was given in respect of such moneys received properly apportionable to the other liabilities. Where an order for

costs in respect of such a judgment has been so assigned moneys received pursuant to the order shall be dealt with in the same manner.

(VI)   EXEMPTIONS/EXCEPTIONS

6 (1)   MIB shall not incur any liability under Clause 2 of this Agreement in a case where—

(a)   the claim arises out of the use of a vehicle owned by or in the possession of the Crown, except where any other person has undertaken responsibility for the existence of a contract of insurance under Part VI of the Road Traffic Act 1972 (whether or not the person or persons liable be in fact covered by a contract of insurance) or where the liability is in fact covered by a contract of insurance;

(b)   the claim arises out of the use of a vehicle the use of which is not required to be covered by a contract of insurance by virtue of s 144 of the Road Traffic Act 1972, unless the use is in fact covered by such a contract;

(c)   at the time of the accident the person suffering death or bodily injury in respect of which the claim is made was allowing himself to be carried in a vehicle and—

(i)   knew or had reason to believe that the vehicle had been taken without the consent of the owner or other lawful authority except in a case where—

(A)   he believed or had reason to believe that he had lawful authority to be carried or that he would have had the owner's consent if the owner had known of his being carried and the circumstances of his carriage; or

(B)   he had learned of the circumstances of the taking of the vehicle since the commencement of the journey and it would be unreasonable to expect him to have alighted from the vehicle; or

(ii)   being the owner of or being a person using the vehicle, he was using or causing or permitting the vehicle to be used without there being in force in relation to such use a contract of insurance as would comply with Part VI of the Road Traffic Act 1972, knowing or having reason to believe that no such contract was in force.

(2)   The exemption specified in sub-para (1)(c) of this Clause shall apply only in a case where the judgment in respect of which the claim against MIB is made was obtained in respect of a relevant liability incurred by the owner or a person using the vehicle in which the person who suffered death or bodily injury was being carried.

(3)   For the purposes of these exemptions—

(a)   a vehicle which has been unlawfully removed from the possession of the Crown shall be taken to continue in that possession whilst it is kept so removed;

(b)   references to a person being carried in a vehicle include reference to his being carried in or upon or entering or getting on to or alighting from the vehicle;

(c)   'owner' in relation to a vehicle which is the subject of a hiring agreement or a hire- purchase agreement, means the person in possession of the vehicle under that agreement.

(VII)   AGENTS

7   Nothing in this Agreement shall prevent MIB performing their obligations under this Agreement by Agents.

(VIII)   OPERATION

8   This agreement shall come into operation on the first day of December 1972 in relation to accidents occurring on or after that date. The agreement made on

1 February 1971 between the Secretary of State and MIB shall cease and determine except in relation to claims arising out of accidents occurring before the first day of December 1972.

IN WITNESS etc

Notes

The following notes are for the guidance of those who may have a claim on the Motor Insurers' Bureau under the Agreement, and of their legal advisers, but they must not be taken as rendering unnecessary a careful study of the Agreement itself. Communications on any matter connected with the Agreement should be addressed to the Motor Insurers' Bureau whose address is [Linford Wood House, 6–12 Capital Drive, Linford Wood, Milton Keynes MK14 6XT (DX 142620 MILTON KEYNES 10].

1   The agreement, which operates from 1 December 1972, supersedes earlier agreements made on 17 June 1946 (which was operative from 1 July 1946) and on 1 February 1971 (which was operative from 1 March 1971) in relation to claims arising out of accidents occurring on or after 1 December 1972.

2   If damages are awarded by a court in respect of death or personal injury arising out of the use of a motor vehicle on a road in circumstances where the liability is one which was, at the time the accident occurred, required to be covered by insurance and such damages, or any part of them, remain unpaid seven days after the judgment becomes enforceable, the Bureau will, subject to the exceptions in Clause 6 of the Agreement, pay the unrecovered amount (including any interest awarded by the court and costs) to the person in whose favour the judgment has been given against an assignment of the judgment debt. This applies whether the judgment debtor is a British resident or a foreign visitor.

3   Nothing in the Agreement affects the position at law of the parties to an action for damages arising out of the driving of a motor vehicle. The Bureau's liability under the Agreement can only arise when the plaintiff has successfully established his case against the person or persons liable in the usual manner and judgment has been given in his favour. There is, of course, nothing to exclude the acceptance of compensation by the plaintiff under a settlement negotiated between the plaintiff and the alleged person liable or the Bureau.

4   WHERE THERE IS A POLICY In cases where it is ascertained that there is in existence a policy issued in compliance with the Road Traffic Act 1972, the insurer concerned will normally act as the agent of the Bureau and, subject to notice being given as provided for in Clause 5(1)(a)(ii), will handle claims within the terms of the Agreement. This will apply even if the use of the vehicle at the time of the accident was outside the terms of the policy or the insurer is entitled to repudiate liability under the policy for any other reason. (In the latter connection, victims and those acting on their behalf are reminded of the requirements as to the giving of notice to the insurer if the protection afforded to third parties by s 149 of the Road Traffic Act is sought.) This arrangement is, of course, without prejudice to any rights insurers may have against their policyholders and, to avoid any possible misapprehension, it is emphasised that there is nothing in this Agreement affecting any obligations imposed on a policyholder by his policy. Policyholders are not released from their contractual obligations to their insurers, although the scheme protects THIRD PARTY VICTIMS from the consequences of failure to observe them. For example, the failure of a policyholder to notify claims to his insurers as required by his policy, although not affecting a victim's right to benefit under the scheme, may leave the policyholder liable to his insurers.

WHERE THERE IS NO POLICY OR THE IDENTITY OF THE INSURER CANNOT BE ASCERTAINED In cases where there is no policy, or for any reason the existence of a policy is in doubt or where there is a policy but the identity of the insurer cannot be ascertained, the victim or those acting on his behalf must notify the Bureau of the claim. It is a condition of the Bureau's liability that they should receive notification before or within seven days after the commencement of proceedings against the alleged person liable. In practice, however, it will be preferable to notify the Bureau in all cases where the name of the insurer is not speedily forthcoming.

5   Claims arising out of the use of uninsured vehicles owned by or in the possession of the Crown will in the majority of cases be outside the scope of the Bureau's liability (see Clause 6 of the Agreement). In such cases the approach should be made to the responsible authority in the usual way. The same benefits in respect of compensation will be afforded by the Crown to the victim in such cases as they would receive were the accident caused by a private vehicle except where the victim is a serviceman or servicewoman whose death or injury gives rise to an entitlement to a pension or other compensation from public funds.

6   The Bureau have no liability UNDER THIS AGREEMENT to pay compensation in respect of any person who may suffer personal injuries or death resulting from the use on a road of a vehicle, the owner or driver of which cannot be traced. However, in relation to accidents occurring ON OR AFTER 1 May 1969 and before 1 December 1972, an Agreement dated 21 April 1969 between the Minister of Transport (now the Secretary of State for the Environment) and the Bureau for the Compensation of Victims of Untraced Drivers applies. In relation to accidents occurring on or after 1 December 1972, an Agreement dated 22 November 1972 between the Secretary of State and the Bureau applies.

COMMENTARY ON THE 1972 AGREEMENT

Clause 1: Liabilities covered by MIB

RELEVANT LIABILITY

[3.6]   In claims brought under the 1972 Agreement, a 'relevant liability' is a liability that is required to be covered by a policy of insurance under the Road Traffic Act 1972. MIB does not have to pay for any other liability. For these purposes, the material sections of the 1972 Act are s 143(1) and s 145, which, as originally enacted, read:

'143.—(1) Subject to the provisions of this Part of this Act, it shall not be lawful for a person to use, or to cause or permit any other person to use, a motor vehicle on a road unless there is in force in relation to the use of the vehicle by that person or that other person, as the case may be, such a policy of insurance or such a security in respect of third-party risks as complies with the requirements of this Part of this Act; and if a person acts in contravention of this section he shall be guilty of an offence.

...

145.—(1) In order to comply with the requirements of this Part of this Act, a policy of insurance must satisfy the following conditions.

(2)   The policy must be issued by an authorised insurer, that is to say, a person or body of persons carrying on motor vehicle insurance business in Great Britain.

(3)   Subject to subsection (4) below, the policy–

(a)   must insure such person, persons or classes of persons as may be specified in the policy in respect of any liability which may be incurred by him or them in respect of the death of or bodily injury to any person caused by, or arising out of, the use of the vehicle on a road; and

(b) must also insure him or them in respect of any liability which may be incurred by him or them under the provisions of this Part of this Act relating to payment for emergency treatment.

(4) The policy shall not, by virtue of subsection (3)(a) above, be required to cover–

(a) liability in respect of the death, arising out of and in the course of his employment, of a person in the employment of a person insured by the policy or of bodily injury sustained by such a person arising out of and in the course of his employment; or

(b) any contractual liability.'

It will be seen from these statutory provisions that under the 1972 Act the obligation to insure against third party risks applied in almost all cases where a motor vehicle was used on a road.

'Motor vehicle' was defined at s 190(1) of the 1972 Act as '… a mechanically propelled vehicle intended or adapted for use on roads'. For something to fall within the definition requires a reasonable person, looking at the vehicle, to take the view that one of its uses would include general use on the road. The courts have been asked to consider the issue on several occasions: see *Daley v Hargreaves* [1961] 1 All ER 552, [1961] 1 WLR 487 (dumper trucks not fitted with windscreens, lamps, reflectors, horns, wings, number plates etc not within the definition); *Burns v Currell* [1963] 2 QB 433, [1963] 2 All ER 297 (mechanical go-kart not within the definition); *Chief Constable of Avon and Somerset v Fleming* [1987] 1 All ER 318 (motorcycle adapted for scrambling not within the definition); *Chief Constable of North Yorkshire Police v Saddington* [2001] RTR 227, [2000] All ER (D) 1530 (petrol-driven motor scooter was within the definition because it was difficult to see on what terrain it might be used other than a road); *Winter v DPP* [2002] All ER (D) 143 (Jul) (electrically powered 'City Bug' within the definition).

'Use' has been interpreted broadly. In *Hardy v Motor Insurers' Bureau* (at para [3.53] below), the court held that the requirement for compulsory insurance (and hence MIB's liability to pay) covered the intentional criminal use of a car as a weapon. See also *Gardner v Moore* (at para [3.54] below). In *Dunthorne v Bentley* [1996] RTR 428, [1996] PIQR P323, CA, a woman's car broke down when it ran out of petrol. Seeing a friend who had stopped on the other side of the road she ran across but was struck by an oncoming vehicle, causing injury to the driver, who claimed damages against her. Her insurers were found liable to pay the driver because the accident arose out of her 'use' of the vehicle. See also *Slater v Buckinghamshire County Council* [2004] EWCA Civ 1478, [2004] All ER (D) 164 (Nov) where it was held a passenger in a vehicle who was employed by the defendant was not using the vehicle when assisting the claimant to cross a road to enter the vehicle.

Section 196(1) of the 1972 Act defined 'road' as '… any highway and any other road to which the public has access'. This definition includes public bridleways and footpaths. In *Bugge v Taylor* [1941] 1 KB 198 the Divisional Court found that a hotel forecourt was a road. The statutory definition survived unchanged on the passing of the Road Traffic Act 1988 and, recently, in *Clarke v Kato; Cutter v Eagle Star Insurance Co* [1998] 4 All ER 417, [1998] All ER (D) 481, [1998] 1 WLR 1647, the House of Lords stated that the issue of whether the place in question was a road is one of fact to be determined after consideration of its physical character and the function it existed to serve. It was held that neither of the two car parks under consideration fell within the definition.

There were however some important exceptions to the requirement to insure. By s 144 of the 1972 Act certain public service vehicles were exempted from the need for third party insurance. The exemption under s 145(4)(a) in relation to cover for an employer's liability for death or injury to one of his employees suffered in a motor accident in the course of the latter's employment, was inserted because that liability should have been the subject of compulsory employer's liability insurance. Such cover did not always exist, however, in which case by virtue of that subsection the unfortunate injured employee had no recourse against MIB either.

It should be noted that the 1972 Act, as enacted, did not oblige motorists to insure against liability for damage to property. MIB was therefore not liable to deal with such a claim under the 1972 Agreement. Such insurance became compulsory on 31 December 1988, upon amendment of the 1972 Act by the Motor Vehicles (Compulsory Insurance) Regulations 1987, SI 1987/2171. On the same day, the 1972 Agreement was superseded by the 1988 Agreement.

In *Cooper v Motor Insurers' Bureau* (at para [3.44] below), the Court of Appeal held that the third party risks that had to be insured under s 143(1) of the 1972 Act did not include injury to the driver of the vehicle at the relevant time, so that where an uninsured owner of a vehicle had asked another person to drive it for him and that other person was injured because of a brake defect in the vehicle of which he was unaware as a result of the owner's negligence, that liability was not a 'relevant liability' and MIB were not responsible to pay the unsatisfied judgment.

Since 1972 it has been compulsory to insure liability for all passengers. The old MIB cases dealing with the issue of use of the vehicle for hire or reward are therefore no longer relevant in the context of a passenger's claim.

Clause 2: Satisfaction of claims by MIB

[3.7]   (*See* Notes 2 and 3 to the Agreement).

The liability of MIB under the Agreement is to the Secretary of State. As there is no privity of contract between a claimant and MIB, the claimant has, at law, no cause of action, but in practice MIB submits to being sued without taking the point and the court turns a blind eye to this legal anomaly.

Indeed, MIB will very often wish to be joined as defendant to the proceedings (see comment under the 1999 Agreement (at para [3.28] below) in order to protect its financial interests and in some cases joinder of MIB will be essential: see, e g *Gurtner v Circuit* (at para [3.31] below), where the driver gave his name but insufficient insurance details after the accident and then became untraceable before proceedings were issued. The evidence indicated that he probably was insured, but, as he could not be found and the identity of his insurer was unknown, the way was open for the victim to obtain an unopposed judgment, which MIB would have been liable to satisfy under the Agreement. MIB therefore sought permission to be joined as defendant. The Court of Appeal agreed that it should be so joined.

However, the power to add parties is a discretionary one and it will not be exercised in MIB's favour in every case. See, for example, *White v London*

Transport Executive (at para [3.60] below). This case involved an application under the Untraced Drivers Agreement, where MIB had required the applicant to bring the action. MIB applied to be joined, being concerned that the case would not be pursued with the required vigour. Joinder was refused on the ground that it was not a necessary step. The action was adequately constituted without MIB's participation. See also *Baker v Francis* (at para [3.36] below), where joinder was permitted but on certain conditions.

Clause 4: Recoveries by insurers acting for MIB/insurer concerned (now Article 75 insurer)

[3.8]   (*See* Note 4 to the Agreement.)
   Nothing in the Agreement prevents an insurer from seeking recovery from a policyholder where he is entitled to do so in contract.
   The words 'insurer concerned' refer to what is currently the 'domestic regulations/Article 75 insurer' under the relevant article of MIB's Memorandum and Articles of Association dealing with the obligations of MIB's members to handle claims on behalf of MIB, as to which see below at para [3.62].

Clause 5: Conditions precedent to MIB's liability

[3.9]

5(1)(A): NOTICE
(*See* Note 4 to the Agreement.)
   The requirement of notice is in similar terms to that of notice to insurers in the Road Traffic Act 1988, s 152(1)(a) and its predecessors. The cases under the Acts (see Chapter 2 of the handbook) are therefore of relevance.
   It should be observed that this condition, like the others in clause 5, is a condition precedent to MIB's liability. Any failure to comply may preclude enforcement against MIB of an unsatisfied judgment obtained against a tortfeasor. Although involving interpretation of the slightly different notice provisions under the 1988 Agreement, the case of *Silverton v Goodall and Motor Insurers' Bureau* (at para [3.40] below) illustrates the strictness with which the notice provisions may be interpreted. There, the claimant's solicitor sent particulars of claim to the court by post together with a request for issue of a summons. The court issued the proceedings on 13 October, but the claimant's solicitor did not receive the sealed documents back from the court until 22 October. Copies were sent to MIB who received them on 29 October. The Court of Appeal held: (i) that time started to run for the purposes of the seven day notice requirement at the date of issue, ie, 13 October; and (ii) that notice was therefore given late. MIB had no liability.
   In the majority of cases, there will have been an intimation by the claimant's advisers of an intent to issue proceedings before that actually took place. In some cases, that intimation may be sufficiently concrete to constitute notice. In others, it may not. Resolution of the issue may therefore turn on an interpretation of the words used in one or more pieces of pre-issue correspondence. In *Stinton v Stinton and Motor Insurers' Bureau* (at para [3.45] below), the Court of Appeal upheld the judge's finding that an initial letter of claim and a later

letter, written after the grant of legal aid but before it was even possible to gauge the value of the claim or to begin to explore the possibilities of settlement, did not constitute notice to MIB of the proceedings that were issued some 18 months after the second letter. The first instance report in *Stinton* (reported at [1993] PIQR P135) contains a useful review of the main authorities dealing with the question of the giving of notice under the analogous Road Traffic Act provisions.

If notice has not been effectively given (and MIB are taking the point) but time remains within the primary limitation period, the claimant's best course is to abandon the original proceedings, re-issue and re-serve. This may be possible even after judgment has been obtained. In *O'Neill v O'Brien and Motor Insurers' Bureau* (at para [3.35] below), a case involving the 1988 Agreement, MIB took the view that they had not been kept properly informed of the proceedings and were not liable to satisfy a judgment obtained in default against the uninsured first defendant. The claimant applied to set aside the judgment so that a fresh action could be commenced. MIB opposed the application. The Court of Appeal upheld the judge's decision to set the judgment aside on the basis that it was in the interests of justice to do so. The case of *Horton v Sadler* (at para [3.38] below) has now made it possible for claimants who have fallen foul of the notice requirements and where the primary limitation period has expired to issue fresh proceedings relying on the Court to exercise discretion under s 33 of the Limitation Act 1980. The decision overrules the previously binding authority of *Walkley v Precision Forgings Ltd* [1979] 2 All ER 548, [1979] 1 WLR 606.

Of course, MIB may not always take notice points if the claimant's response will simply be to re-issue. However, claimants' solicitors need to be aware that MIB is as astute as any other litigant to take tactical points that they think may reasonably be available to them. In *Begum v Ullah* (at para [3.42] below), another 1988 Agreement decision, the claimant's solicitor was aware that she had failed to comply with the seven day notice requirement and rang MIB to ask if they might waive it to avoid the need to re-issue. That was said to have been agreed and the claim proceeded. After the expiry of the limitation period, MIB asserted that no proper notice was given. The question of notice was decided as a preliminary issue and the judge held that an MIB employee had agreed to accept notice over the telephone and found that MIB was estopped from raising the point.

5(1)(C): ANOTHER TORTFEASOR LIABLE

Where some degree of blame might conceivably attach to another driver who is insured, or to another potential defendant who can pay, then a claimant can be required under clause 5(1)(c) to join that other person as a defendant and pursue the claim against him as well as against the uninsured driver.

Should it be established that another insured driver is jointly responsible for the claimant's injuries, MIB will avoid payment. This is because that other driver's insurers will be bound by MIB's Articles of Association (see below at para [3.61]) and will be compelled to satisfy the claim in full. This obligation can be enforced by MIB, hence the need for litigation in such cases rarely arises.

If the other tortfeasor is not a driver but is some other person of means (eg, a highway authority or the Ministry of Defence (MOD)) then it will again be in MIB's interests to ensure that judgment is obtained against that person. MIB is a fund of last resort: its liability to pay extends only to unsatisfied judgments.

MIB is sometimes said to be relying on the 'one percent rule' where it seeks to establish blame against someone else. That other person need only be found 1% to blame for the accident in order for MIB to avoid liability under the Agreement altogether.

Nor can another defendant who is not a driver circumvent the position by attempting to enforce against MIB any judgment for contribution made against the uninsured driver in the proceedings. The liability to make contribution to a fellow tortfeasor arises under the Civil Liability (Contribution) Act 1978 (or, for accidents before 1 January 1979, its predecessor, the Law Reform (Married Women and Tortfeasors) Act 1935). Such a liability is not a 'relevant liability' for MIB purposes, ie it was not one that was required to be covered by insurance by s 143 etc of the Road Traffic Act 1972. See *Campbell v McFarland and Armagh UDC* [1972] NI 31 (para [2.222] of the handbook) for an analogous decision under what has since become s 143 of the Road Traffic Act 1988. See also *Bell v Donnelly and MOD* (13 January 1998, unreported).

An illustration of MIB requiring a claimant to pursue another tortfeasor can be found in *Norman v Ali and Motor Insurers' Bureau* (at para [3.37] below). There the claimant had the option of suing the owner of the vehicle for causing or permitting the tortfeasor driver to use the vehicle on the road. MIB required her to do so but she failed to issue proceedings against him until after the expiry of the three-year limitation period, with the result that the claim failed. It was found that in missing the primary limitation period she had also failed to take 'all reasonable steps to obtain judgment against all the persons liable in respect of the injury'. MIB was not liable.

5(1)(D): ASSIGNMENT
This condition (which must be fulfilled by the claimant on request as a condition precedent to any payment by MIB of an unsatisfied judgment) is to enable MIB to execute the judgment against the uninsured driver.

Clause 6: Exemptions/exceptions

[3.10]

CLAUSE 6(1)(B): ROAD TRAFFIC ACT 1972, S 144
On enactment, this read as follows:

'144.—(1) Section 143 of this Act shall not apply to a vehicle owned by a person who has deposited and keeps deposited with the Accountant General of the Supreme Court the sum of £15,000, at a time when the vehicle is being driven under the owner's control.

(2)   The said section 143 shall not apply–
   (a)   to a vehicle owned by the council of a county, county borough or county district in England or Wales, the Common Council of the City of London, the council of a London borough, the Greater London Council, a county, town or district council in Scotland, or by a joint board or joint committee in England or Wales, or joint committee in Scotland, which is so constituted as to include among its members representatives of any such council, at a time when the vehicle is being driven under the owner's control;

    (b)   to a vehicle owned by a police authority or the Receiver for the Metropolitan Police District, at a time when it is being driven under the owner's control, or to a vehicle at a time when it is being driven for police purposes by or under the direction of a constable, or by a person employed by a police authority, or employed by the said Receiver; or

    (c)   to a vehicle at a time when it is being driven on a journey to or from any place undertaken for salvage purposes pursuant to Part IX of the Merchant Shipping Act 1984;

    (d)   to the use of a vehicle for the purpose of its being furnished in pursuance of a direction under paragraph (b) of section 166(2) of the Army Act 1955 or under the corresponding provision of the Air Force Act 1955;

    (e)   to a vehicle owned by the London Transport Executive or by a body which is within the meaning of the Transport (London) Act 1969 (but disregarding section 51(5) of the Transport Act 1968) a wholly-owned subsidiary of that Executive, at a time when the vehicle is being driven under the owner's control.'

CLAUSE 6(1)(C)(II): 'A PERSON USING THE VEHICLE'

The word 'using' in this context has the same meaning as in the Road Traffic Acts and it is well established that merely being carried as a passenger in a vehicle does not amount to use of it. In *Brown v Roberts* [1965] 1 QB 1, [1963] 2 All ER 263, it was held that for there to be use of the vehicle by the passenger, there had to be an element of 'controlling, managing or operating the vehicle' at the relevant time. Whether those elements existed in a particular case may be a difficult question to answer, such matters invariably being matters of degree. In *Stinton v Stinton and Motor Insurers' Bureau* (at para [3.45] below), the injured passenger and his brother, the uninsured driver, had travelled together in the car during an evening's drinking. They were found to have used the car for a common end and thus the claimant had been involved in a joint enterprise or venture such as to render him a person using the vehicle. This was so even though on the final, fateful journey home from the nightclub, the claimant was so drunk that he had to be put into the passenger seat of the car by his companions. On the other hand, in *Hatton v Hall and Motor Insurers' Bureau* (at para [3.46] below), the Court of Appeal upheld the judge's finding that the injured passenger who rode pillion on the uninsured driver's motorcycle for a trip to the pub was not 'using' the vehicle. In *Hatton*, the decision in *Stinton* was not questioned but was said to have been a decision on extreme facts. However, such extreme facts arose again in *O'Mahoney v Joliffe and Motor Insurers' Bureau* [1999] All ER (D) 151, [1999] RTR 245, where the young, female, injured pillion passenger went out with her uninsured boyfriend on a three hour 'jointly conceived plan to combine periods of illicit joy riding with intervals of dalliance' in the middle of a summer's night. She was found by the Court of Appeal to have been 'using' the motorcycle and her claim against MIB failed.

CLAUSE 6(1)(C)(II): 'KNOWING OR HAVING REASON TO BELIEVE'

See *Porter v Addo*; *Porter v Motor Insurers' Bureau* (at para [3.43] below) – the claimant mistakenly assumed that the driver was insured. The court held that there was nothing in the surrounding circumstances that should have caused her to question that assumption and the exclusion did not therefore apply.

Clause 7: Agents

[3.11] (*See* Note 4 to the Agreement.)

The practice of MIB hitherto has frequently been to appoint an insurance office, the 'investigating member', to make inquiries and, where appropriate, negotiate settlement. (*Note*: the exercise of this function did not mean that the office in question was a 'domestic regulations/article75 insurer', as to which see para [3.61], below.) However, for reasons of efficiency and economy, MIB is currently moving all claims 'in-house' and the involvement of member insurers as claims handlers has ceased in respect of new cases from 1 January 2003.

(C) TEXT OF AGREEMENT DATED 21 DECEMBER 1988

[3.12] In accordance with the Agreement made on 31 December 1945 between the Minister of War Transport and insurers transacting compulsory motor vehicle insurance business in Great Britain (published by HMSO under the title 'Motor Vehicle Insurance Fund') a corporation called the 'Motor Insurers' Bureau' entered into an Agreement on 17 June 1946 to the principle recommended in July 1937 by the Departmental Committee under Sir Felix Cassel (Cmnd 5528), to secure compensation to third party victims of road accidents in cases where, notwithstanding the provisions of the Road Traffic Acts relating to compulsory insurance, the victim is deprived of compensation by the absence of insurance, or of effective insurance. That Agreement was replaced by an Agreement which operated in respect of accidents occurring on or after 1 March 1971 which in turn was replaced by a new Agreement which operated in respect of accidents occurring on or after 1 December 1972. The Agreement of 1972 has now been replaced by a new Agreement which operates in respect of accidents occurring on or after 31 December 1988.

The text of the new Agreement is as follows—

MEMORANDUM OF AGREEMENT made the 21st day of December 1988 between the Secretary of State for Transport and the Motor Insurers' Bureau, whose registered office is at New Garden House, 78 Hatton Garden, London EC1N 8JQ (hereinafter referred to as 'MIB') SUPPLEMENTAL to an Agreement (hereinafter called the 'Principal Agreement') made the 31st day of December 1945 between the Minister of War Transport and the insurers transacting compulsory motor insurance business in Great Britain by or on behalf of whom the said Agreement was signed and in pursuance of paragraph 1 of which MIB was incorporated.

IT IS HEREBY AGREED AS FOLLOWS

(I) DEFINITIONS
   1 In this Agreement—
      'contract of insurance' means a policy of insurance or a security;
      'insurer' includes the giver of a security;
      'relevant liability' means a liability in respect of which a policy of insurance must insure a person in order to comply with Part VI of the Road Traffic Act 1972; and
      references to the Road Traffic Act 1972 are references to that Act as amended by the Motor Vehicles (Compulsory Insurance) Regulations 1987 (SI 1987/2171).

(II) SATISFACTION OF CLAIMS BY MIB
   2 (1) If judgment in respect of any relevant liability is obtained against any person or persons in any court in Great Britain whether or not such a person or

persons be in fact covered by a contract of insurance and any such judgment is not satisfied in full within seven days from the date upon which the person or persons in whose favour the judgment was given became entitled to enforce it then MIB will, subject to the provisions of paragraphs (2), (3) and (4) below and to Clauses 4, 5 and 6 hereof, pay or satisfy or cause to be paid or satisfied to or to the satisfaction of the person or persons in whose favour the judgment given any sum payable or remaining payable thereunder in respect of the relevant liability including any sum awarded by the court in respect of interest on that sum and any taxed costs or any costs awarded by the court without taxation (or such proportion thereof as is attributable to the relevant liability) whatever may be the cause of the failure of the judgment debtor to satisfy the judgment.

(2)   Subject to paragraphs (3) and (4) below and to Clauses 4, 5 and 6 hereof, the MIB shall incur liability under paragraph (1) above in respect of any sum awarded under such a judgment in respect of property damage not exceeding £250,000 or in respect of the first £250,000 of any sum so awarded exceeding that amount.

(3)   Where a person in whose favour a judgment in respect of relevant liability which includes liability in respect of damage to property has been given, has received or is entitled to receive in consequence of a claim he has made, compensation from any source in respect of that damage, MIB may deduct from the sum payable or remaining payable under paragraph (1) above an amount equal to the amount of that compensation in addition to the deduction of £175 by virtue of paragraph (4) below. The reference to compensation includes compensation under insurance arrangements.

(4)   MIB shall not incur liability under paragraph (1) above in respect of any amount payable or remaining payable under the judgment in respect of property damage liability where the total of such amounts is more than £175, in respect of the first £175 of such total.

(III)   PERIOD OF AGREEMENT

3   This Agreement shall be determinable by the Secretary of State at any time or by MIB on twelve months' notice without prejudice to the continued operation of the Agreement in respect of accidents occurring before the date of termination.

(IV)   RECOVERIES

4   Nothing in this Agreement shall prevent insurers from providing by conditions in their contracts of insurance that all sums paid by them or by MIB by virtue of the Principal Agreement or this Agreement in or towards the discharge of the liability of their insured shall be recoverable by them or by MIB from the insured or from any other person.

(V)   CONDITIONS PRECEDENT TO MIB'S LIABILITY

5 (1)   MIB shall not incur any liability under Clause 2 of this Agreement unless—

(a)   notice in writing of the bringing of the proceedings is given within seven days after the commencement of the proceedings—

   (i)   to MIB in the case of proceedings in respect of a relevant liability which is either not covered by a contract of insurance or covered by a contract of insurance with an insurer whose identity cannot be ascertained; or

   (ii)   to the insurer in the case of proceedings in respect of a relevant liability which is covered by a contract of insurance with an insurer whose identity can be ascertained.

Such notice shall be accompanied by a copy of the writ, summons or other document initiating the proceedings;

    (b)   the person bringing the proceedings furnishes to MIB—
        (i)   such information (in such form as MIB may specify) in relation thereto as MIB may reasonably require; and
        (ii)   such information (in such form as MIB may specify) as to any insurance covering any damage to property to which the claim or proceedings relate and any claim made in respect of the damage under the insurance or otherwise and any report which may have been made or notification which may have been given to any person in respect of that damage or the use of the vehicle giving rise thereto, as MIB may reasonably require;

    (c)   the person bringing the proceedings has demanded the information and, where appropriate, the particulars specified in s 151 of the Road Traffic Act 1972 in accordance with that section or, if so required by MIB, has authorised MIB to do so on his behalf;

    (d)   if so required by MIB and subject to full indemnity from MIB as to costs the person bringing the proceedings has taken all reasonable steps to obtain judgment against all the persons liable in respect of the injury or death or damage to property and, in the event of any such person being a servant or agent, against his principal; and

    (e)   the judgment referred to in Clause 2 of this Agreement and any judgment referred to in paragraph (d) of the Clause which has been obtained (whether or not either judgment includes an amount in respect of a liability other than a relevant liability) and any order for costs are assigned to MIB or their nominee.

(2)   In the event of any dispute as to the reasonableness of a requirement by MIB for the supply of information or that any particular step should be taken to obtain judgment against other persons it may be referred to the Secretary of State whose decision shall be final.

(3)   Where a judgment which includes an amount in respect of a liability other than a relevant liability has been assigned to MIB or their nominee in pursuance of paragraph (1)(e) of the Clause MIB shall apportion any moneys received in pursuance of the judgment according to the proportion which the damages in respect of the relevant liability bear to the damages in respect of the other liabilities and shall account to the person in whose favour the judgment was given in respect of such moneys received properly apportionable to the other liabilities. Where an order for costs in respect of such a judgment has been so assigned moneys received pursuant to the order shall be dealt with in the same manner.

(VI)   Exceptions

6 (1)   MIB shall not incur any liability under Clause 2 of this Agreement in a case where—

    (a)   the claim arises out of the use of a vehicle owned by or in the possession of the Crown, except where any other person has undertaken responsibility for the existence of a contract of insurance under Part VI of the Road Traffic Act 1972 (whether or not the person or persons liable be in fact covered by a contract of insurance) or where the liability is in fact covered by a contract of insurance;

    (b)   the claim arises out of the use of a vehicle the use of which is not required to be covered by a contract of insurance by virtue of s 144 of the Road Traffic Act 1972, unless the use is in fact covered by such a contract;

    (c)   the claim is in respect of a judgment or any part thereof which has been obtained by virtue of the exercise of a right of subrogation by any person;

    (d)   the claim is in respect of damage to property which consists of damage to a motor vehicle or losses arising there from if at the time of the use giving rise to the damage to the motor vehicle there was not in force in relation to the use of that vehicle when the damage to it was sustained such a policy of insurance as is required by Part VI of the Road Traffic Act 1972 and the person or persons claiming in respect of the loss or damage either knew or ought to have known that that was the case;

(e) at the time of the use which gave rise to the liability the person suffering death or bodily injury or damage to property was allowing himself to be carried in or upon the vehicle and either before the commencement of his journey in the vehicle or after such commencement if he could reasonably be expected to have alighted from the vehicle he—

   (i) knew or ought to have known that the vehicle had been stolen or unlawfully taken; or

   (ii) knew or ought to have known that the vehicle was being used without there being in force in relation to its use such a contract of insurance as would comply with Part VI of the Road Traffic Act 1972.

(2) The exception specified in sub-paragraph (1)(e) of the Clause shall apply only in a case where judgment in respect of which the claim against MIB is made was obtained in respect of a relevant liability incurred by the owner or a person using the vehicle in which the person who suffered death or bodily injury or sustained damage to property was being carried.

(3) For the purposes of these exceptions—

   (a) a vehicle which has been unlawfully removed from the possession of the Crown shall be taken to continue in that possession whilst it is kept so removed;

   (b) references to a person being carried in a vehicle include references to his being carried in or upon or entering or getting onto or alighting from the vehicle; and

   (c) 'owner' in relation to a vehicle which is the subject of a hiring agreement or a hire- purchase agreement, means the person in possession of the vehicle under that agreement.

(VII) AGENTS

7 Nothing in the Agreement shall prevent MIB performing their obligations under this Agreement by agents.

(VIII) OPERATION

8 This Agreement shall come into operation on the 31st day of December 1988 in relation to accidents occurring on or after that date. The Agreement made on 22nd November 1972 between the Secretary of State and MIB shall cease and determine except in relation to claims arising out of accidents occurring before the 31st day of December 1988.

IN WITNESS etc

Notes

The following notes are for the guidance of those who may have a claim on the Motor Insurers' Bureau under the Agreement, and of their legal advisers, but they must not be taken as rendering unnecessary a careful study of the Agreement itself. Communications on any matter connected with the Agreement should be addressed to the Motor Insurers' Bureau whose address is [Linford Wood House, 6–12 Capital Drive, Linford Wood, Milton Keynes MK14 6XT (DX 142620 MILTON KEYNES 10)].

On the date of coming into force of the Road Traffic Act 1988 references to the provisions of the Road Traffic Act 1972 are by virtue of s 2(4) of the Road Traffic (Consequential Provisions) Act 1988 to be read as references to the corresponding provisions of the Road Traffic Act 1988.

1.   The Agreement, which operates from 31 December 1988 supersedes earlier Agreements made on 17 June 1946 (which was operative from 1 July 1946), on 1 February 1971 (which was operative from 1 March 1971), and on 22 November 1972 (which was operative from 1 December 1972) in relation to claims arising out of accidents occurring on or after 31 December 1988.

2.   If damages are awarded by a Court in respect of death or personal injury or damage to property arising out of the use of a motor vehicle on a road in circumstances where the liability is one which was, at the time the accident occurred, required to be covered by insurance and such damages, or any part of them, remain unpaid seven days after the judgment becomes enforceable, the Bureau will, subject to the limit specified in Clause 2(2), which corresponds with the limited insurance requirement in section 145(4)(b) of the Road Traffic Act 1972, and the exceptions in paragraphs (3) and (4) of Clause 2 and Clause 6 of the Agreement, pay the unrecovered amount (including any interest awarded by the Court and costs) to the person in whose favour the judgment has been given against an assignment of the judgment debt. This applies whether the judgment debtor is a British resident or a foreign visitor.

3.   Clause 1 defines 'relevant liability' as a liability in respect of which a policy of insurance must insure a person in order to comply with Part VI of the Road Traffic Act 1972, which includes liability in respect of property damage caused by, or arising out of, the use of a motor vehicle on a road in Great Britain. This provision gives effect to Article 1.1 of Council Directive (84/5/EEC) of 30 December 1983 on the approximation of the laws of Member States relating to insurance against civil liability in respect of the use of motor vehicles (OJ No.L8, 11.1.84, p.17). In the context of the Directive 'damage to property' means damage to material property. Accordingly in this Agreement the reference to damage to property is understood in that sense. With regard to liability in respect of such damage which is covered by the Agreement, MIB would expect to meet the consequential loss elements of a claim flowing from damage to the claimant's material property which a Court would allow. It must be emphasised that MIB's obligation does not extend to those liabilities not required to be covered by the policy under section 145(4) of the Road Traffic Act 1972.

4.   Nothing in the Agreement affects the position at law of the parties to an action for damages arising out of the driving of a motor vehicle. The Bureau's liability under the Agreement can only arise when the plaintiff has successfully established his case against the person or persons liable in the usual manner and judgment has been given in his favour. There is, of course, nothing to exclude the acceptance of compensation by the plaintiff under a settlement of his claim negotiated between the plaintiff and the alleged person liable or the Bureau.

5.   The purpose of Clause 2(3) is to oblige any claimant in respect of property damage to give credit for compensation which he may have received or be entitled to receive under a claim he has made on another source or sources relative to that damage. The most common instances will involve compensation recovered under comprehensive motor or household policies. Policyholders with these covers cannot be forced to claim under them but will normally wish to do so for their convenience. Furthermore legal liability for the accident will not affect that claim and the MIB excess of £175 (Clause 2(4)) will not apply. Where such a claim has been made successfully MIB will only be concerned with the claimant's uninsured losses, eg, any excess he may have under his own policy, or loss of use of his vehicle subject to legal liability and the MIB excess of £175.

6.   WHERE THERE IS A POLICY. In cases where it is ascertained that there is in existence a policy issued in compliance with the Road Traffic Act 1972, the insurer will act as the agent of the Bureau even if entitled to repudiate liability under the policy and, subject to notice being given as provided for in Clause 5(1)(a)(ii), will handle claims within the terms of the Agreement.

In many cases, particularly where the vehicle was being used without the policyholder's authority, the provisions of the Road Traffic Act preclude repudiation by the insurer of a victim's claim. Victims and those acting on their behalf are expressly reminded of the requirements as to the giving of notice to the insurer if the protection afforded to third parties by section 149 of the Road Traffic Act 1972 is sought.

It must be stressed that the above arrangements are without prejudice to any rights insurers may have against their policyholders and, to avoid any possible misunderstanding, it is emphasised that there is nothing in this Agreement affecting any obligation imposed on a policyholder by his policy. Policyholders are not released from their contractual obligations to their insurers, although the Road Traffic Act and MIB protect THIRD PATRY VICTIMS from the consequences of failure to observe them. For example, if a policyholder fails to notify claims to his insurers as required by his policy or permits an unauthorised person to drive, he may be liable to his insurers.

WHERE THERE IS NO POLICY OR THE IDENTITY OF THE INSURER CANNOT BE ASCERTAINED. In cases where there is no policy, or for any reason the existence of a policy is in doubt or where there is a policy but the identity of the insurer cannot be ascertained, the victim or those acting on his behalf must notify the Bureau, and in practice it is desirable to inform the Bureau in all cases where the name of the insurer is not speedily forthcoming. It is a condition of the Bureau's liability that they should be given notification in writing (with relevant documents) within seven days after the commencement of proceedings against the alleged person liable. It should always be remembered that the requirement for notice of issue of proceedings under Clause 5(1)(a)(i) and (ii) must be complied with strictly. Notice should be given immediately on issue of the proceedings, and such notice must be accompanied by copies of the writ or summons.

7.   Claims arising out of the use of uninsured vehicles owned by or in the possession of the Crown will in the majority of cases be outside the scope of the Bureau's liability (see Clause 6 of the Agreement – Exceptions). In such cases the approach should be made to the responsible authority in the usual way. The same benefits in respect of compensation will normally be afforded by the Crown to the victims in such cases as they would receive were the accident caused by a private vehicle, except where the victim is a serviceman or servicewoman whose death or injury gives rise to an entitlement to a pension or other compensation from public funds.

8.   The purpose of Clause 6(1)(c) is to relieve MIB of liability to meet judgments in respect of damage to property obtained by persons who have compensated the victim such as the victim's own insurers. Such insurers have the right to attempt to recoup their outlay by requiring an insured to lend his name to proceedings against the person responsible, but MIB will not meet such claims as the victim has already been compensated.

9.   Claims for damage to a vehicle or for losses arising therefrom for which a policy of insurance issued in compliance with Part VI of the Road Traffic Act 1972 is required, are excluded from the Agreement if the vehicle was not insured and the claimant knew or ought to have known that it was not. See Clause 6(1)(d). The claim may also be excluded under Clause 6(1)(e).

10.   It should be noted that the monetary limit applicable to property damage claims by virtue of Clause 2(2) corresponding with the insurance limit in s 145(4)(b) of the Road Traffic Act 1972, and the excess prescribed by Clauses 2(3) and (4) of this Agreement will be subject to review from time to time.

11.   The Bureau have no liability UNDER THIS AGREEMENT to pay compensation in respect of any person who may suffer bodily injury or death or may sustain damage to property resulting from the use on a road of a vehicle, the owner or driver of which cannot be traced. A separate Agreement between the Secretary

of State for Transport and the Bureau for Compensation of Victims of Untraced Drivers in respect of bodily injury and death applies, but this Agreement does not embrace damage to property.

COMMENTARY ON THE 1988 AGREEMENT

Clause 1: Liabilities covered by MIB

'RELEVANT LIABILITY'

[3.13]   In claims brought under the 1988 Agreement, a 'relevant liability' is a liability that is required to be covered by a policy of insurance under the Road Traffic Act 1988. MIB does not have to pay for any other liability. For these purposes, the relevant sections of the Road Traffic Act 1988 are s 143(1) and s 145, which, so far as material for the purposes of most claims under the 1988 Agreement, read:

'143 Users of motor vehicles to be insured or secured against third-party risks
(1)   Subject to the provisions of this Part of this Act–
   (a)   a person must not use a motor vehicle on a road unless there is in force in relation to the use of the vehicle by that person such a policy of insurance or such a security in respect of third party risks as complies with the requirements of this Part of this Act, and
   (b)   a person must not cause or permit any other person to use a motor vehicle on a road unless there is in force in relation to the use of the vehicle by that other person such a policy of insurance or such a security in respect of third party risks as complies with the requirements of this Part of this Act.

...

145 Requirements in respect of policies of insurance
(1)   In order to comply with the requirements of this Part of this Act, a policy of insurance must satisfy the following conditions.
(2)   The policy must be issued by an authorised insurer.
(3)   Subject to section (4) below, the policy–
   (a)   must insure such person, persons or classes of persons as may be specified in the policy in respect of any liability which may be incurred by him or them in respect of the death of or bodily injury to any person or damage to property caused by, or arising out of, the use of the vehicle on a road in Great Britain, and
  (aa) must, in the case of a vehicle normally based in the territory of another member State, insure him or them in respect of any civil liability which may be incurred by him or them as a result of an event related to the use of the vehicle in Great Britain, if–
     (i)   according to the law of that territory, he or they would be required to be insured in respect of a civil liability which would arise under that law as a result of that event if the place where the vehicle was used when the event occurred were in that territory, and
    (ii)   the cover required by that law would be higher than that required by paragraph (a) above, and

(b) must in the case of a vehicle normally based in Great Britain, insure him or them in respect of any liability which may be incurred by him or them in respect of the use of the vehicle and of any trailer, whether or not coupled, in the territory other than Great Britain and Gibraltar of each of the member States of the Communities according to–

    (i) the law on compulsory insurance against civil liability in respect of the use of vehicles of the State in whose territory the event giving rise to the liability occurred; or

    (ii) if it would give higher cover, the law which would be applicable under this part of this Act if the place where the vehicle was used when that event occurred were in Great Britain; and

(c) must also insure him or them in respect of any liability which may be incurred by him or them under the provisions of this Part of this Act relating to payment for emergency treatment.

(4) The policy shall not, by virtue of subsection (3)(a) above, be required–

(a) to cover liability in respect of the death, arising out of and in the course of his employment, of a person in the employment of a person insured by the policy or of bodily injury sustained by such a person arising out of and in the course of his employment, or

(b) to provide insurance of more than £250,000 in respect of all such liabilities as may be incurred in respect of damage to property caused by, or arising out of, any one accident involving the vehicle, or

(c) to cover liability in respect of damage to the vehicle, or

(d) to cover liability in respect of damage to goods carried for hire or reward in or on the vehicle or in or on any trailer (whether or not coupled) drawn by the vehicle, or

(e) to cover any liability of any person in respect of damage to property in his custody or under his control, or

(f) to cover any contractual liability.

(4A) In the case of a person–

(a) carried in or upon a vehicle, or

(b) entering or getting on to, or alighting from, a vehicle, the provisions of paragraph (a) of subsection (4) above do not apply unless cover in respect of the liability referred to in that paragraph is in fact provided pursuant to a requirement of the Employers' Liability (Compulsory Insurance) Act 1969.'

It will be seen from these statutory provisions that under the 1988 Act the obligation to insure against third party risks applies in almost all cases where a motor vehicle is used on a road.

'Motor vehicle' is defined at s 185(1) of the 1988 Act as '... a mechanically propelled vehicle intended or adapted for use on roads'. For something to fall within the definition requires a reasonable person, looking at the vehicle, to take the view that one of its uses would include general use on the road. The courts have been asked to consider the issue on several occasions: see *Daley v Hargreaves* [1961] 1 All ER 552, [1961] 1 WLR 487 (dumper trucks not fitted with windscreens, lamps, reflectors, horns, wings, number plates etc not within the definition); *Burns v Currell* [1963] 2 QB 433, [1963] 2 All ER 297 (mechanical go-kart not within the definition); *Chief Constable of Avon and Somerset v Fleming* [1987] 1 All ER 318 (motorcycle adapted for scrambling not within the definition); *Chief Constable of North Yorkshire Police v Saddington* [2001] RTR 227 (petrol-driven motor scooter was within the definition because it was difficult to see on what terrain it might be used other than a road); *Winter v DPP* [2002] All ER (D) 143 (Jul) (electrically powered 'City Bug' within the definition).

'Use' has been interpreted broadly. In *Hardy v Motor Insurers' Bureau* (at para [3.53] below), the court held that the requirement for compulsory insurance (and hence MIB's liability to pay) covered the intentional criminal use of a car as a weapon. See also *Gardner v Moore* (at para [3.54] below). In *Dunthorne v Bentley* [1996] RTR 428, [1996] PIQR P323 CA, a woman's car broke down when it ran out of petrol. Seeing a friend who had stopped on the other side of the road she ran across but was struck by an oncoming vehicle, causing injury to the driver, who claimed damages against her. Her insurers were found liable to pay the driver because the accident arose out of her 'use' of the vehicle. See also *Slater v Buckinghamshire County Council* [2004] EWCA Civ 1478, [2004] All ER (D) 164 (Nov) where it was held a passenger in a vehicle who was employed by the defendant was not using the vehicle when assisting the claimant to cross a road to enter the vehicle.

Section 192 of the Road Traffic Act 1988 defines 'road' as '... any highway and any other road to which the public has access'. This definition includes public bridleways and footpaths. In *Bugge v Taylor* [1941] 1 KB 198 the Divisional Court found that a hotel forecourt was a road. Recently, in *Clarke v Kato; Cutter v Eagle Star Insurance Co* [1998] 4 All ER 417, [1998] All ER (D) 481, [1998] 1 WLR 1647, the House of Lords stated that the question of whether the place in question was a road is one of fact to be determined after consideration of its physical character and the function it existed to serve. It was held that neither of the two car parks under consideration fell within the definition. Note that the requirement to insure was broadened in ss 143 and 145 of the Road Traffic Act 1988 when the words 'or other public place' were inserted after 'road' by the Motor Vehicles (Compulsory Insurance) Regulations 2000, SI 2000/726. Claims under the 1988 Agreement are unaffected by this amendment.

There are however some important exceptions to the requirement to insure. By s 144 (as amended by the Motor Vehicles (Third Party Risks) (Amendment) Regulations 1992, SI 1992/1283 and the Motor Vehicles (Third Party Risks Deposits) Regulations 1992, SI 1992/1284) provision is made for the vehicle owner to deposit £500,000 with the Accountant General of the Supreme Court as an alternative to insurance. The section also exempts certain public service vehicles from the need for third party insurance.

The exemption under s 145(4)(a) in relation to cover for an employer's liability for death or injury to one of his employees suffered in a motor accident in the course of the latter's employment, exists because that liability should be the subject of compulsory employer's liability insurance. Such cover does not always exist, however, and, until 1992, the unfortunate injured employee whose employer was not insured had no recourse against MIB either. This caused obvious injustice and, from 1 January 1993, by virtue of amendment (the Motor Vehicles (Compulsory Insurance) Regulations 1992, SI 1992/3036) in the form of s 145(4A) of the 1988 Act, the exception only applies where the employer's liability cover actually exists.

Following amendment to the Road Traffic Act 1972 and on the passing of the Road Traffic Act 1988, it became compulsory to insure against liability for property damage. Thus under the 1988 Agreement MIB is liable to compensate for such loss also.

In *Cooper v Motor Insurers' Bureau* (at para [3.44] below), the Court of Appeal held that the third party risks that had to be insured under the predecessor of s 143(1) of the 1988 Act did not include injury to the driver of the vehicle at the relevant time, so that where an uninsured owner of a vehicle had asked another person to drive it for him and that other person was injured because of a brake defect in the vehicle of which he was unaware as a result of the owner's negligence, that liability was not a 'relevant liability' and MIB were not responsible to pay the unsatisfied judgment.

Since 1972 it has been compulsory to insure liability for all passengers. The old MIB cases dealing with the issue of use of the vehicle for hire or reward are therefore no longer relevant in the context of a passenger's claim.

Clause 2: Satisfaction of claims by MIB

[3.14] (*See* Notes 2 and 3 to the Agreement.)
The liability of MIB under the Agreement is to the Secretary of State. As there is no privity of contract between a claimant and MIB, the claimant has, at law, no cause of action, but in practice MIB submits to being sued without taking the point and the court turns a blind eye to this legal anomaly.

Indeed, MIB will very often wish to be joined as defendant to the proceedings (see comment in respect of the 1999 Agreement at para [3.28] below) in order to protect its financial interests and in some cases joinder of MIB will be essential: see, e g *Gurtner v Circuit* (at para [3.31] below), where the driver gave his name but insufficient insurance details after the accident and then became untraceable before proceedings were issued. The evidence indicated that he was probably insured, but, as he could not be found and the identity of his insurer was unknown, the way was open for the victim to obtain an unopposed judgment which MIB would have been liable to satisfy under the Agreement. MIB therefore sought permission to be joined as defendant. The Court of Appeal agreed that it should be so joined.

However, the power to add parties is a discretionary one and it will not be exercised in MIB's favour in every case. See, for example, *White v London Transport Executive* (at para [3.60] below). This case involved an application under the Untraced Drivers Agreement, where MIB had required the applicant to bring the action. MIB applied to be joined, being concerned that the case would not be pursued with the required vigour. Joinder was refused on the ground that it was not a necessary step. The action was adequately constituted without MIB's participation. See also *Baker v Francis* (at para [3.36] below), where joinder was permitted but on certain conditions.

Clause 4: Recoveries by insurers acting for MIB/insurer concerned (now Article 75 insurer)

[3.15] (*See* Note 4 to the Agreement.)
Nothing in the Agreement prevents an insurer from seeking recovery from a policyholder where he is entitled to do so in contract.

The words 'insurer concerned' refer to what is currently the 'domestic regulations/Article 75 insurer' under the relevant article of MIB's Memorandum and Articles of Association dealing with the obligations of MIB's members to handle claims on behalf of MIB, as to which see below at para [3.61].

Clause 5: Conditions precedent to MIB's liability

[3.16]

5(1)(A): NOTICE
The requirement of notice is in different terms from that of notice to insurers in the Road Traffic Act 1988, s 152(1)(a) and its predecessors. The cases under the Acts are therefore of limited significance.

It should be observed that this condition, like the others in clause 5, is a condition precedent to MIB's liability. Any failure to comply may preclude enforcement against MIB of an unsatisfied judgment obtained against a tortfeasor. *Silverton v Goodall and Motor Insurers' Bureau* (at para [3.40] below) illustrates the strictness with which the notice provisions may be interpreted. There, the claimant's solicitor sent particulars of claim to the court by post together with a request for issue of a summons. The court issued the proceedings on 13 October, but the claimant's solicitor did not receive the sealed documents back from the court until 22 October. Copies were sent to MIB who received them on 29 October. The Court of Appeal held that time started to run for the purposes of the seven-day notice requirement at the date of issue, ie, 13 October and that notice was therefore given late. MIB had no liability.

In *Cambridge v Motor Insurers' Bureau* [1998] RTR 365 the Court of Appeal took a slightly less strict approach in interpreting clause 5. It was held that the purpose of the requirement to serve documents at the same time of giving the notice was to provide MIB with evidence that the proceedings had been issued. Pre-CPR, in the High Court, that usually meant serving a copy of the stamped writ or, in the county court, a copy of the stamped summons. In *Cambridge*, a county court case, the claimant's solicitors served only a copy of what was then known as an N205 Notice of Issue of Default Summons (Plaint Note). Although not technically a 'document initiating the proceedings', the N205 was clear evidence that proceedings had been issued and was therefore held to satisfy the requirement. Post-CPR, service of a copy of the stamped Claim Form is obviously the best means of complying with the requirement, but, in cases where that is not possible, some other official document which actually evidences the issue of proceedings should suffice.

Under the 1988 Agreement, there can be no question of notice being given before proceedings are issued. Unlike the equivalent provision under the 1972 Agreement, clause 5 of the 1988 Agreement does not allow for this.

If notice has not been effectively given (and MIB is taking the point) but time remains within the primary limitation period, the claimant's best course is to abandon the original proceedings, re-issue and re-serve. This may be possible even after judgment has been obtained. In *O'Neill v O'Brien and Motor Insurers' Bureau* (at para [3.35] below), MIB took the view that it had not been kept properly informed of the proceedings and was not liable to satisfy a judgment obtained in default against the uninsured first defendant. The claimant applied to set aside the judgment so that it could commence a fresh action. MIB opposed the application. The Court of Appeal upheld the judge's decision to set the judgment aside on the basis that it was in the interests of justice to do so. The case of *Horton v Sadler* (at para [3.38] below) has now made it possible for claimants who have fallen foul of the notice requirements and where the primary limitation period has expired to issue fresh proceedings relying on the court to exercise discretion under s 33 of the Limitation Act 1980. The decision overrules the previously binding authority of *Walkley v Precision Forgings Ltd* [1979] 2 All ER 548, [1979] 1 WLR 606.

Of course, MIB may not always take notice points if the claimant's response will simply be to re-issue. However, claimants' solicitors need to be aware that MIB is as astute as any other litigant to take tactical points that it thinks may be available to it. In *Begum v Ullah* (at para [3.42] below), the claimant's solicitor was aware that she had failed to comply with the seven-day notice requirement and rang MIB to ask if it might waive it to avoid the need to re-issue. That was said to have been agreed and the claim proceeded. After the expiry of the limitation period, MIB asserted that no proper notice was given. The question of notice was decided as a preliminary issue and the judge held that an MIB employee had agreed to accept notice over the telephone and that MIB was estopped from raising the point.

5(1)(C): DEMANDED INFORMATION
Section 151 of the Road Traffic Act 1972 became, with amendments, s 154 of the Road Traffic Act 1988. It obliges a person against whom a claim is made to provide the other person with full details of his insurance.

5(1)(D): ANOTHER TORTFEASOR LIABLE
Where some degree of blame might conceivably attach to another driver who is insured, or to another potential defendant who can pay, then a claimant can be required under clause 5(1)(d) to join that other person as a defendant and pursue the claim against him as well as against the uninsured driver.

Should it be established that another, insured driver is jointly responsible for the claimant's injuries, MIB will avoid payment. This is because that other driver's insurers will be bound by MIB's Articles of Association (at para [3.61] below) and will be compelled by the terms of that agreement to satisfy the claim in full. MIB can enforce that obligation hence the need for litigation rarely arises.

If the other tortfeasor is not a driver but is some other person of means (eg, a highway authority) then it will again be in MIB's interests to ensure that judgment is obtained against that person. MIB is a fund of last resort: its liability to pay extends only to unsatisfied judgments.

MIB is sometimes said to be relying on the 'one percent rule' where it seeks to establish blame against someone else. That other person need only be found 1% to blame for the accident in order for MIB to avoid liability under the Agreement altogether.

Nor can another defendant who is not a driver circumvent the position by attempting to enforce against MIB any judgment for contribution made against the uninsured driver in the proceedings. The liability to make contribution to a fellow tortfeasor arises under the Civil Liability (Contribution) Act 1978. Such a liability is not a 'relevant liability' for MIB purposes, ie it is not one that is required to be covered by insurance by s 143 etc of the Road Traffic Act 1988.

See *Campbell v McFarland and Armagh UDC* [1972] NI 31 (para [2.222] of the handbook) for an analogous decision under what has since become s 143 of the Road Traffic Act 1988. See also *Bell v Donnelly and MOD* (13 January 1998, unreported).

An illustration of MIB requiring a claimant to pursue another tortfeasor can be found in *Norman v Ali and Motor Insurers' Board* (at para [3.37] below). There the claimant had the option of suing the owner of the vehicle for causing or permitting the tortfeasor driver to use the vehicle on the road. MIB required her to do so but she failed to issue proceedings against him until after the expiry of the three-year limitation period, with the result that the claim failed. It was found that in missing the primary limitation period she had also failed to take 'all reasonable steps to obtain judgment against all the persons liable in respect of the injury'. MIB were not liable.

5(1)(E): ASSIGNMENT
This condition (which must be fulfilled by the claimant on request as a condition precedent to any payment by MIB of an unsatisfied judgment) is to enable MIB to execute the judgment against the uninsured driver.

Clause 6: Exemptions/exceptions

[3.17]

CLAUSE 6(1)(B)
Section 144 of the Road Traffic Act 1972 has now become s 144 of the Road Traffic Act 1988.

CLAUSE 6(1)(E): 'KNEW OR OUGHT TO HAVE KNOWN'
One of the purposes of the 1988 Agreement was to give effect to the terms of the Second Council Directive 84/5/EEC of 30 December 1983 on the approximation of the laws of the Member States relating to insurance against civil liability in respect of the use of motor vehicles. This Directive includes the following provision at Art 1(4):

'4. Each Member State shall set up or authorize a body with the task of providing compensation, at least up to the limits of the insurance obligation for damage to property or personal injuries caused by an unidentified vehicle or a vehicle for which the insurance obligation provided for in paragraph 1 has not been satisfied.

This provision shall be without prejudice to the right of the Member States to regard compensation by that body as subsidiary or non-subsidiary and the right to make provision for the settlement of claims between that body and the person or persons responsible for the accident and other insurers or social security bodies required to compensate the victim in respect of the same accident.

The victim may in any case apply directly to the body which, on the basis of information provided at its request by the victim, shall be obliged to give him a reasoned reply regarding the payment of any compensation.

However, Member States may exclude the payment of compensation by that body in respect of persons who voluntarily entered the vehicle which caused the damage or injury when the body can prove that they knew it was uninsured.

Member States may limit or exclude the payment of compensation by that body in the event of damage to property by an unidentified vehicle.

They may also authorize, in the case of damage to property caused by an uninsured vehicle an excess of not more than 500 ECU for which the victim may be responsible.

Furthermore, each Member State shall apply its laws, regulations and administrative provisions to the payment of compensation by this body, without prejudice to any other practice which is more favourable to the victim.'

The exception in this Article relating to knowledge refers to those passengers who 'voluntarily entered the vehicle'. The words 'allowing himself to be carried' in clause 6(1)(e) of the 1988 Agreement mirror the words of the Directive. Where the passenger was very drunk when he entered the vehicle, an issue may arise as to whether he was allowing himself to be carried. It is reasonable to suppose that only an extreme state of drunkenness may suffice to enable a passenger to argue that he was not. The case of *Stinton v Stinton and Motor Insurers' Bureau* (at para [3.45] below) may be of indirect assistance here. Although decided under the 1972 Agreement and on a somewhat different issue (whether the very drunk passenger was 'using' the vehicle), there are obvious similarities. Whether or not a passenger had 'voluntarily allowed himself to be carried' was considered in the case of *Pickett v Roberts* (at para [3.50] below). In that case the claimant sought to argue that she had done enough to withdraw her consent to the 'use which gave rise to the liability'. The Court of Appeal disagreed (Pill LJ dissenting) stating that a person who had voluntarily entered a vehicle could not withdraw her consent except by an unequivocal repudiation of the common venture to which she consented when she entered the vehicle. An unequivocal request to alight from the vehicle was enough but an objection to way the vehicle was being driven was not.

The exception allowed for in Art 1(4) only applies to those who 'knew' the vehicle was uninsured, the burden of proving that knowledge resting on MIB. There are no words in the Directive equivalent to the 'or ought to have known' that appear in the 1988 Agreement. On the face of it, the Agreement therefore provides for a much wider exception.

A challenge was made to the terms of clause 6 of the 1988 Agreement in *White v White* (at para [3.48] below). There, the injured passenger was found by the judge at first instance to have been careless in failing to appreciate the true insurance position. He did not have actual knowledge but, as the judge found, he 'ought to have known'. However, the judge also found that the passenger could rely on the terms of the Directive against MIB, the latter being, according to the judge, an emanation of the state. Because the exclusion in the

Directive covered only 'actual' knowledge, the passenger succeeded. On appeal by MIB, the Court of Appeal reversed the judge's decision and applied the wording of clause 6(1)(e) strictly, on the basis that, although there was obvious inconsistency between the words in the Directive and the Agreement, the terms of the Directive were not capable of direct enforcement.

On further appeal by the passenger, the House of Lords held that the Agreement had to be interpreted in accordance with the Directive. The knowledge contemplated by the Directive could not include a state of mind, which, as a result of mere carelessness or negligence, fell short of actual knowledge. Therefore, it was held, the words 'or ought to have known' in the Agreement could not include that state of mind either. The passenger's claim against MIB succeeded. However, the House also stated that knowledge within the terms of the Directive could include the knowledge that an honest passenger would be expected to have. So, where the passenger deliberately refrains from asking obvious questions in order to avoid obtaining confirmation of the true facts, he may be found to have possessed a state of mind tantamount to actual knowledge.

Because it was a case involving a narrow finding of fact as to the state of the passenger's knowledge, the decision in *White* does not set the boundary between the type of knowledge that will be within clause 6(1)(e) and the type that will be without it. As Lord Nicholls of Birkenhead commented, that question would have to be pursued in a case where the facts made it necessary to obtain guidance from the Court of Justice on the precise scope of the exemption permitted by the Directive. Following *White v White* in the case of *Akers v Motor Insurers' Bureau* [2003] EWCA Civ 18, [2003] All ER (D) 16 (Jan), [2003] Lloyd's Rep IR 427 the Court of Appeal confirmed in dismissing the claimant's claim that on the basis of the evidence heard by the lower court the claimant either knew there was no insurance, knew there was a problem with the insurance and ought to have known there was none or deliberately avoided enquiring further about insurance. In that case the evidence was that the claimant was present within a group where the subject of insurance was discussed.

CLAUSE 6(1)(E): 'OR AFTER SUCH COMMENCEMENT IF HE COULD REASONABLY BE EXPECTED TO HAVE ALIGHTED FROM THE VEHICLE'
This exception affords MIB what is sometimes called the 'petrol station' defence. In other words, if the injured passenger found out during the journey that the vehicle had been stolen and/or that the driver was uninsured, MIB could avoid liability if, at any time thereafter, the passenger failed to take any reasonable opportunity to get out of the vehicle.

CLAUSE 6(2): EXTENT OF THE CLAUSE 6(1)(E) EXCEPTION
The exception only applies where the passenger has sued the driver or owner of the vehicle in which he was travelling. It has no application, for example, where the passenger is injured through the fault of the driver of an entirely different vehicle and obtains judgment against that other driver.

Clause 7: Agents

[3.18]   (*See* Note 6 to the Agreement.)
The practice of MIB hitherto has frequently been to appoint an insurance office, the 'investigating member', to make inquiries and, where appropriate, negotiate settlement. (This function did not mean that the office in question was a 'domestic regulations/Article 75 insurer', as to which see para [3.61], below.) However, for reasons of efficiency and economy MIB is currently moving all claims 'in-house' and the involvement of member insurers as claims handlers has ceased in respect of new cases from 1 January 2003.

(D)   TEXT OF AGREEMENT DATED 13 AUGUST 1999

[3.19]   The 1988 Agreement was replaced by a new Agreement, which operates in respect of accidents occurring on or after 1 October 1999.
The text of the new Agreement is as follows—
This agreement is made the thirteenth day of August 1999 between the Secretary of State for the Environment, Transport and the Regions (hereinafter referred to as 'the Secretary of State') and the Motor Insurers' Bureau, whose registered office is at 152 Silbury Boulevard, Milton Keynes MK9 1NB (hereinafter referred to as 'MIB') and is supplemental to an Agreement (hereinafter called 'the Principal Agreement') made the 31st day of December 1945 between the Minister of War Transport and the insurers transacting compulsory motor insurance business in Great Britain by or on behalf of whom the said Agreement was signed and in pursuance of paragraph 1 of which MIB was incorporated.

(Note—The MIB's registered office is now Linford Wood House, 6–12 Capital Drive, Linford Wood, Milton Keynes MK14 6XT (DX 142620 MILTON KEYNES 10).)

It is hereby agreed as follows:—

Interpretation

(I)   GENERAL DEFINITIONS
    1   In this Agreement, unless the context otherwise requires, the following expressions have the following meanings—
    '1988 Act' means the Road Traffic Act 1988;
    '1988 Agreement' means the Agreement made on 21 December 1988 between the Secretary of State for Transport and MIB;
    'bank holiday' means a day which is, or is to be observed as, a bank holiday under the Banking and Financial Dealings Act 1971;
    'claimant' means a person who has commenced or who proposes to commence relevant proceedings and has made an application under this Agreement in respect thereof;
    'contract of insurance' means a policy of insurance or a security covering a relevant liability;
    'insurer' includes the giver of a security;
    'MIB's obligation' means the obligation contained in clause 5;
    'property' means any property whether real, heritable or personal;
    'relevant liability' means a liability in respect of which a contract of insurance must be in force to comply with Part VI of the 1988 Act;
    'relevant proceedings' means proceedings in respect of a relevant liability (and 'commencement', in relation to such proceedings means, in England and Wales,

the date on which a Claim Form or other originating process is issued by a Court or, in Scotland, the date on which the originating process is served on the Defender);

'relevant sum' means a sum payable or remaining payable under an unsatisfied judgment, including—

  (a)   an amount payable or remaining payable in respect of interest on that sum; and

  (b)   either the whole of the costs (whether taxed or not) awarded by the Court as part of that judgment or, where the judgment includes an award in respect of a liability which is not a relevant liability, such proportion of those costs as the relevant liability bears to the total sum awarded under the judgment;

'specified excess' means £300 or such other sum as may from time to time be agreed in writing between the Secretary of State and MIB;

'unsatisfied judgment' means a judgment or order (by whatever name called) in respect of a relevant liability which has not been satisfied in full within seven days from the date upon which the claimant became entitled to enforce it.

(II)   MEANING OF REFERENCES

2 (1)   Save as otherwise herein provided, the Interpretation Act 1978 shall apply for the interpretation of this Agreement as it applies for the interpretation of an Act of Parliament.

(2)   Where under this Agreement, something is required to be done—

  (a)   within a specified period after or from the happening of a particular event, the period begins on the day after the happening of that event;

  (b)   within or not less than a specified period before a particular event, the period ends on the day immediately before the happening of that event.

(3)   Where, apart from this paragraph, the period in question, being a period of seven days or less, would include a Saturday, Sunday or bank holiday or Christmas Day or Good Friday, that day shall be excluded.

(4)   Save where expressly otherwise provided, a reference in this Agreement to a numbered clause is a reference to the clause bearing that number in this Agreement and a reference to a numbered paragraph is a reference to a paragraph bearing that number in the clause in which the reference occurs.

(5)   In this Agreement—

  (a)   a reference (however framed) to the doing of any act or thing by or the happening of any event in relation to the claimant includes a reference to the doing of that act or thing by or the happening of that event in relation to a Solicitor or other person acting on his behalf; and

  (b)   a requirement to give notice to, or to serve documents upon, MIB or an insurer mentioned in clause 9(1)(a) shall be satisfied by the giving of the notice to, or the service of the documents upon, a Solicitor acting on its behalf in the manner provided for.

(III)   CLAIMANTS NOT OF FULL AGE OR CAPACITY

3   Where, under and in accordance with this Agreement—

  (a)   any act or thing is done to or by a Solicitor or other person acting on behalf of a claimant;

  (b)   any decision is made by or in respect of a Solicitor or other person acting on behalf of a claimant; or

  (c)   any sum is paid to a Solicitor or other person acting on behalf of a claimant, then, whatever may be the age or other circumstances affecting the capacity of the claimant, that act, thing, decision or sum shall be treated as if it had been done to or by, or made in respect of or paid to a claimant of full age and capacity.

Principal terms

(IV) DURATION OF AGREEMENT

4 (1) This Agreement shall come into force on 1st October 1999 in relation to accidents occurring on or after that date and, save as provided by clause 23, the 1998 Agreement shall cease and determine immediately before that date.

(2) This Agreement may be determined by the Secretary of State or by MIB giving to the other not less than twelve months' notice in writing but without prejudice to its continued operation in respect of accidents occurring before the date of termination.

(V) MIB's OBLIGATION TO SATISFY COMPENSATION CLAIMS

5 (1) Subject to clauses 6 to 17, if a claimant has obtained against any person in a Court in Great Britain a judgment which is an unsatisfied judgment then MIB will pay the relevant sum to, or to the satisfaction of, the claimant or will cause the same to be so paid.

(2) Paragraph (1) applies whether or not the person liable to satisfy the judgment is in fact covered by a contract of insurance and whatever may be the cause of his failure to satisfy the judgment.

(VI) EXCEPTIONS TO AGREEMENT

6 (1) Clause 5 does not apply in the case of an application made in respect of a claim of any of the following descriptions (and, where part only of a claim satisfies such a description, clause 5 does not apply to that part)—

(a) a claim arising out of a relevant liability incurred by the user of a vehicle owned by or in the possession of the Crown, unless—
  (i) responsibility for the existence of a contract of insurance under Part VI of the 1988 Act in relation to that vehicle had been undertaken by some other person (whether or not the person liable was in fact covered by a contract of insurance); or
  (ii) the relevant liability was in fact covered by a contract or insurance;

(b) a claim arising out of the use of a vehicle which is not required to be covered by a contract of insurance by virtue of section 144 of the 1988 Act, unless the use is in fact covered by such a contract;

(c) a claim by, or for the benefit of, a person ('the beneficiary') other than the person suffering death, injury or other damage which is made either—
  (i) in respect of a cause of action or a judgment which has been assigned to the beneficiary; or
  (ii) pursuant to a right of subrogation or contractual or other right belonging to the beneficiary;

(d) a claim in respect of damage to a motor vehicle or losses arising therefrom where, at the time when the damage to it was sustained—
  (i) there was not in force in relation to the use of that vehicle such a contract of insurance as is required by Part VI of the 1988 Act; and
  (ii) the claimant either knew or ought to have known that that was the case;

(e) a claim which is made in respect of a relevant liability described in paragraph (2) by a claimant who, at the time of the use giving rise to the relevant liability was voluntarily allowing himself to be carried in the vehicle and, either before the commencement of his journey in the vehicle or after such commencement if he could reasonably be expected to have alighted from it, knew or ought to have known that—

    (i)   the vehicle had been stolen or unlawfully taken;

    (ii)   the vehicle was being used without there being in force in relation to its use such a contract of insurance as would comply with Part VI of the 1988 Act;

    (iii)   the vehicle was being used in the course or furtherance of a crime; or

    (iv)   the vehicle was being used as a means of escape from, or avoidance of, lawful apprehension.

(2)   The relevant liability referred to in paragraph (1)(e) is a liability incurred by the owner or registered keeper or a person using the vehicle in which the claimant was being carried.

(3)   The burden of proving that the claimant knew or ought to have known of any matter set out in paragraph (1)(e) shall be on MIB but, in the absence of evidence to the contrary, proof by MIB of any of the following matters shall be taken as proof of the claimant's knowledge of the matter set out in paragraph (1)(e)(ii)—

    (a)   that the claimant was the owner or registered keeper of the vehicle or had caused or permitted its use;

    (b)   that the claimant knew the vehicle was being used by a person who was below the minimum age at which he could be granted a licence authorising the driving of a vehicle of that class;

    (c)   that the claimant knew that the person driving the vehicle was disqualified for holding or obtaining a driving licence;

    (d)   that the claimant knew that the user of the vehicle was neither its owner nor registered keeper nor an employee of the owner or registered keeper nor the owner or registered keeper of any other vehicle.

(4)   Knowledge which the claimant has or ought to have for the purposes of paragraph (1)(e) includes knowledge of matters which he could reasonably be expected to have been aware of had he not been under the self-induced influence of drink or drugs.

(5)   For the purposes of this clause–

    (a)   a vehicle which has been unlawfully removed from the possession of the Crown shall be taken to continue in that possession whilst it is kept so removed;

    (b)   references to a person being carried in a vehicle include references to his being carried upon, entering, getting on to and alighting from the vehicle; and

    (c)   'owner', in relation to a vehicle which is the subject of a hiring agreement or a hire- purchase agreement, means the person in possession of the vehicle under that agreement.

Conditions precedent to MIB's obligation

(VII)   FORM OF APPLICATION

7 (1)   MIB shall incur no liability under MIB's obligation unless an application is made to the person specified in clause 9(1)—

    (a)   in such form;

    (b)   giving such information about the relevant proceedings and other matters relevant to this Agreement; and

    (c)   accompanied by such documents as MIB may reasonably require.

(2)   Where an application is signed by a person who is neither the claimant nor a Solicitor acting on his behalf MIB may refuse to accept the application (and shall incur no liability under MIB's obligation) until it is reasonably satisfied that,

having regard to the status of the signatory and his relationship to the claimant, the claimant is fully aware of the contents and effect of the application but subject thereto MIB shall not refuse to accept such an application by reason only that it is signed by a person other than the claimant or his Solicitor.

(VIII)   SERVICE OF NOTICES ETC

8   Any notice required to be given or documents to be supplied to MIB pursuant to clauses 9 to 12 of this Agreement shall be sufficiently given or supplied only if sent by facsimile transmission or by Registered or Recorded Delivery post to MIB's registered office for the time being and delivery shall be proved by the production of a facsimile transmission report produced by the sender's facsimile machine or an appropriate postal receipt.

(IX)   NOTICE OF RELEVANT PROCEEDINGS

9 (1)   MIB shall incur no liability under MIB's obligation unless proper notice of the bringing of the relevant proceedings has been given by the claimant not later than fourteen days after the commencement of those proceedings—

(a)   in the case of proceedings in respect of a relevant liability which is covered by a contract of insurance with an insurer whose identity can be ascertained, to that insurer;

(b)   in any other case, to MIB.

(2)   In this clause 'proper notice' means, except in so far as any part of such information or any copy document or other thing has already been supplied under clause 7—

(a)   notice in writing that proceedings have been commenced by Claim Form, Writ, or other means;

(b)   a copy of the sealed Claim Form, Writ or other official document providing evidence of the commencement of the proceedings and, in Scotland, a statement of the means of service;

(c)   a copy or details of any insurance policy providing benefits in the case of the death, bodily injury or damage to property to which the proceedings relate where the claimant is the insured party and the benefits are available to him;

(d)   copies of all correspondence in the possession of the claimant or (as the case may be) his Solicitor or agent to or from the Defendant or the Defender or (as the case may be) his Solicitor, insurers or agent which is relevant to—

　(i)   the death, bodily injury or damage for which the Defendant or Defender is alleged to be responsible; or

　(ii)   any contract of insurance which covers, or which may or has been alleged to cover, liability for such death, injury or damage the benefit of which is, or is claimed to be, available to Defendant or Defender;

(e)   subject to paragraph (3), a copy of the Particulars of Claim whether or not indorsed on the Claim Form, Writ or other originating process, and whether or not served (in England and Wales) on any Defendant or (in Scotland) on any Defender; and

(f)   a copy of all other documents which are required under the appropriate rules of procedure to be served on a Defendant or Defender with the Claim Form, Writ or other originating process or with the Particulars of Claim;

(g)   such other information about the relevant proceedings as MIB may reasonably specify.

(3)   If, in the case of proceedings commenced in England or Wales, the Particulars of Claim (including any document required to be served therewith) has not yet

been served with the Claim Form or other originating process paragraph (2)(e) shall be sufficiently compiled with if a copy thereof is served on MIB not later than seven days after it is served on the Defendant.

(X)   NOTICE OF SERVICE OF PROCEEDINGS

10 (1)   This clause applies where the relevant proceedings are commenced in England and Wales.

(2)   MIB shall incur no liability under MIB's obligation unless the claimant has, not later than the appropriate date, given notice in writing to the person specified in clause 9(1) of the date of service of the Claim Form or other originating process in the relevant proceedings.

(3)   In this clause, 'the appropriate date' means the day falling—

   (a)   seven days after—

      (i)   the date when the claimant received notification from the Court that service of the Claim Form or other originating process has occurred;

      (ii)   the date when the claimant receives notification from the Defendant that service of the Claim Form or other originating process has occurred; or

      (iii)   the date of personal service; or

   (b)   fourteen days after the date when service is deemed to have occurred in accordance with the Civil Procedure Rules, whichever of those days occurs first.

(XI)   FURTHER INFORMATION

11 (1)   MIB shall incur no liability under MIB's obligation unless the claimant has, not later than seven days after the occurrence of any of the following events, namely—

   (a)   the filing of a defence in the relevant proceedings;

   (b)   any amendment to the Particulars of Claim or any amendment of or addition to any schedule or other document required to be served therewith, and either—

      (i)   the setting down of the case for trial; or

      (ii)   where the court gives notice to the claimant of the trial date, the date when that notice is received, given notice in writing of the date of that event to the person specified in clause 9(1) and has, in the case of the filing of a defence or an amendment of the Particulars of Claim or any amendment of or addition to any schedule or other document required to be served therewith, supplied a copy thereof to that person.

(2)   MIB shall incur no liability under MIB's obligation unless the claimant furnishes to the person specified in clause 9(1) within a reasonable time after being required to do so such further information and documents in support of his claim as MIB may reasonably require notwithstanding that the claimant may have complied with clause 7(1).

(XII)   NOTICE OF INTENTION TO APPLY FOR JUDGMENT

12 (1)   MIB shall incur no liability under MIB's obligation unless the claimant has, after commencement of the relevant proceedings and not less than thirty-five days before the appropriate date, given notice in writing to the person specified in clause 9(1) of his intention to apply for or to sign judgment in the relevant proceedings.

(2)   In this clause, 'the appropriate date' means the date when the application for judgment is made or, as the case may be, the signing of judgment occurs.

(XIII)   SECTION 154 OF THE 1988 ACT

13   MIB shall incur no liability under MIB's obligation unless the claimant has as soon as reasonably practicable—

(a)   demanded the information and, where appropriate, the particulars specified in section 154(1) of the 1988 Act; and

(b)   if the person of whom the demand is made fails to comply with the provisions of that subsection—

(i)   made a formal complaint to a police officer in respect of such failure; and

(ii)   used all reasonable endeavours to obtain the name and address of the registered keeper of the vehicle. or, if so required by MIB, has authorised MIB to take such steps on his behalf.

(XIV)   PROSECUTION OF PROCEEDINGS

14   MIB shall incur no liability under MIB's obligation—

(a)   unless the claimant has, if so required by MIB and having been granted a full indemnity by MIB as to costs, taken all reasonable steps to obtain judgment against every person who may be liable (including any person who may be vicariously liable) in respect of the injury or death or damage to property; or

(b)   if the claimant, upon being requested to do so by MIB, refuses to consent to MIB being joined as a party to the relevant proceedings.

(XV)   ASSIGNMENT OF JUDGMENT AND UNDERTAKINGS

15   MIB shall incur no liability under MIB's obligation unless the claimant has—

(a)   assigned to MIB or its nominee the unsatisfied judgment, whether or not that judgment includes an amount in respect of a liability other than a relevant liability, and any order for costs made in the relevant proceedings; and

(b)   undertaken to repay to MIB any sum paid to him—

(i)   by MIB in discharge of MIB's obligation if the judgment is subsequently set aside either as a whole or in respect of the part of the relevant liability to which that sum relates;

(ii)   by any other person by way of compensation or benefit for the death, bodily injury or other damage to which the relevant proceedings relate, including a sum which would have been deductible under the provisions of clause 17 if it had been received before MIB was obliged to satisfy MIB's obligation.

Limitations on MIB's liability

(XVI)   COMPENSATION FOR DAMAGE TO PROPERTY

16 (1)   Where a claim under this Agreement includes a claim in respect of damage to property, MIB's obligation in respect of that part of the relevant sum which is awarded for such damage and any losses arising therefrom (referred to in this clause as 'the property damage compensation') is limited in accordance with the following paragraphs.

(2)   Where the property damage compensation does not exceed the specified excess, MIB shall incur no liability.

(3)   Where the property damage compensation in respect of any one accident exceeds the specified excess but does not exceed £250,000, MIB shall incur liability only in respect of the property damage compensation less the specified excess.

(4)   Where the property damage compensation in respect of any one accident exceeds £250,000, MIB shall incur liability only in respect of the sum of £250,000 less the specified excess.

(XVII)   COMPENSATION RECEIVED FROM OTHER SOURCES
17   Where a claimant has received compensation from—
(a)   the Policyholders Protection Board under the Policyholders Protection Act 1975; or
(b)   an insurer under an insurance agreement or arrangement; or
(c)   any other source, in respect of the death, bodily injury or other damage to which the relevant proceedings relate and such compensation has not been taken into account in the calculation of the relevant sum MIB may deduct from the relevant sum, in addition to any sum deductible under clause 16, an amount equal to that compensation.

Miscellaneous

(XVIII)   NOTIFICATIONS OF DECISIONS BY MIB
18   Where a claimant—
(a)   has made an application in accordance with clause 7, and
(b)   has given to the person specified in clause 9(1) proper notice of the relevant proceedings in accordance with clause 9(2), MIB shall—
    (i)   give a reasoned reply to any request made by the claimant relating to the payment of compensation in pursuance of MIB's obligation; and
    (ii)   as soon as reasonably practicable notify the claimant in writing of its decision regarding the payment of the relevant sum, together with the reasons for that decision.

(XIX)   REFERENCE OF DISPUTES TO THE SECRETARY OF STATE
19 (1)   In the event of any dispute as to the reasonableness of a requirement made by MIB for the supply of information or documentation or for the taking of any step by the claimant, it may be referred by the claimant or MIB to the Secretary of State whose decision shall be final.
(2)   Where a dispute is referred to the Secretary of State—
(a)   MIB shall supply the Secretary of State and, if it has not already done so, the claimant with notice in writing of the requirement from which the dispute arises, together with the reasons for that requirement and such further information as MIB considers relevant; and
(b)   where the dispute is referred by the claimant, the claimant shall supply the Secretary of State and, if he has not already done so, MIB with notice in writing of the grounds on which he disputes the reasonableness of the requirement.

(XX)   RECOVERIES
20   Nothing in this Agreement shall prevent an insurer from providing by conditions in a contract of insurance that all sums paid by the insurer or by MIB by virtue of the Principal Agreement or this Agreement in or towards the discharge of the liability of the insured shall be recoverable by them or by MIB from the insured or from any other person.

(XXI) APPORTIONMENT OF DAMAGES, ETC

21 (1)   Where an unsatisfied judgment which includes an amount in respect of a liability other than a relevant liability has been assigned to MIB or its nominee in pursuance of clause 15 MIB shall—

    (a)   apportion any sum it receives in satisfaction or partial satisfaction of the judgment according to the proportion which the damages awarded in respect of the relevant liability bear to the damages awarded in respect of the other liability; and

    (b)   account to the claimant in respect of the moneys received properly apportionable to the other liability.

(2)   Where the sum received includes an amount in respect of interest or an amount awarded under an order for costs, the interest or the amount received in pursuance of the order shall be dealt with in the manner provided in paragraph (1).

(XXII) AGENTS

22   MIB may perform any of its obligations under this Agreement by agents.

(XXIII) TRANSITIONAL PROVISIONS

23 (1)   The 1988 Agreement shall continue in force in relation to claims arising out of accidents occurring before 1st October 1999 with the modifications contained in paragraph (2).

(2)   In relation to any claim made under the 1988 Agreement after this Agreement has come into force, the 1988 Agreement shall apply as if there were inserted after clause 6 thereof—

'6A. Where any person in whose favour a judgment in respect of a relevant liability has been made has—

(a)   made a claim under this Agreement, and

(b)   satisfied the requirements specified in clause 5 hereof, MIB shall, if requested to do so, give him a reasoned reply regarding the satisfaction of that claim.'

IN WITNESS whereof the Secretary of State has caused his Corporate Seal to be hereunto affixed and the Motor Insurers' Bureau has caused its Common Seal to be hereunto affixed the day and year first above written.

Notes for the guidance of victims of road traffic accidents

The following notes are for the guidance of anyone who may have a claim on the Motor Insurers' Bureau under this Agreement and their legal advisers. They are not part of the Agreement, their purpose being to deal in ordinary language with the situations which most readily occur. They are not in any way a substitute for reading and applying the terms of this or any other relevant Agreement, nor are they intended to control or influence the legal interpretation of the Agreement.

At the request of the Secretary of State, these notes have been revised with effect from 15th April 2002 and in their revised form have been agreed by MIB, the Law society of England and Wales, the Law Society of Scotland, the Motor Accident Solicitor's Society and the Association of Personal Injury Lawyers. Any application made under the Agreement after this date (unless proceedings have already been issued) will be handled by MIB in accordance with these notes.

Where proceedings have been issued in Scotland, for the words 'Claimant' and 'Defendant' there shall be substituted in these notes where appropriate the words 'Pursuer' and 'Defender' respectively.

Enquiries, requests for application forms and general correspondence in connection with the Agreement should be addressed to:—

Motor Insurers' Bureau
Linford Wood House
6–12 Capital Drive
Linford Wood
Milton Keynes
MK14 6XT
Tel: 01908 830001
Fax: 01908 671681
DX: 142620 Milton Keynes 10

1   INTRODUCTION – MIB'S ROLE AND APPLICATION OF THE AGREEMENT
1.1   The role of MIB under this Agreement is to provide a safety net for innocent victims of drivers who have been identified but are uninsured. MIB's funds for this purpose are obtained from levies charged upon insurers and so come from the premiums which are charged by those insurers to members of the public.
1.2   MIB has entered into a series of Agreements with the Secretary of State and his predecessors in office. Under each Agreement MIB undertakes obligations to pay defined compensation in specific circumstances. There are two sets of Agreements, one relating to victims of uninsured drivers (the 'Uninsured Drivers' Agreements) and the other concerned with victims of hit and run or otherwise untraceable drivers (the 'Untraced Drivers' Agreements). These Notes are addressed specifically to the procedures required to take advantage of the rights granted by the Uninsured Drivers Agreements. However, it is not always certain which of the Agreements applies. For guidance in such cases please see the note on Untraced Drivers at paragraph 11 below.
1.3   In order to determine which of the Uninsured Drivers Agreements is applicable to a particular victim's claim, regard must be had to the date of the relevant accident. This Agreement only applies in respect of claims arising on or after 1st October 1999. Claims arising earlier than that are covered by the following Agreements:–
    1.3.1 Claims arising in respect of an incident occurring between 1st July 1946 and 28th February 1971 are governed by the Agreement between the Minister of Transport and the Bureau dated 17th June 1946.
    1.3.2 Claims arising in respect of an incident occurring between 1st March 1971 and 30th November 1972 are governed by the Agreement between the Secretary of State for the Environment and the Bureau dated 1st February 1971.
    1.3.3 Claims arising in respect of an incident occurring between 1st December 1972 and 30th December 1988 are governed by the Agreement between the Secretary of State and the Bureau dated 22nd November 1972.
    1.3.4 Claims arising in respect of an incident occurring between 31st December 1988 and 30th September 1999 are governed by the Agreement between the Secretary of State and the Bureau dated 21st December 1988.

2   MIB'S OBLIGATION
2.1   MIB's basic obligation (see clause 5) is to satisfy judgments which fall within the terms of this Agreement and which, because the Defendant to the proceedings is not insured, are not satisfied.
2.2   This obligation is, however, not absolute. It is subject to certain exceptions where MIB has no liability (see clause 6), there are a number of pre-conditions which the claimant must comply with (see clauses 7 to 15) and there are some limitations on MIB's liability (see clauses 16 and 17).
2.3   Nothing in the Agreement is intended to remove the limitation rules applying to claimants not of full age or capacity. Limitation for personal injury remains 3 years from the date of full age or capacity.

2.4   MIB does not have to wait for a judgment to be given; it can become party to the proceedings or negotiate and settle the claim if it wishes to do so.

3   CLAIMS WHICH MIB IS NOT OBLIGED TO SATISFY

MIB is not liable under the Agreement in the case of the following types of claim.

3.1   A claim made in respect of an unsatisfied judgment which does not concern a liability against which Part VI of the Road Traffic Act 1988 requires a vehicle user to insure (see section 145 of the Act). An example would be a case where the accident did not occur in a place specified in the Act. See the definitions of 'unsatisfied judgment' and 'relevant liability' in clause 1.

3.2   A claim in respect of loss or damage caused by the use of a vehicle owned by or in the possession of the Crown (that is the Civil Service, the armed forces and so on) to which Part VI does not apply. If the responsibility for motor insurance has been undertaken by someone else or the vehicle is in fact insured, this exception does not apply. See clause 6(1)(a).

3.3   A claim made against any person who is not required to insure by virtue of section 144 of the Road Traffic Act 1988. See clause 6(1)(b).

3.4   A claim (commonly called subrogated) made in the name of a person suffering damage or injury but which is in fact wholly or partly for the benefit of another who has indemnified, or is liable to indemnify, that person. See clause 6(1)(c). It is not the intention of this Clause to exclude claims by family members or friends for the gratuitous provision of care, travel expenses by family members or friends, or miscellaneous expenses incurred on behalf of the Claimant, where the claimant is entitled to include such claims in his claim for damages.

3.5   A claim in respect of damage to a motor vehicle or losses arising from such damage where the use of the damaged vehicle was itself not covered by a contract of insurance as required by law. See clause 6(1)(d).

3.6   A claim made by a passenger in a vehicle where the loss or damage has been caused by the user of that vehicle if:—

    3.6.1 the use of the vehicle was not covered by a contract of insurance; and

    3.6.2 the claimant knew or could be taken to have known that the vehicle was being used without insurance, had been stolen or unlawfully taken or was being used in connection with crime; See clause 6(1)(e), (2), (3) and (4).

      For an interpretation of 'knew or ought to have known' refer to the House of Lords judgment in *White v White* of 1st March 2001.

3.7   A claim in respect of property damage amounting to £300 or less, £300 being the 'specified excess'. See clause 16(2).

3.8   Where the claim is for property damage, the first £300 of the loss and so much of it as exceeds £250,000. See clause 16(3) and 4 Procedure after the accident and before proceedings

4.1   The claimant must take reasonable steps to establish whether there is in fact any insurance covering the use of the vehicle which caused the injury or damage. First, a claimant has statutory rights under section 154 of the Road Traffic Act 1988 to obtain relevant particulars which he must take steps to exercise even if that involves incurring expense and MIB will insist that he does so. See clause 13(a).

MIB accept that if the MIB application form is completed and signed by the Claimant, the Claimant will have complied with this Clause of the Agreement.

4.2   Other steps will include the following:—

    4.2.1 The exchange of names, addresses and insurance particulars between those involved either at the scene of the accident or afterwards.

    4.2.2 Corresponding with the owner or driver of the vehicle or his representatives. He will be obliged under the terms of his motor policy to inform his insurers and a letter of claim addressed to him will commonly be passed to the insurers who may reply on his behalf. See clause 9(2)(d).

    4.2.3 Where only the vehicle's number is known, enquiry of the Driver and

Vehicle Licensing Agency at Swansea SA99 1BP as to the registered keeper of the vehicle is desirable so that through him the identity of the owner or driver can be established or confirmed.

4.2.4 Enquiries of the police (see clause 13(b) and Note 4.1 above).

4.3   If enquiries show that there is an insurer who is obliged to accept and does accept the obligation to handle the claim against the user of the vehicle concerned, even though the relevant liability may not be covered by the policy in question, then the claim should be pursued with such insurer.

4.4   If, however, enquiries disclose that there is no insurance covering the use of the vehicle concerned or if the insurer cannot be identified or the insurer asserts that it is under no obligation to handle the claim or if for any other reason it is clear that the insurer will not satisfy any judgment, the claim should be directed to MIB itself.

5   WHEN PROCEEDINGS ARE COMMENCED OR CONTEMPLATED

5.1   As explained above, MIB does not have to wait for a judgment to be obtained before intervening. Claimants may apply to MIB before the commencement of proceedings. MIB will respond to any claim which complies with clause 7 and must give a reasoned reply to any request for compensation in respect of the claim (see clause 18) although normally a request for compensation will not be met until MIB is satisfied that it is properly based. Interim compensation payments are dealt with at paragraph 8 below. Application Forms are available from MIB's office or their website: www.mib.org.uk. Where a claim is made by the Claimant in person, who has not received legal advice, then if the claim is first made within 14 days prior to expiry of the limitation period, MIB will require the completed application form within the 21 days after the issue of proceedings.

5.2   It is important that wherever possible claims should be made using MIB's application form, fully completed and accompanied by documents supporting the claim, as soon as possible to avoid unnecessary delays. See clause 7(1). Copies of the form can be obtained on request made by post, telephone, fax or the DX or on personal application to MIB's offices.

5.3   The claimant must give MIB notice in writing that he has commenced legal proceedings. The notice, the completed application form (if appropriate) and all necessary documents must be received by MIB no later than 14 days after the date of commencement of proceedings. See clause 9(1) and (2)(a). The date of commencement is determined in accordance with the definitions of 'relevant proceedings' and 'commencement' given in clause 1. When it is decided to commence legal proceedings, MIB should be joined as a defendant (unless there is good reason not to do so). Once MIB is a defendant, the Court will advise the relevant events direct and Clause 9(3), 11 and 12 will no longer apply.

The form of words set out below should be used for the joinder of MIB:

1.   The Second Defendant is a Company limited by guarantee under the Companies Act. Pursuant to an Agreement with the Secretary of State for the Environment, Transport and the Regions dated 13th August 1999, the Second Defendant provides compensation in certain circumstances to persons suffering injury or damage as a result of the negligence of uninsured motorists.

2.   The Claimant has used all reasonable endeavours to ascertain the liability of an insurer for the First Defendant and at the time of the commencement of these proceedings verily believes that the First Defendant is not insured.

3.   The Claimant accepts that only if a final judgment is obtained against the First Defendant (which judgment is not satisfied in full within seven days from the date upon which the Claimant became entitled to enforce it) can the Second Defendant be required to satisfy the judgment and then only if

the terms and conditions set out in the Agreement are satisfied. Until that time, any liability of the Second Defendant is only contingent.

4.   To avoid the Second Defendant having later to apply to join itself to this action (which the Claimant must consent to in any event, pursuant to Clause 14(b) of the Agreement) the Claimant seeks to include the Second Defendant from the outset recognising fully the Second Defendant's position as reflected in 3. above and the rights of the Second Defendant fully to participate in the action to protect its position as a separate party to the action.

5.   With the above in mind, the Claimant seeks a declaration of the Second Defendant's contingent liability to satisfy the claimant's judgment against the First Defendant.

5.4   This notice must have with it the following:–

5.4.1 a copy of the document originating the proceedings, usually in England and Wales a Claim Form and in Scotland a Sheriff Court Writ of Court of Session Summons (see clause 9(2)(b)); 5.4.2 normally the Particulars of Claim endorsed on or served with the Claim Form or Writ (see clause 9(2)(e), although this document may be served later in accordance with clause 9(3) if that applies); 5.4.3 in any case the documents required by the relevant rules of procedure (see clause 9(2)(f)).

Provided that the documents referred to above are forwarded to MIB, it is not necessary to enclose the Response Pack or the Notice of Issue.

5.5   In addition, other items as mentioned in clause 9(2), e g correspondence with the Defendant (or Defender) or his representatives, need to be supplied where appropriate.

5.6   It is for the claimant to satisfy himself that the notice has in fact been received by MIB. Clause 8 applies to service of documents by post and fax. MIB prefer service by fax as it is almost instantaneous and can be confirmed quickly. Claimants should note that service of documents by DX is not permitted under the Agreement since delivery cannot be proved.

However, where the Claimant proves that service by DX, First Class Post, Personal Service or any other form of service allowed by the Civil Procedure Rules, was effected, MIB will accept that such notice has been served in the same circumstances in which a party to litigation would be obliged to accept that he had been validly served by such means.

5.7   It should be noted that when MIB has been given notice of a claim, it may elect to require the claimant to bring proceedings and attempt to secure a judgment against the party whom MIB alleges to be wholly or partly responsible for the loss or damage or who may be contracted to indemnify the claimant. In such a case MIB must indemnify the claimant against the costs of such proceedings. Subject to that, however, MIB's obligation to satisfy the judgment in the action will only arise if the claimant commences the proceedings and takes all reasonable steps to obtain a judgment. See clause 14(a).

6   SERVICE OF PROCEEDINGS

6.1   If proceedings are commenced in England and Wales the claimant must inform MIB of the date of service (See clause 10(1) and (2)).

6.2   If service of the Claim Form is effected by the Court, notice should be given within 14 days from the earliest of the dates listed in clause 10(3)(a)(i) or (ii) or within 14 days from the date mentioned in clause 10(3)(b) (the date of deemed service under the court's rules of procedure). Claimants are advised to take steps to ensure that the court or the defendant's legal representatives inform them of the date of service as soon as possible. Although a longer period is allowed than in other cases, service may be deemed to have occurred without a Claimant knowing of it until some time afterwards.

6.3   Where proceedings are served personally, notice should be given seven days from the date of personal service (clause 10(3)(a)(iii)).

However, by concession MIB will accept the notice referred to in note 6.1 above if it is received by MIB within 14 days from the dates referred to in notes 6.2 and 6.3.

6.4   In Scotland, proceedings are commenced at the date of service (see clause 1) so notice should already have been given under clause 9 and clause 10 does not apply there.

7   AFTER SERVICE AND BEFORE JUDGMENT

See Note 5.3 above.

7.1   Notice of the filing of a defence, of an amendment to the Statement or Particulars of Claim, and the setting down of the case for trial must be given not later than seven days after the occurrence of such events and a copy of the document must be supplied (clause 11(1)).

7.2   However, by concession MIB will accept the notice referred to in note 7.1 above if it is received by MIB within 14 days after the proven date on which it was received by the claimant.

7.3   MIB may request further information and documents to support the claim where it is not satisfied that the documents supplied with the application form are sufficient to enable it to assess its liability under the Agreement (see clause 11(2)).

7.4   If the claimant intends to sign or apply for judgment he must give MIB notice of the fact before doing so. This notice must be given at least 35 days before the application is to be made or the date when judgment is to be signed (see clause 12). The 35 days notice does not apply where the court enters judgment of its own motion.

7.5   At no time must the claimant oppose MIB if it wishes to be joined as a party to proceedings and he must if requested consent to any application by MIB to be joined. Conflicts may arise between a Defendant and MIB which require MIB to become a Defendant or, in Scotland, a party Minuter if a defence is be filed on its behalf (see clause 14(b)).

8.   INTERIM PAYMENTS

8   In substantial cases, the claimant may wish to apply for an interim payment. MIB will consider such applications on a voluntary basis but otherwise the claimant has the right to apply to the court for an interim payment order which, if granted, will be met by MIB.

9.   AFTER JUDGMENT

9.1   MIB's basic obligation normally arises if a judgment is not satisfied within seven days after the claimant has become entitled to enforce it (see clause 1). However, that judgment may in certain circumstances be set aside and with it MIB's obligation to satisfy it. Sometimes MIB wishes to apply to set aside a judgment either wholly or partially. If MIB decides not to satisfy a judgment it will notify the claimant as soon as possible. Where a judgment is subsequently set aside, MIB will require the claimant to repay any sum previously paid by MIB to discharge its obligation under the Agreement (see clause 15(b)).

9.2   MIB is not obliged to satisfy a judgment unless the claimant has in return assigned the benefit to MIB or its nominee (see clause 15(a)). If such assignment is effected and if the subject matter of the judgment includes claims in respect of which MIB is not obliged to meet any judgment and if MIB effects any recovery on the judgment, the sum recovered will be divided between MIB and the claimant in proportion to the liabilities which were and which were not covered by MIB's obligation (see clause 21).

10.   PERMISSIBLE DEDUCTIONS FROM PAYMENTS BY MIB

10.1   Claims for loss and damage for which the claimant has been compensated or indemnified, e g under a contract of insurance or under the Policyholders Protection Act 1975, and which has not been taken into account in the judgment, may be deducted from the sum paid in settlement of MIB's obligation (see clause 17).

10.2   If there is a likelihood that the claimant will receive payment from such a source after the judgment has been satisfied by MIB, MIB will require him to undertake to repay any sum which duplicates the compensation assessed by the court (see clause 15(b)).

11.   UNTRACED DRIVERS

11.1   Where the owner or driver of a vehicle cannot be identified application may be made to MIB under the relevant Untraced Drivers Agreement. This provides, subject to specified conditions, for the payment of compensation for personal injury. It does not provide for compensation in respect of damage to property.

11.2   In those cases where it is unclear whether the owner or driver of a vehicle has been correctly identified it is sensible for the claimant to register a claim under both this Agreement and the Untraced Drivers Agreement following which MIB will advise which Agreement will, in its view, apply in the circumstances of the particular case.

COMMENTARY ON THE 1999 AGREEMENT

Clause 1: Definitions

[3.20]   In claims brought under the 1999 Agreement, a 'relevant liability' is a liability that is required to be covered by a policy of insurance under the Road Traffic Act 1988. MIB does not have to pay for any other liability under the Agreement. For these purposes, the material sections of the Road Traffic Act 1988 are s 143(1) and s 145, which, as amended, now read:

'143 Users of motor vehicles to be insured or secured against third-party risks
(1)   Subject to the provisions of this Part of this Act–
   (c)   a person must not use a motor vehicle on a road [or other public place] unless there is in force in relation to the use of the vehicle by that person such a policy of insurance or such a security in respect of third party risks as complies with the requirements of this Part of this Act, and
   (d)   a person must not cause or permit any other person to use a motor vehicle on a road [or other public place] unless there is in force in relation to the use of the vehicle by that other person such a policy of insurance or such a security in respect of third party risks as complies with the requirements of this Part of this Act.

...

145 Requirements in respect of policies of insurance
(1)   In order to comply with the requirements of this Part of this Act, a policy of insurance must satisfy the following conditions.
(2)   The policy must be issued by an authorised insurer.
(3)   Subject to section (4) below, the policy–

...

(d) must insure such person, persons or classes of persons as may be specified in the policy in respect of any liability which may be incurred by him or them in respect of the death of or bodily injury to any person or damage to property caused by, or arising out of, the use of the vehicle on a road [or other public place] in Great Britain, and

[(aa) must, in the case of a vehicle normally based in the territory of another member State, insure him or them in respect of any civil liability which may be incurred by him or them as a result of an event related to the use of the vehicle in Great Britain, if–

   (iii) according to the law of that territory, he or they would be required to be insured in respect of a civil liability which would arise under that law as a result of that event if the place where the vehicle was used when the event occurred were in that territory, and

   (iv) the cover required by that law would be higher than that required by paragraph (a) above, and

(e) must [in the case of a vehicle normally based in Great Britain,] insure him or them in respect of any liability which may be incurred by him or them in respect of the use of the vehicle and of any trailer, whether or not coupled, in the territory other than Great Britain and Gibraltar of each of the member States of the Communities according to–

   (i) the law on compulsory insurance against civil liability in respect of the use of vehicles of the State in whose territory the event giving rise to the liability occurred; or

   (ii) if it would give higher cover, the law which would be applicable under this part of this Act if the place where the vehicle was used when that event occurred were in Great Britain; and

(f) must also insure him or them in respect of any liability which may be incurred by him or them under the provisions of this Part of this Act relating to payment for emergency treatment.

(4) The policy shall not, by virtue of subsection (3)(a) above, be required–

(a) to cover liability in respect of the death, arising out of and in the course of his employment, of a person in the employment of a person insured by the policy or of bodily injury sustained by such a person arising out of and in the course of his employment, or

(b) to provide insurance of more than £250,000 in respect of all such liabilities as may be incurred in respect of damage to property caused by, or arising out of, any one accident involving the vehicle, or

(c) to cover liability in respect of damage to the vehicle, or

(d) to cover liability in respect of damage to goods carried for hire or reward in or on the vehicle or in or on any trailer (whether or not coupled) drawn by the vehicle, or

(e) to cover any liability of any person in respect of damage to property in his custody or under his control, or

(f) to cover any contractual liability.

(4A) In the case of a person–

...

(bb) carried in or upon a vehicle, or

(cc) entering or getting on to, or alighting from, a vehicle, the provisions of paragraph (a) of subsection (4) above do not apply unless cover in respect of the liability referred to in that paragraph is in fact provided pursuant to a requirement of the Employers' Liability (Compulsory Insurance) Act 1969.]'

It will be seen from these statutory provisions that under the 1988 Act the obligation to insure against third party risks applies in almost all cases where a motor vehicle is used on a road or other public place.

'Motor vehicle' is defined at s 185(1) of the 1988 Act as '... a mechanically propelled vehicle intended or adapted for use on roads'. For something to fall within the definition requires a reasonable person, looking at the vehicle, to take the view that one of its uses would include general use on the road. The courts have been asked to consider the issue on several occasions: see *Daley v Hargreaves* [1961] 1 All ER 552, [1961] 1 WLR 487 (dumper trucks not fitted with windscreens, lamps, reflectors, horns, wings, number plates etc not within the definition); *Burns v Currell* [1963] 2 QB 433, [1963] 2 All ER 297 (mechanical go-kart not within the definition); *Chief Constable of Avon and Somerset v Fleming* [1987] 1 All ER 318 (motorcycle adapted for scrambling not within the definition); *Chief Constable of North Yorkshire Police v Saddington* [2001] RTR 227, [2000] All ER (D) 1530 (petrol-driven motor scooter was within the definition because it was difficult to see on what terrain it might be used other than a road); *Winter v DPP* [2002] All ER (D) 143 (Jul) (electrically powered 'City Bug' within the definition).

'Use' has been interpreted broadly. In *Hardy v Motor Insurers' Bureau* (at para [3.53] below), the court held that the requirement for compulsory insurance (and hence MIB's liability to pay) covered the intentional criminal use of a car as a weapon. See also *Gardner v Moore* (at para [3.54] below). In *Dunthorne v Bentley* [1996] RTR 428, [1996] PIQR P323, CA, a woman's car broke down when it ran out of petrol. Seeing a friend who had stopped on the other side of the road she ran across but was struck by an oncoming vehicle, causing injury to the driver, who claimed damages against her. Her insurers were found liable to pay the driver because the accident arose out of her 'use' of the vehicle. See also *Slater v Buckinghamshire County Council* [2004] EWCA Civ 1478, [2004] All ER (D) 164 (Nov) where it was held a passenger in a vehicle who was employed by the defendant was not using the vehicle when assisting the claimant to cross a road to enter the vehicle.

Section 192 of the Road Traffic Act 1988 defines 'road' as '... any highway and any other road to which the public has access'. This definition includes public bridleways and footpaths. The words 'or other public place' were added in ss 143, 145 and 146 by the Motor Vehicles (Compulsory Insurance) Regulations 2000, with effect from 3 April 2000, as a result of the House of Lords decision in *Clarke v Kato; Cutter v Eagle Star Insurance Co* [1998] 4 All ER 417, [1998] All ER (D) 481, [1998] 1 WLR 1647 (see commentary notes to the 1972 or 1988 Agreement).

There are however some important exceptions to the requirement to insure. By s 144 of the 1988 Act provision is made for the vehicle owner to deposit £500,000 with the Accountant General of the Supreme Court as an alternative to insurance. The section also exempts certain public service vehicles from the need for third party insurance.

The exemption under s 145(4)(a) in relation to cover for an employer's liability for death or injury to one of his employees suffered in a motor accident in the course of the latter's employment, exists because that liability should be the subject of compulsory employer's liability insurance. Such cover does not always exist, however, and, until 1992, the unfortunate injured employee whose employer was not insured had no recourse against MIB either. This caused obvious injustice and, from 1 January 1993, by virtue of amendment in the form of s 145(4A) of the Act, the exception only applies where the employer's liability cover actually exists.

Following amendment to the Road Traffic Act 1972 and on the passing of the Road Traffic Act 1988, it became compulsory to insure against liability for property damage. Thus under the 1999 Agreement MIB is liable to compensate for such loss also, up to a maximum figure of £250,000 – see clause 16. This figure has not been increased above that provided for in the 1988 Agreement. The reason for this is presumably that the figure remains at £250,000 in s 145(4)(b) of the 1988 Act.

In *Cooper v Motor Insurers' Bureau* (at para [3.44] below), the Court of Appeal held that the third party risks that had to be insured under the predecessor of s 143(1) of the 1988 Act did not include injury to the driver of the vehicle at the relevant time, so that where an uninsured owner of a vehicle had asked another person to drive it for him and that other person was injured because of a brake defect in the vehicle of which he was unaware as a result of the owner's negligence, that liability was not a 'relevant liability' and MIB were not responsible to pay the unsatisfied judgment.

Since 1972 it has been compulsory to insure liability for all passengers. The old MIB cases dealing with the issue of use of the vehicle for hire or reward are therefore no longer relevant in the context of a passenger's claim.

Clause 3: Claimants not of full age or capacity

[3.21]   This clause is designed to enable MIB to avoid the problems of formality that can arise where a claimant lacks full capacity. Conceivably, it could be relied upon to avoid the need for court approval where settlement sums are paid before proceedings have been issued, although MIB have stated that they would always prefer that settlements be approved. More importantly, it allows MIB to rely on the representations of the claimant's representative especially where that representative is an accident management company or adjuster. See also Note 2.3 of the Notes for Guidance, which confirms that this clause does not have the effect in terms of limitation that some feared it might.

Clause 5: Satisfaction of claims by MIB

[3.22]   (*See* Note 2 to the Agreement.)

Technically, the liability of MIB under the Agreement is to the Secretary of State. As there is no privity of contract between a claimant and MIB, the claimant has, at law, no cause of action, but in practice MIB submits to being sued without taking the point and the court turns a blind eye to this legal anomaly.

Clause 6: Exceptions

[3.23]

6(1)(C): ASSIGNMENT AND SUBROGATION

Generally speaking, MIB will not be liable to pay any claim other than one brought by the person injured for his own benefit, except where the claim is of the type described in Note 3.4 to the Agreement. In *Lund v Coran and Motor Insurers' Bureau* (12 June 2002, unreported), MIB tried to argue that success fees recoverable under a conditional fee agreement should not be recoverable by the claimant as they were for the benefit of someone else, ie his lawyers. This argument was described as 'just tenable' by the judge, although the case was disposed of on another point.

6(1)(E): 'ALLOWING HIMSELF TO BE CARRIED' AND 'KNEW OR OUGHT TO HAVE KNOWN'

These words first appeared in the 1988 Agreement and were intended to give effect to the terms of the Second Council Directive 84/5/EEC of 30 December 1983 on the approximation of the laws of the Member States relating to insurance against civil liability in respect of the use of motor vehicles. This Directive includes the following provision at Art 1(4):

'4. Each Member State shall set up or authorize a body with the task of providing compensation, at least up to the limits of the insurance obligation for damage to property or personal injuries caused by an unidentified vehicle or a vehicle for which the insurance obligation provided for in paragraph 1 has not been satisfied.

This provision shall be without prejudice to the right of the Member States to regard compensation by that body as subsidiary or non-subsidiary and the right to make provision for the settlement of claims between that body and the person or persons responsible for the accident and other insurers or social security bodies required to compensate the victim in respect of the same accident.

The victim may in any case apply directly to the body which, on the basis of information provided at its request by the victim, shall be obliged to give him a reasoned reply regarding the payment of any compensation.

However, Member States may exclude the payment of compensation by that body in respect of persons who voluntarily entered the vehicle which caused the damage or injury when the body can prove that they knew it was uninsured.

Member States may limit or exclude the payment of compensation by that body in the event of damage to property by an unidentified vehicle.

They may also authorize, in the case of damage to property caused by an uninsured vehicle an excess of not more than 500 ECU for which the victim may be responsible.

Furthermore, each Member State shall apply its laws, regulations and administrative provisions to the payment of compensation by this body, without prejudice to any other practice which is more favourable to the victim.'

The exception in this Article relating to knowledge refers to those passengers who 'voluntarily entered the vehicle'. The words 'voluntarily allowing himself to be carried' in clause 6(1)(e) of the Agreement mirror the words of the Directive. Where the passenger was very drunk when he entered the vehicle, an issue may arise as to whether he was allowing himself to be carried. However, clause 6(4) may be used by MIB to severely limit the scope for an argument based on intoxication. Note that the exceptions under clause 6(1)(e)(iii) and (iv) are new under the 1999 Agreement. Whether or not a passenger had 'voluntarily allowed himself to be carried' was considered in the case of *Pickett v Roberts* (at para [3.50] below). In that case the claimant sought to argue that she had done enough to withdraw her consent to the 'use which gave rise to the liability'. The Court of Appeal disagreed (Pill LJ dissenting) stating that a person who had voluntarily entered a vehicle could not withdraw her consent except by an unequivocal repudiation of the common venture to which she consented when she entered the vehicle. An unequivocal request to alight from the vehicle was enough but an objection to way the vehicle was being driven was not.

Article 1(4) provides for an exception where the passenger 'knew' there was no insurance. There are no words in the Directive equivalent to the 'or ought to have known' that appear in the Agreement. On its face, the Agreement therefore provides for a much wider exception. A challenge was made to the similar terms of clause 6 of the 1988 Agreement in *White v White* (at para [3.48] below). There, the injured passenger was found by the judge at first instance to have been careless in failing to appreciate the true insurance position. He did not have actual knowledge but, as the judge found, he 'ought to have known'. However, the judge also found that the passenger could rely on the terms of the Directive against MIB, the latter being, according to the judge, an emanation of the state. Because the exclusion in the Directive covered only 'actual' knowledge, the passenger succeeded. On appeal by MIB, the Court of Appeal reversed the judge's decision and applied the wording of clause 6(1)(e) strictly, on the basis that, although there was obvious inconsistency between the words in the Directive and the Agreement, the terms of the Directive were not capable of direct enforcement.

On further appeal by the passenger, the House of Lords held that the Agreement had to be interpreted in accordance with the Directive. The knowledge contemplated by the Directive could not include a state of mind that, as a result of mere carelessness or negligence, fell short of actual knowledge. Therefore, it was held, the words 'or ought to have known' in the Agreement could not include that state of mind either. The passenger's claim against MIB succeeded. However, the House also stated that knowledge within the terms of the Directive could include the knowledge that an honest passenger would be expected to have. So, where the passenger deliberately refrains from asking obvious questions in order to avoid obtain confirmation of the true facts, he may be found to have possessed a state of mind tantamount to actual knowledge.

Because it was a case involving a narrow finding of fact as to the state of the passenger's knowledge, the decision in *White* does not set the boundary between the type of knowledge that will be within clause 6(1)(e) and the type that will be without it. As Lord Nicholls of Birkenhead commented, that question would have to be pursued in a case where the facts made it necessary to obtain guidance from the Court of Justice on the precise scope of the exemption permitted by the Directive. Following *White v White* in the case of *Akers v Motor Insurers' Bureau* [2003] EWCA Civ 18, [2003] All ER (D) 16 (Jan), [2003] Lloyd's Rep IR 427 the Court of Appeal confirmed in dismissing the claimant's claim that on the basis of the evidence heard by the lower court the claimant either knew there was no insurance, knew there was a problem with the insurance and ought to have known there was none or deliberately avoided enquiring further about insurance. In that case the evidence was that the claimant was present within a group where the subject of insurance was discussed.

In *S (a child) v Goldstraw* (at para [3.51] below), the claim of an infant dependant under the Fatal Accidents Act 1976 was dismissed on the basis that the Uninsured Drivers Agreement 1999 had to be construed with regard to its context and to the Second Council Directive 85/5. Therefore clause 6(1)(e) had to be construed to include the dependants of a deceased who knew that there was no insurance. However, the case of *Louise Phillips (as representative of the estate of Neville Phillips, deceased) v Mohammed Rafiq and Motor Insurers' Bureau* (at para [3.52] below) concluded that clause 6(1)(e) did not apply to a claim brought by a dependant where the deceased passenger did have knowledge that the driver was uninsured. This point will have to be determined in the higher courts:

'or after such commencement if he could reasonably be expected to have alighted from [the vehicle]'.

This exception affords MIB what is sometimes called the 'petrol station' defence. In other words, if the injured passenger found out during the journey that the vehicle had been stolen and/or that the driver was uninsured, MIB could avoid liability if, at any time thereafter, the passenger failed to take any reasonable opportunity to get out of the vehicle.

CLAUSE 6(2): EXTENT OF THE CLAUSE 6(1)(E) EXCEPTIONS
The exceptions only apply where the passenger has sued the driver or owner of the vehicle in which he was travelling. It has no application, for example, where the passenger is injured through the fault of the driver of an entirely different vehicle and obtains judgment against that other driver.

CLAUSE 6(3): BURDEN OF PROOF
The burden of proving knowledge rests on MIB. However, under this clause, MIB can rely on proof of certain subsidiary matters to establish the passenger's knowledge that the driver was uninsured. Reliance by MIB on the matters particularly under clause 6(3)(a) and (d) may re-open the difficult issues in *White v White* concerning the definition of knowledge in Directive 84/5/EEC. Take the following hardly unforeseeable example: the injured passenger, who knows that his young friend the driver has no vehicle of his own, is told by the driver that the vehicle in which they are travelling belongs to the driver's mother. Unless the passenger can produce 'evidence to the contrary', which, in

the example, is likely to be limited to his word on oath, he may well be fixed with knowledge that the driver was not insured by virtue of clause 6(3)(d). The passenger would doubtless argue in this example that his state of knowledge fell short of that required by the Directive.

CLAUSE 6(4): DRINK AND DRUGS

Once again, this entirely new clause may give rise to arguments as to the degree of knowledge required by Directive 84/5/EEC.

Clause 7: Form of application

[3.24]   See paragraph 5.2 of the Notes for Guidance attached to the Agreement. The form can also be downloaded from website: www.mib.org.uk.

Clause 9: Notice of relevant proceedings

[3.25]   (*See* Note 5.1 of the Notes for Guidance for the extension granted in the case of a litigant in person and Note 5.3 for MIB's concession as to the method of service.)

Apart from these concessions, it should be observed that the notice conditions are strict conditions precedent to MIB's liability. Any failure to comply is likely to preclude enforcement against MIB of an unsatisfied judgment obtained against a tortfeasor. Decisions under the earlier Agreements, which both provided for shorter seven-day notice periods, illustrate this point: in *Silverton v Goodall and Motor Insurers' Bureau* (at para [3.40] below), the claimant's solicitor sent particulars of claim to the court by post together with a request for issue of a summons. The court issued the proceedings on 13 October, but the claimant's solicitor did not receive the sealed documents back from the court until 22 October. Copies were sent to MIB who received them on 29 October. The Court of Appeal held that time started to run for the purposes of the seven day notice requirement under the 1988 Agreement at the date of issue, ie, 13 October and that notice was therefore given late. MIB had no liability.

Under the 1999 Agreement, there can be no question of valid notice being given before proceedings are issued. Clause 9 does not allow for this. However, insofar as any of the required materials under clause 9(2)(a) to (g) have already been provided under clause 7, they need not be sent to MIB again.

If notice has not been effectively given (and MIB is taking the point) but time remains within the primary limitation period, the claimant's best course is to abandon the original proceedings, re-issue and re-serve. This may be possible even after judgment has been obtained. In *O'Neill v O'Brien and Motor Insurers' Bureau* (at para [3.35] below), MIB took the view that it had not been kept properly informed of the proceedings and was not liable to satisfy a judgment obtained in default against the uninsured first defendant. The claimant applied to set aside the judgment so that it could commence a fresh action. MIB opposed the application. The Court of Appeal upheld the judge's decision to set the judgment aside on the basis that it was in the interests of justice to do so. The case of *Horton v Sadler* (at para [3.38] below) has now made it possible for claimants who have fallen foul of the notice requirements and where the primary limitation period has expired to issue fresh proceedings relying on the court to exercise discretion under s 33 of the Limitation Act 1980. The decision overrules the previously binding authority of *Walkley v Precision Forgings Ltd* [1979] 2 All ER 548, [1979] 1 WLR 606.

Of course, MIB may not always take notice points if the claimant's response will simply be to re-issue. However, claimants' solicitors need to be aware that MIB is as astute as any other litigant to take tactical points that they think may be available to them. In *Begum v Ullah* (at para [3.42] below), the claimant's solicitor was aware that she had failed to comply with the seven day notice requirement and rang MIB to ask if they might waive it to avoid the need to re-issue. That was said to have been agreed and the claim proceeded. After the expiry of the limitation period, MIB asserted that no proper notice was given. The question of notice was decided as a preliminary issue and the judge held that an MIB employee had agreed to accept notice over the telephone and that MIB was estopped from raising the point.

Clause 12: Notice of intention to apply for judgment

[3.26]   These are new requirements and the same general principles as apply to notice of issue will apply here. Note that all notice requirements apply even where MIB is joined as a defendant at the outset of the action. For a successful challenge to an unreasonable and unnecessary demand for information by MIB, see *Dray v Doherty* [1999] CLY 525. In that case, the court refused MIB a declaration that it was not liable because the claimant did not comply precisely with its requests for information. A claimant's remedy where an unreasonable request is made is by way of reference to the Secretary of State under clause 19.

Clause 13: Section 154 of the 1988 Act

[3.27]   This section reads:

'154.—(1) A person against whom a claim is made in respect of any such liability as is required to be covered by a policy of insurance under section 145 of this Act must, on demand by or on behalf of the person making the claim—
  (a) state whether or not, in respect of that liability—
       (i) he was insured by a policy having effect for the purposes of this Part of this Act or had in force a security having effect for those purposes, or
       (ii) he would have been so insured or would have had in force such a security if the insurer or, as the case may be, the giver of the security had not avoided or cancelled the policy or security, and
  (b) if he was or would have been so insured, or had or would have had in force such a security—
       (i) give such particulars with respect to that policy or security as were specified in any certificate of insurance or security delivered in respect of that policy or security, as the case may be, under section 147 of this Act, or
       (ii) where no such certificate was delivered under that section,

> give the following particulars, that is to say, registration mark or other identifying particulars of the vehicle concerned, the number or other identifying particulars of the insurance policy issued in respect of the vehicle, the name of the insurer and the period of the insurance cover.
>
> (2)   If without reasonable excuse, a person fails to comply with the provisions of subsection (1) above, or wilfully makes a false statement in reply to any such demand as is referred to in that subsection, he is guilty of an offence.'

(*See* Note 4.1 of the Notes for Guidance.)

Clause 14: Prosecution of proceedings

[3.28]

14(1)(A): ANOTHER TORTFEASOR LIABLE

Where some degree of blame might conceivably attach to another driver who is insured, or to another potential defendant who can pay, then a claimant can be required under clause 14(a) to join that other person as a defendant and pursue the claim against him as well as against the uninsured driver.

Should it be established that another, insured driver is jointly responsible for the claimant's injuries, MIB will avoid payment. This is because that other driver's insurers will be bound by MIB's Articles of Association and will be compelled by the terms of that agreement to satisfy the claim in full. MIB can enforce this obligation, hence the need for litigation rarely arises.

If the other tortfeasor is not a driver but is some other person of means (eg, a highway authority or the MOD) then it will again be in MIB's interests to ensure that judgment is obtained against that person. MIB is a fund of last resort: its liability to pay extends only to unsatisfied judgments.

MIB is sometimes said to be relying on the 'one percent rule' where it seeks to establish blame against someone else. That other person need only be found 1% to blame for the accident in order for MIB to avoid liability under the Agreement altogether.

Nor can another defendant who is not a driver circumvent the position by attempting to enforce against MIB any judgment for contribution made against the uninsured driver in the proceedings. The liability to make contribution to a fellow tortfeasor arises under the Civil Liability (Contribution) Act 1978. Such a liability is not a 'relevant liability' for MIB purposes, ie it was not one that was required to be covered by insurance by s 143 etc of the Road Traffic Act 1972 (s 143 etc, Road Traffic Act 1988). See *Campbell v McFarland and Armagh UDC* [1972] NI 31 (para [2.222] of the handbook) for an analogous decision under what has since become s 152 of the Road Traffic Act 1988. See also *Bell v Donnelly and MoD* (13 January 1998, unreported).

An illustration of MIB requiring a claimant to pursue another tortfeasor can be found in *Norman v Ali and Motor Insurers' Board* (at para [3.37] below). There the claimant had the option of suing the owner of the vehicle for causing or permitting the tortfeasor driver to use the vehicle on the road. MIB required her to do so but she failed to issue proceedings against him until after the expiry of the three-year limitation period, with the result that the claim failed. It was found that in missing the primary limitation period she had also failed to take 'all reasonable steps to obtain judgment against all the persons liable in respect of the injury'. MIB were not liable.

14(1)(B): JOINDER OF MIB

Technically, MIB cannot be brought into an action at the outset because it has, at most, a contingent liability. However, under previous Agreements it was well established (see, e g *Gurtner v Circuit* at para [3.31] below) that MIB could apply to be joined where necessary to protect its position. Now, pursuant to Note 5.3 of the Notes for Guidance, MIB accepts that it should normally be included as second defendant at the outset in order to save costs and time.

In cases where MIB has not been made second defendant at the outset but where both the claimant and MIB agree to joinder, it is likely that the court will simply approve a consent order to this effect. However, the power to add parties remains a discretionary one and it may not be exercised in MIB's favour in every case. See also *Baker v Francis* (at para [3.36] below), where joinder was permitted but on certain conditions.

Clause 20: Recoveries by insurers acting for MIB/insurer concerned/ Article 75 insurer

[3.29]   The words used here are almost identical to those in the Agreements of 1972 and 1988. See the comments thereunder. The words 'insurer concerned' refer to the domestic regulations/Article 75 insurer under MIB's Memorandum and Articles of Association which set out the obligations of member insurers to MIB, as to which, see further below at para [3.61].

Clause 22: Agents

[3.30]   The practice of MIB hitherto has frequently been to appoint an insurance office, the 'investigating member', to make inquiries and, where appropriate, negotiate settlement. (This function did not mean that the office in question was a 'domestic regulations/Article 75 insurer'.) However, for reasons of efficiency and economy MIB is currently moving all claims 'in-house' and the involvement of member insurers as claims handlers has ceased in respect of new cases from 1 January 2003.

Note—The rules relating to substituted service are now set out in CPR 6.8 – Service by an alternative method.

3.   CASE SUMMARIES

(A)   SERVICE OF PROCEEDINGS, JOINDER AND LIMITATION

[3.31]   Gurtner v Circuit
[1968] 2 QB 587, [1968] 1 All ER 328, [1968] 2 WLR 668, 112 Sol Jo 73, [1968] 1 Lloyd's Rep 171, CA

The plaintiff's solicitors issued a writ against the defendant but were unable to serve it personally because he had gone to Canada and could not be traced.

Although it appeared from the policy report that the defendant had produced a valid insurance certificate after the accident the insurers could not be identified. The plaintiff's solicitors applied to MIB who instructed the Royal Insurance Company to investigate. The solicitors obtained an order for substituted service of the writ on the defendant by sending it to the Royal Insurance Company by ordinary prepaid post.

HELD, ON APPEAL: It was obviously wrong to order service on the defendant at the address of the Royal Insurance Company, since the affidavit did not show that the writ was likely to reach the defendant or come to his notice. The order could be set aside if it would serve any useful purpose. If there was any possibility of tracing the defendant in Canada, substituted service should be ordered by advertisement but that seemed useless in the present case and the order should be allowed to stand. Where it is not possible to ascertain the insurers an order might be made for service at the address of the Bureau but such an order should not be made except on evidence that all reasonable efforts have been made by the plaintiff to trace the defendant and effect personal service.

[3.32]   Clarke v Vedel
[1979] RTR 26, CA

The plaintiffs were injured in a collision with a motorcycle. The motorcyclist gave his name as David Vedel. He disappeared after the accident and could not be traced. The address he gave turned out to be false; he produced no insurance or other documents to the police. The motorcycle, bearing false number plates, had been stolen from its lawful owner some months earlier. The records of the Registrar of Births and Deaths showed no entry for any person named David Vedel at the time of the date of birth he gave. The plaintiffs issued a writ against 'David Vedel' and obtained an order for substituted service at the address of MIB.

HELD: The order should be set aside. *Gurtner v Circuit* (see para [3.31] above) was not an authority for saying that it is proper in every case where the Bureau may be involved to make an order for substituted service on the defendant at the address of the Bureau. The order could not possibly bring the proceedings to the notice of whoever was the motorcyclist. It was an Untraced Drivers Agreement case and should be dealt with under that Agreement.

Per Stevenson LJ: This court recognises that there may be cases where a defendant who cannot be traced and, therefore, is unlikely to be reached by any form of substituted service, can nevertheless be ordered to be served at the address of the insurers or the Bureau in a road accident case. But ... I am not satisfied that it applies to this case.

[3.33]   Mather v Adesuyi and Motor Insurers' Bureau
[1995] PIQR P454

In September 1990 the plaintiff was injured when his motorcycle was struck by a car driven by the defendant. The defendant gave his address to the police but within a year of the accident it became apparent to the plaintiff's solicitors that the defendant had moved from that address and they were unable to obtain any forwarding address. The plaintiff's solicitors then contacted MIB and insurers were nominated to handle the plaintiff's claim on their behalf.

One day before the expiry of the primary limitation period the plaintiff's solicitors sent to the nominated insurers copies of a county court summons, particulars of claim and special damage schedule, indicating that they had asked the court to effect service on the defendant at his original address. MIB in due course were joined to the proceedings and applied to dismiss the action on the grounds that the proceedings had not been properly served on the defendant.

HELD: (1) The proceedings had not been properly served on the defendant – *Willowgreen Ltd v Smithers* [1994] 2 All ER 533, [1994] 1 WLR 832 applied.

   (2)   The court would not exercise its discretion to extend the validity of the summons so as to allow for good service to be effected thereafter by way of substituted service.

Note—The rules relating to service of a claim form are now governed by CPR 7.5 and 7.6.

[3.34]   Daines v King & Chasbikes Ltd and Motor Insurers' Bureau
(13 November 1995, unreported), CA

D appealed against a judgment dismissing his appeal from a decision which ordered that MIB have leave to file a notice of intention to defend on behalf of K and that service on K of the writ and all subsequent proceedings be set aside. The proceedings arose out of a traffic accident in which K, driving a motor car, collided with D on his motorcycle. The writ was issued on the last day of the limitation period and served by first class post. Its deemed service was four days out to time. D's solicitors wrote to MIB stating that the writ was served on the date it was posted, which was misleading. D obtained judgment in default. D argued that the application to set aside the judgment was not made timeously according to the RSC Ord 12, r 8 and the judge should not have exercised his discretion to allow it as it had prejudiced D.

HELD: Dismissing the appeal on the grounds that:
   (1)   the position of MIB was different from that of K because MIB did not know that the service was bad. MIB applied to set aside the writ as soon as it knew of the irregularity; and
   (2)   D was not seriously prejudiced because he was in the same position as when the writ had been served. The limitation period had expired and there were no grounds for extending the validity of the writ.

[3.35]   O'Neill v O'Brien
(1997) Times, 21 March, [1997] PIQR P223

The plaintiff sustained personal injuries in a road traffic accident which was caused by the defendant's negligence. The defendant was uninsured at the time of the accident and the plaintiff commenced proceedings against the defendant and then entered judgment in default of defence pursuant to Ord 9, r 6 of CCR 1981. Damages were then assessed at £10,007. The plaintiff's solicitors sought to obtain payment from MIB but it refused payment on the grounds that it had not been informed of the date when damages were to be assessed as required under the 1988 Agreement. The plaintiff's solicitors then applied to have the judgment in default set aside. The plaintiff's application was granted by a district judge and upheld by a circuit judge and MIB then appealed to the Court of Appeal on the basis that there were no proper grounds for setting aside the judgment.

HELD: CCR Ord 37, r 4 was deliberately drawn in wide terms so as to allow a plaintiff or a court to set aside a judgment if it was appropriate to do so. It was in the interests of justice that the judgment should be set aside so that a needless dispute of a technical nature could be avoided.

[3.36]   **Baker v Francis**

[1997] PIQR P155

The plaintiff was injured in a road traffic accident when the car in which he was travelling as a passenger collided with a bus shelter. Neither the driver nor the owner of the vehicle was insured. The plaintiff's solicitors notified MIB of the potential claim and then commenced proceedings against the defendants. The insurers nominated to act on behalf of MIB twice requested an extension of time for service of their defence as they attempted to trace the defendants. The extension was terminated 18 months after the proceedings had been started and judgment was entered in default. MIB applied to be joined to the proceedings and also for an order that the claim had been automatically struck out under CCR Ord 9, r 10.

HELD: MIB had a right to be joined to the proceedings so that it could deal with issues relating to quantum but the default judgments should stand. It would be unjust for the court's discretion in relation to joinder to be exercised in favour of MIB so as to permit MIB to strike out the plaintiff's claim in circumstances where the delay had been contributed to by MIB's agent.

Note—There is no equivalent provision to CCR Ord 9, r 10 (automatic strike out) in the CPR.

[3.37]   **Norman v Ali and Motor Insurers' Bureau**

[1999] All ER (D) 1416, [2000] RTR 107

The claimant was injured in a road accident caused by the negligent driving of the uninsured first defendant. The claimant commenced proceedings against the first defendant. One month prior to the expiry of the primary three-year limitation period MIB asked the claimant to bring the owner of the vehicle into the proceedings pursuant to clause 5(1)(d) of the 1988 Agreement. The claimant's solicitors failed to join the second defendant correctly and thus commenced separate proceedings against the owner of the vehicle some five years after the material accident. The claimant in the second action sought to argue that a vehicle owner who permitted uninsured use of a vehicle did not cause personal injury but had created a situation in which the injured person was unable to claim damages.

HELD: The damages claimed by the claimant in the second action were 'in respect of' personal injury and were therefore statute barred. Further, MIB was not obliged to compensate the claimant under the terms of the 1988 Agreement as she had failed to comply with the condition precedent in clause 5(1)(d).

[3.38]   **Horton v Sadler**

[2006] UKHL 27

[2006] 3 All ER 1177, [2006] All ER (D) 130 (Jun), [2006] 2 WLR 1346

The claimant was injured in a road traffic accident for which the defendant was wholly responsible. As the defendant was not insured MIB became involved, making an interim payment. The claimant then issued proceedings two days before the expiry of the limitation period but failed to give the MIB appropriate notice. Once joined to the action MIB filed a defence which denied liability due to the failure to give notice of the proceedings, and which counter-claimed for the return of the interim payment. The claimant responded by issuing fresh proceedings but this time giving correct notice to MIB. The Bureau defended this second set of proceedings on the basis that it was statute barred, to which the claimant replied by seeking to disapply the limitation period via s 33 of the Limitation Act 1980. The initial claim and the claimant's appeal were dismissed because the courts were bound by the authority of the House of Lords' decision in *Walkley v Precision Forgings Ltd* [1979] 2 All ER 548, [1979] 1 WLR 606 which prevented discretion from being exercised under s 33 in such circumstances.

HELD, allowing the appeal: (1) the question for the court under s 33 was whether it was equitable or inequitable between the parties to override the time bar. *Walkley*, which had held that a claimant who had commenced proceedings in time could not be prejudiced by s 11 of the 1980 Act and that it was only in exceptional circumstances that the time bar could be disapplied, was overruled. In essence, the House of Lords decided that there should be no distinction between those who commence proceedings within or outside of the limitation period and that s 33 confers a broad discretion on the court to disapply the time bar.

(2) Whilst former decisions of the House of Lords were normally binding, following precedent too closely could cause injustice in individual cases and prevent the development of the law.

(B) PROPER NOTICE

[3.39] **Torres and Papadimos v White Rose Motor Policies Ltd**
(12 October 1994, unreported), Central London County
Court   HHJ Butter QC

Section 151(1) of the Road Traffic Act 1972 provides as follows: 'No sum is payable by an insurer under s 151 of this Act in respect of any judgment unless before or within seven days after the commencement of the proceedings in which the judgment was given the insurer had notice of the bringing of the proceedings'.

At the time when the proceedings were issued the plaintiff believed the defendant to be uninsured. In fact it subsequently transpired that the defendant was insured, his insurers being White Rose Motor Policies Ltd. The plaintiff issued proceedings against the defendant and gave notice to MIB.

HELD: It was not sufficient for a plaintiff simply to give notice to MIB; there was only a liability on an insurer (as opposed to MIB) where that insurer had been validly notified within the terms of s 151.

Note—MIB can accept notice where proper inquiries have failed to trace an insurer. In this case there was no evidence before the court as to what, if any enquiries, had been made by the plaintiff's insurers to establish whether or not the defendant was insured.

[3.40] **Silverton v Goodall and Motor Insurers' Bureau**
[1997] PIQR P451, CA

The plaintiff claimed damages for personal injuries arising out of a road traffic accident that occurred on 26 August 1992. The plaintiff claimed against the first defendant who was uninsured. On 9 October 1992 the plaintiff's solicitors gave MIB notice of intention to commence proceedings. The relevant forms were completed.

On 26 September 1994 the plaintiff's solicitors sent a request for the summons, particulars of claim and medical reports to the county court by post. The court sealed the documents and marked them as issued on Thursday 13 October 1994.

The plaintiff's solicitors stated that they received the summons from the court on 22 October 1994 and sent the documents to MIB on 28 October 1994 and they would have been received by MIB the following day.

The MIB contended that the proceedings had been issued without correct notice being given to them under clause 5(1)(a) of the 1988 Agreement which states that MIB shall not incur liability unless 'notice in writing of the bringing of the proceedings is given within seven days of the commencement of the proceedings'.

The plaintiff argued that the seven-day notice period should commence from the date that the plaintiff's solicitors received the summons from the court office, ie, 22 October 1994. The plaintiff also argued that MIB had waived its rights or was estopped from relying on clause 5 on the basis that it had subsequently been joined as a second defendant and continued with the proceedings.

HELD: The judge concluded that MIB was not liable to satisfy any judgment. The plaintiff appealed.

HELD, ON APPEAL: The appeal was dismissed. The action was commenced 13 October 1994 when the court prepared, issued and sealed the summons for service. The words 'the commencement of the proceedings' in clause 5(1)(a) had their ordinary meaning. MIB was relying on a condition precedent and a party claiming the benefit of a condition precedent is not required to prove any loss or disadvantage as a result of the failure to comply with it.

There was no waiver by MIB and no estoppel could be raised against MIB. The MIB was entitled to maintain and plead the point of failure to give due notice and at the same time to intervene in the action to protect their position if they were wrong on that point.

[3.41]   Cambridge v Callaghan and MIB

(1997) Times, 21 March, CA

The plaintiff was injured in a motor accident caused by the first defendant's negligence. The first defendant was uninsured. The plaintiff's solicitor notified MIB by letter that proceedings had been brought and enclosed a notice of issue of a default summons. MIB disputed that the notice complied with the terms of clause 5 of the 1988 Agreement.

HELD, ON APPEAL: It was a condition precedent of clause 5 that the notice of issue was to be accompanied by a copy of the writ, summons or other document initiating proceedings. When proceedings are commenced in the High Court a copy of the writ stamped by the court officer should be sent to MIB. In the county court, where the plaintiff or his solicitors did not have a stamped copy of the summons, a copy of the notice of issue of default summons was sufficient. Thus on the facts of this case the notice of issue did comply with the terms of clause 5.

[3.42]   Begum v Ullah

[1998] CLY 590

The plaintiff was knocked down by an uninsured driver and suffered serious injuries. The plaintiff's solicitors commenced proceedings and sent the particulars of claim to the court with a request that the summons be issued and served on MIB who had already confirmed that it would accept service. The court failed to give the plaintiff notice of issue until eight days after the summons had been issued. The plaintiff's solicitors said they had telephoned MIB and spoke to an employee who agreed to waive the requirement of notice within seven days of issue. The plaintiff's solicitors then sent notice in writing together with a copy of the summons and these were received by MIB nine days after issue. MIB then rejected the plaintiff's claim on the basis that proper notice had not been given.

HELD: MIB had waived its right to rely on the seven-day limit, it being held that an employee had indeed accepted notice on the phone. MIB was estopped from relying on clause 5(1)(a) of the 1988 Agreement by the oral representation made by its employee – a representation which the plaintiff's solicitors had relied upon to their detriment.

(C) PASSENGER CLAIMS

[3.43] Porter v Addo; Porter v Motor Insurers' Bureau
[1978] RTR 503, [1978] 2 Lloyd's Rep 463, 122 Sol Jo 418   Forbes J

Mrs Porter bought a car in Holland and brought it to England. She was told by Customs she must not drive the car because it was not insured. She told Mr Addo, a television engineer who she knew used a car in the course of his work, about her difficulties and he offered to drive the car for her from Harwich to London. She did not ask him if he was insured to drive but as she had told him Customs had said she must get an insured driver to drive it she assumed his insurance policy covered him to drive other people's cars including hers. On the journey an accident occurred caused by his negligence and she was injured. He was not in fact insured to drive her car. She sued Addo for damages and MIB for a declaration that the Bureau should pay an unsatisfied judgment against Addo. The Bureau relied on clause 6(1)(c)(ii) of the 1972 Agreement, saying that as owner she was permitting the vehicle to be used 'having reason to believe' there was no contract of insurance in force.

HELD: She was entitled to a declaration. 'Having reason to believe' is not the same as 'having reasonable belief' nor as 'having no reason to believe' a contract was in force. 'Having reason to believe' is a reference to a rational process of thought. It placed the onus quite differently. What reason could Mrs Porter have to believe no contract was in force? On the facts as found she could have none.

[3.44] Cooper v Motor Insurers' Bureau
[1985] QB 575, [1985] 1 All ER 449, [1983] 2 WLR 248

A motorcycle owner with no valid motor insurance asked the plaintiff to road test his motorcycle. The plaintiff was injured when the brakes on the motorcycle failed causing him to collide with another vehicle. The plaintiff successfully sued the owner for failing to warn him about the defective brakes but the owner was unable to satisfy the judgment. The plaintiff then sought compensation from MIB under the 1972 Agreement.

HELD: MIB was not liable to compensate the plaintiff because the requirement to insure against 'third party risks' did not include risks to the driver of the vehicle at the relevant time. The term 'any person' in s 145(3)(a) of the Road Traffic Act 1972 was restricted to persons other than the driver of the vehicle.

[3.45] Stinton v Stinton
[1993] PIQR P135; [1995] RTR 167

Christopher Stinton brought an action for damages against his brother Leslie following a road traffic accident caused by his brother's negligent driving. At the time Leslie was uninsured and this was known to Christopher. For MIB to rely upon clause 6(1)(c) of the 1972 Agreement it was necessary to show that the plaintiff was 'using the vehicle'.

HELD: Simon Brown J found that the plaintiff knew he was going to be carried in the uninsured vehicle during the course of the evening's drinking. Clause 6(1)(c) exempted MIB from liability where the plaintiff allowed himself to be carried in a vehicle which he was using or causing or permitting to be used without there being in force in relation to such use a contract of insurance, and in those circumstances the claim against MIB failed.

[3.46]   Hatton v Hall and Motor Insurers' Bureau
[1997] RTR 212, [1999] Lloyd's Rep IR 313, CA

The plaintiff and first defendant were acquaintances and the plaintiff had employed the first defendant to do some work for him. When the work was finished for the day the plaintiff invited the first defendant to have a drink with him and suggested a public house some 10 miles away to which he would direct the first defendant who was unfamiliar with the area. They rode together on the first defendant's motorcycle with the plaintiff riding as pillion passenger. On the return journey the motorcycle crashed and the plaintiff was injured. The plaintiff commenced proceedings against the first defendant and, as he was uninsured, joined MIB as second defendant. MIB claimed that the plaintiff had known that the first defendant had no insurance, and that the plaintiff had been a person using the vehicle at the time of the accident, and that consequently MIB was exempt from liability under the provisions of clause 6(1)(c)(ii) of the 1972 Agreement. The judge gave judgment for the plaintiff against MIB on the ground that, although the plaintiff had had reason to believe that the first defendant was uninsured, the plaintiff had not been a user of the vehicle at the time of the accident.

HELD, ON APPEAL (by MIB): Dismissing the appeal, it was clear from the wording of clause 6(1)(c)(ii) of the 1972 Agreement that the expression 'using' was intended to bear the same meaning as it bore in Part VI, 'Third-party Liabilities Compulsory insurance or Security against Third-party Risks', of what was now the Road Traffic Act 1988. A finding that a passenger was a user of a vehicle under the 1988 Act would carry serious legal consequences, in both criminal and civil law. Consequently 'use' had to be given a restricted meaning limited to circumstances where there was an element of controlling, managing or operating the vehicle by the person concerned. Further, a claim by a passenger under the 1972 Agreement was not defeated under clause 6(1)(c)(iii) merely by the finding that there was no sufficient third-party cover but only if additionally the passenger was liable for failure to provide that cover. Not all plans shared between driver and passenger gave the passenger sufficient control or management of the vehicle to make him a user of the vehicle, it being a question of fact and degree in each case. On the facts the plaintiff had not been a person using the motorcycle.

[3.47]   O'Mahoney v Joliffe and Motor Insurers' Bureau
[1999] All ER (D) 151, [1999] RTR 245, CA

The plaintiff, aged 20, and the first defendant, aged 18, took out the first defendant's motorcycle late at night, despite previous warnings from the first defendant's mother to both individuals that they were not to go out on the motorcycle because it had no tax and MOT and neither party was insured to drive it. The two pushed the motorcycle up the road together, bump started it and then rode it to a nearby industrial estate. On the way home, the first defendant lost control of the motorcycle and crashed it. The plaintiff, who was riding as a pillion passenger, was seriously injured.

HELD, ON APPEAL: The plaintiff was not merely a passive passenger. The parties' venture was not just an agreement to travel somewhere on an uninsured vehicle but was a jointly conceived plan to go out joy riding. The whole venture evolved as one of flagrant criminality which enabled it to be categorised as one involving 'user' on the part of all those who fully participated.

Hatton v Hall and Motor Insurers' Bureau (at para [3.46]) distinguished.

[3.48] White v White and Motor Insurers' Bureau

[2001] 2 All ER 43, [2001] 1 All ER (Comm) 1105, [2001] 1 WLR 481, [2001] RTR 379, HL

The claimant was injured whilst travelling as a passenger in a vehicle being driven by his uninsured brother, Shane. MIB argued that the claimant knew or ought to have known that Shane was uninsured. The trial judge accepted the claimant's evidence that, when they were both in prison shortly before the accident, Shane, who had a history of uninsured driving, had indicated to the claimant his intention to insure in future. The judge found that the claimant did not know but ought to have known that Shane was uninsured. Thus under the 1988 Agreement the claimant could not succeed. However, Art 1 of the Second EEC Motor Insurance Directive 84/5 permits the exclusion of the payment of compensation, in respect of persons who voluntarily enter the vehicle that causes the damage or injury, if it can be proved that they knew it was uninsured. The trial judge held that the terms of the 1988 Agreement were incompatible with the terms of the Directive and that the claimant could recover by virtue of the Directive's direct effect. MIB successfully appealed to the Court of Appeal on the basis that although the UK government had failed to implement the Directive fully, the terms of the Directive were not directly enforceable. The claimant then appealed to the House of Lords.

HELD: Allowing the claimant's appeal, the 1988 Agreement had not been embodied in legislation and therefore UK courts were not required to interpret the provisions of the Agreement as far as possible in a way which gave effect to the Directive – the Marleasing principle. The application of conventional principles of interpretation of documents nevertheless led to the same result. The 1988 Agreement was intended to implement the provisions of the Directive. The phrase 'knew or ought to have known' was intended to be co-extensive with the exception permitted by Art 1. Therefore 'knew or ought to have known' ought to be construed restrictively and should not extend to cases, such as the claimant's, where the lack of knowledge as to the driver's insurance was due to negligence or carelessness on the part of the claimant rather than 'wilful blindness', ie deliberately refraining from asking questions lest suspicions be confirmed.

[3.49] Akers and Others v Motor Insurers' Bureau

[2003] EWCA Civ 18

[2003] All ER (D) 16 (Jan), [2003] Lloyd's Rep IR 427

MIB appealed against that it was liable to A's relatives in respect of A's death in a car accident. A had been one of a number of passengers in a vehicle driven by T. T had lost control of the vehicle and crashed. A was killed and T was uninsured. MIB argued that it was not liable to A's relatives because A knew or ought to have known that the vehicle was uninsured. MIB contended that A had been present in a group when a discussion took place about T not being insured and there was no evidence that A did not hear the comments made. MIB argued that A either knew there was no insurance or, having heard the matter of insurance being discussed, should have enquired as to whether there was insurance or not. The trial judge concluded that although there was evidence that A knew T was uninsured he could not be satisfied of that on the balance of probabilities.

HELD: Allowing the appeal on the basis that given the evidence recorded the judge must have applied too stringent a standard of proof. As the judge seemed to accept that A was one of a group where one or possibly two statements had been made about lack of insurance it would follow that A would have heard those statements. Consequently, either A had accepted the lift knowing that there was no insurance or was aware there was a problem with insurance and ought to have known there was none or, at the very least, deliberately avoided enquiring further about T's insurance. *White v White* (at para [3.48] above) followed.

Note—The case of *Akers* involved the Uninsured Drivers Agreement 1988.

[3.50]   Pickett v Roberts

[2004] EWCA Civ 06

[2004] 2 All ER 685, [2004] All ER (D) 169 (Jan), [2004] 1 WLR 2450, [2004] RTR 476, [2004] Lloyd's Rep IR 513, [2004] PIQR P24

P, a passenger in her own uninsured vehicle, was severely injured. She appealed against a ruling that MIB had no liability to satisfy a judgment obtained against the driver, R. The pair, who lived together, took their dog out for a drive. Whilst travelling on a gravelled mountain track R began performing handbrake turns. P asked him to stop but when he continued she became frightened and asked him to stop the car. P thought R was slowing down so she could get out so she took off her seatbelt. R then accelerated and lost control of the vehicle. The court had to decide whether P was allowing herself to be carried in the vehicle 'at the time of the use giving rise to the liability' for the purposes of clause 6(1)(e) of MIB's 1988 Agreement with the Department of Transport.

HELD: Appeal dismissed. The issue of consent was not normally judged at the moment of entry to the vehicle but 'the use which gave rise to the liability' had to be interpreted in relation to the facts at the time of the accident. A person who had voluntarily entered a vehicle could not withdraw her consent except by an unequivocal repudiation of the common venture to which she consented when she entered the vehicle. An unequivocal request to be allowed to alight was enough but an objection to the manner of the driving was not. Although the judge had not applied the right test it could not be concluded from the evidence that P had done enough to withdraw her consent. *White v White* (at para [3.48] above) considered.

[3.51]   S (a child) v Goldstraw

[2005] 12 CL 286

The claimant child S brought a claim on behalf of her siblings for loss of dependency under the Fatal Accidents Act 1976. S's mother M was riding pillion on a motorcycle driven by her husband G when he collided with a pedestrian. As a result of the collision M was killed. The defendant G was uninsured and MIB was named as second defendants. MIB argued that M knew G was uninsured and as such had no liability to S.

HELD: Clause 6 of the Uninsured Drivers Agreement 1999 was to be construed by reference to its context and to the Second Council Directive 84/5. In the circumstances, it had to be the case that clause 6(1)(e) could be applied to the dependants of a deceased who had the requisite knowledge. It would be absurd if MIB had to satisfy a claim by S where M had died but not a claim by M if she had lived.

[3.52] **Louise Phillips (as representative of the estate of Neville Phillips, deceased) v Mohammed Rafiq and Motor Insurers' Bureau**
[2006] EWHC 1461 (QB), QBD

P's husband (H) had been killed whilst a passenger in his own car. R was driving but was uninsured. The court was asked to determine as a preliminary issue whether MIB had to satisfy any judgment obtained by P against R. MIB argued that as H had allowed himself to be carried in a vehicle and knew the driver was uninsured it had no obligation to satisfy a judgment against R by reason of the exception contained at clause 6(1)(e)(ii) of the 1999 Uninsured Drivers Agreement. The basis of the argument was that as H could not bring a claim against R it followed that H's dependants could not be in any better position to do so. P argued that the exception could not apply as P was not being carried in the car at the time of the accident and that the wording of the 1999 Agreement was different to the wording of the 1988 Agreement. The 1988 Agreement excluded claims arising out of the personal injury or death or damage to property of a passenger who knew that the car was uninsured. However, the 1999 Agreement adopts a different form of words which prevents claims arising where the claimant knew the driver was uninsured.

HELD: The Court held that the different wording of the two Agreements made it clear that there was no intention to create the same effect. The 1988 Agreement was clear as to the effect upon the claims of dependants. It was not relevant that H would not have satisfied the terms of the 1999 Agreement but only whether or not P satisfied the said terms.

(D)   DELIBERATE INJURY

[3.53]   **Hardy v Motor Insurers' Bureau**
[1964] 2 QB 745, [1964] 2 All ER 742, [1964] 3 WLR 433, 108 Sol Jo 422, [1964] 1 Lloyd's Rep 397, CA

The plaintiff was chief security officer at a large metal works. Having seen a stolen road fund licence in a van belonging to a fitter named Phillips he waited at the place where the private road leading from the works joined the main road and stopped the van as it came out. He put his head in at the window and asked Phillips to pull in to the nearside. Instead Phillips drove forward at a fast rate on to the main road dragging the plaintiff along and injuring him. The plaintiff obtained judgment against Phillips for £300 damages but the judgment was unsatisfied. Phillips was uninsured and the plaintiff, having given notice of the proceedings against Phillips to MIB began this action against the Bureau for the amount of the unsatisfied judgment. It was argued for the defendants that liability for a criminal act was not a liability which the Road Traffic Act 1960 required or could require to be covered by insurance.

HELD: Applying the test in *DPP v Smith* [1961] AC 290, [1960] 3 All ER 161, [1960] 3 WLR 546, 124 JP 473, 104 Sol Jo 683 Phillips must be taken to have intended to injure the plaintiff and was guilty of a felony under the Offences Against the Person

Act 1861, s 18. The Road Traffic Act 1960, s 203(3)(a) required Phillips to be covered by a policy of insurance 'in respect of any liability which may be incurred by him in respect of the death of or bodily injury to any person caused by, or arising out of, the use of a vehicle on a road'. This included any use by him of the vehicle, be it an innocent use or a criminal use, or be it a murderous use or a playful use. Such a policy would be good in its inception but the question arises whether the motorist can enforce it when he had made criminal use of the vehicle. Clearly he could not, since no person can claim reparation or indemnity for the consequences of a criminal offence of which his own wicked intent is an essential ingredient – *Beresford v Royal Insurance Co Ltd* [1938] AC 586, [1938] 2 All ER 602, 107 LJKB 464, 158 LT 459, 54 TLR 789, 82 Sol Jo 431, HL. There is a broad rule of public policy that no person can claim reparation or indemnity for his own wilful and culpable crime. Thus if Phillips had himself met the plaintiff's judgment he would have been unable to claim indemnity from an insurer if he had been insured. But this rule of public policy affected only the wrongdoer and would not prevent an innocent third party from claiming the benefit of such a policy against an insurer. Part VI of the 1960 Act gave a third party a direct right of action under s 207 against insurers where there was a liability against which the statute required a motorist to insure. It followed that where, as here, the motorist was not insured the liability was one which the plaintiff could require the defendants to meet under MIB Agreements.

[3.54]   Gardner v Moore

[1984] AC 548, [1984] 1 All ER 1100, [1984] 2 WLR 714, 128 Sol Jo 282, [1984] 2 Lloyd's Rep 135, HL

The defendant, Moore, when driving his car without any insurance cover, deliberately drove on to the pavement, striking and injuring the plaintiff. It was an intentionally criminal act for which Moore was convicted and sentenced to imprisonment. Gardner sued Moore for damages in an action in which Moore took no part. Judgment was given against him for £15,526 damages. MIB (joined as second defendants) denied liability to meet the judgment, maintaining that *Hardy v Motor Insurers' Bureau* (at para [3.53] above) was wrongly decided and/or that the claim should lie against the Criminal Injuries Compensation Board (CICB).

HELD: *Hardy's* case had been correctly decided and the Bureau was liable to satisfy the judgment. The two remedies provided by the CICB and MIB were not mutually exclusive alternatives and were not designed to be so. The general principle that no person can claim indemnity for his own wilful and culpable crime cannot be invoked against an innocent third party whose claim is not through that of the wrongdoer. The MIB Agreement was intended to protect an innocent third party where the wrongdoer was not covered by a relevant policy of insurance; for the Bureau to invoke the doctrine of public policy that a man may not profit by the consequences of his own wrong doing was contrary both to the object and grammatical sense of the Agreement.

(E)   INTERIM PAYMENTS

[3.55]   Powney v Coxage

(1988) Times, 8 March, CA

The plaintiff failed in his appeal from the district judge who had refused to order MIB to make an interim payment in respect of damages for personal injury. The

1972 Agreement between the Secretary of State for Transport and the Bureau only required it to meet judgments against uninsured motorists after the expiry of a seven-day period (subject to the conditions set out in the Agreement). At the time of this application the plaintiff did not have a judgment capable of assignment nor did he fall within the criteria set out in RSC Ord 29, r 9. MIB was not a defendant who had admitted liability and the uninsured motorist could not be considered as 'insured' by the Bureau or in any sense fall within r 11(2)(a).

[3.56] Sharp v Pereria

[1998] 4 All ER 145, [1998] All ER (D) 299, [1999] 1 WLR 195, [1999] RTR 125, CA

An interim payment order can be made in a personal injury action against an uninsured driver whose liability would be met from the Central Fund of MIB.

Under the Motor Insurers' Bureau (Compensation of Victims of Uninsured Drivers) Agreement 1988 if the payment was not met by the insured driver within seven days, MIB was obliged to meet the payment itself.

The Court of Appeal ordered an interim payment of £50,000 to be made. The court had jurisdiction to make an interim payment under RSC Ord 29, r 11 of the old Rules of the Supreme Court.

(F) UNTRACED DRIVERS

[3.57] Persson v London Country Buses

[1974] 1 All ER 1251, [1974] 1 WLR 569, 118 Sol Jo 134, [1974] 1 Lloyd's Rep 415, CA

The plaintiff, a bus conductor, was injured when the bus pulled up sharply. He claimed damages from his employers on the ground that the driver was negligent, but they denied liability; they said the accident was caused by the negligence of a motorist who could not be identified or traced. The plaintiff applied to MIB for an award under the 1969 (untraced drivers) Agreement. After investigation the Bureau decided that no award should be made because the plaintiff had not satisfied clause 1(1)(c). He then began proceedings in the county court against his employers and the Bureau, alleging a failure by the Bureau to compensate him in accordance with the 1969 Agreement. The county court judge ordered the claim against the Bureau to be struck out on the grounds that it disclosed no cause of action.

HELD, ON APPEAL: The judge was right. The agreement is enforceable by the Minister and (by consent of the Bureau) by an applicant, but only in accordance with the terms of the agreement. An award under clause 3 in favour of an applicant is expressly made subject to the provisions of the clause 11, and including clause 7, which prescribes what the Bureau has to do and, when done, requiring the Bureau to decide whether to make an award. The process under clause 7 is subject to a right of appeal under clause 11, but if there is no award there is no right to payment. The Bureau's decision to reject the application was in fulfilment of the terms of the agreement and not a repudiation of it. An applicant cannot bring an action against the Bureau alleging breach of the agreement upon a basis of fact which is reserved by the agreement for the Bureau's decision.

[3.58]   **Elizabeth v Motor Insurers' Bureau**

[1981] RTR 405, CA

The appellant was injured when riding his motorcycle behind a van. The van braked and the appellant ran into it. The van did not stop and was not traced. In an appeal under the Motor Insurers' Bureau Untraced Drivers Agreement the arbitrator said he found it impossible to say that the appellant had proved on the balance of probabilities that the van driver did anything negligent.

HELD, ON APPEAL from the decision of a judge refusing to remit the case to an arbitrator: The burden of proof in the circumstances was not on the appellant. Having regard to the fact that all the evidence was contained in documents a judge should be ready to inquire closely into the proceedings before the arbitrator. Award remitted.

[3.59]   **Evans v (1) Secretary of State for the Environment, Transport and the Regions (2) Motor Insurers' Bureau**

[2003] ECR I-14447, [2004] Lloyd's Rep IR 391, [2005] All ER (EC) 763, [2003] All ER (D) 84 (Dec)

The claimant sued the defendants as a result of his dissatisfaction with an award of damages made to him by an arbitrator under the Untraced Drivers Agreement 1972 which did not include interest on damages or a payment in respect of his costs and also the way that the procedure by which the award was decided. The European Court of Justice had held that procedure by which awards were determined was sufficient but it was necessary for Member States under Directive 84/5 to consider payment of interest when compensating the victims of untraced drivers and also in limited circumstances for costs to be paid as well. The first defendant applied for the claim to be struck out as an abuse of process as the claim had no real prospect of success because the 1972 and 1996 Agreements had been corrected by the 2003 Agreement and, in any event, the claimant could not hope to be awarded more than the £36,000 he owed to the second defendant which MIB had offered to waive if the claimant discontinued proceedings.

The UK court sought a preliminary ruling on the interpretation of Council Directive 84/5.

HELD: The procedural arrangements put in place by the UK in respect of the victims of untraced drivers were sufficient to satisfy Directive 84/5. However, the UK had failed to implement the Directive in respect of payment of interest on a compensation payment and although reimbursement of costs was not required in all cases it was necessary to include a payment of costs where such a payment was necessary to safeguard the rights derived from the directive.

Summary judgment was given for the first defendant because there was no public interest reason for allowing the claim to continue as the Untraced Drivers Agreement 2003 had corrected the criticisms of the Untraced Drivers Agreements of 1972 and 1996 made by the European Court of Justice. Further, MIB had the benefit of a costs order against the claimant in the sum of £36,000 which would outweigh any award the claimant may have received in the proceedings. As MIB had offered to waive the costs order if the claimant discontinued his claim it would be an abuse of process to allow the claim to continue.

Note—The case does show that victims of untraced drivers may have a cause of action for interest and costs in respect of claims under the Untraced Drivers Agreement 1972 and 1996. However, the case also demonstrates an interesting and sensible approach taken by Judge Mackie QC to an application for summary judgment where although the claimant might have succeeded on some limited issues, on the whole, his successes would not outweigh, in financial terms, the monetary debt he owed to MIB even though that debt related to separate proceedings.

(G) SUING POSSIBLE JOINT TORTFEASOR – CLAUSE 6(1)(A), (B)

[3.60] **White v London Transport Executive**
[1971] 2 QB 721, [1971] 3 All ER 1, [1971] 3 WLR 169, 115 Sol Jo 368, [1971] RTR 326, CA

The plaintiff was in a bus when it pulled up sharply and she was injured. The bus driver said the accident was due to the negligence of the driver of a vehicle which had not stopped and could not be traced. The plaintiff applied to MIB under the 1969 Agreement. The Bureau then required the plaintiff under clause 6(1)(b) of the agreement to take proceedings against the bus driver and his employers, London Transport Executive (LTE). When she did so the Bureau applied under RSC Ord 15, r 6(2)(b) to be joined as a party because it was believed that the proceedings would not be pursued with full vigour.

HELD: The application should be rejected. The 1969 Agreement gave the Bureau considerable powers of control over the litigation which it required the plaintiff to conduct, e g clauses 6(1)(a) and (b), 6(2) and 8. Since the plaintiff was bringing this action on the direction of the Bureau she was bound to pursue it with all the vigilance and skill to make the defendants liable, so that all matters in the claim against LTE would be properly and fully investigated without joining the Bureau. Joinder of the Bureau was not 'necessary' within the opening words of RSC Ord 15, r 6(2)(b).

4. DOMESTIC REGULATION/ARTICLE 75 INSURERS

(A) BACKGROUND

[3.61] The liability of MIB under the Uninsured Drivers Agreement, may, in appropriate cases, be passed on to what were previously termed 'Domestic Regulations insurers' but are now known as 'Article 75 insurers'.

Article 75 of MIB's Memorandum and Articles of Association (which replaced the Domestic Regulations in June 2001) establishes a set of rules whereby a member of MIB may be required to pay for what is legally an MIB exposure.

It is important to note that these rules are a private set of rules applicable solely to members of MIB. They are designed to ensure the efficient and expeditious handling of claims by MIB and its members and are unlikely to be of any practical relevance to claimants or their solicitors.

The general principle established by Article 75 is that where there is 'insurance' in existence in respect of the vehicle being used at the time of the relevant accident, even though there may not be in the strict sense a 'contract', the insurer issuing that 'insurance' will meet the claim.

When drivers, or users of a vehicle, are not covered by a policy in respect of the vehicle and the insurers deal with the claim only as an Article 75 insurer, then the insurers cannot claim the benefit of any of the terms of their policy (eg, in defending the action in the name of the defendant driver). The insurers are in precisely the same position as MIB would be if there were not a policy at all, and they deal with the claim under the terms of the relevant MIB Agreement, ie the insurer cannot file notice of acceptance of service of the claim form without obtaining the defendant's express authority or by application to the court under CPR 19.2 in the name of MIB. On the other hand the Article 75 insurer has the protection of the notice requirements under MIB agreements.

(B)   THE TERMS OF ARTICLE 75

[3.62]   Article 75 applies in respect of all cases which fall to be dealt with under any agreements entered into by MIB, both in its capacity as a Guarantee Fund, as the National Green Card Bureau, or as Compensation Body under the 4th Directive.

An Article 75 insurer is defined in clause 1 of Article 75 as:

> 'an Insurer who at the time of the accident which gave rise to the Road Traffic Act liability was providing any insurance against such liability in respect of the vehicle arising out of the use of which the liability of the judgment debtor was incurred, irrespective of whether that insurance was evidenced by documentation as required by the Road Traffic Act or by a record held on the Motor Insurance Database.'

An insurer is an Article 75 insurer within the meaning of Article 75 notwithstanding that:

(1)   the insurance has been obtained by fraud, misrepresentation, non-disclosure of material facts, or mistake.

(2)   the use of the vehicle is other than that permitted under the policy.

An insurer only ceases to be an Article 75 insurer:

(i)   in the case of a short period insurance which shall be defined as any insurance proposed for a term of less than twelve months, where there is no intention on the part of the insurer to renew, nor any renewal document issued and where a new insurance for the same policyholder is not incepted within a period of 15 days of the date of expiry;

(ii)   when the insurance has been cancelled and the certificate of insurance has been recovered, before the date on which the Road Traffic liability was incurred, by specific request of the insured, or strictly in accordance with the power of cancellation contained in the insurer's standard form of contract. Where an intermediary cancels the policy, and the certificate of insurance has been recovered by the intermediary, either as agent for the insurer or because of the term of any independent agreement or contract entered into between the intermediary and the insured, cancellation must be exercised under the same formal strict compliance with the insurer's standard form of contract, and there must be clear evidence that the intermediary is empowered to do so by the policy wording.

(iii)   When before the date on which the Road Traffic Act liability was incurred the insurer has obtained a declaration from the court of competent jurisdiction that the insurance is void or unenforceable.

(iv)   When the insurance has ceased to operate by reason of transfer of interest in the vehicle involved in the accident, which the insurance purports to cover, and which transfer is proved by evidence.

In all cases the burden of proof shall rest upon the insurer who contends not to be the Article 75 insurer.

Where an insurance includes cover for 'driving other vehicles' then unless that cover has been specifically withdrawn and the certificate returned, notwithstanding that the original subject matter of the policy may have ceased to exist or have been the subject of a transfer of interest, the insurer will be an Article 75 insurer unless another member is found to be an Article 75 insurer relative to any cover other than 'driving other vehicles' cover – clause 3.

In the event that there is more than one Article 75 insurer in respect of a particular vehicle then the handling of any claims will be by agreement and the costs of handling and settling claims shall be shared equally between those Article 75 insurers – clause 11.

Disputes between MIB and its members relating to the application of Article 75 are adjudicated on by MIB's Technical Committee – clause 9.

5. THE UNTRACED DRIVERS AGREEMENT

(A) INTRODUCTION

[3.63]   Until 1969, the victim of an untraced driver could expect to receive no more than an ex gratia payment. In that year, the first of a number of formal agreements between MIB and the Secretary of State was established, under which the victim of an untraced driver could apply to the Bureau for a compensation payment.

The 1969 Agreement was replaced by an agreement dated 22 November 1972, which applied to all accidents occurring on or after 1 December 1972. This 1972 Agreement was supplemented by a further agreement dated 7 December 1977, which provided for the speedier disposal of certain types of application. These agreements were in turn replaced by Agreements dated 14 June 1996 and 4 February 2003. The latter is the Agreement currently in force. It applies to all accidents occurring on or after 14 February 2003.

Each of the Agreements required the application for compensation to be made within three years of the date of the accident. It is therefore unlikely that the 1972 or 1977 agreements will be of any immediate relevance to the practitioner. Both the 1972 and 1977 Agreements are reproduced here along with the text of the 1996 and 2003 agreements. The agreements covering the islands of Alderney, Jersey, Guernsey, Sark, Isle of Man and Gibraltar can be obtained via the MIB's website at: www.mib.org.uk.

(B) TEXT OF AGREEMENT DATED 22 NOVEMBER 1972

[3.64]   Text of an Agreement dated 22 November 1972, between the Secretary of State for the Environment and the Motor Insurers' Bureau together with some notes on its scope and purpose.

On 21 April 1969 the Minister of Transport and the Motor Insurers' Bureau entered into an agreement to secure compensation for third party victims of road accidents when the driver responsible for the accident could not be traced. That agreement has now been replaced by a new agreement which operates in respect of accidents occurring on or after 1 December 1972. The text of the new agreement is as follows.

AN AGREEMENT made on 22 November 1972 between the Secretary of State for the Environment and the Motor Insurers' Bureau, whose registered office is at Aldermary house, Queen Street, London, EC4N 1TR (hereinafter referred to as 'MIB').

IT IS HEREBY AGREED as follows:—

1 (1)   Subject to paragraph (2) of this clause, this agreement applies to any case in which an application is made to MIB for a payment in respect of the death of or bodily injury to any person caused by or arising out of the use of a motor vehicle on a road in Great Britain and the case is one in which the following conditions are fulfilled, that is to say,—

(a)   the event giving rise to the death or injury occurred on or after 1 December 1972;

(b)   the applicant for the payment either—

　　(i)   is unable to trace any person responsible for the death or injury; or

　　(ii)   in a case to which clause 5 hereof applies where more than one person was so responsible, is unable to trace one of those persons (any person so untraced is hereby referred to as 'the untraced person');

(c)   the death or injury was caused in such circumstances that on the balance of probabilities the untraced person would be liable to pay damages to the applicant in respect of the death or injury;

(d)   the liability of the untraced person to pay damages to the applicant is one which is required to be covered by insurance or security under Part VI of the Road Traffic Act 1972, it being assumed for this purpose, in the absence of evidence to the contrary, that the vehicle was being used in circumstances in which the user was required by the said Part VI to be insured or secured against third party risks;

(e)   the death or injury was not caused by the use of the vehicle by the untraced person as a weapon, that is to say, in a deliberate attempt to run the deceased or injured person down;

(f)   the application is made in writing within three years from the date of the event giving rise to the death or injury.

(2)   This agreement does not apply to a case in which—

(a)   the death or bodily injury in respect of which such application is made was caused by or arose out of the use of a motor vehicle which at the time of the event giving rise to the death or bodily injury was owned by or in the possession of the Crown, unless the case is one in which some other person has undertaken responsibility for the existence of a contract of insurance under Part VI of the Road Traffic Act 1972;

(b)   at the time of the accident the person suffering death or bodily injury in respect of which the application is made was allowing himself to be carried in a vehicle and—

　　(i)   knew or had reason to believe that the vehicle had been taken without the consent of the owner or other lawful authority, except in a case where—

　　　　(A)   he believed or had reason to believe that he had lawful authority to be carried or that he would have the owner's consent if the owner had known of his being carried and the circumstances of his carriage; or

　　　　(B)   he had learned of the circumstances of the taking of the vehicle since the commencement of the journey and it would be unreasonable to expect him to have alighted from the vehicle; or

　　(ii)   being the owner of or being a person using the vehicle he was using or causing or permitting the vehicle to be used without there being in force in relation to such use a policy of insurance or such security as would comply with Part VI of the Road Traffic Act 1972, knowing or having reason to believe that no such policy or security was in force.

(3)   The exemption from the application of this agreement specified in sub-para (2)(b) of this clause shall apply only in a case where the application is made to MIB in respect of a liability arising out of the use of the vehicle in which the person who suffered death or bodily injury was being carried.

(4)   For the purpose of para (2) of this clause—

(a)   a vehicle which has been unlawfully removed from the possession of the Crown shall be taken to continue in that possession whilst it is kept so removed;

(b)   references to a person being carried in a vehicle include references to his being carried in or upon, or entering or getting on to or alighting from the vehicle;

(c)   'owner' in relation to a vehicle which is the subject of a hiring agreement or a hire purchase agreement means the person in possession of the vehicle under that agreement.

2 (1)   An application to MIB for a payment in respect of the death of or bodily injury to any person may be made either by the person for whose benefit that payment is to be made (hereinafter called 'the applicant') or by any solicitor acting for the applicant or by any other person whom MIB may be prepared to accept as acting for the applicant.

(2)   Any decision, award or payment given or made or other thing done in accordance with this agreement to or by a person acting as aforesaid on behalf of the applicant, or in relation to an application made by such a person, shall, whatever may be the age, or the circumstances affecting the capacity, of the applicant, be treated as having the same effect as if it had been done to or by, or in relation to an application made by, an applicant of full age and capacity.

(3)   Subject to the following provisions of this agreement, MIB shall, on any application made to them in a case to which this agreement applies, award to the applicant in respect of the death or injury in respect of which the application is made a payment of an amount which shall be assessed in like manner as a court, applying English law in a case where the event giving rise to the death or injury occurred in England or Wales or applying the law of Scotland in a case where that event occurred in Scotland, would assess the damages which the applicant would have been entitled to recover from the untraced person in respect of that death or injury if proceedings to enforce a claim for damages in respect thereof were successfully brought by the applicant against the untraced person.

(4)   In making an award in accordance with clause 3 hereof—

(a)   MIB shall not be required to include in the payment awarded any amount in respect of any damages for loss of expectation of life or for pain or suffering which the applicant might have had a right to claim under the Law Reform (Miscellaneous Provisions) Act 1934, or, as the case may be, under any corresponding rule of law in force in Scotland nor, in a case where the application is made in respect of a death, shall MIB be required to include in the payment awarded any amount in respect of solatium for the grief of any relative of the deceased which the applicant might have had a right to claim under any enactment or rule of law in force in Scotland; and

(b)   in assessing the amount to which the applicant is entitled in respect of loss of earnings if the applicant has received his wages or salary in full or in part from his employer, whether or not upon an undertaking given by the applicant to reimburse his employer if he recovers damages, he shall be not to the extent of the amount so received be regarded as having sustained a loss of earnings.

5 (1)   This clause applies to any case to which this agreement applies where the death or bodily injury in respect of which an application has been made to MIB

under this agreement (hereinafter in this clause referred to as 'the relevant death or injury') was caused partly by the untraced person and partly either by an identified person, or by identified persons, or by some other untraced person or persons whose master or principal can be identified and was so caused in circumstances making the identified person or persons or any such master or principal as aforesaid liable to the applicant in respect of the relevant death or injury.

(2)   If in a case to which this clause applies one or other of the conditions specified in the next following paragraph is satisfied, the amount to be awarded by MIB to the applicant in respect of the relevant death or injury shall be determined in accordance with the provisions of para (4) of this clause and their liability to the applicant shall be subject also to the provisions of para (7) of this clause and to clause 6 hereof.

(3)   The conditions referred to in the last foregoing paragraph are—

(a)   that the applicant has obtained a judgment in respect of the relevant death or injury against the identified person or against one or more of the identified persons or against any person liable as their master or principal or the master or principal of any other person which has not been satisfied in full within three months from the date on which the applicant became entitled to enforce it; or

(b)   that the applicant—

(i)   has not obtained and has not been required by MIB to obtain a judgment in respect of the relevant death or injury against the identified person or persons or against any person liable as the master or principal of any such identified person or persons or as the master or principal of any other person; and

(ii)   has not received any payment by way of compensation from any such person or persons.

(4)   The amount to be awarded by MIB to the applicant in a case to which this clause applies shall be determined as follows:

(a)   if the condition specified in para (3)(a) of this clause is satisfied and the judgment mentioned in that paragraph is wholly unsatisfied within the period of three months therein referred to, the amount to be awarded shall be an amount equal to the untraced person's contribution to a full award;

(b)   if the condition specified in para 3(a) of this clause is satisfied but the judgment mentioned in that paragraph is satisfied in part only within the period of three months therein referred to, the amount to be awarded—

(i)   if the unsatisfied part of the said judgment is less than the untraced person's contribution to a full award, shall be an amount equal to that unsatisfied part; or

(ii)   if the unsatisfied part of the said judgment is equal to or greater than the amount of the untraced person's contribution to a full award, shall be an amount equal to the untraced person's said contribution;

(c)   if the condition specified in para (3)(b) of this clause is satisfied, the amount to be awarded shall be an amount equal to the untraced person's contribution to a full award.

(5)   The following provisions of this paragraph shall have effect in any case in which an appeal from or any proceeding to set aside any such judgment as is specified in para (3)(a) of this clause (hereinafter in this clause referred to as 'the original judgment') is commenced within a period of three months beginning on the date on which the applicant became entitled to enforce the original judgment:

(a)   until the said appeal or proceeding is disposed of the foregoing provisions of this clause shall have effect as if for the period of three months referred to in the said para (3)(a) there were substituted a period expiring on the date when the said appeal or proceeding is disposed of;

(b)   if as a result of the said appeal or proceeding the applicant ceases to be entitled to receive any payment in respect of the relevant death or injury from any of the persons against whom he has obtained any such judgment as is specified in the said para (3)(a), the foregoing provisions of this clause shall have effect as if he had neither obtained nor been required by MIB to obtain a judgment against any person or persons;

(c)   if as a result of the said appeal or proceeding, the applicant becomes entitled to recover an amount which differs from that which he was entitled to recover under the original judgment, the foregoing provisions of this clause shall have effect as if for the reference in the said para (3)(a) to the original judgment there were substituted a reference to the judgment under which the applicant became entitled to the said different amount;

(d)   if as a result of the said appeal or proceeding the applicant remains entitled to enforce the original judgment the foregoing provisions of this clause shall have effect as if for the period of three months referred to in the said para (3)(a) there were substituted a period of three months beginning on the date on which the appeal or other proceeding was disposed of. The foregoing provisions of this paragraph shall apply also in any case where any judgment given upon any such appeal or proceeding is itself the subject of a further appeal or similar proceeding and shall apply in such a case in relation to that further appeal or proceeding in the same manner as they apply in relation to the first mentioned appeal or proceeding.

(6)   In this clause—

(a)   'full award' means the amount which would have fallen to be awarded to the applicant under clause 3 thereof in respect of the relevant death or injury if the untraced person had been wholly responsible for that death or injury; and

(b)   'untraced person's contribution' means that proportion of a full award which on the balance of probabilities would have been apportioned by a court as the share to be borne by the untraced person in the responsibility for the event giving rise to the relevant death or injury if proceedings to recover damages in respect of that death or injury had been brought by the applicant against the untraced person and all other persons having a share in that responsibility.

(7)   MIB shall not be under any liability in respect of the relevant death or injury if the applicant is entitled to receive compensation from MIB in respect of that death or injury under the agreement providing for the compensation of victims of uninsured drivers entered into between the Secretary of State and MIB on 22 November 1972.

6 (1)   The following shall be conditions precedent to any liability falling upon MIB upon an application made to them under this agreement in respect of any death or injury, that is to say,—

(a)   the applicant shall give all such assistance as may reasonably be required by or on behalf of MIB to enable any investigation to be carried out under this agreement, including, in particular, the furnishing of statements and information either in writing, or, if so required, orally at an interview between the applicant and any person acting on behalf of MIB;

(b)   if so required by MIB at any time before MIB have communicated their decision upon the application to the applicant, the applicant shall, subject to the following provisions of their liability to the applicant in respect of the death or injury as having caused or contributed to that death or injury as being the master or principal of any person who has caused or contributed to that injury;

(c)   if so required by MIB the applicant shall assign to MIB or to their nominee any judgment obtained by him (whether or not obtained in pursuance of a requirement under sub-paragraph (b) of this paragraph) in respect of the death or injury to which his application to MIB relates upon such terms as will secure that MIB or their nominee shall be accountable to the applicant for any amount by which the aggregate of all sums recovered by MIB or their nominee under the said judgment (after deducting all reasonable expenses incurred in effecting such recovery) exceeds the amount payable by MIB to the applicant under this agreement in respect of that death or injury.

(2)   If MIB require the applicant to bring proceedings against any specified person or persons:

(a)   MIB shall indemnify the applicant against all costs reasonably incurred by the applicant in complying with that requirement unless the result of those proceedings materially contributes to establish that the untraced person did not cause or contribute to the relevant death or injury; and

(b)   the applicant shall, if so required by MIB and at their expense; furnish MIB with a transcript of any official shorthand note taken in those proceedings of any evidence given or judgment delivered therein.

(3)   In the event of a dispute arising between the applicant and MIB as to the reasonableness of any requirement by MIB under para (1)(b) of this clause, or as to whether any such costs as are referred to in para (2)(a) of this clause were reasonably incurred, that dispute shall be referred to the Secretary of State whose decision thereon shall be final. Provided that any dispute arising between the applicant and MIB as to whether MIB are required to indemnify the applicant under para (2)(a) of this clause shall, in so far as it depends on the question whether the result of any proceedings which MIB have required the applicant to bring against any specified person or persons have or have not materially contributed to establish that the untraced person did not cause or contribute to the relevant death or injury, be referred to the arbitrator in accordance with the following provisions of this agreement, whose decision on that question shall be final.

7   MIB shall cause any application made to them for a payment under this agreement to be investigated and, unless MIB decide that the application should be rejected because a preliminary investigation has disclosed that the case is not one to which this agreement applies, they shall cause a report to be made on the application and on the basis of that report MIB shall decide whether to make an award and, if so, the amount of the award which shall be calculated in accordance with the foregoing provisions of this agreement.

8   MIB may before coming to a decision on any application made to them under this agreement request the applicant to furnish them with a statutory declaration to be made by the applicant, setting out to the best of his knowledge, information and belief the facts and circumstances upon which his claim to an award under this agreement is based, or such of those facts and circumstances as may be specified by MIB.

9 (1)   MIB shall notify their decision to the applicant and when so doing shall:

(a)   if the application is rejected because a preliminary investigation has disclosed that it is not one made in a case to which this agreement applies, give their reasons for the rejection; or

(b)   if the application has been fully investigated furnish him with a statement setting out—

(i)   the circumstances in which the death or injury occurred and the evidence bearing thereon;

(ii)   the circumstances relevant to the assessment of the amount to be awarded to the applicant under this agreement and the evidence bearing thereon; and

(iii)   if they refuse to make an award their reasons for that refusal; and

(c)   in a case to which clause 5 of this agreement applies specify the way in which the amount of that award has been computed and its relation to those provisions of clause 5 which are relevant to its computation.

(2)   Where MIB have decided that they will not indemnify the applicant against the costs of any proceedings which they have under clause 6(1)(b) hereof required

the applicant to bring against any specified person or persons on the ground that those proceedings have materially contributed to establish that the untraced person did not cause or contribute to the relevant death or injury, they shall give notice to the applicant of that decision and when doing so they shall give their reasons for it and furnish the applicant with a copy of any such transcript of any evidence given or judgment delivered in those proceedings as is mentioned in clause 6(2)(b) hereof which they regard as relevant to that decision.

10   Subject to the provisions of this agreement MIB shall—

(a)   on being notified by the applicant that MIB's award is accepted; or

(b)   if at the expiration of the period during which the applicant may give notice of an appeal under clause 11 hereof there has not been given to MIB either any such notification as aforesaid of the acceptance of MIB's award or a notice of an appeal under the said clause 11, pay the applicant the amount of that award, and such payment shall discharge MIB from all liability under this agreement in respect of the death or injury in respect of which that award has been made.

11   The applicant shall have a right of appeal to an arbitrator against any decision notified to him under clause 9 hereof on any of the following grounds, that is to say—

(a)   that the case is one to which this agreement applies and that his application should be fully investigated by MIB with a view to their deciding whether to make an award to the applicant and, if so, the amount of that award; or

(b)   where the application has been fully investigated—

(i)   that MIB were wrong in refusing to make an award; or

(ii)   that the amount they have awarded to the applicant is insufficient; or

(c)   in a case where a decision not to indemnify the applicant against the costs of any proceedings has been notified under clause 9(2) hereof, that that decision was wrong, if within six weeks from the date when notice of the decision against which he wishes to appeal was given him, the applicant, not having previously notified MIB that their decision is accepted, gives notice to MIB that he wishes to appeal against their decision.

12   A notice of appeal under clause 11 hereof shall state the grounds of the appeal and shall be accompanied by an undertaking to be given by the applicant or by the person acting on his behalf as provided in clause 2 hereof, that—

(a)   the applicant will accept the decision of the arbitrator; and

(b)   the arbitrator's fee shall be paid to MIB by the applicant or by the person giving the said undertaking in any case where MIB are entitled to reimbursement of that fee under the provisions of clause 22 hereof.

13   The applicant may, when giving notice of his appeal or at any time before doing so, make comments to MIB on their decision and may supply them with such particulars as the applicant may think fit of any other evidence not contained in the written statement supplied to the applicant by MIB which he considers is relevant to the application and MIB may, before submitting the applicant's appeal to the arbitrator, cause an investigation to be made into this further evidence and shall report to the applicant the result of that investigation and of any change in their decision which may result from it. The applicant may, within six weeks from the date on which this report was sent to him, unless he withdraws the appeal, make such comments thereon as he may desire to have submitted to the arbitrator.

14 (1)   In a case where MIB receive from the applicant a notice of appeal in which the only ground of appeal which is stated is that the amount awarded to the applicant is insufficient MIB may before submitting that appeal to the arbitrator give notice to the applicant that if the appeal proceeds they will request the arbitrator to decide whether the case is one in which MIB should make an award at all and if they do so they shall at the same time furnish the applicant with a

statement setting out such comments as they may consider relevant to the decision which the arbitrator should come to on that question.

(2)   Where MIB give a notice under para (1) of this clause, the applicant may within six weeks from the date on which that notice is given make such comments to MIB and supply them with such particulars of other evidence not contained in any written statement furnished to him by MIB as he may consider relevant to the question which the arbitrator is by the notice requested to decide, and clause 13 hereof shall apply in relation to any comments made or particulars supplied by the applicant under this paragraph as it applies in relation to any comments made or particulars supplied under the said clause 13.

15   MIB shall, where they receive notice of an appeal from the applicant under the foregoing provisions of this agreement, unless the appeal is previously withdrawn, submit that appeal (but in a case where they cause such an investigation to be made as is mentioned in clause 13 hereof, not until the expiration of six weeks from the date on which they sent the applicant a report as to the result of that investigation and, in a case where they gave such notice to the applicant as is mentioned in clause 14(1) hereof, not until the expiration of six weeks from the date on which they gave that notice and, if they have caused an investigation to be made into any evidence supplied under clause 14(2) hereof, not until the expiration of six weeks from the date on which they sent the applicant a report as to the result of that investigation) to an arbitrator for a decision, sending to the arbitrator for that purpose the application made by the applicant, a copy of their decision thereon as notified to the applicant and of all statements, declarations, notices, undertakings, comments, transcripts, particulars or reports furnished, given or sent under this agreement either by the applicant or any person acting for him to MIB or by MIB to the applicant or a person so acting.

16   On any such appeal—
  (a)   if the appeal is against a decision by MIB rejecting an application because a preliminary investigation has disclosed that the case is not one to which this agreement applies, the arbitrator shall decide whether the case is or is not one to which this agreement applies and, if he decides that it is such a case, shall remit the application to MIB for full investigation and for a decision by MIB in accordance with the foregoing provisions of this agreement;
  (b)   if the appeal is against a decision by MIB given after an application has been fully investigated by MIB (whether before the appeal or in consequence of its being remitted for such investigation under para (a) of this clause), the arbitrator shall decide, as may be appropriate, having regard to the grounds stated in the notice of appeal and to any notice given by MIB to the applicant under clause 14 thereof, whether MIB should make an award under this agreement to the applicant and, if so, the amount which MIB should award to the applicant under the foregoing provisions of this agreement;
  (c)   if the appeal relates to a dispute which has arisen between the applicant and MIB which is required by the proviso to clause 6(3) hereof to be referred to the arbitrator, the arbitrator shall also give his decision on that dispute.

17   The arbitrator shall decide the appeal on the documents submitted to him as set out in clause 15 hereof and no further evidence shall be produced to him: Provided that—
  (a)   the arbitrator shall be entitled to ask MIB to make any further investigation which he considers desirable and to submit a written report of their findings to him for his consideration; and
  (b)   MIB shall send a copy of any such report to the applicant who shall be entitled to submit written comments on it to MIB within four weeks of the date on which that copy is sent to him; and
  (c)   MIB shall transmit those comments to the arbitrator for his consideration.

18   The arbitrator by whom any such appeal as aforesaid shall be decided shall be an arbitrator to be selected by the Secretary of State from two panels of Queen's Counsel appointed respectively by the Lord Chancellor and the Lord Advocate for the purpose of determining appeals under this agreement, the arbitrator to be selected from the panel appointed by the Lord Chancellor in cases where the event giving rise to the death or injury occurred in England or Wales and from the panel appointed by the Lord Advocate where that event occurred in Scotland.

19   The arbitrator shall notify his decision on any appeal under this agreement to MIB and MIB shall forthwith send a copy of the arbitrator's decision to the applicant.

20   Subject to the provisions of this agreement, MIB shall pay the applicant any amount which the arbitrator has decided shall be awarded to the applicant, and such payment shall discharge MIB from all liability under this agreement in respect of the death or injury in respect of which that decision has been given.

21   Each party to the appeal will bear his own costs.

22   MIB shall pay the arbitrator a fee approved by the Lord Chancellor or the Lord Advocate, as the case may be, after consultation with MIB: Provided that the arbitrator may in his discretion, in any case where it appears to him that there were no reasonable grounds for the appeal, decide that his fee ought to be paid by the applicant and, where the arbitrator so decides, the person giving the undertaking required by clause 12 hereof shall be liable to reimburse MIB the amount of the fee paid by them to the arbitrator except in so far as that amount is deducted by MIB from any amount which they are liable to pay to the applicant in consequence of the decision of the arbitrator.

23   If in any case it appears to MIB that by reason of the applicant being under the age of majority or of any other circumstances affecting his capacity to manage his affairs it would be in the interest of the applicant that all or some part of the amount which would otherwise be payable to him under an award made under this agreement should be administered for him by the Family Welfare Association or by some other body or person under a trust MIB may establish for that purpose a trust of the whole or part of the said amount to take effect for such period and subject to such provisions as may appear to MIB appropriate in the circumstances of the case.

24   This agreement may be determined at any time by the Secretary of State or by MIB by either of them giving to the other not less than 12 months previous notice in writing: Provided that this agreement shall continue to have effect in respect of any case where the event giving rise to the death or injury occurred before the date on which this agreement terminates in accordance with any notice so given.

25   This agreement shall come into operation on 1 December 1972 in relation to accidents occurring on or after that date, and the agreement made on 21 April 1969 between the Secretary of State and MIB shall cease and determine except in relation to applications arising out of accidents which occurred on or after 1 May 1969 and before the said 1 December 1972.

IN WITNESS etc.

Notes

The following notes are for the guidance of those who may wish to make application to the Motor Insurers' Bureau for payment under the agreement, and for the guidance of their legal advisers, but they must not be taken as rendering unnecessary a careful study of the agreement itself. Communications connected with the agreement should be addressed to the Motor Insurers' Bureau, whose address is Aldermary House, Queen Street, London, EC4N 1TR.

1   This agreement replaces a previous one dated 21 April 1969 which put on a formal basis the arrangements which have existed since 1946 under which the

Bureau have made ex gratia payments in respect of death or personal injuries resulting from the use of a motor vehicle the owner or driver of which cannot be traced. Provision is made for an appeal against the Bureau's decision in such cases.

2   The agreement dated 21 April 1969 applies to a death or bodily injury arising out of an accident occurring on a road in Great Britain on or after 1 May 1969, and before 1 December 1972. This agreement applies in relation to accidents occurring on or after 1 December 1972.

3   Subject to the terms of the agreement, the Bureau will accept applications for a payment in respect of the death of, or bodily injury to, any person resulting from the use of a motor vehicle on a road in Great Britain in any case in which:

(a)   the applicant for the payment cannot trace any person responsible for the death or injury (or, in certain circumstances, a person partly responsible) (clause 1(1)(b)); and

(b)   the death or injury was caused in such circumstances that the untraced person would be liable to pay damages to the applicant in respect of the death or injury (clause 1(1)(c)); and

(c)   the untraced persons' liability to the applicant is one which at the time the accident occurred, was required to be covered by insurance or security (clause 1(1)(d)).

The Bureau will not, however, deal with deliberate 'running down' cases (clause 1(1)(e)) nor with certain other cases relating to Crown vehicles and certain categories of 'voluntary' passenger (clause 1(2)–(4)).

4   Application for a payment under the agreement must be made in writing to the Bureau within three years of the date of the accident giving rise to the death or injury (clause 1(1)(f)).

5   Under clause 3, the amount which the Bureau will award will (except for the exclusions of those elements of damages mentioned in clause 4) be assessed in the same way as a court would have assessed the amount of damages payable by the untraced person had the applicant been able to bring a successful claim for damages against him.

6   Clause 5 relates to cases where an untraced person and an identified person are each partly responsible for a death or injury, and defines the conditions under which the Bureau will in such cases make a contribution in respect of the responsibility of the untraced person.

7   Under clause 6(1)(b), the Bureau may require the applicant to bring proceedings against any identified person who may be responsible for the death or injury, subject to indemnifying the applicant as to his costs as provided in clause 6(2) and (3).

8   On receipt of an application, the Bureau will, if satisfied that the application comes within the terms of the agreement, investigate the circumstances and, when this has been done, decide whether to make a payment and, if so, how much (clause 7).

9   The Bureau may request the applicant to make a statutory declaration setting out all, or some, of the facts on which his application is based (clause 8).

10   The Bureau will notify the applicant of their decision, setting out the circumstances of the case and the evidence on which they base their decision and, if they refuse to make a payment, the reasons for that refusal (clause 9).

11   If the applicant does not exercise his right to appeal against the Bureau's decision, the Bureau's decision will be final and the applicant will be entitled to be paid the amount awarded by the Bureau (clause 10).

12   If the applicant wishes to appeal against the decision on the grounds specified in clause 11, he must notify the Bureau within six weeks of being notified of the decision, and give the undertakings set out in clause 12.

13   The Bureau may, as a result of comments made by the applicant on their decision, investigate the application further, and if so they will communicate with

the applicant again. In such a case, the applicant will have six weeks from the date of that further communication in which to decide whether or not to go on with his appeal (clause 13).

14   Where the applicant appeals only on the grounds that the amount awarded to him is too low, the Bureau may give him notice that if the matter proceeds to appeal, they will ask the arbitrator to decide also the issue of the Bureau's liability to make any payment. The applicant will have six weeks from the date of any such notice in which to comment to the Bureau on this intention (clause 14).

15   Appeals will be decided by an arbitrator who will be a Queen's Counsel selected by the Minister of Transport from one of two panels to be appointed by the Lord Chancellor and the Lord Advocate respectively (clause 18).

16   All appeals will be decided by the arbitrator on the basis of the relevant documents (as set out in clause 15) which will be sent to him by the Bureau. If the arbitrator asks the Bureau to make a further investigation, the applicant will have an opportunity to comment on the result of that investigation (clause 17).

17   The arbitrator may, at his decision, award the cost of his fee against the applicant if he considers the appeal unreasonable; otherwise, each party to the appeal will bear their own costs, the Bureau paying the arbitrator's fee (clauses 21 and 22).

In certain circumstances, the Bureau may establish a trust for the benefit of an applicant of the whole or part of any award (clause 23).

[Reproduced by permission of the Controller of HM Stationery Office.]

Note—The 1972 Agreement provides a complete code of practice for such applications. So long as MIB complies with the procedure provided by the agreement its decisions cannot be the subject of litigation.

(C)   TEXT OF AGREEMENT DATED 7 DECEMBER 1977

SUPPLEMENTARY AGREEMENT

[3.65]   A Supplemental Agreement dated 7 December 1977 has been made the object of which is to provide for speedier disposal of certain types of application. It enables the Bureau at its discretion to offer an award in a specified sum furnishing the applicant with particulars of the circumstances and of the evidence on which the offer is based. The applicant can accept the offer at that stage foregoing the right of appeal and discharging the Bureau from all liability. The agreement relates to applications on or after 3 January 1978. There is an upper limit for the operation of the accelerated procedure. As from 19 July 1982 the limit is £20,000. Before that date the limit was £10,000.

Text of an Agreement dated 7 December 1977, between the Secretary of State for Transport and the Motor Insurers' Bureau together with some notes on its scope and purpose.

AN AGREEMENT made 7 December 1977 between the Secretary of State for Transport and the Motor Insurers' Bureau, whose registered office is Aldermary House, Queen Street, London, EC4N 1TR (hereinafter referred to as 'MIB') SUPPLEMEN-TAL to an agreement (hereinafter referred to as the 'Principal Agreement') relating to compensation of victims of untraced drivers and made 22 November 1972 between the Secretary of State for the Environment and MIB.

IT IS HEREBY AGREED as follows:

1 (1)   In any case in which an application has been made to MIB in pursuance of clause 2(1) of the principal agreement on or after the 3 January 1978 and in which a preliminary investigation in pursuance of clause 7 thereof has disclosed that the case is one to which that agreement, but not clause 5 thereof, applies MIB may, instead of causing a report to be made on the application as provided by the said

clause 7, make, or cause to be made, to the applicant an offer to settle his application in a specified sum, assessed in accordance with clause 3 of the principal agreement.

(2)   Where an offer is made in pursuance of paragraph (1) above, there shall be furnished to the applicant (at the same time) in writing particulars of:

   (i)   the circumstances in which the death or injury occurred and the evidence bearing thereon; and

   (ii)   the circumstances relevant to the assessment of the amount to be awarded to the applicant and the evidence bearing thereon.

2   On receipt by MIB or its agent of an acceptance of the offer referred to in the foregoing clause, in the form specified in the Schedule hereto and duly completed by the applicant:

   (a)   the principal agreement shall have effect in relation to the application as if in clause 7 the words 'and unless MIB decide' to the end of that clause, and clauses 9 to 22 inclusive were omitted; and

   (b)   MIB shall pay to the applicant the amount specified in the offer, and such payment shall discharge MIB from all liability under this and the principal agreement in respect of the death or injury in relation to which the payment has been made.

3   In clause 4(a) of the principal agreement after the words 'solatium for the grief of any relative of the deceased' there shall be inserted the words 'or a loss of society award to a member of the immediate family of the deceased under s 1(4) of the Damages (Scotland) Act 1976'.

4   In clause 16 of the principal agreement there shall be added at the end the following proviso: 'Provided that where the arbitrator has dealt with an appeal under paragraph (a) of this clause all the foregoing provisions of this agreement shall apply as if the case were an application to which this agreement applies upon which MIB had not communicated a decision'.

5   This agreement shall be construed as one with the principal agreement and, without prejudice to the operation of clause 6 thereof, shall cease to have effect on the date that that agreement terminates in accordance with clause 24 thereof, and subject to the proviso there mentioned.

6   Clauses 1 and 2 of this agreement may be determined at any time by the Secretary of State or by MIB, by either of them giving to the other not less than 12 months previous notice in writing: Provided that the said clauses shall continue to have effect in respect of any case where the event giving rise to the death or injury occurred before the date on which those clauses terminate in accordance with any notice so given.

SCHEDULE (referred to in clause 2)

Form of Acceptance (under Supplemental Agreement dated 7 December 1977) I, [*full name of applicant*] of [*address*] HEREBY ACCEPT the sum of £... offered, in pursuance of clause 1 of an agreement made between the Secretary of State for Transport and the Motor Insurers' Bureau (hereinafter called 'MIB') and dated 7 December 1977, by or on behalf of MIB in settlement of the application made by me or on my behalf on [*date*] to MIB in pursuance of clause 2(a) of an agreement made between the Secretary of State for the Environment and MIB and dated 22 November 1972 relating to compensation of victims of untraced drivers in respect of: [*particulars of, and circumstances giving rise to, injuries*] AND UNDERSTAND that payment of that sum will discharge MIB from all liability under the aforementioned agreements, and that I shall have no further rights under those agreements (in particular any right of appeal to an arbitrator under clause 11 of the agreement of 22 November 1972).

Name and address and description of witness.

Signature of applicant:

Date:

IN WITNESS etc.

Notes

1   This agreement supplements the agreement dated 22 November 1972 concerning compensation for personal injuries suffered by victims of untraced drivers.

2   The following notes are for guidance only and must not be taken as rendering unnecessary a careful study of this supplemental agreement itself together with the main agreement to which it relates. Communications concerning these agreements should be addressed to the Motor Insurers' Bureau, whose address is Aldermary House, Queen Street, London EC4N 1TR.

3   Clause 1 of the supplemental agreement provides for the use of a shorter form of procedure than that stipulated in the main agreement with the object of securing speedier disposal of certain applications to the Bureau. Except in a case where both an untraced person and an identified person may each partly be responsible for the injuries giving rise to an application, the Bureau may, at its discretion, make an offer of an award in a specified sum furnishing the applicant at the same time with particulars of the circumstances of the case and of the evidence on which the offer is based. If the applicant is prepared to accept the offer and undertake, on payment by the Bureau, to discharge them from all liability and forgo any right of appeal to an arbitrator the Bureau will pay the sum offered forthwith. If the offer is not acceptable the application will thereafter be dealt with in accordance with the full procedure as set out in the main agreement.

4   The purpose of clause 4 of the supplemental agreement is to make clear that the Bureau remain entitled to require any applicant to take proceedings against a known person in accordance with clause 6(1)(b) of the main agreement, notwithstanding that the applicant had successfully appealed against a decision by the Bureau to reject the application after a preliminary investigation.

Note —MIB is now based at 152 Silbury Boulevard, Central Milton Keynes, MK9 1NB (DX 84753 MILTON KEYNES 3).

(D)   TEXT OF AGREEMENT DATED 14 JUNE 1996

[3.66]   Text of an Agreement dated the 14 June 1996 between the Secretary of State for Transport and Motor Insurers' Bureau together with some notes on its scope and purpose.

1   On 21 April 1969 the Minister of Transport and Motor Insurers' Bureau entered into an Agreement ('the First Agreement') to secure compensation for Third party victims of road accidents when the driver responsible for the accident could not be traced.

2   The First Agreement was replaced by a new Agreement ('the Second Agreement') which operated in respect of accidents occurring on or after 1 December 1972.

3   The Second Agreement was added to by a Supplemental Agreement dated 7 December 1977 ('the Third Agreement') which operated in respect of accidents occurring on or after 3 January 1978.

4   The Second Agreement and the Third Agreement have now been replaced by a new Agreement ('this Agreement') which operates in respect of accidents occurring on or after 1 July 1996.

5   The text of this Agreement is as follows:

AN AGREEMENT made the Fourteenth day of June 1996 between the Secretary of State for Transport ('the Secretary of State') and the Motor Insurers' Bureau, whose registered office is at 152 Silbury Boulevard, Milton Keynes, MK9 1NB ('the MIB').

IT IS HEREBY AGREED as follows:—

1 (1)   Subject to paragraph (2) of this Clause, this Agreement applies to any case in which an Application is made to the MIB for a payment in respect of the death

of or bodily injury to any person caused by or arising out of the use of a motor vehicle on a road in Great Britain and the case is one in which the following conditions are fulfilled, that is to say—

    (a)   the event giving rise to the death or injury occurred on or after 1 July 1996;

    (b)   the applicant for the payment either:

        (i)   is unable to trace any person responsible for the death or injury; or

        (ii) in a case to which Clause 5 applies where more than one person was responsible, is unable to trace one of those persons. (Any person so untraced is referred to as 'the untraced person');

    (c)   the death or injury was caused in such circumstances that on the balance of probabilities the untraced person would be liable to pay damages to the applicant in respect of the death or injury;

    (d)   the liability of the untraced person to pay damages to the applicant is one which is required to be covered by insurance or security under Part VI of the Road Traffic Act 1988 ('the 1988 Act'), it being assumed for this purpose, in the absence of evidence to the contrary, that the vehicle was being used in circumstances in which the user was required by the 1988 Act to be insured or secured against third party risks;

    (e)   the death or injury was not caused by the use of the vehicle by the untraced person in any deliberate attempt to cause the death or injury of the person in respect of which an application is made; and

    (f)   the application is made in writing within three years from the date of the event giving rise to the death or injury;

    (g)   the incident was reported to the police within fourteen days or as soon as the applicant reasonably could and the applicant co-operated with the police.

  (2)   This Agreement does not apply to a case in which—

    (a)   the death or bodily injury in respect of which any such application is made was caused by or arose out of the use of a motor vehicle which at the time of the event giving rise to the death or bodily injury was owned by or in the possession of the Crown, unless the case is one in which some other person has undertaken responsibility for the existence of a contract of insurance under the 1988 Act;

    (b)   at the time of the accident the person suffering death or bodily injury in respect of which the application is made was allowing himself to be carried in a vehicle and either before or after the commencement of his journey in the vehicle, if he could reasonably be expected to have alighted from the vehicle, he knew or had reason to believe that the vehicle:

        (i)   had been stolen or unlawfully taken; or

        (ii)   was being used without there being in force in relation to its use a contract of insurance which complied with the 1988 Act; or

        (iii) was being used in the course or furtherance of crime; or

        (iv) was being used as a means of escape from or avoidance of lawful apprehension.

  (3)   For the purpose of paragraph (2) of this Clause—

    (a)   a vehicle which has been unlawfully removed from the possession of the Crown shall be taken to continue in that possession whilst it is kept so removed;

    (b)   references to a person being carried in a vehicle include references to his being carried in or upon, or entering or getting on to or alighting from the vehicle;

    (c)   'owner' in relation to a vehicle which is the subject of a hiring agreement or a hire purchase agreement means the person in possession of the vehicle under that agreement.

2 (1)   An application to the MIB for a payment in respect of the death or bodily injury to any person may be made:

(a) by the person for whose benefit that payment is to be made ('the applicant'); or
(b) by any solicitor acting for the applicant; or
(c) by any other person whom the MIB may be prepared to accept as acting for the applicant.

(2) Any decision made, or award or payment given or made or other thing done in accordance with this Agreement to or by a person acting under paragraph 1(b) and (1)(c) of this Clause on behalf of the applicant, or in relation to an application made by such a person, shall, whatever may be the age, or the circumstances affecting the capacity, of the applicant, be treated as having the same effect as if it had been done to or by, or in relation to an application made by, an applicant of full age and capacity.

3. Subject to the following provisions of this Agreement, the MIB shall, on any application made to it in a case to which this Agreement applies, award to the applicant in respect of the death or injury for which the application is made a payment of an amount which shall be assessed in like manner as a court, applying English law in a case where the event giving rise to the death or injury occurred in England or Wales or applying the law of Scotland in a case where that event occurred in Scotland, would assess the damages which the applicant would have been entitled to recover from the untraced person in respect of that death or injury if the applicant had brought successful proceedings to enforce a claim for such damages against the untraced person.

4. In assessing the level of an award in accordance with Clause 3, the MIB shall be under no obligation to include in such award any sum in respect of loss of earnings suffered by the applicant where and in so far as the applicant has in fact been paid wages or salary or any sum in lieu of the same, whether or not such payments were made subject to an undertaking on the part of the applicant to repay the same in the event of the applicant recovering damages.

5 (1) This Clause applies to any case:
(a) to which this Agreement applies; and
(b) the death or bodily injury in respect of which an application has been made to the MIB under this Agreement ('the relevant death or injury') was caused:
   (i) partly by the untraced person and partly by an identified person, or by identified persons; or
   (ii) partly by the untraced person and partly by some other untraced person or persons whose master or principal can be identified; and
(c) in circumstances making the identified person or persons or any master or principal ('the identified person') liable to the applicant in respect of the relevant death or injury.

(2) If in a case to which this Clause applies one or other of the conditions in paragraph (3) of this Clause is satisfied, the amount of the award to be paid by the MIB to the applicant in respect of the relevant death or injury shall be determined in accordance with paragraph (3) of this Clause and its liability to the applicant shall be subject to paragraph (7) of this Clause and Clause 6 of this Agreement.

(3) The conditions referred to in paragraph (2) of this Clause are:
(a) that the applicant has obtained a judgment in respect of the relevant death or injury against the identified person ('the original judgment') which has not been satisfied in full within three months from the date on which the applicant became entitled to enforce it ('the three month period'); or
(b) that the applicant—
   (i) has not obtained and has not been required by the MIB to obtain a judgment in respect of the relevant death or injury against the identified person; and
   (ii) has not received any payment by way of compensation from the identified person or persons.

(4)   The amount to be awarded by the MIB to the applicant in a case to which this Clause applies shall be determined as follows—

   (a)   if the condition in paragraph (3)(a) of this Clause is satisfied and the original judgment is wholly unsatisfied within the three month period, the amount to be awarded shall be an amount equal to that proportion of a full award attributable to the untraced person;

   (b)   if the condition in paragraph (3)(a) of this Clause is satisfied but the original judgment is satisfied in part only within the three month period, the amount to be awarded—

      (i)   if the unsatisfied part of the original judgment is less than the proportion of a full award attributable to the untraced person, shall be an amount equal to that unsatisfied part; or

      (ii)   if the unsatisfied part of the original judgment is equal to or greater than the proportion of a full award attributable to the untraced person, shall be an amount equal to the untraced person's proportion;

   (c)   if the condition in paragraph (3)(b) of this Clause is satisfied the amount to be awarded shall be an amount equal to the proportion of a full award attributable to the untraced person.

(5)   The following provisions of this paragraph shall have effect in any case in which an appeal from or any proceeding to set aside the original judgment is commenced within a period of three months beginning on the date on which the applicant became entitled to enforce the original judgment—

   (a)   until the said appeal or proceeding is disposed of the provisions of this Clause shall have effect as if for the three month period there were substituted a period expiring on the date when the said appeal or proceeding is disposed of;

   (b)   if as a result of the appeal or proceeding the applicant ceases to be entitled to receive any payment in respect of the relevant death or injury from any person or persons against whom he has obtained the original judgment the provisions of this Clause shall have effect as if he had neither obtained nor been required by the MIB to obtain a judgment against any person or persons;

   (c)   if as a result of the appeal or proceeding, the applicant becomes entitled to recover an amount which differs from that which he was entitled to recover under the original judgment, the provisions of this Clause shall have effect as if for the reference in paragraph (3)(a) to the original judgment there were substituted a reference to the judgment under which the applicant became entitled to the said different amount;

   (d)   if as a result of the said appeal or proceeding the applicant remains entitled to enforce the original judgment the provisions of this Clause shall have effect as if for the three month period there were substituted a period of three months beginning on the date on which the appeal or other proceeding was disposed of. The provisions of this paragraph shall apply also in any case where any judgment given upon any such appeal or proceeding is itself the subject of a further appeal or similar proceeding and shall apply in such a case in relation to that further appeal or proceeding in the same manner as they apply in relation to the first mentioned appeal or proceeding.

(6)   In this Clause—

   (a)   'full award' means the amount which would have fallen to be awarded to the applicant under Clause 3 in respect of the relevant death or injury if the untraced person had been adjudged by a court to be wholly responsible for that death or injury; and

   (b)   'the proportion of a full award attributable to the untraced person' means that proportion of a full award which on the balance of probabilities would have been apportioned by a court in proceedings between the untraced person and any other person liable in respect of the same event as the share to be borne by the untraced person in the responsibility for the event giving rise to the relevant death or injury.

(7)   The MIB shall not be under any liability in respect of the relevant death or injury if the applicant is entitled to receive compensation from the MIB in respect of that death or injury under any Agreement providing for the compensation of victims of uninsured drivers entered into between the Secretary of State and the MIB.

6 (1)   Any liability falling upon the MIB upon an application made to it under this Agreement in respect of any death or injury, shall be subject to the following conditions:

   (a)   the applicant shall give all such assistance as may reasonably be required by or on behalf of the MIB to enable any investigation to be carried out under this Agreement, including, in particular, the provision of statements and information either in writing, or, if so required, orally at an interview or interviews between the applicant and any person acting on behalf of the MIB;

   (b)   at any time before the MIB has communicated its decision upon the application to the applicant, the applicant shall, subject to the following provisions of this Clause, take all such steps as in the circumstances it is reasonable for the MIB to require him to take to obtain judgment against any person or persons in respect of their liability to the applicant for the death or injury as having caused or contributed to that death or injury or as being the master or principal of any person who has caused or contributed to that death or injury; and

   (c)   if required by the MIB the applicant shall assign to the MIB or to its nominee any judgment obtained by him (whether or not obtained in accordance with a requirement under subparagraph (b) of this paragraph) in respect of the death or injury to which his application to the MIB relates upon such terms as will secure that the MIB or its nominee shall be accountable to the applicant for any amount by which the aggregate of all sums recovered by the MIB or its nominee under the judgment (after deducting all reasonable expenses incurred in effecting such recovery) exceeds the amount payable by the MIB to the applicant under this Agreement in respect of that death or injury.

(2)   If the MIB requires the applicant to bring proceedings against any specified person or persons—

   (a)   the MIB shall indemnify the applicant against all costs reasonably incurred by him in complying with that requirement unless the result of those proceedings materially contributes to establishing that the untraced person did not cause or contribute to the relevant death or injury; and

   (b)   the applicant shall, if required by the MIB and at its expense, provide the MIB with a transcript of any official shorthand note taken in those proceedings of any evidence given or judgment delivered therein.

(3)   In the event of a dispute arising between the applicant and the MIB as to the reasonableness of any requirement by the MIB under paragraph (1)(b) of this Clause or as to whether any such costs as are referred to in paragraph (2)(a) of this Clause were reasonably incurred, that dispute shall be referred to the Secretary of State whose decision shall be final:

Provided that any dispute arising between the applicant and the MIB as to whether the MIB are required to indemnify him under paragraph (2)(a) of this Clause shall, in so far as it depends on the question whether the result of any proceedings which the MIB has required the applicant to bring against any specified person or persons has or has not materially contributed to establish that the untraced person did not cause or contribute to the relevant death or injury, be referred to the arbitrator in accordance with the following provisions of this Agreement, whose decision on that question shall be final.

7.   The MIB shall cause any application made to it for a payment under this Agreement to be investigated and, unless it decides that the application should be rejected because a preliminary investigation has disclosed that the case is not one to which this Agreement applies, it shall cause a report to be made on the application and on the basis of that report it shall decide whether to make an award and, if so, the amount of the award which shall be calculated in accordance with the provisions of this Agreement.

8.   The MIB may before coming to a decision on any application made to it under this Agreement request the applicant to provide it with a statutory declaration to be made by the applicant, setting out to the best of his knowledge, information and belief the facts and circumstances upon which his claim to an award under this Agreement are based, or facts and circumstances as may be specified by it.

9 (1)   The MIB shall notify its decision to the applicant and when so doing shall—

(a)   if the application is rejected because a preliminary investigation has disclosed that it is not one made in a case to which this Agreement applies, give its reasons for the rejection; or

(b)   if the application has been fully investigated provide him with a statement setting out:

   (i)   the circumstances in which the death or injury occurred and the relevant evidence;

   (ii)   the circumstances relevant to the assessment of the amount to be awarded to the applicant under this Agreement and the relevant evidence; and

   (iii)   if it refuses to make an award, its reasons for that refusal, and

(c)   in a case to which Clause 5 of this Agreement applies specify the way in which the amount of that award has been computed and its relation to those provisions of Clause 5 which are relevant to its computation.

(2)   Where the MIB has decided that it will not indemnify the applicant against the cost of any proceedings which it has under Clause 6(1)(b) required him to bring against any specified person or persons on the ground that those proceedings have materially contributed to establish that the untraced person did not cause or contribute to the relevant death or injury, it shall give notice to the applicant of that decision together with its reasons for it and shall provide the applicant with a copy of any transcript of any evidence given or judgment delivered in those proceedings as is mentioned in Clause 6(2)(b) hereof which it regards as relevant to that decision.

10 (1)   Subject to the provisions of this Agreement, where the MIB has decided to make an award to the applicant, it shall pay the applicant the amount of that award if:

(a)   it has been notified by the applicant that the award is accepted; or

(b)   at the expiration of the period during which the applicant may give notice of an appeal under Clause 11 the applicant has not given the MIB either any such notification of the acceptance of its award or a notice of an appeal under Clause 11.

(2)   Such payment as is made under paragraph (1) of this Clause shall discharge the MIB from all liability under this Agreement in respect of the death or injury for which that award has been made.

11 (1)   The applicant shall have a right of appeal to an arbitrator against any decision notified to him by the MIB under Clause 9 if:

(a)   he gives notice to the MIB, that he wishes to appeal against its decision ('the notice of appeal');

(b)   he gives the MIB the notice of appeal within 6 weeks from the date when he was given notice of the decision against which he wishes to appeal; and

(c)   he has not previously notified the MIB that he has accepted its decision.

(2)   The grounds of appeal are as follows:

(a)   where the application has not been the subject of a full investigation:
    (i)   that the case is one to which this Agreement applies; and
    (ii)   that the applicant's application should be fully investigated by the MIB with a view to its deciding whether or not to make an award to him and, if so, the amount of that award; or

(b)   where the application has been fully investigated:
    (i)   that the MIB was wrong in refusing to make an award; or
    (ii)   that the amount it has awarded to the applicant is insufficient; or

(c)   in a case where a decision not to indemnify the applicant against the costs of any proceedings has been notified to the applicant by the MIB under Clause 9(2), that the decision was wrong.

12.   A notice of appeal under Clause 11 shall state the grounds of the appeal and shall be accompanied by an undertaking given by the applicant or by the person acting on his behalf under Clause 2(1)(b) and 2(1)(c), that—

(a)   the applicant will accept the decision of the arbitrator; and

(b)   the arbitrator's fee shall be paid to the MIB by the applicant or by the person who has given the undertaking in any case where the MIB is entitled to reimbursement of that fee under the provisions of Clause 22.

13 (1)   When giving notice of his appeal or at any time before doing so, the applicant may:

(a)   make comments to the MIB on its decision; and

(b)   supply it with such particulars as he thinks fit of any further evidence not contained in the written statement supplied to him by the MIB which he considers is relevant to the application.

(2)   The MIB may, before submitting the applicant's appeal to the arbitrator:

(a)   cause an investigation to be made into the further evidence supplied by the applicant under paragraph (1)(b) of this Clause; and

(b)   report to the applicant the result of that investigation and of any change in its decision which may result from it.

(3)   The applicant may, within six weeks from the date on which the report referred to in paragraph (2)(b) of this Clause was sent to him, unless he withdraws his appeal, make such comments on the report as he may desire to have submitted to the arbitrator.

14 (1)   In a case where the MIB receives from the applicant a notice of appeal in which the only ground of appeal which is stated is that the amount awarded to the applicant is insufficient, before submitting that appeal to the arbitrator the MIB may:

(a)   give notice to the applicant that if the appeal proceeds it will request the arbitrator to decide whether the case is one in which the MIB should make an award at all; and

(b)   at the same time as complying with paragraph (1)(a) of this Clause provide the applicant with a statement setting out such comments as it may consider relevant to the decision which the arbitrator should come to on that question.

(2)   Where the MIB gives the applicant notice under paragraph (1)(a) of this Clause, the applicant may, within six weeks from the date on which that notice is given:

(a)   make such comments to the MIB and supply it with particulars of other evidence not contained in any written statement provided to him by the MIB as he may consider relevant to the question which the arbitrator is by that notice requested to decide; and

(b)   Clause 13 shall apply in relation to any comments made or particulars supplied by the applicant under paragraph (2)(a) of this Clause.

15 (1)   Subject to paragraph (2) of this Clause, where the MIB receives a notice of appeal from the applicant under the provisions of this Agreement, unless the appeal is previously withdrawn, it shall:

(a)   submit that appeal to an arbitrator for a decision; and

(b)   send to the arbitrator for the purpose of obtaining his decision:
   (i)   the application made by the applicant;
   (ii)   a copy of its decision as notified to the applicant; and
   (iii)   copies of all statements, declarations, notices, undertakings, comments, transcripts, particulars of reports provided, given or sent to the MIB under this Agreement either by the applicant or any person acting for him under Clause 2(1)(b) or 2(1)(c) by the MIB.

(2)   In a case where the MIB causes an investigation to be made under Clause 13, the MIB shall not comply with paragraph (1) of this Clause until:
   (a)   the expiration of six weeks from the date on which it sent the applicant a report as to the result of that investigation; or
   (b)   the expiration of six weeks from the date on which it gave the applicant notice under Clause 14(1); or
   (c)   the expiration of six weeks from the date on which it sent the applicant a report as to the result of that investigation, if it has caused an investigation to be made into any evidence supplied under Clause 14(2).

16.   On an appeal made by the applicant in accordance with this Agreement:
   (a)   if the appeal is against a decision by the MIB rejecting an application because a preliminary investigation has disclosed that the case is not one to which this Agreement applies, the arbitrator shall decide whether the case is or is not one to which this Agreement applies and, if he decides that it is such a case, shall remit the application to the MIB for full investigation and a decision in accordance with the provisions of this Agreement;
   (b)   if the appeal is against a decision by the MIB given after an application has been fully investigated by it (whether before the appeal or in consequence of its being remitted for such investigation under paragraph (a) of this Clause) the arbitrator shall decide, as may be appropriate, having regard to the grounds stated in the notice of appeal and to any notice given by the MIB to the applicant under Clause 14, whether the MIB should make an award under this Agreement to the applicant and, if so, the amount which it should award to the applicant under the provisions of this Agreement;
   (c)   if the appeal relates to a dispute which has arisen between the applicant and the MIB which is required by the proviso to Clause 6(3) to be referred to the arbitrator, the arbitrator shall also give his decision on that dispute. Provided that where the arbitrator has allowed an appeal under paragraph (a) of this Clause all the provisions of this Agreement shall apply as if the case were an application to which this Agreement applies upon which the MIB had not communicated a decision.

17 (1)   Subject to paragraph (2) of this Clause, the arbitrator shall decide the appeal on the documents submitted to him under Clause 15(1)(b) and no further evidence shall be produced to him;

(2)   The following shall apply where documents have been submitted to the arbitrator under Clause 15(1)(b):
   (a)   the arbitrator shall be entitled to ask the MIB to make any further investigation which he considers desirable and to submit a written report of its findings to him for his consideration; and
   (b)   the MIB shall send a copy of that report to the applicant who shall be entitled to submit written comments on it to the MIB within four weeks of the date on which that copy is sent to him; and
   (c)   the MIB shall transmit those comments to the arbitrator for his consideration.

18.   The arbitrator by whom an appeal made by an applicant in accordance with the provisions of this Agreement shall be considered shall be an arbitrator to be selected by the Secretary of State from two panels of Queen's Counsel appointed respectively by the Lord Chancellor and the Lord Advocate for the purpose of determining appeals under this Agreement, the arbitrator to be selected from the

panel appointed by the Lord Chancellor in cases where the event giving rise to the death or injury occurred in England or Wales and from the panel appointed by the Lord Advocate where that event occurred in Scotland.

19.   The arbitrator shall notify his decision on any appeal under this Agreement to the MIB and the MIB shall forthwith send a copy of the Arbitrator's decision to the applicant.

20.   Subject to the provisions of this Agreement, the MIB shall pay the applicant any amount which the arbitrator has decided shall be awarded to him, and that payment shall discharge the MIB from all liability under this Agreement in respect of the death or injury in respect of which that decision has been given.

21.   Each party to the appeal will bear their own costs.

22.   The MIB shall pay the arbitrator a fee approved by the Lord Chancellor or the Lord Advocate, as the case may be, after consultation with the MIB.

Provided that, in any case where it appears to the arbitrator that there were no reasonable grounds for the appeal, the arbitrator may in his discretion decide:

(a)   that his fee ought to be paid by the applicant; and

(b)   that the person giving the undertaking required by Clause 12 shall be liable to reimburse the MIB the amount of the fee paid by it to the arbitrator, except in so far as that amount is deducted by the MIB from any amount which it is liable to pay to the applicant in consequence of the decision of the arbitrator.

23.   If in any case it appears to the MIB that the reason of the applicant being under the age of majority or of any other circumstances affecting his capacity to manage his affairs it would be in the applicant's interest that all or some part of the amount which would otherwise be payable to him under an award made under this Agreement should be administered for him by the Family Welfare Association or by some other body or person under a trust or by the Court of Protection (or in Scotland by the appointment of a Judicial Factor) the MIB may establish for that purpose a trust of the whole or part of the amount to take effect for a period and under provisions as may appear to it to be appropriate in the circumstances of the case or may initiate or cause any other person to initiate process in that Court and otherwise cause any amount payable under the award to be paid to and administered thereby.

24.   In any case in which an application has been made to the MIB under Clause 2(1) and in which a preliminary investigation under Clause 7 has disclosed that the case is one to which the Agreement, save for Clause 5, applies, the MIB may, instead of causing a report to be made on the application as provided by Clause 7, make, or cause to be made, to the applicant an offer to settle his application in a specified sum, assessed in accordance with Clause 3.

25.   Where an offer is made under Clause 24, there shall be provided to the applicant (at the same time) in writing particulars of:

(a)   the circumstances in which the death or injury occurred and the relevant evidence; and

(b)   the circumstances relevant to the assessment of the amount to be awarded to the applicant and the relevant evidence.

26 (1)   On receipt by the MIB or its agent of an acceptance of the offer referred to in Clause 24:

(a)   this acceptance shall have effect in relation to the application as if in Clause 7 the words 'and, unless the MIB decide' to the end of that Clause, and Clauses 9 to 22 inclusive were omitted; and

(b)   the MIB shall pay to the applicant the amount specified in the offer.

(2)   The payment made by the MIB under paragraph (1)(b) of this Clause shall discharge it from all liability under this Agreement in respect of the death or injury for which the payment has been made.

27.   This Agreement may be determined at any time by the Secretary of State or by the MIB by either of them giving to the other not less than twelve months previous notice in writing:

Provided that this Agreement shall continue to have effect in any case where the event giving rise to the death or injury occurred before the date on which this Agreement terminates in accordance with any notices so given.

28.   From 14 June 1996 the following periods of operation shall apply:

(a)   this Agreement shall come into operation on 1 July 1996 in relation to accidents occurring on or after that date;

(b)   the Second Agreement shall cease and determine except in relation to applications arising out of accidents which occurred on or after 1 December 1972 and before the 3 January 1978; and

(c)   the Third Agreement shall cease and determine except in relation to accidents occurring on or after 3 January 1978 and before the 1 July 1996.

IN WITNESS etc.

Notes

The following Notes are for the guidance of those who may wish to make application to the Motor Insurers' Bureau for payment under the Agreement, and for the guidance of their legal advisers, but they must not be taken as making unnecessary a careful study of the Agreement itself. Communications connected with the Agreement should be addressed to the Motor Insurers' Bureau ('the MIB'), whose address is 152 Silbury Boulevard, Central Milton Keynes, MK9 1NB.

1   This Agreement replaces a previous one dated 22nd November 1972 and a Supplemental Agreement dated 7th December 1977 and continues the arrangements which have existed since 1946 under which the MIB has made ex gratia payments in respect of death or personal injuries resulting from the use on the road of a motor vehicle the owner or driver of which cannot be traced. Provision is made for an appeal against the MIB's decision in such cases.

2   The Agreement dated 22nd November 1972 applies to a death or bodily injury arising out of an accident occurring on a road in Great Britain on or after 1st December 1972 and before 3rd January 1978. The Agreement dated 22nd November 1972 as supplemented by the Supplemental Agreement dated 7th January 1977 applies in relation to accidents occurring on or after 3rd January 1978 and before 1 July 1996.

This Agreement applies in relation to accidents occurring on or after 1 July 1996.

3   Subject to the terms of the Agreement, the MIB will accept applications for a payment in respect of the death of, or bodily injury to any person resulting from the use of a motor vehicle on a road in Great Britain in any cases in which—

(a)   the applicant for the payment cannot trace any person responsible for the death or injury (or, in certain circumstances, a person partly responsible) (Clause 1(1)(b)); and

(b)   the death or injury was caused in such circumstances that the untraced person would be liable to pay damages to the applicant in respect of the death or injury (Clause 1(1)(c)); and

(c)   the untraced person's liability to the applicant is one which at the time the accident occurred, was required to be covered by insurance or security (Clause 1(1)(d)).

The MIB will not deal with the following:

(a)   deliberate 'running down' cases (Clause 1(1)(e));

(b)   certain other cases relating to Crown vehicles; and

(c)   certain categories of 'voluntary' passenger (Clause 1(2)–(4)).

4   Applications for a payment under the Agreement must be made in writing to the MIB within three years of the date of the accident giving rise to the death or injury (Clause 1(1)(f)).

5   Under Clause 3, the amount which the MIB will award will (except for the exclusion of those elements of damages mentioned in Clause 4) be assessed in the

same way as a Court would have assessed the amount of damages payable by the untraced person had the applicant been able to bring a successful claim for damages against him.

6   Clause 5 relates to cases where an untraced person and an identified person are each partly responsible for a death or injury, and defines the conditions under which the MIB will in such cases make a contribution in respect of the responsibility of the untraced person.

7   Under Clause 6(1)(b), the MIB may require the applicant to bring proceedings against any identified person who may be responsible for the death or injury, subject to indemnifying the applicant as to his costs as provided in Clause 6(2) and (3).

8   On receipt of an application, the MIB will, if satisfied that the application comes within the terms of the Agreement, investigate the circumstances and, when this has been done, decide whether to make a payment and, if so, how much (Clause 7). 9 The MIB may request the applicant to make a statutory declaration setting out all, or some, of the facts on which his application is based (Clause 8).

10   The MIB may notify the applicant of its decision, setting out the circumstances of the case and the evidence on which it bases its decision and, if it refuses to make a payment, the reasons for the refusal (Clause 9).

11   If the applicant wishes to appeal against the decision on the grounds specified in Clause 11(2), he must notify the MIB within six weeks of being notified of the decision, and he or any person acting on his behalf shall give the undertakings set out in Clause 12.

12   The MIB may, as a result of the comments made and further evidence submitted by the applicant on its decision, investigate the further evidence, and if so it will communicate with the applicant again. In such a case the applicant will have six weeks from the date of that further communication in which to decide whether or not to go on with the appeal (Clause 13).

13   Where the applicant appeals only on the grounds that the amount awarded to him is too low, the MIB may give him notice that if the matter proceeds to appeal, it will ask the arbitrator to decide also the issue of the MIB's liability to make any payment.

The applicant will have six weeks from the date of any such notice in which to comment to the MIB on this intention (Clause 14).

14   Appeals will be decided by an arbitrator who will be a Queen's Counsel selected by the Secretary of State for Transport from one of two panels to be appointed by the Lord Chancellor and the Lord Advocate respectively (Clause 18).

15   All appeals will be decided by the arbitrator on the basis of the relevant documents
(as set out in Clause 15) which will be sent to him by the MIB. If the arbitrator asks the MIB to make a further investigation, the applicant will have an opportunity to comment on the result of that investigation (Clause 17).

16   The arbitrator may, at his discretion, award the cost of this fee against the applicant if he considers the appeal unreasonable; otherwise, each party to the appeal will bear their own costs, the MIB paying the arbitrator's fee (Clause 21 and 22).

17   In certain circumstances, the MIB may establish a trust for the benefit of an applicant of the whole or part of any award (Clause 23).

18   Clauses 24 to 26 provide for the use of a shorter form of procedure than that stipulated in Clause 7 with the object of securing speedier disposal of certain applications to the MIB. The MIB may, at its discretion, make an offer of an award in a specified sum providing the applicant at the same time with particulars of the circumstances of the case and of the evidence on which the offer is based. If the applicant is prepared to accept the offer, thus undertaking, on payment by the MIB, to forego any right of appeal to an arbitrator, the MIB will pay the sum offered forthwith. If the offer is not acceptable the application will thereafter be dealt with in accordance with the full procedure set out in the Agreement.

The shorter form of procedure does not apply in a case where both an untraced person and an identified person may each partly be responsible for injuries giving rise to an application to the MIB.

COMMENTARY ON 1996 AGREEMENT

Clause 1

[3.67]   An 'untraced driver' is one whose identity is unknown and cannot be established, thus making proceedings against him in a court of law impossible. A driver whose name and address, or other necessary details sufficient to establish his identity and enable proceedings to be served upon him does not become an untraced driver merely because he has disappeared or cannot be found when a claim is made. However, a driver who gave fictitious details at the time of the accident and could not therefore be found, is an 'untraced driver' within the meaning of the agreement: *Clarke v Vedel* (at para [3.32] above).

The agreement applies only to cases of death or personal injury. The Second Council Directive 84/5/EEC of 30 December 1983 on the approximation of the laws of Member States relating to insurance against civil liability in respect of the use of motor vehicles requires each Member State to 'set up or authorize a body with the task of providing compensation, at least up to the limits of the insurance obligation, for damage to property or personal injuries caused by an unidentified vehicle or a vehicle for which the insurance obligation ... has not been satisfied' (Art 1, para 4). However, in the case of an unidentified vehicle, the Member State may 'limit or exclude the payment of compensation by that body in the case of damage to property caused by an unidentified vehicle' (Art 1, para 4). Thus, in this respect at least, there can be no argument that the 1996 Agreement fails to implement fully the terms of the Second Directive.

If any of the conditions of eligibility set out in clause 1(1) of the agreement are not met, the Bureau will reject the claim. An appeal will lie against any such rejection (see below).

The exceptions set out in clause 1(2) of the 1996 Agreement are similar in wording to those which are found in the Uninsured Drivers Agreement. The principal difference is in the use of the phrase 'knew or had reason to believe'. This phrase connotes a 'rational process of thought' (see *Porter v Addo* (at para [3.43] above)). It will thus apply to the passenger who had actual knowledge or who had closed his eyes to the obvious. It will not, for the reasons set out below, apply to the passenger who fails to make the inquiries that a reasonably prudent passenger would have made in the particular circumstances of the case.

In *White v White* (at para [3.48] above) it was held that the phrase 'knew or ought to have known' in the corresponding provisions of the Uninsured Drivers Agreement ought to be construed narrowly, to exclude the case of the careless passenger, in the light of the Second Council Directive (above). That Directive permitted the exclusion of compensation payments to a person 'who voluntarily entered the vehicle', if it is proved that the person 'knew that [the vehicle] was uninsured' (Art 1, para 4). Since the Directive applies equally to cases involving an unidentified or untraced driver, it is submitted that the same narrow construction should be adopted when considering the relevant provisions of the 1996 Agreement.

An appeal will lie against MIB's rejection of an application under either of the exceptions set out in clause 1(2).

The decision whether the 1996 Agreement applies is one for MIB to make. An applicant whose application is rejected on the ground that it does not come within the Agreement cannot bring a claim against MIB alleging a breach of the Agreement, because the factual basis for such an allegation (that the Agreement does, in the circumstances, apply) is reserved by the Agreement for the decision of MIB: see *Persson v London Country Buses* (at para [3.57] above) (a decision on clause 1(1)(c) of the 1969 Agreement which, in its terms, corresponds to clause 1(1)(c) of the 1996 Agreement).

Clause 2

[3.68] The application must be made in writing to MIB: see clause 1(1)(f) above. An application form and accompanying notes can now be downloaded from MIB's website at: www.mib.org.uk.

Clause 3

[3.69] 'Damages' do not include 'interest'; the latter is awarded by a court to compensate the injured party for the delay in receiving his damages. Thus, there is no power under the 1996 Agreement to award interest on any payment of compensation: see *Evans v Motor Insurers' Bureau* (1997) Times, 29 July; [1997] 3 CMLR 1218, QBD (and, for the decision of the Court of Appeal upholding this first instance decision, see [1999] 1 CMLR 1251, [1999] Lloyd's Rep IR 30). In respect of interest, the victim of an untraced driver is in a worse position than the victim of an uninsured driver. In the latter case, the Bureau's obligation is to satisfy any judgment obtained by or on behalf of the victim. Such a judgment will almost invariably include interest and costs. It was partly the existence of this disparity which led the court in the *Evans* case to make the reference to the European Court. The European Court of Justice in the case of *Evans v Secretary of State for the Environment, Transport & the Regions* [2003] ECR I-14447, [2005] All ER (EC) 763, [2003] All ER (D) 84 (Dec) (at para [3.59] above)has held that the non-recovery of interest under the 1996 Agreement amounts to a failure, on the part of the Secretary of State, to implement fully the provisions of the Second Directive (para [3.67] above). However, this has been corrected by the 2003 Agreement.

Clause 4

[3.70] Note that this is an exception to the general provision in clause 3, above. A court assessing compensation according to English law would allow a claimant to recover any wages or salary paid in consequence of the injury but which the claimant is contractually bound to repay to his employer. Again, this gives rise to a disparity between the position of the victim of an untraced driver and that of the victim of an uninsured driver. It is questionable whether, in the circumstances, this exception amounts to a failure fully to implement the terms of the Second Directive (para [3.67] above).

Clause 5

[3.71]   The provisions apply where the applicant's injuries are caused partly by an untraced driver and partly by a driver who has been traced, or whose employer, principal or other person who would be vicariously liable for that driver's acts and omissions has been traced. In such a case, MIB's liability will be determined in accordance with clause 5(4) where either:
(a)   the applicant has obtained a judgment against the traced person which has gone unsatisfied for a period of three months; or
(b)   MIB has not required the applicant to bring proceedings against the traced person, and the applicant has not received a payment of compensation from that person.
The practical effect of these provisions can best be illustrated by an example. Suppose A is injured in a road traffic accident for which B (an untraced driver) and C (whose identity is known and who is insured) are equally liable. A must bring proceedings in the usual way against C, as well as making an application under the 1996 Agreement (in respect of B). Judgment is entered in A's favour against C for £100,000 (the full value of the claim). If A recovers the full amount from C, MIB will be under no liability to A under the 1996 Agreement. If A recovers only £75,000 from C, MIB will be liable for the balance of £25,000 (since that sum is less than MIB's notional liability on behalf of B). If A recovers only £25,000 from C, MIB will be liable to pay a further £50,000 (that being its notional liability on behalf of B). In that last example, A will be left out of pocket. Query whether, in that respect, these provisions fail to implement fully the provisions of the Second Directive, because the applicant in such a case is in a worse position than if he had been the victim of an uninsured driver.

Clause 6

[3.72]   A failure on the part of an applicant to satisfy any of the conditions precedent set out in this clause will justify a rejection of the application by MIB.
Where MIB requires an applicant, pursuant to clause 6(1)(b) to bring proceedings, MIB will have no right to be joined as a party, since it will already exercise sufficient control over the proceedings through the provisions of the Agreement: see *White v London Transport Executive* (at para [3.60] above), where it was held that joinder of MIB in those circumstances was not 'necessary' within the meaning of the opening words of RSC Ord 15, r 6(2)(b) (see now CPR Pt 19).
Note that a dispute as to the reasonableness of any requirement by MIB, or a dispute as to whether costs had been reasonably incurred, is to be referred to the Secretary of State for a final decision. The only exception to this is where the dispute is whether proceedings which MIB required the applicant to take either did or did not materially contribute to establishing whether the untraced person caused or contributed to the relevant injury or death. In such a case, an appeal lies to the arbitrator (for the procedure, see para [3.75] below).

Clause 7

[3.73]　There are four stages once an application is received by MIB:
(1)　the application is investigated;
(2)　if the investigation reveals that the application does not come within the 1996 Agreement, it is rejected;
(3)　if the application comes within the 1996 Agreement, a report is made;
(4)　on the basis of the report, MIB decides whether to make an award, and the amount of any such award.

Clauses 8 and 9

[3.74]　A preliminary rejection by MIB is regarded as one where the information submitted by the applicant is in itself sufficient to justify immediate rejection. (For example an application submitted more than three years after the date of the accident.) Hence there is no need for any documentation to accompany the decision and its explanation.

Clauses 10 to 22

[3.75]　An appeal against a decision by MIB under the 1996 Agreement lies to an arbitrator selected from panels appointed by the Lord Chancellor (for cases where the accident occurred in England or Wales) or the Lord Advocate (for cases where the accident occurred in Scotland). The grounds on which an appeal may be brought are extensive. However, the appeal is conducted on the papers only: the arbitrator will have before him all the material on which the Bureau based its decision, together with such further material as either the applicant or MIB supply under the following provisions of the agreement; the arbitrator will not hear oral evidence or submissions.

In *Evans v Secretary of State for the Environment, Transport & the Regions* (also at para [3.69] above), the claimant argued that the absence of a full appeal hearing, in front of a judge sitting in an ordinary court and hearing oral submissions amounted to a failure, on the part of the Secretary of State to implement fully the provisions of the Second Directive (para [3.67] above). This question (among others) was referred to the European Court of Justice. The particular concerns to the court hearing the claim were:
(a)　the (contested) fact that the applicant did not see MIB's initial report and did not have the opportunity of dealing with any adverse points in it;
(b)　the absence of an oral hearing or any formal exchange of statements of case or submissions; and
(c)　the fact that any further appeal from the arbitrator was constrained by the provisions of the Arbitration Acts 1950 and 1996 and would not involve a rehearing or unfettered review of the evidence.
The European Court of Justice held that the procedural arrangements set up were sufficient to protect the victims of damage or injury.

Where the appeal is solely on the amount of the compensation payment, MIB may invite the arbitrator to consider whether the case is one in which any award should be made. If it does so, it will provide a statement setting out the matters which it wants the arbitrator to consider on that question.

Where an arbitrator allows an appeal against MIB's decision that the application was one to which the 1996 Agreement did not apply, he will remit the application to MIB, for it to carry out a full investigation and prepare a report, in accordance with clause 7 (at para [3.73] above).

Where the case has been fully investigated, the arbitrator will consider whether an award should be made, and if so, the amount of that award.

Where the arbitrator is of the view that there were no reasonable grounds for the appeal, he has a discretion under clause 22 to direct that the applicant should pay his fee. Apart from that, there is no express provision as to costs in the 1996 Agreement. It is, however, MIB's practice (in accordance with an informal agreement with the Law Societies of England and Wales, Scotland and Northern Ireland), to make a small ex gratia payment to an applicant's solicitor and to pay reasonable disbursements (excluding counsel's fees). Again, this could be said to give rise to a disparity between the position of the victim of an untraced driver and that of the victim of an uninsured driver, albeit the process under the Untraced Drivers Agreement is inquisitorial as opposed to adversarial. In the latter case, the sum which MIB is liable to pay under the Uninsured Drivers Agreement in respect of an unsatisfied court judgment includes any taxed costs or costs awarded by the court without taxation. This disparity led the court in *Evans v Secretary of State for the Environment, Transport & the Regions* (above) to doubt whether there had been adequate implementation of the Second Directive. This question (whether the non-recoverability of costs under the 1996 Agreement amounts to a failure to implement fully the terms of the Second Directive) was referred to the European Court of Justice which held that Art 1(4) of the Directive did not require compensation to include reimbursement of costs except in circumstances where such re-imbursement was necessary to safeguard rights derived from the Directive. The 2003 Agreement has since incorporated payment of costs in certain circumstances to the applicant.

Clause 23

[3.76]   This provision applies where the applicant is under a disability. In such a case, the Bureau may either establish a trust to administer any compensation payment or take such steps as may be necessary to secure the involvement of the Court of Protection.

Clauses 24 to 26

[3.77]   Clauses 24 to 26 make provision for a 'fast-track' assessment, where a preliminary investigation has revealed that the application is one to which the 1996 Agreement applies. In such a case, the Bureau can simply proceed to an assessment of the award of compensation, rather than causing a report to be made in accordance with clause 7 (at para [3.73] above).

Acceptance of the offer made by the Bureau under these provisions will deprive the applicant of a right of appeal against the Bureau's decision (cf clause 11(1)(c), where the applicant may appeal only if he has not previously notified the Bureau that he has accepted its decision).

(E)   TEXT OF AGREEMENT DATED 7 FEBRUARY 2003, COMING INTO EFFECT 14 FEBRUARY 2003

[3.78]   THIS AGREEMENT is made the seventh day of February 2003 between the SECRETARY OF STATE FOR TRANSPORT (hereinafter referred to as 'the Secretary of State') and the MOTOR INSURERS' BUREAU, whose registered office is at Linford Wood House 6–12 Capital Drive Linford Wood Milton Keynes MK14 6XT (hereinafter referred to as 'MIB').

IT IS HEREBY AGREED AS FOLLOWS:—

INTERPRETATION

General interpretation

1. (1)   In this Agreement, unless the context otherwise requires, the following expressions have the following meanings—

'1988 Act' means the Road Traffic Act 1988;

'1996 Agreement' means the Agreement made on 14 June1996 between the Secretary of State for Transport and MIB providing for the compensation of victims of untraced drivers;

'1999 Agreement' means the Agreement dated 13th August 1999 made between the Secretary of State for the Environment, Transport and the Regions and MIB providing for the compensation of victims of uninsured drivers;

'applicant' means the person who has applied for compensation in respect of death, bodily injury or damage to property (or the person on whose behalf such an application has been made) and 'application' means an application made by or on behalf of an applicant:

'arbitrator', where the arbitration takes place under Scottish law, includes an arbiter;

'award' means the aggregate of sums which MIB is obliged to pay under this Agreement;

'bank holiday' means a day which is, or is to be observed as, a bank holiday under the Bank and Financial Dealings Act1971;

'judgement' means, in relation to a court in Scotland, a court decree;

'property' means any property whether (in England and Wales)real or personal, or (in Scotland) heritable or moveable:

'relevant proceedings' means civil proceedings brought by the applicant (whether or not pursuant to a requirement made under this Agreement) against a person other than the unidentified person in respect of an event described in clause 4(1);

'specified excess' means £300 or such other sum as many from time to time to be agreed in writing between the Secretary of State and MIB;

'unidentified person' means a person who is, or appears to be, wholly or partly liable in respect of the death, injury or damage to property to which an application relates and who cannot be identified.

(2)   Save as otherwise herein provided, the Interpretation Act 1978 shall apply for the interpretation of this Agreement as it applies for the interpretation of an Act of Parliament.

Where, under this Agreement, something is required to be done within a specified period after a date or the happening of a particular event, the period begins on the day after the happening of that event.

Where, apart from this paragraph, the period in question, being a period of 7 days or less, would include a Saturday, Sunday, bank holiday, Christmas Day or Good Friday, that day shall be excluded.

Save where expressly otherwise provided, a reference in this Agreement to a numbered clause is a reference to the clause bearing that number in this Agreement and a reference to a numbered paragraph is a reference to a paragraph bearing that number in the clause or schedule in which the reference occurs.

In this Agreement—

a reference (however framed) to the doing of any act or thing by or the happening of any event in relation to the applicant includes a reference to the doing of that act or thing by or the happening of that event in relation to a Solicitor or other person acting on his behalf, and shall, where MIB has appointed a Solicitor to act on its behalf in relation to the application, be satisfied by the giving of the notice or the sending of the documents, in the matter herein provided for, to that Solicitor.

APPLICANTS' REPRESENTATIVES

2.　Where, under and in accordance with this Agreement—

　(a)　any notice or other document is given to or by a Solicitor or other person acting on behalf of an applicant;

　(b)　any act or thing is done by or in respect of such Solicitor or other person;

　(c)　any decision is made by or in respect of such Solicitor or other person; or

any payment is made to such Solicitor or other person, then, whatever may be the age or other circumstances affecting the capacity of the applicant, that act, thing, decision or payment shall be treated as if it has been done to or by, or made to or in respect of an applicant of full age and capacity.

APPLICATION OF AGREEMENT

Duration of Agreement

3. (1)　This Agreement shall come into force on 14 February 2003.

(2)　This Agreement may be determined by the Secretary of State or by MIB giving to the other not less than twelve months notice in writing to that effect.

(3)　Notwithstanding the giving notice of determination under paragraph (2) this Agreement shall continue to operate in respect of any application made in respect of death, bodily injury or damage to property arising from an event occurring on or before the date of termination specified in the notice.

Scope of Agreement

4. (1)　Save as provided in Clause 5, this Agreement applies where—

　(a)　the death of, or bodily injury to, a person or damage to any property of a person has been caused by, or arisen out of, the use of a motor vehicle on a road or other public place in Great Britain; and

　(b)　the event giving rise to the death, bodily injury or damage to property occurred on or after fourteenth day February 2003; and

　(c)　the death, bodily injury or damage to property occurred in circumstances giving rise to liability of a kind which is required to be covered by a policy of insurance or a security under Part VI of the 1988 Act; and

it is not possible for the applicant—

　　　(i)　to identify the person who is, or appears to be, liable in respect of the death, injury or damage; or

　　　(ii)　(where more than one person is or appears to be liable) to identify any one or more of those persons; and

　(d)　the applicant has made an application in writing to MIB for the payment of an award in respect of such death, bodily injury or damage to property (and in a case where they are applicable the requirements of paragraph (2)are satisfied); and

the conditions specified in paragraph (3), or such of those conditions as are relevant to the application, are satisfied.

(2)　Where an application is signed by a person who is neither the applicant nor a Solicitor acting on behalf of the applicant MIB may refuse to accept the application (and shall incur no liability under this Agreement) until it is reasonably satisfied that, having regard to the status of the signatory and his relationship with the applicant, the applicant is fully aware of the content and effect of the application but subject thereto MIB shall not refuse to accept an application by reason only of the fact that it is signed by a person other than the applicant or his Solicitor.

The conditions referred to in paragraph (1) (f) are that—

(a) except in a case to which sub-paragraph (b) applies, the application must have been made not later than—
   (i) three years after the date of the event which is the subject of the application in the case of a claim for compensation for death or bodily injury (whether or not damage to property has also arisen from the same event); or
   (ii) nine months after the date of that event in the case of a claim for compensation for damage to property (whether or not death or bodily injury has also arisen from the same event);

(b) in a case where the applicant could not reasonably have been expected to have become aware of the existence of bodily injury or damage to property, the application must have been made as soon as practicable after he did become (or ought reasonably to have become) aware of it and in any case not later than—
   (i) fifteen years after the date of the event which is the subject of the application in the case of a claim for compensation for death or bodily injury (whether or not damage to property has also arisen from the same event); or
   (ii) two years after the date of that event in the case of a claim for compensation for damages to property (whether or not death or bodily injury has also arisen from the same event);

(c) the applicant, or a person acting on the applicant's behalf, must have reported that event to the police—
   (i) in the case of an event from which there has arisen a death or bodily injury alone, not later than 14 days after its occurrence; and
   (ii) in the case of an event from which there has arisen property damage (whether or not a death or bodily injury has also arisen from it), not later than 5 days after its occurrence;
   but where that is not reasonably possible the event must have been reported as soon as reasonably possible.

(d) the applicant must produce satisfactory evidence of having made the report required under sub-paragraph (c) in the form of an acknow-ledgement from the relevant force showing the crime or incident number under which that force has recorded the matter; after making, or author-ising the making of, report to the police the applicant must have co-operated with the police in any investigation they have made into the event.

(4) Where both death or bodily injury and damage to property have arisen from a single event nothing contained in this clause shall require an applicant to make an application in respect of the death or bodily injury on the same occasion as an application in respect of the damage to property and where two applications are made in respect of one event the provisions of this Agreement shall apply separately to each of them.

Exclusions from Agreement

5. (1) This Agreement does not apply where an application is made in any of the following circumstances (so that where an application is made partly in such circumstances and partly in other circumstances, it applies only to the part made in those circumstances)—

(a)   where the applicant makes no claim for compensation in respect of death or bodily injury and the damage to property in respect of which compensation is claimed has been caused by, or has arisen out of, the use of an unidentified vehicle;

(b)   where the death, bodily injury or damage to property in respect of which the application is made has been caused by or has arisen out of the use of a major vehicle which at the time of the event giving rise to such death, injury or damage was owned by or in the possession of the Crown, unless at that time some other person had undertaken responsibility for bringing into existence a policy of insurance or security satisfying the requirements of the 1988 Act;

(c)   where, at the time of the event in respect of which the application is made the person suffering death, injury or damage to property was voluntarily allowing himself to be carried in the responsible vehicle and before the commencement of his journey in the vehicle (or after such commencement if he could reasonably be expected to have alighted from the vehicle) he knew or ought to have known that the vehicle—

  (i)   had been stolen or unlawfully taken; or

  (ii)   was being used without there being in force in relation to its use a contract of insurance or security which complied with the 1988 Act; or

  (iii)   was being used in the course or furtherance of crime; or

  (iv)   was being used as a means of escape from or avoidance of lawful apprehension;

(d)   where the death, bodily injury or damage to property was caused by, or in the course of, an act of terrorism;

(e)   where property damaged as a result of the event giving rise to the application is insured against such damage and the applicant has recovered the full amount of his loss from the insurer on or before the date of the application (but without prejudice to the application of the Agreement in the case of any other claim for compensation made in respect of the same event);

(f)   where a claim is made for compensation in respect of damage to a motor vehicle (or losses arising there from) and, at the time when the damage to it was sustained—

  (i)   there was not in force in relation to the use of that vehicle such a contract of insurance as is required by Part VI pf the 1988 Act; and

  (ii)   the person suffering damage to property either knew or ought to have known that was the case (but without prejudice to the application of the Agreement in the case of any other claim for Compensation made in respect of the same event);

(g)   where the application is made neither by a person suffering injury or property damage nor by the personal representative of such a person nor by a dependant claiming in the respect of the death of another person but is made in any pf the following circumstances, namely—

  (i)   where a cause of action or a judgment has been assigned to the applicant; or

  (ii)   where the applicant is acting pursuant to a right of subrogation or a similar contractual or other right belonging to him.

(2)   The burden of proving that the person suffering death, injury or damage to property knew or ought to have known of any matter set out in paragraph (1) (c) shall be on MIB but, in the absence of evidence to the contrary, proof by MIB of any of the following matters shall be taken as proof of his knowledge of the matter set out in paragraph (1) (c) (ii)—

(a)   that he was the owner or registered keeper of the vehicle or had caused or permitted its use;

(b) that he knew the vehicle was being used by a person who was below the minimum age at which he could be granted a licence authorising the driving of a vehicle of that class;

(c) that he knew that the person driving the vehicle was disqualified for holding or obtaining a driving licence;

(d) that he knew that the user of the vehicle was neither its owner nor registered keeper nor an employee of the owner or registered keeper nor the owner or registered keeper of any other vehicle.

(3) Where—

(a) the application includes a claim for compensation both in respect of death or bodily injury and also in respect of damage to property; and

(b) the death or injury and the property damage has been caused by, or has arisen out of, the use of an unidentified vehicle;

the Agreement does not apply to the claim for compensation in respect of the damage to property.

(4) For the purposes of paragraphs (1) and (2)—

(a) references to a person being carried in a vehicle include references to his being carried in or upon, or entering or getting on to or alighting from the vehicle;

(b) knowledge which a person has or ought to have for the purposes of sub-paragraph (c) includes knowledge of matters which he could reasonably be expected to have been aware of had he not been under the self-induced influence of drink or drugs;

(c) 'crime' does not include the commission of an offence under the Traffic Acts, except an offence under section 143 (use of a motor vehicle on a road without there being in force a policy of insurance), and 'Traffic Acts' means the Road Traffic Regulation Act 1984, the Road Traffic Act 1988 and the Road Traffic Offenders Act 1988;

(d) 'responsible vehicle' means the vehicle the use of which caused (or through the use of which there arose) the death, bodily injury or damage to property which is the subject of the application;

(e) 'terrorism' has the meaning given in section 1 of the Terrorism Act 2000;

(f) 'dependant' has the same meaning as in section 1 (3) of the Fatal Accidents Act 1976.

Limitation on application of Agreement

6. (1) This clause applies where an applicant received compensation or other payment in respect of the death, bodily injury or damage to property otherwise than in the circumstances described in clause 5 (1) (e) from any of the following persons—

(a) an insurer or under an insurance policy (other than a life assurance policy) or arrangement between the applicant or his employer and the insurer, or

(b) a person who has given a security pursuant to the requirements of 1988 Act under an agreement between the applicant and the security giver; or

(c) any other source other than a person who is an identified person for the purposes of clauses 13 to 15 or an insurer of, or a person who has given a security on behalf of, such a person.

(2) Where the compensation or other payment received is equal to or greater than the amount which MIB would otherwise be liable to pay under the provisions of clauses 8 and 9 MIB shall have no liability under those provisions (to the intent that this Agreement shall immediately cease to apply except to the extent that the applicant is entitled to a contribution to his legal costs under clause 10).

(3)   Where the compensation or other payment received is less than the Amount which MIB would otherwise be liable to pay under the provisions of Clauses 8 and 9 MIB's liability under those provisions shall be reduced by an amount equal to that compensation or payment.

PRINCIPAL TERMS AND CONDITIONS

MIB's obligation to investigate claims and determine amount of award
7. (1)   MIB shall, at its own cost, take all reasonable steps to investigate the claim made in the application and—
   (a)   if it is satisfied after conducting a preliminary investigation that the case is not one to which this Agreement applies and the application should be rejected, it shall inform the applicant accordingly and (subject to the following provisions of this Agreement) need to take no further action, or
   (b)   in any other case, it shall conduct a full investigation and shall as soon as reasonably practicable having regard to the availability of evidence make a report on the applicant's claim.
(2)   Subject to the following paragraphs of this clause, MIB shall, on the basis of the report and, where applicable, any relevant proceedings—
   (a)   reach a decision as to whether it must make an award to the applicant in respect of the death, bodily injury or damage to property, and
   (b)   where it decides to make an award, determine the amount of that award.
(3)   Where MIB reaches a decision that the Agreement applies and that it is able to calculate the whole amount of the award the report shall be treated as a full report and the award shall (subject to the following provisions of this Agreement) be treated as a full and final award.
(4)   Where MIB reaches a decision that the Agreement applies and that it should make an award but further decides that it is not at that time able to circulate the final amount of the award (or a part thereof), it may designate the report as an interim report and where it does so—
   (a)   it may, as soon as reasonably practicable, make one or more further interim reports; but
   (b)   it must, as soon as reasonably practicable having regard to the availability of evidence, make a final report.
(5)   Where it makes an interim or final report MIB shall, on the basis of that Report and, where applicable, any relevant proceedings—
   (a)   in the case of an interim report, determine the amount of any interim award it wishes to make, and
   (b)   in the case of its final report, determine the whole amount of its award which shall (subject to the following provisions of this Agreement) be treated as a full and final award.
(6)   MIB shall be under an obligation to make an award only if it is satisfied, on the balance of probabilities, that the death, bodily injury or damage to property was caused in such circumstances that the unidentified person would (had he been identified) have been held liable to pay damages to the applicant in respect of it.
(7)   MIB shall determine the amount of its award in accordance with the Provisions of clauses 8 to 10 and (in an appropriate case) clauses 12 to 14 but shall not thereby be under a duty to calculate the exact proportion of the award which represents compensation, interest or legal costs.

Compensation
8. (1)   MIB shall include in its award to the applicant, by way of compensation for the death, bodily injury or damage to property, a sum equivalent to the amount which a court—
   (a)   applying the law of England and Wales, in a case where the event giving rise to the death, injury or damage occurred in England or Wales; or

(b)   applying the law of Scotland, in a case where that event occurred in Scotland;

would have awarded to the applicant (where applying English law) as general and special damages or (where applying the law of Scotland) as solatium and patrimonial loss if the applicant had brought successful proceedings to enforce a claim for damages against the unidentified person.

(2)   In calculating the sum payable under paragraph (1), MIB shall adopt the same method of calculation as the court would adopt in calculating damages but it shall be under no obligation to include in that calculation an amount in respect of loss of earnings suffered by the applicant to the extent that he has been paid wages or salary (or any sum in lieu of them) whether or not such payments were made subject to an agreement or undertaking on his part to repay the same in the event of his recovering damages for the loss of those earnings.

(3)   Where an application includes a claim in respect of damage to property, MIB's liability in respect of that claim shall be limited in accordance with the following rules—

(a)   if the loss incurred by an applicant in respect of any one event giving rise to a claim does not exceed the specified excess, MIB shall incur no liability to that applicant in respect of the event,

(b)   if the aggregate of all losses incurred by both the applicant and other persons in respect of any one event giving rise to a claim ('the total loss') exceeds the specified excess but does not exceed £250,000—

(i)   MIB's liability to an individual applicant shall be the amount of the claim less the specified excess; and

(ii)   MIB's total liability to applicants in respect of claims arising from that event shall be the total loss less a sum equal to the specified excess multiplied by the number of applicants who have incurred loss through damage to property.

(c)   if the total loss exceeds £250,000—

(i)   MIB's liability to an individual applicant shall not exceed the amount of the claim less the specified excess; and

(ii)   MIB's total liability to applicants in respect of claims arising from that event shall be £250,000 less a sum equal to the specified excess multiplied by the number of applicants who have incurred loss due to property damage.

(4)   MIB shall not be liable to pay compensation to an appropriate authority in respect of any loss incurred by that authority as a result of its failure to recover a charge for the recovery, storage or disposal of an abandoned Vehicle under a power contained in the Refuse Disposal (Amenity) Act 1978 or Part VIII of the Road Traffic Regulation Act 1984 (and in this paragraph 'appropriate authority' has the meaning given in the Act under which the power to recover the charge is exercisable).

Interest

9. (1)   MIB shall in an appropriate case also include in the award a sum representing interest on the compensation payable under clause 8 at a rate equal to that which a court—

(a)   applying the law of England and Wales, in a case where the event giving rise to the death, bodily injury or damage to property occurred in England and Wales; or

(b)   applying the law of Scotland, in a case where that event occurred in Scotland, would have awarded to a successful applicant.

(2)   MIB is not required by virtue of paragraph (1) to pay a sum representing interest in respect of the period before the date which is one month after the date on which MIB received the police report (but, where MIB has failed to seek and

obtain that report promptly after the date of the application, interest shall run from the date which falls one month after the date on which it would have received it had it acted promptly).

Contribution towards legal costs

10. (1)   MIB shall, in a case where it has decided to make a compensation payment under clause 8, also include in the award a sum by way of contribution towards the cost of obtaining legal advise from a Solicitor, Barrister or Advocate in respect of—

(a)   the making of an application under this Agreement;

(b)   the correctness of a decision made by MIB under this Agreement; or

(c)   the adequacy of an award (or a part thereof) offered by MIB under this Agreement.

That sum to be determined in accordance with the Schedule to this Agreement.

(2)   MIB shall not be under a duty to make a payment under paragraph (1) unless it is satisfied that the applicant did obtain legal advise in respect of any one or more of the matters specified in that paragraph.

Conditions precedent to MIB's obligations

11. (1)   The applicant must—

(a)   make his application in such form;

(b)   provide in support of the application such statements and other information (whether in writing or orally at interview); and

(c)   give such further assistance, as may reasonably be required by MIB or by any person acting on MIB's behalf to enable an investigation to be carried out under clause 7 of this Agreement.

(2)   The applicant must provide MIB with written authority to take all such steps as may be reasonably necessary in order to carry out a proper investigation of the claim.

(3)   The applicant must, if MIB reasonably requires him to do so before reaching a decision under clause 7, provide MIB with a statutory declaration, made by him, setting out to the best of his knowledge and belief all the facts and circumstances in relation to the application as MIB may reasonably specify.

(4)   The applicant must, if MIB reasonably requires him to do so before it reaches a decision or determination under clause 7 and subject to the following provisions of the clause—

(a)   at MIB'S option (and subject to paragraph (5)) either—

(i)   bring proceedings against any person or persons who may, in addition or alternatively to the unidentified person, be liable to the applicant in respect of the death, bodily injury or damage to property (by virtue of having caused or contributed to that death, injury or damage, by being vicariously liable in respect of it or having failed to effect third party liability insurance in respect of the vehicle in question) and co-operate with MIB in taking such steps as are reasonably necessary to obtain judgement in those proceedings; or

(ii)   authorise MIB to bring such proceedings and take such steps in the applicant's name;

(b)   at MIB's expense, provide MIB with a transcript of any official shorthand or recorded note taken in those proceedings of any evidence given or judgement delivered therein;

(c)   assign to MIB or to its nominee the benefit of any judgement obtained by him (whether or not obtained in proceedings brought under sub-paragraph (a) above) in respect of the death, bodily injury or damage to property upon such terms as will secure that MIB or its nominee will be accountable to the applicant for any amount by which the aggregate of all sums recovered by MIB or its nominee under the judgement (after deducting all reasonable expenses incurred in effecting recovery) exceeds the award by MIB under this Agreement in respect of that death, injury or damage;

(d) undertake to assign to MIB the right to any sum which is or may be due from an insurer, security giver or other person by way of compensation for, or benefit in respect of, the death, bodily injury or damage to property and which would (if payment had been made before the date of the award) have excluded or limited MIB's liability under the provisions of clause 6.

(5) If, pursuant to paragraph (4)(a), MIB requires the applicant to bring proceedings or take steps against any person or persons (or to authorise MIB to bring such proceedings or take such steps in his name) MIB shall indemnify the applicant against all costs and expenses reasonably incurred by him in complying with that requirement.

(6) Where the applicant, without having been required to do so by MIB, has commenced proceedings against any person described in paragraph (4)—

(a) the applicant shall as soon as reasonably possible notify MIB of such proceedings and provide MIB with such further information about them as MIB may reasonably require; and

(b) the applicant's obligations in paragraph (4)(a) to (c) shall apply in respect of such proceedings as if they had been brought at MIB's request.

JOINT AND SEVERAL LIABILITY

Joint and several liability: interpretation
12. In clauses 13 to 15—
'identified person' includes an identified employer or principal of a person who is himself unidentified;
'original judgement' means a judgement obtained against an identified person at first instance in relevant proceedings;
'three month period' means the period of three months specified in clause 13(3); and
'unidentified person's liability' means the amount of the contribution which (if not otherwise apparent) would, on the balance of probabilities, have been be recoverable from the unidentified person in an action brought—

(a) (i) in England and Wales, under the Civil Liability (Contribution) Act 1978, or
(ii) in Scotland, under the Law Reform (Miscellaneous Provisions) (Scotland) Act 1940,
by an identified person who had been held liable in full in an earlier action brought by the applicant, and

(b) where a court has awarded the applicant interest or costs in addition to damages, an appropriate proportion of that interest or those costs.

MIB's liability where wrongdoer is identified
13. (1) This clause applies where the death, bodily injury or damage to property in respect of which the application is made is caused, or appears on the balance of probabilities to have been caused—

(a) partly by an unidentified person and partly by an identified person; or
(b) partly by an unidentified person and partly by another unidentified person whose employer or principal is identified;
in circumstances making (or appearing to make) the identified person liable, or vicariously liable, to the applicant in respect of the death, injury or damage.

(2)   Where this clause applies, MIB's liability under this Agreement shall not exceed the unidentified person's liability and the following provisions shall apply to determine MIB's liability in specific cases.

(3)   Where the applicant has obtained a judgement in relevant proceedings in respect of the death, injury or damage which has not been satisfied in full by or on behalf of the identified person within the period of three months after the date on which the applicant became entitled to enforce it—

    (a)   if that judgement is wholly unsatisfied within the three month period MIB shall make an award equal to the unidentified person's liability;

    (b)   if the judgement is satisfied in part only within the three month period, MIB shall make an award equal to—

        (i)   the unsatisfied part, if it does not exceed the unidentified person's liability; and

        (ii)   the unidentified person's liability, if the unsatisfied part exceeds the unidentified person's liability.

(4)   A judgement given in any relevant proceedings against an identified person shall be conclusive as to any issue determined in those proceedings which is relevant to the determination of MIB's liability under this Agreement.

(5)   Where the applicant has not obtained (or been required by MIB to obtain) a judgement in respect of the death, injury or damage against the identified person but has received an agreed payment from the identified person in respect of the death, bodily injury or damage to property, that payment shall be treated for the purposes of the Agreement as a full settlement of the applicant's claim and MIB shall be under no liability under this Agreement in respect thereof.

(6)   Where the applicant has not obtained (or been required by MIB to obtain) a judgement in respect of the death, injury or damage against the identified person nor received any payment by way of compensation in respect thereof from the identified person MIB shall make an award equal to the unidentified person's liability.

Appeals by identified persons

14. (1)   This clause applies where an appeal against, or other proceeding to set aside, the original judgement is commenced within the three month period.

If, as a result of the appeal or other proceeding—

    (a)   the applicant ceases to be entitled to receive any payment in respect of the death, bodily injury or damage to property from any identified person, clause 13 shall apply as if he had neither obtained nor been required by MIB to obtain a judgement against the person;

    (b)   the applicant becomes entitled to recover an amount different from that which he was entitled to recover under original judgement the provisions of clause 13(3) shall apply, but as if for each of the references therein to the original judgement there were substituted a reference to the judgement in that appeal or other proceeding;

    (c)   the applicant remains entitled to enforce the original judgement the provisions of clause 13 (3) shall apply, but as if for each of the references therein to the three month period there was substituted a reference to the period of three months after the date on which the appeal or other proceeding was disposed of.

(3)   Where the judgement in the appeal or other proceeding is itself the subject of a further appeal or similar proceedings the provisions of this clause shall apply in relation to that further appeal or proceeding in the same manner as they apply in relation to the first appeal or proceeding.

(4)   Nothing in this clause shall oblige MIB to make a payment to the applicant until the appeal or other proceeding has been determined.

Compensation recovered under Uninsured Drivers Agreements

15. (1)   Where, in case to which clause 13 applies, judgement in the relevant proceedings is given against an identified person in circumstances which render MIB liable to satisfy that judgement under any of the Uninsured Drivers Agreements, MIB shall not be under any liability under this Agreement in respect of the event to which the relevant proceedings relate.

(2)   In this clause 'Uninsured Drivers Agreements' means—

(a)   the Agreement dated 21st December 1988 made between the Secretary of State for Transport and MIB providing for the compensation of victims of uninsured drivers;

(b)   the 1999 Agreement; and

(c)   any agreement made between the Secretary of State and MIB (or their respective successors) which supersedes (whether immediately or otherwise) the 1999 Agreement.

NOTIFICATION OF DECISION AND PAYMENT OF AWARD

Notification of decision

16.   MIB shall give the applicant notice of a decision or determination under clause 7 in writing and when so doing shall provide him—

(a)   if the application is rejected because a preliminary investigation has disclosed that it is not one made in a case to which this Agreement applies, with a statement to that effect;

(b)   if the application has been fully investigated, with a statement setting out—

(i)   all the evidence obtained during the investigation; and

(ii)   MIB's findings of fact from that evidence which are relevant to the decision;

(c)   if it has decided to make an interim award on the basis of an interim report under clause 7(4), with a copy of the report and a statement of the amount of the interim award;

(d)   if it has decided to make a full report under clause 7(3) or a final report under clause 7(4)(b), with a copy of the report and a statement of the amount of the full and final award;

(e)   in a case to which clause 13 applies, with a statement setting out the way in which the amount of the award has been computed under the provisions of that clause; and

(f)   in every case, with a statement of its reasons for making the decision or determination.

Acceptance of decision and payment of award

17. (1)   Subject to the following paragraphs of the clause, if MIB gives notice to the applicant that it has decided to make an award to him, it shall pay him that award—

(a)   in the case of an interim award made pursuant to clause 7(5)(a), as soon as reasonably practicable after the making of the interim report to which the award relates;

(b)   in the case of a full and final award made pursuant to clause 7(3) or (5)(b)—

(i)   where the applicant notifies MIB in writing that he accepts the offer of the award unconditionally, not later than 14 days after the date on which MIB receives that acceptance; or

(ii)   where the applicant does not notify MIB of his acceptance in accordance with sub-paragraph (a) but the period during which he may give notice of an appeal under clause 19 has expired without such notice being given, not later than 14 days after the date of expiry of that period;

that payment shall discharge MIB from all liability under this Agreement in respect of the death, bodily injury or damage to property for which the award is made.

(2)   MIB may, upon notifying an applicant of its decision to make an award offer to pay the award in instalments in accordance with a structure described in the decision letter (the 'structured settlement') and if the applicant notifies MIB in writing of his acceptance of the offer—

(a)   the first instalment of the payment under the structured settlement shall be made not later than 14 days after the date on which MIB receives that acceptance; and

(b)   subsequent payments shall be made in accordance with the agreed structure.

(3)   Where an applicant has suffered bodily injury and believes either that there is a risk that he will develop a disease or condition other than that in respect of which he has made a claim or that a disease or condition in respect of which he has made a claim will deteriorate, he may—

(a)   by notice given in his application; or

(b)   by notice in writing received by MIB before the date on which MIB issues notification of its full or (as the case may be) final report under clause 16;

state that he wishes MIB to make a provisional award and if he does so paragraphs (4) and (5) shall apply.

(4)   The applicant must specify in the notice given under paragraph (3) – each disease and each type of deterioration which he believes may occur, and the period during or within which he believes it may occur.

(5)   Where MIB receives a notice under paragraph (3) it shall, not later than 14 days after the date of such receipt (or within such longer period as the applicant my agree)—

(a)   accept the notice and confirm that any award it makes (other than an interim award made pursuant to clause 7(5)(a)) is to be treated as a provisional award; or

(b)   reject the notice and inform the applicant that it is not willing to make a provisional award.

(6)   Where MIB has notified the applicant that it accepts the notice, an award which would otherwise be treated a full and final award under this Agreement shall be treated as a provisional award only and the applicant may make a supplementary application under this Agreement but—

(a)   only in respect of a disease or a type of deterioration of his condition specified in his notice; and

(b)   not later than the expiration of the period specified in his notice.

(7)   Where MIB has notified the applicant that it rejects the notice, subject to any decision to the contrary made by an arbitrator, no award which MIB makes shall be treated as a provisional award.

APPEALS AGAINST MIB'S DECISION

Right of appeal

18.   Where an applicant is not willing to accept—

(a)   a decision or determination made by MIB under clause 7 or a part thereof;

(b)   a proposal for a structured settlement or a rejection of the applicant's request for a provisional award under clause 17;

he may give notice (a 'notice of appeal') that he wishes to submit the matter to arbitration in accordance with the provisions of clauses 19 to 25.

Notice of appeal

19. (1)   A notice of appeal shall be given in writing to MIB at any time before the expiration of a period of 6 weeks from—
    (a)   the date on which the applicant received notice of MIB's decision under clause 16;
    (b)   where he disputes a notification given under clause 17(5)(b), the date when such notification is given;
    (c)   in any other case, the date on which he is given notification of the decision, determination or requirement.
(2)   The notice of appeal—
    (a)   shall state the grounds on which the appeal is made;
    (b)   shall contain the applicant's observation on MIB's decision;
    (c)   may be accompanied by such further evidence in support of the appeal as the applicant thinks fit; and
    (d)   shall contain an undertaking that (subject, in the case of an arbitration to be conducted England and Wales, to his rights under sections 67 and 68 of the Arbitration Act 1996) the application will abide by the decision of the arbitrator made under this Agreement.

Procedure following notice of appeal

20. (1)   Not later than 7 days after receiving the notice of appeal MIB shall—
    (a)   apply to the Secretary of State for the appointment of a single arbitrator; or
    (b)   having notified the applicant of its intention to do so, cause an investigation to be made into any further evidence supplied by the applicant and report to the applicant upon that investigation and of any change in its decision which may result from it.
(2)   Where the only ground stated in the notice of appeal is that the award is insufficient (including a ground contesting the degree of contributory negligence attributed to the applicant or, as the case may be, the person in respect of whose death the application is made), MIB may give notice to the applicant of its intention, if the appeal proceeds to arbitration, to ask the arbitrator to decide whether its award exceeds what a court would have awarded or whether the case is one in which it would make an award at all and shall in that notice set out such observations on that matter as MIB considers relevant to the arbitrator's decision.
(3)   Where MIB has made a report under paragraph (1)(b) or given to the applicant notice under paragraph (2), the applicant may, not later than 6 weeks after the date on which the report or (as the case may be) the notice was given to him—
    (a)   notify MIB that he wishes to withdraw the appeal; or
    (b)   notify MIB that he wishes to continue with the appeal and send with that notification—
        (i)   any observations on the report made under paragraph (1)(b) which he wishes to have drawn to the attention of the arbitrator;
        (ii)   any observations on the contents of the notice given under paragraph (2), including any further evidence not previously made available to MIB and relevant to the matter, which he wishes to have drawn to the attention of the arbitrator.
(4)   Where the applicant notifies MIB under paragraph (3)(b) of his wish to continue the appeal, or if the applicant fails within the specified period of 6 weeks to give notification of his wish either to withdraw or to continue with the appeal, MIB shall, not later than 7 days after receiving the notification or 7 days after the expiry of the said period (as the case may be)—
    (a)   apply to the Secretary of State for the appointment of an arbitrator; or

(b)   having notified the applicant of its intention to do so, cause a further investigation to be made into the further evidence sent under paragraph (3)(b)(ii).

(5)   Where MIB has caused an investigation to be made into any further evidence supplied by the applicant under paragraph (3)(b)(ii), it shall report to the applicant upon that investigation and of any change in a decision or determination made under clause 7 which may result from it and the applicant may, not later than 6 weeks after the date on which he received the report—

(a)   notify MIB that he wishes to withdraw the appeal; or

(b)   notify MIB that he wishes to continue with the appeal.

(6)   Where the applicant notifies MIB under paragraph (5)(b) of his wish to continue the appeal, or if the applicant fails within the specified period of 6 weeks to give notification of his wish either to withdraw or to continue with the appeal, MIB shall not later than 7 days after receiving the notification or 7 days after the expiry of the said period (as the case may be) apply to the Secretary of State for the appointment of an arbitrator.

(7)   When applying to the Secretary of State for the appointment of an arbitrator MIB may send with the application such written observations as it wishes to make upon the applicant's notice of appeal but must at the same time send a copy of those observations to the applicant.

Appointment of arbitrator

21. (1)   In the event of MIB neither applying to the Secretary of State for the appointment of an arbitrator in accordance with the provisions of clause 20 nor taking such further steps as it may at its discretion take in accordance with that clause, the applicant may apply to the Secretary of State for the appointment of an arbitrator.

(2)   For the purposes of the Arbitration Act 1996 (where the arbitration is to be conducted in England and Wales) the arbitral proceedings are to be regarded as commencing on the date of the making of the application by the Secretary of State or the applicant (as the case may be).

(3)   The Secretary of State shall, upon the making of an application for the appointment of an arbitrator to hear the appeal, appoint the first available member, by rotation, of a panel of Queen's Counsel appointed for the purpose of determining appeals under this Agreement (where the event giving rise to the death, bodily injury or damage to property occurred in England and Wales) by the Lord Chancellor or (where the event giving rise to the death, bodily injury or damage to property occurred in Scotland) by the Lord Advocate and shall forthwith notify the applicant and MIB of the appointment.

Arbitration procedure

22. (1)   Upon receiving notification from the Secretary of State of the appointment of an arbitrator, MIB shall send to the arbitrator—

(a)   the notice of appeal;

(b)   (if appropriate) its request for a decision as to whether its award exceed what a court would have awarded or whether the case is one in which it would make an award at all;

(c)   copies of—

(i)   the applicant's application;

(ii)   its decision; and

(iii)   all statements, declarations, notices, reports observations and transports of evidence made or given under this Agreement by the applicant or MIB.

(2)　The arbitrator may, if it appears to him to be necessary or expedient for the purpose of resolving any issue, ask MIB to make a further investigation and to submit a written report of its findings to him for his consideration and in such a case—

    (a)　MIB shall undertake the investigation and send copies of the report to the arbitrator and the applicant;

    (b)　the applicant may, not later than 4 weeks after the date on which a copy of the report is received by him, submit written observations on it to the arbitrator and if he does so he shall send a copy of those observations to MIB.

(3)　The arbitrator shall, after considering the written submissions referred to in paragraphs (1) and (2), send to the applicant and MIB a preliminary decision letter setting out the decision he proposes to make under clause 23 and his reasons for doing so.

(4)　not later than 28 days after the date of sending of the preliminary decision letter (or such later date as the applicant and MIB may agree) the applicant and MIB may, by written notification given to the arbitrator and copied to the other, either–

    (a)　accept the preliminary decision; or

    (b)　submit written observations upon the preliminary decision or the reasons or both; or

    (c)　request an oral hearing;

and if either of them should within that period fail to do any of those things (including a failure to provide the other person with a copy of his notification) he or it shall be treated as having accepted the decision.

(5)　If the applicant submits new evidence with any written observations under paragraph (4)(b) MIB may at its discretion, but within 28 days or such longer period as the arbitrator may allow, do any of the following—

    (a)　make an investigation into that evidence;

    (b)　submit its own written observations on that evidence; and

    (c)　if it has not already done so, request an oral hearing;

and, expect where an oral hearing has been requested, the arbitrator shall (in exercise of his powers under section 34 of the Arbitration Act 1996 if the arbitration is being conducted in England and Wales) determine whether, and if so how, such evidence shall be admitted and tested.

(6)　If both the applicant and MIB accept the reasoned preliminary decision that decision shall be treated as his final decision for the purposes of clause 23 (so that clause 23(2) shall not then apply) but if either of them submits observations on that decision the arbitrator must take those observations into account before making a final decision.

(7)　If the applicant or MIB requests an oral hearing, the arbitrator shall determine the appeal in that manner and in such a case—

    (a)　the hearing shall be held in public unless the applicant requests that it (or any part of it) be heard in private;

    (b)　the hearing shall take place at a location—

        (i)　in England or Wales, or where the event giving rise to the death, bodily injury or damage to property occurred in England or Wales and the applicant is resident in England or Wales;

        (ii)　in Scotland, where the event giving rise to the death, bodily injury or damage to property occurred in Scotland and the applicant is resident in Scotland; or

        (iii)　in England, Wales or Scotland in any other case, which in the opinion of the arbitrator (after consultation with each of them) is convenient both for the MIB and the applicant as well as for himself;

    (c)　a party to the hearing may be represented by a lawyer or other person of that party's choosing;

(d)   a party to the hearing shall be entitled to address the arbitrator, to call witnesses and to put questions to those witnesses and any other person called as a witness.

Arbitrator's decision

23. (1)   The arbitrator, having regard to the subject matter of the proceedings, may in an appropriate case—

(a)   determine whether or not the case is one to which this agreement applies;

(b)   remit the application to MIB for full investigation and a decision in accordance with the provisions of this agreement;

(c)   determine whether the MIB should make an award under this agreement and if so what the award should be;

(d)   determine such other questions as have been referred to him as he thinks fit;

(e)   (subject to the provisions of paragraph (4) of this clause and clause 24) order that the costs of the proceedings shall be paid by one party or allocated between the parties in such proportions as he thinks fit;

and where the arbitrator makes a determination under sub-paragraph (a) that the case is one to which this Agreement applies, all the provisions of this Agreement shall apply as if the case were one to which clause 7(1)(b) applies.

(2)   The arbitrator shall notify MIB and the applicant of his decision in writing. MIB shall pay to the applicant any amount which the arbitrator has decided shall be awarded to him, and that payment shall discharge MIB from all liability under this Agreement in respect of the death, bodily injury or damage to property in respect of which that decision is given.

(3)   Where an oral hearing has taken place at the request of the applicant and the arbitrator is satisfied that it was unnecessary and that the matter could have been decided on the basis of the written submissions referred to in clause 22(1) and (2) he shall take that into account when making an order under paragraph (1)(e).

Payment of the arbitrator's fee and costs of legal representation

24. (1)   Subject to paragraph (2), MIB shall upon being notified of the decision of the arbitrator pay the arbitrator a fee approved by the Lord Chancellor or the Lord Advocate, as the case may be, after consultation with MIB.

(2)   In a case where it appears to the arbitrator that, having regard to all the surrounding circumstances of the case, there were no reasonable grounds for making the appeal or bringing the question before him, the arbitrator may, in his discretion, order—

(a)   the applicant or;

(b)   where he considers it appropriate to do so, any Solicitor or other person acting on behalf of the applicant;

to reimburse MIB the fee it has paid to the arbitrator or any part thereof.

(3)   Where, pursuant to the paragraph (2), the arbitrator orders—

(a)   the applicant to reimburse MIB, MIB may deduct an amount equal to the fee from any amount which it pays to the applicant to discharge its liability under this Agreement;

(b)   a Solicitor or other person to reimburse MIB, MIB may deduct an amount equal to the fee from any amount which it pays to that Solicitor or other person to discharge its liability to the applicant under this Agreement.

(4)   Where there is an oral hearing and the applicant secures an award of compensation greater then that previously offered, then (unless the arbitrator orders otherwise) MIB shall make a contribution of £500 per half day towards the cost incurred by the applicant in respect of representation by a Solicitor, Barrister or Advocate.

Applicants under a disability

25. (1)   If in any case it appears to MIB that, by reason of the applicant being a minor or of any other circumstance affecting his capacity to manage his affairs, it would be in the applicant's interest that all or some part of the award should be administered for him by an appropriate representative, MIB may establish for that purpose a trust of the whole or part of the award (such trust to take effect for such period and under such provisions as appears to MIB to be appropriate in the circumstances of the case) or, as the case may be, initiate or cause any other person in initiate the proceedings necessary to have the award administrated by an appropriate representative and otherwise cause any amount payable under the award to be paid to and administered by the appropriate representative.

(2)   In this clause 'appropriate representative' means—

    (a)   in England and Wales—

        (i)   the Family Welfare Association, or a similar body or person, as trustee of the trust; or

        (ii)   the Court of Protection; and

    (b)   in Scotland—

        (i)   a Judicial Factor; or

        (ii)   a guardian under the Adults with Incapacity (Scotland) Act 2000; or

        (iii)   (where the applicant is a child) the tutor or curator of the child or a person having parental responsibilities under the Children (Scotland) Act 1995.

ACCELERATED PROCEDURE

Instigation of accelerated procedure

26. (1)   In any case where, after making a preliminary investigation under clause 7, MIB has decided that—

    (a)   the case is one to which this Agreement applies; and

    (b)   it is not one to which clause 13 applies;

MIB may notify the applicant of that decision and, instead of causing a full investigation and report to be made under clause 7, may make to the applicant an offer to settle his claim by payment of an award specified in the offer representing compensation assessed in accordance with clause 8 together, in an appropriate case, with interest thereon assessed in accordance with clause 9 and a contribution towards the cost of obtaining legal advice in respect of the making of the application.

(2)   Where an offer is made under paragraph (1), MIB shall send to the applicant a statement setting out the relevant evidence it has collected disclosing the circumstances in which the death, bodily injury or damage to property occurred, and its reasons for the assessment of the award.

Settlement by accelerated procedure

27. (1)   The applicant shall not later than 6 weeks after he receives an offer under clause 26 notify MIB of his acceptance or rejection thereof.

Where the applicant notifies MIB of his acceptance of the offer—

    (a)   MIB shall not later than 14 days after receipt of the acceptance pay to the applicant the amount of the award; and

    (b)   MIB shall be discharged from all liability under this Agreement in respect of the death, bodily injury or damage to property for which that payment is made.

(2)   In the event of the applicant failing to accept the offer within the specified Period, the application shall be treated as one to which clause 7(1)(b) applies.

MISCELLANEOUS

Referral of disputes to arbitrator
28. (1)   Any dispute between the applicant and MIB concerning a decision, determination or requirement made by MIB under the terms of this Agreement, other than a dispute relating to MIB's decision for which provision is made by clause 18, shall be referred to and determined by an arbitrator.
(2)   Where an applicant wishes to refer such a dispute to arbitration, he shall not later than 4 weeks after the decision, determination or requirement is communicated to him, give notice to MIB that he wishes the matter to be so resolved.
(3)   For the purposes of the Arbitration Act 1996 (where the arbitration is to be conducted in England and Wales) the arbitral proceedings are to be regarded as commencing on the date of such application.
(4)   Upon receipt of the applicant's notice MIB shall apply immediately to the Secretary of State for the appointment of an arbitrator and in the event of MIB failing to do so the applicant may make the application.
(5)   The Secretary of State shall, upon receiving the application for the appointment of an arbitrator to hear the appeal, appoint the first available member, by rotation, of a panel of Queen's Counsel appointed for the purpose of determining appeals under this Agreement (where the event giving rise to the death, bodily injury or damage to property occurred in England Wales) by the Lord Chancellor or (where the event giving rise to the death, bodily injury or damage to property occurred in Scotland) by the Lord Advocate and shall forthwith notify the applicant and MIB of the appointment.
(6)   The applicant and MIB shall, not later than 4 weeks after receiving notification of the appointment of the arbitrator, submit to him a written statement of their respective cases with supporting documentary evidence where available.
(7)   Subject to paragraphs (8) to (10), the arbitrator shall decide the appeal on the documents submitted to him under paragraph (6) and no further evidence shall be produced to him.
(8)   The applicant may, by notice in writing given to the arbitrator and MIB not later than the date on which he submits the statement of his case, ask the arbitrator to determine the appeal by means of an oral hearing and shall submit to the arbitrator and MIB a written statement, with supporting documentary evidence where appropriate, in support of that request.
(9)   The arbitrator shall in such a case seek the view of MIB on the need for an oral hearing and MIB may submit to the arbitrator and the applicant a written statement, with supporting documentary evidence where appropriate, in support of its view.
(10)   If, after considering those written submissions, the arbitrator decides that an oral hearing is necessary to determine the dispute—
  (a)   the hearing shall be held in public unless the applicant request that it (or any part of it) be heard in private;
  (b)   the hearing shall take place at a location—
    (i)   in England and Wales, where the event giving rise to the death, bodily injury or damage to property occurred in England or Wales and the applicant is resident in England or Wales;
    (ii)   in Scotland, where the event giving rise to the death, bodily injury or damage to property occurred in Scotland and the applicant is resident in Scotland; or
    (iii)   in England, Wales or Scotland in any other case, which in the opinion of the arbitrator (after consultation with each of them) is convenient for both MIB and the applicant as well as for himself;
  (c)   a party to the hearing may be represented by a lawyer or other person of that party's choosing;

(d) a party to the hearing shall be entitled to address the arbitrator, to call witnesses and to put questions to those witnesses and any other person called as a witness.

(11) The arbitrator may, having regard to the subject matter of the proceedings and in an appropriate case, order that his fee or the costs of the proceedings (as determined according to clause 10(1)(b) of, and the Schedule to, this Agreement) or both his fee and those costs shall be paid by one party or allocated between the parties in such proportions as he thinks fit.

(12) Unless otherwise agreed, the decision, determination or requirement in respect of which notice is given under paragraph (2) shall stand unless reserved by the arbitrator.

Services of notices, etc, on MIB

29. Any notice required to be served on or any other notification or document required to be given or sent to MIB under the terms of his Agreement shall be sufficiently served or given sent by fax or by Registered or Recorded Delivery post to MIB's registered office and delivery shall be proved by the production of a fax report produced by the sender's fax machine or an appropriate postal receipt.

Agents

30. MIB may perform any of its obligation under this Agreement by agents.

Contracts (Rights of Third Parties) Act 1999

31 (1) For the purposes of the Contracts (Rights of Third Parties) Act 1999 the following provisions shall apply.

(2) This Agreement may be—
(a) varied or rescinded without the consent of any person other than the parties hereto; and
(b) determination under clause 3(2) without the consent of any such person.

(3) Save for the matters specified in paragraph (4), MIB shall not have available to it against an applicant any matter by way of counterclaim or set- off which would have been available to it if the applicant rather than the Secretary of State had been a party to this Agreement.

(4) The matters referred to in paragraph (3) are any counterclaim or set-off arising by virtue of the provisions of—
(a) this Agreement;
(b) the 1996 Agreement;
(c) the 1999 Agreement;
(d) either of the agreements which were respectively superseded by the 1996 Agreement and the 1999 Agreement.

(5) This agreement, being made for the purposes of Article 1 (4) of Council Directive 84/5/EEC of 30th December 1983—
(a) is intended to confer a benefit on an applicant but on no other person; and
(b) to confer such benefit subject to the terms and conditions set out herein.

Enforcement against MIB

32. If MIB fail to pay compensation in accordance with the provisions of this agreement the applicant is entitled to enforce payment through the courts.

Transitional provisions

33.   The 1996 Agreement shall cease to have effect after the 13 February 2003 but shall continue in force in relation to any claim arising out of an event occurring on or before that date.

IN WITNESS whereof the Secretary of State has caused his Corporate Seal to be hereunto affixed and the Motor Insurers' Bureau has caused its Common Seal to be hereunto affixed the day and year first above written.

SCHEDULE

MIB's contribution towards applicant's legal costs

1.   Subject to paragraph 4, MIB shall pay a contribution towards the applicant's costs of obtaining legal advice determined in accordance with paragraph 2.

2.   That amount shall be the aggregate of—
   (a)   the fee specified in column (2) of the table below in relation to the amount of the award specified in column (1) of the table;
   (b)   the amount of value added tax charged on that fee;
   (c)   where the applicant has opted for an oral hearing under clause; and
   (d)   reasonable disbursements.

Table

Amount of the award (1)	Specified fee (2)
Not exceeding £150,000	15% of the amount of the award, subject to a minimum of £500 and a maximum of £3,000
Exceeding £150,000	2% of the amount of the award

3.   For the purposes of paragraph 2—
   (a)   'amount of the award' means the aggregate of the sum awarded by way of compensation and interest under clauses 8 and 9, before deduction of any reimbursement due to be paid to the Secretary of State for Work and Pensions through the Compensation Recovery Unit (CRU) of his Department (or to any successor of that unit), but excluding the amount of any payment due in respect of benefits and hospital charges;
   (b)   'reasonable disbursements' means reasonable expenditure incurred on the applicant's behalf and agreed between the applicant and MIB before it is incurred (MIB's Agreement no having been unreasonably withheld) but includes Counsel's fees only where the applicant is a minor or under a legal disability.

4.   The foregoing provisions of this Schedule are without prejudice to MIB's liability under the provisions of this Agreement to pay the costs of arbitration proceedings or an arbitrator's fee.

THE CORPORATE SEAL of the Secretary of State for Transport hereunto affixed is authorised by:
   Authorised by the Secretary of State
   Richard Jones
   THE COMMON SEAL of the Motor Insurers' Bureau was hereunto affixed in the presence of:

J A Read   R D Snook

Directors of the Board of Management
B Louisy
Secretary

NOTES

The agreement came into force on 14 February 2003 and applies to all accidents involving untraced drivers occurring on or after that date.

Clause 4(3)(ii) confirms that the limitation period for claims for compensation for damage to property is 9 months after the date of the event

More than 1 claim can be made in respect of the same event.

1.   Where the applicant could not reasonably have been expected to be aware of the existence of either a claim for injury or damage to property (clause 4(3)(b)) then the applicant must make the application as soon as possible after he became aware and in the case of death or injury the application must be made no later than 15 years after the accident and where property damage is involved the claim must be made no later than 2 years after the event.

2.   Clause 4(3)(c) requires the applicant to have reported the claim to the police within 14 days of the accident if an injury was sustained or within 5 days if the damage was limited to damage to property. The applicant must be able to prove that the claim was reported and must have co-operated with the police. Practically, the applicant must keep some written proof that the accident was reported rather than assuming the Police will have kept a record.

3.   The Agreement does not apply where the applicant has not been injured but makes a claim for property damage which arises out of the use of an unidentified vehicle. Nor does it apply where death, injury or damage to property was caused or arose out of the use of a vehicle owned or in the possession of the Crown.

4.   Exclusions set out at clause 5 confirm that a payment will not be made where the applicant knew or ought to have known that the vehicle in which he was travelling was stolen (5(1)(c)(i)), uninsured (ii), was being used in furtherance of a crime, not including an offence under the traffic acts, (iii) or was being used to escape arrest (iv). Notably an applicant will not be able to claim compensation where the death, injury or property damage was caused by or in the course of an act of terrorism (5(1)(d)).

5.   Where an applicant is insured and has received payment of the full amount of the claim from an insurer the application will not be successful. Further no payment will made in respect of damage to a motor vehicle if the applicant knew or ought to have known that at the time the damage was sustained the vehicle was uninsured.

6.   An application will not be entertained where the cause of action or judgment has been assigned to the applicant or where the applicant is acting pursuant to any subrogated or contractual right (clause 5(1)(g)(i) and (ii)).

7.   Where compensation is received from another source either through insurance or via the applicant's employer or via a person who has given a security (self insuring) under the requirements of the 1988 Act or from any other source then only if that compensation is less than the MIB would have paid will the MIB pay the difference (clause 6(1)(a)(b)(c) and (2).

8.   The MIB must make a preliminary investigation of all claims to determine whether the Agreement applies. If the claim is one to which the Agreement applies then a full investigation must be carried out and a full report made. The purpose of a full report is to determine whether an award should be made and if so what the award should be.

9.   If it is not possible for the MIB to calculate the amount of any award it may issue an interim report as long as a final report is issued as soon as reasonably practicable.

10.   Issues are determined on the balance of probabilities.

11.   The MIB can award legal costs and interest. Interest is only payable in an 'appropriate case' and from a date 1 month after receipt of the police report. If the report has not been obtained promptly then interest runs from 1 month from the date MIB would have received the report had it acted promptly.

12.   Quantum of damages is determined by the law in England and Wales for accidents occurring in that jurisdiction or by the law of Scotland if the accident occurred there.

13.   The MIB does not have an obligation to pay damages for loss of earnings in respect of payments made to the applicant by his employer which the applicant has agreed to repay.

14.   Property damage claims are subject to a £300 excess and cannot exceed £250,000 less the excess.

15.   Only a contribution to legal costs of an applicant will be made if legal advice was obtained in respect of the making of the application, the correctness of a decision made by MIB or the adequacy of an award made.

16.   If a payment is made to the applicant by an identified person the same being in full and final settlement of the claim then MIB will have no liability. Should a judgment be obtained against an identified person and either the whole of the judgment or part of it remains unsatisfied after 3 months then MIB will make a payment equal to the unsatisfied judgment or the relevant unsatisfied part of the judgment as long as the same does not exceed the unidentified person's liability but only if no payments have been made under the Uninsured Drivers Agreements (clauses 13–15).

17.   MIB must set out a calculation of how an award has been reached (clause 16).

   Clause 17(3) provides for a provisional award.

18.   An applicant has the right to submit the matter to arbitration if he does not agree with the MIB's decision or proposal for a structured settlement. This is done by giving a notice of appeal to MIB within 6 weeks from the date on which the applicant received MIB's decision (clauses 19(1)(a)(b)(c)).

19.   The arbitration procedure is set out through clauses 20–23.

20.   There is now a right to an oral hearing, see clause 22(4)(c)

21.   The arbitrator's fee will be paid by MIB in the first instance but the arbitrator may order that the applicant or solicitors reimburse the fee to MIB.

22.   If the applicant secures an award higher than that previously offered by MIB via arbitration then the MIB shall make a contribution to the costs incurred by the applicant of no more than £500 per half day.

23.   Where the applicant is under a disability or is a minor then under clause 25 MIB may set up a trust to administer all or part of any award made.

24.   The Agreement provides for an accelerated procedure whereby an offer is made to the applicant following a preliminary report and without a full investigation (clause 26). An applicant has 6 weeks from receipt of an offer to accept or reject it.

25.   Where MIB makes a contribution to legal costs where the compensation does not exceed £150,000 then the costs will be 15% of the amount award although the minimum payment will be £500 and the maximum £3,000. Where the award exceeds £150,000 the costs will be 2% of the award.

PART 2

LIABILITY

General Principles of Negligence

1. THE RULE

[4.1]   There are three elements to a cause of action for negligence: a duty to the person injured, a breach of that duty and foreseeability of loss.

There is a duty on the driver of a motor car to observe ordinary care or skill towards persons using the highway whom he could reasonably foresee as likely to be affected.

The concept of negligence has been developed over the course of the last century. There have been many attempts at a precise definition of negligence but in the words of Lord Atkin in *Donoghue v Stevenson* (at para [4.2]):

'To seek a complete logical definition of the general principle is probably to go beyond the function of the judge, for the more general the definition the more likely it is to omit essentials or to introduce non essentials.'

and per Lord Roskill in *Caparo Industries plc v Dickman* (at para [4.8]):

'... There is no simple formula or touchstone to which recourse can be had in order to provide in every case a ready answer to the questions whether, given certain facts, the law will or will not impose liability for negligence or, in cases where such liability can be shown to exist, determine the extent of that liability. Phrases such as "foreseeability", "proximity", "neighbourhood", and "just and reasonable", "fairness", "voluntary acceptance of risk" or "voluntary assumption of responsibility" will be found used from time to time in the different cases. But, as your Lordships have said, such phrases are not precise definitions. At best they are but labels or phrases descriptive of the very different factual situations which can exist in particular cases and which must be carefully examined in each case before it can be pragmatically determined whether a duty of care exists and, if so, what is the scope and extent of that duty.'

Whether or not a duty of care exists depends so much on the particular circumstances of each individual case. Nevertheless, over the years the courts have given certain guidelines:

[4.2]   Donoghue v Stevenson

[1932] AC 562, [1932] All ER Rep 1, 101 LJPC 119, 147 LT, 48 TLR 494, HL

Per Lord Atkin: The rule that you are to love your neighbour becomes, in law, you must not injure your neighbour; and the lawyer's question, who is my neighbour? receives a restricted reply. You must take reasonable care to avoid acts or omissions which you can reasonably foresee would be likely to injure your neighbour. Who, then, in law is my neighbour? The answer seems to be—persons who are so closely and directly affected by my act that I ought reasonably to have them in contemplation as being so affected when I am directing my mind to the acts or omissions which are called in question.

[4.3]   Nance v British Columbia Electric Rly Co Ltd

[1951] AC 601, [1951] 2 All ER 448, [1951] 2 TLR 137, 95 Sol Jo 543, PC

In running down accidents, when two parties are so moving in relation to one another as to involve risk of collision, each owes to the other a duty to move with due care, and that is true whether they are both in control of vehicles, or both proceeding on foot, or whether one is on foot and the other controlling a moving vehicle. A pedestrian crossing the road owes a duty to the owner of a vehicle, eg if his rashness causes the vehicle to pull up so suddenly as to damage its mechanism, or as to result in following traffic running into it from behind, or in damage to the vehicle itself by contact with the pedestrian. When a man steps from a kerb into the roadway, he owes a duty to traffic which is approaching him with a risk of collision to exercise due care.

[4.4]   Berrill v Road Haulage Executive

[1952] 2 Lloyd's Rep 490

Per Slade J: Paraphrasing the words of Lord Uthwatt in *London Passenger Transport Board v Upson* [1949] AC 155, [1949] 1 All ER 60, [1949] LJR 238, 65 TLR 9, 93 Sol Jo 40, HL, a driver is not bound to foresee every extremity of folly which occurs on the road. Equally he is certainly not entitled to drive upon the footing that other users of the road, either drivers or pedestrians, will exercise reasonable care. He is bound to anticipate any act which is reasonably foreseeable, which the experience of a road user teaches that people do, albeit negligently.

Note—See also *Nettleship v Weston* (at para [8.12]) on the duty of care of a driver.

[4.5]   **Hughes v Lord Advocate**

[1963] AC 837, [1963] 1 All ER 705, [1963] 2 WLR 779, 107 Sol Jo 232, HL

Per Lord Guest: In order to establish a coherent chain of causation it is not necessary that the precise details leading up to the accident should have been reasonably foreseeable: it is sufficient if the accident which occurred is of the type which should have been foreseeable by a reasonably careful person.

[4.6]   **Yuen Kun-yeu v A-G of Hong Kong**

[1988] AC 175, [1987] 2 All ER 705

Per Lord Keith: Foreseeability of harm does not of itself automatically lead to a duty of care. All the circumstances of the case, not only the foreseeability of harm, are to be taken into account in determining whether a duty of care arises. There needs to be sufficient close and direct relation between the parties to give rise to the duty of care.

[4.7]   **D & F Estates Ltd v Church Comrs For England**

[1989] AC 177, [1988] 2 All ER 992, HL

See also at para [35.62].

Per Lord Oliver: No cause of action in tort arises in English law for the defective manufacture of an article which causes no injury other than injury to the defective article itself. If I buy a second-hand car to which there has been fitted a pneumatic tyre which, as a result of carelessness in manufacture, is dangerously defective and which bursts, causing injury to me or the car, no doubt the negligent manufacturer is liable in tort on the ordinary application of *Donoghue v Stevenson* [1932] AC 562, [1932] All ER Rep 1, 101 LJPC 119, 147 LT, 48 TLR 494, HL [at para [4.2]]. But if the tyre bursts without causing any injury other than to itself or if I discovered a defect before it bursts, I know of no principle upon which I can claim to recover from the manufacturer in tort the cost of making good the defect which, in practice, could only be the cost of supplying and fitting a new tyre. That would be, in effect, to attach to goods a non-contractual warranty of fitness which would follow the goods in whosoever hands they came. Such concept was suggested, obiter, by Lord Denning MR in Dutton's case, *Dutton v Bognor Regis United Building Co Ltd* [1972] 1 QB 373, [1972] 1 All ER 462 but it was entirely unsupported by any authority and is, in my opinion, contrary to principle.

[4.8]   **Caparo Industries plc v Dickman**

[1990] 2 AC 605, [1990] 1 All ER 568, HL

See also at para [35.65].

Per Lord Bridge of Harwich: What emerges is that, in addition to the foreseeability of damage, necessary ingredients in any situation giving rise to a duty of care are that there should exist between the party owing the duty and the parties to whom it is owed a relationship characterised by the law as one of 'proximity' or 'neighbourhood' and that the situation should be one in which the court considers it fair, just and reasonable that the law should impose a duty of a given scope on the one party for the benefit of the other.

[4.9]   **Murphy v Brentwood District Council**

[1991] 1 AC 398, [1990] 2 All ER 908

Note—See also at para [35.64].

'It is preferable, in my view, that the law should develop novel categories of negligence incrementally and by analogy with established categories, rather than by a massive extension of prima facie duty of care restrained only by indefinable considerations with ought to negative, or to reduce or limit the scope of the duty or the class of persons to whom it is owed': per Brennan J in the Australian High Court case of *Sutherland Shire Council v Heyman* and approved of by the House of Lords.

[4.10]   **Spring v Guardian Assurance plc**

[1995] 2 AC 296, [1994] 3 All ER 129, [1994] IRLR 460, [1994] 3 WLR 354, [1994] ICR 596, HL

Per Lord Goff of Chieveley: The central issue in this appeal is whether a person who provides a reference in respect of another who was formerly engaged by him as a member of his staff ... may be liable in damages to that other in respect of economic loss suffered by him by reason of negligence in the preparation of the reference.

In a series of well known cases, your Lordships' house has commenced a gradual case by case approach to the development of the law of negligence, particularly in cases concerned with claims in respect of pure economic loss. Even so, one broad category of cases has been recognised in which there may be liability in negligence for loss of this kind. These are the cases which spring from, or have been gathered under the umbrella of, the landmark decision of your Lordships' House in *Hedley Byrne & Co Ltd v Heller & Partners Ltd* [1964] AC 465, [1963] 2 All ER 575.

It is my opinion that an employer who provides a reference in respect of one of his employees to a prospective future employer will ordinarily owe a duty of care to his employee in respect of the preparation of the reference. The employer is possessed of special knowledge, derived from his experience of the employee's character, skill and diligence in the performance of his duties while working for the employer. ... Furthermore, when such a reference is provided by an employer, it is plain that the employee relies upon him to exercise due skill and care in preparation of the reference before making it available to the third party. In these circumstances, it seems to me that all the elements requisite for the application of the *Hedley Byrne* principle are present.

[4.11]   **X and others (minors) v Bedfordshire County Council, M (a minor) v Newham London Borough Council, E (a minor) v Dorset County Council**

[1995] 2 AC 633, [1995] 3 All ER 353, [1995] 3 WLR 152, HL

Per Lord Browne-Wilkinson: ... the question whether there is such a common law duty and if so its ambit, must be profoundly influenced by the statutory framework within which the acts complained of were done ... in my judgment, a common law duty of care cannot be imposed on a statutory duty if the observant of such common law duty of care would be inconsistent with, or have a tendency to discourage, the due performance by the local authority of its statutory duties.

[4.12]   **Barrett v Enfield London Borough Council**

[2001] 2 AC 550, [1999] 3 All ER 193, [1999] 3 WLR 79, HL

Per Lord Browne-Wilkinson: In a wide range of cases public policy has lead to the decision that the imposition of liability would not be fair and reasonable in the circumstances, e.g. some activities of financial regulators, building inspectors, ship surveyors, social workers dealing with sex abuse cases. In all these cases and many others the view has been taken that the proper performance of the defendant's primary functions for the benefit of society as a whole will be inhibited if they are required to look over their shoulder to avoid liability in negligence. In English law the decision is whether it is fair, just and reasonable to impose a liability in negligence on a particular class of would-be defendants depend on weighing in the balance the total detriment to the public interest in all cases from holding such class liable in negligence as against the total loss to all would-be plaintiffs if they were not to have a cause of action in respect of the loss they have individually suffered. In English law, questions of public policy and the question of whether it is fair and reasonable to impose liability in negligence are decided as questions of law. Once the decision is taken ... that decision will apply to all future cases of the same kind. The decision does not depend on weighing the balance between the extent of the damage to the plaintiff and the damage to the public in each particular case.

[4.13] S v Gloucestershire County Council, L v Tower Hamlets London Borough Council
[2000] 3 All ER 346, [2001] 2 WLR 909, CA

Per May LJ: It is clear from these principles that in an ordinary case a local authority defendant is unlikely to establish a defence which relies on a blanket immunity ... Remembering always that the critical question is a composite one which embraces the alleged duty of care and its breach in the context of the damage alleged to have been caused, the court has to consider the nature of the actions and the decisions of the local authority which are said to have been negligent.

[4.14] Phelps v Hillingdon London Borough Council, Anderton v Clwyd County Council, Jarvis v Hampshire County Council, Re G (a minor)
[2001] 2 AC 619, [2000] 4 All ER 504, [2000] 3 WLR 776, HL

Per Lord Slynn: I accept that, as was said in X *(minors) v Bedfordshire County Council* [at para [4.11]] there may be cases where to recognise such a vicarious liability on the part of the authority may so interfere with the performance of the local education authorities duties that it would be wrong to recognise any liability on the part of the authorities. It must, however, be for the local authority to establish that: it is not to be presumed and I anticipate that the circumstances where it could be established would be exceptional.

But where an educational psychologist is specifically called in to advise in relation to the assessment and future provision for a specific child, and it is clear that the parents acting for the child and the teachers would follow that advice, prima facie a duty of care arises.

[4.15] D v East Berkshire Community Health NHS Trust
[2003] EWCA Civ 1151
[2004] QB 558, [2003] 4 All ER 796, CA; affd [2005] 2 All ER 443, HL

Per Lord Phillips MR: In the circumstances the recent policy that led the House of Lords [in Bedfordshire] to hold that no duty of care towards a child arises, insofar as those reasons have not largely been discredited by the subsequent decisions of the House of Lords, will largely cease to apply. Substantial damages will be available on proof of individual short comings which will be relevant alike to a claim based on breach of section 6 [of the Human Rights Act 1998] and the claim based on breach of a common law duty of care ... the decision in Bedfordshire cannot survive the 1998 Act ... the absence of an alternative remedy for children who were victims of abuse before October 2000 militates in favour of the recognition of a common law duty of care once the public policy reasons have lost their force.

2. THE DUTY OF CARE

[4.16] Muirhead v Industrial Tank Specialities

[1986] QB 507, [1985] 3 All ER 705, [1985] 3 WLR 993, 129 Sol Jo 855, CA

The claimant, a wholesale fishmonger, wanted to purchase lobsters in the summer and store them in tanks so he could sell them for higher prices at Christmas. The pump which kept the water in the tanks oxygenated continually failed. The claimant depended heavily on advice from the tank installers but neither knew of, nor had any contact with, the pump manufacturers. The judge held that there was sufficient reliance, in the circumstances, by the claimant on the manufacturers for a duty of care to be owed, and that the economic loss suffered, through loss of fish farm stock in stale uncirculated water, was reasonably foreseeable. The manufacturers appealed against this finding. He also held that the actual physical damage (ie the death of the lobsters) was unforeseeable. The claimant contended, on appeal, that this was wrong.

HELD, ON APPEAL: The manufacturers were not liable to the claimant for economic loss. In the circumstances of this case there was no sufficient proximity or reliance by the claimant on the manufacturers to create a duty of care extending to liability for economic loss. But the physical damage (to the lobsters, as stock) was a foreseeable result of the pump motor failure and the manufacturers were liable for the cost of this and the consequential financial losses. *Junior Books Ltd v Veitchi Co Ltd* ([1983] 1 AC 520, [1982] 3 All ER 201, [1982] 3 WLR 477, 126 Sol Jo 538, HL) was very much a decision on its specific facts and represented only a very limited extension in principle.

Note—See also *Simaan General Contracting Co v Pilkington Glass Limited (No 2)* [1988] QB 758, [1988] 1 All ER 791, [1988] 2 WLR 761, 132 Sol Jo 463, CA.

[4.17] Tomlinson v (1) Congleton Borough Council (2) Cheshire County Council

[2003] UKHL 47

[2004] 1 AC 46, [2003] 3 All ER 1122, [2003] 3 WLR 705, HL

The claimant dived into a lake at Brereton Health Park, a site owned and occupied by the first defendant and managed by the second defendant, and sustained a serious injury.

Irrespective of the fact that there were notices by the lake clearly stating 'Dangerous Water, No Swimming' it was still a popular place to swim. The defendants were aware of the danger from previous accidents. The claimant was also aware of the depth of the shallow water having previously stood in it up to the depth of his mid-thigh.

It was not disputed that the claimant had seen and ignored the warning signs and so therefore he became a trespasser rather than a bone fide visitor and the Occupiers Liability Act 1984 applied.

At first instance, Jack J dismissed the claimant's claim but the Court of Appeal held that the risk was one against which the defendants might reasonably be expected to offer trespassers some protection.

To simply post notices was shown to be ineffective and consequently was not enough to discharge the duty of care.

The defendants appealed to the House of Lords.

HELD: The characteristics of the lake and the potential danger were matters which were obvious to the claimant and were ones which did not need to be warned against and in any event, the warning signs gave the claimant no additional information beyond what was already obvious. Accordingly, the defendants owed no duty of care.

Per Lord Hoffmann: ... the law does not provide such compensation simply on the basis that the injury was disproportionately severe in relation to one's own fault or even not one's own fault at all ... The law provides compensation only when the injury was someone else's fault. In order to succeed in his claim that is what Mr Tomlinson had to prove.

[4.18]   Vowles v Evans

[2003] EWCA Civ 318

[2003] All ER (D) 134 (Mar), [2003] 1 WLR 1607, CA

The claimant was playing hooker for Llanharan RFC in an amateur rugby match. Thirty minutes into the game a Llanharan prop was injured. The prop was replaced by a Llanharan flanker. The referee did not ask the flanker about his experience of playing in the position of prop and neither did the referee continue the game with uncontested scrums which was an option for him under the rules by which this particular game was being played. At the very end of the game the claimant was seriously injured when a scrum collapsed. The claimant alleged that the referee (and vicariously, the second defendant) owed him a duty of care and he was in breach of that duty by failing to check the flankers experience or continue the game with uncontested scrums.

At first instance the judge held the referee did owe the claimant a duty of care. The defendants appealed.

HELD, ON APPEAL: The judge's decision was upheld. It was fair, just and reasonable to impose a duty of care on the referee of an adult amateur rugby match. Rugby was a dangerous sport and the rules were there to reduce the risk of injury. The players relied on the referee to exercise reasonable care in enforcing those rules to reduce the risk of injury. The referee was in breach of his duty to exercise this reasonable care and that breach was the cause of the claimant's injury.

[4.19]   Rhind v (1) Astbury Water Park Ltd (2) Maxout Ltd

[2004] EWCA Civ 756

[2004] All ER (D) 129 (Jun)

A claim for personal injury by a swimmer who ignored signs forbidding swimming and dived into shallow water sustained spinal injuries failed. The claimant brought the action against two defendants, both of whom exercised degrees of occupation and control over the lake in a country park. The claimant was found to be a visitor rather than a trespasser. However, the risk of injury from diving into shallow water was so obvious that the defendants owed no duty to warn specifically of that risk or take steps to exclude the public from the water's edge.

Note—See also *Van Oppen v Clerk to the Bedford Charity Trustees* [1989] 1 All ER 273 when it was held that the school did not owe a duty to a pupil to obtain personal accident insurance or advise the pupils' parents to do so.

Per Boreham J: The relationship of proximity which existed between the school and its pupils did not of itself give rise to a duty to insure or to protect the claimant's economic welfare. That was beyond what either party to the relationship contemplated.

[4.20]   Ancell v McDermott
[1993] 4 All ER 355, 137 Sol Jo LB 36, [1993] RTR 235

The police attended the scene of a road accident in which diesel fuel had been spilt. Two officers noted the spillage but left it to attend to the individuals involved in the accident. A car driven by one of the claimants and in which the other claimant was a passenger later skidded on the diesel and collided with another vehicle as a result of which the claimants suffered injury.

The question to be decided was whether individual police officers who, in the course of their employment, come across a potential hazard on the highway caused by a third party, owe a duty to individual members of the public who may subsequently be injured.

HELD: The extent of the duty owed depends on the precise circumstances such as the nature of the hazard, the extent of the danger and the likelihood of injury. In this instance the court did not consider that the officers' duty extended to the warning of an indeterminate number of third parties of an obvious hazard.

3.   FORESEEABILITY

[4.21]   Hay (or Bourhill) v Young
[1943] AC 92, [1942] 2 All ER 396, 111 LJPC 97, 167 LT 261, 86 Sol Jo 349, HL

A woman was at the front of a stationary tramcar on the offside loading a creel on to her back. A motor cyclist passed on the near side of the tramcar and collided with a car 45 to 50ft ahead. The woman did not see the impact but merely heard the noise of the collision. She alleged shock caused by the noise of the collision. It was admitted that her terror did not involve any element of reasonable fear of immediate bodily injury to herself.

HELD: The motorcyclist owed no duty to the woman as he could not reasonably have foreseen the likelihood that she could be affected by his negligent act. She was outside the area of potential danger. The question was one of liability, not remoteness of damage. The mere accidental and unknown presence of a person upon the same street as, and somewhere within earshot of, the occurring of an accident in mid-carriageway, does not per se create any relationship of duty raising liability — some other and special element of immediacy is required.

Per Lord Wright: The breach of duty must be vis-à-vis the claimant. The claimant must sue for a wrong to herself. She cannot build on a wrong to somebody else. A blind or deaf man who crosses the traffic on a busy street cannot complain if he is run over by a careful driver who does not know of and could not be expected to observe and guard against the man's infirmity. These questions go to culpability, not compensation.

Per Lord Thankerton: The duty is to take such reasonable care as will avoid the risk of injury to such persons as he can reasonably foresee might be injured by failure to exercise such reasonable care.

Per Lord Macmillan: The duty to take care is the duty to avoid doing or omitting to do anything the doing or omitting to do which have as its reasonable and probable consequence injury to others, and the duty is owed to those to whom injury may reasonably and probably be anticipated if the duty is not observed.

Note—See also *McLoughlin v O'Brian* (at para [36.23]); *Smith v Littlewoods Organisation Ltd* (at para [35.42]); and *Hevican v Ruane* [1991] 3 All ER 65.

[4.22] Alcock v Chief Constable of South Yorkshire Police
[1992] 1 AC 310, [1991] 4 All ER 907, [1991] 3 WLR 1057, HL

The claimants were relatives and friends of football supporters injured or killed at the Hillsborough Stadium disaster as a result of overcrowding in part of the stadium. The defendant was responsible for policing the football match. The claimants were either present in another part of the stadium; outside the stadium; watching the football match live on television or later watched recorded television pictures. The claimants claimed damages for psychiatric illness.

HELD: The claimants' claims failed. They were either not within the class of persons to whom the defendant owed a duty or they were not sufficiently proximate to the accident in time and space.
   Nolan LJ in the Court of Appeal expressed the view that:

'I would accept at once that no general definition is possible but I see no difficulty in principle in requiring a defendant to contemplate that the person physically injured or threatened by his negligence may have relatives or friends whose love for him is like that of a normal parent or spouse, and who in consequence may similarly be closely and directly affected by nervous shock ... the identification of the particular individuals who come within that category, like that of parents and spouses themselves, could only be carried out *ex post facto*, and would depend on evidence of the "relationship" in a broad sense which gave rise to the love and affection. It is accepted that the proximity to the accident must be close both in time and space ... in the circumstances of this case the simultaneous television broadcasts of what occurred cannot be equated with the "sight or hearing of the evidence or its immediate aftermath". Accordingly, shock sustained by reason of these broadcasts cannot found a claim.'

Note—See also at para [36.28] and case of *Hicks v Chief Constable of the South Yorkshire Police* (at para [36.29]) and Chapter 35 section 3(d) generally.

[4.23]   French and Others v Chief Constable of Sussex
[2006] EWCA Civ 312

(2006) Times, 5 April

Five police officers participated in an armed raid that resulted in a fatal shooting. The shooting was not witnessed by these five officers. Disciplinary and criminal charges were initiated against the officers which they claimed caused them stress and psychiatric damage. The officers brought a claim for negligence against the Chief Constable alleging systemic shortcomings in training with the type of operations that led to the fatal shooting. The claims for psychiatric damage were supported by medical evidence.

HELD: The claim was struck out at first instance on the basis that the allegations had no reasonable prospect of success. The police officers had not witnessed the shootings and were not secondary victims. They had also not established that their employers were on notice that they were vulnerable to stress. The Court of

Appeal upheld the decision. It was not reasonably foreseeable that corporate failings would cause the officers psychiatric injury by reason of disciplinary and criminal proceedings. Police officers who witness shootings cannot claim as secondary victims and therefore the officers in this claim, who were more remotely affected, could not succeed.

[4.24]   Setchell v Snowdon
[1974] RTR 389, CA

Snowdon and Ashton were acquainted with each other by being members of the same football team. Ashton asked Snowdon, who owned a car, to teach him to drive but Snowdon declined. When at a club together on the evening of that day Ashton asked Snowdon to lend him the key of his car, which was parked nearby, so that he could sit in it with a girl he had met. Ashton said expressly he did not want to drive the car. Snowdon lent him the key which was also the ignition key. When Ashton and the girl were in the car Ashton decided to drive it and, losing control, crashed it, severely injuring the girl. She sued Snowdon saying he should have realised Ashton might drive off in the car and was thereby negligent, knowing Ashton had not learned to drive. The judge accepted Snowdon's evidence that it never crossed his mind that Ashton would drive.

HELD: Snowdon was not liable. The test was: would a reasonable man in all the circumstances have realised that there was a real risk of Ashton driving the car? The answer was no; Snowdon had no reason to anticipate that Ashton would do something contrary to what he had promised and which would be in more than one respect a criminal offence.

[4.25]   Denton v United Omnibus Ltd
(1986) Times, 6 May, CA

The defendant garaged its buses in an open depot without doors or gates. Early one morning a thief drove one of the buses away and hit the claimant's parked car. The claimant claimed that even though this person was unidentified and unauthorised, the defendant was in breach of a duty of care to him because it had failed to secure its premises (despite previous incidents) and that this damage was foreseeable.

HELD: The defendant owed no duty of care to the claimant: there was no special relationship and the bus was taken unlawfully by an unauthorised person over whom it had no control. In any event, the defendant had not been negligent. *P Perl (Exporters) Ltd v Camden London Borough Council* [1984] QB 342, [1983] 3 All ER 161, [1983] 3 WLR 769, 127 Sol Jo 581, CA applied.

[4.26]   Topp v London Country Bus (South West) Ltd
[1993] 3 All ER 448, [1992] RTR 254

A public service mini-bus was left unattended, unlocked and with the keys in the ignition. The bus was stolen and driven negligently causing the death of a cyclist.

HELD: No duty of care was owed by the bus operators to the cyclist for:
  (1)   there was no duty to prevent deliberate wrongdoings by a third party;
  (2)   it would be difficult to assess the degree of negligence based on the type of vehicle left and the period for which it was left unattended; and
  (3)   the likelihood of the vehicle being stolen, driven negligently and causing injury was low.

An appeal to the Court of Appeal was dismissed.

4. CONTRIBUTORY NEGLIGENCE

(A) INTRODUCTION

[4.27] 'In order to establish the defence of contributory negligence, the defendant must prove, first, that the claimant failed to take 'ordinary care for himself' or, in other words, such care as a reasonable man would take for his own safety, and, second, that his failure to take care was a contributory cause of the accident': Per du Parcq LJ in *Lewis v Denye* [1939] 1 KB 540, [1939] 1 All ER 310, 108 LJKB 217, 160 LT 224, 55 TLR 391, 83 Sol Jo 192, CA.

A plea of contributory negligence should be treated as setting up want of care by the claimant for his own safety, whether in the circumstances of the accident the claimant owed a duty to the defendant or not.

The statement that, when negligence is alleged as the basis of an actionable wrong, a necessary ingredient in the conception is the existence of a duty owed by the defendants to the claimant to take due care, is, of course, indubitably correct. But when contributory negligence is set up as a defence, its existence does not depend on any duty owed by the injured party to the party sued, and all that is necessary to establish such a defence is to prove that the injured party did not in his own interest take reasonable care of himself, and contributed, by that want of care, to his own injury. Where a man was part author of his own injury, he could not call on the other party to compensate him in full: *Davies v Swan Motor Co (Swansea) Ltd* [1949] 2 KB 291, [1949] 1 All ER 620, 65 TLR 278, CA followed: *Nance v British Columbia Electric Rly Co Ltd* (at para [4.3]).

The test of contributory negligence in the case of a pedestrian is not whether he is under a duty of care towards the defendant, but whether he was acting as a reasonable man and with reasonable care: per Denning LJ in *Davies v Swan Motor Co.*

(B) LAW REFORM (CONTRIBUTORY NEGLIGENCE) ACT 1945

[4.28]
1. Apportionment of liability in case of contributory negligence
(1) Where any person suffers damage as the result partly of his own fault and partly of the fault of any other person or persons, a claim in respect of that damage shall not be defeated by reason of the fault of the person suffering the damage, but the damages recoverable in respect thereof shall be reduced to such extent as the court thinks just and equitable having regard to the claimant's share in the responsibility for the damage:
Provided that—
(a) this subsection shall not operate to defeat any defence arising under a contract;
(b) where any contract or enactment providing for the limitation of liability is applicable to the claim, the amount of damages recoverable by the claimant by virtue of this subsection shall not exceed the maximum limit so applicable.
(2) Where damages are recoverable by any person by virtue of the foregoing subsection subject to such reduction as is therein mentioned, the court shall find and record the total damages which would have been recoverable if the claimant had not been at fault.

(3)   [Repealed by the Civil Liability (Contribution) Act 1978, s 9(2).]

(4)   [Replaced by the Fatal Accidents Act 1976, s 5: see note, below.]

(5)   Where, in any case to which subsection (1) of this section applies, one of the persons at fault avoids liability to any other such person or his personal representative by pleading the Limitation Act 1939, or any other enactment limiting the time within which proceedings may be taken, he shall not be entitled to recover any damages from that other person or representative by virtue of the said subsection.

(6)   Where any case to which subsection (1) of this section applies is tried with a jury, the jury shall determine the total damages which would have been recoverable if the claimant had not been at fault and the extent to which those damages are to be reduced.

2.   [Replaced by the National Insurance (Industrial Injuries) Act 1946, s 89(1) and Sch 9.]

The Consumer Protection Act 1987, s 6 now provides as follows:

'6. Application of certain enactments

(4)   Where any damage is caused partly by a defect in a product and partly by the fault of the person suffering the damage, the Law Reform (Contributory Negligence) Act 1945 and section 5 of the Fatal Accidents Act 1976 shall have effect as if the defect were the fault of every person liable by virtue of this Part for the damage caused by the defect.

(5)   In subsection (4) above "fault" has the same meaning as in the 1945 Act.'

Per Denning LJ in *Davies v Swan Motor Co (Swansea) Ltd* [1949] 2 KB 291, [1949] 1 All ER 620, 65 TLR 278, CA: Speaking generally, the questions in road accidents are simply these: What faults were there which caused the damage? What are the proportions in which the damages should be apportioned having regard to the respective responsibilities of those in fault?

Questions of negligence and contributory negligence are pure questions of fact for the court, and the court finding of fact is binding if there is evidence to support it.

See Chapters 8, 9 and 12 generally.

(C)   EXAMPLES OF CONTRIBUTORY NEGLIGENCE

[4.29]   **Basildon District Council v J E Lesser (Properties) Ltd**

[1985] QB 839, [1985] 1 All ER 20, [1984] 3 WLR 812, 128 Sol Jo 330, [1984] NLJR 330   Judge Newey QC Official Referee

On a clear and exact analysis of ss 1 and 4 of the Law Reform (Contributory Negligence) Act 1945, it does not apply to contracts.

The claimant entered into a standard term contract with Lesser (who were system builders) for the construction of houses and maisonettes. The contract referred to drawings and specifications which had been prepared by or under the control of the claimant's engineers or architects. Lesser subsequently assigned the benefit of the contract to the second defendant; then the third defendant (the holding company of Lesser and the second defendant) agreed to indemnify the claimant against any breach of contract by them both. Defects developed in some of the houses and maisonettes caused, according to the claimant, by foundation movement and inadequately supported cross walls. The claimant sued the third defendant alleging breach of contract on the part of the second defendant. The third defendant alleged that the claimant's architect and clerk of works were at fault and that it could plead contributory negligence in a contractual dispute; alternatively that, where a breach of contract involved a failure to take reasonable care, contributory negligence could be relied upon under the Law Reform (Contributory Negligence) Act 1945.

HELD: The 1945 Act only applied where the claimant's cause of action related to an act or omission for which the defendants would be liable in tort even though they might also be liable in contract. The claimant's claim was founded on the contract with the third defendant so the 1945 Act could not apply; the third defendant could not rely upon the defence of contributory negligence in answer to the local authority's claim for damages for breach of contract.

Note—By contrast, see the following case (at para [4.30]).

[4.30]　**Forsikringsaktieselskapet Vesta v Butcher**

[1989] AC 852, [1988] 2 All ER 43, [1988] 3 WLR 565, 132 Sol Jo 1181, [1988] 1 Lloyd's Rep 19, CA

The claimants, Norwegian insurers, covered the owners of a fish farm against the loss of fish from any cause. They reinsured 90% of the risk through English brokers. The reinsurance policy included a warranty that a 24-hour watch had to be maintained on the site; failure to comply with this warranty would render the policy void. Although the warranty was then incorporated in the policy issued by the claimants to the owners, the claimants knew that it could not be observed and told the reinsurance brokers. These brokers undertook to discuss this matter with the underwriters but failed to do so. When a violent storm occurred, the fish farm suffered substantial damage. The claimants met the claim but when they sought reimbursement the reinsurers refused to pay, depending on the breach of the warranty. The claimants sued the reinsurers and the brokers claiming that if the reinsurers could successfully rely on the breach of warranty, the brokers were in breach of contract in failing to obtain valid and effective reinsurance and negligent in failing to inform the underwriters of the impossibility of providing a 24-hour watch. The brokers, in defending the action, alleged that the claimants were guilty of contributory negligence in failing to ensure that the brokers told the reinsurers.

HELD: On the facts, reinsurers should indemnify insurers (so there was no loss). But the issue of contributory negligence by the claimants was considered; where a defendant's liability arose from breach of a contractual provision which did not require or depend on negligence on his part the Law Reform (Contributory Negligence) Act 1945 would not permit a defence of contributory negligence but where the defendant's liability in contract was tantamount to liability in tort, regardless of the existence of a contract, the Act can apply and liability can be apportioned between claimant and defendant. Per Sir Roger Ormrod: 'The context of the 1945 Act, and the language of section 1, to my mind make it clear that the Act is concerned only with tortious liability and the power to apportion only arises where a defendant is liable in tort and concurrent liability in contract, if any, is immaterial.' The narrow interpretation of the 1945 Act in *Marintrans (A B) v Comet Shipping Co Ltd, The Shinjitsu Maru No 5* (1985) Times, 19 March was criticised by O'Connor LJ.

Note—An appeal to the House of Lords was dismissed: [1989] 1 All ER 402.

(D)   100% CONTRIBUTORY NEGLIGENCE

[4.31]   Note: Section 1 of the Law Reform (Contributory Negligence) Act 1945 only takes effect once the defendant has been fixed with liability. Therefore there can be no finding of 100% contributory negligence. Either the claimant was wholly to blame for the accident or the defendant was to blame subject to a finding of contributory negligence.

See—*Pitts v Hunt* (at para [7.44]) and *Anderson v Newham College of Further Education* [2002] EWCA Civ 505, [2002] All ER (D) 381 (Mar).

5.   CONTRIBUTION BETWEEN TORTFEASORS

[4.32]   *Note*—When an injured party has suffered damage by the negligence of two or more persons, whether acting in concert or not, he may recover the whole of his damage from any one of them, or may sue all of them jointly in the same action. Formerly, joint wrongdoers or those severally liable for the same damage had no right of contribution or indemnity against each other. The rule was altered by the Law Reform (Married Women and Tortfeasors) Act 1935, s 6 of which enabled tortfeasors to recover contribution from any other tortfeasor who was, or would if sued have been, liable in respect of the same damage. This section of the 1935 Act was repealed and replaced with effect from 1 January 1979 by the Civil Liability (Contribution) Act 1978. Under this Act contribution may be claimed even if one or both of those concerned is liable to the claimant otherwise than in tort.

(A)   CIVIL LIABILITY (CONTRIBUTION) ACT 1978

[4.33]
1.   Entitlement to contribution
(1)   Subject to the following provisions of this section, any person liable in respect of any damage suffered by another person may recover contribution from any other person liable in respect of the same damage (whether jointly with him or otherwise).

(2)   A person shall be entitled to recover contribution by virtue of subsection (1) above notwithstanding that he has ceased to be liable in respect of the damage in question since the time when the damage occurred, provided that he was so liable immediately before he made or was ordered or agreed to make the payment in respect of which the contribution is sought.

(3)   A person shall be liable to make contribution by virtue of subsection (1) above notwithstanding that he has ceased to be liable in respect of the damage in question since the time when the damage occurred, unless he ceased to be liable by virtue of the expiry of a period of limitation or prescription which extinguished the right on which the claim against him in respect of the damage was based.

(4)   A person who has made or agreed to make any payment in bona fide settlement or compromise of any claim made against him in respect of any damage (including a payment into court which has been accepted) shall be entitled to recover contribution in accordance with this section without regard to whether or not he himself is or ever was liable in respect of the damage, provided, however, that he would have been liable assuming that the factual basis of the claim against him could be established.

(5)   A judgment in any action brought in any part of the United Kingdom by or on behalf of the person who suffered the damage in question against any person from whom contribution is sought under this section shall be conclusive in the proceedings for contribution as to any issue determined by that judgment in favour of the person from whom the contribution is sought.

(6)   References in this section to a person's liability in respect of any damage are references to any such liability which has been or could be established in an action

brought against him in England and Wales by or on behalf of the person who suffered the damage; but it is immaterial whether any issue arising in any such action was or would be determined (in accordance with the rules of private international law) by reference to the law of a country outside England and Wales.

[4.34]
2. Assessment of contribution

(1) Subject to subsection (3) below, in any proceedings for contribution under section 1 above the amount of the contribution recoverable from any person shall be such as may be found by the court to be just and equitable having regard to the extent of that person's responsibility for the damage in question.

(2) Subject to subsection (3) below, the court shall have power in any such proceedings to exempt any person from liability to make contribution, or to direct that the contribution to be recovered from any person shall amount to a complete indemnity.

(3) Where the amount of the damages which have or might have been awarded in respect of the damage in question in any action brought in England and Wales by or on behalf of the person who suffered it against the person from whom the contribution is sought was or would have been subject to—

(a) any limit imposed by or under any enactment or by any agreement made before the damage occurred;

(b) any reduction by virtue of section 1 of the Law Reform (Contributory Negligence) Act 1945 or section 5 of the Fatal Accidents Act 1976; or

(c) any corresponding limit or reduction under the law of a country outside England and Wales;

the person from whom the contribution is sought shall not by virtue of any contribution awarded under section 1 above be required to pay in respect of the damage a greater amount of those damages as limited or reduced.

Note—See above (at para [4.28]) for the effect of ss 6(4) and 6(5) of the Consumer Protection Act 1987.

[4.35] *Note*—A tortfeasor who wishes to recover contribution from another tortfeasor who is liable for the same damage must bring the action for contribution within two years from the date on which the judgment or award was made against him or on which he admitted liability for the amount in respect of which he claimed contribution: Limitation Act 1980, s 10 (see para [18.77]).

For contribution proceedings between tortfeasors already a party to the same action, see *Kennett v Brown* [1988] 2 All ER 600 and Chapter 20 generally.

(B) CASE LAW

[4.36] The Miraflores and The Abadesa
[1967] 1 AC 826, [1967] 1 All ER 672, [1967] 2 WLR 806, 111 Sol Jo 211, HL

The *Miraflores* and the *Abadesa* collided in the River Scheldt. The *George Livanes*, following the *Miraflores*, was presented with a difficulty and, failing to take action in time to avoid it, ran aground. In actions to determine liability for the damage caused to the vessels the judge first apportioned liability for the collision between the *Miraflores* and the *Abadesa* at one-third and two-thirds respectively. Then to ascertain liability for damage to the *George Livanes* due to grounding he treated the negligence of the other two vessels leading to the collision as one unit and the negligence of the *George Livanes* in running aground as the other. Finding the *George Livanes* one-half to blame for the grounding he awarded the owners one-half of their damages to be paid two thirds by the *Abadesa* and one-third by the *Miraflores*.

HELD, ON APPEAL: The 'unit approach' was wrong. In assessing degrees of fault blameworthiness as well as causation must be considered—it is necessary to weigh the fault of each negligent party against each of the others separately and not conjunctively: by putting the several acts of negligence of the *Abadesa* and the *Miraflores* into one characterless 'unit' the judge did not measure their respective blameworthiness against the blameworthiness of the *George Livanes*. The proportions of fault in the other two ships for the grounding of the *George Livanes* should be assessed at two-fifths to the *Abadesa* and one-fifth to the *Miraflores*.

Per Lord Pearce: The Law Reform (Contributory Negligence) Act 1945, s 1 does not give any support to the unit approach. Its intention was to allow the claimant, though negligent, to recover damages reduced to such an extent as the court thinks just and equitable, having regard to his share in the responsibility for the damage (s 1(1)). But that share can only be estimated by weighing his fault against that of the defendant or, if there are two defendants, against that of each defendant. It is true that apportionment as between the defendants comes theoretically at a later stage (under the Law Reform (Married Women and Tortfeasors) Act 1935). But as a matter of practice the whole matter is decided at one time and the Court weighs up the fault of *each* in assessing liability as between claimant and defendants themselves. And I see nothing in the 1945 Act to show that it intends the Court to treat the joint defendants as a unit whose joint blameworthiness could only, one presumes, be the aggregate blameworthiness of its differing components.

[4.37]   J (a child) v Wilkins (Wynn and Another, third parties)
[2001] PIQR P179, [2001] 7 LS Gaz R 41, (2001) Times, 6 February

The claimant was a child passenger in a motor vehicle. She was seriously injured in an accident as a result of not being properly secured by a suitable seat restraint. The defendant admitted negligence. The judge regarded himself bound by *Froom v Butcher* [1976] QB 286, [1975] 3 All ER 520, CA and apportioned liability 75% to the defendant and 25% to the third parties, the child's mother and aunt. The defendant appealed.

HELD: The Court of Appeal dismissed the appeal and confirmed that the suitable apportionment should be determined by applying the test laid down in s 2(1) of the Civil Liability (Contribution) Act 1978 of what was '*just and equitable*'. In applying the test, *Froom v Butcher* continued to provide valuable guidance. In that case the court had not sought to put a maximum figure on contributory negligence but had provided guidance on what would apply in the vast majority of cases.

[4.38]   Askey v Wood
[2005] EWCA Civ 574
[2005] All ER (D) 286 (Apr), 149 Sol Jo LB 514

The trial judge held that liability was equal in respect of an accident where the car driven by the claimant had straddled the centre line of a country road and a motorcycle driven by the defendant had been travelling in the opposite direction at excessive speed.

HELD: The Court of Appeal found that the trial judge had been faced with a position where both parties had been negligent but it was not easy to say which party was more negligent than the other. Not every judge would have found liability to be equal but the Court of Appeal could not say that the division of liability was not within the reasonable range of apportionment that was open to the trial judge.

[4.39]   **Aer Lingus v Gildacroft and Sentinel Lifts**

[2006] EWCA Civ 4

[2006] 2 All ER 290, [2006] 1 WLR 1173

Aer Lingus had settled a claim against them. In that claim judgment for damages to be assessed was given on 9 May 2001 and a consent order recording the agreed damages was made on 3 October 2003.

Aer Lingus sought a contribution/indemnity from Gildacroft and Sentinel Lifts, and commenced contribution proceedings on 4 February 2004. Both defendants pleaded limitation.

The limitation period in such claims is two years from the date on which the right to recover contribution accrued. The issue was whether the relevant date in this case was the judgment on liability of 9 May 2001 or the final damages order of 3 October 2003.

The High Court decided that the relevant date was the judgment of 9 May 2001 and, since this date was more than two years before the commencement of the contribution proceedings, those proceedings were statute barred.

HELD, ON APPEAL: The Court of Appeal disagreed. The relevant date was the consent order that ascertained the quantum, and not merely the existence, of the tortfeasor's liability. Accordingly, the claim was not statute barred.

6.   RES JUDICATA

[4.40]   **Brunsden v Humphrey**

(1884) 14 QBD 141, [1881–85] All ER Rep 357, 53 LJQB 476, 51 LT 529, 49 JP 4, 32 WR 944, CA

The rule of the ancient common law is that where one is barred in any action real or personal by judgment, demurrer, confession or verdict, he is barred as to that or the like action of the like nature for the same thing for ever. It is a well settled rule of law that damages resulting from one and the same cause of action must be assessed and recovered once for all. One wrong was damage to property. A further wrong was injury to the person.

(A)   TWO ACTIONS, SAME ACCIDENT

[4.41]   **Marginson v Blackburn Borough Council**

[1939] 2 KB 426, [1939] 1 All ER 273, 108 LJKB 563, 160 LT 234, 55 TLR 389, 83 Sol Jo 212, CA

The car of A driven by A's wife, with A and his daughter as passengers, collided with the bus of B and as a result there was damage to the property of C. C sued A and B in the county court. B served a third-party notice on A and counter-claimed against A for damage to the bus. A served a third-party notice on B. The judge found A and B equally to blame. Afterwards A sued B in the High Court for damages for injury to himself, his daughter and death of his wife.

HELD: The claimant was estopped from proceeding with his personal claims but not with claims in his representative capacity as it had been necessary to decide in the first action the question of negligence as between the parties to the second action.

[4.42]   **Townsend v Bishop**

[1939] 1 All ER 805, 160 LT 296, 55 TLR 433, 83 Sol Jo 240   Lewis J

A motor car was driven by the son as servant of the owner and collided with a lorry. The father brought an action in the High Court against the lorry owner for the father's damage in negligence, which was sent to the county court. The judge found the son was negligent and the action failed. The son then brought an action in the High Court against the lorry owner for the son's own damage.

HELD: No *res judicata*. The defendant had failed to prove that the matter now in issue was the same as that previously litigated and between the same parties. The son was not a party, but an agent, in the previous litigation.

[4.43]   **Johnson v Cartledge and Matthews**

[1939] 3 All ER 654   Cassels J

A was a passenger in car of B which collided with the taxi cab of C. C brought a county court action against B, and C was held by the county court judge alone to blame. Afterwards, A sued B and C in the High Court and Cassels J found B alone to blame. B had issued third-party proceedings against C in the action. B contended the issue of negligence between B and C was *res judicata* and he was entitled to indemnity on this ground.

HELD, per Cassels J: C had been found in the High Court proceedings not to be a tortfeasor, and B could not therefore recover indemnity or contribution from C. Furthermore, this was not a case of *res judicata*, as the damage in the two cases was different. For the doctrine of *res judicata* to apply the parties must be the same, and the damage must be the same, and the issues of law and of fact must be the same. (*Marginson v Blackburn Borough Council* (at para [4.41]) distinguished.)

The action in the county court was for damage to property; in the High Court for personal injuries and in the third-party proceedings the claim would not have been possible before the Law Reform (Married Women and Tortfeasors) Act 1935.

[4.44]   **Bell v Holmes**

[1956] 3 All ER 449, [1956] 1 WLR 1359, 100 Sol Jo 801   McNair J

A motor car driven by A collided with a motor car driven by B which had a passenger X on 26 March 1955. A issued a writ against B for personal injuries and B counter-claimed for his own personal injuries. On 7 October 1955, X issued a summons against both A and B as defendants in the county court. The pleadings in the two actions were substantially identical. In the county court action each defendant blamed the other and adopted the allegations made by the claimant against the other. No formal notice of contribution was filed by either defendant against the other but the judge was requested by both defendants to deal with the matter of apportionment between the defendants. On 17 February 1956, the judge found against both defendants and held A five-sixths to blame and B one-sixth. Both judgments were satisfied and the time for appeal had long expired when the action between A and B came on for hearing. By his amended defence B pleaded A was bound by the county court judgment and A by his reply denied that he was so bound. McNair J directed this issue be tried as a preliminary issue.

HELD: (1) It was plain on the authorities, and was common practice, that the court as to apportionment had power to determine the question of contribution between defendants without any formal notice of contribution.

(2) As to *res judicata*, this was a matter of evidence, and included a case where judgment had been given after the issue of the writ, and was a good plea in this case.

(3) As to the plea that the issues were not the same, the issues of fact were identically the same and the fact that they were technically different was immaterial.

(4) As to the contention that a plea of estoppel by record could only be proved by production of the record under CCR 1936, Ord 24 (now CPR Sch 2, CCR Ord 22) whilst not satisfied that this was necessary. A had waived this form of proof by his pleadings. The apportionment was *res judicata*.

[4.45]   Randolph v Tuck

[1962] 1 QB 175, [1961] 1 All ER 814, [1961] 2 WLR 855, 105 Sol Jo 157   Lawton J

The claimant received injuries on 19 July 1957, when riding in a car owned and driven by the first defendant which collided with a car owned by the second defendant and driven by its servant, the third defendant. In a county court action heard on 13 July 1958, in which the first defendant had sued the second and third defendants for damages for his own personal injuries he was found wholly to blame. The claimant issued her writ on 15 October 1959 and on 1 January 1960 the second and third defendants by third-party notice claimed indemnity from the first defendant in the event of their being found liable to pay damages to the claimant. The claim was based on the Law Reform (Married Women and Tortfeasors) Act 1935. They pleaded that the issue between them and the first defendant had been determined by the county court judge and that his decision was binding on the first defendant. The claimant's action was heard on 6 February 1961, when Lawton J held that the damage suffered by the claimant was caused by the negligence of both the first and third defendants and that they were equally to blame.

HELD, in the third-party proceedings:
(1) The second and third defendants were not entitled to claim indemnity as persons entitled to be indemnified under the Law Reform (Married Women and Tortfeasors) Act 1935, s 6(1)(c) since to do so would be to base a cause of action on an estoppel by record. At common law this cannot be done and s 6(1)(c) does not allow that which common law would not.

(2) The first defendant was not estopped by the judgment in the county court from denying his own sole responsibility for the damage suffered by the claimant, since the precise issue decided in the county court was not the same as in the claimant's action. In the county court the issue decided was that the damage suffered by the first defendant was caused, not by any breach of duty owed him by the third defendant, but by his own failure to take proper care for his own safety. In the present action the issue decided was whether the damage suffered by the claimant had been caused by breach of duty owed to her by the first or the third defendant or either of them. These duties were similar but nevertheless separate and distinct (*Hay (or Bourhill) v Young* (at para [4.21])). Moreover the extent of the respective responsibilities of the

first and third defendants for the damage suffered by the claimant, ie blameworthiness as distinct from causation, had never been before the county court.

(3)   *Marginson v Blackburn Borough Council* (at para [4.41]) was distinguished on the ground that in that case the county court judge had made a separate decision in the damage claim between Marginson and the bus company. *Bell v Holmes* (at para [4.44]) not followed.

Note—For the Law Reform (Married Women & Tortfeasors) Act 1935 s 6(1)(c), see now Civil Liability (Contribution) Act 1978 (at para [4.33]).

[4.46]   Wood v Luscombe

[1966] 1 QB 169, [1964] 3 All ER 972, [1965] 3 WLR 996, 109 Sol Jo 833   Streatfield J

L and W, both riding motorcycles, collided. L was injured and so also was W's father who was riding pillion on W's machine. L sued W for damages: at the trial of the action Phillimore J held them both to blame equally for L's injuries. W's father then sued L for damages for his own injuries and L joined W as third party, claiming a contribution. L contended that, as Phillimore J in the previous action had held L and W equally to blame, W was estopped from denying in the present proceedings that they were equally to blame.

HELD: The contention was correct. W's father being an innocent passenger the thing actually in dispute, namely, who was to blame for the damage done in the accident had already been determined by Phillimore J and was *res judicata*. The issue was precisely the same in both actions and the same evidence would support both. *Bell v Holmes* (at para [4.44]) followed: *Randolph v Tuck* (at para [4.45]) not followed. *Marginson v Blackburn Borough Council* (at para [4.41]) not applicable because the facts were different.

(B)   SCOPE OF DOCTRINE

[4.47]   Greenhalgh v Mallard

[1947] 2 All ER 255, CA

Res judicata is not confined to the issues which the court is actually asked to decide, but covers issues of facts which are so clearly part of the subject matter of the litigation and so clearly could have been raised that it would be an abuse of the process of the court to allow a new proceedings to be started in respect of them. In *Green v Weatherill* [1992] 2 Ch 213 at 221, Maugham J quoted some observations by Wigram VC in *Henderson v Henderson* (1843) 3 Hare 100 at 114:

'I believe I state the rule of the court correctly when I say, that, where a given matter becomes the subject of litigation in, and of adjudication by, a court of competent jurisdiction, the court requires the parties to that litigation to bring forward their whole case, and will not (except under special circumstances) permit the same parties to open the same subject of litigation in respect of matter which might have been brought forward as part of the subject in contest, but which was not brought forward only because they have, from negligence, inadvertence, or even accident, omitted part of their case. The plea of *res judicata* applies, except in special cases, not only to points upon which the court was actually required by the parties to form an opinion and pronounce a judgment, but to every point which properly belonged to the subject of litigation and which the parties, exercising reasonable diligence, might have brought forward at the time.'

[4.48]   Re Waring, Westminster Bank Ltd v Burton-Butler

[1948] Ch 221, [1948] 1 All ER 257, [1948] LJR 705, 64 TLR 147   Jenkins J

Where a decision of the Court of Appeal is overruled by a later case in the House of Lords, a person who was a party to the proceedings in the Court of Appeal is bound by the decision of the Court of Appeal on the principle of *res judicata*, but a person who was not a party is not bound and is entitled to take advantage of the decision of the House of Lords.

[4.49]   Wright v Bennett

[1948] 1 All ER 227, 92 Sol Jo 95, CA

The issues need not be identified. The plea will succeed if the issues and facts are in substance the same.

[4.50]   Talbot v Berkshire County Council

[1993] 4 All ER 9, [1993] 3 WLR 708, [1993] RTR 406

The claimant's action for damages for personal injury he suffered in a road traffic accident caused partly as a result of the defendant's negligence could not be pursued where the issues of liability had already been tried in an action brought against Mr Talbot by his passenger. The doctrine of *res judicata* was to be applied in the absence of special circumstances which would have precluded its operation.

[4.51]   Johnson v Gore Wood & Co (a firm)

[2002] 2 AC 1, [2001] 1 All ER 481, [2001] 2 WLR 72

The Court of Appeal held that the claimant's action was an abuse of process under the rule in *Henderson v Henderson* (see [4.47]). The claimant appealed to the House of Lords.

HELD, ON APPEAL: It was correct in principle that a party could not bring a claim or raise a defence if that claim or defence could have been raised in earlier proceedings if it could be raised at all. However it was wrong to be too dogmatic when applying this rule, as the Court of Appeal had been.

What the court had to do was to look at the matter in the round and make a broad, merits based judgment which took account of private and public interests and all the facts of the case.

[4.52]   McNally v McWilliams

[2001] NI 106

Mr McN was killed and his wife, Mrs McN was injured when the car that they were travelling in and Mr McN was driving collided with the defendant's vehicle. The defendant's brought an action against the estate of Mr McN for damages for personal injury. Mrs McN as Mr McN's personal representative brought an action against the defendant for damages pursuant to the Fatal Accidents (Northern Ireland) Order 1977, SI 1977/1251 (NI 18). Those actions were compromised. Mrs McN subsequently brought an action against the defendant for her own injuries arising out of the same accident. The defendant applied to have this action stayed on the basis that it was an abuse of process.

HELD: The defendant's application to stay was refused. Mrs McN had never accepted that her husband had been responsible for the accident so it was sensible for her to wait for the outcome of the first proceedings before commencing her own. There was no *res judicata* where an action was settled on terms. *Johnson v Gore Wood* (see para [4.51]) considered.

[4.53]   Khiaban v Beard

[2002] EWCA Civ 358

[2003] 3 All ER 362, [2003] 1 WLR 1626, [2003] RTR 419, CA

The claimant and defendant were involved in a road traffic accident as a consequence of which the claimant claimed repair costs to his vehicle of £755.89, an excess of £125 and miscellaneous expenses. The parties' insurers reached a memorandum of understanding between themselves to the effect that they would be bound by the liability decision at trial. In the circumstances the claim was only pleaded for the excess and miscellaneous expenses and did not include the sum for the vehicle repair costs.

The district judge struck out the claim on the basis that the particulars of claim did not reflect the full value of the claim because it did not include the full cost of the vehicle repairs. Leave to appeal was given to the Court of Appeal.

HELD, ON APPEAL: The district judge was wrong to strike out the claim. There was nothing in the Civil Procedure Rules which supported the district judge's view that the claim had to include the repair costs and there was no reason for distinguishing between subrogated and non-subrogated claims. The parties were entitled to simplify the claim in the manner that they did.

Per Dyson LJ: A claimant is fully entitled to decide what to include in his claim. If he excludes a head of loss from his claim, and he is awarded judgment on his pleaded claim, he will normally be precluded as a matter of law from subsequently starting proceedings to recover the excluded head of loss: see *Henderson v Henderson* (1843) 3 Hare 100. That is the chance that a claimant must take if excludes from his claim sums which he could claim from the defendant. But there is nothing in the general law which positively obliges a claimant to include in his pleaded case all the claims which he could arguably advance against the defendant.

7.   ESTOPPEL

[4.54]   Greenwood v Martins Bank Ltd

[1933] AC 51, [1932] All ER Rep 318, 101 LJKB 623, 147 LT 441, 48 TLR 601, 75 Sol Jo 544, HL   Lord Tomlin

Per Lord Tomlin: The essential factors giving rise to an estoppel are, I think:

(1)   A representation or conduct amounting to a representation intended to induce a course of conduct on the part of the person to whom the representation is made.

(2)   An act or omission resulting from the representation whether actual or by conduct by the person to whom the representation is made.

(3)   Detriment to such person as a consequence of the act or omission.

Mere silence cannot amount to a representation, but when there is a duty to disclose deliberate silence may become significant and amount to a representation.

[4.55]   **Hayler v Chapman**
[1989] I Lloyd's Rep 490, CA

In 1984, the claimant's and the defendant's cars collided. The claimant's insurer paid out the written-off value of the car, and in April 1985 claimed that amount and the claimant's uninsured losses from the defendant's insurer, who denied liability. Meanwhile, the claimant claimed the uninsured loss from the defendant's insurer in May 1985, and on receiving a denial of liability, commenced proceedings in June 1985. He obtained an arbitrator's award in August 1985, which the defendant's insurer satisfied. The claimant's insurer was unaware that the claimant had obtained the award and in May 1987 issued proceedings in the claimant's name against the defendant for the written-off value of the car. The defendant's insurer applied successfully to the court for an order that the second action should be struck out as an abuse of process, since two actions could not be brought in respect of the same cause of action. The court refused the claimant's insurer's application to have the arbitrator's award set aside. The claimant's insurer appealed against the refusal.

HELD, dismissing the appeal: The judge was entitled to exercise his discretion not to set aside the award. There was no evidence that it would have been unjust or inequitable for it to stand. The claimant had been compensated, and if the insurer had kept in closer contact with the insured, the issue would have been avoided altogether.

[4.56]   **Wall v Radford**
[1991] 2 All ER 741

A passenger in Miss Wall's car established liability against her to the extent of 50% with the balance being recovered against the defendant, Mr Radford. Subsequent to determination of that claim, Miss Wall instituted her own proceedings against Radford for damages for the personal injury she had suffered. Radford successfully argued that Miss Wall's claim was barred by issue estoppel.

Note—Affirmed *Talbot v Berkshire County Council* [1993] 4 All ER 9, [1993] 3 WLR 708, [1993] RTR 406.

[4.57]   **Sellen v Bailey**
[1999] RTR 63

Judgment was entered on claim for uninsured loss. It was not permissible later to issue proceedings for personal injury arising out of the same accident.

[4.58]   **Harvey v McGurran Solkhon**
(13 June 1999, unreported), QBD

The commencement of a second action against the defendant when an earlier action between the same parties had been concluded by a consent judgment in the defendant's favour was an abuse of process. The claimants filed evidence to the effect that they had abandoned the first action because legal aid had been withdrawn after the late service of documents by the defendant had led to a reappraisal of the merits of the claimant's case.

HELD: There was no issue estoppel. The court was required to assess precisely which matters in the first action were essential or fundamental and how they had been determined. This was difficult where there was only a formal consent judgment. The court was entitled to look at all the available evidence to determine whether a party had, by consenting to judgment, conceded defeat upon any particular issue. The consent judgment did not necessarily imply abandonment by the claimants of their case. The second action was an abuse of process. The claimants were in full control of both claims and had ample time to obtain an order that the actions should be consolidated or heard together. The additional burden on the defendant in terms of duplication of cost, effort and time was plain.

CHAPTER 5

Vicarious Liability

1.   LIABILITY FOR EMPLOYERS

(A)   WHO IS AN EMPLOYEE?

[5.1] 'It must now be taken to be firmly established that the question of whether or not the work was performed in the capacity of an employee or as an independent contractor is to be regarded by the appellate court as a question of fact to be determined by the trial court': per Lord Griffiths in *Lee Ting Sang v Chung Chi-Keung* [1990] 2 AC 374, [1990] IRLR 236.

[5.2]   Ready Mixed Concrete Ltd v Minister of Pensions
[1968] 2 QB 497, [1968] 1 All ER 433, [1968] 2 WLR 775, 112 Sol Jo 14   MacKenna J

The owner of a lorry worked for the appellant company under a written contract which described him as an independent contractor. It required him to make his lorry available for the purpose of carrying concrete for the company, to maintain it in good order at his own expense and to hire a driver to drive it when he himself was not available to do so. He was to be paid per mile for the concrete he delivered.

HELD: A contract of service existed if three conditions were fulfilled:
(1)   an agreement by the servant to provide his own work and skill to perform some service in consideration of remuneration;
(2)   agreement that in performance of the service he would be subject to control sufficiently to make the other the master,
(3)   the other provisions of the contract are consistent with a contract of service. In classifying the contract a judge might take into account other matters besides control.

In the present case the driver had ownership of the assets, the chance of profit and the risk of loss. He had sufficient freedom in the performance of the obligations under the contract to qualify as independent contractor. He was a 'small businessman' not a servant.

[5.3]   Challinor v Taylor
[1972] ICR 129, 116 Sol Jo 141, 7 ITR 104

A taxi driver had an agreement with the owner of a taxi whereby he paid to the owner 65% of the fares registered on the clock plus the cost of an employee's national insurance stamp. The owner paid for fuel and maintenance. The driver kept the balance of the takings plus all the tips. He was assessed income tax under Sch D as a self-employed person. No memorandum of the terms of employment was supplied to him under the Contracts of Employment Act 1963. The owner never exercised any control over where or for how long the driver plied for hire. When the owner sold the cab the driver claimed a redundancy payment under the Redundancy Payments Act 1965 as an 'employee'.

HELD: He was not an employee. In deciding whether someone was an employee or an independent contractor many factors had to be taken into account of which actual control or the right to control the way in which the work was performed was only one. Whether the contract was one of service depended in the last resort on whether an ordinary person would so consider it in the light of his experience and knowledge.

[5.4]   Global Plant Ltd v Secretary of State for Health and Social Security
[1972] 1 QB 139, [1971] 3 All ER 385, [1971] 3 WLR 269, 115 Sol Jo 506   Lord Widgery CJ

For a period up to 1968 the appellants, a company which hired out earth-moving machines with drivers, employed Summers as a driver at a weekly wage and on terms which amounted to a contract of service. In that year he asked to be self-employed as a sub-contractor. Thereafter he stamped his own insurance card at the self-employed person's rate, paid his own income tax under Sch D and was paid at a much enhanced hourly rate, but without travelling expenses, sick pay or provision for holidays. He drove the company's machines as before on sites selected by them under the control of the site foreman or agent. He was not expressly under any duty to work at all but the intention was that he should work exactly as he had before. A determination was made by the Secretary of State for Social Services under the National Insurance Act 1965 that Summers was still a person employed under a contract of service.

HELD: There was no error in law in the Minister's decision.

Note—After commenting that 'the idea of the degree of control exercised by the employer over the servant being a decisive factor in this question has been very largely modified'. Lord Widgery quoted with approval a passage from Cooke J's judgment in *Market Investigations Ltd v Minister of Social Security* [1969] 2 QB 173, [1968] 3 All ER 732, [1969] 2 WLR 1, 112 Sol Jo 905: 'factors which may be of importance are such matters as whether the man performing the services provides his own equipment, whether he hires his own helpers, what degree of financial risk he takes, what degree of responsibility for investment or management he had and whether and how far he has an opportunity of profiting from sound management in the performance of his task'.

[5.5]   Roberts v Warne

[1973] RTR 217, Div Ct

Roberts, a hire-car driver, made an agreement with Davies, who ran a hire-car booking office, having the following elements: Roberts would drive Davies's car for the purpose of carrying passengers who booked in at Davies's Need-a-cab office. Roberts would be on call or attend at the office regularly at agreed times on every weekday except Fridays and Saturdays and would then drive a car as directed by Davies's office: Davies would ensure that Roberts was covered by Davies's own insurance: Roberts would be entitled to 50% of the takings from passengers whom he drove and would pay his own national insurance contributions and income tax.

HELD: The question whether Roberts was employed by Davies under a contract of service or not could be decided by asking: whose business was it that was being carried on? What they had agreed was that Davies was to supply the car and booking facilities and Roberts was to do the work and they were to split the proceeds 50–50; the answer to the question was that it was the business of both of them. It was not a contract of service, it was a co-adventure.

[5.6]   Ferguson v Dawson

[1976] 1 Lloyd's Rep 143, Boreham J; aff'd [1976] 3 All ER 817, [1976] 1 WLR 1213, [1976] 2 Lloyd's Rep 669, CA

The claimant was a building worker 'on the lump'. He was injured when working for the defendants who were building contractors. Both the claimant and the defendants regarded and named him as a 'self-employed labour only contractor'. The claimant paid his own national insurance stamp as a self-employed person and his wages were paid free of tax.

HELD: Where all the other indicia mentioned by MacKenna J in *Ready Mixed Concrete v Ministry of Pensions* (at para [5.2] above) point to the relationship being that of master and servant then it was in reality a contract of service.

[5.7]   Massey v Crown Life Insurance Co Ltd

[1978] 2 All ER 576, [1978] 1 WLR 676, 121 Sol Jo 791, CA

From 1971 to 1973 the appellant worked as branch manager for the respondent insurance company which treated him as a servant, paying his wages and deducting tax. From 1973 onwards he carried on doing the same job but as an independent contractor under a new agreement at his own instance to enable him to be taxed under Sch D. Later he was dismissed and sought compensation for unfair dismissal.

HELD: He was not an employee and could not claim compensation. Where a perfectly genuine agreement had been entered into at his instance and for his benefit he could not afterwards claim the relationship was something other than what the agreement stated. *Ferguson v Dawson* (at para [5.6]) was different; there the contract was so unspecific that the way the parties had acted was the only thing to go by.

[5.12]   Mersey Docks and Harbour Board v Coggins and Griffiths (Liverpool) Ltd

[1947] AC 1, [1946] 2 All ER 345, HL

Coggins and Griffiths hired from the Dock Board a crane and driver who was engaged and paid by the Board. A third party employed by a firm of forwarding agents was injured by the negligence of the crane driver and obtained judgment against the Board. The Board appealed.

Per Viscount Simon: In applying the doctrine of *respondeat superior*, prima facie the responsibility for the negligence of servants engaged and paid by a general employer or permanent employer is on that employer, and the burden of proving that the responsibility has shifted to the hirer rests on the general employer. That burden is a heavy one and can only be discharged in quite exceptional circumstances. I prefer, instead of the test applied by the Court of Appeal following *Nicholas v F J Sparkes & Son* [1945] KB 309n, CA, the test where the authority lies to direct, or to delegate to, the workman, the manner in which the vehicle is driven. It is this authority which determines who is the workman's 'superior'.

In this case, the servant was exercising his own discretion as driver, a discretion vested in him by his general employers, and the mistake he made had nothing to do with the hirers. If, however, the hirers had intervened to give directions how to drive and the driver *pro hac vice* had complied with them the hirers might have been liable, as joint tortfeasors.

The contract between the parties provided that the hirers of the crane and workman must take all risks and the workman shall be the servant of the hirers. This contract does not affect the rights of third parties.

Appeal dismissed.

[5.13]   Chowdhary v Gillot

[1947] 2 All ER 541, 63 TLR 569   Streatfield J

The claimant for 10 or 12 years had been a valued customer of the Daimler Co. He was in the habit of taking his Daimler car to their works and leaving it with them for servicing and repairs. Before the War the Daimler Co drove the claimant to the nearest railway station as a courtesy service in their own car with their own driver. During the War, their servant drove the claimant in his own car to the station and would then drive the car back to the works. On the way to the station an accident occurred by the negligence of the servant, and the claimant and a third party were injured.

HELD: Although the burden of proof of transfer of a servant is not so heavy when the servant alone is hired, as opposed to the man plus the machine, it remains a heavy burden. The burden of proof was on the claimant to show that he had abandoned his right to control or had contracted himself out of that right:
(1)   the Daimler Co were in possession of the car as bailees;
(2)   the claimant had no right to control the bailees' servant;
(3)   the claimant was doing no more than receive courtesy service;
(4)   the claimant was not in a position to exercise control.
The fact that the claimant could have ordered the driver to drive more carefully if he was driving dangerously, or more slowly if at an uncomfortable or dangerous speed would be no more than the common prudence that a hirer would exercise towards a taxi driver, who is not the servant of the fare. He could not have ordered the driver to stop and wait half an hour, or deviate and wait while he visited a patient, or drive to a more distant place for his own purposes. If the

Daimler Co had a regulation limiting the driving of customer's cars to a speed of, say, 20mph and the claimant had ordered the driver to drive faster to catch a train, the driver could have refused.

Distinguishing *Pratt v Patrick* [1924] 1 KB 488, [1923] All ER Rep 512, 93 LJKB 174, 130 LT 735 and *Samson v Aitchison* (at para [5.36]), the driver remained the servant of the Daimler Co.

[5.14]   Denham v Midland Employers Mutual Assurance Ltd
[1955] 2 QB 437, [1955] 2 All ER 561, [1955] 3 WLR 84, 99 Sol Jo 417, [1955] 1 Lloyd's Rep 467, CA

Eastwoods Ltd, brickmakers, contracted with Le Grand Co, arterial well engineers, to perform work on their property, and agreed to provide one unskilled labourer to assist two skilled drillers of Le Grand Co free of charge. The labourer was selected by and paid by Eastwoods; they alone could suspend or dismiss him; they kept his insurance cards and paid for his insurance stamps. He was not asked nor did he consent to a transfer of his contract of service; if he was not paid his wages, or was wrongfully dismissed, he could sue Eastwoods and no one else; if he failed to turn up, Eastwoods alone could sue him. The labourer was killed in circumstances whereby Le Grand Co were liable to his widow by reason of negligence of Le Grand Co or their servants.

Le Grand Co had a policy of insurance against employers' liability with the first defendants indemnifying them in respect of injury to any person under a contract of service with them by accident arising out of and in the course of his employment by them. They also had a public liability policy with the second defendants, which excluded liability in respect of any person under a contract of service with them by accident arising out of and in the course of employment by them. Each insurer contended the other was liable to indemnify.

HELD, ON APPEAL: There was no contract of service with Le Grand and they were not entitled to recover from the first insurers. The contract of service was with Eastwoods. The second defendants were liable under the public liability policy.

[5.15]   Savory v Holland, Hannen and Cubitts (Southern) Ltd
[1964] 3 All ER 18, [1964] 1 WLR 1158, 108 Sol Jo 479, CA

The defendants, building contractors, were clearing a large site to build a factory. They encountered rock, and engaged sub-contractors to blast it out. The sub-contractors sent the claimant, a skilled blaster, to do the job. He brought his own equipment but the defendants provided flagmen. The sub-contractors employed him, paid him and had power to dismiss him. The defendants could decide what rock they wanted him to blast but had no right to dictate to him how the actual blasting should be done. He was injured when he slipped whilst walking down a bank after acting as a flagman. He claimed damages on the grounds that the defendants had not provided enough flagmen nor a ladder to climb the bank in spite of his having asked for both. The judge held that he was a servant for the time being of the defendants and that they were liable.

HELD, ON APPEAL: The claimant was not a servant of the defendants either for the time being or at any time. He remained throughout the servant of the sub-contractors, his general employers, and the defendants were not liable.

Per Diplock LJ: The doctrine of master and servant *pro hac vice* today seems to me to be relevant only to a question of vicarious liability: it is a mere adjunct of the doctrine or *respondeat superior* for determining whether A is the superior of B.

Note—See also *Garrard v A E Southey & Co and Standard Telephones and Cables Ltd* [1952] 2 QB 174, [1952] 1 All ER 597, [1952] 1 TLR 630, 96 Sol Jo 166, and *Johnson v A H Beaumont* [1953] 2 QB 184, [1953] 2 All ER 106, [1953] 2 WLR 1153, 97 Sol Jo 389, [1953] 1 Lloyd's Rep 546.

[5.16]   McConkey v Amec plc

(1990) Times, 28 February, CA

The claimant was injured by equipment falling from a crane. His employers ('the hirers') had hired the crane and driver. The claimant sued both the hirers and the owners of the crane and driver.

The terms of the contract between the parties incorporated the model conditions agreed between the Contractors Plant Association and the Federation of the Civil Engineering Contractors. The relevant clauses were:

'5(a) Unless notification ... to the contrary is received ... the plant shall be deemed to be in good order ...'

'8 When a driver or operator is supplied by the owner with the plant, the owner shall supply a person competent in operating the plant and such person shall be under the direction and control of the hirer ...'

'13(a) ... Nothing in this clause affects the operation of clauses 5, 8 ... of this agreement ...'

The judge accepting that the driver of the crane was not at the relevant time a competent operator within the terms of clause 8, nevertheless, found that the owners had a complete indemnity from the hirers. The hirers appealed.

HELD: The driver of the crane was an employee of the owners who were vicariously liable for the damage caused by his negligence. The agreement was to be read to the effect that if the owners supplied an incompetent operator or defective equipment then such operator was not to be regarded as a servant or agent of the hirer and the owner remained vicariously liable for his negligence.

Note—But see the two earlier decisions of *Philips Products Ltd v Hyland* [1987] 2 All ER 620, [1987] 1 WLR 659n, (1984) 129 Sol Jo 47, [1985] LS Gaz R 681, CA and *Thompson v T Lohan (Plant Hire) Ltd* [1987] 2 All ER 631, [1987] 1 WLR 649 [1987] IRLR 148, 131 Sol Jo 358, CA, where the indemnity was effective.

[5.17]   Hawley v (1) Luminar Leisure plc (2) ASE Security Services and Others

[2005] EWHC 5 (QB); aff'd [2006] EWCA Civ 18

[2006] All ER (D) 158 (Jan), 150 Sol Jo LB 163

The claimant was assaulted by a nightclub doorman. The doorman was employed by a security company who had been contracted to provide security services to the nightclub. The claimant claimed that both the security company and the nightclub owner were each liable for the acts of the doorman. It was claimed that the doorman was a temporary deemed employee of the nightclub which was vicariously liable for his actions. The insurers of the security company were alleged to be liable to indemnify the security company for the claimant's injuries pursuant to the policy of insurance.

HELD: The test for determining whether the nightclub could be vicariously liable was one of the nature and extent of control which the nightclub had over the doorman supplied by the security company. It did not matter that the contract stipulated that the doormen were employees of the security company at all times. The nightclub did control the doormen and their work and were therefore vicariously liable to the claimant. The security company's insurers were liable under the policy as the injury was '*accidental*' when viewed from the perspective of the policyholder. This decision was confirmed on appeal.

[5.18] **Viasystems (Tyneside) Ltd v Thermal Transfer (Northern) Ltd and Others**

[2005] EWCA Civ 1151

[2005] 4 All ER 1181, [2006] 2 WLR 428, [2005] IRLR 983, CA

A flood caused damage within the claimant's factory when air-conditioning was installed. Ducting work had been subcontracted to the second defendants ('Darwell'). Darwell in turn contracted with the third defendants ('CAT') to provide fitters and fitters' mates on a labour-only basis. One such fitter was a Mr Megson, who had a mate, Darren Strang. Megson and Strang were thus employed by CAT, but they were operating under the instruction and supervision of Darwell acting through a Mr Horsley.

At the time of the accident, the men were working in the roof space. Megson needed some fittings and sent Darren Strang to get them. He was expected to return by a sensible route. Instead he attempted to return by crawling through some sections of ducting that were in place. These moved and came into contact with part of the fire protection sprinkler system. This fractured resulting in the flood.

At first instance the judge held the permanent general employer of Strang, CAT, vicariously liable for his negligence in causing the flood. It was not suggested by either party at first instance that both 'employers' might be vicariously liable. The parties appealed.

HELD, ON APPEAL: The long-standing assumption that a finding of dual vicarious liability was not legally permissible was technically unsupported by authority binding the Court of Appeal. Revisiting the matter afresh it was held that dual vicarious liability is a legal possibility. On the facts of the case it was appropriate that both Darwell and CAT should be held vicariously liable for Strang's negligence.

Per May LJ: So the core question on the facts of this case is who was entitled, and in theory, if they had had the opportunity, obliged, so to control Darren as to stop him crawling through the duct. In my judgment, the only sensible answer to that question in this case is that both Mr Megson and Mr Horsley were entitled, and in theory obliged, to stop Darren's foolishness. Mr Megson was the fitter in charge of Darren. Mr Horsley was the foreman on the spot. They were both entitled and obliged to control Darren's work, including the act which was his negligence.

2. LIABILITY OF EMPLOYER

[5.19]   Note: The traditional test for the imposition of vicarious liability was set out by Salmond in his Law of Torts 1907:

'a master is not responsible for a wrongful act done by his servant unless it is done in the course of his employment. It is deemed to be so done if it is either (1) a wrongful act authorised by the master, or (2) a wrongful and unauthorised mode of doing some act authorised by the master but a master, as opposed to the employer of an independent contractor, is liable even for acts which he has not authorised, provided they are so connected with acts which he has authorised that they may rightly be regarded as modes – although improper modes-of doing them.'

(A)   SCOPE OF EMPLOYMENT

[5.20]   Lister v Hesley Hall Ltd

[2001] UKHL 22

[2002] 1 AC 215, [2001] 2 All ER 769, [2001] 2 WLR 1311, [2001] ICR 665, [2001] IRLR 472, [2001] 2 FLR 307, [2001] 2 FCR 97, (2001) 3 LGLR 987, [2001] ELR 422, [2001] Fam Law 595, [2001] LS Gaz R 45

The defendant ran a school for boys with emotional and behavioural difficulties. An employee of the defendant, a warden/housekeeper who looked after the boys at the school, systematically abused residents between 1979 and 1982. In 1997 the residents brought personal injury claims against the defendant on the grounds that it was negligent in selecting, appointing and supervising the warden and it was vicariously liable for his tortious acts.

At first instance, the trial judge dismissed the claim in negligence and held that the defendant could not be vicariously liable for the sexual assaults themselves. The judge, however, held that the defendant could be vicariously liable for the employee's failure to report the harm to the boys. The Court of Appeal allowed the defendant's appeal because, if the sexual assaults themselves were outside the course of the warden's employment, then the failure to prevent or report those assaults could not be within the course of his employment. The claimants appealed to the House of Lords.

HELD, ON APPEAL: The defendant was vicariously liable for the warden's assaults. The correct approach in determining liability is to consider whether the employee's torts are so closely connected with his employment that it is fair and just to hold the defendant vicariously liable. 'It is no answer to say that the employee was guilty of intentional wrongdoing, or that his act was not merely tortious but criminal, or that he was acting exclusively for his own benefit, or that he was acting contrary to express instructions, or that his conduct was the very negation of his employer's duty': per Lord Millett.

The school was responsible for the care and welfare of the children and had entrusted the responsibility to perform those functions to the warden. The warden had abused those responsibilities and so there was a very close connection between the warden's torts and his employment.

Note—See also *Dubai Aluminium Co Ltd v Salaam* [2003] 2 AC 366, [2003] 1 All ER 97, HL when it was held that an employee's 'wrongful acts' were not confined to common law torts but extended to the equitable wrong of dishonest participation in a breach of trust:

'... for the purpose of the liability of the firm or the employer to third parties, the wrongful conduct may fairly and properly be regarded as done by the partner while acting in the ordinary course of the firm's business or the employee's employment': per Lord Millett.

[5.21]   Weir v Bettison (sued as the Chief Constable of Merseyside Police)

[2003] EWCA Civ 111

[2003] All ER (D) 273 (Jan)

An off-duty policeman borrowed a police van without permission to assist his girlfriend to move house. He parked outside the girlfriend's house and, in the course of moving, noticed the claimant who appeared to be looking through the girlfriend's belongings. The off-duty policeman challenged the claimant, took hold of him and threw him down the stairs, and then locked him in the police van advising the claimant that he was taking him to the police station. Subsequent criminal proceedings brought against the policeman were unsuccessful. The claimant brought proceedings for personal injury arising out of the assault against the Chief Constable under s 88 of the Police Act 1996.

HELD, ON APPEAL: As a policeman was an office holder rather than an employee he was, as a matter of law, authorised to act without specific instruction from superiors, and that in that sense the liability of a Chief Constable was more extensive than the vicarious liability of an employer. Whilst the officer was off duty he had in all respects behaved as if was acting in the course of his duties as a police officer, specifically in locking the claimant in the police van and taking him to the police station. Therefore it was appropriate that the claimant should recover damages from the Chief Constable.

[5.22]   Mattis v Pollock (t/a Flamingo's Nightclub)

[2003] EWCA Civ 887

[2004] 4 All ER 85, [2003] 1 WLR 2158, CA

The claimant was rendered a paraplegic by stab wounds inflicted upon him by a doorman employed by the defendant nightclub. Earlier in the evening the doorman, who was not licensed as a doorman by the local authority, had started a fight which involved the claimant. Later that same evening the doorman left the club, went home, armed himself with a knife and then returned to an area outside the club where the stabbing of the claimant took place. The judge held that the defendant was not vicariously (and therefore also not personally) liable for the doorman's conduct towards the claimant. The incident had taken place outside the course of the doorman's employment and was akin to an act of personal revenge. The claimant appealed.

HELD, ON APPEAL: The court applied *Lister v Hesley Hall Ltd* (see para 5.20 above) and *Dubai Aluminium Co Ltd v Salaam* (under Comment at para 5.20 above) and held that the defendant was vicariously liable for the doorman's attack as it was so closely connected with what the doorman had been authorised to do by the defendant that it would be fair and reasonable to impose a liability. It was expected that the doorman would use violence and the defendant had encouraged this behaviour. As violence was a part of the doorman's employed role, the likelihood of establishing that a particular act of violence fell within the scope of his employment increased. The defendant's should not have employed this doorman nor should he have encouraged this violent behaviour. For the same reasons the claimant was also personally liable.

[5.23]   **Brown v Robinson**
[2004] UKPC 56
[2004] All ER (D) 208 (Dec)

The appellant appealed to the Privy Council against an order dismissing her action for damages. The appellant's son had been shot by the assailant who was on duty preventing unauthorised entry to a football match. Proceedings were brought against the assailant and his employers. At first instance it was held that whilst the assailant's conduct was unauthorised, it was still within the scope of his employment. Therefore the employers were found to be liable for his conduct and both respondents were held responsible for damages on behalf of the estate of the appellant's son. The employers appealed against the decision and were successful. The Court of Appeal found that the assailant's conduct was outside the scope of his employment.

The Privy Council overturned the Court of Appeal's decision, and applied the test formulated in *Dubai Aluminium Co Ltd v Salaam*, i e whether there was a close connection between the offending act and the employment so as to make it just and reasonable to hold the employers liable. The assailant's acts were so closely connected with his employment and it would be just and reasonable to hold the employer's liable. The shooting was not an act of revenge nor private retaliation.

(B)   OTHER CASES

[5.24]   **Poland v John Parr & Sons**
[1927] I KB 236, 96 LJKB 152, 136 LT 271, CA

A carter employed by the defendants was walking behind a wagon driven by one of the defendants carrying bags of sugar. The carter honestly thought a boy of twelve, walking beside the wagon, was pilfering the sugar, struck the boy on the neck and knocked him under the wagon.

HELD: Master was liable: the servant had implied authority to protect his master's property; the method was mistaken and excessive, and even amounted to a crime; it was not so excessive as to take it outside the authority; it was an unauthorised mode of doing an authorised act.

Per Bankes LJ: A master is not responsible for a wrongful act done by his servant unless it is done in the course of his employment. It is deemed to be so done if it is either:
   (a)   a wrongful act authorised by the master, or
   (b)   a wrongful and unauthorised mode of doing some act authorised by the master.

Per Scrutton LJ: To make an employer liable for the act of a person alleged to be his servant the act must be one of a class of acts which the person was authorised or employed to do. If the act is one of that class the employer is liable, though the act is done negligently or, in some cases even if it is done with excessive violence. But the excess may be so great as to take the act out of the class of acts which the person is authorised or employed to do.

[5.25]   **Crook v Derbyshire Stone Ltd**
[1956] 2 All ER 447, [1956] I WLR 432, 100 Sol Jo 302   Pilcher J

The driver of a motor lorry on a journey stopped shortly before 8 am and crossed the road to a cafe on the other side. A motorcyclist collided with him and both were injured. The practice of drivers stopping at wayside cafes to obtain refreshment was well known to the driver's employers and impliedly sanctioned by them.

HELD: The driver was not employed on the employer's business. When he left the lorry he had no further duty to perform on his employer's account until he returned to the lorry and resumed his journey. The employers were not liable for his negligence.

Century Insurance Co v Northern Ireland Road Transport Board (at para [5.8]) distinguished.

Note—This case was distinguished in the case of *Staton v National Coal Board* (at para [5.26]). See also *British Transport Commission v Maxine & Co Ltd* (1963) 107 Sol Jo 1024.

[5.26] Staton v National Coal Board

[1957] 2 All ER 667, [1957] 1 WLR 893, 101 Sol Jo 592   Finnemore J

A workman was in regular employ of a colliery as a first-aid man. He was on night shift from 10.30 pm to 8 am. Friday afternoon between 1 pm and 5 pm was the proper time for the men employed at the colliery to collect their week's wages. On Friday he finished his shift at 8.30 am. In the afternoon he proceeded to the colliery for his wages. He called at the Time Office in the colliery premises and then proceeded on his cycle to the General Office where the pay office was situated. On the left-hand side of the road was a bus park where some buses were parked waiting to take home the miners who had finished the day shift. The workman left the road to proceed across the bus park and decided to ride through the space between the second and third buses.

A miner employed by the colliery who had finished his work on the day shift, was seated in one of the buses, when he suddenly remembered something which required him to go back across the road to one of the offices. He came round the front of the bus and was knocked down in collision with the cycle, and sustained injuries from which he died.

HELD: The accident arose in the course of the employment of the first-aid man rendering his employers liable to the defendants of the injured man. He had finished his manual work and was riding his cycle across the employers' premises to collect the wages the employers had contracted to pay him and was still in the course of his employment. There had been nothing to break the course of his employment. It was in the interests of the employer as well as the employee that a workman should receive his wages and receive them at a convenient place and at a convenient time. He was not on the Queen's highway on his way to his place of employment to get his wages but was actually on his employers' premises going to the place which the employers had said was the place to which he was required to come in order to draw his wages. The case of *Crook v Derbyshire Stone Ltd* (at para [5.25]) was quite different on the facts.

SEMBLE: If a workman was off the employers' premises, eg on the Queen's highway on his way to his place of employment, he would not be in the course of his employment.

Note—See also *British Transport Commission v Maxine & Co Ltd* (1963) 107 Sol Jo 1024.

[5.27]   Ilkiw v Samuels

[1963] 2 All ER 879, [1963] 1 WLR 991, 107 Sol Jo 680, CA

The defendants' lorry was driven to the premises of the claimant's employers to load bags of sugar. The defendants' driver, Waines, put the lorry under a conveyor and then stood in the back of the lorry to load bags from the conveyor. When sufficiently loaded the lorry had to be moved. Samuels, a fellow employee of the claimant's and not employed by the defendants, offered to move it. Waines allowed him to do so without asking whether he could drive. In fact Samuels could not drive and after starting the lorry could not stop it. It crushed the claimant, who was working nearby, against another conveyor causing him serious injury. Waines remained in the back of the lorry throughout. He had been expressly forbidden by his employers to let anyone other than himself drive the lorry.

HELD: (1) Waines was negligent in allowing Samuels to drive without inquiring whether he was competent: the defendants were vicariously liable for his negligence because it was a mode, though an improper mode, of performing the duties on which he was employed namely, to have charge and control of the lorry. It was therefore a negligent act within the scope of his employment.

'Waines was employed not only to drive but also to be in charge of his vehicle in all circumstances during any such times as he was on duty. That means to say that, even when he was not himself sitting at the controls, he remained in charge of the lorry and in charge as his employers' representative. His employers must remain liable for his negligence so long as the vehicle was being used in the course of their business. As I understand the authorities, the employers escape liability if, but only if, at the time of the negligent act, the vehicle was being used by the driver for the purpose of what had been called a "frolic" of his own. That is not this case. Here, at the material time, this vehicle was in fact being used in the course of the defendants' business. In those circumstances it appears to me that there is no ground on which the defendants can escape liability for Waines' negligence': per Willmer LJ.

(2)   Even if Samuels had been a competent driver but negligent on that occasion, Waines would still have been negligent for the reason given *Ricketts v Tilling* [1915] 1 KB 644, 84 LJKB 342, 112 LT 137, 31 TLR 17, CA that it was his duty to prevent another person from driving, or, if he allowed another person to drive, to see that he drove properly. This also was negligence within the scope of his employment.

(3)   'It was not necessarily negligent of Waines to allow Samuels to drive; even if it were, the employers would not be vicariously liable since the selection of a person to drive was not part of Waines's duties – indeed he was forbidden to let anyone else drive. But the employers were liable to the claimant on the broader ground that the lorry was being driven negligently while being used for the purposes of the defendants' business under the control of their servant Waines, he being employed to take charge and control of the vehicle while engaged on the task being performed when the accident took place. Liability would be the same even if Samuels had been a highly experienced driver, provided his negligent driving on this occasion was the cause of the claimant's injuries': per Diplock LJ.

(4)   The fact that the defendants had expressly forbidden Waines to let anyone else drive was immaterial since it was no more than a direction

as to the mode in which the servant was to perform the duty. *Limpus v London General Omnibus Co* (1862) 1 H & C 526, 32 LJ Ex 34, 7 LT 641 followed.

[5.28]   Morris v C W Martin & Sons Ltd

[1966] 1 QB 716, [1965] 2 All ER 725, [1965] 3 WLR 276, 109 Sol Jo 451, [1965] 2 Lloyd's Rep 63, CA

The claimant's mink fur was sent to the defendants for cleaning. They delegated the task of cleaning it to an employee, who stole it. It was not recovered and the claimant sued for its value. The county court judge held that the employee was not acting in the scope of his employment in stealing the fur and that the defendants were not liable for his wrongful act.

HELD, ON APPEAL: The defendants had accepted the fur as bailees for reward in order to clean it. They put the employee as their agent to clean the fur and take charge of it whilst doing so. The manner he conducted himself in doing that work was to convert it: it was done in the scope or course of his employment and the defendants were liable for his wrongful act.

Lord Denning MR drew attention to the fact that if the owner of a car takes it to a garage to be repaired and it is repaired by a garage hand who then takes it out on a 'frolic of his own' and collides with a motorcycle the owner of the car can sue the garage proprietor for any damage to the car (as in *Central Motors Glasgow Ltd v Cessnock Garage Co* 1925 SC 796, 1925 SN 103, 1925 SLT 563 but the motorcyclist cannot sue the garage proprietor for damage to the motorcycle (citing *Storey v Ashton* (1869) LR 4 QB 476, 10 B & S 337, LLQB 223). He continued: 'I ask myself, How can this be? How can the servant, on one and the same journey, be acting both within and without the course of his employment? Within *qua* the car owner. Without *qua* the motorcyclist. It is time we got rid of this confusion. And the only way to do it, so far as I can see, is by reference to the duty laid by the law on the master. The duty of the garage proprietor to the owner of the car is very different from his duty to the motorcyclist. He owes to the owner of the car the duty of a bailee for reward, whereas he owes no such duty to the motorcyclist on the road. He does not even owe him a duty to use care not to injure him. If you go through the cases on this difficult subject, you will find that, in the ultimate analysis, they depend on the nature of the duty owed by the master towards the person whose goods have been lost or damaged'.

[5.29]   Elleanor v Cavendish Woodhouse Ltd and Comerford

[1973] 1 Lloyd's Rep 313, 117 Sol Jo 14, CA

The second defendant was a salesman employed by the first defendant. He worked ordinary business hours in his employer's shop in Darlington but was also required to do some canvassing during evenings within the radius of 30 miles, using his own car. Sometimes he went with another salesman, a practice known to their employer which led to better results. One evening he took another salesman, Smith, on canvassing some distance from Darlington. The canvassing finished by 8 pm and they then called at one or more public houses for food and drink. On the way home there was an accident at about 9.30 pm caused by the second defendant's negligence.

HELD: The employer was vicariously liable. On the evidence the second defendant was under a duty as an employee to bring his fellow-salesman back to Darlington and was therefore doing something which he was employed to do.

[5.30]   Rose v Plenty

[1976] I All ER 97, [1975] I WLR 141, 119 Sol Jo 592, CA

The second defendant employed the first defendant as a milkman. Notices at the depot made it clear that roundsmen were not allowed to take children on vehicles. Despite this the first defendant took the claimant, a boy of 13, on his milk float, paying him a few shillings for help in delivering milk. Whilst being carried on the vehicle the claimant was injured by the first defendant's negligence.

HELD, ON APPEAL (Lawton LJ dissenting): There was vicarious liability on the second defendant. The prohibited act, namely taking the boy on the float to help him deliver milk was done by the milkman in the course of his service and for the employer's purposes. *Twine v Beans's Express Ltd* (1946) 175 LT 131, 62 TLR 458, CA and *Conway v George Wimpey & Co* [1951] 2 KB 266, [1951] I All ER 363, 95 Sol Jo 156, [1951] I TLR 587, CA were cases where a driver had given a lift to someone else contrary to a prohibition and not for the purposes of the employers. The prohibition on the milkman against employing boys to help him was not one which defined or limited his sphere of employment, which was to go round the rounds delivering milk. This distinguished it from such cases as *Iqbal v London Transport Executive* (1973) 16 KIR 329, CA.

[5.31]   Smith v Stages

[1989] AC 928, [1989] I All ER 833

The first defendant and M, who were based in Staffordshire, were instructed by their employer to drive to Wales for a week's work. They were told to commence work on Tuesday, 23 August 1977 at 8 am. The men travelled down the preceding Monday and were given expenses equivalent to the return rail fare, together with a day's pay. No stipulations were made as to how they should travel and they went in the first defendant's car. The men then worked through the week until 8.30 am on the following Monday morning. The men were paid for sleeping and travel time on their return journey.

They had to report back for work to Staffordshire on the Wednesday morning and they set off on the Monday in the first defendant's car. An accident occurred and M suffered serious injuries. M subsequently died from connected causes. His widow claimed damages against the employers of the driver. At first instance the judge found that the defendant was not acting in the course of his employment when driving and dismissed the widow's claim. She appealed.

HELD: An employee paid by his employer to travel to a workplace different from his usual one to carry out a job, who was also paid wages for the return journey was acting in the course of his employment. It did not matter that the defendant in this case could decide the mode and time of travel. The defendant was acting in the course of his employment when driving the deceased to Pembroke and back. The driver's employer was vicariously liable for his negligence.

(C)   VICARIOUS LIABILITY UNDER THE PROTECTION FROM HARASSMENT ACT 1997

[5.32]   **Majrowski v Guy's and St Thomas' NHS Trust**

[2006] UKHL 34

[2006] All ER (D) 146 (Jul), [2006] IRLR 695, [2006] 3 WLR 125

Mr Majrowski was employed by the Trust as an audit co-ordinator and alleged that he had been unlawfully harassed by his departmental manager in breach of s 1 of the Protection from Harassment Act 1997 and that the employer was vicariously liable. At first instance and on a preliminary issue the court found that an employer could not be vicariously liable and struck out the claim as disclosing no reasonable cause of action. This decision was reversed by a majority of 2:1 in the Court of Appeal on 16 March 2005 and then appealed by the Trust to the House of Lords on 10 and 11 May 2006.

Section 1 of the 1997 Act prohibits a person pursuing a course of conduct which he knows or ought to know amounts to harassment of another.

Under the 1997 Act claimants do not need to prove a recognised psychiatric condition and limitation is extended to six years. However, a claimant has to prove:

- a *course of conduct*, i e more than a single act of harassment or arguably one act together with evidence and fear of repetition;
- that the conduct satisfies the definition of harassment and;
- that there is a sufficiently close connection between the work and alleged harassment for vicarious liability to attach.

There is a defence available to employers if they can show that the conduct was for the purpose of preventing or detecting crime, under a rule of law or that it was reasonable to pursue the conduct.

HELD, ON APPEAL: The Lordships found that Parliament had intended there should be vicarious liability under the 1997 Act. Although not advanced by the claimant's legal advisors in either the Court of Appeal or House of Lords, during the course of submissions Lord Hope considered the limitation provisions of the 1997 Act in Scotland, which are different to those in England and Wales. Section 10 of the Scottish legislation amends the Prescription and Limitation (Scotland) Act 1973 such that the limitation period is three years from:

(i)   the date harassment ceases; or

(ii)   a date when the victim ought reasonably know the identity of the alleged perpetrator of harassment *or the employer or principal* of that person.

It was argued on behalf of the Trust that reference to *'employer or principal'* in the Scottish formulation was only to include situations where an employer is secondarily liable in respect of the harassment, for example where they condone or encourage the conduct.

The majority of the Lordships found the Trust's policy arguments as to why the 1997 Act did not apply compelling but concluded differential interpretation could not apply in Scotland when compared to England and that the amendment made to the Prescription and Limitation (Scotland) Act 1973 was decisive in interpreting the English provisions which were silent on the issue.

Lord Hope said that had it not been for the Scottish provisions he would have found it hard to disagree with Scott Baker's dissenting judgment in the Court of Appeal that the 1997 Act imposed a duty personal to the perpetrator and should not be extended to the blameless employer.

Note—Although there is no definition of harassment under the 1997 Act, Lord Nicholls' leading judgment makes it very clear that conduct which is simply unattractive or unreasonable or regrettable is not sufficient to satisfy the Act. The behaviour must be oppressive and unacceptable and the gravity of the misconduct must be of an order which would sustain criminal liability. Baroness Hale said that harassment is genuinely offensive and unacceptable behaviour. The Act should therefore only apply to cases of the serious misconduct. If courts properly interpret the Act then claimants will be presented with significant hurdles to overcome and claims arising from trivial workplace grievances should not succeed.

3.   OWNER'S LIABILITY FOR DRIVER

(A)   PRIMA FACIE LIABILITY

[5.33]   *Note*—An owner of a vehicle does not incur a liability for damage caused by it, merely by being the owner. It must be established that the driver of the vehicle was driving it as the servant or agent of the owner: see Du Parcq LJ in *Hewitt v Bonvin* (at para [5.43]).

[5.34]   Barnard v Sully
(1931) 47 TLR 557

Where a claimant in an action for negligence proved that damage has been caused by the defendant's motor car, the fact of ownership of the motor car is *prima facie* evidence that the motor car, at the material time, was being driven by the owner, or by his servant or agent.

Per Scrutton LJ: The more usual fact is that a motor car is driven by the owner or the servant or agent of the owner and therefore the fact of ownership is some evidence fit to go to the jury that at the material time the motor car was being driven by the owner of it or by his servant or agent. But it is evidence which is liable to be rebutted by proof of the actual facts.

Note—Applied in *Elliott v Loake* [1983] Crim LR 36, a criminal case, and more recently applied in *Pask v Keefe & Stewarts Garages* (23 April 1985, unreported) (Webster J).

[5.35]   Rambarran v Gurrucharran
[1970] 1 All ER 749, [1970] 1 WLR 556, 114 Sol Jo 244, [1970] RTR 195, PC

The defendant owned a car which he allowed his sons to use at any time. He himself did not drive. An accident occurred when his son Leslie was driving. The defendant gave evidence at the trial, accepted by the trial judge, that he did not know Leslie was out in the car on the day in question; it had not been used for his own purposes on that day and he was not at his home where the car was kept. The Guyana Court of Appeal by a majority held that the defendant had not rebutted the *prima facie* case of agency arising from the fact of ownership of the car, as in *Barnard v Sully* (at para [5.34]), since he had left the court without evidence as to the journey during which the accident occurred.

HELD, ON APPEAL to the Privy Council: The defendant was not liable. A claimant must establish, if he is to make the owner liable, that the driver was driving the car as the servant or agent of the owner and not merely on his own concerns. Although in the absence of other evidence an inference can be drawn from ownership that the driver was the servant or agent of the owner there was evidence from the defendant that the car was not being used for his purposes on the day of the accident and this was sufficient to rebut the inference. It was not necessary additionally that he should prove what Leslie's object was in using the car; once he had proved that Leslie was not driving as his servant or agent then Leslie's actual purpose on that day was irrelevant. Appeal allowed.

(B)   OWNER IN CAR

[5.36]   Samson v Aitchison
[1912] AC 844, 82 LJPC 1, 107 LT 106

Where the owner of a vehicle, being himself in possession and occupation of it, requests or allows another person to drive, this will not of itself exclude his right and duty of control, and therefore, in the absence of further proof that he has abandoned that right by contract or otherwise, the owner is liable as principal for damage caused by the negligence of the person actually driving.

In his judgment which was approved by the Privy Council, the trial judge said:

'I think that where the owner of an equipage, whether a carriage and horses or a motor, is riding in it while it is being driven, and has thus not only the right to possession but the actual possession of it, he necessarily retains the power and the right of controlling the manner in which it is to be driven, unless he has in some way contracted himself out of his right, or is shown by conclusive evidence to have in some way abandoned his right. If any injury happens to the equipage while it is being driven, the owner is the sufferer. In order to protect his own property if, in his opinion, the necessity arises, he must be able to say to the driver, "Do this", or "Don't do that". The driver would have to obey, and if he did not the owner in possession would compel him to give up the reins or the steering wheel. The owner, indeed, has a duty to control the driver ... The duty to control postulates the existence of the right to control. If there was no right to control there could be no duty to control. No doubt if the actual possession of the equipage has been given by the owner to a third person – that is to say, if there has been a bailment by the owner to a third person – the owner has given up his right of control' (quoted in *Chowdhary v Gillot* (at para [5.13]).

[5.37]   Pratt v Patrick
[1924] 1 KB 488, 93 LJKB 174, 130 LT 735   Acton J

The defendant was in his motor car, with him, on his invitation, being two friends, E and P. E drove the car and, owing to his negligence, it collided with another vehicle and P sustained injuries from which he died. P's widow sued defendant under the Fatal Accidents Act for damages.

HELD: As defendant was in the car, and there was no evidence that he had abandoned his right of control, he was liable notwithstanding that by a casual delegation he had entrusted its actual management and mechanical control to E.

Note—In the above case there was a delegation of the control of the car by the owner to a casual driver while the owner himself remained in the car ready to control, if he was so minded, or to direct the driver. There was no question of the car having been handed over to anybody. There was no evidence there of any abandonment by the owner of his right to control it: per Streatfield J in *Chowdhary v Gillot* (at para [5.13]).

[5.38]   **Trust Co Ltd v de Silva**

[1956] I WLR 376, 100 Sol Jo 262, [1956] I Lloyd's Rep 309, PC

The insurers employed canvassers on commission but no salary, and field officers with a small salary and overriding commission who supervised their canvassers. Either selected a doctor to examine proposers for life insurance. A doctor was a passenger with a field officer in a car of the field officer driven by a canvasser, and was injured.

HELD: The field officer was a servant of the insurers and was acting in the course of and for the purposes of his employment; he had the right to exercise control over the driver and was in control of the car. Insurers were liable to the doctor for injuries caused by the negligent driving of the canvasser.

[5.39]   **Haydock v Brown**

(1939) Times, 24 May, (1939) Manchester Guardian, 24 May   Croom-Johnson J

The owner of a car gave permission to A (her son) to drive the car. A was in the car which was being driven by B. A was bailee of the car and had the right to possession of it. There is no difference whether the right to possession is as owner, hirer, or gratuitous bailee. If he is in the car, he must be taken to have retained his right of control, and if he has the right of control, he is liable for a person who must be deemed to be driving on his behalf and under his control.

(C)   OWNER NOT IN CAR

(I)   LOAN OF CAR

[5.40]   **Britt v Galmoye and Nevill**

(1928) 44 TLR 294, 72 Sol Jo 122

A had been in the employment of B as a van driver. B lent A his private car after the day's work was finished to take A's friends to a theatre. A, by his negligent driving, injured the claimant.

HELD: As the journey was not on the master's business, and the master was not in control, he was not liable for his servant's act.

[5.41]   **Hillman v Walls**

(1938) 5 LJCCR 167

The defendant owned a car and lent it to a fellow servant, H, to go home to lunch. H returned by other means. At the owner's request H brought the car back to work next morning, and on the way injured the claimant. H disappeared and the claimant sued the defendant alleging that the defendant had the right to control.

HELD: Following *Higbid v RC Hammett Ltd* (1932) 49 TLR 104, CA, the defendant was not in control and H was not his servant or agent.

[5.42] **Candler v Thomas (t/a London Leisure Lines)**
[1998] RTR 214, CA

A car driven by the claimant was damaged in a collision with the defendant's van. The defendant's van had been borrowed on the basis that the borrower deliver a package for the defendant as a favour and then go on to use the van for the borrower's own purpose.

At an Arbitration hearing the district judge concluded that the collision resulted from the negligence of the driver of the defendant's van and the defendant was vicariously liable for that negligence. The defendant appealed.

HELD, ON APPEAL: The appeal was dismissed. For the owner of the defendant's vehicle to be vicariously liable for any negligence of the driver it had to be shown that the driver was using the vehicle at the time for the owner's purpose. A driver who agreed to do a favour for the owner and was thus using the vehicle partly for the owner's benefit, brought the owner within that principle. Therefore the owner was vicariously liable.

[5.43] **Hewitt v Bonvin**
[1940] 1 KB 188, 109 LJKB 223, 161 LT 360, 56 TLR 43, 83 Sol Jo 869, CA

A son was driving his father's car with the consent of the father. Lewis J held that, as he was driving with the consent of the father, he was the father's agent on that journey. The Court of Appeal reversed the decision.

Per MacKinnon LJ: A man may, of course, be temporarily employed as a servant without remuneration. If I say to a friend, or to my son, 'The chauffeur is ill and cannot come. Will you drive me in my car to the station?' he is no doubt *pro tempore* my servant, and he is doing my work for me. But a servant must at the moment of his act be doing work for his employer. The claimant must establish:
  (1) that the son was employed to drive the car as his father's servant, and
  (2) that he was, when the accident happened, driving the car for the father, and not merely for his own benefit and for his own concerns.

Per du Parcq LJ: It is plain that the ownership of the car cannot of itself impose any liability on the owner. The owner, without further information, is *prima facie* liable, because the court is entitled to draw the inference that the car was being driven by the owner, his servant or agent, but when the facts are given in evidence the court is not left to draw an inference. The owner is liable if the driver had authority, express or implied, to drive on the owner's behalf. This depends not on ownership, but on the delegation of a task or duty. Permission to drive the car is consistent with a mere loan or bailment. The relationship of father and son is not of itself evidence of agency.

HELD: The father was not liable.

Note—See also *Rambarran v Gurrucharran* (at para [5.35]). The following is a form of a Plea in a Defence denying agency:

> 'The driver of the defendant's car was not the servant or agent of the defendant. The defendant lent the car to the said driver, who was driving the car merely for his own benefit and for his own concerns and was not driving the car for the defendant. The defendant disclaims all legal liability for the acts of the said driver.'

[5.44]   Klein v Caluori

[1971] 2 All ER 701, [1971] 1 WLR 619, 115 Sol Jo 228, [1971] 1 Lloyd's Rep 421, [1971] RTR 354   Lyell J

The defendant's car was borrowed and driven away without his knowledge or consent by a friend. An hour or two later the friend telephoned the defendant and told him he had taken the car. The defendant told him curtly to bring it back. On the way back the car collided with the claimant's stationary car and damaged it. The claimant claimed that the defendant was vicariously liable on the ground that his friend was his agent in driving the car because in bringing it back he was driving for the purposes of the owner, the defendant.

HELD: The return journey was part and parcel of the whole enterprise, namely, the borrowing of the car. A mere permission to drive a car does not make the driver the agent of the person giving permission. Whether or not the borrowing had been with consent the return journey was for the purposes of the borrower only. It could make no difference that the defendant told the friend to bring the car back; it was merely a reminder of his duty to do so.

(II)   DRIVING ON OWNER'S BUSINESS

[5.45]   Smith v Moss

[1940] 1 KB 424, [1940] 1 All ER 469, 109 LJKB 271, 162 LT 267, 56 TLR 305, 84 Sol Jo 115   Charles J

B bought a car which was garaged at her son's house and the son was the only driver. The car was used to convey the mother, son and son's wife home from a party. The mother was taken to her house and the son drove the wife in the car to the son's house. The wife was injured and sued the mother.

HELD: The driver was the agent of the owner. It was by her direction that he took her to the party, and it was by her direction that he took her back from the party. He had not ceased to be acting for her. The wife was entitled to recover.

[5.46]   Ormrod v Crosville Motor Services Ltd

[1953] 2 All ER 753, [1953] 1 WLR 1120, 97 Sol Jo 570, CA

The owner of a car who was taking part in the Monte Carlo rally arranged with a friend for the friend to drive the car, with the friend's wife as passenger, in the friend's own time and manner, and meet him at Monte Carlo before the end of the rally, after which the car would be used for a holiday in Switzerland of these three persons. A suitcase belonging to the owner was carried in the car. On the journey in England the car was involved in a collision and the owner of the other vehicle sued the car owner for damages caused by the negligent driving of the friend.

HELD: The friend driving was not the servant of the owner. To render the owner liable there must be something more than the granting of the mere permission but it is not necessary to show a legal contract of agency. It is, however, sufficient where there is a social or moral obligation (per du Parcq LJ in *Hewitt v Bonvin* (at para [5.43])), to drive the owner's car. A request to the friend to drive the car, and compliance with the request, makes the friend the agent of the owner, since the owner has an interest in the request being complied with. The driving was for the owner's benefit, and the owner is liable for the driver's negligence.

Per Singleton LJ: Mere consent is not proof of agency. Here the purpose was that the car should be used by the owner or for the joint purposes of the claimant and the owner when it reached Monte Carlo. The male claimant was driving for the purposes of the owner or the joint purposes of the owner and himself.

Per Denning LJ: An owner may be liable although the driver is not his servant. The owner is also liable if the driver is, with the owner's consent, driving the car on the owner's business or for the owner's purposes. Here it was partly for the driver's own purposes and partly for the owner's purposes. The contention that because the driver started two or three days earlier for his own purposes the owner is not liable fails. The law puts an especial responsibility on the owner who allows it to go on the road in charge of someone else. If it is being used wholly or partly on the owner's business or for the owner's purposes, the owner is liable. He only escapes when it is to be used for purposes in which he has no interest or concern (*Hewitt v Bonvin*). The trip to Monte Carlo must be considered as a whole.

[5.47] Carberry v Davies

[1968] 2 All ER 817, [1968] 1 WLR 1103, 112 Sol Jo 445, CA

The owner of a car was a coal-merchant who had three lorries for delivery of coal one of which was driven by his employee H, who was a servant at a wage. The owner also had a Ford car which he regarded as the family car and which he wanted all his family to use as far as practicable. But he would not allow anyone to drive it except himself and H. When his son aged 16 wanted to go out in the car he could do so provided H drove it. On one such occasion it collided with the claimant and H was held to blame. Was the car-owner vicariously liable for H's negligence?

HELD: The principle was stated by Singleton LJ in *Ormrod v Crosville Motor Services Ltd* (at para [5.46]): 'the driver of a motor car must be doing something for the owner of the car to become an agent of the owner'. The present case turned on how the arrangement was made. Did the car owner make the arrangement with H, so that his son could have the use of the car or was it the son who made the arrangement and simply asked his father's permission? On the facts it was the father who made the arrangement and he was liable for H's negligent driving.

[5.48] Vandyke v Fender

[1970] 2 QB 292, [1970] 2 All ER 335, [1970] 2 WLR 929, 134 JP 487, 114 Sol Jo 205, CA

On the facts set out at para [1.17], the Court of Appeal held, following *Ormrod v Crosville Motor Services Ltd* (at para [5.46]) that Fender was the agent of the second defendants when driving the car owned by them for a purpose in which they had an interest and they were vicariously liable for his negligent driving whether or not he was driving in the course of his employment.

(III)   RESPONSIBILITY OF SPOUSE

[5.49] Morgans v Launchbury

[1973] AC 127, [1972] 2 All ER 606, [1972] 2 WLR 1217, 116 Sol Jo 396, HL

Mrs Morgans, the defendant, owned a car which was registered and insured in her name. Both she and her husband regularly used it, he more than she. She regarded it as being their car jointly, rather than hers. He used it for going to work. One evening he telephoned her from his place of work, saying he was going out for the evening. He visited various public houses and at one of them, conscious that he ought not to drive, asked a friend named Cawfield to act as his chauffeur for the rest of the evening. Later he and Cawfield left a public house in the car with the claimants as passengers and were travelling to a town some miles away, not in a homeward direction, when an accident occurred due to Cawfield's negligent driving. The defendant's husband and Cawfield were killed, the claimants injured. The defendant had been promised by her husband that if ever he had had too much to drink when out with the car he would get someone who was sober to drive. The Court of Appeal held the defendant vicariously liable for Cawfield's negligent driving on the grounds *inter alia* that it was a 'family car' and that she had an 'interest and concern' in the purpose for which it was being driven.

HELD: Allowing the appeal, there was no authority for accepting the 'interest and concern' or 'family car' arguments, which have no validity in English law. An owner's vicarious liability for the negligence of the driver was correctly and accurately stated by MacKinnon LJ and du Parcq LJ in *Hewitt v Bonvin* (at para [5.43]). The understanding between Mr and Mrs Morgans that when unfit he would get someone else to drive was no basis for holding that Cawfield had been delegated to drive as agent for her, and she was not vicariously liable for his negligence.

[5.50]   Norwood v Navan
[1981] RTR 457, CA

Mrs Navan had her husband's consent to use his car. She went out in it for the afternoon with two friends to a neighbouring town, first to visit a fortune-teller and then on a shopping expedition. On the return journey by her negligent driving she caused injury and loss to the claimant. He claimed damages against both Mr and Mrs Navan. She allowed judgment against her to go by default but her husband denied any vicarious liability for her negligence. The county court judge held he was liable in that the shopping she had done was in the interests and for the purpose of both of them. There was a sufficient use of the car for his purposes to make her his agent: he was vicariously liable for her negligent driving.

HELD, ON APPEAL: This was not right. The idea of a 'matrimonial car' formulated by Lord Denning in *Launchbury v Morgans*, sub nom *Morgans v Launchbury* (at para [5.50]) had been rejected by the House of Lords. The law there laid down by the Lords is based on proper proof of agency. The facts in the present case did not amount to such proof. Mrs Navan was at very most doing only general shopping. It would be absurd in such a case for the court to examine the contents of her shopping basket to see what she had bought. There was no vicarious liability on Mr Navan.

(IV)   PRINCIPAL NOT THE OWNER OF VEHICLE

[5.51]   Nottingham v Aldridge
[1971] 2 QB 739, [1971] 2 All ER 751, [1971] 3 WLR 1, 115 Sol Jo 328, [1971] 1 Lloyd's Rep 424   Eveleigh J

The claimant and the first defendant were apprentices employed by the Post Office (the second defendants). They were required by the terms of their service to attend a residential course of training some distance from home. They were allowed home for the weekend but had to be back at the training centre by Sunday night. They were returning on Sunday evening in a car driven by the first defendant when an accident occurred in which the claimant was injured. The car belonged to the first defendant's father. In accordance with Post Office regulations the first defendant was entitled to be, and was, paid 3d per mile for the cost of travel by car and an additional 1d per mile for conveying the claimant. The claimant claimed that the Post Office was vicariously liable for the first defendant's negligence either:

(1)   as their servant; or

(2)   as their agent, driving the car for their benefit.

HELD: (1) Although the first defendant was the servant of the Post Office in that he had a contract of service, he was not at the relevant time acting as such and the relationship of master and servant did not exist.

(2)   The Post Office was not so involved in the carriage of the claimant as to make the first defendant its agent. While ownership of motor vehicle is not essential in all cases to make a principal liable for the acts of his agent in driving it for his benefit the fact of ownership is of value in determining whether or not the driver was driving independently or on behalf of the principal. Where (as here) the principal is not the owner of the vehicle it must be established that the driver was driving in a genuinely representative capacity, that is, as an agent for and on behalf of the principal and as one to whom there has been a delegation of a task or duty. That was not the case here and the Post Office was not liable.

CHAPTER 6

Res Ipsa Loquitur

1.   THE DOCTRINE

[6.1]   **Scott v London and St Katherine Docks Co**

(1865) 3 H & C 596, 34 LJ Ex 220, 13 LT 148, 11 Jur NS 204

Merchandise being lowered in a crane slipped out of its fastenings and fell upon the claimant.

HELD: That where the thing is shown to be under the management of the defendants or his servants, and the accident is such as in the ordinary course of things does not happen if those who have the management use proper care, it affords reasonable evidence, in the absence of explanation by the defendant, that the accident arose from want of care.

[6.2]   **Bennett v Chemical Construction (GB) Ltd**

[1971] 3 All ER 822, [1971] 1 WLR 1571, 115 Sol Jo 550, CA

The claimant, a foreman steel erector, was supervising the installation of electrical control panels. One of the panels started to topple and the claimant rushed forward to steady it; as he was doing so another panel next to it fell on him, causing injuries. At the trial the claimant was unable to show what caused the panel to fall, nor could the defendant suggest any explanation for the accident. The judge said the panels could not have fallen unless their stability had been interfered with or unless there was some lack of care by the workmen working on the first panel. He accordingly held the defendant negligent.

HELD, ON APPEAL: On the evidence before him the judge could not have come to any other conclusion. It was a classic case of *res ipsa loquitur*. It was not necessary for that doctrine to be pleaded when it was proved that the accident could not have happened without negligence on the part of the defendants.

[6.3]   **Aspin v Bretherton**

(1947) Policy Holder Law Supplement, 24 December   Streatfield J

If the defendant gives an explanation consistent with negligence or no negligence, the onus of proof of negligence passes to the claimant.

The defendant is not required to prove exactly how the accident happened. It is sufficient for it to give an explanation which is consistent with no negligence.

Note—See also *Ludgate v Lovett* (at para [6.8]).

[6.4]   Swan v Salisbury Construction Co Ltd
[1966] 2 All ER 138, [1966] 1 WLR 204, 109 Sol Jo 195, PC

The claimant was employed by the defendant as a labourer on pile-driving, which was done by means of a crane. In the course of the work the crane toppled over and the claimant was injured. At the trial the judge accepted the evidence of another servant of the defendant that the cause of the crane falling was that the ground gave way under one of the wheels of the crane and the wheel bolts sheared as a result of the jolt. The judge also found that having regard to the work which had already been done, it was not reasonable to anticipate that the ground would give way or that extra precautions should have been taken against it. He gave judgment for the defendant.

HELD, ON APPEAL: There had been no failure on the part of the judge to apply the principles summarised in the phrase 'res ipsa loquitur'. When once the claimant had proved he was injured by the collapse of the crane he was well on the way to proving his care – res ipsa loquitur. But the mere fact that the crane fell did not establish that the case must inevitably succeed: it was then for the defendants to show that they had not been negligent. The judge had decided on the evidence what caused the crane to fall over and that the defendants had taken reasonable care in positioning it. This was a conclusion of fact and not based on any error in law.

Appeal dismissed.

[6.5]   Ng Chun Pui v Lee Chuen Tat
[1988] RTR 298, (1988) 132 Sol Jo 1244, PC

A coach in Hong Kong skidded, crossed the central reservation of a dual carriageway and collided with a light bus. The claimant relied on the doctrine of *res ipsa loquitur*. The defendant called evidence to show that the accident occurred because an untraced car cut into the fast lane some 6ft ahead of the coach, causing the driver to brake and swerve.

HELD: The claimant's claim failed; it had not proved negligence. The burden of proof remains with the claimant and it is misleading to talk of this shifting to the defendant if *res ipsa loquitur* is pleaded.

[6.6]   Worsley v Hollins
[1991] RTR 252, CA

The claimant was stationary in a line of traffic. The first defendant driving the second defendant's nine-year-old van, failed to stop and drove into the rear of the claimant's vehicle. The claimant brought proceedings against both defendants.

It was ruled by the judge that the maxim *res ipsa loquitur* applied and the defendants gave evidence first. The first defendant claimed that the van's brakes failed and it was established that an essential part was missing. When replaced the brakes operated correctly. This evidence was accepted and the judge found the driver had not been negligent.

The next question to be dealt with was whether the owner had taken reasonable care to have the van properly maintained. In his defence the second defendant produced a valid MOT certificate and a bill from a reputable firm of engineers for a 'full service' carried out some six weeks before the accident. Parts were charged at £13.64 and labour of £28.00. The judge found that on the basis of these charges a full safety check would not have been obtained and, therefore, the second defendant had run a very old vehicle without having it properly checked. The claimant succeeded against the second defendant. The second defendant appealed.

HELD: The production of a valid MOT certificate was not sufficient to discharge the second defendant's burden of proof. However, it was not correct of the judge to reject the second defendant's unchallenged evidence and conclude that on the basis of the amount charged the second defendant had not given instructions for a full service. Therefore the claimant's claim against the second defendant failed.

[6.7]   Widdowson v Newgate Meat
[1998] PIQR P138, CA

The claimant was walking on the unlit northbound carriageway of the A168. He was wearing dark clothing. It was just before midnight on a fine dry July night. The claimant was hit by a van driven by Mr Scullion.

At the trial of the action neither the claimant nor the defendant gave evidence. The claimant called a consultant psychiatrist who gave evidence that the claimant had been suffering from a mental illness for many years. However, the claimant was on medication, had no history of attempting suicide or taking deliberate risks and would be appreciative of danger and aware of road safety.

The trial judge declined to apply the maxim 'res ipsa loquitur' and dismissed the claimant's claim. The claimant appealed.

HELD: The claimant was entitled to walk where he was. The defendant would have had a long clear view of the road in front of him as he approached the claimant. Therefore on the basis of all the evidence in front of the judge it was open to him to find that it was more likely than not that the effective cause of the accident was Mr Scullion's negligence.

In addition, Mr Scullion had not given evidence to rebut the inference of negligence nor had any plausible explanation been suggested to the court consistent with an absence of negligence on Mr Scullion's part. Therefore the maxim 'res ipsa loquitur' applied.

Similarly, in the absence of any evidence from the defendant, a secondary application of the maxim 'res ipsa loquitur' may hold the claimant liable for contributory negligence. In the circumstances the claimant was held 50% contributorily negligent.

[6.8]   Ludgate v Lovett
[1969] 2 All ER 1275, [1969] 1 WLR 1016, 113 Sol Jo 369, CA

The defendant hired a motor van from the claimant. It was in good condition with no mechanical defects. When the defendant was driving along a motorway at speed it suddenly swerved to right and left and turned over. The claimant sued for the damage done, pleading *res ipsa loquitur*. The county court judge accepted the defendant's evidence that he did not go to sleep or fail to pay attention and that he was not negligent. The judge suggested an explanation of the accident which was not supported by any evidence and dismissed the claim.

HELD, ON APPEAL: The claimant was entitled to succeed. In a *res ipsa loquitur* case it is open to the defendant to satisfy the court that he took all reasonable precautions and was not negligent even though he cannot explain why or how the accident happened. But in the present case the presumption of negligence from the facts of the accident was too strong to be overcome merely by the defendant's denial that he had done anything negligent. The judge had accepted the defendant's evidence of no negligence only by advancing an explanation of his own. As this was not acceptable it remained that the defendant had not discharged the onus placed upon him by the plea *res ipsa loquitur*.

2.   VEHICLE COLLISIONS – INFERENCE OF NEGLIGENCE

[6.9]   **Baker v Market Harborough Industrial Co-operative Society Ltd**
Wallace v Richards (Leicester) Ltd
[1953] I WLR 1472, 97 Sol Jo 861, CA

A motor lorry and a motor van, in the hours of darkness, descending hills in opposite directions, met at the bottom. The two vehicles had collided whilst the offside front wheel of one or other, or perhaps both, was over the 'cat's eyes' which demarked the centre of the road. Both drivers were killed. The widow of each sued the employers of the other. One action was dismissed by Ormerod J on the ground that the claimant had failed to prove negligence. In the second, Sellers J differed from Ormerod J in the inference to be drawn from the same facts and held both drivers equally to blame. Appeals in both cases were taken together.

HELD: The inference was that both drivers were negligent in not keeping a proper look-out and hugging the centre of the road. In the absence of evidence that one was more to blame than the other, the blame should be apportioned equally. Assuming that one vehicle was over the centre line a few inches, and thus to blame, why did not the other pull in more to its nearside? The absence of any avoiding action makes that vehicle also to blame. It was not necessary to prove that the other vehicle was over the cat's eyes. It was sufficient to show that the defendant should have taken avoiding action.

Note—See also *Howard v Bemrose* [1973] RTR 32, CA and *Knight v Fellick* [1977] RTR 316, CA and *Hatton v Cooper* [2001] EWCA Civ 623, [2001] All ER (D) 41 (May). These cases established that the case of *Baker* did not create a rule of law concerning how responsibility for road traffic accidents should be apportioned but was concerned with inferences to be drawn from the evidence.

[6.10]   **Bray v Palmer**
[1953] 2 All ER 1449, [1953] I WLR 1455, 97 Sol Jo 830, CA

A motorcyclist with a pillion passenger was proceeding on the main road from Gloucester to Bristol and a small motor car with passengers was proceeding in the opposite direction. The time was about midday on 6 August 1951. The road was approximately 26ft wide. There was no other traffic. There was a pool of water on the car's nearside. The car turned to the off to avoid this pool. The motorcycle also turned to its off side and there was a collision in the middle of the road. Both vehicles were proceeding at a reasonable speed. The motorcyclist alleged that the car turned so far to its off that he had to turn to the off to avoid a collision. The judge decided that the accident was due either to the sole negligence of the car driver or the sole negligence of the motorcyclist and was not prepared to find both to blame. He was unable to decide which was the right story, and on the principle that the claimant must prove his case he dismissed the claim of the motorcyclist and the counterclaim of the motor car driver.

HELD: The possibility of both to blame should not have been excluded. Until a judge has decided that an accident has happened in some particular way, he is not in a position to decide. New trial ordered.

Note—Distinguished in *Salt v Imperial Chemical Industries* (1958) Times, 1 February, CA.

[6.11]   France v Parkinson

[1954] 1 All ER 739, [1954] 1 WLR 581, 98 Sol Jo 214, CA

Two motor cars collided at crossroads of equal status. The driver of the claimant's car had hired the car under a false name and disappeared after the accident. The claimant's only evidence was that of a police officer from whose evidence it was reasonably plain that both cars were on the right side of their respective roads and they collided somewhere where the two crossroads met. He also gave evidence that the defendant said – 'I was going along the road and we met in the middle.' The defendant called no evidence and the judge dismissed the claimant's claim.

HELD, ON APPEAL: Following *Baker v Market Harborough Industrial Co-operative Society Ltd; Wallace v Richards (Leicester) Ltd* (at para [6.9]), the balance of probabilities was in favour of both drivers having been negligent, particularly having regard to the place of collision and the statement to the police officer. There was a *prima facie* case against the defendant on which the court should have found him negligent in the absence of any evidence given by him.

Appeal allowed.

[6.12]   Shiner v Webster

(1955) Times, 27 April 1955

A motorcyclist was riding along a main road in broad daylight at 40mph, and the rider of an auto-cycle was proceeding in the opposite direction and presumably was turning into a side road on his off side. A collision occurred and the auto-cyclist was killed and the motorcyclist suffered severe concussion and was unable to recollect anything about the accident. The only witness was the driver of a motor car following the auto-cyclist. This witness was certain that the deceased was intending to cross the road as he made a circular turn up to the middle of the road, showing that he was going to turn into the side road. It looked to him as though both acted as though the other was not on the road at all.

Finnemore J held there was not enough evidence to show whose negligence caused the accident and as in neither case had it been proved before him that there had been negligence, he gave judgment for the defendant in each of the two actions of the deceased's administrator against the motorcyclist and of the motorcyclist against the administrator. The administrator appealed.

HELD: A court cannot say – we do not know whose fault it was and therefore there is no remedy for anyone. It was impossible to take the view that neither saw the other. The trial judge was wrong in thinking that it was not proved that either were negligent. There was evidence of negligence on the part of both.

Appeal allowed and, by a majority, both held equally to blame.

[6.13]   W and M Wood (Haulage) Ltd v Redpath

[1967] 2 QB 520, [1966] 3 All ER 556, [1966] 3 WLR 526, 110 Sol Jo 673   Ashworth J

Shortly before midnight a lorry and a car collided on the Great North Road, there was no other traffic, visibility was clear and from the point of collision it was possible to see in both directions for 350 yards. The occupants of the car were killed and the lorry driver died later. There were no other witnesses. There was some police evidence as to marks on the road which was inconclusive.

HELD: It was not possible to say with confidence which of the vehicles was over the centre line. In these circumstances the case fell within the principle applied in *Baker v Market Harborough Industrial Co-operative Society Ltd; Wallace v Richards (Leicester) Ltd* (at para [6.9]). There was no cogent evidence suggesting that one driver was more to blame than the other and the drivers must be held equally to blame.

[6.14]   Davison v Leggett
(1969) 133 JP 552, 113 Sol Jo 409, CA

The claimant driving his van on a straight main road overtook a car. The defendant riding a motorcycle in the opposite direction also overtook a car. The van and motorcycle collided in the middle of the road. The judge said he could find no indication who began overtaking first and who was in the wrong: it was feasible that neither was negligent. He dismissed both claim and counterclaim.

HELD, ON APPEAL: Following *Baker v Market Harborough Industrial Co-operative Society Ltd; Wallace v Richards (Leicester) Ltd* (at para [6.9]) where one or both parties were to blame and the court could not decide which, the inference was that both were equally to blame. The principle was not confined to cases where both drivers were dead or could not remember.

[6.15]   Howard v Bemrose
[1973] RTR 32, CA

On a country road in the dark a motorcyclist and car collided at a bend. The car driver did not remember anything of the accident; the motorcyclist was killed. Marks and débris on the road and the final positions of the vehicles were the only evidence. The judge said that having examined all the facts and argument as put to the court he was unable to say whether or not (as had been argued) the car was on its offside of the road or not at the moment of impact. He therefore considered the right course to adopt was to apply the *Baker v Market Harborough Industrial Co-operative Society Ltd; Wallace v Richards (Leicester) Ltd* (at para [6.9]) principle and hold the parties equally to blame. The motorcyclist's personal representative appealed.

HELD: The judge was entitled so to hold. What he was saying was that it was no more probable that the collision took place on the car driver's wrong side than that it took place in the centre of the road at the bend. As he was quite unable without independent evidence to say whether it was caused by the negligence of the motorcyclist rather than of the car driver he was right to divide the blame between them equally.

3. EVENTS IMPLYING NEGLIGENCE

(A)   VEHICLES OVERLAPPING PAVEMENT

[6.16]   Ellor v Selfridge & Co Ltd
(1930) 74 Sol Jo 140, 46 TLR 236

Where a motor van gets on to a pavement intended for foot passengers and injures persons standing there, these facts, in the absence of explanation, constitute evidence of negligence.

[6.17]   McGowan v Stott
(1920) 99 LJKB 357, 143 LT 217, CA

The claimant was walking along a well defined footpath. The defendant's motor vehicle mounted the footpath and struck the claimant. This was considered sufficient evidence of negligence.

[6.18]   Laurie v Raglan Building Co Ltd
[1942] 1 KB 152, [1941] 3 All ER 332, 111 LJKB 292, 166 LT 63, 86 Sol Jo 69, CA

Where a portion of the vehicle sweeps across the pavement, the facts raise a *prima facie* case of negligence just as much as where the wheels mount the pavement. It is a position where it has no right to be. No vehicle has a right so to manoeuvre itself that its tail or its radiator, or whatever it may be, projects over the pavement to the injury of pedestrians lawfully there.

[6.19]   Watson v Thomas S Whitney & Co Ltd
[1966] 1 All ER 122, [1966] 1 WLR 57, 130 JP 109, 110 Sol Jo 73, CA

Shortly after midnight the claimant was walking along the pavement about six inches from the edge and with the roadway on his left. The defendant's van turned in suddenly from the middle of the road to draw in alongside the pavement for a passenger to alight. In doing so it struck the claimant's left arm with the projecting handle of a door, causing him slight injury. The registrar of the Liverpool Court of Passage held the defendant's driver not to blame: he had difficulty in seeing the claimant whom he would not expect to be there.

HELD, ON APPEAL: The registrar was wrong. There was no blame to be attached to the claimant in walking close to the edge of the pavement. The pavement should give security to those who use it from vehicles using the road. There was clear liability on the driver where, as here, the vehicle overlapped the footpath.

Note—See also *Chapman v Post Office* (at para [10.25]).

(B)   TYRE BURSTING

[6.20]   Barkway v South Wales Transport Co Ltd
[1950] AC 185, [1950] 1 All ER 392, 66 TLR 597, 94 Sol Jo 128, HL

A motor omnibus of the defendant was proceeding along the highway when the off-front tyre burst. The omnibus then went to the off side of the road, mounted the pavement, crashed into some railings and fell on its side down an embankment. Four passengers were killed and others injured.

The burst was caused by an impact fracture of the cord of the outer tyre brought about by a blow more severe than in the ordinary course on the external surface of the tyre causing some of the plys to become fractured. The tyre which burst was periodically examined on the rim by an expert fitter of the defendants. He examined it on frequent dates during January and February 1943, the last occasion on 24 February, three days before the accident and on each occasion adjusted the pressure, and he tested the pressure on 20 February and 22 February. There was no evidence when the impact fracture was caused. No instructions were given to drivers to report an unusual and heavy blow on the tyre. There was no examination of the internal surface. A burst in this size of tyres is very rare. The tyre would go in for thorough examination at 25,000 miles. It had not been taken off for examination for nearly 18 months, during which time it had run about 21,750 miles.

HELD, ON APPEAL to the House of Lords:

Per Lord Porter: Adopting the language in *Scott v London and St Katherine Docks Co* (1865) 3 H & C 596, 34 LJ Ex 220, 13 LT 148, 11 Jur NS 204 [at para [6.1]], if the facts are sufficiently known, the question is whether on the established facts, negligence is to be inferred or not.

The decision in favour of the claimant depends on one or other of the grounds (1) whether there was negligence in the system of inspection, or (2) of any of the drivers in not reporting a blow severe enough to cause an impact fracture. The evidence established that a competent driver would recognise the difference between a blow heavy enough to endanger the strength of the tyre and a lesser concussion. If this be so, the fact that he would be unlikely to report it would still leave him negligent in not doing so, and for that negligence his employers must answer. In the second place, it was the duty of the respondents, who were fully aware of the possibility of an impact fracture, to instruct their employees as to the effect which a heavy blow may produce, and to impress upon them the necessity of reporting its incidence. An uninstructed driver might not know nor have experience of such a danger, and that difficulty would be surmounted if proper instructions were given. Such an incident is a rare event but the duty of a transport company is to take all reasonable precautions for the safety of their passengers and not to leave them in danger of a risk against which some precautions, at any rate, can be taken. Although the practice of inspection and overhaul of tyres was adequate in other respects, and was in accordance with the practice of companies carrying on a similar occupation, the respondents did not take all the requisite steps to protect their passengers from risk.

Per Lord Normand: The drivers themselves failed to report impacts which they ought to have reported, the respondents failed to instruct their drivers about impact fractures and to require them to report, and the tyre examiners ought to have been, but were not, informed. The defendants were liable.

[6.21] Elliott v Chiew

(1966) 110 Sol Jo 724, (1966) Times, 24 May, CA

The defendant was driving the claimant's car on the M1 motorway with the claimant as a passenger. When travelling at 70 to 80mph the defendant felt a swaying of the car over the back wheels. It was corrected after a little distance but the defendant said at some point 'I can't hold the car'. After going all right for a few moments the car began to sway again: the defendant applied the brakes but the car went out of control over an embankment, seriously injuring the claimant. A police officer gave evidence that after the accident the rear offside tyre was flat. An expert gave evidence that the tyre had probably deflated gradually and that it should have been possible to bring the car under control. The judge found that the cause of the accident was in all probability a deflated tyre, that when the brakes were applied the car went out of control and that nothing which a reasonably competent driver could have done at that time could have prevented the accident. He dismissed the claim.

HELD, ON APPEAL: It was essentially a matter for the judge who heard the case and saw the witnesses. The principle of *res ipsa loquitur* enabled the claimant to get the case on its legs but at the end the judge had to ask himself: was the defendant negligent or not? It was a matter for regret that he had not referred to the expert's evidence but a judgment was not to be criticised because a judge did not refer to everything which no doubt had passed through his mind. Where there was this evidence from the driver and passengers from which the judge could conclude that the driver was not guilty of negligence the Court of Appeal should not interfere.

CHAPTER 7

Defences

1.   ACCIDENT: DEFINITION

[7.1]   Fenton v Thorley & Co Ltd
[1903] AC 443, 72 LJKB 787, 89 LT 314, HL

The definition of accident was explained as: an unlooked-for mishap or an untoward event which is not expected or designed; any unintended and unexpected occurrence which produces hurt or loss, or such hurt or loss apart from its cause especially if the cause is not known.

[7.2]   R v Morris
[1972] 1 All ER 384, [1972] 1 WLR 228, 136 JP 194, 116 Sol Jo 17, Div Ct

'Accident' in the present context (Road Safety Act 1967, s 2(2)) means an unintended occurrence which has an adverse physical result.

[7.3]   Chief Constable of West Midlands Police v Billingham
[1979] 2 All ER 182, [1979] 1 WLR 747, 123 Sol Jo 98, [1979] RTR 446, QBD

It would not be right to treat the definition of 'accident' in *R v Morris* (at para [7.2]) as if it were written into the statute (now the Road Traffic Act 1972, s 8(2)). Where a man deliberately entered a police car, released the brake, steered it round a parked car and then let it run downhill and crash down an embankment 25ft deep there was an 'accident' for the purposes of the section. The test was whether an ordinary man would say in the circumstances that an accident had occurred.

Note—Section 8(2) of the Road Traffic Act 1972 has been replaced by s 7(2) of the Road Traffic Act 1988.

[7.4]   Chief Constable of Staffordshire v Lees
[1981] RTR 506, QBD

The defendant deliberately drove his car through a locked gate, smashing it.

HELD: Applying *Chief Constable of West Midlands Police v Billingham* (at para [7.3]) an 'accident' could be said to have occurred within the meaning of the Road Traffic Act 1972, s 8 (2). It was relevant to note that among the meanings to be found in the Oxford English Dictionary is 'an unfortunate event, a mishap'.

[7.5]   Churchill Insurance v Charlton
Sub nom Charlton v Fisher
[2001] EWCA Civ 112
[2002] QB 578, [2001] 1 All ER (Comm) 769, [2001] 3 WLR 1435, CA

Within the confines of a pub car park, Fisher deliberately reversed into a vehicle in which the claimant, Charlton, was a rear seat passenger. Charlton suffered significant injuries. Fisher pleaded guilty to causing criminal damage but there was no evidence that he had deliberately intended to cause Charlton injury. Charlton issued proceedings against Fisher. Fisher's insurer, the Churchill, was joined as second defendant to dispute liability to indemnify Fisher on the basis that the incident which caused injury to Charlton was not an 'accident' within the meaning of the policy and public policy precluded Fisher for making a claim in respect of damage arising out of his own deliberate criminal act.

HELD, ON APPEAL: The word 'accident' should not be given a narrow meaning. The circumstances should be considered within the context of the statutory background of the Road Traffic Act 1988 and on that basis the word 'accident' might well extend to any incident involving Fisher's car. However public policy precluded Fisher, and therefore Charlton, from making a claim in respect of damage suffered as a result of Fisher's criminal act. *Gardner v Moore* [1984] AC 548 considered.

(A)   WIND RECORDS

[7.6]   Note—A weather report that can be used in court proceedings can be obtained from the Legal Consultancy department of the Met Office at: Legal Consultancy, Customer Centre, Met Office, Fitzroy Road, Exeter, EX1 3PB; telephone: 0870 900 0100; fax: 0870 900 5050; email: enquiries@metoffice.gov.uk. The Met Offices website is: www.metoffice.com.

2.   ACT OF GOD/AGONY OF THE MOMENT

[7.7]   Nugent v Smith
(1876) 1 CPD 423, 45 LJQB 697, 34 LT 827, 41 JP 4

A direct, violent, sudden and irresistible act of nature, which could not, by any reasonable care, have been foreseen or resisted.

[7.8] Trent and Mersey Navigation Co v Wood

(1785) 4 Doug KB 287, 3 Esp 127

The act of God is natural necessity, as winds and storms, which arise from natural causes, and is distinct from inevitable accident.

[7.9] Greenock Corpn v Caledonian Rly Co

[1917] AC 556, 86 LJPC 185, 117 LT 483, 81 JP 269, HL

Circumstances which no human foresight can provide against, and of which human prudence is not bound to recognise the possibility.

[7.10] Brandon v Osborne, Garrett & Co

[1924] 1 KB 548, 93 LJKB 304, 130 LT 670, 40 TLR 235, 68 Sol Jo 460   Swift J

Where a person or a third party is placed in danger by the wrongful act of the defendant, that person is not negligent if he exercises such care as may reasonably be expected of him in the difficult position in which he is so placed. He is not to blame if he does not do quite the right thing in the circumstances.

Note—See also *Tocci v Hankard (No 2)* (1966) 110 Sol Jo 835, CA (at para [9.7]). 'Alternative danger' has a somewhat similar principle to 'agony of the moment'. See the cases of *Jones v Boyce* (1816) 1 Stark 493, 18 RR 812, *Adams v Lancashire and Yorkshire Railway Company* (1869) LR 4 CP 739, 20 LT 850, 17 WR 884.

3.   INEVITABLE ACCIDENT

[7.11]   *Note*—See also 'Act of God' at para [7.7].
    In an unreported case where a wasp entered a car and settled on the driver's eye (*Gilson v Kidman* (28 October 1938, unreported), Lewis J adopted the definition of inevitable accident of Sir James Colville in *The Marpesia* (1872) LR 4 PC 212. Nothing was done or omitted to be done which a person exercising ordinary care, caution and maritime skill, in the circumstances, either would not have done, or would not have left undone, as the case may be.
    The judge held that the defence of inevitable accident had not been made out and gave a verdict for the claimant.
    Per Fry LJ (in *The Merchant Prince* [1892] P 179): The burden rests on the defendants to show inevitable accident. To sustain that, the defendants must do one of two things. They must either show what was the cause of the accident, and show that the result of that cause was inevitable; or they must show all the possible causes, one or other of which produced the effect, and must further show with regard to every one of these possible causes that the result could not have been avoided. Unless they do one or other of these two things, it does not appear to me that they have shown inevitable accident.
    The principles were followed in *The Saint Angus* [1938] P 225.

[7.12] McBride v Stitt

[1944] NI 7, CA   Andrews CJ

'Inevitable accident' was defined by Dr Lushington in the Admiralty case of *The Virgil* (1843) 2 Wm Rob 201 in terms which have since received general acceptance – 'that which the party charged with the offence could not possibly prevent by the exercise of ordinary care, caution and maritime skill'. Omitting the word 'maritime' the definition is as applicable to Courts of Common Law as to the Court of Admiralty.

[7.13]   **Barry v Pugh**

[2005] EWHC 2555 (QB)

[2005] All ER (D) 239 (Nov)

The claimant was riding a motorcycle along a narrow country lane when he collided with the defendant's vehicle which was towing a horse box in the opposite direction. The defendant argued that she had either stopped or had been at the point of stopping when the incident occurred, but in any event there was insufficient time for both vehicles to stop.

HELD: The claimant motorcyclist had been travelling too fast and the defendant had adopted the best course possible, even if that meant that the defendant was still moving at the point of impact. It was sufficient that the defendant made a reasonable choice. The claim was dismissed.

4.   INVOLUNTARY ACT

(A)   DRIVER OVERCOME BY ILLNESS/DEATH

[7.14]   **Ryan v Youngs**

[1938] I All ER 522, 82 Sol Jo 233, CA

The driver died whilst driving a lorry, which ran on and injured the claimant. The driver appeared to be in sound health but suffered from fatty degeneration of the heart. Medical examination would not have indicated any liability to sudden collapse.

HELD: (I) The man appeared to be in good health; medical examination would not have disclosed any defect; the defendant was under no obligation to have the driver medically examined; and the defendant was not negligent.
(2)   There was no defect in the lorry and it was not a nuisance.
(3)   The accident was due to an act of God.

[7.15]   **Waugh v James K Allan Ltd**

[1964] 2 Lloyd's Rep I, 1964 SC (HL) 102, 1964 SLT 269

The driver of a lorry was suddenly disabled by an attack of coronary thrombosis which killed him. The lorry mounted the pavement and struck the appellant injuring him. Fifteen minutes before the accident the driver had been taken ill when loading the lorry but had recovered, at least partially, and had driven off. He had driven a quarter of a mile when the accident occurred. He had had gastric attacks from time to time in the past but had otherwise enjoyed good health.

HELD: A motor vehicle is potentially a dangerous and lethal instrument; there rests upon every driver of such a vehicle a serious duty owed to his fellow human beings not to drive the vehicle on a public highway if he has or should have any reasonable ground for thinking that, from illness or otherwise, his skill or judgment as a driver may have been impaired. Nevertheless, on the facts of this case, the driver was not negligent in taking the lorry out; he had no reason to suppose that his illness was not another gastric attack which, when it passed off, had left no serious disability. The respondent, his employer, was not liable.

[7.16]   **Jones v Dennison**

[1971] RTR 174, CA

The defendant was driving his car when it ran out of control on to the pavement, striking the claimant and injuring her. His defence to her claim for damages was that he had temporarily lost control due to a 'blackout', i e a loss of consciousness. His medical history included a coronary thrombosis six years earlier and a slight cerebral thrombosis. His doctor had not advised he should not drive. He had also had four short blackouts in the previous ten months but had been unaware of them: his wife knew of them but did not tell him of them until after the accident. In the court below the judge accepted the defendant's evidence that he did not know of the blackouts before the accident and held that he had discharged the burden of proof on him. His wife was not called to give evidence because of illness. On appeal it was argued that without the wife's evidence as to when, where and how the blackouts had taken place it was an undefended case.

HELD: The judge had properly directed himself that the real issue was whether the defendant ought to have realised from what had happened in the past that he ought not to have been driving. On the evidence of the defendant and his doctor there was no ground for saying he ought reasonably to have suspected that he was or might be subject to an attack such as he had. The onus was on the defendant and he had established his case.

Appeal dismissed.

(B)   DRIVER OVERCOME BY SLEEP

[7.17]   **Kay v Butterworth**

(1945) 173 LT 191, 61 TLR 452, 89 Sol Jo 381

The driver of a motor car who had been working all night until 7.45 am at an aircraft factory, was driving a car at about 9 am and was overcome by sleep or drowsiness and ran into the rear of a party of soldiers marching in column in the same direction. The police prosecuted under the Road Traffic Act 1930, ss 11 and 12 (now the Road Traffic Act 1988, ss 2 and 3).

HELD, by Divisional Court, allowing appeal from justices: If a driver allows himself to drive while he is asleep, he is guilty of driving without due care and attention, because it is his business to keep awake; if drowsiness overtakes him whilst at the wheel, he should stop and wait until he shakes it off and is wide awake again. If a person through no fault of his own becomes unconscious while driving, e g by being struck by a stone, or being taken ill, he ought not to be held liable at criminal law. The respondent must have known that drowsiness was overtaking him.

[7.18]   **Henderson v Jones**

(1955) 119 JP 304, 53 LGR 319, Div Ct

The defendant was charged with driving without due care and attention. She contended she was not 'driving' the car because she was admittedly asleep, she had no control over her actions.

HELD: Driving while asleep was at least driving without due care and attention. Being asleep was no excuse.

(C) STATE OF AUTOMATISM

[7.19] Watmore v Jenkins
[1962] 2 QB 572, [1962] 2 All ER 868, 126 JP 432, 106 Sol Jo 492, 60 LGR 325, Div Ct

The defendant was a diabetic. Whilst driving home in the evening he was seen at several points en route to be swerving about in the road and finally collided with a parked car. He remembered nothing of the last five miles of the journey. He had injected himself with a normal dose of insulin that morning but medical investigation showed that he was suffering from a hypoglycaemic episode due to the effects of recovery from a recent illness. The episode resulted from an excess of bodily and injected insulin. When the episode overtook him he was driving his car and continued to perform the functions of driving after a fashion until the accident happened. He was charged with:
  (1)   driving a vehicle on a road whilst unfit to drive through drugs;
  (2)   dangerous and careless driving.
The charges were dismissed. On the first charge the justices held that the defendant's unfitness to drive was not directly due to the dose of insulin: on the other charges they held that the defendant had been driving in a state of automatism.

HELD: On case stated:
  (1)   the justices were entitled on the evidence to entertain a reasonable doubt whether the injected insulin was more than a predisposing or historical cause of the hypoglycaemic episode;
  (2)   the justices had not defined 'a state of automatism'. The expression is no more than a catch phrase to connote the involuntary movement of the body or limbs of a person. It was not reasonable to conclude that the defendant's condition was such that throughout the five miles when he was 'driving after a fashion' the whole of such performance was involuntary or unconscious.
There must be a conviction on the charge of dangerous driving.

[7.20] Farrell v Stirling
[1978] Crim LR 696, Sheriff Ct

After a collision with another car the defendant continued to drive his car for a distance of four miles and collided with two other cars. His defence to a charge of careless driving was that he was diabetic and had been in a state of hypoglycaemia.

HELD: The test to determine whether he was 'driving' was whether at the material time he was in conscious control and whether his movements were voluntary. On the evidence he was convicted but given an absolute discharge.

Note—See also *Broome v Perkins* [1987] RTR 321 in which the defendant was charged with driving without due care and attention and relied upon a very similar defence. He was also convicted. Sections 87 and 170 of the Road Traffic Act 1972 have been replaced by ss 92 and 174 respectively of the Road Traffic Act 1988.

[7.21] Roberts v Ramsbottom
[1980] 1 All ER 7, [1980] 1 WLR 823, 124 Sol Jo 313, [1980] RTR 261   Neill J

The defendant, a man of 73, was driving his car when it collided with a parked van. He continued on his journey and shortly afterwards collided with a stationary car, injuring the claimant. He told the police 'I felt a bit queer before I ran into the van. I went away and felt all right. After that I felt a bit queer again and I hit the other car.' He was found on medical examination to have suffered a stroke just before starting his journey. The defendant had no previous symptoms or warning signs. After its onset his consciousness was impaired, but he was sufficiently in possession of his faculties to have some awareness of his surroundings and of traffic conditions and to make deliberate and voluntary though inefficient movements of hands and legs to manipulate the controls. He was not aware that he was unfit to drive.

HELD: In civil as well as in criminal matters (following *Watmore v Jenkins* (at para [7.19])) a state of automatism means in law a complete loss of consciousness; a driver will escape liability only if his actions at the relevant time were wholly beyond his control. If he retained some control, albeit imperfect, he remains liable. The defendant was liable on this ground, and liable also in having continued to drive when he should have been aware of his unfitness.

[7.22] Moses v Winder

[1981] RTR 37, QBD

The defendant drove his car into collision with another in circumstances justifying a conviction for careless driving. He pleaded automatism, being a diabetic of 20 years' duration. He called no medical evidence.

HELD: (1) Cases must be exceedingly rare where a defence of automatism can succeed without medical evidence.
(2)   The defendant was well aware of the danger of his going into a coma. He felt he was about to have an attack and took sugar sweets to ward it off; he then drove off and the attack became worse. In those circumstances he failed to take those precautions which he should, both in his own interests and in the interests of public safety. The justices must convict.

[7.23] Attorney-General's Reference (No 2 of 1992)

[1994] QB 91, [1993] 4 All ER 683, [1994] Crim LR 692, [1993] RTR 337, CA

The respondent was a HGV driver. Over the course of a 12-hour period he had driven for 6 hours and covered 343 miles. Throughout the day he had taken the appropriate breaks to comply with regulations. After passing junction 7 on the M5 the respondent drove deliberately onto the hard shoulder. He continued to drive along the hard shoulder for some 700 m until he collided with a stationary white van which was positioned just behind a recovery vehicle. The white van had its hazard warning lights on and the recovery vehicle was displaying a rotating yellow light. The collision caused two fatalities and the respondent was charged with causing death by reckless driving.

At the trial the prosecution alleged that the respondent had fallen asleep at the wheel. The defence produced expert evidence from a chartered psychologist who contended that the respondent was 'driving without awareness', a condition in which a driver's capacity to avoid a collision ceased to exist. The defence argued that the respondent was in a state of automatism and, therefore, could not be regarded as driving at all. On this basis the judge left the jury the defence of automatism and they acquitted the claimant.

The Attorney-General sought the opinion of the Court of Appeal as to whether the state described as 'driving without awareness' should, as a matter of law, be capable of founding a defence of automatism.

HELD: The defence of automatism requires that there be a total destruction of voluntary control on the defendant's part. Impaired, reduced or partial control is not enough. The defendant's expert had conceded that the driver's unawareness was not total. His awareness was only reduced or imperfect. There remained the ability to steer the vehicle straight and a capacity to react to stimuli appearing on the road ahead. In his evidence the respondent had admitted he had seen the flashing lights some quarter of a mile from the scene of the collision. Therefore the answer to the Attorney-General's question was no.

[7.24]   Chelsea Girl v Alpha Omega Electrical Services

[1995] CLY 3644   Mr Recorder Collins QC

Chelsea Girl brought proceedings against the defendant for damages arising out of a motor traffic accident that occurred on 23 July 1990. The defendant's driver had caused an accident just outside the Dartford Tunnel and caused damage to eight vehicles, one of which belonged to the claimant.

The defendant alleged that its driver, who was a diabetic, had suffered from an attack of hypoglycaemia which he could not have foreseen or guarded against. Therefore the defence was one of automatism.

HELD: The defence of automatism was not available to the defendant. The defendant had to establish that there was a total destruction of voluntary control and that evidence of impairment, to whatever extent, was insufficient. Evidence of the defendant's driving at the time of the accident suggested that there could not have been a complete absence of voluntary control. Thus, total loss of control had not occurred at the time of the accident as the defendant was capable of swerving to avoid traffic. The legal requirements for the defence of automatism, however artificial they may be, had not been established.

[7.25]   Mansfield v Weetabix Ltd

[1998] 1 WLR 1263, [1998] RTR 390, [1997] PIQR 526, CA

Mr T was the driver of the defendant's lorry when it failed to negotiate a left-hand bend and crashed into the claimant's shop causing extensive damage. At the time of the accident Mr T had an impaired degree of consciousness because of a malfunction of his brain caused by deficiency in glucose, a condition known as malignant insulinoma. This was the cause of the accident.

It was accepted that Mr T was a careful and considerate driver who would not have driven had he appreciated that his ability to drive was impaired. However one of the features of the condition is that the affected individual would not be aware that his senses were impaired.

The judge applied the criminal test. On the basis that the claimant had retained control of his limbs his driving fell below the required standard and the defendant was found liable. The defendant appealed.

HELD: The appeal was allowed. The judge was wrong to apply the criminal test of automatism. There was no reason in principle why a driver should not escape liability where the disabling event was gradual rather than sudden and provided that the driver was unaware of it.

Per Leggatt LJ: In my judgment the standard of care that Mr T was obliged to show in the circumstances was that which is to be expected of a reasonably competent driver unaware that he is or may be suffering from a condition that impairs his ability to drive. To apply an objective standard in a way that did not take account of Mr T's conditions would be to impose strict liability but that is not the law.

Note: Applied by *C (a child) v Burcombe* [2003] CLY 3030

(D)   EPILEPSY

[7.26]   Balmer v Hayes
1950 SC 477, 1950 SLT 388, Ct of Sess, Scot

A motor omnibus collided with a motor lorry and a passenger in the motor omnibus was injured. She brought an action against the driver of the omnibus, who averred that immediately before the accident he suffered a temporary loss of consciousness owing to a fit of epilepsy. The pursuer replied averring that it was the driver's duty when applying for a driving licence to disclose that he suffered from lapses of consciousness which were likely to cause his driving to be a danger to the public.

The Road Traffic Act 1930, s 5(1) enacts that an applicant for a licence shall make a declaration as to whether or not he is suffering from any such disease or physical disability specified in the form or any other disease or physical disability which would be likely to cause his driving to be a source of danger to the public. Subsection (2) allows an application for a test except in prescribed cases. The Motor Vehicles (Driving Licences) Regulations 1947, SR&O 1947/925, reg 5 prescribes as an exception epilepsy, liability to sudden attacks of disabling giddiness or fainting.

Section 112(2) of the 1930 Act provides a penalty for false statement on application for a licence and for a false statement or withholding of material information on application for a certificate.

Note—The Road Traffic Act 1930, ss 5 and 112 have been replaced so far as they affect this case by the Road Traffic Act 1988, ss 92 and 173.

[7.27]   Green v Hills
(1969) 113 Sol Jo 385, (1969) Times, 22 April   James J

The claimants, man and wife, were injured when they were knocked off their moped by the defendant, a woman, who stepped off the kerb in a state of automatism after an attack of *petit mal*. She suffered from two different forms of epileptic attacks, major attacks of which she received warning and which occurred once or twice a year, and minor attacks which were more frequent and some of which were accompanied by periods of time when she was not conscious of what was going on or afterwards of what had gone on. She remembered going out on the afternoon of the accident and going into a shop but did not remember the accident. She had not been advised by her doctor not to go out alone. A neurologist said in evidence he did not think it reasonable to forbid a person such as the defendant from going into the street.

HELD: The defendant was not liable. She had first to satisfy the court on the balance of probabilities that she was in a state of automatism: on her own evidence she had discharged this burden. The issue was then whether it was reasonable for her to have gone out alone. Clearly there was some risk but one could not 'chain' an epileptic person to his house. A reasonable person, knowing her life history, would be prepared to balance the risk of causing injury with the need to go out and live as normal a life as possible.

5.   VOLENTI NON FIT INJURIA

(A)   THE MAXIM

[7.28]   *Note*—A person who has expressly or impliedly assented to an act cannot claim for its consequences, but the principle is *volenti*, not *scienti*, that is, consent as distinct from mere knowledge.

[7.29]   Cutler v United Dairies (London) Ltd
[1933] 2 KB 297, 102 LJKB 663, 149 LT 436, CA

A man who, without being under any duty, went into a field to help to catch a runaway horse, was held to be a volunteer.

[7.30]   Haynes v Harwood
[1935] 1 KB 146, 104 LJKB 63, 152 LT 121, 51 TLR 100, 78 Sol Jo 801, CA

If the act of the claimant is pursuant to duty, or is a reasonable act to avoid injury to others, the principle does not apply. The claimant, a police constable, was on duty inside a police station in a street in which, at the material time, were a large number of people, including children. Seeing the defendant's runaway horses with a van attached coming down the street he rushed out and eventually stopped them, sustaining injuries in consequence, in respect of which he claimed damages.

HELD: (1) That on the evidence the defendant's servant was guilty of negligence in leaving the horses unattended in a busy street.
   (2)   That as the defendant must or ought to have contemplated that someone might attempt to stop the horses in an endeavour to prevent injury to life and limb, and as the police were under a general duty to intervene to protect life and property, the act of, and injuries to, the claimant were the natural and probable consequences of the defendant's negligence:
   (3)   That the maxim *volenti non fit injuria* did not apply to prevent the claimant recovering.

Note—Followed in *The Gusty and The Daniel M* [1940] P 159, 109 LJP 71, 164 LT 271, 56 TLR 785, 84 Sol Jo 454. Considered in *Smith v Littlewoods Organisation Ltd* (at para [35.42]).

[7.31]   Morgan v Aylen
[1942] 1 All ER 489   Cassels J

The claimant was escorting a child of three-and-a-half years, and when they reached a crossroad, the child was a little way in front of her and ran forward and began to cross the road. The defendant was riding a motorcycle along the road about 7ft from the near side. He was about 7 yards from the corner when the child ran into the road and about 5 yards from the child. The claimant ran out to save the child. If the claimant had been alone, an attempt by her to cross the road in front of the defendant might have been negligent. Here the circumstances were different. The American rule is that the doctrine of the assumption of risk does not apply where the claimant has, under an exigency caused by the defendants' wrongful misconduct, consciously and deliberately faced a risk, even death, to rescue another from imminent danger of personal injury or death, whether the person endangered is one to whom he owes a duty of protection, as a member of his family, or is a mere stranger to whom he owes no such special duty. What the claimant did here was, in the circumstances, natural and proper. The initial wrongful act was on the part of the defendant, who was approaching the crossroads at too great a speed. The claimant saw the danger and ran out to save the child, which was a natural and proper thing to do, and there was no contributory negligence on her part. The defendant was in law solely responsible for the accident.

Note—See also 'Rescue cases' at para [7.41].

[7.32]   White v Blackmore
[1972] 2 QB 651, [1972] 3 All ER 158, [1972] 3 WLR 296, 116 Sol Jo 547, CA

The defendant organised a race meeting for jalopy cars. The claimant's husband took his car and entered his name as a competitor. He brought his wife, child and mother-in-law to the meeting as spectators. He competed in a race but during the next race, in which he was not a competitor, he stood near a post to which safety ropes were fastened talking to his family. The ropes were arranged in a faulty manner and on being fouled by a car in that race, pulled out the post and caused the claimant's husband injuries from which he died. He had seen the notices around the track: 'Warning to the Public. Motor racing is dangerous. It is a condition of admission that all persons having connection with the promotion and/or organisation and/or conduct of the meeting are absolved from all liabilities arising out of accidents causing damage or personal injury (whether fatal or otherwise) howsoever caused to spectators or ticket holders.'

HELD: (1) The deceased was at the time of the accident a spectator not a competitor.
(2)   The defence of *volenti non fit injuria* was available only against one who had impliedly agreed, with full knowledge of the nature and extent of the risk, to incur it. It was not obvious to the deceased that he was standing in a particularly dangerous place and the defence of *volenti* did not apply.
(3)   The warning notice applied to the deceased as a spectator at the time of the accident and the action failed.

[7.33]   Latchford v Spedeworth International Ltd
(1983) 134 NLJ 36   Hodgson J

The claimant was a competitor at a 'hot rod' car racing stadium. He had often raced there and was aware of the danger presented to drivers by two concrete flower beds within the area of the race track. He was not aware until the evening of the accident of the organiser's practice of marking the edge of the track with small tyres. The organiser (the defendant company) knew that the practice was potentially hazardous and that larger tyres would have been safer. The claimant did not know this. During a race another competitor dislodged some of the tyres of which one jammed under the back axle of the claimant's car causing him to crash into one of the concrete flowerbeds. He was seriously injured.

HELD: The accident resulted from the defendant's negligence with regard to the tyres and as the claimant was unaware of that danger the defence of *volenti non fit injuria* could not avail in respect of it. The defendant had also pleaded that the claimant was on his own admission aware of the danger presented by the flowerbeds and had consented to run that risk. However, the defendant had failed to prove that the claimant actually had a full appreciation of the nature and extent of the risk. The plea of *volenti non fit injuria* thus failed entirely.

[7.34]   Cook v Cook

[1987] 41 SASR 1

A learner driver was involved in a collision; her passenger sustained personal injury, and sued the driver. At the time of the accident the passenger was aware that the learner had minimal experience – she had not yet passed the examination to obtain a learner's permit.

HELD: The passenger was fully aware of the driver's inexperience and had waived the right to legal remedy. *Volenti non fit injuria* applied. (Australian case.)

[7.35]   North v TNT Express (UK) Ltd

[2001] EWCA Civ 853

[2001] All ER (D) 358 (May), CA

The claimant was with a group of friends outside a wine bar at one in the morning waiting for a taxi to take him home. The defendant's driver and mate were travelling in their employer's lorry and came across the claimant and his group of friends. The claimant jumped in front of the defendant's lorry forcing it to stop. The claimant asked for a lift home. The defendant's driver refused whereupon the claimant climbed onto the front bumper of the lorry and grabbed hold of one of the windscreen wipers. After twice requesting the claimant to get off, which he failed to do, the defendant driver drove off slowly and after a short distance the claimant fell off and was run over by the defendant's lorry causing serious internal injuries. The claimant brought proceedings against the defendant.

The judge at first instance found, that as a matter of fact, the claimant had deliberately and vigorously pulled the windscreen wiper off and that had caused him to fall off the lorry. Nevertheless the judge found the defendant 25% to blame for the accident on the basis that the defendant's driver did not have to take the risk of driving with the claimant hanging on the lorry and he did not stop driving at varying speeds until the claimant fell off. The defendant appealed.

HELD, ON APPEAL: The driver of the defendant's vehicle had done all he could in the circumstances. He had been placed in a difficult position by the claimant who was drunk and was acting in a stupid and irresponsible way. It was accepted that the defendant driver had not braked sharply at any point and it was reasonable for him to drive away from the claimant's friends who may have been aggressive. There was no breach of duty on the part of the defendant and the claimant's claim failed.

[7.36]   Wattleworth v Goodwood Road Racing Co Ltd and Others

[2004] EWHC 140 (QB)

[2004] All ER (D) 51 (Feb)

The deceased, an experienced amateur racing driver, died when he crashed his car at the first defendant's racing track. The claimant alleged that the owner of the race track (Goodwood) breached its common duty of care under the Occupiers Liability Act 1957. It was further contended that several of the sports licensing bodies breached their duty of care to the claimant by failing to exercise proper skill and care in inspections and recommended changes to the track which had been approved prior to the accident.

Goodwood accepted that it owed a duty of care but contended that it discharged that duty by following the safety recommendations. The defences of '*volenti non fit injuria*' and contributory negligence were also raised.

HELD: The claim was dismissed and it was held that Goodwood did not breach its duty of care. It had reasonably relied upon the advice of the various licensing bodies. One of the licensing bodies owed both the claimant and Goodwood a duty of care and it had discharged that duty as the crash barrier had met a reasonable standard of safety. The claimant failed to establish causation. Other bodies were found to owe no duty.

It was held that although the deceased had consented to the risks involved in motor racing, he would have relied on the reasonable safety measures. Therefore, the court would have rejected the '*volenti non fit injuria*' defence. Contributory negligence would have been assessed at 20% had the defendant been found negligent.

[7.37]   Pemberton v West Devon Borough Council
[2004] CLY 4358

P, who was disabled, brought a claim under the Occupiers' Liability Act 1957 against the local authority, W, after slipping on water and urine which was on the floor of a men's toilets owned by W. P had used the main section of the toilets rather than the disabled toilet which would have required a key to be obtained from a nearby leisure centre. P claimed W had failed to ensure that his visit to the toilets was reasonably safe. There was a cleaning system in place which involved cleaning early in the morning and a check clean after lunchtime. There was also an inspection system in place.

HELD: Claim dismissed. There was a reasonable cleaning system in place and W was not negligent. P had voluntarily accepted the risk of using the main section of the toilets. It would have taken him six minutes to obtain the key which was a reasonable time to wait to use the disabled toilets.

(B)   DRUNKEN DRIVER

[7.38]   Winnik v Dick
1984 SC 48, 1984 SLT 185, Ct of Sess

The claimant accepted a lift from a friend who he knew was drunk. En route an accident occurred, injuring the claimant. The defendant driver pleaded *volenti non fit injuria*.

HELD: The maxim did not negative negligence: it merely absolved a party from the consequences of his negligence. In the present case the claimant had to be taken as having appreciated and consented to the defendant's lack of reasonable care. However, the Road Traffic Act 1972, s 148(3) expressly provided that the fact that a passenger had willingly accepted the risk that the driver may be negligent was not to be treated as negating the driver's liability. The subsection excluded the operation of the maxim. The claimant was entitled to damages subject to 50% deduction for contributory negligence.

Note—Section 148(3) of the Road Traffic Act 1972 has been replaced by s 149 of the Road Traffic Act 1988 from 15 May 1989

[7.39] Dann v Hamilton

[1939] 1 KB 509, [1939] 1 All ER 59, 83 Sol Jo 155   Asquith J

The claimant was injured while travelling as a non-paying passenger in a car driven by one H. Prior to the accident H had been drinking, and this had markedly affected his driving, which thereafter was fast and erratic. During a stop to let down a passenger, the claimant, who by then knew that H, while far from being dead drunk, was not sober, and that there was a certain danger in being a passenger in a car driven by him, had an opportunity of leaving the car, but elected to continue the journey. Shortly afterwards, the accident occurred, and it was contended for the defence that the maxim *volenti non fit injuria* applied.

HELD: The claimant was entitled to succeed. By voluntarily travelling in the car with knowledge that through drink H had materially reduced his capacity for driving safely, she did not impliedly consent to, or absolve H from liability for, any subsequent negligence on his part which might cause injury to the claimant.

Note—Comments on this decision in 55 LQR 184 and 65 LQR 20 and elsewhere suggested that even if the plea of '*volenti*' did not apply, there was a cast-iron defence on the ground of contributory negligence. Lord Asquith wrote (69 LQR 817) that contributory negligence was not pleaded and counsel for the defendant declined a suggestion from the judge that he should apply for leave to amend and add this plea. The Law Reform (Contributory Negligence) Act 1945 was still in the future. See also the Road Traffic Act 1972, s 148(3). See also 'Consent to Drunken Driving' 17 NLJ 1079.
    In *Slater v Clay Cross Co Ltd* [1956] 2 QB 264, [1956] 2 All ER 625, [1956] 3 WLR 232, 100 Sol Jo 450, Denning LJ said of the judgment of Asquith J in *Dann v Hamilton* and of the note written by Lord Asquith. 'In so far as he decided that the doctrine of *volenti* did not apply, I think the decision was quite correct. In so far as he suggested that the plea of contributory negligence might have been available, I agree with him.' Parker and Birkett LJJ agreed.
    See also *Dawrant v Nutt* (at para [12.2]).
    Section 148(3) of the Road Traffic Act 1972 has been replaced by s 149 of the Road Traffic Act 1988 from 15 May 1989.

[7.40] Morris v Murray

[1991] 2 QB 6, [1990] 3 All ER 801, [1991] 2 WLR 195, 134 Sol Jo 1300

The claimant and defendant, having been drinking in each others' company for some time, decided to go on a joy ride in the defendant's light aeroplane. The claimant drove the defendant to the aerodrome, assisted in starting the engine and was generally anxious to commence the ride. The weather was bad. The local flying club had suspended flying. The defendant just managed to take off but a few minutes later the aeroplane crashed killing the defendant and seriously injuring the claimant. An autopsy of the defendant found that he had consumed the equivalent of 17 whiskies or three times the limit permitted for a car driver. The judge awarded the claimant damages with reduction of 20% for his contributory negligence. The defendant, through his estate, appealed.

HELD: The claimant's claim failed by virtue of the defence of *volenti non fit injuria*. The claimant knew that he was going on a flight, he knew the plane was to be flown by the defendant and he knew that the defendant had been drinking heavily that afternoon. The claimant co-operated fully in the joint activity and did all he could to assist it. By embarking on the flight with the defendant the claimant had implicitly waived his rights in the event of injury consequent upon the defendant's failure to fly with reasonable care.

Assistance was derived from the dictum of Asquith J in the case of *Dann v Hamilton* (at para [7.39]) and particularly at p 518 where Asquith J mentions the example of the case where:

'The drunkenness of the driver at the material time is so extreme and so glaring that to accept a lift from him was like engaging in an intrinsically and obvious dangerous occupation ...'

(C)   RESCUE CASES

[7.41]   Baker v T E Hopkins & Son
[1959] 3 All ER 225, [1959] 1 WLR 966, 103 Sol Jo 812, CA

The defendants, a builder and contractor, had arranged to clean out a well at a farm. Two workmen in the defendant's employ went down the well and were overcome by poisonous gases. A doctor was summoned by telephone, and, though warned of the danger, went down the well to see what he could do for them. He was overcome and died.

The court held the defendant liable in negligence in respect of the deaths of the two workmen. The defendant contended that it owed no duty to the doctor; that his conduct was unreasonable and amounted to a *novus actus interveniens*; and it was a case of *volenti non fit injuria*.

HELD, ON APPEAL: It was a natural and proper consequence of the defendant's negligence that someone would attempt to rescue, and the defendant should have foreseen that consequence; accordingly the defendants was in breach of duty towards the doctor (*Donoghue v Stevenson* (at para [4.2])).

It was not a case of *novus actus interveniens*. The act in question was the very kind of thing that was likely to happen as a result of the negligence.

The maxim *volenti non fit injuria* could not be successfully invoked as a defence by a person who had negligently placed others in a situation of such peril that it was foreseeable that someone would attempt their rescue.

Appeal dismissed.

[7.42]   Videan v British Transport Commission
[1963] 2 QB 650, [1963] 2 All ER 860, [1963] 3 WLR 374, 107 Sol Jo 458, CA

Per Lord Denning: The right of the rescuer is an independent right, and is not derived from that of the victim. The victim may have been guilty of contributory negligence – or his right may be excluded by contractual stipulation—but still the rescuer can sue. Foreseeability is necessary, but not foreseeability of the particular emergency that arose. Suffice it that he ought reasonably to foresee that, if he did not take care, some emergency or other might arise, and that someone or other might be impelled to expose himself to danger in order to effect a rescue. Whoever comes to the rescue, the law should see that he does not suffer for it. It seems to me that, if a person by his fault creates a situation of peril, he must answer for it to any person who attempts to rescue the person who is in danger.

He owes a duty to such a person above all others. The rescuer may act instinctively out of humanity or deliberately out of courage. But whichever it is, so long as it is not wanton interference, if the rescuer is killed or injured in the attempt, he can recover damages from the one whose fault has been the cause of it.

[7.43]   Harrison v British Railways Board

[1981] 3 All ER 679   Boreham J

The claimant was the guard on a passenger train. At a station en route he gave the ready-to-start signal to the driver and the train began to move. An off-duty member of the station staff, Howard, then attempted to board the train by seizing the handrail at the guard's door. The claimant saw him but failed to apply the emergency brake as he could and should have done. Instead he attempted to help Howard off his feet and he fell between the train and the platform, causing the claimant to fall down with him. The claimant was injured.

HELD: As an experienced railwayman, Howard was negligent in attempting to board the train when it was moving. Moreover he knew the claimant had seen him and would try to help him if he got into trouble. He should have foreseen that by intervening the claimant would probably endanger himself. A duty is owed to a rescuer if his intervention is reasonably foreseeable even if the defendant owes no duty to the person being rescued (*Videan v British Transport Commission* (at para [7.42])). A duty must likewise be owed to a rescuer when the person being rescued is the person who created the peril. Howard was liable to the claimant; but he was himself guilty of contributory negligence to the extent of 20% in failing to apply the emergency brake and thus reduce the chance of injury to himself.

Note—See also *Chadwick v British Transport Commission* (at para [36.22]).

6   EX TURPI CAUSA NON ORITUR ACTIO

(No action arises out of a base cause)

[7.44]   Pitts v Hunt

[1991] 1 QB 24, [1990] 3 All ER 344, [1990] 3 WLR 542, 134 Sol Jo 834, CA

The claimant was a pillion passenger on the first defendant's motorcycle. The claimant and the first defendant had been drinking together that evening. After the accident the first defendant's blood alcohol was twice the legal limit for driving. The claimant was aware that the first defendant was not even licensed to drive the motorcycle, nor insured. The judge accepted evidence from witnesses that on the way home the first defendant, encouraged by the claimant, drove the motorcycle in a fast, haphazard manner deliberately intending to frighten members of the public. The motorcycle collided with the car driven by the second defendant. The first defendant was killed and the claimant seriously injured. The claimant brought an action for personal injuries against both defendants.

The judge at first instance dismissed the claimant's claim on the basis that:

(1)   The maxim *ex turpi causa non oritur actio* applied for the claimant and the first defendant were engaged on a joint illegal enterprise.

(2)   It would be against public policy for the claimant to succeed.

(3)   The nature of the joint enterprise was such that it precluded the court from finding that the defendant owed any duty of care to the claimant.

(4)   The claimant was 100% contributorily negligent.

The claimant appealed against the dismissal of the claim against the first defendant.

HELD: The claimant's claim failed. The judge's findings at (1), (2) and (3) were upheld. The application of the maxim ex *turpi causa* was not to be judged by the degree of moral turpitude or illegal character involved in the joint enterprise but whether the conduct of the person claiming, the character of the enterprise and hazards involved made it impossible for the court to determine the appropriate standard of care because the joint illegal purpose had displaced the ordinary standard of care.

The judge's finding at (4) above was disapproved. A finding of 100% contributory negligence is logically unsupportable for the Law Reform (Contributory Negligence) Act 1945 operates on the premise that there is fault on the part of both parties which has caused the damage. Thus responsibility must be shared.

Note—The judge at first instance held that the claimant's claim would also have been defeated by the doctrine of *volenti non fit injuria* but for the operation of s 148(3) of the Road Traffic Act 1972. This provides that an 'agreement or understanding' between a driver and passenger of a motor vehicle has no effect so far as it purports to negative or restrict the drivers liability to the passenger. Section 148(3) of the Road Traffic Act 1972 has been replaced by s 149 of the Road Traffic Act 1988.

[7.45]   Mighell v Reading & MIB
(21 February 1997, unreported), QBD   Gage J

The claimant was a front seat passenger in a vehicle owned by him but driven by the first defendant. The first defendant drove the car into a stationary vehicle causing the claimant to suffer severe head injuries. The claimant could remember nothing about the accident. The first defendant took no part in the proceedings.

For some hours prior to the accident both the claimant and first defendant had been drinking heavily. The judge was not prepared to find that the claimant was in a coma or comatose at the beginning of the fateful journey but that he was able to get into the car and apply his seat-belt. The claimant was aware that the first defendant was going to drive, allowed him to do so and must have known that the first defendant had drunk a great deal.

The first defendant raised the defence of ex *turpi causa non oritur actio* and contributory negligence.

HELD: *Pitts v Hunt* (at para [7.44]) could be distinguished on the basis that in this case there was no evidence that the claimant had encouraged the first defendant to drive recklessly. The defence of ex *turpi causa* was rejected.

The claimant knew that the first defendant had drunk a great deal of alcohol during the course of that evening and he could have refused to allow the claimant to drive his car and taken a taxi home. Contributory negligence was assessed at 45%.

[7.46]   Vellino v Chief Constable of Greater Manchester Police
[2001] EWCA Civ 1249

[2002] 3 All ER 78, [2002] 1 WLR 218, [2001] NLJR 1441

The claimant suffered brain damage and tetraplegia when he jumped out of a window attempting to evade arrest by the police. The police had arrived at the claimant's home to enforce an arrest warrant knowing that in the past the claimant had frequently evaded arrest in this way. The claimant alleged the police had negligently stood idly by and allowed him to jump as he was making his escape.

HELD: The police were not under a duty to take care that the claimant was not injured in this way. The claimant's claim arose out of his own criminal conduct in escaping lawful custody, and consequently the claim failed.

[7.47] Edwards v German

[2004] CLY 2743

Just prior to a road traffic collision involving the claimant and defendant, the claimant had been driving up a hill having accelerated from 40mph to 60mph up to the top of the hill. As the claimant crested the hill he noticed the defendant's vehicle which was travelling on the wrong side of the road. The claimant braked but was unable to stop in time to avoid the collision. After the accident the claimant was breathalysed and found to be over the drink-driving limit. As a consequence of this, the defendant argued the maxim *ex turpi causa non oritur actio* applied as the claimant was engaged in an illegal activity at the time of the accident, ie drink driving which should, therefore, preclude him recovering damages.

HELD: The maxim *ex turpi causa non oritur actio* did not apply as the claimant did not have to rely on his illegal act to found his cause of action. The court did make a 25% finding of contributory negligence on the basis that the claimant was driving too fast and the effect of the alcohol in his blood may have increased his reaction time.

CHAPTER 8

Liability of Road Users

1. THE HIGHWAY CODE

[8.1]   The Highway Code is issued with the authority of Parliament as laid down before both Houses of Parliament in June 1998. The Road Traffic Act 1999, s 38(7) provides:

> 'A failure on the part of a person to observe a provision of the Highway Code shall not of itself render that person liable to criminal proceedings of any kind, but any such failure may in any proceedings (whether civil or criminal ...) be relied upon by any party to the proceedings as tending to establish or negative any liability which is in question in those proceedings.'

The current edition of the Highway Code was published in April 2006. Paragraphs 1 to 33 relate to pedestrians and paragraphs 45 to 226 relate to drivers, motorcyclists and cyclists. There are also rules relating to those people in charge of animals (paragraphs 34 to 44), paragraphs 227 to 254 deal with driving on the motorway.

This edition of the Highway Code follows the trend of emphasising the need for motorists to drive slowly and carefully and to take into account the need of vulnerable road users. Emphasis is again placed upon the fact that the code is essential reading for everyone, pedestrians, cyclists and horse-riders, as well as motorists.

2. OBSTRUCTING THE HIGHWAY

[8.2]   **Wallwork v Rowland**
[1972] I All ER 53

The defendant stopped on the hard shoulder of a motorway to eat sandwiches. He was charged with unlawfully causing his vehicle to remain at rest on a 'carriageway'.

327

HELD: The hard shoulder of a motorway is part of the 'verge' and not of the 'carriageway'. The 'marginal strip' in the Motorways Traffic Regulations 1959, SI 1959/1147 refers not to the hard shoulder but to the white line which borders the running surface of the nearside lane.

[8.3] Lloyds Bank Ltd v Budd

[1982] RTR 80, CA

A lorry broke down with clutch trouble on the A1 and was left all night in a lay-by. Early the following morning, in daylight but foggy conditions, the driver, Lake, returned with a mechanic to repair the vehicle. They found it capable of being driven and decided to take it to a place more convenient for them to do the repairs. After a short distance the lorry again broke down and came to a halt on the carriageway causing an obstruction. Because of the foggy conditions the mechanic went to the rear of the vehicle to warn other road users. A police car leading a line of vehicles came to a stop when the mechanic waved it down. The police officers went to the front of the lorry to attach a tow rope. Three or four minutes later there was a series of collisions at the back of the stationary convoy as vehicles came through the fog and failed to pull up in time. A car in which the claimant's husband was a passenger struck a stationary vehicle in front of it and was then struck very violently by a lorry driven by the first defendant, Budd. The claimant's husband was killed. The judge said it was negligent of Lake to take his lorry out on to the carriageway and that it created a nuisance, but he considered that Lake's actions were not causative of the accident as they were too remote. He found the first defendant alone to blame for the death of the claimant's husband.

HELD, ON APPEAL: Lake's negligence was not too remote. Despite the interval between the convoy coming to a halt and the subsequent collisions the broken down vehicle was a cause of the collisions. The court held Budd the first defendant more blameworthy, in driving much too fast in foggy conditions, and apportioned liability: Budd 60%, Lake 40%.

Note—See also *Rouse v Squires* [1973] QB 889, [1973] 2 All ER 903, [1973] 2 WLR 925, 117 Sol Jo 431, CA.

[8.4] Wright v Lodge

[1993] 4 All ER 299, [1993] RTR 123

It was a foggy night and visibility was poor when Mrs Shepherd's mini broke down on the nearside lane of a dual carriageway a short way from Cambridge. It would have been an easy task to push the mini on to the verge. Mr Lodge was driving his Scania lorry at about 60mph and crashed into the rear of Mrs Shepherd's mini injuring her passenger. The lorry then veered out of control across the central reservation coming to rest on the opposite carriageway whereupon it was struck by other vehicles injuring Mrs Wright and Mr Kerek. Mrs Shepherd's passenger, Mrs Wright and Mr Kerek brought proceedings against Mrs Shepherd and Mr Lodge. Mr Lodge admitted liability but claimed a contribution from Mrs Shepherd. The trial judge held that Mrs Shepherd should contribute 10% in respect of her passenger's claim but not to the claims of Wright and Kerek. Mr Lodge appealed on the basis that the judge should have held Mrs Shepherd also 10% responsible for the injuries to Wright and Kerek.

HELD: Appeal dismissed. Mr Lodge's driving was not just negligent but reckless. The presence of Mr Lodge's lorry on the opposite carriageway was wholly attributable to his reckless speed which resulted in the swerve, loss of control and overturn on that carriageway. The presence of Mrs Shepherd's mini did not necessarily become a legally operative cause of the subsequent collision.

Mention was made of the case of *Rouse v Squires* [1973] QB 889, [1973] 2 All ER 903, [1973] 2 WLR 925, 117 Sol Jo 431, CA which established that reckless driving is a different category from negligent driving and that an obstruction which is only a danger to a reckless driver does not constitute a relevant danger.

[8.5]   Howells v Trefigen Oil and Trefigen Quarries Ltd
(2 December 1997, unreported), CA

The claimant was cycling at about 25mph when he hit the rear of the defendant's lorry which was parked on a bend in the road. It was raining heavily, there was a strong wind and the claimant was cycling with his head down, occasionally glancing up to check the traffic in front. He saw the defendant's lorry at the last minute and could not avoid a collision. The defendant's lorry protruded into the road some 2–3ft and was clearly visible from 5m.

At first instance the judge held that the claimant was 75% contributory negligent and the defendant 25% negligent for parking his lorry in the position he did. The defendant appealed.

HELD, ON APPEAL: The Court of Appeal said that the question the judge had to decide in this case was whether by leaving the lorry, parked as it was, this presented a danger to other road users. The answer to this question was no. The court found the claimant to blame as he failed to keep sufficient lookout or moderate his speed so that he could have avoided the presence of the lorry. Appeal allowed.

[8.6]   Bramley v Pipes and Another
(29 April 1998, unreported), CA

The claimant was an innocent passenger in the second defendant's vehicle which the second defendant was driving, at some speed, along a wide main road. The first defendant was attempting to cross the main road from a minor road. He saw the second defendant's vehicle some 300m away and began his manoeuvre. Upon realising that he had under-estimated the second defendant's speed the first defendant stopped at a point where the front wheels of his vehicle were just over the give way line markings on the minor road.

The second defendant swerved around the first defendant's car, braked, lost control and crashed causing serious injuries to the claimant.

At first instance the judge apportioned liability 80/20 in the second defendant's favour. The first defendant appealed.

The Court of Appeal allowing the appeal held that the position where the first defendant had stopped his car did not create a hazard or even an obstacle and was not in itself negligent. Therefore as no hazard had been created there was nothing to contribute causally to the occurrence of the accident. Any car approaching the junction would not have had any difficulty either in retaining control nor successfully passing the first defendant's vehicle.

'The cause of the accident is fully explained by the conduct of the second defendant and the second defendant alone. On the evidence which the judge accepted, the conduct of the first defendant did not contribute in any legally recognisable way to the occurrence of the accident' (per Hobhouse LJ).

[8.7]   Billington v Maguire

[2001] EWCA Civ 273

[2001] All ER (D) 107 (Feb)

The claimant cyclist struck the defendant's stationary vehicle which was parked in a cycle lane on the A584. The Court of Appeal held that the defendant owed a duty of care to the claimant, and that he was in breach of that duty of care in failing to park elsewhere, and that the breach had led to the claimant suffering injury. The claimant's damages would be reduced by 70% by reason of the fact that the defendant's vehicle was there to be seen and the claimant had not been keeping a proper lookout.

[8.8]   Houghton v Stannard

[2003] EWHC 2666 (QB)

[2003] All ER (D) 91 (Dec), QB

The claimant was travelling south on the A13 towards Southend on a wet but clear day, when his car broke down and became stationary in the nearside lane. It was positioned approximately 1ft from the white line marking the edge of the carriageway. On the left hand side of the white line was an unprotected verge. The line and the verge were separated by 1m of tarmac. The claimant remained in the vehicle and put on his hazard lights.

The defendant was travelling in the same nearside lane heading south at a speed of around 60mph. Although the defendant had seen the claimant's vehicle at around 250 yards, it was not until he was 50 yards away that he noticed that it was stationary. Although he braked he was unable to avoid colliding with the rear of the claimant's vehicle. The defendant admitted primary liability but alleged contributory negligence stating *inter alia* that the failure by the claimant to remove the vehicle from the highway after the breakdown, and his failure to exit the vehicle were matters to take into account when considering liability.

McKinnon J held that the claimant had his hazard warning lights displayed and that they were visible from a distance of 250 yards. The judge found that the defendant had failed to see them. He further stated that other road users had seen the claimant and were able to take steps to avoid a collision. As such the judge did not find the claimant's position in the road hazardous and found the defendant guilty of negligence with no deduction for contributory negligence.

3.   SPECIAL ROADS

(A)   MOTORWAY

[8.9]   *Note*—The motorways are special roads provided under the Special Roads Act 1949, or the Highways Act 1959, limited to certain classes of vehicles. The special rules applying to traffic on motorways are contained in the Motorways Traffic (England and Wales) Regulations 1982, SI 1982/1163 as amended by the SI 1992/1364, reg 6(2). The use of motorways is restricted to traffic of Classes I and II specified in the Second Schedule to the Special Roads Act 1949, as amended by the Special Roads (Classes of Traffic) Order 1959, SI 1959/1280.

The Special Roads Act 1949, s 12, under which the Motorways Traffic Regulations 1959, SI 1959/1147, was repealed by the Road Traffic Act 1960 and its provisions are now contained in s 17 of the Road Traffic Regulation Act 1984. Vehicles excluded from motorways include pedal cycles, motorcycles not exceeding 50 cc capacity, invalid carriages, certain vehicles carrying oversize loads and agricultural vehicles. Vehicles must be driven in one direction only. Stopping, turning or reversing on a carriageway are forbidden. If a vehicle has to be stopped for certain specified emergencies it must be driven on to the nearside verge and shall not remain there longer than necessary. Learner drivers are forbidden to drive on motorways. No person must go on foot on a motorway except for certain necessary purposes. There are exceptions to and relaxation of the rules in certain specified circumstances, e g to avoid or prevent an accident.

There is a general speed limit of 70mph (SI 1974/502).

(B)   NARROW ROAD

[8.10]   Thrower v Thames Valley Bus Co Ltd
[1978] RTR 271, CA

The claimant on a dark December evening was driving his car along a narrow lane when he collided with the offside of the defendants' bus travelling in the opposite direction. The lane was 9ft wide to the centre line on the defendants' side and 8ft 6 on the claimant's side. The judge found that the bus may have been an inch or two over the centre line but acquitted the driver of any negligence. There was a restriction order in force prohibiting vehicles more than 6ft 6 inches wide from using the road although public service vehicles were exempt. The court held the defendants negligent in failing to give their driver some form of special training or instruction so that he could take special precautions when driving a bus on this narrow road. The defendant appealed.

HELD, ON APPEAL: That the defendants were not negligent, in that the road was perfectly adequate to take two vehicles of the width of the two vehicles concerned. Other vehicles ahead of the claimant had got past safely and it was perfectly possible for the claimant to have done so as well.

4.   LEARNER DRIVERS

[8.11]   *Note*—By the Motor Vehicles (Driving Licences) Regulations Act 1981, SI 1981/952, reg 8, a provisional licence is subject to the condition that the holder shall use it only when under the supervision of a person who holds a licence, not being a provisional licence, authorising him to drive a motor vehicle of the same class as that being driven by the holder of the provisional licence. This person shall, except in the case of a motor cycle or invalid carriage, be present with him in or on the vehicle.

[8.12]   Nettleship v Weston
[1932] AC 562, [1932] All ER Rep 1, 101 LJPC 119, 147 LT, 48 TLR 494, HL

The defendant asked the claimant to teach her how to drive, although he was not a professional driving instructor. He agreed, having first asked about insurance cover. The defendant advised that comprehensive insurance cover was in place, which covered the claimant as a passenger.

During the defendant's third lesson the claimant told her to move off from a halt sign and turn left. She did so but failed to straighten up. Despite the claimant's efforts to apply the handbrake and move the steering wheel the car mounted the pavement and struck a lamp-post. The claimant was injured. The judge dismissed his claim for damages saying that the only duty the defendant owed him was to do her best and this she had done.

HELD, ON APPEAL: This was not right. The standard of care owed by any driver, whether a learner or not, is that of a driver of skill, experience and care, who is sound in mind and limb, eyesight and hearing, makes no errors of judgment and is free from infirmity. The duty of care is the same to all persons on or near the highway, whether passengers or not and is the same to an instructor, with the exception, that there would be no liability if he had voluntarily agreed to take the risk of injury. The defence of *volenti non fit injuria* is not available unless the claimant expressly or impliedly agreed to waive any claim for injury that may befall him. In the present case the claimant did not agree to waive any claim. This was clear as he had asked about insurance to make sure that he was covered. However, an instructor could be guilty of contributory negligence if for example, he was not quick enough to correct errors. Moreover, an instructor and learner are jointly concerned in driving the car and together must maintain the same measure of control over the car as an experienced and skilful driver. If an accident happens one or both must have been at fault, and in the absence of evidence to distinguish between them they should be held equally to blame. That was the case here and the claimant was entitled to half his damages.

Note—Salmon LJ disagreed that the defence of *volenti* was not available against an instructor in the absence of agreement to waive any claim. He held that as an instructor knows the learner has practically no driving experience or skill he is not owed the duty of care to be expected from a skilled driver: the instructor voluntarily agrees to run the risk of injury. But he held that this claimant's enquiry about insurance had altered the whole relationship to one in which the defendant accepted responsibility for any injury. Megaw LJ dissented on the question of contributory negligence: he could not see that, on the facts, the claimant had done anything wrong.

Volenti is not now a defence available in road accident cases. See *Pitts v Hunt* [1991] 1 QB 24, [1990] 3 All ER 344, 3 WLR 542, 134 Sol Jo 834, CA.

[8.13]   Rubie v Faulkner

[1940] 1 KB 571, [1940] 1 All ER 285, 109 LJKB 241, 163 LT 212, 104 JP 161, 56 TLR 303, 84 Sol Jo 257, Div Ct

The appellant, while in a motor vehicle driven by the holder of a provisional licence was in a position to see that the driver was about to overtake another vehicle by pulling considerably to the offside at a pronounced bend in the road, but neither said nor did anything to prevent the learner driver's actions. An accident occurred, and the driver was convicted of driving without due care and attention.

HELD: That the appellant was rightly convicted of aiding and abetting the driver in the commission of the offence. Not relevant for the summary

Per Hilbery J: The Regulations were framed to make some provision for the protection of the public against the dangers presented by leaner drivers. The Regulations place a duty on the supervisor to ensure that the learner driver is properly supervised in order to prevent the learner driver from acting unskilfully or carelessly or in a manner likely to cause danger to others. That duty includes participating in driving if necessary.

[8.14]   R v Clark

(1950) Daily Telegraph, 30 May   Sheriff Substitute, Dundee

The supervisor of an 'L' driver of a lorry was held to be the person in charge of the vehicle and convicted of being under the influence of drink to such an extent as to be incapable of having proper control. There was a continuing duty on the part of the supervisor to control the learner's driving which was not interrupted because the learner was driving properly. *Rubie v Faulkner* [1940] 1 KB 571, [1940] 1 All ER 285, 109 LJKB 241, 163 LT 212, 104 JP 161, 56 TLR 303, 84 Sol Jo 257 followed.

[8.15]   Gibbons v Priestley

[1979] RTR 4   Judge Lymberry QC, QBD

After 18 lessons in a driving school car which had dual controls, the claimant a woman of 51, went out with the instructor in her husband's car which did not have dual controls. At a T-junction the claimant came to a halt before turning left. On starting forward and turning left she let the clutch out too fast, failed to straighten up and crashed into a tree. The whole incident from start to finish lasted about five seconds. The claimant sustained injury and sued the instructor for damages, claiming that he was negligent in letting her drive on the highway in a car without dual controls and failing at the time of the accident to take any proper steps to avoid the collision.

HELD: The instructor was not liable because:
   (1)   it was not wrong to allow the claimant to drive without dual controls in light of the knowledge he had of her tuition;
   (2)   the passenger supervisor of a learner driver, whether he is a driving instructor or not is not a mere passenger, and has a responsibility jointly with the learner driver to other road users in relation to the safe conduct and control of the car. Further, the supervisor and the learner each have a responsibility to the other in the exercise of control over the car. The degrees of negligence between learner and supervisor will vary dependent upon the circumstances. In the short time available the instructor could not reasonably have done more than he did, namely, to shout 'Brake, brake' and pull on the handbrake;
   (3)   the instructor was negligent in failing to recommend the claimant wear her seat belt but this was not a cause of the collision.

[8.16]   Verney v Wilkins

(1962) 106 Sol Jo 879, [1962] Crim LR 840   Winn J

The infant claimant a passenger in a car driven by the defendant was injured when the car overturned. The defendant a learner driver only held a provisional licence and was not accompanied by a qualified driver.

HELD, Winn J awarding damages to the claimant for personal injury: That there was no actionable claim against the defendant merely on the ground that the injury had been caused by him driving without a full driver's licence or having a fully licensed driver in the vehicle.
   A breach of the statutory requirements with regard to learner drivers did not give rise to any cause of action, even if a more skilful driver might have avoided an accident which occurred. On the facts, however, the defendant was liable in negligence.

[8.17]   British School of Motoring Ltd v Simms

[1971] 1 All ER 317, [1971] RTR 190   Talbot J

A learner driver was undergoing a driving test by a Ministry of Transport examiner. She approached a road junction governed by a 'Give Way' sign and broken white lines. She failed to see them and drove into the junction. The examiner saw a car

approaching and applied the brake. The test car stopped in the path of the other car and was struck, causing another collision with the claimant's car. They sued the learner and examiner, alleging negligence against him on the grounds:
  (1)   that he failed to ensure that the learner paid regard to the 'Give Way' sign and lines and failed to apply the brake soon enough; and
  (2)   that he applied the brakes when it was unsafe and stopped the car in the path of the other car.

HELD: The examiner was not negligent because:
  (1)   he is not in the position of a driving instructor but is there to observe if mistakes are made: he should not interfere with the driving except where it is essential in the interests of safety;
  (2)   his application of the brakes was done in the agony of the moment and following the principle in *Jones v Boyce* (1816) 1 Stark 493, 18 RR 812 and *The Bywell Castle* (1879) 4 PD 219, he was not to be blamed if what he reasonably did in the circumstances turned out to be wrong.

[8.18]   Lovelace v Fossum

(1971) 24 DLR (3d) 561

This is a British Columbian case which considered the authority of *Nettleship v Weston* (at para [8.12]) The claimant a friend was giving driving lessons to C who was nearly ready to take his driving test. On approaching a bend in wet slippery conditions the claimant warned C to slow down, which he did. Approximately 90 feet from the bend the claimant again told C to slow down which C failed to hear. In negotiating the corner C lost control and skidded off the road injuring the claimant.

HELD: That both the claimant and C were equally to blame, as the duty of the instructor is to instruct the pupil in the correct and safe management of a vehicle. It is also the duty of the pupil to use the best skill he has to obey the instructor in so far as he has acquired the skill to do so, and in the absence of any stipulation to the contrary the instructor accepts those risks associated with a learner driver.

CHAPTER 9

Driving, Manoeuvring and Parking

1. FINDING OF LIABILITY IN MOTOR CASES

In a case involving two vehicles where both drivers provide diametrically opposed versions of the material accident, the court must find one or both drivers are at fault.

[9.1] Hatton v Cooper

[2001] EWCA Civ 623

[2001] All ER (D) 41 (May), [2001] RTR 544

Where the court had little evidence on which to decide whether one party was more culpable than the other in the case of a road traffic accident, the responsibility was shared equally. Evidence from the third party employer relating to the driving ability was not relevant in the circumstances. The judge's conclusion that the defendant was wholly responsible for the accident was wrongly based on the weight he attached to the evidence of the claimant's employer. Without this evidence the court could not have concluded that the defendant was solely responsible for the accident. The only reasonable and proper inference that could be drawn from the available evidence was that each party was partly responsible.

[9.2] Cooper v Floor Cleaning Machines

[2003] EWCA Civ 1649

[2003] All ER (D) 322 (Oct), [2004] RTR 254

The accident arose when the trailer on the defendant's vehicle struck the nearside wheel arch of the claimant's car. Both parties gave different views as to how the accident occurred and the judge at first instance held that neither party had proved their case and dismissed both the claim and the counter-claim.

The defendant appealed.

HELD, ON APPEAL: That the accident could not have happened without at least one of the drivers being at fault. The Court of Appeal held that the judge failed to properly analyse the evidence and decide which one of the two accounts was the more likely.

On the facts the court held the claimant liable, and entered judgment for the defendant.

Appeal allowed.

2. OVERTAKING

[9.3] Holdack v Bullock Bros (Electrical) Ltd

(1964) 108 Sol Jo 861; affd (1965) 109 Sol Jo 238, CA

In daylight on a straight road a motor scooter was overtaking a van when the van swerved to the offside and the scooter collided with the offside front wing of the van. The van driver had not seen the scooter in spite of having two outside mirrors and an interior mirror. The judge held the van driver was negligent in changing course without warning when it was extremely dangerous to do so, but held the scooter rider one-third to blame for having failed to hoot to show his intention to overtake. The scooter rider appealed.

HELD: There was no ground on which the Court of Appeal should interfere. In the ordinary way if a motor scooter was overtaking another vehicle which was going straight along a road there was no need for the scooter to hoot before overtaking if the scooter was giving reasonable clearance. In this case the judge must have come to the conclusion that the movement of the van was such as to put the scooter rider on enquiry as to what the van was going to do.

[9.4] Rothwell v Davies Bros Haulage Ltd
[1963] Crim LR 577, 107 Sol Jo 436, CA

The second defendant was in his stationary car when it was struck and damaged by the first defendant's lorry which did not stop. The second defendant, incensed, followed the lorry trying to attract the driver's attention. He drove alongside the lorry flashing his lights, sounding his horn and shouting. The lorry driver's attention was distracted and as a result the lorry collided with the claimant's car and injured the claimant. The judge found the lorry driver one-quarter to blame and the second defendant three-quarters.

HELD, ON APPEAL by the second defendant: The apportionment could not be disturbed. Motorists must not distract the attention of a driver of a heavy vehicle on a busy road. The second defendant's conduct, though understandable, was foolish and was the substantial cause of the accident.

[9.5] Powell v Moody
(1966) 110 Sol Jo 215, Times, 10 March, CA

Riding his motorcycle along a busy road, the claimant came up to the tail of a stationary line of traffic consisting of vehicles two abreast. The claimant proceeded along the offside of the line of traffic, overtaking the stationary vehicles. The defendant, driving a car, came out of a side road on the nearside of the line of traffic to pass through a gap and turn right to go along the main road in the opposite direction. He was given a signal by the driver of a milk tanker to come out and as he was inching his way out the claimant, who had not seen the side road, collided with him. The judge held both parties to blame but attributed 80% of the blame to the claimant. The claimant appealed.

HELD, ON APPEAL: The judge's apportionment was reasonable. Any vehicle which jumped a queue of stationary vehicles was undertaking an operation fraught with great hazard and which had to be carried out with great care. There was always difficulty in such circumstances in seeing what was happening, especially when emerging from gaps.

[9.6] Gregory v Kelly
[1978] RTR 426   Jones J

The defendant was driving his Mini car at a time when the footbrake was completely inoperative because part of the hydraulic system was missing. The claimant, a passenger in the defendant's car, knew the brakes did not work; furthermore, he was not wearing the seat belt provided. The defendant, driving at about 40mph on a narrow country road, was confronted, on rounding a bend, with a vehicle parked partly on the roadway on his nearside. Being unable to brake he pulled out to overtake and crashed into a car coming in the opposite direction.

HELD: (1) The defendant's negligence was of a high order in driving too fast and in so driving when he knew he had no footbrake.

(2)   The claimant was negligent in not wearing a seat belt and additionally in travelling in the car as a passenger when he knew from the start it had no operative footbrake.

In assessing the respective fault or blameworthiness of the two parties it would not be right to assess the percentages of negligence or contributory negligence separately and add them up. The matter must be looked at generally. Apportionment of blame was 60% on the defendant, 40% on the claimant.

[9.7]   Tocci v Hankard (No 2)

(1966) 110 Sol Jo 835, CA

The claimant was riding his moped in a main London street when the defendant's vehicle travelling from the opposite direction swerved across the road and struck him. The reason the defendant swerved was that he was in the act of overtaking a scooter travelling in the same direction as himself when the scooter swung to the right to enter a side road. The scooter rider did not stop and could not be identified.

HELD, ON APPEAL: The defendant was not to blame. The rule in the Highway Code not to overtake at road junctions did not apply to side roads such as this of which there were so many in London. One ought not to be critical of what was done on the spur of the moment when a dangerous situation had been created by someone else.

[9.8]   *Note*—The Highway Code formerly contained a hand signal denoting that the driver was ready to be overtaken. The signal was omitted from the 1959 and subsequent editions of the Highway Code, but as some drivers still use it the following case may sometimes be useful.

[9.9]   White v Broadbent and British Road Services

[1958] Crim LR 129, Times, 29 November, CA

A woman was walking along the pavement at 3.30 pm on a wet and misty afternoon. The driver of a motor lorry, which was stationary at the time gave a 'passing' signal to a van approaching from the rear. The van struck the claimant who was crossing in front of the lorry. He had not seen the woman who had actually started to cross the road when he gave the signal.

The county court judge found the claimant one-third to blame; of the remaining two-thirds, the lorry driver 80% and the van driver 20%. The second defendant appealed.

HELD: The overtaking signal did not amount to an authority to the van driver to pass, but it was probable the van driver would proceed, and with greater confidence. The lorry would to some extent obscure the view of pedestrians seeking to cross. The lorry driver's duty was to be on the look-out for pedestrians before he gave the signal.

Appeal dismissed; no interference with the apportionment.

[9.10]   Grange Motors (Cymbran) Ltd v Spencer

[1969] 1 All ER 340, [1969] 1 WLR 53, 112 Sol Jo 908, CA

The defendant in his car was approaching a bend in the road. A Post Office van was parked at the bend partly on the roadway. A postman who had returned to his van saw the defendant's car approaching, and looked in the opposite direction before signalling to the defendant to pass. The defendant who saw the postman look in the opposite direction took the signal to mean that it was safe to proceed. The defendant had to go over the centre line of the road to overtake the van. The claimant who was travelling in the opposite direction came round the bend colliding with the defendant's vehicle. The county court judge held the postman wholly to blame for the accident.

HELD, ON APPEAL: That the judge was entitled to find the postman responsible, as the postman owed a duty of care to the defendant. The Court of Appeal found the postman was negligent in giving an invitation to the defendant to pass at a time when it was unsafe to give such an invitation. As was said in *White v Broadbent and British Road Services* (at para [9.9]) the driver of a vehicle on a road who makes a signal to another vehicle must have regard to other road users before giving that signal and owes a duty to other drivers to that effect. However, to what extent the driver to whom the signal is addressed is entitled to rely on the gesture is a question of fact and degree according to each case. As there was no evidence that the defendant had been negligent the appeal was dismissed.

[9.11]   Hillman v Tompkins

(22 February 1995, unreported), CA   Simon Brown, Ward LJJ

The defendant was driving her Ford Sierra in a slow moving line of traffic held up by temporary traffic signals. The claimant was riding a motorcycle in the same direction, overtaking the slow moving traffic. The defendant reached Godwin Way, a junction to her offside, into which she wished to turn. She signalled her intention, failed to see the motorcyclist approaching from her rear, turned and the collision occurred.

The defendant's case was that she was positioned at the crown of the road, clear of the line of traffic and visible to the claimant. The claimant alleged that the defendant commenced her turn from within the line of traffic and so he was unable to see her indicator until the turn had commenced.

In the face of this and other conflicting witness accounts the judge found the defendant's vehicle had not moved to a position clear of the line of traffic or otherwise to enable the motorcyclist to see her flashing indicator before she commenced the turn. The claimant was probably travelling between 30–40mph at or near the centre of the opposite carriageway in the overtaking position. The judge held both parties equally to blame. The defendant appealed.

HELD: There was no reason to interfere with the judge's findings. The defendant was negligent for failing to see the claimant's approach: '... undesirable as it may be, motorcyclists do and can be expected to overtake in circumstances of this kind and in my judgment the defendant was negligent in failing to see the claimant as he approached'. The claimant was approaching a road junction overtaking slow moving and stationary traffic. In the circumstances he increased the standard of care required to be exercised by him. The speed which he was doing was too fast to discharge that standard of care.

Per Simon Brown LJ: This court will rarely interfere with a trial judge's assessment of the respective degrees of blame to be attached to those involved in road traffic accidents. There has to be something quite exceptional before we would think it appropriate to adjust respective contributions in such a case.

Appeal dismissed.

[9.12]   Broocks v Ward and Another

(14 July 1997, unreported), CA

The claimant was driving his Post Office van around a very sharp left hand bend and collided with the first defendant's transit van which was being driven on the wrong side of the road. The claimant had no opportunity to avoid the collision.

The first defendant's van had been forced to overtake the second defendant's Sierra which was stationary on the road, just prior to the bend blocking most, if not all, of the first defendant's carriageway. The second defendant's vehicle had developed a sudden electrical fault of which there had been no advance warning. It was accepted that the second defendant's vehicle created a serious danger.

HELD: Both the first and second defendant were equally to blame for the accident. The first defendant was overtaking when it was unsafe to do so. Such was the danger of the hazard that the first defendant ought to have stopped and, if necessary, assisted other drivers to remove or reduce the hazard. The second defendant should have made more effort to give vehicles approaching from the claimant's direction some advance warning of the serious hazard around the sharp left hand bend.

The judge's apportionment of liability was upheld on appeal.

[9.13]   Pell v Moseley

[2003] EWCA Civ 1533

[2003] All ER (D) 338 (Oct)

The accident happened on 18 April 1999, when the claimant aged 39 was riding his motorcycle along the Milton Malsor Road in Northamptonshire. Milton Malsor Road was a single lane carriageway with one lane of traffic in each direction. A speed limit of 60mph was in operation.

The claimant was travelling behind the defendant whom he intended to overtake. The defendant intended to turn right into a field to attend a motor cross event. As she attempted the right turn, a collision occurred between the claimant and defendant.

At first instance the judge found in favour of the claimant with no deduction to take account of contributory negligence. The defendant appealed.

HELD, ON APPEAL: That both parties were equally to blame and liability was apportioned 50/50. The court found the defendant negligent in that she failed to indicate, and notice the presence of the defendant's vehicle before attempting to turn right.

The claimant was negligent in that he failed to notice that the defendant's vehicle would have needed to slow down before turning right, a fact which should have been apparent despite her failure to indicate. Further, as the claimant was aware of the motor cross event and considered the possibility that the defendant may wish to turn into the field he should not have attempted to overtake as he did.

Appeal allowed.

[9.14]   Farley v Buckley

(June 2006, unreported)

The defendant insured was emerging from a side road intending to turn right into a major road. There was a wagon on the main road waiting to turn left into the side road. A line of stationary traffic had built up behind the wagon. The claimant motorcyclist was on the main road overtaking the line of stationary traffic. As the defendant was making his manoeuvre, the claimant overtook the wagon and collided with the defendant on the crown of the road.

The facts were very similar to those in *Powell v Moody* (at para [9.5]) in which the defendant was held 20% liable.

Swift J, sitting in the High Court, held that the claimant was wholly liable for the accident. The defendant had proceeded slowly and with caution. The claimant had overtaken the wagon at 30mph whilst on or over the centre white line. The claimant could not see what was ahead of the wagon and his actions in the circumstances were held to be reckless.

(A)   U-TURNS AND THREE-POINT TURNS

[9.15]   **Bingham v Fuller**
(5 November 1997, unreported), CA

The claim involved an accident on the A645 road from Knottingley to Pontefract, when the claimant was returning home from work. The claimant intended to leave the A645 on to the A1 towards Sheffield. Unfortunately he missed his turning and continued for a mile before realising.

It was the claimant's intention to undertake a U-turn in order to proceed in the right direction.

The claimant was followed by two cars with the defendant's motorcycle positioned behind them.

As the defendant was overtaking the two cars positioned behind the claimant, he collided with the claimant's vehicle.

The claimant stated that he had checked his mirrors before commencing his manoeuvre. The defendant was unsighted by the claimant although he heard the motorcycle. The claimant alleged that the defendant had gone on to the wrong side of the road to overtake the other vehicles, and that this was the cause of the accident. The defendant denied this blaming the cause of the accident on the claimant in failing to see him.

The judge found in favour of the claimant on the basis of the witness evidence provided by the drivers of the two vehicles travelling behind the claimant. The witnesses, who had a good view of the accident, confirmed that the defendant had overtaken them on the wrong side of the road, and proceeded to continue on that side of the road until colliding with the claimant's vehicle. They also confirmed that the claimant was travelling at an excessive speed prior to impact.

The defendant appealed.

HELD, ON APPEAL: That the judge was correct to find in favour of the claimant. The court accepted that by the claimant undertaking a U-turn in the position he did contravened the Highway Code, although they agreed with the judge that this was not causative. The appeal was therefore dismissed.

[9.16]   **Jenkins v Holt**
[1999] RTR 411

The claim arose following a collision which occurred on River Road, Barking near the junction of Long Reach Road. The claimant was travelling south along River Road on his way to work. The defendant who was travelling in the same direction executed a U-turn into the path of the claimant's vehicle which resulted in a collision.

The defendant did not see the claimant's vehicle and the claimant only had time to brake hard before colliding with the defendant's vehicle.

The judge held the claimant entirely to blame and entered judgment for the defendant in both the claim and the counter-claim.

The claimant appealed against the judge's findings as to the claimant's speed, and also on the basis that the judge was wrong in finding no negligence against the defendant.

HELD, ON APPEAL: Allowing the appeal that the claimant was travelling too quickly and had failed to notice the presence of the defendant's vehicle. The court also found that the defendant had embarked upon a U-turn without looking. Therefore the court said that the 'defendant had created the danger and ... the plaintiff had failed to avoid it'. As both parties were equally to blame liability was apportioned 50/50 in both the claim and the counter-claim.

[9.17]   Stotardt v South East London and Kent Bus Co Ltd

[2003] EWHC 2135 (QB)

[2003] All ER (D) 315 (Jul)

The claimant was injured when a single decker bus owned by the first defendant went into shop premises in Well Hall Road, Eltham. Prior to colliding with the shop, the bus was involved in a collision with a Proton motor vehicle, driven by the second defendant, who the first defendant alleged negligently performed a U-turn immediately prior to collision. The second defendant denied that he had undertaken a U-turn.

HELD: There was insufficient evidence to support the first defendant's allegation that the second defendant had performed a U-turn. In the circumstances the court held the first defendant alone at fault and entered judgment against him.

[9.18]   Warren v Cole and Lunn

(25 October 2004, unreported)

The claimant a pedal cyclist brought a claim following a collision in the southbound lane of the A1024 Mile Cross Road in Norwich. The first defendant who was in the northbound lane wished to continue in a southerly direction. The second defendant was driving a lorry in the southbound lane which was heavily congested and moving intermittently. Having come to a stop, the second defendant signalled to the first defendant who wished to undertake a U-turn.

The claimant who was cycling along the nearside of the second defendant's lorry between the second defendant's vehicle and the kerb collided with the first defendant's vehicle as he was completing his U-turn manoeuvre. The claimant issued proceedings alleging that the first and second defendant were negligent, the former in undertaking an inherently dangerous manoeuvre and relying upon the signal given by the second defendant; and the latter in that he indicated to the first defendant that it was safe to proceed, and failed to check his nearside before giving such indication.

HELD: The claims were dismissed on the basis that it was not negligent to carry out a U-turn in the circumstances where the first defendant's car was turning across a stationary line of traffic, proceeding slowly and with caution. Although it would be negligent to rely on the signal of a third party without checking, the first defendant had checked for himself that it was safe to perform the U-turn and continued to keep a lookout as he carried out his manoeuvre at a very low speed. The first defendant was not liable for turning when his view of the claimant's approach was obstructed by the line of stationary vehicles. The claimant was under a duty in these circumstances to exercise a very high degree of care because he was overtaking on the nearside when his vision to the right was almost totally obscured.

The second defendant was not liable as he had checked both mirrors before signalling to the first defendant. In any event the signal did not mean that all was safe as the first defendant was still required to take all reasonable steps to ensure that it was safe to proceed (see *Clarke v Winchurch* at para [9.65]).

The judge found the cyclist to blame in that he was travelling too fast in the circumstances and had failed to keep a proper lookout or brake in time as he overtook the second defendant on the nearside.

3. SPEED

[9.19]   *Note*—There is a general speed limit of 70mph on dual carriageway roads (not being motorways), and a general speed limit of 60mph on single carriageway roads (not being motorways) (SI 1978/1548).

The speed limit of 30mph on restricted roads is imposed by the Road Traffic Regulation Act 1984, s 81. A restricted road is a road with street lamps 'placed not more than two hundred yards apart' (s 82(1)) but the section provides for various exceptions.

Speed limits on roads other than restricted roads are authorised by s 84, and for vehicles of different classes by s 86. The speed limits at present applicable to various classes of vehicle are contained in the Road Traffic Regulation Act 1984, Sch 5.

(A)   SPEED TABLES

[9.20]

Distance covered in one second at various speeds

Miles per hour	Feet per second	Metres per second
10	14.66	4.39
15	22.00	6.60
20	29.33	8.79
25	36.66	10.99
30	44.00	13.20
35	51.33	15.39
40	58.66	17.59
45	66.00	19.80
50	73.33	21.99
60	88.00	26.40

Braking tests

Appropriate minimum stopping distances

Four-wheel brakes, pneumatic tyres

Stopping distances in feet

Road surface	Dry smooth Concrete	Macadam Dry	Asphalt Dry	Wet	Low adhesion surface (Wet)
Co-efficient of:					
Friction	0.9	0.8	0.7	0.5	0.4
SPEEDS WHEN BRAKES APPLIED IN MPH:					
20	15	17	19	27	33
25	23	27	30	42	52
30	33	38	43	60	75
35	45	50	59	82	102
40	60	67	76	107	133
45	75	85	97	135	170
50	93	105	120	167	207
55	112	127	145	202	251
60	134	152	172	240	298

Time lag not allowed for.

Two-wheel brakes – approximately double the distance, subject to correction for weight distribution.

Smooth tyres – add about 25%.

Solid tyres – add about 33%.

For approximate stopping distances in metres multiply by 0.30.

Note—The Highway Code (2006), para 105 gives the following stopping distances in perfect conditions, ie good weather – broad daylight – good dry roads.

Speed	Thinking distance		Braking distance		Overall stopping distance	
mph	ft	m	ft	m	ft	m
70	70	21	245	75	315	96
60	60	18	180	55	240	73
50	50	15	125	38	175	53
40	40	12	80	24	120	36
30	30	9	45	14	75	23
20	20	6	20	6	40	12

(B)   SPEED AND NEGLIGENCE

[9.21]   Barna v Hudes Merchandising Corpn

[1962] Crim LR 321, 106 Sol Jo 194, CA

The claimant, driving his car, wished to turn right from a minor road into a major road. Another car was waiting on the crown of the major road to turn into the minor road. The claimant's view to his right was obscured by parked cars. He moved out slowly at a time when the defendant's car was approaching from his right at a speed between 30 and 40mph, though the road was subject to a 30mph speed limit. The defendant was unable to pull up in time and ran into the claimant's car.

HELD: The defendant was not to blame for the accident. To exceed the speed limit, though an offence, was not in itself negligence imposing civil liability. In the circumstances the defendant's speed was not excessive. He had no reason to suppose that the road would be blocked as it was.

[9.22]   Hurlock v Inglis

(1963) 107 Sol Jo 1023   Havers J

The defendant was driving at a speed of 100mph or more along the M1 motorway when his car got out of control and struck the claimant's lorry, causing him injuries. There were skid and tyre marks over 950ft long. The defendant said he was about to overtake a car travelling in the centre lane when a van swerved in front of it: in trying to avoid the car he was unable to avoid striking the claimant's lorry.

The judge found the defendant liable. It was not in itself negligent to drive on the M1 at 100mph but the defendant had not satisfactorily explained what happened. He had for some reason jammed on his brakes when he was in the outside lane and his car got out of control and for a considerable distance went backwards. Some explanation was called for to account for this extraordinary behaviour. In the absence of a satisfactory explanation he must be held to have been negligent.

[9.23]   Quinn v Scott

[1965] 2 All ER 588, [1965] 1 WLR 1004, 109 Sol Jo 498   Glyn-Jones J

On a straight level main road 32ft wide the defendant was driving his Jaguar car at 70 to 75mph. He was overtaking another car when he saw, 50 yards ahead, a tree falling across the road from the left. He instinctively swerved to the offside towards the thinner part of the tree, applying his brakes. He crashed into the foliage and lost control of the car due to the windscreen breaking, the car being filled with leaves and the steering wheel spinning out of his hands. The claimant driving a minibus from the opposite direction had seen the tree falling and had pulled up about 40 yards from the centre of the tree. The defendant, coming through the tree out of control, collided with the minibus and the claimant was injured.

HELD: The defendant was not negligent. High speed alone is not evidence of negligence unless the particular conditions at the time preclude it. There were no conditions present to make the defendant negligent in overtaking the two cars on his nearside at a speed of 70 to 75mph. Fifty yards was not at that speed sufficient distance in which to pull up when the tree began to fall: the 'thinking distance' shown on the diagrams on the back of the Highway Code could not be applied as a universal rule of thumb where so alarming an event occurs as the unexpected fall of a tree.

[9.24]   **Cornwell v Automobile Association**

(2 June 1989, unreported)

The defendant, driving an AA van, was travelling along the hard shoulder of a motorway accompanying a car that was experiencing carburettor problems. When the hard shoulder ran out because of a bridge crossing the motorway, the defendant pulled out from the hard shoulder into the inside lane at a speed of 15mph. The claimant, travelling at 60mph, collided with the rear of the defendant's van.

HELD: The claimant succeeded against the defendant. In the circumstances the defendant's speed was too slow. The claimant was not found contributorily negligent.

[9.25]   **Arnott v Sprake**

[2001] EWCA Civ 341

[2001] All ER (D) 287 (Feb)

The defendant appealed a finding of negligence following an accident where he had been driving a crop sprayer, which was pulling a trailer.

   The judge at first instance found the defendant negligent on the basis that he should have placed a red triangle on the road to warn other road users, sounded his horn, and turned on his flashing lights.

HELD, ON APPEAL: There was nothing about the vehicle or the junction to warrant the defendant taking exceptional steps. There is nothing to suggest that by sounding the horn the accident would have been avoided or to suggest that the defendant was unreasonable in failing to flash his lights. The court held that the accident was caused by the speed of the claimant's approach to the corner where the incident occurred.

   Appeal allowed.

[9.26]   **Macklin v Baird**

[2002] CLY 3269

The claimant had been riding a motorcycle along a trunk road, when he collided with the offside rear of a tractor pulling a trailer as it emerged on the trunk road.

   The claimant contended that the defendant had been negligent in that he should have used an alternative access route to the trunk road, where visibility of the junction was better. The defendant contended that his actions were reasonable and that the accident was caused by the claimant's excessive speed.

HELD: The claimant had been driving too fast, and knew the area, therefore he was aware of the presence of agricultural vehicles. Judgment was given for the defendant with no deduction for contributory negligence.

[9.27]   **Russell v Smith**

[2003] EWHC 2060 (QB)

147 Sol Jo LB 1118

The claimant, 10¼ years of age at the time of the accident, cycled across the junction of Graham Road and Churchbury Lane and collided with a car driven by the first defendant.

The claimant was seriously injured and had no recollection of the events leading to the accident. The judge was assisted by accident reconstruction evidence in determining the speed of both the defendant's vehicle and the claimant's bicycle leading up to the collision.

HELD: The defendant was travelling within the speed limit at a speed of no less than 27.5mph at the point of impact. The judge also found that the claimant was travelling at a speed of no more than 10mph when he emerged into the path of the defendant's vehicle.

It was held that the defendant had failed to apply her brakes before impact which evidenced a lack of attention. Given the number of parked cars and reduced visibility the judge found the defendant's speed excessive in the circumstances and her lack of attention amounted to evidence of negligence.

As the claimant emerged into the defendant's path the judge held him 75% to blame for the accident although he only reduced damages by 50% to take account of the fact that the claimant was a vulnerable road user.

[9.28]   Grealis v Opuni

[2003] EWCA Civ 177

[2003] All ER (D) 254 (Jan), [2004] RTR 97

The claimant who was working as a pizza delivery boy was travelling along the A5 in a southerly direction, where he intended to turn right into Camrose Avenue. There was a queue of traffic also waiting to turn into Camrose Avenue and instead of waiting for the traffic to clear, the claimant jumped the queue by passing along the right of the centre bollard. The defendant travelling in a northerly direction across the junction collided with the rear wheel of the claimant's vehicle. The claimant's speed at the time of impact was around 10mph whilst the defendant's speed was around 37–39mph which was in excess of the 30mph speed limit.

The judge held that the defendant owed no duty of care to the claimant and was not negligent even though he was travelling at a speed in excess of the speed limit. The claimant appealed.

HELD, ON APPEAL: Although it does not necessarily follow that negligence is to be imputed to a driver who breaks the speed limit, there is no doubt that evidence of the speed limit being broken may provide evidence of negligence. The judge found that had the defendant been driving within the speed limit that the accident would have been avoided. Therefore the defendant's speed was the cause of the accident.

The court went on to state that a prudent driver would have been aware that the vehicles waiting to turn right in the opposite carriageway were merely waiting for a gap to appear before commencing their manoeuvre, and therefore would have adjusted his speed accordingly.

[9.29]   Hussain v Jones

[2004] CLY 2747

The claimant had been driving his car when he lost control and crossed the centre white line into the path of the defendant's vehicle. The accident reconstruction evidence demonstrated that the defendant's car had been travelling at between 39 and 44mph in a 30mph zone.

HELD: Judgment was entered in favour of the claimant in that had the defendant been driving at or within the speed limit he would have been able to bring his vehicle to a halt between 7 and 13 metres before the point of impact. Therefore in all probability the accident would have been avoided or at worst a minor shunt. The judge found the claimant 80% liable for the accident, and ordered the defendant to meet 20% of the claim.

[9.30]   Lamoon v Fry

[2004] EWCA Civ 591

[2004] All ER (D) 323 (Apr)

This case involves a collision between the claimant a cyclist and the defendant who was driving a Nissan Primera. The judge found as a fact that the claimant was travelling on the wrong side of the road immediately before impact. The defendant who was travelling in the opposite direction approached the shallow bend where the incident occurred at 40mph without slowing down. The hedges, which were on either side of the road, were considerable and foliage extended into the road. The parties were approximately 20m apart when they first saw each other, and attempted to avoid each other at the last minute.

The judge found both the claimant and defendant liable and apportioned liability 60/40 in the defendant's favour.

The defendant appealed. One of the grounds for appeal was that as he was travelling below the 60mph speed limit he was not negligent. He further contented that his speed was not causative of the accident, as the accident occurred because the claimant was travelling on the wrong side of the road.

HELD, ON APPEAL: The judge was right to find the defendant negligent. The court was satisfied that there was sufficient evidence to support the judges findings that the defendant's speed was causative in that he was travelling too fast in the circumstances at the point of impact. The court also made reference to para 132 of the Highway Code which stated 'Take extra care on country roads and reduce your speed at approaches to bends ... Be prepared for pedestrians, horse riders and cyclists'. As the defendant did not slow down on his approach to the bend the judge was right to find him negligent.

Appeal dismissed.

[9.31]   Askey v Wood

[2005] EWCA Civ 574

[2005] All ER (D) 286 (Apr)

The claimant was driving a Renault Clio motorcar and the defendant riding a 750cc Honda motorcycle, along a country road with a speed limit of 60mph. A collision occurred between the two vehicles at a 90-degree blind bend.

The judge found as a fact that the claimant's vehicle was on the wrong side of the road and that the defendant was on the correct side of the road at the point of impact. The judge also found that the defendant was travelling at an excessive speed of around 60mph on his approach to the blind bend. The judge held that the defendant's speed and the claimant's positioning in the road were the cause of the accident, and found both parties equally to blame. The defendant appealed.

HELD, ON APPEAL: The defendant's speed had caused him to lose control of his vehicle before he even saw the claimant. Therefore there was nothing further he could have done to avoid the accident. As the defendant was unable to control his motorcycle he was unable to take any evasive action and as such the judge was right to find the defendant partially responsible.

[9.32]   Bland v Morris

[2006] EWCA Civ 56

[2006] All ER (D) 87 (Jan)

On 21 August 2004 an accident occurred on the A1 just north of the Wittering service station, when the claimant's coach driven by Simon Bland collided with the rear of a stationary coach driven by Jeanette Morris. The defendant had been involved in a collision only minutes earlier when the coach was struck by a lorry driven by Mr Penarrubia.

Following the collision between the defendant and Mr Penarrubia the defendant stopped the coach approximately 90m beyond the point of impact. None of her passengers had been injured following this incident. The defendant exited the coach which was parked on the verge, to speak to Mr Penarrubia. They returned to her vehicle and she asked her passengers to alight the coach.

Although traffic was light, vehicles were passing regularly. The claimant saw Mr Penarrubia's lorry protruding from the exit of the service station into the carriageway. However, the claimant did not see the coach until it was too late and collided with the rear of the coach, killing three of the passengers and injuring a number of others.

The claimant therefore sought a contribution from the defendant having admitted liability in respect of those passengers killed and injured following the accident.

The defendant brought Part 20 proceedings against Mr Penarrubia.

At first instance the judge found the defendant 60% to blame and Mr Penarrubia 40% responsible in connection with the first collision.

In connection with the second collision the judge held the claimant one-third responsible and the defendant two-thirds responsible. He also ordered Mr Penarrubia to contribute 20% towards the defendant's share of the blame in connection with the second accident.

The defendant appealed on the basis that the claimant should bear the greater share of the blame for colliding with the rear of the defendant's vehicle.

HELD, ON APPEAL: There was a lay-by, which the defendant was aware of following the incident with Mr Penarrubia. The lay-by was positioned a short distance away from where the defendant had parked and would have been a safer place to park the coach before seeking to obtain details from Mr Penarrubia. The judge found that the defendant was more motivated with trying to prevent Mr Penarrubia from getting away than the safety of her passengers. Further, the defendant failed after parking the coach to arrange the safe evacuation of her passengers, which would have reduced the risk to them.

It was the failure of the defendant to give regard to the safety of the passengers in her charge which outweighed the general responsibility of the claimant to drive carefully.

The court accepted that the claimant was clearly negligent in failing to see the defendant's coach when it was visible for a distance of 100m and also of driving in excess of the speed limit.

The court also considered that although it was not binding, the fact that the defendant was convicted of a more serious offence than the claimant was something the judge could consider in reaching his conclusions on apportionment of liability.

However, the failure to consider the safety of the passengers was one of the major factors in the judge deciding as he did.

Appeal dismissed.

(C)   POLICE VEHICLES AND FIRE ENGINES

[9.33]   Gaynor v Allen

[1959] 2 QB 403, [1959] 2 All ER 644, [1959] 3 WLR 221, 103 Sol Jo 677   McNair J

A pedestrian was injured by a police motorcyclist who was on a road where a 40mph speed limit was in force. The policeman who was travelling at 60mph in the course of his duties was killed as a result of the accident. The claimant issued proceedings seeking damages for personal injury. The defendant contended that there was a difference between a police officer and an ordinary motorcyclist, especially when the vehicle was being used on an emergency call out.

The court held that in respect of civil liability the police driver was to be judged in exactly the same way as any other civilian driver, and that he owed a duty to the public to drive with due care and attention without exposing members of the public to undue danger. The defendant was guilty of negligence and so was the claimant, to a lesser extent. Liability was apportioned one-third to the claimant and two-thirds to the defendant.

[9.34]   Dyer v Bannell

(1965) 109 Sol Jo 216   Glyn-Jones J

The claimant was injured when a van she was driving was struck by a police car driven by the defendant, a police constable. The claimant wished to turn right from a main road into a side turning. She switched on her flashing indicators and also made a hand signal. She saw in her driving mirror a taxicab some distance behind and the reflection of the defendant's car lights behind that. She then began to turn. The defendant was answering a call and was travelling at 45mph in a built-up area. He overtook the taxi and collided with the claimant's van as she turned across his path.

HELD: It was not negligent of a police officer in the execution of his duty to drive at a fast speed; but he must exercise a degree of care and skill proportionate to the speed at which he was driving. He must remember that the ordinary road user in a built-up area would not expect vehicles to drive at that speed and should give audible warning of his approach or otherwise make known the presence of a police car. The defendant had not appreciated what the van was doing as quickly as he should have done. The claimant as a reasonable motorist was entitled to suppose it was safe to turn, and need not contemplate that a vehicle still further away was travelling at such a speed that it would be dangerous to turn. Judgment was entered for the claimant with no deduction for contributory negligence.

Note—The Road Traffic Regulation Act 1984, s 87 provides:

'No statutory provision imposing a speed limit on motor vehicles shall apply to any vehicle on an occasion when it is being used for fire brigade, ambulance or police purposes, if the observance of that provision would be likely to hinder the use of the vehicle for the purpose for which it is being used on that occasion.'

[9.35]   Wood v Richards

[1977] RTR 201, 65 Cr App Rep 300, [1977] Crim LR 295, Div Ct

A police patrol driver on a motorway when answering an emergency call decided to overtake a large vehicle by driving on the hard shoulder. In doing so he collided with a lorry standing on the hard shoulder. He was convicted of driving without due care contrary to the Road Traffic Act 1972, s 3. On appeal he claimed that a special standard was applicable to a police officer driving to an emergency.

HELD: Not so. If the 1972 Act had meant a different standard to apply it would have said so – as does the Road Traffic Regulation Act 1984 on speed limits by s 87 – and it does not.

Note—Section 3 of the Road Traffic Act 1972 is repeated as s 3 of the Road Traffic Act 1988.

[9.36]   Marshall v Osmond

[1983] QB 1034, [1983] 2 All ER 225, [1983] 3 WLR 13, 127 Sol Jo 309, [1983] RTR 475, CA

The claimant was a passenger in a car which he knew was stolen. A police car set off in pursuit and stopped alongside the stolen car when the occupants were getting out and running away. The claimant was struck by the police car and sustained injury which he claimed was caused by the negligent driving of the defendant, the driver of the police car.

HELD: The claimant was not entitled to succeed. A police officer on an emergency call out does not owe a person suspected of having committed an arrestable offence the same duty of care which he owes to a lawful and innocent road user. However he must not deliberately injure such a person unless it is reasonably necessary to do so in order to arrest him.

On appeal by the claimant per Sir John Donaldson MR: 'I do not believe that the defence of *volenti non fit injuria* is really applicable in the case of the police pursuing a suspected criminal. I think that the duty owed by a police driver to the suspect is … the same duty as that owed to anyone else, namely to exercise such care and skill as is reasonable in all the circumstances. The vital words in that proposition of law are "in all the circumstances" and of course one of the circumstances was that the claimant bore all the appearance of having been somebody engaged in a criminal activity for which there was a power of arrest. There had been an error of judgment by police driver but he had not been negligent'.

Appeal dismissed.

[9.37]   Langley v Dray and MT Motor Policies at Lloyds

[1997] PIQR P508; affd [1998] PIQR P314

The first defendant, Dray, had stolen the vehicle and was driving through the streets of Birmingham. Dray was driving at excessive speeds, ignoring traffic signals and endangering pedestrians. He was being pursued by police vehicles who were flashing headlights, sounding their horns and displaying their blue lights. The claimant, a police officer, was driving one of the police vehicles in pursuit.

It was clear throughout the chase that Dray's objective was to escape from the pursuing police officers. Later, in evidence provided to the police, Dray acknowledged that he knew that for virtually the whole of the chase he was being pursued by the police cars.

Dray and his pursuers approached a T junction. Unbeknown to all drivers there was a patch of black ice on the road. Due to the black ice neither Dray nor the claimant were able to control their vehicles at the junction. Dray's vehicle crossed the junction and ended up in a field opposite but the claimant's vehicle hit a lamp post, causing the claimant serious injuries.

HELD: The duty of care owed by Dray to the claimant was the ordinary duty of care owed to other road users, ie a duty to drive with the skill and care of the ordinary driver so as to minimise the risk of reasonably foreseeable injury to others using the highway lawfully.

The claimant knew that he was being pursued by police cars and he realised, or should have realised, that the speeds at which he was being pursued would increase the risk of injury to those pursuing him.

The black ice on the road was wholly unexpected but had the claimant been driving at a normal speed he would have been able to brake more effectively and avoid hitting the lamp post.

Therefore Dray was in breach of his duty towards the claimant and that breach caused the injuries sustained by the claimant.

Per John Mitting QC: If by careless or reckless driving a defendant creates circumstances in which he foresees, or should foresee, that he will be pursued by police officers in a manner which increases the risk of injury to those police officers, or to other road users, and he is pursued in that manner without negligence on the part of the pursuer, then, if in consequence injury is caused to a pursuing officer or other road user, the defendant will be liable.

[9.38] **Aldridge v Metropolitan Police Commissioner**
(6 March 1998, unreported), CA

The claimant was crossing Oxford Street at about 5 pm on a dark winters' evening in December. She crossed between stationary vehicles to get to the central reservation where she stopped and checked the road to her left. The road was clear so she began to cross and at that moment became aware of a police vehicle travelling on the wrong side of the road towards her. A collision occurred and the claimant was injured and brought proceedings against the defendant.

The defendant driver, a rapid response police officer, was entitled to travel up the wrong side of the road as long as he did so in a manner that was not likely to endanger any person (reg 15(2) of the Traffic Signs Regulations and General Directions 1994, SI 1994/1519). The defendant driver had switched on the blue flashing lights, automatic headlights and the two-tone sirens. The vehicle was travelling at a speed of around 25mph for 75 yards on the wrong side of the road for some six seconds before hitting the claimant.

HELD: The defendant was 100% to blame. The police driver should have proceeded on the right-hand side of the road at such a speed that he could have stopped if a pedestrian walked out in front of him having not been alerted to his presence. The defendant appealed.

HELD, ON APPEAL: The claimant was aware of the presence of the police vehicle before crossing the road and had recalled thinking that this vehicle would have difficulty negotiating the heavy traffic on the first carriageway. Furthermore, other pedestrians with the claimant on the central reservation had not stepped out into the road. The judge had failed to take into account adequately the finding that the police car's siren was sounding, the lights were flashing and it had travelled some 75 yards up the wrong side of the road for nearly six seconds. The claimant was found one-third contributorily negligent.

[9.39]   Wardell-Yerburgh v Surrey County Council

[1973] RTR 462   Brabin J

On a three-lane road in fog with visibility limited to 50 yards the claimant's husband was driving a mini-van in the centre lane, slowly overtaking a lorry and trailer 52ft long. He was following at least one other car. The defendant's fire engine was being driven in the opposite direction in the centre lane at 50mph with headlights on and blue light flashing on an emergency call out. A car ahead of the fire engine moved into its nearside lane to let it through, as did the car ahead of the claimant. The fire engine collided with the claimant's vehicle, killing the claimant's husband. It was argued by the defendants that a fire engine on an emergency could be driven in a way which fell below the standard of an ordinary vehicle.

HELD: Following *Gaynor v Allen* (at para [9.33]) the driver of the fire engine owed to the public the same duty of care as any other driver: he was negligent in driving too fast in fog and not keeping a proper look-out. But the mini-van driver was more blameworthy in the manner of his overtaking. To overtake as the last of three vehicles in fog is negligent. The claimant's husband should have delayed overtaking until he could see what was ahead of him. Instead he was moving forward at a slow differential speed in relation to the lorry he was overtaking and could move neither to right nor left when the fire engine came in sight. The court apportioned liability two-thirds/one-third in favour of the defendant.

[9.40]   Griffin v Mersey Regional Ambulance

[1998] PIQR P34, CA

The claimant was driving across a junction controlled by traffic lights. His speed was 25mph and the lights were green in his favour. The defendant's ambulance was crossing the junction from the claimant's offside against red lights. The ambulance was on an emergency call. A collision occurred and the claimant was injured.

The ambulance had its klaxon blaring and had already travelled approximately some 20 yards against the lights. A van ahead of the claimant had stopped to allow the ambulance across.

HELD: The claimant was negligent in having failed to hear the ambulance, failing to see the ambulance and for failing to appreciate that other vehicles had stopped to allow the ambulance to pass. The ambulance driver should have waited a little longer to ensure that the remaining part of the junction was clear and had moved across in front of the claimant rather too fast. On this basis the judge apportioned liability at 60/40 in the defendant's favour. The claimant's appeal was dismissed.

Note—The effect of the Traffic Signals Regulations and General Directions 1994, SI 1994 No 1519, reg 33 is to designate the red light as, effectively, a 'give way' sign.

[9.41]   Methven v Metropolitan Police Commissioner

(10 October 2000, unreported), CA

On 14 September 1996, the claimant was driving a van which collided with a police dog van which was proceeding to an emergency call, and passed through a red light. The sirens on the police vehicle were activated and the blue lights were flashing.

Neither driver had seen the other until it was too late, although the claimant stated that he had heard the police vehicle he was unable to ascertain its location prior to impact.

The claimant mistakenly believed that a vehicle which had it lights on were the police vehicle and he intended to go through the green lights before pulling over to allow the vehicle to pass.

The judge accepted that the claimant's reaction was an agony of the moment and that his decision although wrong was understandable. The driver of the defendant's vehicle had no such excuse for failing to see the claimant's vehicle and was held liable.

The defendant appealed on the basis that the claimant should have been equally to blame.

HELD, ON APPEAL: The recorder was entitled to have preferred the claimant's evidence. The court further stated that although neither driver had seen the other this was not a ground for apportioning blame equally especially as the claimant had an explanation for his actions, whereas the driver of the defendant's vehicle was unable to explain his.

Appeal dismissed.

[9.42]   Nelson v Chief Constable of Cumbria
[2000] CLY 4217

The claimant driving a distinctive car was being followed by a police transit van, which indicated for him to stop. Both vehicles were travelling at approximately 40mph with the police vehicle five to six car lengths behind the claimant's vehicle. Suddenly the claimant performed an emergency stop and the police vehicle collided with the rear of his vehicle. The claimant brought a claim for compensation in respect of the damage to his vehicle and for personal injury.

HELD: The police officer owed the same duty as any other road user and in the circumstances of no pursuit or overly excessive speed the collision was *prima facie* evidence of negligence. However, as the claimant had performed an unexplained emergency stop he was also negligent and liability was apportioned 75/25 in favour of the claimant.

[9.43]   Scutts v Keyse
[2001] EWCA Civ 715
[2001] All ER (D) 236 (May)

A police driver appealed against a finding of 75% negligence when he was involved in a collision with a pedestrian when proceeding to an emergency call out. The police vehicle had been displaying flashing blue lights and the sirens were activated. As the officer approached traffic lights at a road junction he slowed down to 20mph. As the lights were green and the road was clear the officer speeded up to around 50mph. The claimant stepped off the kerb and the officer attempted to stop. He unfortunately collided with the claimant. At first instance the court found the defendant liable.

HELD, ON APPEAL: The police driver was not negligent for injuring a pedestrian who stepped onto the road as the police car accelerated through a green light with its sirens and lights on. It was held that speed alone is not evidence of negligence and that drivers of emergency vehicles are entitled to expect other road users to be aware of their approach and react accordingly.

[9.44] **Purdue v Devon Fire & Rescue Service**

[2002] EWCA Civ 1538

[2002] All ER (D) 125 (Oct)

The claimant was involved in road traffic accident on 27 June 1999, on the A361 Braunton Road in Barnstaple. The claimant had stopped at a red traffic light where he intended to turn right. The defendant's vehicle was travelling from the claimant's right on an emergency call out towards the traffic lights. The road was a long dual carriageway with good visibility. The road was clear. The defendant's vehicle had activated its flashing lights although the sirens were not. As the traffic lights changed from red to green the claimant moved forward and collided with the defendant's vehicle, which was proceeding through a red light.

At first instance the judge found in favour of the claimant, as the defendant's driver would have seen the claimant's stationary vehicle at the traffic lights before proceeding through the red light. Further, the driver of the defendant's vehicle was negligent to assume that the claimant had seen him before the he proceeded. The judge also found the defendant's driver negligent in not sounding his sirens.

The defendant appealed as there was no finding of contributory negligence.

HELD, ON APPEAL: The claimant was negligent in failing to glance to his right before proceeding through a green light. The court also held that it was difficult to understand how the claimant did not see the oncoming fire appliance with it lights flashing, as a properly observant driver would and should have seen it. Liability was therefore reduced by 20% to take account of the claimant's negligence.

[9.45] **Gilfillan v Barbour**

2003 SLT 1127, 2004 SCLR 92

This Scottish case considers some of the issues considered by English courts in respect of accident involving police vehicles.

The claimant a police constable in the traffic division issued proceedings following a road traffic accident in which the defendant's wife died. The defendant who issued a counterclaim had been driving along a major thoroughfare when he approached a junction intending to turn right. The defendant heard the police siren although his view of the carriageway was restricted by another vehicle facing him. The defendant attempted to turn right when he thought it was safe which is when he saw the police vehicle approaching at speed on its way to an emergency call out. The claimant unable to avoid the collision struck the defendant's vehicle.

HELD: Apportioning liability equally, that although the defendant was in breach of his duty of care, in that he failed to give regard to the Highway Code, and failed to notice the police vehicle until immediately prior to the collision, it is probable that a driver keeping a proper lookout especially for an emergency vehicle would have seen the police car approaching, or waited at the junction.

It was further stated that although police officers owed a duty of care to other road users it was not clear whether this duty was the same as that required by an ordinary road user.

As the claimant's driving failed to meet the standard to be expected of a reasonable driver despite his being on an emergency call, with sirens and blue lights activated. This is because although the claimant was on an emergency call there was a danger that traffic may cross his path at the junction. Therefore by approaching the junction at 60mph in damp conditions with a restricted view meant that the claimant was negligent as he simply needed to slow down on his approach. As the court had little to choose between the parties in terms of liability it was apportioned equally.

4.   SKIDDING

[9.46]   Custins v Nottingham Corpn
[1970] RTR 365, CA

The claimant was waiting for a bus; it was freezing weather and the road was covered with snow. She was standing not on the pavement but about three feet out in the road. The bus driver saw her when he was 70 yards away; he was moving at only 10mph and slowed down gradually to the place where the claimant was standing. He applied slight pressure to the brake and managed to stop the bus, but then it slid sideways and knocked the claimant down. The Commissioner of Assize held that as the bus had stopped without difficulty and then slipped sideways the driver had failed to keep the bus under control and was negligent.

HELD: It was impossible to draw an inference of negligence from the evidence accepted by the Commissioner. What more could the driver have done than drive very slowly, keep a proper look-out and apply his brakes gently? There was a camber on the road; when a vehicle starts to skid on an icy road it may take the most unpredictable of courses. It is common knowledge that if you are unlucky when you are driving on an icy road, whatever care you may take, it sometimes by mischance occurs that the vehicle does slide and gets out of control. In these circumstances it does not mean that there is any negligence on the part of the driver.

Appeal allowed.

[9.47]   London Transport Executive v Foy, Morgan & Co
(7 July 1955, unreported)

The claimant's coach had just pulled up on a particularly bad winter night when there had been ice on the road because of previous snow. It had been snowing and the snow had turned to a certain degree of sleet. It was freezing as well and the road was in such a condition that a police officer had some difficulty in standing. It was a very bad and a very dangerous road. The defendant was driving at 25mph. He realised that he was on a dangerous road and he was coming to a bend and he had no chance to stop. He was therefore driving in a way that was not showing the care which he ought to have been showing and in such a way as would reasonably avoid a skid.

Per Lord Goddard CJ: People are apt to think that if only they can show that their car skidded, because of certain decisions given a very long time ago, there is an end of the matter. When the cases are examined carefully, it will always be seen that it is only where the skid occurs unavoidably that the driver cannot be held responsible. If he is driving in a way which is asking for a skid, then he is liable.

[9.48]   Richley v Faull
[1965] 3 All ER 109, [1965] 1 WLR 1454, 129 JP 498, 109 Sol Jo 937   MacKenna J

On a road which was wet, but not slippery from any other cause, the defendant was driving his Bentley car when it went into a skid. It skidded across the road, turning as it went, into the path of a Hillman car in which the claimant was a passenger. The Hillman collided with the Bentley and the claimant was injured. The defendant gave no explanation of the reason why his car skidded. He said the same thing had happened two years before when he was driving the same car: he could not explain why.

HELD: The collision was caused by the defendant's negligence. Adopting Lord Greene's reasoning in *Laurie v Raglan Building Co* [1942] 1 KB 152, [1941] 3 All ER 332, 111 LJKB 292, 166 LT 63, 86 Sol Jo 69, CA, where a vehicle moves on to the wrong side of the road into the path of another car there is a *prima facie* case of negligence which is not displaced merely by proof that the defendant's car skidded. But Lord Greene's dictum that a skid by itself is neutral is not acceptable; the unexplained and violent skid is in itself evidence of negligence. It is hardly consistent to hold that the skid which explains the presence of the vehicle on the wrong side of the road is neutral but that the defendant must fail unless he proves that this neutral event happened without his default. On either view, however, the conclusion is the same: the defendant fails if he does not prove that the skid which took him to the wrong place happened without his default.

(A)   RACING COMPETITIONS

[9.49]   O'Down v Frazer-Nash
[1951] WN 173, 95 Sol Jo 269   McNair J

The course of a road race in Jersey and the regulations were approved by the RAC. The deceased, a doctor, gave his services as a first aid official. He was provided with an RAC handbook for officials giving warning not to set foot on the course, the pavement or road except where their duty required them to do so.

On a practice run the deceased took up a position on the pavement at a road junction opposite a bend where the course took a sharp right-hand bend. The brakes of a car failed and the deceased was killed. There had been no neglect to maintain the car in a fit condition. There was no negligence of the driver. The organisers had performed their duty of protecting their officials against reasonably foreseeable perils. There was no inadequacy in any of their arrangements. The warning in the handbook was adequate. It was a case of familiarity having bred contempt.

[9.50]   Wilks v Cheltenham Home Guard Motor Cycle and Light Car Club
[1971] 2 All ER 369, [1971] 1 WLR 668, 115 Sol Jo 309, CA

The claimant was a spectator at a motorcycle scramble when he was struck and injured by a machine of a competitor, the second defendant. The machine and rider somehow surmounted a 'wrecking rope', crossed a space of 10ft and then went under or over another rope barrier before striking the claimant. The judge of assize acquitted the organisers (the first defendant) of any blame but held the second defendant negligent on the ground that he lost control of his machine because of excessive speed, inadequate skill or reckless driving. The second defendant appealed.

HELD, ON APPEAL: He was not to blame. A competitor in a race must use reasonable care – but as a competitor he is expected to go all out to win and the degree of care required is that which a reasonable competitor would take in those circumstances. In a race a reasonable man would do everything he could to win but he would not be foolhardy, that is, conduct himself as to show a reckless disregard for the safety of spectators. There was no evidence of greatly excessive speed on the part of the second defendant. The fact that he had somehow crossed the two rope barriers did not bring into play the doctrine of *res ipsa loquitur*; the circumstances were vastly different from a case such as *Ellor v Selfridge & Co Ltd* (1930) 46 TLR 236, 74 Sol Jo 140 where a motorist mounts the pavement.

Appeal allowed.

[9.51]   Harrison v Vincent
[1982] RTR 8, CA

In a motorcycle and combination race the claimant was a sidecar passenger. At a point on the course the machines had to be brought down from speeds of 100mph or more to 30mph to negotiate a hairpin bend. The rider of the machine applied the brake but due to a defect it failed adequately to slow the machine which went off the course into an escape road. It struck a vehicle projecting into the road injuring the claimant severely. The vehicle was placed there to clear away any broken-down equipment. The claimant sued the rider and the organisers.

HELD: He was entitled to succeed:
(1)   against the rider of the machine, since he owed the normal duty of care to the claimant, the defect in the brake being one which should have been rectified beforehand; and
(2)   against the race organisers for not keeping the escape road clear of obstruction.

Note—See also *White v Blackmore* (at para [7.32]) and *Latchford v Spedeworth International Ltd* (1983) 134 NLJ 36.

5.   LEADING AND FOLLOWING VEHICLE

[9.52]   Sharp v Avery and Kerwood
[1938] 4 All ER 85, 82 Sol Jo 908, CA

A motorcyclist in company with another motorcyclist carrying a pillion passenger was proceeding from London to Southend. The two motorcyclists agreed that one of them, 'A', should lead the other because he knew the way. The other followed at a distance of about eight yards. The leading motorcyclist mistook the road and drove on to some waste ground. He then applied his brakes and skidded forward gradually slowing down. The second motorcyclist followed on to the waste ground and collided with the first motorcycle and the pillion passenger on the second motorcycle was injured.

HELD: The first motorcyclist was negligent and in the circumstances there was a duty on him not to mislead the motorcyclist who was following. Verdict against 'A' upheld.

[9.53]   Smith v Harris
[1939] 3 All ER 960, 83 Sol Jo 730, CA

Five motorcyclists were engaged in a treasure hunt. P was apparently clever at finding clues, and it was agreed that he should lead the hunt. They were proceeding at about 25 to 30mph with about eight yards between each of them. P overshot a turning and braked hard. He did not swerve either to the left or right to give those behind him a chance of avoiding him. O, who was next, was spread eagled on the ground to the right of P, and M, who was third, was spread eagled to the left. H, with the claimant as pillion passenger, who was fourth, swerved out to avoid M but ran into O and overturned, injuring the claimant. The county court judge held that P was negligent in the way he drew up, and H for not having proper control of his machine, and found each equally to blame.

HELD, ON APPEAL: It was a question of fact. The case *Sharp v Avery and Kerwood* (at para [9.52]) laid down no fresh principle of law.

Appeal dismissed.

[9.54]   Brown and Lynn v Western Scottish Motor Traction Co Ltd
1945 SC 31, 1944 SN 59, Ct of Sess

A motor lorry was travelling along a public street followed at a distance of 25 to 30ft by a motor omnibus, the speed of both vehicles being approximately 15mph. The driver of the lorry, in order to avoid a pedestrian, swerved suddenly to the left and pulled up almost instantaneously, and the driver of the omnibus, when he realised that the lorry was stopping, swerved to the right and applied his brakes, but, although he acted with reasonable promptitude, he did not succeed in avoiding a collision. The driver of the lorry had no time to give any signal, and the driver of the omnibus had not seen, and had no reasonable chance of seeing, the pedestrian.

HELD: (Lord Stevenson dissenting): The fact that the driver of the omnibus, although allowing a sufficient space between the vehicles in which to deal with the ordinary exigencies of traffic, had followed the lorry so closely that he could not cope with its exceptionally abrupt stop did not amount to negligence upon his part, and, accordingly, the owners of the omnibus were not liable to the owners of the lorry.

Per Lord Cooper: The distance which should separate two vehicles travelling one behind the other must depend upon many variable factors – their speed, the nature of the locality, the other traffic present or to be expected, the opportunity available to the following driver of commanding a view ahead of the leading vehicle, the distance within which the following vehicle can be pulled up, and many other things. The following driver is, in my view, bound, so far as reasonably possible, to take up such a position and to drive in such a fashion, as will enable him to deal successfully with all traffic exigencies reasonably to be anticipated: but whether he has fulfilled this duty must in every case be a question of fact whether, on any emergency disclosing itself, the following driver acted with the alertness, skill and judgment reasonably to be expected in the circumstances.

[9.55]   Jungnikel v Laing
(1966) 111 Sol Jo 19, CA

Lorry A was travelling in the slow lane of the M1 motorway at night when it was run into from behind by lorry B. As a result of the collision lorry B crossed the central island on to the other carriageway and turned over. The claimant's husband driving a mini-truck ran into it and was killed.

As between the two lorry drivers the judge held the driver of lorry B 90% to blame for not keeping a proper look-out but said the driver of lorry A was 10% to blame because he had effected a sudden reduction of speed without warning, as if changing gear.

HELD, ON APPEAL: The driver of lorry A was not at all to blame. Even on the M1 deceleration without warning is not an act of negligence. If a driver was going to make a sudden heavy stop he was under a duty to give warning to traffic behind, but not if he was merely decelerating. Moreover his failure to warn had no causative effect since the driver of lorry B was not keeping a look-out and would not have seen a signal.

[9.56]   Brown v Thompson

[1968] 2 All ER 708, [1968] 1 WLR 1003, 112 Sol Jo 464, CA

Mrs Brown was injured when a car driven by her husband collided with the rear of the defendant's lorry. The accident occurred at about 3 am in winter on an unlighted road. The lorry had no lights and was without reflectors. Mr Brown did not see the lorry until just before the accident and was turning out to avoid it when he hit it. The judge apportioned liability 80% to the defendant and 20% to Mr Brown. The defendants appealed contending that 50% responsibility should be apportioned to Mr Brown.

HELD: Dismissing the appeal, regard must be had not only to the causative potency of the acts or omissions of each of the parties but to their relative blameworthiness (citing *The Miraflores and The Abadesa* [1967] 1 AC 826, [1967] 1 All ER 672, [1967] 2 WLR 806, 111 Sol Jo 211, HL). The act of driving in such a manner that the driver failed to turn out and ran into the back of a stationary vehicle was in a high degree potently causative of the injuries suffered by Mrs Brown. Equally it was potently causative of the collision that the lorry was left in the position it was without lights. But when one looked at the blameworthiness then it seemed plain that Mr Brown's fault was really quite small.

Note—See also *Baker v Willoughby* [1970] AC 467, [1969] 3 All ER 1528, [1970] 2 WLR 50, 114 Sol Jo 15, HL.

[9.57]   Thompson v Spedding

[1973] RTR 312, CA

The claimant was riding her moped in a moving line of traffic. There was a Triumph car ahead of her, and in front of that, a Morris driven by the defendant. The Morris pulled up sharply turning right. The Triumph was able to pull up safely without colliding with the Morris but the claimant could not pull up in time and in trying to avoid the Triumph collided with it and was injured. The judge held the defendant wholly to blame, saying that the claimant was not required to ride her moped on the basis that the defendant was suddenly going to stop and put her and the driver in front in jeopardy.

HELD, ON APPEAL: The judge had failed to express correctly the duty of persons driving in a line of traffic; it was to drive at such a distance behind the car in front as to be prepared for foreseeable emergencies. The claimant's blame was equal to that of the defendant.

[9.58]   Clift v (1) Hawes (2) Motor Insurers' Bureau

(24 November 1999, unreported), CA   Judge Bowsher

There were two accidents involving five vehicles travelling in the same direction. The first defendant caused the first accident and there was debris left on the road, being a dual carriageway, which lead to the second accident.

The claimant was riding a 200cc motorcycle following a Renault Clio. The Clio was driven at 60–70mph in the offside lane and on approaching the debris, the Clio braked and slowed to 10mph or possibly to a halt. The claimant then struck the Clio violently, and was thrown from his bike suffering serious injuries.

HELD, at first instance: The first defendant was liable for all the loss and damage that occurred and there was no contributory negligence on behalf of the claimant.

HELD, ON APPEAL: The duty of persons who are driving in a line of traffic is such that they must drive at such a distance behind the vehicle in front as to be prepared for foreseeable emergencies which arise. The claimant was partly at fault in failing to stop without colliding with the Clio and this showed a lack of care. Contributory negligence on the part of the claimant was assessed at 30%.

The remainder of the liability rests on the first defendant as the second collision was caused by his negligence, which led to the debris being on the road. The driver of the Renault Clio was not negligent, his actions were caused by the negligence of the first defendant, and his conduct was within the band of foreseeability.

[9.59]   Scott v Warren

[1974] RTR 104, [1974] Crim LR 117, Div Ct

The defendant was driving a car behind a van, both travelling at about 20 to 25mph. The van driver braked suddenly to avoid a large piece of metal which dropped off a lorry in front. The defendant did not see the metal fall, his vision being obstructed by the van, and he had no warning that the van driver was about to make an emergency stop. He braked but was unable to avoid colliding with the back of the van. The prosecution, on a charge of driving without due care, presented it as a matter of settled law that if a driver did not leave sufficient space between himself and the vehicle in front to avoid a collision whatever the circumstances, he was guilty of the offence charged; the Highway Code (1968), rr 34 and 35 were relied on.

HELD: The proposition could not be accepted. The words of Lord Cooper in *Brown and Lynn v Western Scottish Motor Traction Co Ltd* (at para [9.54]) indicated a standard to be observed by a following driver appropriate in civil cases. The obligation could not be higher on a criminal charge. In the present case it could not be said the justices were perverse in finding the defendant not guilty of the offence.

Note—The Highway Code (1968), ss 34 and 35 are repeated as para 105 of the Highway Code (2006).

[9.60]   Arnesen v Heffey

[2002] EWCA Civ 1058

[2002] All ER (D) 124 (Jul)

The defendant motorist had a blow out on a two-lane motorway. The car drivers immediately behind managed to avoid a collision, although the claimant, a motor-cyclist, crashed into the rear of the defendant's vehicle.

The judge at first instance found the defendant negligent as she either had time to pull into the hard shoulder or should have stopped the car near the central crash barrier. The defendant appealed on the basis that the judge failed to analyse any of the witness evidence when reaching his conclusion.

It was held that there was no justification for the judge's finding that the defendant could easily move to the hard shoulder, or move the car to the central reservation. There was no basis on which to reject the defendant's evidence and accordingly the judge's principal conclusion was flawed and unsustainable.

Appeal allowed.

6.   SIGNALLING AND TURNING

(A)   OVERTAKING TURNING VEHICLE

[9.61]   Sorrie v Robertson
1944 JC 95, 1944 SN 14, 1944 SLT 332, Ct Jus

The Road Traffic Act 1930, s 12, (now section 3 of the Road Traffic Act 1988) made it an offence to drive 'a motor vehicle on a road without due care and attention or without reasonable consideration for other persons using the road'.

The driver of a motor lorry, who knew that he was being overtaken gradually by a motorcycle, signalled in the appropriate manner that he was about to turn across the road to his right – his intention being to enter a garage 50 yards further on. At that moment he saw the motorcyclist in his driving mirror, but after giving the signal he concentrated his whole attention on turning into the garage. He took no steps to ascertain whether his signal had been observed, and, when he made the turn, the cyclist, who had not observed the signal, was about to pass him, which resulted in a collision. The lorry driver having been convicted of an offence under s 12 of the Act of 1930.

HELD: That the conviction was warranted, in respect that the accused, in view of his knowledge of the overtaking motorcycle, had a duty to observe whether his own signal had been appreciated.

[9.62]   Clark v Wakelin
(1965) 109 Sol Jo 295   Roskill J

The claimant on a pedal cycle turned right from the nearside of the road and was struck by the defendant who was about to overtake a motorcycle. The claimant's statement to the police was 'I looked behind me, let a car go by, put out my hand and turned right.' The defendant said he was about to overtake when the claimant put out his hand, turned and never gave him a chance to avoid the accident. The claimant said in evidence that the car he let go by was coming towards him from the opposite direction. He relied on the provision in the Highway Code 'Never overtake unless you know you can do so without danger to yourself and others.'

The judge said the defendant's version of the accident was to be accepted. A driver was entitled to assume that he could overtake without danger if what he was overtaking gave not the slightest sign that it was going to do something other than what another ordinary careful motorist or motorcyclist might expect. The claimant was solely to blame.

Note—See also *Dyer v Bannell* (at para [9.34]).

[9.63]   Goke v Willett
[1973] RTR 422, 117 Sol Jo 468, CA

On a busy three-lane road in daylight a mini-van pulled out into the centre lane to overtake a lorry and trailer travelling in the nearside lane. The mini driver whilst still in the centre lane decided to enter a service station on the offside of the road. He put on his offside indicator and braked, slowing down sharply to enter the further of the two entrances. The mini-van was then struck from behind by a heavily-laden lorry which was travelling behind the mini-van in the centre lane. The lorry driver had been about 100 yards behind the mini-van when it braked but the driver had not seen the mini's brake light or indicator. The mini driver was unaware of the presence behind him of the lorry until after the impact.

HELD: As the mini driver was undertaking an undesirable manoeuvre it was incumbent upon him to ensure that he was able to undertake this without risk to other road users. In these particular circumstances the mini driver ought to have given a hand signal; if he had the lorry driver who was travelling behind him would probably have seen his signal and avoided a collision. The Highway Code, insofar as it appears to say that hand signals need never be used when indicators and brake lights are in good working order, contains unwise advice. There may still be circumstances, as in this case, where the utmost warning to other road users of one's intentions should be adopted Liability was apportioned mini driver one-third, lorry driver two-thirds.

Note—But see now the Highway Code (2006).

[9.64]   Barry v Pugh

[2005] EWHC 2555 (QB)

[2005] All ER (D) 239 (Nov)

The claimant motorcyclist was rendered paraplegic as a result of contact between his motorcycle and the rear mudguard of a horse trailer being towed by an Isuzu Trooper vehicle driven by the defendant.

The accident scene was an undulating country lane in Montgomeryshire, Wales. The lane was 2.8m wide and the total width of the motorcycle and trailer combined amounted to 2.915m.

The claimant accepted he had been negligent in attempting to get past the trailer at 15mph. The claimant alleged, however, that the defendant had also been negligent as she was possibly still moving at the point of impact and should have stopped sooner than she did. The claimant also alleged the trailer had swung out in to the path of the claimant's oncoming motorcycle as a result of the defendant pulling on to the verge.

The court held that the defendant had braked and had stopped or was in the process of stopping at the point of impact. She had pulled over on to a verge as far as she could and had taken all necessary steps to avoid a collision.

She had been faced with a motorcyclist who was going far too fast at the point that she saw him. Nothing in her actions could be regarded as negligent. Her decision to move across to the verge had avoided a head on collision.

(B)   TURNING OUT OF MINOR ROAD

[9.65]   Clarke v Winchurch

[1969] 1 All ER 275, [1969] 1 WLR 69, 112 Sol Jo 909, CA

The first defendant's car was parked on the offside of the road, facing the direction in which the first defendant wished to travel. A continuous line of traffic was travelling in the opposite direction and he had to pass through this to proceed on his way. The third defendant, a bus driver driving the second defendants' bus, saw that the first defendant wished to come out and stopped to allow him to do so. The bus driver flashed his headlights at the first defendant who then came out slowly across the front of the bus. When the front of the car was about a yard beyond the offside of the bus the car was struck by a moped ridden by the claimant who had overtaken the bus on the offside. The bus driver had looked in his mirror but had not seen the claimant. The judge of assize accepted the first defendant's evidence that he was only just crawling out and acquitted him of any blame. He found the claimant two-thirds to blame and the bus driver one-third for not giving a hand signal to warn the claimant which he said he would have done if he had seen him.

HELD, ON APPEAL: The claimant was to blame but the first defendant and the bus driver were not. A cyclist or moped rider is entitled to overtake stationary traffic but to do this warrants a very high degree of care and he must ride in such a way that he can immediately deal with an emergency.

When he saw that the bus had stopped the claimant ought to have realised that something was going on in front of it and driven accordingly. With regard to the bus driver his flashing his headlights meant merely 'Come on so far as I am concerned'. Having stopped he was under no duty to do anything else and the flashing of the headlights was not a representation that it was clear for the car driver to pull out beyond the offside of the bus. Nor was the bus driver under a duty to give a signal to the moped rider. With regard to the first defendant, the judge's finding that he was moving very, very slowly and that he could not have done more justified his being acquitted of negligence.

Note—In a dissenting judgment, Russell LJ said the car driver should have stopped with only the tip of his bonnet showing beyond the bus as an indication to overtaking traffic of his presence and should then have paused and listened for any horn sounding before going any further out. He would have held him 20% to blame. The other members of the court also felt there was a good deal of difficulty in finding no blame on the part of the driver but were unwilling to hold that there was anything more the driver could do once the judge's finding was accepted that he came out very, very slowly. In *Worsfold v Howe* (at para [9.68]) the Court of Appeal held that *Clarke v Winchurch* laid down no principle of law.

[9.66] Harding v Hinchcliffe

(1964) Times, 8 April, CA

The claimant was riding his motorcycle to school along a class B road when he came up behind a bus travelling in the same direction. The bus driver signalled his intention to turn left into a minor road. The claimant, wishing to continue along the main road, overtook the bus as it was turning. He was hit by the defendant's car which came out of the minor road as the bus turned into it. The defendant had stopped at the mouth of the lane, intending to turn right into the main road. He had seen the bus approaching for about 150 yards and had waited but when the bus driver showed he was now going to turn into the lane the defendant had driven out. He had not seen the claimant, who had been masked by the bus until the moment of collision, nor had the claimant seen the defendant. The judge held that the defendant had not been negligent, since he could not have anticipated a motorcyclist being masked by the bus for all that time and distance.

HELD, ON APPEAL: Coming out from a lane into a major road the defendant ought to have waited the few extra seconds necessary to let the bus get completely into the lane because there was always the possibility of a vehicle being masked by the bus. The proper inference was that he was negligent and the boy was not negligent at all.

[9.67] MacIntyre v Coles

[1966] 1 All ER 723, [1966] 1 WLR 831, 130 JP 189, 110 Sol Jo 315, CA

On a Sunday morning in pouring rain the defendant was driving a heavy lorry along Spon End in the city of Coventry towards a Y junction where The Butts forked off to the right and Spon Street to the left. He intended bearing right into The Butts. There were no road signs indicating the relative importance of these streets but the defendant passed along this route regularly and knew that traffic entering Spon End from Spon Street on his left usually paused at the mouth of Spon Street where there was a 'Keep Left' sign. The claimant's husband who did not know the district was riding a motorcycle along Spon Street towards the junction intending to bear right into Spon End along which the defendant was approaching. The claimant's husband rode out of Spon Street across the path of the defendant's lorry, which was taking the right fork into The Butts, and was struck by it and killed. The judge held the defendant to be free from blame.

HELD, ON APPEAL: The claimant could not succeed. The defendant had given a proper signal that he was turning right, had seen the claimant's husband and was proceeding round in the ordinary way. Although it was most unfortunate there were no road signs to indicate how traffic should manoeuvre, the configuration of the road and the 'Keep Left' sign in the mouth of Spon Street did indicate that traffic on Spon End should have priority. Moreover the deceased had the lorry coming from his right: it is a well-recognised and conventional practice that where there is a doubt as to priority, the vehicle which has the other on its right-hand side is the give-way vehicle.

Note—Lang v London Transport Executive (at para [9.130]) was not cited.
  The alleged 'well recognised and conventional practice' of giving way to vehicles on the right was said not to exist by Streatfield J but this, like *Lang's* case, was apparently not brought to the attention of the court.

[9.68]   Worsfold v Howe
[1980] 1 All ER 1028, [1980] 1 WLR 1175

The defendant wished to drive his car out of a minor road and turn right into the southbound carriageway of a major road. Due to heavy traffic a petrol tanker had stopped leaving a gap in front. The defendant's view of traffic in the northbound lane was obscured due to the position of the tanker. The defendant began to edge forward and inch past the tanker.

The front of the defendant's vehicle had reached about between one to two feet beyond the tanker when the claimant motorcyclist who was travelling within the right hand lane collided with the defendant's vehicle. The trial judge held both the claimant and defendant responsible as the claimant was travelling too quickly to stop or avoid the collision. The defendant was responsible as he proceeded beyond his line of vision. The judge said that he was bound by the authority of *Clarke v Winchurch* (at para [9.65]) and had to absolve the defendant from any liability as he had discharged his duty to other drivers by inching out.

The claimant appealed and the Court of Appeal held that there was no principle of law which entitled a driver to emerge blind from a minor road onto a major road by inching forward beyond his line of vision, even if he did so slowly. The appeal was allowed with judgment apportioned equally between the claimant and defendant.

[9.69]   Hamied v Eastwick
1 November 1994, CA   Bingham MR, Hobhouse, Morritt LJJ

The claimant was travelling along the main Streatham Road. The defendant was attempting to turn right into Streatham Road from Lynx Road in the direction from which the claimant was travelling.

The claimant could remember nothing of the incident. There were no independent witnesses. The defendant was, therefore, the only witness and provided the police, his advisers, and the court three different versions of events. The claimant did not challenge the finding that he must have been travelling between 35–40mph. The speed limit was 30mph. There was no evidence that the claimant had braked prior to the collision. Doing the best he could the judge found that the defendant drove out of the minor road, possibly paused, and then started moving forward again, slowly and not taking very long. The judge found the defendant primarily liable and the claimant 20% contributory negligent. The claimant appealed on the finding of contributory negligence.

HELD, ON APPEAL: The judge was fully entitled to come to the decision that he did. The fact that the claimant was exceeding the speed limit did not, necessarily, point to negligence but it is necessary to consider all the circumstances. Streatham Road was in a built up area and a main road carrying a lot of traffic with a number of side roads. A prudent driver must bear in mind the real possibility that someone may emerge from the side road, even one which provides that the driver should stop and give way. By driving faster than he should have done in the circumstances the claimant deprived himself of the time and opportunity to take avoiding action by braking or swerving in front of the defendant's vehicle.

Appeal dismissed.

[9.70] **Kenfield Motors Ltd v Hayles and Reece**
[1998] 1 CL 429
8 October 1997, Uxbridge County Court

The claimant was driving along a main road and intended to turn right into a side road. He crossed to the wrong side of the road 40 yards before the junction intending to pass the entrance to the side road and reversed into it.

As the claimant's driver passed the entrance to the side road the defendant pulled out and collided with the claimant's vehicle. The defendant had looked to the left briefly and did not recall seeing the claimant's vehicle. He then looked to the right for four to five seconds before turning his head again to the left as he pulled out into the junction.

HELD: The claimant's driver must bear some responsibility for the accident having undertaken a dangerous manoeuvre. However the defendant had not looked sufficiently to the left before pulling out. The district judge apportioned blame on a two-thirds/one-third basis in the claimant's favour.

[9.71] **Downes v (1) Crane (2) Villers**
(13 December 1999, unreported)   Beldam LJ, Ward LJ

The claimant was driving along a road with the first defendant travelling towards him in the opposite direction. The second defendant turned right into the path of the first defendant's vehicle. The first defendant braked to prevent his vehicle from colliding with the second defendant's vehicle. The first defendant lost control, and skidded onto the claimant's side of the road resulting in a head-on collision. The judge found the second defendant wholly responsible. The second defendant appealed.

HELD, ON APPEAL: The Court of Appeal said that the judge should have asked himself: when the second defendant emerged from the side road, was the first defendant a sufficient distance away that a reasonable driver keeping a proper lookout would have been able to brake without losing control? The court found that the evidence suggested that had the first defendant been keeping a proper lookout it would not have been necessary for him to brake so hard and skid across the road into the path of the claimant's vehicle. Therefore the first defendant was negligent. However, the second defendant's actions were more causative and as such liability was apportioned 25% against the first defendant with the second defendant being found 75% liable.

(C) TURNING INTO MINOR ROAD

[9.72] Simpson v Peat
[1952] 2 QB 24, [1952] 1 All ER 447, [1952] 1 TLR 469, 96 Sol Jo 132, Div Ct

The driver of a motor car on a main road turned to enter a road on his offside and a collision occurred with a motorcyclist coming in the opposite direction. He was prosecuted for driving without due care and attention. The justices found that the defendant had committed an error of judgment in thinking he had left room for the motorcyclist to get through. The defendant contended he could not be guilty for a mere error of judgment, and was acquitted. The prosecutor appealed.

HELD: The expression 'error of judgment' was not a term of art and was of the vaguest possible description. It could mean either a negligent act or one which, though mistaken, is not negligent. A driver might not be using due care and attention although his lack of care may be due to something which could be described as an error of judgment. If he is driving without due care and attention it is immaterial what caused him to do so. The question was whether he was exercising that degree of care and attention which a reasonable and prudent driver would exercise in the circumstances. The question was one of fact and not of law. On the facts, the defendant was cutting across the line of traffic coming from the opposite direction. It was for him to take care that he could execute the manoeuvre in safety.

Case remitted to justices with a direction to convict.

[9.73] Patel v Edwards
[1970] RTR 425, CA

At a crossroads in town the claimant on a pedal cycle wished to turn off the main road into the minor road on his right. He looked behind him and saw a car signalling a left turn and slowing down. He moved towards the centre of the road to make his turn just as the defendant, on a motorcycle, overtook the car, which was then almost stationary. The defendant ran into the claimant knocking him on to the pavement on the far corner. The claimant had not seen the defendant, nor did the defendant see the claimant until he came out in front of him; by that time the defendant was already level with the rear side window of the car. The trial judge said the parties were equally to blame; the claimant for his failure to make absolutely certain that it was safe to cross by coming out gently, the defendant overtaking the car when he could not see what was happening ahead of it.

HELD, ON APPEAL: The blame should be apportioned two-thirds to the claimant, one-third to the defendant. The judge had not given sufficient weight to the factor that the pedal cyclist was moving in front of a substantially stationary car across a main and important road. Anyone making such a move must naturally take special care to see that he does not get into the path of other traffic. Failure to take such care imports a high degree of culpability.

[9.74]   **Challoner v Williams and Croney**

[1975] 1 Lloyd's Rep 124, CA

At night on an unlighted road Williams was driving the first of three cars, the other two being driven by friends whom he was leading. He discovered he had taken the wrong route and, seeing a turning on the right, put on his offside indicator. He slowed and moved towards the centre of the road. He looked in his mirror when he first indicated and looked in the mirror again before turning. He began to turn right without actually stopping. When he was about halfway across the offside half of the road, his car was struck by a car driven by Croney which had overtaken both the other cars, Croney not having seen Williams's car ahead until too late. The judge held both drivers equally to blame: he said Williams should have satisfied himself that there was no car overtaking the other two and should have stopped before crossing the offside half of the road.

HELD, ON APPEAL: Williams had done nothing wrong; Croney was wholly to blame.

(D)   BRAKE LIGHTS AND HAND SIGNALS

[9.75]   **Flack v Withers**

(1960) Times, 22 March (reported on another point at [1961] 3 All ER 388, HL), CA

The infant claimant was riding his pedal cycle behind a car driven by the defendant, W, when the latter pulled up to allow the defendant, S, to pass him in the opposite direction. The claimant ran into the rear bumper of W's car, was thrown to the right and was hit by S's car, sustaining severe injuries. W gave evidence that he looked into his inside mirror but not the wing mirror as he was slowing down, but did not see the claimant or any other traffic. His car was fitted with the usual red lights at the back which came on as soon as any pressure was applied to the brake pedal. He had not regarded a hand signal as necessary in the circumstances particularly having regard to his slow speed. At the trial the jury found W 17% to blame for the accident.

HELD, ON APPEAL: There was no evidence to support a finding of negligence against W. A driver would not give more than an occasional glance into his driving mirror. As to the lack of hand signal, W's car was fitted with the usual red lights at the back. It was difficult to accept the view that that might properly be regarded by a jury as evidence of want of care on W's part. The onus of proof on the claimant had not been discharged.

Note—The 2006 edition of the Highway Code at para 85 accepts that brake light signals can be used to mean 'I am slowing down or stopping'.

[9.76]   **Moss v Dixon**

(19 March 1998, unreported), CA

The claimant was cycling along a normal road. Her intention was to turn right into a track. On her evidence she signalled to turn right, moved to the centre of the road and then cycled a further 50 yards down the road to the junction intending to turn right but without maintaining her hand signals. The defendant overtook her on the offside and there was a collision. The defendant contended that the claimant had been in the centre or nearside of her lane and had pulled out, intending to turn right, without any hand signals.

The judge found the defendant wholly liable and did not consider that the claimant had been contributorily negligent. The defendant appealed.

HELD, ON APPEAL: The judge was entitled to prefer the claimant's evidence. In accordance with the Highway Code, paras 193 and 198 the claimant was only obliged to signal and look behind her during the course of the manoeuvre from the nearside to the centre of the road. Once at the centre of the road the paragraphs did not apply and the claimant would be concentrating on her intention of crossing the oncoming line of traffic. The claimant's position in the road would have made it obvious to the defendant that it was the claimant's intention to turn right.

(E)   MISLEADING SIGNALS

[9.77]   Pratt v Bloom
(1958) Times, 21 October, Div Ct

Per Streatfield J: The duty of a driver changing direction is:
  (1)   to signal; and
  (2)   to see that no one was inconvenienced by his change of direction and the duty is greater if he first gives a wrong signal and then changes it.

[9.78]   Another v Probert
[1968] Crim LR 564, Div Ct

The defendant was driving a car along a main road: the 'left turn' indicator was flashing. A police car waiting in a side turning moved out into the main road in reliance on the flashing signal. The defendant drove straight on, colliding with the police car. He defended a charge of careless driving on the ground that the police driver should not have relied on the indicator signal.

HELD: On the prosecutor's appeal, it was careless driving to give misleading signals; the justices must convict.

The Highway Code (2006), para 146 says 'You should … not assume, when waiting at a junction, that a vehicle coming from the right and signalling left will actually turn, wait and make sure'.

(F)   TRAVELLING IN THE WRONG LANE

[9.79]   Grace v Tanner
[2003] EWCA Civ 354
[2003] All ER (D) 377 (Feb)

The claimant was riding a motorcycle southwards on the A23. The A23 is a dual carriageway which has two lanes.
  The claimant was in the outside lane and the defendant in the inside lane. Both vehicles entered the roundabout, and retained their lane positions. The defendant inadvertently went past the required exit and instead of attempting a sharp left-hand turn carried on.
  The claimant who thought that the defendant was intending to leave the roundabout at that exit attempted to turn left and collided with the defendant's

vehicle. The judge found the claimant at fault and the claimant appealed, as the court did not make a finding of contributory negligence.

HELD, ON APPEAL: Both parties were to blame. The defendant was to blame in that although by going past her intended exit by mistake this was not negligent, she was negligent in failing to take account of the potential danger she presented to other road users. Therefore as the defendant was unaware of the claimant, and failed to become aware of her until it was too late she was liable.

Appeal allowed with liability apportioned 50/50.

7.   LIGHTING OF VEHICLES

[9.80]   Note—Paragraph 93 of the Highway Code (2006) states that you must:
1.   Use headlights at night, except on restricted roads (those with street lights not more than 185 metres (600 feet) apart and which are generally subject to a speed limit of 30mph).
2.   Use headlights where visibility is seriously reduced.
3.   Ensure all sidelights and rear registration plate lights are lit at night.
Paragraph 94 states that you must not:
1.   Use any lights which would dazzle or cause discomfort to other road users.
2.   Use front or rear fog lights unless visibility is seriously reduced. You must switch them off when visibility improves to avoid dazzling other users.
Paragraph 95 states that you should also:
1.   Use dipped headlights, or dim-dip if fitted, at night in built up areas and in dull daytime weather, to ensure that you can be seen.
2.   Keep your headlights dipped when overtaking until you are level with the other vehicle and then change to main beam if necessary, unless this would dazzle oncoming traffic.
3.   Slow down, and if necessary stop, if you are dazzled by oncoming headlights.

(A)   LIGHTS ON VEHICLES

[9.81]   **Sieghart v British Transport Commission**
(1956) 106 L Jo 185   Finnemore J

On a dark and rainy night the defendant's driver stopped his lorry for the purpose of adjusting his windscreen wiper. He stopped on a straight length of road with a visibility of not less than 20 to 30 yards and parked correctly on his nearside. The driver did not know and had no reason to suspect that at the time his rear lamp was unlit. The lorry had been checked at the depot a few miles back. Having glanced in both directions and seen that no traffic was approaching the driver descended from his cab. As he reached up to move the windscreen wiper, the car driven by the claimant struck the back of the lorry and he and his wife, the second claimant, received injuries.

HELD: The statement regarding stopping at night in the Highway Code (p 65 in 1978 edition) 'see that your side and tail lamps are alight' did not require that a driver who was stopping only for a minute or two and had no reason to suspect that his lamps were not alight should, immediately after stopping, examine the vehicle's rear lights. In the circumstances the lorry driver was not guilty of negligence and had not created a nuisance on the highway. Judgment for defendants.

Note—See the Highway Code (2006).

[9.82]   **Chisman v Electromotion (Export) Ltd**

(1969) 6 KIR 456, 113 Sol Jo 246, CA

In the hours of darkness on a straight main road the defendant's lorry was parked on the wrong side of the road with its headlights on. It was visible 700 yards away. The claimant driving a Mini struck the lorry full tilt. The judge said it was a case of almost maximum negligence on the part of both parties and apportioned liability equally.

HELD, ON APPEAL: The court declined to alter the judge's decision. The attempt to plead that the claimant should be found wholly to blame was just one more attempt to bring into the law the doctrine of last opportunity. The court would decline to administer the kiss of life to that doctrine. To put a lorry with its lights on on the wrong side of the road was plain and obvious negligence. There was also negligence on the part of the claimant. The court had the power to apportion the damages if it was satisfied that the apportionment was wrong but started with the presumption that the judge was right. In this case he was.

[9.83]   **Saville v Bache**

(1969) 113 Sol Jo 228, Times, 28 February, CA

The first defendant was driving along an unlighted B road at night, using dipped headlights. The second defendant was approaching in the opposite direction, also on dipped headlights. When he was about 100 yards from the first defendant he (as the judge found) turned his headlights on to main beam. The first defendant was dazzled and collided with the claimant whom he had not seen and who was standing with his bicycle at the side of the road. The second defendant denied that he had put his headlights on full beam; he said they were dipped all the time. The judge, rejecting his evidence, held him one-third to blame. The second defendant appealed.

HELD: Dismissing his appeal, it was good manners and good driving to approach another vehicle with headlights dipped. There could be circumstances when a driver had to put his lights on full beam but the second defendant was negligent unless he had a good reason for doing so. He had not given a reason; he had merely denied it.

[9.84]   **Burgess v Hearn**

(1965) Guardian, 25 March, CA

The claimant, riding a motorcycle combination, was injured when he collided with the offside wing of the defendant's car, which was travelling in the opposite direction. The accident happened in thick fog with visibility of 10 to 15 yards. The claimant was travelling at 25mph and the defendant at 15mph. The claimant had a dipped headlight on but the defendant was showing sidelights only. There had been a collision shortly before on the claimant's side of the road between a van and a car. The claimant ignored the wave of a man who had come to wave people down and had to swerve round the car and then pass the van. It was at this point when the bulk of his motorcycle was on the wrong side of the road that he saw the defendant's car at very short range. The judge found the parties equally to blame, holding the defendant negligent for not having his headlights on and the claimant for his speed and for blindly pulling out on to the wrong side of the road.

HELD, ON APPEAL by the defendant: The judge was justified in finding the defendant negligent in not having dipped headlights on. He referred to para 111 of the

Highway Code (1978) which recommended headlights in mist or fog and although not of statutory force it was of assistance in assessing proper road usage. Moreover, there was evidence at trial that it was police policy to use headlights in foggy conditions. There was also evidence from witnesses at the trial who had confirmed that they were using dipped headlights.

However, the court held that even if the defendant had his headlights on it would not have prevented the accident as the claimant would not have been able to see the defendant's headlights in any event.

Appeal allowed.

[9.85]   *Note*—As from 30 April 1972 all rules and regulations relating to parking without lights were standardised. Cars and goods vehicles not exceeding 1,525 kg unladen, invalid carriages and motorcycles may be parked without lights on a road provided that:

(a)   the road is subject to a speed limit of 30mph or less;

(b)   the vehicle is parked at least 10m (32ft) away from any junction, close to the kerb and facing in the direction of the flow of traffic; or

(c)   in a recognised parking place.

Other vehicles and trailers, and all vehicles with projecting loads, must not be left on a road at night without lights.

The current regulations are contained in the Road Vehicles Lighting Regulations 1989, SI 1989/1796 and at paras 213–226 of the Highway Code (2006).

For the lighting-up time at any particular place and date, apply to: Nautical Almanac Office, Space Science and Technology Dept, Rutherfod Appleton Laboratory, Chilton, Didcot, OX11 OQX (tel: 01235 446 503; fax: 01235 446 667) marked 'Attention HM Nautical Almanac Office'.

(B)   FAILURE OF LIGHTS

[9.86]   Henley v Cameron

[1948] WN 468, [1949] LJR 989, 65 TLR 17, CA

The defendant's car ran out of petrol on the road from Market Drayton to Newcastle about midnight. By 1 am the batteries had run down and there were no lights on the car. The road was 19ft wide with a three-inch kerb and a 5ft grass verge in a cutting with hedges and trees 15ft high. The car was left with its rear near wheel close to the kerb and front near wheel about 1ft out, the front wheels being turned in slightly to the offside. There was a turning into a lane 20 or 30 yards away. Lighting up time was 4.20 pm to 7.50 am. At about 6 am the deceased riding a motorcycle combination collided with the car. A police officer said the car could have been placed in the mouth of the lane or on the verge. Henn Collins J found the deceased alone to blame.

HELD, ON APPEAL, per Tucker LJ: The defendant was negligent in leaving the car unlighted in that position in the hours of darkness when it could have been moved, and said that the car constituted a nuisance. The absence of a light was *prima facie* a cause contributing to the accident. The fact that a car driver runs into a stationary unlighted vehicle does not establish that he is solely to blame. It is a question of fact depending on the particular circumstances.

Per Singleton LJ: There was evidence from two witnesses of the difficulty seeing a car in that position. The negligence of both parties continued up to the time of the accident.

HELD by a majority: Liability was apportioned: defendant – two-thirds; deceased – one-third to blame.

[9.87]   Hill-Venning v Beszant

[1950] 2 All ER 1151, 49 LGR 12, 94 Sol Jo 760, 66 (pt 2) TLR 921, CA

A motorcyclist was riding along the road from Guildford to Farnham when his lights failed. He thought it would only mean changing the bulb in the headlight, but discovered that the tail light was also out, and that there was a fault in the electric wiring. Still thinking the fault could be quickly repaired, he did not move his motorcycle, which was standing with its offside some three feet from a wide grass verge. The road was wide and straight and he would have had no difficulty in removing it on to the verge which was level with the highway. While repairing the wiring, he observed some five minutes after stopping, the light of a vehicle coming from behind, which was the dipped headlight of the claimant's motorcycle. The claimant failed to see the defendant's motorcycle in time to avoid it. It was not disputed that the claimant was negligent, but the claimant contended that the defendant was negligent in not removing the motorcycle on to the grass verge and leaving an obstacle on the road. Parker J held the defendant had not been guilty of negligence. The claimant appealed.

Per Cohen LJ: It might not have been negligent not to have moved the motorcycle merely to change the bulb, but when he found the breakdown in the electric wiring, it was his duty to move it on to the grass verge, and when he saw a light and knew a vehicle was coming, he should have taken the precaution of moving it off the road. A court has to be very careful before taking the view that there is no negligence in leaving an obstacle on the road after lighting up time when it is not plainly visible to approaching vehicles without the aid of full headlights and when it could easily be moved off the road. I think the defendant was responsible to the extent of one-third.

Per Denning LJ: It is clear beyond controversy that his unlighted motorcycle was a danger on the road. Any unlighted bicycle on a fast motor road is a danger to traffic. This is a proposition not of law, but of common sense. It is *prima facie* evidence of negligence and the onus is on him to show how it came to be unlighted and why he could not move it out of the way or give warning to on-coming traffic. I should have been inclined to apportion the responsibility two-thirds to the unlighted vehicle as in *Henley v Cameron*, but in deference to my brothers I do not dissent from the proportions suggested by Cohen LJ.

Appeal allowed.

[9.88]   Moore v Maxwells of Emsworth Ltd

[1968] 2 All ER 779, [1968] 1 WLR 1077, 112 Sol Jo 424, CA

On a clear evening in the hours of darkness the defendant's lorry was being driven along an unlit dual-track road by their driver when a passing motorist signalled that there was something wrong. The driver stopped at the nearside of the road and found his rear light was out. In checking whether a plug was connected he fused all the obligatory lights. He began to repair the plug whilst his mate stood at the back of the lorry to warn approaching vehicles. The claimant failed to see the lorry until too late and crashed into the back of it. The defendant's driver had checked his lights before starting the journey and again at lighting-up time and found them working properly.

HELD: The defendant was not liable. The presence of an unlighted vehicle on the highway called for an explanation from the defendant and to that extent the onus of proof was on it, but the driver had given an explanation, namely, the failure of the lighting system. There was no further onus of proving regular servicing of the vehicle. Nor was the defendant negligent in not supplying torches or flashing warning lights, there being no evidence that it was customary to do so. The driver was not negligent in not driving on to the verge as it was soft and the lorry heavy. He acted reasonably in assuming it would not take long to mend the fuse rather than drive on with no lights to a place where there was street lighting.

Note—See also *Brown v Thompson* [1968] 2 All ER 708, [1968] 1 WLR 1003, 112 Sol Jo 464, CA and *Parish v Judd* (at para [9.97]). And see *Jordan v North Hampshire Plant Hire Ltd* (at para [9.92]).

[9.89]   Lee v Lever
[1974] RTR 35, CA

The claimant's car developed an electrical fault and as a result came to a stop at night by the nearside verge (to which the claimant had steered it) of a well-lighted road which was a clearway. There were no lights on the car; he took the battery to a garage on the other side of the road for recharging. Twenty minutes later the defendant driving his car at about 30mph did not see the claimant's car in time and crashed into the back of it. The county court judge held the claimant wholly to blame; he said the claimant had not discharged the onus of proof placed on him by Denning LJ's ruling in *Hill-Venning v Beszant* (at para [9.87]).

HELD, ON APPEAL: The claimant was negligent in failing to borrow a red lamp from the garage to put by his car and perhaps (as the county court judge held) for failing earlier to see the warning red light on the dashboard and failing to push the car to the verge; but the defendant was also to blame for not seeing the claimant's car in time to pull up. The proper proportions of blame were 50–50.

Per Buckley LJ: I do not think normal experience leads one to the conclusion that it is safe to assume that no one will ever park in a part of the roadway which is classified as a 'Clearway', and it is incumbent upon every user of such a roadway to drive in a way which enables him to meet an emergency or hazard presented by the fact that someone has parked – it may be for unavoidable reasons, such as a breakdown – in the 'Clearway'.

(C)   ILL-LIT LORRY ACROSS HIGHWAY

[9.90]   Harvey v Road Haulage Executive
[1952] 1 KB 120, 96 Sol Jo 759, CA

On a foggy morning in November 1949, shortly after sunrise, the defendant's lorry, 22ft long and 7ft wide was towed from a car park on to the highway in order to start the engine. The towing vehicle left, and the lorry remained standing with the engine running for about five minutes to warm up. The road was 30ft wide, divided into three 10ft strips by two white lines. The lorry was on the slant diagonal to the road, the near rear wheel being 5ft from the nearside kerb, the near front wheel 7ft from the kerb and the off-front wheel 14ft out into the road nearly half-way across, straddling across the nearside white line. Visibility only extended to 11 or 12 yards. The claimant was riding a motorcycle at 18 or 20mph along the nearside white line, came from behind, saw the lorry when within 11 or 12 yards and thought it was moving. It was impossible to overtake it on the offside, since he could not see a clear way through on-coming traffic. There was a dispute whether the red rear light was on, and without coming to a firm conclusion, the judge assumed the light was on. Slade J found the claimant was driving too fast in the fog and that he was also negligent in failing to avoid the impact when he had seen the lorry. He made no finding whether the lorry driver was also at fault in leaving the lorry in a dangerous position diagonal to the road. The position of the defendant's vehicle created a static position which the claimant could have avoided. He dismissed the action.

HELD, ON APPEAL: The lorry driver was at fault. He ought to have brought the lorry wholly within the nearside lane. If a motorist sees an obstruction on the road and purposely and recklessly runs into it, he could not recover, but if he were merely negligent in not taking steps to avoid the vehicle then both parties were equally to blame.

[9.91]   Barber v British Road Services
(1964) Times, 18 November, CA

The defendant's driver, stopping at a lorry drivers' cafe on the Oxford–Banbury road at 3 am on a dark and rainy morning, decided to turn his lorry round and back it into the car park. The lorry was 30ft long and the road 32ft wide. The manoeuvre took one and a half minutes and involved having the lorry at right angles covering the whole road in both directions. Whilst the lorry was across the road the claimant driving a lorry from Banbury failed to see it in time and crashed into it, sustaining serious injuries. The judge held that the defendant's driver was not negligent.

HELD, ON APPEAL: If at night there was an obstruction across a fast main road, that was *prima facie* evidence of negligence and it was up to the person who put it there to explain how it came there without negligence. The defendant's driver had not given any sufficient explanation. The length of time required to reverse a lorry of this size made the manoeuvre inevitably dangerous. The defendant was not entitled to assume that any person driving along that road at that time of night would be driving at a moderate speed and keeping a good look-out. Permanent lights showing sideways were contrary to the law but some temporary lateral light could have been shown either by torches carried by someone from the cafe or at the side of the vehicle. Blame should be apportioned as to two-thirds to the claimant and one-third to the defendants.

[9.92]   Jordan v North Hampshire Plant Hire Ltd
[1970] RTR 212, CA

After a stop at a cafe on the west side of a fast and busy main road in the hours of darkness the defendant's driver wished to resume his journey south. The lorry was an articulated vehicle 35ft long. It had a flashing light on the cab roof but no other lights showing to the side. There were three reflectors on the side of the trailer. The driver had to drive slowly across the road which had double white lines in the middle and then turn right using the grass verge on the other side to get enough room to make the turn. The manoeuvre would take 10 to 15 seconds during which the lorry would block the carriageway. The claimant, driving his car from the south at about 60mph approached the scene round a slight left hand bend which limited visibility to about 300 yards. He failed to see the lorry in time and struck the back end of the trailer. The county court judge found the two drivers equally to blame. The defendants appealed.

HELD, by the Court of Appeal: (1) It was quite wrong for the defendant's driver to have pulled into a cafe on his offside of the road when the curve was such that only rarely, if at all, could he pull out again without creating grave risks.

(2)   The lorry was quite insufficiently lit to give proper warning to a driver coming from the south. The flashing light might confuse, and at the time of the accident was in the other traffic lane; the three reflectors had swung round by the time the claimant arrived and would not show, and there was no other light which showed.

(3)   The lorry driver's mate could have flashed a torch as a warning. There have been changes in outlook since *Moore v Maxwells of Emsworth Ltd* (at para [9.88]) and the defendant was negligent in not using warning lights in such circumstances as the present.

The appeal was hopeless. The claimant (who had not cross-appealed) was unlucky to have had his damages docked by as much as one-half.

[9.93]   Butland v Coxhead

(1968) 112 Sol Jo 465, Times, 8 May   Browne J

The claimant, a learner, was riding a scooter on a clearway on the main London–Portsmouth road in the hours of darkness when he ran into the back of the defendant's stationary lorry. The lorry had broken down and could not be moved. Before the claimant's accident another vehicle had collided with the lorry's offside rear and damaged the rear lamp, but the lamp had been repaired and when the claimant ran into the lorry both rear lamps were on and visible from a reasonable distance.

HELD: The defendant was not liable. Though a stationary lorry, even with normal tail lights, was a danger to traffic on a fast road and on a bad night, the lorry could not move after it had broken down and the defendant was not negligent in not parking in a side road or on the verge. There was no evidence of a practice among lorry owners to provide torches or flashing lamps. The case of *Moore v Maxwells of Emsworth Ltd* (at para [9.88]) was stronger than the present case. It would be a very good thing if heavy lorries were required to carry some form of warning lamp but no regulations existed to that effect; there was no negligence on the part of the defendant.

[9.94]   Rouse v Squires

[1973] QB 889, [1973] 2 All ER 903, [1973] 2 WLR 925, 117 Sol Jo 431, CA

On the M1 motorway at night an articulated lorry driven by Allen got out of control and came to a stop in a position blocking the middle and fast lanes. A car collided with it in the centre lane and remained there with rear lights on. Another lorry stopped in the nearside lane short of Allen's lorry with its headlights on to illuminate the stationary vehicles. Squires then came along driving his employer's lorry, he saw the vehicles ahead when 400 yards away but did not realise two lanes were obstructed. At 150 yards away he saw the vehicle in the nearside lane, braked and moved into the centre lane. He then realised that lane was also blocked; he applied the brake harder, went into a skid and hit the lorry on the nearside, killing the claimant's husband who was standing in front of it. The judge held Squires wholly to blame; the fact that Allen caused an obstruction was not, bearing in mind the circumstances, a factor which contributed to the fatal accident.

HELD, ON APPEAL: There was no break in the chain of causation between the negligent driving of Allen and the death of the claimant's husband. If a driver so negligently manages his vehicle as to obstruct the highway and constitute a danger to other road users including those who are driving too fast or not keeping a proper look-out (but not those who deliberately or recklessly drive into an obstruction as in *Dymond v Pearce* [1972] 1 QB 496, [1972] 1 All ER 1142, then the first driver's negligence may be held to have contributed to the causation of the accident of which the immediate cause was the negligent driving of a vehicle which collided with it. Where a party guilty of prior negligence has created a dangerous situation which is still continuing to a substantial degree at the time of the accident which would not have happened but for the continuing danger he is responsible as well as the subsequently negligent party. Liability was apportioned with Allen held 25% to blame.

[9.95]   Lancaster v HB and H Transport Ltd
[1979] RTR 380, CA

The defendant's driver had to deliver a lorry load of potatoes to a farm on the east side of the A1 road. To do so he came to the A1 from the west on a side road and wished to cross to a road on the opposite side of the double carriageway. It was early on a February morning, still getting light. Mist reduced visibility to between 50 and 100 yards; the roadway was wet. The articulated lorry had its headlights on but only a small marker light and orange reflector on the side. It crossed the north-bound carriageway and stopped in the intersection to allow cars to pass before starting to cross the southbound carriageway. When he started forward the driver could see no headlights to his left but when part-way over he saw the headlights of a car approaching at quite a fast speed. He thought it best to continue; the car did not stop but crashed into and underneath the trailer. It left no brake marks. The car driver was killed. The lorry would take 12 seconds to cross the carriageway. The judge at first instance considered the lorry driver not to blame.

HELD, ON APPEAL: The lorry driver was negligent in taking the lorry across the A1 in such poor conditions of visibility. He knew that vehicles coming towards him and which he could not see – even 150 yards away at 30mph – would be on him before he could get clear of the carriageway. He could have found out, had he asked, that he could cross the A1 by slip roads and a bridge a couple of miles to the north. Allegations of contributory negligence on the grounds of excessive speed and the car driver's failure to brake were not adequately established by the defendant's evidence. It was too much to expect of the car driver that he should realise that disembodied headlights passing from the right to left across his front indicated no less than 50ft of a slow moving vehicle blocking the carriageway.

(D)   UNLIGHTED VEHICLE ON ROAD

[9.96]   Drew v Western Scottish Motor Traction Co
1947 SC 222, 1947 SLT 92

On a dark morning in December, just before daybreak and the end of lighting-up time, a bread van was delivering bread at a shop situated on a main road in a built-up area. The van was drawn up facing west close to the south kerb. Although its rear lamp was lit, it was completely obscured by the lower half of the open back door which folded downwards. An omnibus coming from the east ran into the back of the van and inflicted fatal injuries on a boy who was unloading bread. The court found the owners of the omnibus to blame in that their driver had failed to maintain a proper look-out, The van owners were also found liable in that they had allowed their vehicle to be on the road during lighting-up time with a rear light which was invisible to other road users. Liability was apportioned on a 50–50 basis.

[9.97]   Parish v Judd

[1960] 3 All ER 33, [1960] 1 WLR 867, 124 JP 444, 104 Sol Jo 664, CA

On a dark night at about 10 pm the defendant was driving along a main road when without negligence on his part the lighting system of his car failed completely. A passing lorry stopped and the driver offered him a tow to a service station. The defendant accepted and the lorry began to tow the defendant's car. Before reaching the service station the lorry driver stopped to see if the defendant was all right. He chose a place just beyond a street lamp, which illuminated the rear of the defendant's car. When the two vehicles had been stationary about a minute a car driven by the claimant's husband ran into the back of the defendant's car and the claimant, who was a passenger, was injured.

HELD: (1) The mere fact that an unlighted vehicle is found at night on a road is not sufficient to constitute a nuisance; there must also be some fault on the part of the person responsible for the vehicle.

   (2)   The presence on a dark road at night of a wholly unlit vehicle is *prima facie* evidence of negligence on the part of the person responsible for the vehicle.

   (3)   the whole basis of the claim, both in negligence and in nuisance, must be the existence of danger. On the facts, no danger was presented by the presence of the defendant's motor car on that road at that place at that time.

[9.98]   Fotheringham v Prudence

[1962] CLY 2036, CA

The defendant was driving a lorry after dark when a wheel came off. He had to draw in on the nearside of the road just past a bridge. There were no rear lights on the lorry and no reflectors. The nearest street lamp was 12 yards away on the other side of the road. The claimant riding a motorcycle at 10 to 12mph ran into the back of the stationary lorry and was injured. Elwes J found the defendant wholly to blame. The Court of Appeal refused to disturb the finding: there was ample evidence of negligence and causation and the claimant was not guilty of contributory negligence.

[9.99]   Hill v Phillips

(1963) 107 Sol Jo 890, CA

The claimant was injured when a car in which she was a passenger collided with a stationary trailer during the hours of darkness. The trailer had broken down and had been pushed by the driver of the towing lorry on to a 4ft 6in grass verge. As the trailer was 8ft wide it protruded 3ft 6in into the roadway. The lorry driver had gone in the lorry to find a garage and left the trailer unlighted. The driver of the car, driving with dipped headlights at 30mph, did not see the trailer until he was a car's length away. The judge held the lorry driver wholly to blame, saying that a motorist was not negligent if he did not see what was not visible.

On appeal, the drivers were held equally to blame. The car driver was plainly negligent in failing to keep a proper look-out. When driving with dipped headlights in country roads motorists should drive so that they can see unlighted obstructions. Although unlighted obstructions should not be on country roads their presence was to be anticipated, eg cyclists without lights or men in dark clothes.

The lorry driver was negligent in leaving an unlighted obstruction which was a danger to oncoming traffic. He should have done something to illuminate the trailer; he could have left the lorry behind it with the lights on. It might be that drivers of heavy lorries should have lamps with them as a precaution in case their lights failed.

[9.100]   Young v Chester
[1974] RTR 70, CA

The defendant was driving his car on a fast, wide road at night when the engine stopped and he came to a standstill by the nearside verge but not on it. He then attempted to re-start the engine by operating the self-starter. The claimant driving his van in the nearside lane from the same direction at 45 to 50mph saw the two rear lights of the defendant's car when he was about 400 yards away and they seemed to him to disappear. He thought the car must have turned off on to a slip road. He did not see it again until he was quite close. He applied his brakes heavily but struck the car, pushing it 57ft. The judge concluded that the apparent disappearance of the car's rear lights was due to the defendant's use of the self-starter, causing the lights to dim or go out and that the defendant was 60% to blame.

HELD, ON APPEAL by the defendant: The judge was entitled to find as he did.

[9.101]   Hannam v Mann
[1984] RTR 252, CA

The claimant, riding a motorcycle in the hours of darkness, followed a car out of a side road turning left into a well-lit major road. When in the major road the car's offside traffic indicator light came on. The claimant, watching the car and thinking it about to turn right, took his eyes momentarily off the road ahead and crashed into the defendant's car parked without lights against the nearside kerb. The car driver was not turning right; he was merely indicating to show that he was moving out to pass the defendant's car. Although the defendant's car was illuminated by a street lamp opposite it was illegally parked since it was only five yards from a road junction, contrary to the Road Vehicles Lighting (Standing Vehicles) (Exemption) General Regulations 1975, reg 4. The judge found the defendant 25% to blame on the ground that if the rear lights of his car had been on they might just have drawn the claimant's attention to the car and enabled him to avoid it. The defendant appealed.

HELD: The appeal should be dismissed. The car, was unlit and in the position where it constituted a nuisance. The judge had asked himself the right question, would the accident have been avoided if the car had been lit? He was entitled to draw the inference that it might and it would be wrong to interfere with that decision or, alter the assessment of blame.

Note—The Road Vehicles Lighting (Standing Vehicles) (Exemption) General Regulations 1975 have been superseded by the Road Vehicles Lighting Regulations 1989, SI 1989/1796. See also paras 222–224 of the Highway Code (2006).

8.   NEGLIGENT PARKING/OPENING DOOR OF VEHICLE

[9.102]   **Waller v Levoi**
(1968) 112 Sol Jo 865, Times, 16 October, CA

The defendant was driving his car on a main road in daylight when he came to a left-handed bend where a side road went off to the left. He had been intending to turn off on to the side road but missed it and went beyond it a little way. He stopped at the kerb on the nearside of the bend to look back at the signpost and his car was run into from behind by the claimant on a motorcycle. The county court judge found the claimant 80% to blame and the defendant 20%.

HELD, ON APPEAL: The judge's apportionment of blame should stand. The claimant was negligent in failing to see the car in time. The defendant was to blame in stopping on the bend. It was a distinct bend though not sharp; he could have driven on to a straight part of the road and walked back to see the signpost. A car parked on a bend should not cause danger to a person driving carefully but one also owed a duty to careless drivers. A motorist who drove too fast or was temporarily inadvertent could be put in difficulty by a car parked on a bend.

[9.103]   **Rugg v Marriott**
(6 October 1999, unreported), CA   Otton LJ, Mummery LJ, Simon Brown LJ

The defendant's vehicle broke down on the road and the defendant tried to push it to a garage but was unable to do so. He then left it between two lamp posts on the left-hand side of the road, locked it and went home. The vehicle was clearly visible from a distance of approximately 300 metres.

The claimant was riding his motorbike home in the same direction in which the defendant's vehicle had been pushed. He collided with the stationary vehicle and suffered grave head injuries. The county court judge found the claimant 70% to blame and the defendant 30% to blame.

HELD, ON APPEAL: The defendant was in no way negligent and the judgment against the defendant was set aside. The question was if the possibility of the danger of the car being parked in that position was reasonably apparent, then to take no precautions was negligent, but if the possibility of the danger was only a mere possibility, which would never occur to the mind of a reasonable man, then there is no negligence in not having taken extraordinary precautions. The possibility of danger emanating from the position of the parked car was not reasonably apparent, it was only a mere possibility.

[9.104]   **Chop Seng Heng v Thevannasan s/o Sinnapan**
[1975] 3 All ER 572, [1976] RTR 193, PC

At 3 am on a winding road in rather misty conditions A was driving his employer's lorry when he required to stop. He chose a spot about 30ft beyond the exit from a blind left-hand bend. He parked the lorry at the nearside with its lights on. There was plenty of room for other vehicles to pass. B drove a lorry round the bend at about 25mph and crashed into the back of A's lorry, causing severe injuries to the claimant, a passenger in B's lorry. The judge at first instance held A 75% to blame and B 25%. On appeal the Federal Court held by a majority that B was wholly to blame. The dissenting member considered A wholly to blame.

HELD, ON APPEAL to the Privy Council: (1) The proposition that a driver who parks a vehicle at night with its lights on where there is room to pass cannot be guilty of negligence is unacceptable. A was to blame for parking too close to the corner. *Waller v Levoi* (at para [9.102]) applied.

(2)   B was also to blame for taking the bend too fast. Had he been travelling more slowly the impact would have been less heavy and the claimant's injuries less severe.

(3)   As the judge at first instance had not misdirected himself when apportioning blame his 75:25 apportionment should be restored.

[9.105]   Stevens v Kelland

[1970] RTR 445   Waller J

In a quiet street V left his van parked on the inside of a bend without lights. C, without noticing the van, parked his car on the outside of the bend near a street lamp a short distance to the north of the van. The gap between the two vehicles, measured along the road, was about 20 feet. S, riding a scooter from the south, saw V's van on his offside and C's car on his nearside and also saw a car driven by Z approaching from the opposite direction on its correct side of the centre line. S saw he could pass C's car safely without himself crossing the centre line and carried on. Z did not see S until he, Z, had pulled over the centre line to pass through the gap. He collided with the scooter as it was passing C's car, jamming it against the car and severely injuring the pillion rider.

HELD: (1) S was not to blame because by the time Z pulled over to pass through the gap he could do nothing to avoid the accident.

(2)   Z was mainly to blame because he had not seen S in time; he should not have pulled over without ensuring that it was safe to do so.

(3)   V and C were each partly to blame; V for having parked his van near the elbow of the bend where it blocked the view and was a potential cause of danger, C because by parking his car where he did without noticing the van he had created a hazard.

(4)   Apportionment of blame was 60% to Z and 20% each to V and C.

[9.106]   Watson v Heslop

[1971] RTR 308, 115 Sol Jo 308, CA

The defendant parked his car by the nearside kerb of a busy main road 22ft wide in the hours of darkness. There were no street lights and no speed restrictions. He turned out the lights of the car except for a parking light on the offside. The claimant driving his car at 40mph with dipped headlights failed to see the defendant's car because of the dazzling headlights of approaching traffic and drove straight into it from the rear. The judge of assize held the defendant solely to blame.

HELD, ON APPEAL by the defendant: He was negligent in parking his car where traffic was passing at speed in both directions: he could foresee that a stationary car might well put traffic in a difficulty. But the claimant was also to blame. When he found himself dazzled by approaching headlights he should at once have slowed down to a very slow pace in case there should be someone or something in his path. Moreover, if he had been keeping a proper look-out he should have seen the parking light. He was 30% to blame.

Per Sachs LJ: The defendant should have put his car at least partly on the footway. A parking light was not as good as normal lights.

[9.107] **Lemon v Ilfield & Barrett Roofing Ltd**

(24 March 1998, unreported), Guildford County Court

The defendant parked on a dual carriageway to ask for directions. The weather was fine and the road was clear and the vehicle was partially obstructing the near-side lane. The claimant drove into the rear of the defendant's van. There was a gap of approximately 20 seconds between the defendant's vehicle stopping and the accident occurring. The defendant was not displaying his hazard warning lights.

HELD: The claimant was primarily responsible for the accident. The judge found the defendant 10% liable for not displaying his hazard warning lights.

[9.108] *Note*—Claims for damages for personal injuries or for damage to passing vehicles caused by the opening of the offside door of a stationary car are extremely common but, perhaps because the negligence is self evident, they rarely result in a reported decision. For examples where a passenger was to blame, see *Brown v Roberts* [1965] 1 QB 1, [1963] 2 All ER 263, [1963] 3 WLR 75, 107 Sol Jo 666, [1963] 1 Lloyd's Rep 314.

Prosecutions were at one time laid under the Highway Act 1835, s 77 or 78. They are now brought under the Road Vehicles (Construction and Use) Regulations 1986, SI 1986 No 1078, reg 105 which provides:

'No person shall open or cause or permit to be opened any door of a motor vehicle or trailer on a road so as to cause injury or danger to any person.'

The regulation does not give a right of action to a person injured by the breach – see *Barkway v South Wales Transport Co Ltd* [1950] 1 All ER 392 and *Phillips v Britannia Hygienic Laundry Co* [1923] 1 KB 539; affd [1923] 2 KB 832, 93 LJKB 5, 129 LT 777, 39 TLR 530, 68 Sol Jo 102, CA. For a case in which justices were held on a prosecutor's appeal to the divisional courts to have been entitled to hold that there was a doubt whether opening a car door had caused danger, see *Sever v Duffy* [1977] RTR 429.

[9.109] **Atkins v Metropolitan Police**

8 February 1994, London Crown Court   Philpott J

The driver, after parking in a hurry on the Kings Road, opened her door wide enough to get her foot out. The motorcyclist collided with the door. The car driver was convicted of an offence under the Road Traffic Act 1972 as amended by reg 125 of the Road Vehicles (Construction and Use) Regulations 1978, SI 1978/1017. (This offence is now covered by the Road Vehicles (Construction and Use) Regulations 1986, SI 1986/1078, reg 105.)

The car driver appealed the decision on the basis that the motorcyclist was driving too close to the car on the basis of the decision in *Sever v Duffy* [1977] RTR 429. The car driver's appeal failed. She was at fault although she had not shown 'thoughtlessness'.

9. TRAFFIC LIGHTS

[9.110] *Note*—The current regulations providing for traffic light signals are the Traffic Signs Regulations and General Directions 1981, SI 1981/859, of which reg 31 describes the size, colour and type and reg 34 sets out their significance.

(A) VEHICLE CROSSING AGAINST RED LIGHT

[9.111] Eva Ltd v Reeves
[1938] 2 KB 393, [1938] 2 All ER 115, CA

At a crossing controlled by traffic lights, R approached on his offside at 25 to 30mph and lights changed to green when he was 20 to 30 yards away. The nearside was occupied by traffic and R passed these vehicles on offside of road just as they were starting to move. A van was crossing from his left against the red lights. R could not avoid collision.

HELD: R was not negligent. He owed no duty to traffic crossing against the red light beyond a duty, if in fact he saw such traffic, to take reasonable care to avoid a collision. He was entitled to assume no traffic would be crossing against the lights and could therefore overtake on offside provided no danger to traffic in opposite direction or to traffic turning right. The Traffic Signs Regulations provide that the red signal shall be taken as prohibiting vehicular traffic to proceed until the green signal is shown. The Highway Code – 'Never overtake at cross roads'– distinguished where traffic is regulated by lights.

Note—Though criticised from time to time this decision has never been overruled. It has been considered or explained in the following two cases. See also *Godsmark v Knight Bros (Brighton) Ltd* (at para [9.116]).

[9.112] Knight v Wiper Supply Services Ltd
(1965) 109 Sol Jo 358   Havers J

The claimant was riding his moped along Brixton Hill when he came to traffic lights controlling a junction with a road on his left. When he passed the traffic light, the judge found, it was at green but immediately afterwards turned to amber. The defendant's vehicle came out of the side road and struck the claimant, injuring him.

HELD: As the light had only just turned amber it must still have been showing red for the defendant's driver when he came out and he was therefore negligent. On the issue of contributory negligence *Eva Ltd v Reeves* (at para [9.111]) decided that the driver of a motor vehicle entering a crossroads with the traffic lights in his favour was not guilty of contributory negligence in colliding with a vehicle entering the crossroads with the lights against it, since the driver with the lights in his favour was not under any obligation to assume that a driver might be entering the crossroads with the lights against him. The decision had never been criticised in any subsequent decision and accordingly it was unnecessary in this case to consider any question of contributory negligence. The defendant was solely liable.

[9.113] Davis v Hassan
(1967) 117 NLJ 72, CA

The claimant drove across a junction controlled by traffic signals with the green light in her favour. The defendant drove out from the road on her left against a red light and there was a collision. The county court judge held himself bound by

Eva Ltd v Reeves (at para [9.111]) to find wholly in favour of the claimant but said that if he had not been so bound he would have held the claimant one-third to blame.

HELD, ON APPEAL: (1) It was not necessary in this case to consider whether *Eva v Reeves* was right or wrong. Every case of negligence and certainly every case of traffic accidents had to be decided on its own particular facts. The judge was wrong in thinking himself bound by *Eva v Reeves*.

    (2)   On the facts the judge's finding of the blame against the claimant was not justified. The question was whether having the green light in her favour the claimant was negligent in not seeing the defendant's car come out of the road on the left. Her attention was focused on the lights and it was a very large junction: it would be wrong to hold her guilty of negligence merely because she did not see the car until the last moment.

Note—Willmer LJ said he wished to make it clear that he was approaching the matter as a jury question and not seeking to lay down a proposition of law. The effect of the decision seems to be that cases which might formerly have been regarded as governed by the principle of *Eva v Reeves* are now simply to be treated as questions of fact.

[9.114]   Sudds v Hanscombe
[1971] RTR 212, CA

The defendant's car entered a crossroads from the east when the traffic lights were in his favour. He passed the primary light but before reaching the centre of the crossroads he had to stop because of an altercation between the drivers of two cars which had stopped there. Those two cars were eventually driven away and the defendant then drove forward to continue over the crossroads. Meanwhile the traffic lights had changed and were red for the road along which he was travelling. The claimant's car came to the crossroads from the south: when it was about 10 yards short of the crossing the traffic lights changed to green and he drove straight on. He did not see the defendant's car which had begun to move forward again and there was a collision. The county court judge found against the defendant and held there was no contributory negligence on the part of the claimant.

HELD, ON APPEAL: The claimant was entitled to assume when approaching lights which had already changed in his favour that no fresh traffic would enter the junction from the east because the lights there must have been red. On the other hand, he was not discharged from his duty of looking to his front to see where he was going and to look out for traffic already in the junction which might obtrude into his path. The crucial question was whether or not the defendant was in a position where a reasonably careful motorist in the claimant's position might regard him as a hazard. On the evidence the judge was right in holding the defendant was far enough back from the centre of the crossing that the claimant would not suppose he would continue over the junction.

Note—No cases were referred to in the judgments nor were any cited in argument.

[9.115]   Hopwood Homes Ltd v Kennerdine
[1975] RTR 82, CA

The claimant, driving a lorry, approached a cross roads where he intended to turn right. The traffic lights were green for him and changed to amber just as he passed the primary light. He came to a stop in the centre of the junction angled to the right ready to continue to make his turn. He looked to his left and saw the defendant's car approaching about 25 yards away. Knowing the traffic lights had turned to red and seeing the car had time to pull up he began to move forward. The car did not stop but continued on past the red light and collided with the lorry. The county court judge held the claimant 10% to blame for not having apprehended that the car might not stop at the lights.

HELD, ON APPEAL: The claimant was not at all to blame. He had good reason to suppose the car would pull up at the traffic signal. Although as Lord du Parcq said in *Grant v Sun Shipping Co* [1948] AC 549, 'a prudent man will guard against the possible negligence of others when experience shows such negligence to be common', one's experience does not lead one to think that it is a common folly for a driver who has time to pull up at traffic lights to fail to do so. The claimant was correct in his assessment when he first saw that car that it had time to stop at the lights which were red and that it was safe for him to move forward.

(B)   DUTY OF DRIVERS WHEN LIGHTS CHANGING

[9.116]   **Godsmark v Knight Bros (Brighton) Ltd**

(1960) Times, 12 May 1960   Barry J

A, driving a large lorry over 30ft long, and B, driving a car, were approaching a crossroads controlled by traffic lights – A from the south, B from the east. When A was well short of the stop line the lights changed from green to amber. He could not safely stop on or short of the line, however, and carried on, though the stop line was about 40ft from the crossroads and he could have pulled up within the 40ft. As B approached the crossroads the lights changed from red to red-and-amber and were showing green when he entered the crossroads. Thus neither driver disobeyed the rules in the Traffic Signs Regulations as to the significance of light signals. The two vehicles collided at the crossroads.

HELD: A was two-thirds and B one-third to blame. It must have been obvious to A when the lights changed to amber before he reached the stop line that, if he proceeded, he would for a considerable time be blocking traffic on the east–west road which had received the green light. He should have taken steps to avoid obstruction of traffic lulled into a sense of security by green lights.

[9.117]   **Radburn v Kemp**

[1971] 3 All ER 249, [1971] 1 WLR 1502, 115 Sol Jo 711, CA

The claimant, riding a bicycle, came to a large road junction controlled by traffic lights. He wished to enter a street on the opposite side of the junction but the lights were red. When the lights changed to green he started forward but by the time he had reached a point about two-thirds of the way over the junction, he noticed the light at the mouth of the street he was aiming for had changed to amber. He was then struck by the defendant's car which had emerged from a street on his left. The defendant had started from this street when the light there changed to green: he had not seen the claimant at all. It was admitted that he was negligent but the judge also held the claimant 50% to blame because he had not seen the defendant's car and if he had, could have stopped. The claimant appealed.

HELD, ON APPEAL: The claimant was not at all to blame. As in *Godsmark v Knight Bros (Brighton) Ltd* (at para [9.116]) the defendant, for whom the light had just changed to green, was under a duty to see that there were no vehicles on the crossing which might still be passing across. He had no business, despite the light being in his favour, to enter the junction at all unless he was satisfied that it was safe for him to do so. Once having entered it he had no right to proceed further without taking the utmost care to save harmless people who rightly were already on the junction before he entered it. The defendant had failed to prove that the claimant if he had seen the car before the collision could have done anything effective to avoid it.

[9.118]   Smithers v H & M Transport (Oxford) and Hodgkinson

(1983) 133 NLJ 558   Stocker J

The defendant's van was stationary in a crossroads junction controlled by traffic lights, waiting to turn right when the lights should change. A motorcyclist was approaching from the opposite direction. The lights had changed for him from green to amber as he crossed the stop line. The van moved into his path and there was a collision.

HELD: The van driver was liable. He had not seen the motorcycle until a split second before impact though he could have seen it if he had looked. It must have been visible before the van was driven off from its angled and stationary position. He should not have driven forward at all so long as the lights were green for traffic coming from the opposite direction over the crossroads.

[9.119]   Connaire v McGuire

[1994] CLY 3343   Wright J

The claimant and his friend were attempting to cross an eight lane carriageway at Dagenham late one evening. There was a footbridge which would have only taken them 150m out of their way but they decided to cross at the traffic light controlled junction with Thames Avenue. The speed limit was 40mph but it was accepted that, at night, traffic travelled much faster than this.

The traffic lights were red. The claimant and friend made it across the first four carriageways and then the claimant's friend completed the crossing. However when the claimant reached the third of the final four carriageways the lights turned from red to green.

The defendant had been dawdling in second gear in the fourth lane waiting for the lights to change. His intention was to accelerate hard so as to get a flying start on all the other traffic at the lights. The defendant did so and hit the claimant.

HELD: The claimant was 40% to blame. It was not negligent to cross where he did, but having chosen to do so he had a duty to take appropriate care. Before venturing onto the final lane he should have checked to see if there was any traffic moving in reliance on the green light.

The defendant was 60% to blame. It was his duty to make sure that the junction was clear before crossing. He could not proceed blindly relying only on the green signal on the traffic light and he could have seen the pedestrian had he looked. The defendant's driving demonstrated a total disregard for the safety of other road users.

(C)   PRESUMPTION THAT LIGHTS ARE WORKING CORRECTLY

[9.120]   **Wells v Woodward**
(1956) 54 LGR 142, Div Ct

Where a court finds that traffic lights are showing green one way, the court is entitled to infer, unless the contrary is proved, that they are showing red the other way.

[9.121]   **Tingle Jacobs & Co v Kennedy**
[1964] 1 All ER 888, [1964] 1 WLR 638, 108 Sol Jo 196, CA

At a crossroads controlled by traffic lights a car belonging to the claimants collided with a car owned and driven by the defendant. In evidence the claimant's driver said that when travelling westwards he saw the traffic light was green in his favour and was crossing the junction when the defendant's car came across his path from the south and ran into it. Two independent witnesses supported the claimants' driver's evidence that the light was green in his favour when he entered the crossing. The defendant and his wife gave evidence that they saw the light in their road change from red to amber and then green and they then went forward into the crossing. There was evidence from a police officer of inspections of the lights on dates before and after the accident when they were working properly. The county court judge accepted that both parties were telling the truth and concluded that the traffic lights could not have been working properly. Liability was apportioned equally on the ground that the drivers had failed to keep a proper look-out.

HELD, ON APPEAL: It was plain that one side or the other must have been mistaken. The police evidence was that there had been no trouble with the lights. When you have a device of this kind set up for the public use in active operation the presumption should be that it is in proper working order unless there is evidence to the contrary and there was none here. The case must be decided on the basis that the lights were working properly and there must be a new trial.

(D)   LIGHTS NOT WORKING CORRECTLY

[9.122]   **Ramoo, son of Erulapan v Gan Soo Swee**
[1971] 3 All ER 320, [1971] 1 WLR 1014, 115 Sol Jo 445, PC

At a crossroads controlled by traffic lights a lorry was approaching from the east and a taxicab (in which the claimant was a passenger) from the north. The lights were not functioning properly: those facing the lorry were showing only a green-amber-green sequence with no red phase; those facing the cab were changing in normal sequence but too rapidly. The lorry driver said he first looked at the lights when he was 40 to 50ft away and saw them at green only; he was unaware of any malfunction. The claimant said he first saw the lights facing the cab when it was 15ft away and they were green. The cab driver did not give evidence. Both vehicles drove on to the junction at speed and the cab was hit by the lorry, injuring the claimant.

HELD: The question was whether either driver should have realised the lights were not working properly and proceeded with caution. The cab driver should have noticed that the lights were changing rapidly and have realised that they were out of order. He should have slowed down but did not. The natural inference in the absence of evidence from him was that he was not keeping a proper look-out. If the lorry driver did not, as he said, see the lights until he was 40 to 50ft away he too was not keeping a proper look-out. He could not shelter behind the possibility that even if he had looked at them much earlier he may not have been able to deduce that they were out of order. Both drivers were negligent.

[9.123]   Clough v Bussan, ex p West Yorkshire Police Authority
[1990] 1 All ER 431, [1990] RTR 178

A collision occurred at a road junction controlled by traffic lights that were malfunctioning. This malfunction had been reported to the police 34 minutes before the collision. The passenger in one of the vehicles sued the drivers of the two vehicles involved in the collision and one of these obtained leave to join the Police Authority as a third party. This was on the basis that the police had not responded as they should have done. The Police Authority applied to the registrar to strike out the third party notice as disclosing no reasonable cause of action. The registrar dismissed the application. The Police Authority appealed.

HELD: It was established law that the police are under a duty to preserve law and order and to protect life and property because this is their continuing obligation. However, nothing had happened to give rise to a particular duty of care towards this particular individual which he could rely on in respect of the claim made against him by the injured passenger. The fact that the police were informed of the malfunction was not sufficient to impose upon them a duty of care to every motorist who might subsequently use the junction.

See also *Hill v Chief Constable of West Yorkshire* [1989] AC 53, [1988] 2 All ER 238, [1988] 2 WLR 1049, HL for another discussion about the ambit of the police authorities duty of care.

10.   TRAFFIC SIGNS

(A)   REGULATIONS

[9.124]   *Note*—The Road Traffic Regulation Act 1984, s 65 authorises a highway authority to place traffic signs and s 36 of the Road Traffic Act 1988 makes it an offence for the driver of any vehicle who fails to conform to the sign.

[9.125]   *Note*—The current traffic signs regulations are the Traffic Signs Regulations and General Directions 1994, SI 1994/1519, replacing earlier regulations. The principle of these Regulations is to use symbols to replace words wherever possible in traffic signs. The symbols adopted are, in general, those in use on the continent of Europe.

To understand some of the older cases it is necessary to know that 'Stop' replaces the old 'Halt at Major Road Ahead' sign. It appears on a minor road where traffic emerges into a major road and requires every vehicle:

(a)   to stop at the major road; and

(b)   not to proceed into the major road 'in such a manner or at such a time as is likely to cause danger to the driver of any other vehicle on the major road or as to necessitate the driver of any such other vehicle to change its speed or course in order to avoid an accident with the first mentioned vehicle.'

'Give Way' replaces the old 'Slow Major Road Ahead' sign. Its meaning is the same as that of the 'Stop' sign with the omission of requirement (a).

The Traffic Signs (Speed Limits) Regulations and General Directions 1969, SI 1969/1487, deal with traffic signs relating to speed limits.

[9.126]   **Coote v Stone**

[1971] I All ER 657, [1971] I WLR 279, 115 Sol Jo 79, CA

The Various Trunk Roads (Prohibition of Waiting) (Clearways) Order 1963, art 4 provides that 'no person shall … cause or permit any vehicle to wait on a clearway'. On a straight stretch of main road which had been designated a clearway, the defendant stopped his car close in to the nearside to attend to his small daughter who was feeling sick. After two minutes or so the claimant came along in his car from the same direction as the defendant. Being dazzled by the sun he failed to see the defendant's car and crashed into the back of it. The judge held the defendant in breach of the regulation, and said that as the collision would not have occurred if he had not stopped there he was liable.

HELD, ON APPEAL: That was not right. As in *Clarke v Brims* [1947] KB 447, [1947] I All ER 242 and *Phillips v Britannia Hygienic Laundry Co* [1923] I KB 539; affd [1923] 2 KB 832, 93 LJKB 5, 129 LT 777, 39 TLR 530, 68 Sol Jo 102, CA the question was whether the regulation was intended to give a civil remedy to a person injured by the breach or whether it imposed only a public duty. The primary object of the Clearways Regulations was to facilitate the passage of traffic, and though this object is not unconnected with the avoidance of danger it was not intended to give rise to any private liability.

[9.127]   **Brazier v Alabaster**

(1962) Times, 16 January, Div Ct, QBD

A motorist approached a roundabout on a dual-track road. The central intersection of the road ended 62ft 9in from the roundabout. Instead of going round the roundabout the motorist made a U-turn between the end of the intersection and the roundabout to get on to the other track of the road. There was a 'Keep Left' sign on the roundabout. He was convicted of failing to conform to an indication given by a traffic signal contrary to s 14 of the Road Traffic Act 1960 (s 36 of the Road Traffic Act 1988).

HELD, ON APPEAL: The conviction could not stand. A traffic sign could only indicate that if a motorist were to pass it he must obey it. As there was not a 'No Entry' sign in the intersection the motorist had the right to use that part of the highway.

[9.128]   **Buffel v Cardox (Great Britain) Ltd**

[1950] 2 All ER 878, 114 JP 564, CA

A cyclist crossing a main road was injured by a lorry on the main road. About 95 yards from the crossing there were in the main road three warning signs consisting of studs in the road with the word 'slow', a cross-roads sign and a flashing beacon. The lorry did not slow down before the crossing. Parker J held the cyclist alone to blame.

HELD, ON APPEAL:
  Per Bucknill LJ: I do not think that 'slow' means any more than 'proceed with caution' – 'proceed at such a speed that you can stop if, when you get to the crossing, you find somebody, or something, in the process of crossing, or about to cross.'
  Per Singleton LJ: It is not easy to define the word 'slow'. Its meaning must depend on a variety of circumstances. That which may appear slow to some motorists may strike a pedestrian as fast. I think the fairest way to look on it is that the sign is an

indication to the motorist that he is approaching a place of potential danger, and that, therefore, he ought to be driving more slowly than he would drive on a normal open road without any such sign. In other words, his speed ought to be such that he can pull up fairly quickly if someone or something appears from one or other of the crossroads.

Appeal allowed.

(B)   TRAFFIC ENTERING MAJOR ROAD FROM MINOR ROAD

[9.129]   **Brown v Central Scottish Motor Traction**
1949 SC 9, 1949 SLT 66, Ct of Sess

A motorcyclist with pillion passenger was proceeding along a minor road which had a 'Slow, Major Road Ahead" sign and formed the left arm of a Y junction with a major road. He collided with a bus proceeding along the major road at about 25mph. Each vehicle should have been clearly visible to the other driver. The bus driver did not slow down until the motorcycle emerged from the minor road. As soon as the bus driver noticed the motorcyclist, he braked and swerved. The pillion passenger was killed, and his father brought proceedings against the bus company. The jury found the bus driver negligent.

HELD, ON APPEAL: There was no evidence of negligence against the bus driver. On the evidence, the bus driver had no opportunity of observing what the motorcyclist was going to do.

Note—Compare *Lang v London Transport Executive* (at para [9.130]). See also *MacIntyre v Coles* (at para [9.67]).

[9.130]   **Lang v London Transport Executive**
[1959] 3 All ER 609, [1959] 1 WLR 1168   Havers J

A motorcyclist was riding along a minor side road approaching a major main road. The minor road continued along the line of the major road from the junction, where the major road changed direction. On the minor road about 180ft from the junction there was a 'Slow, Major Road Ahead' sign. Traffic on the major road was clearly visible from the side road for a distance of 40 yards from the junction. There was a 'Slow' sign painted on the major road about 190ft away from the junction. Just after passing the 'Slow' sign, the bus driver glanced in the direction of the side road and saw some cyclists, but did not look in the direction of the side road again. The bus driver was aware of the 'Slow' sign in the minor road, and he knew that people would suddenly emerge from a side road when it was unwise to do so. The motorcyclist was proceeding at a speed of 20mph. and was killed when he emerged from the side road. His widow sued the bus driver and his employers.

HELD: The deceased was guilty of a high degree of negligence. The bus driver was negligent in not taking the precaution of looking at the traffic in the side road. The judge found the deceased was two-thirds to blame and the bus driver one-third.

Note—See comments of Sachs LJ in *Watkins v Moffatt* (at para [9.136]).

[9.131]   **Walsh v Redfern**
[1970] RTR 201   Lyell J

The defendant was driving an army lorry and trailer along the main Bath Road late at night. His speed was 35mph. A car containing six people was being driven along a narrow lane at great speed towards the Bath Road from his left. The defendant saw from the light cast by the car's headlight on the tall hedges on each side of the lane that a car was approaching but owing to the rain and darkness he could form no clear impression of speed and gave no further thought to it. The driver of the car did not stop or slow down but drove straight out on to the main road at speed. The defendant was unable to avoid the car and in the collision four of its occupants were killed.

HELD: The defendant was not at all to blame. There was nothing he could have done to avoid the collision short of slowing right down to such a speed that he could have stopped the lorry and let the car pass across its front when he saw it emerge from behind the hedge. It would be unreasonable to expect him to do so. He was driving on one of the main trunk roads from London to the West of England; it is common knowledge that every minor road which debouches on to a road of this importance has warning signs to approach the major road at slow speed. There was nothing known to the defendant to put him on guard against a lunatic driver who would wholly disregard the warning signs.

[9.132]   Garston Warehousing Co v O F Smart (Liverpool) Ltd
[1973] RTR 377, CA

On a November evening after dark the claimant's car was being driven out of a side street across a main road, which was 26ft wide and well-lit, into a street opposite. The main road was a one-way street with traffic travelling only from the car driver's right. As he was about to leave the side street there was on his immediate right against the kerb in the main road a bus which obscured his view to the right. The bus driver gave a flash of his headlights and a hand signal to the car driver to come on. After looking along the nearside of the bus and seeing nothing approaching the car driver switched on his headlights and drove out slowly across and beyond the front of the bus without stopping. When about to enter the street opposite the car was struck violently on its offside by the defendant's van which had overtaken the bus. The van driver had not seen the car until he was 12 to 15ft away, nor had he noticed a slow-down signal given by the bus driver. The judge held the van driver two-thirds to blame for driving at a speed excessive in the circumstances and failing to see the car earlier; he held the car driver one-third to blame for not stopping when the car was just past the bus and when he would have seen the van approaching.

HELD, ON APPEAL: The apportionment should not be disturbed.

[9.133]   Davis v Swinwood
[2003] CLY 3029

The claimant brought an action following a collision with the defendant after he exited a minor road into a major road. He contended that he was relying upon the defendant's left hand indicator and the position of the defendant's vehicle in the road as well as his speed at the material time.

The defendant denied that he had indicated and stated that he intended to proceed along the major road.

HELD: Although the court found as a fact that the defendant's indicator had been displayed, the court held that this was not the relevant issue, as the claimant had been seeking to enter a major road from a minor road. As the defendant had precedence on the road the onus was clearly on the person entering the major road to enter safely. This, the claimant failed to do. The claim was dismissed with judgment entered in favour of the defendant. There was no deduction to take account of contributory negligence. (*Wadsworth v Gillespie* [1978] CLY 2534 distinguished.)

(C)   CROSSROADS COLLISION

[9.134]   *Note—See* Brown v Central Scottish Motor Traction (at para [9.129]).

[9.135]   Gooder v Taylor and Yorkshire Tar Distillers Ltd
(1966) Times, 18 October, CA

At a crossroads where a minor road crossed a major road a van was travelling along the minor road and a tanker along the major road. As the van approached the crossroads the driver slowed down almost to a stop. He looked along the major road but saw nothing coming, pressed the accelerator again and proceeded to cross. The tanker-driver had seen the van approaching the crossroads. He took his foot off the accelerator but, seeing the van slow down as if to stop, put his foot on again to go over the crossroads. When at the last moment the van moved forward on to the crossroads the tanker driver was unable to avoid hitting it. The judge of assize held the van driver five-sixths to blame for the collision and the tanker-driver one-sixth.

HELD: Allowing the tanker-driver's appeal, he was not to blame at all. He had seen the van slow down and was justified in thinking that the van driver had seen him and was going to let him pass. For the same reason he was not negligent in not sounding his horn. The tanker driver was not negligent in not reducing his speed, for only by slowing down to a very considerable extent could he have avoided the consequences of the van pulling out at the last moment. As he had seen the van slow down as if to allow him to pass he was under no duty to take such drastic action.

[9.136]   Watkins v Moffatt
[1970] RTR 205n, 111 Sol Jo 719, CA

The claimant, a passenger, was injured in a crossroads collision between a Ford van in which he was travelling and an Austin car. The Ford was travelling on the minor road on which there was a 'Slow, Major Road Ahead' sign. The Austin was on the major road. The judge held that the Ford driver was guilty of a high degree of negligence in coming out faster than he should have done but the possibility of danger should have been reasonably apparent to the driver of the Austin if he had been keeping a proper look-out. He held the Austin driver one-third to blame.

HELD, ON APPEAL: It could not be inferred that the driver of the Austin was not keeping a proper look-out. The Ford was on a side road with 'Major Road Ahead' signs and must have been coming so fast that the driver of the Austin, keeping a reasonable look-out on both sides of the road might well not have seen it, and he was not to blame.

Per Sachs LJ: The case is another in which the authority of *Lang v London Transport Executive* (at para [9.130]) is prayed in aid on behalf of a driver of a vehicle emerging from a side road on to a main road. Whatever may be the correct view of that case on its own facts, a matter on which I would wish to reserve judgment,

Lang's case is not a charter in favour of motorists emerging from a side road at speed. That would entail a somewhat unrealistic view of the way reasonably driven traffic uses main roads and would derogate from the great responsibility of those emerging from side roads in relation to main road traffic.

[9.137]   Barclays Bank Ltd v Gaughan and Toole
(8 June 1970, unreported)   James J

Approaching a crossroads in a rural area in daylight the second defendant was driving his car along the main road at 25 to 30mph. He knew the minor road on his left had a 'Halt' sign at its mouth. From a point about 35 yards from the junction there was a view through an open fence along the minor road for a similar distance from the junction. The first defendant approaching the crossroads along the minor road at about 50mph ignored the 'Halt' sign and drove straight on to the junction striking the second defendant's car and killing a passenger. The second defendant, who was paying attention to some horses approaching from the far side of the junction, said he had only a fleeting glimpse of the other car before the collision.

HELD: The second defendant was not at all to blame. He was driving quietly and sensibly on a main road with knowledge of the 'Halt' sign in the minor road. He was faced with the presence of horses. His obligation was to behave reasonably. It was doubtful whether he would have seen anything in the minor road but he had every reason to believe a car in the minor road would stop. The sole responsibility for the accident lay on the first defendant.

[9.138]   Humphrey v Leigh
[1971] RTR 363, CA

The second defendant was driving his car at a steady pace up Gipsy Hill in south London when the first defendant drove out of a side road to cross into a road opposite without stopping or slowing down. There was a collision resulting in injury to the claimant. There were no road signs to show that Gipsy Hill was the major road but there was no doubt that it was and that traffic in the side road would as a matter of course slow down and stop. The judge attributed all the blame to the first defendant, who appealed.

HELD: The appeal should be dismissed – the second defendant was in no way negligent.

Per Russell LJ: The question is whether it can be propounded as a matter of law that a person in the position of the second defendant has a duty, if he is to avoid a charge of negligence every time he comes across a side road of this kind leading out of Gipsy Hill, to take his foot off the accelerator and poise his foot over the brake, being prepared to stop short of the crossing. In so far as anything to that effect was said by Ormerod LJ in the case of *Williams v Fullerton* (1961) 105 Sol Jo 280, CA [at para [9.139]] it was an *obiter dictum* and I personally would not follow it at all; otherwise you would approach a situation in which no traffic moves about the country at any reasonable speed whatsoever.

[9.139]   Williams v Fullerton
(1961) 105 Sol Jo 280, CA

A was driving a car along Richmond Avenue, near King's Cross, London: B was driving a car along Hemingford Road, a minor road which crosses Richmond

Avenue at an ordinary cross-roads junction. Hemingford Road had a sign 'Slow—Major Road Ahead'. Despite this B drove on to the crossroads at a speed estimated between 30 and 60mph and collided with A's car causing fatal injuries to a passenger. A had approached the junction, which had a conventional cross-roads sign, at a reasonable speed, looked right and left and did not see anything. The trial judge held A 25% to blame and B 75%. A appealed. It was argued on his behalf that a driver on a major road approaching a crossing had no duty to keep a look-out except to see what might reasonably be seen and that there was no obligation to look out for what travelled at an excessive speed.

HELD: The trial judge's finding could not be disturbed. If A's failure had consisted merely in failing to take into account the outrageous driving of B it was at least doubtful if he could be considered negligent. But although he had looked left and right at the crossing he had not, as indicated by the Highway Code, looked right again. Had A looked at the right time or looked properly he must have seen the other car and could have taken avoiding action.

Per Ormerod LJ: If a driver exercised proper care he would approach a crossing with his foot off the accelerator and ready to brake and deal with any traffic from the minor road by slowing down or stopping.

Note—For comment on this decision see *Humphrey v Leigh* [1971] RTR 363, CA (at para [9.138]).

[9.140]   Butters v J H Fenner & Co Ltd

(1967) 117 NLJ 213   MacKenna J

At a crossroads in a built-up area the first defendant's servant was driving a car along a minor road. He failed to see a 'Slow, Major Road Ahead' sign and a large 'Slow', painted on the roadway. He drove straight on to the crossroads where the car was hit by the second defendant's lorry travelling on the major road. The lorry driver had not looked to his offside as he crossed the junction nor had he slowed down.

HELD: The lorry driver was 25% to blame. He should have looked to his right and slowed down before entering the junction. If he had done so he would have been able to avoid the collision or at least reduce its force.

[9.141]   There is no rule or custom in this country requiring a driver approaching crossroads to give way to traffic on his right and allowing him to take precedence over traffic on his left. It would be quite disastrous if some users of the highway observed that practice while others did not. Users of roads of equal importance which crossed one another owed a duty to each other to take care. Even the driver on a major road was not acquitted altogether of the duty of taking care, even though there might be a greater duty on the driver on the minor road. The question of negligence is one of fact (per Streatfield J (1954) 98 Sol Jo 380, Times, 29 May).

(D)   WHITE LINES AND DOTTED LINES

[9.142]   The Road Traffic Regulation Act 1984, s 64 provides that: 'In this Act "traffic sign" means ... any line or mark on a road for' conveying to traffic on roads warnings, information, requirements, restrictions or prohibitions of any kind specified by regulations.

[9.143]   **Day v Smith**
(1983) 133 NLJ 726, QBD

The claimant was injured when the car he was driving collided with another on a bend. The deceased's administrator counter-claimed, alleging negligence on the part of the claimant. There were no eye witnesses of the accident but there was evidence of some marks on the road. The bend on which the accident occurred was a left hand bend for the claimant, the road being 24 feet wide divided by a single central white line.

HELD: On the evidence the claimant's car was 3 to 4ft on the wrong side of the white line at the time of the collision. He was negligent in allowing that to happen and the deceased was not to blame. Judgment for the defendant administrator on the counter-claim.

[9.144]   *Note*—The Traffic Signs Regulations and General Directions 1981, SI 1981/859 provide by regs 21 and 22 that transverse broken white lines across the mouth of a road at a road junction have the effect of a 'Give Way' sign whether or not used in conjunction with a sign.
   See *Hardy v Walder* [1984] RTR 312, CA.

[9.145]   *Note*—The Traffic Signs Regulations and General Directions 1981, SI 1981/859, reg 23 contains the rules of the 'double white line' system of traffic control. Vehicles must not stop on any length of road having a double white line, nor must a vehicle cross a continuous line when it is on the left of a dotted or continuous line as viewed in the direction of travel of the vehicle. There are exceptions to the rule against stopping, including a stop for a person to board or alight, or for the purposes of loading or unloading. It is permissible to cross a continuous line for, *inter alia*, the purpose of passing a stationary vehicle or entering another road. When the dotted line is on the left a vehicle may cross it provided it is seen by the driver to be safe to do so.

[9.146]   **R v Blything Justices, ex p Knight**
[1970] RTR 218, Div Ct

The defendant was following two cars and an articulated lorry. He decided to overtake. He did not know he was approaching the beginning of a double white line. He was unable to get back to the nearside until he had driven 40 or 50 yards on the offside of the double white line. He was charged with failing to comply with the Traffic Signs Regulations 1964, SI 1964/1857, reg 23 (now reg 23 of the 1981 Regulations). He said the first of the two cars had accelerated and prevented him from getting back to the nearside in time and that this was an accident giving him a defence under reg 23(4)(a). The magistrate's clerk advised the bench that this defence was not available to a driver who had not first had the double white lines on his offside before crossing them. He was convicted.

HELD, ON APPEAL: The conviction should stand because a driver could not, after putting himself in the wrong by beginning to overtake in such circumstances, claim that he had to continue in the wrong because of some accident. Even so, the magistrate's clerk's advice had been too narrow and was bad. There may be cases (eg when overtaking stationary vehicles) when a man through no fault of his own approaches the double white line on the wrong side of it and never gets back on to his nearside until some distance of the white line has been passed.

(E) CLAIMANT MOTORCYCLIST NOT WEARING CRASH HELMET

[9.147] *Note*—The Road Traffic Act 1962, s 41 (now the Road Traffic Act 1988, s 16(2)) empowering the Minister of Transport to make regulations requiring persons driving or riding on motorcycles to wear protective headgear was brought into force as from 1 October 1971 by the Road Traffic Act 1962 (Commencement No 7) Order 1971, SI 1971/1335.

The wearing of helmets by riders of motorcycles, scooters and mopeds was made compulsory by the Motor Cycles (Wearing of Helmets) Regulations 1973, SI 1973/180 which came into force on 1 June 1973. Paragraph 29 of the Highway Code (1978) says 'when on a motorcycle, scooter or moped you must wear a safety helmet of approved design.' A Sikh is excused from wearing a helmet while he is wearing a turban. This is reiterated at para 67 of the Highway Code (1999). See also the Motor Cycles (Protective Helmets) Regulations 1998, SI 1998/1807.

[9.148]   **O'Connell v Jackson**

[1972] 1 QB 270, [1971] 3 All ER 129, [1971] 3 WLR 463, 115 Sol Jo 742, CA

The claimant was riding his moped to work along a busy street when the defendant drove out in his car from a side street and collided with him. The claimant was thrown off and struck his head violently on the roadway sustaining a severe fracture of the skull. He was not wearing a crash helmet: he had intended buying one but had not done so. There was evidence from three doctors that the injury would have been less serious had he been wearing one. The judge held the defendant solely to blame for the accident. He also found that if the claimant had been wearing a helmet it would have reduced the gravity of the head injuries but he declined to hold that the failure to wear one was contributory negligence.

HELD, ON APPEAL by the defendant: The Law Reform (Contributory Negligence) Act 1945 required damages to be reduced according to 'the claimant's share in the responsibility for the damage.' In *Jones v Livox Quarries Ltd* [1952] 2 QB 608, [1952] 1 TLR 1377, 96 Sol Jo 344, CA, Denning LJ had said a person was guilty of contributory negligence if he ought reasonably to have foreseen that if he did not act as a reasonably prudent man he might be hurt himself, and in his reckonings he must take into account the possibility of others being careless. Applying this test the claimant ought to have foreseen when travelling through a busy traffic area the possibility of an accident occurring even though he himself drove carefully and that he could well sustain greater hurt if he failed to wear a helmet. He knew as was clear from his own evidence, that it was a sensible practice to wear one. The claimant was partly to blame for the additional injury he sustained by not wearing a helmet and the reduction of damages should amount to 15% of the whole.

Pedestrians

1.   DRIVERS

(A)   DRIVER NOT LIABLE

[10.1]   **Kayser v London Passenger Transport Board**

[1950] 1 All ER 231, 114 JP 122   Humphreys J

A bus driver stopped at a compulsory stop some distance from a pedestrian crossing near where two wide thoroughfares joined the main road. When about one and a half bus lengths from the traffic lights, the driver saw the claimant, a girl of 14, another girl, and a man, hurrying across the road, holding hands and talking. An air raid shelter obstructed the driver's vision and he proceeded very slowly in first gear. The pedestrians scattered, including the claimant when she was struck by the driver of the defendant's vehicle. According to the evidence, the claimant was half-way across, when she suddenly ran back, probably as a result of the traffic in the opposite carriageway, and ran into the defendant's bus.

HELD: Where the driver of a vehicle is satisfied that persons who are lawfully entitled to cross the road, whether they are on a pedestrian crossing or not, are out of danger, he is entitled to proceed but only at such a pace as will enable him to stop almost immediately should the persons who are crossing do anything dangerous or negligent.

There was no negligence on the part of the driver. Judgment for defendants.

Note—Compare *Foskett v Mistry* [1984] RTR 1, [1984] LS Gaz R 2683, CA.

[10.2]   Brophy v Shaw

(1965) Times, 25 June, CA

Shortly before midnight the claimant and a friend had taken part in a street brawl. The police were about to apprehend them when the claimant and his friend ran away. They ran along the pavement past a bus which was just pulling away from a stop and darted out into the road which was a dual carriageway. The defendant was driving his car at about 30mph keeping close to the offside. He failed to see the men crossing from his left, even though his headlights were on, until they had got a substantial way across the road. They ran right across in front of his car which resulted in a collision. The claimant was seriously injured and his friend killed.

HELD: The defendant was not liable. It had been alleged that he should have seen the men running along the pavement, but his duty, like that of any other road user, was to exercise reasonable care. He was not under a duty to be a perfectionist. It was going too far to say he should have observed the negligence and irresponsible action of the two men earlier than he did.

[10.3]   Pollard v Curcic

[1994] CLY 3402, Watford County Court   HHJ Stockdale

The claimant was delivering newspapers. He parked his van next to a bus stop with the intention of crossing the road. He chose not to make use of the pedestrian crossing a short distance away. The bus driver indicated to the claimant that he could cross. The claimant began crossing but was hit by a motorcycle overtaking the bus and ridden by the defendant. Despite applying his brakes and attempting to manoeuvre to the offside the defendant motorcyclist was unable to avoid the claimant.

HELD: The claimant's claim was dismissed. There was nothing to indicate that the defendant was travelling at any more than 15mph. He was riding in a proper manner and at a proper speed and had no chance of avoiding the claimant.

[10.4]   Barlow v Entwistle

15 May 2000, QBD

A2/99/0922   Roach LJ, Latham LJ

The claimant was larking about on the grass beside an A road with two of his friends. The claimant ran out into the road heading for the other side. The claimant was then struck by the defendant's car which was travelling at about 25mph. At first instance it was held that the defendant had failed to keep a proper look out as he had not seen any pedestrian prior to impact. Therefore the defendant was liable but contributory negligence was assessed at 50%.

HELD, ON APPEAL: No driver could anticipate that the claimant would, without warning or reason, run across this busy road. As such, the defendant's failure to keep a proper look out was not a causative factor of the accident and the accident would have happened even if the defendant had seen the claimant and his friends. Judgment was ordered in the defendant's favour.

[10.5]   North v TNT Express UK Ltd
[2001] EWCA Civ 853

[2001] All ER (D) 358

The claimant climbed onto the front bumper of the defendant's lorry while it was stationary at a roundabout and, holding onto one of the windscreen wipers, requested that the defendant's driver provide him with a lift home. The claimant remained on the lorry despite two requests from the driver to dismount. The claimant, who had been drinking, did not do so. The manner in which the driver then drove off (with the claimant still positioned on the lorry) was disputed, but in any event the court held that when the claimant came to fall off, it was on account of his vigorous and deliberate pulling off of the windscreen wiper. Nonetheless, the judge held that the defendant was liable for 25% of the damages which resulted when the lorry struck the claimant after he fell from the front of the lorry as the defendant's driver failed to act properly and reasonably in driving as he did. The defendant appealed.

HELD, ON APPEAL: The judge had applied too high a standard of care. The defendant's driver had been presented with a difficult dilemma and in the circumstances it was very difficult to know what to do. Taking all the circumstances, including the fact that the claimant's friends were around and that they too had been drinking, the driver had behaved reasonably. The defendant was not liable for the results of the claimant's stupid acts.

[10.6]   Das International Ltd v Manley
[2002] EWCA Civ 1638

[2002] All ER (D) 195 (Oct)

The claim involved two successive road traffic accidents on the A55 dual carriageway on 2 November 1998. The defendant was travelling in the eastbound carriageway when he saw a pedestrian walking along the side of the road. He swerved to his offside, collided with the central reservation and ended up down an embankment in a ditch. The defendant alighted from his vehicle and returned to the roadside to obtain assistance. A vehicle owned by the claimant approached the accident site. The driver saw the defendant standing on the roadside waving his arms around. As the driver swerved to avoid the defendant he skidded, hit the central reservation with the vehicle ending up on a ditch in the embankment.

It was found that the defendant had moved from the roadside into the nearside lane. The judge felt that it was appropriate for the defendant to seek assistance as he did. The claimant appealed.

HELD, ON APPEAL: That the judge should measure the defendants actions against those of a 'reasonable person'. The court of appeal held that the defendant's actions in the circumstances were not reasonable regardless of his circumstances and allowed the appeal.

[10.7]   **Roda Sam (previously Al-Sam) v Atkins**

[2005] EWCA Civ 1452

[2005] All ER (D) 113 (Nov)

The claim arose following a road traffic accident on 12 February 2001, on a busy four lane street. It was dark although street lights were on. The claimant, a pedestrian, intended to cross from the south side of the road onto the north side.

The defendant travelling west in the offside lane was in the process of overtaking a transit van which was stationary in the nearside lane. The defendant was travelling at no more than 20mph when the claimant stepped out into her path from the front of a stationary transit van, and was struck by the defendant's vehicle.

At first instance the judge found that although the defendant had been negligent, this was not the cause of the accident, and dismissed the claim. The claimant appealed.

HELD, ON APPEAL: That the judge was wrong to find the defendant negligent as the claimant had stepped out into her path giving no opportunity to stop. Further, her speed was not excessive as the claimant emerged unexpectedly into her path. The court held that as the defendant had not been negligent the judge was right to find in favour of the defendant, and dismissed the appeal.

(B)   CONTRIBUTORY NEGLIGENCE

[10.8]   **Snow v Giddins**

(1969) 113 Sol Jo 229, CA

The claimant began to cross the road near a road junction and not far from a pedestrian crossing which had a central refuge. He threaded his way through the north-bound traffic, which was stationary and then stood in the middle of the road just over the centre line looking to his left for any approaching south-bound traffic. Whilst standing there he was struck from his right by a motorcycle ridden by the defendant, who was travelling north overtaking the stationary vehicles. The county court judge held the defendant wholly to blame, rejecting, *inter alia*, a suggestion that the claimant was negligent in not using the pedestrian crossing.

HELD, ON APPEAL: The claimant was not negligent in failing to use the pedestrian crossing, but he was negligent in taking on himself the hazard of being marooned in the centre of the road at the mercy of on-coming traffic instead of crossing where there was a central refuge: He was 25% to blame. A pedestrian who elected not to use a crossing took upon himself a higher standard of care.

[10.9]   **Baker v Willoughby**

[1970] AC 467, [1969] 3 All ER 1528, [1970] 2 WLR 50, 114 Sol Jo 15, HL

The claimant wished to cross a main road 33ft wide in open country. He saw a car approaching from his right about 100 yards away and assumed he had time to cross. He walked out into the centre of the road, paused to look left, and was struck by the defendant's car coming from his right. The defendant had overtaken two other cars at least 200 yards before the point of collision and had the claimant in view over that distance. The judge found both parties to blame: the defendant three-quarters because, having the claimant in view for 200 yards and taking no evasive action he must have been either driving too fast or not keeping a proper look-out; the claimant one-quarter for not waiting for the approaching cars to pass and not looking to his right a second time. The Court of Appeal altered the apportionment to 50–50 on the ground that each party had a view of each other throughout the time the claimant was crossing the road to the point of collision and neither did anything about it.

HELD, ON APPEAL to the House of Lords: The judge's apportionment of blame should be restored. There were two elements in an assessment of liability, causation and blameworthiness. A pedestrian had to look to both sides as well as forwards. He was going at perhaps three miles an hour and was rarely a danger to anyone else. A motorist had not got to look sideways and if he was going at a considerable speed must not relax his observation otherwise the consequences might be disastrous. It was quite possible for a motorist to be very much more to blame than the pedestrian.

[10.10]   Mulligan v Holmes
[1971] RTR 179, CA

Two pedestrians began to cross a wide brightly-lit street at night. The distance from the kerb to the central island was 35ft. There was no satisfactory evidence whether they looked to their right or not. Two cars were approaching. The driver of the first, travelling at 30–40mph, saw the pedestrians begin to cross when he was about 60 yards away. He slowed slightly but they presented no problem to him and passed across his front. The second car driven by the defendant at a very fast speed, overtook the first car when it was 10 to 15 yards from the pedestrians. The defendant had not seen them before though he could have seen them from 100 yards away if he had looked. They were by that time quite near the central island. They were struck by his car and injured, one fatally. The judge at first instance held that the pedestrians could not have looked to their right and were 50% to blame.

HELD, ON APPEAL: The proportion of contributory negligence should be reduced to 20%. The evidence did not warrant the conclusion that the pedestrians did not look to their right. Nevertheless, they were not blameless: if they had exercised all reasonable care they would have realised that the second car was being driven very quickly and that there was a risk that the driver might not see them and would run them down.

[10.11]   Hurt v Murphy
[1971] RTR 186   Talbot J

The claimant's wife began to cross the road at a place where her visibility to her left was restricted by a bend to 100 yards. There was no vehicle in sight when she left the pavement. She walked across, looking ahead. The defendant driving his car at a speed very much greater than the 30mph limit came round the bend and though he applied his brakes he was unable to avoid striking and killing her. She was then just beyond the centre of the road. The defendant admitted his own negligence but alleged contributory negligence.

HELD: The claimant's wife was not negligent when she left the pavement because there was then nothing in sight, but there was lack of care on her part in not looking to her left again as she was crossing the road. She was one-fifth to blame.

[10.12]   Williams v Needham
[1972] RTR 387, QBD

The claimant at night but in a well-lit street parked her car with its nearside to the kerb so that she could cross to a shop on the other side. She stood in the roadway on the offside of the car with her back to it and looked to her right. She saw nothing approaching and then looked to her left. She saw three cars approaching and waited until they had passed. Then without looking again to her right she stepped forward to cross the road and was at once hit by the defendant's car coming from her right. The defendant had seen her standing by her car looking away from him and had guessed that she intended crossing the road. He assumed she would look to her right before beginning to cross and he took no precautions against her not doing so. When she stepped forward he was too near to avoid hitting her.

HELD: The claimant must bear two-thirds of the blame but one-third must rest with the defendant. He knew that people sometimes began crossing without looking and, realising the claimant was about to cross, should have drawn her attention to the presence of his car or taken some other precautions against the possibility of her taking a risky step.

[10.13]   Liddell v Middleton

[1996] PIQR P36, CA

The claimant and his wife were attempting to cross Holderness Road, Hull at 11.45 at night. The weather was fine and dry and the road was well lit. There was a reasonable flow of traffic although it was spaced out with gaps between the vehicles. The claimant and his wife reached the centre of the road in safety and both waited there for about ten seconds. The claimant's wife said she saw a car coming in the distance and ran across the remaining half of the road to the opposite pavement. The claimant did not immediately follow but waited, took one or two steps and was hit by the offside front corner of the defendant's car. The claimant's injuries were serious enough for him to be prevented from giving any evidence.

The defendant's evidence was that he was travelling in a line of cars, never saw the claimant, never saw the claimant's wife and the first thing he knew of the accident was when there was a bang. The judge found that the claimant and his wife were there to be seen in the centre of the road and that the defendant should have seen them, was driving too fast and should have sounded his horn.

The judge held the defendant 75% to blame and the claimant 25% contributory negligent. The defendant appealed.

HELD: The defendant had failed to keep a proper look out. Furthermore, had he seen these pedestrians, the defendant, on his own admission, would have altered the manner of his driving by slowing his speed and steering further to the nearside. Had he done so the accident would have been avoided. However, the judge was wrong to conclude that the defendant should have sounded his horn simply if he had seen the claimant standing in the middle of the road. As to the apportionment of liability, both parties were to blame. The claimant's action in attempting to cross the carriageway when he did was an extremely dangerous one. The car was almost upon him and in the circumstances it gave the defendant very little opportunity to avoid the accident. The judge's apportionment of 25% contributory negligence was wrong in principle and too lenient. Liability should be apportioned on a 50/50 basis.

Note—The Court of Appeal criticised the use of expert evidence: 'We do not have a trial by expert in this country; we have trial by judge. In my judgment, the expert witnesses contributed nothing to the trial in this case except expense. For the reasons I have indicated their evidence was largely if not wholly irrelevant and inadmissible ... in road traffic accidents it is the exception rather than the rule that expert witnesses are required': per Stuart-Smith LJ.

[10.14] Bertoli v Farrell

(12 January 1995, unreported), CA

It was just after 11 pm. The claimant, a 19-year-old overseas student from Spain was standing on the highway talking to a friend who was sitting in a taxi. The taxi was parked at the edge of the defendant's carriageway with other taxis outside a public house. The claimant moved away from the taxi and was hit by the defendant seconds later. It was accepted by the judge that at the moment of impact the claimant had embarked on his journey from the parked taxi. Unfortunately, being Spanish, he had looked in the wrong direction. The defendant only saw the claimant at the last minute and this was endorsed by a fellow passenger. The defendant could not swerve as there was a car coming in the opposite direction. She could only brake.

The judge held the claimant 75% to blame for the accident. The defendant was 25% responsible on the basis that even though she did not see the claimant, the claimant was 'there to be seen'. The situation of the taxis and the public house was a potential hazard. Furthermore, a driver of a vehicle coming in the opposite direction had the claimant in her sights for about 250m.

Both parties appealed but the Court of Appeal did not interfere with the judge's findings.

[10.15] Eagle v Chambers

[2003] EWCA Civ 1107

[2003] All ER (D) 411 (Jul), [2004] RTR 115

The claimant who was 17 at the time of the accident was walking along unsteadily in the centre of a dual carriageway. She was in a highly emotive state. The defendant who was travelling along at 35mph struck the claimant causing severe injuries. The defendant failed a roadside breath test, although when retested at the station was found to be below the legal limit.

At first instance, the claimant was found to be 60% responsible for the accident and her damages were reduced accordingly.

HELD, ON APPEAL: That it was rare for a pedestrian to be found more culpable than a driver unless it could be shown that she moved suddenly into the driver's path. As there was no evidence that the claimant had done this, the court adopted the traditional approach in placing a higher burden on the driver particularly as a car is potentially a 'dangerous weapon'. The court held the drivers conduct was more blameworthy than that of the claimant, although there was sufficient evidence to justify a finding of contributory negligence. The claimant's liability was therefore reduced to 40%.

[10.16] Adjei v King

[2003] EWCA Civ 414

[2003] All ER (D) 280 (Mar)

The claimant was a pedestrian who when attempting to cross a carriageway was struck by a coach driven by the defendant.

There was one eye witness, who felt that the defendant had failed to see the claimant until the point of impact. The eye witness was positioned along side the defendant's vehicle. As the witness approached a set of traffic lights, she noticed that the claimant was attempting to cross the road and stopped. However, the defendant continued thereafter colliding with the claimant.

There was expert evidence from an accident reconstruction expert who concluded that the defendant was travelling at a speed of 25mph before he started to skid. The speed limit was 30mph. The judge felt that the defendant was travelling too fast and that had he been travelling slower the accident could have been avoided.

The defendant appealed on two counts:

(1)   that the evidence did not support the finding of excessive speed; and

(2)   that the judge should have made a finding of contributory negligence.

HELD, ON APPEAL: That the defendant was not travelling too fast. However, the Court of Appeal felt that it would have been appropriate for the defendant to slow down given the actions of the eye witness. Therefore the finding of liability was correct.

However, as the road conditions were good with clear visibility the conduct of the claimant meant that he was partly responsible and therefore damages were reduced by 40% to reflect his negligence.

[10.17]   Green v Bannister

[2003] EWCA Civ 1819

[2003] All ER (D) 279 (Dec), 148 Sol Jo LB 27

The claimant had collapsed in a drunken stupor in the roadway of a residential cul-de-sac outside his parent's house.

The defendant had reversed from a parking space outside her home in the cul-de-sac, looking over her right shoulder. She continued to reverse for about 35 yards, before running over the claimant.

The court at first instance found in favour of the claimant, but with a deduction of 60% to reflect contributory negligence. The defendant appealed on the basis that the trial judge was applying a driving standard of perfection.

HELD, ON APPEAL: The defendant should have checked her nearside mirror and had she done so, she would probably have seen the claimant lying in the road and stopped. The care required for revering in the cul-de-sac called for particular attention as to what was in the car's path. The court dismissed the appeal and upheld the 60% contributory negligence as this was not unfair to the defendant.

[10.18]   Rose v South East London and Kent Bus Co Ltd
[2004] EWHC 1106 (QB), QB

The claimant was struck by a bus operated by the defendant whilst she attempted to cross a road divided by a traffic island. The traffic island was surrounded by a railing that left a roadside strip of 18 inches of pavement. The sole break in the railing was a pelican crossing, some 30m away. The claimant crossed the road up to the traffic island and then walked along the narrow roadside strip up to the pelican crossing. At that time traffic on the road was very heavy and a bus operated by the defendant was stationary in a line of traffic queuing to go through the crossing. The bus driver noticed the claimant walking along the strip. The claimant slipped just before she reached the crossing and was struck by the defendant's bus as it started up to go through the crossing.

HELD: On the evidence the bus driver was a careful driver but had suffered a momentary lapse in concentration which was sufficient to amount to a failure to take care, as the onus was on him to check that the claimant was out of an area of risk before he moved forward. The judge found the claimant 50% to blame for placing herself in a position of risk.

[10.19]   **Parkinson v Chief Constable of Dyfed Powys Police**
[2004] EWCA Civ 802

The claimant was injured when he walked out into the road past a parked taxi and into the path of a passing police car. The claimant was under the influence of alcohol and stepped into the road when he should have been aware of the presence of a motor car. The police car was travelling at 40mph when it was passing the stationary taxi and collided with the claimant.

The accident happened in a built up area late at night. The judge found that the driver of the defendant's vehicle should have anticipated that there might be pedestrians in the sort of condition of the claimant and should have adjusted his speed accordingly. Liability was apportioned 35/65 in the claimant's favour. The Court of Appeal refused the defendant's application for permission to appeal.

(C)   DRIVER AT FAULT

[10.20]   **Boss v Litton**
(1832) 5 C & P 407

All persons, paralytic as well as others, have a right to walk on the road and are entitled to the exercise of reasonable care on the part of persons driving carriages upon it.

Note—See *Kite v Nolan* (1982) 126 Sol Jo 821, [1983] RTR 253, CA.

[10.21]   **Parkinson v Parkinson**
[1973] RTR 193n, CA

The defendant was driving his car along a straight unlighted road at night. He saw ahead of him on the nearside of the road two women pedestrians walking in the same direction as he was travelling, but failed to see until it was too late, two men walking about 20 yards behind them. One of the men was approximately 4 ft 6 inches away from the edge of the road. The road was 25ft wide. There was a grass verge on the left of the road but only a hedge on the right. The judge found the defendant wholly to blame. On appeal it was argued that the pedestrians were negligent in not following the advice in the Highway Code to walk on the right of the road so as to face the oncoming traffic.

HELD: There were no grounds for finding contributory negligence. Even if the outside pedestrian was 4ft 6 inches away from the edge of the road, this did not amount to negligence on a road which was 25ft wide. It is depriving pedestrians of their natural rights as highway users to say they must walk on the right and are not entitled to walk on the nearside. The mere fact that a pedestrian walks on the left side of a country road is not necessarily negligent; it depends on the circumstances. In the present case there was a grass verge on the left where pedestrians could move onto when faced with an emergency. There was only a hedge on the right.

[10.22]   **Tremayne v Hill**
[1987] RTR 131, CA

The defendant drove into a junction past a red traffic light and struck the claimant, a pedestrian who had not used the nearby light-controlled pelican crossing, but was crossing the junction diagonally. He alleged that the claimant was contributorily negligent for failing to keep a proper lookout and failing to cross at the pelican crossing. The judge held that the accident was entirely caused by the defendant's negligence.

HELD, ON APPEAL: The defendant was wholly to blame. The claimant had no reason to anticipate that he would ignore the traffic lights. The defendant was seriously careless and any possible failure to keep a proper lookout was not a contributory factor. *Per curiam*: There is no legal duty on a pedestrian to cross a junction only at a light-controlled pedestrian crossing. He (or she) is entitled to cross anywhere he wishes provided he takes reasonable care for his own safety.

Note—See also *Fitzgerald v Lane* [1989] AC 328, [1988] 2 All ER 961, [1988] 3 WLR 356, 132 Sol Jo 1064, HL.

[10.23]   Carter v Sheath
[1990] RTR 12, CA

The defendant who was a good careful driver was approaching a pelican crossing which was showing a green light in his favour. Somewhere close to the pelican crossing the defendant's car struck the claimant, a 13-year-old boy, who suffered serious injuries. The claimant could remember nothing about the accident. Neither the defendant nor his wife, who was sitting in the front passenger seat, saw the claimant at all. The judge at first instance commented on the unusual difficulties of the case because of the 'curious paucity of direct evidence as to what exactly happened'. The judge held the defendant 50% to blame for not seeing the claimant who was there to be seen and the claimant 50% contributorily negligent. Both parties appealed.

HELD: The defendant's appeal was allowed. The claimant had not discharged the burden of proving that his injuries were caused by the defendant's negligence. Therefore no question of contributory negligence arose. Lord Brandon of Oakbrooks dictum in *Rhesa Shipping Co SA v Edmunds* [1985] 2 All ER 712, [1985] 1 WLR 948 applied.

[10.24]   Adamson v Roberts
1951 SC 681, 1951 SLT 355, 101 L Jo 511, Ct of Sess

A pedestrian was walking in daylight along a pavement at a point where it was narrowed by a projecting building, and had to put one foot over the edge of the pavement into the gutter in order to pass other pedestrians. As she did so, she was struck from behind by a motor van. The van did not encroach upon or over the kerb. In the Outer House of the Court of Session the action was dismissed ((1951) 101 LJ 330).

HELD, ON APPEAL: In the circumstances a special duty was imposed upon the driver in relation to the speed at which he travelled, the warning which he gave and the part of the road on which he directed his vehicle. Appeal allowed.

[10.25]   Chapman v Post Office
[1982] RTR 165, CA

The claimant was struck by the projecting driver-mirror of a passing vehicle when standing on the kerb at a bus stop. She sustained a severe blow to her arm. At the trial of her claim for damages the judge said she must have been leaning over the carriage way and found her equally to blame with the driver of the vehicle.

HELD, ON APPEAL: She was not at all to blame. A person standing on a kerb is not guilty of negligence if struck even if leaning out or having her back to the traffic, nor even if she went an inch or two into the roadway.

[10.26]   Powell v Phillips

[1972] 3 All ER 864, [1973] RTR 19, 116 Sol Jo 713, CA

The claimant and a friend were walking along a poorly-lit street at night on the left-hand pavement. From time to time because of snow and slush on the pavement they walked in the roadway near the kerb. Whilst so doing, the claimant was hit from behind by the defendant's car, which was travelling at speed and did not stop. It was argued for the defendant that the claimant was guilty of 25% contributory negligence because she was not complying with the rules for pedestrians in the Highway Code: she was walking next to the kerb with her back to traffic, not wearing or carrying anything white.

HELD: She was not, on the facts, guilty of contributory negligence. Though the Road Traffic Act 1960, s 74(5) (now s 38(7) of the 1988 Act) enables a party to rely upon a breach of the Highway Code as tending to establish or negative liability, a breach creates no presumption of negligence calling for an explanation, still less a presumption of negligence contributing to or causing an accident or injury. A breach is just one of the circumstances on which a party can rely in establishing the negligence of the other and its contribution to causing the accident or injury. A breach of the Highway Code must not be elevated into a breach of statutory duty. In the present case, the claimant had not failed to take reasonable care for her own safety in walking a few feet out in the road for about 20 yards when it got too slushy; even if it did amount to negligence it made no real contribution to the accident.

[10.27]   Kerley v Downes

[1973] RTR 188, CA

The claimants were father and son, the latter aged 13. At night they left the lighted entrance to a fairground adjoining a straight country road and walked along a grass verge alongside the road for a distance and then along the left hand edge of the road for 20 yards or so preparatory to crossing to the other side at a place where there was an isolated street lamp. Before they reached it they were struck from behind by the defendant's car. The judge declined to find the claimant father negligent either for his own safety or in respect of his son's.

HELD: The judge was right. Following *Parkinson v Parkinson* and *Powell v Phillips* [1972] 3 All ER 864, 116 Sol Jo 713, CA mere contravention of the recommendation in the Highway Code to walk on the right of the road and not to walk with your back to the traffic did not create a presumption of negligence.

[10.28]   Thomas v Kostanjevec

[2004] EWCA Civ 1782

[2005] All ER (D) 39 (Jan)

The deceased was a pedestrian who was killed when he was struck by the claimant's motorcycle on the A4042. The road is a single carriageway which is approximately 8m wide. The claimant was travelling north towards Abergavenny and was riding down a hill towards a bend. The deceased was attempting to cross the road from east to west on his way home when he was struck by the claimant's motorcycle.

The claimant's speed immediately prior to impact was 50mph which was below the 60mph speed limit. The judge at first instance found in favour of the claimant and dismissed the counterclaim. The basis of the judge's findings was that the claimant's speed was not excessive. Also as he did not see the deceased until the last moment he was unable to avoid the collision. The defendant appealed.

HELD, ON APPEAL: The claimant was riding a powerful heavy motorcycle which when approaching the bend at 50mph made it difficult for him to brake safely. The area was well known to both parties and the deceased had crossed at that section of the road on previous occasions in the past. The court found that the claimant had been travelling too quickly in the circumstances, as he could not stop within the limit of his visibility, and failed to keep a proper lookout, or take account of a pedestrian who may have been attempting to cross the road. The appeal was allowed with the deceased not being held liable.

[10.29]   **Dickens v Bearman**

[2003] EWCA Crim 1397

[2003] All ER (D) 23 (Oct)

The claimant was positioned on the nearside kerb. The defendant driving a Mitsubishi Shogun was in the process of reversing when he struck the claimant. The judge at first instance apportioned liability 50/50. The claimant appealed.

HELD, ON APPEAL: The defendant had called no evidence and relied upon CCTV footage. The claimant who suffered a brain injury had no recollection of events. The Court of Appeal held that the CCTV footage showed the claimant returning to the defendant's vehicle. He was standing by the nearside door when the defendant reversed colliding with the claimant in the process. As neither the defendant nor his passengers attended court to give evidence, the court was unable on the available evidence to find the claimant at fault. Appeal allowed.

[10.30]   **Sang v Cornes**

[2005] EWHC 203 (QB), QB

The claimant was injured when she was struck by the defendant's vehicle as she attempted to cross Shiel Road in Liverpool. The accident occurred near the junction of Kensington Road, which is a junction governed by traffic lights which has a green filter for traffic turning right from Prescott Road (which becomes Kensington Road). Primary liability was admitted, but the issue of contributory negligence had to be addressed. The court was asked to decide whether the place where the claimant decided to cross the road was dangerous, and also whether the filter light was in the defendant's favour when he went through it.

HELD: The filter light was off when the defendant entered Shiel Road, and it was also held that the claimant had crossed the road at the safest point in the road. As the claimant was not in any way at fault the defendant was found 100% liable. The court further found that as the claimant had been careful and observant she exercised extreme care, which was supported by independent evidence.

2. PEDESTRIAN CROSSINGS/ZEBRA CROSSINGS

[10.31] Crank v Brooks

[1980] RTR 441, QBD

A person who is walking across a pedestrian crossing pushing a bicycle having started on the pavement on one side on foot and pushing the bicycle with both feet on the ground is a 'foot passenger' within the meaning of the 'Zebra' pedestrian crossings.

(A) THE STATUTORY REGULATIONS

(I) ROAD TRAFFIC REGULATION ACT 1984

[10.32]

25

(1)   The Secretary of State may make regulations with respect to the precedence of vehicles and pedestrians respectively, and generally with respect to the movement of traffic (including pedestrians), at and in the vicinity of crossings.

(2)   Without prejudice to the generality of subsection (1) above, regulations under that subsection may be made:

    (a)   prohibiting pedestrian traffic on the carriageway within 100 yards of a crossing, and

    (b)   with respect to the indication of the limits of a crossing, or of any other matter whatsoever relating to the crossing, by marks or devices on or near the roadway or otherwise, and generally with respect to the erection of traffic signs in connection with a crossing.

(3)   Different regulations may be made under this section in relation to different traffic conditions, and in particular (but without prejudice to the generality of the foregoing words) different regulations may be made in relation to crossings in the vicinity of, and at a distance from, a junction of roads, and in relation to traffic which is controlled by the police, and by traffic signals, and by different kinds of traffic signals, and traffic which is not controlled.

(4)   Regulations may be made under this section applying only to a particular crossing or particular crossings specified in the regulations.

(5)   A person who contravenes any regulations made under this section shall be guilty of an offence.

(6)   In this section 'crossing' means a crossing for pedestrians established:

    (a)   by a local authority under section 23 of this Act, or

    (b)   by the Secretary of State in the discharge of the duty imposed on him by section 24 of this Act, and (in either case) indicated in accordance with the regulations having effect as respects that crossing; and, for the purposes of a prosecution for a contravention of the provisions of a regulation having effect as respects a crossing, the crossing shall be deemed to be so established and indicated unless the contrary is proved.

(II) ZEBRA, PELICAN AND PUFFIN PEDESTRIAN CROSSINGS REGULATIONS AND GENERAL DIRECTIONS 1997, SI 1997/2400

[10.33] *Note*—The 'Zebra' Pedestrian Crossings Regulations 1971, SI 1971/1524, reg 8, which *inter alia* gave precedence to foot passengers only on an uncontrolled zebra crossing, was revoked and updated by SI 1997/2400, reg 25.

25   Precedence of pedestrians over vehicles at Zebra crossings

(1)   Every pedestrian, if he is on the carriageway within the limits of a Zebra crossing, which is not for the time being controlled by a constable in uniform or traffic warden, before any part of a vehicle has entered those limits, shall have

precedence within those limits over that vehicle and the driver of the vehicle shall accord such precedence to any such pedestrian.

(2)   Where there is a refuge for pedestrians or central reservation on a Zebra crossing, the parts of the crossing situated on each side of the refuge for pedestrians or central reservation shall, for the purposes of this regulation, be treated as separate crossings.

[10.34]   Scott v Clint

(1960) Times, 28 October, Div Ct

A lorry was approaching a pedestrian crossing at 15–20mph. When it was only 10 yards from the crossing two children stepped on to the crossing without looking to their right and started to cross. The driver did his best to avoid them but was unable to avoid hitting one of them.

HELD: Regulation 4 of the Pedestrian Crossings Regulations 1954, SI 1954/370 laid down an absolute duty (now regulation 25 of SI 1997/2400) Once a pedestrian is on a crossing the driver of any vehicle approaching that crossing must accord him precedence, however unexpectedly or suddenly he crosses. The driver was found guilty of an offence.

[10.35]   Hughes v Hall

[1960] 2 All ER 504, [1960] 1 WLR 733, 124 JP 411, 104 Sol Jo 566, Div Ct

The respondent was driving a car, at a reasonable and proper speed towards a pedestrian crossing. He had passed over the studs indicating the approach to the crossing when a woman stepped off the nearside pavement on to the crossing without looking to right or left and began to walk over the crossing. The respondent applied his brakes at once but was unable to pull up in time to avoid hitting her. On a charge under the Pedestrian Crossings Regulations 1954, SI 1954/370, reg 4 (now regulation 25 of SI 1997/2400) the respondent pleaded that:

(1)   in passing over the approach studs he had come within the limits of the crossing before the woman stepped on to it and there was no case to answer;

(2)   on the authority of *Leicester v Pearson* [1952] 2 All ER 71, the duty imposed by reg 4 was not absolute.

HELD: (1) The limits are not the approach studs but the studs which border the striped crossing.

(2)   On the latest decisions of the Divisional Court in *Gibbons v Kahl* [1956] 1 QB 59, [1955] 3 All ER 345 and *Lockie v Lawton* (1959) 124 JP 24, regulation 4 imposes an absolute duty and it is quite immaterial whether there is any evidence of negligence or failure to take reasonable care.

Offence proved.

[10.36]   Levy v Hockey

(1961) 105 Sol Jo 157   Nield J

The claimant was knocked down and injured on an uncontrolled pedestrian crossing by a car driven by the defendant who overtook three other cars that were slowing down. The defendant pleaded that his failure to pull up in time was due to a latent defect in the braking system of his car, not discoverable by the exercise of reasonable care, so that the brakes failed to operate properly when he applied them.

HELD: In so far as the claim was based on a breach of the Pedestrian Crossings Regulations 1954, SI 1954/370, reg 4 (now reg 25 of SI 1997/2400), the question arose of impossibility. If the court were satisfied that, owing to a latent defect, a situation arose in which it was impossible for a driver to accord precedence to a foot passenger there would be no breach of the statutory duty so as to give rise to a right to damages. On the particular facts of this case, however, there was no latent defect.

[10.37]   Neal v Bedford

[1966] 1 QB 505, [1965] 3 All ER 250, [1965] 3 WLR 1008, 129 JP 534, Div Ct

Two pedestrians began to walk across a pedestrian crossing. When they were about a third of the way across they stopped to allow a car coming from their right to pass over the crossing in front of them. The defendant was driving a car behind the one which the pedestrians had allowed to pass and he began to follow it over the crossing. As he did the pedestrians started to walk forward again and one was struck by his car on the crossing. A charge against him of failing to accord precedence to the pedestrians on the crossing was dismissed, the magistrates being of the opinion that the pedestrians had waived their precedence. The prosecutor appealed.

HELD: Regulation 4 of the Pedestrian Crossings Regulations 1954, SI 1954/370 imposed an absolute duty on motorists to accord precedence to pedestrians on an uncontrolled crossing. The justices had taken the view that the defendant was misled into thinking that the pedestrians had stopped to let him pass. Whether he genuinely thought they would let him pass was irrelevant. His absolute duty was to allow the pedestrians to cross. They had not waived their precedence by signalling him to pass; they had started walking. There must be a conviction.

[10.38]   Burns v Bidder

[1967] 2 QB 227, [1966] 3 All ER 29, [1966] 3 WLR 99, 130 JP 342, 110 Sol Jo 430, Div Ct

The defendant was charged with failing to accord precedence to a pedestrian on a pedestrian crossing contrary to regulation 4 of the Pedestrian Crossings Regulations 1954, SI 1954/370 (now regulation 25 of SI 1997/2400). When driving his car he had overtaken a bus which was waiting at a pedestrian crossing for people to cross, and had gone straight over the crossing without stopping, striking a pedestrian. He alleged that his brakes had failed, though a police officer testing them afterwards found nothing wrong. The magistrate said he was not satisfied the brakes had not failed but that the duty under the regulation was absolute and the defendant was guilty of the offence charged.

HELD, ON APPEAL: Regulation 4 does not impose an absolute duty come what may; there is no breach of the obligation under the regulation in circumstances where the driver fails to accord precedence to a pedestrian on the crossing solely because his control of the vehicle is taken from him by the occurrence of an event which is outside his possible or reasonable control and in respect of which he is in no way at fault. As Nield J said in *Levy v Hockey*, regulation 4 must be read subject to the principle as to impossibility. Examples include a driver stung by a swarm of bees or suffering a sudden epileptic form of disabling attack, or a vehicle being knocked forward on to the crossing by another vehicle hitting it from behind, or a sudden removal of control occasioned by a latent defect of which the driver did not and could not reasonably know. But beyond that limited sphere the obligation of the driver can properly be described as absolute. In the present case the magistrate was not satisfied the brakes had not failed and the conviction must be quashed.

[10.39] Moulder v Neville

[1974] RTR 53, Div Ct

The defendant was driving his car towards an uncontrolled (ie 'Zebra') crossing and was within the area marked by the zig-zag lines when a pedestrian stepped on to the crossing. The defendant continued over the crossing, missing the pedestrian by a foot. On a charge of failing to give precedence he claimed that the area between the zig-zag lines was part of the crossing and that when a vehicle was within the controlled area (ie between the zig-zag lines) no pedestrian should move on to the crossing.

HELD: The roadway between the zig-zag lines was not part of the crossing. If a pedestrian gets on to the striped area before the car gets on to the striped area the driver must give the pedestrian priority.

Note—See SI 1997/2400, reg 25 at para [10.32], which sets out the regulations relating to precedence of pedestrians on zebra crossings.

(B)   DRIVER NOT LIABLE

[10.40] Jankovic v Howell

[1970] CLY 1863   Ormerod J

The claimant, crossing a road by a pedestrian crossing, walked over the central island without pausing and on to the other half of the crossing, where he was struck by the defendant's scooter.

HELD: It was superfluous to hoot or take evasive action every time a pedestrian approaches a refuge. Judgment for the defendant.

(C)   CONTRIBUTORY NEGLIGENCE

[10.41] Lawrence v W M Palmer (Excavations) Ltd

(1965) 109 Sol Jo 358   Phillimore J

The claimant, aged 77 and deaf, was crossing the road on a pedestrian crossing when she was struck by the rear nearside of the defendant's lorry, which came from her right. She was found after the accident lying on the road 11ft from the pavement and 8 or 9ft from the crossing.

HELD: Her injuries indicated a considerable impact from which one might have expected her to be thrown backwards towards the direction from which she came. The defendant was found negligent as the court were satisfied that the lorry driver could not have been keeping a proper lookout as the claimant must have been on the crossing before the lorry. As the claimant had precedence over the lorry driver, he was found negligent as well as being in breach of statutory duty. The claimant was also found contributory negligent in failing to see the lorry and proceeding without regard to whether there was other traffic on the road. Liability was apportioned two-thirds to one-third in favour of the claimant.

[10.42] **Maynard v Rogers**

[1970] RTR 392   Mocatta J

Shortly after midnight in a not very well-lit street the claimant, aged 19, stepped on to a pedestrian crossing without first looking to her right. She was hit by the defendant's car coming from her right. She was not far from the pavement she had left and the defendant had very little opportunity of avoiding the accident. The claimant must have been able to see his car if she had looked.

HELD: Although the major proportion of the blame must rest on the claimant it was possible that if the defendant had sounded his horn she might have been able to jump back. The claimant was found two-thirds to blame, the defendant one-third.

[10.43] **Clifford v Drymond**

[1976] RTR 134, CA

Whilst walking across the road on a zebra crossing, the claimant was struck by a car coming from her right. She was thrown or carried 45ft and sustained serious injuries. She was 10ft on to the crossing when hit. The judge found on the available evidence that the car, travelling not more than 30mph had been about 75ft away when the claimant began to cross. He considered whether the claimant was guilty of contributory negligence in stepping on to the crossing when the approaching car was within 75ft to 80ft and decided she was not.

HELD, ON APPEAL: The claimant should bear 20% of the blame. The Highway Code required a pedestrian not only to allow vehicles plenty of time to slow down or stop before starting to cross, but also to look right and left while crossing. If the claimant did not look at the approaching car she was negligent; if she did look she should have seen the car was near enough to make it doubtful whether it would pull up. She must also have been guilty of a measure of negligence in having failed to keep the car under observation as she proceeded to cross the road. If she had she would have seen that it was not going to stop and could have allowed it to pass.

[10.44] **Judge (by her mother and litigation friend Gwen Judge) v Brown**

(26 March 2001, unreported), QBD

The claimant was 12 years old at the date of the accident. The claimant was walking home from school with friends and as she stepped out onto a zebra crossing, a vehicle driven by the defendant collided with her. The claimant brought an action against the defendant alleging he was negligent in failing to keep a lookout for pedestrians on the zebra crossing.

HELD, at trial: The judge found that had the defendant been keeping a proper look out he ought to have seen the claimant. The judge submitted that a reasonably careful driver should have been ready to slow down or stop to let children cross. The judge also stated that a girl of the claimant's age ought reasonably to have appreciated that she was stepping out when the defendant's vehicle was close. Judgment was entered with liability split between the parties at 50/50.

3.   TRAFFIC LIGHTS (PUSH BUTTON CONTROLLED CROSSINGS)

(A)   THE STATUTORY REGULATIONS

[10.45]   *Note*—The Zebra, Pelican and Puffin Pedestrian Crossings Regulations and General Directions 1997, 1997/2400, reg 12.

12   Significance of vehicular light signals at Pelican crossings

(1)   The significance of the vehicular light signals prescribed by regulation 5(2)(a) and paragraph 3 of Schedule 2 for the purpose of indicating a Pelican crossing shall be as follows-

(a)   the green signal shall indicate that vehicular traffic may proceed beyond the stop line and across the crossing;

(b)   the green arrow signal shall indicate that vehicular traffic may proceed beyond the stop line and through the crossing only for the purpose of proceeding in the direction indicated by the arrow;

(c)   except as provided by sub-paragraph (e) [and sub-paragraph (ea)] [and sub-paragraph (eb)] the steady amber signal shall convey the same prohibition as the red signal except that, as respects a vehicle which is so close to the stop line that it cannot safely be stopped without proceeding beyond the stop line, it shall convey the same indication as the green signal or, if the amber signal was immediately preceded by a green arrow signal, as that green arrow signal;

(d)   except as provided in sub-paragraph (e) [and sub-paragraph (ea)] [and sub-paragraph (eb)], the red signal shall convey the prohibition that vehicular traffic shall not proceed beyond the stop line;

(e)   when a vehicle is being used for [relevant authority (as defined in section 6 of the Fire (Scotland) Act 2005 (asp 5))] [or, in England, fire and rescue authority], ambulance, national blood service or police purposes and the observance of the prohibition conveyed by the steady amber or the red signal in accordance with sub-paragraph (c) or (d) would be likely to hinder the use of that vehicle for the purpose for which it is being used, then those sub-paragraphs shall not apply to the vehicle, and the steady amber and the red signal shall each convey the information that the vehicle may proceed beyond the stop line if the driver-

(i)   accords precedence to any pedestrian who is on that part of the carriageway which lies within the limits of the crossing or on a central reservation which lies between two crossings which do not form part of a system of staggered crossings; and

(ii)   does not proceed in a manner or at a time likely to endanger any person or any vehicle approaching or waiting at the crossing, or to cause the driver of any such vehicle to change its speed or course in order to avoid an accident; and

[(ea) as regards England and Wales, and so far as relating to the functions of the Serious Organised Crime Agency which are exercisable in or as regards Scotland and which relate to reserved matters (within the meaning of the Scotland Act 1998), when a vehicle is being used for Serious Organised Crime Agency purposes and the observance of the prohibition conveyed by the steady amber or the red signal in accordance with sub-paragraph (c) or (d) would be likely to hinder the use of that vehicle for those purposes, then those sub-paragraphs shall not apply to the vehicle, and the steady amber and the red signal shall each convey the information that the vehicle may proceed beyond the stop line if the driver-

(i)   accords precedence to any pedestrian who is on that part of the carriageway which lies within the limits of the crossing or on a central reservation which lies between two crossings which do not form part of a system of staggered crossings; and

(ii)   does not proceed in a manner or at a time likely to endanger any person or any vehicle approaching or waiting at the crossing, or to cause the driver of any such vehicle to change its speed or course in order to avoid an accident; and]

[(eb) so far as relating to the functions of the Serious Organised Crime Agency which are exercisable in or as regards Scotland and which do not (within the meaning of the Scotland Act 1998) relate to reserved matters, when a vehicle is being used for Serious Organised Crime Agency purposes and the observance of the prohibition conveyed by the steady amber or the red signal in accordance with sub-paragraph (c) or (d) would be likely to hinder the use of that vehicle for those purposes, then those sub-paragraphs shall not apply to the vehicle, and the steady amber and the red signal shall each convey the information that the vehicle may proceed beyond the stop line if the driver-

    (i)   accords precedence to any pedestrian who is on that part of the carriageway which lies within the limits of the crossing or on a central reservation which lies between two crossings which do not form part of a system of staggered crossings;

    (ii)   does not proceed in a manner or at a time likely to endanger any person or any vehicle approaching or waiting at the crossing, or to cause the driver of any such vehicle to change its speed or course in order to avoid an accident; and]

    (f)   the flashing amber signal shall convey the information that traffic may proceed across the crossing but that every pedestrian who is on the carriageway or a central reservation within the limits of the crossing (but not if he is on a central reservation which lies between two crossings forming part of a system of staggered crossings) before any part of a vehicle has entered those limits, has the right of precedence within those limits over that vehicle, and the requirement that the driver of a vehicle shall accord such precedence to any such pedestrian.

(2)   Vehicular traffic proceeding beyond a stop line in accordance with paragraph (1) shall proceed with due regard to the safety of other road users and subject to any direction given by a constable in uniform or a traffic warden or to any other applicable prohibition or restriction.

(3)   In this regulation, references to the 'stop line' in relation to a Pelican crossing where the stop line is not visible are to be treated as references to the post or other structure on which the primary signal is mounted.

[10.46]   Oakley-Moore v Robinson

[1982] RTR 74, Div Ct

The defendant's car ran out of petrol. He stopped it within the limits of a Pelican crossing and went away. He was convicted of leaving it within the approach limits of the crossing. On appeal he contended he had been 'prevented from proceeding by circumstances beyond his control' (the 'Pelican' Pedestrian Crossing Regulations, reg 9(2)).

HELD: Though a latent defect unknown to the driver could be a defence, the present case was not one of latent defect. The amount of petrol in a motor car is something which is at all times plainly within the control of the driver.

(B)   DRIVER NOT LIABLE

[10.47]   Turner v Arriva North East Ltd

[2006] EWCA Civ 410

[2006] All ER (D) 369 (Mar)

The deceased was killed by a bus driver when she attempted to cross a road whilst the pedestrian lights were red against her. It was the bus drivers evidence that his speed was 15mph, although expert evidence suggested that his speed was in the region of 24mph (which was within the speed limit). At first instance the judge found in favour of the bus driver as his speed was not excessive, and he was travelling in a clear lane with traffic lights in his favour. The judge also found that given the size and angle of the bus, the driver's view of the pedestrian crossing was restricted. The claimant appealed.

The Court of Appeal held that the judge was justified in finding that no liability rested with the bus driver as there was no reason why he could not proceed and there was no way he could have seen the pedestrian until it was too late.

(C) CONTRIBUTORY NEGLIGENCE

[10.48] Goddard and Walker v Greenwood

[2002] EWCA Civ 1590

[2002] All ER (D) 285 (Oct), [2003] RTR 159

The claimants were jogging on the eastern side of the A20 carriageway in Dover, which is made up of three lanes. The defendant was approaching a junction controlled by traffic lights when the lights changed from red to green. The defendant therefore continued to drive and collided with the claimants as they passed in front of him.

At first instance, the judge found that no liability should attach to the defendant as he was under no obligation to stop or slow down as the signal had changed to green. The judge further commented that if he was wrong on primary liability that he would have reduced the claim for damages by 80% to reflect the claimants level of contributory negligence.

HELD, ON APPEAL: That the judge was not entitled to make a finding of no liability as although the lights were green, this did not mean that the defendant had discharged his duty of care. Further, as there was a lorry to the defendant's left, which had remained stationery, this should have alerted him to the fact that pedestrians might have been crossing especially as the lights had just changed.

The court held that a prudent driver would have realised this and would have acted accordingly.

The court therefore held that the defendant was liability but accepted the level of contributory negligence found by the judge at first instance.

[10.49] Lunt v Khelifa

[2002] EWCA Civ 801

[2002] All ER (D) 352

A defendant motorist, who was driving within the speed limit, knocked down the claimant who was a pedestrian crossing the road at a junction normally controlled by traffic signals. At the time neither the main traffic lights nor the pedestrian lights were working. The claimant was three-and-a-half times over the drink-driving limit for drivers.

HELD: The Court of Appeal upheld an apportionment of liability of two-thirds/one-third in the claimant's favour as the defendant breached his duty of care in failing to brake and failing to see the claimant in an area near an Underground station where he should have known there were likely to be pedestrians.

(D)   DRIVER AT FAULT

[10.50]   Shepherd v H West & Son Ltd
(1962) 106 Sol Jo 391   Paull J

The claimant and her 13-year-old daughter wished to cross the road at a junction controlled by traffic lights. They ensured that the traffic lights were showing red and then began to cross in front of a bus which was stationary at the traffic light on the nearside of the road. Whilst they were passing in front of the bus the light changed to red-amber and the bus driver 'revved-up' his engine preparatory to moving off. This alarmed the claimant who looked to her right along the offside of the bus and took a step forward to clear the bus in case it moved forward. She was at once struck by the defendant's lorry which was overtaking the bus. The lorry driver's evidence was that the traffic lights were red when he approached, changed to red-amber before he reached the bus and to green as he came alongside it.

HELD: The lorry driver was clearly negligent. A reasonable driver in such circumstances would not have let the front wheels of his lorry get level with the bus until the bus had got half-way across the crossing. To pass a stationary vehicle under such circumstances was a dangerous practice: the danger ought to be realised by all motorists. It was natural for the claimant to have tried to get out of the way of the bus when she heard its engine 'revving-up': she could not have taken more than one step forward and was not in any way negligent.

[10.51]   Frank v Cox
(1967) 111 Sol Jo 670, CA

At a crossroads controlled by traffic lights Frank began walking across the road on the south side from east to west. The traffic lights had changed and were in his favour. Cox was in his car in the road at the west side of the junction. As soon as the lights changed he drove into the junction and turned right, knocking down Frank who had then almost reached the centre refuge.

HELD: Cox's driving was not only careless, it verged on the monstrous, and Frank was not at all to blame. There is a paramount duty on motorists turning at junctions when the lights show in their favour to be sure that no pedestrians are crossing the road they are entering. They must observe the Highway Code which requires drivers when turning at junctions to give precedent to pedestrians who are crossing.

[10.52]   White v Saxton
11 PMIL 10
January 1996

The claimant was a 17-year-old pedestrian. At 6 pm in November she was attempting to cross a single carriageway using a designated pedestrian crossing. She pressed the button and waited for the traffic lights to change to red, and for the green man to appear.
  A car travelling from her left stopped at the crossing. The claimant started to cross, and in the course of crossing noticed some headlights coming from her right. This vehicle driven by the defendant struck the claimant causing injury. Primary liability was conceded and the trial was limited to the issue of contributory negligence.

HELD: The claimant was not contributorily negligent. When the claimant commenced her crossing there was either no traffic to her right or if there was a vehicle approaching she was correct to assume that the vehicle would see the changing lights and come to a halt. Therefore it was reasonable for the claimant to assume that it was safe to cross when the lights permitted her to do so.

4. SCHOOL CROSSINGS

(A) THE STATUTORY REGULATIONS

[10.53] *Note*—The Traffic Signs Regulations and General Directions 2002, SI 2002/3113, reg 50, governs warning lights at school crossing places.
Signs prescribed by SI 1982/859.

(I) ROAD TRAFFIC REGULATION ACT 1984

[10.54]
26 Arrangements for patrolling school crossings
    (1)   Arrangements may be made by the appropriate authority for the patrolling of places where children cross roads on their way to or from school, or from one part of a school to another, ... by persons appointed by or on behalf of the appropriate authority, other than constables.
    [(1A)   Arrangements under subsection (1) above may be made for patrolling places at such times as the authority thinks fit.]
    (2)   For the purposes of this section, in its application to England and Wales, the appropriate authority—
        (a)   as respects places [outside Greater London], shall be the council of the county [or metropolitan district] in which the places in question are;
        (b)   as respects places in the City of London, shall be the Common Council of the City; and
        [(c)   as respects places in a London borough, shall be the council for the borough,] and for the purposes of this section, in its application to Scotland, the appropriate authority shall be the [council constituted under section 2 of the Local Government etc (Scotland) Act 1994].
    (3)   The functions of the appropriate authority for the purposes of arrangements under subsection (1) above shall include the duty to satisfy themselves of the adequate qualifications of persons appointed to patrol, and to provide requisite training of persons to be appointed.
    (4)   In taking decisions as to making arrangements under subsection (1) above ... in England or Wales, the council of a county [or metropolitan district], ... shall have regard to any representations made to them ... by local authorities for localities in the county [or] [, metropolitan district ..., as the case may be, ...
    [(4A)   Before making arrangements under subsection (1) above for the patrolling of places where children cross GLA roads, a London borough council or the Common Council of the City of London must consult Transport for London and take account of any representations made by Transport for London.]
    (5)   Any arrangements under subsection (1) above ... if made in England or Wales by the council of the county[, London borough] [or metropolitan district as respects places in the county[, London borough] or district], may include an agreement between that council and the police authority for the police area in which those places are, ... for the performance by the police authority, ... on such terms as may be specified in the agreement, of such functions for the purposes of the arrangements as may be so specified.

Note—That section 27 of the 1984 Act was repealed by the Greater London Authority Act 1999, ss 288(6).

[10.55]
28   Stopping of vehicles at school crossings
(1)   When ... a vehicle is approaching a place in a road where [a person is] crossing or seeking to cross the road, a school crossing patrol wearing a uniform approved by the Secretary of State shall have power, by exhibiting a prescribed sign, to require the person driving or propelling the vehicle to stop it.
(2)   When a person has been required under subsection (1) above to stop a vehicle—
    (a)   he shall cause the vehicle to stop before reaching the place where the [person is] crossing or seeking to cross and so as not to stop or impede [his] crossing, and
    (b)   the vehicle shall not be put in motion again so as to reach the place in question so long as the sign continues to be exhibited.
(3)   A person who fails to comply with paragraph (a) of subsection (2) above, or who causes a vehicle to be put in motion in contravention of paragraph (b) of that subsection, shall be guilty of an offence.
(4)   In this section—
    (a)   'prescribed sign' means a sign of a size, colour and type prescribed by regulations made by the Secretary of State or, if authorisation is given by the Secretary of State for the use of signs of a description not so prescribed, a sign of that description;
    (b)   'school crossing patrol' means a person authorised to patrol in accordance with arrangements under section 26 of this Act; and regulations under paragraph (a) above may provide for the attachment of reflectors to signs or for the illumination of signs.
(5)   For the purposes of this section—
    (a)   where it is proved that a sign was exhibited by a school crossing patrol, it shall be presumed, unless the contrary is proved, to be of a size, colour and type prescribed, or of a description authorised, under subsection (4)(b) above, and, if it was exhibited in circumstances in which it was required by the regulations to be illuminated, to have been illuminated in the prescribed manner; [and]
    (b)   where it is proved that a school crossing patrol was wearing a uniform, the uniform shall be presumed, unless the contrary is proved, to be a uniform approved by the Secretary of State; ...
    (c)   ...

(II)   TRAFFIC SIGNS REGULATIONS AND GENERAL DIRECTIONS 2002, SI 2002/3113

[10.56]
50   Warning lights at school crossing places
A sign for conveying a warning to vehicular traffic that a school crossing place lies ahead and is being patrolled by a school crossing patrol or is otherwise in use by such children—
    (a)   shall be a light signal of the size, colour and type shown in diagram 4004, each lamp of which when operated shall show an intermittent amber light at a rate of flashing of not less than 60 nor more than 90 flashes per minute and in such a manner that one light is always shown when the other light is not shown; and
    (b)   may be erected on or near part of the road in advance of a crossing place in relation to oncoming traffic.

(B)   DUTY OF TRAFFIC PATROL OFFICER

[10.57]   Hoy v Smith

[1964] 3 All ER 670, [1964] 1 WLR 1377, 129 JP 33, 108 Sol Jo 841, 62 LGR 661, Div Ct

'Exhibiting' does not necessarily mean that the sign should be held full face to the oncoming traffic; it is sufficient if the sign is held in such a way that the driver can see the words 'Stop: children crossing' on the sign.

[10.58]   Toole v Sherbourne Pouffes Ltd

[1971] RTR 479, CA

The claimant, aged six, came out of school, which was beside a busy main road, and was taken by a teacher with other children to a pedestrian crossing. At the crossing was a school crossing patrol officer. He stood at the side of the road with the children, waiting until he could step forward with his sign board to stop the traffic. The first defendant's van was approaching. The driver saw the patrol officer waiting at the side of the crossing so he carried on to pass over the crossing at about 30mph. Suddenly the claimant darted across the road on the crossing and was hit by the van. The judge held the first defendant's driver free from blame and held the second defendants, the school authority who employed the patrol officer, liable by reason of his negligence.

HELD: Dismissing the appeal, the patrol officer had not done enough to keep the children under control. If he had been exercising proper charge and keeping the children back the claimant would not have run suddenly into the road. Moreover, the second defendants, on this most critical part of the case, had not called the patrol officer to give evidence.

[10.59]   Franklin v Langdown

[1971] 3 All ER 662, 135 JP 615, 115 Sol Jo 688

When the crossing patrol is correctly displaying the 'Stop: children crossing' sign a motorist must stop and not move on again until the sign has been removed.

[10.60]   Wall v Walwyn

[1974] RTR 24, [1973] Crim LR 376.

An offence is committed if the driver fails to stop whether the children are impeded or not.

CHAPTER 11

Liability of Children

1.   CHILD NOT NEGLIGENT

[11.1]   Gough v Thorne

[1966] 3 All ER 398, [1966] 1 WLR 1387, 110 Sol Jo 529, CA

The claimant aged 13½ was waiting with her brothers aged 17 and 10 to cross the road. A lorry stopped to allow them to cross. The driver put his right hand out to warn other traffic and beckoned the children to cross. They had got across just beyond the lorry when a car driven by the defendant came past the lorry at speed and hit the claimant. The judge held the defendant negligent but said the claimant was one-third to blame for having advanced past the lorry into the open road without pausing to see whether there was any traffic coming from her right.

HELD, ON APPEAL: The claimant was not to blame at all. Though there was no age below which it could be said that a child could not be guilty of contributory negligence age was a most material fact to be considered. The question whether the claimant could be said to be guilty of contributory negligence depended on whether any ordinary child of 13½ could be expected to do any more than she did. If she had been a good deal older she might have wondered whether a proper signal had been given and looked to see whether any traffic was coming, but it was quite wrong to suggest that a child of 13½ should go through such mental processes.

[11.2]   Andrews v Freeborough

[1967] 1 QB 1, [1966] 2 All ER 721, [1966] 3 WLR, 110 Sol Jo 407, CA

An eight-year-old girl and her brother, aged four, were standing on the pavement edge waiting to cross the road. The defendant was driving her car at 15–20mph close to the kerb (because of oncoming traffic) and saw the children when she was about 40 yards away. She thought they were waiting to cross although they did not look in her direction. She did not slacken speed or sound her horn. As the car passed the children the girl's head came into violent contact with the windscreen.

At the trial of the action the defendant said she saw the girl step off the pavement into the side of the car but the judge did not accept this evidence. He held the defendant to blame:

(1)   for not sounding her horn;
(2)   for failing to reduce her speed and if necessary stop on seeing the children;
(3)   for driving too close to the kerb.

He found no contributory negligence on the part of the child. On appeal, the defendant did not dispute the finding of negligence in not sounding the horn but disputed the judge's other findings including that of no contributory negligence.

The appeal was dismissed.

Per Willmer LJ: I confess I find it quite difficult to appreciate just how the accident happened if the child remained on the kerb throughout. But [the judge's] finding that the child did not step off the kerb was a finding of primary fact, based largely on his view of the quality of the evidence he had heard. In my judgment it is not a finding with which this Court could properly interfere ... I would only add that if I thought that we could properly find that this child did step off the kerb into the road, I should have needed a good deal of persuasion before imputing contributory negligence to the child having regard to her tender age.

Per Davies LJ: So far as concerns the finding that the defendant was negligent in driving too close to the kerb, it is not easy to see the justification for it save in the light of the judge's conclusion that the little girl while still on the pavement was caught up by the car. Failure to slow or stop is another matter: in the light of the fact that the defendant had seen the children and had failed to call their attention to her presence the judge was entitled to make this finding. On the question whether, as the judge found, the child was caught up by the car or, as the defendant said, she stepped off from the kerb into the side of the car I am bound to say that I am of the view that it was more probable that the child did step off the kerb into the side of the car. But it is not necessary to express any decided view on this point for the little girl was only eight years of age. Even if she did step off into the car it would not be right to count as negligence on her part such a momentary, though fatal, act of inattention or carelessness.

[11.3]   Prudence v Lewis

(1966) Times, 21 May   Brabin J

The infant claimant aged just under-three years old was struck by the defendant's car on a pedestrian crossing. His mother had been waiting to cross, holding her youngest child in a push chair poised on the edge of the kerb at the crossing: while she looked round for her third child the claimant ran on to the crossing and was hit when about 7ft from the kerb.

HELD: The defendant was wholly to blame. He had seen the mother and children but, though realising that any child was likely to run out, did not blow his horn, thought that they should wait for him and drove on. A child of just under-three years old was incapable of being guilty of contributory negligence.

[11.4]   Jones v Lawrence

[1969] 3 All ER 267

The claimant, a boy aged seven, ran across a street 22ft wide from behind a parked van. The defendant was riding his motorcycle near the crown of the road and was unable to avoid striking the claimant, who had failed to see the motorcycle approaching. There was a 30mph speed limit but the judge found from independent evidence that the defendant's speed was about 50mph.

HELD: By travelling at such a speed the defendant had deprived himself of the opportunity to avoid the collision by swerving or braking and was negligent. The claimant's behaviour was such as one could expect in a normal child of his age momentarily forgetful of the perils of crossing a road and no finding of contributory negligence could be made against him.

[11.5]   Puffett (a minor by his litigation friend Joyce Ann Puffett) v Hayfield

[2005] EWCA Civ 1760

[2005] All ER (D) 256 (Dec)

The claimant aged 6 at the time of the accident was seriously injured after he was struck by the defendant's vehicle whilst driving on Glenmare in Essex. The road was a residential road where both the claimant and defendant lived. The accident occurred at 7.00 pm when it was dark although street lights were on. The road was dry and weather conditions were good. Children regularly played in the street.

The accident occurred when the claimant emerged between two parked vehicles, one of which was a van, into the path of the defendant's vehicle. The claimant's presence would have at first been obscured from the defendant.

The defendant was found to be liable at first instance, and appealed.

HELD, ON APPEAL: The judge was right to find the defendant negligent in that her speed was excessive in the circumstances.

[11.6]   M (a child) v Rollinson

[2003] 2 QR 14

The claimant who was aged 5 at the date of the accident, was taken by her father to purchase an ice cream from an ice cream van. The claimant was given the ice cream and went around the front of the van whilst the father was paying for it. The claimant ran into the side of the defendant's vehicle which was driving at no more than 15mph. It was held that whilst it was generally not negligent to pass a vehicle at 15mph, consideration had to be given to the fact that the vehicle in question was an ice cream van and the van carried a warning to its rear. Any reasonable person should have been aware of that hazard and 15mph was not slow enough to avoid the impact. The accident occurred in a residential area. The defendant had not been sufficiently careful and was liable to M in damages.

Note—Compare to *Kite v Nolan* (1982) 126 Sol Jo 821, [1983] RTR 253, CA.

2.   NEGLIGENCE OF CHILDREN

(A)   CONTRIBUTORY NEGLIGENCE

[11.7]   Gough v Thorne

[1966] 3 All ER 398, [1966] 1 WLR 1387, 110 Sol Jo 529, CA

Per Lord Denning MR: A very young child cannot be guilty of contributory negligence. An older child may be, but it depends on the circumstances. A judge should only find a child guilty of contributory negligence if he or she is of such an age as to be expected to take precautions for his or her own safety: and then he or she is only to be found guilty if blame should be attached to him or her. A child has not the road sense or the experience of his or her elders. He or she is not to be found guilty unless he or she is blameworthy.

[11.8]   Morales v Eccleston

[1991] RTR 151, CA

The claimant, an 11-year-old boy, was playing with a football along the pavement adjacent to a busy London road. The traffic was heavy but moving at 20–30mph on both sides of the road. The weather was fine, the road was dry and the visibility was good. The defendant was travelling at 20mph on the opposite side of the road to which the claimant was walking. The claimant lost control of his football and, without looking in either direction, followed it across the first carriageway into the path of the defendant's vehicle. The claimant suffered serious injuries and sued the defendant. The trial judge held that the defendant was 80% to blame. The defendant appealed.

HELD: McCowan LJ: On the evidence presented to the trial judge the defendant could not have had much more than two seconds in which to see the claimant. Despite this there was some evidence upon which the judge could have arrived at the view that the defendant was not keeping a proper lookout. The claimant showed a reckless disregard for his own safety and must bear a higher proportion of blame for the accident than the defendant. Blame was apportioned at 25% to the defendant and 75% to the claimant.

[11.9]   Foskett v Mistry

[1984] RTR 1, [1984] LS Gaz R 2683, CA

The claimant, a boy of 16½, ran down a parkland slope on to a busy road and collided with the nearside of the defendant's car near the windscreen, sustaining serious injury. The defendant had not seen him before he ran into the car. A driver coming in the opposite direction had seen the claimant and thought he was going to run into the road. The judge at first instance dismissed the claim.

HELD, ON APPEAL: The root of liability was negligence, which depended on the facts: reference to authorities in simple running-down cases was unnecessary. Could the defendant be shown to have failed to take reasonable care in all the circumstances? The defendant taking reasonable care ought to have glanced at the open parkland on his left and should have seen the claimant when he emerged into his view. A reasonably careful driver would have sounded his horn in the circumstances; if the defendant had seen the claimant and sounded his horn the accident would probably have been prevented. The defendant was plainly negligent, though the claimant was guilty of contributory negligence to the extent of 75%.

Appeal allowed.

[11.10]   Armstrong v Cottrell

(1993) 2 PIQR P109, CA

The claimant attempted to cross a road, hesitated, and was struck by the defendant's vehicle. The defendant had seen the claimant and her friends 'hovering' at the side of the road. The claimant's claim had failed. The claimant appealed.

HELD: The appeal was allowed as the defendant had seen the claimant, she should have slowed down and sounded her horn. The claimant's contributory negligence was assessed at one-third.

[11.11] **Willbye v Gibbons**

(16 July 1997, unreported), CA

The claimant, aged 12, was attempting to cross a road and ran into the side of the defendant's vehicle. Prior to this collision the defendant had driven past a group of jostling boys. He was concerned enough about their behaviour to hoot his horn. The defendant then stopped behind parked cars on his side of the road to allow vehicles in the opposite direction to pass. As the defendant moved away he saw a child on his left moving in and out of the parked cars. He then saw the claimant standing on the kerb to his right 'poised' as if to run across the road and looking in his direction. The next time the defendant saw the claimant was as the collision occurred.

It was accepted on the evidence that the defendant had accelerated to about 25mph over 20–25 yards from his stationary position behind the parked cars.

The recorder found the defendant was not negligent and that the claimant was wholly to blame for the accident. The claimant appealed.

HELD, ON APPEAL: The recorder applied the proper test as follows: 'Did the defendant's driving fall below the standard of the reasonable driver, not the perfect driver who takes every imaginable precaution, but the reasonable driver judged by reasonable standards of skill and ability'. However the recorder did not properly assess the evidence of the defendant himself. The defendant was not keeping a proper look out. He failed to see the claimant crossing the road at all despite the fact there must have been at least two seconds from the moment that she took off from the kerb until the moment she ran into the side of the car.

Secondly, from his stationary position, the defendant took off with greater acceleration than was called for in these particular circumstances. Had the defendant been paying proper attention and accelerated more moderately he could have braked and sounded his horn and, probably, the accident would not have occurred. The defendant was 25% responsible for the accident.

[11.12] **Melleney v Wainwright**

(3 December 1997, unreported), CA

The claimant, aged 11, ran into the path of the defendant's vehicle. The claimant's two friends had already crossed the road and the claimant was attempting to join them. The defendant was travelling on a road with a 60mph limit. He had seen the claimant and braked momentarily to reduce his speed to 30mph. The judge found that the defendant had foreseen the possibility that the claimant might cross.

HELD: The defendant was negligent. Given that he was not aware that the claimant had definitely seen him, he should have taken the precaution of sounding his horn and slowing down substantially. The claimant's contributory negligence was assessed at one third. *Armstrong v Cotterell* (1993) PIQR 109, CA was followed.

The defendants appeal was dismissed: 'I do not think it can be overstated, that when motorists are driving near to a group of young children, and especially young boys, a very high standard of caution indeed is required. Here were three 11 year old lads, two had crossed the road, their companion, the plaintiff, was left stranded on the side from which they had come. The risk of him doing something silly in order to rejoin them ought to have been foreseen as a very high risk. The precautions the defendant did take were simply not adequate, in my view, to discharge his duty as the driver of a motor vehicle approaching the situation that he had seen' (as per the Vice Chancellor).

[11.13]   **Britland v East Midland Motor Services Ltd**
(1 April 1998, unreported), CA

The claimant was a 12-year-old boy on his way to school. A Mr G was driving the defendant's school bus along Rock Crescent. The claimant ran along the pavement of Rock Crescent for between 10–12 yards before veering right through parked cars to run across the road into the path of the defendant's bus.

HELD: The claimant would have known that he should not have run into the road. He was thoughtless and reckless for his own safety. He was largely to blame. However the defendant driver ought to have noticed the claimant running along Rock Crescent for those 10–12 yards and slowed his speed or covered his brakes in anticipation of the claimant running out.
   The defendant was 25% to blame.

[11.14]   **Wells v Trinder**
[2002] EWCA Civ 1030
[2002] All ER (D) 122

The pedestrian claimant was hit by the defendant's vehicle while crossing a road. The claimant's mother had just dropped her off and had seen the approaching defendant's vehicle and shouted to warn her daughter. The judge at first instance found in favour of the claimant. The defendant appealed on the grounds that the judge had failed to attach contributory negligence or should not have found against the defendant at all.

HELD, ON APPEAL: The judge at first instance had found that the defendant approached the scene very fast. The judge was therefore entitled to find negligence against the defendant on the basis of his speed and failure to have his full lights on. With regards to the issue of contributory negligence, the Court of Appeal held that it could not see how the claimant could be acquitted of all responsibility in the case, as the claimant's mother had seen the oncoming car and therefore there was no reason why the claimant should not have seen it. The claimant was held 25% liable for her own injuries.

[11.15]   **Honnor v Lewis**
[2005] EWHC 747 (QB)
[2005] All ER (D) 374 (Apr), QB

The claimant who was almost 12 years old at the time of the accident, was attempting to cross North Road Hetton-le-Hole in Tyne and Wear to get to school when he was struck by the defendant's motor vehicle. The school was directly opposite where the claimant attempted to cross the road and the road was known to be highly populated with school children at that time of the morning.
   It was the defendant's case that he did not see the claimant until immediately prior to the collision and that he was travelling well within the speed limit. The claimant, who had red hair, was seen by a witness who was travelling immediately behind the defendant's vehicle. Although the claimant did not have any recollection of events, the evidence suggested that the claimant had not seen the defendant's vehicle before the collision.

HELD: That the defendant was negligent for failing to slow down, failing to notice the school warning sign, failing to sound his horn and failing to notice the presence of the claimant. As the claimant stepped out into the road without noticing the presence of the defendant's vehicle the claimant was found to be 20% responsible for his own injuries.

[11.16]   Ehrari v Curry

[2006] EWHC 1319 (QB)

[2006] All ER (D) 61 (Jun), QB

The 13-year-old claimant, was struck by the defendant's truck when she walked out from behind a parked Volvo with furniture on the roof. The passenger saw the claimant a fraction before impact but the driver did not.

HELD: Because the passenger saw the claimant prior to the impact, the defendant's attention must have been elsewhere. The defendant's attention did not always have to be fixed in front but had it been, he could have blown his horn which might have avoided such a serious accident. Liability was apportioned 70/30 in the defendant's favour because the primary cause of the accident was the claimant walking into the road.

(B)   DRIVER NOT AT FAULT

[11.17]   Moore v Poyner

[1975] RTR 127, CA

The defendant was driving his car at 25–30mph along a street in a poor district in Birmingham on a Sunday afternoon. There was no other traffic. A coach 30ft long was parked against the nearside pavement and concealed from the defendant an opening between the houses on that side of the road just beyond the front of the coach. As the defendant's car was passing the coach the claimant, a child of six, ran from the opening across the front of the coach into the defendant's path and was struck by the nearside front of the car. The judge held the defendant liable: he should have slowed down or sounded his horn.

HELD, ON APPEAL: The defendant was not liable. The test to be applied to the facts was would it have been apparent to a reasonable man, armed with common sense and experience of the way pedestrians, particularly children, behave in certain circumstances to have slowed down or sounded his horn, or both? What course of action would he have taken if he was going to make quite certain that no accident would occur? Ought he to have slowed down to such an extent that there could have been no possibility of a child's running out at any moment in front of him and his being unable to stop without striking the child? In the present case for the defendant to do so he would have had to slow down to something like 5mph. Such a duty of care would be unreasonable; the chance that a child would run out at the precise moment the defendant was passing the coach was so slight as not to require him to slow down to that extent. As for sounding the horn, drivers in traffic are constantly exposed to the danger of pedestrians stepping out in front of parked vehicles. It would be an impossible burden for drivers to sound their horns every time they passed a parked vehicle.

[11.18]   Davies v Journeaux

[1976] RTR 111, [1975] 1 Lloyd's Rep 483, CA

The claimant, aged 11½, was struck by the defendant's car when running across the road from the pavement on the defendant's nearside. She had come down a flight of steps to the pavement, which was 3ft wide. The entrance to the steps was 3 or 4ft wide. She was struck by the offside front of the car which, after the accident, was parallel with the pavement and 4 ft 9 inches from it. There was a mark on the road behind the nearside rear wheel 22ft long indicating heavy application of the brakes. The passenger in the nearside front seat of the car saw the claimant as she stood momentarily in the entrance to the steps and then dashed across. The defendant did not see her until she was in the act of dashing across; he was then 50 to 60ft away, travelling at 20 to 25mph. The judge held him 40% to blame for having failed to see the claimant at the moment when his passenger did and failing to sound his horn. The defendant appealed.

HELD ON APPEAL: The fact that the passenger saw the claimant a split second before the defendant did not establish a lack of proper care on the defendant's part; he was driving and needed to switch his eyes from one direction to another. Even if he had seen the claimant at the same instant it could not be said he should then have sounded his horn; what he did do was to apply his brakes heavily. Having regard to the brake marks he had acted promptly and efficiently. The judge's decision seemed to place a duty on motorists to sound the horn virtually whenever they see a pedestrian, regardless of whether the pedestrian is manifesting an intention of leaving the pavement and dashing across the road.

Appeal allowed.

[11.19]   Kite v Nolan
[1983] RTR 253, (1982) 126 Sol Jo 821, CA

The defendant was driving his car on a hot afternoon when he saw an ice-cream van parked on the offside of the road in front of him. He also saw three cars parked on the nearside ahead of the van. He slowed almost to a standstill to allow an approaching car to pass between the van and the parked cars. He then accelerated to about 15mph. The claimant, aged five, ran out in front of him from between the parked cars and was struck by the defendant's car. The judge found that the defendant could not have avoided striking the claimant unless travelling at not more than 5mph. He held that the defendant was not negligent, referring to *Moore v Poyner* (at para [11.17]). On appeal it was argued that the defendant should have realised the serious risk of a child running out bearing in mind the weather and the attraction of the ice-cream van.

HELD: The judge had decided correctly. He had to determine what was a reasonable standard of care in all the circumstances of the particular case. He would have regard to many factors including the following:
(1)   the likelihood of a pedestrian crossing the road, considering the allurement of the ice-cream van;
(2)   the nature of the pedestrian likely to cross, child or adult;
(3)   the likely degree of injury if struck;
(4)   the adverse consequences to the public and to the defendant of taking whatever precautions are under consideration.
    The application of the principles must always depend on the particular circumstances of the case; any decision applying the general standard to particular facts is unlikely to, produce a precedent. The judge had not treated *Moore v Poyner* as a precedent. He had correctly applied the general principle.

[11.20] **Saleem v Drake**

(1993) 2 PIQR P129, CA

The claimant was a six-year-old pedestrian who was severely injured, having been struck by the defendant's mini-bus. The claimant had suddenly run out into the road. The defendant had noticed the claimant playing at the side of the road and had slowed down. The defendant had not sounded his horn. The claimant's claim failed. The claimant appealed.

HELD: The appeal was dismissed. The defendant had satisfied his duty of care towards the claimant by slowing down. There was no indication that the claimant would rush out and, therefore, the defendant was under no duty to sound his horn.

[11.21] **Brooking v Stuart-Buttle** (deceased)

(30 March 1995, unreported), CA   Russell, Hobhouse, Morritt LJJ

The defendant was travelling along Roehampton Lane, a main road, at 10.45 pm. It was a fine night, the road was appropriately lit and the defendant's speed was 30mph which was found to be acceptable in the circumstances. The claimant aged 9 years 8 months and his friend James were on their way to a fish and chip shop on the other side of Roehampton Lane. James crossed the road first. He ran across the road in front of the defendant's vehicle. The defendant saw him, cried out and began to take evasive action. James made it to the central reservation. The claimant did not. He ran into the path of the defendant's vehicle, was hit and suffered serious injuries as a result.

The trial judge found for the defendant on the basis that she could not have been expected to have seen the claimant until shortly before he emerged into the road and, as such, the collision was unavoidable. The claimant appealed.

HELD: The claimant argued that the defendant, having seen James run across the road, should have immediately reduced her speed in anticipation of the claimant running out behind him. The Court of Appeal held that this was not reasonable. There was nothing to suggest that the defendant should have anticipated the emergence of a second child.

Secondly, the claimant argued that the defendant did not keep a proper look out. The Court of Appeal held that this was not correct. On the facts the defendant could not have been expected to have seen the claimant until shortly before he emerged onto the roadway. In addition, the defendant was faced with the distracting presence of James. The fact that James had run across relatively close to her oncoming car and only just made it to the central reservation would inevitably lead the defendant to pay attention to the presence of James.

A motorist is expected to be reasonably prudent, but not expected to be a perfectionist assisted by hindsight.

[11.22] **Ebanks v Collins and Motor Insurers' Bureau**

[1994] CLY 3401, CA   Butler-Sloss, Mann, Saville LJJ

The claimant aged 6, in the company of his uncle, had just bought some sweets. He detached himself from his uncle, ran across a road from between parked cars and was hit by the defendant's vehicle travelling on the opposite carriageway. The judge held that the defendant had no opportunity of avoiding the collision and gave judgment for the defendant. The claimant appealed.

HELD: The fact that the defendant managed to stop shortly beyond the place of the accident indicated that he was driving at a very moderate speed. The claimant ran out from between parked cars. Children with sweets in their pockets on their way home can run extremely fast. The defendant could not avoid the collision with the claimant.

Per Butler-Sloss LJ: The fact that he was unable to stop in time because a child was running out between parked cars, even though he was on the other side of the road, is not in itself a reason for saying that in every case of that sort the driver should have been able to take action to prevent an accident.

[11.23]   James v Fairley
[2002] EWCA Civ 162

[2002] All ER (D) 298 (Feb), [2002] RTR 341

The claimant, an eight-year-old child at the time of the accident, was struck by the car that the defendant was driving as the claimant crossed the second of two lanes of an A-road. The trial judge found on the facts that the defendant was not negligent. The claimant appealed.

HELD: The trial judge's findings of fact were entirely proper. When the claimant was standing on the pavement before crossing the road, she had not been behaving in a manner which would have alerted a prudent driver to the possibility of anything unusual or dangerous occurring. The judge had been entitled to find that the defendant would not have seen the claimant before he collided with her even though she had crossed one of the two lanes of the road. The fact that the trial judge had expressed, obiter dictum, that had he found the defendant to be liable he would also have found the claimant 60% contributory negligent, was irrelevant for the purposes of the appeal.

[11.24]   Miller v C & G Coach Services Ltd
[2002] EWHC 1361 (QB)

[2002] All ER (D) 120 (Jul), QB

The claimant, a 15-year-old schoolgirl, alighted from her school bus and passed behind it to cross the road when she was hit by a coach owned by the defendant. The claimant alleged that the defendant had failed to keep a proper look out, drove too fast and failed to slow down. The defendant's case was that the driver had no reason to expect passengers to run into the road, he slowed down and the accident was caused by the claimant's negligence in not checking that it was safe for crossing.

HELD: It could not be proved that the coach driver had driven negligently. He did not see the claimant before the moment of impact. His speed was appropriate to conditions and he had kept a proper look out. The claimant had stepped out from behind the departing bus into the path of the coach, which she had not previously seen.

[11.25]   Palmer v Lawley and Another
[2003] CLY 2976

The claimant brought an action against two defendants following a road traffic accident. The claimant had been driving down a suburban road when the first defendant who was travelling in the opposite direction swerved to avoid hitting a two-year-old child.

The child had escaped from a house when her eight-year-old sister failed to properly secure the latch. It was alleged by the claimant that the child's mother had been negligent in allowing her to escape.

HELD: The court gave judgment in favour of the defendants on the following terms. Namely, that the first defendant (Lawley) had not been driving negligently in swerving to avoid the child. It was further held that if the child's mother were to be found negligent, then this would place too high a burden on parents. Therefore nobody was liable.

[11.26]   Goundry v Hepworth

[2005] EWCA Civ 1738

[2005] All ER (D) 405 (Nov)

The claimant who was four years old at the time of the accident attempted to cross the road with a number of adults. The claimant was in the middle of the road when two cars approached. The first car passed by. However, when the second car approached and drew level the claimant ran out into the road where a collision occurred. At trial the judge held the defendant liable on the basis that she should have stopped or slowed down to allow the claimant to cross. The defendant's appeal was successful as the court held that the judge's proposition was incorrect as, if the defendant was obliged to stop or slow down, so was the car in front.

CHAPTER 12

Passengers

1.   GENERAL LIABILITY TO, AND OF, PASSENGERS

(A)   DUTY TO PASSENGERS

[12.1]   *Note*—A person who undertakes to carry another person in a vehicle either gratuitously or for reward will be liable to that other party if he causes him damage by negligence. The duty is to use reasonable care and skill for the safety of the passengers during the period of carriage. There is no absolute duty.

[12.2]   Dawrant v Nutt
[1960] 3 All ER 681, [1961] 1 WLR 253

The claimant was a passenger in a vehicle driven by her husband. It was late and the front lights of the vehicle were not working – a fact known to both husband and wife. The car was involved in a head on collision with the defendant's vehicle. The claimant was seriously injured and her husband was killed.

The court held that both the claimant and her husband were guilty of contributory negligence, although not to the same degree. The court held that a passenger in a vehicle owes the same duty to other users of the highway to take reasonable care for his own safety as does the driver. The apportionment of damages would depend on the circumstances of the case.

[12.3] McKee v Jones
(1984) 7 NIJB

The claimant was injured when the brakes on the school bus in which he was a passenger failed whilst descending a hill. The bus driver was not held liable as he was unaware that the brakes were maladjusted. The claimant succeeded against the manufacturers of the bus as the brakes contained a design fault.

[12.4] Sweeney v Westerman and Burton Coaches
[1993] CLY 2941

The court found that the second defendant was not liable to the claimant as the duty of care owed by the coach driver did not include chaperoning passengers across the road, as the driver's duty did not extend beyond the inside of the coach and its exit.

[12.5] Griffiths v Brown
[1999] PIQR P131

The claimant was injured when he was struck by a vehicle when attempting to cross the road after being set down.

The court held that a taxi driver did not owe a duty of care to an intoxicated passenger he set down 30 to 40 yards from his destination, on the other side of the road, close to a pedestrian crossing. The taxi driver's duty came to an end once the passenger alighted his vehicle. It was neither reasonable nor practicable for the taxi driver to make an assessment of the passenger's state before setting him down.

2. CONTRIBUTORY NEGLIGENCE

[12.6] Madden v Quirk
[1989] 1 WLR 702, [1989] RTR 304, 133 Sol Jo 752

The claimant was one of several passengers in the open back of a pick-up truck being driven along a main road by the first defendant. As the pick-up truck went to overtake a vehicle a car emerged from its offside. The emerging car swerved and avoided a collision with the truck. However, a second vehicle driven by the second defendant following behind this car took no evasive action and collided with the truck. As a result of this collision the claimant was thrown from the back of the truck and severely injured.

The first defendant pleaded guilty to carrying passengers in a dangerous manner contrary to s 40(5) of the Road Traffic Act 1972 and reg 100(1) of the Road Vehicles (Construction and Use) Regulations 1986, SI 1986/1078. The first defendant was also convicted of driving without due care and attention.

The claimant accepted that he was 5% contributory negligent and the trial judge found that both defendants were negligent. The judge then considered the question of contribution as between the defendants.

HELD: The negligence of the first defendant was to be assessed at 80% and that of the second defendant at 20%. However, in considering the Civil Liability (Contribution) Act 1978 the judge felt that the primary duty of care was on the driver rather than the passenger pursuant to reg 100(1) of the 1986 Regulations. Therefore he regarded the first defendant as additionally negligent and in the circumstances the first defendant's contribution was increased to 85% and that of the second defendant reduced to 15%.

Note—Section 40(5) of the Road Traffic Act 1972 is now found at s 42(1) of the 1988 Act.

[12.7]   Priestley v McKeown

(3 August 1998, unreported), QBD, Plymouth District Registry

The infant claimant's mother was killed as a consequence of the defendant's driving. The mother and a female friend had been given a lift by the defendant driver to a late night petrol station. On the way to the petrol station the defendant had deliberately driven dangerously with total disregard to other road users.

On reaching the petrol station both women complained about his dangerous driving but, nevertheless, they got back in the car for the return journey. On the return journey the defendant crashed the car killing the claimant's mother and seriously injuring her friend.

The defendant was sober and admitted that he was simply trying to impress the women.

HELD: An agreement to reduce the claimant's damages by 10% for contributory negligence was approved by the court. There was clear evidence that on the way to the petrol station the defendant had been driving dangerously and yet the women got back into the car for the return journey.

(A)   WHEN DRIVERS AFFECTED BY DRINK

[12.8]   Owens v Brimmell

[1977] QB 859, [1976] 3 All ER 765, [1977] 2 WLR 943, 121 Sol Jo 338, [1977] RTR 82   Tasker Watkins J

The claimant and defendant were friends, both about 20 years of age, who at times drank together in public houses and clubs. One evening they went together visiting various public houses and a club, which they left in the defendant's car at about 2 am. By that time each had drunk about eight pints of beer. A short distance from the club the defendant overtook another car and in bringing his car to the nearside lost control and ran into a lamp post. The claimant was very seriously injured.

HELD: (1) It must be inferred that the effect of alcohol on the defendant's ability to drive was the cause of his losing control.

(2)   It was a clear case of contributory negligence on the part of the claimant either on the ground that the minds of both parties behaving recklessly were so befuddled by drink as to rid them of clear thought and perception or that the claimant should have foreseen the risk of being hurt by riding as a passenger with the defendant. But in such a case the driver, who alone controls the car and therefore has it in him whilst in drink to do great damage must bear by far the greater responsibility. The claimant's damages would be reduced by 20%.

[12.9]   **Thomas v Fuller**

(7 February 1977, unreported)   Cantley J

The claimant, defendant and a friend spent an evening at a public house drinking. They were all habitual drinkers there, and on this evening, just before Christmas, they drank even more than usual, mainly spirits, amounting to about £45 worth. The claimant and defendant in the course of the evening began to think it a good idea to drive to Scotland on the M1. They borrowed the friend's car. They called at the claimant's house where they had more to drink and then set off. A few miles along the M1 the car ran into the back of a lorry. Each man said the other was driving; the driver was in fact the defendant. The claimant was seriously injured.

HELD: The cause of the accident was drink and the parties were on a drunken frolic. In putting himself as a passenger in a car driven by his drinking companion at the end of such an evening the claimant showed recklessness for his own safety. But although it was a joint venture it would be wrong to apportion the damages equally between them. The driver of a car is in control and it is he who is primarily responsible for its being properly driven. A fair adjustment even though this was a bad case of its type would be to hold the claimant 25% to blame for his injuries.

[12.10]   **Buckingham v D'Souza**

(18 July 1978, unreported)

The claimant aged 16 ½ and the defendant aged 19 went out together for the evening in the defendant's car. Despite his being the younger, the claimant was the dominant partner in the expedition; they were out to find girls. After pints of lager in two public houses they went to a dance hall at about 10 pm. Between bouts of dancing they bought drinks and sat at a table drinking. They had further pints of lager as well as vodka and lime. They left the hall at 2 am, with two girls in the back of the car. On a clear road with no other traffic present the car, driven by the defendant, ran off the road and overturned: the claimant suffered injury causing permanent paralysis below neck level. At about 5.30 am a blood test showed the defendant's alcohol level to be 150 mg. At trial expert evidence was given that it must have been at least 190 mg at the time of leaving the dance hall.

HELD: The amount the boys had had to drink by the time they left the dance hall was enough to have considerably affected the defendant's ability to drive and for it to be visible to anyone who was watching out for it. A passenger knows, or should know, that any drinking substantially beyond the permitted limit is likely to result in an accident. The claimant must bear some responsibility; his damages should be reduced by 20%. If it had been a case of two boys setting out on a pub-crawl a higher degree of contributory negligence would have been appropriate: per Jupp J.

[12.11]   **Traynor v Donovan**

[1978] CLY 2612   Sheldon J

The claimant suffered severe injuries when travelling as a front seat passenger in a car driven by the defendant. She had first met him in a public house only half an hour previously. The defendant was found to have a blood/alcohol level of 168 mg but she had not noticed before accepting a lift any sign that his driving ability might be impaired. She called police evidence to confirm that symptoms of such excessive consumption of alcohol were not necessarily apparent to a lay person. There was medical evidence that her injuries had she been wearing a seat belt would have been different but no less serious.

HELD: There should be no deduction for contributory negligence from the claimant's damages.

[12.12]   Malone v Rowan
[1984] 3 All ER 402   Russell J

At about 8.15 pm the defendant was driving his small van with five friends as passengers when he lost control of the vehicle. One of his passengers, the claimant's husband, was thrown out and killed. The party had been out since morning. Between 12.30 and 3.30 pm they had been in public houses where the defendant drank four pints of lager; in the evening he had a further three half-pints. A blood-alcohol test showed that at the time of the accident he would have had at least 148 mg per 100 ml of blood. The surviving passengers said in evidence they knew the defendant had been drinking but not how much; they did not consider him unfit to drive and said there was nothing unusual in his manner of driving.

HELD: The facts were far removed from those of *Owens v Brimmell* (at para [12.8]). There was no direct evidence of the deceased's knowledge of what the defendant had consumed or whether he appreciated the risk he was running. The burden of proof was on the defendant. There should be no reduction of damages for contributory negligence.

[12.13]   Meah v McCreamer
[1985] 1 All ER 367, [1985] NLJ Rep 80

The claimant was seriously injured when a car in which he was a passenger, driven by the defendant, crashed into a tree. The two men had been out drinking before the accident: the claimant ought to have realised that the defendant was unfit to drive. The defendant was tested and found to have excess alcohol in his blood. Subsequently he disappeared and could not be found; his insurer through its solicitors contested the action. They pleaded that the claimant was negligent in accepting a lift when he knew the defendant was drunk. It was argued on behalf of the claimant that the plea was an admission of a criminal offence on the part of the defendant and that as the solicitor had received no express instructions from him he was not able to make such a plea.

HELD: The insurance policy gave the insurer 'full discretion' in the conduct of proceedings. Although *Groom v Crocker* [1939] 1 KB 194, [1938] 2 All ER 394, 108 LJKB 296, 158 LT 477, 54 TLR 861, 82 Sol Jo 374, 60 Ll L Rep 393, CA showed that a solicitor was nevertheless bound in such case by a general duty to his client it was not inconsistent with that duty to plead contributory negligence. It was merely a plea that if the defendant were found to have been negligent the claimant was negligent in accepting a lift; indeed not so to plead would be inconsistent with the duty to the defendant not to incur more damages than justice required. The claimant's damages should be reduced by 25%.

Note—See also *Morris v Murray* (at para [7.40]) and *Pitts v Hunt* (at para [7.44]).

[12.14]   Stinton v Stinton
(1992) Times, 5 August

The claimant was injured when a passenger in a car belonging to and driven by his brother. The claimant's brother had just acquired the car but had not acquired any insurance. The claimant was aware that his brother did not have any insurance and that he and his brother would be using the car as a joint means of transport during an evening over the course of which much drink was consumed. The claimant's brother lost control of the car due to his inebriated condition and the claimant sued his brother and the Motor Insurers' Bureau (MIB).

HELD: The claimant obtained a judgment against his brother with a one-third deduction for contributory negligence but his claim against the MIB failed.

[12.15]   Brignall v Kelly

(17 May 1994, unreported), CA   Balcombe, McCowan, Rose LJJ

The claimant was a passenger in the defendant's vehicle. The defendant lost control of his vehicle, crashed and as a result the claimant suffered serious injuries. No other vehicle was involved. The defendant provided a blood sample two and a half hours after the accident which showed that his blood alcohol level was slightly more than twice the permitted maximum for driving. The issue before the court was whether the claimant's damages should be reduced for contributory negligence on the basis that the claimant knew or ought to have known it was not safe to drive with the defendant because he was obviously drunk.

The defendant relied on evidence from a professor of forensic pathology. By a process of back calculation the professor estimated that at the start of the journey the defendant would have been well into the 'obviously drunk' state. However he did concede that there could be a great personal variation in the effect of alcohol on different people. The claimant relied on five witnesses who saw the defendant just prior to the accident and stated that the defendant was behaving normally. The claimant (who the judge accepted was sober) gave evidence that he saw the defendant drink one pint of lager, he had a sensible conversation with the defendant and when walking to the defendant's vehicle, he saw no overt signs to suggest to him that the defendant was drunk. The defendant himself gave evidence to the effect that he had drunk a maximum of four pints of lager in a two hour period, was used to drinking much greater amounts on a regular basis and felt perfectly capable of driving safely.

The judge held that the defendant had not established that the claimant was in any way guilty of a want of proper care for his own safety. The defendant appealed.

HELD: The judge was perfectly entitled to prefer the lay witness evidence over the professor. Furthermore as to the defendant's argument that the claimant should have taken some steps to enquire of the defendant how much he had consumed.

Per McCowan LJ: For my part I refuse to accept the proposition that if a man in a public house observes another man drink one pint of lager and give no sign of intoxication, he cannot accept a lift from him without interrogating him as to exactly how much he has had to drink.

[12.16]   Donelan v General Accident Fire and Life Assurance

[1993] PIQR P205   HHJ Astill

The claimant was a passenger in a vehicle driven by the defendant, his wife. No other vehicles were involved. The facts accepted by the court were as follows. Both claimant and defendant were very drunk. The vehicle driven by the defendant was the claimant's. It was a powerful automatic car which the defendant had never driven before. The claimant knew this. The defendant admitted that the cause of the accident was the power of the car. The claimant was the dominant member of the partnership and the defendant would probably not have driven had the claimant not made the decision that she should.

HELD: The claimant was the instigator and cause of the defendant's drunken driving. He put the defendant in a position of great difficulty. He knew or ought to have known and recognised the great risks involved in her driving. The defendant must bear some responsibility and this was assessed at 25%. The claimant's contributory negligence was assessed at 75%.

Per HHJ Astill: This is a departure from the line of authorities that I have considered, but I consider the facts of this case to be wholly exceptional.

[12.17]   Akers v Motor Insurers' Bureau

[2003] EWCA Civ 18

[2003] All ER (D) 16 (Jan), [2003] Lloyd's Rep IR 427

A rear seat passenger was killed in a road traffic accident when travelling in a vehicle driven by the uninsured first defendant. MIB was joined as second defendant. MIB alleged that the death was caused or contributed to by the negligence of the deceased in that he knew or ought to have known that the driver was impaired by alcohol and/or drugs so as to affect his ability to drive safely. The deceased was further negligent in failing to wear a seat belt. MIB sought to refuse indemnity on the basis that the deceased knew or ought to have known that the driver was uninsured.

HELD: The deceased knew the driver had been drinking alcohol and smoking cannabis and therefore ought to have realised there was a risk in accepting a lift. Accordingly a reduction of 20% was appropriate. A further 25% reduction was applied for the deceased failure to wear a seat belt. The judge was not satisfied that the deceased knew that the driver was not insured and therefore MIB was obliged to meet the claim.

[12.18]   Booth v White

[2003] EWCA Civ 1708

[2003] All ER (D) 245 (Nov), 147 Sol Jo LB 1367

The claimant was drinking with the defendant at the Morning Star public house, where he bought the defendant a pint of lager. The defendant left the pub to play football and the claimant remained consuming approximately two or three pints of lager an hour.

On the defendant's return, the claimant bought him another pint of lager. The claimant was unaware of exactly how much alcohol the defendant had consumed although he knew the defendant was habitually a heavy drinker. The claimant and defendant left the pub and the claimant allowed himself to be carried as a front seat passenger in the defendant's vehicle. The defendant subsequently lost control of his vehicle and collided with a telegraph pole, and went through three fences before coming to a halt.

The claimant although wearing a seat belt was badly injured. The defendant who was tested for alcohol was found to be nearly twice over the legal limit. Primary liability was admitted and the defendant argued that there should be a finding of contributory negligence, as the claimant has elected to be driven in a vehicle when he knew or ought to have known that the defendant was drunk. At first instance the judge made no deductions to take account of contributory negligence for the claimant's failure to make enquiries of the defendant as to how much alcohol he had consumed. The defendant appealed.

HELD, dismissing the appeal: The duty on passengers did not include making enquiries of the driver to ascertain how much alcohol had been consumed before he set out on his journey. The law was that the passenger had to assess the driver, when deciding 'whether in the interests of his own safety he should have a lift'.

(B)   SEAT BELT

(1)   *Froom v Butcher*

[12.19]   *Note*—The question whether the omission to wear a seat belt was reason for reducing the claimant's damages was argued in a number of cases heard in courts of first instance and gave rise to several conflicting decisions. The question eventually came before the court in *Froom v Butcher* (at para [12.20]) on 21 July 1975.

[12.20]   Froom v Butcher

[1976] QB 286, [1975] 3 All ER 520, [1975] 3 WLR 379, 119 Sol Jo 613, CA

A head-on collision occurred, wholly by the negligence of the defendant, between his car and a car driven by the claimant. The injuries sustained by the claimant included an abrasion of the scalp, fracture of the fourth right rib and fracture of a bone in the right hand. He was not wearing the seat belt fitted in the car for his use. He said he did not like wearing one and had heard of cases where belts had caused danger. The judge held on the medical evidence that the injuries might have been slighter if the belt had been worn; the issue was whether the driver's omission to wear the belt constituted negligence or lack of care. There were two bodies of opinion of which the dominant opinion was that belts should be worn. Nevertheless proper respect should be paid to the minority view; the courts were not justified in invading the freedom of choice of a motorist by holding it to be negligence or lack of care or fault to act on an opinion firmly and honestly held and shared by many other sensible people. The claimant's damages should not be reduced ([1974] RTR 528).

HELD, ON APPEAL: The judge's view was not right. In determining responsibility the law took no notice of the views of the particular individual. It required everyone to exercise all such precautions as a man of ordinary prudence would observe. As it is compulsory for every motor car to be fitted with seat belts Parliament must have thought it sensible to wear them. The material before the court about the value of wearing a seat belt showed plainly that everyone in the front seats of a car should wear one. The Highway Code advised wearing them. Wearing them only when there was a high risk as on a motorway in a fog was not enough; every time a car went out on the road there was a risk of accident. Forgetfulness was no excuse but there might be exceptional cases where a person might be excused from wearing a belt – for example, an unduly fat man or pregnant women. Apart from such cases a person failing to wear a seat belt should accept some share of responsibility for the damage if it could have been prevented or lessened by wearing one. The question how much the share should be should not be prolonged by an expensive inquiry into the degree of blameworthiness. If the injuries would have been prevented altogether by wearing a seat belt the reduction should be 25%. If the evidence merely showed that the injuries would have been a good deal less by wearing a belt damages should be reduced by 15%. In the present case 20% would be right. In the case of passengers a driver might have a duty to invite his passenger to fasten the seat belt but adult passengers should know they ought to wear a seat belt without being told.

[12.21]   **Condon v Condon**

[1978] RTR 483   Bristow J

The claimant, a front seat passenger in the defendant's car, sustained injury to her right eye when the car struck a telephone pole. She was not wearing a seat belt. In a medical report a doctor said she would probably not have sustained such a severe injury had she been wearing a seat belt. The defendant called no evidence on the point. The claimant said she could not bear to wear a seat belt because of her fear of being trapped in the event of an accident.

HELD: If the defence wished to rely on a seat belt contributory negligence plea then in the absence of a clear admission it must elicit some evidence at the trial to enable the court to form a conclusion about it. The doctor had not said on what basis he expressed his opinion. On the available evidence it was unlikely that not wearing a seat belt had anything to do with the eye injury at all. Even if it had the damages should not be reduced because the claimant's phobia made her an 'extraordinary case' such as Lord Denning had visualised in *Froom v Butcher* (at para [12.20]). Her not wearing a seat belt was not a failure on her part to take reasonable care for her own safety.

[12.22]   **Patience v Andrews**

[1983] RTR 447, CA   Croom-Johnson J

Where a claimant who was not wearing a seat belt suffered injuries the court had to examine the injuries actually suffered, assess compensation and then make a deduction depending on the extent to which those injuries had been caused or contributed to by the failure to wear the seat belt. It was not open to the court to reduce that percentage by speculating upon what other injuries the claimant might have suffered had he been wearing a seat belt, otherwise there would be 'an imponderable diminution' of the effect of the rule set out in *Froom v Butcher* (at para [12.20]).

[12.23]   **Salmon v Newland**

(1983) Times, 16 May   Michael Davies J

The claimant suffered a perforating injury to his right eye resulting in total loss of useful vision in that eye, multiple facial injuries resulting in scarring and a continuing anxiety state. The injuries were sustained in a head-on collision of cars in one of which the claimant was a passenger. She was not wearing a seat belt.

HELD: She was guilty of contributory negligence. Even though there was no medical evidence on the point, her injuries would have been a good deal less severe if she had been wearing a seat belt. Although Lord Denning had said in *Froom v Butcher* (at para [12.20]) that 15% was an appropriate reduction in such cases it was not high enough in this case; the reduction should be 20%. Additionally the cost of a convalescent holiday was recoverable in damages when, without it, her general condition might now be a good deal worse. Award for pain suffering and loss of amenity £18,500; loss of future earnings £54,000, special damages £11,414 all subject to 20% reduction for contributory negligence.

[12.24]   **Eastman v South West Thames Regional Health Authority**

[1991] RTR 389, [1991] 2 Med LR 297, 135 Sol Jo LB 99, CA

A passenger travelling in the front seat of an ambulance who sustained injuries for which the driver was in no way to blame, and which would have been avoided had she worn a seat belt was not entitled to recover damages from the health authority for the ambulance driver's failure to advise her to wear a belt. Seats in the rear part of the ambulance are equipped with seat belts: the claimant chose to occupy a seat in the front which did not have a belt. Above the seats was a notice which read 'For your own safety use the seat belts provided'. The question was whether in the circumstances it could fairly be said that the defendant had not exercised reasonable care in failing to draw attention to the seat belts, which were there to be seen. Russell LJ could not accept the judge's decision at first instance that the ambulance attendant was under any obligation to point out the seat belts and the notice. In his Lordship's view no negligence had been demonstrated.

[12.25]   Cross v Smith

(1998) (unreported), QB

The claimant who was seated in the rear load area of a van which was not fitted with rear seats or seat belts, was injured when the defendant lost control of the vehicle before colliding with a wall. The judge found in favour of the claimant without making any deductions to take account of contributory negligence. The defendant appealed.

HELD, dismissing the appeal: Two questions arose:
(1)   was the claimant at fault; and
(2)   if at fault was this the cause of his injury.
The Court of Appeal held that the judge was entitled on the facts to reach the conclusion that he did. *Froom v Butcher* (at para [12.20]), did not apply, as the claimant did not deliberately chose not to wear a seat belt. The court also accepted that if the claimant had accepted a lift in a car not fitted with rear seat belts, he would not have been negligent, and therefore the same principle applies to this case. As the court was unable to determine that the injuries had resulted from the claimant being unrestrained there should be no reduction of his damages for causation.

[12.26]   Barot v Morling

[2002] CLY 3528

The court dismissing an application to rely upon the evidence of a seat belt expert, held that as the expert had concluded that even if the child had been restrained he would have suffered different but equally as serious injuries, the allegations of contributory negligence for failing to wear a seat belt were bound to fail.

(II)   STATUTORY REGULATIONS – ROAD TRAFFIC ACT 1988, SS 14 AND 15

[12.27]
14.   Seat belts: adults
(1)   The Secretary of State may make regulations requiring, subject to such exceptions as may be prescribed, persons who are driving or riding in motor vehicles on a road to wear seat belts of such description as may be prescribed.
(2)   Regulations under this section—
    (a)   may make different provisions in relation to different classes of vehicles, different descriptions of persons and different circumstances,
    (b)   shall include exceptions for—
        (i)   the users of vehicles constructed or adapted for the delivery of goods or mail to consumers or addresses, as the case may be, while engaged in making local rounds of deliveries,

(ii)   the drivers of vehicles while performing a manoeuvre which includes reversing,

(iii)   any person holding a valid certificate signed by a medical practitioner to the effect that it is inadvisable on medical grounds for him to wear a seat belt,

(c)   may make any prescribed exceptions subject to such conditions as may be prescribed, and

(d)   may prescribe cases in which a fee of a prescribed amount may be charged on an application for any certificate required as a condition of any prescribed exception.

(3)   A person who drives or rides in a motor vehicle in contravention of regulations under this section is guilty of an offence; but, notwithstanding any enactment or rule of law, no person other than the person actually committing the contravention is guilty of an offence by reason of the contravention.

(4)   If the holder of any such certificate as is referred to in subsection (2)(b) above is informed by a constable that he may be prosecuted for an offence under subsection (3) above, he is not in proceedings for that offence entitled to rely on the exception afforded to him by the certificate unless—

(a)   it is produced to the constable at the time he is so informed, or

(b)   it is produced—

(i)   within seven days after the date on which he is so informed, or

(ii)   as soon as is reasonably practicable,

at such police station as he may have specified to the constable, or

(c)   where it is not produced at such police station, it is not reasonably practicable for it to be produced there before the day on which the proceedings are commenced.

(5)   For the purposes of subsection (4) above, the laying of the information or, in Scotland, the service of the complaint on the accused shall be treated as the commencement of the proceedings.

(6)   Regulations under this section requiring the wearing of seat belts by persons riding in motor vehicles shall not apply to children under the age of fourteen years.

[12.28]
15.   Restrictions on carrying children not wearing seat belts in motor vehicles

(1)   Except as provided by regulations, where a child under the age of fourteen years is in the front of a motor vehicle, a person must not without reasonable excuse drive the vehicle on a road unless the child is wearing a seat belt in conformity with regulations.

(2)   It is an offence for a person to drive a motor vehicle in contravention of subsection (1) above.

(3)   Except as provided by regulations, where a child under the age of fourteen years is in the rear of a motor vehicle and any seat belt is fitted in the rear of that vehicle, a person must not without reasonable excuse drive the vehicle on a road unless the child is wearing a seat belt in conformity with regulations.

(4)   It is an offence for a person to drive a motor vehicle in contravention of subsection (3) above.

(5)   Provision may be made by regulations—

(a)   excepting from the prohibition in subsection (1) or (3) above children of any prescribed description, vehicles of a prescribed class or the driving of vehicles in such circumstances as may be prescribed,

(b)   defining in relation to any class of vehicle what part of the vehicle is to be regarded as the front of the vehicle for the purposes of subsection (1) above or as the rear of the vehicle for the purposes of subsection (3) above,

(c)   prescribing for the purposes of subsection (1) or (3) above the descriptions of seat belt to be worn by children of any prescribed description and the manner in which such seat belt is to be fixed and used.

(6)   Regulations made for the purposes of subsection (3) above shall include an exemption for any child holding a valid certificate signed by a medical practitioner to the effect that it is inadvisable on medical grounds for him to wear a seat belt.

(7)   If the driver of a motor vehicle is informed by a constable that he may be prosecuted for an offence under subsection (4) above, he is not in proceedings for that offence entitled to rely on an exception afforded to a child by a certificate referred to in subsection (6) above unless—

(a)   it is produced to the constable at the time he is so informed, or

(b)   it is produced—

(i)   within seven days after the date on which he is so informed, or

(ii)   as soon as is reasonably practicable,

at such police station as he may have specified to the constable, or

(c)   where it is not produced at such police station, it is not reasonably practicable for it to be produced there before the day on which the proceedings are commenced.

(8)   For the purposes of subsection (7) above, the laying of the information or, in Scotland, the service of the complaint on the accused shall be treated as the commencement of the proceedings.

(9)   In this section—

'regulations' means regulations made by the Secretary of State under this section, and

'seat belt' includes any description of restraining device for a child and any reference to wearing a seat belt is to be construed accordingly.

(10)   This section is affected by Schedule 5 to the Road Traffic (Consequential Provisions) Act 1988 (transitory modifications).

Note—The Motor Vehicles (Wearing of Seat Belts) Regulations 1993, SI 1993/176 made it compulsory for rear seat passengers including children to wear seat belts.

The Motor Vehicles (Wearing of Seat Belts) (Amendment) Regulations 2006, SI 2006/1892 which came into force in September 2006 update the 1993 Regulations.

[12.29]   Webb v Crane

[1988] RTR 204, QBD

A newsagent driving to collect bundles of newspapers and returning to his premises must wear a seat belt as he is not 'making local rounds of deliveries' for the purposes of the exception under s 14 of the Road Traffic Act 1988. The word 'rounds' means a series of visits or calls such as those made by milkmen, bakers or postmen. It does not include a newsagent driving to collect bundles of newspapers for distribution and returning to his premises.

[12.30]   Jones v Morgan

[1994] CLY 3344, High Court, Cardiff   Dison J

The claimant was a taxi driver carrying a female fare-paying passenger late at night. There was a collision. The claimant was not wearing a seat belt. The claimant admitted that if he had been wearing a seat belt then his rib injuries would have been pretty minor and reversible. As it was they were not.

The claimant argued that there were three points preventing a finding of contributory negligence against him. Firstly, the Motor Vehicles (Wearing of Seat Belts) Regulations 1993, SI 1993/176 stated that taxi drivers were exempt from wearing a seat belt when taking a fare-paying passenger. Secondly, the claimant's employers had advised taxi drivers not to wear a seat belt when carrying fare-paying passengers at night. Thirdly, the claimant's colleagues had advised him for his own safety it was easier to escape from an aggressive fare paying passenger when the seat belt was not done up.

HELD: The first reason was obviously something that the court had to take into account. The second and third points had been established on the evidence. Even when the passenger was female she could still pose a threat. Therefore there was no reduction for contributory negligence.

[12.31]   Biesheuvel v Birrell

(21 January 1998, unreported), QBD

The claimant was a rear seat passenger in a motor car driven by the defendant. Seat belts were fitted but the claimant was not wearing one.

An accident occurred which was as a result of the defendant's negligence. The claimant suffered serious injuries which rendered him a tetraplegic. None of the other rear passengers in the car, who were also not wearing seat belts, were seriously injured.

The defendant argued that had the claimant been wearing a seat belt his injuries would have been much less severe and that the principles in the case of *Froom v Butcher* (at para [12.20]) should apply.

The claimant argued that the claimant's injuries would not have been prevented by the wearing of a seat belt and that the wearing of rear seat belts was not a common or publicly accepted practice.

HELD: The authority of *Froom v Butcher* applied to rear seat belts as well as front seat belts. A person of ordinary prudence would and should wear a seat belt if travelling as a rear seat passenger. However in this case there was no convincing evidence that the wearing of a rear seat belt would have reduced the extent of the claimant's injuries. Therefore there was no finding of contributory negligence.

(III)   TRIPPING ON SEAT BELT

[12.32]   Donn v Schacter

[1975] RTR 238   Phillips J

The defendant's car had seat belts for the front seats, fitted in the usual position on the central door pillar on each side. They were rarely used and were normally left hooked up on each pillar. The claimant when being given a lift home by the defendant was travelling in the rear offside seat; at the end of the journey when alighting she caught her foot in the nearside seat belt and fell, sustaining injury.

HELD: The defendant was not liable. On the evidence that the seat belt was probably hooked up the driver was not in breach of duty to the passenger either in allowing it to remain in that condition or failing to warn the claimant about it. Even if the belt was not hooked up but was on this isolated occasion lying loose on the floor there was no obligation on the driver to make a visual check or to warn the passenger to make sure the seat belt was satisfactory.

[12.33]   McCready v Miller

[1979] RTR 186, CA

The claimant, a woman of 53, travelled home at night in the defendant's mini-cab. She occupied the rear nearside seat. The car was an ordinary saloon car with a seat belt on the nearside central pillar properly hooked up out of use. When alighting at the end of the journey the claimant's left foot caught in the belt and she fell out on to the pavement, breaking her ankle. The street lighting was poor and the interior light of the car was not on. The judge held that the defendant was under no duty to see that the seat belt was not loose or warn the claimant or switch the interior light on, but was entitled to assume that a passenger would do what was necessary to avoid the hazard.

HELD, ON APPEAL: This was not right. The driver of a car carrying passengers has a duty to take reasonable care to provide a vehicle which is safe for them when getting into it, riding in it and getting out of it. The duty depends on the circumstances but it cannot be lower than the common duty of care defined in the Occupiers' Liability Act 1957, s 2(2) and may be higher on a driver who carries passengers for hire. The decision in *Donn v Schacter* (at para [12.32]) may have been right on the facts but is no authority for saying that the driver's duty does not include a duty to see that the hazard or obstruction caused by a seat belt is avoided or reduced. The defendant was under a duty to reduce the reasonably foreseeable risk by switching on the interior light or by warning the claimant or both.

3.   CONTRACTING OUT OF LIABILITY

(A)   PUBLIC PASSENGER VEHICLES ACT 1981

[12.34]
29.   Avoidance of contracts so far as restrictive of liability in respect of death of or injury to passengers in public service vehicles
A contract for the conveyance of a passenger in a public service vehicle shall, so far as it purports to negative or to restrict the liability of a person in respect of a claim which may be made against him in respect of the death of, or bodily injury to, the passenger while being carried in, entering or alighting from the vehicle, or purports to impose any conditions with respect to the enforcement of any such liability, be void.

[12.35]
1.   Definition of 'public service vehicle'
   (1)   Subject to the provisions of this section, in this Act 'public service vehicle' means a motor vehicle (other than a tramcar) which–
      (a)   being a vehicle adapted to carry more than eight passengers, is used for carrying passengers for hire or reward, or
      (b)   being a vehicle not so adapted, is used for carrying passengers for hire or reward at separate fares in the course of a business of carrying passengers.

Note—s 149 of the Road Traffic Act 1988. Note also the provisions of s 2(1) of the Unfair Contract Terms Act 1977.

[12.36]   Wilkie v London Passenger Transport Board
[1946] 1 All ER 650, 175 LT 331, 110 JP 215, 62 TLR 327, 90 Sol Jo 249; affd [1947] 1 All ER 258, [1947] LJR 846, 177 LT 71, 111 JP 89, 63 TLR 115, 45 LGR 170   Lord Goddard CJ, CA

The claimant was a clerk in the employ of the London Passenger Transport Board (LPTB) and was given a free pass for use on their omnibuses. The pass contained the following condition: 'No 6. It is issued and accepted on condition that neither the London Passenger Transport Board nor their servant are to be liable to the holder or his or her representative for loss of life, injury or delay or other loss of or damage to property howsoever caused.' The pass was subject to the right of the

Board at any moment to cancel it if it thought fit. The condition did not apply in the case of an employee while using the pass in the course of his or her employment or on the business of the Board.

The claimant was injured as a passenger whilst on vacation.

HELD: There was no contract and the Road Traffic Act 1930, s 97 (which was in the same terms as the Public Passenger Vehicles Act 1981, s 29) did not apply. The pass was a mere privilege or licence and no part of the claimant's contract of employment.

HELD, ON APPEAL: The condition came into operation as soon as the claimant began to enjoy any of the benefits and included taking such steps as would enable him to obtain those benefits and included boarding the bus. The pass was nothing but a licence subject to a condition and s 97 had no application.

Per Bucknill LJ: There must be some limitation on the wide terms of the condition. It would be reasonable that it should only apply when the pass-holder is using the pass.

[12.37]   Cosgrove v Horsfall
(1945) 175 LT 334, 62 TLR 140, CA

An omnibus driver in the employ of the Board was travelling for his own purposes as passenger on one of the Board's buses with a similar pass. He sued and recovered against the driver. The condition did not avail the driver who was not a party to the contract nor were the Board his agents in making the contract.

Per du Parcq LJ: It is, to say the least, doubtful whether the deposit under s 35(4) of the Road Traffic Act 1930 (now the Road Traffic Act 1972, s 144(1)) can be made available to meet the judgment.

Note—Section 144(1) of the Road Traffic Act 1972 has now been replaced by s 144(1) of the Road Traffic Act 1988.

[12.38]   Mayor v Ribble Motor Services Ltd
(1958) Times, 16 October, CA

A bus conductress was injured whilst a passenger in an omnibus belonging to her employers by the negligence of the bus driver. She was a member of a darts team and was being carried gratuitously subject to the express condition that the employers should be under no duty to carry her with care or safety and were to be free from all liability to her arising from personal injuries or loss or damage to her property, however caused. They had agreed to provide transport for sporting events.

HELD: Section 97 of the Road Traffic Act 1930 did not apply, since there was no contract. The document containing the condition used the word 'agreed' but this did not of itself have a contractual import and did not make the document a term of the claimant's contract of employment. It merely expressed willingness to provide transport, and was not taking any obligation on itself. The same defence applied to the claim based on the Law Reform (Personal Injuries) Act 1948, s 1(3).

Note—The provisions of the Road Traffic Act 1930, s 97 are now contained in the Public Passenger Vehicles Act 1981, s 29.

[12.39]   Genys v Matthews

[1965] 3 All ER 24, [1966] 1 WLR 758, 110 Sol Jo 332, Liverpool Court of Passage

The Liverpool Corporation granted the claimant a free pass on Corporation buses on the following conditions: 'The pass is issued and accepted on the understanding that it merely constitutes and grants a licence to the holder to travel on the Liverpool Corporation's buses with and subject to the conditions that neither the Liverpool Corporation nor any of their servants or agents ... are to be liable to the holder ... for ... injury ...'. The claimant was injured when travelling on a Corporation bus due to the negligence of the defendant, the driver of the bus, who was a servant of the Corporation.

HELD: Following *Cosgrove v Horsfall* (at para [12.37]) the defendant was not protected by the terms on which the pass was issued. Even though the pass may be only a licence and not a contract, the condition could only be enforced by a party to it. This was the effect, *inter alia*, of *Scruttons v Midland Silicones* [1962] AC 446, [1962] 1 All ER 1, [1962] 2 WLR 186, 106 Sol Jo 34, [1961] 2 Lloyd's Rep 365, HL and *Adler v Dickson* [1955] 1 QB 158, [1954] 3 All ER 397, [1954] 3 WLR 696, 98 Sol Jo 787, [1954] 2 Lloyd's Rep 267, CA.

[12.40]   Gore v Van der Lann

[1967] 2 QB 31, [1967] 1 All ER 360, [1967] 2 WLR 358, 110 Sol Jo 928, CA

The claimant was an old-age pensioner who had been given a free pass by the Liverpool Corporation to travel on its buses. The defendant was a bus conductor employed by the Corporation. Due to his negligence the claimant was injured when boarding a bus. The Corporation intervened in the action claiming an order to stay on the ground that the free pass was issued on the express condition that the Corporation and its servants should be under no liability for injury to the claimant.

HELD: (1) The free pass in this case, unlike that in *Wilkie v London Passenger Transport Board* (at para [12.36]) was a contract. It was issued in response to a written application, was couched in the language of contract, calculated to impress upon the claimant that she was entering into a legally binding agreement. Consequently the exclusion of liability was void under the Road Traffic Act 1960, s 151.
   (2)   A stay could be granted (under the Supreme Court of Judicature (Consolidation) Act 1925, s 41) only if the prosecution of the action amounted to a fraud on the Corporation either:
   (a)   because the claimant had agreed with the Corporation for good consideration not to bring the action; or
   (b)   because the Corporation would in law be obliged to indemnify the defendant against liability to the claimant.
   As to (a) no express or implied agreement had been made out. As to (b) there was no such legal obligation on the Corporation. It was not entitled to a stay.

Note—The Road Traffic Act 1960, s 151 is repealed and is repeated in the Public Passenger Vehicles Act 1981, s 29. The provisions of the Supreme Court of Judicature (Consolidation) Act 1925, s 41 relating to a stay of proceedings are now contained in the Supreme Court Act 1981, s 49(3).

(B)   EXCLUSION OF PASSENGER LIABILITY INEFFECTIVE

ROAD TRAFFIC ACT 1988, S 149

[12.41]
149.   Avoidance of certain agreements as to liability towards passengers
   (1)   This section applies where a person uses a motor vehicle in circumstances such that under section 143 of this Act there is required to be in force in relation to his use of it such a policy of insurance or such a security in respect of third-party risks as complies with the requirements of this part of this Act.
   (2)   If any other person is carried in or upon the vehicle while the user is so using it, any antecedent agreement or understanding between them (whether intended to be legally binding or not) shall be of no effect so far as it purports or might be held—
   (a)   to negative or restrict any such liability of the user in respect of persons carried in or upon the vehicle as is required by section 145 of this Act to be covered by a policy of insurance, or
   (b)   to impose any conditions with respect to the enforcement of any such liability of the user.
   (3)   The fact that a person so carried has willingly accepted as his the risk of negligence on the part of the user shall not be treated as negativing any such liability of the user.
   (4)   For the purposes of this section—
   (a)   references to a person being carried in or upon a vehicle include references to a person entering or getting on to, or alighting from, the vehicle, and
   (b)   the reference to an antecedent agreement is to one made at any time before the liability arose.

See also *Winnick v Dick* 1984 SC 48, 1984 SLT 185, Ct of Sess.

4.   PASSENGERS ON PUBLIC TRANSPORT

(A)   DUTY OF DRIVER

[12.42]   **Parkinson v Liverpool Corpn**
[1950] 1 All ER 367, [1950] WN 43, 66 TLR 262, 94 Sol Jo 161, CA

The driver of an omnibus applied his brakes with some suddenness to avoid running over a dog. The dog came from the nearside and the driver saw it about 20 yards away. It appeared to be crossing in front of the bus and the driver took his foot off the accelerator and passed behind the dog. Having cleared the bus, the dog suddenly came back across the front of the bus when the driver was some 5 or 6 yards away, whereupon the driver applied his brakes with some suddenness and stopped the bus. A male passenger aged 65 had risen from his seat to be ready to alight and was walking along the gangway. He was thrown to the floor and broke two ribs. The conductor was also thrown to the floor but the seated passengers were not inconvenienced.

   Pritchard J held the test was not whether the driver owed a duty to the dog and a greater duty to the passengers. The test was: Did the driver act reasonably or unreasonably by doing something which a reasonable person would do? The judge held that the driver acted as a reasonable person in an emergency and there was no negligence.

HELD, ON APPEAL: If there had been no explanation there was a *prima facie* inference of negligence but the driver had given an explanation. The proper test had been applied of an ordinary, reasonable, careful driver. The argument based upon *Glasgow Corpn v Sutherland* (at para [12.43]) that there was a paramount duty to the passengers and that it is not an answer to say it was to avoid a dog, was not accepted. There were two differences on the facts:

(1)   the passengers had not had time to get to their seats;

(2)   it was a case of a magnetic brake on a tramway car which had extremely sudden consequences. Although drivers act instinctively they are required to go through some process of reasoning. The driver's evidence was that he would try to save the animal's life without endangering anybody else. He had applied his mind to the question of endangering anyone else when faced with an emergency of this kind.

Appeal dismissed.

[12.43]   Glasgow Corpn v Sutherland

[1951] WN 111, 95 Sol Jo 204, HL

A passenger boarded a tramcar at a stopping place and soon after it moved off a dog which had been running alongside darted in front. The driver applied his magnetic brake and brought the car to a sudden stop. The passenger had not had time to take her seat and was thrown to the ground and injured.

Per Lord Simmonds: It was a question of fact whether the driver had acted with the skill and care of a reasonable driver and the findings showed that he had not. This opinion did not either doubt or affirm *Parkinson v Liverpool Corpn* [1950] 1 All ER 367, [1950] WN 43, 66 TLR 262, 94 Sol Jo 161, CA.

[12.44]   Challen v Bell and London Transport Executive

(1954) Times, 6 February   Pilcher J

A pedestrian stepped in front of an omnibus causing it to stop suddenly. The claimant was a passenger and was thereby injured. The claimant sued London Transport Executive (LTE) and the pedestrian. The pedestrian was found alone to blame; judgment against the pedestrian and for LTE.

[12.45]   Wooller v London Transport Board

[1976] RTR 206n, CA

The defendant's bus was being driven along Lewisham Way in the rush hour at about 25mph. It was about half a bus-length behind a lorry. Some passengers in the bus, of whom the claimant was one, were standing ready to get off at a stop 150 yards ahead. Suddenly a pedestrian stepped off the pavement on to a pedestrian crossing in front of the lorry. The lorry pulled up suddenly and the bus driver applied his brakes hard and stopped without hitting the lorry. The claimant, who was not holding on, was thrown over by the sudden stop and injured. The judge held the bus driver two-thirds to blame for driving too close to the lorry.

HELD, ON APPEAL: The bus driver was not to blame at all. It was a case like *Parkinson v Liverpool Corpn* (at para [12.42]). The bus was a reasonable distance behind the lorry and the driver was able to pull up in this emergency without hitting it. The suggestion that the bus should keep such a distance from the lorry that it could pull up without having to brake suddenly was a counsel of perfection which ignored modern traffic conditions.

[12.46]   **Barry v Greater Manchester Passenger Transport Executive**
(19 January 1984, unreported), CA

As the driver of a bus approached a bus stop where he intended to stop he saw ahead on the pavement three girls with two dogs, one on a lead, the other not. He was driving slowly, at about 15mph, because he was approaching the stop. Just as he was about to pass the girls and dogs one of the dogs dashed out into the road in front of him. Instinctively he stepped on the brake; the claimant passengers who had risen from their seats intending to alight were thrown to the floor and injured. The judge held the driver not to blame; he had acted on instinct – the instinct to preserve life whether of a dog or of a child or whatever it may be. 'Anybody who has driven for any length of time knows perfectly well that when such an emergency arises you go for the brakes.' It was argued on appeal that the judge should not have equated the attitude of a driver to a dog as it should be to a child; the driver should have taken a conscious decision as he approached the group that if a dog ran out he would drive on rather than risk injuring his passengers.

HELD: This would be a totally unrealistic expectation utterly divorced from the way in which reasonable people conduct their affairs. Three young people and two dogs standing on a pavement do not call for any special adjustment of the driving of a bus. A dog suddenly dashing out is an uncovenanted happening. The judge approached the case on the right lines: the driver was taken by surprise and reacted instinctively. Passengers on public transport take the risk that the driver may effect emergency braking causing inconvenience. Although the facts in *Parkinson v Liverpool Corpn* (at para [12.42]) were different the judge was right to have regard to that decision as a guide.

Appeal dismissed.

[12.47]   **Gardner v United Counties Omnibus Co Ltd**
[1996] CLY 4477

The claimant was a 78-year-old passenger travelling in one of the defendant's buses. The bus had to travel around a number of bends and in the course of negotiating one of these bends the claimant was thrown from her seat and sustained injuries. The claimant was sitting with her husband and had not been properly seated.

The claimant argued that the defendant bus company had been negligent on the basis that it had failed to warn the claimant by means of a sign or otherwise that it was dangerous to sit where she was; that she should brace her feet or hold onto a handrail; that the claimant should choose a different seat from the one she did and, lastly, the bus company had failed to advise the claimant that it was unsafe to sit with her husband.

HELD: The claimant's claim was dismissed. It would place an impossible burden on the defendant if its bus drivers owed a duty to ensure that passengers did not sit inappropriately and if the driver had to check that the passengers were properly seated and were properly safeguarding themselves before a journey commenced.

[12.48]   **Bradbury v Midland Fox Ltd**
(10 December 1999, unreported), Nottingham County Court   Mr Recorder Goodchild

A bus belonging to the defendant and being driven by Mr Glover was due to take the regular trip from Leicester City Centre to Enderby where there was a hospital for the mentally ill. In the queue was a drunk who managed to get on to the bus without the driver realising his condition. The drunk sat upstairs where there were a number of youths and the claimant.

The drunk gulped down undiluted vodka on the bus; he then appeared to fall asleep. When he woke up he became aggressive and was making indecent suggestions and propositions to the young lads on the bus. The driver of the bus was unaware of what was happening. Two of the lads came down to get off the bus and told the driver that there was a 'nutter' upstairs. This did not appear to be a complaint but a statement, which was usual given that the bus took residents back to the hospital.

The claimant had seen the drunk assault a youth and protested verbally. The drunk then turned on the claimant by pulling his hair, and swinging the claimant around. A lady then went and told the driver what was happening and asked him to do something. The claimant had got the better of the drunk and was restraining him. The bus driver carried on until he found somewhere to pull up but no phone could be located. He then drove to the nearest public house where a phone was located and called the police. When the police arrived, the drunk had died as he had choked on his own vomit.

As a consequence of this experience, the claimant suffered significant mental illness and brought proceedings against the defendant company.

HELD: The defendant, through Mr Glover, was not negligent as the drunk did not display sufficient signals that he was drunk when boarding the bus. Once notified of the disturbance Mr Glover could have done no more than he did.

[12.49]   Phillips-Turner v Reading Transport Ltd
[2000] CLY 4207

The claimant was injured as she was making her way to the far end long seat between the entry and the exit doors, as the bus moved off. The claimant brought an action against the defendant alleging that there driver was negligent in that he:

(1)   failed to ensure that she was seated before moving off; and
(2)   moved the bus with a jerk so as to cause a danger to the passengers.

The claim was dismissed as the court held that the bus driver did not owe a duty to wait for all passengers to be seated where safety supports are provided. However, different considerations may apply where a passenger is elderly or infirm. As the claimant was a fit and healthy 63-year-old who could not be described as vulnerable and the accident occurred because the claimant failed to hold on to the supports, the claim was dismissed.

[12.50]   Glarvey v Arriva North West Ltd
[2002] CLY 3263

The claimant aged 72 at the time of the accident brought an action for damages after he was injured when he attempted to sit down on the rear facing seat on the bus. As he attempted to sit down the bus pulled away with a sudden jerk throwing him to the floor causing him to sustain facial injuries.

The claimant had been carrying two shopping bags at the time which when he paid the fare, he was able to carry in one hand. The incident was not reported to the driver at the time by the claimant or any other passengers.

The court held that there was no breach of duty, as the driver was not required to wait until all the passengers were safely seated as this was too high a duty, and would unnecessarily slow down the bus services.

This duty was higher in respect of vulnerable passengers.

(B)   ENTERING THE VEHICLE

[12.51]   Degan v Borough of Dundee
(1940) 190 LT Jo 15

A passenger was thrown off balance by a number of workmen who boarded an omnibus as he was making his way towards a seat. The court held the bus company not liable. The plea that the presence in an omnibus of 20 or 30 workmen placed on the bus company a duty for special measures of caution by police or a special staff was fantastic.

Note—See also *Glasgow Corpn v Sutherland* (at para [12.43]).

[12.52]   Davies v Liverpool Corpn
[1949] 2 All ER 175, 93 Sol Jo 373, CA

Five women were waiting to board a tramcar at a request stop. Three of them had boarded it and the claimant had one foot on the step, when an unidentified and unauthorised passenger rang the bell to restart the car and the claimant was injured. The conductor was collecting fares on the upper deck. The judge found that the conductor made no endeavour to come from the top deck for the purpose of restarting the car and, notwithstanding the number of persons waiting to board it, showed gross indifference to the safety of the passengers. The car was stopped for an appreciable time and the conductor could have come down to see that it was safe, and in breach of his admitted duty and without sufficient excuse was absent from the place where he should have been.

HELD, ON APPEAL: It is desirable, unless there are some special circumstances which make it impracticable or impossible, for the conductor to be on the platform at a stopping place, because he is the only person authorised to give the starting signal. The conductor might reasonably have foreseen such a happening if he did not come down quickly.
   Appeal dismissed.

[12.53]   Guinnear v London Passenger Transport Board
(1948) 92 Sol Jo 350, Times, 10 April   Lynksey J

The claimant signalled a Green Line bus to stop at a request stop in Limpsfield. The bus driver slowed down and drew in towards the claimant, but signalled to him that he was going to stop farther on. The claimant failed to see the signal and attempted to board the bus while it was still moving at 3 or 4mph. The bus then accelerated and the claimant fell from it into a trench, which had been dug in the road just in front of the request stop, and suffered personal injuries.

HELD: The driver of the bus was negligent in accelerating before he had made sure of the claimant's safety, and the claimant was negligent in boarding a moving bus; each party was equally to blame. An award of one-half of assessed damage was made.

(C)   PASSENGERS INJURED EN ROUTE

[12.54]   Baird v South London Tramways Co
(1886) 2 TLR 756, 190 LT Jo 15

A conductor who calls out the name of a stopping place which a tramcar is approaching does not thereby invite a passenger to alight.

[12.55]   Folkes v North London Rly Co
(1892) 8 TLR 269

A passenger who stood by an open door of a tram as it slowed down and was thrown out because it stopped with a jerk was held not entitled to recover.

Note—This case was afterwards doubted but not reversed, 190 LTJ 15.

[12.56]   Hall v London Tramways Co Ltd
(1896) 12 TLR 611, 190 LT Jo 15, CA

If, after a bell is rung, the driver slows down 'almost to a standstill' he is bound to look round and see whether the passenger is safe.

[12.57]   Western Scottish Motor Traction v Allam
[1943] 2 All ER 742, 60 TLR 34, 87 Sol Jo 399, HL

A passenger was standing in a motor omnibus near the doorway which was in the forward part just behind the driver's cabin. The door had not been closed. There were no vacant seats, but he was not holding on to any part of the vehicle. The vehicle was not provided with rails or straps. He was thrown through the doorway into the road while it was being driven round a curve.

HELD: The driver was negligent in driving round the bend at high speed and there was no contributory negligence. The decision was upheld in the House of Lords.

Per Viscount Simon LC: The driver was not entitled to sway round the corner at what speed he liked so long as that speed was safe for passengers who were seated or holding on to some portion of the vehicle. The duty of reasonable care owed by the driver to those on board extends to all passengers whether they are 'holding on' or not. There may well be a case, eg of a person with a baby in his arms, where a standing passenger had no free hand with which to hold on.

[12.58]   Wragg v Grout and London Passenger Transport Board
(1966) 116 L Jo 752, Times, 21 April, CA

The claimant boarded a bus at a request stop and decided to go upstairs. As she was mounting the stairs the conductor rang the bell and the bus started. It had covered about 40 yards and had reached a speed of about 20mph when on rounding a slight right-hand bend it swayed to the left. The claimant had not quite reached the top of the stairs; she was not holding on and fell back down the stairs breaking her leg. The road had a camber so that as the bus started from the bus stop it would tend to be leaning to the left. On passing the mouth of a side road it would straighten up and would sway to the left again after passing the side road and on entering upon the right-hand bend.

HELD: It must be common knowledge that when a bus was being driven in a normal fashion movements of the body of the bus could be felt and that as it went round the bend even at a moderate speed it would not be unusual for it to sway to the left. Anyone standing or just about to sit down would be inconvenienced by the sway and might momentarily lose his balance; that was even more true of anyone mounting the stairs whilst holding two bags in one hand as the claimant did and momentarily not holding on to the rail. It was impossible to say that if a person did fall down that that was evidence of negligence against the bus driver. If there was evidence of an extraordinary swerve or sway, that might be evidence of negligence on the basis of *res ipsa loquitur. Western Scottish Motor Traction v Allam* (at para [12.57]) was no authority for saying that if there was any movement of the bus while people were standing or walking to their seats it was evidence that the driver was not driving the bus carefully. In the absence of a finding that the driver was driving too fast or that the movement or sway was wholly exceptional there was no ground for holding the driver negligent. *Allam's* case was quite different. In that case the bus was going too fast.

[12.59]   Fletcher v United Counties Omnibus Co Ltd
[1998] PIQR P154

The claimant, a 22-year-old woman, boarded the defendant's bus. She moved towards the rear of the bus so that she could sit with a friend. Before she was seated the driver, having consciously chosen to do so without waiting for the claimant to sit down, pulled out gently at a reasonable speed. Before the claimant was seated the driver was obliged to make an emergency stop. There was no suggestion that he was at fault in that manoeuvre. The claimant fell and sustained injury.

HELD: The driver was found to have been negligent in driving the bus from a stationary position without first ensuring the claimant was seated. The claimant was found 30% contributory negligent for failing to use the available supports to steady herself. The defendant appealed.

HELD, ON APPEAL: The appeal was allowed. The driver had not been negligent. Drivers of public buses cannot sensibly be expected to wait for all boarding passengers to take their seats, wherever they may choose to sit, before they can properly drive away. Bus drivers and companies must take steps to ensure the reasonable safety of their passengers but that duty is satisfied by the provision within buses of appropriate safety supports.

The driver was entitled to drive away from the bus stop as he did, gently and at a reasonable speed. Different considerations may have applied if elderly or infirm passengers or passengers encumbered by luggage or children were boarding. If there is some particular risk of accident then special steps may need to be taken.

(D)   ALIGHTING FROM VEHICLE

[12.60]   Hett v McKenzie
1939 SC 350

A passenger, while getting out of the rear of a car, put his hand on the pillar between the rear and front door. The driver slammed the front door and injured the passenger's fingers, not knowing they were there. The driver was held liable.

[12.61] Mottram v South Lancashire Transport Co

[1942] 2 All ER 452, 86 Sol Jo 321, CA

About 10.30 pm on 7 September 1941, the claimant followed a male passenger down the stairs from the upper deck of a bus to dismount at a request stop. The male passenger rang the bell once, and the bus slowed down, but just as he was getting off, he rang the bell twice (the signal to proceed). The claimant proceeded to alight after him but the bus did not stop and gathered speed, and claimant was thrown and injured. The conductress was collecting fares on the upper deck.

HELD: No negligence of conductress; it was putting the duty too high to say that she should go down to the platform to see people off safely.

[12.62] Massie v Edinburgh Corpn

(1950) 100 L Jo 665, Ct of Sess

A man boarded a bus which had a door at the front, and sat beside a friend on the front nearside seat next the gangway. In front of him was a metal shield and an upright stretching to the roof for passengers to hold on to. He got up to leave, holding the upright with his left hand, and, as the bus turned a corner, he fell out of the open door and was killed.

HELD: The conductor was not under an absolute obligation to keep the door shut; he had no reason to anticipate that the deceased might fall through the open door, there being no standing passengers. Nor was there evidence that it should have been apparent to the conductor that the deceased was unwell and might fall. The owners of the bus were not liable.

[12.63] Prescott v Lancashire United Transport Co

[1953] 1 All ER 288, [1953] 1 WLR 232, 97 Sol Jo 64, CA

The claimant and her husband were passengers on the defendants' single-decker bus, which was full. All the seats were occupied and some five or eight people were standing. The door was at the front. The husband told the conductor that they wished to alight at the next request stop. The conductor rang the bell and told them to wait until the bus stopped. Owing to road works, marked with red lights, and driving conditions, the bus stopped 20 or 25 yards short of the request stop right into the kerb. Unknown to the driver and conductor, but known to the claimant and her husband, it had for some time been customary for other buses to stop for passengers to alight at that point short of the request stop on account of the road works. The claimant and her husband assumed the bus had stopped for them to alight. The husband alighted and as the claimant was alighting, the bus re-started and the claimant was injured. The driver was unaware of the accident. The conductor had closed the door at the previous stop and had not noticed anyone opening the door.

HELD: There was no evidence of negligence of the driver. The conductor was negligent. His statement to the husband to 'wait until the bus stops' was a clear invitation to the claimant and her husband to alight when the bus did stop. When the bus stopped short of the request stop, the conductor ought either to have warned the passengers or communicated with the driver. The conductor could see the husband had got off and that there were others waiting to get off.

Adopting the statement of Goddard LJ in *Mottram v South Lancashire Transport Co* (at para [12.61]):

'After the man had given the signal for the bus to stop, and if the bus had stopped, it would have been the duty of the conductress to see that no one else was getting off before giving the signal for the bus to start again. In this case the bus never did stop.'

Before it could stop, the officious passenger gave the signal for the bus to start again. The conductor was negligent and the defendants were liable.

[12.64] **Wyngrove v Scottish Omnibuses Ltd**
1966 SC (HL) 47

The appellant's bus was of a type having a rear door which gave access from and to a rear platform. The doorway was 3ft 3in wide. The door was kept open along parts of the route where stops were frequent. There was no central pillar in the doorway but there were nine handholds available to passengers on the platform. The respondent's husband came on to the platform ready to alight at the next stop. The door was open. There were two handholds on the right but he failed to grasp either and fell out. The bus was being driven smoothly at the time. In the courts below the judges took the view that if there had been a central pillar the accident would have been prevented and the appellants were negligent.

HELD, ON APPEAL: The well established principles of law on the duty of a person towards passengers showed that he must take all precautions for their safety and anticipate such degree of inadvertence on their part as experience showed to be not uncommon. But he was entitled to have regard to his own experience and that of others in a similar situation with regard to what precautions had been found hitherto to be adequate. It was clearly foreseeable that a person leaving his seat in a moving bus may lose his balance and, if near the door, may fall out. The recognised means of enabling him to save himself was to provide handholds, of which there were nine on the platform of this bus. Over a period of years no accident had been attributed to the absence of a central pillar and it would have been unreasonable to fit one.

Appeal allowed.

Defective Vehicles

1.   STATUTORY DUTIES

(A)   ROAD TRAFFIC ACT 1988, S 41

[13.1]

41   Regulation of construction, weight, equipment and use of vehicles

(1)   The Secretary of State may make regulations generally as to the use of motor vehicles and trailers on roads, their construction and equipment and the conditions under which they may be so used.

Subsections (2) to (4) below do not affect the generality of this subsection.

(2)   In particular, the regulations may make provision with respect to any of the following matters—

(a)   the width, height and length of motor vehicles and trailers and the load carried by them, the diameter of wheels, and the width, nature and condition of tyres, of motor vehicles and trailers,

(b)   the emission or consumption of smoke, fumes or vapour and the emission of sparks, ashes and grit,

(c)   noise,

(d)   the maximum weight unladen of heavy locomotives and heavy motor cars, and the maximum weight laden of motor vehicles and trailers, and the maximum weight to be transmitted to the road or any specified area of the road by a motor vehicle or trailer of any class or by any part or parts of such a vehicle or trailer in contact with the road, and the conditions under which the weights may be required to be tested,

(e)   the particulars to be marked on motor vehicles and trailers,

(f)   the towing of or drawing of vehicles by motor vehicles,

(g)   the number and nature of brakes, and for securing that brakes, silencers and steering gear are efficient and kept in proper working order,

   (h)   lighting equipment and reflectors,

   (j)   the testing and inspection, by persons authorised by or under the regulations, of the brakes, silencers, steering gear, tyres, lighting equipment and reflectors of motor vehicles and trailers on any premises where they are (if the owner of the premises consents),

   (k)   the appliances to be fitted for—

       (i)   signalling the approach of a motor vehicle, or

      (ii)   enabling the driver of a motor vehicle to become aware of the approach of another vehicle from the rear, or

     (iii)   intimating any intended change of speed or direction of a motor vehicle,

      and the use of any such appliance, and for securing that any such appliance is efficient and kept in proper working order,

   (l)   for prohibiting the use of appliances fitted to motor vehicles for signalling their approach, being appliances for signalling by sound, at any times, or on or in any roads or localities, specified in the regulations.

(3)   The Secretary of State may, as respects goods vehicles, make regulations under this section—

   (a)   prescribing other descriptions of weight which are not to be exceeded in the case of such vehicles,…

(4)   Regulations under this section with respect to lighting equipment and reflectors—

   (a)   may require that lamps be kept lit at such times and in such circumstances as may be specified in the regulations, and

   (b)   may extend, in like manner as to motor vehicles and trailers, to vehicles of any description used on roads, whether or not they are mechanically propelled.

(B) ROAD VEHICLES (CONSTRUCTION AND USE) REGULATIONS 1986

[13.2] *Note*—These Regulations are intended to conform with European Community law. They came into force on the 11 August 1986. As appears from cases set out below, breach of the Regulations does not give rise of a cause of action for damages.

Part I of the new Regulations deals with preliminaries and interpretation. Part IIA deals with dimensions of vehicles, Part IIB with brakes, Part IIC with wheels and tyres, Part IID with steering, Part IIE with vision, Part IIF with instruments and equipment, Part IIG with fuel, Part IIH with minibuses, Part II.I with power to weight ratio, Part IIJ with protective systems, and Part IIK with control of exhausts. Part III deals with plates and markings, Part IVA deals with laden weight, Part IVB with dimensions of laden vehicles, Part IVC with trailers and sidecars, Part IVD with gas propulsion systems, Part IVE with control of noise, and Part IVF with avoidance of danger. The Parts are supplemented by 12 Schedules.

Included are regulations which require that a vehicle must not be driven backwards further than may be requisite for the safety or reasonable convenience of the occupants or of other vehicles on the road (reg 106); that during the hours of darkness vehicles must not stand on a road otherwise than with the nearside of the vehicle as close as may be to the edge of the carriageway (reg 101); that a motor vehicle not attended by a person licensed to drive it must (subject to some necessary exceptions) have the engine stopped and the brake set (reg 107); and that no person shall open any door of a motor vehicle so as to cause injury or danger to any person (reg 105). Part III gives power to a police officer or vehicle examiner to test and inspect the brakes, silencers, steering gear, tyres, lighting equipment and reflectors either on 48 hours' notice or in any event within 48 hours of an accident in which the vehicle had been involved.

[13.3] **Phillips v Britannia Hygienic Laundry Co**

[1923] 2 KB 832, [1923] All ER Rep 127, 93 LJKB 5, 129 LT 777, 39 TLR 530, 68 Sol Jo 102, CA

The axle of the defendants' motor lorry broke, causing a wheel to come off and damage the claimant's van. He claimed damages for breach of a clause of the Motor Cars (Use and Construction) Order 1904 made under the Locomotives on Highways Act 1896: 'The motor car and all the fittings thereof shall be in such a condition as not to cause ... danger to any person on the motor car or on any highway.'

HELD: Breach of the regulation did not give rise to a civil cause of action because (per Bankes LJ) it was a rule for the protection of the public at large and not a particular class: the public using the highway is not a class; it is itself the public: per Atkin LJ. Whether a person aggrieved by a breach of the duty has a right of action depends on the intention of the Act. The duty the Regulations were intended to impose was not a duty enforceable by individuals injured, but a public duty only, the sole remedy for which was the remedy provided by way of fine.

[13.4] **Tan Chye Choo v Chong Kew Moi**

[1970] 1 All ER 266, [1970] 1 WLR 147, 113 Sol Jo 1000, PC

The respondent bought a taxi as an investment in November 1960. It was driven and maintained by an employee. In October 1961 it was examined by the registrar of motor vehicles who reported that it was satisfactory in all respects. On 28 January 1962 it suddenly swerved out of control when being driven by the respondent's servant, colliding with a car travelling in the opposite direction and killing two of the occupants. The cause of the swerve was the collapse of the nearside ball joint of the steering gear due to excessive strain placed upon it by the modification to the spring seating done when the original petrol engine was replaced by a heavier diesel engine. This modification had been done before the respondent bought the car and was not of a kind which any ordinary inspection would have revealed.

HELD: The respondent had not been negligent and was not liable. On an alternative claim that she was liable in damages for breach of a statutory rule requiring the condition of the car to be at all times 'such that no danger is caused or likely to be caused to any person' the case was impossible to differentiate from *Phillips v Britannia Hygienic Laundry Co* (at para [13.3]). The statutory rule was not one which gave a civil cause for action.

(C) MOT INSPECTION

[13.5] *Note*—Section 43 of the Road Traffic Act 1972 has been replaced by s 45 of the 1988 Act: s 44 of the 1972 Act has been replaced by ss 47–48 of the 1988 Act.

The Road Traffic Act 1972, s 43, replacing the Road Traffic Act 1960, s 65, contains provisions for the purpose of ascertaining whether the prescribed statutory requirements relating to the construction and condition of motor vehicles are complied with. Subsection 2 of the section enables the Secretary of State to make provision by regulations for the examination of vehicles and the issue of test certificates. Section 44 makes it an offence to use on a road a vehicle to which the section applies and in respect of which no test certificate has been issued within the previous 12 months. The section applies to vehicles registered more than ten years but enables the Minister by regulation to substitute a shorter period. The period is at present three years.

The Motor Vehicles (Tests) Regulations, SI 1981/1694, have been made under s 43. They provide, *inter alia*, for examiners to be authorised to carry out tests at vehicle testing stations, requirements as to vehicles submitted for examinations and the manner of carrying out the examinations. Regulation 14 provides that when a vehicle has been submitted for examination the authorised examiner shall have the same responsibility for loss of or damage to the vehicle or to any other property, or personal injury, arising out of the use of the vehicle in connection with the carrying out of the examination as would rest on a person who had undertaken for payment to accept the custody of the vehicle and to carry out the same examination under a contract making no express provision with respect to the incidence of liability as between the parties thereto for any such loss, damage or injury.

This provision would appear to exclude the operation of any 'owners risk' notices or other exemptions from liability which may be displayed at garages and service stations which are also authorised vehicle testing stations whilst a vehicle is being tested or is in the custody of the examiner for the purpose of carrying out the test.

[13.6]   Rowley v Chatham

[1970] RTR 462   Shaw J

On 6 March the defendant, an authorised examiner under the Motor Vehicles (Test) Regulations 1960, SI 1960/1083, issued a test certificate relating to the claimant's husband's motor van. On 31 March the claimant's husband was driving the van when it steered into the path of an approaching lorry and he was killed. It was found that the upper and lower ball race cages of the steering column had broken down. There was evidence that this state of affairs had existed at the time of the test on 6 March.

HELD: (1) On the evidence adduced by the defendant, the tests required by the 1960 Regulations were properly and duly applied and would not have revealed that there was a fault or defect in the steering.

(2)   The relationship between the examiner and the owner of the vehicle is a contractual one but the duty owed by the examiner is prescribed by the Regulations and is limited to certifying the condition of the vehicle at the date of the examination. Any representation expressed or implicit in the certificate cannot be relied upon (as in the present case) some weeks later. The purpose of the Road Traffic Act 1960, s 66 is to protect the public from unroadworthy vehicles, not to provide motorists with a cheap means of being advised on the condition of their own vehicles.

Judgment for the defendant.

Note—See also *Rees v Saville* [1983] RTR 332.

[13.7]   Artingstoll v Hewen's Garages Ltd

[1973] RTR 197   Kerr J

On 13 December 1967, the claimant delivered his car to the defendants, who were authorised examiners for the annual MOT test. After the test they issued a notification of refusal of a certificate saying that the nearside front hub bearing needed renewal. The claimant obtained a new bearing and the defendants fitted it. Without further test they then issued a test certificate on 14 December. Five weeks later during which the claimant had driven the car 700 miles it suddenly veered across a busy main road and collided with an approaching vehicle, injuring the claimant. It was found that steering joints were loose. The claimant sued the defendants for damages for personal injury.

HELD: Following *Rowley v Chatham* (at para [13.6]:

(1)   there is a duty on an examiner in contract to carry out the test properly and with reasonable skill and care and the issue of a test certificate bearing the prescribed wording also imports a warranty that the statutory requirements prescribed by the regulations were complied with at the date of the examination;

(2)   though a claim for damages either in contract or tort may be difficult to establish because of the lapse of time, there is no reason in principle (contrary to the view expressed in *Rowley's* case) why substantial (as distinct from nominal) damages should not be recovered by a claimant who can prove a failure to carry out the examination with proper skill and care and the issue of a test certificate which should not have been issued and that loss and damage were thereby caused;

(3)   if a claimant himself was guilty of some degree of carelessness in driving at the time of the accident the court can make an apportionment as between the causative faults under the Law Reform (Contributory Negligence) Act 1945 even if the claim is regarded as lying solely in contract;

(4)   on the facts of the present case the claimant had failed to prove any breach of contract or duty in relation to the brakes or steering.

Action dismissed.

Note—But see *Basildon District Council v J E Lesser (Properties) Ltd* [1985] QB 839, [1985] 1 All ER 20, [1984] 3 WLR 812, 128 Sol Jo 330, [1984] NLJR 330 and *Marintrans (A B) v Comet Shipping Co Ltd, The Shinjitsu Maru No 5* [1985] Times, 19 March.

Section 66 of the Road Traffic Act 1960 is now s 188 of the Road Traffic Act 1988.

[13.8]   **Rees v Saville**

[1983] RTR 332, CA

The defendant was driving his car when it suddenly swerved to the right and struck the claimant's parked car causing substantial damage for which the claimant claimed. The accident was caused by the failure of a ball joint on the steering mechanism of the front offside wheel of the defendant's car. The car was eight years old but he had owned it only a month or less; he had bought it privately. He was not an engineer but he had inspected it before purchase and found no defects. It had an MOT certificate three or four months old. Expert evidence suggested that the worn condition of the ball joint was not easily discoverable on inspection, but should have been detected on the MOT test. The defendant said in evidence that he had noticed no symptoms of wear on the ball joint which might be shown by uneven tyre wear or otherwise and that 'it was a natural assumption from the MOT certificate that the vehicle was okay'. The judge said the test of negligence was what a reasonable motorist could be expected to do. He held there was no negligence on the part of the defendant.

HELD, ON APPEAL: The judge was entitled so to hold:

(1)   the question of onus matters only when there is a question of fact on which no evidence is called on one side or the other. In this case credibility of the evidence was established at the trial and it merely remained for the court to decide whether, on the facts proved or admitted, the defendant was negligent. *Henderson v Henry E Jenkins & Sons and Evans* (see para [13.23]), and *Barkway v South Wales Transport Co Ltd* [1950] AC 185, [1950] 1 All ER 392, 66 TLR 597, 94 Sol Jo

128, HL were distinguishable. In *Henderson's* case the claimant established the cause of the corrosion but the defendants called no evidence. In *Barkway's* case negligence was proved against the defendant's servants or agents;

(2)   it had been said against the present defendant that he should have placed no reliance on the MOT certificate. A valid MOT certificate was a factor which must be taken into account in deciding whether or not it was necessary for the defendant himself to submit the car to an expert for inspection.

On the facts of the present case the defendant was not negligent in failing to have a further inspection of the vehicle.

2.   DEFENDANT LIABILITY

[13.9]   Herschtal v Stewart and Ardern Ltd

[1940] 1 KB 155, [1939] 4 All ER 123, 161 LT 331, 56 TLR 48, 84 Sol Jo 79   Tucker J

The claimant who was a director of, and had a controlling interest in, a company known as UP Ltd acquired on its behalf a reconditioned motor car from a company known as S & A Services Ltd. The latter company acquired the car from the defendants for the purpose of hiring it out on hire purchase terms to UP Ltd. The defendants knew that the car was going to be used chiefly by the claimant, and they knew that it was going to be so used immediately. On the morning after the delivery of the car, before it had been driven more than a few miles, and while it was being driven by the claimant, the nearside rear wheel came off, whereby the claimant suffered damage. There was no evidence that anything had happened between the time when the car was delivered by the defendants and the time of the accident. At the time of delivery the claimant had signed, for and on behalf of UP Ltd, a form of receipt stating that the car was accepted as being in good condition and as seen, tried and approved.

HELD: (1) The form of receipt did not protect the defendants in a claim of negligence by the claimant, however it might affect their contractual liability with UP Ltd.

(2)   The defendants were liable in negligence under the rule in *Donoghue v Stevenson* because, although the claimant was given an opportunity to examine the car for the purpose of discovering any defects, yet the defendants never anticipated that there would be any such examination.

Note—In the above case the Motor Vehicles (Construction and Use) Regulations 1937, reg 67 (now the Road Vehicles (Construction and Use) Regulations 1986, SI 1986/1078, and the Road Traffic Act 1934, s 8 were referred to, but counsel for the claimant conceded that the claimant could not succeed without proof of negligence in view of *Phillips v Britannia Hygienic Laundry Co* (at para [13.3]). See also *Andrews v Hopkinson* (at para [13.10]).

[13.10]   Andrews v Hopkinson

[1957] 1 QB 229, [1956] 3 All ER 422, [1956] 3 WLR 732, 100 Sol Jo 768   McNair J

On 11 September 1952, the claimant arranged to obtain from the defendant, a dealer in second hand cars, a 1934 car. The claimant told the defendant that he did not know a great deal about cars. The defendant took the claimant and a friend for a drive for about five miles in the car and said 'It's a good little bus. I would stake my life on it. You will have no trouble with it'. The claimant agreed to a price of £150 for the car, payable as to £50 the next day, the balance to be by hire purchase. On 12 September 1952, the £50 was paid and a hire-purchase agreement completed. This agreement provided that acceptance of delivery should be conclusive evidence that the car was complete and in good order and condition and in every way satisfactory, and the claimant signed the agreement.

On 19 September 1952, the claimant was driving the car when it suddenly swerved and collided with a lorry. The car was wrecked and the claimant seriously injured. The claimant sued the defendant for damage to the car and personal injuries. The judge found that the defective condition of the drag-link joint was the cause of the accident.

HELD: The words used amounted to a warranty that the car was in good condition and reasonably safe for use on the highway. There was an implied warranty similar to that implied on a sale of goods and the claimant had acted on this warranty in entering into the agreement and could enforce the warranty. The claimant's personal injuries were a direct and natural result of the breach and the claimant was entitled to recover on this ground. The defendant was also liable for negligence in delivering the car in a dangerous condition when he could have discovered the condition by reasonable care and he had failed to have the car examined or warn the claimant that it had not been examined. *Herschtal v Stewart and Ardern Ltd* followed (see para [13.9]).

Judgment for claimant.

[13.11]   Lexmead (Basingstoke) Ltd v Lewis
[1982] AC 225, [1981] 1 All ER 1185, [1981] 2 WLR 713, 125 Sol Jo 310, [1981] 2 Lloyd's Rep 17, [1981] RTR 346, HL

The first defendant was the owner of a Land Rover and trailer being driven by his employee, the second defendant, when the trailer became detached and ran out of control into collision with a car in which the claimants were travelling. The coupling which failed had been designed and manufactured by the third defendants and sold to the first defendant by retailers, the fourth defendants. The judge found, on the evidence, that the coupling was defective in design and dangerous in use and that the defects were readily foreseeable by an appropriately skilled engineer; the manufacturers were negligent and liable to the claimants in tort for the personal injuries sustained. He also found the owner liable in that he had allowed the coupling to be used for some months in a damaged condition without having it repaired or even finding out if it was safe to use in such condition. Apportionment: 75% blame on the manufacturers, 25% on the owner. The retailers were not liable to the claimants because:
(1)   the coupling in question was a standard fitting for a Land Rover and the defects would call for a knowledge of design they did not possess; and
(2)   when servicing the vehicle they were not required without specific mention to inspect the coupling.
In third party proceedings the owner claimed indemnity from the retailers for breach of the Sale of Goods Act 1893, s 14, the retailers having supplied the coupling as fit and suitable for the owner's requirements. The judge held that there was a breach of s 14(1) of the 1893 Act in that the coupling was unsuitable and unfit for the purpose, but the owner's act in continuing to use the coupling when he realised, or ought to have realised, that it was broken was not within the

contemplation of the parties when the contract was made. *Mowbray v Merry-weather* [1895] 2 QB 640 was authority for saying that the owner's liability to pay damages to the claimants was a natural consequence of the breach of s 14 and entitled the owner to indemnity, but not where the damage was also due to an act not within the contemplation of the parties, namely, the use of the coupling in a damaged condition. The owner's claim against the retailers failed. The Court of Appeal disagreed, holding that as the owner's conduct was not so unreasonable as to be beyond the contemplation of the retailers there was no break in the chain of causation and the dealers were liable to indemnify him.

HELD, in the House of Lords: This was not right. The first inquiry to be made was what were the terms of the warranty which was said to have been broken? It was that the coupling as fixed to the Land Rover should be reasonably fit for towing trailers fitted with the appropriate type of attachment. This warranty was continuing up to the time when the owner learnt of its damaged condition. After this damage became apparent to him the only warranty he could have relied on was one which warranted that the coupling could continue to be safely used even in a damaged state – an obvious impossibility. The issue of causation on which the owner's claim against the dealers depended was whether it resulted from the dealer's breach of warranty, and manifestly it did not; it resulted from his own negligence in using the coupling in a damaged state.

3.   MANUFACTURER/REPAIRER/SELLER LIABLE

(A)   STATUTORY REGULATIONS

(I)   CONSUMER PROTECTION ACT 1987

[13.12]

The Consumer Protection Act 1987, Part I, ss 1–9 implements provisions contained in Council Directive 85/374/EEC of 25 July 1985 on the approximation of the laws, regulations and administrative provisions of the Member States concerning liability for defective products. Section 1 defines the meaning of products and producers. Section 2 imposes civil liability on producers and importers into the EEC for damage caused by defective products. Section 3 provides that there is a defect in a product if its safety is not such as persons are generally entitled to expect. Section 4 provides certain defences to liability under the 1987 Act. Section 5 limits liability under the 1987 Act to damage in respect of death, personal injury, or damage to property intended for private use exceeding £275. Section 6 causes the 1987 Act to apply to certain enactments, including the Law Reform (Miscellaneous Provisions) Act 1934, and the Fatal Accidents Act 1976. The 1987 Act also applies to the Congenital Disabilities (Civil Liability) Act 1976 and the Limitation Act 1980, among others. Section 7 prohibits a person who is liable for damage caused by a defective product from limiting or excluding his liability by any contract term or similar provision. Section 8 contains the power for Part I of the 1987 Act to be modified if modifications are made to the Directive. The Crown is bound by Part I of the 1987 Act under s 9.

Note—The Road Traffic Act 1930, s 3(1) (now replaced by s 42(1) of the Road Traffic Act 1988) made it unlawful to use a motor vehicle which does not comply with the regulations as to construction, weight and equipment.

The Road Traffic Act 1934, s 8(1) (now replaced by s 75 of the 1988 Act) made it unlawful to sell or supply a motor vehicle in such a condition that its use would be unlawful under s 3 of the 1930 Act.

Section 30 of the 1930 Act (now replaced by s 41(1) of the 1988 Act) empowered the Minister to make regulations as to the number and use of brakes, and for securing their efficiency and maintenance.

Section 113 of the 1930 Act provided penalties for offences under that Act.

The Road Vehicles (Construction and Use) Regulations 1986, SI 1986/1078, regs 15 and 18 set out the legal requirements for vehicle braking systems including their maintenance and efficiency levels.

[13.13] Vaile Bros v Hobson Ltd
[1933] All ER Rep 447, [1933] 149 LT 283, Div Ct

The claimants had sent a carburettor to the defendants for repair. In use one of the connecting rods broke, the engine raced out of control, the flywheel broke and extensive damage was done. The county court judge found that the engine switch was not connected to the dashboard, with the result that the damage could not be prevented by switching off the engine. He held this to be contributory negligence and absolved the defendants from liability. On appeal, this was reversed and it was held that the repairer could not escape liability for a defective repair by pointing to another defect for which he was not liable.

[13.14] Malfroot v Nozal
(1935) 51 TLR 551, 74 Sol Jo 610   Lewis J

While the male claimant, the owner of a motorcycle to which a few days previously the defendants had fitted a side-car, was driving the combination along a public road, the side-car became detached from the motor cycle. Both the male claimant and the female claimant who was a passenger in the side-car, sustained personal injuries. An action was brought for damages.

HELD: That the defendants were guilty of negligence in fitting the side-car to the motorcycle, that they were liable to the male claimant in contract and in tort, and to the female passenger in tort. The principles enunciated in *Donoghue v Stevenson* [1932] AC 562, [1932] All ER Rep 1 were applied: per Lewis J.

[13.15] Stennett v Hancock and Peters
[1939] 2 All ER 578, 83 Sol Jo 379   Branson J

The owner of a motor lorry took a wheel of the lorry, the flange of which had come off, to a motor repairer with instructions to reassemble it. The repairer's assistants reassembled and replaced it on the lorry, and the lorry owner's servant drove the lorry away. An hour or two later, the flange came off while the lorry was being driven on the highway by the lorry owner's servant, and, bowling along the road, it mounted the pavement and hit the female claimant, injuring her. There was no evidence that anything had happened between the time when the lorry was taken out of the garage and the time of the accident which might have caused the wheel to become dislodged.

HELD: (1) Following *Phillips v Britannia Hygienic Laundry Co* (at para [13.3]) the lorry owner having entrusted the repair of the lorry to a competent repairer, he was not liable for either negligence or nuisance to a person who suffered injury upon the road by reason of the competent repairer having been negligent.

(2)   The lorry owner, or the person who was going to take the vehicle on

the road, was not under a duty to ascertain for himself, in so far as his capabilities allowed him to do so, whether the competent repairer had competently repaired the lorry.

(3)   Following *Donoghue v Stevenson* [1932] AC 562, [1932] All ER Rep 1 and distinguishing *Earl v Lubbock* [1905] 1 KB 253 the repairer was liable to the persons who suffered injury on the road as a result of his negligence, as he was in the same position as that of the manufacturer of an article sold by a distributor in circumstances which prevented the distributor or ultimate purchaser or consumer from discovering by inspection any defect in the article.

[13.16]   Aspin v J Bretherton & Sons

(1947) Policy Holder Law Supplement

24 December 1947   Streatfield J

On 24 June 1946, the owners sent their lorry to the repairers to have the brakes relined, which involved dismantling, reassembling and replacement as necessary. The following day the repairers fitted a new drum and replaced roller bearings. On 22 July 1946, the owners sent the lorry to the repairers for special greasing. The owners did the maintenance work and greased once a week and tested for end play. On 24 July 1946, the lorry had travelled 2,059 miles, when the front offside wheel came off causing the lorry to collide with a bus. A passenger in the bus was injured and sued the lorry owners and the repairers.

HELD: The owners' explanation excluded them from liability. The lorry driver was not negligent. The condition of the thrust washer put the repairers on inquiry. There was not anticipation of examination by the owners and they were not bound to inspect after 2,059 miles and within a month. Time and distance were questions of fact. The repairers were negligent and were liable to the passenger.

[13.17]   Vinall v Howard

[1954] 1 QB 375, [1954] 1 All ER 458, [1954] 2 WLR 314, 98 Sol Jo 143, CA

The claimant sold to the defendant a second hand motor car which had defects in the speedometer, brake and silencer. Both parties were aware of the defects at the date of sale. The defendant gave a cheque in payment but stopped payment of the cheque and the claimant sued for the amount of the cheque. Streatfield J held the sale was unlawful under s 8(1) of Road Traffic Act 1934 Act (now s 75(1) of the 1988 Act).

HELD, ON APPEAL by the defendant: The defects were not in the original construction and equipment of the car but neglect of proper maintenance, a failure to keep in working order. They did not come under Part II of the Act made under s 3 of the Road Traffic Act 1930, but arose under Part III made under s 30 of the 1930 Act. The defects did not fall within s 3 and the contract was not unlawful under s 8(1) of the 1934 Act.

Note—The Road Traffic Act 1988, s 75(7) provides: 'Nothing in the preceding provisions of this section shall affect the validity of a contract or any rights arising under a contract.' There was no such provision in the 1930 Act.

[13.18]

(B)   LATENT DEFECT

The Latent Damage Act 1986 has no application to personal injury cases.

If an accident is due to a latent defect which was not discoverable by reasonable care, there is no negligence. For example, it is sufficient that a carrier should adopt the best known apparatus, kept in perfect order and worked without negligence by the servants he employs. If the carrier does this then he is not responsible for the consequences of an extremely rare and obscure accident which could not have been prevented by any reasonable means. Having said that, there is a higher degree of duty on the carrier. (See *Readhead v Midland Rly Co* (1869) LR 4 QB 379, 38 LJQB 169, *Hyman v Nye* (1881) 6 QBD 685, 44 LT 919, 45 JP 554 and *Newberry v Bristol Tramways and Carriage Co Ltd* (1912) 107 LT 801, 29 TLR 177, 57 Sol Jo 172.

[13.19]   R v Spurge
[1961] 2 QB 205, [1961] 2 All ER 688, [1961] 3 WLR 23, 125 JP 502, 105 Sol Jo 469, CCA

The appellant was driving his sports car round a very sharp and dangerous left hand bend. The car went over the double white lines in the centre of the road and collided with an oncoming motor scooter. His defence was that he decided to take the bend at a snail's pace and applied the brakes somewhat vigorously; the application of the brakes pulled the car on to its wrong side of the road in such a fashion that it was impossible for him to control it. Expert witnesses gave evidence that the brakes were in very bad condition and that vigorous application at 30mph pulled the car fairly violently to its offside. The appellant had taken delivery of the car only a few days before.

HELD: (1) There is no real distinction between a man being suddenly deprived of all control of a motor car by some sudden affliction to his person and being so deprived by some defect suddenly manifesting itself in the motor car.
  (2)   Cases in which a mechanical defect can be relied on as a defence to a charge of dangerous driving must be rare. The defence has no application where the defect is known to the driver or should have been discovered by him had he exercised reasonable prudence;
  (3)   The appellant could not succeed because he admitted he was aware of the tendency of the car to pull to the right when its brakes were applied.

[13.20]   Davie v New Merton Board Mills
[1959] AC 604, [1959] 1 All ER 346, [1959] 2 WLR 331, 103 Sol Jo 177, [1959] 2 Lloyd's Rep 587, HL

The claimant a maintenance fitter, was knocking out a metal key by using a drift and a hammer, when a piece of metal flew off and went into his eye. The drift was provided by the claimant's employers and although in good condition was of excessively hardness, which made it dangerous. The drift was negligently made by reputable manufacturers.

HELD: The Court of Appeal found in favour of the employers, not holding them negligent. However, the manufacturers were negligent and therefore liable to the claimant.

[13.21]   Hougham v Martin
(1964) 108 Sol Jo 138, Div Ct

The defendant was driving a Ford Anglia car along a main road when it gradually moved over to its offside of the road and collided with a vehicle travelling in the opposite direction. The defendant said she had no recollection of the accident. In answer to a charge of driving without due care and attention it was argued in her favour that the accident might have been caused by a mechanical defect to which modern mass-produced vehicles were prone but which it was not possible to specify. The justices dismissed the information.

HELD: On a case stated the Divisional Court directed the justices to convict. The mere suggestion that modern mass-produced vehicles were prone to mechanical defects did not give rise to a reasonable doubt and was merely fanciful.

[13.22]   Pearce v Round Oak Steel Works Ltd
[1969] 3 All ER 680, [1969] 1 WLR 595, 113 Sol Jo 163, CA

The claimant, a factory worker, was injured when a piece of a machine fell on his foot. The fall was caused by the breakage of a bolt due to a latent defect not discoverable by reasonable inspection. The claimant pleaded *res ipsa loquitur* and called as a witness a metallurgist who said the machine had been made in 1930 and bought by the defendants in 1959. He said there may have been drawings which would have given information about the material from which the bolt was made. The defendants called no evidence. The county court judge said the claimant had given sufficient evidence to put the burden on the defendants to show they had taken reasonable precautions. They had called no evidence and the claimant was entitled to succeed.

HELD, ON APPEAL: The judge's approach to the problem was right. Even though there is a latent defect the defendants must prove that the accident happened despite all reasonable care on their part: this means reasonable care not only in inspection and maintenance but also when they bought the machine. They must prove that in acquiring the machine and in their dealings with it they had taken reasonable care to see that it was in good order and condition. They ought to have called evidence about the circumstances in which they acquired the machine.

Appeal dismissed.

[13.23]   Henderson v Henry E Jenkins & Sons and Evans
[1970] AC 282, [1969] 3 All ER 756, [1969] 3 WLR 732, 113 Sol Jo 856, HL

A lorry driver applied the brakes of the lorry on a steep hill but they failed to operate. As a result the lorry struck and killed a man who was emerging from a parked vehicle. His widow sued the lorry owners who denied liability on the ground that the brake failure was due to latent defect not discoverable by reasonable care on their part. The lorry was five years old and had done at least 150,000 miles. The brakes were hydraulically operated. It was found after the accident that the brake failure was due to a steel pipe bursting at a point where corrosion had reduced the thickness of the wall of the pipe from 7mm to 1mm. The corrosion had occurred where it could not be seen except by removing the pipe completely from the vehicle and this had never been done. Expert evidence showed that it was not a normal precaution to do this if, as was the case, the visible parts of the pipe were not corroded. The corrosion was unusual and unexplained. An expert witness said it must have been due to chemical action of some kind such as exposure to salt from the roads in winter or on journeys near the sea or from leakage of corrosive liquids from particular kinds of loads. The judge of assize held there was no negligence on the part of the lorry owners. The Court of Appeal, by majority, agreed.

HELD, ON APPEAL to the House of Lords: The defendants had not discharged the burden of proof which lay on them of showing they had taken all reasonable care and that despite this the defect remained hidden. The evidence showed that something unusual must have happened to cause this corrosion – it was caused by some chemical agent. So it was necessary for the defendants to show that they neither knew nor ought to have known of any unusual occurrence to cause the breakdown. They had given no evidence at all of the history of the vehicle or the loads it had carried. It might have been sufficient for them to prove that they had a proper system for drivers reporting all occurrences but they had not done this. They chose to leave the case in a state where, for all they knew, the lorry might have been carrying carboys of acid regularly or had been coming into contact with sea water or salt frequently or had been engaged in carrying cattle. They had to prove that in all the circumstances of which they knew or ought to have known they had taken all proper steps to avoid danger. They had failed to do that and the claimant must succeed.

Note—See also *Barkway v South Wales Transport Co Ltd* [1950] AC 185, [1950] 1 All ER 392, 66 TLR 597, 94 Sol Jo 128, HL.

[13.24]   Carroll v Fearon

(1998) Times, 26 January, CA

Mr Bent was a passenger in a motor car owned by him but driven by his friend, Mr Fearon. Mr Fearon was driving along the M4. He lost control of the vehicle and careered through a gap in the central reservation coming into collision with a motor car being driven in the opposite direction.

The cause of the accident was a sudden and complete tread strip of a tyre on Mr Bent's car. The tyre was manufactured by Dunlop in 1988. There was overwhelming evidence that the manufacturing process had been defective. Inadequate rubber penetration of cords had fatally weakened the tyre which led to its failure.

HELD: The tyre failure should have been prevented by the exercise of due care by Dunlop in the manufacture of the tyre. Dunlop was assessed to be 80% liable.

Mr Fearon (driver) was assessed 8% liable for driving between 85–90mph and Mr Bent (owner) was assessed to be 12% liable for not adequately checking his vehicle's tyre pressures. Each defendant appealed against the finding of negligence made against them.

HELD, ON APPEAL: Dunlop argued that there was no presumption of negligence nor any justification for applying the maxim *res ipsa loquitur*. This submission was rejected. There was ample evidence that Dunlop was negligent.

There is no evidence to suggest that the speed that Mr Fearon was driving nor the tyre pressures of the other tyres would have had any significant impact on a properly manufactured tyre. Fearon's and Bent's appeals were successful. Dunlop was found to be 100% liable.

[13.25]   **Girbash v Main Line Auto Engineering Ltd**

[2004] EWCA Civ 614

[2004] All ER (D) 344 (May)

The claimant was seriously injured when she lost control of the car she was driving, swerved and collided with another vehicle. It was the claimant's case that the accident was caused by the defective rear offside brakes.

Before the accident, the claimant brought the car into the defendant's garage for repair and inspection and said that the defendant was negligent in failing to detect the problem with the brakes. The judge at first instance found in favour of the claimant, and the defendant appealed.

HELD, ON APPEAL: The judge was entitled to find that the defective brakes caused or contributed to the initial swerve, which caused the loss of control, and also that on balance the claimant had brought the vehicle into the defendant's premises for a service.

4.   DEFENDANT NOT LIABLE

[13.26]   **Hurley v Dyke**

[1979] RTR 265, HL

The defendant was a garage owner near Malvern. On 28 September a man named Halford driving an old Reliant three-wheeled car called at the garage because the carburettor was leaking. Both looked at the car and noticed it was down on one side. The defendant said Halford could not drive it like that. Halford said he would scrap the car and the defendant then paid him £10 for it. On 8 October, the carburettor having been repaired, the defendant took the car to a car auction at Tewkesbury, putting a reserve of £40 on it. It was offered for sale at auction on the terms 'To be sold as seen and with all its faults and without warranty'. Jones, a motor dealer, bought it for £40 intending to use it for spares, but after the sale Nigel Clay, a young man who had tried unsuccessfully to bid for the car, offered Jones a further £10 and Jones sold it to him. Clay drove it to Coventry where he lived and a week later to Surrey to see a friend. On 16 October he was driving the car with the claimant as passenger when the nearside of the chassis collapsed causing the car to go out of control. Clay was killed and the claimant very seriously injured. The judge at first instance held the defendant liable on the ground that, knowing the car was dangerous to drive, he had not ensured that the auctioneer made it clear that what was being sold was an unroadworthy vehicle. The Court of Appeal held there was no liability on the defendant. The warning given by the auctioneer was sufficient to bring home to the mind of any reasonable immediate buyer from the defendant that the car should not be put upon the road without intermediate examination. The defendant's duty did not extend beyond any first buyer from him.

HELD, ON APPEAL to the House of Lords: The defendant was not liable. The case turned on the question of fact as to the extent of the defendant's knowledge of the nature of the defect in the car when he put it up for auction. The highest that the defendant's knowledge could be put was an awareness of the public danger of driving the car without further examination. The warning given at auction that it was to be sold 'as seen and with all its faults' was adequate to satisfy any duty of care owed by the defendant to the claimant.

[13.27]   **Sidey v Olsen Bros**

[1984] CLY 2304

In June 1974 a coach operator bought a brand new coach which operated until September 1974. The coach manufacturer had raised a campaign about a design defect, and had provided the coach operator with the replacement part.

The part had not been fitted and the coach was repossessed and sold on to the defendant. The coach was thereafter involved in an accident injuring the claimant and 14 others. At first instance judgment was found against the defendant on the basis that they should have made enquiries of the coach operator as to whether there were any problems. The defendant appealed.

HELD, ON APPEAL: The trial judge had placed too high a duty of care on the defendant, as it was unreasonable to expect the defendant to make such enquiries with the coach operator. As the defendant was able to show on the facts that it had taken all reasonable care, the appeal was allowed.

Ownership of Vehicle

1.   INTRODUCTION

[14.1]   *Note*—The majority of motor policies indemnify in respect of the loss of or damage to the car insured, without any qualification or limitation, so that they are somewhat similar to an all-risks policy in this respect. Other policies limit the indemnity, so far as conversion is concerned to loss by theft.

A common cause for claims for loss of vehicles arises where the insured takes a cheque in payment on the sale of the car and the cheque is dishonoured on presentation. In the absence of circumstances such as in the cases of *Cundy v Lindsay* [1878] 3 App

Cas 459, 47 LJQB 481, 38 LT 573, 42 JP 483, 26 WR 406, HL and *Pearson v Rose and Young Ltd* (at para [14.32]), this is a case of loss of the proceeds of sale and not of loss of the car.

Where insurers are liable and have paid the loss, they are subrogated to the rights of the insured in respect of recovery of the car or of damages, and this involves tracing the property, as distinct from the possession, in the car. It is therefore necessary to consider the subjects of theft, sale of goods and hire purchase.

Where the car is in the possession of the police, there is a right to proceed in the magistrates' court for its return.

If the car is not in police possession, the proceedings are in the civil court for delivery up of the car or payment of its value and damages for detention. There is also the right to claim damages for conversion against any intermediate purchaser. The question is whether the title has passed to a subsequent purchaser.

[14.2]   Lancashire and Yorkshire Rly Co v MacNicoll

(1918) 88 LJKB 601, 118 LT 596, 34 TLR 280, 62 Sol Jo 365

Dealing with goods in a manner inconsistent with the right of the true owner amounts to a conversion, provided that it is also established that there is an intention on the part of the defendant in so doing to deny the owner's right or to assert a right which is inconsistent with the owner's right.

[14.3]   Webster v General Accident Assurance Corpn

[1953] 1 QB 520, [1953] 1 All ER 663, [1953] 2 WLR 491, 97 Sol Jo 155, [1953] 1 Lloyd's Rep 123   Parker J

A comprehensive policy on a motor car included the following words: 'Section 1 Loss of or damage to the insured motor car. The corporation will indemnify the policyholder against loss of ... any motor car described in the schedule hereto.'

The car owner entered his car for sale with a reserve of £325, which was not reached. He was about to collect his car, when Taylor (who had arranged the auction) said to him 'Don't go' and told him he had an offer to buy the car privately for £335. The owner then left the car with Taylor on the understanding that it would be sold as soon as Taylor had communicated to the private buyer that his offer was accepted. There was no such buyer. Taylor sent the car to another auction sale and the car was sold to A at auction and afterwards by A to B. Taylor sent cheques for varying amounts in purported payment, all of which were dishonoured, and the last returned 'account closed'. The arbitrator found that there was no larceny by a trick, nor larceny by a bailee, but that the owner had been swindled out of the car by the fraud and false pretences of Taylor. The arbitrator found that the purchaser had acquired a good title and it was not unreasonable for the owner to refrain from attempting to claim the car from the purchaser. He considered that 'loss' could be fairly defined as 'an effective deprivation in circumstances making recovery uncertain'.

If a chattel is handed over to an agent, whether or not as a result of a fraudulent misrepresentation, and the agent then proceeds to deal with the chattel in a way which amounts to a conversion of the chattel, there may be a loss. The claimant had taken all reasonable steps to recover his car and recovery was, to say the least, uncertain. There was a loss within the meaning of the policy.

The judge declined the argument that the loss was of the proceeds of sale and not the loss of the chattel. Following *London and Provincial Leather Processes v Hudson* (at para [14.19]), award affirmed.

Note—69 LQR 163 points out that the fact that the claimant had voluntarily handed the car to T did not mean that a loss could not be established. If the owner of a chattel hands it over to X for sale, X having honestly represented that he has a buyer, and the chattel is duly sold by X who misappropriates the proceeds, there would not be a loss of the chattel but a loss of the proceeds of sale. Here, however, the loss occurred when T sent it to the auction for sale, for at that moment he deprived the claimant of his title without authority.

[14.4] Eisinger v General Accident Fire and Life Assurance Corpn Ltd

[1955] 2 All ER 897, [1955] 1 WLR 869, 99 Sol Jo 511, [1955] 2 Lloyd's Rep 95 Lord Goddard CJ

The owner of a motor car agreed to sell the car to a purchaser and accepted a cheque in payment and parted with the car and the log book. The purchaser never had any intention of paying for the car and the cheque was worthless. The car was insured against loss or damage and the owner claimed from insurers for a loss of the car.

HELD: The car had been obtained by false pretences and the property in the car had passed to the purchaser. The consent of the owner was real consent induced by fraud and not an appearance of consent induced by fraud produced by a trick. The transaction amounted to obtaining a car by false pretences and not that of larceny by a trick. The loss was the value of the cheque and not the loss of the car. Parting with the property as well as the possession distinguished it from *Webster v General Accident Assurance Corpn* (at para [14.3]). The owner had not lost the car. He had lost the proceeds of sale. There was no loss within the meaning of the policy.

[14.5] Dobson v General Accident Fire and Life Assurance Corpn plc

[1990] 1 QB 274, [1989] 3 All ER 927

The claimant held home insurance cover for, among other things, 'loss or damage caused by theft'. The claimant advertised for sale his Rolex watch and diamond ring. A rogue expressed an interest and a sale was agreed. In exchange for the jewellery the rogue handed over a building society cheque which the claimant subsequently found had been stolen and was worthless. The claimant claimed under his insurance policy. The defendant insurer refused to indemnify on the basis that the loss of the jewellery did not constitute theft within the meaning of the Theft Act 1968. The claimant commenced proceedings and succeeded at first instance. The defendant insurer appealed.

HELD, ON APPEAL: The defendant's appeal failed. The four elements of the offence of theft were satisfied. There had been a dishonest appropriation of property belonging to another with the intention of permanently depriving the owner of it. The fact that the claimant had consented to the property being taken away was irrelevant.

[14.6] Ballett v Mingay

[1943] KB 281, [1943] 1 All ER 143, 112 LJKB 193, 168 LT 34, CA

The claimant loaned goods to an infant who agreed to pay a weekly sum for the loan. The claimant demanded the return of the goods. The defendant had meanwhile parted with possession of the goods. The claimant sued the infant in detinue, ie in tort. The infant pleaded that the claim was for breach of contract and infancy was a defence.

HELD: The terms of the bailment did not permit the infant to part with the possession of the goods. The action of the infant in parting with the goods fell outside the contract altogether. The act was one of tort, distinct from the contract, and the infant was liable in tort.

2.   REMEDIES OF OWNER

(A)   THE TORTS (INTERFERENCE WITH GOODS) ACT 1977, S 3

[14.7]
3.   Form of judgment when goods are detained
(1)   In proceedings for wrongful interference against a person who is in possession or in control of the goods relief may be given in accordance with this section, so far as appropriate.
(2)   The relief is—
   (a)   an order for delivery of the goods, and for payment of any consequential damages, or
   (b)   an order for delivery of the goods, but giving the defendant the alternative of paying damages by reference to the value of the goods, together in either alternative with payment of any consequential damages, or
   (c)   damages.
(3)   Subject to rule of court—
   (a)   relief shall be given under only one of paras (a), (b) and (c) of subsection (2),
   (b)   relief under paragraph (a) of subsection (2) is at the discretion of the court, and the claimant may choose between the others.
(4)   If it is shown to the satisfaction of the court that an order under subsection (2)(a) has not been complied with, the court may—
   (a)   revoke the order, or the relevant part of it, and
   (b)   make an order for payment of damages by reference to the value of the goods.
(5)   Where an order is made under subsection (2)(b) the defendant may satisfy the order by returning the goods at any time before execution of judgment, but without prejudice to liability to pay any consequential damages.
(6)   An order for delivery of the goods under subsection (2)(a) or (b) may impose such conditions as may be determined by the court, or pursuant to rules of court, and in particular, where damages by reference to the value of the goods would not be the whole of the value of the goods, may require an allowance to be made by the claimant to reflect the difference.
   For example, a bailor's action against the bailee may be one in which the measure of damages is not the full value of the goods, and then the court may order delivery of the goods, but require the bailor to pay the bailee a sum reflecting the difference.
(7)   Where under subsection (1) or subsection (2) of s 6 an allowance is to be made in respect of an improvement of the goods, and an order is made under subsection (2)(a) or (b), the court may assess the allowance to be made in respect of the improvements, and by the order require, as a condition for delivery of the goods, that allowance to be made by the claimant.
(8)   This section is without prejudice—
   (a)   to the remedies afforded by s 133 of the Consumer Credit Act 1974, or
   (b)   to the remedies afforded by ss 35, 42 and 44 of the Hire-Purchase Act 1965, or to those sections of the Hire-Purchase Act (Northern Ireland) 1966 (so long as those sections respectively remain in force), or
   (c)   to any jurisdiction to afford ancillary or incidental relief.

[14.8]   *Note*—An owner can lawfully reclaim and take possession of a car wrongfully detained wherever he happens to find it, so long as it is not in a riotous manner or attended with breach of the peace, and may even justify an assault to recapture the car if the person in possession refuses to return it (*Blades v Higgs* (1861) 10 CBNS 713 at p 720 per Erle CJ). In that event it seems that if the person wrongfully in possession has spent money on improving the car, this money might not be recoverable from the owner.

See *Greenwood v Bennett* (at para [14.28]), and s 6 of the Torts (Interference with Goods) Act 1977.

[14.9]   Butterworth v Kingsway Motors

[1954] 2 All ER 694, [1954] 1 WLR 1286, 98 Sol Jo 717   Pearson J

A hire-purchase (HP) company as owners hired a car to R on a usual hire-purchase agreement on 3 January 1951. Before R had paid all the instalments or exercised the option to purchase, she purported on 1 August 1951 to sell the car to a motor dealer, K, for £350 cash and a car valued at £650. On 11 August 1951 K sold the car to H for £1,015. The same day H sold it to M for £1,030. On 15 August 1951, M sold it to B for £550 cash and a car valued at £725 (£1,275). B continued to use the car until but not after 16 July 1952. R meanwhile continued to pay the instalments until she learned she had no right to sell and she then informed the HP company of the position. On 15 July 1952, the HP company wrote to B stating that the car was their property and calling for its delivery up, adding without prejudice, that they would accept £175 14s 2d to validate the title. On 17 July 1952, B's solicitors wrote to K claiming the return of the money paid for the car, and to the HP company for a copy of the HP agreement. On 23 July 1952 the HP company's solicitors wrote to B's solicitors that they had received a cheque from R which when met would discharge their interest. The cheque was met on 25 July. On 9 August B's solicitors wrote to M for the return of the purchase price of £1,275 and for instructions with regard to the return of the car. On 14 August the HP company wrote to B's solicitors that their interests had been completed and on 18 August M's solicitors wrote to the same effect to B's solicitors, who on 22 August wrote to B's solicitors referring to their letter of 17 July. The reply was on 22 August that they had nothing to add to their letter of 18 August. On 12 September 1952 a specially indorsed writ was issued claiming £1,275.

M issued a third-party notice against H; H issued a fourth-party notice against K; and K issued a fifth-party notice against R.

HELD: B had effectively rescinded the contract of sale and was entitled to recover £1,250: *Rowland v Divall* (at para [14.10]). On 25 July 1952 R had acquired a good title and this fed the previously defective title of the subsequent buyers: *Whitehorn Bros v Davison* [1911] 1 KB 463, 80 LJKB 425, 104 LT 234. CA, *Blundell-Leigh v Attenborough* [1921] 3 KB 235, 90 LJKB 1005, 125 LT 356, 37 TLR 567, 65 Sol Jo 474, CA, *Robin and Rambler Coaches v Turner* [1947] 2 All ER 284. M was entitled to damages from H assessed on the value of the car in July 1952, assessed by the court at £800; judgment for £475. H was entitled to £475 from K and K to £475 from R.

[14.10]   Rowland v Divall

[1923] 2 KB 500, 92 LJKB 1041, 129 LT 757, 67 Sol Jo 703, CA

If the person wrongfully in possession has purchased the car from a third party, he can recover his full loss from the third party.

[14.11]   Mason v Burningham

[1949] 2 KB 545, [1949] 2 All ER 134, [1949] LJR 1430, 65 TLR 466, 93 Sol Jo 496, CA

A person in wrongful possession of a car who then recovers his losses from a third party from whom he made the purchase, would be limited to money expended in the ordinary course of events and not fancy expenditure at the buyer's whim.

Note—If the owner sues for delivery up, but the court does not order the return of the car and awards damages, then on recovery from the third party, of all the damage suffered, the car would become the property of the third party. See the Torts (Interference with Goods) Act 1977, s 5(1):

[14.12]
5.   **Extinction of title on satisfaction of claim for damages**
   (1)   Where damages for wrongful interference are, or would fail to be, assessed on
   the footing that the claimant is being compensated—
      (a)   for the whole of his interest in the goods, or
      (b)   for the whole of his interest in the goods subject to a reduction for
            contributory negligence, payment of the assessed damages (under all
            heads), or as the case may be settlement of a claim for damages for the
            wrong (under all heads), extinguishes the claimant's title to that interest.

(B)   SALE

[14.13]   Curtis v Maloney

[1951] 1 KB 736, [1950] 2 All ER 982, [1950] WN 525, 66 (pt 2) TLR 869, 94 Sol Jo 761, CA

The owner of a motor cabin cruiser left it in the care of a firm of boatwrights. In execution of a writ of *fieri facias* against the boatwrights, the sheriff seized the boat and sold it by public auction. The sale was advertised, and no claim was made to the sheriff in respect of the boat before the sale. The owner sued the purchaser for the return of the boat or its value and damages for detention.
   The Bankruptcy and Deeds of Arrangement Act 1913, s 15 provides:

'Where any goods in the possession of an execution debtor at the time of seizure by a sheriff, high bailiff, or other officer charged with the enforcement of a writ, warrant, or other process of execution, are sold by such sheriff, high bailiff, or other officer, without any claim having been made to the same, the purchaser of the goods so sold shall acquire a good title to the goods so sold, and no person shall be entitled to recover against the sheriff, high bailiff, or other officer, or anyone lawfully acting under the authority of either of them, except as provided by the Bankruptcy Acts 1883 and 1890, for any sale of such goods or for paying over the proceeds thereof, prior to the receipt of a claim to the said goods unless it is proved that the person from whom recovery is sought had notice, or might by making reasonable inquiry have ascertained that the goods were not the property of the execution debtor. Provided that nothing in this section contained shall affect the right of any claimant who may prove that at the time of sale he had a title to any goods so seized and sold to any remedy to which he may be entitled against any person other than such sheriff, high bailiff, or other officer as aforesaid.'

The claimant contended that as he had a title to the goods at the time of the sale and as the purchaser was a person other than such sheriff, high bailiff, or other officer, the proviso preserved the claimant's rights.

The defendant contended that the first part of the section gave a good title to the purchaser, and the proviso reserved the rights against the execution creditor.

HELD: By Finnemore J [1950] 2 All ER 201, 66 (Pt 2) TLR 147, the purchaser acquired a good title and the action failed.

The decision was upheld on appeal.

Per Somervell LJ: A good title means a good title against everybody. The proviso cannot be read so as to contradict and make these express words meaningless by excluding from them the true owner at the time of the sale.

Per Cohen LJ: The proviso preserves the true owner's rights against the execution creditor, and removes any doubts as to the right of the true owner to sue the execution creditor for money he had received.

Per Denning LJ: The proviso preserves the rights of the original owner against the execution creditor or any wrongdoer who had converted the goods prior to the sale.

Note—Approved in *Dyal Singh v Kenyan Insurance Ltd* [1954] AC 287, [1954] 1 All ER 847, [1954] 2 WLR 607, 98 Sol Jo 231, PC. On 'notice' and 'reasonable inquiry', see *Observer Ltd v Gordon* [1983] 2 All ER 945, [1983] 1 WLR 1008, 127 Sol Jo 324.

[14.14]   Bulbruin Ltd v Romanyszyn

[1994] RTR 273, CA

A local authority used its statutory power under ss 99 and 101 of the Road Traffic Regulation Act 1984 and reg 15(1) of the Removal and Disposal of Vehicles Regulations 1986, SI 1986/183 to collect a van abandoned at the roadside and sell it to the defendant. The van belonged to the claimant. It had been stolen and abandoned with false number plates. The claimant demanded the return of the van and the defendant refused. The claimant then brought proceedings against the defendant for the return of the van and the defendant, by way of third party proceedings against the local authority, sought an indemnity under the contract of sale. The judge at first instance held that the title of the van had not passed to the defendant. The defendant appealed.

HELD, ON APPEAL: The defendant's appeal succeeded. The provision of s 21(1) of the Sale of Goods Act 1979 did not affect a statutory power of sale. The exercise of the powers of sale provided by s 101 of the 1984 Act effected a transfer of title despite the absence of an express provision in this statute.

3.   DAMAGES

(A)   MEASURE OF DAMAGES

[14.15]   Caxton Publishing Co v Sutherland Publishing Co

[1939] AC 178, [1938] 4 All ER 389, 108 LJ Ch 5, 160 LT 17, 55 TLR 123, 82 Sol Jo 1047, HL

Per Lord Roche: The measure of damages for conversion is the value of the thing converted at the date of conversion. In *Reid v Fairbanks* (1853) 13 CB 692, 43 Dig 509, there was a list of value available, because the true owner had contracted to sell a ship under construction for £x. It was held, or rather, agreed (because the actual decision was on another point) that the damage was £x–£y representing the cost of finishing the construction. I entirely accept the view that expenses incurred after the conversion should come off [the damages]. As the appellants in fact used the material, the proper inquiry is as to its fair value.

Per Lord Porter: Damages to the full value of the property converted may be given against two persons for successive conversions of the same chattel, and, until payment in full of the sum awarded is made by one of the defendants, the judgment remains in force against the other. In neither case, however, would the claimant be permitted to recover more than the sum awarded for the injuries received or the value of the chattel, as the case might be, because the law will not permit any greater sum to be recovered than that representing the actual damage suffered. Mere possession of the property of others is not conversion, since, by a fiction, the original possession is regarded as lawful.

[14.16]   The Mediana

[1900] AC 113, 69 LJP 35, 82 LT 98, 48 WR 398, HL

Even the loss of the use for a time of a chattel which the owner would not have used during that time may give rise to substantial damages, whether in an action for damages or in an action for conversion.

[14.17]   Sachs v Miklos

[1948] 2 KB 23, [1948] 1 All ER 67, [1948] LJR 1012, 64 TLR 118, CA

While the measure of damages for conversion is usually the value of the goods at the date of judgment, if the bailor knew or ought to have known at an earlier date that the conversion had taken place or was about to take place and took immediate steps to recover the goods, the measure of damages was the value of the goods at the date of his knowledge or supposed knowledge.

Note—The Torts (Interference with Goods) Act 1977, s 2 (which came into force on the 1 June 1978) states as follows:

[14.18]
2.   Abolition of detinue
   (1)   Detinue is abolished.
   (2)   An action lies in conversion for loss or destruction of goods which a bailee has allowed to happen in breach of his duty to his bailor (that is to say it lies in a case which is not otherwise conversion, but would have been detinue before detinue was abolished).

[14.19]   London and Provincial Motor and Tractor Co Ltd v Boundary Garage

[1948] WN 267, 92 Sol Jo 499   Birkett J

B bought A a motor car for £350 on the faith of statements made with utter recklessness and without any inquiry whether they were true or false and therefore fraudulent. B entered into a hire-purchase agreement with C. The car was a stolen car and had to be returned to the true owner.

HELD, in an action by B against A: B was entitled to recover the £350 from A and a declaration (following *Household Machines Ltd v Cosmos Exporters Ltd* [1947] KB 217, [1946] 2 All ER 622, [1947] LJR 578, 176 LT 49, 62 TLR 757) that the claimants were entitled to recover from the defendants such damages as the claimants may be held liable to pay and/or may reasonably pay to C in consequence of any breach by claimants of the hire purchase agreement with C, in so far as such breaches were attributable to B's fraudulent/reckless statements.

[14.20] Strand Electric and Engineering Co Ltd v Brisford Entertainments Ltd

[1952] 2 QB 246, [1952] 1 All ER 796, [1952] 1 TLR 939, 96 Sol Jo 260, CA

The defendant, the owner of a theatre, allowed possession to a prospective purchaser, who obtained lighting equipment from the claimant on hire at £9 6s 8d per week. The prospective purchaser was unable to complete and notified the claimant to collect the equipment. The defendant refused to allow the claimant to take possession of the goods. The judge assessed damages on the prospective receipts from hire if the goods had been returned.

HELD, ON APPEAL: The defendant had used the goods for its own benefit and was liable for the payments payable under the hire agreement.

Per Denning LJ: If a car used in business is detained, and the owner has to hire another car at an increased rate, he can recover the cost of the substitute, ie the actual loss. If a car is put out of action during repair, the wrongdoer is only liable for the loss suffered by the claimant.

[14.21] Hillesden Securities Ltd v Ryjak Ltd

[1983] 2 All ER 184, [1983] 1 WLR 959, [1983] RTR 491, 127 Sol Jo 521   Parker J

R, the owner of a Rolls Royce car, leased it on the 11 June 1979 to V for a term of 36 months. On 13 September 1980 V purported to sell the car to E and a company of which E was a director and shareholder. V paid no leasing instalments after October 1980 and R accordingly sought the return of the car. Having failed he assigned his rights in the car to the claimant who began proceedings against E and his company. On 11 March 1982 E ceased to be a director or shareholder in the company. The action came on for trial on 30 November 1982. The car was returned to the claimant on 3 December 1982. On the issue of damages it was argued on behalf of E that s 3 of the Torts (Interference with Goods) Act 1977 had no application as he had not been in possession and control of the car after 11 March 1982.

HELD: E plainly converted the car on the 13 September 1980 and was liable for conversion. The parties had agreed that a proper figure for the use of the car which the defendant had enjoyed was £115 per week. Section 3 of the 1977 Act referred to relief which may be given 'in proceedings ... against a person who is in possession or control of the goods'. This meant persons who were in possession and control of the goods when the proceedings were launched. Following the decision in *Strand Electric and Engineering Co Ltd v Brisford Entertainments Ltd* (at para [14.20]) in the case of a profit-earning chattel which a defendant has used for his own benefit the owner can recover by way of damages a hire charge plus either the return of the chattel or, if there has been a subsequent conversion by disposal, the value of the chattel at the date of such conversion. The claimants had lost the use of the car over the whole period from the original conversion to the 3 December 1982. Though E had ceased to have any connection with the company on the 11 March 1982 he could not be heard to say that by putting it out of his power to return the car he terminated his liability. Judgment against both defendants for the hire charge at the agreed weekly figure for the whole period to 3 December 1982, namely, £13,280, plus interest from 23 February 1981 the date when R first made a written demand for return of the car.

[14.22] IBL Ltd v Coussens

[1991] 2 All ER 133, CA

The claimant company purchased two vehicles for the defendant's use in his capacity as chairman and managing director of the company. Subsequently, the defendant was dismissed. The claimant company gave the defendant the option of returning the two vehicles or purchasing them for a total cost of £62,000. The defendant neither returned the vehicles nor took up the option to purchase and the claimant brought proceedings against him seeking the delivery of the vehicles and damages for conversion. The Master, giving judgment for the claimant, ordered that the vehicles be returned to the claimant without the option to purchase. On appeal to the deputy High Court judge the defendant managed to vary the order to allow him the option of purchasing the vehicles for the original sum of £62,000.

The claimant appealed. The claimant did not seek an order returning the vehicles but argued that: firstly, the offer to sell at £62,000 was only valid at the time that it was made and this offer was refused; secondly, the value of the vehicles had increased since the time that the offer was made and, thirdly, there was a continuing conversion of the vehicles by the defendant and, thus, damages should be assessed on the basis of the value of the vehicles at the time of judgment rather than original conversion.

The defendant argued that the vehicle had been converted at the time the offer to sell at £62,000 was made and so this was the value to be taken for the purposes of the assessment of damages.

HELD: Although the tort of detinue had been abolished by s 2(1) of the Torts (Interference with Goods) Act 1977, the remedies available for detinue subsisted. There were many competing considerations to be taken into account when considering the provisions of the 1977 Act thus 'if one takes account of all these considerations and the fact that several different remedies are available under s 3 of the 1977 Act it is not possible, or indeed appropriate, to attempt to lay down any rule which is intended to be of universal application as to the date by reference to which the value of goods is to be assessed. The method of valuation and the date of valuation will depend on the circumstances' (per Neill LJ).

On the facts of the case it was held that the damages were to be assessed by reference to the value of the vehicles at the date of judgment and not at the date of the initial conversion. The case was referred back to the Master for the assessment of damages.

Note—But contrast *BBMB Finance (Hong Kong) Ltd v Eda Holdings Ltd* (at para [14.23]).

[14.23] BBMB Finance (Hong Kong) Ltd v Eda Holdings Ltd

[1991] 2 All ER 129, [1990] 1 WLR 409

The defendant received a share certificate to be held on trust for the claimants. Subsequently, the defendant disposed of the shares (and handed over the share certificate) to a third party for a value of $5.75 per share receiving a cheque in return which was never presented for payment. About six months later the defendant replaced these shares by purchasing an equivalent number on the open market at a price of $2.40 per share. The claimant sued the defendant for conversion and was awarded damages equivalent to the difference between the value of the shares at the time of conversion and the value of the replacement shares. The defendant appealed to the Privy Council.

HELD: Per Lord Templeman: The general rule is that a claimant whose property is irreversibly converted has vested in him a right to damages for conversion measured by the value of the property at the date of conversion.

The defendant had sold and irreversibly converted the claimant's shares and at that stage the claimant became entitled to damages for conversion equal to the market price. It was irrelevant that the defendant had failed to present the cheque from the third party.

(B)   ALLOWANCE FOR IMPROVEMENT OF GOODS

[14.24]   *Note*—See s 6 of The Torts (Interference with Goods) Act 1977 below:
6.   Allowance for improvement of the goods
  (1)   If in proceedings for wrongful interference against a person (the 'improver') who has improved the goods, it is shown that the improver acted in the mistaken but honest belief that he had a good title to them, an allowance shall be made for the extent to which, at the time at which the goods fall to be valued in assessing damages, the value of the goods is attributable to the improvement.
  (2)   If, in proceedings for wrongful interference against a person ('the purchaser') who has purported to purchase the goods—
    (a)   from the improver, or
    (b)   where after such a purported sale the goods passed by a further purported sale on one or more occasions, or any such occasion,
  it is shown that the purchaser acted in good faith, an allowance shall be made on the principle set out in subsection (1).
    For example, where a person in good faith buys a stolen car from the improver and is sued in conversion by the true owner the damages may be reduced to reflect the improvement, but if the person who bought the stolen car from the improver sues the improver for failure of consideration, and the improver acted in good faith, subsection (3) below will ordinarily make a comparable reduction in the damages he recovers from the improver.
  (3)   If in a case within subsection (2) the person purporting to sell the goods acted in good faith, then in proceedings by the purchaser for recovery of the purchase price because of failure of consideration, or in any other proceedings founded on that failure of consideration, an allowance shall, where appropriate, be made on the principles set out in subsection (1).
  (4)   This section applies, with the necessary modifications, to a purported bailment or other disposition of goods as it applies to a purported sale of goods.

[14.25]   **Munro v Willmott**
[1949] 1 KB 295, [1948] 2 All ER 983, [1949] LJR 471, 64 TLR 627, 92 Sol Jo 662   Lynskey J

The defendant allowed the claimant to leave her car in the yard of the premises of which he was licensee without charge in 1942. In 1945 he wanted the car moved. He tried but failed to get in touch with the claimant. The car was not roadworthy and he had it repaired at a cost of £85, and sold it by auction for £105. In 1946 the claimant sued for the full value of the car without any allowance for the £85 spent on repairs.

HELD: The defendant was not an agent of necessity and was liable. He was entitled to credit, not because he had made the payment, but to ascertain the true value of the property which the claimant had lost. If the car had not been repaired, it would at the time of the judgment have realised something in the nature of £25 as scrap. Judgment awarded to claimant for £35 (£120 being the value of the car, and crediting the £85).

[14.26]   Wilson v Lombank Ltd

[1963] 1 All ER 740, [1963] 1 WLR 1294   Hinchcliffe J

The claimant, a dealer, bought a car and took it for repairs to a garage where he had a monthly account. After the repairs were done the garage staff put the car on the forecourt to await collection. A representative of the defendant, a finance company, saw it there and took it away. Both parties thought themselves to have a good title to the car but neither in fact was the owner: it really belonged to another finance company to whom the defendants delivered it when satisfied that this was so. The claimant sued for damages for trespass on the ground that he had possession of the car and the defendants had no right to take it away.

HELD: The claimant was entitled to immediate possession of the car at the time when it was on the forecourt since he could at any moment demand its return. The garage had no lien for the costs of repairs having regard to the course of dealing, i e the monthly account. The claimant having never lost possession of the car meant that the defendant had wrongfully taken it and must pay damages. Delivery to the true owner did not defeat the claimant's claim. The measure of damages was the full value of the car at the time the tort was committed, namely, the price the claimant paid for the car plus the cost of repairs.

[14.27]   Wickham Holdings Ltd v Brooke House Motors Ltd

[1967] 1 All ER 117, [1967] 1 WLR 295, CA

When a finance company sues in conversion (eg when the hirer under a hire-purchase agreement wrongfully sells the goods or the benefit of the agreement) it can recover its actual loss and no more. It does not recover the full value of the goods but only the balance outstanding on the hire-purchase price.

Note—Followed in *Belvoir Finance Co Ltd v Stapleton* [1971] 1 QB 210, [1970] 3 All ER 664, [1970] 3 WLR 530, 114 Sol Jo 719, CA. Both *Wickham* and *Belvoir* were considered in *Chubb Cash Ltd v John Crilley & Son* [1983] 2 All ER 294, [1983] 1 WLR 599, 127 Sol Jo 153, CA. Per Bush J:

> 'These cases decided that the measure of damages was the market value of the goods, or the amount still owing under the hire-purchase agreement, whichever was the lower as at the date of the conversion. It was a limited decision, not a decision which entitled the claimants, if the amount outstanding on the hire-purchase agreement was greater than the value of the goods, to claim that.'

[14.28]   Greenwood v Bennett

[1973] QB 195, [1972] 3 All ER 586, [1972] 2 WLR 691, [1972] RTR 535, CA

Bennett wishing to have some work done to a car to prepare it for sale entrusted it to Searle to do the work. Searle used the car for his own purposes and in doing so damaged it. He wrongfully 'sold' it in its damaged state to Harper who in good faith paid him £75 for it. Harper spent £226 on it to put it in good order and then sold it for £450 to a finance company. When Searle's misdealing with the car was discovered the police seized the car and brought interpleader proceedings to determine the ownership. The judge ordered the car to be delivered up to Bennett and held that Harper was not entitled to be paid by Bennett for the £226 worth of work done to the car.

HELD: The judge should have required Bennett to pay Harper the £226 as a condition of being given delivery of the car. The principle that lay to hand to meet the case was derived from the law of restitution – that the owners should not be allowed to enrich themselves at the expense of a person who has done work to a property of which he honestly believes himself to be the owner.

[14.29] Highland Leasing v Field
[1986] CLY 3224

The claimant owned a tractor worth £20,000.00. The defendant came into possession of it after it was burnt out in 1981. The defendant offered the insurers £1,000.00 for the salvage. The offer was refused. Two months later a salvage agent appointed by the insurers attempted to recover the tractor to assess its salvage value. The defendant refused, and subsequently rebuilt the tractor later selling it for £15,150.00.

HELD: The claimant sought to claim damages as at the date of sale by the defendant, which would have resulted in a substantial windfall. The defendant retained the tractor believing he had a valid claim against the insurers, however, he did not believe he had good title. The court held that the material act of conversion amounted to the salvage value of the tractor in the aftermath of the fire, which did not take account of the improvements made by the defendant.

4. OWNER'S RIGHTS AGAINST PURCHASERS IN GOOD FAITH

(A) STATUTE LAW

(I) THE FACTORS ACT 1889, SS 1, 2

[14.30]
1. Definitions
For the purposes of this Act—
    (1) The expression 'mercantile agent' shall mean a mercantile agent having in the customary course of his business as such agent authority either to sell goods, or to consign goods for the purpose of sale, or to buy goods, or to raise money on the security of goods.
    (2) A person shall be deemed to be in possession of goods or of the documents of title to goods, where the goods or documents are in his actual custody or are held by any other person subject to his control or for him or on his behalf.
    (3) The expression 'goods' shall include wares and merchandise.
    (4) The expression 'document of title' shall include any bill of lading, dock warrant, warehouse-keeper's certificate, and warrant or order for the delivery of goods, and any other document used in the ordinary course of business as proof of the possession or control of goods, or authorising or purporting to authorise, either by endorsement or by delivery, the possessor of the document to transfer or receive goods thereby represented.
    (5) The expression 'pledge' shall include any contract pledging, or giving a lien or security on, goods, whether in consideration of an original advance or of any further or continuing advance or of any pecuniary liability.
    (6) The expression 'person' shall include any body of persons corporate or unincorporate.

[14.31]
2. Powers of mercantile agent with respect to disposition of goods
    (1) Where a mercantile agent is, with the consent of the owner, in possession of goods or of the documents of title to goods, any sale, pledge, or other disposition

of the goods, made by him when acting in the ordinary course of business of a mercantile agent, shall, subject to the provisions of this Act, be as valid as if he were expressly authorised by the owner of the goods to make the same; provided that the person taking under the disposition acts in good faith, and has not at the time of the disposition notice that the person making the disposition has not authority to make the same.

(2)   Where a mercantile agent has, with the consent of the owner, been in possession of goods or of the documents of title to goods, any sale, pledge, or other disposition, which would have been valid if the consent had continued, shall be valid notwithstanding the determination of the consent: provided that the person taking under the disposition has not at the time thereof notice that the consent has been determined.

(3)   Where a mercantile agent has obtained possession of any documents of title to goods by reason of his being or having been, with the consent of the owner, in possession of the goods represented thereby, or of any other documents of title to the goods, his possession of the first-mentioned documents shall, for the purposes of this Act, be deemed to be with the consent of the owner.

(4)   For the purposes of this Act the consent of the owner shall be presumed in the absence of evidence to the contrary.

[14.32]   Pearson v Rose and Young Ltd

[1951] 1 KB 275, [1950] 2 All ER 1027, 66 (pt 2) TLR 886, 94 Sol Jo 778, CA

The claimant on 15 March 1949 was told by a mercantile agent that the agent could obtain a new motor car for the claimant for £467 in six months, but required a deposit of £100. Three days later the claimant saw the agent and discussed whether the claimant could sell his car because of the covenant against resale, and to clear up this point the claimant produced his log book and handed it to the agent. Whilst the agent had it, he asked the claimant to accompany the agent's wife to hospital, which the claimant did and forgot about the log book. Later the same day the agent sold the claimant's car and handed the log book to the purchaser. The purchaser sold the car, and his purchaser in turn also sold it. The agent was afterwards convicted of fraud in connection with this and other cars. The claimant sued the ultimate purchaser for damages for conversion.

Devlin J held the agent was in possession of the car with the consent of the claimant, that the agent had tricked the claimant out of possession of the log book, and dismissed the claimant's claim.

HELD, ON APPEAL: On the sale of a second-hand car the purchaser would ordinarily require delivery of the log book. Cars could be sold without a log book but the price would be substantially reduced, and the sale of a car without a log book was not a sale in the ordinary course of business. The sale of a car with its log book is a more valuable subject matter than a car without its log book. The agent was never in possession of the log book with the consent of the claimant.

Appeal allowed with costs.

[14.33]   Stadium Finance Ltd v Robbins

[1962] 2 QB 664, [1962] 2 All ER 633, [1962] 3 WLR 453, 106 Sol Jo 369, CA

The defendant was the owner of a car which he wished to sell. He took it to a dealer who agreed to put it in his showroom and to report any inquiries. The defendant kept the ignition key but, probably by accident, left the log book locked in the glove box. The dealer obtained an ignition key and also opened the glove box, finding the log book. He arranged for his salesman to take the car on hire purchase and sold it to the claimant, a hire-purchase company. The salesman failed to make the first monthly payment and the claimant sought to take possession of the car. It found that the defendant had already seized it as his property. It claimed the return of the car or its value and damages.

HELD: The claimant could succeed only if it could show that the sale of the car to it by the dealer was made by him when acting in the ordinary course of business of a mercantile agent, ie within the terms of the Factors Act 1889, s 2(1). The car, with or without the ignition key and the log book, was 'goods' within the meaning of the 1889 Act but the dealer was not acting in the ordinary course of his business as a mercantile agent. The car had been put in possession of the dealer with no key and no registration book easily available: a dealer who sells motor cars in the ordinary course of his business sells those which are in a condition to be used as cars and the sale of a car deficient both of log book and ignition key could not be in the ordinary course of business of a mercantile agent. The provision in s 2(4) of the 1889 Act that consent of the owner shall be presumed in the absence of evidence to the contrary did not affect the case because the defendant's retention of the key was evidence of his intention to control the sale.

[14.34]   Lambert v G and C Finance Corpn Ltd

(1963) 107 Sol Jo 666   Havers J

The claimant advertised his car for sale. E agreed to buy it and offered a cheque in payment of the price. The claimant was unwilling to let E have the car except for cash but eventually agreed to let E take the car away in exchange for the cheque on the terms that he, the claimant, retained the log book, which he would send on when the cheque was cleared. In fact the cheque was dishonoured and the claimant reported the matter to the police. The car was subsequently sold by a dealer to the defendant, a hire-purchase company. The claimant sued for damages for its conversion. The defendant contended that he was not the owner, having sold it to E.

HELD: The Sale of Goods Act 1893, s 18(1) provides that unless a different intention appears the property in specific goods passes when the contract is made. Section 25(2) of the 1883 Act provides that where a person agrees to buy goods and is given possession of them by the owner he has the same power to give a good title as a mercantile agent under the Factors Act 1889 (see para [14.33] above). In the present case, a different intention was shown for the purposes of s 18(1) by the claimant's retaining the log book. The defendant could not rely on s 25(2) because a sale of a car without a log book is not a sale in the ordinary course of business. The claimant was still the owner and was entitled to damages.

Note—The Sale of Goods Act 1893, s 18(1) is repeated in the Sale of Goods Act 1979, s 18(1) and s 25(2) of the 1893 Act in s 25(1) of the 1979 Act.

[14.35]   Newtons of Wembley Ltd v Williams

[1965] 1 QB 560, [1964] 3 All ER 532, [1964] 3 WLR 888, 108 Sol Jo 619, CA

On 15 June the claimant sold a car to Andrew who gave them a cheque for £735 for it. He drove it away and registered it in his name on the same day. On 18 June the claimant heard from the bank that the cheque would not be met. It at once made extensive though unsuccessful enquiries to find Andrew, sent a 'Stop' notice to the Hire-Purchase Information Bureau and informed the police. On 6 July in Warren Street, London, Andrew sold the car to Biss, a dealer, for £550 cash. Biss took the car to Wincanton and on 12 July sold it to the defendant for £505, which was all the defendant would give him for it. Later in July as a result of an effort by the defendant to sell the car, the Hire-Purchase Information Bureau became aware of its whereabouts and told the claimant. On 14 September Andrew pleaded guilty at Middlesex Sessions to a charge of obtaining a car by false pretences. The claimant claimed the return of the car or its value on the ground that like the defendant in *Car and Universal Finance Co v Caldwell* (at para [14.52]) it had rescinded the contract before the car was sold by the fraudulent party who could thus pass no title to it.

HELD: The unequivocal acts of the claimant on finding that the cheque would not be met were effective to rescind the contract as in *Caldwell's* case so that after 20 June at the latest Andrew had at common law no title to pass. But the Factors Act 1889, s 9 provided that when a buyer of goods obtained possession of them with the seller's consent, delivery of the goods on sale to any person acting in good faith without notice of the original seller's rights in respect of them had the same effect as if the person making the delivery were a mercantile agent in possession of the goods with the consent of the owner. Section 2 of the 1889 Act provides that a sale of goods by a mercantile agent in possession of the goods with the consent of the owner (which has not, to the knowledge of the person taking under the sale, been determined) shall be valid if made when acting in the ordinary course of business of a mercantile agent. Biss took the car in good faith without notice of the claimants' rights. Andrew was acting in the ordinary course of business of a mercantile agent in that the sale to Biss was made at the well-known kerbside market for cash dealing in second-hand cars in Warren Street. Accordingly Biss received a valid title to the car which he later passed to the defendant.

[14.36]   George v Revis

(1966) 111 Sol Jo 51   Megaw J

The claimant advertised his car for sale. A man named Robinson called and agreed to buy it, subject to a satisfactory engineer's report. He was allowed by the claimant to take the car away for an engineer's inspection. After he had gone the claimant discovered he had taken the log book also, though the claimant had not consented to his having possession of it. Robinson did not return and a month later sold the car to the defendant, who bought in good faith.

HELD: The Factors Act 1889 protected an innocent purchaser if:
  (1)   there had been an agreement by the owner to sell;
  (2)   the original purchaser (here Robinson) had obtained the goods with the consent of the seller;
  (3)   the ultimate purchaser (the defendant) had acted in good faith and without notice of any rights of the original seller.
Conditions (1) and (3) were fulfilled. Condition (2) was fulfilled as far as the car alone was concerned if the facts as to the log book were disregarded, but the log book was of vital significance in the sale of a car. *Pearson v Rose and Young Ltd* (at para [14.32]) was clear authority for this and was sufficient to decide the case. The claimant had not consented to Robinson having possession of the log book; he was entitled to a return of the car or damages.

Note—See also *Bentworth Finance Ltd v Lubert* (at para [14.67]).

(II)   SALE OF GOODS ACT 1979

[14.37]
11.   When condition to be treated as warranty
  (1)   (Applies to Scotland only.)
  (2)   Where a contract of sale is subject to a condition to be fulfilled by the seller, the buyer may waive the condition, or may elect to treat the breach of the condition as a breach of warranty and not as a ground for treating the contract as repudiated.
  (3)   Whether a stipulation in a contract of sale is a condition, the breach of which may give rise to treat the contract as repudiated, or a warranty, the breach of which may give rise to a claim for damages but not to a right to reject the goods and treat the contract as repudiated, depends in each case on the construction of the contract; and a stipulation may be a condition, though called a warranty in the contract.
  (4)   Where a contract of sale is not severable and the buyer has accepted the goods or part of them, the breach of a condition to be fulfilled by the seller can only be treated as a breach of warranty, and not as a ground for rejecting the goods and treating the contract as repudiated, unless there is an express or implied term of the contract to that effect.
  (5)   (Applies to Scotland only.)
  (6)   Nothing in this section affects a condition or warranty whose fulfilment is excused by law by reason of impossibility or otherwise.

[14.38]
21.   Sale by person not the owner
  (1)   Subject to this Act, where goods are sold by a person who is not their owner, and who does not sell them under the authority or with the consent of the owner, the buyer acquires no better title to the goods than the seller had unless the owner of the goods is by his conduct precluded from denying the seller's authority to sell.
  (2)   Nothing in this Act affects—
      (a)   the provisions of the Factors Acts, or any enactment enabling the apparent owner of the goods to dispose of them as if he were their true owner;
      (b)   the validity of any contract of sale under any special common law or statutory power of sale, or under the order of a court of competent jurisdiction.

[14.39]
22.   Market overt
  (1)   Where goods are sold in market overt, according to the usage of the market, the buyer acquires a good title to the goods, provided he buys them in good faith and without notice of any defect or want of title on the part of the seller.
  …

Note—Market overt has been abolished by the Sale of Goods (Amendment) Act 1994.

[14.40]
23.   Sale under voidable title
When the seller of goods has a voidable title to them, but his title has not been avoided at the time of the sale, the buyer acquires a good title to the goods, provided he buys them in good faith and without notice of the seller's defect of title.

[14.41]
24.   Seller in possession after sale
Where a person, having sold goods, continues or is in possession of the goods, or of the documents of title to the goods the delivery or transfer by that person, or by a mercantile agent acting for him, of the goods or documents of title under any sale,

pledge, or other disposition thereof, to any person receiving the same in good faith and without notice of the previous sale, has the same effect as if the person making the delivery or transfer were expressly authorised by the owner of the goods to make the same.

[14.42]

25.   Buyer in possession after sale

(1)   Where a person, having bought or agreed to buy goods, obtains, with the consent of the seller, possession of the goods or the documents of title to the goods, the delivery or transfer by that person, or by a mercantile agent acting for him, of the goods or documents of title, under any sale, pledge or other disposition thereof, to any person receiving the same in good faith and without notice of any lien or other right of the original seller in respect of the goods, has the same effect as if the person making the delivery or transfer were a mercantile agent in possession of the goods or documents of title with the consent of the owner.

[14.43]

26.   Supplementary to section 24 and 25

In ss 24 and 25 above 'mercantile agent' means a mercantile agent having in the customary course of business as such agent authority either—

(a)   to sell goods, or

(b)   to consign goods for the purpose of sale, or

(c)   to buy goods, or

(d)   to raise money on the security of goods.

Note—See *Lambert v G and C Finance Corpn Ltd* (at para [14.34]) and *Newtons of Wembley Ltd v Williams* (at para [14.35]).

[14.44]

29.   Rules about delivery

(1)   Whether it is for the buyer to take possession of the goods or for the seller to send them to the buyer is a question depending in each case on the contract, express or implied, between the parties.

(2)   Apart from any such contract, express or implied, the place of delivery is the seller's place of business if he has one, and if not, his residence; except that, if the contract is for the sale of specific goods, which to the knowledge of the parties when the contract is made are in some other place, then that place is the place of delivery.

(3)   Where under the contract of sale the seller is bound to send the goods to the buyer, but no time for sending them is fixed, the seller is bound to send them within a reasonable time.

(4)   Where the goods at the time of sale are in the possession of a third person, there is no delivery by seller to buyer unless and until the third person acknowledges to the buyer that he holds the goods on his behalf; but nothing in this section affects the operation of the issue or transfer of any document of title to goods.

(5)   Demand or tender of delivery may be treated as ineffectual unless made at a reasonable hour; and what is a reasonable hour is a question of fact.

(6)   Unless otherwise agreed, the expenses of and incidental to putting the goods into a deliverable state must be borne by the seller.

[14.45]   Shaw v Metropolitan Police Comr (Natalegawa, claimant)

[1987] 3 All ER 405, [1987] 1 WLR 1332, 131 Sol Jo 1357, [1987] LS Gaz R 3011, CA

The claimant, Mr Natalegawa, was a student from Indonesia who acquired a red Porsche in December 1982 for £16,750. In March 1984 he decided to return to Indonesia and advertised the car for sale. On 15 April a man called London contacted Mr Natalegawa who let London have the car on 16 April, and on 1 May gave him a letter purporting to certify that he had no further legal responsibility connected with the car. London gave a post-dated cheque which proved to have no value.

On 1 May London agreed to sell the car to the claimants.

The claimant gave London a draft for the purchase price, but when London's bank refused to cash it, London disappeared. The car was left with the claimant, who subsequently commenced proceedings against the police claiming that the car belonged to it. Mr Natalegawa discovered the location of the car, and also claimed it. The police issued an interpleader summons to determine who was entitled to the vehicle. The claimant submitted that the property in the car had passed to them firstly because London had bought or agreed to buy the car from Mr Natalegawa and secondly in reliance on s 25 of the Sale of Goods Act 1979.

HELD, ON APPEAL: The case was most unusual because if the claimant succeeded, it would have obtained a car without having had to pay for it. However, since it was found as a fact at first instance that there was no purported sale between Mr Natalegawa and London, s 25 of the Sales of Goods Act 1979 did not apply. Section 25 could only apply when there had been an actual sale or agreement to sell the goods. Therefore, London could not pass good title to the claimants. Further, although s 21 of the 1979 Act provided that the buyer acquires no better title to goods than the seller had, unless the owner of the goods is by his conduct precluded from denying the seller's authority to sell, this section could not apply, again because there had been no proper sale or agreement to sell. Indeed, nothing in ss 21 to 26 of the 1979 Act, or the general law of estoppel could alter the simple fact that London never purported to transfer the property in the car on the evidence before the court.

[14.46] **National Employers Mutual General Insurance Association Ltd v Jones**
[1990] 1 AC 24, [1988] 2 All ER 425, [1988] 2 WLR 952, [1988] RTR 289, 132 Sol Jo 658, HL

On 3 February 1983, a Ford Fiesta was stolen from Miss H who later assigned her rights in the car to the claimant, her insurer, in return for a cash payment. After the theft the car had passed through a number of hands before it was sold to the defendant, who purchased it in good faith. The claimant claimed from the defendant the return of the car or its monetary value, plus damages for its detention. The defendant claimed that he was entitled to retain possession of the car under s 9 of the Factors Act 1889. (Section 25(1) of the Sale of Goods Act 1979 is in the same terms.) The claimant maintained in reply that s 9 of the 1889 Act had no application to the purported purchase by the defendant of the car. The judge at first instance and the Court of Appeal gave judgment for the claimant.

HELD, ON APPEAL to the House of Lords by the defendants: The terms 'owner' and 'seller' in s 9 should not be equated. On a historical view of the Factors Act, there was no indication that the legislature had ever intended to depart from the basic principle of '*nemo dat quod non habet*' to enable a factor or agent, entrusted with goods from a thief or a purchaser from a thief, to give title to a bona fide purchaser and override the title of the true owner. The proper approach was to go back along the chain of transactions until the initial defect in title was located, ie the thief who sold the car to the first innocent purchaser. This was not a sale under the Factors Act since there had been no transfer of title. The first purchaser from the thief did not get a good title to the car, and could not pass one on.

Appeal dismissed.

(B) CONTRACT

[14.47] Ingram v Little

[1961] 1 QB 31, [1960] 3 All ER 332, [1960] 3 WLR 504, 104 Sol Jo 704, CA

The claimants were the owners of a car which they advertised for sale. A swindler called on them and made them an offer which they were willing to accept, but on it appearing that he intended to pay by cheque the claimants said that they would accept only cash. The swindler then said he was a Mr PGM Hutchinson of Stanstead Road, Caterham. Whilst the matter was being discussed, one of the claimants went to the post office nearby and found that there was a Mr PGM Hutchinson at the address mentioned. She returned and told the co-claimant and as a result the claimants agreed to accept a cheque. The swindler took the car away in exchange for the cheque and sold it to the defendants. He was not PGM Hutchinson of Caterham and the cheque was dishonoured.

HELD: There was no contract for sale between the claimants and the swindler and the property in the car had not passed to him. The claimants were the offerors and the swindler was the offeree. In making their offer to sell the car not for cash but for a cheque the claimants were under the belief that they were dealing with, and therefore making their offer to, the honest Mr PGM Hutchinson of Caterham. The swindler knew what was in the minds of the claimants for he had put it there and he knew that their offer was intended for Mr PGM Hutchinson of Caterham and not for him. There was no offer which he (the swindler) could accept and therefore there was no contract.

[14.48] Milford Mutual Facilities Ltd v HW Hidson Ltd

(1962) Guardian, 7 December

The defendant was a motor dealer. A man came to the dealer with a Ford car and asked to exchange it for an Austin which was in the showroom. He said he was R Ashworth of Cheadle. He produced a log book for the car in that name and a driving licence in the same name. He was allowed to take away the Austin and collected the log book of that car four days later. The defendant sold the Ford but it was later found to be a stolen car and the defendant had to reimburse the purchaser. Meanwhile the man had offered the Austin for sale to a Mr Wright. As the latter required hire-purchase facilities both he and the man (who was still representing himself to be R Ashworth of Cheadle) went in person to the office of the claimant, a hire-purchase company. The log book of the Austin showed the defendant as owner and the man produced a receipt showing the exchange for the Ford. The claimant then bought the Austin for £480, entering into a hire-purchase agreement with Wright. The defendant, having found that the Ford was stolen traced the Austin to Wright and repossessed itself of it by driving it away from outside his house. In this action the claimant claimed its return and damages for detinue and conversion. The defendant contended that the car was not the property of the claimant as there had been no contract of sale: the claimant had intended to contract with R Ashworth of Cheadle and not with the man who had brought the car for sale. There was a real R Ashworth of Cheadle but he was entirely unconnected with the transactions.

HELD: The court was bound by *Ingram v Little* (at para [14.47]) which had to be applied to this case. When parties contracted in each others' presence there was a presumption that the offeror intended to contract with the person physically before him and it was a difficult presumption to rebut. The vital question was whether the person contracted with the man or with the real Mr Ashworth. Did the physical presence in the offices preponderate over the personality of the real person who was fraudulently misrepresented? On the facts of this case it was contracting with the person present before it: not a man who represented himself to be Mr R Ashworth but a man who represented himself as owner of the car. There was accordingly a voidable, not a void, contract and the property passed. The claimant was entitled to succeed.

[14.49]   Lewis v Averay

[1972] 1 QB 198, [1971] 3 All ER 907, [1971] 3 WLR 603, 115 Sol Jo 755, CA

The claimant advertised his car for sale. A man came to see it: he said he was Richard Green and led the claimant to believe he was a well-known film actor of that name. Eventually he said he would like to buy the car and proffered a cheque for the price. The claimant agreed to sell but was unwilling to let the man take the car until the cheque had been cleared. He asked if he had anything to prove he was Richard Green. The man produced a pass of admission to a film studio bearing his photograph and the name 'RA Green'. The claimant was satisfied and let the man take the car and log book in exchange for the cheque. On presentation the cheque was found to be from a stolen cheque book and was worthless. A day or two later the man, under the name of the claimant, sold the car to the defendant who bought it in good faith. The claimant, on discovering what had happened, sued the defendant for a return of the car and damages for its retention.

HELD: The claimant could not succeed. The facts were very similar to those in *Ingram v Little* (at para [14.47]) and *Phillips v Brooks Ltd* (at para [14.51]) but those two cases could not be reconciled with one another. The true principle is that when two parties have come to what appears to be a contract the fact that one party is mistaken as to the identity of the other does not mean that there is no contract, but merely that the contract is voidable and liable to be set aside provided it is done before a third party has in good faith acquired rights under it. The claimant had made a contract with the man who was before him: the misrepresentations as to his identity merely made the contract voidable and it had not been avoided when the defendant acquired the car.

Note—Megaw LJ said he found it 'difficult to understand the basis, either in logic or in practical considerations, of the test laid down by the majority of the court in *Ingram v Little*' by which the validity of the offer 'is made to depend on the view which some rogue should have formed ... as to the state of mind of the opposite party ... who does not know that he is dealing with a rogue'.

See also *Dennant v Skinner and Collom* (at para [14.53]).

[14.50]   Four Point Garage Ltd v Carter

[1985] 3 All ER 12, QBD

On 2 October 1984 the defendant agreed with a garage called Freeway to purchase a new Ford Escort XR3i. On 8 October he posted the contract sum to Freeway, who agreed to deliver the car to him on 10 October. Freeway did not have the car in stock, and ordered it from the claimant, who sold it to Freeway but delivered it direct to the defendant. The defendant was unaware that it was not Freeway who had delivered the car to him. The claimant, for its part, was under the impression that Freeway was intending to lease the car to the defendant, not to sell it. On 13 October the claimant discovered that Freeway was insolvent and going into liquidation. Soon afterwards, it took proceedings against the defendant for the return of the car, which was subject to a reservation of title (Romalpa) clause as between the claimant and Freeway.

HELD: (1) The defendant could rely on s 25 of the Sale of Goods Act 1979. There was no difference between a seller delivering the goods directly to the sub-purchaser, and the seller delivering the goods to the purchaser for on-sale to the sub-purchaser. In both circumstances the sub-purchaser received good title under s 25 of the 1979 Act.

  (2)   There was also an implied term in the contract between the claimant and Freeway that the car could be sub-sold to the defendant. The wording of the retention of title clause was sufficient to rebut this term. The fact that the claimant believed that he was delivering the car to the defendant for leasing purposes was irrelevant and the title to the car had validly passed to the defendant.

[14.51]   Phillips v Brooks Ltd

[1919] 2 KB 243, 88 LJKB 953, 121 LT 249, 35 TLR 470, 24 Com Cas 263

If A, fraudulently assuming the name of a person of credit and stability, buys, in person, and obtains delivery of, goods from B, the property in the goods passes to A, and he can therefore give a good title thereto to a third party who, acting bona fide and without notice, has given value therefore, unless in the meantime B has taken steps to dis-affirm the contract with A.

Note—See *Lewis v Averay* (at para [14.49]) and *Ingram v Little* (at para [14.47]).

[14.52]   Car and Universal Finance Co Ltd v Caldwell

[1965] 1 QB 525, [1964] 1 All ER 290, [1964] 2 WLR 600, 108 Sol Jo 15, CA

On 12 January the defendant sold his car to a swindler, Norris, accepting for it a cheque for £975. On the following day he presented the cheque to the bank and was told it was worthless. He at once went to the police so as to recover the car and telephoned the AA for the same purpose. On 20 January the police found the car in the possession of Motobella Ltd, who claimed to have bought it in good faith and to have sold it on 15 January to G & C Finance Corpn Ltd, a finance company. On 29 January Norris was arrested and pleaded guilty to obtaining the car by false pretences. On 13 August the car was transferred from G & C Finance to the claimant, another finance company. After the defendant had obtained judgment against Motobella Ltd by default for the return of the car the claimant claimed in this action that the title in the car was vested in it.

HELD: The question was whether G & C Finance obtained a good title to the car from Norris. The sale to Norris was voidable by the defendant: could he avoid it without communicating his rescission to Norris? Normally the rule is that an election to avoid a contract is not complete until the decision has been communicated to the other party, but in the circumstances of the present case where a fraudulent rogue would know that the defendant would want his car back as soon as he discovered the fraud it would not be right to hold that such a man could claim to have the rescission communicated to him. The position has to be viewed as between Norris and the defendant, who could not have made his position plainer. In circumstances such as the present case the innocent party may evince his intention to disaffirm the contract by overt means falling short of communication or repossession. The claimant had not obtained any title to the car as against the defendant.

(1)   AUCTION

[14.53]   **Dennant v Skinner and Collom**

[1948] 2 KB 164, [1948] 2 All ER 29, [1948] LJR 1576   Hallett J

The claimant carried on business as the South London Motor Auctions and was a certified auctioneer. He held an auction sale of 35 vehicles and knocked down six vehicles to a man named King. When the first vehicle, a Commer van, was knocked down, the claimant asked the buyer his name. The man said it was King and that he was from King's Motors of Oxford and the son of the proprietor. This firm was known to the claimant as a highly reputable one. A later vehicle was a Standard car. When King went to the claimant's office after the sale, the claimant asked how he meant to pay, and King said he would like to pay by cheque. The claimant said he did not accept cheques from people he did not know. King was in possession of trade plates and had drivers there to drive away the vehicles. He repeated that he was the son of the proprietor of King's of Oxford and said he was running the Portsmouth branch and produced a cheque book showing by the counterfoils he had been paying large sums to other auctioneers. The claimant believed these representations and accepted the cheque on King signing a form certifying that the cheque would be met on presentation and agreeing that the ownership of the vehicles would not pass until the cheque was met. The cheque was dishonoured and King was convicted of obtaining the vehicles by false pretences and with intent to defraud.

King had meanwhile sold the Standard car to Collom, who sold it to Skinner. The claimant sued Skinner for possession of the car on the ground that the transaction was larceny by a trick. Skinner brought in Collom as third party.

HELD: The sale was complete on the fall of the hammer (Sale of Goods Act 1893, s 58(2)). The property passed on the sale (Sale of Goods Act 1893, s 18, r 1). It was not a case of larceny by a trick but obtaining goods by false pretences. The distinction stated in *Archbold* is that in larceny the owner does not intend to part with the property but only the possession; in false pretences he intends to part with the property. Lord Haldane in *Lake v Simmons* [1927] AC 487 at 501, HL adopting Fry J in *Smith v Wheatcroft* (1878) 9 Ch D 223, 47 LJ Ch 745, 39 LT 103, 27 WR 42, when consideration of the person is an element in the contract, error with regard to the person destroys consent and annuls the contract, but where it does not and the vendor is willing to sell to any person, the contract stands. Here the sale was irrespective of the identity of the buyer. The claimant did not sell to King because of the false statements. The car was sold before King's identity was mentioned. The case was indistinguishable from *Phillips v Brooks Ltd* (at para [14.51]). In *Lake v Simmons* the goods were handed to the swindler as bailee and the vendor did not intend to enter into any contract of sale. In *Heap v Motorists' Advisory Agency Ltd* [1923] 1 KB 577, 92 LJKB 553, 129 LT 146, 39 TLR 150, 67 Sol Jo 300, the claimant never intended to part with the property to the fraudulent person but merely the custody to sell to a person who was imaginary.

By parting with the property, the claimant lost his rights of lien or re-sale (Sale of Goods Act 1893, s 39(1)(a) and (c)), but the property had already passed. The signed agreement that the property would not pass could not affect the fact that the property had already passed. It did not divest King of the property and re-vest it in the claimant.

The defendant was acting reasonably in joining the third party.

Judgment was passed for the defendant, and for the third party against the defendant with costs: defendant's costs against claimant to include all costs of third-party proceedings.

Note—See also *Lewis v Averay* (at para [14.49]) (The Sale of Goods Act 1893, s 58(2) has been replaced in the same terms by the Sale of Goods Act 1979, s 57(2) and s 18 of the 1893 Act by s 18 of the 1979 Act. Section 39(1)(a) and (c) of the 1893 Act was repeated in s 39(1)(a) and (c) of the 1979 Act.)

[14.54]   RH Willis & Son v British Car Auctions Ltd

[1978] 2 All ER 392, [1978] I WLR 438, [1978] RTR 244, 122 Sol Jo 62, 246 EG 134, CA

Where goods are sold by the intervention of an auctioneer, under the hammer or as a result of a provisional bid, then if the seller has no title, the auctioneer is liable in conversion to the true owner.

(II)   SALE BY INTERMEDIARIES

[14.55]   Eastern Distributors Ltd v Goldring (Murphy, third party)

[1957] 2 QB 600, [1957] 2 All ER 525, [1957] 3 WLR 237,101 Sol Jo 553, CA

The owner of a motor van authorised a motor dealer to sell the van to a hire-purchase finance company, to obtain an agreement by the company to sell it to him on hire-purchase terms and to apply the proceeds of sale in paying the deposits on the van and on a car which he desired to purchase from the dealer. He signed in blank a proposal form and memorandum of hire-purchase agreement in respect of both vehicles and gave them to the dealer to complete. The dealer certified in the proposal form that the van was his (the dealer's) absolute property. The dealer sold the van to the claimant, a hire-purchase finance company, who accepted the owner's proposal and sent him a counterpart of the agreement. The hire-purchase transaction in respect of the car was not implemented and the dealer told the owner that the whole transaction was cancelled. The owner afterwards sold the van, believing it to be his own property, to a third party who bought it in good faith and without knowledge of the dealer's action. The owner made no payments under the hire-purchase agreement to the claimant, who terminated the agreement and claimed the van or its value from the third party.

HELD: The claimant was entitled to recover.
  (1)   The owner had clothed the dealer with apparent authority to sell and was precluded from denying authority within the Sale of Goods Act 1893, s 21(1).
  (2)   Although the agreement had not been 'made and signed by the hirer' as required by the Hire-Purchase Act 1938, s 2(2)(a), neither that section nor s 17 of that Act took away the claimant's rights against any person other than the hirer.
  (3)   The judge assumed the owner to be the seller under s 25(1) of the 1893 Act and he had not remained in possession; the hire-purchase agreement was effective to change his possession as seller to possession as bailee.

5. HIRE PURCHASE

(A) HIRE-PURCHASE AGREEMENTS

[14.56] Lowe v Lombank Ltd

[1960] 1 All ER 611, [1960] 1 WLR 196, 104 Sol Jo 210, CA

The claimant, a widow aged 65, went to a motor car dealer to buy a second-hand car. She was offered a car at £200 which the dealer said was in perfect condition. She wanted hire-purchase facilities and was required by the dealer to sign a form of hire-purchase agreement issued by the defendant. She signed without reading it. The car was later delivered to her and she signed a delivery receipt. The car turned out to be utterly unroadworthy, though to the claimant the defects would not have been apparent on reasonable inspection. The claimant sued for damages for breach of the implied condition of fitness in the Hire-Purchase Act 1938, s 8(2).

HELD: (1) Clauses in the hire-purchase agreement which purported to exclude conditions and warranties, express or implied, were not brought to the claimant's notice as required by s 8(3) of the 1938 Act and the defendants could not rely on them.

    (2)   The claimant had made known to the owner the particular purpose for which the goods were required since the agreement itself contained terms appropriate to the use of the car as a means of transport.

    (3)   There was a breach of the implied warranty of fitness in s 8(2) of the 1938 Act.

    (4)   The claimant was not estopped from relying on the defects as proof of the breach of warranty by having signed a delivery receipt acknowledging that the car was in good order and condition, because it was not the case that the defendants had entered into the hire-purchase agreement in reliance on the terms of the receipt.

Note—For implied term as to fitness in hire-purchase agreements see, sections 17 (2) and (3) of the Supply of Goods and Services Act 1982.

[14.57] Astley Industrial Trust Ltd v Grimley

[1963] 2 All ER 33, [1963] 1 WLR 584, 107 Sol Jo 474, CA

The defendant, a haulage contractor in a fair way of business, went to a dealer to obtain a tipping lorry on hire purchase. He said he had not done tipping before and that he could afford to take a lorry in the £500–£700 range. The dealer recommended him to take a Bedford lorry, six years old, and the defendant agreed to do so. The dealer sold the vehicle to the claimant, a hire-purchase company, from whom the defendant agreed to hire it under a hire-purchase agreement which expressly excluded any warranty as to description, repair, quality or fitness for any purpose. The defendant noticed defects in the clutch, starter and tipping mechanism which the dealer said he would put right. After the lorry had been left with him on two occasions the defects were still not put right and the defendant took the lorry away, under protest, and began to use it for carrying hardcore. He drove it 150 miles to a place where for some weeks he used it to carry hardcore from a quarry. This was very heavy work which could quickly wear out even a new vehicle. A number of defects showed themselves and breakdowns occurred requiring repairs which cost the defendant a total of £55 in three months.

HELD: The claimant was entitled to succeed: there was an implied condition or fundamental term that it was letting on hire a Bedford tipper, but the vehicle, though not free from defects, complied with that description and was capable of use as such. There was no fundamental breach and the claimant was entitled to rely on the express exclusion of warranties in the hire-purchase agreement.

[14.58] G Montague (Southern) Ltd v Warren

(1965) Times, 5 February, CA

The defendant, a chauffeur, took on hire purchase a Ford car. He paid three monthly instalments and drove the car 1,200 miles before beginning to complain about the condition of the car. His complaint was that he had to keep having the car repaired. He took the car back to the dealers from whom he had obtained it and paid no further instalments. To an action for recovery of arrears he pleaded a fundamental breach in that the condition of the car made it unroadworthy.

HELD: He had driven it 1,200 miles: there was no fundamental breach.

[14.59] Porter v General Guarantee Corpn Ltd

[1982] RTR 384   Kilner Brown J

The claimant took a second-hand car on hire purchase from motor dealers. The dealers represented that the car was in excellent condition, knowing that he wished to use it as a minicab. The car was not in fact in excellent condition.

HELD: The representation in the context of intended use as a minicab was sufficiently important in the minds of both parties to make it a fundamental term, breach of which entitled the claimant to repudiate the contract. He was entitled to judgment against the hire-purchase company as the contract was between him and them, they having utilised the services of the dealers and being bound by any representations made by them. As the agreement was a consumer credit agreement under the Consumer Credit Act 1974 the hire-purchase company were entitled as creditors to be indemnified by the dealers who were suppliers to the debtor.

(B)   'SALE' BY HIRER

[14.60] North Central (or General) Wagon and Finance Co v Graham

[1950] 2 KB 7, [1950] 1 All ER 780, 66 (pt 1) TLR 707, CA

The claimant, a hire-purchase company, let a motor car on hire purchase under an agreement which contained obligations on the hirer:
'1.	not to do anything prejudicially to affect the ownership or financial position of the owner;
2.	not to attempt to sell or otherwise dispose of the car;
3.	
   (a)	if the hirer shall fail to pay any sum due or to observe or perform any stipulation on his part herein contained the owner may terminate the hiring;
   (b)	if this hiring be terminated for any reason the owner may by written notice put an end to the hiring under any other agreement between the parties;
4.	this agreement is only a contract of bailment.'

The hirer instructed an auctioneer to sell the car, and the auctioneer sold it. The claimant sued the auctioneer for damages for conversion.

Lewis J dismissed the action, being influenced by the absence of a clause that breach *ipso facto* put an end to the agreement. He held the claimant was not entitled to possession at the time of sale.

HELD, ON APPEAL: It was essential for the claimant to show that it was entitled at the time of the sale to immediate possession. The case was similar to *Jelks v Hayward* [1905] 2 KB 460, 74 LJKB 717, 92 LT 692, 53 WR 686, except that the right to determine the hiring and take possession did not include the words 'without previous notice'. There could be no implied term requiring notice, because such notice was required in the case of other agreements. There is, apparently, no direct authority on the construction of the words 'may terminate the hiring', and it is a little startling that there should not be because it is the commonest form of expression in hire-purchase agreements. The claimants could terminate the hiring without notice, and the moment a breach occurred the owner had the right to immediate possession. The claimant therefore had the right to terminate the hiring at will the moment after the breach occurred. It therefore had an immediate right to possession and could sue the defendant in conversion.

The general principle of law is that a bailee who does something inconsistent with the terms of the contract, or any act or disposition which is wholly repugnant to or an absolute disclaimer of the holding as bailee, terminates the bailment and re-vests the bailor's right to possession. Here that general law does not apply because the contract makes special provision.

Appeal allowed.

[14.61]   Moorgate Mercantile Co Ltd v Finch
[1962] 1 QB 701, [1962] 2 All ER 467, [1962] 3 WLR 110, 106 Sol Jo 284, CA

The claimant was a finance company who let a car on hire purchase to the first defendant. At a time when he was in arrears with payments under the agreement he lent the car to the second defendant at his request though without knowing for what purpose it was required. The second defendant loaded the car with uncustomed watches and was subsequently caught by Customs men with the watches in the car. As a result he was convicted and the car was forfeited to the Customs authorities under the relevant statutory provisions. The claimant claimed damages for conversion of the car by the second defendant. The hire-purchase agreement contained the words 'in case of any and every breach of any term or condition hereof the owners shall forthwith without notice or demand become entitled immediately to recover possession of the vehicle'.

HELD: (1) The second defendant knew that forfeiture of the car was a natural and probable consequence of his conduct and there was a conversion of the car.
   (2)   As the first defendant was in arrear with payments under the hire-purchase agreement this was a breach which entitled the claimants to immediate possession (following *North Central (or General) Wagon and Finance Co v Graham* (at para [14.60])) and the second defendant was therefore liable to the claimants for conversion of the vehicle.

[14.62]   Union Transport Finance v British Car Auctions Ltd
[1978] 2 All ER 385, 246 Estates Gazette 131, CA

Smith took a car on hire purchase from the claimant. The contract gave the claimant the right at any time to declare the hiring terminated on breach of its terms or default in rental payments on notice given to the hirer at his last known address. Smith took the car to the defendant auctioneer without disclosing the hire-purchase contract and the auctioneer sold it at auction to an innocent purchaser. The claimant sued the defendant in conversion for damages. The defendant contended that the claimant had no right to immediate possession of the car at the time of the sale, not having served notice, and could not sue in conversion. It was not disputed that for a bailor or lessor on hire purchase to sue in conversion he must show that he is entitled at the time of the sale to immediate possession of the goods.

HELD: The defendant could not succeed. At common law a bailor becomes entitled at once to bring the contract to an end and acquire the right to immediate possession if the bailee acts in a way which destroys the basis of the contract. The express term of the contract enabling the claimant to terminate the hiring by notice did not oust the common law rule and deprive the claimant of its rights at common law. Smith had torn up the contract of bailment by fraudulently selling the car through an auctioneer to an innocent third party. It would require very clear language to deprive the bailor of his common law rights in such circumstances and the language used in the present contract was nothing like strong enough. *North Central (or General) Wagon and Finance Co v Graham* (at para [14.60]) applied.

(C)   HIRER'S DUTY ON TERMINATION OF HIRE

[14.63]   **Capital Finance Co Ltd v Bray**
[1964] 1 All ER 603, [1964] 1 WLR 323, 108 Sol Jo 95, CA

The defendant hired a car from the claimant under a hire-purchase agreement. He fell behind with his instalments and the claimant repossessed the car by taking it from outside his house in the middle of the night. This was unlawful since the contract was one within the Hire-Purchase Act 1938 and the defendant had paid more than one-third of the hire-purchase price. Perhaps realising the error, the claimant returned the car on the following day. The defendant paid no further instalments though there was evidence that he made some use of the car. The claimant wrote to the defendant requiring him to return the car by delivering it to one of three specified addresses. The defendant did not do so: the claimant then sued him for instalments due and for damages in detinue for the period subsequent to its letter demanding a return of the car.

HELD: (1) The hire-purchase agreement was determined by the illegal retaking of the car and was not revived by returning it, since this was merely an implied offer to revive it which the defendant had not accepted.

(2)   The defendant's failure to return the car, following the claimant requiring him to deliver it to one of the specified addresses, did not give the claimant any cause of action in detinue. He was not bound to take the car to the company but only to let it have it if it came for it. No one, except by contract, is under a duty to take a chattel to its owner. In this case the contract, that is, the hire-purchase agreement, was already at an end.

[14.64]   **Kelly v Sovereign Leasing**
[1995] CLY 720, Chichester County Court   Assistant Recorder IKR Wilson

The claimant entered into a lease purchase agreement with the defendant leasing company for a prestigious motor car. The Consumer Credit Act 1974 did not apply.

The claimant missed two instalments whereupon the defendant repossessed the car and sold it. The claimant claimed damages for conversion.

The defendant argued that the contract made it clear that time for the payment of the instalments was of the essence and that, accordingly, the failure on the claimant's part to pay the instalments was a repudiatory breach.

HELD: It was not clear from the contract when the payment of instalments should be made and so it could not be said that time for payment was of the essence. In any event, non-payment of two instalments was not in itself a repudiatory breach. The defendant was liable in conversion and the claimant was entitled to damages.

[14.65] Bowmaker Ltd v Wycombe Motors Ltd

[1946] KB 505, [1946] 2 All ER 113, 115 LJKB 411, 175 LT 133, 62 TLR 437, 90 Sol Jo 407, Div Ct

A hire-purchase company determined the hire of a car for default in payment of instalment, but the hirer retained possession of the car. After the determination the hirer instructed repairers to repair the car. Repairers claimed a lien against the hire-purchase company. The hire-purchase agreement contained a condition that the hirer had no authority from the company to create a lien for repairs.

HELD: Whilst the hiring was in existence and the hirer entitled to possession, the lien would have been good, and the condition would not affect the repairer, but when the hire had been determined, the hirer has no right to the car and there is no lien.

6. REGISTRATION DOCUMENTS

[14.66] Bishopsgate Motor Finance Corpn Ltd v Transport Brakes Ltd

[1949] 1 KB 322, [1949] 1 All ER 37, [1949] LJR 741, 65 TLR 66, 93 Sol Jo 71, CA

Per Denning LJ: Whilst the log book was not a document of title, it was the best evidence of title and a transfer was open to suspicion if the log book was not handed over. If not produced, or containing the wrong name, or if obviously tampered with, the buyer was put on enquiry, and purchased at his own risk. The claimant here did not keep the log book in its own hands or in its own name. It was a finance company who allowed the hirer to have the car and take the log book in his own name. By reason of that fact, he was able to dispose of the car to an innocent purchaser.

[14.67] Bentworth Finance Ltd v Lubert

[1968] 1 QB 680, [1967] 2 All ER 810, [1967] 3 WLR 378, 111 Sol Jo 272, CA

The defendant signed a hire-purchase agreement with the claimant, a finance company for a car. The car was delivered to her house but not a log book. She did not use the car, not being able to tax it, and did not pay any instalments. The claimant took possession of the car and sued for arrears of instalments.

HELD: There was an implied condition that there should be a log book and as no log book had been supplied the contract of hire purchase had never come into effect and the claimant could not sue on it.

Per Lord Denning MR: It is the common understanding of people that, if a car is bought or is taken on hire purchase, the log book will be provided. There is a great difference between the price of a car *with* the log book and the price of a car *without* the log book. The absence of it gives rise to the suspicion that the seller has a doubtful title. In short, the log book, though not a document of title, is very good evidence of title.

7.   BAILMENT

[14.68]   *Note*—Bailment is a delivery of goods from one person, called the bailor, to another person called the bailee, for some purpose, upon a condition, express or implied, that, after the purpose has been fulfilled, they shall be redelivered to the bailor, or otherwise dealt with according to his directions, or kept till he reclaims them.

Bailments are of three kinds:

(1)   those for the exclusive benefit of the bailor; as, if A leaves plate with B to keep safely and securely without reward. He, the bailee, is only responsible in respect of gross negligence;

(2)   those for the mutual benefit of bailor and bailee; as, if C lets a horse to D for so much per hour; or if E gives F (a tailor) clothes to repair, in the course of his trade, etc. The bailee must exercise ordinary care;

(3)   those for the exclusive benefit of the bailee; as, if G lends H a book to read, without reward. The bailee is responsible for even slight negligence.

Questions of bailment may arise in the case of a car park, of a carrier, of owner's risk and contracting out of negligence, or garage of cars, and of repairs to car, as well as in keeper cases.

The onus is on the bailee to prove that loss or damage to the goods has occurred without negligence on his part.

[14.69]   Metaalhandel JA Magnus BV v Ardfields Transport Ltd and East-fell Ltd (t/a Jones Transport)
[1988] 1 Lloyd's Rep 197, [1987] 2 FTLR 319

The defendant was asked to collect goods on behalf of the claimant and store them at its warehouse. In fact it took them to the second defendant's premises from where they were subsequently stolen.

Gatehouse J concluded on the evidence that the defendant was not bailee of the goods, as they were never actually in its possession. The defendant had entered into an authorised subcontract and thus became 'quasi-bailees'. Whilst that entitled the defendant to subcontract performance of a contract, it remained responsible for the faults of the subcontractor, and in this case the defendant was liable to the claimant.

[14.70]   Transcontainer Express Ltd v Custodian Security Ltd
[1988] 1 Lloyd's Rep 128, [1988] 1 FTLR 54, CA

The claimant subcontracted part of a carriage of goods contract to Crossland Haulage Limited. Those subcontractors deposited the sealed load at premises protected by the defendant security company. The container was subsequently stolen whilst there and the claimant brought an action for breach of the duty of care they were owed by the defendant or in the alternative for breach of duty as sub-bailee to take all reasonable care of the container and its contents.

Boreham J dismissed the claimant's claim. The defendant was not bailee and its duty to the owner of the goods was in contract only. It therefore followed that the defendant was not sub-bailee and its limited duty only extended to the owner. The Court of Appeal dismissed the appeal for there was no evidence that Crossland were anything other than subcontractors, and the claimant had failed to establish 'possessory title' in the goods, as defined by Lord Brandon in *Leigh & Sullivan Ltd v Aliakmon Shipping Ltd, The Aliakmon* [1986] 2 Lloyd's Rep 1.

(A) BAILEE'S LIABILITY FOR LOSS OR DAMAGE

(1) ONUS OF PROOF ON BAILEE

[14.71] **Global Dress Co Ltd v WH Boase & Co Ltd**
[1966] 2 Lloyd's Rep 72, CA

The defendants, master porters, received 30 cases of dresses for the claimant at their dockside shed. A few days later one case was found to be missing. The county court judge found that the defendants' security system was good but said he could not understand how the case could have been removed without being seen if the watchman, checkers or others of the defendants' servants were doing their duty properly. He held the defendants had not discharged the onus on them as bailees.

HELD, ON APPEAL: The judge's decision should not be upset. The onus was on the defendants as bailees to show that they had taken reasonable care of the claimant's goods. It was not sufficient for them to prove that their system was to have a watchman on duty. There was evidence on which the judge could find that the watchman had not been sufficiently vigilant but even if he had been left in doubt on this point the defendants still could not have succeeded because the onus was upon them.

[14.72] **British Road Services Ltd v AV Crutchley & Co Ltd**
[1968] 1 All ER 811, [1968] 1 Lloyd's Rep 271, CA

The claimant arranged for the defendant to receive a lorry load of whisky worth £9,000 at its warehouse preparatory to being loaded on board ship for export. The whisky was unloaded from the lorry on to a trailer which was left overnight, with tractor attached, facing the doors of the warehouse ready to be driven to the ship on the following morning. During the night thieves entered the warehouse through a skylight, opened the doors and drove away the whole load. The defendant had a contract with a third party to send a patrolman to the premises from time to time during the night but he had failed to make all the visits required of him.

HELD: The onus was on the defendant to prove that the loss did not result from negligence on its part (*Coldman v Hill* [1919] 1 KB 443, 88 LJKB 491, 120 LT 412, CA). On the facts, the defendant's system of protection was not adequate in relation to the special risks involved and it had failed to discharge the burden on it of proving that the loss was not caused by negligence on its part. The defendant must accept responsibility for the negligence of the third party's patrolman even though they were independent contractors. A bailee cannot escape from the responsibility for taking proper care of the goods bailed merely by employing sub-contractors for that purpose.

[14.73] **Transmotors Ltd v Robertson Buckley & Co Ltd**
[1970] 1 Lloyd's Rep 224   Mocatta J

The defendant, a road haulier, contracted with the claimant to deliver consignments of food by lorry from Liverpool to places in the London area. The defendant's driver, Davenport, left Liverpool at 5 am; late in the afternoon he reported to Plumstead Police Station that his lorry and load had been hijacked when he stopped on a lay-by on the A4 near Maidenhead at about 1 pm. He said he had been forced into a van and dumped four hours later at Woolwich. His lorry was found empty at Bow the following day. There was no evidence to corroborate his story but it was not positively disproved. He had been convicted of theft when working as a docker some months earlier and his employer knew of this when it engaged him. His account of his movements up to the time of the hijacking was unsupported by any other evidence. Nine months after the hijacking he was sacked by the defendant after another conviction for theft. The claimant claimed for the loss of the goods.

HELD: If the servant of a bailee in the course of his employment stole goods bailed, then the bailee was liable to the bailor for the loss of the goods – *Morris v C W Martin & Sons Ltd* [1966] 1 QB 716, [1965] 2 All ER 725, [1965] 3 WLR 276, 109 Sol Jo 451, [1965] 2 Lloyd's Rep 63, CA. In order for a bailee to escape liability he had to prove he had taken all reasonable care in relation to the goods including proof that the goods had not been stolen by his employees (though it was highly desirable that the bailors should give specific notice of their intention to allege theft, if that was their case, either in the pleadings or otherwise). It was not necessary for the court to decide positively whether Davenport was a party to the theft but merely whether on the balance of probabilities the defendant had exercised reasonable care in regard to the goods and their safety and had negatived Davenport having acted as an accomplice. On the evidence the defendant had not discharged the burden of proof upon it.

Judgment for the claimants.

(II) REPAIRER

[14.74]   Cowan v Blackwill Motor Caravan Conversions Ltd
[1978] RTR 421, CA

The claimant took his motor caravan to the defendant for repair. It was difficult to engage any of the forward gears and the reverse gear could not be engaged at all. The defendant told him to leave it in a side street alongside its wired-in compound. He was told it would put it in the compound as soon as possible. The side street was a cul-de-sac; the vehicle was left facing downhill towards the dead end. It was not put in the compound on the following day because other vehicles were put there in preference to the claimant's, since it could not be taken away except by pushing it backwards uphill. On the second night there it was stolen.

HELD: The issue was whether the defendant, as bailee of the vehicle, had discharged the onus of showing that the vehicle was lost without negligence on its part. The standard of care required of the defendant was that which was to be expected in the relevant circumstances from a prudent owner, and was no greater than the standard exhibited by thousands of vehicle owners who immobilise their vehicles appropriately by steering locks, locking doors, removing the distributor arm or by other means. On the facts the defendant had not been negligent.

[14.75]   Idnani v Elisha (t/a Grafton Service Station)
[1979] RTR 488, CA

The defendant was proprietor of a service station on a main route out of London, comprising a forecourt, two petrol pumps, a kiosk and two repair bays. The enclosed premises where vehicles would be under lock and key could accommodate only three vehicles: the defendant handled many more than this and there were often seven or eight vehicles left out on the forecourt overnight. The claimant, a motor dealer for whom the defendant had previously repaired vehicles, took a Jaguar E-type car to him for repair. The defendant removed the cylinder head in the course of the repairs; consequently the car could not be moved under its own power. It was left locked on the forecourt. Overnight someone towed it away; when subsequently recovered it had been severely damaged by the removal of components. The claimant sued for the damage done. In the pleadings both parties pleaded contractual terms; the claimant that it was an express term of their dealings with each other that no car of his would be left out on the forecourt overnight; the defendant that there was a term to be implied from their dealings that he was at liberty to keep a car entrusted to him by the claimant on the forecourt overnight. In the course of the hearing both these pleas were expressly abandoned. The county court judge nevertheless held as a fact that the claimant did tell the defendant that he wanted his cars kept in at night. The judge said it was in every way foreseeable that someone would come on the forecourt and help itself to components from the car. He held that the defendant had not discharged the burden of proof on him to show that he had discharged the duty of care he owed as bailee.

HELD, ON APPEAL: This was not right. The finding of the judge that the claimant had asked for his cars to be kept in at night, taken with his express abandonment of the alleged contractual term, must imply that the defendant had not given the claimant reason to believe that he would do so. Whether there was negligence or not depended on the circumstances of any particular case; the degree of risk on the one hand had to be balanced against the degree of practicability of taking effective steps to prevent that loss on the other. Was it in all the circumstances reasonably practicable for lock-up accommodation? The decisive consideration was that the car was not placed inside because it was immobile and difficult to manoeuvre in the morning to get out. The judge had given too little consideration to the practical difficulties confronting the defendant of which the claimant was well aware.

Appeal allowed. *Cowan v Blackwill Motor Caravan Conversions Ltd* (at para [14.74]) applied.

Note—See also *Smith v Taylor* [1966] 2 Lloyd's Rep 231.

(III) OTHER BAILEES

[14.76] Adams (Durham) Ltd and Day v Trust Houses Ltd
[1960] 1 Lloyd's Rep 380

The second claimant, driving a car owned by the first claimant, arrived at the defendant's hotel some time after 10 pm to stay the night. The night porter unlocked the hotel garage for him and he put the car in. The night porter locked the garage and remained in possession of the keys. There was a charge of 2s for using the garage. During the night the night porter took the car out for some purpose of his own, ran into a traffic island and wrecked it.

HELD: (1) There was a bailment of the car to the defendant, not a mere licence to park the car on the defendant's premises. *Ashby v Tolhurst* [1937] 2 KB 242, [1937] 2 All ER 837, 106 LJKB 783, 156 LT 518, 53 TLR 770, 81 Sol Jo 419, CA distinguished.

(2) As bailee for safe custody for reward the defendant was under a legal

obligation to take all reasonable care of the claimant's car. It had delegated the safe custody of the car to its night porter and was liable not so much as being vicariously responsible for his torts when driving about the streets, but on the basis that it had entrusted to him the fulfilment of its own contractual duty and that duty was not performed. *Central Motors, Glasgow Ltd v Cessnock Garage Co* 1925 SC 796, 1925 SN 103, 1925 SLT 563, followed.

(3)   On the facts, clauses excluding liability for the defendant had not been brought to the notice of the second claimant and did not form part of the contract, but even if they had, there was a fundamental breach of the contract of bailment bringing it to an end along with any conditions forming part of it.

[14.77]   Houghland v RR Low (Luxury Coaches) Ltd
[1962] 1 QB 694, [1962] 2 All ER 159, [1962] 2 WLR 1015, 106 Sol Jo 243, CA

The claimant was a passenger in the defendant's motor coach on a journey from Southampton to Hoylake. Her suitcase was put with other passengers' luggage in the boot of the coach at Southampton and the boot was locked. When the coach stopped during the journey for the passengers to take tea it could not be restarted. The defendant's driver telephoned the defendants who sent a relief coach. Whilst the driver of the relief coach was having his tea the driver of the first coach with the help of the passengers transferred the luggage from the boot of his coach to the boot of the other which was then locked. When the relief coach arrived at Hoylake the claimant's suitcase was not in the boot and could not be found. She claimed the value of the case and contents from the defendant.

HELD: The defendant was liable. It was bailee of the suitcase and had failed to discharge the onus which was on it of proving that the suitcase had been lost without default on its part. It made no difference whether the case was put in detinue or whether it was treated as an action for negligence. It had been admitted in argument that the claimant, by proving the delivery of the suitcase at Southampton and its non-return on the arrival of the coach at Hoylake, made out a *prima facie* case. That *prima facie* case stood unless and until it was rebutted. The burden was on the defendant to adduce evidence in rebuttal. It could discharge that burden by proving that what in fact did happen happened without any default on its part or by showing that, although it could not put its fingers on what actually did happen to the suitcase, nevertheless, whatever did occur occurred notwithstanding all reasonable care having been exercised by it throughout the journey. The first coach had stood for three hours in the dark waiting for the relief coach and the luggage had then been transferred by passengers and stowed in the relief coach by one driver only, with no supervision at all over the unloading of the first coach. The defendant had failed to discharge the onus of proof on it.

(B)   BAILEE'S OWN LOSS

[14.78]   O'Sullivan v Williams
[1992] 3 All ER 385, [1992] RTR 402

The defendant's excavator badly damaged the first claimant's car (which at the time was parked outside the second claimant's home) when it fell off his trailer. The first claimant sought to recover the value of the car and damages for loss of use. The second claimant (his girlfriend) who had borrowed the vehicle whilst he was on holiday claimed for loss of use and for nervous shock.

The trial judge dismissed the nervous shock claim but awarded £400 in respect of the loss of use, despite the fact that the first claimant's claim had already been settled. The Court of Appeal allowed the defendant's appeal, for a bailee could not recover damages in circumstances where that loss had already been recovered by the bailor. It was for the bailor to account to the bailee if there were an enforceable agreement between them.

Note—The Court of Appeal accepted that the second claimant had 'possessory title' in the vehicle as bailee at the time of the damage.

[14.79]   Preston v Ascot Central Car Park Ltd

(1954) Times, 28 January   Pilcher J

The claimant on 18 June 1952, went to Ascot races and left his car in the car park of the Ascot Central Park Ltd, to whom he had paid 15s and received a ticket with the words on it 'The proprietor does not hold himself responsible for any damage to the motor car, or loss by fire or theft of any property stored here, but all due care will be taken.' The car was stolen.

HELD: There was no sufficient delivery to constitute a contract of bailment; the claimant had locked the doors and closed the windows to prevent the car being tampered with. There was only a licence to park and no duty was owed to the car owner. The words 'all due care will be taken' merely meant that the attendant would be careful in parking and unparking cars, and no more; *Ashby v Tolhurst* [1937] 2 KB 242, [1937] 2 All ER 837, 106 LJKB 783, 156 LT 518, 53 TLR 770, 81 Sol Jo 419, CA followed.

[14.80]   BRS (Contracts) Ltd v Colney Motor Engineering Co Ltd

(1958) Times, 27 November, CA

A lorry which was carrying cigarettes worth £32,000 from Ashton-under-Lyme to London, stopped for the night at the defendant's car park. The place where the lorry had been parked consisted of a large floodlit yard surrounded by a fence 6ft high, topped with barbed wire. There was an adjacent petrol station, and an attendant was on duty night and day. Whilst the lorry was parked, part of the load, of the value of £312, was stolen. A standard charge of 1s 6d a night was made for parking irrespective of the value of the contents of the lorry, which was locked up by the driver, who kept the keys and who drove away when he liked. At the trial of an action by the lorry owners the judge held the lorry had been bailed and awarded them £312.

HELD, ON APPEAL: The defendant exercised no control over the lorry. There was no bailment. The facts pointed to the place being a car park rather than a place in the nature of a closed garage.

Appeal allowed.

Note—See also *Cooper v Dempsey* (1961) 105 Sol Jo 320.

[14.81]   BG Transport Service v Marston Motor Co

[1970] 1 Lloyd's Rep 371   Bean J

The defendant was the owner of a large garage with a car park at the rear enclosed by fencing. Drivers could leave vehicles in the car park on payment or by

509

pre-arrangement. A driver on parking a vehicle paid a charge and received a ticket which bore a printed notice relieving the defendant of liability for all risks and losses and containing the words 'On production of this ticket by any person, the vehicle be released to the bearer. No responsibility can be accepted by us for any delay in releasing the vehicle resulting from the loss of this ticket.' The claimant's driver left a loaded van in the car park overnight having paid the charge and received a ticket. On returning the following morning he found the van had gone. The defendant's night watchman, who had come on duty at midnight, said that at about 2 am he was in the petrol pump attendant's office where the keys of parked vehicles were kept when a man knocked and asked for the keys of the vehicle, mentioning the number of the ticket. The man had then taken the keys and driven the vehicle away. He had not surrendered, nor been asked for, the driver's part of the ticket. There was evidence that not all drivers left their keys in the office nor, if they were regular parkers, did they always have tickets. The claimant claimed the value of the load, which was stolen, on the basis that there was a bailment and that the defendant was at fault in parting with the vehicle without receiving or seeing the ticket. It cited an Australian case of *City of Sydney v West* (1965) 144 CLR 481 in which there was held to have been a bailment where the attendant at the exit from a parking station was under a duty not to permit vehicles to proceed out of the parking station except on production of a ticket.

HELD: The present case was one of a licence only and not a bailment. The case of *Ashby v Tolhurst* [1937] 2 KB 242, [1937] 2 All ER 837, 106 LJKB 783, 156 LT 518, 53 TLR 770, 81 Sol Jo 419, CA was on one side of the line between licences and bailments and the Australian case was on the other. The *Ashby v Tolhurst* style of parking, with a nominal payment and no formalities to collect the car, would result in a licence; equally, parking within a bounded area in circumstances under which there is no access to the vehicle except through a special entrance, and where the vehicle can be withdrawn by presentation of a ticket and not otherwise, is a bailment. The present case was similar to *BRS (Contracts) Ltd v Colney Motor Engineering Co Ltd* (at para [14.80]). The words on the ticket did not mean that a vehicle would only be handed over in exchange for a ticket; nor, on the evidence, did the ticket play but a small part in the running of the car park.

[14.82]   Fred Chappel Ltd v National Car Parks Ltd
(1987) Times, 22 May, QBD

The claimant's employee parked a vehicle in a car park run by the defendant. The car park had two attendants but no barrier; ready access to the cars could be gained through the perimeter of the car park. The claimant's employee paid a charge of £2, and parked the vehicle subject to the defendant's standard terms and conditions which purported to transfer custody of the vehicle to them. The vehicle was stolen and the claimant sued the defendant for negligence and breach of contract.

HELD: The claim failed. Despite the wording of the standard terms and conditions, the contract was merely a licence to park, not a bailment of the vehicle. Custody of the vehicle had not been transferred to the defendant. The defendant had reserved the right not to release the vehicle without production of the ticket, but this did not imply a positive obligation to the claimant not to allow the vehicle to leave the car park without production of the ticket. It appeared that the vehicle had been stolen by an expert thief. In the circumstances the defendant was not negligent or in breach of contract.

8.   CARRIERS

[14.83]   WLR Traders Ltd v B & N Shipping Agency Ltd

[1955] 1 Lloyd's Rep 554   Pilcher J

The claimant contracted with forwarding agents, who sub-contracted with private carriers, to collect three cartons of nylon stockings from the claimant's London warehouse and deliver at Millwall Docks. The goods, with other goods, were taken on an open lorry, which was left by the driver in Euston Road while he went to a nearby shop on a private errand to buy a hammer. He removed the ignition key pursuant to his employer's instructions and was absent for three or four minutes during which time the lorry with its load was stolen.

HELD: The carriers as bailees of the goods had failed to prove that the loss occurred without their negligence. Lorries containing goods are often stolen when left unattended. The driver ought to have anticipated that the load was probably valuable. He had no reason to stop. He must be taken to have known that lorry thieves are active in London; that ignition keys are easily procurable; that removing the ignition key would not foil a thief for more than half a minute; he might have removed a vital part of the electrical mechanism. His employer should have taken further precautions by instructions to drivers if obliged to leave their lorries unattended. The carriers were liable to the claimant for the loss of its goods.

[14.84]   Lee Cooper Ltd v CH Jeakins & Sons Ltd

[1967] 2 QB 1, [1965] 1 All ER 280, [1965] 3 WLR 753, [1964] 1 Lloyd's Rep 300, 109 Sol Jo 794   Marshall J

The claimant instructed a firm of shipping agents with whom it normally did business to forward some goods from London to Eire. For a part of the journey the shipping agents engaged the defendants, who were hauliers, to carry the goods in their lorry. The driver stopped on the journey and left the lorry unattended. As a result the goods were stolen. The contracts between the claimant and the shippers, and between the shippers and the defendants, both contained exclusion clauses. The judge found that the theft was due to the driver's negligence and that, there being no contractual relationship between the claimant and defendants, the defendants had no protection from the exclusion clauses, nor were claimants owed any duties by the defendants in contract. Could the claimant succeed in tort?

HELD: Lord Atkin's famous dictum in *Donoghue v Stevenson* (at para [4.2]) was wide and flexible and the claimant's case was within it: 'The law of torts exists to prevent men from hurting one another, whether in respect of their property, their persons, their reputation or anything else that is theirs.' The defendants were bailees for reward of the claimant's goods though their contractual duty was owed to the shippers. They knew from previous trading that the shippers were continuously handling their customers' goods and not their own. They knew from the delivery notes that the claimant was the owner of the goods. They owed the claimant a duty of care which was breached by their driver's negligence.

Judgment for the claimant.

[14.85]   Learoyd Bros & Co Ltd v Pope & Sons Ltd

[1966] 2 Lloyd's Rep 142   Sachs J

The claimant wished to send 12 bales of worsted from Huddersfield to London Docks. It contracted for the carriage with Hanson Haulage Ltd who, for the last stage of the journey hired a lorry and driver from the defendant. The lorry was loaded with the bales and other goods some of which were for Mark Brown's Wharf, off Tooley Street. The driver parked his vehicle in Tooley Street and left it unattended whilst he went to the wharf office 75 yards away, which he knew would not be open for another 10 minutes or so. When it did open he took 15 minutes to transact his business. When he returned to the place where he had left the lorry it had gone. When it was found later the bales had been stolen.

HELD: (1) The defendant was bailee of the goods in relation to the claimant.
   (2)   Whatever were the terms of the contract between Hanson Haulage and the defendant, the driver, so far as the claimant was concerned, remained a servant of the defendant who was liable for his negligence.
   (3)   The driver was negligent in leaving the vehicle when he knew the office was not yet open, not keeping it under observation and locking it properly.
   (4)   The defendants was negligent in not fitting the vehicle with brake lock devices. The defendant was liable to the claimant for the value of the goods lost.

9.   LIEN OF REPAIRER

[14.86]   Hatton v Car Maintenance Co Ltd
[1915] 1 Ch 621, 84 LJCh 847, 110 LT 765, 30 TLR 275, 58 Sol Jo 361

The owner of a motor car had an agreement with a company under which the latter was for three years to maintain the car and its accessories, provide a driver who was to be the company's servant, and do the necessary repairs. The owner was to pay the company a fixed annual sum up to a limited mileage and at a rate for every mile beyond the limit. The car when in London was kept at the company's garage, and whether the owner was in London or elsewhere she took the car out when and as she liked. An amount having become due by the owner under the agreement, the company took possession of the car and claimed a lien on it for the amount due.

HELD: (1) Inasmuch as what the company did to the car was not to improve it, but only to maintain it in its former condition, the company had no lien on the car.
   (2)   Even if the company had a lien, its lien would have been lost by the arrangement acted on, under which the owner was entitled to take away the car as and when she pleased.

[14.87]   Re Southern Livestock Producers Ltd
[1963] 3 All ER 801, [1964] 1 WLR 24, 108 Sol Jo 15

Per Pennycuick J: It is perfectly clear that unless a bailee can establish improvement he has no lien. If this matter were free from authority it would, I think, be tempting to draw the line in rather a different place so as to cover the case where a person by the exercise of labour and skill prevents a chattel from deteriorating ... However, it is quite impossible for me at this time of day to introduce that sort of modification into a well-established principle.

[14.88]   Tappenden v Artus
[1964] 2 QB 185, [1963] 3 All ER 213, [1963] 3 WLR 685, 107 Sol Jo 572, CA

The claimant, a motor dealer, owned a motor vehicle which A wished to take on hire purchase. A wanted to use the car at once for his business but had insufficient cash to pay the necessary deposit, but was allowed by the claimant to take it away and use it pending completion of a hire-purchase agreement. It was also stipulated by the claimant that A should tax and insure the vehicle and he did so. Two days later A was using the vehicle when it broke down. He arranged for a repairer to take it to its garage and repair it. After doing so the repairer rendered an account for £40 to A which was unpaid. After some weeks (the bailment to A having been terminated) the claimant traced the vehicle to the repairer who refused to give it up whilst the bill for repairs remained unpaid, claiming to exercise its repairer's lien. The claimant sued the repairer for a return of the van and damages for its detention.

HELD: The repairer was entitled to assert his lien against the claimant. Where possession of goods is given to a repairer not by the owner but by a bailer the test whether the repairer can assert his lien against the owner is whether the owner authorised the bailee either expressly or as a necessary incident of the bailment to give possession of the goods to the repairer. A had received the vehicle from the claimant as a bailee with the right to use it for all reasonable purposes and in all reasonable ways, and among those ways was the right to get the vehicle repaired when necessary (*Bowmaker Ltd v Wycombe Motors Ltd* (at para [14.65]) per Goddard CJ). There was consideration for the bailment in that A had taxed and insured the vehicle. On the day in question A lawfully had possession of the vehicle and could not use it for the purposes of the bailment unless he were to have it repaired: the giving of actual and lawful possession of the vehicle to the repairer for the purpose of effecting repairs necessary to render it roadworthy was an act reasonably incidental to his use of the vehicle.

CHAPTER 15

Highways

1.   DEFINITION OF A HIGHWAY

(A)   THE STATUTORY DEFINITION

[15.1]   The statutory definition of a highway is set out at s 328 of the Highways Act 1980:

(1)   In this Act, except where the context otherwise requires, 'highway' means the whole or part of a highway other than a ferry or waterway.

(2)   Where a highway passes over a bridge or through a tunnel, that bridge or tunnel is to be taken for the purposes of this Act to be part of the highway.

(3)   In this Act, 'highway maintainable at the public expense' and any other expression defined by reference to a highway is to be construed in accordance with the foregoing provisions of this section.

Section 329(1) of the Highways Act 1980 defines a carriageway as, 'a way of constituting or comprised in a highway, being a way (other than a cycle track) over which the public have a right of way for the passage of vehicles.'

Pavements by the side of roads are 'footways': s 329(1) of the Highways Act 1980. Paths for pedestrians that run by the side of roads, which form part of the road, are repairable by the body or person liable to repair the road: *Derby County Council v Matlock Bath and Scarthin Nick Urban District* [1896] AC 315.

Section 329(1) of the Highways Act 1980 also defines footpaths as highways that carry only a public right of way on foot and are not footways.

(B)   COMMON LAW

[15.2]   Common law definitions may assist in establishing the status of the place where an accident occurs. It was held in the case of *Ex p Lewis* (1888) 21 QBD 191 that a highway is a way over which there exists a public right of passage.

(C)   THE ADOPTION OF HIGHWAYS

[15.3]   This is governed by ss 36 to 40 of the Highways Act 1980.

2.   THE HIGHWAYS ACT 1980

(A)   APPLICATION OF SECTION 41

(1)   DEFINITION

[15.4]
41.   Duty to maintain highways maintainable at public expense

(1)   The authority who are for the time being the highway authority for a highway maintainable at the public expense are under a duty ... to maintain the highway.

By s 329(1) of the 1980 Act 'maintain' includes 'repair'.

Highways that are maintainable at the public expense are further defined by s 6 of the 1980 Act. These in essence, comprise all highways which were maintainable at the public expense before the 1980 Act and in addition:

(a)   any highway constructed by or on behalf of the highway authority;

(b)   any highway constructed by the Council pursuant to Part II of the Housing Act 1985;

(c)   any highway which is not designated a trunk road or special road; and

(d)   a footpath or bridle-way created by specific order or dedicated as a highway for the purposes of the Act.

(II)   NATURE OF DUTY

[15.5]   Griffiths v Liverpool Corpn

[1967] 1 QB 374, [1966] 2 All ER 1015, [1966] 3 WLR 467, 110 Sol Jo 548, CA

The claimant was walking along the pavement of a street when she slipped or tripped on a flagstone and fell, sustaining injury. The flagstone rocked when walked on and when at rest one of its edges protruded half an inch above the adjacent flagstone. She brought a claim against the highway authority. The county court judge on the evidence of a surveyor and of a highway superintendent found as a fact that the flagstone was dangerous. The highway superintendent said there was no system of inspection and that inspection should be done every three months. The reason it was not was that it was not possible to get tradesmen to do the repair work, though there was no difficulty in getting sufficient labourers to do the inspection. If the flagstone in question had been discovered it could have been made safe even by a labourer.

HELD: The Highways Act 1959, s 44, imposed a duty on the defendant, the highway authority, to keep the pavement in repair. This action was based on a breach of that duty. The Highways (Miscellaneous Provisions) Act 1961, abrogated the old rule exempting highway authorities from liability for non-repair of highways and therefore, since the flagstone was dangerous, the defendant was liable to the claimant absolutely and without proof of negligence unless it could establish a defence under s 1(2) and (3) of the 1961 Act. To establish the defence it was not necessary that the highway authority should prove it had taken such care as was reasonably necessary to make the highway safe: it would be sufficient for it to prove that it had taken such care as, in all the circumstances, it reasonably could. If through no fault of its own it had been unable to take steps to make the highway safe, it would escape liability. In the present case the defendant, though unable to get tradesmen, could have employed labourers to deal with dangers such as the one in question and had not established a defence under s 1(2) and (3).

Judgment for the claimant upheld.

Note—The finding of fact that the flagstone was dangerous was not appealed. All the appeal judges expressed doubts whether they themselves would have made such a finding. See *Meggs v Liverpool Corpn* (at para [15.6]) and *Littler v Liverpool* (at para [15.7]). The Highways Act 1959 was repealed as from 1 January 1981 by the Highways Act 1980. Section 44(1) of the 1959 Act is re-enacted in s 41(1) of the 1980 Act.

[15.6]   Meggs v Liverpool Corpn

[1968] 1 All ER 1137, [1968] 1 WLR 689, 132 JP 207, 111 Sol Jo 742, 65 LGR 479, CA

The claimant tripped on uneven flagstones of a pavement in the highway. One of them had sunk three-quarters of an inch. She brought a claim against the highway authority. The judge found as a fact that the state of the pavement was not such as to indicate a failure by the highway authority to discharge its duty.

HELD: The claimant's appeal was dismissed. The Highways Act 1959 put the duty to maintain on the highway authority and the Act of 1961 had abrogated the non-feasance rule. If a highway was in a dangerous condition so that it was not reasonably safe for traffic or people going along it there was *prima facie* a breach of the obligation to maintain or repair. But in order to get a claim going the claimant must at least show that the highway or pavement was not reasonably safe and that it was dangerous to traffic. The judge had examined the evidence and, having regard to the fact that thousands had used the pavement and no one had reported the defect, had said he was not satisfied the highway authority was in breach of its duty. That was a finding of fact: everyone had to take account of unevenness in a pavement here and there, and there was no reason for discharging the judge's finding.

Note—Section 44 of the 1959 Act is now replaced by the Highways Act 1980, s 41(1) in similar terms.

[15.7]   Littler v Liverpool Corpn

[1968] 2 All ER 343n, 66 LGR 660   Cumming-Bruce J

The claimant, aged 19, was running along the pavement of a street when he tripped and fell. The pavement was of York stone about 80 years old. The only defect was a triangular depression half-an-inch deep measuring about three inches along its longest side. He alleged against the defendant, the highway authority, a failure to maintain contrary to the Highways Act 1959, s 44, and negligence.

HELD: To establish a cause of action for failing to maintain the highway the claimant must prove that it was dangerous to relevant traffic (*Meggs v Liverpool Corpn* (at para [15.6])). The test is reasonable foreseeability of danger. It is a mistake to isolate and emphasise differences in level between the flagstones of a pavement unless the difference is such that a reasonable person who considered it would regard it as a real source of danger. Differences of about an inch may cause a stumble but they have to be accepted. A pavement is not to be judged by the standards of a bowling green. The evidence in the present case did not establish that the pavement was dangerous.

Note—See also *Ford v Liverpool Corpn* (1972) 117 Sol Jo 167 where the highway authority was held not liable when a pedestrian slipped over on a one inch ridge where tarmac of the roadway abutted on a metal grid. See also *Griffiths v Liverpool Corpn* (at para [15.5]).

[15.8]   Rider v Rider

[1973] QB 505, [1973] 1 All ER 294, [1973] 2 WLR 190, 117 Sol Jo 71, CA

The claimant was badly injured when a car in which she was a passenger on a narrow lane at night swung across the road and collided with an approaching vehicle. The lane was commonly used as a secondary traffic route but the highway authority had done no repair work for at least six months. The edges of the tarmac had broken away in places causing gaps where the nearside wheels of vehicles would pass; the judge accepted that the driver's loss of control was due to this state of disrepair. He held the highway authority two-thirds to blame.

HELD: The highway authority's appeal was dismissed. It had failed to perform its statutory duty under the Highways Act 1959, s 44 to keep the highway in repair. It had further failed to discharge the duty implied in the Highways (Miscellaneous Provisions) Act 1961, s 1(2), to maintain the road in such a way as to secure that there was no danger for traffic. Whether part of the highway is a danger for traffic is a question of fact to be decided in a common sense way, but it was not correct that the test of danger is the risk to a careful driver. The duty of maintaining the highway free of danger is owed to all users who use the highway in the way normally to be expected of it – including some who may be rated as negligent. In the present case a finding of one-third negligence on the part of the car driver was justified on the ground that, with knowledge of the state of the lane he should have been going more slowly.

[15.9] Pitman v Southern Electricity Board

[1978] 3 All ER 901, 143 JP 156, 122 Sol Jo 300, 76 LGR 578, CA

The claimant, aged 78, was walking at dusk along the pavement in the village where she lived when she tripped on a metal sheet which the defendant's employees had placed over a hole. It was only ⅛ inch proud of the surrounding surface. The place was not lit.

HELD: The claim was successful. The difference between this case and those of *Meggs v Liverpool Corpn* (at para [15.6]) and *Littler v Liverpool Corpn* (at para [15.7]) was that she tripped on an unexpected condition and level of the pavement – unexpected because as an inhabitant of the village she had become accustomed to the state of affairs there and on the evening in question was faced with a new and unexpected hazard.

Note—However, a breach of this duty only gives rise to an action for damages for personal injury or as a result of damage to property and does not include economic loss.

[15.10] Mills v Barnsley Metropolitan Borough Council

[1992] PIQR P291, 157 JPN 831

The claimant tripped when the heel of her shoe became caught in a depression left by a missing piece of paving brick in a pedestrianised area. The missing piece of brick was triangular in shape and measured two inches at its widest point. At first instance, the judge found in favour of the claimant and held that the highway was in a dangerous condition, which was likely to expose a lady to a risk of injury.

The defendant appealed the county court decision.

Steyn LJ in the Court of Appeal held that in order for a claimant to succeed in a claim for personal injury against a highway authority for failure to maintain the highway he has to show that:

(a) the condition of the highway was such that it was dangerous to traffic or pedestrians in the sense that, in the ordinary course of human affairs, danger may have reasonably have been anticipated from its continued use by the public;

(b) the dangerous condition was created by the failure to maintain or repair the highway; and

(c) the injury or damage resulted from such a failure.

Only if the claimant fulfils the above criteria does it become necessary to turn to the highway authority's reliance on the defence under s 58 of the Highways Act 1980, namely that the highway authority had taken such care as in all the circumstances was reasonably required to ensure that the highway was not dangerous.

Steyn LJ accepted that the judge at first instance had these principles well in mind but his reasoning and conclusions were not supported by the photographic evidence.

The claimant's shoe heel was half an inch, making a total drop from the top of the brick of one and a half inches. The question was whether the judge was right to regard this as a danger to women. It was not right to say that a depression of less than an inch will never be dangerous but above one inch will always be dangerous.

Such mechanical jurisprudence is not be encouraged. The test of dangerousness is one of reasonable foresight of harm to users of the highway and each case will turn on its facts.

Steyn LJ held that the photographs showed a wholly remarkable scene. The public must expect minor irregularities. The missing corner of the paving brick was a minor defect. A balance had to be reached between private and public interest.

Appeal allowed.

Note—Applied in *Pazinas v Kent County Council* (24 July 1997, unreported), CA, *Dibb v Kirklees Metropolitan Council* (15 April 1999, unreported), CA, *Brett v Lewisham London Borough Council* [2000] LGR 443, *Winterhalder v Leeds County Council* (18 July 2000, unreported), CA.

[15.11]   James and Another v Preseli Pembrokeshire District Council
[1993] PIQR P114

On 10 February 1989 the claimant tripped on an uneven paving stone with a defect measuring approximately three quarters of an inch. On 2 March 1989 a second claimant tripped on a nearby paving stone with a defect measuring approximately half and inch to one inch. Both claimants brought claims against the local authority alleging breach of s 41 of the Highways Act 1980, or alternatively in nuisance.

The first claimant was unsuccessful but the second claimant was successful. In the second claimant's claim the court held that the defect was dangerous, as the defect had been on a slope and the highway inspector considered the area was dangerous.

The first claimant appealed the decision of his claim and the defendant appealed the decision of the second claimant's claim.

The Court of Appeal dismissed the first claimant's appeal and allowed the defendant's appeal of the second claimant's claim.

The question was not whether the pavement as a whole was in a poor condition, but whether the particular spot where the claimant tripped was dangerous.

First claimant: The Court of Appeal upheld the decision that the pavement could not properly be said to have been in a dangerous condition and provided a reasonable foreseeability of danger. The trial judge commented that each case turns on its own facts.

Second claimant: The Court of Appeal held that the trial judge had fallen into error and that his judgment in favour of the second claimant could not stand. The trial judge had identified no particular defect in the footway as the probable cause of fall. The Court of Appeal followed *Mills v Barnsley Metropolitan Borough Council* (at para [15.10]). Lloyd LJ commented that:

'In one sense, it is reasonably foreseeable that any defect in the highway, however slight, may cause an injury. But that is not the test of what is meant by "dangerous" in this context. It must be the sort of danger which an authority may reasonably be expected to guard against. There must, as Steyn LJ says, be a reasonable balance between private and public interest in these matters. In the present case, I am driven to the conclusion that the judge ignored that balance. He has imposed a standard which is much too high and has thus reached a conclusion which was plainly wrong on the facts'.

[15.12]   **Stovin v Wise**

[1996] AC 923, [1996] 3 All ER 801, [1996] 3 WLR 388, [1996] RTR 354

The claimant was knocked off his motorcycle by a car turning right out of a road called Cemetery Lane. The junction was known by Norfolk Council to be extremely dangerous. Visibility was very limited for vehicles turning right out of Cemetery Lane. Prior to the claimant's accident the council had written to the owner of the land, British Rail, suggesting that part of the bank be removed to improve visibility. The council would do the work at its own expense. A site meeting took place and British Rail agreed to seek the necessary internal approval. However, British Rail did not get in touch with the council again and the council did not send a reminder. The matter was left to go to sleep and as such the work was never completed.

The claimant was then involved in the accident. The court held the defendant car driver 70% to blame for the accident and Norfolk Council, which the defendant had joined as a third party, was 30% to blame for the accident. The Court of Appeal dismissed the council's appeal, although rejected the contention that the council was in breach of s 41 of the Highways Act 1980, as the land in question did not constitute part of the highway. Keane LJ held, 'it would be stretching the meaning of both "highway" and "maintain" if this court were to say that in order to comply with its duty to maintain the highway authority had to remove an obstruction to visibility situated on adjoining land'. The Court of Appeal's decision on s 41 was not contested by the claimant before the House of Lords.

The council further appealed to the House of Lords on whether the council owed the claimant any common law duty in respect of its failure to take action. The council has responsibilities for maintaining and improving the highway, including powers to remove potential sources of danger. Section 79 of the Highways Act 1980 is such a power. Where a highway authority deems it necessary for the prevention of danger arising from obstruction to the view of road users, the authority has power to serve a notice on the owner of the land directing him to alter a fence, wall or bank.

HELD, ON APPEAL: The House of Lords, by a majority of three to two, allowed the council's appeal. There were no grounds upon which a public law duty should give rise to an obligation to compensate persons who have suffered loss because it was not performed. The alleged negligence involved an omission and as such no duty of care ought to be imposed on the highway authority.

[15.13]   **Galloway v London Borough of Richmond Upon Thames**

(20 February 2003, unreported), QBD   Eady J

The claimant tripped on a gap in a kerbstone sustaining injury. At first instance it was held that the defect had been dangerous and the defendant was in breach of its duty under s 41 of the Highways Act 1980 to maintain the highway. The defendant appealed submitting that too high a standard had been imposed and that the defect had only been minor giving rise to a low order risk.

HELD, ON APPEAL: Although the gap gave rise to some risk of harm, that is true of any gap, hollow or irregularity into which a pedestrian's foot may be placed. Eady J held that the photographs of the scene showed the defect to be unremarkable and not such as to give rise to a real source of danger. A sensible compromise must be achieved between public and private interest. Eady J believed that the decision at first instance had tilted the balance too far in favour of the unfortunate pedestrian. There was no need for s 58 of the Highways Act 1980 to be considered.

[15.14]   **Gorringe v Calderdale Metropolitan Borough Council**

[2002] EWCA Civ 595

[2002] RTR 446, (2002) 22 LS Gaz R 36, CA; affd [2004] 2 All ER 326, [2004] 1 WLR 1057, HL

The claimant suffered personal injuries when the car she was driving collided head on with a bus while making her way up a hill. The claimant was on the opposite carriageway at the time of the accident, and alleged that the council was at fault for not clearly indicating the dangers of that particular area of road. At the top of the hill where the collision took place the road bent sharply to the left and it was not possible to see oncoming traffic until one was virtually at the crest itself. The claimant had been travelling at 50mph and had stamped on her brakes to negotiate the turn, but lost control and was sent skidding onto the opposite carriageway and into the path of the oncoming bus. An 'uneven road' warning sign marked the area, as did a painted 'SLOW' sign on the road's surface, although this had heavily worn away and was held to be no longer visible.

Judgment was given for the claimant with no finding of contributory negligence on the basis that:
(1)   the failure to repaint the 'SLOW' sign was a breach by the defendant of s 41 of the Highways Act 1980;
(2)   a visible marking would have caused the claimant to slow and avoid the accident;
(3)   the claimant had been induced to drive at 50mph by the absence of sufficient warning signs or markings;
(4)   the defendant was in breach of its common law duty arising from s 39 of the Road Traffic Act 1988 per *Larner v Solihull Metropolitan Borough Council* [2001] RTR 32 and ought to have appreciated the clear and obvious danger presented by the road conditions.

The council appealed.

HELD, ON APPEAL: (1) There was no breach of s 41 of the 1980 Act following the House of Lords decision in *Goodes v East Sussex County Council* (at para [15.18]) as a road marking did not constitute part of the physical or structural condition of the roadway.
(2)   The defendant was not in breach of its duty of care under s 39 of the 1988 Act (Potter LJ dissenting). The accident location did not have a history suggestive of being an accident black spot, and if the defendant had given proper consideration to the question of warnings it would not have been irrational not to have placed them – there were no special circumstances suitable for *Larner* to apply.
(3)   The trial judge had made serious and material errors of fact and inference.
(4)   The judge's finding of no contributory negligence was unsupportable. Although no consensus was reached by the court on the degree of contributory negligence, it would not have been less than 50%.

Appeal allowed.

Note—In *Larner v Solihull Metropolitan Borough Council* [2001] RTR 32 the claimant was involved in an accident when she emerged from a minor road to a major road without stopping at the junction. The claimant alleged that the council should have provided additional advance warning and that the council was negligent and/or in breach of its statutory duty under section 39 of the Road Traffic Act 1988. The Court of Appeal held that although a common law duty of care might be imposed under section 39 in exceptional circumstances, it would have to be shown that the default of the authority was outside the ambit of the discretion given to that authority by that section, for example where the authority has acted wholly unreasonable.

[15.15]   Thompson v Hampshire County Council
[2004] EWCA Civ 1016

[2004] All ER (D) 468 (Jul), [2005] LGR 467

The claimant had been walking along the verge of a highway when she strayed from the path by perhaps no more than a step and fell into a ditch sustaining injury. At first instance the judge held that the path was safe for those who used it and that s 41 of the Highways Act 1980 did not impose a duty to avoid the risk of harm that could be created where pedestrians walked to the side of the path. The claimant submitted that the fault of the highway authority lay in the juxtaposition of path and ditch, and further that the ditch represented a hole in the highway itself.

HELD: The Court of Appeal dismissed the claimant's appeal on the basis that a highway authority was not responsible for the layout of a highway. The duty was no more than a duty to repair the structure of the highway if it was out of repair: *Gorringe v Calderdale Metropolitan Borough Council* [2004] UKHL 15, [2004] 1 All ER 326 and *Goodes v East Sussex County Council* (at para [15.18]) applied. However, the court maintained that a duty in common law negligence may go further, where such negligence amounts to a positive act of entrapment or ensnarement, although in the present case, no such allegation was advanced.

The claimant's complaint with regard to the juxtaposition of path and ditch concerned layout rather than lack of repair.

(III)   SNOW AND ICE

[15.16]   Haydon v Kent County Council
[1978] QB 343, [1978] 2 All ER 97, [1978] 2 WLR 485, 121 Sol Jo 849, CA

The claimant was descending a steep footpath coated with snow and ice when she slipped and broke her ankle. She claimed damages from the highway authority, relying on the duty in the Highways Act 1959, s 44 'to maintain the highway'. Section 295 says 'Maintain' includes repair'. (The Highways Act 1980, s 329 says 'maintenance' includes repair and 'maintain' and 'maintainable' are to be construed accordingly'.)

HELD: The duty under s 44 of the 1959 Act was to repair and also maintain. The statutory obligation included clearing snow and ice or providing temporary protection by gritting, but whether there had been a breach of that duty was a question of fact and degree on the facts of each case. The claimant must prove either that the authority was at fault apart from merely failing to take steps to deal with the ice, or that having regard to the nature and importance of works sufficient time had elapsed to make it prima facie unreasonable for the authority to have failed to take remedial measures. In the present case insufficient time had elapsed after the onset of the icy conditions having regard to the authority's heavy commitments to keep major roads in its area safe and clear.

[15.17]   Scottish Omnibuses Ltd v Midlothian County Council
(1955) 105 L Jo 90, Outer House, Ct of Sess

A motor omnibus was proceeding along a road which turned to the right, and 90 yards further on, going downhill, crossed a bridge over a river. The outer side of the turn was 2ft higher than the inner side making a gradient of about one in ten across the road. The road was icebound and at the turn the bus skidded and slipped down the road, collided with the parapet of the bridge and fell into the river.

HELD: The highway authority was under no duty to construct a roadway to prevent such an occurrence.

[15.18]   Goodes v East Sussex County Council

[2000] 3 All ER 603, [2000] 1 WLR 1356, [2000] RTR 366, [2000] BLGR 465, [2000] PIQR PI48, [2000] EGCS 75, (2000) 26 LS Gaz R 38, [2000] NLJR 949, [2000] NPC 65

The claimant was driving along a public highway at about 7.00 am on a frosty morning when his car skidded on black ice causing him to crash into the parapet of a bridge sustaining serious injuries.

At first instance the court held that the defendant had not been in breach of its duty under s 41 of the Highways Act 1980 to maintain the highway.

On appeal the Court of Appeal held that the highway authority was in breach of s 41 of the Highways Act 1980. Where preventative rather than remedial action was required the question was whether once the highway authority had become aware of the need for preventative measures it had acted with appropriate diligence in carrying out those measures. The pre-salting of the highway was a preventative action that could have been commenced at a time that would have achieved that objective.

The defendant appealed to the House of Lords.

HELD, ON APPEAL: A highway authority's duty under s 41 was an absolute duty to maintain the road so that it is safe for the passage of those who use the highway. Section 41 has to be read with s 58 of the 1980 Act, which provides a defence that reasonable care has been taken by the authority. However, the duty under s 41 did not include a duty to prevent the formation of ice or remove the accumulation of ice on the road. The removal of ice may be maintaining the use of the highway or facilitating or easing the access that the highway provides, but it is not a maintaining of the highway itself.

Note—The decision of the House of Lords in *Goodes* has now been effectively reversed by s 111 of the Railways and Transport Safety Act 2003, which has added to s 41 of the Highways Act 1980 a duty 'to ensure, so far is reasonably practicable, that safe passage along a highway is not endangered by snow or ice'.

[15.19]   Sandhar v Department of Transport, Environment and the Regions
[2004] EWCA Civ 1440

[2004] All ER (D) 105 (Nov), [2005] 1 WLR 1632, [2005] RTR 119

The claimant's husband died in a road traffic accident when his car skidded on frost. The defendant had delegated the performance of its functions of snow clearing and salting relating to such roads to Bedfordshire County Council. The local authority had in place a winter maintenance programme in accordance with the defendant's Trunk Roads Maintenance Manual.

The road had not been salted during the previous day or evening. If it had been salted the accident probably would not have occurred. The judge held that the defendant owed no relevant duty of care. There could be no liability for breach of statutory duty in light of *Goodes v East Sussex County Council* (at para [15.18]) and the accident occurred prior to the coming into force of the statutory amendment to s 41 of the Highways Act 1980, which reversed the effect of *Goodes*. Furthermore, liability at common law did not arise since the deceased did not have a more proximate relationship with the defendant than any other road user or potential road user choosing to drive at that time.

The claimant submitted that a common law duty in negligence arose because the evidence established a public expectation at the time of the deceased's accident whereby the local authority had assumed responsibility to perform the salting operations that it had undertaken to perform in its agreement with the defendant.

HELD: The Court of Appeal held that the claimant had not established the existence of a relevant common law duty of care (*Gorringe v Calderdale Metropolitan Borough Council* [2004] UKHL 15, [2004] 2 All ER 326). The defendant could not properly be taken to have assumed a general responsibility to all road users to ensure that all or any trunk roads would be salted in freezing conditions. It is the primary responsibility of motorists to take care for their own safety and that of their passengers and other road users. The existence of the delegation agreement, the Trunk Roads Maintenance Manual, and the highway authority's Winter Maintenance Programme does not predicate an assumption of responsibility by the defendant to motorists generally that the system for salting roads will always be carried out without fail. An assumption of responsibility sufficient to create a duty of care normally requires a particular relationship with an individual or individuals, as indicated in *Barrett v London Borough of Enfield* [2001] 2 AC 550, [1999] 3 All ER 193, [1999] LGR 473 and *Phelps v Hillingdon London Borough* [2001] 2 AC 619, [2000] 4 All ER 504, [2000] LGR 651. A general expectation cannot alone support an assumption of responsibility.

Further, there was no evidence that the deceased had relied on an expectation that the road had been salted. The deceased was not entitled to rely on the defendant to have salted the road. The fact that the road was not salted was not to be regarded as a trap. The deceased had a primary duty to have regard for his own safety.

Appeal dismissed.

(IV)   FLOODING

[15.20]   **Burnside v Emerson**
[1968] 3 All ER 741, [1968] 1 WLR 1490, 133 JP 66, 112 Sol Jo 565, CA

The claimant and first defendant were driving their cars in opposite directions on a main road and were about to pass each other. It had been raining hard for some hours and a pool of water had formed extending half-way across the road on the first defendant's side. He was travelling at about 50mph. As his car struck the water it swerved across the road into collision with the claimant's car. The second defendant was the highway authority. Prior to the accident the highway authority's attention had been drawn to the tendency of the road to become flooded at that point in wet weather, due to bad positioning of a drain and a failure by the second defendant's employees to keep the grips or gulleys in good condition and to keep the ditch cleaned out.

HELD: The second defendant was liable for its failure to fulfil the duty to maintain the highway placed upon it by the Highways Act 1959, s 44(1). An action under the section requires three things:
   (1)   the claimant must show the road was dangerous for traffic, that is to

say, in a state in which injury may reasonably be anticipated to persons using the highway: foreseeability is an essential element;

(2)   the claimant must prove that the dangerous condition was due to a failure to maintain which includes a failure to repair;

(3)   If there is a failure to maintain, the highway authority is prima facie liable but can escape liability if it proves that it took such care as in all the circumstances was reasonable, having regard to the Highways (Miscellaneous Provisions) Act 1961, s 1(3).

The pool of water was admitted by the second defendant's surveyor at the trial to be a danger to traffic and the existence of the pool was due to its failure to maintain the drainage system in a satisfactory condition. The highway authority was liable, but the first defendant was also negligent in driving too fast. Blame was apportioned two-thirds to the first defendant and one-third to the second defendant.

[15.21]   Morris v Thyssen (GB) Ltd

[1983] Abr 2418   Booth J

A van driver lost control of his vehicle when it hit a large pool of water on the road caused by flooding. He blamed the highway authority.

HELD: The flooding was a serious hazard which was reasonably predictable from the low-lying nature of the road and the weather conditions. The authority had direct knowledge of the serious extent of the flood from the police and their own employees. The one flood sign displayed in a nearby lay-by was not an adequate warning. The authority was found two-thirds liable, the van driver one-third.

[15.22]   Department for Transport, Environment and the Regions v Mott McDonald

[2006] EWHC 928 (QB), QB

Between August 1999 and September 2000 three claimants were involved in road traffic accidents as a consequence, it was claimed, of the presence of water on the road.

The Department for Transport, Environment and the Regions ('the defendant') and its predecessor was the relevant highways authority with a duty to maintain the highway pursuant to s 41 of the Highways Act 1980.

The Department settled all three claims and subsequently brought proceedings against three contractors to whom it had sub-contracted responsibility for the maintenance of the highway claiming an indemnity against or contribution towards the sums paid to the three claimants.

It was directed that the court should decide as a preliminary issue whether, on the facts pleaded by the claimants the Department would have been liable in law to them. In essence the court was asked to consider whether the decision of the Court of Appeal in *Burnside v Emerson* (see para [15.20]) had been overruled by the House of Lords in *Goodes v East Sussex County Council* (see para [15.18]) and *Gorringe v Calderdale Metropolitan Borough Council* (see para [15.28]).

HELD: The Court of Appeals decision in *Burnside* cannot stand with the decision of the House of Lords in *Goodes* and *Gorringe*. The duties of a highway authority in respect of the roads for which it is responsible are confined to the repair and keeping in repair of the surface of those roads. The highway authority had power under the Highways Act 1980, s 100, to provide drains for the purpose of draining a highway and also power to keep the drains clear, but it had no duty to exercise these powers.

'The word "repair" ... does not extend to dealing with obstructions which rendered the highway less commodious, but do not damage the surface', per Seymour J.

Note—This decision was overturned on appeal. See [2006] EWCA Civ 1089, [2006] All ER (D) 400 (Jul). It was held on appeal that the highway authority was liable to the original claimants for failing to maintain the drains in good repair. *Burnside* followed.

(V)   SIGNS AND VISIBILITY

[15.23]   Rider v Rider

[1973] QB 505, [1973] 1 All ER 294, [1973] 2 WLR 190, 117 Sol Jo 71, CA

See para [15.8].

[15.24]   Bird v Pearce (Somerset County Council third party)

[1979] RTR 369, 77 LGR 753, CA

At a crossroads where Downs Lane crossed the Bruton Road, the first defendant's car entering the crossroads from Downs Lane was struck by the second defendant's car travelling along the Bruton Road. Both roads were unclassified. The traffic system laid out by the highway authority gave priority to the Bruton Road by double dotted white lines at the mouth of side roads, but at this crossroads the white lines had been obliterated by resurfacing about a month before the accident and not yet repainted. As between the defendants the first defendant was found 90% to blame. In third-party proceedings he sought contributions from the highway authority.

HELD: It was foreseeable that there was a risk of drivers misunderstanding their priorities at a crossroads junction – a greater risk than in the days before there had been any signs at all at the mouths of the side roads along a major road. The highway authority had created a pattern of traffic flow which did not exist before it placed white lines on the roads, a pattern which drivers could be expected to rely on. The highway authority was under a duty of care to the claimant to prevent injury from the potentially dangerous situation resulting from the removal of the white lines. It failed to erect any warning sign. The authority should contribute one-third to the damages paid by the first defendant.

Note—See also *Murray v Nicholls* 1983 SLT 194.

[15.25]   Lavis v Kent County Council

(1992) 90 LGR 416, CA

The claimant motorcyclist suffered severe injuries when he collided with a kerbstone on Waterloo Road, near Vigo, Kent. The road markings were minimal and, in the claimant's submission, inadequate in warning of the potential danger to road users.

On appeal from the Master, the Statement of Claim was struck out for failing to disclose a reasonable cause of action. The Court of Appeal, considering the Road Traffic Regulation Act 1984, concluded that although the Act did not impose upon a local authority a duty to erect traffic signs, it did require them to implement the regulations with reasonable care. It was a question of fact whether in this instance they were justified in taking no further steps and it was only right that the claimant be allowed to investigate the matter by way of discovery.

[15.26]   **Stovin v Wise**

[1996] AC 923, [1996] 3 All ER 801, [1996] 3 WLR 388, [1996] RTR 354

See para [15.12].

[15.27]   **King v Department of Transport, Local Government and the Regions**
[2003] EWCA Civ 730
[2003] All ER (D) 352 (May)

The claimant was a motorcyclist who was severely injured when he drove his motorcycle into a roundabout. The defendant was the highway authority that had designed and built the roundabout.

At first instance, the judge found for the claimant on the basis that the design of the roundabout was negligent. Specifically the judge held that the 'entry angle' at which the claimant entered the roundabout was in excess of the design recommendations. The claimant's damages were reduced by 50% for contributory negligence. The defendant appealed.

HELD, ON APPEAL: The defendant's appeal was upheld. The entry angle to the roundabout was on the high side but it could not be found that the defendant's failure to design the roundabout with a marginally smaller entry angle, which would have been compliant with the regulations, was the cause of the accident. The roundabout was well lit and preceded by hazard warning lines, give way lines and three left turn signals as well as being well sign posted. The cause of the accident was entirely the claimant's failure to register the warning signs and the roundabout itself sufficiently or at all.

[15.28]   **Gorringe v Calderdale Metropolitan Borough Council**
[2002] EWCA Civ 595
[2002] RTR 446, (2002) 22 LS Gaz R 36, CA; affd [2004] 2 All ER 326, [2004] 1 WLR 1057, HL

See para [15.14].

(VI)   STATUTORY UNDERTAKERS

[15.29]   **Nolan v Merseyside County Council and North West Water Authority**
(15 July 1982, unreported), CA

On 30 May 1979 the claimant tripped in a hole created by a missing stopcock box that had been removed by vandals. The box was the property of the water authority. The box had been inspected by the water authority between 26 March 1979 and 2 April 1979 and found to be in order. The claimant brought claims against both the water authority and the highway authority.

The trial judge found against the water authority and dismissed the claim against the highway authority. The water authority appealed and contended that the judgment be set aside and entered for the claimant against the first defendant, or in the alternative that judgment be entered for the claimant against both defendants with liability apportioned between the defendants as the court believed just. The highway authority did not invoke the statutory defence.

May LJ in the Court of Appeal held that on the facts, in whatever way the stopcock box came to lose its lid, the highway authority was clearly in breach of its duty to maintain the highway under the Highway Act 1959. Similarly, the water authority was in breach of its duty under the Water Act 1945 to carry out any necessary works of maintenance or repair.

May LJ held that the claimant was entitled to judgment against both defendants. May LJ also noted that:

'In some cases, where for instance a highway authority draws the attention of a water authority to the absence of a lid to a stopcock box which renders the highway unsafe and the water authority takes no steps to replace the lid and in consequence a user of the highway has an accident, the particular facts may give rise to causes of action in negligence and nuisance, in addition to the breaches of the basic statutory duties ... This must depend on the evidence given in the particular case and the facts found by the trial judge'.

However, this was not the position in the present case, where the facts proved and found were that the lid of the stopcock box was missing.

The position with regard to the apportionment of liability was governed by ss 1(1) and 2(1) of the Civil Liability (Contribution) Act 1978. These two subsections provide that any person liable in respect of damage suffered by a claimant may recover contribution from any other person liable in respect of the same damage and that the amount of such contribution 'shall be such as may be found by the court to be just and equitable having regard to the extent of that person's responsibility for the damage in question'.

HELD, ON APPEAL: The Court of Appeal allowed the appeal and ordered that judgment be entered for the claimant against both defendants on a mutual basis.

(B)   STATUTORY DEFENCE

(I)   DEFINITION

[15.30]   Section 58 of the Highways Act 1980 provides a defence where the highway authority can show that it took reasonable care to ensure that the highway was not hazardous to users of the highway.

Highways Act 1980, s 58

[15.31]
58.   Special defence in action against a highway authority for damages for non-repair of highway
(1)   In an action against a highway authority in respect of damage resulting from their failure to maintain a highway maintainable at the public expense, it shall be a defence (without prejudice to any other defence or the application of the law relating to contributory negligence) to prove that the authority had taken such care as in all the circumstances was reasonably required to secure that the part of the highway to which the action relates was not dangerous for traffic.
(2)   For the purposes of a defence under subsection (1) above, the court shall in particular have regard to the following matters:
(a)   the character of the highway, and the traffic which was reasonably to be expected to use it;
(b)   the standard of maintenance appropriate for a highway of that character and used by such traffic;
(c)   the state of repair in which a reasonable person would have expected to find the highway;

    (d)   whether the highway authority knew, or could reasonably have been expected to know, that the condition of the part of the highway to which the action relates was likely to cause danger to users of the highway;

    (e)   where the highway authority could not reasonably have been expected to repair that part of the highway before the cause of action arose, what warning notices of its condition had been displayed;

but for the purposes of such a defence it is not relevant to prove that the highway authority had arranged for a competent person to carry out or supervise the maintenance of the part of the highway to which the action relates unless it is also proved that the authority had given him proper instructions with regard to the maintenance of the highway and that he had carried out the instructions.

    (3)   This section binds the Crown.

Subsection (4) excludes the operation of the section from damage following the breakage or opening of a street and resulting from an event before the completion of reinstatement required by the Public Utilities Street Works Act 1950, s 7(2).

Note—Section 7(2) of the Public Utilities Street Works Act 1950 has now been replaced by s 70 of the New Roads and Street Works Act 1991.

(II)   APPLICATION

[15.32]   Pridham v Hemel Hempstead Corpn

(1970) 114 Sol Jo 884, 69 LGR 523, CA

The claimant was pushing a pram along the pavement of a residential road when she caught her foot in a hole and was injured. In answer to her claim for damages for breach of the Highways Act 1959, s 44, the defendant, the highway authority, pleaded the statutory defence in s 1(2) of the 1961 Act. They gave evidence that two men were employed full time on inspection of roads and that residential roads were inspected every three months. The judge concluded on examination of the figures of mileage of roads and hours of work that residential roads could have been inspected monthly and held that the defendants had not established the statutory defence.

HELD, ON APPEAL: It was wrong to depart from the words of the section, in which the test is reasonableness. The system was reasonable and the fact that it was practicable to inspect more frequently did not make the system unreasonable. Appeal allowed.

Note—The duties imposed on the highway authority to inspect the highway have been tightened by the Code of Practice for Inspections (1992) which came into force on 1 January 1993. See also ss 70–72 of the New Roads and Street Works Act 1991.

[15.33]   Meggs v Liverpool Corpn

[1968] 1 All ER 1137, [1968] 1 WLR 689, 132 JP 207, 111 Sol Jo 742, 65 LGR 479, CA

See para [15.6].

[15.34]   Jacobs v Hampshire County Council

(1984) Times, 28 May   Skinner J

A cyclist was injured when the front wheel of his cycle went into a hole at the edge of the road caused by water penetration. The highway authority had inspected the road at six-monthly intervals, having regard to the type of area in which the road lay and the likely extent and type of use of the road.

HELD: To establish a defence under the Highways Act 1980, s 58 the authority should have also taken into account in deciding the frequency of inspections, the design of the road. Tarmac adjoining cobbles at the edge made it especially vulnerable to water penetration, capable of causing damage within two months. The defence was not established.

[15.35]   Mills v Barnsley Metropolitan Borough Council
[1992] PIQR P291, 157 JPN 831

See para [15.10].

[15.36]   Allen v Newcastle City Council
(29 June 1995, unreported), Newcastle upon Tyne County Court   Mr Recorder Hurst

The claimant tripped in the course of descending the defendant's steps and suffered injuries to her knee, shoulder and neck. The steps were defective to the extent that a fallen flagstone created a raised defect of one inch when descending the staircase and the front edge of the step had sunk by approximately three inches.

The defendant relied on the statutory defence pursuant to the Highways Act 1980, s 58. The steps had been inspected three times in the course of the six months prior to the claimant's accident. Appropriate documentation was produced. The steps had been repaired on a previous occasion.

HELD: It was only necessary for the highway authority to establish that the steps had been inspected regularly. The evidence proved that they had and were afforded the section 58 defence.

(III)   SECTION 58 AND UTILITY COMPANIES

[15.37]   Reid v British Telecommunications plc
(1987) Times, 27 June, CA

The claimant tripped on a protruding manhole cover, which protruded 12 millimetres above the level of the pavement. At first instance the claim succeeded. The defendant appealed the decision and contended that it was not negligent, as it had relied on the half-yearly inspections of the pavement carried out by the highway authority.

The appeal was dismissed. It was not negligent for a statutory undertaker to rely on the inspections of a local highway authority, but if the statutory undertaker did so rely it would be assumed to have the knowledge of the condition of the manholes had it carried out its own inspections.

3. NEGLIGENT REPAIR

[15.38]   Newsome v Darton Urban District Council
[1938] 3 All ER 93, 159 LT 153, 54 TLR 945, 82 Sol Jo 520, CA

In July 1933, the defendant had made a trench in a highway for the purpose of executing certain drainage work. The excavation was filled in, and in 1935, it was resurfaced and the surface was said to be level. In 1936, a depression or hole had formed at the place where the work had been carried out, and the jury found that the highway at this place was dangerous to those using it with due care. The jury also found that, although the original work was executed without negligence, the dangerous condition was due to the work of the defendant, and that the defendant was negligent in not discovering and taking steps to remedy the danger. The claimant having been thrown from his bicycle and injured by reason of the subsidence of the road at the place in question, brought an action against the defendant as the highway authority responsible for the repair of the road.

HELD: There was a duty on the defendant to make good the inevitable subsidence from its work in 1933, and it was negligent in not discovering, and in not taking steps to remedy, the danger. The jury had found that the subsidence was due to the excavations made by the highway authority. If the authority interferes with the structure of the road, then the operation of restoring it to the condition in which it was before such interference includes the remedying of a subsequent subsidence, although the subsidence was two years after the excavation and the accident three years after the excavation.

[15.39]   **Birmingham v East Ham Corpn**

(1961) 60 LGR 111, CA

The claimant was injured when walking across a public highway for which the defendant was the appropriate authority. His foot went into a hole 9 inches wide by 6 inches deep. Four days previously the highways superintendent of the defendant had noticed a depression at the same spot. He had at once arranged for repairs, which had been carried out. The loose earth beneath the surface was taken out until a solid base was reached. The sides of the excavation were made firm and the hole filled and made firm. An asphalt topping was applied and levelled. There was evidence that rats were active in the vicinity.

HELD: The defendant was not liable. The mere fact that the surface had sunk so soon after the work was done was not conclusive that the work had not been satisfactorily carried out. There was direct evidence that the work had been properly done and there was evidence of a rat run, which could provide an explanation as to how the cavity arose. The defendant was not under a further duty in the circumstances to take special precautions against the rats, eg by mixing broken glass with the filling.

[15.40]   **Bright v Ministry of Transport**

(1971) 115 Sol Jo 226, [1971] RTR 253, 69 LGR 338, [1971] 2 Lloyd's Rep 68, CA

The claimant was riding his motorcycle down a road which had formerly been part of the A1 road when he lost control due to longitudinal ridges on the road surface and was injured. The road had ceased to be a trunk road about two years earlier and the Ministry of Transport had instructed the local authority as its agent to remove double white lines which had divided two lanes of traffic. The local authority had done so about four months before the accident by covering the lines with asphalt. Summer traffic had compacted the asphalt between the lines, creating the ridges. An expert gave evidence that the groove between the ridges presented a serious and foreseeable danger to motorcycles. The judge at first instance held the Ministry to blame for not having given instructions to the local authority on how the work should be done.

HELD, ON APPEAL: The case turned on its own special facts. The Ministry was not negligent since the local authority was quite capable of doing the work properly.

The negligence was that of the workmen who had failed to chip off the lines but had merely covered them up. The local authority was liable for the negligence of its workmen and the Ministry, as principals, must accept responsibility.

Per Lord Denning: If it were not for the special circumstances of this case I would have held the defendant not liable. The law still is that a highway is not to be considered to be dangerous simply because it is uneven, or not level, or has patches or undulations, or has been dug up for pipes and been filled in, or because the surface is bad. Road users cannot expect it to be as level as a bowling green. They must take the rough with the smooth. A highway is only to be considered dangerous when there is something which may be regarded as a trap into which an ordinary careful person may fall.

Note—In *Rider v Rider* (see para [15.8]) members of the Court of Appeal disagreed with the final sentence of the passage from Lord Denning's judgment in *Bright's* case; they did not accept as a matter of law that a danger for traffic cannot exist unless the road conditions constituting it would be a trap for the careful driver. Highway authorities must not provide only for those who use reasonable care.

[15.41]   McLaughlin v Strathclyde Regional Council
1992 SLT 959

The claimant brought an action for damages against the defendant when she fell and injured herself as she crossed the road. At some point after the construction of the road, a metal framed drainage gully had been placed in the road surface, and the area around it had been infilled and tarmac reapplied. Over the years the infill had subsided and at the time of the accident there was a difference in height between the existing roadway and the replaced tarmac of between 1–2 inches. In the court's view that was insufficient to create a liability for the local authority.

Per Lord Coulsfield: I think it is clear that a road authority is not required to keep all pavements, far less all parts of the road surface, absolutely flat and even.

4.   COMMON LAW

(A)   GENERAL

[15.42]   Some of the previous cases illustrate that some breaches of duty will *not* be considered as a failure to maintain. This leaves negligence claims at common law. Diplock LJ's discussion of the difference between a common law claim and a claim for breach of statutory duty can be found in *Griffiths v Liverpool Corporation* (see para [15.5]).

The courts have restricted the scope of the common law duty of care in cases in which the highway authority did not positively create a danger. See *Gorringe v Calderdale Metropolitan Borough Council* (see para [15.14]). Not simply a pure omission.

The following cases show that common law cannot be imposed:

Gorringe v Calderdale Metropolitan Borough Council (see para [15.14]) – failure to provide a warning sign; *Sandhar v Department of Transport* (see para [15.19]) – ice; *Stovin v Wise* (see para [15.26]) – obstruction to visibility; *Sheppard v Glossop* (see para [15.53]) – street lighting; *Baxter v Stockon-on-Tees* [1959] 1 QB 441 – reconstruct road; and *Price v Rhondda* [2000] CLY 4232 – no visible warning signs.

(B)   DANGER INTRODUCED TO THE HIGHWAY

[15.43]   Fisher v Ruislip-Northwood Urban District Council and Middlesex County Council

[1945] KB 584, [1945] 2 All ER 458, 173 LT 161, 62 TLR 1, 89 Sol Jo 434, CA

The defendant local authority had lawfully erected a surface shelter in the highway under the Civil Defence Act 1939, s 9. There was a warning light at each corner which could be turned on and off by a switch inside the shelter. It was the duty of the air-raid wardens to switch on the lights at the appointed time. The shelter was sometimes lighted and sometimes not lighted. The claimant was driving a car in the hours of darkness with due care and on the proper side of the road collided with the shelter which was unlighted. He was a complete stranger to the district and had never been in the road before.

HELD, by the Court of Appeal: On undertakers, who were given statutory power to construct works, a legal duty was imposed that reasonable care should be taken to construct and maintain the works as to render them safe and not dangerous to the public though no such duty was imposed by the statute itself or by the common law; except in cases where the statute excluded the duty of taking care. The duty to take reasonable care to prevent danger to the public was present throughout; the date of the erection of an obstruction and the purpose for which it was intended to be used (apart from special circumstances or special language in the statute), were immaterial. So long as the streets were properly lit, the duty was *ipso facto* performed, but when the street lighting was suspended for any reason, whether by lighting restrictions, the exercise of an option on the part of the local authority not to light, or accidental breakdown, it became the duty of the local authority to take such steps to safeguard the public by special danger lights or otherwise, as in the circumstances of the case were reasonably possible.

The respondents were responsible for the shelter and were under a duty to take reasonable steps to warn the public of its existence and that duty was not performed, and they were liable to the appellant.

Appeal allowed.

[15.44]   Whiting v Middlesex County Council and Harrow Urban District Council

[1948] 1 KB 162, [1947] 2 All ER 758, [1948] LJR 242, 112 JP 74, 63 TLR 614, 92 Sol Jo 41, 46 LGR 136   Croom-Johnson J

A motorcyclist during the hours of darkness when public lighting was unrestricted, collided with an air-raid shelter which was built partially on the footway to the extent of about 1ft and jutted out into the roadway for about another 6ft. It was near a street lamp which threw a shadow into the roadway causing a pool of darkness. An electric bulb showing a red light was built in, protected from outside by a wire mesh grill, and inside two screws would have to be removed to remove the red glass covering the lamp. The lamp was for some reason extinguished. The light had been destroyed over and over again by mischievous persons, and other accidents had occurred. The defendants ordered workpeople to put the light back, but it was repeatedly destroyed to the knowledge of the defendants.

HELD: The defendants had not taken reasonable steps. What they did was equivalent to taking no steps at all. The duty is not a duty to light but a duty to take reasonable steps to prevent the obstruction becoming a danger to the public; to ensure that a warning is given. Lighting is no doubt the obvious and simplest measure of precautions during the hours of darkness.

'Properly lit' (see *Fisher v Ruislip-Northwood Urban District Council and Middlesex County Council* (at para [15.43])) applies when the street lighting is effective to fulfil the duty. Here the public lighting resulted in something like a trap and the structure remained a danger. The defendants could not say – we will put the lighting back and, until somebody destroys it again, we have performed our duty. The defendants were liable.

[15.45] Murray v Southwark Borough Council

(1966) 65 LGR 145   MacKenna J

In a street in Rotherhithe, London, reasonably well lit by sodium lighting of orange colour, the claimant saw lines of red lamps dividing the road into two lanes. He was using only the sidelights of his car. He drove into the nearside lane, which was out of use for repairs, and though finding the surface rough drove on for ten yards or so until the front wheels fell into an excavation a foot deep. Some hooligans had removed a trestle and lamps which had been placed across the entrance to the nearside lane by the defendant highway authority to divert traffic into the offside lane.

HELD: The claimant was not negligent either in not using headlights or in failing to see the excavation. The defendant was negligent in not providing enough watchmen in an area where hooliganism was common.

[15.46] Lilley v British Insulated Callenders Construction Co Ltd

(1968) 67 LGR 224, CA

The claimant was injured when at about 10.50 pm his car collided with an obstruction left in the road by the defendant. The claimant said there were no lights or guard rails round the obstruction. The defendant brought evidence that at 8.30 pm barriers were in position and lights were burning.

HELD, ON APPEAL: The real issue was whether the defendant ought to have had a man to inspect the lights periodically during the night. There was evidence that the defendant did so at their main sites, but this accident had taken place in a quiet residential road. The defendant had taken reasonable precautions and was under no obligation to send a man to inspect the site.

[15.47] Maher v Hurst

(1969) 113 Sol Jo 167, 67 LGR 367, CA

On the Watford by-pass, which was a road wide enough to take three lines of traffic, asphalting contractors were spreading asphalt by means of a large machine which spread a strip 10ft wide. It operated on one lane at a time leaving the other two lanes open for traffic. The contractors had put the usual warning signs out to warn oncoming traffic and so placed as to funnel the traffic into the two open lanes. The claimant, an employee of the contractors was standing at the side of the strip being spread, on the road surface of the middle lane which was being used by traffic. A lorry began to pass the roadworks using the middle lane with the spreader on its nearside. The driver saw a coach approaching at a time when a cloud of steam came up from the hot asphalt causing serious injury. The judge said the driver was going too fast but accepted the suggestion that the contractors should have put up a barrier of tripods on the middle lane to protect the claimant. He held the contractors three-quarters to blame.

HELD: The contractors were not to blame at all. They were carrying out the usual system for such work by which two lanes were left clear for traffic. There was no evidence of similar accidents. If tripods were put in the middle lane traffic, on this very important road, would be reduced to one line. It would cause such inconvenience to the public that it should not be done unless the risk to the men was so great as to warrant it. There was no evidence of such risk. The accident was caused solely by the driver's negligence in driving too fast.

(C)   CONSTRUCTION OF HIGHWAY

[15.48]   **Great North Eastern Railway Ltd v Hart**
[2003] EWHC 2450 (QB)
[2003] All ER (D) 506 (Oct), QB

The defendant was the driver of the vehicle that caused the Selby rail crash in February 2001. The defendant had fallen asleep at the wheel of his Land Rover, which veered off the motorway and landed on railway tracks in the path of an oncoming train. Proceedings were brought by the claimant against the defendant for damage to rolling stock, rail infrastructure and consequential losses.

The defendant's insurers paid out approximately £22 million to various claimants and sought a contribution under s 1(1) of the Civil Liability (Contribution) Act 1978 from the Secretary of State for negligence in failing to erect sufficient crash barriers along the motorway.

The defendant's expert contended that the barrier should have been up to 100m long. The barrier in place at the time of the accident measured 62.7m. The minimum length of safety fence prescribed by the Department of Transport standards was 30m. The bridge that carried the motorway over the railway line had been constructed in 1974.

The department submitted that they owed no duty of care to prevent the egress of a vehicle from the carriageway to avoid either physical injury or property damage to those off the highway.

HELD: The court dismissed the claim for contribution. The court held that the reasonably safe length for the safety fence was site specific. The expert's submission did not establish that the professional judgment made in 1974 with regard to the length of the barrier was negligent.

However, the court highlighted that the main railway line presented an exceptionally high hazard and if the department had erected no safety fence or an unreasonably short safety fence, having regard to the foreseeable consequences of the egress of a vehicle from the motorway onto the railway line, the department would have been in breach of duty.

[15.49]   **King v Department of Transport, Local Government and the Regions**
[2003] EWCA Civ 730
[2003] All ER (D) 352 (May)

See para [15.27].

(D)   ROAD SIGNS

[15.50]   **Bird v Pearce (Somerset County Council third party)**
[1979] RTR 369, 77 LGR 753, CA

See para [15.24].

[15.51]   **Gorringe v Calderdale Metropolitan Borough Council**

[2002] EWCA Civ 595

[2002] RTR 446, (2002) 22 LS Gaz R 36, CA; affd [2004] 2 All ER 326, [2004]
1 WLR 1057, HL

See para [15.14].

(I)   DANGEROUS POSITION OF ROAD SIGNS

[15.52]   **Levine v Morris**

[1970] 1 All ER 144, [1970] 1 WLR 71, 113 Sol Jo 798, [1970] RTR 93, CA

The first defendant driving a car on a main road towards a roundabout in heavy
rain skidded and crashed into massive concrete columns supporting a road sign
erected by the Ministry of Transport, killing a passenger. He was held 75% to blame
and the Ministry 25%.

HELD: The Ministry's appeal was dismissed. They owed a duty to take reasonable
care, when there were sites for signs equally good as regards visibility, not to select
the one which involved greater hazards to the motorist. It was well known that at
high speeds there was a risk of motorists going off the road in bad weather. The
chances of such accidents should always be borne in mind by the Ministry and the
extent of such chances assessed. In the present case anyone skilled in road design
would foresee that drivers who had not the fullest degree of skill might leave the
road. The danger could have been averted by siting the sign where the risk was
diminished.

(E)   LIGHTING

[15.53]   **Sheppard v Glossop Corpn**

[1921] 3 KB 132, [1921] All ER Rep 61, CA

The defendant had placed a lamp in a position that was dangerous when not
lighted. The lamp was extinguished every night soon after 9.00pm in accordance
with a resolution passed by the authority.

HELD: The legislation confers upon urban authorities a discretion, but imposes on
them no obligation to light the streets in their districts; consequently the defendant
was not bound to continue to light the street; and having done nothing to make
the street dangerous they were under no obligation whether by lighting or
otherwise, to give warning of danger.

Note—See also *Burton v West Suffolk CC* (see para [15.54]).

[15.54]   **Burton v West Suffolk County Council**

[1960] 2 QB 72, [1960] 2 All ER 26, [1960] 2 WLR 745, 124 JP 273, 104 Sol Jo
349, 58 LGR 175, CA

The claimant was injured when his car skidded, without negligence on his part, on
a road covered, at the place of the accident, by a thin film of ice. The defendant,
who was the highway authority, had carried out some road drainage work some
months previously by which the drainage had been improved, but there was still a
tendency to flooding and the road surface tended to be damp from water which

ran off the adjoining land. If more drainage work had been done this tendency would have been reduced and the accident would probably not have occurred. The claimant claimed damages on the grounds:

(1)   that the failure to complete the drainage work amounted to misfeasance;

(2)   that the defendant failed to give warning of the dangerous state of the road.

HELD: (1) If a highway authority does work on a road by way of repair or reconstruction, it must be done properly and in such a way as not to cause danger on the road, but this does not mean that where some work has been done and done properly to improve the drainage of the road the defendant should be held liable for failing to do further work, which would result in further improvement of the drainage. It was not misfeasance but non-feasance.

(2)   The defendant was under no duty to warn the claimant of the icy conditions of the road.

(F)   OBSTRUCTIONS TO VISIBILITY

Section 79 of Highways Act 1980

[15.55]
79   Prevention of obstruction to view at corners

(1)   Where, in the case of a highway maintainable at the public expense, the highway authority for the highway deem it necessary for the prevention of danger arising from obstruction to the view of persons using the highway to impose restrictions with respect to any land at or near any corner or bend in the highway or any junction of the highway with a road to which the public has access, the authority may, subject to the provisions of this section, serve a notice, together with a plan showing the land to which the notice relates—

(a)   on the owner or occupier of the land, directing him to alter any wall (other than a wall forming part of the structure of a permanent edifice), fence, hoarding, paling, tree, shrub or other vegetation on the land so as to cause it to conform with any requirements specified in the notice; or

(b)   on every owner, lessee and occupier of the land, restraining them either absolutely or subject to such conditions as may be specified in the notice from causing or permitting any building, wall, fence, hoarding, paling, tree, shrub or other vegetation to be erected or planted on the land.

[15.56]   Stovin v Wise
[1996] AC 923, [1996] 3 All ER 801, [1996] 3 WLR 388, [1996] RTR 354

See para [15.26].

[15.57]   Gorringe v Calderdale Metropolitan Borough Council
[2002] EWCA Civ 595

[2002] RTR 446, (2002) 22 LS Gaz R 36, CA; affd [2004] 2 All ER 326, [2004] 1 WLR 1057, HL

See para [15.14].

(G)   DEFENCE TO STATUTORY OBSTRUCTION

[15.58]   Great Central Rly Co v Hewlett
[1916] 2 AC 511, 85 LJKB 1705, 115 LT 349, 32 TLR 707, 60 Sol Jo 678, HL

A railway company erected in the public highway gate posts from which collapsible steel gates could be run across the road so as to close the entrance to the station yard. These posts were erected by the company in contravention of their special Act and in 1901 were judicially held to be an obstruction to the highway. In 1902 the company obtained an Act which empowered them to 'maintain' the posts and gates and to replace them when necessary on the same site. A licensed taxicab driver, while lawfully driving his cab on a dark rainy night along the public highway into the station yard, collided with one of these posts, which was practically invisible owing to the darkening of the street in compliance with the Reduction of Lighting Regulations and thereby damaged his cab. The post was in the condition in which it was at the time of the passing of the Act in 1902. An action was brought by the cab driver against the railway company for damages for negligence.

HELD: The accident arose, not from any overt act of the company, but from the existence of the gate post which had been legalised by the Act of 1902, coupled with the diminution of light necessitated by the exigencies of the War; the mere power to maintain the post imposed no obligation on the company to take reasonable precautions to warn the public of its existence; and the company was not guilty of negligence.

(H)   OTHER DANGERS

[15.59]   Manchester Corpn v Markland
[1936] AC 360, [1935] All ER Rep 667, 104 LJKB 480, HL

The Manchester Corporation was the statutory authority for the supply of water. A service pipe in a road burst and caused a pool of water to form in the road. The water lay unheeded for three days. On the third day a frost occurred, the water froze and ice formed and a motor car skidded and knocked down and killed a man. The Corporation was not informed until after this accident that the service pipe had burst.

HELD: The driver of the car was not guilty of negligence, but the Corporation was liable for not having taken prompt steps to attend to the leak and so to prevent the road from becoming dangerous to traffic.

[15.60]   Caseley v Bristol Corpn
[1944] 1 All ER 14, CA

The duty of an occupier of land is to fence any dangerous excavation adjoining the highway, and this may extend to a danger close to, though not actually adjoining the highway.
   A man wandered in a fog from the highway and fell into a dock basin 47ft from the highway.

HELD: There was no duty to fence unless the danger was so near to the highway that a man making a false step, or overcome by temporary giddiness, would fall into the excavation.

[15.61] **Lambie v Western Scottish Motor Traction Co**
1944 SC 415

Ice formed on the pavement from washing of buses in a neighbouring garage. A pedestrian slipped on the ice and was injured.

HELD: The bus company were liable.

[15.62] **Almeroth v W E Chivers & Sons Ltd**
[1948] 1 All ER 53, 92 Sol Jo 71, CA

Contractors left a small pile of slates by the kerb, which was between 4 and 6 inches high. The pile did not overtop the kerb. The claimant crossing the road in daylight tripped over the pile which he had not previously seen and did not notice as he was stepping up on to the kerb, and was injured. There was no evidence that the defendant's work could not be carried on in any other way.

Lewis J held the heap constituted a nuisance but that the accident was due solely to the negligence of the claimant because he did not see the pile.

HELD, ON APPEAL: A pedestrian is not bound to keep his eyes on the ground or look constantly down to his feet to see whether or not there was any obstacle in his path. The small heap did not cause an obstruction in that it prevented or impeded the flow of traffic or the passage of pedestrians, but it constituted a nuisance which might easily not be noticed by a reasonably careful person. There was no evidence of negligence of the claimant. The defendant was liable for negligence and nuisance.

Appeal allowed.

[15.63] **Holling v Yorkshire Traction Co Ltd**
[1948] 2 All ER 662   Oliver J

The second defendant was the owner of coke ovens on the north side of and about 50 yards from the main road from Sheffield to Manchester. The operations produced masses of steam and smoke about every three-quarters of an hour. In normal weather the clouds of vapour rose and blew over the road at a height which did not inconvenience traffic, but on comparatively rare occasions they passed low over the road.

On 22 February 1947, at about 3.00 pm, an omnibus of the first defendant's and a private car travelling in opposite directions collided in the middle of a particularly dense cloud of grey smoke and steam, which amounted to complete obscurity. The omnibus driver could not see the car even after he had run into it. Two passengers in the car were killed and their widows brought proceedings against both defendants.

HELD: There was no negligence of the driver of the private car.

With regard to the second defendant, the discharge of vapour was a nuisance. It was not an incident of the ordinary and lawful use of land, nor a case of lawful user of the highway. The smoke clouds had persisted all day and were obvious. The second defendant was also negligent. They could have posted a man at each of the affected areas to warn traffic.

As to the first defendant, the accident occurred during one of the most severe winters in human memory. The road surface was extremely treacherous and dangerous demanding the utmost care from drivers. Any sudden application of the brakes unless the speed was very moderate would certainly precipitate a skid. Visibility apart from the smoke was quite good. The omnibus driver was negligent:

(1)   in driving on the wrong side of the road;
(2)   in going too fast; and
(3)   in failing to observe and guard against the vapour cloud in time to take effective action.

[15.64]   Rollingson v Kerr

[1958] CLY 2427

A collision occurred between two vehicles going in opposite directions on a straight stretch of road. The defendant's servant had lit a bonfire of hedge clippings, causing dense smoke to blow across the road, and it was in the midst of this that the collision took place. The judge found the defendant guilty of negligence and the defence of *volenti non fit injuria* failed. Neither driver was guilty of contributory negligence.

Holling v Yorkshire Traction Co Ltd (at para [15.63]) followed; *Heywood v London North Eastern Rly Co* (1926) Times, 1 December not followed.

[15.65]   Hall & Co Ltd v Ham Manor Farms Ltd

(1966) 116 L Jo 838, Chichester CC   Judge Talbot

The claimant's lorry collided with another lorry in thick smoke on the main Worthing-Chichester road. The smoke came from the defendant's adjacent field where stubble was being burnt; it was patchy but in one area visibility on the road was reduced practically to nil.

HELD: (1) In so far as the claim lay in negligence it failed because the defendant's servants had taken all reasonable precautions to avoid any dangers and the enveloping of the road with thick smoke was not only foreseen but was of short duration and was a temporary hazard, which could be seen by those travelling along the road.

(2)   If an action lay in nuisance it could do so only as a public nuisance from which the claimant had suffered damage. It was impossible to hold that the thick smoke, which covered the road for such a short space of time could be classed as such an interference with the public right as to warrant it being classed as a public nuisance; the facts were wholly different from *Holling v Yorkshire Traction Co Ltd* (at para [15.63]).

(3)   The rule in *Rylands v Fletcher* was not applicable where the defendants were making an ordinary and proper use of their land.

Judgment for the defendant.

[15.66]   Amos v Glamorgan County Council

(1967) 66 LGR 166, CA

The claimant, a youth of 19, was riding his motorcycle when he collided with the defendant's stationary fire engine. The accident happened in broad daylight. The fire engine was properly parked at the kerb, having been called to a fire at a nearby house. It had been there only two minutes or so and had two blue flashing lights on top. The claimant had a view of it for at least 80 yards. There was heavy rain and the claimant was not wearing his spectacles. The Commissioner of Assize found the defendant one-half to blame for omitting to put a red warning light on the road to give oncoming traffic early warning of the presence of the fire engine.

HELD, ON APPEAL: The defendant was not to blame at all. The fire brigade had to give priority to those in peril from fire and in the circumstances the flashing signal from the fire engine was a sufficient warning of its presence. Bad weather conditions did not justify a motorcyclist for failing to keep a proper look-out; they required him to proceed more carefully.

[15.67]   Salsbury v Woodland

[1970] 1 QB 324, [1969] 3 All ER 863, [1969] 3 WLR 29, 113 Sol Jo 327, CA

The first defendant was the owner of a house adjoining a public highway. He wished to have a hawthorn tree removed, which stood in the front garden 28ft from the roadway. His wife found some tree-fellers and engaged one of them (the second defendant) to do the job. He failed to lop the branches sufficiently before bringing the tree down and as a result it fell and broke two telephone wires running to the house from a post on the other side of the road. The wires hung across the roadway and the claimant, a bystander, went to remove them. Before he reached them he saw the third defendant coming in his car at fast speed towards the wires. He flung himself down on the grass verge to avoid being struck by the wires and injured his back. The second defendant did not contest the action. The judge held the first defendant was liable for the second defendant's negligence even though he was an independent contractor. He said that when the very act which is required to be done by the independent contractor contains a risk of injury to others, the principal is liable if injury results from negligence in performing it.

HELD, ON APPEAL: The judge's statement of principle was too wide. The first defendant was not himself negligent and could not be liable unless the case was within the special categories of case in which the principal was liable for the contractor's lack of care in doing the work. Only two such categories were relevant to the present case:
   (1)   'extra hazardous acts' – those acts so hazardous that the law has seen fit to impose direct liability on the principal. The present case did not come into that category. The job, if done with elementary caution by skilled men, presented no hazard to anyone at all;
   (2)   dangers created in a highway. Such cases are all found on analysis to be cases where the work being done was in a highway and of a character that would have been a nuisance unless authorised by statute. This case was not one of work done in a highway. There was no sound authority for saying that there is an additional class of case of liability where the principal commissions work to be done *near* a highway.

[15.68]   Davies v Carmarthenshire County Council

[1971] RTR 112, CA

The claimant was driving her car up a hill at about 17mph into the setting sun. The road had recently been widened by the defendant, who had left a lamp post in its original position about 5ft out from the new edge of the road. The claimant completely failed to see it and drove straight into it. The county court judge held the defendant wholly to blame. The case was appealed on the issue of contributory negligence.

HELD: The claimant was not so dazzled by the sun that she had no visibility at all. If she were then it was negligent to go ahead except at a minimal pace. She was not driving completely blind and should have seen the lamp post at the speed she was travelling and avoided it. But the blameworthiness of the defendant in leaving the obstacle in the road without any sufficient warning to motorists was very much greater. Liability was apportioned 80% to the defendant, 20% to the claimant.

[15.69] **Perkins v Glyn**

[1976] RTR ixn, [1976] CLY 1883

The claimant, riding a motorcycle, collided with a stationary car when his vision was obscured by smoke from stubble burning in a field owned by the defendant. The smoke was blowing in gusts across the road for a distance of 150 yards or so.

HELD: (1) Burning stubble was not a non-natural use of land.
    (2)   The defendant was not negligent. He could not always wait until the wind was blowing away from the road; warning was not necessary as the smoke was visible a mile away and the claimant had already ridden through 100 yards of it.
    (3)   On the question of nuisance, a motorist must expect to be obstructed occasionally and the defendant could not be said to have set a trap. The claim failed (per Judge Pennant).

[15.70] **Hilder v Associated Portland Cement Manufacturers Ltd**

[1961] 3 All ER 709, [1961] 1 WLR 1434, 105 Sol Jo 725, 179 Estates Gazette 445 Ashworth J

The defendant allowed its field adjoining a busy road to be used as a playing field by children. The field was separated from the road by a 3ft wall and a line of poplar trees. Two boys aged nine and ten were playing with a football using a poplar tree as one goal post and a stick as the other. In the course of the game one of the boys kicked the ball on to the road. The claimant's husband was riding by on a motorcycle and was thrown off as a result of the ball and was killed.

HELD: The defendant was liable in negligence. The test was whether the defendant was shown to have failed to take reasonable care in all the circumstances. The relevant circumstances included the situation of the field and the road, the amount of traffic using the road, the ages of the children using the field, the nature of their amusements and the frequency with which the field was used. A reasonable man would come to the conclusion, on the facts given in evidence, that there was a risk of damage to persons using the road which was not so small that he could disregard it.

5.   NEW ROADS AND STREET WORKS ACT 1991

[15.71]   *Note*—The duty to maintain the highway under s 41(1) of the Highways Act 1980 is absolute and cannot be delegated. Nevertheless, where *prima facie* liability is established against the highway authority it may be entitled to an indemnity if contractors were working on site at the time of the accident. The highway authority will need to demonstrate that:
    (a)   it used independent contractors to carry out the works;
    (b)   it exercised reasonable care when choosing the contractors;
    (c)   the contractors were *de facto* responsible for any alleged negligent act or omission; and
    (d)   the contractors were competent.

[15.72]   The Public Utilities Street Works Act 1950 has now been repealed and replaced by the New Roads and Street Works Act 1991. The 1991 Act brought changes for both local authorities and public utilities and their sub-contractors. The Act came into force on 1 January 1993 together with three codes of practice:

(i)   Specification for the Reinstatement of Openings in Highways.

(ii)   Measures necessary where apparatus is affected by Major Works (Diversionary Works).

(iii)   Code of Practice of Inspection.

(A)   REINSTATEMENT

New Roads and Street Works Act 1991, s 70

[15.73]
70.   Duty of undertaker to reinstate

(1)   It is the duty of the undertaker by whom streetworks are executed to reinstate the street.

(2)   The undertaker shall begin the reinstatement as soon after the completion of any part of the street works as is reasonably practicable and shall carry on and complete the reinstatement with all such dispatch as is reasonably practicable.

 (iii)   He shall before the end of the next working day after the day on which the reinstatement is completed inform the street authority that he has completed the reinstatement of the street stating whether the reinstatement is permanent or interim.

 (iv)   If it is interim he shall complete the permanent reinstatement of the street as soon as reasonably practicable and in any event within six months (or such other period as may be prescribed) from the date on which the interim reinstatement was completed; and he shall notify the street authority when he has done so.

 (v)   The permanent reinstatement of the street shall include in particular the reinstatement of features designed to assist people with a disability.

Interim reinstatement is defined in the Codes of Practice as 'the orderly placement and proper compaction of reinstatement layers to finished surface level including some temporary materials'.

Permanent reinstatement is defined as 'the orderly placement and proper compaction of reinstatement layers up to and including the finished level'.

Under s 71 of the 1991 Act the standard of reinstatement must conform with the Approved Code of Practice (the Specification for the Reinstatement of Openings in Highways) which sets out general performance requirements and detailed reinstatement, inspections, methods and materials for various types of roads.

(1)   GUARANTEE PERIOD

[15.74]   Section 1.2.1 of the Specification for the Reinstatement of Openings in Highways requires the undertaker to ensure that:

(a)   the interim reinstatement conforms to prescribed standards until the permanent reinstatement is completed; and that

(b)   the permanent guarantee period shall run for two years following completion of the reinstatement or for three years in the case of deep openings.

The effect of the new legislation therefore is to shift the burden of responsibility for reinstatement from the highway authority to the undertaker.

Notwithstanding that, the street authority may still be at risk for any residual responsibility they have retained for supervising or signing off the temporary or permanent reinstatement works or for carrying out periodical inspections.

CHAPTER 16

Nuisance, Level Crossings and Trees

1.   MEANING OF NUISANCE

(A)   PUBLIC NUISANCE

[16.1]   *R v Mathias* (1861) 2 F & F 570, per Byles J:
(a)   an act or omission which makes the highway dangerous or less convenient for public passage;
(b)   causing or permitting an unreasonable obstruction to the highway.

(B)   WHAT CONSTITUTES A NUISANCE?

[16.2]   Pope v Fraser and Southern Rolling and Wire Mills Ltd
(1938) 55 TLR 324, 83 Sol Jo 135

A lorry was on a highway loaded with carboys of sulphuric acid. Without the driver's knowledge and without negligence, one carboy became cracked and the acid ran into the road. After going some distance, the driver was told of the leakage, but did not return for nearly half an hour and took no steps to warn persons on the highway of the danger. In the interval, the claimant on a motorcycle saw the patch of acid extending across the road, but thought it was water. His machine skidded in the acid and he fell and was burned.

HELD: The driver could have discovered the leakage when he stopped and it was his duty to go back and warn traffic, and the defendant was liable.

[16.3]   Dymond v Pearce

[1972] I QB 496, [1972] I All ER 1142, [1972] 2 WLR 633, 116 Sol Jo 62, [1972] RTR 169, CA

The defendant's driver fetched a large loaded lorry from its depot at 6.00 pm and parked it near his home ready for an early start the next morning. It was parked on the outside of a shallow bend on an urban road that had two carriageways each 25ft wide. Prior to it becoming light, the driver turned on the lights. The lorry was under a streetlight and was visible for at least 200 yards to approaching traffic. It was 7½ft wide leaving at least 16ft of the carriageway unobstructed. After light a motorcyclist, looking round at someone on the pavement, failed to see the lorry and crashed into it. The motorcyclist's passenger was injured. He based his claim on two grounds:
  (1)   that the lorry was negligently parked; and
  (2)   that the lorry was an obstruction and amounted to a common law nuisance, actionable without proof of negligence.
The trial judge held that:
  (1)   in the manner in which the lorry was parked there was no foreseeable danger and no negligence;
  (2)   the mere parking of the lorry on the nearside of the road where it was not foreseeably dangerous did not amount to nuisance at common law;
  (3)   the sole cause of the accident was the motorcyclist's failure to look where he was going.

HELD, ON APPEAL: (1) The judge was right in finding that the defendant and its driver had not been negligent in parking the lorry at that place.

(2) There were two categories of nuisance on a highway, an obstruction which constituted a danger and an obstruction without danger. It was important to remember the two categories when looking at the authorities. In neither category was it necessary to prove negligence as an ingredient, and in both, proof of what was *prima facie* a nuisance laid the onus on the defendant to prove justification. Neither category was actionable unless the claimant could prove damage had been caused to him. Leaving aside the special position of frontagers (and the driver in this case was not a frontager) the common law rights of users of the highway were normally confined to use for passage and repassage and incidents reasonably associated with such use. Leaving a large vehicle on the highway *prima facie* resulted in a nuisance, for it narrowed the highway: in the present case the lorry constituted a nuisance at the time the motorcyclist ran into it but that did not render the defendant liable to the claimant because, as the judge had found, the nuisance was not the cause of the accident – the sole cause was the motorcyclist's negligence. In most cases that was an inevitable conclusion once negligence on the part of a stationary vehicle was negatived.

HELD: Edmund Davies LJ held that a person creating a highway obstruction must be alert to the possibility that weather changes or the actions of third parties might convert what was originally a danger-free obstruction into a grave traffic hazard. In the present case the lorry parked as it was did not present a danger to those using the highway in the manner in which they could be reasonably expected to use it.

Appeal dismissed.

Note—In *Dymond v Pearce* Sachs LJ considered that there were two categories of nuisance: either an obstruction which was not dangerous, or one which was. Edmund Davies LJ in the same case thought an obstruction in a highway did not become a nuisance unless it was shown to be dangerous. This difference of view was alluded to in the cases of *Wills v T F Martin (Roof Contractors) Ltd* (Forbes J) (see para [16.5]) and *Drury v Camden Borough Council* (May J) (see para [16.6]).

[16.4] Saper v Hungate Builders Ltd

[1972] RTR 380 Cantley J

A driver was driving his car in the hours of darkness along a residential road with the claimant as passenger when he collided with a builder's skip, which he did not see in time to avoid. The skip had been placed partly on the grass verge and partly on the roadway by the owners who had delivered it on the instructions of the hirers. The hirers were builders doing work on a nearby house. They arranged for the house-owner, their customer, to put a lamp at each offside corner of the skip. Two motorists passing the skip two to three hours before the accident had seen the skip only just in time to swerve and avoid it.

HELD: The provision of two lamps that so many persons failed to see was not adequate lighting. An object like a skip was very dangerous unless proper warning was given by lighting, which would be readily and instantly apparent. This skip in its position and condition was a nuisance in the highway. The fact that the driver failed to see it was not fatal to his claim, but driving at a reasonable speed and being alert as a driver should be at night; he should have seen it. The driver was 40% to blame. The builders were liable as having taken detailed charge of the safety precautions. The owners of the skip were equally to blame with the builders having put the obstruction in the carriageway and left it there; they were under a duty to light it and could not escape liability by delegating the duty to someone else. The house owner was not liable; he had merely done what he was asked to do.

Note—In *Dymond v Pearce* (at para [16.3]) Sachs LJ considered there were two categories of nuisance: either an obstruction which was not dangerous, or one which was. Edmund Davies LJ in the same case thought an obstruction in a highway did not become a nuisance unless it was shown to be dangerous. This difference of view was alluded to in the following two cases.

[16.5] Wills v TF Martin (Roof Contractors) Ltd

[1972] RTR 368, (1972) 116 Sol Jo 145 Forbes J

Whilst riding a moped in the hours of darkness along a residential road, which was poorly lit, the claimant collided with a skip that he had not seen. It was on the nearside of the roadway and the claimant said it was unlighted. He was injured and claimed damages in nuisance and negligence against the roofing contractors who had put it there.

HELD: Applying *Dymond v Pearce* (at para [16.3]), you have first to consider whether the presence of the skip on the highway is a nuisance. If the claimant satisfies that burden he has still to show, according to Edmund Davies LJ (in *Dymond's* case), that the obstruction was also a dangerous obstruction. The last link in the chain is that the claimant must satisfy the court that the obstruction was at least a cause of the accident. A skip placed on a highway is in a different category from a parked vehicle. It has no business to be on a highway at all; to deposit a container of that character on the highway creates a nuisance. The skip was a nuisance because it was occupying a section of the highway which ought not to have been obstructed in that way. If unlit in this position on the road it would be potentially dangerous, but on the evidence it was not established that it was unlighted. The sole cause of the accident was the claimant's failure to look where he was going and the claim failed.

[16.6]   Drury v Camden Borough Council

[1972] RTR 391   May J

The defendant council had placed a skip against the nearside kerb of a one-way street 35ft wide. It was 6ft wide and of much the same colour as the road surface and unlighted. The street lighting was adequate but not good. The claimant riding a scooter in the early morning before it was light failed to see the skip in time and collided with it.

HELD: As a matter of law, adopting Sachs LJ's view in *Dymond v Pearce* (at para [16.3]), the skip was an obstruction and as such constituted a nuisance; it did not matter either that it occupied only 6ft of a 35ft wide road, nor that the street lighting was or was not good. If the view of Edmund Davies LJ in *Dymond's* case was correct, and in any event on the alternative claim in negligence, it was necessary to decide further whether the obstruction was dangerous. On the facts and the evidence it was. The final question was one of causation; did the presence of the skip play any causative part in the occurrence of the accident or was the claimant's failure to keep a proper lookout the sole cause? Bearing in mind all the circumstances, the nature of the road, the lighting and the amount of traffic which had avoided the skip, the existence of the nuisance did play a part but the claimant was 50% to blame in failing to keep as good a lookout as he should.

[16.7]   Tysoe v Davies

[1984] RTR 88, [1983] Crim LR 684   Skinner J

The defendant was driving a horsebox which was emitting dense clouds of smoke. A Land Rover was travelling behind the horsebox. The claimant riding a moped came up behind the Land Rover and, thinking it was that vehicle that was causing the smoke, overtook it. Because of the smoke he failed to see the horsebox and crashed into it, sustaining injury. He claimed in negligence and public nuisance.

HELD: The defendant was negligent in driving the horsebox when it was dangerous to do so. It would have been neither difficult nor expensive to have it towed. As to public nuisance the claimant was entitled to sue because:
   (1)   the clouds of smoke made the highway less commodious to other road users;
   (2)   they were a dangerous obstruction; and
   (3)   the defendant had acted unreasonably. The claimant was 20% to blame for failing to keep a proper look out.

2.   HIGHWAY NUISANCES

[16.8]   Highways Act 1980, s 130
130   Protection of public rights
   (1)   It is the duty of the highway authority to assert and protect the rights of the public to the use and enjoyment of any highway for which they are the highway authority, including any roadside waste which forms part of it.

(2)   Any council may assert and protect the rights of the public to the use and enjoyment of any highway in their area for which they are not the highway authority, including any roadside waste which forms part of it.

(3)   Without prejudice to subsections (1) and (2) above, it is the duty of a council who are a highway authority to prevent, as far as possible, the stopping up or obstruction of—

(a)   the highways for which they are the highway authority, and

(b)   any highway for which they are not the highway authority, if, in their opinion, the stopping up or obstruction of that highway would be prejudicial to the interests of their area.

(4)   Without prejudice to the foregoing provisions of this section, it is the duty of a local highway authority to prevent any unlawful encroachment on any roadside waste comprised in a highway for which they are the highway authority.

(5)   Without prejudice to their powers under section 222 of the Local Government Act 1972, a council may, in performance of their functions under the foregoing provisions of this section, institute legal proceedings in their own name, defend any legal proceedings and generally take such steps as they deem expedient.

(6)   If the council of a parish or community or, in the case of a parish or community which does not have a separate parish or community council, the parish meeting or a community meeting, represent to a local highway authority—

(a)   that a highway as to which the local highway authority have the duty imposed by subsection (3) above has been unlawfully stopped up or obstructed, or

(b)   that an unlawful encroachment has taken place on a roadside waste comprised in a highway for which they are the highway authority,

it is the duty of the local highway authority, unless satisfied that the representations are incorrect, to take proper proceedings accordingly and they may do so in their own name.

(7)   Proceedings or steps taken by a council in relation to an alleged right of way are not to be treated as unauthorised by reason only that the alleged right is found not to exist.

3.   LEVEL CROSSINGS

(A)   PUBLIC CROSSINGS

(I)   NATURE OF PROTECTION OF PUBLIC CROSSINGS

[16.9]   Law v Railway Executive and Chigwell Urban District Council
[1949] WN 172, 65 TLR 288, 93 Sol Jo 251   Hallett J

A cyclist at 10.00 pm on 5 October 1949, collided with a pavement and wall which formed part of a sub-way substituted under statutory authority for a public level crossing. By agreement the county council built the wall and pavement; the railway company were responsible for maintenance of the sub-way and the council for lighting.

HELD: The railway company would not have been under any legal liability to light the gates, but that did not apply to the wall and pavement; there was no obligation on the council to light the road, the council and railway company were partners in the works and therefore shared in any liability. They had not taken all reasonable precautions to render it safe, and were liable. The claimant knew the obstruction was there and was also negligent. Liability was apportioned 50–50.

(B)   PRIVATE CROSSINGS

[16.10]   Knight v Great Western Rly Co
[1943] 1 KB 105, [1942] 2 All ER 286   Tucker J

There is a duty to take reasonable precautions, but the nature of the precaution and the degree of care required are not the same as for a public crossing and may vary very considerably. The difference is merely in the degree of care that is required in the circumstances. There may be cases where, owing to a sharp turn in the railway or the presence of a large number of trees in a cutting obstructing the view, precautions should be taken, but there is no rule that at any private crossing the railway company is bound to use special precautions of some kind.

The distance of vision owing to fog was limited to a space of from 30 to 50 yards, and the engine was proceeding at 30mph. The driver knew of the crossing and that cows were driven across it daily. He had blown his whistle at the whistle board 440 yards from the crossing. He had received the appropriate fog signal, that the line was clear from the railway point of view.

HELD: It was not negligent that the driver could not pull up within the distance of his vision.

Citing *Cliff v Midland Rly Co* (1870) LR 5 QB 258, 22 LT 382:

'The railway company are to work the railway in a reasonably proper manner; and in crossing a footway on a level the company are bound, as to the mode of working their railway, as to the rate of speed, the provision of men to give warning of approach, the position of warning signals such as a whistle board, and signalling or whistling, or other ordinary precautions to do everything reasonably necessary for the safety of persons crossing.'

[16.11]   Liddiatt v Great Western Rly Co
[1946] KB 545, [1946] 1 All ER 731, CA

The claimant's servant was driving eight cattle across a private accommodation crossing over a single track railway line. This crossing was 160 yards east of a public level crossing. There was a signal box, 1,030 yards and a signal 700 yards west of the public crossing. The public crossing gate and the signal were operated by a crossing keeper. The gate of the accommodation crossing on the south side, but not on the north side, was visible to the crossing keeper. The crossing keeper did not have any regard to the accommodation crossing.

HELD: The railway company was under no duty to place a watchman or keeper at the accommodation crossing; nor was there any evidence that the crossing was so placed as to impose on the railway company the duty to take some greater precaution at this spot than is usual in the normal working of a railway. The fact that it was only 160 yards from a public crossing did not enlarge or extend the obligations or duties of the company or the crossing keeper.

[16.12]   Smith v Smith and Railway Executive
[1948] WN 276, 92 Sol Jo 499   Hilbery J

The claimant was a passenger in a car driven by the first defendant in a private lane over a railway line of the second defendant's at an accommodation crossing. The gates were open to the lane. A train ran into the motor car and the claimant was injured. The lane had been regularly used by occupiers of the adjacent land and their servants and visitors. The railway company had constructed the gates to close the lane when a train was approaching and provided a hut for a servant whose duty was to open and shut the gates. The servant left duty at 6.00 pm and the accident occurred in daylight about 9.40 pm on 10 July 1941. About two years before the accident a swimming pool had been constructed about 100 yards from the crossing and the lane was largely used by private motorists visiting the pool and this must have been known to the railway company's servants, but they took no action to prevent it except to put up a notice near the crossing marked 'Beware of the trains.'

HELD: Citing Pickford J, in *Jenner v South East Rly Co* (1911) 105 LT 131, there was a duty cast on a railway company to take reasonable precautions at an accommodation crossing. The judge rejected the contention of the railway company that its only duty was to refrain from obstructing a right of way. *Johnson v London Midland and Scottish Rly Co* (7 May 1926, unreported) distinguished. In that case the claimant was the occupier of land adjacent to the road, he knew about the crossing and was guilty of contributory negligence. The judge found both defendants to blame, and apportioned the blame as to three-fifths to the railway company and two-fifths to the motor driver.

[16.13] Smith v London Midland and Scottish Rly
1948 SC 125, 1948 SLT 235, Ct of Sess

A railway company has a duty at every level crossing where members of the public have a right to be, to take all reasonable precautions in train operations (and perhaps in other respects) to reduce the danger to a minimum. The nature of the precautions required and the question whether the duty has been fulfilled depend on the circumstances of each case. *Cliff v Midland Rly Co* (1870) LR 5 QB 258, 22 LT 382, 34 JP 357, 18 WR 456 applied.

[16.14] Lloyds Bank Ltd v British Transport Commission
[1956] 3 All ER 291, [1956] 1 WLR 1279, 100 Sol Jo 748, CA

A railway built about one hundred years ago crossed a lane to a farm and four cottages and an accommodation crossing was provided for the occupants. Gates were installed, which were regularly closed but were occasionally left open. A ganger who patrolled the line daily inspected the gates and closed them if open. There was a distance of vision to the left for about 350 yards. Owing to the acute angle, a car driver would have the difficult task of looking behind across his left shoulder to see if anything was coming along the line.

The accident occurred when the driver of a car drove, with his headlights on, straight through the gates, which had been left open. When crossing the second line of rails the car was hit broadside by a train coming from his left, and the driver was killed. His widow brought a claim against the railway authorities and contended that the crossing had special peculiarities, which called for safeguards; that there was negligence in the management of the railway and also negligence of the engine driver; that there ought to have been a whistle board; that the driver ought to have seen the headlights of the car, and that the bend in the railway line and the crossing called for special precautions.

HELD: The railway authority had fulfilled its duty; the engine driver's look-out was properly directing his attention to the signals; he did whistle 175 yards from the crossing; the bend was immaterial as the car driver could see for 350 yards; the driving of a train and of a motor car were two different things. The learned judge was correct in finding that the engine driver was not negligent and that the accident was due solely to the negligence of the car driver in failing to stop in the 30ft between the gate and the actual line. The facts in the cases of *Smith v London Midland and Scottish Rly Co* (at para [16.13]) and *Lloyds Bank Ltd v Railway Executive* (at para [16.14]) were different.

Appeal dismissed.

[16.15]   Hazell v British Transport Commission

[1958] 1 All ER 116, [1958] 1 WLR 169, 102 Sol Jo 124   Pearson J

A farm tractor was being driven across an accommodation crossing, on a single branch line. On a stretch of 16 miles there were 33 level crossings most of which were accommodation crossings. Possibly two or three farm vehicles used the crossing each day. The gates were padlocked except when opened by a user. The crossing was so wide that the tractor could stand between the gates and the railway line. Shortly before the crossing the line ran round a left-hand bend with a slow down gradient of about 1 in 500. In ordinary weather the train could be seen several hundred yards away.

There was a bad fog with visibility varying from place to place. As the tractor was being driven over the line a train ran into it. The train driver had shut off steam and was coasting, there being a station about a mile or one and a half miles ahead, so that the sound of the exhaust blast had ceased; the line was wet so that the train made less noise than usual, and the effect of the fog was to smother the sound to some extent, but the train could have been heard by anyone at the crossing if there was no other noise, and the judge drew the inference that the tractor driver failed to switch off his engine.

HELD: The principle to be applied is that in the absence of special circumstances, the engine driver is not expected to reduce speed or whistle, and the Commission is not expected to erect a whistle-board. An engine driver is not expected to reduce speed to 5mph because of fog. If the engine driver is aware of something on, or likely to come on, the line, he must take proper steps to avoid an accident. There are no special circumstances in this case, and no liability on the Commission or the engine driver, and the action fails.

[16.16]   Kemshead v British Transport Commission

[1958] 1 All ER 119, [1958] 1 WLR 173, 102 Sol Jo 122, CA

An accommodation level crossing for a road leading to a farm and some farm cottages had a notice on the gates requiring users to shut and fasten the gates. The claimant was a passenger in a car going to the farm. He had used the crossing on at least twenty occasions and knew of the notice. The gates had been left open by some unknown person and apparently the car driver crossed without stopping. It was a foggy morning and as the car crossed the railway lines, a train ran into it. The claimant and driver were severely injured and another passenger was killed. The claimant alleged that no whistle was sounded and no indication was given of the approach of the train.

HELD: At an accommodation crossing there is no obligation on a railway company to supply watchmen or have signals or bells, nor to whistle unless there are special circumstances where people may reasonably be expected. Citing Scrutton LJ in *Burrows v Southern Rly Co* (1933) unreported (read by Tucker J in *Knight v Great Western Rly Co* (at para [16.10])) a sharp turn in the railway, or the presence of a large number of trees in a cutting obstructing the view might call for some reasonable precautions even at a private crossing. There was nothing calling for special precautions. The presence of fog calls for special precautions by the person crossing. There were no special conditions applying to this crossing. There must be judgment for the Commission.

[16.17]   Skeen v British Railways Board

[1976] RTR 281   Latey J

Three cottages were reached by crossing a railway at an accommodation crossing approached down a lane from which the railway could not be seen. At the crossing the visibility to the right along the railway was limited to 100 yards by a sharp curve. On 14 June a van was being driven over the crossing when it was hit by a train from the right travelling at about 50mph. The van driver and passenger were both killed. Though there had been no previous accidents the occupier of one of the cottages had complained to British Railways about seven weeks earlier about the danger at the crossing. A meeting had been held with British Railways representatives when it was agreed that the crossing was dangerous. Various safety precautions were canvassed such as the erection of whistle boards or the provision of a telephone to the signal box, but nothing had been done. The defendant pleaded that both the van driver and passenger were negligent in not having the passenger cross the line on foot and direct the driver from the other side, from which visibility of trains was 200 yards.

HELD: There was a duty on the defendant to take reasonable care not to imperil those using the crossing. What is reasonable depends on the particular circumstances of the crossing, its layout and any special dangers. The fact of there having been no previous accident was immaterial since the danger was admitted seven weeks earlier. Precautionary measures should have been taken as a matter of urgency. The direct telephone to the signal box was the best method as was in fact done after the accident. The defendant was liable in negligence. The passenger was not negligent since decisions are in the hands of the driver of a motor vehicle. The driver was not negligent in not sending the passenger across the line to direct him because the increase in visibility would have reduced the danger so minimally as to be insignificant.

4.   TREES

(A)   GENERAL

[16.18]   Noble v Harrison

[1926] 2 KB 332, 95 LJKB 813, Div Ct

A branch of a beech tree growing on the defendant's land overhung a highway at a height of 30ft above the ground. In fine weather the branch suddenly broke and fell upon the claimant's vehicle, which was passing along the highway. In an action by the claimant claiming in respect of the damage to his vehicle, the county court judge found that neither the defendant nor his servants knew that the branch was dangerous, and that the fracture was due to a latent defect not discoverable by any reasonably careful inspection, but he held that the defendant was liable:
   (1)   upon the principle of *Rylands v Fletcher* (1868) LR 3 HL 330; and
   (2)   for a nuisance.

HELD: Reversing the decision of the county court judge:

(1)   that the *Rylands v Fletcher* principle had no application, inasmuch as a tree was not in itself a dangerous thing, and to grow trees was one of the natural uses of the soil;

(2)   that the mere fact that the branch overhung the highway did not make it a nuisance seeing that it did not obstruct the free passage of the highway, and although the branch proved to be a danger the defendant was not liable, inasmuch as he had not created the danger and had no knowledge, actual or imputed, of its existence. (*Barker v Herbert* [1911] 2 KB 633 applied.) (Observations of Best J in *Earl of Lonsdale v Nelson* (1823) 2 B & C 302 and *Tarry v Ashton* (1876) 1 QBD 314, distinguished.)

[16.19]   Coachcraft v Lancegays Safety Glass Co
(1938) City Press, 15 July, City of London Ct

Repairers placed a car under a lime tree. Lime pollen fell or was driven on to the car by rain. The acid concentration from the lime pollen pitted and damaged the cellulose and lacquer treatment of the car body.

HELD: Repairers were negligent as bailees and liable for damage.

[16.20]   Brown v Harrison
[1947] WN 191, 177 LT 281, 63 TLR 484, CA

The claimant was walking along the highway when he was injured by the fall of a tree growing in a spinney on the side of the road. At about the time of the accident there was a gust of wind at 58mph registered at an observatory 10 or 15 miles away, and two other perfectly sound trees in the neighbourhood were blown down.

   The defendant owner of the tree was in the habit of passing the spinney daily and it never occurred to him that the tree was a source of danger or he would have removed the danger. It did not occur to anyone that there was any real likelihood of danger.

HELD: The tree was in a defective and, therefore, dangerous condition. There is no duty on the landowner to have a periodical examination by an expert. It is impossible to define the duty to call in expert advice and have expert examination. However, in the ordinary case a landlord discharges his duty if he takes reasonable steps to remove any dangers of which he becomes aware, but if there is a danger which is apparent, not only to the expert but to the ordinary layman, which the ordinary layman can see with his own eyes if he chooses to use them, and he fails to do so, and injury is occasioned to someone on the highway, the owner is responsible.

   The tree had the appearance of being dead at the top for many years. It was not quite dead all the way down, but the leaf in spring was very restricted and less than a normal healthy tree and did not blossom. The ordinary layman with ordinary powers of observation would have noted this, and that it could fall across the highway. In *Noble v Harrison* (at para [16.18]) it was said a tree in decay may become a dangerous object. If the owner knew of the danger and did not remedy it, his liability would be established beyond controversy. This tree by reason of its decay had become a dangerous object, sufficiently apparent to impose on the landowner the duty of taking precautionary measures. The defendant was liable: (1946) Birmingham Assizes, 11 December (Stable J).

HELD, ON APPEAL: The landowner's duty was correctly stated that if there was a danger apparent, not only to the expert, but to the ordinary layman, if he chose to notice it, the owner should take precautionary measures. A dying tree at a certain stage became a danger, which should be apparent to the ordinary landowner.

[16.21]   Caminer v Northern and London Investment Trust Ltd

[1951] AC 88, [1950] 2 All ER 486, 66 TLR (pt 2) 184, [1950] WN 361, 94 Sol Jo 518, HL

A large elm tree in the forecourt of a block of flats fell on a car passing along the highway. The wind was blowing in strong squally gusts from time to time but was not exceptional. The defendant became owners of the tree in 1940. The tree was a large, well-grown elm between 120 and 130 years old. After it fell it was evident that the base of the tree had been affected by a disease not uncommon in an elm tree of elm butt rot. The disease was of long standing and must have been in the roots long before the defendant became owners. There was nothing in the appearance of the tree to indicate that it was in any way diseased. The tree carried a crown of about 35ft. It had not been trimmed or lopped for a great many years. Elms are shallow-rooted trees and notoriously treacherous and apt to fall. The owners shortly before the accident had given orders to lop and top the trees in the forecourt and, but for the Easter holidays this tree would probably have been pollarded or topped before the accident. There was evidence that elm trees should be inspected every five to seven years.

HELD, ON APPEAL to the House of Lords: The defendant was not liable.

Per Lord Porter: I cannot accept the view that the defendants were negligent merely because they failed to call in an expert to advise as to the possible existence of an unsuspected and undiscoverable disease, even though an expert, if called in, might have recommended topping and lopping.

I do not regard the evidence as establishing that elm trees are so plainly a danger as to require their being lopped and topped lest they should fall, though to all external appearance they are sound and no inspection would raise a doubt as to their general condition.

Per Lord Oaksey: The defendant had performed its duty by employing a well-known firm of estate agents to manage this property and they in turn employed a timber contractor.

[16.22]   Quinn v Scott

[1965] 2 All ER 588, [1965] 1 WLR 1004, 109 Sol Jo 498   Glyn-Jones J

At a place where the Doncaster-Nottingham road runs alongside Clumber Park a belt of trees inside the park bordered the road. They included a beech tree about 200 years old having four or five limbs growing 70ft or so almost vertically from the top of a bole about 20ft high. On a windy day part of the tree split away from the rest and fell across the road causing a collision of vehicles in which the claimant was injured. The tree had reached an age at which decay could be apprehended. There was, before the accident, some appearance of unhealthiness in the thinness of the foliage and indications of die-back, but these had not been reported to the owners, the National Trust.

HELD: (1) A landowner on whose land this belt of trees stood, adjoining a busy highway, was under a duty to provide himself with skilled advice about the safety of the trees;

(2)   The National Trust had fulfilled this duty by employing a forestry adviser, a land agent, a forester and seven woodmen who inspected the tree several times a year; but

(3)   There had been a failure to report the signs of decay to the land agent and the Trust should have known of them;

(4)   A reasonable landowner with knowledge of these signs would have had the tree felled.

The National Trust must be held liable.

[16.23]   Lynch v Hetherton

[1991] 2 IR 405

The claimant was driving along the defendant's land when a tree fell and damaged his car. Externally this tree showed no signs of decay but was rotten on the inside. The trial judge found the defendant liable to the claimant but reduced the claimant's award for contributory negligence. The defendant appealed.

HELD: The claimant's claim should fail. The defendant regularly inspected his trees and exercised the degree of care which a reasonable and prudent landowner would have exercised in ensuring his trees were not a danger to the users of the highway.

[16.24]   Chapman v London Borough of Barking & Dagenham

[1998] CLY 4053, [1997] 2 EGLR 141

The claimant was severely injured when the cab of the van he was driving was crushed by a falling limb from a horse-chestnut tree. The limb had broken off the tree during high winds. At first instance the judge found in favour of the claimant on the basis that a defendant is liable for nuisance constituted by the state of his property if, by neglect of some duty he allowed it to arise and if, when it has arisen without his own act or default, he omits to remedy it within a reasonable time after he became aware of it.

The leading case relied on was *Noble v Harrison* (at para [16.18]).

The defendant appealed the decision on the judge's findings as to fact.

The tree, planted in the 1930s by the Borough, was beside a busy minor traffic route in East London. It stood between the road and the pavement in the verge. It had been catalogued in 1987 but not pruned thereafter. Substantial branches had fallen from the tree previously on at least four occasions. The defendant was also the highway authority and was under a duty to inspect the tree. There had been no programme of inspection for approximately ten years and the defendant had a reactive but not proactive programme in respect of tree maintenance. The tree was later found to be diseased.

HELD: The Court of Appeal held that there was evidence to justify the trial judge reaching the conclusions he did. Although it was the responsibility of the Court of Appeal to review the decision on the evidence, the court would not lose sight of the fact that the trial judge was in the best position to weigh conflicting evidence and arrive at the truth. The defendant had failed to carry out formal inspections of trees in high-risk areas between 1987 and the accident. The judge had preferred expert evidence that a climbing inspection should have been carried out. The criticisms of the judge's approach and reasoning were rejected summarily.

Appeal dismissed.

(B) VEHICLES COLLIDING WITH TREES

[16.25] Radley v London Passenger Transport Board

[1942] 1 All ER 433, 166 LT 285, 106 JP 164, 58 TLR 364, 86 Sol Jo
147 Humphreys J

On a country road an overhanging branch of a tree on the side of the road broke a window in a bus and injured a passenger. The accident occurred at midday, and the tree was clearly visible along the road. A witness said he had seen the defendant's buses brush against the trees on the road on several occasions. The defendant submitted no case and called no evidence.

HELD: This was a *prima facie* case of negligence and defendant was liable. It was immaterial that the obstruction was not on the ground. It was visible to the driver. It might be different if a branch broke off suddenly in a gale.

[16.26] Hale v Hants and Dorset Motor Services Ltd

[1947] 2 All ER 628, 46 LGR 50, CA

The claimant was a passenger on top of a bus. Just after the bus moved off from a stop, the near side upper deck came in contact with the branches of a tree standing on the edge of the pavement and glass on the upper deck was broken. A splinter entered the claimant's eye. He brought a claim against the bus company and the corporation.

The judge held that the corporation ought to have contemplated that a bus would pull close to the tree near a bus stop, and should have pruned a badly shaped tree leaning towards the highway. The road camber caused the bus to tilt slightly, but the bus would hit the overhanging branch in any event.

He held the corporation two-thirds, and the bus company one-third, to blame.

Both defendants appealed. On appeal it appeared from the evidence that the projection of the branches was 7½ and 6½ inches respectively. It was at night. There was a brilliant street lamp between the driver and the tree as he came round a roundabout.

HELD, ON APPEAL: The corporation had planted the tree on the side of the highway under the provisions of the Road Improvement Act 1925, s 1(1) (now replaced by the Highways Act 1980, s 96) which empowers a highway authority to cause trees to be planted in any highway maintainable by them. Section 1(2) (now replaced by the Highways Act 1980, s 96(6)) is as follows: 'No such tree ... shall be planted, laid out or erected ... allowed to remain in such a situation as to hinder the reasonable use of the highway by any person entitled to the use thereof.'

HELD: The passengers on the omnibus were persons entitled to the use of the highway, the omnibus was making reasonable use of it, the tree hindered reasonable use and the corporation had allowed the tree to remain in that position. It was not unreasonable for the driver to drive very close to the kerb. It was only the tree that made the danger. The driver was not to be blamed for not observing and estimating the overhang, but he knew the trees were potential sources of danger and should have acted on the footing that it might overhang and give it a wide berth.

Both appeals dismissed.

[16.27]   Lambourn v London Brick Co

(1950) 156 EG 146

The claimant's husband was killed in a collision with elm trees that had been blown across a road from the defendant's land.

HELD: There was nothing to indicate to the defendant that the trees were dangerous; the defendant was not liable.

[16.28]   J H Dewhurst Ltd v Ratcliffe

(1951) 101 L Jo 361   Judge Reid

The claimants' motor car, in daylight and clear weather, was being driven along a road 16 to 18ft wide at 20 to 25mph, when a single-deck omnibus approached from the opposite direction. The car driver in passing brushed the hedge on the near side with the car and collided with a tree stump nearly 4ft high which was 1 or 2 inches inside the hedge and hidden by the leaves and foliage. The claimants sued the defendant who was the owner and occupier of the farm adjoining the road. The tree stump was wholly on the defendant's land but did not overhang the road although it was less than 6 inches clear of it. The defendant trimmed the top and inside of the hedge and the local council cut back the hedge from the road.

HELD: The claim in negligence failed because the defendant owed no legal duty to the claimants. As regards nuisance, the car driver was not entitled to brush innocent looking leaves and twigs at the roadside and complain if he sustained damage because of something lying behind them. The court found in favour of the defendant.

[16.29]   Cunliffe v Bankes

[1945] 1 All ER 459   Singleton J

A motor cyclist riding along a road in the dark collided with a tree that had fallen across the road. It was an elm, 50 years old, about 40ft high, growing about 20ft inside a park wall 6ft high. It had been attacked by honey fungus. The estate agent in performing his duty had inspected each year when the trees were in foliage, but the tree showed no sign of danger.

HELD: There was no evidence of negligence. As to nuisance, the defendant was not liable unless:
  (1)   he caused the nuisance; or
  (2)   by the neglect of some duty he allowed it to arise; or
  (3)   when it has arisen without his own act or default, he omits to remedy it within a reasonable time after he became or ought to have become aware of it.

[16.30]   British Road Services Ltd v Slater

[1964] 1 All ER 816, [1964] 1 WLR 498, 108 Sol Jo 357   Lord Parker CJ

A lorry belonging to the claimant was being driven at night along the A41 road at a place where it adjoined farmland belonging to the defendant. The roadway was 20ft wide and along the side of it was a strip of gravel a foot wide beyond which was a grass verge or bank. Standing in the verge about 2ft 6 inches from the gravel edge was an oak tree of considerable age, which had a stout branch growing towards the road for about 2ft and then turned upwards. The driver of the lorry on approaching this place had to keep well to the nearside to avoid another of the claimant's lorries, which was approaching from the opposite direction. As the first lorry passed the tree a packing case stacked on the back of the lorry struck the branch causing another packing case to fall off into the path of the second lorry. Damage was caused both to this lorry and the packing case, for which the claimants claimed against the defendant on the ground that he had created or continued a nuisance in the form of the branch of the tree. The defendant had owned the land on both sides of the road since 1936 but the tree had been sown long before that, but not before the highway. Neither the defendant nor the highway authority nor the driver of the lorry (who had very frequently passed along the road) had ever considered the branch to be a hazard.

HELD: (1) Looked at objectively, the branch prevented the convenient use of the highway and was a nuisance.

(2) Even though the highway authority might have a right or duty to remove obstructions, the defendant was not sufficiently dispossessed of the verge or of the tree to exonerate him from liability for an obstruction created by the branch.

(3) Although the branch was a nuisance the defendant could not be presumed to know of it because no one had ever thought it was a hazard. Only the fortuitous circumstance that two heavy lorries happened to meet at that point in the dark had shown this. The defendant had not created the nuisance since the tree was already there when he acquired the land. He could be liable for continuing the nuisance only if he had knowledge or means of knowledge so that he knew or should have known of the nuisance in time to correct it and obviate its mischievous effects (quoting Lord Wright in *Sedleigh-Denfield v O'Callaghan* [1940] AC 880). This rule was not limited to cases where the nuisance was due to a hidden defect but applied also where, as here, the defendant had no reason to suppose it was a nuisance.

The defendant was not liable.

[16.31]   **Poll v Viscount and Viscountess Asquith of Morley**
[2006] All ER (D) 158 (May), (2006) 150 Sol Jo LB 706

The claimant, a motorcyclist, sustained injury and consequential losses when he collided with a tree that had fallen from the defendants' land. The defendants were responsible for the maintenance of the tree and had employed an independent forestry contractor to undertake 'drive by' examinations.

It was agreed between the parties that the tree had fallen as a result of a combination of a structural defect and an undetected fungal defect. The claimant submitted that if a competent inspector had examined the tree, he would have detected the visible structural defect and appreciated that a closer and more detailed inspection was necessary to detect decay and, as a result, the fungal defect would have been discovered.

HELD: On the balance of probabilities the fungal defect would have been discovered on a proper inspection by an appropriate, competent inspector. The forestry contractor employed by the defendants was not an inspector of the requisite expertise and to that extent the defendants were in breach of their duty.

CHAPTER 17

Animals on Highway

1. INTRODUCTION

[17.1]   The common law rules relating to the strict liability of keepers for damage caused by animals were replaced by ss 2 to 5 Animals Act 1971, which came into force on 1 October 1971. General principles of negligence, however, continue to apply.

The common law rule in *Searle v Wallbank* [1947] 1 All ER 12, HL that a landowner is under no duty to fence or maintain existing fences on land adjoining highways so as to prevent animals straying onto them, was abolished by s 8 of the Animals Act 1971.

The Dangerous Dogs Act 1991, which came into force on 12 August 1991, made further provision for the liability of keepers for damage caused by dogs belonging to certain species.

Those sections of the Acts which are or may be relevant to motor claims are as follows.

2. STATUTORY PROVISIONS

(A)   ANIMALS ACT 1971

[17.2]
1.   New provisions as to strict liability for damage done by animals
   (1)   The provisions of sections 2 to 5 of this Act replace—

(a)   the rules of the common law imposing a strict liability in tort for damage done by an animal on the ground that the animal is regarded as ferae naturae or that its vicious or mischievous propensities are known or presumed to be known;

(b)   ...

(c)   ...

(2)   Expressions used in those sections shall be interpreted in accordance with the provisions of section 6 (as well as those of s 11) of this Act.

2.   Liability for damage done by dangerous animals

(1)   Where any damage is caused by an animal which belongs to a dangerous species, any person who is a keeper of the animal is liable for the damage, except as otherwise provided by this Act.

(2)   Where damage is caused by an animal which does not belong to a dangerous species, a keeper of the animal is liable for the damage, except as otherwise provided by this Act, if-

(a)   the damage is of a kind which the animal, unless restrained, was likely to cause or which, if caused by the animal, was likely to be severe; and

(b)   the likelihood of the damage or of its being severe was due to characteristics of the animal which are not normally found in animals of the same species or are not normally so found except at particular times or in particular circumstances; and

(c)   those characteristics were known to that keeper or were at any time known to a person who at that time had charge of the animal as that keeper's servant or, where that keeper is the head of a household, were known to another keeper of the animal who is a member of that household and under the age of sixteen.

5.   Exceptions from liability under sections 2 to 4

(1)   A person is not liable under sections 2 to 4 of this Act for any damage which is due wholly to the fault of the person suffering it.

(2)   A person is not liable under section 2 of this Act for any damage suffered by a person who has voluntarily accepted the risk thereof.

(3)   A person is not liable under section 2 of this Act for any damage caused by an animal kept on any premises or structure to a person trespassing there, if it is proved either-

(a)   that the animal was not kept there for the protection of persons or property; or

(b)   (if the animal was kept there for the protection of persons or property) that keeping it there for that purpose was not unreasonable.

6.   Interpretation of certain expressions used in sections 2 to 5

(1)   The following provisions apply to the interpretation of sections 2 to 5 of this Act.

(2)   A dangerous species is a species—

(a)   which is not commonly domesticated in the British Islands; and

(b)   whose fully grown animals normally have such characteristics that they are likely, unless restrained, to cause severe damage or that any damage they may cause is likely to be severe.

(3)   Subject to subsection (4) of this section, a person is a keeper of an animal if—

(a)   he owns the animal or has it in his possession; or

(b)   he is the head of a household of which a member under the age of sixteen owns the animal or has it in his possession;

and if at any time an animal ceases to be owned by or to be in the possession of a person, any person who immediately before that time was a keeper thereof by virtue of the preceding provisions of this subsection continues to be a keeper of the animal until another person becomes a keeper thereof by virtue of those provisions.

(4)   Where an animal is taken into and kept in possession for the purpose of preventing it from causing damage or of restoring it to its owner, a person is not a keeper of it by virtue only of that possession.

(5)   Where a person employed as a servant by a keeper of an animal incurs a risk incidental to his employment he shall not be treated as accepting it voluntarily.

8.   Duty to take care to prevent damage from animals straying on to the highway

(1)   So much of the rules of the common law relating to liability for negligence as excludes or restricts the duty which a person might owe to others to take such care as is reasonable to see that damage is not caused by animals straying on to a highway is hereby abolished.

(2)   Where damage is caused by animals straying from unfenced land to a highway a person who placed them on the land shall not be regarded as having committed a breach of the duty to take care by reason only of placing them there if—

(a)   the land is common land, or is land situated in an area where fencing is not customary, or is a town or village green; and

(b)   he had a right to place the animals on that land.

10.   Application of certain enactments to liability under sections 2 to 4

For the purposes of the [Fatal Accidents Act 1976], the Law Reform (Contributory Negligence) Act 1945 and the [Limitation Act 1980] any damage for which a person is liable under sections 2 to 4 of this Act shall be treated as due to his fault.

11.   General interpretation

In this Act—

'common land' and 'town or village green' have the same meanings as in the Commons Registration Act 1965;

'damage' includes the death of, or injury to, any person (including any disease and any impairment of physical or mental condition);

'fault' has the same meaning as in the Law Reform (Contributory Negligence) Act 1945;

'fencing' includes the construction of any obstacle designed to prevent animals from straying;

'species' includes sub-species and variety.

12.   Application to Crown

(1)   This Act binds the Crown, but nothing in this section shall authorise proceedings to be brought against Her Majesty in her private capacity.

(2)   Section 38(3) of the Crown Proceedings Act 1947 (interpretation of references to Her Majesty in her private capacity) shall apply as if this section were contained in that Act.

(B)   DANGEROUS DOGS ACT 1991

[17.3]   The relevant sections of this Act were brought into force on 12 August 1991 by the Dangerous Dogs Act 1991, SI 1991/1742.

3.   Keeping dogs under proper control

(1)   If a dog is dangerously out of control in a public place—

(a)   the owner; and

(b)   if different, the person for the time being in charge of the dog,

is guilty of an offence, or, if the dog while so out of control injures any person, an aggravated offence, under this subsection.

(2)   In proceedings for an offence under subsection (1) above against a person who is the owner of a dog but was not at the material time in charge of it, it shall be a defence for the accused to prove that the dog was at the material time in the charge of a person whom he reasonably believed to be a fit and proper person to be in charge of it.

(3)   If the owner or, if different, the person for the time being in charge of a dog allows it to enter a place which is not a public place but where it is not permitted to be and while it is there—

(a)   it injures any person; or

(b)   there are grounds for reasonable apprehension that it will do so,

he is guilty of an offence, or, if the dog injures any person, an aggravated offence, under this subsection.

(4)   A person guilty of an offence under subsection (1) or (3) above other than an aggravated offence is liable on summary conviction to imprisonment for a term not exceeding six months or a fine not exceeding level 5 on the standard scale or both; and a person guilty of an aggravated offence under either of those subsections is liable—

(a)   on summary conviction, to imprisonment for a term not exceeding six months or a fine not exceeding the statutory maximum or both;

(b)   on conviction on indictment, to imprisonment for a term not exceeding two years or a fine or both.

(5)   It is hereby declared for the avoidance of doubt that an order under section 2 of the Dogs Act 1871 (order on complaint that a dog is dangerous and not kept under proper control)—

(a)   may be made whether or not the dog is shown to have injured any person; and

(b)   may specify the measures to be taken for keeping the dog under proper control, whether by muzzling, keeping on a lead, excluding it from specified places or otherwise.

(6)   If it appears to a court on a complaint under section 2 of the said Act of 1871 that the dog to which the complaint relates is a male and would be less dangerous if neutered the court may under that section make an order requiring it to be neutered.

(7)   The reference in section 1(3) of the Dangerous Dogs Act 1989 (penalties) to failing to comply with an order under section 2 of the said Act 1871 to keep a dog under proper control shall include a reference to failing to comply with any other order made under that section; but no order shall be made under that section by virtue of subsection (6) above where the matters complained of arose before the coming into force of that subsection.

6.   Dogs owned by young persons

Where a dog is owned by a person who is less than sixteen years old any reference to its owner in section 1(2)(d) or (e) or 3 above shall include a reference to the head of the household, if any, of which that person is a member or, in Scotland, to the person who has his actual care and control.

10.   Short title, interpretation, commencement and extent

(2)   In this Act—

'advertisement' includes any means of bringing a matter to the attention of the public and 'advertise' shall be construed accordingly;

'public place' means any street, road or other place (whether or not enclosed) to which the public have or are permitted to have access whether for payment or otherwise and includes the common parts of a building containing two or more separate dwellings.

(3)   For the purposes of this Act a dog shall be regarded as dangerously out of control on any occasion on which there are grounds for reasonable apprehension that it will injure any person, whether or not it actually does so, but references to a dog injuring a person or there being grounds for reasonable apprehension that it will do so do not include references to any case in which the dog is being used for a lawful purpose by a constable or a person in the service of the Crown.

(C) DANGEROUS DOGS (AMENDMENT) ACT 1997

[17.4]
4. Extended application of 1991 Order
(1)   Where an order is made under section 4A(1) or 4B(3) of the 1991 Act, Part III of the Dangerous Dogs Compensation and Exemption Schemes Order 1991 (exemption scheme) shall have effect as if—
    (a)   any reference to the appointed day were a reference to the end of the requisite period within the meaning of section 4A or, as the case may be, section 4B of the 1991 Act;
    (b)   paragraph (a) of Article 4 and Article 6 were omitted; and
    (c)   the fee payable to the Agency under Article 9 were a fee of such amount as the Secretary of State may by order prescribe.
(2)   The power to make an order under this section shall be exercisable by statutory instrument which shall be subject to annulment in pursuance of a resolution of either House of Parliament.
5. Transitional provisions
(1)   This Act shall apply in relation to cases where proceedings have been instituted before, as well as after, the commencement of this Act.
(2)   In a case where, before the commencement of this Act—
    (a)   the court has ordered the destruction of a dog in respect of which an offence under section 1, or an aggravated offence under section 3(1) or (3), of the 1991 Act has been committed, but
    (b)   the dog has not been destroyed,
that destruction order shall cease to have effect and the case shall be remitted to the court for reconsideration.
(3)   Where a case is so remitted, the court may make any order in respect of the dog which it would have power to make if the person in question had been convicted of the offence after the commencement of this Act.

(D) ROAD TRAFFIC ACT 1988

[17.5]
27. Control of dogs on roads
(1)   A person who causes or permits a dog to be on a designated road without the dog being held on a lead is guilty of an offence.
(2)   In this section 'designated road' means a length of road specified by an order in that behalf of the local authority in whose area the length of road is situated.
(3)   The powers which under subsection (2) above are exercisable by a local authority in England and Wales are, in the case of a road part of the width of which is in the area of one local authority and part in the area of another, exercisable by either authority with the consent of the other.
(4)   An order under this section may provide that subsection (1) above shall apply subject to such limitations or exceptions as may be specified in the order, and (without prejudice to the generality of this subsection) subsection (1) above does not apply to dogs proved—
    (a)   to be kept for driving or tending sheep or cattle in the course of a trade or business, or
    (b)   to have been at the material time in use under proper control for sporting purposes.
(5)   An order under this section shall not be made except after consultation with the chief officer of police.
(6)   The Secretary of State may make regulations—
    (a)   prescribing the procedure to be followed in connection with the making of orders under this section, and

   (b)   requiring the authority making such an order to publish in such manner as
         may be prescribed by the regulations notice of the making and effect of
         the order.
(7)   In this section 'local authority' means—
   (a)   in relation to England and Wales, the council of a county, metropolitan
         district or London borough or the Common Council of the City of
         London, and
   (b)   (*applies to Scotland only*).
(8)   The power conferred by this section to make an order includes power,
exercisable in like manner and subject to the like conditions, to vary or revoke it.

3.   CASE LAW

(A)   NEGLIGENCE

[17.6]   Heath's Garage Ltd v Hodges
[1916] 2 KB 370, 85 LJKB 1289, 115 LT 129, 32 TLR 570, 60 Sol Jo 554, CA

An owner or occupier of land adjoining a highway (leaving aside cases where,
either by a local Enclosure Act, or by prescription, or otherwise, a duty to fence
was imposed) was not bound to fence so as to prevent animals like sheep straying
upon the highway.
   While the claimant's motor car was being driven along a highway in the daylight
at the rate of 16 to 20mph, the driver saw in front of him on the road a number of
sheep untended. He put on his brakes and almost immediately thereafter two
sheep, which had apparently been left behind by the others, jumped from the bank
on the near side and one of them ran in front of the car and broke part of the
steering gear. The driver lost control and the car ran into a bank and was damaged.
The sheep were the property of the defendant, who was subsequently prosecuted
and fined under the Highways Act 1864, s 25, for having allowed them to stray on
the highway. In an action against the defendant by the claimant in respect of the
damage to the car, the county court judge found:
   (1)   the sheep escaped on to the highway from the defendant's field owing
         to a defective hedge;
   (2)   it was the natural tendency of sheep which were untended to run
         across or otherwise endanger vehicles in a road and it was common
         knowledge that when sheep found themselves separated from the
         flock, they have almost a mania for rejoining it, regardless of intervening
         traffic;
   (3)   the defendant was negligent, or had committed a nuisance, in allowing
         sheep to stray on to the highway and the accident was the natural
         consequence thereof therefore the defendant was liable.

HELD, ON APPEAL: (1) Whether the action was sought to be based on negligence or
on a nuisance to the highway, it was not a breach of duty by the defendant by not
keeping his sheep from straying on to the highway.
   (2)   An animal like a sheep, by nature harmless, could not fairly be regarded
         as likely to collide with a motor car and defendant could not be held
         liable on that footing.
   (3)   (Per Avory J) the tendencies of sheep as found by the county court
         judge were not a vicious or mischievous propensity within the decided
         cases.
(But see *Hoskin v Rogers* at para [17.30].)

[17.7]   Fardon v Harcourt-Rivington

[1932] All ER 81, (1932) 146 LT 391, 48 TLR 215, 76 Sol Jo 81, HL

The defendant parked his car in a street with its back against the pavement. The car was left shut with a dog inside it. There was no evidence that the dog had a vicious propensity. When the claimant was walking past the defendant's car, the dog, which had been barking and jumping about, jumped up against a window in the rear of the car and smashed a panel. A glass splinter flew out and entered claimant's eye, with the result that he lost the eye. An action for damages for personal injuries was brought.

HELD: The danger of a piece of glass being knocked by a dog out of a small window at the back of the car and of a splinter of glass hitting a passer-by on the pavement, was such an unforeseeable event that no reasonable man could say that a person ought to be found liable of negligence for not taking any precautions against it. A person must guard against reasonable probability of danger; he was not bound to guard against a fantastic possibility.

[17.8]   Frazer v Pate

1923 SC 748, 60 SLR 470

A motorcyclist was injured by a collision in daylight with a sheep upon a public road. The claimant averred the defendant was negligent in knowingly failing to keep his fences in such repair as would prevent his sheep from straying on to the road and allowing his sheep to graze upon the road.

HELD: The accident was not the natural and probable result of the negligence alleged.

[17.9]   Deen v Davies

[1935] 2 KB 282, [1935] All ER 9, 104 LJKB 540, 153 LT 90, 51 TLR 398, 79 Sol Jo 381, CA

The defendant, a farmer, rode his pony into a neighbouring large town and stabled it there whilst he did business in the town. Instead of tethering it to a staple provided for the purpose, he tied it to a piece of wood which he believed to be firmly nailed to the wall of the stable. Whilst he was away the pony broke the piece of wood away from the wall and went out into the street to return home. Though of docile disposition, it caused the claimant to fall when stepping from the pavement and she sustained injury. The county court found that the pony, whilst not exhibiting any savage tendencies, had acted in a way in which a pony might be expected to when unattended on a roadway in a town. The defendant had been negligent in not tying up the pony properly in the stall and his negligence had led to the pony getting on to the roadway unattended and injuring the claimant.

HELD, ON APPEAL: This was not a case of an animal being depastured on land adjoining the highway and escaping or straying on to it: it was one of a different class of case in which the owner himself has brought the animal upon the highway. In this type of case the owner had a duty to take reasonable care that the animal did not damage third parties. Reasonable care in the country may not be reasonable care in the town. The defendant had brought his horse upon the highway and rode it into a town. When he tethered it in the stable he had not secured it properly and thereby failed to discharge the duty he owed to the public. The duty began when he took the horse on to the highway and did not come to an end when he tethered it in the stable. Appeal dismissed.

[17.10]   Ludlam v Peel

(1939) Times, 10 October

Cattle belonging to a farmer were customarily driven from the farm for about a mile along the Great North Road to a field. Six cows were being driven along the grass verge at the side of the road. A motor car was being driven along the road in the opposite direction. When the car was a few yards away, one cow suddenly ran out across the road in front of the car and a collision occurred. The county court judge decided, based on the judgment of Lord Moncrieff in *Harpers v GNR of Scotland* (1886) 13 R (Ct of Sess) 1139, that it was not necessary to prove actual negligence, there was a duty to control the cows on the highway and the farmer had failed to keep them under proper control.

HELD, ON APPEAL: It was necessary to prove negligence. The owner had employed a competent drover and there was no evidence of failure to take reasonable care. The county court judge had sought to impose an absolute duty which did not exist at common law.

[17.11]   Imrie v Clark

(24 October 1939, unreported)   Lord Patrick

A motorcyclist at 5.45 am whilst it was dark, collided with cattle on the road. The owner of the cattle had opened a gate between the field and the road to allow the cattle to emerge and proceed along the road to the farm. The owner remained in the field and took no steps to warn drivers of vehicles in the road.

HELD: The cattle were entitled to use the road for passage as much as motor cars or pedestrians. The law did not require or custom prescribe that warnings should be given of cattle on the road or that in the dark the cattle owner must place lights on the road or give signals to warn traffic.
   (But see *Harrison v Jackson* at para [17.12] below.)

[17.12]   Harrison v Jackson

(1947) 14 LJNCCR 242   Judge Peel KC

About 5.45 am on 12 October 1946, the claimant was driving his motor car along the highway from Kirkby Lonsdale to Carnforth. On the nearside ahead was an open gate to a field and about 30 or 40 yards inside the gate, about 30 cows. On the offside nearly opposite the field gate was the gate from the farmyard to the road. This gate was open. The claimant inferred that the cows had just come from the farm to the field. There was no one on the road. A high wall prevented the claimant seeing into the farmyard. The claimant reduced his speed to 10 or 15mph in case any other cows emerged. Just short of the farm gate two other cows came out at a fast speed close together and side by side. One cow was probably playing with the other. The claimant applied his brakes. One cow went straight into the car at the offside end of the windscreen and the other landed across the bonnet. What was taking place was a routine operation of the farm. Whether the car had actually come to rest at the moment of impact was immaterial.

HELD: This was not a case of cattle straying on to the highway but of their being put on to and across the highway and of being sent by the defendant's men across it. The defendant was not any the less liable by letting his cattle wander back unattended than if they had been driven. Following Romer LJ's dictum in *Deen v Davies* (see para [17.9]) which was approved by Lord Porter in *Searle v Wallbank*

[1947] I All ER 12, the defendant had failed in his duty to users of the highway to ensure that reasonable care was taken in the control of his cows crossing the highway. It would have been reasonable to have a man on the road to warn approaching traffic, especially as the corner at the gateway was blind. A man placed in the roadway would have been able to prevent the cows dashing out, or halt the claimant's car. Judgment for claimant.

See also *Andrews v Watts* at para [17.27].

[17.13]   Landau v Railway Executive
(1949) 99 L Jo 233, Clerkenwell CC   Judge Earengey

A railway carman took his horse and cart on his usual collection and delivery round into a manufacturer's yard. The yard was paved with stone sets and sloped down to an archway, where there was a gatekeeper. The cart was backed up to a loading bank at right angles to the slope, a nosebag was put on the horse and a chain on the rear wheel, but without the brake applied. The horse had been bought about two years previously with a warranty that it was quiet. It had been driven frequently by the carman who had never known it to bolt before. After the horse had been left unattended for about five minutes, it ran through the archway into the highway and caused damage.

HELD: The brake was fitted for the obvious purpose of reinforcing the chain on difficult ground, or in cases of emergency and the yard was clearly dangerous ground. *Deen v Davies* (see para [17.9]) was not doubted by the Court of Appeal in *Brackenborough v Spalding UDC* [1942] I All ER 34 and was approved by Lord Porter in *Searle v Wallbank* [1947] AC 341, [1947] I All ER 12, HL. The defendant was liable.

[17.14]   Wright v Callwood
[1950] 2 KB 515, 66 TLR (pt 2) 72, 94 Sol Jo 420, CA

The defendant, a farmer, drove two calves out of a field on to the highway, then to the right for a few yards along the highway and then to the left through a gateway 14ft wide and 50ft long into a drive to a farm. A lorry was stationary in the farm yard and the engine was started which frightened the calves and they ran back down the drive, the defendant following close behind with a stick attempting to get in front of them. The claimant was cycling along the highway passing the gateway. One of the calves ran out about a yard in front of her cycle and the second knocked her off. A veterinary surgeon gave evidence that a calf ran away just like a young horse and more men were needed to drive them. The county court judge considered there were special circumstances which imposed a special duty, referred to the judgment of Greer LJ in *Sycamore v Ley* (1932) 147 LT 342 and decided the defendant ought to have closed the gates or had a man to assist. The defendant appealed.

HELD, ON APPEAL: There was no evidence the defendant knew that the lorry was in the yard and that its engine might be started and therefore were no special circumstances. Appeal allowed.

[17.15]   McGowan v Gilmore
[1953] CLY 117, Cty Ct

A farmer's ram escaped on to the highway in the hours of darkness. The defendant went in his car in pursuit and, whilst chasing it, the ram collided with and damaged the claimant's car.

HELD: The defendant had not brought the ram on to the highway. He was reasonably and properly attempting to take possession and control of it but had not succeeded in doing so at the time of the accident. The defendant was not negligent.

[17.16] Howarth v Straver

(16 November 1953, unreported)   Croom-Johnson J

The claimant was riding a motorcycle with a pillion passenger at 10.40 pm on 14 October 1951, along Bagshot Road, Cobham at not more than 40mph. The defendant's golden retriever dog was loose and uncontrolled and roaming about the road. It ran across the road from the right, swerved to go behind the motorcycle and then came back and hit the motorcycle. The claimant in trying to avoid it ran into a hedge on the left-hand side of the road and was injured. He sued the defendant for damages alleging that the dog was of a mischievous nature. A cyclist gave evidence that the dog had previously got in his way and a woman that the dog ran round bicycles and people and that she had complained to the defendant.

HELD: The dog was not vicious in the ordinary sense of the term. Citing *Deen v Davies* [1935] 2 KB 282 at 295 (see para [17.9]), if an animal owner knows that it has a tendency to run into cyclists or other passengers on the highway, it cannot avail him to say that it was not vice, but a frolicsome disposition, or perhaps mere blundering, which caused the harm. The dog was a nuisance to people and a potential source of danger and the defendant was liable.

[17.17] Adam v Chiddingfold Farmers Foxhounds

(1955) Times, 5 November

A motorist driving at 35 to 40mph along the Portsmouth Road near Wisley, saw a fox run across the road 20 or 30 yards ahead of him. He did not realise it was a fox until a pack of hounds dashed into the road after it, when he was about 10 to 15 yards away. He could not avoid them and sustained damage to his car and sued for £22 10s 6d.

HELD: All reasonable precautions had been taken. The huntsmen and hounds were legitimate users of the highway and there was nothing improper in allowing hounds on a road of this sort.
   Judgment for the defendants.

[17.18] Thorp v King Bros

(1957) Times, 23 February   Stable J

A cow unloaded from a transport vehicle at Guildford Market ran away without any negligence in the unloading. It turned into a cul-de-sac where it was frightened by a number of people shouting and waving their arms and it turned into the main street and trotted quietly along and turned into a car park. The sound of a motor horn sent it into another road and over a pedestrian crossing. A pedestrian on the crossing was knocked down by the cow and injured. He claimed damages from the owner of the cow and the transporters.

HELD: The cow had never shown any sign of vice. It had been driven frantic by the behaviour of the people.
   Judgment for the defendants.

[17.19] **Annells v Warneford**

[1958] CLY 104, (1958) Times, 7 May, CA

Two children were trying to catch a pony which was in a field, but the pony slipped past one of them, ran down a lane and into a main road where it collided with a motor car. The driver of the car sued in negligence.

HELD, ON APPEAL: Although the children had been under a duty to take reasonable care to prevent the pony going down the lane and into the road, they had fulfilled that duty.

[17.20] **Martin v Zinn**

(1960) Times, 9 March, CA

The claimant, riding a 1935 motorcycle with a light which shone for 50 yards, collided in the dark with one of the defendant's cows which was crossing a narrow public road which divided two of the defendant's fields. The defendant's practice was to allow his cows to cross in threes. He stood by the gate holding a lamp until the third cow was in the road, when he would follow behind.

HELD: The claimant was to blame for the accident. He was riding an old fashioned motorcycle with a headlamp, which for country lanes was inadequate. The defendant had stationed himself by the gateway of his farm and was holding a lamp which could be seen by traffic on the road. The claimant knew the locality and should have anticipated that cows might be on the road.

[17.21] **Friend v Facey**

(1963) Times, 19 March, CA

The claimant was driving his car along the main Ilfracombe to Barnstaple road at about 40mph when a cow suddenly galloped out of a gateway on his nearside whilst being taken to the farm for milking. He jammed on his brakes at once but struck the cow, injuring it and damaging the car. The county court judge found the farmer to blame for not having two men to take the cows home to milk: it was not sufficient to leave the job to his 17-year-old son as he had done. He found the claimant equally to blame for not avoiding the cow by swerving to the offside.

HELD, ON APPEAL: The farmer was negligent for the reasons given by the county court judge but the claimant was free from blame. His speed was not too fast on that road, he received no warning and it would be asking too much to say he was negligent because he did not swerve.

[17.22] **Gomberg v Smith**

[1963] 1 QB 25, [1962] 1 All ER 725, [1962] 2 WLR 749, 106 Sol Jo 95, CA

At about 6.30 pm at Roman Road, Bow, London, the defendant opened the door of his shop. His dog, a large St Bernard, shot out and ran across the road. The defendant followed, shouting at the dog, which eluded him and ran back across the road, colliding with the claimant's van and causing damage. In a solicitor's letter and in his defence of the action, the defendant alleged, untruthfully, that he had the dog on a lead. In the county court the judge held, following *Searle v Wallbank* [1947] AC 341, [1947] 1 All ER 12, HL, that there was no liability on the defendant if the dog escaped on to the highway and there was no evidence either how the dog got out or that the defendant was taking it on to the highway. The claimant appealed.

HELD, ON APPEAL: The evidence of a witness that the defendant and dog came out together and the fact that the defendant had not alleged in his defence that the dog escaped, amounted to evidence that he had brought the dog on to the highway. He had failed to keep it under control and was liable, following *Deen v Davies* [1935] 2 KB 282 at 295 (see para [17.9]).

[17.23]   Fitzgerald v E D and A D Cooke Bourne (Farms) Ltd

[1964] 1 QB 249, [1963] 3 All ER 36, [1963] 3 WLR 522, 107 Sol Jo 459, 188 EG 209, CA

The claimant was crossing a field by a public footpath when she was knocked down by a filly belonging to the defendants. She did not receive serious physical injury but was frightened and subsequently suffered a nervous breakdown. The filly was one of two normally pastured in the field. It had not attacked the claimant but galloped up to her, swerving and prancing in a playful way, striking her with its shoulders and knocking her down. There was some evidence of similar behaviour to a person on the footpath on a previous occasion. The judge held that the horses were not vicious but had a natural propensity to gallop up to people who walked across the field: their behaviour was what could be expected of young animals of that sort of breeding. The defendants were liable on the basis that they knew of the potential danger of the horse doing to the claimant what it did.

HELD, ON APPEAL: The claimant's case was put in two ways:
(1)   that the filly was a dangerous animal to the knowledge of the defendants and that accordingly they were strictly liable for an animal regarded as *ferae naturae*;
(2)   that they were liable in negligence on the ground that they ought reasonably to have foreseen and guarded against an accident of the kind that occurred.

On the first point, the filly was not vicious but was merely indulging its natural propensity to be playful. It was not attacking or showing hostility. The fact that its conduct was frightening to the claimant or others did not make it a dangerous animal so as to place the defendants under strict liability.

On the second point the footpath was similar to a highway in the unfenced condition in which highways existed when the common law developed. *Searle v Wallbank* (see para [17.1]) made it clear beyond doubt that the owner of animals pastured in the vicinity had no duty to prevent them from straying on to the highway, but it was envisaged in that case that an action for negligence might lie if, in the particular circumstances of the particular case, the owner of a particular animal ought reasonably to foresee that, having regard to its peculiar propensities, it may cause injury otherwise than by merely straying if it escaped on to a highway. To establish such a case in negligence, it was not sufficient to show a 'reasonable possibility' of injury: it must be shown that there was a real likelihood of injury which ought to have been foreseen. In the present case the evidence did not establish that the defendants ought reasonably to have foreseen the likelihood of injury except in so far as they must be taken to have had a general knowledge of the behaviour of fillies of this class; this was not sufficient to make them liable.

[17.24]   **Lister v Vergette**

(1964) Times, 12 June   Thompson J

The claimant was injured when he was knocked off his moped by the defendant's dog, which emerged suddenly from the gateway of the defendant's house. It was the dog's habit to accompany tractor drivers on their rounds to nearby fields. A tractor was being manoeuvred and the dog probably thought it was being left out and ran to join the tractor driver. The claimant's case was based on *Brock v Richards* [1951] 1 KB 529, [1951] 1 All ER 261 and *dicta* of Pearson LJ in *Ellis v Johnstone* [1963] 2 QB 8, [1963] 1 All ER 286.

HELD: The defendant was not aware of the dog's 'unwelcome attitude to users of the highway' nor of any previous incidents it may have caused. In the circumstances, the defendant had not acted unreasonably in failing to take measures to prevent the dog running out. The claim failed.

[17.25]   **Burns v Ellicott**

(1969) 113 Sol Jo 490   Paull J

The claimant was riding her horse on a path at the side of a narrow road. Her right leg was over the edge of the kerb. The defendant driving his car in the same direction as the claimant saw another car approaching him from the opposite direction. He slowed down and passed the claimant almost brushing her horse. The horse took fright and reared or turned catching its hoofs under the front bumper of the defendant's car. It was badly injured and had to be destroyed.

HELD: The defendant was negligent. If a horse was being ridden in a narrow road a car driver must exercise great caution in passing it. His duty was to slow down and give the horse a wide berth. If he could not do that because a car was coming from the other direction his duty was to wait until the other car had passed.

[17.26]   **Bativala v West**

[1970] 1 QB 716, [1970] 1 All ER 332, [1970] 2 WLR 8, 113 Sol Jo 856   Bridge J

The defendant, the proprietor of a riding school, organised a gymkhana in a field. The part of the field used was some distance from a road and separated from it first by a rope to control spectators and then by a hedge with an open gateway in it. In a race in which competitors had to saddle their ponies, a saddle slipped and caused a pony to bolt, clearing the rope and running out into the road where it collided with the claimant's car.

HELD: The defendant was liable. She was aware of the risk; a slipping saddle was a well-known hazard and if this happened the horse would probably run away in fear. Each link in the chain of causation was reasonably foreseeable and she was negligent by ordinary standards. She had relied on the rule as laid down in *Searle v Wallbank* (see para [17.1]) that there was no duty to prevent the escape of animals on to the highway, but an owner could still be liable if he could be shown to have failed in his duty to take care. Most cases in which the rule in *Searle v Wallbank* had been held to apply were cases in which the animal had strayed from a situation in which it had been properly left to its own devices. Different considerations arose when the animal escaped from a situation in which it was under direct human control. The present case could be decided in accordance with the ordinary principles of negligence and the claimant was entitled to damages.

[17.27]   Andrews v Watts

[1971] RTR 484   Karminski LJ

The owner of some cattle wanted to fetch them from a field some distance from her farm. She took two men to help her. It was a dark evening in November. They got the cattle out from the field on to the road, one man walking at the front and the other at the rear of the herd. Neither man was carrying a light of any kind. The owner had parked her car in the road at the gateway with dipped headlights on facing away from the herd. She stood there herself to warn approaching traffic. A car came along at about 40mph and the cattle owner waved it down. The driver, a 19-year-old girl took fright; she was dazzled by the headlights and seeing nothing beyond thought it must be some kind of hold-up. Her own headlights were dipped. She went on faster and ran into the man at the rear of the herd who by that time was about 50 yards from the gateway. He was killed and his widow sued the driver and cattle owner.

HELD: Both the driver and the cattle owner were to blame. The driver should have realised that the waving-down and the headlights might be a warning of an obstruction; she should have reduced her speed and put her headlights on full beam. The cattle owner had brought the cows on to the road, had failed to provide the men with any lights (contrary to the advice in the Highway Code) and had pointed the headlights away from the cattle instead of illuminating them. The cattle owner was two-thirds to blame and the driver one-third. The deceased was not to blame at all.

[17.28]   Haimes v Watson

[1981] RTR 90, CA

The defendant counterclaimed for damages sustained when his car collided with a horse ridden by the claimant. He was driving along a road 20ft wide at about 30mph. The horse was being ridden in the same direction in the nearside gutter when it shied and moved broadside across the road: the collision was unavoidable. The claimant admitted that the shy took the horse temporarily out of his control. There was no plea of *scienter* in the counterclaim.

HELD, ON APPEAL: The defendant could not succeed. He had established that the horse had suddenly moved sideways across his bows and that called for an explanation; but the claimant had given one which was adequate to negative any inference of negligence. The county court judge's view that a rider must so control his horse that it will not move sideways if startled and that not so to control the horse was negligence was not the law.

[17.29]   Carryfast Ltd v Hack

[1981] RTR 464, QB

The defendant, an experienced horsewoman, was riding her horse along the narrow grass verge on the nearside of a main road 21ft wide. The claimant's van was being driven by its employee in the same direction at about 30mph. When the van had almost reached the horse, the driver saw the horse begin to 'dance'; he swerved to the offside, crashing into a lorry approaching from the opposite direction. The claimant claimed against the defendant for the damage to the van. She admitted in evidence that her horse was nervous in traffic but said she could keep the animal under control and that it was on the grass verge all the time before the accident.

HELD: The defendant was not liable. The accident was caused by the claimant's driver's negligence in not being able to slow down sufficiently and stop when he saw the horse 'dancing'. Every case turned on its own facts. It was not negligent of a rider to go on the highway on a horse simply because the rider knows that the horse did not like some traffic noises and may on occasion act as if unsettled, but such a rider may be negligent in taking a horse on to the highway if there was a reasonable risk of the horse getting out of control.

Note—Horses have a right of way on the highway.

[17.30]   Hoskin v Rogers

[1985] LS Gaz R 848, (1985) Times, 25 January, CA

The claimant motorcyclist was injured when he collided with the body of a heifer killed by another vehicle. It had strayed on to the highway through inadequate fencing from adjoining land owned by the second defendant. The accident occurred in October; the land had been let to the first defendant on a 'grass purchase' agreement since May, when the fence was reasonably stockproof. The judge held the first defendant solely liable.

HELD, ON APPEAL: The duty of care of the second defendants as owners of the land was to take reasonable care to see that the land was fenced adequately so as to prevent stock they knew was going to be on the land from straying on to the highway. There was no breach of that duty by the second defendants in May when the agreement was negotiated. Thus the question was whether it had been shown that by the date of the accident they had been put on notice that the fencing was by then inadequate. The evidence did not establish that this was so; the second defendants were not in breach of their duty of care. Appeal dismissed.

[17.31]   Matthews v Taylor

(25 January 1995) LEXIS, CA

The defendant was a Cornish sheep farmer. With assistance from his son, two farm workers and a couple of sheep dogs, the defendant was herding a flock of about 300 sheep along a country road. A number of vehicles were stationary or very slow moving behind the sheep. The claimant drove over the brow of a hill, saw the stationary or slow moving vehicles ahead of him, lost control, crashed into a wall and then into a vehicle approaching from the opposite direction. Just prior to the accident the defendant's son had been positioned at the brow of the hill to warn traffic of the sheep ahead and eventually decided that the danger to oncoming traffic had passed and left his post. Subsequently the accident occurred. In the face of much contradictory evidence, the trial judge accepted that the distance between the brow of the hill and the last of the line of stationary vehicles behind the sheep was approximately 50 to 75m. The judge found for the claimant subject to a discount of 40% for contributory negligence. The defendant appealed.

HELD, ON APPEAL: The judge was wrong to rely on the one witness who gave evidence of a distance of 50 to 75m in the face of other witness evidence to the contrary. Furthermore and in any event, the expert evidence demonstrated that even the distance of 75m between the brow of the hill and the last stationary vehicle should have given the claimant sufficient time to negotiate the situation safely. The claimant was driving too fast and lost control in the agony of the moment. The claim failed.

Per Russell LJ: In my judgment, Mr Taylor did all that could reasonably be expected of him. He positioned his son who remained at his post until such time as all ordinary and to be anticipated circumstances had resolved themselves and the vehicles held up by the herd of sheep had moved down the road a sufficient distance as no longer to present a hazard.

[17.32]   **James v Barther (t/a Highbarn Riding Stables)**
(31 January 1995) LEXIS, CA

The claimant and her two children were on horseback riding up a steep and narrow country lane accompanied by the first defendant, also on horseback, who owned all the horses and who had chosen the route. The second defendant, aged 14, was riding a bicycle down the hill towards the horses. He turned a corner, saw the horses, braked and stopped about 20ft from them without falling off his bicycle and keeping to his side of the road. As a result of the appearance of the second defendant on his bicycle and the reaction of the first defendant's horse, the claimant's horse went out of control and the claimant fell off and suffered injury. The trial judge found for the claimant and apportioned liability between the two defendants as to two thirds to the first defendant and one third to the second defendant. Both defendants appealed.

HELD, ON APPEAL: The first defendant had used this lane on many occasions for similar rides over a four year period without any problems. She had never previously come across a cyclist coming down the hill. The horses were not particularly nervous. It would be putting too high a burden on someone in the position of the first defendant to say that she should have foreseen the possibility of a cyclist coming down a hill at a speed which would frighten these horses. There was nothing to suggest that the second defendant was riding his bicycle too fast. He stopped without colliding with any of the horses. He did not skid or fall off his bicycle and remained on his side of the road.
  Appeals granted.

Per Balcombe LJ: It needs to be said that there are still such things as true accidents and that not every accident can be attributed to the negligence of some person or persons. Riding, as everybody knows, is a sport and all sports necessarily carry some degree of risk.

[17.33]   **Cooke v Jackson**
(1999) LTL, 30 November, CA

The defendant was exercising her dog by riding a bicycle through a park, the dog following on behind. The dog was approximately 30ft behind the defendant when it ran into the claimant.

HELD: The defendant had negligently created a situation of hazard by riding along a path which pedestrians used and that situation caused the injury. The defendant had a duty to control the dog on the path which she had failed to do.

[17.34]   **Tierney v Barbour**
[2001] All ER (D) 37 (Feb)

The claimant, a motorcyclist, collided with the defendant's dog which had escaped from the defendant's property and run into the road. Shortly before the accident, the claimant had accelerated away from road works at high speed and pulled a wheelie.

HELD: The defendant was negligent for allowing the dog to escape onto a busy road and it was reasonably foreseeable that, if the dog escaped, injury was likely to result. The claimant was riding in a reckless manner but neither his behaviour nor his speed was a material cause of the accident. He had regained proper control of his motorcycle before the dog ran across and accordingly a deduction for contributory negligence was not appropriate.

[17.35]   Gardner v Wharton (t/a Charles Wharton Partners)

(14 January 2004, unreported), Norwich County Court

The claimant drove into a cow which had suddenly appeared onto the road. The claimant alleged that the defendant was negligent and allowed cattle to get onto the road. The defendant counter-claimed against the claimant averring that the cows were properly secured by gates which were checked several times a day and the accident occurred as the claimant was travelling too fast and as a result did not see the cow until the last moment and was unable to stop in time.

HELD: The cows were in a field with a properly secured gate and the claimant had been driving too fast and failed to keep a proper look out in a rural area particularly given that there were cattle warning signs on the road. The claimant would have seen the cow had he been driving at a proper speed. The claimant was liable in negligence.

[17.36]   Donaldson v Wilson

[2004] EWCA Civ 972

[2004] All ER (D) 165 (Jul), 148 Sol Jo LB 879, CA

Cattle in the defendant's field escaped as a result of a gate being left open by walkers. The cattle were able to wander into the neighbouring farm which was in a dilapidated state, had no useful gates and led the cattle directly onto the highway. At first instance the court found the defendant should have been aware of the state of the neighbouring farm and taken adequate precautions to prevent the cattle from reaching the highway, given that the gate was the last defence.

HELD, ON APPEAL: The first instance decision was upheld because the defendant should have made provision for the risk of walkers leaving the gate open.

(B)   ANIMALS ACT 1971

(I)   SECTION 2(1)

[17.37]   Behrens v Bertram Mills Circus Ltd

[1957] 2 QB 1, [1957] 1 All ER 583, [1957] 2 WLR 404

An animal will be defined as dangerous if it is not commonly domesticated in the United Kingdom and if any damage it causes is likely to be severe. It is not open to the owner of the animal to argue that the particular animal in question was domesticated if it belongs to a non-domesticated species in this case, elephants.

[17.38]   Tutin v M Chipperfield Promotions Ltd

(1980) 130 NLJ 807, (1980) Times, 23 May, QB

Whilst taking part in a charity camel race, the claimant, a distinguished actress, fell from the defendant's camel and sustained injuries.

HELD: A camel is a dangerous species within the meaning of s 6(2) of the Animals Act 1971, because:

(1)   it is an animal which is not commonly domesticated in the British Islands, and

(2)   any damage it may cause is likely to be severe.

Therefore the defendant was strictly liable under s 2(1) of the 1971 Act. The defendant was also negligent in letting go of the camel before the race was due to begin, catching the claimant off guard.

(II)   SECTION 2(2)

[17.39]   Cummings v Granger

[1977] QB 397, [1977] 1 All ER 104, [1976] 2 WLR 842, CA

See also at para [17.56].

The claimant entered a yard containing scrap metal owned by the defendant and occupied by a guard dog who was running loose. The claimant was a trespasser and the dog bit the claimant.

HELD, ON APPEAL: The guard dog's characteristics, i e barking and running around its territory, were not normally found in Alsatian dogs, except in the particular circumstances, in which they were used as guard dogs. This brought the case within s 2(2)(b) of the Animals Act 1971. The damage caused by the dog was likely to be severe if an intruder did enter on its territory and the characteristics in this case were known to the keeper.

[17.40]   Burley v Gilbert

[1981] CLY 5

The defendant's dog bit a five-year-old child. Although the dog was known to have attacked children, the question was whether the keeper knew of the dog's characteristic at all material times.

HELD: On the facts the owners did know of the characteristics and were therefore liable under the Animals Act 1971.

[17.41]   Wallace v Newton

[1982] 2 All ER 106, [1982] 1 WLR 375, 126 Sol Jo 101   Park J

The claimant was employed as a groom, handling horses belonging to her employer which were used for show jumping. On an occasion when she was leading a horse into a horsebox it suddenly leaped or lunged forward, crushing her arm against a bar in the trailer. The injury was serious. She claimed damages under the Animals Act 1971, s 2(2).

HELD: Under s 2(2)(b), the claimant had to establish that the likelihood of the damage was due to characteristics of the animal which were not normally found in horses. This did not mean the horse had to be shown to have a vicious tendency to injure people by attacking them; it was sufficient to show that it had characteristics of a kind not usually found in horses. There was evidence that during the period the claimant had the horse in her charge its behaviour was unpredictable and unreliable and that the owner, the defendant, knew of it. The defendant was liable under s 2(2).

[17.42]   **Smith v Prendergast**

(1981) Times, 18 October, CA

The defendant took custody of a stray Alsatian which visited its premises. The defendant kept it and used it as a guard dog and the dog bit a child.

HELD: Although the defendant had no knowledge of the dog's characteristics, he should have observed it and kept it on a lead until he was satisfied that it was docile. There was no liability under the Animals Act 1971 due to lack of knowledge. However, the defendant was in breach of his duty of care at common law and was negligent as he should have attempted to train or control the dog until he knew of its characteristics.

[17.43]   **Breeden v Lampard**

(21 March 1985, unreported)

The claimant and the defendant were out hunting. The claimant was riding close behind the defendant when the defendant's horse, Raffles, moved to the left and kicked out, breaking the claimant's leg. Although Raffles was a young and exuberant horse, the defendant did not know of any propensity of Raffles to kick out, even when followed too closely behind.

HELD: Owing to the defendant's lack of knowledge of any propensity of Raffles to kick out, the claim was dismissed.

[17.44]   **Curtis v Betts**

[1990] 1 All ER 769, [1990] 1 WLR 459, CA

The ten-year-old claimant was injured in an attack by his neighbours' bull mastiff as the dog was being loaded in a Land Rover for its usual walk in the park.

HELD: The defendants were liable under s 2(2) of the Animals Act 1971 even though there had been no failure on their part to control the dog. The second limb of s 2(2)(a) was satisfied by showing that damage from a bite was likely to be severe in view of the type of breed. On the evidence, the dog was territorially possessive, in particular of the area near to the Land Rover. This was a characteristic not normally found in bull mastiffs except at particular times or in particular circumstances. This was sufficient to bring the claim within the second limb of s 2(2)(b). The dog's nature was known to the defendant owner and therefore s 2(2)(c) was satisfied.

[17.45]   **Smith v Ainger**

(1990) Times, 5 June, [1990] CLY 3297, CA

The claimant sustained a fractured left leg after being knocked over by Sam, an aggressive dog, owned by the defendant, which had lunged to attack the claimant's dog. The defendant knew that his dog had a propensity to attack other dogs. The claimant relied on s 2(2)(a) of the Animals Act 1971 on the basis that the damage caused was likely if the dog was not restrained, or was likely to be severe. Neill LJ said that the two issues to consider were:

(1)   Was personal injury to a human a kind of damage which the defendant's dog unless restrained, was likely to cause?

(2)   Was personal injury to a human, if caused by that dog likely to be severe?

HELD, ON APPEAL: The judge at first instance had been satisfied on the evidence that Sam was likely to attack another dog even without provocation. If Sam did attack the other dog there was a 'material risk' that the owner of the other dog would seek to defend his animal and would be injured as a result of that intervention. The fact that previous injuries inflicted by Sam were quite minor, was considered irrelevant as damage caused by a large dog such as an Alsatian was likely to be severe within the meaning of s 2(2)(a).

Judgment for the claimant.

[17.46]   Hunt v Wallis

[1994] PIQR P128, QB

The claimant was injured when the defendant's border collie collided with him.

HELD: The dog was not likely to cause physical injury. Section 2(2)(b) of the Animals Act 1971 did not require the court to compare the characteristics of a border collie with dogs in general. The proper test was to look at the nature of other dogs of that breed, where a particular breed could be identified, to see whether it had unusual characteristics. The defendant had no knowledge of the dog's propensity to collide with people.

Judgment for the defendant.

[17.47]   Jaundrill v Gillett

(1996) Times, 30 January, QBD

Several of the defendant's horses had been released from a field at night by persons unknown. One of those horses collided with a car. At first instance it was held that the damage was due to the characteristics of the horse which were not normally found in animals of the same species or were not normally so found except at particular times and in particular circumstances. Accordingly, the defendant was found liable.

HELD, ON APPEAL: The real and effective cause of the accident was the release of the animals onto the highway. It was the presence of the horses on the highway that was the cause of the damage sustained. Therefore there was no causal link between the animal's characteristic and the damage.

Appeal allowed.

[17.48]   Chauhan v Paul

(1998) LTL, 19 February, CA

The claimant, a postman, whilst delivering letters to the defendant's address, was attacked by the defendant's rottweiler dog. The claimant fell and sustained injury. At first instance it was held that if the dog had run up to the postman, it was because it wanted to greet him and play. The judge rejected evidence that the dog had reached or touched the claimant.

HELD, ON APPEAL: Even if the dog had chased the claimant in a friendly way, there was no evidence that it had a propensity to do so, nor that the defendant was aware of any such propensity. Therefore there was no liability.

[17.49]   Gloster v Chief Constable of Greater Manchester Police

[2000] All ER (D) 389, (2000) LTL, 24 March, CA

The claimant was in a police car chasing an allegedly stolen vehicle. When that vehicle stopped, and the driver ran off, the claimant gave chase. The police dog handler slipped whilst holding the dog which then slipped its leash. Police dogs, once set loose, were unable to differentiate between friend and foe, and will chase whichever running target they first set eyes upon. Unfortunately, the dog ran after the claimant police officer and bit him twice.

HELD, ON APPEAL: A dog's training is different from its characteristics or natural inclination, such that the claimant could not succeed under s 2(2)(b) of the Animals Act 1971. The act of attacking, or biting, was not a characteristic in itself, but merely a manifestation of the dog's characteristic of being able to respond to instruction.

[17.50]   Flack v Hudson

[2001] QB 698, [2000] All ER (D) 1701, [2001] 2 WLR 982, CA

See also at para [17.58].

The claimant's wife was exercising the defendant's horse. The horse had a propensity to be frightened by agricultural machinery, of which the defendant was aware but the claimant's wife was not. On the approach of a tractor, the horse bolted and the claimant's wife fell, resulting in fatal injuries.

HELD, ON APPEAL: The horse's propensity to bolt when near agricultural machinery was an abnormal characteristic of the horse for which the defendant was liable under s 2(2)(b) of the Animals Act 1971. The fact that the claimant's wife was a keeper of the horse did not prevent an action against the defendant, another keeper.

[17.51]   Mirvahedy v Henley

[2003] UKHL 16

[2003] 2 AC 491, [2003] 2 All ER 401, [2003] 2 WLR 882

The defendants' three horses escaped from their field and made their way onto the nearby road. One of the horses collided with the claimant's car, causing damage and serious personal injuries. The judge concluded that the horses had escaped because of some unknown event that had caused them to panic and to trample the fences, posts and vegetation that were adequate for containing normally docile horses.

HELD, ON APPEAL: The accident had been caused by the horses' panic which led to their escape. The panic constituted a temporary characteristic in particular circumstances which were normal for horses. Therefore the defendants were liable under s 2(2)(b) of the Animals Act 1971.

[17.52]   Hole v Ross-Skinner

[2003] EWCA Civ 774

[2003] All ER (D) 272 (May)

In a case very similar to *Mirvahedy* (at para [17.51]), the claimant was injured when his vehicle collided with a horse on a dual carriageway. The horse was kept at a stud on the defendant's land which was run by his wife. The trial judge found the defendant liable both in negligence and pursuant to s 2(2) of the Animals Act 1971. The defendant accepted the finding of strict liability under the 1971 Act, but appealed the finding in negligence as he intended to pursue a claim for contribution against the owners of the horse, Mr and Mrs Woollaston.

HELD, ON APPEAL: The defendant was not liable in negligence and the appeal was allowed. On the night of the accident the horse was left secure in its field and the defendant was not responsible for its escape. The fact there was general scruffiness of the gates and fences on the defendant's property was inadequate evidence to establish liability for negligence. What mattered was not the quality of the fences and gates generally on this property, but the state of the fences and gates on the fields in question.

Note—The defendant having successfully appealed the finding in negligence was then able to pursue a claim for contribution against the owners of the horse, unencumbered by a finding in negligence against him. This case demonstrates a person in possession of an animal may be jointly liable under the Animals Act 1971 even if not the owner, for example, the owner of stables where a horse is kept on livery.

[17.53]   Elliott v Town Foot Stables

(3 September 2003, unreported), Newcastle Upon Tyne County Court

An 8-year-old claimant fell from a pony during a riding lesson at the defendant's premises.

HELD: The defendant was not liable in negligence as the instructor was competent, the lesson was conducted appropriately and the pony was suitable for the claimant. The claim also failed under s 2 because, following the comments of Lord Scott in *Mirvahedy* (at para [17.51]), damage was not 'reasonably to be expected'.

[17.54]   Livingstone v Armstrong

(11 December 2003, unreported), Newcastle County Court

The claimant drove into a cow which was standing in the middle of the road at 4 am.

HELD: At the time of the collision, the cow was standing still and there was no evidence it was frightened or was panicking. There was no evidence as to what the characteristic of the cow was. The case was distinguished from *Mirvahedy* (at para [17.51]). The defendant was not liable for negligence as the fencing was found to be sufficient on the farm and the claim also failed under s 2 of the Animals Act 1971.

[17.55]   Burrow v Metropolitan Police Comr

[2004] EWHC 1435 (QB)

[2004] All ER (D) 170 (May), QB

The claimant was a mounted police officer who was riding a horse on Wimbledon Common. It was alleged that the horse suddenly 'bolted' into a wooded area causing the claimant to strike his face on low branches. The defendant conceded that if the accident occurred as the claimant alleged then there would be a breach of s 2(2) of the Animals Act 1971 and the defendant would be liable. However, the defendant contended that the claimant's evidence regarding the circumstances of the accident was not true.

HELD: Having reviewed the accident circumstances carefully, the claimant had over exaggerated the history of the horse and had not been truthful about his account of the accident. A colleague who was with him at the time supported the claimant's version of events, but mentioned shortly after the accident to two other police officers that the accident occurred as the claimant had been smoking a cigarette, only had the reins in one hand and the horse who had been cantering on soft ground was not sufficiently controlled by the claimant causing him to enter into the wooded area.

Accordingly, the claim was dismissed.

(III) SECTION 5

[17.56] **Cummings v Granger**
[1977] QB 397, [1977] 1 All ER 104, [1976] 2 WLR 842, CA

See also at para [17.39] where the facts of this case are set out.

The keeper of the dog was strictly liable under s 2(2) of the Animals Act 1971. However, the court considered the exceptions from liability available under s 5 of the 1971 Act.

HELD, ON APPEAL: Section 5(1) did not apply because the bite was not wholly due to the fault of the claimant but only partly so. Section 5(2) applied because the claimant knew the dog was loose in the yard, she had seen the warning notice 'Beware of the Dog' and in the circumstances had voluntarily accepted the risk of injury. In relation to s 5(3), the court observed 'This was a yard in the East End of London where persons of the roughest type come and go ... the only reasonable way of protecting the place was to have a guard dog.' Therefore, it was found under s 5(3) that the claimant was a trespasser and it had been reasonable to have guard dog there.

[17.57] **Canterbury City Council v Howletts & Port Lympne Estates Ltd**
[1997] ICR 925, 95 LGR 798, [1997] JPIL 51

In this case, a zoo-keeper was killed by a tiger.

HELD: The defence of *volenti* was not open to an employer, even where the employee was employed expressly to assume hazardous duties

[17.58] **Flack v Hudson**
[2001] QB 698, [2000] All ER (D) 1701, [2001] 2 WLR 982, CA

See also at para [17.50] where the facts of this case are set out.

The defendant was strictly liable under s 2(2) of the Animals Act 1971. However, the court considered the exception from liability available under s 5(2) of the 1971 Act.

HELD, ON APPEAL: Section 5(2) did not apply because the defendant did not give the claimant a sufficient warning about the horse's particular characteristic and accordingly the claimant was not alerted to the specific risk of injury to which she was exposed.

(IV) SECTION 8

[17.59] **Davies v Davies**
[1975] QB 172, [1974] 3 All ER 817, [1974] 3 WLR 607, 118 Sol Jo 717, CA

Alongside a main road was a large area of common land. Owners of a nearby farm were entitled to put animals on the common for grazing and were registered for that purpose under the Commons Registration Act 1965. Sheep got on the road from the common and the claimant in his car collided with them without negligence on his part and his car was damaged. The defendant was a son of the owner of the farm who was licensed to have sheep on the farm and pleaed guilty to a charge under s 135 of the Highways Act 1959.The claimant sued for the damage to his car.

HELD: The defendant was not liable. He had the right to place sheep on the common and so was protected by the Animals Act 1971, s 8(2).A conviction under the Highways Act 1959 did not make him liable for a civil offence. Being licensed to put sheep on the common was sufficient to apply s 8(2); the protection was not limited to persons actually having title to the land.

PROCEDURE

Limitation

1. BACKGROUND

[18.1] A general rule for limitation of actions in tort and simple contract requiring such actions to be commenced within six years from the cause of action arising was established by the Statute of Limitation of 1623, which remained in force (with some accretion of exceptions and amendments) until supplanted by the Limitation Act 1939. The six-year period was maintained by s 2 of the 1623 Act. A proviso was added to that section by the Law Reform (Limitation of Actions) Act 1954 reducing the limitation period to three years in actions of negligence, nuisance and breach of duty for damages in respect of personal injuries. The 1954 Act also abolished or amended to three years a variety of special periods of limitation contained in particular statutes.

The Limitation Act 1963 gave the court power to disapply the limitation period of three years so as to enable a claimant to pursue an action for damages for personal injury when material facts 'of a decisive character' were proved to have been outside his knowledge, in effect, when the cause of action arose. The 1963 Act also by s 4, prescribed a time limit of two years for contribution proceedings.

The Limitation Act 1975 simplified the elaborate provisions of the 1963 Act for disapplying or extending the three-year period and, by ss 2A, 2B and 2C added to the 1939 Act, made rules for determining the date from which time began to run in personal injury and fatal accident cases. A further section inserted as s 2D in the 1939 Act provided a new and more liberal rule by which to disapply the three-year period in certain cases. The Limitation Act 1980 (in force from 1 May 1981) repealed and re-enacted with some amendments and additions the surviving provisions of the earlier Acts and are considered below so far as they relate to the subject matter of this book.

The Law Commission has recently reviewed the law relating to limitation periods in its Report No. 270, 2001, and recommended that there should be a simplified core regime for civil actions. The special rules for personal injury action and disapplying the limitation period is expected to remain, but changes are recommended in most other areas to remove some of the uncertainty, unfairness and confusion which has developed through the case law. Since the report was finalised, little has been done to put it into effect, but it remains an issue about which the Law Commission are concerned.

The Latent Damage Act 1986 (amending the Limitation Act by inserting sections 14A and 14B) added an alternative limitation period in situations where damage could not be discovered until after the ordinary limitation period had expired. These provisions are discussed in more detail below at para [18.90].

As some cases in this chapter refer to provisions of the Limitation Acts before 1980 the following destination table may be useful:

Limitation Act 1963	*Limitation Act 1980*
s 4	s 10

Limitation Act 1939	*Limitation Act 1980*
s 2	s 2 (tort), s 5 (contract)
s 2A	ss 11, 14
s 2B	ss 2, 14
s 2C	s 13
s 2D	s 33

A few cases dealing with the provisions of s 35 of the Limitation Act 1980 have been reported. What guidance has been provided by the courts can be found at paras [18.2]–[18.9]. Useful general points are as follows:

(1) a defendant wishing to rely on the Statute of Limitation 1623 must plead it (CPR PD 16 para 1);

(2) 'damage only' claims have a six-year limitation period (Statute of Limitation 1623, s 2);

(3) the day on which the cause of action arose is excluded from the computation of the limitation period;

(4) in the case of claimants under age, time does not begin to run until their 18th birthday;

(5) the limitation period for trespass to persons is six years.

2. LIMITATION ACT 1980

[18.2]
2. Time limit for actions founded on tort
An action founded on tort shall not be brought after the expiration of six years from the date on which the cause of action accrued.

[18.3]
5. Time limit for actions founded on simple contract
An action founded on simple contract shall not be brought after the expiration of six years from the date on which the cause of action accrued.

(A) ACTIONS IN RESPECT OF WRONGS CAUSING PERSONAL INJURIES OR DEATH

[18.4]
11. Special time limit for actions in respect of personal injuries
(1) This section applies to any action for damages for negligence, nuisance or breach of duty (whether the duty exists by virtue of a contract or of provision made by or under a statute or independently of any contract or any such provision) where the damages claimed by the plaintiff for the negligence, nuisance or breach of duty consist of or include damages in respect of personal injuries to the plaintiff or any other person.
(2) None of the time limits given in the preceding provisions of this Act shall apply to an action to which this section applies.
(3) An action to which this section applies shall not be brought after the expiration of the period applicable in accordance with subsection (4) or (5) below.
(4) Except where subsection (5) below applies, the period applicable is three years from—
    (a) the date on which the cause of action accrued; or
    (b) the date of knowledge (if later) of the person injured.
(5) If the person injured dies before the expiration of the period mentioned in subsection (4) above, the period applicable as respects the cause of action surviving for the benefit of his estate by virtue of section 1 of the Law Reform (Miscellaneous Provisions) Act 1934 shall be three years from—
    (a) the date of death; or
    (b) the date of the personal representative's knowledge;
whichever is the later.
(6) For the purposes of this section 'personal representative' includes any person who is or has been a personal representative of the deceased, including an executor who has not proved the will (whether or not he has renounced probate) but not anyone appointed only as a special personal representative in relation to settled land; and regard shall be had to any knowledge acquired by any such person while a personal representative or previously.
(7) If there is more than one personal representative, and their dates of knowledge are different, subsection (5)(b) above shall be read as referring to the earliest of those dates.

[18.5]
12. Special time limit for actions under Fatal Accidents legislation
(1) An action under the Fatal Accidents Act 1976 shall not be brought if the death occurred when the person injured could no longer maintain an action and recover damages in respect of the injury (whether because of a time limit in this Act or in any other Act, or for any other reason).
    Where any such action by the injured person would have been barred by the time limit in section 11 of this Act, no account shall be taken of the possibility of that time limit being overridden under section 33 of this Act.

(2)   None of the time limits given in the preceding provisions of this Act shall apply to an action under the Fatal Accidents Act 1976, but no such action shall be brought after the expiration of three years from—

(a)   the date of death; or

(b)   the date of knowledge of the person for whose benefit the action is brought;

whichever is the later.

(3)   An action under the Fatal Accidents Act 1976 shall be one to which sections 28, 33 and 35 of this Act apply, and the application to any such action of the time limit under subsection (2) above shall be subject to section 39; but otherwise Parts II and III of this Act shall not apply to any such action.

[18.6]
13.   Operation of time limit under section 12 in relation to different dependants

(1)   Where there is more than one person for whose benefit an action under the Fatal Accidents Act 1976 is brought, section 12(2)(b) of this Act shall be applied separately to each of them.

(2)   Subject to sub-s (3) below, if by virtue of subsection (1) above the action would be outside the time limit given by subsection 12(2) as regards one or more, but not all, of the persons for whose benefit it is brought, the court shall direct that any person as regards whom the action would be outside that time limit shall be excluded from those for whom the action is brought.

(3)   The court shall not give such a direction if it is shown that if the action were brought exclusively for the benefit of the person in question it would not be defeated by a defence of limitation (whether in consequence of section 28 of this Act or an agreement between the parties not to raise the defence, or otherwise).

[18.7]
14.   Definition of date of knowledge for purposes of sections 11 and 12

(1)   In section 11 of this Act references to a person's date of knowledge are references to the date on which he first had knowledge of the following facts—

(a)   that the injury in question was significant; and

(b)   that the injury was attributable in whole or in part to the act or omission which is alleged to constitute negligence, nuisance or breach of duty; and

(c)   the identity of the defendant; and

(d)   if it is alleged that the act or omission was that of a person other than the defendant, the identity of that person and the additional facts supporting the bringing of an action against the defendant;

and knowledge that any acts or omissions did or did not, as a matter of law, involve negligence, nuisance or breach of duty is irrelevant.

(2)   For the purposes of this section an injury is significant if the person whose date of knowledge is in question would reasonably have considered it sufficiently serious to justify his instituting proceedings for damages against a defendant who did not dispute liability and was able to satisfy a judgment.

(3)   For the purposes of this section a person's knowledge includes knowledge which he might reasonably have been expected to acquire—

(a)   from facts observable or ascertainable by him; or

(b)   from facts ascertainable by him with the help of medical or other appropriate expert advice which it is reasonable for him to seek;

but a person shall not be fixed under this subsection with knowledge of a fact ascertainable only with the help of expert advice so long as he has taken all reasonable steps to obtain (and, where appropriate, to act on) that advice.

[18.8]
14A.   Special time limit for negligence actions where facts relevant to cause of action are not known at date of accrual

(1)   This section applies to any action for damages for negligence, other than one to which section 11 of this Act applies, where the starting date for reckoning the period of limitation under subsection (4)(b) below falls after the date on which the cause of action accrued.

(2)   Section 2 of this Act shall not apply to an action to which this section applies.

(3)   An action to which this section applies shall not be brought after the expiration of the period applicable in accordance with subsection (4) below.

(4)   That period is either—
(a)   six years from the date on which the cause of action accrued; or
(b)   three years from the starting date as defined by subsection (5) below, if that period expires later than the period mentioned in paragraph (a) above.

(5)   For the purposes of this section, the starting date for reckoning the period of limitation under subsection (4)(b) above is the earliest date on which the claimant or any person in whom the cause of action was vested before him first had both the knowledge required for bringing an action for damages in respect of the relevant damage and a right to bring such an action.

(6)   In subsection (5) above 'the knowledge required for bringing an action for damages in respect of the relevant damage' means knowledge both—
(a)   of the material facts about the damage in respect of which damages are claimed; and
(b)   of the other facts relevant to the current action mentioned in subsection (8) below.

(7)   For the purposes of subsection (6)(a) above, the material facts about the damage are such as would lead a reasonable person who had suffered such damage to consider it sufficiently serious to justify his instituting proceedings for damages against a defendant who did not dispute liability and was able to satisfy a judgment.

(8)   The other facts referred to in subsection (6)(b) above are—
(a)   that the damage was attributable in whole or in part to the act or omission which is alleged to constitute negligence; and
(b)   the identity of the defendant; and
(c)   if it is alleged that the act or omission was that of a person other than the defendant, the identity of that person and the additional facts supporting the bringing of an action against the defendant.

(9)   Knowledge that any acts or omissions did or did not, as a matter of law, involve negligence is irrelevant for the purposes of subsection (5) above.

(10)   For the purposes of this section a person's knowledge includes knowledge which he might reasonably have been expected to acquire—
(a)   from facts observable or ascertainable by him; or
(b)   from facts ascertainable by him with the help of appropriate expert advice which it is reasonable for him to seek;

but a person shall not be taken by virtue of this subsection to have knowledge of a fact ascertainable only with the help of expert advice so long as he has taken all reasonable steps to obtain (and, where appropriate, to act on) that advice.

[18.9]
14B.   Overriding time limit for negligence actions not involving personal injuries

(1)   An action for damages for negligence, other than one to which section 11 of this Act applies, shall not be brought after the expiration of fifteen years from the date (or, if more than one, from the last of the dates) on which there occurred any act or omission—
(a)   which is alleged to constitute negligence; and
(b)   to which the damage in respect of which damages are claimed is alleged to be attributable (in whole or part).

(2)   This section bars the right of action in a case to which subsection (1) above applies notwithstanding that—

    (a)   the cause of action has not yet accrued; or

    (b)   where section 14A of this Act applies to the action, the date which is for the purposes of that section the starting date for reckoning the period mentioned in subsection (4)(b) of that section has not yet occurred;

before the end of the period of limitation prescribed by this section.

3.   CALCULATING THE PERIOD

(A)   WHEN TIME BEGINS TO RUN: S 14 'DATE OF KNOWLEDGE'

[18.10]   Davis v Ministry of Defence

[1985] CLY 2017, [1985] CA Transcript 413, [1985] LS Gaz R 3265, CA

Davis had been employed as a welder by the Ministry of Defence (MOD) since 1955. In April 1969 he suffered a localised attack of dermatitis. In August 1971 he suffered a generalised outbreak and left MOD's employment. Over ten years later, on 10 November 1981, he sued the MOD. Evidence showed that Davis had believed strongly throughout that his dermatitis had been caused by his working conditions and that he had a good claim against the MOD. The statement of claim pleaded that before 10 November 1978 he had been unaware that the general outbreak was 'attributable' to the MOD's negligence and breach.

HELD: The action should not be struck out. Section 14(1)(b) of the Limitation Act 1980 required the court to ask when did Davis first know (not reasonably believe or suspect) that his dermatitis was capable of being attributed to his working conditions. It could not certainly be said that the combined state of mind of Davis and (applying s 14(3)), his doctors and lawyers was such that they knew this, prior to 10 November 1978.

Note—Contrast *Wilkinson v Ancliff (BLT) Ltd* (at para [18.11]).

[18.11]   Wilkinson v Ancliff (BLT) Ltd

[1986] 3 All ER 427, [1986] 1 WLR 1352, 130 Sol Jo 766, [1986] LS Gaz R 3248, CA

The claimant was employed as a road-tanker driver based at Felixstowe; the tankers carried Toluene Di-Isocyanate (TDI). In April 1981 he suffered wheezing, coughing and shortness of breath. In August 1981 he stopped work due to ill-health; he claimed DHSS benefit showing his cause of incapacity as 'chest congestion due to inhalation of chemicals'. In November 1981 he was medically examined; the hospital registrar concluded that he had developed bronchial asthma due to sensitisation to TDI. He immediately consulted solicitors about claiming compensation from his employers. On 7 March 1984 a writ was issued stating that he first discovered his asthma was 'attributable to the defendants in November 1981'. In June 1984 a consultant chemist was instructed; his report, in December 1984, made a number of criticisms of the defendants' handling procedures for TDI and concluded that there was little doubt that the claimant's asthma had been brought about by his continued exposure to TDI. The writ and statement of claim were served on 29 March 1985. In considering whether the validity of the writ should be extended or that its service be set aside, the court had (applying the principle in *Heaven v Road & Rail Wagons Ltd* [1965] 2 QB 355) to assess whether the defendant might be deprived of a limitation defence. The crucial question for these purposes was did the claimant have the relevant knowledge referred to in s 14 of the Limitation Act 1980 by 6 March 1982 (three years before the writ expired)?

HELD: The service of the writ should be set aside and the action dismissed. On the basis of the claimant's own evidence he well knew, after his visit to hospital in November 1981, that his injuries were capable of being attributed to the defendants' failure to provide him with safe working conditions.

Note—Section 14A (added by Latent Damage Act 1986, s 1) which relates only to non-personal injury actions reads, in subsection (5): 'the starting date for reckoning the period of limitation ... is the earliest date on which the plaintiff ... had both the knowledge required for bringing an action for damages in respect of the relevant damage and a right to bring such an action'.

[18.12]   Davis v City and Hackney Health Authority

[1991] 2 Med LR 366, QBD

The claimant, who suffered from cerebral palsy, was born on 16 June 1963. Immediately before his birth his mother had been given the drug Ergometrine by the defendants. He left home on 3 February 1983. As a result of meeting a helpful law student in August 1985 he instructed solicitors on 13 September 1985. Shortly after receiving an expert's report, on 26 November 1986, the claimant was fully informed of his rights of action. A writ was issued on 1 April 1987.

HELD: For the purposes of s 14(1) of the Limitation Act 1980, he acquired relevant knowledge in late November 1986, or alternatively for personal and domestic reasons could not reasonably have been expected to acquire this knowledge before about December 1984. To decide when a claimant should have acquired knowledge for the purposes of s 14(3) of the 1980 Act, the test was not what a reasonable man would have known, but what an individual of the claimant's age, background, intelligence and disabilities would have been expected to have known.

[18.13]   Stephen v Riverside Health Authority

[1990] 1 Med LR 261

The claimant underwent a mammography on 11 March 1977. She was aware that the radiographer was not operating the equipment properly. The claimant had trained (though not qualified) as a radiographer in her teens, but had not worked in this capacity for the 20 years prior to this mammography. Following the examination the claimant suffered from various distressing symptoms for some months but was continually reassured by the defendant that the mammography had been carried out satisfactorily and the symptoms arose from unrelated causes. Despite the assurances and her recovery the claimant continued to worry about the possibility that she had received an overdose of radiation which might cause her harm in the future. An expert was instructed in 1980 but was unable to arrive at any reasonably favourable conclusion until further tests had been undertaken. He had attended a conference with counsel on 20 February 1985. The writ was issued on 15 February 1988.

HELD: The claimant's date of knowledge was 20 February 1985. Mere anxiety about an increased risk of cancer founded at most on the claimant's suspicion did not amount to knowledge of injury for the purpose of s 14(1)(a) of the Limitation Act 1980. The claimant's symptoms after the mammography were not sufficiently serious to justify instituting proceedings for damages. Further, the claimant's suspicion or belief that the mammography had been carried out incompetently was not sufficient to impute to her the knowledge that the symptoms could be attributable to excessive exposure to radiation. The claimant's past experience in radiography did not make her an expert in this field so as to transform the suspicion or conviction into the knowledge of attributability. Her action was not statute-barred.

Note—See also the cases of *Bentley v Bristol & Western Health Authority* [1991] 2 Med LR 359 and *Broadley v Guy Clapham & Co* [1994] 4 All ER 439, (1993) Times, 6 July, CA. In the *Bentley* case it was held that broad knowledge that the injury was caused by an operation was insufficient to set the limitation running. The limitation period did not arise until the claimant had knowledge of an act or omission that could constitute negligence. However, Balcombe LJ in the *Broadley* case expressed the view that *Bentley* had been wrongly decided. In the *Broadley* case it was held that the claimant's cause of action in a medical negligence case arose when she could have known with the help of medical advice reasonably obtainable, that her injury had been caused by damage resulting from something done or not done by the surgeon during her operation. Knowledge detailed enough to plead the statement of claim was not required before the time limit began to run.

[18.14]   Guidera v NEI Projects Ltd (India)

(1990) Independent, 19 February, CA

The court considered the definition of 'attributable' in s 14 (1)(b) of the Limitation Act 1980. It was held on appeal that the word 'attributable' meant 'capable of being attributed to'. Thus, the attribution of the injury to the accident need only be a possibility, though a real possibility rather than a fanciful one.

Per Sir David Croom-Johnson: The act or omission of the defendant must be a possible cause as opposed to a probable cause of injury. One is dealing here with knowledge, actual or imputed, and not with proof of liability.

[18.15]   Halford v Brookes

[1991] 3 All ER 559, [1991] 1 WLR 428, CA

The claimant was the mother of Lyn Halford who was murdered on 3 April 1978. The second defendant was tried and acquitted of murder though confessed to inflicting injuries on the deceased at the instigation of the first defendant. After the trial further evidence came to light implicating the first defendant, but despite a vigorous campaign by the deceased's family the authorities refused to prosecute him.

In July 1985 the claimant consulted new solicitors. Counsel advised that a civil action claiming damages on behalf of the estate was feasible and on the 1 April 1987 a writ was issued against both defendants. The defendants pleaded that the action was statute barred.

HELD, ON APPEAL: 'Appropriate expert advice' referred to in s 14(3) of the Limitation Act 1980 did not include the legal advice that the claimant received from her solicitors in 1985. *Fowell v National Coal Board* [1986] CILL 294, (1986) Times, 28 May followed.

The claimant did not require expert advice in order to invest her with the necessary knowledge contemplated by s 14. She was capable of acquiring that knowledge herself and did so at the conclusion of the second defendant's trial in 1978. Whilst the claimant's action was statute barred, the Court of Appeal overturned the lower court's refusal to exercise discretion under s 33 of the 1980

Act. The case did not depend on the accuracy of recollection but upon the extent to which it could be discerned whether or not the first and second defendant were telling the truth. The claimant's ignorance of her legal rights was also considered by the court to be a relevant consideration exercising discretion under s 33.

[18.16]   Driscoll-Varley v Parkside Health Authority
[1991] 2 Med LR 346

The claimant suffered injuries to her right leg on 18 April 1984. The leg was put in traction for 12 days. It did not heal and throughout the next few years she had to undergo many additional operations. In mid-1985 she was told by her surgeon that there was some dead bone in the leg causing problems. This was removed but it was not possible to obtain a satisfactory union at the fracture site and so the problems and treatment continued.

In late 1986 the claimant was becoming profoundly dissatisfied with her treatment and consulted solicitors with a view to commencing proceedings against the defendant. However, she was reluctant to do so fearing that her consultant surgeon, in whom she had confidence, would cease to treat her. In June 1988 expert evidence was obtained which stated that the cause of the claimant's problems was the premature removal of her right leg from traction. The writ was issued on 4 May 1989.

HELD: The injury was 'significant' within the meaning of s 14(1)(a) of the Limitation Act 1980 in September 1985 at the stage when the dead bone was discovered. However, the claimant did not have actual knowledge that the failure of her leg to respond to treatment was attributable to the premature removal from traction until June 1988. Neither did the claimant have constructive knowledge. The claimant's fear that her surgeon might have ceased to treat her was a reasonable one. Thus, it was reasonable for the claimant to defer seeking legal assistance until she did.

[18.17]   Hendy v Milton Keynes Health Authority
[1992] 3 Med LR 114

On 27 February 1985 the claimant underwent two operations one of which was a hysterectomy. Complications developed and a further operation was performed on 26 March 1985. The claimant met a doctor on 12 November 1986 who explained what had gone wrong during the first operation in February.

The claimant's solicitors, instructed in 1987, obtained a favourable expert's report in July 1988. The writ was issued on the 21 November 1988.

HELD: The claimant received sufficient information from the doctor on 12 November 1986 to know in general terms that her problem was attributable to the operation in February 1985. It did not matter that she was still unaware of the specific errors. In a relatively straightforward case such as this 'broad knowledge' was sufficient to start time running and therefore the claimant's claim was statute barred.

[18.18]   Stubbings v Webb
[1993] AC 498, [1993] 1 All ER 322, HL

The claimant who alleged she had been sexually abused and raped by the defendants (her adoptive father and brother) as a young girl issued a writ claiming damages for mental illness and psychological disturbance caused by the abuse. The claimant was born on 29 January 1957 so she reached her majority 18 years later on 29 January 1975. The writ was issued on 18 August 1987.

The claimant argued that she was not aware she had suffered any significant injury attributable to the abuse until she received the advice of a psychiatrist in September 1984.

This view was rejected by the master but accepted on appeal to the judge and by the Court of Appeal. It was previously thought that these actions for trespass to person were actions in respect of personal injuries within s 11(1) of the Limitation Act 1980. The defendants appealed to the House of Lords.

HELD: The House of Lords accepted the defendants' arguments that s 11(1) did not apply to a cause of action based on indecent assault or rape. The claimant's cause of action was governed by s 2 of the 1980 Act and therefore had a six-year limitation period without any provision for extension. The claimant's claim was statute-barred.

Note—The House of Lords derived assistance from the recommendations of the Tucker Committee Report prepared in 1949 which were given effect to by the Law Reform (Limitation of Actions) Act 1954. Hansard was also referred to.

Per Lord Griffiths: The terms in which the Bill had been introduced made it clear beyond peradventure that the intention was to give effect to the Tucker recommendation that the limitation period in respect of trespass to the person was not to be reduced to three years but should remain at six years.

[18.19]   Dobbie v Medway Health Authority
[1994] NLJR 828, CA

In 1973, the claimant underwent a mastectomy. The surgeon performing the operation believed that an excision of a lump in her breast was cancerous. He had not conducted any microscopic examination. The growth was subsequently found to be benign. The claimant gave evidence to the effect that she knew, within hours, days or months after the operation that it had been carried out unnecessarily. However, at this stage, the claimant did not pursue any claim against the health authority. It was not until 1988 that she sought legal advice, having been prompted by publicity about a similar case. The writ was served in October 1990.

The judge dismissed the claimant's claim, stating that pursuant to s 14(1) of the Limitation Act 1980, time ran from the date of the operation and not from 1988. The judge also refused to exercise his discretion under s 33 of the 1980 Act. The claimant appealed.

HELD: It was irrelevant that at the time of the operation, the claimant might not have been aware that the act or omission of the defendant was negligent. To start time running, it was only necessary that the claimant knew that she had suffered significant injury and that this injury was capable of being attributed to something done or not done by the defendant authority. This she knew very shortly after the operation. The lack of appreciation that this act or omission was arguably negligent did not stop time running. The Court of Appeal also upheld the judge's refusal to exercise his discretion under s 33.

[18.20]   Hallam-Eames v Merrett Syndicates Ltd
(1995) Times, 25 January

The claimants, names at Lloyd's, claimed damages against the defendants who were either management agents of Lloyd's syndicates or their members' agents. The claimants alleged that the defendants were negligent in that they had written certain run-off policies between 1978 and 1983 and involved the names in reinsurance to close (RITC) contracts for the periods 1979 to 1984 without possessing material upon which to make any rational assessment of the potential liabilities to which they were exposing the claimants.

The first writ was issued in January 1993 by which time the claims were statute-barred by the six-year limitation period. The claimants sought to rely on s 14A of the Limitation Act 1980.

The defendants argued that all the claimants could reasonably have expected to acquire was the knowledge required to bring an action from documents distributed to the claimants between 1981 and 1988, and in particular a letter dated 18 April 1985.

The judge at first instance found that these documents would have told the claimants that they had suffered losses significantly serious to justify instituting proceedings within the meaning of s 14A(7) and the knowledge required at s 14A(6)(a) was therefore satisfied. The claimants appealed.

HELD, ON APPEAL: This was an over-simplification of the reasoning and analysis of s 14A in *Broadley v Guy Clapham & Co* [1994] 4 All ER 439, (1993) Times, 6 July, CA and *Dobbie v Medway Health Authority* (at para [18.19]). 'If all that was necessary was that a plaintiff should have known that the damage was attributable to an act or omission of the defendant, the statute would have said so. Instead, it speaks of the damage being attributable to the act or an omission which is alleged to constitute negligence. In other words, the act or omission of which the plaintiff must have knowledge must be that which is causally relevant for the purposes of an allegation of negligence': per Hoffmann LJ.

[18.21]   Henderson v Temple Pier Co Ltd
[1998] 3 All ER 324, [1998] 1 WLR 1540

On 28 January 1993 the claimant suffered an injury in the course of walking down the gangway to visit a bar and restaurant situated on a moored ship on the Thames. She instructed solicitors on 22 February 1993, but these solicitors did not identify the owners of the ship until July 1994. Proceedings were commenced on 30 April 1997 and the Particulars of Claim averred that the claimant's date of knowledge was not more than three years prior to the commencement of the proceedings since the claimant had not known, at the time of the accident, that the defendant was the owner and occupier of the ship and gangway.

The defendant applied for an order that the claimant's claim be struck out on the basis that it was statute barred pursuant to the provisions of s 11 of the Limitation Act 1980.

HELD: The county court judge dismissed the defendant's application. The judge found that the claimant's solicitors had not provided a competent service. They could and should have found out the identity of the defendant at a much earlier stage. However the claimant had no constructive knowledge in accordance with the proviso contained in section 14(3) of the 1980 Act which provided that a claimant should not be fixed with knowledge of facts only ascertainable with the help of expert advice. The county court judge accepted that expert advice included legal advice from a solicitor. The defendant appealed.

HELD, ON APPEAL: The identity of the defendant was knowledge that the claimant could have acquired from facts attainable or ascertainable by her. Furthermore, even if the solicitor was an appropriate expert the facts were ascertainable by that solicitor without the use of legal expertise. The claimant was fixed with constructive knowledge which her solicitors ought to have acquired. The defendant's appeal was allowed.

'The proviso is not intended to give an extended period of limitation to a person whose solicitor acts dilatory in requiring information which is obtainable without particular expertise', per Bracewell J.

[18.22]   Warren v Middlebrook Mushrooms Ltd
6 May 1998, CA

The claimant was employed by the defendant. On 27 November 1990 she suffered an injury which was diagnosed as a minor crush fracture to one of the bones of her spine. After about three months she returned to work and she had pain in her back on a regular basis. She visited her GP in November 1992, April 1993 and November 1994 complaining of back pain. Finally in December of 1995 she underwent an x-ray when it was then discovered that she had developed degenerative changes around her old fracture site and would not be able to continue with her work.

She commenced proceedings on 4 March 1997. The defendant pleaded limitation and the case proceeded to a trial on this preliminary issue.

HELD: The county court judge found for the claimant. He accepted that the claimant reasonably did not regard her injury as significant during the first three months up to her return to work. Furthermore, from February 1991 until December 1995 the claimant reasonably did not attribute her continuing back symptoms to her accident and therefore by a combination of paragraphs (a) and (b) of s 14(1) of the Limitation Act 1980, the claimant's date of knowledge was not until December 1995. The defendant appealed.

HELD, ON APPEAL: There was not sufficient evidence upon which the judge could properly conclude that between February 1991 and December 1995 the claimant had failed to make any connection between the fracture of the spine and her continuing back problems. Therefore it is not possible to contend that the injury was not significant within the meaning of s 14. It was perfectly obvious that it was significant. The claimant's claim was statute barred.

[18.23]   Various claimants v Bryn Alyn Community Homes Ltd
[2003] EWCA Civ 85
[2003] QB 1441, [2004] 2 All ER 716, [2003] 3 WLR 107, CA

The claimants suffered sexual and/or physical abuse between 1973 and 1991 while children in the care of the first defendant's children's home. The claimants commenced proceedings many years later and after the expiry of their primary limitation periods.

The trial judge found the first defendant liable to most of the claimants, but held that all the successful claimants were out of time and not saved by the 'date of knowledge' provisions in ss 11 and 14 of the Limitation Act 1980. Nevertheless, the judge exercised his discretion in favour of the claimants under s 33 of the 1980 Act to disapply the limitation period. The judge also found that in the light of the House of Lords decision in *Lister v Hesley Hall* (see Chapter 5 Vicarious Liability, para [5.20]) that he had no power under s 33 of the 1980 Act to extend the limitation period to tortuous conduct in respect of which the defendant was vicariously responsible, but which was not in itself negligent.

Both parties appealed the judge's various findings on the limitation.

HELD, ON APPEAL: *Section 14 – Date of knowledge:* The trial judge had taken the view that the claimants knew when they left the defendant's care they had suffered significant injury and that they had the relevant knowledge for the purposes of the Limitation Act 1980 at that time. The Court of Appeal disagreed. The Court of Appeal asked the question 'What is the action about?' and took the view that the action was about long-term post traumatic psychiatric injuries.

These were cases where substantial abuse was experienced whilst the claimants were minors and there was a subsequently diagnosed psychiatric condition. There was the added complexity of abuse suffered before the claimant's period of care with the first defendant. The legislation required the court 'to ask whether such an already damaged child would reasonably turn his mind to litigation as a solution to his problems?' This was a fact sensitive question that had to be considered individually and in detail. The judge had not done that.

Furthermore, increasing public awareness through public enquiries, such as the Waterhouse Report, and the high profile criminal prosecutions and civil claims for child abuse had ushered in a 'generation more sensitive to its seriousness and its significance'. Such sensitivity did not exist in the period immediately after the claimants' period of residence with the first defendant in these cases. This impacted directly on the question of an individual turning to litigation. Emphasis should be placed on when the claimant acquired knowledge that he had a psychiatric injury rather than simply being aware of an injury at the time of the abuse, or shortly thereafter.

Section 33 – Discretion: The trial judge was incorrect to exercise his discretion in favour of the claimants at the trial. The overall issue for the court was one of fairness, i e would it be 'equitable' to disapply limitation provisions having regard to 'the balance of potential prejudice weighed with a regard to all the circumstances of the case' including those specifically mentioned in s 33(3)? Generally speaking, the longer the delay the greater the likelihood that a court should refrain from exercising section 33 discretion in favour of a claimant. In particular, if a date of knowledge argument had been successful, the weight to be given to the reasons for the delay thereafter would be limited.

The Lister point: The trial judge's finding was upheld. Where s 11 of the 1980 Act was under consideration, claims for personal injuries in respect of deliberate conduct, whether in the context of the carer's liability or not, were not caught by these provisions. In the absence of some provable allegation of systemic negligence, the first defendant's employees deliberate abuse did not fall within s 11 and was, therefore, governed by the non-extendable six-year period of limitation from the act or the age of majority, whichever is later.

[18.24]   Jan Collins v Tesco Stores

[2003] EWCA Civ 1208

The claimant was employed by the defendants as a petrol kiosk attendant. Whilst re-stocking the kiosk with goods she allegedly sustained an injury to her right shoulder. The symptom first appeared in 1996, but she was not absent from work as a result until 26 June 1998. She remained off work until 13 November 1999, but thereafter only worked for short periods. Proceedings were issued in January 2001. The defendant pleaded that the claim was statute barred, but the claimant stated that she only acquired knowledge in 1998 when she was told by her physiotherapist that her injury had been caused by heavy lifting. The judge found in favour of the claimant at first instance.

HELD, ON APPEAL: the claimant's symptoms, treatment and absence from work meant that by January 1998 she did know that her injury was significant under s 14(2) of the Limitation Act 1980. She was also deemed to know, by that date, that the injury had been caused at work.

[18.25]   Rowe v Kingston upon Hull City Council

[2003] EWCA Civ 1281

[2003] All ER (D) 426 (Jul)

Between 1979 and 1989 the claimant attended a school within the defendant local authority. In March 1991 the claimant was diagnosed with dyslexia and in October 1992 he attained the age of 18.

The claimant did not commence proceedings until September 1998 claiming that it was not until the decision in *Phelps v Hillingdon LBC* [2000] 4 All ER 504 that he knew he could bring a claim against the local authority and that dyslexia would be agreed as an injury. At first instance the judge found in favour of the claimant and found that his claim was not statute barred, on the basis that he had only acquired the relevant knowledge when the decision in *Phelps* had been given.

The defendants appealed claiming the claimant did know that he had suffered a significant injury by the time of his 18th birthday.

HELD: Appeal allowed. Identifying an injury in such cases is not easy, but the claimant knew by his 18th birthday that he was dyslexic and that he had not received any help. The court refused to use their discretion under s 33 of the Limitation Act 1980 because the prejudice to the defendants who would not be able to trace any of the claimants teachers, was too great.

[18.26]   Godfrey v Gloucestershire Royal Infirmary NHS Trust

[2003] EWHC 549 (QB)

[2003] All ER (D) 346 (Mar), QB

On 1 March 1995 the claimant's daughter was born with significant brain damage and cerebral palsy. Prior to her birth, the claimant had a number of scans which indicated there were abnormalities, but the claimant decided against a termination. After the birth the claimant alleged she had not been given sufficiently accurate information to enable her to make an informed decision about a termination and she claimed general damages and the cost of looking after her daughter. Proceedings were commenced on 25 April 2002 and the claimant relied on s 14 of the Limitation Act 1980 saying that she had only, within the previous three years, become aware that she had been given inaccurate information.

Limitation was tried as a preliminary issue and the judge held that the claimant had known from the outset about her daughter's condition, but concluded that it was appropriate and equitable to disapply s 11 of the 1980 Act and use the court's discretion under s 33 of the same Act to allow the action to proceed. The claimant had written a detailed letter of complaint to the defendants only a few weeks after her daughter's birth and it could not therefore be said that the claim had been unexpected.

[18.27]   McCarroll v Statham Gill Davies

[2003] EWCA Civ 425

[2003] All ER (D) 12 (Apr), [2003] Lloyd's Rep PN 167

The appellant, a former member of the band Oasis, appealed against an order that his claim was statute barred. In 1993 the appellant signed a contract between Oasis and Sony. In 1995 he was summarily dismissed from the band and he claimed that at the time of signing the contract, it had not been properly explained to him, by the respondent solicitors, that there were provisions within the contract which enabled him to be summarily expelled without compensation.

The relevant period of limitation was six years, but proceedings were not commenced until April 2001. The appellant considered that he had only suffered damage when he left the band but the respondents believed it was when the contract had been signed.

The first instance judgment was upheld by the Court of Appeal. The judge held that the risk of dismissal, which existed from the moment the contract was signed, was an actual loss. The appellant was unable to rely upon s 32 of the Limitation Act 1980 as there had not been a deliberate concealment of any relevant facts.

[18.28]   Buckler v J F Finnegan Ltd and Sheffield City Council
[2004] EWCA Civ 920

[2004] All ER (D) 214 (Jun)

Between 1969 and 1970 the claimant had been employed by the first defendants as a joiner. From 1970 to 1974 he was employed by the second defendants, also as a joiner. He left the second defendants in 1974, but returned in 1975 when he was employed as an asbestos assessor. The claimant had been exposed to asbestos dust during both periods of employment in the 1970s. In 1991 the claimant was diagnosed as having pleural thickening of his left lung. He was advised by his doctor that he could sue for this condition, but the claimant decided not to, as his condition was only mild. The claimant was regularly screened through the 1990s and his condition remained static. In 1999 the claimant's condition was referred to as 'pleural plaques' and the claimant mistakenly believed his condition had worsened. He commenced proceedings in April 2003.

HELD: At first instance the judge held that the claimant had actual knowledge for the purposes of s 14(2) of the Limitation Act 1980 and constructive knowledge under s 14(3) in 1991. The judge exercised her discretion under s 33 of the 1980 Act to disapply the limitation period as the claimant had shown a real and substantial reason for not commencing proceedings between 1991 and 1999, when he did not consider his condition to be very serious.

HELD, ON APPEAL: The second defendants appealed and the appeal was dismissed. The burden was on the claimant to show that it would be equitable to disapply the limitation period. The judge should have considered the length of the delay and the prejudice to the parties. The claimant had made a conscious decision in 1991 not to commence proceedings and his mistaken belief as to his condition was not a significant reason for s 33 to be applied.

[18.29]   Gravgaard v Aldridge & Brownlee
[2004] EWCA Civ 1529

[2004] All ER (D) 134 (Dec), 149 Sol Jo LB 27

In 1988 the appellant and her husband instructed the respondent to deal with the obtaining of a mortgage for the purposes of discharging the appellant's husband's business debts. Their home was in the appellant's sole name, but it was transferred by deed into joint names.

Over the following six months the appellant's husband built up further debts and the appellant reluctantly agreed to a second charge over the home, by way of a guarantee. Five years later the bank obtained a possession order. The appellant commenced proceedings in 2002 alleging that she had been negligently advised and that she had not needed to transfer the home into joint names in order to obtain the mortgage. By doing so she had allowed the home to become available to her husband's creditors.

HELD: At first instance it was held that the claim was statute barred by s 13A of the Limitation Act 1980 because the appellant should reasonably have obtained legal advice more than three years before she commenced proceedings. The respondent claimed that her date of knowledge was 1988 when the property was transferred. The appellant appealed stating that she had not known of the negligence until January 2001.

HELD, ON APPEAL: Appeal dismissed. The appellant did not have actual knowledge, but she did have constructive knowledge in 1988 when she should have taken legal action. To reach such conclusion under s 14A of the 1980 Act the test is objective and the court should take into account all external circumstances. At the very latest the appellant knew in 1996 that she had a claim against her former solicitors and she should have taken advice then, if not before.

[18.30]   C v Middlesbrough Council
[2004] EWCA Civ 1746

[2005] 1 FCR 76, [2004] All ER (D) 339 (Dec)

Between 1982 and 1988 the appellant attended a school run by the respondents and alleged that during his time there he had been sexually abused by one of his teachers. Shortly before he left school he complained to a social worker about the abuse, but he did not commence proceedings until 2002. At first instance the judge dismissed the appellant's claim stating that the claim was for trespass to the person and therefore subject to a non-extendable limitation period under s 2 of the Limitation Act 1980. He also concluded that there was no evidence the appellant had suffered any harm. The appellant appealed.

HELD, ON APPEAL: The judge was right to have concluded that the appellant had not suffered any harm. Where an action based on vicarious liability of an employer consisted of deliberate abuse, the relevant limitation period was that set out in s 2, not s 11 of the 1980 Act.

[18.31]   Miller v Thames Valley Strategic Health Authority
[2005] EWHC 3281 (QB)

[2005] All ER (D) 299 (Oct)

The claimant, aged 61 at the date of trial, alleged that the defendant health authority had been negligent when between July 1963 and February 1964 they failed to diagnose the claimant's brain tumour. The tumour was only discovered in November 1968 when he attended an optician due to a deterioration in his sight.

The claimant commenced proceedings in November 2003 and the issue of whether the claim was statute barred was determined as a preliminary issue.

The claimant alleged that his date of knowledge was when he had received copies of his medical records in November 2000. The defendants argued the claimant had constructive knowledge in 1969 when he knew he had a tumour and should have investigated its cause and diagnosis.

HELD: that the claimant, being a reasonable man of moderate intelligence could not have considered the failure to diagnose the tumour to be negligence. The claim was not statute barred.

[18.32]   A v Hoare

[2006] EWCA Civ 395

[2006] All ER (D) 203 (Apr), [2006] 1 WLR 2320

Four appellants appealed against the dismissal of their claim for damages and psychiatric harm which they claimed they had suffered following sexual abuse, whilst at the respondents schools. Following *Stubbings v Webb* [1993] AC 498, [1993] 1 All ER 322, the court held that each incident was an intentional sexual assault and therefore subject to a strict six-year limitation period under s 2 of the Limitation Act 1980.

The appellants claimed that *Stubbings* should not be followed as the Law Commission had recommended that the limitation period should be extendable, as it should not apply to local authorities, and because it could be distinguished on its facts.

HELD, ON APPEAL: The Court of Appeal were bound to follow the decision in *Stubbings v Webb*. These were not negligence, nuisance or breach of duty cases which could be brought within s 11(1) of the 1980 Act. Appeals dismissed.

Note—The judgment in this case gave a very thorough and helpful review of the case law to date in this area.

(B)   LIMITATION DEFENCE

[18.33]   Ronex Properties Ltd v John Laing Construction Ltd

[1983] QB 398, [1982] 3 All ER 961, [1982] 3 WLR 875, 126 Sol Jo 727, CA

A writ or third party notice cannot be struck out as disclosing no cause of action merely because the defendant has a defence under the Limitation Act 1980. 'Where it is thought to be clear that there is a defence under the Limitation Act, the defendant can either plead that defence and seek the trial of a preliminary issue, or, in a very clear case, seek to strike out the claim on the ground that it is frivolous, vexatious and an abuse of the process of the court. But in no circumstances can he seek to strike out on the ground that no cause of action is disclosed' (per Stephenson LJ).

[18.34]   Harris v Newcastle Health Authority

[1989] 2 All ER 273, [1989] 1 WLR 96, 133 Sol Jo 47, CA

The claimant, who was born on 30 October 1959, underwent two operations on her left eye in an attempt to correct a squint. The operations in 1961 and 1965 made the condition worse. In February 1987 it was suggested to the claimant that she might have a claim for compensation. The claimant's solicitors made an application for pre-action disclosure on 30 June 1987 which was refused by the district judge and on appeal to the judge. The defendant had made it quite clear that they would be relying on limitation.

HELD, ON APPEAL: If it is plain beyond doubt that a defence of limitation will be raised and will succeed then this is a matter the court may take into account when exercising its discretion whether or not to order pre-action disclosure. However, a court can never be so certain in most personal injury cases because of the existence of s 33 of the Limitation Act 1980. On the basis of limited information about limitation issues at such a pre-trial hearing it is difficult for the court to conclude that the proposed action was bound to fail. Therefore, in general, issues relevant to limitation should not be considered at an application for pre-trial disclosure.

[18.35]   Ketteman v Hansel Properties Ltd

[1987] AC 189, [1988] 1 All ER 38, [1987] 2 WLR 312, HL

The claimants purchased houses built by the first defendants between 1973 and 1975. The foundations were defective and cracking appeared in 1976. The claimants sued the first defendants in 1980. The first defendants joined the architects as third parties, and the architects joined the local authority as fourth parties. In 1982, the claimants obtained leave to join both the architects and the local authority as defendants. Neither party attempted to plead any defence of limitation until the closing stages of the trial, when the effect of a recent judgment might have made such a defence feasible.

HELD, ON APPEAL: The parties' application to amend their defences should be dismissed. Regardless of the existence of new authority, they could have pleaded a defence of limitation if they had chosen long before the hearing had reached its closing stages. Late amendments should only be allowed if they clarified the issues, rather than giving defendants the opportunity of creating a different defence. A defence of limitation is a procedural bar. It has nothing to do with the merits of the case. In the absence of a plea of limitation the claimants' claims succeeded on the merits.

(C)   PERSONS UNDER A DISABILITY

LIMITATION ACT 1980, S 28

[18.36]
28.   Extension of limitation period in case of disability
   (1)   Subject to the following provisions of this section if, on the date when any right of action accrued for which a period of limitation is prescribed by this Act, the person to whom it accrued was under a disability, the action may be brought at any time before the expiration of six years from the date when he ceased to be under a disability or died (whichever first occurred) notwithstanding that the period of limitation has expired.
   (2)   This section shall not affect any case where the right of action first accrued to some person (not under a disability) through whom the person under a disability claims.
   (3)   When a right of action which has accrued to a person under a disability accrues, on the death of that person while still under a disability, to another person under a disability, no further extension of time shall be allowed by reason of the disability of the second person.

LIMITATION ACT 1980, S 38

[18.37]
38.   Interpretation
   (2)   For the purposes of this Act a person shall be treated as under a disability while he is an infant, or of unsound mind.

(3)   For the purposes of subsection (2) above a person is of unsound mind if he is a person who, by reason of mental disorder within the meaning of the Mental Health Act 1959, is incapable of managing and administering his property and affairs.

[18.38]   Penrose v Mansfield

(1970) Times, 8 October (Waller J); affd (1971) 115 Sol Jo 309, Times, 19 March, CA

The claimant was badly injured as a result of the negligence of the defendant on 10 November 1965. The writ was issued on 12 December 1968. He claimed that the action was not out of time because due to his injuries, he was not in a fit state to manage his own affairs until after 12 December 1965 and that he was entitled to the protection of s 22 of the Limitation Act 1980, as amended.

HELD: Following *Kirby v Leather* [1965] 2 QB 367, CA the problem for consideration was whether it had been shown on a balance of probabilities that the claimant was for some five weeks or more of unsound mind, that is, 'by reason of mental illness incapable of managing his affairs in relation to the accident as a reasonable man would do.' On the evidence, especially the fact that he had himself on 10 December 1965 signed a consent for operative treatment, he had failed to show that his mental state until after 12 December was such as to bring himself within the terms of s 22. The action was statute-barred.

[18.39]   Turner v Malcolm Ltd

(1992) 136 Sol Jo LB 236, 15 BMLR 40, CA

The claimant was involved in an accident on 21 October 1980 which left him of unsound mind within the meaning of s 38(2) and (3) of the Limitation Act 1980 and, thus, under a disability for the purposes of that Act.

A writ was issued on 5 August 1981 and the statement of claim served on 25 November 1981. In December 1988, the defendants made an application to the district judge to strike out the claimant's claim for want of prosecution. The district judge dismissed the application and the matter went to an appeal judge who upheld the district judge's decision but on terms disadvantageous to the claimant. The claimant appealed to the Court of Appeal.

HELD: Sections 28 and 38 of the 1980 Act in effect provided that there was no limitation period for a claimant who was under a permanent disability. The effect of striking out this action or imposing any condition on its progress would only extend the period before the claimant's claim was finally resolved. The claimant's appeal was successful and the claimant's claim was allowed to proceed.

Note—See also Chapter 16 generally.

[18.40]   Thomas v Plaistow

[1997] PIQR P540, CA

On 14 July 1984 the claimant and defendant were riding on the defendant's motorcycle. The defendant was uninsured. An accident occurred and the claimant suffered serious personal injuries, including a head injury causing epilepsy. There was a dispute as to who was the rider and pillion passenger. The claimant was prosecuted on the basis that she was the rider, but the prosecution collapsed for lack of evidence.

The writ was issued on 14 October 1994 some seven years and three months out of time. The claimant stated that she had not commenced proceedings earlier because she did not know of the existence of the Motor Insurers' Bureau until 1992; the seriousness of her injuries and resulting disability (although she was not suffering from a mental disorder to make her a patient within the meaning of the Mental Health Act 1983) made it difficult for her to seek legal advice; until some recovery of memory in 1994 she could not remember whether or not she was the rider or passenger and at the criminal proceedings she had not received any legal advice about the possibility of a civil claim.

The district judge granted his discretion under s 33 of the Limitation Act 1980. The defendant appealed.

HELD, ON APPEAL: The defendant's appeal was dismissed and the claimant's claim was allowed to proceed. The court considered the meaning of 'disability' within s 33(3)(d) of the 1980 Act. The district judge had construed 'disability' within that section as including not only mental disorder within the meaning of the Mental Health Act 1983, but also a wider definition of disability including the claimant's condition which involved memory problems, forgetfulness, depression and an inability to concentrate.

This interpretation was incorrect. The word 'disability' within the subsection only referred to that as defined by the Mental Health Act 1983 and not any lesser mental disability. However, any other lesser disability could be relevant under s 33(3)(a) or as part of 'all the circumstances of the case' for the purposes of s 33(3).

Despite the district judge's misinterpretation he had nevertheless exercised his judicial discretion correctly.

4. EXTENDING THE STATUTORY PERIOD

(A) LIMITATION ACT 1980, S 33

[18.41]
33. Discretionary exclusion of time limit for actions in respect of personal injuries or death

(1) If it appears to the court that it would be equitable to allow an action to proceed having regard to the degree to which—

    (a) the provisions of section 11 or 12 of this Act prejudice the plaintiff or any person whom he represents; and

    (b) any decision of the court under this subsection would prejudice the defendant or any person whom he represents;

the court may direct that those provisions shall not apply to the action, or shall not apply to any specified cause of action to which the action relates.

(2) The court shall not under this section disapply section 12(1) except where the reason why the person injured could no longer maintain an action was because of the time limit in section 11.

If, for example, the person injured could at his death no longer maintain an action under the Fatal Accidents Act 1976 because of the time limit in Article 29 in Schedule 1 to the Carriage by Air Act 1961, the court has no power to direct that section 12(1) shall not apply.

(3) In acting under this section the court shall have regard to all the circumstances of the case and in particular to—

    (a) the length of, and the reasons for, the delay on the part of the plaintiff;

    (b) the extent to which, having regard to the delay, the evidence adduced or likely to be adduced by the plaintiff or the defendant is or is likely to be

less cogent than if the action had been brought within the time allowed by
section 11 or (as the case may be) by section 12;

(c)   the conduct of the defendant after the cause of action arose, including the
extent (if any) to which he responded to requests reasonably made by the
plaintiff for information or inspection for the purpose of ascertaining
facts which were or might be relevant to the plaintiff's cause of action
against the defendant;

(d)   the duration of any disability of the plaintiff arising after the date of the
accrual of the cause of action;

(e)   the extent to which the plaintiff acted promptly and reasonably once he
knew whether or not the act or omission of the defendant, to which the
injury was attributable, might be capable at that time of giving rise to an
action for damages;

(f)   the steps, if any, taken by the plaintiff to obtain medical, legal or other
expert advice and the nature of any such advice he may have received.

(4)   In a case where the person injured died when, because of section 11, he could
no longer maintain an action and recover damages in respect of the injury, the
court shall have regard in particular to the length of, and the reasons for, the delay
on the part of the deceased.

(5)   In a case under subsection (4) above, or any other case where the time limit,
or one of the time limits, depends on the date of knowledge of a person other than
the plaintiff, subsection (3) above shall have effect with appropriate modifications,
and shall have effect in particular as if references to the plaintiff included
references to any person whose date of knowledge is or was relevant in determining
a time limit.

(6)   A direction by the court disapplying the provisions of section 12(1) shall
operate to disapply the provisions to the same effect in section 1(1) of the Fatal
Accidents Act 1976.

(7)   In this section 'the court' means the court in which the action has been
brought.

(8)   References in this section to section 11 include references to that section as
extended by any of the preceding provisions of this Part of this Act or by any other
provisions of Part III of this Act.

[18.42]   Donovan v Gwentoys Ltd

[1990] 1 All ER 1018, [1990] 1 WLR 472, 134 Sol Jo 910, HL

The claimant suffered an injury at work on 3 December 1979 when she was aged
16. She made a claim for four weeks' industrial injury benefit on the basis of an
injury to her wrist and returned to work. She left the defendant's employment in
1980 having never indicated her intention to make a claim for damages. The
claimant consulted solicitors in 1984 who issued the writ on 10 October 1984
some five and a half months after the expiry of the limitation period, her date of
birth being 25 April 1963.

The defendant argued that the court should not exercise its discretion under
s 33 of the Limitation Act 1980 in favour of the claimant in view of the fact that
they were unaware of the claimant's claim until some five and a half years after the
accident, and it was not until January of 1986 when the defendant became aware of
the circumstances of the alleged accident and the nature of the injuries sustained.

The trial judge exercised his discretion in favour of the claimant on the basis that
he was confined to consider the prejudice to the defendant caused by the five and
a half months delay between the expiration of the limitation period and the issue
of the writ. This delay was minimal. The Court of Appeal agreed.

HELD, ON APPEAL to the House of Lords: Section 33 provides the judge with an
unfettered discretion to allow an action in respect of personal injuries or death to

proceed despite the expiry of the limitation period if he considers it fair and equitable to do so having regard to the prejudice suffered by both the claimant and the defendant. This section does not prevent the court from considering other matters which experience has shown need to be evaluated by a judge when exercising his discretion. In particular an extremely important consideration to take into account is the date on which the claim is first made against the defendant. The judge had misdirected himself by concentrating only on the five and a half months delay after the limitation period had expired. In this case the degree of prejudice suffered by the defendant was greater than that suffered by the claimant who would only suffer the slightest prejudice if she was required to pursue her remedy against her solicitors.

[18.43]   Howe v David Brown Tractors (Retail) Ltd
[1991] 4 All ER 30, CA

The claimant ran a family firm together with his father. On 23 January 1985 the claimant was injured as a result of the failure of a piece of farming equipment purchased from the defendant in 1982. The primary limitation period expired on the 22 January 1988 and on the 8 July 1988 the claimant issued a writ claiming damages for personal injuries and losses and expenses incurred. The claim was pleaded in tort.

An order was made by consent on 19 December 1988 disapplying the three-year limitation period in respect of the personal injury claim. Thereafter, on the 14 November 1989 the claimant applied to amend the writ and statement of claim to add the firm as second claimant and to include a claim for damages for breach of contract.

It was necessary for the court to decide (*inter alia*) whether the limitation period for the new contract claim was three or six years, ie whether or not s 11 of the Limitation Act 1980 applied.

HELD: The firm's claim was subject to the statutory provisions of s 11 of the Limitation Act 1980. The supply of dangerous machinery constituted a breach of duty in tort to the claimant causing him personal injury. Similarly, the supply of dangerous machinery constituted the breach of contractual duty owed to the firm causing loss.

Per Stuart Smith LJ: The same facts which give rise to the personal injury and breach of statutory duty to the claimant gives rise to the breach of duty albeit a different duty, owed to the firm.

Having decided that, it was for the claimant to apply under s 33 of the Limitation Act 1980 to disapply the limitation period applicable in respect of the firm's claim before or at the same time as seeking leave under RSC Ord 15 r 6(5)(b) to add the firm as a claimant.

[18.44]   Re Workvale Ltd (No 2)
[1992] 2 All ER 627, [1992] 1 WLR 416, [1992] BCLC 544, CA

The claimant was injured on 27 September 1983 and notice was given to his employers that a claim would be made against them. The employer company went into liquidation in 1984 and was dissolved in July 1986. The claimant commenced his action against the company just over three weeks before the expiry of the limitation period. The action then proceeded normally and by September 1988 the case was nearly ready for trial. However, at that stage the defendant's solicitors informed the claimant's solicitors that the defendant company had been dissolved and in 1990 the defendant's solicitors managed to strike out the claimant's claim on the basis that the defendant company no longer existed.

In the meantime, the claimant died and his widow pursued the claim by seeking a declaration that the dissolution of the company was void and a direction under s 651(5) of the Companies Act 1985 that the company be restored to the register and that the period between the dissolution of a company and its restoration on a register be disregarded pursuant to s 651(6). The claimant succeeded before the judge and the defendant's insurers appealed.

The insurers of the defendant company argued that, on the true construction of s 651(5) of the Companies Act 1985, s 33 of the Limitation Act 1980 was to be disregarded. Secondly, if s 33 was not to be disregarded, the court was required to consider whether at trial s 33 was likely to be invoked and on the present facts this was not so.

HELD: It was necessary to look at the entirety of the Limitation Act 1980 when considering whether the claimant's application under s 651(5) should succeed. This consideration included the consideration of s 33. It was enough for the widow to satisfy the court that there was an arguable case that s 33 would be used to disapply the limitation period.

As these proceedings had been commenced within the limitation period the necessity of a s 33 application could be avoided by seeking a declaration under s 651(6) of the Companies Act 1985 that the period between the dissolution of the company and the making of the order shall not count.

[18.45]   Nash v Eli Lilly & Co

[1993] 4 All ER 383, [1993] 1 WLR 782, 14 BMLR 1, CA

The principles to apply when considering s 33 of the Limitation Act 1980 remain the same whether considering an ordinary single case or multi-party litigation.

Per Hidden J: It would not be well for there to be two different sets of principles, one for an ordinary run of the mill case and the other for multi party litigation.

Note—See above at para [18.10] for a general discussion of the whole of s 14 of the Limitation Act 1980.

[18.46]   Walkin v South Manchester Health Authority

[1995] 4 All ER 132, [1994] 1 WLR 1543, 25 BMLR 108, CA

After the birth of her third child, the claimant was admitted to the defendant's hospital and a sterilisation operation was performed. The operation failed and the claimant discovered that she was pregnant in February 1987. She gave birth to a healthy child in September 1987. A writ was issued on 10 October 1991 claiming damages for negligent treatment and advice about the failure of the operation and economic loss, namely, the cost of bringing up the child.

The writ specifically did not claim damages for personal injuries, but despite this the defendant pleaded in the defence that the action was one for personal injuries and was therefore statute-barred.

The judge held that the claimant's claim was statute-barred and the claimant appealed.

HELD, ON APPEAL: The court had to look at the substance of the claim rather than how it was pleaded. Damages for the claimant's own physical injury and for economic loss stemming from the cost of rearing a child arose from one cause of action, namely, the unwanted pregnancy. The claimant had suffered a personal injury. The unwanted conception was a personal injury in the sense of 'impairment' and the economic loss derived from this injury. Therefore the claimant's claim was subject to s 11(1) of the Limitation Act 1980 and was time-barred. The claimant's appeal was dismissed.

[18.47]   Barrand v British Cellophane plc
(1995) Times, 16 February, CA

The claimant claimed damages against the defendant for noise-induced deafness arising during the course of his employment at the defendant's factory between 1958 and 1980. The claimant sought the judge's discretion under s 33 of the Limitation Act 1980. The judge allowed the claimant's claim to proceed and awarded him damages. The defendant appealed.

HELD, ON APPEAL: When exercising his discretion under s 33 the judge had considered the criteria applicable to striking out for want of prosecution. This was wrong.

There were two vital differences between the two exercises. In a strike out application the onus was on the defendant not merely to show the delay but that he had been prejudiced by it. With an application under s 33 the onus was on the claimant.

Secondly, s 33(3) sets out the criteria which the court must consider when exercising discretion. A judge does not have to refer specifically to each of the criteria, but it would be a useful exercise to do so.

The delay in this case was entirely the fault of the claimant. As a result the defendant had suffered significant prejudice and this outweighed the prejudice the claimant would suffer in not being able to pursue his claim.

[18.48]   Coad v Cornwall and Scilly Isles Health Authority
[1997] 1 WLR 189, [1997] 8 Med LR 154, CA

The claimant was employed by the defendant as a nurse. She injured her back in 1983, but did not issue proceedings until 1993. The judge at first instance disapplied the time barring effect of s 11 of the Limitation Act because he accepted that it was only in 1990 that the claimant realised that she could claim against the defendant when her back condition prevented her from returning to work. She was ignorant of her legal rights.

The judge, in exercising his discretion under s 33 of the Limitation Act 1980 had regard to all the circumstances of the case and in particular 'the length of and reasons for the delay on the part of the claimant'. The judge at first instance considered that this was to be read subjectively.

HELD, ON APPEAL: The Court of Appeal agreed and as the genuineness of the claimant's belief was accepted that she did not realise she could bring a claim, the Judge at first instance had proceeded on the correct basis.

[18.49]   Dale v Michelin Tyre plc
(3 March 1999, unreported), CA

The judge erred in exercising his discretion under s 33 of the Limitation Act 1980 to disapply s 11 by having regard to the substantive claim, in respect of which the judge had already heard evidence. The judge overlooked the inevitable conse-quences of an eight-year delay and was wrong in finding that there was no prejudice.

[18.50]   Robinson v St Helens Metropolitan Borough Council

[2002] EWCA Civ 1099

[2002] All ER (D) 388 (Jul)

The claimant was born on 12 June 1967 and at the time of his appeal he was 35. The claimant suffered from educational difficulties during his school years and had had extra tuition. He eventually went on to obtain a second-class degree in art and design, but his parents considered that he would have achieved much more if his literary skills had not been so poor.

In 1992 the claimant went to see an educational psychologist who diagnosed dyslexia. The claimant went to see solicitors in November 1997. A claim was issued in November 2000 and in February 2001 the particulars of claim were served. The claimant alleged that the local education authority had failed to investigate his problems fully by referring him for psychological assessment. The claim form stated that it was a claim for personal injury but there was no claim for physical or psychiatric loss. The claim for special damages consisted of the cost of tuition and loss of earnings.

At first instance the judge held that the action was not one for personal injury and therefore the six-year limitation applied. This had expired in June 1991, some ten years before the claim had been issued. Allowing for the fact that he might be wrong on that point, the judge also held that the date of knowledge was November 1992, after the claimant had received the psychologist's report. Had he been required to deal with section 33 discretion, the judge would have declined to exercise discretion in the claimant's favour. The claimant appealed.

HELD, ON APPEAL: Dyslexia may in itself be an 'impairment of a person's mental condition'. Although not caused by the defendant, a negligent failure to ameliorate the consequences of dyslexia by appropriate teaching may be said to continue the injury. Furthermore, any loss of enjoyment of life or loss of amenity is more appropriately to be considered as damages for personal injury rather than economic loss. Although the claimant had not relied on any medical evidence the Court of Appeal considered that the claimant's evidence was just sufficient to establish a claim for personal injuries as well as one for economic loss.

The Court of Appeal agreed with the first-instance judge that the date of knowledge was November 1992, after the receipt of the psychologist's report. The court then considered the exercise of discretion under s 33 of the Limitation Act 1980 and found no grounds for interfering with the judge's exercise of his discretion in the defendant's favour.

'The question of proportionality is now important in the exercise of any discretion, none more so than under section 33. The court should be slow to exercise its discretion in favour of a claimant in the absence of cogent medical evidence showing a serious effect on the claimant's health or enjoyment of life and employability. The likely amount of an award is an important factor to consider, especially if, as is usual in these cases, they are likely to take a considerable time to try': per Sir Murray Stuart-Smith.

[18.51]   Fletcher v Containerbase

[2003] EWCA Civ 1635

[2003] All ER (D) 516 (Oct)

The claimant was employed by the defendants between 1977 and 1984 and alleged that during that time he had been exposed to hazardous chemicals which led to the claimant developing bladder cancer. The claimant's cancer was diagnosed in 1990 but proceedings were not commenced until December 2003.

The judge at first instance held that the claimant's date of knowledge was 1995 but he exercised his discretion under s 33 of the Limitation Act 1980 and allowed the claim to proceed. He took into account all of the relevant factors and examined in particular the prejudice to the defendants. All of the documents had been retained by them and their witness evidence was still available.

HELD, ON APPEAL: the decision was upheld as there were no grounds for interfering with the decision.

[18.52]   T v Boys & Girls Welfare Service
[2004] EWCA Civ 1747

[2004] All ER (D) 361 (Dec)

Between 1975 and 1976 the appellant attended an assisted community home run by the respondent. He alleged that during his time there he had been sexually abused by a member of staff. That member of staff was imprisoned in 1986 for offences of buggery and gross indecency. In June 2002, the appellant commenced proceedings based on negligence in failing to protect the respondent from harm.

At a preliminary hearing as to limitation the judge held that although the primary limitation period expired in May 1984, three years after he reached maturity, the appellant's date of knowledge for s 14 of the Limitation Act 1980 was June 1997. The judge declined to use his discretion under s 33 of the 1980 Act and the appellant appealed.

HELD, ON APPEAL: The judge was correct to have taken the length of delay, here 28 years, into account. Section 33 should only be used in special cases and it is for a claimant to show that his is one of those special cases. The older the claim, the greater the prejudice on a defendant. The judge had been correct not to apply s 33 in this case and the appeal was dismissed.

(B)   DISCRETION EXERCISED IN THE CLAIMANT'S FAVOUR

[18.53]   Hartley v Birmingham City District Council
[1992] 2 All ER 213, [1992] 1 WLR 968, CA

The claimant suffered an accident on 10 December 1986. The limitation period expired on 11 December 1989 due to the fact that 9 December was a Saturday. The claimant's solicitor did not manage to issue the writ until the morning of 12 December. The claimant applied to the District Registry for the time limit under s 11 of the Limitation Act 1980 to be disapplied. The claimant's application failed and on appeal to the judge. The claimant appealed to the Court of Appeal.

HELD: The court exercised its discretion under s 33 of the 1980 Act in the claimant's favour. A judge had to take into account all the circumstances of the case as well as the specific matters mentioned in s 33(3).

Per Parker LJ: If in this case the discretion is not to be exercised in favour of the plaintiff I find it difficult to envisage circumstances in which it could ever be so exercised.

Note—Parker LJ reviewed the law and held that recent cases of *Thompson v Brown Construction Ltd* [1981] 2 All ER 296, [1981] 1 WLR 744, 125 Sol Jo 377, HL and

Donovan v Gwentoys Ltd (at para [18.42]) affirmed most of what was said in *Firman v Ellis* (at para [18.72]). Thus, if there is a short delay which is not due to the claimant but to a slip on the part of his solicitor, which did not affect the ability of the defendants to defend the claim because of earlier notification, the exercise of discretion in favour of the claimant will be justified even if the claimant, if not allowed to proceed, had a cast iron action against his solicitor.

See also the case of *Ramsden v Lee* [1992] 2 All ER 204, CA where it was held that although it was highly relevant that a claimant had a case against his solicitors, it would be contrary to the requirements of s 33(3) of the 1980 Act to discount entirely the fact that the claimant would suffer some prejudice in pursuing that claim.

But, see *Hashtroodi v Hancock* [2004] EWCA Civ 652, [2004] 3 All ER 530 – solicitor incompetence in not serving in time, the judge allowed the claim to continue, but the defendants appealed and the appeal was allowed.

[18.54]   Steeds v Peverel Management Services Ltd

[2001] EWCA Civ 419

(2001) Times, 16 May

The claimant slipped on a patch of ice on 26 December 1996 sustaining serious injuries and sought damages against the defendant. The three-year limitation period expired on 26 December 1999. Owing to an oversight by the claimant's solicitors, it was not until 49 days after the expiry of the limitation period that a claim was issued. An application was made to the District Judge to disapply s 11 of the Limitation Act 1980 pursuant to s 33 of the 1980 Act. The District Judge found that delay in the case had to be looked at as a whole and if he had given permission for the action to proceed it would in effect be excusing the solicitors for not taking greater care in attending to the limitation period. The claim was therefore statute-barred. On first appeal, although the circuit judge criticised the judgment of the district judge, it was held the claim was statute-barred for different reasons. The claimant appealed to the Court of Appeal.

HELD: The fault on the part of the claimant was a relevant factor in exercising the court's discretion under s 33, but the solicitor's fault was not to be attributed to the claimant personally. The existence of a claim by the claimant against his solicitors was not an irrelevant factor. In weighing the degree of prejudice offered by a defendant in not being able to rely upon the limitation period as a defence, it is always relevant to consider when the defendant first had notification of the claim. Potential prejudice to a defendant must be regarded as a highly relevant factor in a case where the limitation period is an issue, but in this case the claim was not stale and the claimant had acted reasonably. The claimant's solicitors could be fairly criticised for their admitted negligence, but this could not be held against the claimant for the purposes of the exercise of the court's discretion. Any injustice that might be suffered by the defendants was substantially less than the injustice that the claimant would suffer if his claim against them was barred as a result of his solicitor's negligence.

[18.55]   Burke v Ashe Construction Ltd

[2003] EWCA Civ 717

[2003] All ER (D) 353 (May)

In 1994 the claimant was injured in an accident at work when he fell off a temporary platform. The claimant's first solicitors failed to issue the claim within three years and the claimant consulted a second firm in 1998. In 1999 they instructed counsel to consider the strength of a claim against the first solicitor, but counsel recommended that the main claim be commenced and an application under s 33 of the Limitation Act 1980 should be made.

Proceedings were issued in 2001 and the application duly made.

HELD: The judge held that the claimant's solicitors had been incompetent and that was the reason for the delay. He also held that a fair trial was still possible and he allowed the claim to proceed.

HELD, ON APPEAL: On appeal the court found that the judge had considered all relevant matters and had been right to conclude that the prejudice to the defendants was only slight. Appeal dismissed.

[18.56]   Adam v Ali

[2006] EWCA Civ 91

[2006] All ER (D) 276 (Feb), [2006] 1 WLR 1330

The appellant sustained whiplash injuries in a road traffic accident but her claim was struck out because proceedings had been issued outside the three-year limitation period and the particulars of claim had not been served within four months or at all. The appellant subsequently issued a further claim. At first instance the judge held that he could not disapply the limitation period in accordance with *Walkley v Precision Forgings* [1979] 1 WLR 606 because the first claim had not been issued within the relevant period.

HELD, ON APPEAL: The appeal was allowed. *Walkley* was distinguished as in that case the first action had been brought within the three-year period. The discretion under s 33 of the Limitation Act 1980 was a complete discretion and the judge had to consider a balance of prejudice between the claimant and defendants. As liability had been admitted there was little prejudice to the defendants.

[18.57]   Smith v Ministry of Defence

[2005] EWHC 682 (QB)

[2005] All ER (D) 254 (Apr)

The deceased died in May 1991 of mesothelioma. He had been employed by the defendant cleaning floors in a hanger between 1960 and 1962 during which time he had been exposed to asbestos. It was common ground that the primary limitation period for the purposes of the Limitation Act 1980 started in May 1995. The claimant, in fact, commenced proceedings in May 2004, some nine years out of time. The defendant alleged that the claim was statute barred and the claimant sought the court's discretion in her favour under s 33 of the Limitation Act 1980.

In May 1995 the claimant first instructed solicitors to pursue her claim against the defendant having seen a TV programme about asbestos related illness, spoken to an ex-colleague of her husband's and taken advice from the local Citizens Advice Bureau.

Shortly after the claimant had instructed the solicitors she received a bill from them which she could not pay. Non-payment of this bill was followed by threatening letters from the solicitors which frightened the claimant. The claimant obtained legal aid but had difficulty paying the contributions. During this time the claimant was under significant financial pressures and had a young family to bring up on her own. At no time during this period did the claimant receive clear advice that she had a good, or even reasonably good, claim against the defendant.

In the circumstances the claimant stopped paying her legal aid contributions and did not pursue her claim until she instructed a second set of solicitors in 2002. This instruction followed the claimant watching a further television programme about mesothelioma sufferers receiving compensation and receiving positive advice about the prospects of her claim succeeding.

HELD: In the unusual circumstances of this case the claimant had good reasons for the delay in commencing proceedings from 1995 to 2004. In particular the claimant had acted 'reasonably' when she ceased to pay her legal aid contributions in late 1995.

Furthermore, the viewing of the second television programme and the positive advice received in 2002 was a change in the claimant's knowledge of the circumstances which prompted the claimant to resurrect her claim.

The defendant had not been prejudiced in any material way in investigating the claim, as any evidence available to the defendant was no more or less cogent in 2004 as it was in 1995. In particular documents relating to the deceased's employment by the defendant would have been destroyed by the start of the primary limitation period in May 1995 in any event.

In all the circumstances the judge held that the claimant had discharged the heavy burden on her in order to show that the primary limitation period should be disapplied.

(C)   DISCRETION EXERCISED IN THE DEFENDANT'S FAVOUR

[18.58]   **Adams v Bracknell Forest Borough Council**
[2004] UKHL 29
[2005] 1 AC 76, [2004] 3 All ER 897, [2004] 3 WLR 89

The claimant alleged that between 1981 and 1988, when he attended one of the defendant's schools, his educational needs had not been properly assessed and they had failed to diagnose and treat his dyslexia. As a result the claimant suffered from depression and was disadvantaged in the labour market. The claimant believed he only became aware of his dyslexia in November 1999 when he spoke to an educational psychologist. He issued proceedings in June 2002. At first instance the judge held that he did not have knowledge before November 1999 and he had acted reasonably in not investigating the reason for his literacy difficulties. The Court of Appeal agreed and the defendants appealed.

HELD, ON APPEAL: The House of Lords unanimously held that the claimant knew he had reading and writing difficulties many years before 1999 and that he should have been curious about the cause of it. It would be unreasonable for there not to be an expectation that a person would enquire about their injury as it would allow limitation to run indefinitely. The defendants would be significantly prejudiced if the claim proceeded and the claimant's award would only be modest. Section 33 discretion under the Limitation Act 1980 was not therefore invoked.

[18.59]   **Jude v Elliott Medway Ltd**
(12 January 1999, unreported), CA

In considering whether it was equitable to allow an action which was statute barred by virtue of s 11 Limitation Act 1980 to proceed, the court had to have regard to s 33(1) which required the balancing of the prejudice that might be caused to the claimant if he were not allowed to continue as against the prejudice to the defendant if the claimant were allowed to continue the action.

(D)   FATAL ACCIDENTS

[18.60]   Ward v Foss, Heathcote v Foss

(1993) Times, 29 November, CA

The claimant brought a claim on behalf of the deceased's estate arising out of a fatal accident that occurred in July 1982. The writ was issued in November 1989 and the claimant sought to rely on s 33 of the Limitation Act 1980 to disapply the limitation period. Part of the claimant's claim was for damages for lost years, a head of damage which had been abolished by the Administration of Justice Act 1982 which applied to causes of action accruing after 1 January 1983. The Act provided that no claims might be brought on behalf of the deceased's estate for loss of income in respect of any period of the deceased's death.

The defendant argued that it was inequitable to disapply the limitation period when it would have the affect of allowing the claimant to pursue a claim which had been abolished. The claimant succeeded at first instance and the defendant appealed.

HELD: The defendant's appeal was dismissed. The Court of Appeal accepted that a claim for lost years could result in the claimant benefiting from double recovery and that it was specifically this element of over compensation that the 1982 Act was designed to avoid. However, s 33 did not require the court to look at the fairness or otherwise of the laws of England at the time that the cause of action arose. The court had to consider whether or not it was equitable to disapply the limitation period by reference to the specific criteria mentioned in the section. Looking at the case from this point of view the defendants' arguments were unconvincing.

[18.61]   Young v Western Power Distribution (South West) plc

[2003] EWCA Civ 1034

[2003] All ER (D) 328 (Jul), [2003] 1 WLR 2868

In 1993 Mr Young was diagnosed with mesothelioma as a result of exposure to asbestos between 1959 and 1994 when he was employed by the defendants. Mr Young issued proceedings in 1995 but discontinued them in 1997 when the original diagnosis became questionable. Mr Young died in 1991 and it was then discovered that the original diagnosis of mesothelioma was correct. Mr Young's widow brought proceedings under the Fatal Accidents Act 1976 and the Law Reform (Miscellaneous Provisions) Act 1934, outside the limitation period. The claimant sought the judges' discretion under s 33 of the Limitation Act 1980 and he allowed the claim to proceed. The defendants appealed.

HELD, ON APPEAL: It was held that an action could not be brought under the 1976 Act because the *Walkley v Precision Forgings* [1979] 2 All ER 548 principle prevented further proceedings once the original claim was aborted. The 1934 Act could also not be relied upon as there was no cause of action vested in Mr Young's widow when he died, and the claimant could not therefore rely on s 33 of the 1980 Act. The appeal was allowed.

[18.62]   Piggott v Aulton (decd)

[2003] EWCA Civ 24

[2003] All ER (D) 271 (Jan), [2003] RTR 540

The claimant was injured in a road accident in June 1997 and claimed against the defendant's estate, as he had died in the accident. Proceedings were issued in June 2000 and served on the defendant's insurers, but the proceedings were discontinued as there had not been a personal representative appointed for the defendant as required by CPR 19.8(2)(b)(ii). An underwriter was duly appointed and new proceedings were issued in June 2001. The judge at first instance exercised his discretion under s 33 of the Limitation Act 1980 and allowed the claim to proceed, distinguishing *Walkley v Precision Forgings*.

The defendant appealed.

HELD, ON APPEAL: In the first action there was no real defendant who could be identified and the second proceedings were not against the same defendant. *Walkley* was distinguishable and the judge had been correct in his decision. Appeal dismissed.

5. NEW CLAIMS IN PENDING ACTION

(A) LIMITATION ACT 1980, S 35

[18.63]
35. New claims in pending actions: rules of court

(1)   For the purposes of this Act, any new claim made in the course of any action shall be deemed to be a separate action and to have been commenced—

(a)   in the case of a new claim made in or by way of third party proceedings, on the date on which those proceedings were commenced; and

(b)   in the case of any other new claim, on the same date as the original action.

(2)   In this section a new claim means any claim by way of set-off or counter-claim, and any claim involving either—

(a)   the addition or substitution of a new cause of action; or

(b)   the addition or substitution of a new party;

and 'third party proceedings' means any proceedings brought in the course of any action by any party to the action against a person not previously a party to the action, other than proceedings brought by joining any such person as defendant to any claim already made in the original action by the party bringing the proceedings.

(3)   Except as provided by section 33 of this Act or by rules of court, neither the High Court nor any county court shall allow a new claim within subsection (1)(b) above, other than an original set-off or counterclaim, to be made in the course of any action after the expiry of any time limit under this Act which would affect a new action to enforce that claim.

For the purposes of this subsection, a claim is an original set-off or an original counterclaim if it is a claim by way of set-off or (as the case may be) by way of counterclaim by a party who has not previously made any claim in the action.

(4)   Rules of court may provide for allowing a new claim to which subsection (3) above applies to be made as there mentioned, but only if the conditions specified in subsection (5) below are satisfied, and subject to any further restrictions the rules may impose.

(5)   The conditions referred to in subsection (4) above are the following—

(a)   in the case of a claim involving a new cause of action, if the new cause of action arises out of the same facts or substantially the same facts as are already in issue on any claim previously made in the original action; and

(b)   in the case of a claim involving a new party, if the addition or substitution of the new party is necessary for the determination of the original action.

(6)   The addition or substitution of a new party shall not be regarded for the purposes of subsection (5)(b) above as necessary for the determination of the original action unless either—

(a) the new party is substituted for a party whose name was given in any claim made in the original action in mistake for the new party's name; or

(b) any claim already made in the original action cannot be maintained by or against an existing party unless the new party is joined or substituted as plaintiff or defendant in that action.

(7) Subject to subsection (4) above, rules of court may provide for allowing a party to any action to claim relief in a new capacity in respect of a new cause of action notwithstanding that he had no title to make that claim at the date of the commencement of the action. This subsection shall not be taken as prejudicing the power of rules of court to provide for allowing a party to claim relief in a new capacity without adding or substituting a new cause of action.

(8) Subsections (3) to (7) above shall apply in relation to a new claim made in the course of third party proceedings as if those proceedings were the original action, and subject to such other modifications as may be prescribed by rules of court in any case or class of case.

Note—See CPR 17.4 and 19.5 and commentary in the *The Civil Court Practice*, published by LexisNexis Butterworths, paras 17.4[1]–17.4[7].

[18.64]   Liff v Peasley

[1980] 1 All ER 623, [1980] 1 WLR 781, 124 Sol Jo 360, CA

The claimant was injured in a road accident on 25 October 1973 by the negligence of the defendant Peasley. He issued a writ against him on 14 August 1975. In 1978 he was required by the Motor Insurers' Bureau (Peasley being uninsured) to join another defendant, Spinks. The Statement of Claim was amended for this purpose by order of 5 October 1978 and a copy of the amended writ was sent to Spinks's solicitors. They entered unconditional appearance and served a defence which pleaded that the action against Spinks was statute-barred. They then applied for an order under RSC Ord 15 r 6 that Spinks should cease to be a party in that he was joined after the expiry of the limitation period.

HELD: (1) There were no grounds for exercising the discretion of the court under the Limitation Act 1939, s 2D in favour of the claimant since he was not disadvantaged by s 2A: he already had a cast iron case against Peasley.

(2) It was an established rule of practice that the court will not allow a person to be added as a defendant to an existing action if the claim sought to be made against him is already statute-barred and he relies on it as a defence.

(3) The preferable basis, both on the rules of the court and on the decided cases, on which the rule can be justified is that the action against the added party is deemed to begin against him on the date of the amendment of the writ, not the date of the original writ.

(4) Spinks was not precluded from obtaining an order that he cease to be a party by his solicitors having entered unconditional appearance. When it became apparent that he intended to rely on the claim being statute-barred he became a party who had been improperly added, or who had ceased to be a proper party, within the meaning of RSC Ord 15 r 6(2)(a).

Note—Note from the Supreme Court Practice 1988, p 349, Ord 20/5-8/2:

'In relation to an action to which the Limitation Act 1939 applies (this will of course be progressively more rare), an amendment to add a defendant takes effect, not by way of relating back to the date of the original writ but on the date on which he is effectively joined as a party, i e the date of the service of the amended writ on him or serving his own defence (*Ketteman v Hansel Properties Ltd* [1988] 1 All ER 38, HL approving the dictum of Brandon LJ in *Liff v Peasley* [1980] 1 All ER 623, [1980] 1 WLR 781, and see *Gawthrop v Boulton* [1978] 3 All ER 615, [1979] 1 WLR 268).

On the other hand, in actions to which the Limitation Act 1980 applies, the relation back theory of amendment is expressly provided for by statute. By s 35(1), it is provided that any new claim made in the course of the action will be deemed to be a separate action and except in the case of third party proceedings will be deemed to have been commenced on the same date as the original action and for this purpose s 35(2) provides that 'a new claim' means any claim by way of set-off or counteraction and any claim involving either (a) the addition or substitution of a new cause of action or (b) the addition or substitution of a new party (see Vol 2, Limitation Act 1980, para 6160).'

[18.65]   Kennett v Brown
[1988] 2 All ER 600, [1988] 1 WLR 582, 132 Sol Jo 752, CA

The claimant, a pillion passenger on Mr Brown's motorcycle, was injured in a collision with Mr Teagle's motorcycle. The plaintiff sued Brown who in turn blamed Teagle, who was subsequently joined as second defendant. Teagle served a contribution notice on Brown; after the three-year limitation period had passed, Brown also served a contribution notice in which he sought both an indemnity against the claimant's claim and damages for his own personal injuries. The District Registrar (relying upon s 35 of the Limitation Act 1980) held that Brown's claim for his own injuries could not be considered until he had made an application under s 33 to set aside the limitation period. Brown appealed and it was held that before an application under s 33 was necessary, Teagle had to plead the limitation point. Teagle then appealed to the Court of Appeal.

HELD: Brown's claims were both new claims made in the course of the action and not new claims by way of third party proceedings. The effect of s 35(1) of the 1980 Act was to relate these back to the date of the original action so it was for Teagle to plead s 35(3), whereupon s 33 could be considered and the court's discretion exercised.

Note—But see *Welsh Development Agency v Redpath Dorman Long* [1994] 4 All ER 10, [1994] 1 WLR 1409.

[18.66]   Leicester Wholesale Fruit Market Ltd v Grundy
[1990] 1 All ER 442, [1990] 1 WLR 107, CA

The claimant issued a writ on 5 December 1984 against six defendants claiming damages for negligence or breach of statutory duty arising out of the construction of a fruit market. On 28 February 1985 and before the writ was served it was amended to include the seventh defendant. The seventh defendant argued that it should not be a party to the action on the basis that the writ was amended to add them after the limitation period of six years had expired.

HELD: The effect of s 35(1) of the Limitation Act 1980 was that after the amendment of the writ, the proceedings against the seventh defendant were deemed to have commenced on the date when the writ was initially issued (ie 5 December 1984). However, if the seventh defendant could have availed himself of a limitation defence if a new writ had been issued at the time of amendment then they should not be joined as a defendant because it would have been deprived of this defence. In this case time ran for the seventh defendant from early 1982 so the case against this defendant was not statute-barred at the time of the original writ or amendment.

Per Glydewell LJ: In my judgment the proper approach in the circumstances such as these is for the court to ask itself: if at the time when the writ was amended the plaintiff had instead issued a fresh writ against the said defendant, could that defendant have successfully applied to strike out the action on the grounds that the limitation period had expired and the action was thus an abuse of the process of the court? If the answer to that question is 'no' then I can see no reason why exactly the same result should not be achieved by amending the writ to add the defendant as a defendant instead of issuing a new piece of paper.

Note—See also *Holland v Yates Building Co Ltd* (1989) Times, 5 December, CA.

[18.67]   **Balfour Beatty Construction Ltd v Parsons Brown & Newton Ltd**
(1991) 7 Const LJ 205, (1990) Financial Times, 7 November

The claimant's writ and statement of claim claimed damages for breach of contract and negligence arising out of an agreement that came into effect in about mid-1982. In January and May 1990 the claimant applied for leave to amend the writ and statement of claim to include breaches of contract and negligence arising out of a prior agreement entered into by the parties in 1981.

HELD: The effect of s 35 of the Limitation Act 1980 was to allow a new cause of action which would otherwise be statute-barred to be raised in an existing action provided, in the first instance, that it 'arises out of the same facts or substantially the same facts as or are already in issue in any claim previously made in the original action' (see s 35(5)(a)). If this condition is not satisfied then the claimant's pleadings cannot be amended.

On the facts of this case the allegations raised in the original writ and statement of claim could not be read to extend to cover the earlier period. The new allegations did not arise out of the same facts or substantially the same facts as were already in issue in the original proceedings. As there was no jurisdiction to allow the amendments under s 35 the judge did not examine the appropriate rules of the court or consider whether it would be proper to allow the amendments.

Note—In *Steamship Mutual Underwriting Association Ltd v Trollope & Collis Ltd* (1985) 6 Con LR 11, 2 Const LJ 75; affd (1986) 33 BLR 77, 6 Con LR 11, 2 Const LJ 224, CA, the Court of Appeal refused to allow a re-amendment of the statement of claim to add a new cause of action because this was not based on substantially the same facts. For the purposes of s 35 of the Limitation Act 1980 the question to be asked was whether an amendment amounted to an addition of a new cause of action. This required an assessment of the issues raised in the statement of claim and the proposed amendment 'avoiding unnecessary subtleties'.

[18.68]   **Bank of America National Trust & Savings Association v Chrismas, The Kyriaki**
[1993] 1 Lloyd's Rep 137

The claimants obtained an order granting them leave to amend the writ to join six new defendants outside the limitation period. The defendants sought an order setting aside the amended writ on the grounds that pursuant to s 35(3) of the

Limitation Act 1980 the court was debarred from allowing a new claim involving the additional substitution of a new party to be made after the expiry of the relevant limitation period.

HELD: The defendant was successful. Section 35(3) precluded the court from allowing any amendment to be made at a date after the expiry of the limitation period. An order which permitted service on a new defendant outside the limitation period was wrong. It was unjust to join a new party as a defendant when the effect of the amendment would be to deprive the defendant of a limitation defence.

[18.69]   **Welsh Development Agency v Redpath Dorman Long Ltd**
[1994] 4 All ER 10, [1994] 1 WLR 1409, CA

The defendants were consulting engineers who had designed the substructure of a number of factory units in Cardiff for the claimant. The construction of the units was completed by about 1981. In 1985 and 1987 the claimant complained of settlement of floor slabs. On both occasions the defendants produced reports stating that although there had been settlement this was not due to any defect in their design. The claimant commenced proceedings in July 1990 claiming damages for breach of contract and negligence.

In July 1992 the claimant issued an application seeking leave to make a claim for damages for negligent misstatement arising out of the reports produced by the defendants in 1985 and 1987. The summons was heard in May 1993. The judge refused permission and the claimant appealed to the Court of Appeal.

HELD, ON APPEAL: (1) The claims for damages arising out of negligent misstatement were clearly new claims and thus the claimant was seeking the addition of new causes of action under s 35 of the 1980 Act and RSC Ord 20 r 5 (now CPR 17.4).

(2)   On this basis the amendments would only be allowed if the defendants could not reasonably argue that they would be deprived of a limitation defence. With respect to the 1985 report the limitation period for negligent misstatement expired in September 1992 (six years after the expiry of the primary limitation period in contract on 18 September 1986). Although the claimant's summons was issued in July 1992 it was not heard until May 1993 and so allowing the amendments would give the claimant an unfair advantage under s 35(1).

With regard to the second report, the limitation period had not expired by the time of the claimant's summons. However the judge at first instance was of the view that the amendments should not be allowed because the issues arising out of the two reports in 1985 and 1987 were so closely bound up. This decision of the judge was correct.

(3)   It made no difference that the claimant's application was issued in July 1992 before the expiry of the limitation period. The relevant date, as far as s 35 was concerned, was the date upon which the amendment was actually made which by definition must be no earlier than the date at which leave was granted to make the amendment.

(4)   *Kennett v Brown* (at para [18.65]) had been wrongly decided. The reasoning was based on a misinterpretation of s 35(3) which disregarded the affects of s 35(1).

Appeal dismissed.

[18.70]   Kesslar v Moore & Tibbits

[2004] EWCA Civ 1551

[2004] All ER (D) 53 (Nov)

In August 1991 the respondent firm of solicitors acted for the appellant in a conveyancing matter. In September 2002 the appellant alleged that the conveyancing, handled by fee earner X, had been negligently carried out, resulting in her becoming involved in a dispute with her neighbours.

Six days before the limitation period expired the appellant issued proceedings against the firm of solicitors, naming X in the particulars of claim. Three weeks later she applied to add X as a party pursuant to CPR 19.5. At first instance the judge refused the substitution and struck the claim out as the mistake had been as to the legal liability of the firm of solicitors and did not fall within CPR 19.5.

HELD, ON APPEAL: The Court of Appeal held that it was clear from the beginning that the appellant had intended to sue X and that there had been a simple mistake. The substitution should be allowed. *Horne-Roberts v Smithkline Beecham* [2001] EWCA Civ 2006, [2001] All ER (D) 269 (Dec) distinguished.

[18.71]   Morgan Est (Scotland) Ltd v Hanson Concrete Products Ltd

[2005] EWCA Civ 134

[2005] 3 All ER 135, [2005] 1 WLR 2557

Within the limitation period the respondent issued proceedings against the appellant for breach of contract. It was alleged that the appellant had supplied defective pipes used on a construction project and that they were liable in contract. The appellant company changed its name and legal position on a number of occasions and the respondents applied to add two further claimants pursuant to CPR 17.4 or 19.5. CPR 17.4 and 19.5 allow the addition or substitution of a party outside of the primary limitation period. CPR 19.5 implements s 35 of the Limitation Act 1980. The judge allowed the claimants to be added and the defendants appealed.

HELD, ON APPEAL: The Court of Appeal held that post CPR, it was not bound by the *Sardinia Sulcis* [1991] 1 Lloyd's Rep 201 test. CPR 19.5 and 17.4 had to be applied having regard to the overriding objective. There had been a clear mistake as to who was named on the claim form and the mistake could and should be rectified by the substitution.

6.   COMMENCING SECOND ACTION OUT OF TIME

[18.72]   Firman v Ellis
Down v Harvey
Pheasant v Smith (Tyres) Ltd

[1978] QB 886, [1978] 2 All ER 851, [1978] 2 WLR 1, 122 Sol Jo 147, CA

The claimants claimed damages for injuries sustained in a road accident. In each case no issue arose on liability: the only issue was the amount of damages to be awarded and when the claimants should be sufficiently recovered to enable this to be done. In each case the plaintiffs' solicitors issued writs but allowed them by inadvertence to expire before service. When three years had elapsed the defendants' insurers refused to entertain the claims because they had become statute-barred. The claimants began new actions by issuing writs out of time and applied under the Limitation Act 1939, s 2D that the limitation period in s 2A should not apply.

HELD: The court could properly exercise its discretion under s 2D in favour of the claimants. Section 2D was not limited to exceptional cases: it gave discretion to extend time in all cases where the three-year limitation had expired before the issue of the writ. The solicitors' slip had not prejudiced the defendants at all. On subsidiary points:

(1)   under the Limitation Act 1975 the negligence of the claimant's solicitor was an admissible consideration; it might tip the scale where the defendant had been substantially prejudiced by the delay;

(2)   the words 'the plaintiff' in s 2D(3) included his solicitor or agent except where the context confined it to the claimant personally;

(3)   'the court' in subsection (2) meant a judge hearing an application as a preliminary issue, but not a master in the High Court or a registrar in the county court.

Note—But see *Walkley v Precision Forgings Ltd* (at para [18.73]).

[18.73]   Walkley v Precision Forgings Ltd

[1979] 2 All ER 548, [1979] I WLR 606, 123 Sol Jo 354, HL

In 1966 the claimant found himself to be suffering from Reynaud's disease, possibly caused by vibration of machine tools at work. He issued a writ in October 1971 and served it. The employers' solicitors entered an acknowledgement. Nothing more was done because the claimant's solicitors advised him that he did not have a good claim. A second firm of solicitors revived the claim in 1973 but the defendants' solicitors wrote saying that if the claimant intended to proceed with the action they would apply to dismiss it for want of prosecution. Nothing more was done in the action. In December 1976 a third firm of solicitors issued a new writ for the claimant and served it with a statement of claim. The defendants' solicitors applied for the second action to be struck out under RSC Ord 18 r 19 as an abuse of the process of the court*. It was conceded by the claimant that the first action would be likely to have been dismissed for want of prosecution. On appeal from the master, the judge declined to strike out the second action on the claimant's undertaking to discontinue the first action. The Court of Appeal said the judge was right and that the claimant was entitled to have the question whether his second action should be allowed to proceed tested under the Limitation Act 1939, s 2D by reference to the criteria there set out.

HELD, on the defendants' appeal to the House of Lords: The second action should be struck out. The affidavit of the defendants' solicitor had been directed to the issue under s 2D and the claimant had not answered it; no answer was possible for on the facts before the court it was clear that since the claimant had begun an action within the period limited by s 2A he had not been prejudiced by it. *Birkett v James* [1978] AC 297, [1977] 2 All ER 801, [1977] 3 WLR 45, 121 Sol Jo 444, HL had no relevance; all that case decided was that when a claimant had allowed an action to go to sleep it would be an improper exercise of the court's discretion to dismiss it for want of prosecution before the expiry of the limitation period: it had no application to a personal injury action after the primary limitation period had expired.

Per Lord Diplock: Once a plaintiff has started an action (the first action) within the primary limitation period it is only in the most exceptional circumstances that he would be able to bring himself within s 2D in respect of a second action brought to enforce the same cause of action. If the first action is still in existence ... he has not been prevented from starting his action by s 2A or s 2B at all, so the provisions of those sections cannot have caused him any prejudice. Does it make any difference that the first action is no longer in existence at the time of the application under s 2D either because it has been struck out for want of prosecution or because it has been discontinued by the plaintiff of his own volition? In my view it does not. The only exception ... where it might be proper to give a direction under s 2D ... would be a case in which the plaintiff had been induced to discontinue by a misrepresentation or other improper conduct by the defendant.

Note—Firman v Ellis (at para [18.72]) was not cited. But see *Horton v Sadler* (at para [18.76]).

    *   Note: now dealt with as a defendant's application for summary judgment under CPR Pt 24.

[18.74]   Deerness v John R Keeble & Son (Brantham) Ltd

[1983] 2 Lloyd's Rep 260, [1983] Com LR 221, 133 NLJ 641, HL

On 7 October 1977 the claimant was very seriously injured in a road accident. The defendants were to blame. Their insurers embarked on negotiations for settlement of the claim. The claimant's solicitors issued a writ on 23 August 1979 but did not serve it. On 4 August 1980 the insurers paid by agreement the sum of £5,000 as an interim payment. A few days still remained for service of the writ but it was not served, the claimant's solicitors apparently regarding the interim payment as an admission of liability and believing the limitation period would date from that payment. Later, appreciating their error, the solicitors issued a second writ on 23 April 1981 and served it on 12 May: they applied for an order under the Limitation Act 1980, s 33 that the action should be allowed to proceed notwithstanding s 11 of the 1980 Act.

HELD: The action could not proceed. The decision in *Walkley v Precision Forgings Ltd* (at para [18.73]) was binding on the court. No waiver or agreement that the limitation period would not be insisted upon could be made out of the fact that an interim payment had been made. An appeal to the House of Lords was dismissed. The fatal obstacle to the application under s 33 of the Limitation Act 1980 was the fact that the claimant's solicitors did cause a writ to be issued within the primary limitation period. The claimant had not been prejudiced by s 11 of the 1980 Act. She had brought the first action within the normal limitation period; if she suffered any prejudice it was by her own solicitors' inaction and not by operation of the Act.

[18.75]   White v Glass

(1989) Times, 18 February, CA

The claimant suffered an injury on 7 April 1984. The writ was issued on 16 February 1987. The defendant was incorrectly sued as Corby Hazeltree Football Club. This error could have been corrected in a number of ways, but instead on 8 September 1987 the claimant's solicitors consented to have the writ set aside on the grounds that the pleadings were improperly constituted and ineffective. A fresh writ naming the correct defendant was issued on 23 September 1987. The question for the court was whether the claimant was entitled to rely on s 33 of the Limitation Act 1980 to have the three-year limitation period disapplied in view of the decision in *Walkley v Precision Forgings Ltd* (at para [18.73]).

HELD: Although in the *Walkley* case the only exception was where there has been improper conduct on the part of the defendant, this was not the only circumstance and each case has to be looked at on its facts. In the *Walkley* case there was a subsisting properly constituted action against the same defendants as in the first writ. However, in this case the defendant sued in the second action was not the same as that sued in the first. The defendant in the first action was non-existent. There was no action in being against the defendant in the second writ at the time that the limitation period expired. Therefore, the claimant was prejudiced by s 11 of the Limitation Act 1980 and could avail themselves of s 33. It was irrelevant that the initial error could have been remedied by other means.

[18.76] Horton v Sadler

[2006] UKHL 27

[2006] 3 All ER 1177, [2006] 2 WLR 1346

The appellant was involved in a road traffic accident on 12 April 1998, for which the respondent was wholly liable. The respondent was not insured and the Motor Insurers' Bureau (MIB) was therefore involved.

On 10 April 2001 proceedings were issued against the respondent but the appellant failed, as required, to give notice to the MIB. Proceedings were correctly re-issued in September 2001 and the MIB was joined as a party to the proceedings in October 2001. They entered a defence claiming the matter was statute barred. The appellant applied under s 33 of the Limitation Act 1980 for the limitation period to be disapplied.

HELD: At first instance: the judge held himself bound by the decision in *Walkley v Precision Forgings* and was unable to extend the limitation period as, whilst the first action had been brought in time, the second had been brought out of time.

This decision was upheld by the Court of Appeal.

HELD, by the House of Lords: *Walkley* unduly restricts the unfettered discretion which the court has under s 33. It has lead to a number of cases being distinguished on very irrational grounds and the Lords had been wrong to reach the decision they did in that case. Appeal allowed.

7. THIRD PARTY CASES

[18.77]

(A) THE LIMITATION ACT 1980, S 10

10. Special time limit for claiming contribution

(1) Where under section 1 of the Civil Liability (Contribution) Act 1978 any person becomes entitled to a right to recover contribution in respect of any damage from any other person, no action to recover contribution by virtue of that right shall be brought after the expiration of two years from the date on which that right accrued.

(2) For the purposes of this section the date on which a right to recover contribution in respect of any damage accrues to any person (referred to below in this section as 'the relevant date') shall be ascertained as provided in subsections (3) and (4) below.

(3) If the person in question is held liable in respect of that damage—

    (a) by a judgment given in any civil proceedings; or

    (b) by an award made on any arbitration;

the relevant date shall be the date on which the judgment is given, or the date of the award (as the case may be).

For the purposes of this subsection no account shall be taken of any judgment or award given or made on appeal in so far as it varies the amount of damages awarded against the person in question.

(4)   If, in any case not within subsection (3) above, the person in question makes or agrees to make any payment to one or more persons in compensation for that damage (whether he admits any liability in respect of the damage or not), the relevant date shall be the earliest date on which the amount to be paid by him is agreed between him (or his representative) and the person (or each of the persons, as the case may be) to whom the payment is to be made.

(5)   An action to recover contribution shall be one to which sections 28, 32 and 35 of this Act apply, but otherwise Parts II and III of this Act (except sections 34, 37 and 38) shall not apply for the purposes of this section.

[18.78]   Knight v Rochdale Healthcare NHS Trust

[2003] EWHC 1831 (QB)

[2003] 4 All ER 416, [2004] 1 WLR 371

The claimant, a consultant orthopaedic surgeon, sought an indemnity from the NHS Trust in relation to the sum which he had been found liable to pay a former patient, as a result of his alleged negligence. The action was settled on 24 October 2000 and the consent order was made on 8 November 2000. The claim for an indemnity was issued on 1 November 2002.

The court considered, as a preliminary issue, whether the claim for indemnity had been commenced within two years or not. It was held that the consent order constituted a 'judgment' within the meaning of s 10(3) of the Limitation Act 1980 but that time began to run from when an agreement had been made, being 24 October 2000.

[18.79]   Baker & Davies plc v Leslie Wilks Associates

[2005] EWHC 1179 (TCC)

[2005] 3 All ER 603

The claimant, a building contractor, employed the defendant as a consulting engineering to advise upon cracks which had appeared in a block of housing association flats. As a result of the defendant failing to correctly recommend remedial work, the claimant incurred expense in having the building underpinned and reached a settlement with the housing authority. The claimant claimed a contribution or indemnity from the defendants. The court was asked to consider as a preliminary issue, when time began to run under s 10 of the Limitation Act 1980.

HELD, ON APPEAL: The Court of Appeal held that time began to run from the date of the deed which set out the terms of the settlement between the claimant and the housing association.

[18.80]   Aer Lingus v Gildacroft

[2006] EWCA Civ 4

[2006] 2 All ER 290, [2006] 1 WLR 1173

On 27 January 1998, Mr Smyth, an employee of the appellant company, was injured at work as a result of a malfunctioning document lift. The lift had been installed by Gildacroft as primary contractors and Sentinel as subcontractors. Mr Smyth claimed against his employers and the two respondents but an agreement was reached in relation to damages with his employers, the appellants, only.

The appellants issued a claim for contribution and indemnity from the respondents within two years of the final judgment but more than two years from the liability judgment. The court was asked to consider when the two-year limitation period for such claims began to run.

HELD, ON APPEAL: The Court of Appeal held that time ran from the judgment on quantum, and the terms of s 10 of the Limitation Act 1980 should be construed to that effect.

8. WAIVER OF LIMITATION DEFENCE

[18.81] Lubovsky v Snelling

[1944] KB 44, [1943] 2 All ER 577, 113 LJKB 14, 170 LT 2, 60 TLR 52, CA

A defence that the action is statute-barred can be waived by agreement or conduct.

In a claim under the Fatal Accidents Acts, the defendants' insurers agreed with the claimant's solicitors before the limitation period expired:

(1)   that they had no defence, and that the negotiations should proceed 'on the basis of admission of liability', but

(2)   that 'a writ would have to be issued in any event because whether they agreed about the quantum of damages or not, the court would have to approve and apportion it.' This amounted to a contract not to plead the Fatal Accidents Act 1846, s 3.

Appeal from Tucker J (reported 75 Ll L Rep 165) allowed.

Note—The practical result of this decision seems to be that an insurer should never admit liability as distinct from admitting negligence. It was cited and distinguished in the following case, where it was pointed out that in *Lubovsky's* case it was an essential part of the bargain made between the parties that liability for the cause of action was definitely accepted and that the defendants were thereafter precluded from putting forward any defence whatever which would impeach that liability and was a contract not to plead the statute of limitations. They were debarred from raising the point.

[18.82] The Sauria and the Trent

[1957] 1 Lloyd's Rep 396, CA

The claimant's motor vessel was lying moored at a wharf when it was struck and damaged by a barge which was being towed by a tug. Correspondence took place between solicitors of the parties and eventually the solicitors for defendants admitted liability. Attempts were then made to arrange an arbitration to fix the amount of damages, but agreement was not reached, and in January 1957, the claimants began an action. The collision took place on 16 June 1953; the admission of liability was by letter dated 19 January 1955. The defendants took a preliminary objection that the claim was barred by the Maritime Conventions Act 1911, s 8 which required proceedings within two years from the date of damage. Judge Block in the City of London Court held that the action was barred. The claimant submitted the admission was qualified and not absolute; while the matter was still under discussion the admission was withdrawn. The claimants appealed.

HELD: There was an admission of liability but there was no undertaking to waive the right of defendants to rely on the section. The case of *Lubovsky v Snelling* (at para

[18.81]) was distinguishable on its facts. There was no ground for exercising the discretion given to the court by the proviso to the section. Appeal dismissed.

[18.83]   The Owenbawn

[1973] 1 Lloyd's Rep 56   Brandon J

A collision occurred between two vessels on 28 August 1969. Negotiations for settlement of the claims begun between solicitors 10 September 1970 and were still continuing on 2 July 1971 when claimants' solicitors issued a writ and notified the defendants' solicitors that this was to protect the two-year time limit which would otherwise expire in August. Further discussions took place at long intervals. On 3 August 1972, the writ having expired and the latest offer from the defendants being still outstanding, the claimants' solicitors applied ex parte for, and were granted, a renewal to 27 August 1972. The defendants applied for renewal to be set aside.

HELD: On the facts, there was an agreement that service of the claimants' writ should be deferred so long as negotiations were continuing and the writ was rightly renewed. *Re Chittenden, Chittenden v Doe* [1970] 3 All ER 562, [1970] 1 WLR 1618, 114 Sol Jo 954 applied.

[18.84]   Seechurn v Ace Insurance SA NV

[2002] EWCA Civ 67

[2002] 2 Lloyd's Rep 390, [2002] Lloyd's Rep IR 489

Following an injury on a bus in 1988, before which the claimant had taken out two disability insurance policies with the defendant, there was an appeal from a preliminary decision that although proceedings were commenced over ten years since the date of accrual of the cause of action for payment under the two policies, the action was not statute-barred because the defendant insurers were estopped from relying on s 5 of the Limitation Act 1980. The insurers argued that they never promised not to rely on their rights and that no detriment could be shown after the period of limitation had expired.

HELD, ON APPEAL: The Court of Appeal allowed the appeal emphasising that it was important that the unequivocal, unambiguous promise or representation had to be that the parties did not intend to enforce strict legal rights and it considered the relevant questions as to what such a promise constituted. The court agreed with the judge's conclusions that the insurers intended to keep the door open, but that was not enough to enable the claimant to establish a promise that satisfied their requirements. In the circumstances, the claimant had failed to establish the requirement which was fatal to any estoppel operating against the insurers.

9.   FRAUD

(A)   LIMITATION ACT 1980, S 32

[18.85]
32.   Postponement of limitation period in case of fraud, concealment or mistake
  (1)   ... where in the case of any action for which a period of limitation is prescribed by this Act, either—
    (a)   the action is based upon the fraud of the defendant; or

(b)   any fact relevant to the plaintiff's right of action has been deliberately concealed from him by the defendant; …

the period of limitation shall not begin to run until the plaintiff has discovered the fraud [or] concealment … or could with reasonable diligence have discovered it.

[18.86]   Johnson v Chief Constable of Surrey

(1992) Times, 23 November, CA

The claimant, relying on s 32 of the Limitation Act 1980 brought an action against the defendant long after the limitation period had expired. He alleged that new facts had emerged which had been deliberately concealed by the defendants.

HELD: A distinction had to be drawn between those facts which made the cause of action complete and those facts which improved the claimant's chances of success in that action. In this case the new facts were of the latter rather than the former kind and the claimant's case was struck out as statute-barred.

[18.87]   Sheldon v RHM Outhwaite (Underwriting Agencies) Ltd

[1994] 4 All ER 481, [1994] 1 WLR 754

The claimant alleged that there had been deliberate concealment by the defendants after the claimant's cause of action arose and argued under s 32 of the Limitation Act 1980 that the limitation should be extended accordingly. The defendants argued that s 32 only applied to deliberate concealment at the time that the cause of action arose and not to any later concealment.

HELD: The defendants' arguments were rejected. A deliberate concealment could have the affect of preventing the limitation period from running as provided under s 2 of the 1980 Act even when it occurred after the claimant's cause of action arose.

Note—The judge's findings were overturned by the Court of Appeal ([1994] 4 All ER 481) but restored by the House of Lords on a majority of three to two [1996] AC 102, [1995] 2 All ER 558, 43 Con LR 56, [1995] 2 WLR 570, [1995] 2 Lloyd's Rep 197, HL.

[18.88]   Cave v Robinson Jarvis & Rolf

[2002] UKHL 18

[2003] 1 AC 384, [2002] 2 All ER 641, [2002] 2 WLR 1107

The claimant alleged professional negligence against a firm of solicitors who acted for him on a commercial transaction in March 1989. In February 1994 the claimant discovered that he did not have the rights he thought he held and contacted another firm of solicitors who issued proceedings in January 1998.

The claimant alleged that his date of knowledge was March 1996 and, pursuant to s 32(2) of the Limitation Act 1980, the defendants breach of duty had been intentional and limitation did not run until the claimant could have discovered the breach of duty, which was February 1994.

HELD, ON APPEAL: The Court of Appeal followed the case of *Brocklesby v Armitage & Guest* [2001] 1 All ER 172, [2002] 1 WLR 598, but the House of Lords found the approach in that case to be incorrect. The words of s 32 require a 'deliberate commission of a breach of duty' and cannot extend to a breach of duty which the defendant did not know he was committing.

The appeal was allowed.

[18.89]   Skerratt v Linfax Ltd

[2003] EWCA Civ 695

[2003] All ER (D) 49 (May)

On 4 April 1997 the claimant was involved in an accident whilst using the defendants karting track. In November 2001 the claimant was informed that he may have a claim against the track owners and he issued proceedings on 15 January 2002. Until November 2001 the claimant had thought that he had used the track at this own risk because he had signed a form to that effect at the time.

At a preliminary hearing the defendants argued that the claim was statute barred. The claimant stated that his date of knowledge was November 2001 and that there had been a concealment of information. The judge held that under s 31 and 32 of the Limitation Act 1980 the claimant could and should have taken legal advice earlier and the defendants would be prejudiced by a claim which was five years old.

The claim was dismissed and the claimant appealed.

HELD, ON APPEAL: There had not been a deliberate concealment of any facts as all matters relied on by the claimant had taken place before the accident. The judge was entitled to take into account the claimant's failure to take legal advice and he had been correct in his approach to s.33. Appeal dismissed.

10.   THE LATENT DAMAGE ACT 1986

[18.90]   The Latent Damage Act 1986 added ss 14A and 14B to the Limitation Act 1980. Section 14A allows a claim to be brought within three years from the date of discovery of a defect subject to the long stop of 15 years from the date of negligence (s 14B). The 1986 Act came into effect on the 18 September 1986. It was intended to remedy the perceived injustice where hidden damage could remain hidden long past the expiry of the relevant limitation period. See the case of *Pirelli General Cable Works v Oscar Faber & Partners* (at para [18.94]) where the House of Lords ruled that the relevant date was not that of discovery or discoverability but that at which the damage actually occurred.

[18.91]   Iron Trade Mutual Insurance Co Ltd v J K Buckenham Ltd

[1990] 1 All ER 808, [1989] 2 Lloyd's Rep 85

In this case it was argued (*inter alia*) that s 14A of the Limitation Act 1980 provided an alternative limitation period for an action framed in contract. It was held that the words 'any action for damages for negligence' set out in s 14A did not apply to an action for breach of contract founded on an allegation of negligent or careless conduct.

[18.92]   Horbury v Craig Hall & Rutley

[1991] CILL 692

The defendant's surveyor carried out a survey for the claimant. The survey was negligently carried out, but the errors which first came to the knowledge of the claimant were minor and rectified by her without recourse to legal action. More serious errors manifested themselves over three years after the survey was carried out and as a consequence of these the claimant commenced proceedings.

HELD: The three-year limitation period under the Latent Damage Act 1986 began to run as soon as the defendant knew (or was taken to have known) that the survey was negligently carried out and so the claimant's claim was time barred. The claimant did not succeed in arguing that there was a separate limitation period in relation to the other more serious defects which came to light only at a later stage, nor was she permitted to abandon her earlier claims in favour of the later claims.

Note—See also *Felton v Gaskill Osborne & Co* (at para [18.93]).

[18.93] Felton v Gaskill Osborne & Co

(1993) 43 EG 118, Liverpool County Court

The claimant purchased a house on 6 June 1983 relying on the defendant surveyor's report which despite including the need to remedy dampness, failed to report on three particular defects namely cracking over a bay window, a serious bulge in a gable end and a leaning chimney stack.

The claimant was already aware of the leaning chimney stack and remedied this personally. However, it was not until the claimant attempted to sell the property in 1989 that he discovered the problems with the bay window and bulging gable end.

The claimant originally claimed damages for the problem with the bay window, the bulge in the gable end, the lean in the chimney stack and the damp which had been much more extensive than originally reported.

Following an indication by the defendant that limitation would be an issue, the claimant amended his claim to delete reference to problems with the chimney and damp.

HELD per Judge O'Donoghue QC: The judge found for the claimant. The wording of s 14A of the Limitation Act 1980 was different from that of s 14. The limitation period for the purposes of s 14A ran from the date when the claimant knew of the material facts of the damage giving rise to the claim that is made.

[18.94] Pirelli General Cable Works Ltd v Oscar Faber & Partners

[1983] 2 AC 1, [1983] 1 All ER 65, [1983] 2 WLR 6, 127 Sol Jo 16, 265 EG 979, HL

The defendants were consulting engineers who advised the claimants on the construction of a chimney. It was built in July 1969. The material used was unsuitable and cracks occurred not later than April 1970. The damage was not discovered by the claimants until 1977 and they could not with reasonable diligence have discovered it before October 1972. The writ was issued in October 1978.

HELD, ON APPEAL to the House of Lords: The action was statute-barred. In cases of latent defects to buildings the cause of action will not accrue until damage occurs, which will commonly consist of cracks coming into existence as a result of defect even though the cracks or the defect may be undiscovered and undiscoverable. The principle of the decision, in *Cartledge v E Jopling & Sons Ltd* [1963] AC 758, [1963] 1 All ER 341, [1963] 2 WLR 210, 107 Sol Jo 73, [1963] 1 Lloyd's Rep 1, HL was applicable. It was not correct (as had been held in *Sparham-Souter v Town and Country Planning Developments (Essex) Ltd* [1976] QB 858, [1976] 2 All ER 65, [1976] 2 WLR 493, 120 Sol Jo 216, 74 LGR 355, CA) that a claimant suffers damage only when he discovers, or ought with reasonable diligence to have discovered, damage to the buildings.

[18.95]   **Bell v Peter Browne & Co**

[1990] 2 QB 495, [1990] 3 All ER 124, CA

The claimant retained the defendant, a firm of solicitors, to act on his behalf in respect of divorce proceedings. An arrangement was agreed between the claimant and his wife whereby the matrimonial home would not be sold for the time being but transferred solely into the wife's name and he would receive a sixth share of the proceeds upon sale. The house was transferred into Mrs Bell's name on 1 September 1978 but the defendant failed to register the claimant's interest.

In December 1986 the claimant learned that his wife had sold the former matrimonial home and had spent all the proceeds. The claimant sued the defendant in both contract and tort. The writ was issued on 20 August 1987. The defendant argued that the claimant's claim was statute barred.

HELD, ON APPEAL: The claimant's claim was dismissed. With respect to the claim in contract the six-year limitation period ran from the date of breach which was when the defendant failed to register the claimant's continuing interest in the former matrimonial home. This occurred on or shortly after 1 September 1978 and the failure to make good this breach thereafter did not constitute a further or continuing breach.

The claim in tort was also statute barred. The claimant suffered damage when he signed the transfer document over to his wife and at the point when the defendant failed to register his interest in the proceeds of sale within a reasonable time thereafter. The fact that the claimant had no knowledge of the damage and would have been able to easily remedy it if he had was irrelevant.

Note—This case now has to be read in the light of the Latent Damage Act 1986.

CHAPTER 19

Introduction to Civil Procedure

1.   INTRODUCTION

(A)   OVERVIEW

[19.1]   Civil procedure in the courts of England and Wales is governed by the Civil Procedure Rules 1998. The Civil Procedure Rules replaced the Rules of the Supreme Court and the County Court Rules with an entirely new code.

The Civil Procedure Rules (CPR) came into effect on 26 April 1999. Cases concerning procedure decided before that date are generally of no relevance, although the courts have in some limited instances found it useful to refer to such cases for guidance.

The CPR also brought into effect a number of pre-action protocols, including a pre-action protocol for personal injury claims. The protocols are designed to encourage co-operation between the parties, early investigation of liability, and exchange of documents and information, so that issues can be resolved and narrowed, and claims settled without recourse to formal litigation.

The pre-action protocol for personal injury claims only applies to personal injury claims with a value of less than £15,000.

However, regardless of the value of a personal injury claim, parties are obliged to comply with the spirit of the protocol.

(B) A NOTE ON THE FORMAT OF CHAPTERS 19 TO 34

[19.2] Each chapter in the handbook dealing with the CPR follows a similar format – a statement of the relevant CPR rule and/or statutory authority, together with case summaries. Only those sections of the CPR directly relevant to the practice and procedure being discussed are reproduced. The full text of the CPR can be found in *The Civil Court Practice*, published by LexisNexis Butterworths. The extracts from the CPR and the practice directions to the CPR incorporate the 41st update which came into force on 6 April 2006.

2. THE PERSONAL INJURY PRE-ACTION PROTOCOL

(A) TEXT OF THE PROTOCOL

[19.3]

1. INTRODUCTION
1.1 Lord Woolf in his final Access to Justice Report of July 1996 recommended the development of pre-action protocols:

'To build on and increase the benefits of early but well informed settlement which genuinely satisfy both parties to dispute.'
1.2   The aims of pre-action protocols are:
● more pre-action contact between the parties
● better and earlier exchange of information
● better pre-action investigation by both sides
● to put the parties in a position where they may be able to settle cases fairly and early without litigation
● to enable proceedings to run to the court's timetable and efficiently, if litigation does become necessary
● to promote the provision of medical or rehabilitation treatment (not just in high value cases) to address the needs of the claimant
1.3   The concept of protocols is relevant to a range of initiatives for good litigation and pre-litigation practice, especially:
● predictability in the time needed for steps pre-proceedings
● standardisation of relevant information, including documents to be disclosed.

1.4 The Courts will be able to treat the standards set in protocols as the normal reasonable approach to pre-action conduct. If proceedings are issued, it will be for the court to decide whether non-compliance with a protocol should merit adverse consequences. Guidance on the court's likely approach will be given from time to time in practice directions.

1.5 If the court has to consider the question of compliance after proceedings have begun, it will not be concerned with minor infringements, e.g. failure by a short period to provide relevant information. One minor breach will not exempt the 'innocent' party from following the protocol. The court will look at the effect of non-compliance on the other party when deciding whether to impose sanctions.

2. NOTES OF GUIDANCE

2.1 The protocol has been kept deliberately simple to promote ease of use and general acceptability. The notes of guidance which follows relate particularly to issues which arose during the piloting of the protocol.

Scope of the protocol

2.2 This protocol is intended to apply to all claims which include a claim for personal injury (except those claims covered by the Clinical Disputes and Disease and Illness Protocols) and to the entirety of those claims: not only to the personal injury element of a claim which also includes, for instance, property damage.

2.3 This protocol is primarily designed for those road traffic, tripping and slipping and accident at work cases which include an element of personal injury with a value of less than £15,000 which are likely to be allocated to the fast track. This is because time will be of the essence, after proceedings are issued, especially for the defendant, if a case is to be ready for trial within 30 weeks of allocation. Also, proportionality of work and costs to the value of what is in dispute is particularly important in lower value claims. For some claims within the value 'scope' of the fast track some flexibility in the timescale of the protocol may be necessary, see also paragraph 3.8.

2.4 However, the 'cards on the table' approach advocated by the protocol is equally appropriate to higher value claims. The spirit, if not the letter of the protocol, should still be followed for multi-track type claims. In accordance with the sense of the civil justice reforms, the court will expect to see the spirit of reasonable pre-action behaviour applied in all cases, regardless of the existence of a specific protocol. In particular with regard to personal injury cases worth more than £15,000, with a view to avoiding the necessity of proceedings parties are expected to comply with the protocol as far as possible e.g. in respect of letters before action, exchanging information and documents and agreeing experts.

2.5 The timetable and the arrangements for disclosing documents and obtaining expert evidence may need to be varied to suit the circumstances of the case. Where one or both parties consider the detail of the protocol is not appropriate to the case, and proceedings are subsequently issued, the court will expect an explanation as to why the protocol has not been followed, or has been varied.

Early notification

2.6   The claimant's legal representative may wish to notify the defendant and/or his insurer as soon as they know a claim is likely to be made, but before they are able to send a detailed letter of claim, particularly for instance, when the defendant has no or limited knowledge of the incident giving rise to the claim or where the claimant is incurring significant expenditure as a result of the accident which he hopes the defendant might pay for, in whole or in part. If the claimant's representative chooses to do this, it will not start the timetable for responding.

The letter of claim

2.7   The specimen letter of claim at Annex A will usually be sent to the individual defendant. In practice, he/she may have no personal financial interest in the financial outcome of the claim/dispute because he/she is insured. Court imposed sanctions for non-compliance with the protocol may be ineffective against an insured. This is why the protocol emphasises the importance of passing the letter of claim to the insurer and the possibility that the insurance cover might be affected. If an insurer receives the letter of claim only after some delay by the insured, it would not be unreasonable for the insurer to ask the claimant for additional time to respond.

2.8   In road traffic cases, the letter of claim should always contain the name and address of the hospital where the claimant was treated and, where available, the claimant's hospital reference number.

2.9   The priority at letter of claim stage is for the claimant to provide sufficient information for the defendant to assess liability. Sufficient information should also be provided to enable the defendant to estimate the likely size of the claim.

2.10   Once the claimant has sent the letter of claim no further investigation on liability should normally be carried out until a response is received from the defendant indicating whether liability is disputed.

Reasons for early issue

2.11   The protocol recommends that a defendant be given three months to investigate and respond to a claim before proceedings are issued. This may not always be possible, particularly where a claimant only consults a solicitor close to the end of any relevant limitation period. In these circumstances, the claimant's solicitor should give as much notice of the intention to issue proceedings as is practicable and the parties should consider whether the court might be invited to extend time for service of the claimant's supporting documents and for service of any defence, or alternatively, to stay the proceedings while the recommended steps in the protocol are followed.

Status of letters of claim and response

2.12   Letters of claim and response are not intended to have the same status as a statement of case in proceedings. Matters may come to light as a result of investigation after the letter of claim has been sent, or after the defendant has responded, particularly if disclosure of documents takes place outside the recommended three-month period. These circumstances could mean that the 'pleaded' case of one or both parties is presented slightly differently than in the letter of claim and response. It would not be consistent with the spirit of the protocol for a party to 'take a point' on this in the proceedings, provided that there was no obvious intention by the party who changed their position to mislead the other party.

Disclosure of documents

2.13   The aim of the early disclosure of documents by the defendant is not to encourage 'fishing expeditions' by the claimant, but to promote an early exchange of relevant information to help in clarifying or resolving issues in dispute. The claimant's solicitor can assist by identifying in the letter of claim or in a subsequent letter the particular categories of documents which they consider are relevant.

Experts

2.14   The protocol encourages joint selection of, and access to, experts. The report produced is not a joint report for the purposes of CPR Part 35. Most frequently this will apply to the medical expert, but on occasions also to liability experts, e.g. engineers. The protocol promotes the practice of the claimant obtaining a medical report, disclosing it to the defendant who then asks questions and/or agrees it and does not obtain his own report. The Protocol provides for nomination of the expert by the claimant in personal injury claims because of the early stage of the proceedings and the particular nature of such claims. If proceedings have to be issued, a medical report must be attached to these proceedings. However, if necessary after proceedings have commenced and with the permission of the court, the parties may obtain further expert reports. It would be for the court to decide whether the costs of more than one expert's report should be recoverable.

2.15   Some solicitors choose to obtain medical reports through medical agencies, rather than directly from a specific doctor or hospital. The defendant's prior consent to the action should be sought and, if the defendant so requests, the agency should be asked to provide in advance the names of the doctor(s) whom they are considering instructing.

Negotiations / Settlement

2.16   Parties and their legal representatives are encouraged to enter into discussions and/or negotiations prior to starting proceedings. The protocol does not specify when or how this might be done but parties should bear in mind that the courts increasingly take the view that litigation should be a last resort, and that claims should not be issued prematurely when a settlement is in reasonable prospect.

Stocktake

2.17   Where a claim is not resolved when the protocol has been followed, the parties might wish to carry out a 'stocktake' of the issues in dispute, and the evidence that the court is likely to need to decide those issues, before proceedings are started. Where the defendant is insured and the pre-action steps have been conducted by the insurer, the insurer would normally be expected to nominate solicitors to act in the proceedings and the claimant's solicitor is recommended to invite the insurer to nominate solicitors to act in the proceedings and do so 7–14 days before the intended issue date.

3.   THE PROTOCOL

Letter of Claim

3.1   The claimant shall send to the proposed defendant two copies of a letter of claim, immediately sufficient information is available to substantiate a realistic claim and before issues of quantum are addressed in detail. One copy of the letter is for the defendant, the second for passing on to his insurers.

3.2   The letter shall contain **a clear summary of the facts** on which the claim is based together with an indication of the **nature of any injuries** suffered and of **any financial loss incurred**. In cases of road traffic accidents, the letter should provide the name and address of the hospital where treatment has been obtained and the claimant's hospital reference number. Where the case is funded by a conditional fee agreement (or collective conditional fee agreement), notification should be given of the existence of the agreement and where appropriate, that there is a success fee and/or insurance premium, although not the level of the success fee or premium.

3.3   Solicitors are recommended to use a **standard format** for such a letter – an example is at Annex A: this can be amended to suit the particular case.

3.4   The letter should ask for **details of the insurer** and that a copy should be sent by the proposed defendant to the insurer where appropriate. If the insurer is known, a copy shall be sent directly to the insurer. Details of the claimant's National Insurance number and date of birth should be supplied to the defendant's insurer once the defendant has responded to the letter of claim and confirmed the identity of the insurer. This information should not be supplied in the letter of claim.

3.5   **Sufficient information** should be given in order to enable the defendant's insurer/solicitor to commence investigations and at least put a broad valuation on the 'risk'.

3.6   The **defendant should reply within 21 calendar days** of the date of posting of the letter identifying the insurer (if any) and, if necessary, identifying specifically any significant omissions from the letter of claim. If there has been no reply by the defendant or insurer within 21 days, the claimant will be entitled to issue proceedings.

3.7   The **defendant**('s insurers) will have a **maximum of three months** from the date of acknowledgment of the claim **to investigate**. No later than the end of that period the defendant (insurer) shall reply, stating whether liability is denied and, if so, giving reasons for their denial of liability including any alternative version of events relied upon.

3.8   Where the accident occurred outside England and Wales and/or where the defendant is outside the jurisdiction, the time periods of 21 days and three months should normally be extended up to 42 days and six months.

3.9 Where **liability is admitted**, the presumption is that the defendant will be bound by this admission for all claims with a total value of up to £15,000. Where the claimant's investigation indicates that the value of the claim has increased to more than £15,000 since the letter of claim, the claimant should notify the defendant as soon as possible.

Documents

3.10 If the **defendant denies liability**, he should enclose with the letter of reply, **documents** in his possession which are **material to the issues** between the parties, and which would be likely to be ordered to be disclosed by the court, either on an application for pre-action disclosure, or on disclosure during proceedings.

3.11 Attached at Annex B are **specimen**, but non-exhaustive, **lists** of documents likely to be material in different types of claim. Where the claimant's investigation of the case is well advanced, the letter of claim could indicate which classes of documents are considered relevant for early disclosure. Alternatively these could be identified at a later stage.

3.12 Where the defendant admits primary liability, but alleges contributory negligence by the claimant, the defendant should give reasons supporting those allegations and disclose those documents from Annex B which are relevant to the issues in dispute. The claimant should respond to the allegations of contributory negligence before proceedings are issued.

3.13 No charge will be made for providing copy documents under the Protocol.

Special Damages

3.14 The claimant will send to the defendant as soon as practicable a Schedule of Special Damages with supporting documents, particularly where the defendant has admitted liability.

Experts

3.15 Before any party instructs an expert he should give the other party a list of the **name**(s) of **one or more experts** in the relevant speciality whom he considers are suitable to instruct.

3.16 Where a medical expert is to be instructed the claimant's solicitor will organise access to relevant medical records – see specimen letter of instruction at Annex C.

3.17 **Within 14 days** the other party may indicate **an objection** to one or more of the named experts. The first party should then instruct a mutually acceptable expert (which is not the same as a joint expert). It must be emphasised that if the Claimant nominates an expert in the original letter of claim, the defendant has 14 days to object to one or more of the named experts after expiration of the period of 21 days within which he has to reply to the letter of claim, as set out in paragraph 3.6.

3.18 If the second party objects to all the listed experts, the parties may then instruct **experts of their own choice**. It would be for the court to decide subsequently, if proceedings are issued, whether either party had acted unreasonably.

3.19   If the **second party does not object to an expert nominated**, he shall not be entitled to rely on his own expert evidence within that particular speciality unless:
(a)   the first party agrees;
(b)   the court so directs, or
(c)   the first party's expert report has been amended and the first party is not prepared to disclose the original report.
3.20   **Either party may send to an agreed expert written questions** on the report, relevant to the issues, via the first party's solicitors. The expert should send answers to the questions separately and directly to each party.
3.21   The cost of a report from an agreed expert will usually be paid by the instructing first party: the costs of the expert replying to questions will usually be borne by the party which asks the questions.

4.   REHABILITATION
4.1   The claimant or the defendant or both shall consider as early as possible whether the claimant has reasonable needs that could be met by rehabilitation treatment or other measures.
4.2   The parties shall consider, in such cases, how those needs might be addressed. The Rehabilitation Code (which is attached at Annex D) may be helpful in considering how to identify the claimant's needs and how to address the cost of providing for those needs.
4.3   The time limit set out in paragraph 3.7 of this Protocol shall not be shortened, except by consent to allow these issues to be addressed.
4.4   The provision of any report obtained for the purposes of assessment of provision of a party's rehabilitation needs shall not be used in any litigation arising out of the accident, the subject of the claim, save by consent and shall in any event be exempt from the provisions of paragraphs 3.15 to 3.21 inclusive of this protocol.

5.   RESOLUTION OF ISSUES
5.1   Where the defendant admits liability in whole or in part, before proceedings are issued, any medical reports obtained under this protocol on which a party relies should be disclosed to the other party. The claimant should delay issuing proceedings for 21 days from disclosure of the report (unless such delay would cause his claim to become time-barred), to enable the parties to consider whether the claim is capable of settlement.
5.2   The Civil Procedure Rules Part 36 permit claimants and defendants to make offers to settle pre-proceedings. Parties should always consider before issuing if it is appropriate to make Part 36 Offer. If such an offer is made, the party making the offer must always supply sufficient evidence and/or information to enable the offer to be properly considered.
5.3   Where the defendant has admitted liability, the claimant should send to the defendant schedules of special damages and loss at least 21 days before proceedings are issued (unless that would cause the claimant's claim to become time-barred).

Note–Annexes A to D are not reproduced here – reference should be made to *The Civil Court Practice*, published by LexisNexis Butterworths.

(B)   TEXT OF THE PRACTICE DIRECTION TO THE
PRE-ACTION PROTOCOLS

[19.4]

PRACTICE DIRECTION TO THE PRE-ACTION PROTOCOLS

1.1   This Practice Direction applies to the pre-action protocols which have been approved by the head of Civil Justice.

1.2   The pre-action protocols which have been approved are set out in para 5.1. Other pre-action protocols may subsequently be added.

1.3   This Practice Direction applies to the pre-action protocols which have been approved by the Head of Civil Justice.

1.4   Pre-action protocols outline the steps parties should take to seek information from and to provide information to each other about a prospective legal claim.

1.5   The objectives of pre-action protocols are:

   (a)   to encourage the exchange of early and full information about the prospective legal claim,

   (b)   to enable parties to avoid litigation by agreeing a settlement of the claim before the commencement of proceedings,

   (c)   to support the efficient management of proceedings where litigation cannot be avoided.

2.1   The Civil Procedure Rules enable the court to take into account compliance or non-compliance with an applicable protocol when giving directions for the management of proceedings (see CPR rules 3.1(4) and (5) and 3.9(e)) and when making orders for costs (see CPR rule 44.3(a)).

2.2   The court will expect all parties to have complied in substance with the terms of an approved protocol.

2.3   If, in the opinion of the court, non-compliance has led to the commencement of proceedings which might otherwise not have needed to be commenced, or has led to costs being incurred in the proceedings that might otherwise not have been incurred, the orders the court may make include:

   (1)   an order that the party at fault pay the costs of the proceedings, or part of those costs, of the other party or parties;

   (2)   an order that the party at fault pay those costs on an indemnity basis;

   (3)   if the party at fault is a claimant in whose favour an order for the payment of damages or some specified sum is subsequently made, an order depriving that party of interest on such sum and in respect of such period as may be specified, and/or awarding interest at a lower rate than that at which interest would otherwise have been awarded;

   (4)   if the party at fault is a defendant and an order for the payment of damages or some specified sum is subsequently made in favour of the claimant, an order awarding interest on such sum and in respect of such period as may be specified at a higher rate, not exceeding 10%; above base rate (cf. CPR rule 36.21(2), than the rate at which interest would otherwise have been awarded.

2.4   The court will exercise its powers under paragraphs 2.1 and 2.3 with the object of placing the innocent party in no worse a position than he would have been in if the protocol had been complied with.

3.1 A claimant may be found not to have complied with the protocol by, for example:

    (a) not having provided sufficient information to the defendant, or

    (b) not having followed the procedure required by the protocol to be followed (e.g. not having followed the medical expert instruction procedure set out in the Personal Injury Protocol).

3.2 A defendant may be found to have failed to comply with a protocol by, for example:

    (a) not making a preliminary response to the letter of claim within the time fixed for that purpose by the relevant protocol (21 days under the Personal Injury Protocol, 14 days under the Clinical Negligence Protocol),

    (b) not making a full response within the time fixed for that purpose by the relevant protocol (3 months of the letter of claim under the Clinical Negligence Protocol, 3 months from the date of acknowledgement of the letter of claim under the Personal Injury Protocol),

    (c) not disclosing documents required to be disclosed by the relevant protocol.

3.3 The court is likely to treat this practice direction as indicating the normal, reasonable way of dealing with disputes. If proceedings are issued and parties have not complied with this practice direction or a specific protocol, it will be for the court to decide whether sanctions should be applied.

3.4 The court is not likely to be concerned with minor infringements of the practice direction or protocols. The court is likely to look at the effect of non-compliance on the other party when deciding whether to impose sanctions.

3.5 This practice direction does not alter the statutory time limits for starting court proceedings. A claimant is required to start proceedings within those time limits and to adhere to subsequent time limits required by the rules or ordered by the court. If proceedings are for any reason started before the parties have followed the procedures in this practice direction, the parties are encouraged to agree to apply to the court for a stay of the proceedings while they follow the practice direction.

PRE-ACTION BEHAVIOUR IN OTHER CASES

4.1 In cases not covered by any approved protocol, the court will expect the parties, in accordance with the overriding objective and the matters referred to in CPR 1.1(2)(a), (b) and (c), to act reasonably in exchanging information and documents relevant to the claim and generally in trying to avoid the necessity for the start of proceedings.

4.2 Parties to a potential dispute should follow a reasonable procedure, suitable to their particular circumstances, which is intended to avoid litigation. The procedure should not be regarded as a prelude to inevitable litigation. It should normally include–

    (a) the claimant writing to give details of the claim;

    (b) the defendant acknowledging the claim letter promptly;

    (c) the defendant giving within a reasonable time a detailed written response; and

(d) the parties conducting genuine and reasonable negotiations with a view to settling the claim economically and without court proceedings.

4.3 The claimant's letter should–

(a) give sufficient concise details to enable the recipient to understand and investigate the claim without extensive further information;

(b) enclose copies of the essential documents which the claimant relies on;

(c) ask for a prompt acknowledgement of the letter, followed by a full written response within a reasonable stated period;

(For many claims, a normal reasonable period for a full response may be one month.)

(d) state whether court proceedings will be issued if the full response is not received within the stated period;

(e) identify and ask for copies of any essential documents, not in his possession, which the claimant wishes to see;

(f) state (if this is so) that the claimant wishes to enter into mediation or another alternative method of dispute resolution; and

(g) draw attention to the court's powers to impose sanctions for failure to comply with this practice direction and, if the recipient is likely to be unrepresented, enclose a copy of this practice direction.

4.4 The defendant should acknowledge the claimant's letter in writing within 21 days of receiving it. The acknowledgement should state when the defendant will give a full written response. If the time for this is longer than the period stated by the claimant, the defendant should give reasons why a longer period is needed.

4.5 The defendant's full written response should as appropriate–

(a) accept the claim in whole or in part and make proposals for settlement; or

(b) state that the claim is not accepted.

If the claim is accepted in part only, the response should make clear which part is accepted and which part is not accepted.

4.6 If the defendant does not accept the claim or part of it, the response should–

(a) give detailed reasons why the claim is not accepted, identifying which of the claimant's contentions are accepted and which are in dispute;

(b) enclose copies of the essential documents which the defendant relies on;

(c) enclose copies of documents asked for by the claimant, or explain why they are not enclosed;

(d) identify and ask for copies of any further essential documents, not in his possession, which the defendant wishes to see; and

(The claimant should provide these within a reasonably short time or explain in writing why he is not doing so.)

(e) state whether the defendant is prepared to enter into mediation or another alternative method of dispute resolution.

4.7 The parties should consider whether some form of alternative dispute resolution procedure would be more suitable than litigation, and if so, endeavour to agree which form to adopt. Both the Claimant and Defendant may be required by the Court to provide evidence that alternative means of resolving their dispute were considered. The Courts take the view that litigation should be a last resort, and that claims should not be issued prematurely when a settlement is still actively being explored. Parties are warned that if the protocol is not followed (including this paragraph) then the Court must have regard to such conduct when determining costs.

It is not practicable in this protocol to address in detail how the parties might decide which method to adopt to resolve their particular dispute. However, summarised below are some of the options for resolving disputes without litigation:

- Discussion and negotiation.
- Early neutral evaluation by an independent third party (for example, a lawyer experienced in that filed or an individual experienced in the subject matter of the claim).
- Mediation – a form of facilitated negotiation assisted by an independent neutral party.

The Legal Services Commission has published a booklet on 'Alternatives to Court', CLS Direct Information Leaflet 23 (www.clsdirect.org.uk/ legalhelp/leaflet23.jsp), which lists a number of organisations that provide alternative dispute resolution services.

It is expressly recognised that no party can or should be forced to mediate or enter into any form of ADR.

(C)   FLOW CHART SUMMARY

[19.5]

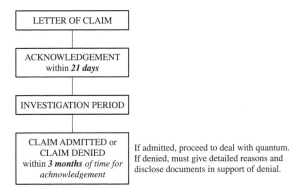

3.   THE CIVIL PROCEDURE RULES

(A)   APPLICATION OF THE RULES

[19.6]

CPR 2.1 – APPLICATION OF THE RULES

(1)   Subject to paragraph (2), these Rules apply to all proceedings in–
   (a)   county courts;
   (b)   the High Court; and
   (c)   the Civil Division of the Court of Appeal.

(B)   JUDGES

[19.7]

CPR 2.4 – POWERS OF JUDGE, MASTER OR DISTRICT JUDGE TO PERFORM FUNCTIONS OF THE COURT

Where these Rules provide for the court to perform any act then, except where an enactment, rule or practice direction provides otherwise, that act may be performed–
   (a)   in relation to proceedings in the High Court, by any judge, Master or district judge of that Court; and
   (b)   in relation to proceedings in a county court, by any judge or district judge.

(C)   COURT STAFF

[19.8]

CPR 2.5 – COURT STAFF
   (1)   Where these Rules require or permit the court to perform an act of a formal or administrative character, that act may be performed by a court officer.
   (2)   A requirement that a court officer carry out any act at the request of a party is subject to the payment of any fee required by a fees order for the carrying out of that act.

(D)   CALCULATION OF TIME

[19.9]

CPR 2.8 – TIME
   (1)   This rule shows how to calculate any period of time for doing any act which is specified–
      (a)   by these Rules;
      (b)   by a practice direction; or
      (c)   by a judgment or order of the court.
   (2)   A period of time expressed as a number of days shall be computed as clear days.
   (3)   In this rule 'clear days' means that in computing the number of days–
      (a)   the day on which the period begins; and
      (b)   if the end of the period is defined by reference to an event, the day on which that event occurs are not included.

EXAMPLES
   (i)   Notice of an application must be served at least 3 days before the hearing.
      An application is to be heard on Friday 20 October.
      The last date for service is Monday 16 October.
   (ii)   The court is to fix a date for a hearing.
      The hearing must be at least 28 days after the date of notice.

If the court gives notice of the date of the hearing on 1 October, the earliest date for the hearing is 30 October.

(iii)   Particulars of claim must be served within 14 days of service of the claim form.

The claim form is served on 2 October.

The last day for service of the particulars of claim is 16 October.

(4)   Where the specified period–

(a)   is 5 days or less; and

(b)   includes–

(i)   a Saturday or Sunday; or

(ii)   a Bank Holiday, Christmas Day or Good Friday,

that day does not count.

EXAMPLE

Notice of an application must be served at least 3 days before the hearing.

An application is to be heard on Monday 20 October.

The last date for service is Tuesday 14 October.

(5)   When the period specified–

(a)   by these Rules or a practice direction; or

(b)   by any judgment or court order,

for doing any act at the court office ends on a day on which the office is closed, that act shall be in time if done on the next day on which the court office is open.

CPR 2.8 only applies to the calculation of a period of time 'for doing any act'

[19.10]   Anderton v Clwyd County Council

[2002] EWCA Civ 933

[2002] 3 All ER 813, [2002] 1 WLR 3174

The Court of Appeal emphasised that the several time calculation provisions in CPR 2.8 do not apply whenever there is a reference in the CPR to the calculation of time. The rule only applies to the calculation of any period of time 'for doing any act' which is so specified.

Per Mummery LJ: CPR 2.8 is about the calculation of any period of time for doing any act which is specified by the rules or by a practice direction or by a judgment or order of the court. Under CPR 2.8(4), where the specified period is five days or less and includes a Saturday or Sunday or a bank holiday, Christmas Day or Good Friday, that day does not count ... [CPR 2.8] only applies to the calculation of any period of time 'for doing any act' which is specified in the Civil Procedure Rules, by a practice direction or court order. CPR 6.7 [which concerns deemed service of a claim form] does not specify a period of time for doing any act under the Civil Procedure Rules. It sets out the methods of calculating the days on which the event of service is deemed to happen as a result of doing other acts under other rules involving the use of the various available methods of service of a claim form.

[19.11]

CPR 2.9 – Dates for compliance to be calendar dates and to include time of day
(1)   Where the court gives a judgment, order or direction which imposes a time limit for doing any act, the last date for compliance must, wherever practicable–
   (a)   be expressed as a calendar date; and
   (b)   include the time of day by which the act must be done.
(2)   Where the date by which an act must be done is inserted in any document, the date must, wherever practicable, be expressed as a calendar date.

[19.12]

CPR 2.10 – Meaning of 'month' in judgments, etc.

Where 'month' occurs in any judgment, order, direction or other document, it means a calendar month.

(E)   VARYING TIME LIMITS

[19.13]

CPR 2.11 – Time limits may be varied by parties

Unless these Rules or a practice direction provide otherwise or the court orders otherwise, the time specified by a rule or by the court for a person to do any act may be varied by the written agreement of the parties.

Note to CPR 2.11 – Time limits which may not be varied by agreement

(Rules 3.8 (sanctions have effect unless defaulting party obtains relief), 28.4 (variation of case management timetable – fast track) and 29.5 (variation of case management timetable – multi-track), provide for time limits that cannot be varied by agreement between the parties)

(F)   CONFLICT BETWEEN THE CPR AND PRACTICE DIRECTIONS

The general rule – CPR to prevail over Practice Directions

[19.14]   **Binks v Securicor Omega Express Ltd**
[2003] EWCA Civ 993
[2003] All ER (D) 266 (Jul), [2003] 1 WLR 2557

Per Maurice Kay J: To the extent that the Practice Direction suggests otherwise, I give precedence to the rule over the Practice Direction.

[19.15]   Godwin v Swindon Borough Council

[2001] EWCA Civ 1478

[2001] 4 All ER 641, [2002] 1 WLR 997

Practice Directions supplement the CPR and are 'at best a weak aid to the interpretation of the rules themselves'.

THE GENERAL RULE MUST BE APPLIED IN ACCORDANCE WITH THE OVERRIDING OBJECTIVE

[19.16]   Hormel Foods Corpn v Antilles Landscape Investments NV

[2003] EWHC 1912 (Ch)

[2003] All ER (D) 104 (Jul)

The claimant, the manufacturer of the meat product Spam, issued proceedings against the defendant in respect of breach of trademark. The claimant applied to strike out the defence on the basis that the defendant had not filed an acknowledgement of service, only a defence: CPR 8.3(1) provides that 'the defendant must file an acknowledgement of service in the relevant practice form not more than 14 days after service of the claim form'. The defendant relied upon the Practice Direction to CPR Pt 8, which provides at 3.2 'Where a defendant who wishes to respond to a CPR 8 claim form is required to file an acknowledgement of service that acknowledgement of service should be in practice form N210, but can alternatively be given in an alternative document such as a letter'.

HELD: Whilst it was argued that where there was conflict between the provisions of the Rules and the provisions of the Practice Direction then the Rules must prevail, the court was not prepared to criticise a defendant who put in a defence rather than an acknowledgement of service when the practice direction would allow a letter to stand as sufficient acknowledgement.

4.   THE OVERRIDING OBJECTIVE

(A)   WHAT IS THE OVERRIDING OBJECTIVE?

[19.17]

CPR 1.1 – THE OVERRIDING OBJECTIVE
   (1)   These Rules are a new procedural code with the overriding objective of enabling the court to deal with cases justly.
   (2)   Dealing with a case justly includes, so far as is practicable–
     (a)   ensuring that the parties are on an equal footing;
     (b)   saving expense;
     (c)   dealing with the case in ways which are proportionate–
       (i)   to the amount of money involved;
       (ii)   to the importance of the case;
       (iii) to the complexity of the issues; and
       (iv)   to the financial position of each party.
     (d)   ensuring that it is dealt with expeditiously and fairly; and
     (e)   allotting to it an appropriate share of the court's resources, while taking into account the need to allot resources to other cases.

[19.18]

CPR 1.2 – APPLICATION BY THE COURT OF THE OVERRIDING OBJECTIVE

The court must seek to give effect to the overriding objective when it–
  (a)   exercises any power given to it by the Rules; or
  (b)   interprets any rule subject to rule 76.2.

[19.19]

CPR 1.3 – DUTY OF THE PARTIES

The parties are required to help the court to further the overriding objective.

[19.20]

CPR 1.4 – COURT'S DUTY TO MANAGE CASES
  (1)   The court must further the overriding objective by actively managing cases.
  (2)   Active case management includes–
    (a)   encouraging the parties to co-operate with each other in the conduct of the proceedings;
    (b)   identifying the issues at an early stage;
    (c)   deciding promptly which issues need full investigation and trial and accordingly disposing summarily of the others;
    (d)   deciding the order in which issues are to be resolved;
    (e)   encouraging the parties to use an alternative dispute resolution procedure if the court considers that appropriate and facilitating the use of such procedure;
    (f)   helping the parties to settle the whole or part of the case;
    (g)   fixing timetables or otherwise controlling the progress of the case;
    (h)   considering whether the likely benefits of taking a particular step justify the cost of taking it;
    (i)   dealing with as many aspects of the case as it can on the same occasion;
    (j)   dealing with the case without the parties needing to attend at court;
    (k)   making use of technology; and
    (l)   giving directions to ensure that the trial of a case proceeds quickly and efficiently.

(B)   APPLICATION OF THE OVERRIDING OBJECTIVE
IN PRACTICE

RELEVANCE OF PRE-CPR AUTHORITIES

[19.21]   **Biguzzi v Rank Leisure plc**
[1999] 4 All ER 934, [1999] I WLR 1926

The claimant suffered an injury at work, and two years later commenced proceedings against the defendant. The claimant failed to comply with directions and the defendant applied successfully to have the claim struck out. The claimant appealed. The appeal was heard shortly after the CPR came into effect. The judge held that, whilst there had been delay, there could still be a fair trial of the issues, and he reinstated the case. The defendant appealed.

HELD, ON APPEAL: Under the CPR, the court had to have regard to the overriding objective, and there were alternative ways in which the court could make it clear to the parties that delay and failure to comply with directions would not be tolerated. A judge was not to be constrained by decisions made under the rules prevailing prior to the introduction of the CPR.

[19.22] Vinos v Marks & Spencer plc
[2001] 3 All ER 784

Per May LJ: Interpretation to achieve the overriding objective does not enable the court to say provisions which are quite plain mean what they do not mean, nor that the plain meaning should be ignored ... The Civil Procedure Rules are a new procedural code, and the question for this court in this case concerns the interpretation and application of the relevant provisions of the new procedural code as they stand untrammelled by the weight of authority that accumulated under the former Rules.

Note—For the facts of this case, see para [22.39].

[19.23] Godwin v Swindon Borough Council
[2001] EWCA Civ 1478
[2001] 4 All ER 641, [2002] 1 WLR 997

Per May LJ: On a preliminary matter, it is not, in my view, generally helpful to seek to interpret the Civil Procedure Rules by reference to the rules which they replaced and to cases decided under former rules ... The new procedural code of the Civil Procedure Rules is positively packed with instances where the court has a wide discretion to manage cases to achieve substantial justice in accordance with the overriding objective. But there are some instances where the court has no discretion or only a limited discretion.

Note—For the facts of this case, see para [22.29].

PARTIES ON AN EQUAL FOOTING

[19.24] Maltez v Lewis
[1999] All ER (D) 425, (1999) Times, 4 May

The claimant made an application seeking an order that the defendant be debarred from instructing leading counsel, in pursuance of the court's duty to further the overriding objective by 'ensuring that the parties are on an equal footing' – CPR 1.1(2)(a).

HELD: It was a fundamental right of any litigant to choose his own counsel, and the CPR should not be interpreted so as to remove that right. The purpose of CPR 1.1 was to ensure that a party was not exposed unfairly to excessive costs because the opposing party had instructed unreasonably expensive advisers. The court could also make orders in the course of case management to ensure a 'level playing field', for example, allowing a smaller firm more time to comply with orders, or requiring a larger firm to prepare court bundles even though the responsibility was that of the smaller firm.

[19.25]   Rowland v Bock

[2002] EWHC 692 (QB)

[2002] 4 All ER 370

The claimant was a Swedish national who was subject to a request for extradition to the United States and who would have been arrested had he entered the UK. He made an application for permission to give his evidence at trial by video link. The master refused permission, and held that for one party to give evidence by video link and one in court meant that the parties were not on an equal footing. The claimant appealed to the Court of Appeal.

HELD, ON APPEAL: Whilst it was preferable for all witnesses to give live evidence at court, the overriding objective was concerned with making use of new technology. Furthermore, if the claimant was required to attend court in the UK and thereby would be at risk of being arrested, the parties would clearly not be on an equal footing. The only other alternative would be for the claimant's witness statement to be read out pursuant to a Civil Evidence Act notice, and again, the parties would not be on an equal footing. The appeal was allowed.

SAVING EXPENSE

[19.26]   Burrows v Vauxhall Motors Ltd
Mongiardi v IBC Vehicles Ltd

[1997] NLJR 1723, [1998] PIQR P48

In June 1993, the claimant suffered personal injury in the course of his employment with the defendant. Liability was admitted. The claimant was examined by a medical expert, and a report was produced in October 1994. It was not sent to the defendant. In May 1995 the claimant issued proceedings, appending the medical report. The claim was settled in December 1995. The defendant issued an application seeking to exclude the claimant's entitlement to costs on the basis that had been no need to issue proceedings, since if the medical report had been disclosed before the issue of proceedings, the claim would have settled.

HELD, ON APPEAL: It was unreasonable for the claimant to withhold plainly relevant medical evidence, and it was unreasonable to disclose such evidence for the first time with the proceedings. Accordingly, it was appropriate to give consideration to disallowing costs unnecessarily incurred.

Note—Whilst this authority predates the introduction of the CPR, and to some extent its relevance is nullified by the introduction of the pre-action protocols, it nevertheless provides a useful example of how the courts will approach a failure to save unnecessary expense.

[19.27]   **Norwich Union Linked Life Assurance Ltd v Mercantile Credit Co Ltd**

[2003] EWHC 3064 (Ch)

[2003] All ER (D) 376 (Dec)

The deputy master refused the claimant's application to strike out two allegations in the defence because he ruled that the application was likely to add to the costs and extend the trial. The claimant appealed:

HELD, ON APPEAL: The court was permitted to refuse to consider the merits of an application if the court considered that the actual making of the application was in itself contrary to the overriding objective. If an application would delay resolution of the case, increase costs, or take up court time unnecessarily, then the court had jurisdiction to refuse to consider it.

[19.28]   **Khiaban v Beard**

[2002] EWCA Civ 358

[2003] 3 All ER 362, [2003] 1 WLR 1626, [2003] RTR 419

The claimant and the defendant were involved in a road traffic accident. Both were comprehensively insured. The claimant issued proceedings in respect of his policy excess in the sum of £125. To minimise costs, the respective insurers, who each had repair costs, entered into a memorandum of understanding, agreeing to abide by the court's decision in the proceedings brought by the claimant. The district judge ordered the claimant to amend the particulars of claim to clarify the full extent of the claim made and include the repair costs. The claimant failed to amend the particulars of claim and the case was struck out. The matter was referred by the circuit judge to the Court of Appeal.

HELD, ON APPEAL: A claimant was entitled to decide what to include in his claim, and the CPR did not give the court jurisdiction to require a claimant to include losses in a claim which the claimant had chosen not to.

Per Dyson LJ: The real issue between the parties was liability. The parties were entitled to simplify the claim, and limit the amount claimed to £125. In so doing, they have acted in accordance with the overriding objective in that expense has been saved and the case can be dealt with proportionately.

PROPORTIONALITY

[19.29]   **Baghdadi v Sunderland**

(27 August 1999, unreported)

The court will give effect to agreements made between the parties regarding the progress of the case, only if consistent with the overriding objective. In the pursuit of proportionality the court will encourage the use of consent orders so that the parties do not need to attend a directions hearing, but only if lodged and approved before the hearing.

[19.30]   **Warner Brothers Productions Ltd v Telegraph Group Ltd**

(19 November 1999, unreported)

Proportionality is not an excuse for not complying with court orders.

[19.31]   Lownds v Home Office

[2002] EWCA Civ 365

[2002] 4 All ER 775, [2002] 1 WLR 2450

HELD, ON APPEAL: Litigation should be conducted in a proportionate manner and, where possible, at a proportionate cost. Parties should recognise from the outset that a case may result in disproportionate costs being incurred, and in recognition of that should plan litigation with a view to minimising expense. When considering costs, the court should apply a two-stage approach. Firstly, consideration should be given to whether the total sum claimed is proportionate. If it is found that the total sum claimed is disproportionate, the court should then go on to consider in relation to each item claimed whether it was reasonable and necessary.

[19.32]   King v Telegraph Group Ltd

[2004] EWCA Civ 613

[2004] All ER (D) 242 (May), [2004] NLJR 823, [2005] 1 WLR 2282

Per Brook LJ: In this judgment I am not concerned to give more than general guidance as to the procedure that should be followed in future cases to mitigate the evils of which [the defendant was] right to complain ... It will be sufficient only to say that the claimant's lawyers appear to have advanced their client's claim from time to time in a manner wholly incompatible with the philosophy of the CPR, and that I would expect a costs judge to take an axe to certain elements of their charges if the matter ever proceeds to an assessment ... There are three main weapons available to a party who is concerned about extravagant conduct by the other side, or the risk of such extravagance. The first is a prospective costs capping order ... The second is a retrospective assessment of costs conducted in accordance with CPR principles. The third is a wasted costs order against the other party's lawyers ...

DEALING WITH CASES EXPEDITIOUSLY AND FAIRLY

[19.33]   Jenkins v Grocott

(30 July 1999, unreported), QBD

The defendant's care expert's report had not been disclosed (owing to genuine mistake) to the claimant's advisers until 18 June 1999, four weeks before the trial and far too late for the claimant to commission his own report.

HELD: (1) The overriding objective required that the parties should be on an equal footing. That would scarcely be the case if one party could spring upon the other party expert evidence which could not reasonably have been foreseen and which there was no realistic opportunity of countering.

(2)   Generally under the CPR it would be unjust to exclude relevant evidence, however this case was a good example of a situation where it could be unjust to allow evidence. Although the defendant was not deliberately taking a tactical advantage and the late disclosure was a genuine mistake, it put the claimant at some disadvantage.

(3)   In considering the balance of fairness however, it was necessary to look at the particular evidence in the context of the present case. In the present case it was narrowly appropriate to admit the evidence of the expert even at a very late stage, in order to allow the court to deal

fairly with the issue of care costs. The evidence in the expert report was not so prejudicial to the claimant's case that the only fair solution would be to exclude it.

[19.34]   Chilton v Surrey County Council
1999 CPLR 525

The claimant sustained personal injury when he fell over an unfenced and unlit pile of earth on a footpath which was the responsibility of the defendant. Some two weeks before trial, the claimant applied to the court for permission to file and serve an amended schedule of loss which increased the value of his claim from £5,000 to £400,000. Permission was refused, and the claimant appealed.

HELD, ON APPEAL: The value of the claim was foreshadowed in the medical evidence upon which the claimant relied. The CPR required that the court deal with the case justly, to further the overriding objective, and in this instance the case could only be dealt with justly if the claimant was permitted to serve an amended schedule of loss.

[19.35]   Hannigan v Hannigan
[2000] All ER (D) 693, [2000] 2 FCR 650

The claimant issued proceedings in respect of a dispute relating to her late husband's will. She issued proceedings pursuant to CPR Pt 8, when in fact the proceedings should have been issued pursuant to CPR Pt 7. Furthermore, the particulars of claim were not verified with a statement of truth. The defendants applied to the court for an order that the claim be struck out. The district judge made such an order, and the designated civil judge refused the claimant's appeal. The claimant appealed to the Court of Appeal.

HELD, ON APPEAL: Whilst it had to be accepted that the proceedings had been instituted using the wrong form and although the form contained numerous defects, nevertheless the defendants were given all the information they required to understand the relief sought by the claimant. The overriding objective would have been better served if the defendants' solicitors had pointed out the defects rather than attempted to take a technical point, and had the claimant's solicitor accepted his incompetence and agreed to meet the expense caused by that incompetence.

[19.36]   Hertsmere Primary Care Trust v Administrators of Balasubramanium's Estate
[2005] EWHC 320 (Ch)
[2005] 3 All ER 274

The claimant brought proceedings against the estate of a deceased optician, who had falsely claimed fees in respect of eye tests. The claimant obtained a freezing order, and then an order for an account of payments made to the deceased. The claimant made an offer to settle its claim, expressed to be made under CPR Pt 36. The letter did not comply with CPR Pt 36 because it did not state that the offer was to remain open for 21 days, and thereafter could only be accepted if the parties agreed their liability for costs or if the court gave permission. The estate advised that the offer did not comply with the terms of CPR Pt 36 but did not elaborate further, despite being asked to do so.

At trial, the claimant was awarded a sum in excess of the offer made, and sought an order for interest at 10% above base rate on the judgment sum, and indemnity costs. The court found that both parties were represented by lawyers, and that the error in the offer was obvious and purely a technicality, and accordingly the claimant should have the benefit of such an order. The estate appealed.

HELD, ON APPEAL: CPR 1.3 provides that the parties are required to help the court to further the overriding objective. CPR 1.4 provides that the court must further the overriding objective by actively managing cases and active case management includes encouraging the parties to cooperate with each other. Accordingly, the estate was obliged to give to the claimant the information requested, namely how the offer failed to comply with CPR 36. Its failure to do was reason for the court to make an order for penalty interest and indemnity costs.

[19.37]   Holmes v SGB Services plc
[2001] EWCA Civ 354

The claimant sustained an injury while unloading scaffolding using a hydraulic crane on the trailer of his lorry. Following the issue of proceedings, directions were given including a direction that the parties have permission to jointly instruct an expert. The evidence of the expert did not support the claimant's assertions, but did suggest an alternative reason why the accident might have happened. The claimant applied to vacate the trial date, amend his particulars of claim, and obtain a further report from the joint expert dealing with the new allegations in the amended particulars of claim.

The judge granted the claimant's request and made an order accordingly. The defendant appealed to the Court of Appeal.

HELD, ON APPEAL: The judge was exercising his discretion and making a case management decision. He had applied the overriding objective and considered and balanced the relevant criteria. These were matters in which the Court of Appeal would not interfere, unless the judge had erred in principle. It was not enough to argue that the judge could have come to a different conclusion.

[19.38]   Roberts and Roberts v Williams and Williams
[2005] CP Rep 44

The claimants alleged that their neighbours, the defendants, had encroached upon a right of way by erecting a wall. Witness statements were exchanged on 4 July 2003, and the first defendant served a statement. On 27 March 2004, an application was made on behalf of the second defendant to serve a witness statement. The application was refused.

HELD, ON APPEAL: The witness statement did not raise any new issues. The court should have applied the overriding objective, and balanced the competing interests of and potential prejudice to the parties of the case management decision. The trial judge should have been permitted to hear all relevant evidence, and late service of the witness statement did not necessarily jeopardise the trial date.

ALLOCATING THE COURT'S RESOURCES

[19.39]   **Arbuthnot Latham Bank Ltd and Others v Trafalgar Holding Ltd and Others**

[1998] 2 All ER 181, [1998] 1 WLR 1426

Per Lord Woolf MR: 'Litigants and their legal advisers must ... recognise that any delay which occurs ... will be assessed, not only from the point of view of the prejudice caused to the particular litigants whose case it is, but also in relation to the effect it can have on other litigants who are wishing to have their cases heard and the prejudice which is caused to the due administration of civil justice.'

THE OVERRIDING OBJECTIVE AND HUMAN RIGHTS

[19.40]   **Daniels v Walker**

[2000] All ER (D) 608, [2000] 1 WLR 1382

The claimant was injured in a road traffic accident, sustaining serious injuries which resulted in a need for long-term care. The parties agreed that evidence was required from an occupational therapist and jointly instructed such an expert. The defendant was unhappy with the resulting report and applied for permission to obtain his own report. In support of that application, it was argued that Art 6 of the European Convention of Human Rights would be breached if the application was refused because the defendant would be barred from an essential or fundamental part of his defence.

HELD, ON APPEAL, Per Lord Woolf MR: ' ... if the court is not to be taken down blind alleys it is essential that counsel ... take a responsible attitude as to when it is right to raise a Human Rights Act point ... Article 6 could not possibly having anything to add to the issue on this appeal. The provisions of the CPR, to which I have referred, make it clear that the obligation on the court is to deal with cases justly.'

[19.41]   **Jones v University of Warwick**

[2003] EWCA Civ 151

[2003] 3 All ER 760, [2003] 1 WLR 954

The claimant was injured during the course of her employment with the defendant. The defendant's advisors obtained surveillance evidence from enquiry agents who posed as market researchers and obtained access to the claimant's home. The defendant's medical expert viewed the resulting footage and concluded that the claimant was able to function fully. The defendant applied for permission to rely upon the footage. The claimant opposed the application, arguing that the enquiry agents' trespass infringed her right to privacy under Article 8 of the European Convention of Human Rights.

HELD, ON APPEAL, per Lord Woolf MR: "Once the court has decided the order, which it should make in order to deal with the case justly, in accordance with the overriding objectives set out in CPR 1.1, in the exercise of its discretion under CPR 32.1 [to not exclude evidence unlawfully obtained by a party], then it is required or it is necessary for the court to make that order."

ENCOURAGING ALTERNATIVE DISPUTE RESOLUTION

[19.42]   **Dyson (1) Field (2) v Leeds City Council**
(22 November 1999, unreported), CA

Per Ward LJ: Damages are substantially agreed. It seems to me therefore that this is pre-eminently the category of case in which, consistent with the overriding objective of the Civil Procedure Rules and the court's duty to manage cases as set out in CPR 1.4(2)(e), that we should encourage the parties to use an alternative dispute resolution procedure ... I would also add the reminder that the court has powers to take a strong view about the rejection of [the court's suggestion that the parties should engage in mediation], if necessary by imposing eventual orders for indemnity costs or indeed ordering that a higher rate of interest be paid on damages which might at the end of the day be recoverable.

[19.43]   **Dunnett v Railtrack plc**
[2002] EWCA Civ 302
[2002] All ER (D) 314 (Feb), CA

The claimant issued proceedings against the defendant seeking damages for negligence arising from the death of three of her horses which had been struck by a train on the Swansea to London railway line. During the course of proceedings, the court advised the claimant, who was acting in person, that she should explore the possibility of alternative dispute resolution (ADR). The claimant expressed a wish to proceed by way of ADR, but the defendant turned the option down. The claimant's claim was dismissed at trial, and she appealed. The appeal was unsuccessful, and the defendant applied for the costs of the appeal.

HELD, ON APPEAL: The parties had an obligation to further the overriding objective, and any party who turned down out of hand a referral to ADR when suggested by the court might face 'uncomfortable costs consequences'.

[19.44]   **Shirayama Shokusan Co Ltd and Others v Danovo Ltd**
[2004] All ER (D) 442 (Feb), [2004] 1 WLR 2985

The claimants brought an action in trespass against the defendant in respect of display of signage and artwork in County Hall. The defendant had previously suggested to the claimants that the dispute could be resolved by way of mediation. The claimants refused, saying that the issue in dispute could not be resolved by mediation – either the defendant was trespassing or it was not.

HELD: The court has power to order the parties to submit to ADR, even in circumstances where one party is unwilling, in pursuance of CPR 1.4(2).

[19.45]   **Halsey v Milton Keynes General NHS Trust**
[2004] EWCA Civ 576
[2004] 4 All ER 920, [2004] 1 WLR 3002

The claimant brought a claim against the defendant NHS Trust in respect of the death of her husband arising out of negligent medical treatment. The claim was dismissed, but the trial judge refused to award costs to the defendant because the defendant had refused invitations from the claimant to submit to mediation. The defendant appealed.

HELD, ON APPEAL: Parties sometimes needed to be encouraged to submit to ADR, and the court's role should be to encourage but not compel ADR. The question of whether a party has acted unreasonably in refusing ADR depends upon the circumstances of the case, and the court will have regard to the nature of the dispute, the merits of the case, the extent to which other settlement methods have been attempted, whether the costs of ADR would be disproportionately high, whether any delay in going to ADR would be prejudicial, and whether ADR would have a reasonable prospect of success.

Furthermore, per Dyson LJ: [the] compulsion of ADR [is likely to be regarded] as an unacceptable constraint on the right of access to the court and, therefore, a violation of Article 6 [of the European Convention on Human Rights] … [and] even if the court does have jurisdiction to order unwilling parties to refer their disputes to mediation, we find it difficult to conceive of circumstances in which it would be appropriate to exercise it.

5.   CASE MANAGEMENT

(A)   COURT'S POWERS

[19.46]

CPR 3.1 – THE COURT'S GENERAL POWERS OF CASE MANAGEMENT
(1)   The list of powers in this rule is in addition to any powers given to the court by any other rule or practice direction or by any other enactment or any powers it may otherwise have.
(2)   Except where these Rules provide otherwise, the court may–
   (a)   extend or shorten the time for compliance with any rule, practice direction or court order (even if an application for extension is made after the time for compliance has expired);
   (b)   adjourn or bring forward a hearing;
   (c)   require a party or a party's legal representative to attend the court;
   (d)   hold a hearing and receive evidence by telephone or by using any other method of direct oral communication;
   (e)   direct that part of any proceedings (such as a counterclaim) be dealt with as separate proceedings;
   (f)   stay the whole or part of any proceedings or judgment either generally or until a specified date or event;
   (g)   consolidate proceedings;
   (h)   try two or more claims on the same occasion;
   (i)   direct a separate trial of any issue;
   (j)   decide the order in which issues are to be tried;
   (k)   exclude an issue from consideration;
   (l)   dismiss or give judgment on a claim after a decision on a preliminary issue;
   (ll)   order any party to file and serve an estimate of costs;
   (m)   take any other step or make any other order for the purpose of managing the case and furthering the overriding objective.
(3)   When the court makes an order, it may–
   (a)   make it subject to conditions, including a condition to pay a sum of money into court; and

   (b)   specify the consequence of failure to comply with the order or a condition.

(4)   Where the court gives directions it may take into account whether or not a party has complied with any relevant pre-action protocol.

(5)   The court may order a party to pay a sum of money into court if that party has, without good reason, failed to comply with a rule, practice direction or a relevant pre-action protocol.

(6)   When exercising its power under paragraph (5) the court must have regard to–

   (a)   the amount in dispute; and

   (b)   the costs which the parties have incurred or which they may incur.

(6A)   Where a party pays money into court following an order under paragraph (3) or (5), the money shall be security for any sum payable by that party to any other party in the proceedings, subject to the right of a defendant under rule 37.2 to treat all or part of any money paid into court as a Part 36 payment.

(7)   A power of the court under these Rules to make an order includes a power to vary or revoke the order.

[19.47]   Omega SA v Omega Engineering Inc

[2003] EWHC 1482 (Ch)

[2003] All ER (D) 267 (May)

On 13 March 2003, Pomfrey J made an order refusing permission to the claimant to register a trademark unless the specification of goods to which the trademark applied was amended within 28 days of the order. The claimant filed an appellant's notice with the Civil Appeals Office, and applied to the court for a stay of the order of 13 March 2003.

HELD: The court had no power to stay an order, but could extend time for compliance with the order under CPR 3.1(2)(a). In the instant case, time was extended until 14 days after disposal of the appeal by the Court of Appeal.

[19.48]   Watford Petroleum Ltd v Interoil Trading SA and Others

[2003] EWCA Civ 1417

[2003] All ER (D) 175 (Sep)

A commercial dispute arose out of a joint venture between two parties. The claimant issued proceedings and an order for directions was made which provided for disclosure of certain documents. The claimant made an application without notice, and obtained an order to delay provision of those documents until after exchange of witness statements. The defendant sought to set this order aside, and when unsuccessful, appealed.

HELD, ON APPEAL: The overriding objective required that, in the normal course of events, disclosure should take place prior to exchange of witness statements, because the witnesses will often be required to comment upon the documents that have been disclosed. To order otherwise would result in expense and delay, and would also be unfair. The courts should encourage a 'cards on the table' approach to evidence. The court has jurisdiction when exercising case management powers to make an order postponing disclosure until after exchange of witness statements, but that jurisdiction should only be exercised in wholly exceptional cases. This was not such a case.

(B)   COURT ORDER

[19.49]

CPR 3.3 – THE COURT'S POWER TO MAKE AN ORDER OF ITS OWN INITIATIVE
(1)   Except where a rule or some other enactment provides otherwise, the court may exercise its powers on an application or of its own initiative.
(2)   Where the court proposes to make an order of its own initiative–
  (a)   it may give any person likely to be affected by the order an opportunity to make representations; and
  (b)   where it does so it must specify the time by and the manner in which the representations must be made.
(3)   Where the court proposes–
  (a)   to make an order of its own initiative; and
  (b)   to hold a hearing to decide whether to make the order,
it must give each party likely to be affected by the order at least 3 days' notice of the hearing.
(4)   The court may make an order of its own initiative, without hearing the parties or giving them an opportunity to make representations.
(5)   Where the court has made an order under paragraph (4) -
  (a)   a party affected by the order may apply to have it set aside, varied or stayed; and
  (b)   the order must contain a statement of the right to make such an application.
(6)   An application under paragraph (5)(a) must be made–
  (a)   within such period as may be specified by the court; or
  (b)   if the court does not specify a period, not more than 7 days after the date on which the order was served on the party making the application.
(7)   If the court of its own initiative strikes out a statement of case or dismisses an application, (including an application for permission to appeal or for permission to apply for judicial review) and it considers that the claim or application is totally without merit–
  (a)   the court's order must record that fact; and
  (b)   the court must at the same time consider whether it is appropriate to make a civil restraint order.

(C)   STRIKING OUT

[19.50]

CPR 3.4 – THE COURT'S POWER TO STRIKE OUT A STATEMENT OF CASE
(1)   In this rule and rule 3.5, reference to a statement of case includes reference to part of a statement of case.
(2)   The court may strike out a statement of case if it appears to the court–
  (a)   that the statement of case discloses no reasonable grounds for bringing or defending the claim;
  (b)   that the statement of case is an abuse of the court's process or is otherwise likely to obstruct the just disposal of the proceedings; or

   (c)   that there has been a failure to comply with a rule, practice
         direction or court order.
(3)   When the court strikes out a statement of case it may make any
consequential order it considers appropriate.
(4)   Where–
   (a)   the court has struck out a claimant's statement of case;
   (b)   the claimant has been ordered to pay costs to the defendant; and
   (c)   before the claimant pays those costs, he starts another claim
         against the same defendant, arising out of facts which are the same
         or substantially the same as those relating to the claim in which the
         statement of case was struck out,
the court may, on the application of the defendant, stay that other claim
until the costs of the first claim have been paid.
(5)   Paragraph (2) does not limit any other power of the court to strike
out a statement of case.
(6)   If the court strikes out a claimant's statement of case and it
considers that the claim is totally without merit–
   (a)   the court's order must record that fact; and
   (b)   the court must at the same time consider whether it is appropriate
         to make a civil restraint order.

[19.51]   Loutchansky v Times Newspapers Ltd

(2000) The Independent, 4 December

The defendant newspaper sought to dismiss a libel action pursued by the claimant
on the basis that whilst the claim had a reasonable prospect of success any award
of damages was likely to be minimal. The defendant sought to rely on the court's
powers of active case management under CPR 3.4 to strike out.

HELD: The court only had power to strike out under CPR 3.4 if:
   (1)   there were no reasonable grounds for pursuing the claim;
   (2)   there was an abuse of the court's process; or
   (3)   there was failure to comply with a rule, direction or court order.
Accordingly the defendant's application was dismissed.

[19.52]   Atos Consulting Ltd v Avis Europe plc

[2005] EWHC 982 (TCC)

[2005] All ER (D) 183 (Nov), [2005] CP Rep 43

The claimant and defendant entered into a contract. Neither was satisfied with the
others conduct, and eventually the claimant issued proceedings. The claimant's
claim amounted to £10 million, the defendant's counterclaim to £30 million. Given
the discrepancy in the two claims, the defendant took the view that they should be
the claimant, and that the claimant's particulars of claim were inadequate, and
applied to strike out the particulars of claim.

HELD: '[The] court will only strike out a statement of case pursuant to the second
limb of CPR 3.4(2)(b) if the statement of case is such as to prevent the just
disposal of the proceedings or, alternatively, such as to create a substantial
obstruction to the just disposal of the proceedings'.

[19.53] Jeffrey v Jeffrey

[2005] EWHC 1697 (Ch)

[2005] All ER (D) 440 (Jul)

The defendant applied to strike out the claimant's claim on the grounds that it was an abuse of process, under CPR 3.4(2)(b). The basis of the claim was known in 1998 but proceedings were not issued until January 2004. A defence was served and directions given. The directions provided for permission to the claimant to amend the particulars of claim. It took some six and a half months from the date of the order for directions for the claimant to file and serve amended particulars of claim. As a consequence, the trial window had to be vacated.

HELD: The delay was not sufficient to amount to an abuse of process such that the claim should be struck out. However, the delay had caused the vacation of the trial window and delayed the disposal of the proceedings. Accordingly, the defendant was awarded the costs of the application on an indemnity basis. Furthermore, the court directed that the trial judge should consider disallowing interest on damages during the period of delay.

(D)   SANCTIONS

[19.54]

CPR 3.8 – SANCTIONS HAVE IMMEDIATE EFFECT
(1)   Where a party has failed to comply with a rule, practice direction or court order, any sanction for failure to comply imposed by the rule, practice direction or court order has effect unless the party in default applies for and obtains relief from the sanction.
(2)   Where the sanction is the payment of costs, the party in default may only obtain relief by appealing against the order for costs.
(3)   Where a rule, practice direction or court order–
   (a)   requires a party to do something within a specified time, and
   (b)   specifies the consequence of failure to comply,
the time for doing the act in question may not be extended by agreement between the parties.

(E)   APPLYING FOR RELIEF FROM SANCTIONS – THE CPR 3.9 CHECKLIST

[19.55]

CPR 3.9 – RELIEF FROM SANCTIONS
(1)   On an application for relief from any sanction imposed for a failure to comply with any rule, practice direction or court order the court will consider all the circumstances including–
   (a)   the interests of the administration of justice;
   (b)   whether the application for relief has been made promptly;
   (c)   whether the failure to comply was intentional;
   (d)   whether there is a good explanation for the failure;

    (e)   the extent to which the party in default has complied with other rules, practice directions, court orders and any relevant pre-action protocol;

    (f)   whether the failure to comply was caused by the party or his legal representative;

    (g)   whether the trial date or the likely trial date can still be met if relief is granted;

    (h)   the effect which the failure to comply had on each party; and

    (i)   the effect which the granting of relief would have on each party.

  (2)   An application for relief must be supported by evidence.

EXTENDING TIME FOR COMPLIANCE WHEN THE TIME PERIOD PROVIDED BY THE RULE HAS ELAPSED

[19.56]   **Sayers v Clarke Walker (a firm)**

[2002] EWCA Civ 645

[2002] 3 All ER 490

Following a trial, the defendant failed to file an appellant's notice with the Civil Appeals Office within the appropriate time limit, and applied for an extension of time in which to file an appellant's notice. The application was refused, and the defendant appealed to the Court of Appeal.

HELD, ON APPEAL: When a court is considering whether to grant an extension of time, and the time period provided by the rule has elapsed by the time the application is made, the exercise of discretion should be considered as if the failure to comply with the time period had resulted in a sanction. Accordingly, the court should have regard to the checklist set out in CPR 3.9 when considering whether it should exercise discretion to extend time. CPR 3.9 was preferable to use rather than the judge-made checklists set out in pre-CPR cases.

[19.57]   **Price v Price (t/a Poppyland Headware)**

[2003] EWCA Civ 888

[2003] 3 All ER 911

The claimant sustained injury during the course of his employment with the defendant. A claim form was issued on 4 April 2001 without any particulars of claim, medical report or schedule of loss. The claimant made an application to extend time in respect of service of these documents, but not until 14 months had elapsed following the time period within which he should have filed and served the documents. The delay was in large part due to the claimant obtaining medical evidence with which he was not satisfied, and then seeking the advice of an alternative expert. This second expert supported a claim of dramatically different value from that which would have been presented had the first medical expert's evidence been filed with the claim form.

HELD, ON APPEAL: The claimant was in serious default in relation to his duty to help the court deal with the case fairly. The defendant had complied with its duty. In applying the CPR 3.9 checklist, the relief that the claimant sought should be granted, but the interests of justice demanded that the claimant's claim should be restricted in value to that which could have been established had the claimant complied with the rules in April 2001.

[19.58]   **Primus Telecommunications Netherlands BV v Pan European Ltd and Others**

[2005] EWCA Civ 273

[2005] All ER (D) 359 (Feb)

The first defendant company owed the claimant company a sum of money in respect of the supply of pre-paid telephone calling cards. The first defendant company and the other defendants, all officers of the first defendant, entered into a compromise agreement which provided for the payment of the debt in instalments over an 18-week period. The claimant issued debt proceedings, and the defendants responded with a defence reciting the terms of the compromise agreement. The first defendant was then the subject of a winding-up order, and proceedings against that defendant were stayed. The claimant's solicitors proceeded with the action against the remaining defendants who because they did not provide instructions to the solicitor on the court record for the first defendant, failed to exchange witness evidence and only became aware of the trial date the day before it took place. The defendants applied for an adjournment, but the trial judge refused, and gave judgment to the claimant. The defendants appealed seeking relief from sanctions under CPR 3.9 and arguing that the judge should have adjourned the case with directions and given the defendants an opportunity to submit evidence.

HELD, ON APPEAL: The trial judge should have considered all the factors set out in CPR 3.9(1). Had he done so, he would have properly weighed the relatively minor prejudice to the claimant of allowing the adjournment as against the significant prejudice to the defendants of refusing the adjournment. The appeal was allowed, subject to a costs order and a payment into court.

[19.59]   **Smith and Hutchinson v Brough**

[2005] EWCA Civ 261

On 4 September 2001, judgment was given against the defendants in a boundary dispute. Between October 2001 and June 2002, the defendants sought to obtain new lay witness evidence in relation to the boundary. Thereafter, in April 2003 they obtained evidence from a surveyor. Between April 2003 and November 2004 the defendants were in discussion with the surveyor. On 6 December 2004, an application was made which sought, *inter alia*, an extension of time within which to apply for permission to appeal. It was submitted on behalf of the defendants that the court should have regard to the factors set out at CPR 3.9.

HELD: The defendants had wrongly conflated the need to obtain new evidence with the need to file a notice of appeal within the requisite time period. The delay in filing the application was 'unprecedented'. Furthermore, there is a public interest in the closure of litigation.

Per Brooke LJ: ... it is a fundamental principle of our common law that the outcome of litigation should be final ... the law exceptionally allows appeals out of time ... [in] ... rare and limited cases ... In interpreting CPR 3.9 in any case where an extension of time for appealing in excess of say two months has been sought, the court will bear in mind [these] matters ... in determining where the interests of the administration of justice truly lie.

[19.60]   **Chapple v Williams and Emmett**

[1999] CPLR 731, CA

The claimant claimed damages for an alleged wrongful termination of his employment contract by the defendants. The defendants initially represented themselves, and later were granted legal aid. The defendants failed to comply with an unless order, and applied for an extension of time within which to comply with the order. The judge considered the provisions of CPR 3.9. His judgment indicated that the extension of time should not be granted. However, he considered that there was merit in the defendants' defence, and therefore granted the extension of time, subject to the condition that the sum of £4,000 be paid into court. Given the granting of legal aid, the defendants were not able to comply with the condition. The claimant appealed, arguing that the judge should not have considered the merits of the defence, and had in any event failed to give proper regard to CPR 3.9.

HELD, ON APPEAL: The checklist at CPR 3.9 is not exhaustive, and in an appropriate case the court can and should consider the merits of a party's case when considering all the circumstances. However, in the instant case, the judge had been wrong to exercise his discretion to extend time, and in all probability he would not have done so had he not felt able to order a payment into court.

[19.61]   **RC Residuals Ltd v Linton Fuel Oils Ltd**

[2002] EWCA Civ 911

[2002] All ER (D) 32 (May), [2002] 1 WLR 2782

The claimant issued proceedings against the defendant. Liability was admitted. On 8 February 2002, the judge made an order which required that the claimant should serve its expert reports by 4 pm on 12 April 2002, failing which it would be debarred from calling expert evidence. The fax sending the first of two reports to the defendant did not arrive until 4:10 pm, and the courier delivering the second report did not arrive until 4:20 pm. The defendant took no issue with late service. However, at the pre-trial review, the circuit judge held that the claimant had failed to comply with the unless order and refused permission to appeal. The claimant renewed its application to appeal, and the matter came before the Court of Appeal.

HELD, ON APPEAL: The judge had failed to exercise his discretion by reference to CPR 3.9(1), and it was apparent from his judgment that he had not carried out the necessary balancing exercise. There was no question that the judge had been right to attach importance to ensuring that parties take unless orders seriously. However, there had been no intentional default on the part of the claimant, and the effect of the unless order was to deprive the claimant of the chance of pursuing a substantial claim. Accordingly, the appeal would be allowed.

EXTENDING TIME FOR COMPLIANCE – APPLICATION MADE WITHIN TIME PERIOD, CPR 3.9 CHECKLIST SHOULD NOT BE APPLIED

[19.62]   **Robert v Momentum Services Ltd**

[2003] EWCA Civ 299

[2003] 2 All ER 74, [2003] 1 WLR 1577

The claimant brought a claim in respect of injuries she had suffered on 5 March 1998 during the course of her employment with the defendant. A claim form was issued on 1 March 2001 within the primary limitation period, and served on or by

1 July 2001, without particulars of claim. On 13 June 2001, the claimant issued an application to extend time for service of the particulars of claim. The defendant objected to the application. The district judge granted an extension of time, saying that if he did not, he 'would not be taking into account the overriding objective'. In his judgment, he set out the factors which he had balanced when considering whether to exercise his discretion. On appeal, the judge said that the district judge had failed to carry out a 'systematic analysis of the situation in accordance with CPR 3.9'. In those circumstances, the judge considered that he was entitled to exercise discretion afresh. Considering the checklist provided by CPR 3.9, the judge decided that the claimant's application should be refused. The claimant appealed to the Court of Appeal.

HELD, ON APPEAL: The issue for the court to resolve was how the discretion provided by CPR 3.1(2)(a) to extend or shorten time for compliance with any rule, practice direction or court order should be exercised. Since the application to extend time had been made within the time period permitted by the rule, this was neither a relief from sanctions case nor analogous to such a case. There was therefore no need for the court to consider the CPR 3.9 checklist, and discretion should be exercised only by reference to the overriding objective. The appeal would be allowed.

(F) THE COURT'S POWER TO RECTIFY ERRORS

[19.63]

CPR 3.10 – GENERAL POWER OF THE COURT TO RECTIFY MATTERS WHERE THERE HAS BEEN AN ERROR OF PROCEDURE

Where there has been an error of procedure such as a failure to comply with a rule or practice direction–
    (a)   the error does not invalidate any step taken in the proceedings unless the court so orders; and
    (b)   the court may make an order to remedy the error.

[19.64] Steele v Mooney and Others
[2005] EWCA Civ 96
[2005] 2 All ER 256, [2005] 1 WLR 2819

The claimant made a claim in respect of alleged clinical negligence on behalf of the defendants. The claim form was issued within the primary limitation period. Having failed to identify and instruct a liability expert, the claimant made an application to extend time for service of particulars of claim and supporting documentation, and the court made an order in those terms. It was only after obtaining a second order for a further extension in the same terms that the claimant realised that no extension of time had been sought in respect of the claim form, which had still not been served. The claimant made an application under CPR 3.10 to rectify the error. The district judge allowed the application, but the judge on appeal refused it. The claimant appealed to the Court of Appeal.

HELD, ON APPEAL: On the facts, it was clear that a genuine error had been made, and that the claimant's two applications for an extension of time, which had been made within their respective time limits, had been made with the intention of extending time in respect of the claim form as well as the particulars of claim and supporting documents. The court was not precluded from correcting the error, in accordance with the case management powers conferred by CPR 3.10, by the rules which limited the court's discretion to grant retrospective extensions of time for service of claim forms.

6. STATEMENTS OF TRUTH

(A) WHAT IS A STATEMENT OF TRUTH?

[19.65]

CPR 22.1(4)–(6) – DOCUMENTS TO BE VERIFIED BY A STATEMENT OF TRUTH
    (4)   Subject to paragraph (5), a statement of truth is a statement that–
        (a)   the party putting forward the document;
        (b)   in the case of a witness statement, the maker of the witness statement; or
        (c)   in the case of a certificate of service, the person who signs the certificate,
believes the facts stated in the document are true.
    (5)   If a party is conducting proceedings with a litigation friend, the statement of truth in–
        (a)   a statement of case;
        (b)   a response; or
        (c)   an application notice,
is a statement that the litigation friend believes the facts stated in the document being verified are true.
    (6)   The statement of truth must be signed by–
        (a)   in the case of a statement of case, a response or an application–
            (i)   the party or litigation friend; or
            (ii)   the legal representative on behalf of the party or litigation friend; and
        (b)   in the case of a witness statement, the maker of the statement.

(B) DOCUMENTS WHICH REQUIRE A STATEMENT OF TRUTH

[19.66]

CPR 22.1(1)–(3) – DOCUMENTS TO BE VERIFIED BY A STATEMENT OF TRUTH
    (1)   The following documents must be verified by a statement of truth–
        (a)   a statement of case;
        (b)   a response complying with an order under rule 18.1 to provide further information;
        (c)   a witness statement;
        (d)   an acknowledgement of service in a claim begun by way of the Part 8 procedure;

(e)   a certificate stating the reasons for bringing a possession claim or a landlord and tenant claim in the High Court in accordance with rules 55.3(2) and 56.2(2);

(f)   a certificate of service; and

(g)   any other document where a rule or practice direction requires.

(2)   Where a statement of case is amended, the amendments must be verified by a statement of truth unless the court orders otherwise.

(3)   If an applicant wishes to rely on matters set out in his application notice as evidence, the application notice must be verified by a statement of truth.

(C)   WHO MAY SIGN A STATEMENT OF TRUTH

[19.67]

PRACTICE DIRECTION – STATEMENTS OF TRUTH

WHO MAY SIGN THE STATEMENT OF TRUTH

3.1   In a statement of case, a response or an application notice, the statement of truth must be signed by:

(1)   the party or his litigation friend, or

(2)   the legal representative or the party or litigation friend.

...

3.4   Where a document is to be verified on behalf of a company or other corporation, subject to paragraph 3.7 below, the statement of truth must be signed by a person holding a senior position in the company or corporation. That person must state the office or position he holds.

3.5   Each of the following persons is a person holding a senior position:

(1)   in respect of a registered company or corporation, a director, the treasurer, secretary, chief executive, manager or other officer of the company or corporation, and

(2)   in respect of a corporation which is not a registered company, in addition to those persons set out in (1), the mayor, chairman, president or town clerk or other similar officer of the corporation.

3.5   Where the document is to be verified on behalf of a partnership, those who sign the statement of truth are:

(1)   any of the partners, or

(2)   any person having the control or management of the partnership business.

3.6A   An insurer or the Motor Insurers' Bureau may sign a statement of truth in a statement of case on behalf of a party where the insurer or the Motor Insurers' Bureau has a financial interest in the result of proceedings brought wholly or partially by or against that party.

3.6B   If insurers are conducting proceedings on behalf of many claimants or defendants a statement of truth in a statement of case may be signed by a senior person responsible for the case at a lead insurer, but–

(1)   the person signing must specify the capacity in which he signs;

(2)   the statement of truth must be a statement that the lead insurer believes that the facts stated in the document are true; and

    (3)   the court may order that a statement of truth also be signed by one or more of the parties.

3.6   Where a party is legally represented, the legal representative may sign the statement of truth on his behalf. The statement signed by the legal representative will refer to the client's belief, not his own. In signing he must state the capacity in which he signs and the name of his firm where appropriate.

3.7   Where a legal representative has signed a statement of truth, his signature will be taken by the court ask his statement:

    (1)   that the client on whose behalf he has signed had authorised him to do so,

    (2)   that before signing he had explained to the client that in signing the statement of truth he would be confirming the client's belief that the facts stated in the document were true, and

    (3)   that before signing he had informed the client of the possible consequences to the client if it should subsequently appear that the client did not have an honest belief in the truth of those facts (see rule 32.14).

3.8   The individual who signs a statement of truth must print his full name clearly beneath his signature.

3.9   A legal representative who signs a statement of truth must sign in his own name and not that of his firm or employer.

[19.68]   **Carlco Ltd v Chief Constable of the Dyfed and Powys Police**

[2002] EWCA Civ 1754

[2002] All ER (D) 244 (Nov)

The claimant company was ordered, through its properly authorised officer, to disclose documents or, if there were none, to serve a statement to that effect. This statement was to be verified by a statement of truth. The statement was signed by someone who was not an authorised officer of the company. The court at first instance held there were gross breaches of the order and struck out the claimant's claim.

HELD, ON APPEAL: CPR Pt 22 stated that where a document was to be verified on behalf of a company the statement of truth must be signed by a person holding a senior position in the company or corporation. This was a reference to an individual person and not to a corporate entity. Although there had been a breach of the disclosure order (as the statement had not been made through the claimant's proper officer) it did not amount to a gross breach of the order such as to merit striking out the claim.

(D)   EFFECT OF FAILURE TO SIGN A STATEMENT OF TRUTH

[19.69]

CPR 22.2 – FAILURE TO VERIFY A STATEMENT OF CASE

    (1)   If a party fails to verify his statement of case by a statement of truth–

    (a)   the statement of case shall remain effective unless struck out; but

    (b)   the party may not rely on the statement of case as evidence of any of the matters set out in it.

(2)   The court may strike out a statement of case which is not verified by a statement of truth.

(3)   Any party may apply for an order under paragraph (2).

[19.70]

CPR 22.3 – FAILURE TO VERIFY A WITNESS STATEMENT
22.3   If the maker of a witness statement fails to verify the witness statement by a statement of truth the court may direct that it shall not be admissible as evidence.

[19.71]

CPR 22.4 – POWER OF THE COURT TO REQUIRE A DOCUMENT TO BE VERIFIED
(1)   The court may order a person who has failed to verify a document in accordance with rule 22.1 to verify the document.

(2)   Any party may apply for an order under paragraph (1).

(E)   ADVANCING ALTERNATIVE CASES

[19.72]   Clarke v Marlborough Fine Art (London) Ltd
[2001] All ER (D) 286 (Nov), [2002] I WLR 1731

The claimant sought permission to make an amendment to the particulars of claim to introduce a plea of actual undue influence in the alternative to the originally pleaded case.

HELD, ON APPEAL: Whilst the claimant would not be permitted to allege two mutually contradictory allegations, CPR Pt 22 was not intended to exclude the possibility of pleading inconsistent factual alternatives. Provided the alternative set of facts was supported by evidence and not pure speculation or invention then a statement of truth could be signed.

[19.73]   Binks v Securicor Omega Express Ltd
[2003] EWCA Civ 993
[2003] All ER (D) 266 (Jul), [2003] I WLR 2557

The claimant issued proceedings in respect of an accident which occurred at work. At trial, he advanced the case set out in his particulars of claim, which he had verified with a statement of truth. After hearing the defendant's evidence, the claimant's counsel sought to advance an alternative case. The trial judge refused permission, on the basis that the alternative case conflicted with the version of events described in the particulars of claim which the claimant had verified, and the claimant could not sign a statement of truth to the conflicting version of events.

HELD, ON APPEAL: CPR 22.1(2) permits the court to dispense with verification by a statement of truth when particulars of claim are amended. Accordingly, since the evidence before the court clearly established liability on the part of the defendant employer, subject to contributory negligence, the court would exercise its discretion to permit the claimant to rely upon the alternative version of events.

CHAPTER 20

Parties

1. CLAIMANTS

(A) CHILDREN AND PATIENTS

[20.1]

CPR 21 – CHILDREN AND PATIENTS: THE LITIGATION FRIEND

21.1
  (1) This Part–
    (a) contains special provisions which apply in proceedings involving
       children and patients; and
    (b) sets out how a person becomes a litigation friend.
  (2) In this Part–
    (a) 'child' means a person under 18; and
    (b) 'patient' means a person who by reason of mental disorder within
       the meaning of the Mental Health Act 1983 is incapable of
       managing and administering his property and affairs.

21.2
  (1) A patient must have a litigation friend to conduct proceedings on his
behalf.
  (2) A child must have a litigation friend to conduct proceedings on his
behalf unless the court makes an order under paragraph (3).
  (3) The court may make an order permitting the child to conduct
proceedings without a litigation friend.
  (4) An application for an order under paragraph (3)–
    (a) may be made by the child;
    (b) if the child already has a litigation friend, must be made on notice
       to the litigation friend; and
    (c) if the child has no litigation friend, may be made without notice.
  (5) Where–
    (a) the court has made an order under paragraph (3); and
    (b) it subsequently appears to the court that it is desirable for a
       litigation friend to conduct the proceedings on behalf of the child,
the court may appoint a person to be the child's litigation friend.

21.3

(1)   This rule does not apply where the court has made an order under rule 21.2(3).

(2)   A person may not, without the permission of the court–

   (a)   make an application against a child or patient before proceedings have started; or

   (b)   take any step in proceedings except–

      (i)   issuing and serving a claim form; or

      (ii)   applying for the appointment of a litigation friend under rule 21.6,

   until the child or patient has a litigation friend.

(3)   If a party becomes a patient during proceedings, no party may take any step in the proceedings without the permission of the court until the patient has a litigation friend.

(4)   Any step taken before a child or patient has a litigation friend shall be of no effect unless the court otherwise orders.

21.4

(1)   This rule does not apply if the court has appointed a person to be a litigation friend.

(2)   A person authorised under Part VII of the Mental Health Act 1983 to conduct legal proceedings in the name of a patient or on his behalf is entitled to be the litigation friend of the patient in any proceedings to which his authority extends.

(3)   If nobody has been appointed by the court or, in the case of a patient, authorised under Part VII, a person may act as a litigation friend if he–

   (a)   can fairly and competently conduct proceedings on behalf of the child or patient;

   (b)   has no interest adverse to that of the child or patient; and

   (c)   where the child or patient is a claimant, undertakes to pay any costs which the child or patient may be ordered to pay in relation to the proceedings, subject to any right he may have to be repaid from the assets of the child or patient.

21.5

(1)   If the court has not appointed a litigation friend, a person who wishes to act as a litigation friend must follow the procedure set out in this rule.

(2)   A person authorised under Part VII of the Mental Health Act 1983 must file an official copy of the order or other document which constitutes his authorisation to act.

(3)   Any other person must file a certificate of suitability stating that he satisfies the conditions specified in rule 21.4(3).

(4)   A person who is to act as a litigation friend for a claimant must file–

   (a)   the authorisation; or

   (b)   the certificate of suitability,

at the time when the claim is made.

(5)   A person who is to act as a litigation friend for a defendant must file–

   (a)   the authorisation; or

   (b)   the certificate of suitability,

at the time when he first takes a step in the proceedings on behalf of the defendant.

(6)   The litigation friend must–

    (a)   serve the certificate of suitability on every person on whom, in accordance with rule 6.6 (service on parent, guardian etc.), the claim form should be served; and

    (b)   file a certificate of service when he files the certificate of suitability.

21.6

(1)   The court may make an order appointing a litigation friend.

(2)   An application for an order appointing a litigation friend may be made by–

    (a)   a person who wishes to be the litigation friend; or

    (b)   a party.

(3)   Where–

    (a)   a person makes a claim against a child or patient;

    (b)   the child or patient has no litigation friend;

    (c)   the court has not made an order under rule 21.2(3) (order that a child can act without a litigation friend); and

    (d)   either–

        (i)   someone who is not entitled to be a litigation friend files a defence; or

        (ii)   the claimant wishes to take some step in the proceedings,

    the claimant must apply to the court for an order appointing a litigation friend for the child or patient.

(4)   An application for an order appointing a litigation friend must be supported by evidence.

(5)   The court may not appoint a litigation friend under this rule unless it is satisfied that the person to be appointed complies with the conditions specified in rule 21.4(3).

21.7

(1)   The court may–

    (a)   direct that a person may not act as a litigation friend;

    (b)   terminate a litigation friend's appointment;

    (c)   appoint a new litigation friend in substitution for an existing one.

(2)   An application for an order under paragraph (1) must be supported by evidence.

(3)   The court may not appoint a litigation friend under this rule unless it is satisfied that the person to be appointed complies with the conditions specified in rule 21.4(3).

21.8

(1)   An application for an order under rule 21.6 or 21.7 must be served on every person on whom, in accordance with rule 6.6 (service on parent, guardian etc.), the claim form should be served.

(2)   Where an application for an order under rule 21.6 is in respect of a patient, the application must also be served on the patient unless the court orders otherwise.

(3)   An application for an order under rule 21.7 must also be served on–

    (a)   the person who is the litigation friend, or who is purporting to act as the litigation friend, when the application is made; and

(b)   the person who it is proposed should be the litigation friend, if he is not the applicant.

(4)   On an application for an order under rule 21.6 or 21.7, the court may appoint the person proposed or any other person who complies with the conditions specified in rule 21.4(3).

21.9

(1)   When a child who is not a patient reaches the age of 18, a litigation friend's appointment ceases.

(2)   When a party ceases to be a patient, the litigation friend's appointment continues until it is ended by a court order.

(3)   An application for an order under paragraph (2) may be made by–
    (a)   the former patient;
    (b)   the litigation friend; or
    (c)   a party.

(4)   The child or patient in respect of whom the appointment to act has ceased must serve notice on the other parties–
    (a)   stating that the appointment of his litigation friend to act has ceased;
    (b)   giving his address for service; and
    (c)   stating whether or not he intends to carry on the proceedings.

(5)   If he does not do so within 28 days after the day on which the appointment of the litigation friend ceases the court may, on application, strike out any claim or defence brought by him.

(6)   The liability of a litigation friend for costs continues until–
    (a)   the person in respect of whom his appointment to act has ceased serves the notice referred to in paragraph (4); or
    (b)   the litigation friend serves notice on the parties that his appointment to act has ceased.

21.10

(1)   Where a claim is made–
    (a)   by or on behalf of a child or patient; or
    (b)   against a child or patient,
no settlement, compromise or payment and no acceptance of money paid into court shall be valid, so far as it relates to the claim by, on behalf of or against the child or patient, without the approval of the court.

(2)   Where–
    (a)   before proceedings in which a claim is made by or on behalf of, or against a child or patient (whether alone or with any other person) are begun, an agreement is reached for the settlement of the claim; and
    (b)   the sole purpose of proceedings on that claim is to obtain the approval of the court to a settlement or compromise of the claim,
the claim must–
    (i)   be made using the procedure set out in Part 8 (alternative procedure for claims); and
    (ii)   include a request to the court for approval of the settlement or compromise.

(3)   In proceedings to which Section II of Part 45 applies, the court shall not make an order for detailed assessment of the costs payable to the child or patient but shall assess the costs in the manner set out in that Section.

21.11

(1)   Where in any proceedings–
   (a)   money is recovered by or on behalf of or for the benefit of a child or patient; or
   (b)   money paid into court is accepted by or on behalf of a child or patient, the money shall be dealt with in accordance with directions given by the court under this rule and not otherwise.

(2)   Directions given under this rule may provide that the money shall be wholly or partly paid into court and invested or otherwise dealt with.

21.11A

(1)   In proceedings to which rule 21.11 applies, a litigation friend who incurs expenses on behalf of a child or patient in any proceedings is entitled to recover the amount paid or payable out of any money recovered or paid into court to the extent that it–
   (a)   has been reasonably incurred, and
   (b)   is reasonable in amount.

(2)   Expenses may include all or part of–
   (a)   an insurance premium, as defined by rule 43.2(1)(m), or
   (b)   interest on a loan taken out to pay an insurance premium or other recoverable disbursement.

(3)   No application may be made under this rule for expenses that–
   (a)   are of a type that may be recoverable on an assessment of costs payable by or out of money belonging to a child or patient, but
   (b)   are disallowed in whole or in part on such an assessment.

(4)   In deciding whether the expense was reasonably incurred and reasonable in amount, the court must have regard to all the circumstances of the case including the factors set out in rule 44.5(3).

(5)   When the court is considering the factors to be taken into account in assessing the reasonableness of expenses incurred by the litigation friend on behalf of a child or patient, it will have regard to the facts and circumstances as they reasonably appeared to the litigation friend or child's or patient's legal representative when the expense was incurred.

(6)   Where the claim is settled or compromised, or judgment is given, on terms that an amount not exceeding £5,000 is paid to the child or patient, the total amount the litigation friend may recover under paragraph (1) of this rule shall not exceed 25% of the sum so agreed or awarded, unless the Court directs otherwise. Such total amount shall not exceed 50% of the sum so agreed or awarded.

21.12

(1)   The court may appoint the Official Solicitor to be a guardian of a child's estate where–
   (a)   money is paid into court on behalf of the child in accordance with directions given under rule 21.11 (control of money received by a child or patient);
   (b)   the Criminal Injuries Compensation Board or the Criminal Injuries Compensation Authority notifies the court that it has made or intends to make an award to the child;
   (c)   a court or tribunal outside England and Wales notifies the court that it has ordered or intends to order that money be paid to the child;

(d) the child is absolutely entitled to the proceeds of a pension fund; or

(e) in any other case, such an appointment seems desirable to the court.

(2) The court may not appoint the Official Solicitor under this rule unless–

(a) the persons with parental responsibility (within the meaning of section 3 of the Children Act 1989 agree; or

(b) the court considers that their agreement can be dispensed with.

(3) The Official Solicitor's appointment may continue only until the child reaches 18.

AGREEMENT WITH CHILD OR PATIENT NOT BINDING UNTIL APPROVED BY THE COURT

[20.2]   Dietz v Lennig Chemicals Ltd

[1969] 1 AC 170, [1967] 2 All ER 282, [1967] 3 WLR 165, HL

A widow brought a dependency claim on behalf of her child and herself, following the death of her husband. She accepted a settlement offer, subject to court approval. The settlement was approved by the court but before the order was drawn up it transpired the widow had remarried. The defendant's solicitors applied to set aside the order approving settlement.

HELD, ON APPEAL: Acceptance of an offer involving a child or a patient did not amount to a binding agreement unless it had been approved by the court and it was open to either party to repudiate it at any time, prior to the court giving approval.

[20.3]   Black v Yates

[1992] QB 526, [1991] 4 All ER 722, [1991] 3 WLR 90, QBD

The claimant's husband was killed in a motorcycle accident in Spain. The Spanish court awarded damages to both the claimant and her children. The claimant then issued dependency proceedings in England.

HELD, ON APPEAL: The claimant was barred from pursuing her claim pursuant to s 34 of the Civil Jurisdiction and Judgment Acts 1982. Her children's claims were not barred as no court approval had been given to validate the settlements. The children had been unaware of the Spanish proceedings and had not given their consent or authority in respect of the same. The English court retained jurisdiction to protect the children if that judgment was not in their interest. The Spanish award of damages was likely to be lower than the amount awarded in England and the children's claims were permitted to proceed.

[20.4]   Drinkall v Whitwood

[2003] EWCA Civ 1547

[2004] 4 All ER 378, [2004] 1 WLR 462

A 14-year-old girl was cycling home from school when she was struck by the defendant's motor car, suffering serious injury. The parties had agreed a liability split of 80/20 in the claimant's favour. The defendant then sought to withdraw from the agreement on liability.

HELD, ON APPEAL: Following *Dietz v Lennig* (at para [20.2]), a settlement involving an infant or person with a disability could be repudiated at any time prior to court approval. As the agreement in respect of liability had not been approved by the court, in accordance with CPR 21.10, the agreement was not binding and the defendant was entitled to renege on the agreement. The agreement was only a partial settlement until such time as court approval had been obtained.

MEANING OF 'CAPACITY' FOR THE PURPOSES OF THE MENTAL HEALTH ACT 1983

[20.5]   **Masterman-Lister v (1) Brutton & Co (2) Jewell & Home Counties Dairies**

[2002] EWCA Civ 1889

[2003] 3 All ER 162, [2003] 1 WLR 1511

The claimant commenced proceedings to re-open an earlier settlement of a personal injury claim. He claimed that, as a result of the accident, he was a patient within the definition of CPR Pt 21 and that the earlier settlement had not been approved by the court in accordance with the court rules.

HELD, ON APPEAL: The test as to whether a person had capacity to manage and administer his property and affairs was an issue-specific test. The question of capacity should be considered in relation to the nature and complexity of the particular transaction in respect of which the decision as to capacity had to be made.

Per Chadwick LJ: Capacity must be approached in a common sense way.

[20.6]   **Bailey v Warren**

[2006] EWCA Civ 51

[2006] All ER (D) 78 (Feb)

The claimant suffered head injuries when he crossed a dual carriageway and was struck by the defendant's vehicle. Liability was agreed on a 50/50 basis and judgment was later entered on this basis. Two years later the claimant was assessed as lacking mental capacity and a litigation friend was appointed. The issue then arose as to whether the claimant had been a patient when liability had been agreed on a 50/50 basis and whether the judgment entered for the claimant should stand or be set aside. At first instance it was held that the claimant was not a patient at the time of the agreement of liability and the judgment should stand.

HELD, ON APPEAL: The appropriate test for capacity was the issue-specific test laid down in *Masterman-Lister* (at para [20.5]). When considering capacity, it was necessary to establish whether the claimant had understood all aspects of the proceedings. Capacity could not be judged on a piecemeal basis. If a claimant understood what was meant by a 50/50 split of liability but failed to understand his award of damages would be halved then he lacked capacity to conduct the proceedings. A compromise made by an individual who was subsequently proved to have been a patient at the time of the compromise was of no binding effect until the approval of the court was obtained (*Dietz v Lennig*, at para [20.2]). When considering the question of retrospective approval, the appropriate test was: 'what is in the claimant's interests?'.
    Appeal dismissed.

[20.7] **Folks v Faizey**

[2006] EWCA Civ 381

[2006] All ER (D) 83 (Apr)

The claimant sustained serious injuries in a road traffic accident. Liability was agreed on a 79/21 basis in favour of the claimant. An application was made for the claimant's sister to be appointed as the claimant's litigation friend. The defendant objected to the application. The court adjourned the application pending the trial of a preliminary issue as to whether the facts justified the appointment of a litigation friend.

HELD: The purpose of an application to appoint a litigation friend was to protect the patient and those advising him. Whilst evidence was required to support such an application it was not open to the other party to the litigation to put in evidence disputing the basis for such an order. The court was critical of the defendant's attempt to interfere with a procedure with which he was only minimally concerned. An order should be made where both the proposed patient and litigation friend consented to the appointment, there was sufficient evidence to support the appointment, and there was no evidence to suggest that the appointment was not bona fide.

(B)   EXECUTORS AND ADMINISTRATORS

[20.8] **Littlechild v Holt**

[1950] 1 KB 1, [1949] 1 All ER 933

Per Lord Goddard CJ: It is always the case that a claim by an executor or administrator, as executor or administrator, can be joined with a claim by the executor or administrator personally. So, too, if there is a claim by the executor personally, it can be joined with a claim by him or her as executor. It is open to a person who obtains an order to continue proceedings as administrator or executor to join a claim by himself or herself in his or her personal capacity with the claim that is made in the representative capacity. At any rate, it is within the discretion of the court to allow those two claims to be made at the same time. Where the two claims are of a very similar nature, I see no reason at all why they should not be joined.

(C)   MISCELLANEOUS MATTERS

DUTY TO REMAIN CONTACTABLE

[20.9] **Neufville v Papamichael**

(23 November 1999, unreported), CA

A claimant who brings an action must remain contactable by the court or by his solicitors and if he does not do so, and an order is made in his absence, the court is not ordinarily prepared to set it aside.

DEFENDANT'S DUTY TO CLAIMANT IN PERSON

[20.10] **Horry v Tate & Lyle Refineries Ltd**

[1982] 2 Lloyd's Rep 416 Pain J

The claimant sustained a hernia at work. There was a 15% chance of recurrence. He accepted £1,000 in settlement of his claim for damages. The employer's insurer negotiated the settlement; the claimant was not professionally represented nor independently advised. He signed what purported to be a final discharge. Later, following a recurrence, he sought advice and in proceedings based on the original accident the employer by its insurer pleaded a release by way of accord and satisfaction based on the settlement.

HELD: The claimant was not bound by the settlement. He had relied on the insurer's advice and the insurer knew it. It had a fiduciary duty of care which it could have discharged by advising the claimant to obtain independent advice. There was a duty on the insurer to specify what deduction was made for contributory negligence. It should have supplied him with a copy of the medical report and ensured he understood that no further claim could be made. Their interest conflicted with his. The relationship imposed on the insurer was a fiduciary duty.

(D)   VEXATIOUS LITIGANTS

[20.11]

CPR 2.3(1) – INTERPRETATION
   (1)   In these Rules–
      'civil restraint order' means an order restraining a party–
      (a)   from making any further applications in current proceedings (a limited civil restraint order);
      (b)   from issuing certain claims or making certain applications in specified courts (an extended civil restraint order); or
      (c)   from issuing any claim or making any application in specified courts (a general civil restraint order).

[20.12]

CPR 3.11 – POWER OF THE COURT TO MAKE CIVIL RESTRAINT ORDERS

A practice direction may set out–
   (a)   the circumstances in which the court has the power to make a civil restraint order against a party to proceedings;
   (b)   the procedure where a party applies for a civil restraint order against another party; and
   (c)   the consequences of the court making a civil restraint order.

[20.13]

Practice Direction – Civil Restraint Orders

This Practice Direction supplements CPR 3.11

Introduction
   1.   This practice direction applies where the court is considering whether to make–
      (1)   a limited civil restraint order;
      (2)   an extended civil restraint order; or
      (3)   a general civil restraint order.

against a party who has issued claims or made applications which are totally without merit.

Limited Civil Restraint Orders

2.1 A limited civil restraint order may be made by a judge of any court where a party has made 2 or more applications which are totally without merit.

2.2 Where the court makes a limited civil restraint order, the party against whom the order is made–

(1) will be restrained from making any further applications in the proceedings in which the order is made without first obtaining the permission of a judge identified in the order;

(2) may apply for amendment or discharge of the order provided he has first obtained the permission of a judge identified in the order; and

(3) may apply for permission to appeal the order and if permission is granted, may appeal the order.

2.3 Where a part who is subject to a limited civil restraint order–

(1) makes a further application in the proceedings in which the order is made without first obtaining the permission of a judge identified in the order, such application will automatically be dismissed–

(a) without the judge having to make any further order; and

(b) without the need for the other party to respond to it;

(2) repeatedly makes applications for permission pursuant to that order which are totally without merit, the court may direct that if the party makes any further application for permission which is totally without merit, the decision to dismiss the application will be final and there will be no right of appeal, unless the judge who refused permission grants permission to appeal.

2.4 A party who is subject to a limited civil restraint order may not make an application for permission under paragraphs 2.2(1) or 2.2(2) without first serving notice of the application on the other party in accordance with paragraph 2.5.

2.5 A notice under paragraph 2.4 must–

(1) set out the nature and grounds of the application; and

(2) provide the other party with at least 7 days within which to respond.

2.6 An application for permission under paragraphs 2.2(1) or 2.2(2)–

(1) must be made in writing;

(2) must include the other party's written response, if any, to the notice served under paragraph 2.4; and

(3) will be determined without a hearing.

2.7 An order under paragraph 2.3(2) may only be made by–

(1) a Court of Appeal judge;

(2) a High Court judge or master; or

(3) a designated civil judge or his appointed deputy.

Where a party makes an application for permission under paragraphs 2.2(1) or 2.2(2) and permission is refused, any application for permission to appeal–

(1) must be made in writing; and

will be determined without a hearing.

2.9 A limited civil restraint order–

(1) is limited to the particular proceedings in which it is made;

(2) will remain in effect for the duration of the proceedings in which it is made, unless the court otherwise orders; and

(3) must identify the judge or judges to whom an application for permission under paragraphs 2.2(1), 2.2(2) or 2.8 should be made.

Extended Civil Restraint Orders

3.1 An extended civil restraint order may be made by–
(1) a judge of the Court of Appeal;
(2) a judge of the High Court; or
(3) a designated civil judge or his appointed deputy in the county court,
where a party has persistently issued claims or made applications which are totally without merit.

3.2 Unless the court otherwise orders, where the court makes an extended civil restraint order, the party against whom the order is made–
(1) will be restrained from issuing claims or making application in–
  (a) any court if the order has been made by a judge of the Court of Appeal;
  (b) the High Court or any county court if the order has been made by a judge of the High Court; or
  (c) any county court identified in the order if the order has been made by a designated civil judge or his appointed deputy,
concerning any matter involving or relating to or touching upon or leading to the proceedings in which the order is made without first obtaining the permission of a judge identified in the order;
(2) may apply for amendment or discharge of the order provided he has first obtained the permission of a judge identified in the order; and
(3) may apply for permission to appeal the order and if permission is granted, may appeal the order.

3.3 Where a party who is subject to an extended civil restraint order–
(1) issues a claim or makes an application in a court identified in the order concerning any matter involving or relating to or touching upon or leading to the proceedings in which the order is made without first obtaining the permission of a judge identified in the order, the claim or application will automatically be struck out or dismissed–
  (a) without the judge having to make any further order; and
  (b) without the need for the other party to respond to it;
(2) repeatedly makes applications for permission pursuant to that order which are totally without merit, the court may direct that if the party makes any further application for permission which is totally without merit, the decision to dismiss the application will be final and there will be no right of appeal, unless the judge who refused permission grants permission to appeal.

3.4 A party who is subject to an extended civil restraint order may not make an application for permission under paragraphs 3.2(1) or 3.2(2) without first serving notice of the application on the other party in accordance with paragraph 3.5.

3.5 A notice under paragraph 3.4 must–
(1) set out the nature and grounds of the application; and
(2) provide the other party with at least 7 days within which to respond.

3.6 An application for permission under paragraphs 3.2(1) or 3.2(2)–
(1) must be made in writing;
(2) must include the other party's written response, if any, to the notice served under paragraph 3.4; and
(3) will be determined without a hearing.

3.7 An order under paragraph 3.3(2) may only be made by–

(1) a Court of Appeal judge;

(2) a High Court judge; or

(3) a designated civil judge or his appointed deputy.

3.8 Where a party makes an application for permission under paragraphs 3.2(1) or 3.2(2) and permission is refused, any application for permission to appeal–

(1) must be made in writing; and

(2) will be determined without a hearing.

3.9 An extended civil restraint order–

(1) will be made for a specified period not exceeding 2 years;

(2) must identify the courts in which the party against whom the order is made is restrained from issuing claims or making applications; and

(3) must identify the judge or judges to whom an application for permission under paragraphs 3.2(1), 3.2(2) or 3.8 should be made.

3.10 The court may extend the duration of an extended civil restraint order, if it considers it appropriate to do so, but it must not be extended for a period greater than 2 years on any given occasion.

3.11 If he considers that it would be appropriate to make an extended civil restraint order–

(1) a master or a district judge in a district registry of the High Court must transfer the proceedings to a High Court judge; and

(2) a circuit judge or a district judge in a county court must transfer the proceedings to the designated civil judge.

General Civil Restraint Orders

4.1 A general civil restraint order may be made by–

(1) a judge of the Court of Appeal;

(2) a judge of the High Court; or

(3) a designated civil judge or his appointed deputy in the county court,

where the party against whom the order is made persists in issuing claims or making applications which are totally without merit, in circumstances where an extended civil restraint order would not be sufficient or appropriate.

4.2 Unless the court otherwise orders, where the court makes a general civil restraint order, the party against whom the order is made–

(1) will be restrained from issuing any claim or making any application in–

(a) any court if the order has been made by a judge of the Court of Appeal;

(b) the High Court or any county court if the order has been made by a judge of the High Court; or

(c) any county court identified in the order if the order has been made by a designated civil judge or his appointed deputy,

without first obtaining the permission of a judge identified in the order;

(2) may apply for amendment or discharge of the order provided he has first obtained the permission of a judge identified in the order; and

(3) may apply for permission to appeal the order and if permission is granted, may appeal the order.

4.3 Where a party who is subject to a general civil restraint order–

(1) issues a claim or makes an application in a court identified in the order without first obtaining the permission of a judge identified in the order, the claim or application will automatically be struck out or dismissed–

        (a)   without the judge having to make any further order; and

        (b)   without the need for the other party to respond to it;

(2)   repeatedly makes applications for permission pursuant to that order which are totally without merit, the court may direct that if the party makes any further application for permission which is totally without merit, the decision to dismiss that application will be final and there will be no right of appeal, unless the judge who refused permission grants permission to appeal.

4.4   A party who is subject to a general civil restraint order may not make an application for permission under paragraphs 4.2(1) or 4.2(2) without first serving notice of the application on the other party in accordance with paragraph 4.5.

4.5   A notice under paragraph 4.4 must–

   (1)   set out the nature and grounds of the application, and

   (2)   provide the other party with at least 7 days within which to respond.

4.6   An application for permission under paragraphs 4.2(1) or 4.2(2)–

   (1)   must be made in writing;

   (2)   must include the other party's written response, if any, to the notice served under paragraph 4.4; and

   (3)   will be determined without a hearing.

4.7   An order under paragraph 4.3(2) may only be made by–

   (1)   a Court of Appeal judge;

   (2)   a High Court judge; or

   (3)   a designated civil judge or his appointed deputy.

4.8   Where a party makes an application for permission under paragraphs 4.2(1) or 4.2(2) and permission is refused, any application for permission to appeal–

   (1)   must be made in writing; and

   (2)   will be determined without a hearing.

4.9   A general civil restraint order–

   (1)   ill be made for a specified period not exceeding 2 years;

   (2)   must identify the courts in which the party against whom the order is made is restrained from issuing claims or making applications; and

   (3)   must identify the judge or judges to whom an application for permission under paragraphs 4.2(1), 4.2(2) or 4.8 should be made.

4.10 The court may extend the duration of a general civil restraint order, if it considers it appropriate to do so, but it must not be extended for a period greater than 2 years on any given occasion.

4.11 If he considers that it would be appropriate to make a general civil restraint order–

   (1)   a master or a district judge in a district registry of the High Court must transfer the proceedings to a High Court judge; and

   (2)   a circuit judge or a district judge in a county court must transfer the proceedings to the designated civil judge.

5.1   The other party or parties to the proceedings may apply for any civil restraint order.

5.2   An application under paragraph 5.1 must be made using the Part 23 procedure unless the court otherwise directs and the application must specify which type of civil restraint order is sought.

COURT'S POWERS TO IMPOSE RESTRAINT ORDERS

[20.14] **Bhamjee v Forsdick and Others (No 2)**
[2003] EWCA Civ 1113
[2003] All ER (D) 429 (Jul), [2004] 1 WLR 88, CA

The claimant issued three separate sets of proceedings against barristers who had been on the other side in previous cases. The court considered that the applications were entirely without merit, and dismissed them and subsequent applications. As a consequence, the defendants themselves had not been inconvenienced, but the court's resources had been diverted and wasted.

HELD, ON APPEAL: The court had power to take appropriate action whenever its functions were being abused.

Per Lord Phillips, MR: All we are doing in this judgment is to provide a modern incarnation of the protection described by Bowen LJ in *Willis v Earl Beauchamp* [1886] 11 PD 59 in these words: '... [T]he rules ... do not ... deprive the court in any way of the inherent power which every court has to prevent the use of legal machinery which will occur, if for no possible benefit the defendants are to be dragged through litigation which must be long and expensive.' Today it is also the resources of the courts themselves that require protection.

Note—The different types of restraint order set out in the judgment in *Bhamjee* are now incorporated in the Practice Direction to CPR Pt 3 set out above.

[20.15] **Wickramaratna v Cambridge University Chemistry Department**
[2004] EWCA Civ 1532
[2004] All ER (D) 36 (Nov)

The claimant appealed from a limited civil restraint order (CRO) order refusing to set aside an order made in the claimant's absence.

HELD: A High Court Master had jurisdiction to make a limited CRO, although not an extended CRO.

(E) GROUP LITIGATION

[20.16]

CPR 19.10 – DEFINITION

A Group Litigation Order ('GLO') means an order made under rule 19.11 to provide for the case management of claims which give rise to common or related issues of fact or law (the 'GLO issues').

[20.17]

CPR 19.11 – GROUP LITIGATION ORDER
    (1)   The court may make a GLO where there are or are likely to be a number of claims giving rise to the GLO issues.

(2)   A GLO must–
    (a)   contain directions about the establishment of a register (the 'group register') on which the claims managed under the GLO will be entered;
    (b)   specify the GLO issues which will identify the claims to be managed as a group under the GLO; and
    (c)   specify the court (the 'management court') which will manage the claims on the group register.
(3)   A GLO may–
    (a)   in relation to claims which raise one or more of the GLO issues–
        (i)   direct their transfer to the management court;
        (ii)   order their stay until further order; and
        (iii) direct their entry on the group register;
    (b)   direct that from a specified date claims which raise one or more of the GLO issues should be started in the management court and entered on the group register; and
    (c)   give directions for publicising the GLO.

[20.18]

CPR 19.12 – EFFECT OF THE GLO
(1)   Where a judgment or order is given or made in a claim on the group register in relation to one or more GLO issues–
    (a)   that judgment or order is binding on the parties to all other claims that are on the group register at the time the judgment is given or the order is made unless the court orders otherwise; and
    (b)   the court may give directions as to the extent to which that judgment or order is binding on the parties to any claim which is subsequently entered on the group register.
(2)   Unless paragraph (3) applies, any party who is adversely affected by a judgment or order which is binding on him may seek permission to appeal the order.
(3)   A party to a claim which was entered on the group register after a judgment or order which is binding on him was given or made may not–
    (a)   apply for the judgment or order to be set aside, varied or stayed; or
    (b)   appeal the judgment or order,
but may apply to the court for an order that the judgment or order is not binding on him.
(4)   Unless the court orders otherwise, disclosure of any document relating to the GLO issues by a party to a claim on the group register is disclosure of that document to all parties to claims–
    (a)   on the group register; and
    (b)   which are subsequently entered on the group register.

[20.19]

CPR 19.13 – CASE MANAGEMENT

Directions given by the management court may include directions–
    (a)   varying the GLO issues;
    (b)   providing for one or more claims on the group register to proceed as test claims;

(c)   appointing the solicitor of one or more parties to be the lead solicitor for the claimants or defendants;

(d)   specifying the details to be included in a statement of case in order to show that the criteria for entry of the claim on the group register have been met;

(e)   specifying a date after which no claim may be added to the group register unless the court gives permission; and

(f)   for the entry of any particular claim which meets one or more of the GLO issues on the group register.

[20.20]

CPR 19.14 – REMOVAL FROM THE REGISTER

(1)   A party to a claim entered on the group register may apply to the management court for the claim to be removed from the register.

(2)   If the management court orders the claim to be removed from the register it may give directions about the future management of the claim.

[20.21]

CPR 19.15 – TEST CLAIMS

(1)   Where a direction has been given for a claim on the group register to proceed as a test claim and that claim is settled, the management court may order that another claim on the group register be substituted as the test claim.

(2)   Where an order is made under paragraph (1), any order made in the test claim before the date of substitution is binding on the substituted claim unless the court orders otherwise.

2.   DEFENDANTS

(A)   DIRECT RIGHT OF ACTION AGAINST INSURANCE COMPANY

MOTOR CLAIMS AND THE FOURTH EUROPEAN MOTOR INSURANCE DIRECTIVE

[20.22]   The Fourth European Motor Insurance Directive 2000/26/EC introduced a right of direct action against insurers where the injured person is involved in an accident in a Member State other than his Member State of residence.

The UK implemented the provisions of the Fourth Directive by way of the European Communities (Rights against Insurers) Regulations 2002, SI 2002/3061 which came into force on 19 January 2003.

The UK Parliament's implementation of the Fourth Directive went beyond the requirements of the Directive, to the extent that under the 2002 Regulations, an injured person has a right of direct action against an insurer even if the accident takes place in the injured person's Member State of residence.

Insurers are 'directly liable to the entitled party to the extent that [they are] liable to the insured person' (cl 3(2)), so policy and indemnity issues can still be raised.

Insurers are required to appoint claims representatives in each Member State.

The victim of an accident caused by a negligent motorist can obtain the name, address and policy number of the insurer of the negligent motorist, as well as the identity of the insurer's local claims representative, from the local 'information centre' (in the UK, the Motor Insurers' Information Centre). If appropriate, the information centre will also provide the victim with details of the registered keeper.

Victims are entitled to confirmation from insurers of cover within 21 days of presenting the claim. Offers where there are no issues on liability are to be made within three months. If there are issues on liability then a reasoned response is required within the same time frame.

If insurers do not comply with the time frames then a fine must be paid. The amount is determined by the insurer's own national authority. In the UK, additional liability in respect of failure to comply has been imposed by the Financial Services Authority.

The relevant law of the Member State in which the accident occurred must be applied.

Claims against insured drivers

[20.23]
- If the insurer fails to respond within three months, or if the insurer has failed to appoint a claims representative, then the injured person can bring his claim against the Member State's 'compensation body'. In the UK, the Motor Insurers' Bureau (MIB) has been given the role of acting as compensation body.
- The compensation body is required to advise the insurer, the compensation body in the Member State where the insurer is established, and the person who caused the accident, that it has received a claim.
- The compensation body must within two months of presentation of the claim set out a reasoned response.
- If the compensation body makes a payment, then the compensation body is entitled to an indemnity from the compensation body in the Member State where the insurer is established. That compensation body is in turn entitled to an indemnity from the insurer and/or its insured.

Claims against uninsured drivers or untraced drivers

[20.24]
- If it is impossible to identify the vehicle or if, within two months following the accident, it is impossible to identify the insurer, the injured party may apply for compensation from the compensation body in the Member State where he resides.
- If the compensation body makes a payment, the compensation body is entitled to an indemnity from the guarantee fund in the Member State where the accident took place.

THIRD PARTIES (RIGHTS AGAINST INSURERS) ACT 1930

[20.25]
1   Rights of third parties against insurers on bankruptcy, etc., of the insured
(1)   Where under any contract of insurance a person (hereinafter referred to as the insured) is insured against liabilities to third parties which he may incur, then–

(a)   in the event of the insured becoming bankrupt or making a composition or arrangement with his creditors; or

(b)   in the case of the insured being a company, in the event of a winding-up order or an administration order being made, or a resolution for a voluntary winding-up being passed, with respect to the company, or of a receiver or manager of the company's business or undertaking being duly appointed, or of possession being taken, by or on behalf of the holders of any debentures secured by a floating charge, of any property comprised in or subject to the charge or of a voluntary arrangement proposed for the purposes of Part I of the Insolvency Act 1986 being approved under that Part;

if, either before or after that event, any such liability as aforesaid is incurred by the insured, his rights against the insurer under the contract in respect of the liability shall, notwithstanding anything in any Act or rule of law to the contrary, be transferred to and vest in the third party to whom the liability was so incurred.

(2)   Where the estate of any person falls to be administered in accordance with an order under section 421 of the Insolvency Act 1986, then, if any debt provable in bankruptcy is owing by the deceased in respect of a liability against which he was insured under a contract of insurance as being a liability to a third party, the deceased debtor's rights against the insurer under the contract in respect of that liability shall, notwithstanding anything in any such order, be transferred to and vest in the person to whom the debt is owing.

(3)   In so far as any contract of insurance made after the commencement of this Act in respect of any liability of the insured to third parties purports, whether directly or indirectly, to avoid the contract or to alter the rights of the parties thereunder upon the happening to the insured of any of the events specified in paragraph (a) or paragraph (b) of subsection (1) of this section the contract shall be of no effect.

(4)   Upon a transfer under subsection (1) or subsection (2) of this section, the insurer shall, subject to the provisions of section three of this Act, be under the same liability to the third party as he would have been under to the insured, but–

(a)   if the liability of the insurer to the insured exceeds the liability of the insured to the third party, nothing in this Act shall affect the rights of the insured against the insurer in respect of the excess; and

(b)   if the liability of the insurer to the insured is less than the liability of the insured to the third party, nothing in this Act shall affect the rights of the third party against the insured in respect of the balance.

(5)   For the purposes of this Act, the expression 'liabilities to third parties', in relation to a person insured under any contract of insurance,

shall not include any liability of that person in the capacity of insurer under some other contract of insurance.

[20.26]
2   Duty to give necessary information to third parties

(1)   In the event of any person becoming bankrupt or making a composition or arrangement with his creditors, or in the event of the estate of any person falling to be administered in accordance with an order under section 421 of the Insolvency Act 1986, or in the event of a winding-up order or an administration order being made, or a resolution for a voluntary winding-up being passed, with respect to any company or of a receiver or manager of the company's business or undertaking being duly appointed or of possession being taken by or on behalf of the holders of any debentures secured by a floating charge of any property comprised in or subject to the charge it shall be the duty of the bankrupt, debtor, personal representative of the deceased debtor or company, and, as the case may be, of the trustee in bankruptcy, trustee, liquidator, administrator, receiver, or manager, or person in possession of the property to give at the request of any person claiming that the bankrupt, debtor, deceased debtor, or company is under a liability to him such information as may reasonably be required by him for the purpose of ascertaining whether any rights have been transferred to and vested in him by this Act and for the purpose of enforcing such rights, if any, and any contract of insurance, in so far as it purports, whether directly or indirectly, to avoid the contract or to alter the rights of the parties thereunder upon the giving of any such information in the events aforesaid or otherwise to prohibit or prevent the giving thereof in the said events shall be of no effect.

(2)   If the information given to any person in pursuance of subsection (1) of this section discloses reasonable ground for supposing that there have or may have been transferred to him under this Act rights against any particular insurer, that insurer shall be subject to the same duty as is imposed by the said subsection on the persons therein mentioned.

(3)   The duty to give information imposed by this section shall include a duty to allow all contracts of insurance, receipts for premiums, and other relevant documents in the possession or power of the person on whom the duty is so imposed to be inspected and copies thereof to be taken.

[20.27]
3   Settlement between insurers and insured persons

Where the insured has become bankrupt or where, in the case of the insured being a company, a winding-up order has been made or a resolution for a voluntary winding up has been passed, with respect to the company, no agreement made between the insurer and the insured after liability has been incurred to a third party and after the commencement of the bankruptcy or winding up, as the case may be, nor any waiver, assignment, or other disposition made by, or payment made to the insured after the commencement aforesaid shall be effective to defeat or affect the rights transferred to the third party under this Act, but those rights shall be the same as if no such agreement, waiver, assignment, disposition or payment had been made.

[20.28]
3A   Application to limited liability partnerships

This Act applies to limited liability partnerships registered under the Limited Liability Partnerships Act 2005 as it applies to companies.

[20.29]
4   Short title
This Act may be cited as the Third Parties (Rights Against Insurers) Act.

Third-party right against insolvent's insurer

[20.30]   The Third Parties (Rights Against Insurers) Act 1930 confers on a third party claimant the right to claim directly against the insurer of an insolvent insured.

In the case of an insured company, a claimant will have the benefit of the 1930 Act when:
- a winding-up order is made;
- the company enters administration;
- a resolution for voluntary winding up is passed;
- a receiver is appointed;
- the holder of a debenture secured by a floating charge takes possession of property subject to that charge; or
- a voluntary arrangement is approved.

In the case of an insured individual the 1930 Act applies where:
- a bankruptcy order or insolvency administration order is made; or
- a composition or arrangement is entered into with creditors.

The 1930 Act covers third party liabilities which are incurred either before or after the insolvency.

In order to succeed in an action against the insurer, the claimant must first establish a claim against the insured. Both the existence of the claim and the amount of the liability must be established by judgment, arbitration or agreement.

This statutory transfer of rights is an exception both to the general rule of privity of contract and to the principle of insolvency law that all unsecured creditors are to be treated equally.

The 1930 Act imposes a duty on the insolvent insured to provide such information as the third party claimant may require for the purposes of ascertaining whether he has any rights under the Act – s 2(3).

If a company has been dissolved following winding up, the claimant will need to apply to the court to have the company restored to the register of companies. Where the claim relates to a fatal accident or personal injury, an action can be brought at any time; otherwise the application must be made within two years of the dissolution. Further, see para [20.32]) below.

[20.31]   Nigel Upchurch Associates v Aldridge Estates Investments Co Ltd
[1993] 1 Lloyd's Rep 535

The duty to provide the information described in s 2 of the Third Parties (Rights Against Insurers) Act 1930 only arises when the liability of the insolvent insured to the claimant has been established by judgment, arbitration or agreement.

(B)   COMPANIES

COMPANIES ACT 1985, S 651

[20.32]
651   Power of court to declare dissolution of company void
(1)   Where a company has been dissolved, the court may at any time within 2 years of the date of the dissolution, on an application made for the purpose by the liquidator of the company or by any other person appearing to the court to be interested, make an order, on such terms as the court thinks fit, declaring the dissolution to have been void.
(2)   Thereupon such proceedings may be taken as might have been taken if the company had not been dissolved.
(3)   It is the duty of the person on whose application the order was made, within 7 days after its making (or such further time as the court may allow), to deliver to the registrar of companies for registration an office copy of the order. If the person fails to do so, he is liable to a fine and, for continued contravention, to a daily default fine.

[20.33]   Re Roehampton Swimming Pool Ltd
[1968] 3 All ER 661, [1968] 1 WLR 1693

On 30 August 1965 an infant sustained injury when diving into a swimming pool in the occupation of a limited company. In July 1967 the company went into voluntary liquidation and on 12 April 1968, the company was deemed to have been dissolved. No proceedings had been issued against the company. In August 1968 the infant's solicitor applied in her own name to resuscitate the company so that it could be sued.

HELD: If the application had been made by the [claimant] himself there would have been no difficulty in granting it since he, with a claim for damages against the company, plainly fell within the words 'any other person appearing to the court to be interested'. But the solicitor was not a 'person … interested', since those words meant a person having a pecuniary or proprietary interest.

[20.34]   Re BBH (Middletons) Ltd
(1970) 114 Sol Jo 431

On 31 December 1965 the company passed special resolution for voluntary winding-up. On 15 February 1966 the applicant, an employee of the company, was injured in a road accident when driving the company's van. On 21 March 1968 the company was dissolved. On 14 February 1969 the applicant issued a writ against the company for damages for personal injury. On 19 March 1970 the applicant began proceedings to have the company's dissolution declared void.

HELD: Assuming time under the Limitation Acts was running in favour of the company during the period until the dissolution it could not have continued to run after 21 March 1968, because the company had been dissolved and there was no one in whose favour it could have run. As the claim was not necessarily statute-barred, or would be barred if an order were made under the section, the dissolution should be declared void but without prejudicing any defence the company cared to put forward in any further action the applicant might bring against it.

COMPANIES ACT 1985, S 653

[20.35]
653 Objection to striking off by person aggrieved
 (1)   The following applies if a company or any member or creditor of it feels aggrieved by the company having been struck off the register.
 (2)   The court, on an application by the company or the member or creditor made before the expiration of 20 years from publication in the Gazette of notice under section 652, may, if satisfied that the company was at the time of the striking off carrying on business or in operation, or otherwise that it is just that the company be restored to the register, order the company's name to be restored.
 (3)   On an office copy of the order being delivered to the registrar of companies for registration the company is deemed to have continued in existence as if its name had not been struck off; and the court may by the order give such directions and make such provisions as seem just for placing the company and all other persons in the same position (as nearly as may be) as if the company's name had not been struck off.

[20.36]   Re Harvest Lane Motor Bodies Ltd
[1969] I Ch 457, [1968] 2 All ER 1012, [1968] 3 WLR 220

The widow of a man killed in a road accident on 16 July 1961 issued proceedings on 26 April 1963 claiming damages against the limited company whose servant she alleged was to blame. In June 1965 whilst the action was still proceeding the company's name was struck off the register under the Companies Act as being a defunct company.

HELD: The widow was a 'creditor' and entitled to apply. The Act was concerned with a grievance on the part of some person whether a company, a member or a creditor. The petitioner had an action in being when the company was struck off. The Act could not have intended to differentiate between those creditors whose debts were fixed and ascertained and those whose debts were contingent and prospective. The company's name should be restored to the register.

[20.37]   Re Regent Insulation Co Ltd
(1981) Times, 4 November

The company was struck off the register in May 1976. A former employee who had worked for the company from November 1964 to January 1967 using asbestos was found in 1976 to be suffering from asbestosis. He applied in January 1981 for the company to be restored to the register to enable him to institute proceedings against it. The registrar made an order in February 1981 restoring the company to the register and directing that the period between its being struck off in 1976 and its restoration should not be counted for the purposes of any Statute of Limitation. An appeal in the name of the company by its insurers was dismissed.

(C)   ESTATE OF DECEASED TORTFEASOR

[20.38]

Practice Direction to CPR 7, paragraph 5.5

5.5   Where it is sought to start proceedings against the estate of a deceased defendant where probate or letters of administration have not been granted, the claimant should issue the claim against 'the personal representatives of A.B. deceased'. The claimant should then, before the expiry of the period for service of the claim form, apply to the court for the appointment of a person to represent the estate of the deceased.

[20.39]

PROCEDURE AGREED BETWEEN THE OFFICIAL SOLICITOR AND THE MOTOR INSURERS' BUREAU, AS APPROVED BY THE SENIOR MASTER ON 11 MARCH 2003

1.   This procedure applies to damages claims brought against the estate of a deceased driver, where no grant of probate or administration of the estate of the deceased has been obtained, and the claimant contends that the Motor Insurers Bureau is interested under its uninsured drivers agreement.

2.   Immediately following the issue of a claim form pursuant to CPR 19.8(2)(b)(i), brought against 'the estate of' the deceased, the claimant should write to the MIB enclosing a copy of the issued claim form and enquiring if the MIB is willing to be appointed to represent the estate of the deceased in the claim pursuant to CPR 19.8(2)(b)(ii).

3.   If the MIB replies agreeing to accept such an appointment, their letter to that effect should be produced to the court in support of an application to give effect to that agreement.

4.   In certain circumstances the MIB may feel unable to accept such appointment, in which the case the Official Solicitor should be approached. He will usually be willing to accept the appointment in such circumstances, subject to payment of his proper costs. His involvement will usually be limited to the acceptance of service only and he will not take any subsequent part in proceedings.

THE OFFICIAL SOLICITOR

[20.40]   The Official Solicitor may act on behalf of an estate in two capacities.

(a)   If the Official Solicitor is the personal representative of an estate he can defend a claim in the same way as any other personal representative.

(b)   Where a proposed defendant has died before proceedings are issued and the cause of action survives, but probate or letters of administration have not been granted, then proceedings can be issued against the personal representatives of the deceased. Application can then be made to the court pursuant to CPR 19.8(2)(b)(ii) for the Official Solicitor to be represented.

(D)   THE CROWN

[20.41]

66.1
(1)   This Part contains rules for civil proceedings by or against the Crown, and other civil proceedings to which the Crown is a party.
(2)   In this Part–
    (a)   'the Act' means the Crown Proceedings Act 1947;
    (b)   'civil proceedings by the Crown' means the civil proceedings described in section 23(1) of the Act, but excluding the proceedings described in section 23(3);
    (c)   'civil proceedings against the Crown' means the civil proceedings described in section 23(2) of the Act but excluding the proceedings described in section 23(3);
    (d)   'civil proceedings to which the Crown is a party' has the same meaning as it has for the purposes of Parts III and IV of the Act by virtue of section 38(4).

66.2   These Rules and their practice directions apply to civil proceedings by or against the Crown and to other civil proceedings to which the Crown is a party unless this Part, a practice direction or any other enactment provides otherwise.

Crown Proceedings Act 1947

[20.42]
2   Liability of the Crown in tort
(1)   Subject to the provisions of this Act, the Crown shall be subject to all those liabilities in tort to which, if it were a private person of full age and capacity, it would be subject:
    (a)   in respect of torts committed by its servants or agents;
    (b)   in respect of any breach of those duties which a person owes to his servants or agents at common law by reason of being their employer; and
    (c)   in respect of any breach of the duties attaching at common law to the ownership, occupation, possession or control of property,
Provided that no proceedings shall lie against the Crown by virtue of paragraph (a) of this subsection in respect of any act or omission of a servant or agent of the Crown unless the act or omission would apart from the provisions of this Act have given rise to a cause of action in tort against that servant or agent of his estate.
(2)   Where the Crown is bound by a statutory duty which is binding also upon persons other than the Crown and its officers, then subject to the provisions of this Act, the Crown shall, in respect of a failure to comply with that duty, be subject to all those liabilities in tort (if any) to which it would be so subject if it were a private person of full age and capacity.
(3)   Where any functions are conferred or imposed upon an officer of the Crown as such either by any rule of the common law or by statute, and that officer commits a tort while performing or purporting to perform those functions, the liabilities of the Crown in respect of the tort shall be

such as they would have been if those functions had been conferred or imposed solely by virtue of instructions lawfully given by the Crown.

(4)   Any enactment which negatives or limits the amount of the liability of any Government department or officer of the Crown in respect of any tort committed by that department or officer shall, in the case of proceedings against the Crown under this section in respect of a tort committed by that department or officer, apply in relation to the Crown as it would have applied in relation to that department or officer if the proceedings against the Crown had been proceedings against the department or officer.

(5)   No proceedings shall lie against the Crown by virtue of this section in respect of anything done or omitted to be done by any person while discharging or purporting to discharge any responsibilities which he has in connection with the execution of judicial process.

(6)   No proceedings shall lie against the Crown by virtue of this section in respect of any act, neglect or default of any officer of the Crown, unless that officer has been directly or indirectly appointed by the Crown wholly out of the Consolidated Fund of the United Kingdom, moneys provided by Parliament, the Road Fund, or any other Fund certified by the Treasury for the purposes of this subsection or was at the material time holding an office in respect of which the Treasury certify that the holder thereof would normally be so paid.

[20.43]
4   Application of law as to indemnity, contribution, joint and several tortfeasors, and contributory negligence

(1)   Where the Crown is subject to any liability by virtue of this Part of this Act, the law relating to indemnity and contribution shall be so enforceable by or against the Crown in respect of the liability to which it is so subject as if the Crown were a private person of full age and capacity.

(2)   [Repealed by Civil Liability (Contribution) Act 1978, s 9(2) and Sch 2.]

(3)   Without prejudice to the general effect of s 1 of this Act, the Law Reform (Contributory Negligence) Act 1945 (which amends the law in relation to contributory negligence) shall bind the Crown.

Note—Section 5 of the Civil Liability (Contribution) Act 1978 reads:

'Without prejudice to s 4(1) of the Crown Proceedings Act 1947 (indemnity and contribution), this Act shall bind the Crown, but nothing in this Act shall be construed as in any way affecting Her Majesty in Her private capacity (including in right of Her Duchy of Lancaster) or the Duchy of Cornwall.'

(E)   THE ARMED FORCES

[20.44]

Practice Direction to CPR 6, paragraph 5

5   The Lord Chancellor's Office issued a memorandum on 26 July 1979 as to service on members of H.M. Forces and guidance notes as to service on members of the United States Air Force. The provisions annexed to this practice direction are derived from that memorandum and guidance notes.

Note: the Annex is not reproduced here – reference should be made to *The Civil Court Practice*, published by LexisNexis Butterworths.

3.   REPRESENTATIVE ACTIONS

[20.45]

CPR 19.6 – REPRESENTATIVE PARTIES WITH SAME INTEREST
   (1)   Where more than one person has the same interest in a claim–
      (a)   the claim may be begun; or
      (b)   the court may order that the claim be continued,
by or against one or more of the persons who have the same interest as
representatives of any other persons who have that interest.
   (2)   The court may direct that a person may not act as a representative.
   (3)   Any party may apply to the court for an order under paragraph (2).
   (4)   Unless the court otherwise directs any judgment or order given in a
claim in which a party is acting as a representative under this rule–
      (a)   is binding on all persons represented in the claim; but
      (b)   may only be enforced by or against a person who is not a party to
           the claim with the permission of the court.
   (5)   This rule does not apply to a claim to which rule 19.7 applies.

[20.46]

CPR 19.7 – REPRESENTATION OF INTERESTED PERSONS WHO CANNOT BE
ASCERTAINED ETC.
   (1)   This rule applies to claims about–
      (a)   the estate of a deceased person;
      (b)   property subject to a trust; or
      (c)   the meaning of a document, including a statute.
   (2)   The court may make an order appointing a person to represent any
other person or persons in the claim where the person or persons to be
represented–
      (a)   are unborn;
      (b)   cannot be found;
      (c)   cannot easily be ascertained; or
      (d)   are a class of persons who have the same interest in a claim and–
           (i)   one or more members of that class are within sub-para-
               graphs (a), (b) or (c); or
           (ii)   to appoint a representative would further the overriding
               objective.
   (3)   An application for an order under paragraph (2)–
      (a)   may be made by–
           (i)   any person who seeks to be appointed under the order; or
           (ii)   any party to the claim; and
      (b)   may be made at any time before or after the claim has started.
   (4)   An application notice for an order under paragraph (2) must be
served on–
      (a)   all parties to the claim, if the claim has started;
      (b)   the person sought to be appointed, if that person is not the
           applicant or a party to the claim; and
      (c)   any other person as directed by the court.
   (5)   The court's approval is required to settle a claim in which a party is
acting as a representative under this rule.

(6)   The court may approve a settlement where it is satisfied that the settlement is for the benefit of all the represented persons.

(7)   Unless the court otherwise directs, any judgment or order given in a claim in which a party is acting as a representative under this rule–

    (a)   is binding on all persons represented in the claim; but

    (b)   may only be enforced by or against a person who is not a party to the claim with the permission of the court.

[20.47]

CPR 19.8 – DEATH

(1)   Where a person who had an interest in a claim has died and that person has no personal representative the court may order–

    (a)   the claim to proceed in the absence of a person representing the estate of the deceased; or

    (b)   a person to be appointed to represent the estate of the deceased.

(2)   Where a defendant against whom a claim could have been brought has died and–

    (a)   a grant of probate or administration has been made, the claim must be brought against the persons who are the personal representatives of the deceased;

    (b)   a grant of probate or administration has not been made–

        (i)   the claim must be brought against 'the estate of' the deceased; and

        (ii)   the claimant must apply to the court for an order appointing a person to represent the estate of the deceased in the claim.

(3)   A claim shall be treated as having been brought against 'the estate of' the deceased in accordance with paragraph (2)(b)(i) where–

    (a)   the claim is brought against the 'personal representatives' of the deceased but a grant of probate or administration has not been made; or

    (b)   the person against whom the claim was brought was dead when the claim was started.

(4)   Before making an order under this rule, the court may direct notice of the application to be given to any other person with an interest in the claim.

(5)   Where an order has been made under paragraphs (1) or (2)(b)(ii) any judgment or order made or given in the claim is binding on the estate of the deceased.

[20.48]

CPR 19.8A – POWER TO MAKE JUDGMENTS BINDING ON NON-PARTIES

(1)   This rule applies to any claim relating to–

    (a)   the estate of a deceased person;

    (b)   property subject to a trust; or

    (c)   the sale of any property.

(2)   The court may at any time direct that notice of–

    (a)   the claim; or

    (b)   any judgment or order given in the claim,

be served on any person who is not a party but who is or may be affected by it.

(3)   An application under this rule–
   (a)   may be made without notice; and
   (b)   must be supported by written evidence which includes the reasons why the person to be served should be bound by the judgment in the claim.
(4)   Unless the court orders otherwise–
   (a)   a notice of a claim or of a judgment or order under this rule must be–
      (i)   in the form required by the practice direction;
      (ii)   issued by the court; and
      (iii)   accompanied by a form of acknowledgment of service with any necessary modifications;
   (b)   a notice of a claim must also be accompanied by–
      (i)   a copy of the claim form; and
      (ii)   such other statements of case, witness statements or affidavits as the court may direct; and
   (c)   a notice of a judgment or order must also be accompanied by a copy of the judgment or order.
(5)   If a person served with notice of a claim files an acknowledgment of service of the notice within 14 days he will become a party to the claim.
(6)   If a person served with notice of a claim does not acknowledge service of the notice he will be bound by any judgment given in the claim as if he were a party.
(7)   If, after service of a notice of a claim on a person, the claim form is amended so as substantially to alter the relief claimed, the court may direct that a judgment shall not bind that person unless a further notice, together with a copy of the amended claim form, is served on him.
(8)   Any person served with a notice of a judgment or order under this rule–
   (a)   shall be bound by the judgment or order as if he had been a party to the claim; but
   (b)   may, provided he acknowledges service–
      (i)   within 28 days after the notice is served on him, apply to the court to set aside or vary the judgment or order; and
      (ii)   take part in any proceedings relating to the judgment or order.
(9)   The following rules of Part 10 (acknowledgment of service) apply–
   (a)   rule 10.4; and
   (b)   rule 10.5, subject to the modification that references to the defendant are to be read as references to the person served with the notice.
(10)   A notice under this rule is issued on the date entered on the notice by the court.

[20.49]

CPR 19.9 – DERIVATIVE CLAIMS
(1)   This rule applies where a company, other incorporated body or trade union is alleged to be entitled to claim a remedy and a claim is made by one or more members of the company, body or trade union for it to be given that remedy (a 'derivative claim').

(2)   The company, body or trade union for whose benefit a remedy is sought must be a defendant to the claim.

(3)   After the claim form has been issued the claimant must apply to the court for permission to continue the claim and may not take any other step in the proceedings except–

(a)   as provided by paragraph (5); or

(b)   where the court gives permission.

(4)   An application in accordance with paragraph (3) must be supported by written evidence.

(5)   The–

(a)   claim form;

(b)   application notice; and

(c)   written evidence in support of the application,

must be served on the defendant within the period within which the claim form must be served and, in any event, at least 14 days before the court is to deal with the application.

(6)   If the court gives the claimant permission to continue the claim, the time within which the defence must be filed is 14 days after the date on which the permission is given or such period as the court may specify.

(7)   The court may order the company, body or trade union to indemnify the claimant against any liability in respect of costs incurred in the claim.

[20.50]   Chubb Insurance Company of Europe SA v Davies

[2004] EWHC 2138 (Comm)

[2004] 2 All ER (Comm) 827, [2005] Lloyd's Rep IR

The claimant, an insurance company, sought summary judgment pursuant to CRP Pt 24 for a declaration that it was not liable to indemnify the defendant, Mr Davies. Mr Black and two companies – American Iron & Metal Co Inc and Lito Trade Inc – sought permission to be joined as defendants so that they could contest the claimant's application. The claimant argued that the intervening parties had no legal or equitable interest in the insurance policy and therefore could not be joined. They could only establish a prospective interest.

HELD: CPR 19.9(2) does not require that a 'new party' should have a cause of action. The rule should be interpreted generously in order to ensure that the overriding objective was satisfied. The intervening parties were given permission to be added as defendants.

4.   ADDITIONAL PARTIES

[20.51]   Reference should be made to Chapter 31, para [31.62] for the addition and substitution of parties.

Reference should be made to Chapter 25 for additional claims against original parties and additional parties.

(B)   CONTENTS OF THE CLAIM FORM

[21.4]

CPR 16.2 – CONTENTS OF THE CLAIM FORM
  (1)   The claim form must–
    (a)   contain a concise statement of the nature of the claim;
    (b)   specify the remedy which the claimant seeks;
    (c)   where the claimant is making a claim for money, contain a statement of value in accordance with rule 16.3; and
    (d)   contain such other matters as may be set out in a practice direction.
  (2)   In civil proceedings against the Crown, as defined in rule 66.1(2), the claim form must also contain–
    (a)   the names of the government departments and officers of the Crown concerned; and
    (b)   brief details of the circumstances in which it is alleged that the liability of the Crown arose.
  (3)   If the particulars of claim specified in rule 16.4 are not contained in, or are not served with the claim form, the claimant must state on the claim form that the particulars of claim will follow.
  (4)   If the claimant is claiming in a representative capacity, the claim form must state what that capacity is.
  (5)   If the defendant is sued in a representative capacity, the claim form must state what that capacity is.
  (6)   The court may grant any remedy to which the claimant is entitled even if that remedy is not specified in the claim form.

[21.5]   **McPhilemy v Times Newspapers Ltd and Others**
[1999] 3 All ER 775, [1999] EMLR 751

HELD, per Lord Woolf MR: 'The need for extensive pleadings including particulars should be reduced by the requirement that witness statements are now exchanged. This does not mean that pleadings are now superfluous. Pleadings are still required to mark out the parameters of the case that is being advanced by each party. In particular they are still critical to identify the issues and the extent of the dispute between the parties. No more than a concise statement of those facts is required'.

[21.6]   **Wilding v Commissioner of Police for the Metropolis**
[2004] EWHC 3042 (QB)
[2004] All ER (D) 181 (Nov)

HELD: CPR 16.2 states that the claim form must contain a concise statement of the nature of the claim. 'It is a matter of elementary pleading to specify independently each and every cause of action ... A defendant should not be left to guess at the cause or causes of action pursued against him' and was 'entitled to know from the claim form the nature of the claim or claims he has to meet'.

[21.7]

Practice Direction to CPR 16, paragraph 2

The claim form

2.1   Rule 16.2 refers to matters which the claim form must contain. Where the claim is for money, the claim form must also contain the statement of value referred to in rule 16.3.

2.2   The claim form must include an address at which the claimant resides or carries on business. This paragraph applies even though the claimant's address for service is the business address of his solicitor.

2.3   Where the defendant is an individual, the claimant should (if he is able to do so) include in the claim form an address at which the defendant resides or carries on business. This paragraph applies even though the defendant's solicitors have agreed to accept service on the defendant's behalf.

2.4   Any address which is provided for the purpose of these provisions must include a postcode, unless the court orders otherwise. Postcode information may be obtained from www.royalmail.com or the Royal Mail Address Management Guide.

2.5   If the claim form does not show a full address, including postcode, at which the claimant(s) and defendant(s) reside or carry on business, the claim form will be issued but will be retained by the court and will not be served until the claimant has supplied a full address, including postcode, or the court has dispensed with the requirement to do so. The court will notify the claimant.

2.6   The claim form must be headed with the title of the proceedings, including the full name of each party. The full name means, in each case where it is known:

   (a)   in the case of an individual, his full unabbreviated name and title by which he is known;

   (b)   in the case of an individual carrying on business in a name other than his own name, the full unabbreviated name of the individual, together with the title by which he is known, and the full trading name (for example, John Smith 'trading as' or 'T/as"JS Autos');

   (c)   in the case of a partnership (other than a limited liability partnership (LLP))–

      (i)   where partners are being sued in the name of the partnership, the full name by which the partnership is known, together with the words '(A Firm)'; or

      (ii)   where partners are being sued as individuals, the full unabbreviated name of each partner and the title by which he is known;

   (d)   in the case of a company or limited liability partnership registered in England and Wales, the full registered name, including suffix (plc, limited, LLP, etc), if any;

   (e)   in the case of any other company or corporation, the full name by which it is known, including suffix where appropriate.

(C)   STATEMENT OF VALUE

[21.8]

CPR 16.3 – STATEMENT OF VALUE TO BE INCLUDED IN THE CLAIM FORM
  (1)   This rule applies where the claimant is making a claim for money.
  (2)   The claimant must, in the claim form, state–
    (a)   the amount of money which he is claiming;
    (b)   that he expects to recover–
        (i)   not more than £5,000;
        (ii) more than £5,000 but not more than £15,000; or
        (iii) more than £15,000; or
    (c)   that he cannot say how much he expects to recover.
  (3)   In a claim for personal injuries, the claimant must also state in the claim form whether the amount which he expects to recover as general damages for pain, suffering and loss of amenity is–
    (a)   not more than £1,000; or
    (b)   more than £1,000.
  (4)   ...
  (5)   If the claim form is to be issued in the High Court it must, where this rule applies–
    (a)   state that the claimant expects to recover more than £15,000;
    (b)   state that some other enactment provides that the claim may be commenced only in the High Court and specify that enactment;
    (c)   if the claim is a claim for personal injuries state that the claimant expects to recover £50,000 or more; or
    (d)   state that the claim is to be in one of the specialist High Court lists and state which list.
  (6)   When calculating how much he expects to recover, the claimant must disregard any possibility–
    (a)   that he may recover–
        (i)   interest;
        (ii) costs;
    (b)   that the court may make a finding of contributory negligence against him;
    (c)   that the defendant may make a counterclaim or that the defence may include a set-off; or
    (d)   that the defendant may be liable to pay an amount of money which the court awards to the claimant to the Secretary of State for Social Security under section 6 of the Social Security (Recovery of Benefits) Act 1997.
  (7)   The statement of value in the claim form does not limit the power of the court to give judgment for the amount which it finds the claimant is entitled to.

[21.9]   **Khiaban v Beard**
[2002] EWCA Civ 358
[2003] 3 All ER 362, [2003] 1 WLR 1626, [2003] RTR 419, CA

The claimant issued proceedings against the defendant to recover his policy excess and miscellaneous expenses. The parties insurers had entered into a memorandum of understanding whereby they agreed to be bound by any liability decision. No claim had been included for the repair costs. At first instance the claimant was ordered to amend the particulars of claim to reflect the true value of the claim (ie to include the repair costs). Following the claimant's refusal to do so his claim was struck out by the court.

HELD, ON APPEAL: There was no requirement in CPR 16.3 to include all of the heads of damage to which a claimant might be entitled. 'There is nothing in the general law which positively obliges a claimant to include in his pleaded case all the claims which he could arguably advance against a defendant'.

3.   PARTICULARS OF CLAIM

(A)   CONTENTS OF THE PARTICULARS OF CLAIM

[21.10]

CPR 16.4 – CONTENTS OF THE PARTICULARS OF CLAIM
  (1)   Particulars of claim must include–
    (a)   a concise statement of the facts on which the claimant relies;
    (b)   if the claimant is seeking interest, a statement to that effect and the details set out in paragraph (2);
    (c)   if the claimant is seeking aggravated damages or exemplary damages, a statement to that effect and his grounds for claiming them;
    (d)   if the claimant is seeking provisional damages, a statement to that effect and his grounds for claiming them; and
    (e)   such other matters as may be set out in a practice direction.
  (2)   If the claimant is seeking interest he must–
    (a)   state whether he is doing so–
      (i)   under the terms of a contract;
      (ii)   under an enactment and if so which; or
      (iii)   on some other basis and if so what that basis is; and
    (b)   if the claim is for a specified amount of money, state–
      (i)   the percentage rate at which interest is claimed;
      (ii)   the date from which it is claimed;
      (iii)   the date to which it is calculated, which must not be later than the date on which the claim form is issued;
      (iv)   the total amount of interest claimed to the date of calculation; and
      (v)   the daily rate at which interest accrues after that date.

'CONCISE STATEMENT OF FACTS'

[21.11]   Brown v Barclays Bank plc
[2003] EWHC 2438 (QB)
[2003] All ER (D) 377 (Oct)

The defendant applied to strike out the claimant's particulars of claim, which had been written on the reverse of the claim form and on a document headed 'draft order', and applied for summary judgment.

HELD: The particulars of claim was a 'long, repetitious and rambling document' and did not include 'a concise statement of the facts on which the claimant [relied] as required by CPR 16.4(1)(a)'. In addition the particulars of claim included allegations of fraud and illegality but proper details had not been set out as required by CPR 16 PD 8.2. The particulars of claim was struck out.

INTEREST

[21.12] Johnson v Deglos
(2 October 2001, unreported)

The claimant served the particulars of claim which included a claim for interest. The claim for interest did not state the date from which interest was to be calculated, nor the daily rate at which interest accrued.

HELD: The purpose of CPR 16.4(2)(b) was to allow a defendant to calculate the value of the claim and the defendant could not do so in this case until standard disclosure had been given, when he first become aware of the date upon which interest started to accrue. Accordingly interest was not allowed from the date of the accident until the date of disclosure.

(B)   MATTERS WHICH MUST BE INCLUDED IN THE PARTICULARS OF CLAIM IN CERTAIN TYPES OF CLAIM

[21.13]

Practice Direction to CPR 16, paragraphs 4 and 5

Personal injury claims
    4.1   The particulars of claim must contain:
      (1)   the claimant's date of birth, and
      (2)   brief details of the claimant's personal injuries.
    4.2   The claimant must attach to his particulars of claim a schedule of details of any past and future expenses and losses which he claims.
    4.3   Where the claimant is relying on the evidence of a medical practitioner the claimant must attach to or serve with his particulars of claim a report from a medical practitioner about the personal injuries which he alleges in his claim.
    4.4   In a provisional damages claim the claimant must state in his particulars of claim:
      (1)   that he is seeking an award of provisional damages under either section 32A of the Supreme Court Act 1981 or section 51 of the County Courts Act 1984,
      (2)   that there is a chance that at some future time the claimant will develop some serious disease or suffer some serious deterioration in his physical or mental condition, and
      (3)   specify the disease or type of deterioration in respect of which an application may be made at a future date.

Fatal accident claims
    5.1   In a fatal accident claim the claimant must state in his particulars of claim:
      (1)   that it is brought under the Fatal Accidents Act 1976,
      (2)   the dependants on whose behalf the claim is made,
      (3)   the date of birth of each dependant, and
      (4)   details of the nature of the dependency claim.

5.2   A fatal accident claim may include a claim for damages for bereavement.

5.3   In a fatal accident claim the claimant may also bring a claim under the Law Reform (Miscellaneous Provisions) Act 1934 on behalf of the estate of the deceased.

(C)   MATTERS WHICH MUST BE SPECIFICALLY SET OUT IN THE PARTICULARS OF CLAIM IF RELIED ON

[21.14]

Practice Direction to CPR 16, paragraph 8

8.1   A claimant who wishes to rely on evidence:

(1)   under section 11 of the Civil Evidence Act 1968 of a conviction of an offence,

(2)   …

must include in his particulars of claim a statement to that effect and give the following details:

(1)   the type of conviction, finding or adjudication and its date,

(2)   the court or Court-Martial which made the conviction, finding or adjudication, and

(3)   the issue in the claim to which it relates.

8.2   The claimant must specifically set out the following matters in his particulars of claim where he wishes to rely on them in support of his claim:

(1)   any allegation of fraud,

(2)   the fact of any illegality;

(3)   details of any misrepresentation,

(4)   details of all breaches of trust,

(5)   notice or knowledge of a fact,

(6)   details of unsoundness of mind or undue influence,

(7)   details of wilful default, and

(8)   any facts relating to mitigation of loss or damage.

[21.15]

CPR 16.8 – COURT'S POWER TO DISPENSE WITH STATEMENTS OF CASE

If a claim form has been–

(a)   issued in accordance with rule 7.2; and

(b)   served in accordance with rule 7.5,

the court may make an order that the claim will continue without any other statement of case.

[21.16]   Totty v Snowden

[2001] EWCA Civ 1415

[2001] 4 All ER 577, [2002] 1 WLR 1384

HELD: CPR 16.8 provides that if a claim form has been issued in accordance with CPR 7.2 and served in accordance with CPR 7.5 the court may make an order that the claim will continue without any other statement of case. The particulars of claim are not an integral part of the claim form.

4.   ALTERNATIVE PROCEDURE UNDER CPR PT 8

(A)   CLAIMS WHERE PART 8 PROCEDURE MAY BE USED

[21.17]

CPR 8.1 – TYPES OF CLAIM IN WHICH PART 8 PROCEDURE MAY
BE FOLLOWED
  (1)   The Part 8 procedure is the procedure set out in this Part.
  (2)   A claimant may use the Part 8 procedure where–
     (a)   he seeks the court's decision on a question which is unlikely to
          involve a substantial dispute of fact; or
     (b)   paragraph (6) applies.

Practice Direction to CPR 8, paragraph 1

Types of claim in which Part 8 procedure may be used
  1.1   A claimant may use the Part 8 procedure where he seeks the court's
        decision on a question which is unlikely to involve a substantial dispute
        of fact.
  1.2   A claimant may also use the Part 8 procedure if a practice direction
        permits or requires its use for the type of proceedings in question.
  1.3   The practice directions referred to in paragraph 1.2 above may in some
        respects modify or disapply the Part 8 procedure and, where that is so,
        it is those practice directions that must be complied with.
  1.4   The types of claim for which the Part 8 procedure may be used include:
     (1)   a claim by or against a child or patient which has been settled before
          the commencement of proceedings and the sole purpose of the claim
          is to obtain the approval of the court to the settlement,
     (2)   a claim for provisional damages which has been settled before the
          commencement of proceedings and the sole purpose of the claim is
          to obtain a consent judgment, and
     (3)   provided there is unlikely to be a substantial dispute of fact, a claim for
          a summary order for possession against named or unnamed defend-
          ants occupying land or premises without the licence or consent of the
          person claiming possession.
  1.5   Where it appears to a court officer that a claimant is using the Part 8
        procedure inappropriately, he may refer the claim to a judge for the
        judge to consider the point.
  1.6   The court may at any stage order the claim to continue as if the
        claimant had not used the Part 8 procedure and, if it does so, the court
        will allocate the claim to a track and give such directions as it considers
        appropriate.

CPR PT 8 NOT APPROPRIATE FOR RESOLVING SUBSTANTIVE DISPUTES

[21.18]   **UCB Group Ltd v Hedworth**

(7 November 2001, unreported)

The defendant applied for summary judgment under CPR Pt 8. The case involved a
dispute as to the terms of an agreement entered into by the defendant.

HELD: CPR Pt 8 was not designed to meet cases where there was a substantial dispute of fact. In this case there was a fundamental issue to be determined and it was not in the interests of justice to deal with the matter under CPR Pt 8.

(B)   ISSUE OF A PART 8 CLAIM

[21.19]

CPR 8.2 – CONTENTS OF THE CLAIM FORM

Where the claimant uses the Part 8 procedure the claim form must state–
(a)   that this Part applies;
(b)   (i) the question which the claimant wants the court to decide; or
   (ii)   the remedy which the claimant is seeking and the legal basis for the claim to that remedy;
(c)   if the claim is being made under an enactment, what that enactment is;
(d)   if the claimant is claiming in a representative capacity, what that capacity is; and
(e)   if the defendant is sued in a representative capacity, what that capacity is.

[21.20]

CPR 8.2A – ISSUE OF CLAIM FORM WITHOUT NAMING DEFENDANTS
(1)   A practice direction may set out circumstances in which a claim form may be issued under this Part without naming a defendant.
(2)   The practice direction may set out those cases in which an application for permission must be made by application notice before the claim form is issued.
(3)   The application notice for permission -
   (a)   need not be served on any other person; and
   (b)   must be accompanied by a copy of the claim form that the applicant proposes to issue.
(4)   Where the court gives permission it will give directions about the future management of the claim.

[21.21]   Re Owens Corning Fibreglass (UK) Pension Plan Ltd
[2002] All ER (D) 191 (Jun), [2002] Pens LR 323

The trustees of an employees' pension plan entered into a compromise agreement with the employers under the pension plan. The trustees applied to the court for approval of the compromise agreement. Proceedings were issued under CPR 8.2A without identifying or naming any respondents. The court was asked to approve the compromise affecting the company's employees without them being present to make submissions on the compromise.

HELD: In most cases it would be desirable for potential beneficiaries to be informed about the application made to the court. On the facts of this case, though, the agreement represented an attractive compromise and approval of the compromise was subject to very severe time constraints. In the circumstances the application was granted.

[21.22]

CPR 8.5 – FILING AND SERVING WRITTEN EVIDENCE
(1)   The claimant must file any written evidence on which he intends to rely when he files his claim form.
(2)   The claimant's evidence must be served on the defendant with the claim form.
(3)   A defendant who wishes to rely on written evidence must file it when he files his acknowledgment of service.
(4)   If he does so, he must also, at the same time, serve a copy of his evidence on the other parties.
(5)   The claimant may, within 14 days of service of the defendant's evidence on him, file further written evidence in reply.
(6)   If he does so, he must also, within the same time limit, serve a copy of his evidence on the other parties.
(7)   The claimant may rely on the matters set out in his claim form as evidence under this rule if the claim form is verified by a statement of truth.

5.   PROCEDURE IN RESPECT OF CLAIMS ARISING OUT OF THE JURISDICTION

[21.23]   Reference should be made to Chapter 20, at para [20.22], which sets out the procedure in respect of motor claims arising in EU Member States.

Claims in respect of general torts committed outside the UK and motor claims arising outside EU territory are matters beyond the scope of this book, and reference should be made to *The Civil Court Practice*, published by LexisNexis Butterworths.

Service

1.   SERVICE GENERALLY

(A)   SERVICE OF DOCUMENTS GENERALLY, INCLUDING THE CLAIM FORM

[22.1]

CPR 6.2 – METHODS OF SERVICE – GENERAL
(1)   A document may be served by any of the following methods–
   (a)   personal service, in accordance with rule 6.4;
   (b)   first class post (or an alternative service which provides for delivery on the next working day);
   (c)   leaving the document at a place specified in rule 6.5;
   (d)   through a document exchange in accordance with the relevant practice direction; or
   (e)   by fax or other means of electronic communication in accordance with the relevant practice direction.

[22.2]

CPR 6.4 – PERSONAL SERVICE
(1)   A document to be served may be served personally, except as provided in paragraphs (2) and (2A).
(2)   Where a solicitor–
   (a)   is authorised to accept service on behalf of a party; and
   (b)   has notified the party serving the document in writing that he is so authorised,
a document must be served on the solicitor, unless personal service is required by an enactment, rule, practice direction or court order.
(2A)   In civil proceedings by or against the Crown, as defined in rule 66.1(2), documents required to be served on the Crown may not be served personally.

(3)   A document is served personally on an individual by leaving it with that individual.

(4)   A document is served personally on a company or other corporation by leaving it with a person holding a senior position within the company or corporation.

(5)   A document is served personally on a partnership where partners are being sued in the name of their firm by leaving it with–

(a)   a partner; or

(b)   a person who, at the time of service, has the control or management of the partnership business at its principal place of business.

FIRST CLASS POST

[22.3]   Petford v Saw

[2002] CLY 478

The claimant's solicitor served a claim form on the defendant's nominated solicitor by special delivery. The defendant argued that special delivery was an invalid method of service for the purpose of the Civil Procedure Rules (CPR).

HELD: 'Special delivery' by the Royal Mail was valid service as a species of first class post for the purpose of CPR 6.2(1).

DOCUMENT EXCHANGE

[22.4]

Practice Direction to CPR 6, paragraph 2

Service by non-electronic means

Service by Document Exchange

2.1   Service by document exchange (DX) may take place only where:

(1)   the party's address for service includes a numbered box at a DX, or

(2)   the writing paper of the party who is to be served or of his legal representative sets out the DX box number, and

(3)   the party or his legal representative has not indicated in writing that they are unwilling to accept service by DX.

2.2   Service by DX is effected by leaving the document addressed to the numbered box:

(1)   at the DX of the party who is to be served, or

(2)   at a DX which sends documents to that party's DX every business day.

FACSIMILE

[22.5]

Practice Direction to CPR 6

Service by electronic means

Service by Facsimile

3.1   Subject to the provisions of paragraph 3.3 below, where a document is to be served by electronic means–

(1)   the party who is to be served or his legal representative must previously have expressly indicated in writing to the party serving –

(a)   that he is willing to accept service by electronic means; and

(b)   the fax number, e-mail address or electronic identification to which it should be sent; and

(2)   the following shall be taken as sufficient written indication for the purposes of paragraph 3.1(1)–

(a)   a fax number set out on the writing paper of the legal representative of the party who is to be served; or

(b)   a fax number, e-mail address or electronic identification set out on a statement of case or a response to a claim filed with the court.

3.2   Where a party seeks to serve a document by electronic means he should first seek to clarify with the party who is to be served whether there are any limitations to the recipient's agreement to accept service by such means including the format in which documents are to be sent and the maximum size of attachments that may be received.

3.3   An address for service given by a party must be within the jurisdiction and any fax number must be at the address for service. Where an e-mail address or electronic identification is given in conjunction with an address for service, the e-mail address or electronic identification will be deemed to be at the address for service.

3.4   Where a document is served by electronic means, the party serving the document need not in addition send a hard copy by post or document exchange.

[22.6]   Asia Pacific (HK) Ltd v Hanjin Shipping Company Ltd and Another
[2005] EWHC 2443

The claimant's solicitors faxed a letter to the defendant's solicitors, enclosing a copy of the claim form. The fax did not state that the claim form was faxed by way of service. The claim form was not acknowledged. The claimant's solicitors sought a declaration that the claim form was served on the defendant.

HELD: The CPR did not define what was meant by service, other than prescribing how it might be effected. The despatch of the fax did constitute service of the claim form. The claimant's solicitors had delivered the claim form to the defendant's solicitors by a permitted method of service of a claim form. When a claim form was delivered to the recipient in a manner provided for by the Rules it was thereby served, unless it was made clear by the person who delivered it that he was not in fact serving it. The fact that no response pack was served, that the claim form was marked as a copy and that the fax did not state that it was sent 'by way of service', did not demonstrate that no service was intended.

[22.7]   Kuenyehia v International Hospitals Group Ltd
[2006] EWCA Civ 21

[2006] All ER (D) 169 (Jan)

On 19 December 2003 the claimant's solicitors issued proceedings. On 19 April 2004 the proceedings were sent to the defendant's solicitors by courier, although the defendant had not nominated solicitors to accept service. The proceedings were also sent by fax on the same day to the defendant's legal department (although no permission had been obtained to serve the proceedings by fax). The defendant objected to service, and the claimant applied for an order that there had been effective service. The court held that the failure to obtain the defendant's consent to serve proceedings by fax was a comparatively minor departure from the requirements of the CPR, and service was held to have been effected. The defendant appealed to the Court of Appeal.

HELD, ON APPEAL: The question to be decided was whether, in light of the principles and approach laid down by the Court of Appeal in previous cases, service of the claim form had properly been dispensed with. The time limits in the CPR were to be strictly observed. Failure to comply with paragraph 3.1(1) of the Practice Direction to CPR Pt 6 represented more than a minor departure from CPR 6.2(1)(e). This was not an exceptional case. The court's power to dispense with service '[was] unlikely to be exercised, save where the claimant has either made an ineffective attempt in time to serve by one of the methods permitted by CPR 6.2 or has served in time in a manner which involved a minor departure from one of those permitted methods of service.' The defendant's appeal was allowed.

[22.8]

CPR 6.2(2) – SERVICE ON A COMPANY

...

(2)   A company may be served by any method permitted under this Part as an alternative to the methods of service set out in–
  (a)   section 725 of the Companies Act 1985 (service by leaving a document at or posting it to an authorised place);
  (b)   section 695 of that Act (service on overseas companies); and
  (c)   section 694A of that Act (service of documents on companies incorporated outside the UK and Gibraltar and having a branch in Great Britain).

[22.9]   Murphy v Staples UK Ltd
[2003] EWCA Civ 656
[2003] 3 All ER 129, [2003] 1 WLR 2441

The defendant's insurers nominated solicitors to accept service of proceedings on behalf of the defendant. Proceedings were served on the defendant at its registered office instead of upon the nominated solicitors. The defendant's solicitors applied to set aside service on the grounds that it was not in accordance with CPR 6.5 and succeeded at first instance. The claimant's subsequent appeal was allowed.

HELD, ON APPEAL: Service on a company under s 725 of the Companies Act 1985 was a permitted alternative method of service, as was made clear by CPR 6.2(2). Although parties could make a binding contract, whereby the claimant agreed to serve the claim form pursuant to the CPR instead of s 725, no such contract existed in this case. *Nanglegan v Royal Free Hospital NHS Trust)* (at para [22.38]) was distinguished as the defendant in that case was not a company.

[22.10]

CPR 6.6 – SERVICE OF DOCUMENTS ON CHILDREN AND PATIENTS
(1)   The following table shows the person on whom a document must be served if it is a document which would otherwise be served on a child or a patient–

Type of document	Nature of party	Person to be served
Claim form	Child who is not also a patient	One of the child's parents or guardians; or If there is no parent or guardian, the person with whom the child resides or in whose care the child is.
Claim form	Patient	The person authorised under Part VII of the Mental Health Act 1983 to conduct the proceedings in the name of the patient or on his behalf; or If there is no person so authorised, the person with whom the patient resides or in whose care the patient is.
Application for an order appointing a litigation friend, where a child or patient has no litigation friend	Child or patient	See rule 21.8.
Any other document	Child or patient	The litigation friend who is conducting proceedings on behalf of the child or patient.

(2)   The court may make an order permitting a document to be served on the child or patient, or on some person other than the person specified in the table in this rule.

(3)   An application for an order under paragraph (2) may be made without notice.

(4)   The court may order that, although a document has been served on someone other than the person specified in the table, the document is to be treated as if it had been properly served.

(5)   This rule does not apply where the court has made an order under rule 21.2(3) allowing a child to conduct proceedings without a litigation friend.

[22.11]

CPR 6.3 – WHO IS TO SERVE

(1)   The court will serve a document which it has issued or prepared except where–

(a)   a rule provides that a party must serve the document in question;

(b)   the party on whose behalf the document is to be served notifies the court that he wishes to serve it himself;

(c)   a practice direction provides otherwise;

(d)   the court orders otherwise; or

(e)   the court has failed to serve and has sent a notice of non-service to the party on whose behalf the document is to be served in accordance with rule 6.11.

(2)   Where the court is to serve a document, it is for the court to decide which of the methods of service specified in rule 6.2 is to be used.

(3)   Where a party prepares a document which is to be served by the court, that party must file a copy for the court, and for each party to be served.

(B)   ADDRESS FOR SERVICE

[22.12]

CPR 6.5 – ADDRESS FOR SERVICE
  (1)   ...
  (2)   A party must give an address for service within the jurisdiction. Such address must include a full postcode, unless the court orders otherwise.
  (3)   Where a party–
  (a)   does not give the business address of his solicitor as his address for service; and
  (b)   resides or carries on business within the jurisdiction,
he must give his residence or place of business as his address for service.
  (4)   Any document to be served–
  (a)   by first class post;
  (b)   by leaving it at the place of service;
  (c)   through a document exchange; or
  (d)   by fax or by other means of electronic communication,
must be sent or transmitted to, or left at, the address for service given by the party to be served.
  (5)   Where–
  (a)   a solicitor is acting for the party to be served; and
  (b)   the document to be served is not the claim form;
the party's address for service is the business address of his solicitor.
  (6)   Where–
  (a)   no solicitor is acting for the party to be served; and
  (b)   the party has not given an address for service,
the document must be sent or transmitted to, or left at, the place shown in the following table.

Nature of party to be served	Place of service
Individual	Usual or last known residence.
Proprietor of a business	Usual or last known residence; or Place of business or last known place of business.
Individual who is suing or being sued in the name of a firm	Usual or last known residence; or Principal or last known place of business of the firm.
Corporation incorporated in England and Wales other than a company	Principal office of the corporation; or Any place within the jurisdiction where the corporation carries on its activities and which has a real connection with the claim.

Nature of party to be served	Place of service
Company registered in England and Wales	Principal office of the company; or Any place of business of the company within the jurisdiction which has a real connection with the claim.
Any other company or corporation	Any place within the jurisdiction where the corporation carries on its activities; or Any place of business of the company within the jurisdiction.

(7)   This rule does not apply where an order made by the court under rule 6.8 (service by an alternative method) specifies where the document in question may be served.

(8)   In civil proceedings by or against the Crown, as defined in rule 66.1(2)–

   (a)   service on the Attorney General must be effected on the Treasury Solicitor;

   (b)   service on a government department must be effected on the solicitor acting for that department as required by section 18 of the Crown Proceedings Act 1947.

[22.13]

CPR 6.13 – SERVICE OF CLAIM FORM BY THE COURT – DEFENDANT'S ADDRESS FOR SERVICE

(1)   Where a claim form is to be served by the court, the claim form must include the defendant's address for service.

(2)   For the purposes of paragraph (1), the defendant's address for service may be the business address of the defendant's solicitor if he is authorised to accept service on the defendant's behalf but not otherwise.

DOCUMENT TO BE SERVED MUST BE SENT TO THE ADDRESS GIVEN FOR SERVICE

[22.14]   McManus v Sharif

[2003] EWCA Civ 656

[2003] 3 All ER 129, [2003] 1 WLR 2441

The last date for service of the claim form was 19 June 2001. The claimant's solicitor sent an unsigned and unsealed draft claim form to the defendant's insurer on 15 June 2001. Service was later effected on the defendant on 25 June 2001.

HELD: Service of a draft claim form on the defendant's insurer, who had no authority to accept service on behalf of the defendant, did not comply with CPR 6.5 as the document had not been sent to an address given for service. This was a significant departure from the Rules as to the permitted mode of service and the court held that the power to dispense with service of the claim form should not be exercised in such a case.

SERVICE ON A SOLICITOR

[22.15]   Nanglegan v Royal Free Hospital NHS Trust
[2001] EWCA Civ 127
[2001] 3 All ER 793, [2002] 1 WLR 1043

HELD, ON APPEAL: If a defendant has nominated solicitors to accept service of proceedings, the claim form should be served on the solicitors. If solicitors have been nominated, then service upon the defendant at the defendant's own address is invalid.

For full summary of this case, see para [22.38] below.

[22.16]   Horn v Dorset Healthcare NHS Trust
(4 May 2004, unreported), Southampton CC

The defendant's claims manager wrote to the claimant's solicitors to nominate solicitors to accept service. The DX address contained in that letter was incorrect. The claimant's solicitors served the claim form directly on the defendant and not on the nominated solicitors. The deputy district judge declared the claim form had not been validly served. The claimant appealed.

HELD, ON APPEAL: Although the defendant had not actually instructed its solicitors to accept service of the proceedings and had only notified the claimant's solicitors of the solicitors that it was intending to instruct, the court held that 'the validity … of service of a claim form ought not to depend on whether or not the solicitors nominated by a defendant to accept service had, at the moment of service, actual, as opposed to some other form of authority to do so'. The letter sent by the defendant constituted a representation to the claimant's solicitors that the named solicitors acting for the defendant had an ostensible authority to accept service on behalf of the defendant. *Nanglegan v Royal Free Hospital NHS Trust* (at para [22.38]) followed.

Appeal dismissed.

[22.17]   Firstdale Ltd v Quinton
[2004] EWHC 1926 (Comm)
[2005] 1 All ER 639

HELD, per Colman J: 'An indication by a potential defendant's solicitor that he is authorised to accept service of proceedings … cannot ordinarily be taken to have indicated his authority to accept service of a document relating to different proceedings or to a different claim'. The scope of the solicitor's authority to accept service was defined by reference to the claim and the identity and capacity of the claimant. Service on the defendant's residential address was good service and the defendant's application was dismissed. *Nanglegan v Royal Free Hospital NHS Trust* (at para [22.38]) considered.

[22.18] **Collier v Williams**

[2006] EWCA Civ 20

[2006] All ER (D) 177 (Jan), [2006] 1 WLR 1945

Proceedings were served on solicitors who had been nominated by the defendant's insurer to accept service of proceedings. The defendant argued that there had not been valid service as the nominated solicitors had not confirmed they were instructed to accept service. The defendant's application was dismissed at first instance and the defendant appealed.

HELD, ON APPEAL: The party to be served must give an address for service and any documents to be served must be sent or transmitted to or left at the address for service given by the defendant. Where a defendant gives the claimant his solicitor's address for service, the claim form may be validly served at that address by one of the permitted methods of service. There was no necessity for the nominated solicitors themselves to notify the claimant that they had authority to accept service. CPR 6.4(2) related only to personal service, and did not have general application.

  Appeal dismissed.

[22.19] **Marshall and Rankine v Maggs**

[2005] EWHC 200 (QB)

[2005] All ER (D) 172 (Jan)

The claimants sent a letter of claim to an address at which they believed the defendant was residing. The defendant's solicitors acknowledged the letter, advising that they acted for the defendant and that they were taking instructions. Subsequently, proceedings were served on the address where the letter of claim had been sent.

HELD, ON APPEAL: As neither the defendant nor his solicitors had confirmed that the solicitors were authorised to accept service, and the defendant had not nominated solicitors for service, there was no solicitor 'acting' for the defendant, and the claimants were therefore permitted to serve the defendant at his last known address.

PARTY TO BE SERVED MUST BE IN THE JURISDICTION

[22.20] **Chellaram v Chellaram (No 2)**

[2002] EWHC 632 (Ch)

[2002] 3 All ER 17

The claimants were beneficiaries of a trust and brought proceedings against the defendants for breach of trust. None of the defendants were domiciled in England. However, one of the defendants was served by first class post at the address he stayed at occasionally when he visited London.

HELD: Service on the defendant at an address in England was not valid service as the defendant had not been present in England at the time of service. There was no evidence that the address was his residence and it could not therefore be his last known residence. The introduction of CPR 6.5 had not changed "the fundamental rule of English procedure and jurisdiction that a defendant may be served within the jurisdiction only if he was present in the jurisdiction at the time of service'.

[22.21]   Lakah Group v (1) Al Jazeera Satellite Channel (2) Mansour

[2003] EWHC 1297 (QB)

[2003] All ER (D) 141 (Jun)

The claimant served proceedings on the first defendant by serving them on an employee of the first defendant's English company.

HELD, ON APPEAL: Service was not effected on the first defendant as the employee upon whom proceedings had been served was not a person holding a senior position within the company. The claimant had not established that the address at which the proceedings were served was a place where the first defendant carried out its activities, nor was it the first defendant's place of business under CPR 6.5(6) or an established place of business under s 695 of the Companies Act 1985. 'Service on an address with which the company has no more than a transient or irregular connection will not be valid'.

[22.22]   Fairmays (a firm) v Palmer

[2006] EWHC 96 (Ch)

[2006] All ER (D) 248 (Jan), Ch

The claimant served proceedings on the defendant by posting them to the defendant's property in England where the defendant used to live before he had left England to work in Ethiopia. The claimant obtained judgment in default. The defendant applied to set aside the judgment on the basis that proceedings had not been validly served. He appealed against the subsequent dismissal of his application.

HELD, ON APPEAL: Following *Chellaram v Chellaram* (at para [22.20]), proceedings issued for service within the jurisdiction could not be properly served when, at the time of deemed service, the defendant was physically out of the jurisdiction. If the claimant was having difficulties in serving proceedings on a defendant, who it was suspected might be absent abroad, he could issue concurrent proceedings for service abroad and obtain an order for alternative service on the last known address of the defendant within the jurisdiction.

Appeal allowed.

MEANING OF 'LAST KNOWN RESIDENCE' AND 'LAST KNOWN PLACE OF BUSINESS'

[22.23]   Smith v Hughes and Another

[2003] EWCA Civ 656

[2003] 3 All ER 129, [2003] 1 WLR 2441

The claimant served proceedings by first class post on the defendant at an address which enquiry agents had ascertained was the defendant's last known address. The Motor Insurers' Bureau applied to the court for a ruling as to whether the claim form had been validly served. At first instance it was held that it had not been validly served.

HELD, ON APPEAL: The words of CPR 6.5(6) in relation to service on an individual at his last known residence were 'plain and unqualified'. If there was no solicitor acting for the party to be served and the party had not given an address for service, then service of a document was effected by being sent, or transmitted to, or left at the individual's usual or last known residence. The Rules did not state that it would not be good service if the defendant did not receive the document, or if the claimant knew, or believed, the defendant was no longer living at the last known residence.

[22.24]   Akram v Adam

[2004] EWCA Civ 1601

[2005] 1 All ER 741, [2005] 1 WLR 2762

The claimant's solicitor posted the claim form and particulars of claim to the defendant at his usual residence. No response was received, and the claimant entered judgment in default. The defendant claimed he had not received service of the proceedings and judgment was set aside. The claimant's subsequent appeal was allowed and the defendant appealed to the Court of Appeal.

HELD, ON APPEAL: The claim form had been properly served under CPR 6.5(6) as it had been sent to the defendant at his usual residence by first class post. There had been no finding that the claim form had been returned undelivered. The subsequent judgment had been regularly entered and the defendant's appeal was dismissed.

[22.25]   O'Hara v McDougal

[2005] EWCA Civ 1623

[2005] All ER (D) 275 (Nov)

The claimant served proceedings on the defendant at 24 Dover Road, a property owned by the defendant but let to tenants. Judgment in default was entered. When the defendant became aware of the proceedings he applied to have the judgment set aside. The court refused his application and on subsequent appeal it was held that the defendant was being sued in his personal capacity so service on his place of business was not appropriate and, in any event, as the defendant rented out 24 Dover Road this did not render it a place of business. The claimant appealed to the Court of Appeal.

HELD, ON APPEAL: A property does not become a place of business merely because rent is collected from a tenant or because the property is let out. Landlords have limited rights of entry to a property and the idea that a defendant could be served at a property where he had no rights of entry seemed wrong. Service had not taken place at the defendant's place of business and the appeal was dismissed.

[22.26]   Marshall and Rankine v Maggs

[2006] EWCA Civ 20

[2006] All ER (D) 177 (Jan), [2006] 1 WLR 1945

The defendant had instructed solicitors to act on his behalf, but neither the defendant nor his solicitors had indicated that the solicitors had instructions to accept service. The claimant's solicitors served proceedings on the defendant at 47 Hays Mews. The defendant's solicitors applied to set aside the order that the claim form had been validly served. It was held that there was valid service as there was no solicitor authorised to accept service and 47 Hays Mews was the defendant's last known address. On appeal it was held that, as the defendant had never lived at 47 Hays Mews, it was not the defendant's usual or last known address, and that the defendant's solicitors were acting for the defendant within the meaning of CPR 6.5(6), even though they did not have instructions to accept service.

HELD, ON APPEAL: As the defendant's solicitors had not confirmed they were authorised to accept service, there was no solicitor 'acting' for the defendant within the meaning of CPR 6.5(6) and service in accordance with CPR 6.5(6) was justified. Knowledge referred to the serving party's actual or constructive knowledge. 'Last known residence' could not refer to an address at which an individual had never resided and therefore service on the defendant at 47 Hays Mews was not effective. The Court of Appeal dismissed the claimant's application for an extension of time.

[22.27]   Mersey Docks Property Holdings v Kilgour

[2004] EWHC 1638 (TCC)

[2004] All ER (D) 303 (Jun)

The claimant's solicitor sent a letter to the defendant enclosing a claim form and draft particulars of claim four days before the four-month period after the date of issue. The letter was sent to the defendant's former business address which he had left four years previously. The issue was whether the claim form had been validly served on the defendant.

HELD: The proper construction of 'last known place of business' was the 'last place of business known to the claimant'. To acquire the requisite knowledge, reasonable steps had to be taken to ascertain the current or last place of business. 'It will be a matter of evidence whether a party has discharged the obligation to have the requisite knowledge at the time of service'. The court held that the claimant had not taken reasonable steps to acquire the requisite knowledge as searches should have been made of the relevant professional directories or Yellow Pages. The claim form had not been validly served.

2.   DEEMED SERVICE

[22.28]

CPR 6.7 – DEEMED SERVICE
   (1)   A document which is served in accordance with these rules or any relevant practice direction shall be deemed to be served on the day shown in the following table–

Method of service	Deemed day of service
First class post	The second day after it was posted.
Document exchange	The second day after it was left at the document exchange.
Delivering the document to or leaving it at a permitted address	The day after it was delivered to or left at the permitted address.
Fax	If it is transmitted on a business day before 4 p.m., on that day; or In any other case, on the business day after the day on which it is transmitted.
Other electronic method	The second day after the day on which it is transmitted.

   (2)   If a document is served personally–
      (a)   After 5 p.m., on a business day; or

(b)   At any time on a Saturday, Sunday or a Bank Holiday,
it will be treated as being served on the next business day.
(3)   In this rule–
'business day' means any day except Saturday, Sunday or a bank
holiday;
and
'bank holiday' includes Christmas Day and Good Friday.

(A)   DEEMED DATE OF SERVICE NOT REBUTTABLE BY EVIDENCE OF ACTUAL DATE OF SERVICE

[22.29]   Godwin v Swindon Borough Council

[2001] EWCA Civ 1478

[2001] 4 All ER 641, [2002] 1 WLR 997, CA

The claimant issued a claim for damages for personal injury sustained at work shortly before the expiry of the limitation period. The time for service of the claim form was 8 September 2000. On 7 September 2000 the claimant posted the claim form, particulars of claim and the response pack to the defendant's solicitors. Under CPR 6.7(1) service was deemed to be effected on 9 September 2002. In fact, the letter and its enclosures were received by the defendant on 8 September 2000. The issue for the court was whether evidence of the date of actual service was admissible to displace the effect of CPR 6.7(1).

HELD, ON APPEAL: The wording of CPR 6.7(1) clearly required that the date specified as the deemed date of service had to be treated as the date of service, irrespective of proof of the date of actual service.

[22.30]   Anderton v Clwyd County Council

[2002] EWCA Civ 933

[2002] 3 All ER 813, [2002] 1 WLR 3174

HELD, ON APPEAL: The date of deemed service was not rebuttable by evidence of earlier or later receipt by a defendant. The position was unaffected by the Human Rights Act 1998. The court held that *Godwin* (at para [22.29]) was not incompatible with Art 6 of the European Convention on Human Rights. Certainty as to the day of service of the claim form was an important requirement for the efficient performance of the case management functions of the court. The object of the rules was to reduce uncertainty. If a claimant was debarred by this rule, that was a consequence of the claimant waiting until the end of the respective periods rather than the effect of disproportionately strict procedural rules.

Saturday and Sunday were not to be excluded from the calculation of deemed service under CPR 6.7. The court disagreed with *obiter* to the contrary in *Godwin*. The court accepted CPR 2.8 excluded Saturday and Sunday but determined that this rule was not applicable to CPR 6.7 which set out the method of calculation of deemed service. The term 'business day' was not specifically used in CPR 6.7 which only referred to 'day' which logically included Saturday and Sunday. The court accepted this gave rise to an anomaly in that postal service after 5pm on a Friday would be deemed served upon a Sunday whereas personal or faxed service would be deemed to be on the next 'business day', ie Monday. The Court of Appeal stated that it was a matter for consideration whether CPR 6.7 should be amended.

3. SERVICE BY AN ALTERNATIVE METHOD

[22.31]

CPR 6.8 – SERVICE BY AN ALTERNATIVE METHOD
(1) Where it appears to the court that there is a good reason to authorise service by a method not permitted by these Rules, the court may make an order permitting service by an alternative method.
(2) An application for an order permitting service by an alternative method–
  (a) must be supported by evidence; and
  (b) may be made without notice.
(3) An order permitting service by an alternative method must specify–
  (a) the method of service; and
  (b) the date when the document will be deemed to be served.

[22.32]   Elmes v Hygrade Food Products plc
[2001] EWCA Civ 121
[2001] All ER (D) 158 (Jan)

On the last date stipulated for service, the claimant's solicitors faxed the claim form to the defendant's insurer instead of to the defendant. Having effected service, but on the wrong party, the claimant sought to rely on CPR 3.9 and CPR 3.10, which allows the court to remedy procedural errors, and CPR 6.8 which empowers the court to permit service by an alternative method.

HELD, ON APPEAL: The claimant's argument was rejected on the basis that it implied that CPR 6.8 could be applied retrospectively. CPR 6.8 was a prospective provision and, as no order had been made, it could not be applied to cure an error already made in effecting service. There was no power to correct the consequences of service on the wrong party.

4. DISPENSING WITH SERVICE

[22.33]

CPR 6.9 – POWER OF COURT TO DISPENSE WITH SERVICE
(1) The court may dispense with service of a document.
(2) An application for an order to dispense with service may be made without notice.

[22.34]   Anderton v Clwyd County Council
[2002] EWCA Civ 933
[2002] 3 All ER 813, [2002] 1 WLR 3174

HELD, ON APPEAL: There was power to dispense with service of the claim form both retrospectively and prospectively, but only in exceptional cases. The court distinguished between cases where no attempt had been made to serve the claim form in time and those cases where an ineffective attempt had been made to serve the claim form in time.

CPR 6.9 should not be used as a means of circumventing what was forbidden by CPR 7.6(3) (extending time for service). The cases that would not be allowed would be those where the claimant had not even attempted to serve the claim form within the time permitted and was asking for a retrospective extension of time.

The court considered a situation where the defendant and/or defendant's legal advisors had received the claim form and had their attention drawn to it within the time for service but that there had been an ineffective attempt actually to serve the documents. In those circumstances there was no need to serve the claim form to bring it to the attention of the relevant party and therefore the need to prove service could be excused. In those circumstances the defendant would not normally suffer prejudice, especially where it was accepted that the claim form had been received before the end of the period. In exercising this discretion, the court would take into account other relevant circumstances such as the explanation for late service, whether any criticism could be made of the claimant and/or their advisors, and whether there was any possible prejudice to the defendant.

[22.35]   Wilkey v British Broadcasting Corpn

[2002] EWCA Civ 1561

[2002] 4 All ER 1177, [2003] 1 WLR 1

The claimant issued proceedings two days before the expiry of the limitation period and served them on the last day of the four-month period by hand delivering them to the defendant's legal department, which had agreed to accept service. The date of deemed service was therefore one day outside the four month time period. The defendant appealed to have service set aside and the action dismissed. At first instance the court held that service was good, but the defendant succeeded on subsequent appeal.

HELD, ON APPEAL: The court could dispense with service in cases where the claimant had sought to serve the claim form by a permitted method of service and the claim form had actually been received by the defendant before the end of the period of service. The appeal was confined to an application under CPR 6.9 for service to be dispensed with. There was no good reason for not exercising the court's dispensing power in the claimant's favour and allowing the claim to proceed as the defendant had suffered no prejudice by the deemed late service, nor were there any other good reasons why service should not be dispensed with.

Obiter: Simon Brown LJ suggested that, rather than exercising power to dispense with service in the claimant's favour unless the defendant could establish prejudice or some other good reason, the power to dispense with service should not be ordinarily exercised in the claimant's favour and a strict approach should be adopted.

5.   EXTENDING TIME FOR SERVICE

(A)   TIME FOR SERVICE OF THE CLAIM FORM

[22.36]

CPR 7.5 – SERVICE OF A CLAIM FORM
   (1)   After a claim form has been issued, it must be served on the defendant.
   (2)   The general rule is that a claim form must be served within 4 months after the date of issue.

(3)   The period for service is 6 months where the claim form is to be served out of the jurisdiction.

(B)   EXTENDING TIME FOR SERVICE OF THE CLAIM FORM

[22.37]

CPR 7.6 – EXTENSION OF TIME FOR SERVING A CLAIM FORM
(1)   The claimant may apply for an order extending the period within which the claim form may be served.
(2)   The general rule is that an application to extend the time for service must be made–
  (a)   within the period for serving the claim form specified by rule 7.5; or
  (b)   where an order has been made under this rule, within the period for service specified by that order.
(3)   If the claimant applies for an order to extend the time for service of the claim form after the end of the period specified by rule 7.5 or by an order made under this rule, the court may make such an order only if–
  (a)   the court has been unable to serve the claim form; or
  (b)   the claimant has taken all reasonable steps to serve the claim form but has been unable to do so; and
  (c)   in either case, the claimant has acted promptly in making the application.
(4)   An application for an order extending the time for service–
  (a)   must be supported by evidence; and
  (b)   may be made without notice.

TO OBTAIN A RETROSPECTIVE EXTENSION OF TIME FOR SERVICE, THE
CLAIMANT MUST SATISFY ALL THE REQUIREMENTS OF CPR 7.6(3)

[22.38]   Nanglegan v Royal Free Hospital NHS Trust

[2001] EWCA Civ 127

[2001] 3 All ER 793, [2002] 1 WLR 1043

The defendant nominated solicitors to accept service of proceedings. Despite the nomination, the claimant served proceedings upon the defendant direct. The defendant objected. The claimant made a retrospective application to extend time for service under CPR 7.6(3) so that the proceedings could be served on the nominated solicitors.

HELD, ON APPEAL: If a defendant has nominated solicitors to accept service of proceedings, the claim form should be served on the solicitors. In such circumstances, service upon the defendant was invalid.
  The claimant could only proceed further if his application for a retrospective extension of time for service of the claim form satisfied the requirements of CPR 7.6(3): namely, the court or claimant must have been unable to serve the claim form, the claimant must have taken all reasonable steps to do so, and must have acted promptly in making the application. In the present case, none of the requirements of CPR 7.6(3) had been satisfied, and accordingly there was no discretion to extend time for service of the claim form.

[22.39] **Vinos v Marks & Spencer plc**

[2001] 3 All ER 784

The claimant's solicitors issued proceedings a week before the expiry of the limitation period. Service of the claim form took place nine days after the expiry of the four-month period. The defendant applied to set aside service and the claimant applied for an extension of time. The district judge at first instance held he had no discretion to extend time and his decision was upheld by the circuit judge.

HELD, ON APPEAL: 'The meaning of CPR 7.6(3) was plain. The court has power to extend the time for serving the claim form after the period for its service has run out "only if" the stipulated conditions are fulfilled. That means that the court does not have a power to do so otherwise'. An exercise of discretion pursuant to CPR 3.1(2)(a) was not appropriate. CPR 3.10 (the court's power to remedy an error) could not be utilised to enable the court to do what CPR 7.6(3) specifically forbade. The plain meaning of CPR 7.6(3) should not be ignored.

Appeal dismissed.

[22.40] **Chaudri v Post Office**

(26 April 2001, unreported), QBD

On 12 May 2000 the claimant's solicitors attended court to issue the claim form. The claimant's solicitors instructed the court not to serve the claim form until the court was provided with the particulars of claim. On 11 September 2000 the claimant's solicitors sent the claim form and particulars of claim to the defendant by DX. The defendant was not a member of the Document Exchange. The claimant's solicitors served a copy of the particulars of claim on 15 September 2000 but omitted to serve the claim form. There was no evidence the claim form had ever been sent by the court to the defendant. The defendant applied to set aside service of the claim form on the basis it was not served within the four-month period. An application was made by the claimant for an extension of time for service of the claim form.

HELD: The failure to serve had not been caused by the court as the claimant had requested the court not to serve. The claimant's solicitors could not show that they had taken all reasonable steps to serve the proceedings, nor that their application was made promptly, so the application was dismissed.

[22.41] **Mason v First Leisure Corpn plc**

[2003] EWHC 1814 (QB)

[2003] All ER (D) 516 (Jul)

The claim form was issued on 23 April 2002. The time for service of the claim form was extended to 23 December 2002 and the claim form was served on 19 December 2002. Following the defendant's application, the order extending time for service of the claim form was set aside.

HELD, ON APPEAL: Although the claimant had taken the wrong course of action by applying for an extension of time for service of the claim form, instead of serving the claim form and applying for an order extending time for service of the particulars of claim and accompanying documents, to set aside service of the claim form would be disproportionate and unjust, given that the claimant's solicitors believed they were taking a reasonable and appropriate course of action. This was a substantial claim and the defendant could not point to any prejudice.

[22.42]   Cranfield v Bridgegrove Ltd

[2003] EWCA Civ 656

[2003] 3 All ER 129, [2003] 1 WLR 2441

The claimants sent two claim forms to the court for issue and service on 12 February 2001. Time for service expired on 15 April 2001. On 24 August 2001 the claimants were informed by the court that, although the proceedings had been issued, they had not been served. The claimants subsequent application to extend time for service was dismissed at first instance but granted on appeal. The defendant appealed.

HELD, ON APPEAL: The real cause of the failure to serve in time was the court's neglect. The court had a discretion under CPR 7.6(3)(a) to extend time for service if 'the court has been unable to serve the claim form'. The words 'unable to serve' should be given an unrestricted meaning, so as to include all cases where the court had failed to serve, including mere oversight. In most cases the court's discretion to extend time would be exercised where the real cause of the failure to serve was the court's neglect and a prompt application had been made. If the real cause of the failure not to serve was the claimant's solicitors' conduct, the court's discretion was unlikely to be exercised.

[22.43]   Claussen v Yeates

[2003] EWCA Civ 656

[2003] 3 All ER 129, [2003] 1 WLR 2441

The claimant issued proceedings on 5 October 1999. The time for service expired on 5 February 2000 but due to administrative errors at the court office, service was not effected within the time limit. On 21 September 2000 the action was struck out and the claimant's subsequent appeal was refused.

HELD, ON APPEAL: The reason the claim form was not served within the four-month period was due to the claimant's solicitors' failure to provide the court with the defendant's solicitors' letter confirming they would accept service, until four days prior to the expiry of the four-month period, and even then not asking the court to deal with service as a matter of urgency. The Court of Appeal was not prepared to extend time for service under CPR 7.6(3), nor to make an order under CPR 6.9 dispensing with service, as the case did not fall within the exception identified in *Anderton v Clwyd County Council* (at para [22.30])

THE REASON FOR THE APPLICATION TO EXTEND TIME HAS TO BE EXPLAINED TO THE COURT'S SATISFACTION

[22.44]   Hashtroodi v Hancock

[2004] EWCA Civ 652

[2004] 3 All ER 530, [2004] 1 WLR 3206

The claim form was issued on 13 January 2003. On 9 May 2003 the claimant applied for an extension of time for service of the claim form until 3 June 2003. The claimant's solicitors proceeded to serve the defendant's solicitors but the claim form was never received. The defendant issued an application to set aside the order extending time for service and to strike out the claim.

HELD: The only reason for the failure to serve the claim form within the four-month period was the incompetence of the claimant's solicitors. Where the only reason for failure to serve was incompetence this was a powerful reason for refusing to grant an extension of time. The defendant's appeal was allowed.

The court considered the principles by which it should be determined whether an application to extend the time for service of a claim form should be granted where the application was made within the period for serving the claim form specified by CPR 7.5 and the claim had become statute barred within that period. The court's power to grant an extension of time under CPR 7.6(2) could not have been intended to be construed as being subject to a condition that a 'good reason' had to be shown for failure to serve within the specified period, and the court's power had to be exercised in accordance with the overriding objective. However, the reason for the failure to serve within the specified period was a highly material factor and 'the weaker the reason, the more likely the court [would] be to refuse to grant the extension'.

[22.45]   Glass v Surrendran

[2006] EWCA Civ 20

[2006] All ER (D) 177 (Jan), [2006] 1 WLR 1945

The claim form was issued on 3 September 2004. The claimant's solicitor applied to extend time for service 13 days before the four-month period expired. The application was dealt with by the court on 4 January 2006 and was refused. The claimant applied to set aside this order and for a further extension, which was granted. The defendant then applied to set aside the order extending time. The application was dismissed both at first instance and on appeal.

HELD, ON APPEAL: There was no justification for the delay in serving the claim form. Although the claimant's solicitors were awaiting receipt of an accountant's report before serving the claim form, the appropriate application would have been to extend the time for service of the particulars of claim and not the claim form. The defendant's appeal was allowed.

[22.46]   Dickins v Solicitors Indemnity Fund

[2005] EWHC 2754 (Ch)

[2005] All ER (D) 298 (Oct)

The claimant issued a claim form on 25 October 2004, three days prior to the expiration of the limitation period. On the day before the validity of the claim form for service expired, the claimant issued a without notice application seeking an extension of time for validity of four months, on the basis that he was not yet able to quantify his claim. The master took the view that the claimant was in a position to serve the claim form that day, but agreed to make an order extending time, not by four months but by seven days. On appeal, the judge asked himself whether it would be unjust to set aside the order of the master, and concluded that it would be. The defendant appealed.

HELD, ON APPEAL: The issue which should have been considered was whether the claimant should have been granted an extension of time by the master. If it was right that there was no justification for an extension of four months, then there was no justification for an extension of seven days.

[22.47]   **Leeson v Marsden and United Bristol Health Care NHS Trust**

[2006] EWCA Civ 20

[2006] All ER (D) 177 (Jan), [2006] I WLR 1945

The claim form was issued on 24 November 2003, three days before the expiry of the limitation period. The claimant obtained a retrospective extension of time for service of the claim form until 15 April 2004. The claim form was served on 8 April 2004. The defendant applied to set aside the order extending time for service and for a declaration that the claim form had been served out of time.

HELD: There was no good reason for the claimant's solicitors' failure to serve the claim form before 24 March 2004. The failure of the defendant to respond to a letter of claim was not a reason for the failure to serve the claim form. In the court's view the claimant's solicitors had not acted reasonably and quickly when applying to extend time. *Hashtroodi v Hancock* (at para [22.44]) required the court to determine and evaluate the reason why the claim form was not served within the specified time period. If there was no reason to justify the failure to serve the claim form in time then it was not necessary to go through the checklist under CPR 1.1(2). If 'there is no reason, or only a very weak reason, for not serving the claim form in time, the court is most unlikely to grant an extension of time'.

[22.48]

CPR 7.7 – APPLICATION BY DEFENDANT FOR SERVICE OF CLAIM FORM
(1)   Where a claim form has been issued against a defendant, but has not yet been served on him, the defendant may serve a notice on the claimant requiring him to serve the claim form or discontinue the claim within a period specified in the notice.
(2)   The period specified in a notice served under paragraph (1) must be at least 14 days after service of the notice.
(3)   If the claimant fails to comply with the notice, the court may, on the application of the defendant–
　　(a)   dismiss the claim; or
　　(b)   make any other order it thinks just.

(C)   EXTENDING TIME FOR SERVICE OF PARTICULARS OF CLAIM

[22.49]

CPR 7.4 – PARTICULARS OF CLAIM
(1)   Particulars of claim must–
　　(a)   be contained in or served with the claim form; or
　　(b)   subject to paragraph (2) be served on the defendant by the claimant within 14 days after service of the claim form.
(2)   Particulars of claim must be served on the defendant no later than the latest time for serving a claim form.
(3)   Where the claimant serves particulars of claim separately from the claim form in accordance with paragraph (1)(b), he must, within 7 days of service on the defendant, file a copy of the particulars together with a certificate of service.

[22.50]

CPR 7.8 – FORM FOR DEFENCE ETC. MUST BE SERVED WITH PARTICULARS
OF CLAIM
(1)   When particulars of claim are served on a defendant, whether they
are contained in the claim form, served with it or served subsequently, they
must be accompanied by–
    (a)   a form for defending the claim;
    (b)   a form for admitting the claim; and
    (c)   a form for acknowledging service.
(2)   Where the claimant is using the procedure set out in Part 8 (alternative procedure for claims)–
    (a)   paragraph (1) does not apply; and
    (b)   a form for acknowledging service must accompany the claim form.

CPR 7.6 DOES NOT APPLY TO PARTICULARS OF CLAIM

[22.51]   Totty v Snowden
[2001] EWCA Civ 1415
[2001] 4 All ER 577, [2002] 1 WLR 1384

On 28 September 1999, one day before the expiry of the limitation period, the
claim form was issued. Two days before the expiry of the four-month currency of
the claim form, the claimant's solicitors served the claim form. Fourteen days later
they served the particulars of claim. The defendant applied to strike out the claim
on the basis this was in breach of CPR 7.4(2) which states the particulars of claim
have to be served on the defendant no later than the latest time for serving a claim
form.

HELD, ON APPEAL: The court had no discretion to extend time for serving the claim
form after the period set down in CPR 7.5(2) unless the conditions stipulated in
CPR 7.6(3) were fulfilled. However, the court did not accept that the particulars of
claim were an integral part of the claim form, and so held that CPR 7.6(1) did not
apply to the particulars of claim. As there were no express words to prevent
consideration of the overriding objective, the court had discretion to consider the
circumstances having regard to the overriding objective. Accordingly, a retrospective extension of time for service of the particulars of claim was granted.

COURT'S REGARD TO THE OVERRIDING OBJECTIVE WHEN CONSIDERING
APPLICATIONS MADE BEFORE THE EXPIRY OF THE TIME PERIOD FOR
SERVICE OF PARTICULARS OF CLAIM

[22.52]   Robert v Momentum Services Ltd
[2003] EWCA Civ 299
[2003] 2 All ER 74, [2003] 1 WLR 1577

The claim form was issued on 1 March 2001 and served without the particulars of
claim. On 13 June 2001 the claimant applied for an extension of time pursuant to
CPR 3.1(2)(a) for service of the particulars of claim as the claimant had not yet
obtained her medical evidence. Her application was granted at first instance and
refused on subsequent appeal.

HELD, ON APPEAL: CPR 3.1(2)(a) contained no list of criteria for the exercise of discretion to grant an extension of time. This was in contrast to CPR 7.6 and CPR 3.9. The court had no doubt this was deliberate and 'saw no reason to import the CPR 3.9(1) checklist by implication into CPR 3.1(2)(a) where an application for an extension is made before the expiry of the relevant time period'. 'By not spelling out a checklist in CPR 3.1(2)(a) ... the draftsman's intention was for the court to exercise their discretion simply by having regard to the overriding objective'.

Appeal allowed.

COURT'S REGARD TO THE CPR 3.9 CHECKLIST WHEN CONSIDERING APPLICATIONS MADE AFTER THE EXPIRY OF THE TIME PERIOD FOR SERVICE OF PARTICULARS OF CLAIM

[22.53]   **Price v Price (t/a Poppyland Headware)**

[2003] EWCA Civ 888

[2003] 3 All ER 911

The claimant sustained injury during the course of his employment with the defendant. A claim form was issued on 4 April 2001 without any particulars of claim, medical report or schedule of loss. The claimant made an application to extend time in respect of service of these documents, but not until 14 months had elapsed following the time period within which he should have filed and served the documents. The delay was in large part due to the claimant obtaining medical evidence with which he was not satisfied, and then seeking the advice of an alternative expert. This second expert supported a claim of dramatically different value than that which would have been presented had the first medical expert's evidence been filed with the claim form.

HELD, ON APPEAL: The claimant was in serious default in relation to his duty to help the court deal with the case fairly. The defendant had complied with its duty. In applying the CPR 3.9 checklist, the relief that the claimant sought should be granted, but the interests of justice demanded that the claimant's claim should be restricted in value to that which could have been established had the claimant complied with the rules in April 2001.

6.   SERVICE OUT OF THE JURISDICTION

[22.54]   Reference should be made to Chapter 20 (at para [20.22]), which sets out the procedure in respect of motor claims arising in EU Member States.

Claims in respect of general torts committed outside the UK and motor claims arising outside EU territory are matters beyond the scope of this book, and reference should be made to *The Civil Court Practice* published by Lexis Nexis Butterworths.

7.   CERTIFICATE OF SERVICE

[22.55]

CPR 6.14 – CERTIFICATE OF SERVICE RELATING TO THE CLAIM FORM
(1)   Where a claim form is served by the court, the court must send the claimant a notice which will include the date when the claim form is deemed to be served under rule 6.7.
(2)   Where the claim form is served by the claimant–
    (a)   he must file a certificate of service within 7 days of service of the claim form; and
    (b)   he may not obtain judgment in default under Part 12 unless he has filed the certificate of service.

[22.56]

CPR 6.10 – CERTIFICATE OF SERVICE

Where a rule, practice direction or court order requires a certificate of service, the certificate must state the details set out in the following table.

Method of service	Details to be certified
Post	Date of posting
Personal	Date of personal service
Document exchange	Date of delivery to the document exchange
Delivery of document to or leaving it at a permitted place	Date when the document was delivered to or left at the permitted place
Fax	Date and time of transmission
Other electronic means	Date of transmission and the means used
Alternative method permitted by the court	As required by the court

CHAPTER 23

Defence

1. RESPONDING TO PARTICULARS OF CLAIM

(A) GENERALLY

[23.1]

CPR 9.1 – RESPONDING TO PARTICULARS OF CLAIM – GENERAL
(1) This Part sets out how a defendant may respond to particulars of claim.
(2) Where the defendant receives a claim form which states that particulars of claim are to follow, he need not respond to the claim until the particulars of claim have been served on him.

[23.2]

CPR 9.2 – DEFENCE, ADMISSION, OR ACKNOWLEDGEMENT OF SERVICE

When particulars of claim are served on a defendant, the defendant may -
  (a) file or serve an admission in accordance with Part 14;
  (b) file a defence in accordance with Part 15,

(or do both, if he admits only part of the claim); or
  (c) file an acknowledgment of service in accordance with Part 10.

(B) ACKNOWLEDGEMENT OF SERVICE

[23.3]

CPR 10.1 – ACKNOWLEDGEMENT OF SERVICE
(1) This Part deals with the procedure for filing an acknowledgment of service.
(2) Where the claimant uses the procedure set out in Part 8 (alternative procedure for claims) this Part applies subject to the modifications set out in rule 8.3.
(3) A defendant may file an acknowledgment of service if–
  (a) he is unable to file a defence within the period specified in rule 15.4; or
  (b) he wishes to dispute the court's jurisdiction.

[23.4]

CPR 10.5 – CONTENTS OF ACKNOWLEDGMENT OF SERVICE
(1) An acknowledgment of service must–
  (a) be signed by the defendant or his legal representative; and
  (b) include the defendants' address for service.

[23.5]

CPR 10.2 – CONSEQUENCES OF NOT FILING AN ACKNOWLEDGEMENT OF SERVICE

If–

(a)   a defendant fails to file an acknowledgment of service within the period specified in rule 10.3; and
(b)   does not within that period file a defence in accordance with Part 15 or serve or file an admission in accordance with Part 14,

the claimant may obtain default judgment if Part 12 allows it.

[23.6]

CPR 10.3 – THE PERIOD FOR FILING AN ACKNOWLEDGEMENT OF SERVICE
(1)   The general rule is that the period for filing an acknowledgment of service is–
    (a)   where the defendant is served with a claim form which states that particulars of claim are to follow, 14 days after service of the particulars of claim; and
    (b)   in any other case, 14 days after service of the claim form.
(2)   The general rule is subject to the following rules–
    (a)   rule 6.22 (which specifies how the period for filing an acknowledgment of service is calculated where the claim form is served out of the jurisdiction);
    (b)   rule 6.16(4) (which requires the court to specify the period for responding to the particulars of claim when it makes an order under that rule); and
    (c)   rule 6.21(4) (which requires the court to specify the period within which the defendant may file an acknowledgment of service calculated by reference to Practice Direction 6B when it makes an order giving permission to serve a claim form out of the jurisdiction).

[23.7]   Roberts v Luton & Dunstable Hospital NHS Trust

[2000] CLY 610

The claimant served a claim form but failed to serve particulars of claim. The defendant applied to strike out the claimant's claim.

HELD: The claimant's submission that the defendant could not bring an application to strike out the claim because no acknowledgement of service had been filed was not accepted. CPR 10.3(1)(a) clearly stated that an acknowledgement was to be filed 14 days after service of the particulars of claim. Where no particulars of claim had been served, time did not run.

Note—For the position regarding service of particulars of claim, see *Totty v Snowden* (at para [22.51]).

2.   DEFAULT JUDGMENT

(A)   BASIS FOR SEEKING A DEFAULT JUDGMENT

[23.8]

CPR 12.1 – MEANING OF 'DEFAULT JUDGMENT'

In these Rules, 'default judgment' means judgment without trial where a defendant–

(a)   has failed to file an acknowledgment of service; or

(b)   has failed to file a defence.

[23.9]

CPR 12.3 – CONDITIONS TO BE SATISFIED

(1)   The claimant may obtain judgment in default of an acknowledgment of service only if–

    (a)   the defendant has not filed an acknowledgment of service or a defence to the claim (or any part of the claim); and

    (b)   the relevant time for doing so has expired.

(2)   Judgment in default of defence may be obtained only–

    (a)   where an acknowledgement of service has been filed but a defence has not been filed;

    (b)   in a counterclaim made under rule 20.4, where a defence has not been filed,

and, in either case, the relevant time limit for doing so has expired.

(3)   The claimant may not obtain a default judgment if–

    (a)   the defendant has applied–

        (i)   to have the claimant's statement of case struck out under rule 3.4; or

        (ii)   for summary judgment under Part 24,

    and, in either case, that application has not been disposed of;

    (b)   the defendant has satisfied the whole claim (including any claim for costs) on which the claimant is seeking judgment; or

    (c)

        (i)   the claimant is seeking judgment on a claim for money; and

        (ii)   the defendant has filed or served on the claimant an admission under rule 14.4 or 14.7 (admission of liability to pay all of the money claimed) together with a request for time to pay.

[23.10]   Coll v Tattum

[2001] All ER (D) 320 (Nov), (2001) Times, 3 December

The claimant applied for judgment in default, but prior to the hearing the defendant filed an acknowledgement of service and a defence.

HELD: Refusing the claimant's application, the issue was not covered by the Civil Procedure Rules (CPR). In a case when no application for default judgment had been made, the court would generally accept the late acknowledgement of service or defence. Here, the issue of whether to grant the claimant's application for judgment in default was a matter for the court's discretion, which would usually be exercised to extend time for service with an order for at least some costs against the defendant, where there was a bona fide defence. However, if the application had been made after the late acknowledgement of service or the defence had been served, then it could be refused with costs.

[23.11]   Boeing Capital Corp v Wells Fargo Bank and Another

[2003] EWHC 1364

The claimant applied for judgment in default, in circumstances where an acknowledgement of service had not been filed. The defendant applied for an adjournment.

HELD: The court was likely to permit a late filing of an acknowledgement of service, but only in circumstances where there was a genuine defence which could be brought against the claim. Since there was no defence to the claim the defendant's application for an adjournment was denied.

(B)   PROCEDURE

[23.12]

CPR 12.4 – PROCEDURE FOR OBTAINING DEFAULT JUDGMENT
   (1)   Subject to paragraph (2), a claimant may obtain a default judgment by filing a request in the relevant practice form where the claim is for–
      (a)   a specified amount of money;
      (b)   an amount of money to be decided by the court;
      (c)   …
      (d)   …
   (2)   The claimant must make an application in accordance with Part 23 if he wishes to obtain a default judgment–
      (a)   on a claim which consists of or includes a claim for any other remedy; or
      (b)   where rule 12.9 or rule 12.10 so provides,
   and where the defendant is an individual, the claimant must provide the defendant's date of birth (if known) in Part C of the application notice.
   (3)   …
   (4)   In civil proceedings against the Crown, as defined in rule 66.1(2), a request for a default judgment must be considered by a Master or district judge, who must in particular be satisfied that the claim form and particulars of claim have been properly served on the Crown in accordance with section 18 of the Crown Proceedings Act 1947 and rule 6.5(8).

[23.13]

CPR 12.10 – CIRCUMSTANCES WHERE AN APPLICATION MUST BE MADE

The claimant must make an application in accordance with Part 23 where–
   (a)   the claim is–
      (i)   a claim against a child or patient; or
      (ii)   a claim in tort by one spouse or civil partner against the other.
   (b)   he wishes to obtain a default judgment where the defendant has failed to file an acknowledgment of service–
      (i)   against a defendant who has been served with the claim out of the jurisdiction under rule 6.19(1) or (1A); (service without leave under the Civil Jurisdiction and Judgments Act 1982(4));
      (ii)   against a defendant domiciled in Scotland or Northern Ireland or in any other Convention territory or Regulation State;
      (iii)   against a State;
      (iv)   against a diplomatic agent who enjoys immunity from civil jurisdiction by virtue of the Diplomatic Privileges Act 1964(5); or
      (v)   against persons or organisations who enjoy immunity from civil jurisdiction pursuant to the provisions of the International Organisations Acts 1968 and 1981(6).

[23.14]

CPR 12.5 – NATURE OF JUDGMENT WHERE DEFAULT JUDGMENT OBTAINED
BY FILING A REQUEST
(1) Where the claim is for a specified sum of money, the claimant may
specify in a request filed under rule 12.4(1)–
    (a) the date by which the whole of the judgment debt is to be paid; or
    (b) the times and rate at which it is to be paid by instalments.
(2) Except where paragraph (4) applies, a default judgment on a claim
for a specified amount of money obtained on the filing of a request, will
be judgment for the amount of the claim (less any payments made) and
costs–
    (a) to be paid by the date or at the rate specified in the request for
        judgment; or
    (b) if none is specified, immediately.
(3) Where the claim is for an unspecified amount of money a default
judgment obtained on the filing of a request will be for an amount to be
decided by the court and costs.
(4) ...

[23.15]

CPR 12.8 – CLAIM AGAINST MORE THAN ONE DEFENDANT
(1) A claimant may obtain a default judgment on request under this Part
on a claim for money ...against one of two or more defendants, and
proceed with his claim against the other defendants.
(2) Where a claimant applies for a default judgment against one of two
or more defendants–
    (a) if the claim can be dealt with separately from the claim against the
        other defendants–
        (i) the court may enter a default judgment against that defend-
            ant; and
        (ii) the claimant may continue the proceedings against the other
            defendants;
    (b) if the claim cannot be dealt with separately from the claim against
        the other defendants–
        (i) the court will not enter default judgment against that defend-
            ant; and
        (ii) the court must deal with the application at the same time as it
            disposes of the claim against the other defendants.
(3) ...

(C) SUBSEQUENT PROCEDURAL STEPS

[23.16]

CPR 27 – PROCEDURE FOR DECIDING AN AMOUNT OR VALUE
(1) This rule applies where the claimant obtains a default judgment on
the filing of a request under rule 12.4(1) and judgment is for–
    (a) an amount of money to be decided by the court;
    (b) the value of goods to be decided by the court; or
    (c) an amount of interest to be decided by the court.

(2) Where the court enters judgment it will–
   (a) give any directions it considers appropriate; and
   (b) if it considers it appropriate, allocate the case.

[23.17]

CPR 12.6 – ENTITLEMENT TO INTEREST ON DAMAGES
(1) A default judgment on a claim for a specified amount of money obtained on the filing of a request may include the amount of interest claimed to the date of judgment if–
   (a) the particulars of claim include the details required by rule 16.4;
   (b) where interest is claimed under section 35A of the Supreme Court Act 1981(2) or section 69 of the County Courts Act 1984(3), the rate is no higher than the rate of interest payable on judgment debts at the date when the claim form was issued; and
   (c) the claimant's request for judgment includes a calculation of the interest claimed for the period from the date up to which interest was stated to be calculated in the claim form to the date of the request for judgment.
(2) In any case where paragraph (1) does not apply, judgment will be for an amount of interest to be decided by the court.

3. SETTING ASIDE OR VARYING DEFAULT JUDGMENT

(A) DEFAULT JUDGMENTS SET ASIDE AS OF RIGHT

[23.18]

CPR 13.2 – CASES WHERE THE COURT MUST SET ASIDE JUDGMENT ENTERED UNDER PART 12

The court must set aside a judgment entered under Part 12 if judgment was wrongly entered because–
   (a) in the case of a judgment in default of an acknowledgment of service, any of the conditions in rule 12.3(1) and 12.3(3) was not satisfied;
   (b) in the case of a judgment in default of a defence, any of the conditions in rule 12.3(2) and 12.3(3) was not satisfied; or
   (c) the whole of the claim was satisfied before judgment was entered.

[23.19] Credit Agricole Indosuez v Unicof Ltd

[2002] EWHC 77 (Comm)

[2003] All ER (D) 21 (Feb)

The claimant entered judgment under CPR 12. The ninth defendant applied to set aside the judgment, on three grounds:
- the proceedings had not been served upon it;
- the judgment should be set aside under CPR 13.3 in any event as the ninth defendant had a reasonable prospect of successfully defending the claim, and;
- the claimant had obtained permission to serve out of the jurisdiction on the basis of untrue evidence.

HELD: CPR 13.2(a) compelled the court to set aside judgment in default where the conditions set out in CPR 12.3(1) were not satisfied, namely that the defendant had not filed an acknowledgement of service and that the time for doing so had expired. Since the claim form had not been served upon the defendant, time had not begun to run for the purposes of CPR 10.3, and therefore the conditions of CPR 12.3(1) were not satisfied.

(B) THE COURT'S DISCRETION TO SET ASIDE OR VARY DEFAULT JUDGMENTS

[23.20]

CPR 13.3 – CASES WHERE THE COURT MAY SET ASIDE OR VARY JUDGMENT ENTERED UNDER PART 12
 (1) In any other case, the court may set aside or vary a judgment entered under Part 12 if–
  (a) the defendant has a real prospect of successfully defending the claim; or
  (b) it appears to the court that there is some other good reason why–
   (i) the judgment should be set aside or varied; or
   (ii) the defendant should be allowed to defend the claim.
 (2) In considering whether to set aside or vary a judgment entered under Part 12, the matters to which the court must have regard include whether the person seeking to set aside the judgment made an application to do so promptly.

JUDGMENT WHERE THE DEFENDANT HAS NO NOTICE OF PROCEEDINGS IS A REGULAR JUDGMENT

[23.21] Akram v Adam
[2004] EWCA Civ 1601
[2005] 1 All ER 741, [2005] 1 WLR 2762

A claim form and particulars of claim were served on the defendant at his last known place of residence, by first class post. The defendant did not come to be aware of the proceedings until he returned to the address to find a warrant for possession had been executed. He applied for judgment in default to be set aside. The court at first instance found, given the circumstances, that proceedings had not been properly served.

HELD: There was a difference between a default judgment wrongly entered and any other default judgment, and the latter could only be set aside if the conditions set out in CPR 13.3(1) were satisfied. A judgment entered where the defendant had no notice of the proceedings was therefore a regular judgment, provided that the claimant had complied with the rules. Accordingly, the defendant would need to apply under CPR 13.3 rather than under CPR 12.

THE TEST (1) – DEFENDANT MUST ESTABLISH 'A REAL PROSPECT OF SUCCESS'

[23.22] Swain v Hillman
[2001] 1 All ER 91

HELD, ON APPEAL: The correct test was whether the defendant had a defence which had a real prospect of success. The use of the word 'real' directed the court to the need to see whether there was a 'realistic' rather than a 'fanciful' prospect of success.

[23.23]   International Finance Corpn v Utexafrica Sprl

[2001] All ER (D) 101 (May), [2001] CLC 1361

The defendant applied to set aside a judgment in default.

HELD: The phrase in CPR 13(3)(1)(a) – 'real prospect of successfully defending the claim' – had the same meaning as in *The Saudi Eagle* [1986] 2 Lloyd's Rep 221. A case which had a real prospect of success was one which was better than merely arguable. There was a significant difference between a defence which had no realistic prospect of success and one which had a real prospect of success. Something more than a 'merely arguable' case was needed to tip the balance of justice in favour of setting the judgment aside.

[23.24]   ED & F Man Liquid Products v Patel

[2003] EWCA Civ 472

[2003] All ER (D) 75 (Apr)

The first defendant's application to set aside judgment in default of acknow-ledgement of service was rejected on the basis there was no real prospect of a successful defence. The first defendant appealed.

HELD, ON APPEAL: The test for setting aside a judgment in default under CPR 13.3(1) was whether the defendant had a real prospect of success. This was similar to the test in CPR 24.2, the distinction being the burden of proof was on the claimant to prove the defendant had no real prospect of successfully defending in the latter, and on the defendant to prove he had a good reason to set aside the judgment in the former. The test 'real prospect of success' meant that the defence sought to be argued must carry some degree of conviction, as opposed to a case which was merely arguable as under the old rules. The court should not conduct a mini-trial but it was not obliged to accept all assertions of fact by a party without question.

THE TEST (2) – DEFENDANT MUST SHOW 'SOME OTHER GOOD REASON'

[23.25]   Manx Electricity Authority v JP Morgan Chase Bank

[2002] EWHC 867 (Comm)

[2002] All ER (D) 187 (May)

The defendant applied to set aside judgment in default. The defendant had clearly not received the claim form and particulars of claim. The conduct of the claimant gave no notice of the proceedings to the defendant other than the original letter of claim, and no notice was given of the intention to seek judgment in default.

HELD: Judgment was set aside. It was unreasonable to conclude that the defendant was content not to respond and have judgment in default entered against it. The CPR was not intended to enable a party to obtain a benefit from a judgment obtained in inappropriate circumstances.

APPLICATION MUST BE MADE 'PROMPTLY'

[23.26] **Manolakaki v Constantinides**

[2003] EWHC 401 (Ch)

[2003] All ER (D) 95 (Mar)

The defendant appealed from an order rejecting his application to set aside judgment in default.

HELD: Although in the instant case the application to set aside was found to have been made promptly for the purpose of CPR 13.3(2), even if such an application was not made promptly for the purposes of the Rule, it would be unjust to deprive a defendant who had a reasonable prospect of defending the claim the opportunity to do so simply because of delay in issuing an application to set aside promptly.

[23.27] **Ali v Car Nation**

[2004] CLY 225

A defendant, six months after admitting liability, obtained a favourable expert's report, and applied to resile from the admission, or alternatively set aside a judgment in default obtained by the claimant two months after the expert report was obtained.

HELD: The defendant had failed to act promptly in the six-month period in attempting to resile from the admission, and in the two-month period before making the application to set aside the judgment in default. There would be prejudice to the claimant and the application was rejected.

[23.28] **MacDonald v Thorn plc**

(1999) Times, 15 October, CA

Proceedings were issued on 7 January 1999 and served on the defendant at its registered office. The defendant failed to serve its defence and judgment in default of a defence was entered on 29 January 1999. The defendant instructed solicitors on 1 February 1999 and a notice of acting was sent to the claimants' solicitors. The defendant applied to have the judgment set aside on 10 February 1999. The defendant's application was dismissed by the district judge on 16 March 1999 on the ground that there had been delay by the defendant before the issue of proceedings for which the defendant had offered no explanation. The defendant appealed but the circuit judge dismissed the appeal.

The defendant appealed contending that the judge was wrong in law in holding that unexplained or substantially unexplained delay before issue of the claim form was a relevant factor in deciding whether to set aside the default judgment.

HELD: (1) It was clear that the judge had not been directed to the Court of Appeal decision of *Mortgage Corpn v Sandoes* (1997) 141 Sol Jo LB 30.

    (2)   The judge was not entitled to add together the nine-day period of delay and the pre-action delay. Bearing in mind that the defendant had established that the defence had real prospects of success, the preju-dice caused to the claimants was minimal and the period of delay, even

though unexplained, amounted to nine days, and the court was of the opinion that justice demanded that the default judgment be set aside.

SETTING ASIDE JUDGMENT WITH CONDITIONS

[23.29]   **Lloyds Investment (Scandinavia) Ltd v Agerr-Hansen**
(7 January 2001, unreported)

The defendant applied to set aside a judgment in default.

HELD: Judgment was set aside following a consideration of the defendant's explanation for the delay in filing a defence, noting that a draft defence was served promptly after the defendant had discovered the need to do so. The court considered the merits of the case and found that the defendant had a real prospect of success for the purposes of the CPR. Nevertheless questions remained about the credibility of the defendant's evidence, and so judgment was set aside on the basis that 50% of the value of the claimant's claim was paid into court.

[23.30]   **Osbourne v Leighton**
(30 April 1999, unreported)

The judge was entitled to order the claimant to pay the defendant's costs on an indemnity basis of her application to set aside a judgment which had been irregularly obtained.

(C)   PROCEDURE

[23.31]

CPR 13.4 – APPLICATION TO SET ASIDE OR VARY JUDGMENT – PROCEDURE

13.4
  (1)   Where–
    (a)   the claim is for a specified amount of money;
    (b)   the judgment was obtained in a court which is not the defendant's home court;
    (c)   the claim has not been transferred to another defendant's home court under rule 14.12 (admission – determination of rate of payment by judge) or rule 26.2 (automatic transfer); and
    (d)   the defendant is an individual
  the court will transfer an application by a defendant under this Part to set aside or vary judgment to the defendant's home court.
  (1A)   Omitted
  (2)   Paragraph (1) does not apply where the claim was commenced in a specialist list.
  (3)   An application under rule 13.3 (cases where the court may set aside or vary judgment) must be supported by evidence.

13.5   Omitted

4 ADMISSIONS

(A)   CPR PT 14

[23.32]

CPR 14.1 – MAKING AN ADMISSION
(1)   A party may admit the truth of the whole or any part of another party's case.
(2)   He may do this by giving notice in writing (such as in a statement of case or by letter).
(3)   Where the only remedy which the claimant is seeking is the payment of money, the defendant may also make an admission in accordance with–
    (a)   rule 14.4 (admission of whole claim for specified amount of money);
    (b)   rule 14.5 (admission of part of claim for specified amount of money);
    (c)   rule 14.6 (admission of liability to pay whole of claim for unspecified amount of money); or
    (d)   rule 14.7 (admission of liability to pay claim for unspecified amount of money where defendant offers a sum in satisfaction of the claim).
(4)   Where the defendant makes an admission as mentioned in paragraph (3), the claimant has a right to enter judgment except where–
    (a)   the defendant is a child or patient; or
    (b)   the claimant is a child or patient and the admission is made under rule 14.5 or 14.7.
(5)   The court may allow a party to amend or withdraw an admission.

[23.33]

CPR 14.2 – PERIOD FOR MAKING AN ADMISSION
(1)   The period ... is–
    (a)   where the defendant is served with a claim form which states that particulars of claim will follow, 14 days after service of the particulars; and
    (b)   in any other case, 14 days after service of the claim form.
(2)   Paragraph (1) is subject to the following rules–
    (a)   rule 6.22 (which specifies how the period for filing or returning an admission is calculated where the claim form is served out of the jurisdiction); and
    (b)   rule 6.16(4) (which requires the court to specify the period for responding to the particulars of claim when it makes an order under that rule).
(3)   A defendant may return an admission ... or file it ... after the end of the period for returning or filing it specified in paragraph (1) if the claimant has not obtained default judgment under Part 12.
(4)   If he does so, this Part shall apply as if he had made the admission within that period.

[23.34]

CPR 14.3 – Admission by notice in writing – application
for judgment
(1)   Where a party makes an admission under rule 14.1(2) (admission by
notice in writing), any other party may apply for judgment on the
admission.
(2)   Judgment shall be such judgment as it appears to the court that the
applicant is entitled to on the admission.

Note—Rules 14.4 to 14.7 are not set out – reference should be made to *The Civil Court
Practice*, published by LexisNexis Butterworths.

[23.35]

CPR 14.8 – Allocation of claims in relation to
outstanding matters

Where the court enters judgment … for an amount to be decided by the court it
will–
(a)   give any directions it considers appropriate; and
(b)   if it considers it appropriate, allocate the case.

(B)   THE PRESUMPTION THAT AN ADMISSION IS BINDING IN
FAST TRACK CLAIMS

[23.36]

Pre-action Protocol for Personal Injury Claims, paragraph 3.9
3.9   Where **liability is admitted**, the presumption is that the defendant will
be bound by this admission for all claims with a total value of up to
£15,000. Where the claimant's investigation indicates that the value of the
claim has increased to more than £15,000 since the letter of claim, the
claimant should notify the defendant as soon as possible.

(C)   APPLICATIONS TO WITHDRAW AN ADMISSION

Evidential burden on party seeking to withdraw admission

[23.37]   Walsh v Liverpool City Council
(2004) CLW, 19 November

The court considered the interplay between paragraph 3.9 of the Pre-action
Protocol for Personal Injury Claims (the presumption that admissions are binding
where the claim does not exceed £15,000) and CPR 14.1(5) (which permits a
party to withdraw an admission).

HELD: The presumption set out in paragraph 3.9 of the Protocol placed the burden upon the party attempting to withdraw the admission to show why the court should disapply the presumption, and prejudice to the claimant would be a relevant consideration.

TEST TO BE APPLIED

[23.38] **Braybrook v Basildon and Thurrock University NHS Trust**
[2004] EWHC 3352 (QB)
[2005] All ER (D) 320 (Apr), QB

A defendant applied to withdraw an admission.

HELD: When considering a defendant's application to withdraw an admission, the court should conduct the exercise of discretion by considering all the circumstances of the case, and in particular should consider the following issues:
  (1)   whether the application has been made in good faith;
  (2)   the reasons and justification for the application;
  (3)   the balance of prejudice;
  (4)   whether a party has been the cause of any prejudice it has suffered;
  (5)   the prospects of success of any issue arising from the withdrawal of an admission; and
  (6)   whether the withdrawal of the admission will result in further litigation and a consequent impact on the resources of the court.
Furthermore, the nearer in time that the application was to the trial date, the less likely it was that the application would succeed, even if prejudice to the applying party could be shown. This could be a decisive consideration if the application was made only shortly before the final hearing.

[23.39] **Barnard v Sappi Europe Ltd**
[2005] EWHC 2169 (QB)
[2005] All ER (D) 223 (Jul)

The defendant applied to withdraw an admission.

HELD: Although the defendant sought to withdraw the admission within a few months of it being made, it was not a short time in relation to the claimant, who was dying from mesothelioma. It was not clear why the admission had originally been made, but to allow it to be withdrawn would represent serious prejudice to the claimant. Furthermore, allowing the defendant to withdraw the admission could deprive the claimant of a trial within his lifetime.

[23.40] **Burden v Harrods Ltd**
[2005] EWHC 410

The defendant applied to withdraw from an admission of primary liability. The claimant argued that correspondence amounted to a binding compromise.

HELD: There was little case law to assist in deciding an issue regarding the interplay between CPR Pt 14 and the law on binding compromise. The fact that the defendant, which now sought to withdraw an admission, had stated in the letter making its admission that it had completed 'preliminary' enquiries indicated it was happy to settle despite its enquiries being incomplete. Later correspondence did not refer to the issue and the defendant did not seek to withdraw the admission for over two years. Permission to withdraw was denied.

[23.41] Sowerby v Charlton

[2005] EWCA Civ 1610

[2005] All ER (D) 343 (Dec), [2006] 1 WLR 568, CA

HELD, ON APPEAL: CPR 14 does not apply to an admission made before the issue of proceedings. CPR 14.1(1) stated that 'a party may admit the truth of the whole or a part of another party's case', which case could not be formulated until proceedings were issued. It was also clear that the pre-action protocol did not intend pre-litigation admissions to be binding for multi-track cases. Accordingly, in a multi-track case, the court was not concerned to control the withdrawal of an admission made before proceedings. However, on the facts, the defendant was likely to be considered at least partly liable for the injury and summary judgment was granted on primary liability.

The majority decision in *Gale v Superdrug Stores plc* [1996] 3 All ER 468, [1996] 1 WLR 1089 was held to be unreliable in light of the introduction of the CPR.

Note—Until *Sowerby v Charlton*, the courts had dealt with applications for permission to withdraw an admission in accordance with the majority decision in *Gale v Superdrug Stores plc*, even though *Gale* was decided before the introduction of the CPR. The Court of Appeal had held that the discretion to allow a party to withdraw an admission was a general one in which all the circumstances of the case had to be taken into account. A balance was to be struck between the prejudice suffered by one party if the admission was withdrawn, and that suffered by the other if it was allowed to stand. Disappointment suffered by the claimant was to be taken into account but was not a major head of prejudice.

ADMISSION NOT BINDING ON NON-CONTRACTING PARTIES

[23.42] Thomasson v Wilkinson

[2003] CLY 294

The insurer of a motorcyclist in a claim for vehicle damage made a binding admission. The motorcyclist claimed against a second driver involved in the same incident, who argued that the admission should bind him in respect of the second set of proceedings.

HELD: The admission did not bind the motorcyclist in the claim against the second driver involved in the same incident. The admission had not been made by the motorcyclist in response to any letter in the claim by him against the second driver.

CPR PT 14 NOT APPLICABLE FOLLOWING THE ENTRY OF JUDGMENT

[23.43] Baker v Sussex Police Authority

[2001] CLY 548

The defendant had filed a defence admitting liability but alleging contributory negligence. However following an interlocutory hearing at which judgment had been entered by consent, the defendant located favourable witnesses and sought to set the judgment aside.

HELD: CPR Pt 14 applied to proceedings prior to judgment being granted. The judgment was valid and made with the consent of legally represented parties. There was no provision in the CPR which could assist the defendant.

MISTAKE OF LAW

[23.44] **Turton v Helier and Environment Agency**
(1 November 2005, unreported)

The defendant's insurer admitted liability, based on a misunderstanding of the effect of the law following the Court of Appeal judgment in *Mirvahedy v Henley* [2001] EWCA Civ 1749, [2002] QB 769, which was not clear until a later House of Lords judgment ([2003] 2 AC 491, [2003] 2 All ER 401).

HELD: A defendant should be permitted to withdraw an admission in these circumstances. The withdrawal of the admission was not a tactical manoeuvre, and the prejudice suffered by the claimant in allowing the defence to stand (both financial and evidential) was not sufficient to deny the defendant, which had acted meritoriously, the opportunity to defend the claim. The admission was not an admission for the purposes of CPR 14.1.

ADMISSION PERMITTED TO ARGUE ALTERNATIVE DEFENCE

[23.45] **Flaviss v Pauley (t/a Banjax Bike Hire)**
(29 October 2002, unreported)

A defendant had hired an unroadworthy motorcycle to the claimant who lost control, fell and injured himself. The defendant admitted liability following an unsuccessful argument in relation to contributory negligence. It later transpired that the claimant had hired the motorcycle on the basis of a false passport, and the defendant argued that it would not have hired the motorcycle out had it known the truth, and the accident would not have occurred.

HELD: It was held that although it would be unjust and disproportionate to allow the defendant to withdraw the whole admission, the admission could be withdrawn to the extent that was necessary for the defendant to be able to put forward the defence that the contract was illegal as formed.

5. DEFENCE

(A) FILING AND SERVING THE DEFENCE

[23.46]

CPR 15.2 – FILING A DEFENCE

A defendant who wishes to defend all or part of a claim must file a defence.

[23.47]

CPR 15.4 – THE PERIOD FOR FILING A DEFENCE
(1)   The general rule is that the period for filing a defence is–

  (a)   14 days after service of the particulars of claim; or
  (b)   if the defendant files an acknowledgment of service under Part 10,
       28 days after service of the particulars of claim.
 (2)   ...

[23.48]

CPR 15.5 – AGREEMENT EXTENDING THE PERIOD FOR FILING A DEFENCE
 (1)   The defendant and the claimant may agree that the period for filing a
defence specified in rule 15.4 shall be extended by up to 28 days.
 (2)   Where the defendant and the claimant agree to extend the period for
filing a defence, the defendant must notify the court in writing.

[23.49]   SSQ Europe SA v Johann and Backes

(30 November 2001, unreported), QBD

The defendant made an application to challenge the court's jurisdiction outside of
the time period allowed for doing so, having previously been granted an extension
of time for serving a defence.

HELD: An extension of time for service of a defence did not extend the time for
challenging the court's jurisdiction.

[23.50]

CPR 15.6 – SERVICE OF COPY OF DEFENCE

A copy of the defence must be served on every other party.

(B)   CONTENT OF THE DEFENCE

[23.51]

CPR 16.5 – CONTENT OF DEFENCE
 (1)   In his defence, the defendant must state–
  (a)   which of the allegations in the particulars of claim he denies;
  (b)   which allegations he is unable to admit or deny, but which he
       requires the claimant to prove; and
  (c)   which allegations he admits.
 (2)   Where the defendant denies an allegation–
  (a)   he must state his reasons for doing so; and
  (b)   if he intends to put forward a different version of events from that
       given by the claimant, he must state his own version.
 (3)   A defendant who–
  (a)   fails to deal with an allegation; but
  (b)   has set out in his defence the nature of his case in relation to the
       issue to which that allegation is relevant,
shall be taken to require that allegation to be proved.
 (4)   Where the claim includes a money claim, a defendant shall be taken
to require that any allegation relating to the amount of money claimed be
proved unless he expressly admits the allegation.

(5)   Subject to paragraphs (3) and (4), a defendant who fails to deal with an allegation shall be taken to admit that allegation.

(6)   If the defendant disputes the claimant's statement of value under rule 16.3 he must–

(a)   state why he disputes it; and

(b)   if he is able, give his own statement of the value of the claim.

(7)   If the defendant is defending in a representative capacity, he must state what that capacity is.

(8)   If the defendant has not filed an acknowledgment of service under Part 10, he must give an address for service.

[23.52]   **Kearsley v Klarfeld**

[2005] EWCA Civ 1510

[2005] All ER (D) 98 (Dec)

The claimant claimed damages for a whiplash injury following a low velocity road traffic accident. The defendant relied upon both engineering and medical evidence to suggest the claimant's injury could not have been caused by the accident.

HELD, ON APPEAL: 'The defendant does not have to put forward a substantive case of fraud in order to succeed. So long as a defendant follows the rules set out in CPR 16.5 ... there is no need for a substantive plea of fraud or fabrication'.

[23.53]

Practice Direction to CPR 16 – The defence

General

10.1   Rule 16.5 deals with the contents of the defence.

10.2   A defendant should deal with every allegation in accordance with rule 16.5(1) and (2).

10.3   Rule 16.5(3), (4) and (5) sets out the consequences of not dealing with an allegation.

10.4   Where the defendant is an individual, and the claim form does not contain an address at which he resides or carries on business, or contains an incorrect address, the defendant must provide such an address in the defence.

10.5   Where the defendant's address for service is not where he resides or carries on business, he must still provide the address required by paragraph 11.4.

10.6   Any address which is provided for the purpose of these provisions must include a postcode, unless the court orders otherwise. Postcode information may be obtained from www.royalmail.com or the Royal Mail Address Management Guide.

10.7   Where a defendant to a claim or counterclaim is an individual, he must provide his date of birth (if known) in the acknowledgment of service, admission, defence, defence and counterclaim, reply or other response.

Statement of truth

11.1   Part 22 requires a defence to be verified by a statement of truth.

11.2   The form of the statement of truth is as follows:

'[I believe][the defendant believes] that the facts stated in the defence are true.'

11.3   Attention is drawn to rule 32.14 which sets out the consequences of verifying a statement of case containing a false statement without an honest belief in its truth.

[23.54]

Practice Direction to CPR 16 – Matters which must be included in the defence

Personal injury claims

12.1   Where the claim is for personal injuries and the claimant has attached a medical report in respect of his alleged injuries, the defendant should:

(1)   state in his defence whether he—

    (a)   agrees,

    (b)   disputes, or

    (c)   neither agrees nor disputes but has no knowledge of,

    the matters contained in the medical report,

(2)   where he disputes any part of the medical report, give in his defence his reasons for doing so, and

(3)   where he has obtained his own medical report on which he intends to rely, attach it to his defence.

12.2   Where the claim is for personal injuries and the claimant has included a schedule of past and future expenses and losses, the defendant should include in or attach to his defence a counter-schedule stating:

(1)   which of those items he—

    (a)   agrees;

    (b)   disputes, or

    (c)   neither agrees nor disputes but has no knowledge of, and

(2)   where any items are disputes, supplying alternative figures where appropriate.

Other matters

13.1   The defendant must give details of the expiry of any relevant limitation period relied on.

13.2   Rule 37.3 and paragraph 2 of the practice direction which supplements Part 37 contains information about a defence of tender.

13.3   A party may:

(1)   refer in his statement of case to any point of law on which his claim or defence, as the case may be, is based,

(2)   give in his statement of case the name of any witness he proposes to call, and

(3)   attach to or serve with this statement of case a copy of any document which he considers is necessary to his claim or defence, as the case may be (including any expert's report to be filed in accordance with Part 35).

6. REPLY

[23.55]

CPR 15.8 – REPLY TO DEFENCE

If a claimant files a reply to the defence, he must–
    (a)   file his reply when he files his allocation questionnaire; and
    (b)   serve his reply on the other parties at the same time as he files it.

[23.56]

CPR 16.7 – REPLY TO DEFENCE
    (1)   A claimant who does not file a reply to the defence shall not be taken to admit the matters raised in the defence.
    (2)   A claimant who–
        (a)   files a reply to a defence; but
        (b)   fails to deal with a matter raised in the defence, shall be taken to require that matter to be proved.

7. PROCEDURE IN RESPECT OF PROCEEDINGS UNDER CPR PT 8

[23.57]

CPR 8.3 – ACKNOWLEDGEMENT OF SERVICE
    (1)   The defendant must–
        (a)   file an acknowledgment of service in the relevant practice form not more than 14 days after service of the claim form; and
        (b)   serve the acknowledgment of service on the claimant and any other party.
    (2)   The acknowledgment of service must state–
        (a)   whether the defendant contests the claim; and
        (b)   if the defendant seeks a different remedy from that set out in the claim form, what that remedy is.
    (3)   The following rules of Part 10 (acknowledgment of service) apply–
        (a)   rule 10.3(2) (exceptions to the period for filing an acknowledgment of service); and
        (b)   rule 10.5 (contents of acknowledgment of service).
    (4)   Omitted

[23.58]

CPR 8.4 – CONSEQUENCES OF NOT FILING AN ACKNOWLEDGEMENT OF SERVICE
    (1)   This rule applies where–
        (a)   the defendant has failed to file an acknowledgment of service; and
        (b)   the time period for doing so has expired.
    (2)   The defendant may attend the hearing of the claim but may not take part in the hearing unless the court gives permission.

[23.59]

CPR 8.5 – FILING AND SERVING WRITTEN EVIDENCE
(1)   The claimant must file any written evidence on which he intends to rely when he files his claim form.
(2)   The claimant's evidence must be served on the defendant with the claim form.
(3)   A defendant who wishes to rely on written evidence must file it when he files his acknowledgment of service.
(4)   If he does so, he must also, at the same time, serve a copy of his evidence on the other parties.
(5)   The claimant may, within 14 days of service of the defendant's evidence on him, file further written evidence in reply.
(6)   If he does so, he must also, within the same time limit, serve a copy of his evidence on the other parties.
(7)   The claimant may rely on the matters set out in his claim form as evidence under this rule if the claim form is verified by a statement of truth.

[23.60]   **Hormel Foods Corpn v Antilles Landscape Investments NV**

[2003] EWHC 1912 (Ch)

[2003] All ER (D) 104 (Jul)

The claimant issued proceedings under CPR Pt 8 for a declaration. The defendant did not serve an acknowledgement of service within 14 days as required by CPR Pt 8 but instead served a 'home made' defence. The claimant applied for the defence to be struck out for failure to comply with CPR 8.3 and CPR 8.5(3).

HELD: Upon reading the Practice Direction to CPR Pt 8 it was apparent that an informal document, such as a letter, could be used to acknowledge service. The defendant's procedural infringements were minor and un-prejudicial and to deny the defendant an early merits hearing was unjust.

CHAPTER 24

Summary Judgment

1.   SUMMARY JUDGMENT

(A)   GENERALLY

INTRODUCTION

[24.1]   CPR Pt 24 provides for a procedure whereby a claim can be disposed of without the need for a trial, either because the claim has no real prospect of success, or the defendant has no real prospect of establishing a defence to the claim.

Summary disposal is only appropriate in certain circumstances, but where it is appropriate, it can lead to an overall saving in costs and court time.

Practice Direction to CPR Pt 24 – Basis for application for summary judgment

1.3   An application for summary judgment under rule 24.2 may be based on:
   (1)   a point of law (including a question of construction of a document),
   (2)   the evidence which can reasonably be expected to be available at trial or the lack of it, or
   (3)   a combination of these.

(B)   THE TEST – 'NO REAL PROSPECT OF SUCCESS'

[24.2]

CPR 24.2 – GROUNDS FOR SUMMARY JUDGMENT

The court may give summary judgment against a claimant or defendant on the whole of a claim or on a particular issue if–
   (a)   it considers that–
      (i)   that claimant has no real prospect of succeeding on the claim or issue; or
      (ii)   that defendant has no real prospect of successfully defending the claim or issue; and
   (b)   there is no other compelling reason why the case or issue should be disposed of at a trial.

MEANING OF 'REAL PROSPECT OF SUCCESS'

[24.3]   Swain v Hillman
[2001] 1 All ER 91

HELD, ON APPEAL: The correct test was whether the defendant had a defence which had a real prospect of succeeding. The use of the word 'real' directed the court to the need to see whether there was a 'realistic' rather than a 'fanciful' prospect of success; summary judgment would not be granted simply because the court decided success was improbable.

[24.4]   Merelie v Newcastle Primary Care Trust
[2006] EWHC 150 (QB)
[2006] All ER (D) 279 (Feb), QB

The claimant issued proceedings against the defendant Trust in respect of personal injury, specifically psychological injuries, allegedly sustained in the course of her employment. In the course of proceedings the claimant served a witness statement setting out her allegations and describing her alleged symptoms. Both parties instructed psychiatrists who prepared a joint report. The experts agreed that the appropriate diagnosis was obsessive-compulsive personality disorder, that symptoms were unlikely to have arisen by reason of her account of events whilst at work, and that any symptoms suffered which could be attributed to the workplace were insufficient to amount to a recognisable psychiatric condition. The defendant applied for summary judgment on two grounds, firstly that the claimant had no real prospect of success in the light of the joint statement of issues, and secondly that it was not foreseeable to the defendant that she would suffer any injury as a result of any breach of duty on its part.

HELD: It was clear that the claimant had no real prospect of success and could not prove that she had suffered psychiatric injury caused by the breaches of duty she had pleaded. However, she had a real prospect of success in proving that she had suffered mental distress leading to loss of income, and the evolving nature of the law in relation to harassment was such that it would be inappropriate to grant summary judgment. Insofar as the question of foreseeability was concerned, the content of the claimant's witness statement was not conclusive and summary judgment was an inappropriate mechanism for considering the issue – the case should proceed to trial. The defendant's application was dismissed.

(C) TYPES OF PROCEEDINGS IN WHICH SUMMARY JUDGMENT IS AVAILABLE

[24.5]

CPR 24.3 – TYPES OF PROCEEDINGS IN WHICH SUMMARY JUDGMENT IS AVAILABLE

(1)   The court may give summary judgment against a claimant in any type of proceedings.

(2)   The court may give summary judgment against a defendant in any type of proceedings except–
    (a)   proceedings for possession of residential premises against–
        (i)   a mortgagor; or
        (ii)   a tenant or a person holding over after the end of his tenancy whose occupancy is protected within the meaning of the Rent Act 1977 or the Housing Act 1988 and;
    (b)   proceedings for an admiralty claim in rem.
    (c)   Omitted

FACTS MUST BE STRAIGHTFORWARD

[24.6]   Bridgeman v Brown
[2000] CLY 498

Following a road traffic accident, proceedings were issued against the defendant just before limitation expired. The defendant claimed that his wife had been driving the car at the time, and applied for the claim to be struck out on the basis that the claimant had proceeded against the wrong party. The claimant applied to join the defendant's wife. The claimant's application was refused and the defendant was granted summary judgment. The claimant appealed.

HELD, ON APPEAL: The summary judgment procedure was not appropriate for this case. The issue of who was driving the car was not straightforward. Neither the defendant nor his insurer had corrected the claimant's mistaken belief that the defendant was the correct party to proceed against, which belief had been evident in correspondence. Defendants should not seek to take points such as this where little injustice would be done to them or their insurers by the mistake, but serious injustice would be done to claimants if they could not pursue their claim.

[24.7]   Shyam Jewellers Ltd v Cheeseman

[2001] EWCA Civ 1818

[2001] All ER (D) 423 (Nov)

At an application for summary judgment, the judge directed that the arguments on which a party had repudiated a contract would be heard as a preliminary issue. Despite protestations from counsel, who had not had the opportunity to prepare arguments, the judge directed that the issue be determined by reference to the witness statements.

HELD, ON APPEAL: A court dealing with a CPR Pt 24 application should be wary of trying issues of fact on evidence where there was a conflict between the parties in relation to those issues of fact. Choosing between them was the function of the trial judge, not the judge on an interim application, unless there was some inherent improbability being asserted.

COMPLEX QUESTIONS OF FACT OR LAW NOT APPROPRIATE FOR
SUMMARY JUDGMENT

[24.8]   Arkin v Borchard Lines Ltd

[2001] CP Rep 108

In complex cases, particularly involving complex questions of law, or in cases involving very detailed facts, applications for summary judgment at an early stage in the proceedings might well fail and might have to proceed to trial on the basis that the claimant had a right to a fair trial, and in order to comply with the overriding objective.

2.   PROCEDURE

(A)   WHEN AN APPLICATION CAN BE MADE

[24.9]

CPR 24.4 – PROCEDURE
(1)   A claimant may not apply for summary judgment until the defendant against whom the application is made has filed–
   (a)   an acknowledgement of service; or
   (b)   a defence,
unless–
    (i)   the court gives permission; or
    (ii)   a practice direction provides otherwise.
(1A)   In civil proceedings against the Crown, as defined in rule 66.1(2), a claimant may not apply for summary judgment until after expiry of the period for filing a defence specified in rule 15.4.

(2)   If a claimant applies for summary judgment before a defendant against whom the application is made has filed a defence, that defendant need not file a defence before the hearing.

(3)   Where a summary judgment hearing is fixed, the respondent (or the parties where the hearing is fixed of the court's own initiative) must be given at least 14 days' notice of–

    (a)   the date fixed for the hearing; and

    (b)   the issues which it is proposed that the court will decide at the hearing.

(4)   A practice direction may provide for a different period of notice to be given.

(B)   CONTENT OF THE APPLICATION NOTICE

[24.10]

Practice Direction to CPR 24 – Procedure for making an application

2 (1)   Attention is drawn to rules 24.4(3) and 23.6.

    (2)   The application notice must include a statement that it is an application for summary judgment made under Part 24.

    (3)   The application notice or the evidence contained or referred to in it or served with it must –

        (a)   identify concisely any point of law or provision in a document on which the applicant relies, and/or

        (b)   state that it is made because the applicant believes that on the evidence the respondent has no real prospect of succeeding on the claim or issue or (as the case may be) of successfully defending the claim or issue to which the application relates,

and in either case state that the applicant knows of no other reason why the disposal of the claim or issue should await trial.

    (4)   Unless the application notice itself contains all the evidence (if any) on which the applicant relies, the application notice should identify the written evidence on which the applicant relies. This does not affect the applicant's right to file further evidence under rule 24.5(2).

    (5)   The application notice should draw the attention of the respondent to rule 24.5(1).

    (6)   Where the claimant has failed to comply with any relevant pre-action protocol, an action for summary judgment will not normally be entertained before the defence has been filed or, alternatively, the time for doing so has expired.

(C)   EVIDENCE

[24.11]

CPR 24.5 – EVIDENCE FOR THE PURPOSES OF A SUMMARY JUDGMENT HEARING

(1)   If the respondent to an application for summary judgment wishes to rely on written evidence at the hearing, he must–

    (a)   file the written evidence; and

    (b)   serve copies on every other party to the application,

at least 7 days before the summary judgment hearing.

(2)   If the applicant wishes to rely on written evidence in reply, he must–

(a)   file the written evidence; and

(b)   serve a copy on the respondent,

at least 3 days before the summary judgment hearing.

(3)   Where a summary judgment hearing is fixed by the court of its own initiative–

(a)   any party who wishes to rely on written evidence at the hearing must–

(i)   file the written evidence; and

(ii)   unless the court orders otherwise, serve copies on every other party to the proceedings,

at least 7 days before the date of the hearing;

(b)   any party who wishes to rely on written evidence at the hearing in reply to any other party's written evidence must–

(i)   file the written evidence in reply; and

(ii)   unless the court orders otherwise serve copies on every other party to the proceedings,

at least 3 days before the date of the hearing.

(4)   This rule does not require written evidence–

(a)   to be filed if it has already been filed; or

(b)   to be served on a party on whom it has already been served.

STANDARD OF PROOF ON AN APPLICATION FOR SUMMARY JUDGMENT

[24.12]   Royal Brompton Hospital NHS Trust v Hammond (No 5)

[2001] EWCA Civ 550

[2001] All ER (D) 130 (Apr)

HELD: On an application for summary judgment, the court should consider the witness statements and what evidence was likely to be available at trial. However, it should not apply the standard of proof required at trial, ie the balance of probabilities. The proper test was whether there was a real prospect of success.

COURT IS NOT TO CONDUCT A 'MINI-TRIAL'

[24.13]   Swain v Hillman

[2001] 1 All ER 91

On a summary judgment application, the detailed facts of the case should be left to the trial judge to consider and proper disposal of an issue under CPR Pt 24 does not involve the judge conducting a mini-trial.

[24.14]   Three Rivers DC v Bank of England

[2001] UKHL 16

[2001] 2 All ER 513

HELD, ON APPEAL: (1) Cases were not suitable for summary disposal where they were highly complex and merited the hearing of oral evidence at trial.

(2)   The court must have regard to evidence available to the parties at present but also that evidence likely to be available following disclosure and exchange of witness statements.

(3) The question of whether a claim has no real prospect of success must be answered having regard to the overriding objective.

(4) 'Real' prospect of success meant prospects which were more than simply 'fanciful'.

[24.15]   Sharma v Jay

[2003] EWHC 1230 (QB)

[2003] All ER (D) 284 (Apr)

HELD: Although it was not open to a judge to conduct a mini-trial on an application for summary judgment, it was open to a judge at the interlocutory stage to make findings of fact adverse to the party against whom summary judgement was sought, if the judge was of the opinion that the evidence, taken at its highest, was such that a jury properly directed could not find facts properly in favour of that party.

[24.16]   Beiersdorf AG v Ramlort Ltd

[2004] EWHC 118 (Ch)

[2004] All ER (D) 82 (Jan), [2004] ETMR 15

The claimants applied for summary judgment in an action to restrain trademark infringement and passing off.

HELD: It was not for the court to conduct a mini-trial on an application for summary judgment. Documents before the court might have appeared forged but the court should not make findings of fact regarding the authenticity of those documents without trial. If the documents were genuine then a defence could be put forward. The application for summary judgment was dismissed on that ground.

[24.17]   Arkin v Borchard Lines Ltd and Others (No 2)

(21 June 2001, unreported), QBD

The defendants applied to strike out certain parts of the amended particulars of claim, and for summary judgment in respect of certain issues. The claimant cross-applied to strike out or dismiss the application.

HELD: The facts of the case were complex and it could not be assumed that all the relevant evidence was before the court. There was a risk that relevant facts could later come to light. It would not be appropriate to dismiss facets of the claim which were factually related to other parts of the claim, and the issues should be determined at a full trial. A mini-trial approach should be avoided. In respect of the claimant's cross-application, an application to strike out was not the appropriate way to deal with an allegedly misconceived application; the claimant should simply have opposed it in the ordinary way.

[24.18]   Wootton v Telecommunications UK Ltd

(4 May 2000, unreported), CA

The claimant claimed an account and a declaration in respect of a contract between himself and the defendant relating to a telephone service. He applied for summary judgment, which was not granted. A conditional order was instead made requiring the defendant to pay monies into court. The claimant appealed and was granted his appeal, and part of the monies in court were paid out to the claimant. The defendant appealed.

HELD: A summary judgment application should not be conducted as a mini-trial. However, if there was a matter of construction to which no factual evidence would be material, it was perfectly proper to resolve that matter by way of a summary procedure. In this case it would not be just to use the summary judgment procedure as investigation of the facts of the case was required.

CROSS EXAMINATION OF WITNESSES

[24.19] Wallis v Valentine

[2002] EWCA Civ 1034

[2002] All ER (D) 275 (Jul)

The parties were neighbours and the claimant claimed he had been libelled in three documents, in particular an affidavit published to the claimant's partner and 'other persons'. Summary judgment was given on this issue, the judge finding that the document had not been published to any other persons, and the entire claim was struck out as an abuse of process.

HELD, ON APPEAL: It might be preferable, where there was written evidence before the court in the form of a witness statement prepared with the aim of vindicating the reputation of an individual, to invite cross-examination where that statement was challenged. This might not be necessary where the judge had already had an opportunity to form an opinion about the subject of the witness statement during the course of proceedings. The correct procedure had been adopted as to summary judgment and the claimant's appeal was dismissed.

(D) THE HEARING

HEARING TO BE BEFORE A MASTER OR DISTRICT JUDGE

[24.20]

Practice Direction to CPR Pt 24

The hearing
    3 (1) The hearing of the application will normally take place before a Master or a district judge.
    (2) The Master or district judge may direct that the application be heard by a High Court Judge (if the case is in the High Court) or a circuit judge (if the case is in a county court).

ORDERS THE COURT MAY MAKE

[24.21]

The court's approach

4   Where it appears to the court possible that a claim or defence may succeed but improbable that it will do so, the court may make a conditional order, as described below.

Orders the court may make

5.1   The orders the court may make on an application under Part 24 include:

(1)   judgment on the claim,

(2)   the striking out or dismissal of the claim,

(3)   the dismissal of the application,

(4)   a conditional order.

CONDITIONAL ORDERS

[24.22]

5.2   A conditional order is an order which requires a party:

(1)   to pay a sum of money into court, or

(2)   to take a specified step in relation to his claim or defence, as the case may be, and provides that that party's claim will be dismissed or his statement of case will be struck out if he does not comply.

Note—The court will not follow its former practice of granting leave to a defendant to defend a claim, whether conditionally or unconditionally.

[24.23]   **Olatawura v Abiloye**

[2002] EWCA Civ 998

[2002] 4 All ER 903, [2003] I WLR 275

Following an application for summary judgment, a conditional order was made which permitted the claimant's claim to proceed, but subject to him paying money into court as security for costs under CPR 3.1(2) and the Practice Direction to CPR Pt 24. The claimant appealed, arguing that the court only had jurisdiction to make such an order under CPR Pt 25 (security for costs).

HELD, ON APPEAL: It was readily apparent that the court had jurisdiction to make a conditional order consequent upon a summary judgment application – CPR 3.1(2) and the Practice Direction to CPR Pt 24. The Court of Appeal recognised that granting summary judgment subject to a conditional order requiring a payment into court was tantamount to requiring security for costs outside the ambit of CPR Pt 25. When exercising discretion, the court should be alert to the fact that it could be denying the party concerned access to the court. The court should have regard to the party's ability to pay, his conduct in the proceedings (including compliance with rules, practice directions and protocols) and the strength of his case. If, as a condition of pursuing an unpromising defence it was appropriate to secure the claim, why not the claimant's costs? Conversely, if a claimant put forward an unpromising claim, why should he not be required to secure the defendant's costs?

[24.24]   **Anglo-Eastern Trust v Kermanshahchi**

[2002] EWCA Civ 198

[2002] All ER (D) 321 (Feb)

In an action for repayment of loans, the judge refused to grant summary judgment on the basis that he did not consider that the defendant had no real prospect of successfully defending the claim. Instead, the judge made a conditional order for the defendant to make a payment into court of £1m, breach of which order would result in the defence being struck out and the claimant being able to enter judgment in default.

HELD: A claimant who seeks to ask the court to make a conditional order should put the defendant on notice of that fact. The court should not require the defendant to make a payment as a condition of continuing to defend the action where that payment was so large the defendant would be unable to pay it. The effect would be to stifle the defence, the effect being the same as if summary judgment had been granted – despite the defence having a real prospect of success.

[24.25]   **Jordan Grand Prix Ltd v Tiger Telematics Inc**

[2005] EWHC 76 (QB)

[2005] All ER (D) 284 (Jan)

The claimant, a Formula 1 Grand Prix motor racing team, brought proceedings against the defendant company, which had agreed to sponsor the claimant, in respect of non-payment of sponsorship fees. The claimant applied for summary judgment under CPR Pt 24. The master considered that the defendant's defence was unlikely to succeed but could not be excluded, and he therefore made a conditional order requiring a payment into court.

HELD, ON APPEAL: When dismissing an application for summary judgment, a master was entitled to make a conditional order requiring a payment into court where the master considered the defence was so weak it was improbable that it would succeed.

Additional Claims

1.   PRELIMINARY MATTERS

(A)   INTRODUCTION

[25.1]   A defendant may have a claim which can be made against the claimant – a counterclaim.

A defendant may also have a claim against another defendant, for an indemnity and/or contribution in respect of the claimant's claim.

A defendant may also have a claim against a person who is not already a party to proceedings. For example, the defendant may consider that another person should meet the claimant's claim, and that the defendant is entitled to an indemnity and/or contribution in respect of the claimant's claim from that person. Alternatively, the defendant may have grounds for making a counter-claim against another person.

Such claims, which are closely associated with the claim brought by the claimant against the defendant, are dealt with by CPR Pt 20.

On 6 April 2006, the version of CPR Pt 20 which had governed such claims was entirely replaced, together with a new Practice Direction, to simplify the terminology associated with such claims.

(B)   THE CPR FRAMEWORK

[25.2]

PREAMBLE TO PRACTICE DIRECTION TO CPR 20

An additional claim is any claim other than the claim by the claimant against the defendant.

Claims under this Part were formerly known as 'Part 20 claims'. As a result of the amendments to Part 20, introduced by Civil Procedure (Amendment No.4) Rules 2005, they are now called 'additional claims'.

However, they are described as 'Part 20 claims' on a number of court forms. For the present, some of those forms will continue to refer to Part 20 claims. These references should be construed as being additional claims under this Part. Any reference to a Part 20 claimant or a Part 20 defendant means a claimant or defendant in an additional claim under this Part.

[25.3]

CPR 20.2 – SCOPE AND INTERPRETATION
  (1)   This Part applies to–
    (a)   A counterclaim by a defendant against the claimant or against the claimant and some other person;
    (b)   An additional claim by a defendant against any person (whether or not already a party) for contribution or indemnity or some other remedy; and
    (c)   Where an additional claim has been made against a person who is not already a party, additional claim made by that person against any other person (whether or not already a party).
  (2)   In these Rules–
    (a)   'Additional claim' means any claim other than the claim by the claimant against the defendant; and

(b)   Unless the context requires otherwise, references to a claimant or defendant include a party bringing or defending an additional claim.

COMPLIANCE WITH PRE-ACTION PROTOCOL

[25.4]   Daejan Investments Ltd v Park West Club Ltd and Part 20 defendant Buxton Associates

[2003] EWHC 2872 (TCC)

[2004] BLR 223

Per: HHJ David Wilcox: A claimant [bringing an additional claim] is not relieved of the obligation to comply in substance with the terms of the [pre-action] protocol, otherwise parties to litigation brought otherwise than in accordance with the protocol might be subject to unfair commercial advantage and to threats of litigation and persist in litigation based on allegation without any real substance ... [If the protocol had been complied with] ... there would have been an informed and supported claim to deal with from a professional and commercial point of view. The option of avoiding litigation altogether would have been available to the defendant [against whom the additional claim is made]."

2.   COUNTERCLAIMS

[25.5]

CPR 20.4 – DEFENDANT'S COUNTERCLAIM AGAINST THE CLAIMANT
(1)   A defendant may make a counterclaim against a claimant by filing particulars of the counterclaim.
(2)   A defendant may make a counterclaim against a claimant–
(a)   Without the court's permission if he files it with his defence, or
(b)   At any other time with the court's permission.
(3)   Part 10 (acknowledgment of service) does not apply to a claimant who wishes to defend a counterclaim.

[25.6]

CPR 20.5 – COUNTERCLAIM AGAINST A PERSON OTHER THAN
THE CLAIMANT
(1)   A defendant who wishes to counterclaim against a person other than the claimant must apply to the court for an order that that person be added as an additional party.
(2)   An application for an order under paragraph (1) may be made without notice unless the court directs otherwise.
(3)   Where the court makes an order under paragraph (1), it will give directions as to the management of the case.

[25.7]

Practice Direction to CPR 20, paragraph 6

Form of counterclaim
6.1   Where a defendant to a claim serves a counterclaim, the defence and

counterclaim should normally form one document with the counter-claim following on from the defence.

6.2   Where a claimant serves a reply and a defence to counterclaim, the reply and the defence to counterclaim should normally form one document with the defence to counterclaim following on from the reply.

3.   CONTRIBUTION OR INDEMNITY

[25.8]

CPR 20.6 – DEFENDANT'S ADDITIONAL CLAIM FOR CONTRIBUTION OR INDEMNITY FROM ANOTHER PARTY

(1)   A defendant who has filed an acknowledge of service or a defence may make an additional claim for contribution or indemnity against a person who is already a party to the proceedings by–
   (a)   filing a notice containing a statement of the nature and grounds of his additional claim; and
   (b)   serving the notice on that party

(2)   A defendant may file and serve a notice under this rule–
   (a)   without the court's permission, if he files and serves it–
      (i)   with his defence; or
      (ii) if his additional claim for contribution or indemnity is against a party added to the claim later, within 28 days after that party files his defence, or
   (b)   at any other time with the court's permission

4.   ANY OTHER ADDITIONAL CLAIMS

[25.9]

CPR 20.7 – PROCEDURE FOR MAKING ANY OTHER ADDITIONAL CLAIMS

(1)   This rule applies to any additional claim except–
   (a)   a counterclaim only against an existing party; and
   (b)   a claim for contribution or indemnity made in accordance with rule 20.6.

(2)   An additional claim is made when the court issues the appropriate claim form.

(3)   A defendant may make an additional claim–
   (a)   without the court's permission if the additional claim is issued before or at the same time as he files his defence;
   (b)   at any other time with the court's permission

(4)   Particulars of an additional claim must be contained in or served with the additional claim.

(5)   An application for permission to make an additional claim may be made without notice unless the court directs otherwise.

5.   PROCEDURAL MATTERS COMMON TO ALL ADDITIONAL CLAIMS

(A)   CPR TO APPLY TO ADDITIONAL CLAIMS

[25.10]

CPR 20.3 – APPLICATION OF THESE RULES TO ADDITIONAL CLAIMS
(1)   An additional claim shall be treated as if it were a claim for the purposes of these Rules except as provided by this Part.
(2)   The following rules do not apply to additional claims–
(a)   Rules 7.5 and 7.6 (time within which a claim form may be served);
(b)   Rule 16.3(5) (statement of value where claim to be issued in the High Court); and
(c)   Part 26 (case management – preliminary stage).
(3)   Part 12 (default judgment) applies to a counterclaim but not to other additional claims.
(4)   Part 14 (admissions) applies to a counterclaim, but only–
(a)   Rules 14.1(1) and 14.1(2) (which provide that a party may admit the truth of another party's case in writing); and
(b)   Rule 14.3 (admission by notice in writing – application for judgment); apply to other additional claims.

[25.11]

Practice Direction to CPR 20, paragraph 3

General
3.   The Civil Procedure Rules apply generally to additional claims as if they were claims. Parties should be aware that the provisions relating to failure to respond to a claim will apply.

(B)   APPLICATION FOR PERMISSION TO MAKE AN ADDITIONAL CLAIM

[25.12]

Practice Direction to CPR 20, paragraph 2

Applications for permission to issue an additional claim
2.1   An application for permission to make an additional claim must be supported by evidence stating:
(1)   the stage which the proceedings have reached,
(2)   the nature of the additional claim to be made or details of the question or issue which needs to be decided,
(3)   a summary of facts on which the additional claim is based, and
(4)   the name and address of any proposed additional party.
2.2   Where delay has been a factor contributing to the need to apply for permission to make an additional claim an explanation of the delay should be given in evidence.
2.3   Where possible the applicant should provide a timetable of the proceedings to date.
2.4   Rules 20.5(2) and 20.7(5) allow applications to be made to the court without notice unless the court directs otherwise.

(C)   SERVICE OF AN ADDITIONAL CLAIM

[25.13]

CPR 20.8 – SERVICE OF THE CLAIM FORM
(1)   Where an additional claim may be made without the court's permission, any claim form must–
  (a)   in the case of a counterclaim against an additional party only, be served on every other party when a copy of the defence is served;
  (b)   in the case of any other additional claim, be served on the person against whom it is made within 14 days after the date on which the additional claim is issued by the court.
(2)   Paragraph (1) does not apply to a claim for contribution or indemnity made in accordance with rule 20.6.
(3)   Where the court gives permission to make an additional claim it will be at the same time give directions as to its service.

[25.14]

CPR 20.10 – EFFECT OF SERVICE OF AN ADDITIONAL CLAIM
(1)   A person on whom an additional claim is served becomes a party to the proceedings if he is not a party already.
(2)   When an additional claim is served on an existing party for the purpose of requiring the court to decide a question against that party in a further capacity, that party also becomes a party in the further capacity specified in the additional claim.

[25.15]

CPR 20.11 – SPECIAL PROVISIONS RELATING TO DEFAULT JUDGMENT ON AN ADDITIONAL CLAIM OTHER THAN A COUNTERCLAIM OR A CONTRIBUTION OR INDEMNITY NOTICE
(1)   This rule applies if–
  (a)   the additional claim is not–
    (i)   a counterclaim; or
    (ii)   a claim by a defendant for contribution or indemnity against another defendant under rule 20.6; and
  (b)   the party against whom an additional claim is made fails to file an acknowledgment of service or defence in respect of the additional claim.
(2)   The party against whom the additional claim is made–
  (a)   is deemed to admit the additional claim, and is bound by any judgment or decision in the proceedings in so far as it is relevant to any matter arising in the additional claim;
  (b)   subject to paragraph (3), if default judgment under Part 12 is given against the additional claimant, the additional claimant may obtain judgment in respect of the additional claim by filing a request in the relevant practice form.
(3)   An additional claimant may not enter judgment under paragraph (2)(b) without the court's permission if–
  (a)   he has not satisfied the default judgment which has been given against him; or

(b)   he wishes to obtain judgment for any remedy other than a contribution or indemnity.

(4)   An application for the court's permission under paragraph (3) may be made without notice unless the court directs otherwise.

(5)   The court may at any time set aside or vary a judgment entered under paragraph (2)(b).

[25.16]

CPR 20.12 – PROCEDURAL STEPS ON SERVICE OF AN ADDITIONAL CLAIM FORM ON A NON-PARTY

(1)   Where an additional claim form is served on a person who is not already a party it must be accompanied by–

(a)   a form for defending the claim;

(b)   a form for admitting the claim;

(c)   a form for acknowledging service; and

(d)   a copy of–

(i)   every statement of case which has already been served in the proceedings; and

(ii)   such other documents as the court may direct.

(2)   A copy of the additional claim form must be served on every existing party.

(D)   CASE MANAGEMENT OF ADDITIONAL CLAIMS

[25.17]

CPR 20.13 – CASE MANAGEMENT WHERE A DEFENCE TO AN ADDITIONAL CLAIM IS FILED

(1)   Where a defence is filed to an additional claim the court must consider the future conduct of the proceedings and give appropriate directions.

(2)   In giving directions under paragraph (1) the court must ensure that, so far as practicable, the original claim and all additional claims are managed together.

[25.18]

Practice Direction to CPR 20, paragraph 5

Case management where there is a defence to an additional claim

5.1   Where the defendant to an additional claim files a defence, other than to a counterclaim, the court will arrange a hearing to consider case management of the additional claim. This will normally be at the same time as a case management hearing for the original claim and any other additional claims.

5.2   The court will give notice of the hearing to each party likely to be affected by any order made at the hearing.

5.3   At the hearing the court may:

(1)   treat the hearing as a summary judgment hearing,

(2)   order that the additional claim be dismissed

(3)   give directions about the way any claim, question or issue set out in or arising from the additional claim should be dealt with

(4)   give directions as to the part, if any, the additional defendant will take at the trial of the claim,

(5)   give directions about the extent to which the additional defendant is to be bound by any judgment or decision to be made in the claim.

5.4   The court may make any of the orders in 5.3(1) to (5) either before or after any judgment in the claim has been entered by the claimant against the defendant.

(E)   SHOULD THE ADDITIONAL CLAIM BE TREATED SEPARATELY FROM THE CLAIM?

[25.19]

CPR 20.9 – MATTERS RELEVANT TO QUESTIONS OF WHETHER AN ADDITIONAL CLAIM SHOULD BE SEPARATE FROM THE CLAIM

(1)   This rule applies where the court is considering whether to–

(a)   permit an additional claim to be made;

(b)   dismiss an additional claim; or

(c)   require an additional claim to be dealt with separately from the claim by the claimant against the defendant.

(2)   The matters to which the court may have regard include–

(a)   the connection between the additional claim and the claim made by the claimant against the defendant;

(b)   whether the additional claimant is seeking substantially the same remedy which some other party is claiming from him; and

(c)   whether the additional claimant wants the court to decide any question connected with the subject matter of the proceedings–

(i)   not only between existing parties but also between existing parties and a person not already a party; or

(ii)   against an existing party not only in a capacity in which he is already a party but also in some further capacity.

CHAPTER 26

Allocation

1. GENERALLY

(A) PROCEDURAL TABLE

[26.1]

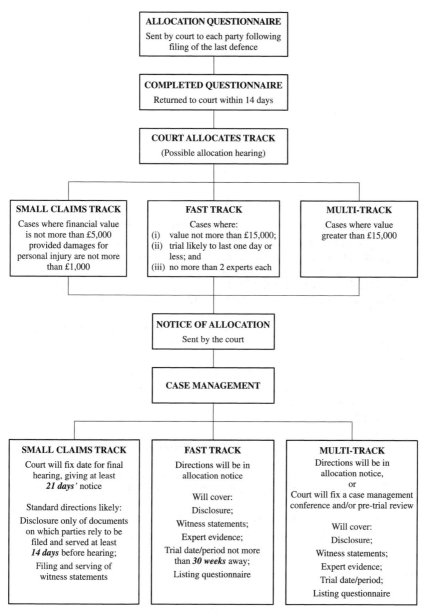

(B) PRELIMINARY MATTERS

[26.2]

CPR 26.1 – CASE MANAGEMENT – PRELIMINARY STAGE
(1)   This Part provides for–
   (a)   the automatic transfer of some defended cases between courts; and
   (b)   the allocation of defended cases to case management tracks.
(2)   There are three tracks–
   (a)   the small claims track;
   (b)   the fast track; and
   (c)   the multi-track.

[26.3]

CPR 26.2 – AUTOMATIC TRANSFER OF CLAIMS FOR A SPECIFIED SUM
(1)   This rule applies to proceedings where–
   (a)   the claim is for a specified amount of money;
   (b)   the claim was commenced in a court which is not the defendant's home court;
   (c)   the claim has not been transferred to another defendant's home court under rule 13.4 (application to set aside or vary default judgment – procedure) or rule 14.12 (admission – determination of rate of payment by judge); and
   (d)   the defendant is an individual.
(2)   This rule does not apply where the claim was commenced in a specialist list.
(3)   Where this rule applies, the court will transfer the proceedings to the defendant's home court when a defence is filed, unless paragraph (4) applies.
(4)   Where the claimant notifies the court under rule 15.10 or rule 14.5 that he wishes the proceedings to continue, the court will transfer the proceedings to the defendant's home court when it receives that notification from the claimant.
(5)   Where–
   (a)   the claim is against two or more defendants with different home courts; and
   (b)   the defendant whose defence is filed first is an individual,
proceedings are to be transferred under this rule to the home court of that defendant.
(6)   The time when a claim is automatically transferred under this rule may be varied by a practice direction in respect of claims issued by the Production Centre.

[26.4]

CPR 26.3 – ALLOCATION QUESTIONNAIRE
(1)   When a defendant files a defence the court will serve an allocation questionnaire on each party unless–
   (a)   rule 15.10 or rule 14.5 applies; or
   (b)   the court dispenses with the need for a questionnaire.

(2) Where there are two or more defendants and at least one of them files a defence, the court will serve the allocation questionnaire under paragraph (1)–

    (a) when all the defendants have filed a defence; or

    (b) when the period for the filing of the last defence has expired,

whichever is the sooner.

(3) Where proceedings are automatically transferred to the defendant's home court under rule 26.2, the court in which the proceedings have been commenced will serve an allocation questionnaire before the proceedings are transferred.

(4) Where–

    (a) rule 15.10 or rule 14.5 applies; and

    (b) the proceedings are not automatically transferred to the defendant's home court under rule 26.2,

the court will serve an allocation questionnaire on each party when the claimant files a notice indicating that he wishes the proceedings to continue.

(5) The court may, on the application of the claimant, serve an allocation questionnaire earlier than it would otherwise serve it under this rule.

(6) Each party must file the completed allocation questionnaire no later than the date specified in it, which shall be at least 14 days after the date when it is deemed to be served on the party in question.

(6A) The date for filing the completed allocation questionnaire may not be varied by agreement between the parties.

(7) The time when the court serves an allocation questionnaire under this rule may be varied by a practice direction in respect of claims issued by the Production Centre.

[26.5]

CPR 26.4 – STAY TO ALLOW FOR SETTLEMENT OF THE CASE

(1) A party may, when filing the completed allocation questionnaire, make a written request for the proceedings to be stayed while the parties try to settle the case by alternative dispute resolution or other means.

(2) Where–

    (a) all parties request a stay under paragraph (1); or

    (b) the court, of its own initiative, considers that such a stay would be appropriate,

the court will direct that the proceedings either in the whole or in part, to be stayed for one month, or for such specified period as it considers appropriate.

(3) The court may extend the stay until such date or for such specified period as it considers appropriate.

(4) Where the court stays the proceedings under this rule, the claimant must tell the court if a settlement is reached.

(5) If the claimant does not tell the court by the end of the period of the stay that a settlement has been reached, the court will give such directions as to the management of the case as it considers appropriate.

[26.6]

CPR 26.5 – Allocation
(1)   The court will allocate the claim to a track–
   (a)   when every defendant has filed an allocation questionnaire, or
   (b)   when the period for filing the allocation questionnaires has expired,
whichever is the sooner, unless it has–
      (i)   stayed the proceedings under rule 26.4; or
      (ii)   dispensed with the need for allocation questionnaires.
(2)   If the court has stayed the proceedings under rule 26.4, it will allocate the claim to a track at the end of the period of the stay.
(3)   Before deciding the track to which to allocate proceedings or deciding whether to give directions for an allocation hearing to be fixed, the court may order a party to provide further information about his case.
(4)   The court may hold an allocation hearing if it thinks it is necessary.
(5)   If a party fails to file an allocation questionnaire, the court may give any direction it considers appropriate.

[26.7]

CPR 26.6 – Scope of each track
(1)   The small claims track is the normal track for–
   (a)   any claim for personal injuries where–
      (i)   the financial value of the claim is not more than £5,000; and
      (ii)   the financial value of any claim for damages for personal injuries is not more than £1,000;
   (b)   any claim which includes a claim by a tenant of residential premises against his landlord where–
      (i)   the tenant is seeking an order requiring the landlord to carry out repairs or other work to the premises (whether or not the tenant is also seeking some other remedy);
      (ii)   the cost of the repairs or other work to the premises is estimated to be not more than £1,000; and
      (iii)   the financial value of any other claim for damages is not more than £1,000.
(2)   For the purposes of paragraph (1) 'damages for personal injuries' means damages claimed as compensation for pain, suffering and loss of amenity and does not include any other damages which are claimed.
(3)   Subject to paragraph (1), the small claims track is the normal track for any claim which has a financial value of not more than £5,000.
(4)   Subject to paragraph (5), the fast track is the normal track for any claim–
   (a)   for which the small claims track is not the normal track; and
   (b)   which has a financial value of not more than £15,000.
(5)   The fast track is the normal track for the claims referred to in paragraph (4) only if the court considers that–
   (a)   the trial is likely to last for no longer than one day; and
   (b)   oral expert evidence at trial will be limited to–
      (i)   one expert per party in relation to any expert field; and
      (ii)   expert evidence in two expert fields.

(6)   The multi-track is the normal track for any claim for which the small claims track or the fast track is not the normal track.

[26.8]

CPR 26.7 – GENERAL RULE FOR ALLOCATION
(1)   In considering whether to allocate a claim to the normal track for that claim under rule 26.6, the court will have regard to the matters mentioned in rule 26.8(1).
(2)   The court will allocate a claim which has no financial value to the track which it considers most suitable having regard to the matters mentioned in rule 26.8(1).
(3)   The court will not allocate proceedings to a track if the financial value of the claim, assessed by the court under rule 26.8, exceeds the limit for that track unless all the parties consent to the allocation of the claim to that track.
(4)   The court will not allocate a claim to the small claims track, if it includes a claim by a tenant of residential premises against his landlord for a remedy in respect of harassment or unlawful eviction.

[26.9]

CPR 26.8 – MATTERS RELEVANT TO ALLOCATION TO A TRACK
(1)   When deciding the track for a claim, the matters to which the court shall have regard include–
   (a)   the financial value, if any, of the claim;
   (b)   the nature of the remedy sought;
   (c)   the likely complexity of the facts, law or evidence;
   (d)   the number of parties or likely parties;
   (e)   the value of any counterclaim or other Part 20 claim and the complexity of any matters relating to it;
   (f)   the amount of oral evidence which may be required;
   (g)   the importance of the claim to persons who are not parties to the proceedings;
   (h)   the views expressed by the parties; and
   (i)   the circumstances of the parties.
(2)   It is for the court to assess the financial value of a claim and in doing so it will disregard–
   (a)   any amount not in dispute;
   (b)   any claim for interest;
   (c)   costs; and
   (d)   any contributory negligence.
(3)   Where–
   (a)   two or more claimants have started a claim against the same defendant using the same claim form; and
   (b)   each claimant has a claim against the defendant separate from the other claimants,
the court will consider the claim of each claimant separately when it assesses financial value under paragraph (1).

[26.10]

CPR 26.9 – NOTICE OF ALLOCATION
   (1)   When it has allocated a claim to a track, the court will serve notice of allocation on every party.
   (2)   When the court serves notice of allocation on a party, it will also serve–
      (a)   a copy of the allocation questionnaires filed by the other parties; and
      (b)   a copy of any further information provided by another party about his case (whether by order or not).

[26.11]

CPR 26.10 – RE-ALLOCATION

The court may subsequently re-allocate a claim to a different track.

[26.12]   Lagden v O'Connor
[2003] UKHL 64
[2004] 1 AC 1067, [2004] 1 All ER 277, [2003] 3 WLR 1571

Cases allocated to the small claims track may be transferred to the fast track if special orders, for example for an interim payment, are required.

[26.13]   Maguire v Molin
[2002] EWCA Civ 1083
[2002] 4 All ER 325, [2003] 1 WLR 644

The claimant issued proceedings in respect of a claim for personal injuries limited to £15,000. Following the filing of a defence, the claim was allocated to the fast track. Directions were given and the case listed for trial. It was apparent from the medical evidence that the claim had a value significantly in excess of £15,000. At trial, the claimant's solicitors advised the court that the medical evidence was out of date. The judge elected to proceed with the trial but only in relation to liability. The trial on liability was adjourned part-heard. During the adjournment, the claimant's solicitor applied to amend the claimant's pleadings on the basis that the claim had a value in excess of the fast-track limit. The district judge refused the application and the claimant appealed. The matter came before the Court of Appeal.

HELD, ON APPEAL: The district judge was wrong to hold that he was only entitled to either allow the application, abort the liability trial, and reallocate to the multi-track, or refuse the application and proceed. A claim did not cease to be in the fast track simply because its financial value had exceeded £15,000. CPR 26.10 allowed the court unfettered discretion.

[26.14]   **Khiaban v Beard**

[2002] EWCA Civ 358

[2003] 3 All ER 362, [2003] 1 WLR 1626, [2003] RTR 419

The claimant and the defendant were involved in a road traffic accident. Both were comprehensively insured. The claimant issued proceedings in respect of his policy excess in the sum of £125. To minimise costs, the respective insurers, who each had repair costs, entered into a memorandum of understanding, agreeing to abide by the court's decision in the proceedings brought by the claimant. The district judge ordered the claimant to amend the particulars of claim to clarify the full extent of the claim made and include the repair costs. The claimant failed to amend the particulars of claim and the case was struck out. The matter was referred by the circuit judge to the Court of Appeal.

HELD, ON APPEAL: A claimant was entitled to decide what to include in his claim, and the Civil Procedure Rules (CPR) did not give the court jurisdiction to require a claimant to include losses in a claim which the claimant had chosen not to. The real issue between the parties was liability, and they were entitled to limit quantum to ensure an allocation to the small claims track. If the issue of liability was particularly complex, it was open to the court to allocate the case to a different track.

[26.15]   **Kearsley v Klarfeld**

[2005] EWCA Civ 1510

[2005] All ER (D) 98 (Dec), (2006) 103(2) LSG 33

The claimant alleged suffering personal injury as a result of a road traffic accident. The defendant admitted that the accident had been caused by his negligence but disputed causation. The defendant obtained a report from an expert who concluded that the collision had occurred at less than 3mph, and that the collision would not have caused any unusual forces to be applied to the claimant. The claim was allocated to the fast track. The defendant made an application seeking permission to call oral evidence from the expert and also from the claimant's medical expert, and that the matter be reallocated to the multi-track.

HELD, ON APPEAL, per Brooke LJ: '... it appears to us that until some of the issues that arise in these disputes have been authoritatively dissected and analysed at High Court level, it would not be wrong or disproportionate to allocate what would ordinarily be a fast track claim (by reason of its low value) into the multi-track on the grounds that the criteria for the admission of oral expert evidence are satisfied and the trial is therefore likely to last more than one day.'

2.   THE SMALL CLAIMS TRACK

(A)   GENERALLY

[26.16]

CPR 27.1 – CLAIMS WHICH ARE NORMALLY ALLOCATED TO THE SMALL CLAIMS TRACK
  (1)   This Part–
    (a)   sets out the special procedure for dealing with claims which have been allocated to the small claims track under Part 26; and

    (b)   limits the amount of costs that can be recovered in respect of a claim which has been allocated to the small claims track.

  (2)   A claim being dealt with under this Part is called a small claim.

(Rule 26.6 provides for the scope of the small claims track. A claim for a remedy for harassment or unlawful eviction relating, in either case, to residential premises shall not be allocated to the small claims track whatever the financial value of the claim. Otherwise, the small claims track will be the normal track for–

●   any claim which has a financial value of not more than £5,000 subject to the special provisions about claims for personal injuries and housing disrepair claims;

●   any claim for personal injuries which has a financial value of not more than £5,000 where the claim for damages for personal injuries is not more than £1,000; and

●   any claim which includes a claim by a tenant of residential premises against his landlord for repairs or other work to the premises where the estimated cost of the repairs or other work is not more than £1,000 and the financial value of any other claim for damages is not more than £1,000)

INFANT CLAIMS NOT TO BE ALLOCATED TO SMALL CLAIMS TRACK

[26.17]   W (a child) v Robinson
[2002] CLY 389

At the conclusion of an infant settlement approval hearing, the defendant argued that because the claimant had recovered a sum less than the limit for small claims, the claim should have been allocated to the small claims track and costs limited to fixed costs only.

HELD: An infant claimant cannot reach any settlement without the approval of the court by way of CPR Pt 8 proceedings. Accordingly, CPR Pt 8 claims for approval are to be treated as allocated to the multi-track and costs assessed accordingly even if the amount of the award might otherwise have justified an allocation to the small claims track.

RULES THAT DO NOT APPLY TO CLAIMS ALLOCATED TO THE SMALL CLAIMS TRACK

[26.18]

CPR 27.2 – EXTENT TO WHICH OTHER PARTS APPLY

  (1)   The following Parts of these Rules do not apply to small claims–

    (a)   Part 25 (interim remedies) except as it relates to interim injunctions;

    (b)   Part 31 (disclosure and inspection);

    (c)   Part 32 (evidence) except rule 32.1 (power of court to control evidence);

    (d)   Part 33 (miscellaneous rules about evidence);

    (e)   Part 35 (experts and assessors) except rules 35.1 (duty to restrict expert evidence), 35.3 (experts – overriding duty to the court), 35.7

(court's power to direct that evidence is to be given by single joint expert) and 35.8 (instructions to a single joint expert);

(f) Subject to paragraph (3), Part 18 (further information);

(g) Part 36 (offers to settle and payments into court); and

(h) Part 39 (hearings) except rule 39.2 (general rule – hearing to be in public).

(2) The other Parts of these Rules apply to small claims except to the extent that a rule limits such application.

(3) The court of its own initiative may order a party to provide further information if it considers it appropriate to do so.

(B)   DIRECTIONS

[26.19]

CPR 27.4 – PREPARATION FOR THE HEARING

(1) After allocation the court will–

(a) give standard directions and fix a date for the final hearing;

(b) give special directions and fix a date for the final hearing;

(c) give special directions and direct that the court will consider what further directions are to be given no later than 28 days after the date the special directions were given;

(d) fix a date for a preliminary hearing under rule 27.6; or

(e) give notice that it proposes to deal with the claim without a hearing under rule 27.10 and invite the parties to notify the court by a specified date if they agree the proposal.

(2) The court will–

(a) give the parties at least 21 days' notice of the date fixed for the final hearing, unless the parties agree to accept less notice; and

(b) inform them of the amount of time allowed for the final hearing.

(3) In this rule–

(a) 'standard directions' means–

(i) a direction that each party shall, at least 14 days before the date fixed for the final hearing, file and serve on every other party copies of all documents (including any expert's report) on which he intends to rely at the hearing; and

(ii) any other standard directions set out in the relevant practice direction; and

(b) 'special directions' means directions given in addition to or instead of the standard directions.

(C)   FINAL HEARING

[26.20]

CPR 27.5 – EXPERTS

No expert may give evidence, whether written or oral, at a hearing without the permission of the court.

[26.21]

CPR 27.8 – CONDUCT OF THE HEARING
(1)   The court may adopt any method of proceeding at a hearing that it considers to be fair.
(2)   Hearings will be informal.
(3)   The strict rules of evidence do not apply.
(4)   The court need not take evidence on oath.
(5)   The court may limit cross-examination.
(6)   The court must give reasons for its decision.

[26.22]

CPR 27.9 – NON-ATTENDANCE OF PARTIES AT A FINAL HEARING
(1)   If a party who does not attend a final hearing–
    (a)   has given written notice to the court and the other party at least 7 days before the hearing date that he will not attend;
    (b)   has served on the other party at least 7 days before the hearing date any other documents which he has filed with the court; and
    (c)   has, in his written notice, requested the court to decide the claim in his absence and has confirmed his compliance with paragraphs (a) and (b) above,
the court will take into account that party's statement of case and any other documents he has filed and served when it decides the claim.
(2)   If a claimant does not–
    (a)   attend the hearing; and
    (b)   give the notice referred to in paragraph (1),
the court may strike out the claim.
(3)   If–
    (a)   a defendant does not–
        (i)   attend the hearing; or
        (ii)   give the notice referred to in paragraph (1); and
    (b)   the claimant either–
        (i)   does attend the hearing; or
        (ii)   gives the notice referred to in paragraph (1),
the court may decide the claim on the basis of the evidence of the claimant alone.
(4)   If neither party attends or gives the notice referred to in paragraph (1), the court may strike out the claim and any defence and counterclaim.

[26.23]

CPR 27.11 – SETTING JUDGMENT ASIDE AND RE-HEARING
(1)   A party–
    (a)   who was neither present nor represented at the hearing of the claim; and
    (b)   who has not given written notice to the court under rule 27.9(1),
may apply for an order that a judgment under this Part shall be set aside and the claim re-heard.

(2)   A party who applies for an order setting aside a judgment under this rule must make the application not more than 14 days after the day on which notice of the judgment was served on him.

(3)   The court may grant an application under paragraph (2) only if the applicant–
  (a)   had a good reason for not attending or being represented at the hearing or giving written notice to the court under rule 27.9(1); and
  (b)   has a reasonable prospect of success at the hearing.

(4)   If a judgment is set aside–
  (a)   the court must fix a new hearing for the claim; and
  (b)   the hearing may take place immediately after the hearing of the application to set the judgment aside and may be dealt with by the judge who set aside the judgment.

(5)   A party may not apply to set aside a judgment under this rule if the court dealt with the claim without a hearing under rule 27.10.

[26.24]   Nasair v Hill

[2002] CLY 397

The claimant issued proceedings in respect of damage to his motor vehicle sustained in a road traffic accident. The defendant entered a defence denying liability. The claimant failed to attend the small claims hearing.

HELD: The claimant's claim was dismissed. He had given no good reason for his non-attendance. If he could establish a good reason, then the judgment could be set aside. The claimant's failure to attend court without good reason amounted to unreasonable conduct within CPR Pt 27, and the defendant was awarded costs.

(D)   COSTS

FIXED COSTS

[26.25]

CPR 27.14 – COSTS ON THE SMALL CLAIMS TRACK
  (1)   This rule applies to any case which has been allocated to the small claims track unless paragraph (5) applies.
  (2)   The court may not order a party to pay a sum to another party in respect of that other party's costs except–
    (a)   the fixed costs attributable to issuing the claim which–
      (i)   are payable under Part 45; or
      (ii)   would be payable under Part 45 if that Part applied to the claim;
    ...
  (3)   The court may also order a party to pay all or part of–
    (a)   any court fees paid by another party;
    (b)   expenses which a party or witness has reasonably incurred in travelling to and from a hearing or in staying away from home for the purposes of attending a hearing;
    (c)   a sum not exceeding the amount specified in the relevant practice direction for any loss of earnings or loss of leave by a party or

witness due to attending a hearing or to staying away from home for the purpose of attending a hearing; and

(d)   a sum not exceeding the amount specified in the relevant practice direction for an expert's fees.

(4)   The limits on costs imposed by this rule also apply to any fee or reward for acting on behalf of a party to the proceedings charged by a person exercising a right of audience by virtue of an order under section 11 of the Courts and Legal Services Act 1990(a lay representative).

[26.26]

CPR 27.14(2), (2A) – Unreasonable conduct

(2)   The court may not order a party to pay a sum to another party in respect of that other party's costs except–

...

(d)   such further costs as the court may assess by the summary procedure and order to be paid by a party who has behaved unreasonably.

(2A)   A party's rejection of an offer in settlement will not of itself constitute unreasonable behaviour under paragraph (2)(d) but the court may take it into consideration when it is applying the unreasonable test.

[26.27]   Clohessy v Homes
[2004] CLY 418

The claimant issued proceedings following a road traffic accident. The proceedings were allocated to the small claims track. The facts of the collision were clear from the outset. The defendant made an offer to settle on a 75/25 basis in the claimant's favour. The claimant refused the offer. At the small claims hearing, the case was dismissed and the defendant applied for an order for costs on the basis that the claimant's conduct was unreasonable.

HELD: On an objective assessment, it was abundantly clear that the claim would fail. Proceedings ought not to have been issued, but given that they had been, then an offer favourable to the claimant should have been accepted. Accordingly, the claimant's conduct had been unreasonable under CPR 27.14(2)(d).

[26.28]   Hayes v Airtour Holidays Ltd (Costs)
[2001] CLY 512

The claimant, acting in person, brought proceedings alleging breach of the Package Tours Regulations 1992, SI 1992/3288. His claim was allocated to the small claims track, but his particulars of claim were incomprehensible and extensive. At a case management conference, the court ordered the claimant to remedy procedural defects but he failed to do so. At trial, he sought to rely upon 40 documents which related to other claims and which the court held to be irrelevant. The hearing lasted for two days and required a reserved judgment. The claim failed and the defendant applied for costs.

HELD: Whilst allowance had to be made for the fact that the claimant was acting in person, his conduct had been unreasonable and disproportionate, and the defendant was therefore entitled to costs.

[26.29]   **Fox v Murray**
[2000] CLY 448

The claimant's vehicle was in collision with the defendant's vehicle. The accident was caused by the defendant's negligence. Nevertheless, a defence was entered that disputed liability. The claim was allocated to the small claims track. The defendant made an offer to settle 50/50 which was rejected, then made an offer to settle 75/25 in the claimant's favour which was also rejected. Eventually, the defendant agreed to meet the whole of the claimant's claim.

HELD: The defendant's conduct had amounted to 'drip feeding' and amounted to unreasonable conduct, and the claimant should therefore have the benefit of a costs order.

[26.30]   **Owen v Burnham**
[2001] CLY 534

The claimant issued proceedings in respect of losses sustained as a consequence of a road traffic accident including a claim for credit hire. The claim was allocated to the small claims track. The claimant served a witness statement wherein she stated that the hire company was able to recover the hire charges from her 'at any time'. On cross examination, she admitted that she had been assured by the hire company that she would never have to repay the hire charges. The claim was dismissed and the defendant applied for a costs order under CPR 27.14(2)(d) on the basis that the claimant's conduct had been unreasonable.

HELD: The claimant's witness statement had been misleading and the claim advanced on the basis of a false premise. This amounted to unreasonable conduct and the defendant's application for costs would be allowed.

(E)   APPEALS

[26.31]

Practice Direction to CPR 27 – Small claims – Appeals

8.1   Part 52 deals with appeals and attention is drawn to that Part and the accompanying practice direction.

8A   An appellant's notice in small claims must be filed and served in Form N164.

8.2   Where the court dealt with the claim to which the appellant is a party:
  (1)   under rule 27.10 with a hearing; or
  (2)   in his absence because he gave notice under rule 27.9 requesting the court to decide the claim in his absence.
an application for permission to appeal must be made to the appeal court.

8.3   Where an appeal is allowed the appeal court will, if possible, dispose of the case at the same time without referring the claim to the lower court or ordering a new hearing. It may do so without hearing further evidence.

[26.32]

Practice Direction to CPR 52

Small claims

5.8

  (1)   This paragraph applies where–
     (a)   the appeal relates to a claim allocated to the small claims track; and
     (b)   the appeal is being heard in a county court or the High Court.
  (1A) An appellant's notice must be filed and served in Form N164.
  (2)   The appellant must file the following documents with his appellant's notice–
     (a)   a sealed copy of the order being appealed; and
     (b)   any order giving or refusing permission to appeal, together with a copy of the reasons for that decision.
  (3)   The appellant may, if relevant to the issues to be determined on the appeal, file any other document listed in paragraph 5.6 or 5.6A in addition to the documents referred to in sub-paragraph (2).
  (4)   The appellant need not file a record of the reasons for judgment of the lower court with his appellant's notice unless sub-paragraph (5) applies.
  (5)   The court may order a suitable record of the reasons for judgment of the lower court (see paragraph 5.12) to be filed–
     (a)   to enable it to decide if permission should be granted; or
     (b)   if permission is granted to enable it to decide the appeal.

Note—For grounds of appeal, please refer to Chapter 34.

3.   THE FAST TRACK

(A)   GENERALLY

[26.33]

CPR 28.2 – GENERAL PROVISIONS
  (1)   When it allocates a case to the fast track, the court will give directions for the management of the case and set a timetable for the steps to be taken between the giving of the directions and the trial.
  (2)   When it gives directions, the court will–
     (a)   fix the trial date; or
     (b)   fix a period, not exceeding 3 weeks, within which the trial is to take place.
  (3)   The trial date or trial period will be specified in the notice of allocation.
  (4)   The standard period between the giving of directions and the trial will be not more than 30 weeks.
  (5)   The court's power to award trial costs is limited in accordance with Part 46.

(B) DIRECTIONS

STANDARD DIRECTIONS

[26.34]

CPR 28.3 – DIRECTIONS
(1)   The matters to be dealt with by directions under rule 28.2(1) include–
   (a)   disclosure of documents;
   (b)   service of witness statements; and
   (c)   expert evidence.
(2)   If the court decides not to direct standard disclosure, it may–
   (a)   direct that no disclosure take place; or
   (b)   specify the documents or the classes of documents which the parties must disclose.

PARTIES CAN AGREE TO VARY DIRECTIONS SAVE IN RESPECT OF TRIAL

[26.35]

CPR 28.4 – VARIATION OF CASE MANAGEMENT TIMETABLE
(1)   A party must apply to the court if he wishes to vary the date which the court has fixed for–
   (a)   the return of a pre-trial check list under rule 28.5;
   (b)   the trial; or
   (c)   the trial period.
(2)   Any date set by the court or these Rules for doing any act may not be varied by the parties if the variation would make it necessary to vary any of the dates mentioned in paragraph (1).

(C) FINAL HEARING

LISTING FOR HEARING

[26.36]

CPR 28.5 – PRE-TRIAL CHECK LIST (LISTING QUESTIONNAIRE)
(1)   The court will send the parties a pre-trial check list (listing questionnaire) for completion and return by the date specified in the notice of allocation unless it considers that the claim can proceed to trial without the need for a pre-trial check list.
(2)   The date specified for filing a pre-trial check list will not be more than 8 weeks before the trial date or the beginning of the trial period.
(3)   If no party files the completed pre-trial checklist by the date specified, the court will order that unless a completed pre-trial checklist is filed within 7 days from service of that order, the claim, defence and any counterclaim will be struck out without further order of the court.
(4)   If–
   (a)   a party files a completed pre-trial checklist but another party does not;

   (b) a party has failed to give all the information requested by the pre-trial checklist; or

   (c) the court considers that a hearing is necessary to enable it to decide what directions to give in order to complete preparation of the case for trial,

the court may give such directions as it thinks appropriate.

[26.37]

CPR 28.6 – FIXING OR CONFIRMING THE TRIAL DATE AND GIVING DIRECTIONS

(1) As soon as practicable after the date specified for filing a completed pre-trial check list the court will–

   (a) fix the date for the trial (or, if it has already done so, confirm that date);

   (b) give any directions for the trial, including a trial timetable, which it considers appropriate; and

   (c) specify any further steps that need to be taken before trial.

(2) The court will give the parties at least 3 weeks' notice of the date of the trial unless, in exceptional circumstances, the court directs that shorter notice will be given.

[26.38]

CPR 28.7 – CONDUCT OF TRIAL

Unless the trial judge otherwise directs, the trial will be conducted in accordance with any order previously made.

4.   THE MULTI-TRACK

(A)   CASE MANAGEMENT AND THE CASE MANAGEMENT CONFERENCE

[26.39]

CPR 29.2 – CASE MANAGEMENT

(1) When it allocates a case to the multi-track, the court will–

   (a) give directions for the management of the case and set a timetable for the steps to be taken between the giving of directions and the trial; or

   (b) fix–

      (i)   a case management conference; or

      (ii) a pre-trial review,

or both, and give such other directions relating to the management of the case as it sees fit.

(2) The court will fix the trial date or the period in which the trial is to take place as soon as practicable.

(3) When the court fixes the trial date or the trial period under paragraph (2), it will–

   (a) give notice to the parties of the date or period; and

(b)   specify the date by which the parties must file a pre-trial check list.

[26.40]

CPR 29.3 – CASE MANAGEMENT CONFERENCE AND PRE-TRIAL REVIEW
   (1)   The court may fix–
      (a)   a case management conference; or
      (b)   a pre-trial review, at any time after the claim has been allocated.
   (2)   If a party has a legal representative, a representative–
      (a)   familiar with the case; and
      (b)   with sufficient authority to deal with any issues that are likely to arise, must attend case management conferences and pre-trial reviews.

[26.41]

CPR 29.4 – STEPS TAKEN BY THE PARTIES

If–
(a)   the parties agree proposals for the management of the proceedings (including a proposed trial date or period in which the trial is to take place); and
(b)   the court considers that the proposals are suitable,

it may approve them without a hearing and give directions in the terms proposed.

[26.42]

CPR 29.5 – VARIATION OF CASE MANAGEMENT TIMETABLE
   (1)   A party must apply to the court if he wishes to vary the date which the court has fixed for–
      (a)   a case management conference;
      (b)   a pre-trial review;
      (c)   the return of a pre-trial check list under rule 29.6;
      (d)   the trial; or
      (e)   the trial period.
   (2)   Any date set by the court or these Rules for doing any act may not be varied by the parties if the variation would make it necessary to vary any of the dates mentioned in paragraph (1).

(B)   FINAL HEARING

[26.43]

CPR 29.6 – PRE-TRIAL CHECK LIST (LISTING QUESTIONNAIRE)
   (1)   The court will send the parties a pre-trial check list (listing questionnaire) for completion and return by the date specified in directions given under rule 29.2(3) unless it considers that the claim can proceed to trial without the need for a pre-trial check list.

(2)   Each party must file the completed pre-trial check list by the date specified by the court.

(3)   If no party files the completed pre-trial checklist by the date specified, the court will order that unless a completed pre-trial checklist is filed within 7 days from service of that order, the claim, defence and any counterclaim will be struck out without further order of the court.

(4)   If–

(a)   a party files a completed pre-trial checklist but another party does not;

(b)   a party has failed to give all the information requested by the pre-trial checklist; or

(c)   the court considers that a hearing is necessary to enable it to decide what directions to give in order to complete preparation of the case for trial,

the court may give such directions as it thinks appropriate.

[26.44]

CPR 29.7 – PRE-TRIAL REVIEW

If, on receipt of the parties' pre-trial check lists, the court decides–

(a)   to hold a pre-trial review; or

(b)   to cancel a pre-trial review which has already been fixed,

it will serve notice of its decision at least 7 days before the date fixed for the hearing or, as the case may be, the cancelled hearing.

TRIAL TIMETABLE

[26.45]

CPR 29.8 – SETTING A TRIAL TIMETABLE AND FIXING OR CONFIRMING THE TRIAL DATE OR WEEK

As soon as practicable after–

(a)   each party has filed a completed pre-trial check list;

(b)   the court has held a listing hearing under rule 29.6(3); or

(c)   the court has held a pre-trial review under rule 29.7,

the court will–

(i)   set a timetable for the trial unless a timetable has already been fixed, or the court considers that it would be inappropriate to do so;

(ii)   fix the date for the trial or the week within which the trial is to begin (or, if it has already done so, confirm that date); and

(iii) notify the parties of the trial timetable (where one is fixed under this rule) and the date or trial period.

[26.46]

CPR 29.9 – CONDUCT OF TRIAL

Unless the trial judge otherwise directs, the trial will be conducted in accordance with any order previously made.

5. ALTERNATIVE DISPUTE RESOLUTION/MEDIATION

[26.47]   **Vahidi v Fairstead House School Trust Ltd**

[2005] EWCA Civ 765

[2005] All ER (D) 55 (Jun)

Per Longmore LJ: As the courts have settled many of the principles in stress at work cases, litigants really should mediate cases … Of course, mediation before trial is infinitely preferable to mediation before appeal. But it is a great pity that neither form of mediation has taken place in this case or, if it has, that it has not produced a result.

[26.48]   **Al-Khatib v Masry**

[2004] EWCA Civ 1353

[2004] 3 FCR 573, [2005] 1 FLR 381

Per Thorpe LJ: From the point of view of the Court of Appeal, [this case] supports our conviction that there is no case, however conflicted, which is not potentially open to successful mediation, even if mediation has not been attempted or has failed during the trial process. It also demonstrates how vital it is for there to be judicial supervision of the process of mediation.

[26.49]   **Halsey v Milton Keynes General NHS Trust**
Steel v Joy & Halliday

[2004] EWCA Civ 576

[2004] 4 All ER 920, [2004] 1 WLR 3002, 81 BMLR 108

In *Halsey*, the claimant brought a claim in respect of her husband's death alleged to have arisen out of the negligent treatment provided by the defendant NHS Trust. From an early stage, her solicitors invited the defendant to engage in mediation in respect of the claim. The defendant refused. At trial, the claim was dismissed. The court held that the defendant's refusal to mediate was reasonable, and made a costs order in favour of the defendant.

In *Steel*, separate proceedings, which were subsequently consolidated, were brought against two defendants in respect of two accidents. Both defendants admitted negligence, but causation remained in issue. The first defendant invited both the claimant and the second defendant to engage in mediation. The second defendant refused. The trial judge determined the issue of causation in favour of the second defendant. Again, it was held that the second defendant's refusal to mediate was reasonable, and the appropriate costs order was made.

HELD, ON APPEAL: The Court of Appeal upheld the orders made in both cases, and then took the opportunity to set out the matters to be considered when a court is asked to decide whether a party has acted unreasonably in refusing mediation or alternative dispute resolution (ADR).

The factors to be considered are:

(a)   the nature of the dispute;
(b)   the merits of the case;
(c)   whether other settlement methods have been attempted;
(d)   whether the costs of mediation would be disproportionately high;
(e)   delay;
(f)   whether the mediation has a reasonable prospect of success; and
(g)   whether the court has encouraged the parties to consider mediation.

Accordingly, in some circumstances, the court will use CPR 44.3 to deprive a successful party of its costs if there is an unreasonable refusal to mediate.

CHAPTER 27

Disclosure

1.   PRE-ACTION DISCLOSURE

(A)   TEXT OF THE PRE-ACTION PROTOCOL FOR PERSONAL INJURY CLAIMS RELEVANT TO DISCLOSURE

[27.1]

NOTES OF GUIDANCE

DISCLOSURE OF DOCUMENTS

2.13   The aim of the early disclosure of documents by the defendant is not to encourage 'fishing expeditions' by the claimant, but to promote an early exchange of relevant information to help in clarifying or resolving issues in dispute. The claimant's solicitor can assist by identifying in the letter of claim or in a subsequent letter the particular categories of documents which they consider are relevant.

THE PROTOCOL

DOCUMENTS

3.1   If the **defendant denies liability**, he should enclose with the letter of reply, **documents** in his possession which are **material to the issues** between the parties, and which would be likely to be ordered to be disclosed by the court, either on an application for pre-action disclosure, or on disclosure during proceedings.

3.2   Attached at Annex B are **specimen**, but non-exhaustive, **lists** of documents likely to be material in different types of claim. Where the claimant's investigation of the case is well advanced, the letter of claim could indicate which classes of documents are considered relevant for early disclosure. Alternatively these could be identified at a later stage.

3.3   Where the defendant admits primary liability, but alleges contributory negligence by the claimant, the defendant should give reasons supporting those allegations and disclose those documents from Annex B which are relevant to the issues in dispute. The claimant should respond to the allegations of contributory negligence before proceedings are issued.

3.4   No charge will be made for providing copy documents under the Protocol.

Note—Annex B is not reproduced here – reference should be made to *The Civil Court Practice*, published by LexisNexis Butterworths.

(B)   APPLICATION TO THE COURT FOR PRE-ACTION DISCLOSURE

[27.2]

CPR 31.16 – DISCLOSURE BEFORE PROCEEDINGS START
(1)   This rule applies where an application is made to the court under any Act for disclosure before proceedings have started.
(2)   The application must be supported by evidence.
(3)   The court may make an order under this rule only where–
   (a)   the respondent is likely to be a party to subsequent proceedings;
   (b)   the applicant is also likely to be a party to those proceedings;
   (c)   if proceedings had started, the respondent's duty by way of standard disclosure, set out in rule 31.6, would extend to the documents or classes of documents of which the applicant seeks disclosure; and
   (d)   disclosure before proceedings have started is desirable in order to–
      (i)   dispose fairly of the anticipated proceedings;
      (ii)   assist the dispute to be resolved without proceedings; or
      (iii)   save costs.
(4)   An order under this rule must–
   (a)   specify the documents or the classes of documents which the respondent must disclose; and
   (b)   require him, when making disclosure, to specify any of those documents–
      (i)   which are no longer in his control; or
      (ii)   in respect of which he claims a right or duty to withhold inspection.
(5)   Such an order may–
   (a)   require the respondent to indicate what has happened to any documents which are no longer in his control; and
   (b)   specify the time and place for disclosure and inspection.

GENERALLY

[27.3]   Bermuda International Securities Ltd v KPMG
[2001] EWCA Civ 269
[2001] All ER (D) 337 (Feb)

HELD, ON APPEAL: Under CPR 31.16, an order for pre-action disclosure could only be made where the respondent and the applicant were likely to be parties to proceedings and where, if proceedings were started the documents sought would fall within the category of those required by way of standard disclosure.
   It was part of a judge's case management role to establish whether pre-action disclosure was 'desirable' in order to dispose fairly of anticipated proceedings, assist resolution of the dispute without proceedings, and to save costs.

Further, whilst the costs of pre-action disclosure would normally be paid by the applicant, an order for costs could be varied where such an application was unreasonably resisted.

MEANING OF 'LIKELY TO BE A PARTY TO SUBSEQUENT PROCEEDINGS'

[27.4]   Black v Sumitomo Corpn

[2001] EWCA Civ 1819

[2003] 3 All ER 643, [2002] 1 WLR 1562, CA

Pre-action disclosure was ordered against the defendant, who appealed.

HELD, ON APPEAL: For the purpose of CPR 31.16(3)(a) and (b), an applicant/ respondent was 'likely to be a party to subsequent proceedings' where it was established that he might well be a party to proceedings if they were issued. The jurisdictional threshold was not intended to be high and it was likely to be a matter for the court's discretion.

NOT NECESSARY TO ASCERTAIN THE MERITS OF THE CASE

[27.5]   Rose v Lynx Express Ltd

[2004] EWCA Civ 447

[2004] 1 BCLC 455, [2004] All ER (D) 143 (Apr)

An order for pre-action disclosure was not granted since, on examining an element of the prospective claimant's case as a preliminary issue, the court found CPR 31.16(3)(c) and (d) were not satisfied. The applicant appealed.

HELD, ON APPEAL: In the context of an application for pre-action disclosure, it was not necessary to do any more than ascertain whether the applicant had a properly arguable case. Full consideration of the arguments to be advanced at trial was not helpful, as these arguments would have to be put again at trial (subject to change flowing from pre-action disclosure). Disclosure would be ordered on a limited basis.

2   STANDARD DISCLOSURE

(A)   WHAT IS STANDARD DISCLOSURE

[27.6]

CPR 31.2 – MEANING OF DISCLOSURE

A party discloses a document by stating that the document exists or has existed.

[27.7]

CPR 31.4 – MEANING OF DOCUMENT

In this Part–
   'document' means anything in which information of any description is recorded; and

'copy', in relation to a document, means anything onto which information recorded in the document has been copied, by whatever means and whether directly or indirectly.

[27.8]

CPR 31.5 – DISCLOSURE LIMITED TO STANDARD DISCLOSURE
(1)   An order to give disclosure is an order to give standard disclosure unless the court directs otherwise.
(2)   The court may dispense with or limit standard disclosure.
(3)   The parties may agree in writing to dispense with or to limit standard disclosure.

[27.9]

CPR 31.6 – STANDARD DISCLOSURE – WHAT DOCUMENTS ARE TO BE DISCLOSED

Standard disclosure requires a party to disclose only–
(a)   the documents on which he relies; and
(b)   the documents which–
  (i)   adversely affect his own case;
  (ii)   adversely affect another party's case; or
  (iii)   support another party's case; and
(c)   the documents which he is required to disclose by a relevant practice direction.

[27.10]   Paddick v Associated Newspapers Ltd

[2003] EWHC 2991 (QB)

[2003] All ER (D) 179 (Dec)

The claimant gave standard disclosure of extracts from witness statements, and stated that the undisclosed parts were irrelevant. The defendant applied for disclosure of those parts which had not been disclosed.

HELD: Disclosure of these parts was refused, the claimant's own witness statement being conclusive as to their relevance.

(B)   DUTY IN RESPECT OF STANDARD DISCLOSURE

[27.11]

CPR 31.7 – DUTY OF SEARCH
(1)   When giving standard disclosure, a party is required to make a reasonable search for documents falling within rule 31.6(b) or (c).
(2)   The factors relevant in deciding the reasonableness of a search include the following–
  (a)   the number of documents involved;
  (b)   the nature and complexity of the proceedings;
  (c)   the ease and expense of retrieval of any particular document; and
  (d)   the significance of any document which is likely to be located during the search.

(3)   Where a party has not searched for a category or class of document on the grounds that to do so would be unreasonable, he must state this in his disclosure statement and identify the category or class of document.

[27.12]

CPR 31.8 – DUTY OF DISCLOSURE LIMITED TO DOCUMENTS WHICH ARE OR HAVE BEEN IN A PARTY'S CONTROL
(1)   A party's duty to disclose documents is limited to documents which are or have been in his control.
(2)   For this purpose a party has or has had a document in his control if–
  (a)   it is or was in his physical possession;
  (b)   he has or has had a right to possession of it; or
  (c)   he has or has had a right to inspect or take copies of it.

[27.13]

CPR 31.11 – DUTY OF DISCLOSURE CONTINUES DURING PROCEEDINGS
(1)   Any duty of disclosure continues until the proceedings are concluded.
(2)   If documents to which that duty extends come to a party's notice at any time during the proceedings, he must immediately notify every other party.

(C)   PROCEDURAL MATTERS

[27.14]

CPR 31.10(1)–(4) – PROCEDURE FOR STANDARD DISCLOSURE
(1)   The procedure for standard disclosure is as follows.
(2)   Each party must make and serve on every other party, a list of documents in the relevant practice form.
(3)   The list must identify the documents in a convenient order and manner and as concisely as possible.
(4)   The list must indicate–
  (a)   those documents in respect of which the party claims a right or duty to withhold inspection; and
  (b)
    (i)   those documents which are no longer in the party's control; and
    (ii)   what has happened to those documents.

[27.15]

CPR 31.10(5)–(9) – DISCLOSURE STATEMENT
(5)   The list must include a disclosure statement.
(6)   A disclosure statement is a statement made by the party disclosing the documents–
  (a)   setting out the extent of the search that has been made to locate documents which he is required to disclose;
  (b)   certifying that he understands the duty to disclose documents; and

(c) certifying that to the best of his knowledge he has carried out that duty.

(7) Where the party making the disclosure statement is a company, firm, association or other organisation, the statement must also–

(a) identify the person making the statement; and

(b) explain why he is considered an appropriate person to make the statement.

(8) The parties may agree in writing–

(a) to disclose documents without making a list; and

(b) to disclose documents without the disclosing party making a disclosure statement.

(9) A disclosure statement may be made by a person who is not a party where this is permitted by a relevant practice direction.

[27.16]

CPR 31.23 – FALSE DISCLOSURE STATEMENTS

(1) Proceedings for contempt of court may be brought against a person if he makes, or causes to be made, a false disclosure statement, without an honest belief in its truth.

(2) Proceedings under this rule may be brought only–

(a) by the Attorney General; or

(b) with the permission of the court.

(D) INSPECTION

[27.17]

CPR 31.3 – RIGHT OF INSPECTION OF A DISCLOSED DOCUMENT

(1) A party to whom a document has been disclosed has a right to inspect that document except where–

(a) the document is no longer in the control of the party who disclosed it;

(b) the party disclosing the document has a right or a duty to withhold inspection of it; or

(c) paragraph (2) applies.

(2) Where a party considers that it would be disproportionate to the issues in the case to permit inspection of documents within a category or class of document disclosed under rule 31.6(b)–

(a) he is not required to permit inspection of documents within that category or class; but

(b) he must state in his disclosure statement that inspection of those documents will not be permitted on the grounds that to do so would be disproportionate.

[27.18]

CPR 31.14 – DOCUMENTS REFERRED TO IN STATEMENTS OF CASE ETC

(1) A party may inspect a document mentioned in–

(a) a statement of case;

(b) a witness statement;

(c) a witness summary; or

(d) an affidavit.

(e) Revoked.

(2) Subject to rule 35.10(4), a party may apply for an order for inspection of any document mentioned in an expert's report which has not already been disclosed in the proceedings.

[27.19] Rigg v Associated Newspapers

[2003] EWHC 710 (QB)

[2003] All ER (D) 97 (Apr)

In defamation proceedings, the defence quoted at length and in detail from notes of an interview, which the defendant maintained was an accurate record of the interview. The notes were not specifically referred to. The claimant made an application for disclosure pursuant to CPR 31.14, which was granted. The defendant appealed.

HELD, ON APPEAL: The notes were not 'mentioned' within the meaning of CPR 31.14; there was no direct and specific reference. Quoting extensively from a document did not amount to mentioning or directly alluding to it (within the meaning of *Dubai Bank Ltd v Galadari (2)* [1990] 2 All ER 738, [1990] 1 WLR 731). However, in the circumstances, an order for specific disclosure could be made under CPR 31.12.

[27.20]

CPR 31.15 – INSPECTION AND COPYING OF DOCUMENTS

Where a party has a right to inspect a document–

(a) that party must give the party who disclosed the document written notice of his wish to inspect it;

(b) the party who disclosed the document must permit inspection not more than 7 days after the date on which he received the notice; and

(c) that party may request a copy of the document and, if he also undertakes to pay reasonable copying costs, the party who disclosed the document must supply him with a copy not more than 7 days after the date on which he received the request.

3. SPECIFIC DISCLOSURE

[27.21]

CPR 31.12 – SPECIFIC DISCLOSURE OR INSPECTION

(1) The court may make an order for specific disclosure or specific inspection.

(2) An order for specific disclosure is an order that a party must do one or more of the following things–

(a) disclose documents or classes of documents specified in the order;

(b) carry out a search to the extent stated in the order;

(c) disclose any documents located as a result of that search.

(3) An order for specific inspection is an order that a party permit inspection of a document referred to in rule 31.3(2).

4. NON-PARTY DISCLOSURE

[27.22]

CPR 31.17 – ORDERS FOR DISCLOSURE AGAINST A PERSON NOT A PARTY
 (1)   This rule applies where an application is made to the court under any Act for disclosure by a person who is not a party to the proceedings.
 (2)   The application must be supported by evidence.
 (3)   The court may make an order under this rule only where–
   (a)   the documents of which disclosure is sought are likely to support the case of the applicant or adversely affect the case of one of the other parties to the proceedings; and
   (b)   disclosure is necessary in order to dispose fairly of the claim or to save costs.
 (4)   An order under this rule must–
   (a)   specify the documents or the classes of documents which the respondent must disclose; and
   (b)   require the respondent, when making disclosure, to specify any of those documents–
     (i)   which are no longer in his control; or
     (ii)   in respect of which he claims a right or duty to withhold inspection.
 (5)   Such an order may–
   (a)   require the respondent to indicate what has happened to any documents which are no longer in his control; and
   (b)   specify the time and place for disclosure and inspection.

[27.23]   **Three Rivers DC v Bank of England**
[2002] EWCA Civ 1182
[2002] 4 All ER 881, [2003] 1 WLR 210

HELD: A document 'likely' to support the applicant's case or adversely affect another party's case, for the purpose of an application for non-party disclosure, was a document which 'may well' do so.

5. PRIVILEGE

(A)   PROCEDURAL MATTERS

[27.24]

CPR 31.19 – CLAIM TO WITHHOLD INSPECTION OR DISCLOSURE OF
A DOCUMENT
 (1)   A person may apply, without notice, for an order permitting him to withhold disclosure of a document on the ground that disclosure would damage the public interest.
 (2)   Unless the court orders otherwise, an order of the court under paragraph (1)–
   (a)   must not be served on any other person; and
   (b)   must not be open to inspection by any person.

(3)   A person who wishes to claim that he has a right or a duty to withhold inspection of a document, or part of a document, must state in writing–

(a)   that he has such a right or duty; and

(b)   the grounds on which he claims that right or duty.

(4)   The statement referred to in paragraph (3) must be made–

(a)   in the list in which the document is disclosed; or

(b)   if there is no list, to the person wishing to inspect the document.

(5)   A party may apply to the court to decide whether a claim made under paragraph (3) should be upheld.

(6)   For the purpose of deciding an application under paragraph (1) (application to withhold disclosure) or paragraph (3) (claim to withhold inspection) the court may–

(a)   require the person seeking to withhold disclosure or inspection of a document to produce that document to the court; and

(b)   invite any person, whether or not a party, to make representations.

(7)   An application under paragraph (1) or paragraph (5) must be supported by evidence.

(8)   This Part does not affect any rule of law which permits or requires a document to be withheld from disclosure or inspection on the ground that its disclosure or inspection would damage the public interest.

[27.25]

CPR 31.20 – RESTRICTION ON USE OF A PRIVILEGED DOCUMENT INSPECTION OF WHICH HAS BEEN INADVERTENTLY ALLOWED

Where a party inadvertently allows a privileged document to be inspected, the party who has inspected the document may use it or its contents only with the permission of the court.

(B)   LEGAL ADVICE PRIVILEGE

[27.26]   Birmingham v Kelly

(26 April 1979, unreported)   Jupp J

The claimant alleged that he was injured in a road traffic accident. As the proposed defendant's whereabouts could not be ascertained, the claimant's solicitors notified his claim to the Motor Insurers' Bureau (MIB). The MIB appointed an insurer to investigate the claim who communicated with the claimant's solicitors. The insurer denied liability on MIB's behalf. The claimant applied for specific disclosure of correspondence and recorded notes of telephone conversations between MIB and the insurer.

HELD: The documents were privileged. Although MIB had not instructed solicitors during the period in question, everything it did was to prepare the case for settlement or defence, whichever would prove appropriate.

[27.27] **Balabel v Air India**

[1988] Ch 317, [1988] 2 All ER 246, [1988] 2 WLR 1036

The claimant sought an order for specific disclosure of certain classes of documents relating to a lease. The defendant claimed privilege but disclosure was nevertheless ordered following an appeal to the High Court. The defendant appealed against this decision.

HELD, ON APPEAL: Legal advice was not confined to telling the client the law; it also included advice as to what should be done in the relevant legal context. Where information was passed by the solicitor or client to the other as part of the continuing process of keeping each other informed, so advice might be given, and privilege would attach. The relationship had an implication that advice would be sought or given at each relevant stage. Approved in *Three Rivers DC v Governor & Company of the Bank of England* (see para [27.29]).

[27.28] **(1) Parry (2) Whelan v News Group Newspapers**

[1990] NLJR 1719, CA

In a defamation claim, the parties' respective solicitors discussed on the telephone the issue of whether a written apology published in the defendant's newspaper would resolve the dispute between the parties. Disagreement arose as to the content of the telephone conversation and what, if any, agreement had been reached. The solicitor for the claimants disclosed his note of the telephone conversation. The defendant argued that the note was privileged, and that in disclosing it, the claimants had waived privilege and should disclose all other documents relevant to the issue.

HELD: An attendance note was merely a record of what occurred during the course of a conversation. It mattered not whether the discussion was 'without prejudice', the attendance note was not protected by legal advice privilege. Accordingly, it was not privileged, and its disclosure did not entitle the defendant to see documents which were protected by privilege.

[27.29] **Three Rivers DC v Governor & Company of the Bank of England (No 6)**

[2004] UKHL 48

[2005] 1 AC 610, [2005] 4 All ER 948, [2004] 3 WLR 1274

HELD, ON APPEAL: Legal advice privilege only applies where the advice is given within a 'relevant legal context'. If the solicitor is a client's 'man of business' responsible for advising on all elements of business, only advice in a relevant legal context, ie objectively relating to the rights, liabilities, obligations or remedies of the client, will be protected by the privilege.

[27.30] **Three Rivers DC v Governor & Company of the Bank of England (No 5)**

[2003] EWCA Civ 474

[2003] QB 1556, [2003] All ER (D) 59 (Apr), [2003] 3 WLR 667

HELD: Legal advice privilege does not extend to communications between lawyers and third parties. The dominant purpose of the communication must have been seeking or giving legal advice if the communication is to be protected by legal advice privilege.

[27.31]   Sumitomo Corpn v Credit Lyonnais Rouse Ltd
[2001] EWCA Civ 1152
[2002] 4 All ER 68, [2002] 1 WLR 479

The claimant appealed against an order rejecting its claim to legal professional privilege in relation to translated documents. No claim to privilege was made in relation to the original documents, but the claimant claimed privilege in respect of the translations on the basis that they were created for the purpose of legal proceedings, and that the selection of the documents might give a clue as to the advice being given to the claimant.

HELD, ON APPEAL: The principle in *Lyell v Kennedy (No 3)* (1884) 27 Ch D 1 – that documents copied by a solicitor are privileged as they represent the work of the solicitor's mind and may give an indication of the advice being given to his client – does not apply to selections from privileged own client documents, only third party documents. If production was resisted by the party in question, it was a matter for the court's discretion whether to order production.

[27.32]   South Coast Shipping Co Ltd v Havant Borough Council
[2002] 3 All ER 779, [2002] NLJR 59

At a detailed costs assessment following three orders in favour of the claimant, the judge ruled there had been no breach of the indemnity principle and the claimant was entitled to claim costs from the respondents. The claimant, during the hearing of this preliminary issue, had disclosed privileged documents to the costs judge but not to the defendant.

HELD: At a detailed assessment, a costs judge could require production of privileged documents but could not order them. The receiving party must be put to an election of waiving privilege and being allowed to rely on the privileged documents, or claiming privilege and not being allowed to do so. If the party elected to waive privilege in those circumstance, privilege was thereby waived only for the purpose of the costs proceedings.

[27.33]   Dickinson (t/a Dickinson Equipment Finance) v Rushmer (t/a FJ Associates)
[2001] All ER (D) 369 (Dec), [2002] 1 Costs LR 128

The defendant appealed against a decision by a costs judge not to allow the defendant to see documents upon which the court had based a finding that there had been no breach of the indemnity principle.

HELD: The costs judge's decision not to allow the paying party to see documents on which he had based his decision was a breach of natural justice. The receiving party had chosen to prove his point on an issue by reference to certain documents; fairness required him to disclose those documents to the paying party.

[27.34]   Somatra Ltd v Sinclair Roche & Temperley
[2000] All ER (D) 1055, [2000] 1 WLR 2453

The court had to decide whether without prejudice material had lost its without prejudice status through waiver.

HELD: Legal professional privilege may be waived unilaterally, however, without prejudice privilege is a joint privilege which may not be waived by one party alone.

(C) WITHOUT PREJUDICE COMMUNICATIONS

[27.35]   Paddock v Forrester
(1842) 3 Man & G 903, 3 Scott NR 715

Where a letter written by one of the parties to a dispute to the other, is expressed to be 'without prejudice', neither that letter nor the answer to it can be given in evidence on the part of the writer of the first letter, although the answer is not expressed to be 'without prejudice'.

[27.36]   Hoghton v Hoghton
(1852) 15 Beav 278, 21 LJ Ch 482, 17 Jur 99

Where letters are written 'without prejudice' with a view to a compromise, they cannot be given in evidence.

[27.37]   India Rubber, Gutta Percha and Telegraph Works Ltd v Chapman
(1926) 20 BWCC 184, CA

Letters following a letter written 'without prejudice' should be treated as being 'without prejudice' and therefore inadmissible unless there was a clear break in the chain of correspondence to indicate that the ensuing letters were open.

[27.38]   Tomlin v Standard Telephones and Cables Ltd
[1969] 3 All ER 201, [1969] 1 WLR 1378, CA

In dealing with a claim for damages for personal injury the defendants' insurers wrote the claimant's solicitor a letter marked 'without prejudice' saying 'We are only prepared to deal with the case on a 50–50 basis'. The solicitor replied 'my client has instructed me to say that he will agree to settle his case on a 50–50 basis as you propose and accordingly this leaves only the question of quantum to be disposed of'. In subsequent letters the insurers referred to 'the agreement come to between us' and eventually wrote 'It has already been agreed that this is a 50–50 case and accordingly we are prepared to pay £625 in settlement'. All the insurers' letters were marked 'without prejudice'. The claimant rejected the offer and sued for damages to be assessed, on the basis that there was a concluded agreement to pay him one-half.

HELD: There was a binding agreement. The court was entitled to look at letters marked 'without prejudice' to see if an agreement had been reached. There was a concluded agreement on the issue of liability leaving over for further negotiation the separate and severable question of quantum of damages.

[27.39]   Rush & Tompkins Ltd v Greater London Council
[1989] AC 1280, [1988] 3 All ER 737, [1988] 3 WLR 939

HELD: The underlying purpose of the 'without prejudice' rule was to protect a litigant from being embarrassed by any admissions made purely in an attempt to achieve settlement. The privilege remained in force even after the compromise had been reached. Any admissions made on a without prejudice basis were protected from discovery by other parties to the same litigation and remained privileged for any subsequent litigation connected with the same subject matter.

[27.40]   Cheddar Valley Engineering Ltd v Chaddlewood Homes Ltd

[1992] 4 All ER 942, [1992] I WLR 820

Where one party wished to change the basis of discussions from 'without prejudice' to 'open' then the burden was on him to bring this to the attention of the other parties. The test was whether a reasonable man would realise that there had been a change in the basis of how the negotiations were being carried out. The use of the word 'open' during a telephone conversation was not sufficient.

[27.41]   Dixons Stores Group Ltd v Thames Television plc

[1993] I All ER 349

The claimant commenced proceedings against the defendant alleging that a television programme broadcast by the defendant was defamatory to the claimant. Proceedings were issued on 11 July 1991 and between February and June 1992 the parties exchanged 'without prejudice' correspondence in an attempt to negotiate a settlement. The negotiations came to nothing.

On 1 and 9 July the defendant wrote two letters to the claimant offering a settlement. The first was not marked 'without prejudice' and the second was marked 'open letter'. At the trial of the action the defendant sought to refer to the terms of these two letters and the claimant objected on the basis that the letters were privileged.

HELD: It was clear that the two letters written were written with the intention that they should be referred to at the trial of the action. The letters were not written as part of continuing without prejudice negotiations. Without prejudice negotiations had occurred between February and June 1992 and had come to nothing and were at an end. A letter containing an offer to settle could be written as an open letter with the intention that it be referred to at trial provided that it was relevant to the issues. The letters were not privileged.

Per Drake J: The policy of the law is clearly to encourage settlement of actions and I think it is quite clear that the modern tendency has been to enlarge the cloak under which negotiations may be conducted without prejudice.

[27.42]   Family Housing Association (Manchester) Ltd v Michael Hyde & Partners

[1993] 2 All ER 567, [1993] I WLR 354, CA

The claimant brought proceedings against a number of defendants claiming loss and damage arising out of alleged defects in the construction and design of the claimant's premises. The first and third defendants applied for an order striking out the claimant's claim for want of prosecution. In response the claimant's solicitor filed an affidavit referring to and setting out the nature and content of without prejudice discussions which had taken place between 1986 and 1991. The defendants acknowledged that the claimant could refer to the fact without prejudice negotiations had taken place and the period of the negotiations but argued that the claimant was not permitted to refer to the details of what was offered. They argued that this was privileged information, inadmissible without the consent of the parties. The defendants brought an application to have the affidavit struck out. The judge refused to do so and the defendants appealed.

HELD, ON APPEAL: The defendants' application failed. There was nothing in reported authorities which excluded the use of without prejudice correspondence in applications of this kind. The unreported authorities recognised a practice of allowing without prejudice correspondence to be admitted in applications of this kind. There was also evidence of a convention permitting the use of such documents for this purpose. As to public policy, there was a public policy consideration in favour of admitting the evidence in these sorts of applications.

Per Hirst LJ: I am unable to see how exposure of the course of negotiations in this narrow context is in any way harmful to either side. If the application succeeds, the action will be at an end. If it fails, and the case proceeds to trial, the material will not be available to the trial judge and he will not be in any way embarrassed.

[27.43]   Unilever plc v Procter & Gamble Co
[2001] 1 All ER 783, [2000] 1 WLR 2436

HELD, ON APPEAL: The protection given to without prejudice communications applied to all statements made without prejudice, and not simply admissions. In the context of without prejudice meetings, parties must be able to speak freely without concern as to whether each statement will be without prejudice.

[27.44]   Reed Executive plc v Reed Business Information Ltd
[2004] EWCA Civ 887
[2004] 4 All ER 942, [2004] 1 WLR 3026

HELD: The court does not have the power to order disclosure of any of the detail of without prejudice negotiations for the purposes of assessing costs, particularly where related litigation or negotiations are ongoing. Adverse inferences should not be drawn against a party refusing disclosure of without prejudice documents, as this would be contrary to the basis of without prejudice negotiations.

[27.45]   Somatra Ltd v Sinclair Roche & Temperley
[2000] All ER (D) 1055, [2000] 1 WLR 2453

HELD: Legal professional privilege may be waived unilaterally. However, without prejudice privilege is a joint privilege which may not be waived by one party alone.

[27.46]   Berry Trade Ltd v Moussavi (No 3)
[2003] EWCA Civ 715
[2003] All ER (D) 315 (May)

On the application of the claimant, statements made by a defendant at a without prejudice meeting were permitted to be admitted as evidence at a later hearing. The defendant appealed.

HELD, ON APPEAL: The correct test for making an exception to the rule that without prejudice communications are privileged from disclosure was whether there had been 'unambiguous impropriety' and a clear abuse of the privilege. In the instant case, the risk of perjury did not qualify as an exception to the rule.
   Appeal allowed.

[27.47]   Alizadeh v Nibkin
(1993) Times, 19 March, CA

The general rule was that admissions made in the course of negotiations for settlement should not be admitted in evidence. (see *Rush & Tompkins Ltd v Greater*

London Council (at para [27.39])). However a tape recording of a without prejudice negotiation could become admissible if there was an unambiguous admission of impropriety during the course of the recorded discussion.

(D)   PUBLIC INTEREST PRIVILEGE

[27.48]   Conway v Rimmer
[1968] AC 910, [1968] 1 All ER 874, [1968] 2 WLR 998, HL

A probationary constable claimed damages from the defendant police superintendent for malicious prosecution. On disclosure of documents the defendant claimed privilege in respect of reports submitted to his superior officer on the ground that they were of a class of documents which it was contrary to the public interest to disclose. The claimant submitted that where the objection was to production of a document because of the class to which it belonged as opposed to its content, the court might examine the document and, if satisfied that the interests of justice so demanded, overrule the Crown objection.

HELD, ON APPEAL: The court had an inherent right to decide for itself on the information supplied, or if necessary, by inspection of the document itself, whether it came within a class of document which must as a class be withheld from production.

'The police are carrying on an unending war with criminals, many of whom are highly intelligent. So it is essential that there should be no disclosure of anything which might give useful information to those who organise criminal activities and it would be generally wrong to require a disclosure in a civil case of anything which might be material in a pending prosecution; but after the verdict has been given or it has been decided to take no proceedings there is not the same need for secrecy'.

[27.49]   Sharples v Halford
(1991) Times, 9 October, EAT

Police disciplinary files, documents relating to the private lives of chief police officers and positive vetting documentation in the files of the Association of Chief Police Officers were privileged on the grounds of public interest immunity.

[27.50]   Goodwin v Chief Constable of Lancashire
(1992) Times, 3 November, CA

The Public Order manuals of police authorities are subject to public interest immunity.

(E)   DOMINANT PURPOSE

[27.51]   Waugh v British Railways Board
[1980] AC 521, [1979] 2 All ER 1169, [1979] 3 WLR 150, HL

The claimant's husband, an engine driver, was killed when two locomotives collided. She claimed damages under the Fatal Accident Act. Soon after the accident a joint internal report was prepared by two officers of the defendant, as was the normal practice after an accident, to assist in establishing the cause of the accident and equally for the purpose of providing the board's solicitor with material on which he could advise the defendant in respect of any proceedings arising out of the accident. Proceedings were to be anticipated in the present case.

The report was headed 'For the information of the board's solicitor ... for the purpose of enabling him to advise the BRB in relation thereto'.

The claimant requested a copy of the report. The defendant refused, asserting that the report was subject to legal professional privilege.

HELD: The report should be disclosed. Unless the purpose of submission to the legal adviser was at least the *dominant* (but not necessarily the sole) purpose for which the relevant document was prepared, the reasons which required privilege to be extended to it could not apply. Here the two purposes for which the report had been prepared were of equal rank or weight.

[27.52]   **Neilson v Laugharne**

[1981] QB 736, [1981] 1 All ER 829, [1981] 2 WLR 537, CA

In an action against the police for wrongful arrest the claimant sought disclosure of statements taken by the police for the purposes of an inquiry under section 49 of the Police Act 1964 into a complaint made by the claimant arising from the same incident. The police claimed legal professional privilege against disclosure.

HELD: Following *Waugh v British Railways Board* (at para [27.51]), the dominant purpose of the police in taking the statements was to carry out the statutory duty to investigate required by section 49 and there was no privilege in respect of those statements.

(F)   CROWN PRIVILEGE

[27.53]   **Re Grosvenor Hotel, London**

[1964] Ch 464, [1964] 1 All ER 92, [1964] 2 WLR 184, CA

HELD, ON APPEAL: It has been clear law since the decision of the House of Lords in *Duncan v Cammell Laird & Co Ltd* [1942] AC 624, [1942] 1 All ER 587 that an objection to production properly taken by a public department on the ground that to produce the document would be injurious to the public interest is conclusive. Viscount Simon said in *Duncan's* case:

'The essential matter is that the decision to object should be taken by the minister who is the political head of the department and that he should have seen and considered the contents of the documents and himself have formed the view that on grounds of public interest they ought not to be produced either because of their actual contents or because of the class of documents, eg departmental minutes to which they belong'.

When an objection to production is supported by a minister's affidavit, the affidavit must:
  (1)   contain evidence from which the court can judge whether the minister came to a fresh decision of his own on the question whether the documents should be withheld, without any regard to a previous decision taken by his subordinates; and

(2)   specify the class of documents to which those for which he claims privilege belong. It is important that the public should know the principles on which ministers purport to act on these cases.

[27.54]   Re Grosvenor Hotel, London (No 2)

[1965] Ch 1210, [1964] 3 All ER 354, [1964] 3 WLR 992, CA

HELD, ON APPEAL: (1) If Crown privilege is to be successfully claimed, the objection must be taken in proper form, in the ordinary way by the minister himself after considering the documents himself.

(2)   A document may be privileged either because of its contents or because it is one of a class of documents privileged, apart from their contents, by the source from which they proceed.

(3)   There is a residual power in the courts to override the executive in cases where Crown privilege is unreasonably claimed for a class of document, eg comprising routine communications between civil servants, and the court may ask to see the documents to make a decision.

(4)   Where a minister is objecting to production of all documents in a particular class which is not privileged by reason of the contents he must justify his objection with reasons, describing the nature of the class and the reason why the documents should not be disclosed.

CHAPTER 28

Witnesses

1.   WITNESS STATEMENTS

(A)   FORM OF WITNESS STATEMENTS

[28.1]

CPR 32.8 – FORM OF WITNESS STATEMENT

A witness statement must comply with the requirements set out in the relevant Practice Direction.

Practice Direction to CPR 32 – Witness statements

Witness statements

Heading
  17.1   The witness statement should be headed with the title of the proceedings …
  17.2   At the top right hand corner of the first page there should be clearly written:
    (1)   the party on whose behalf it is made,
    (2)   the initials and surname of the witness,
    (3)   the number of the statement in relation to that witness,
    (4)   the identifying initials and number of each exhibit referred to, and
    (5)   the date the statement was made.

Body of the witness statement
  18.1   The witness statement must, if practicable, be in the intended witness's own words, the statement should be expressed in the first person and should also state:
    (1)   the full name of the witness,
    (2)   his place of residence or, if he is making the statement in his professional, business or other occupational capacity, the address at which he works, the position he holds and the name of his firm or employer,
    (3)   his occupation, or if he has none, his description, and
    (4)   the fact that he is a party to the proceedings or is the employee of such a party if it be the case.
  18.2   A witness statement must indicate:
    (1)   which of the statements in it are made from the witness's own knowledge and which are matters of information or belief, and
    (2)   the source for any matters of information or belief.
  18.3   An exhibit used in conjunction with a witness statement should be verified and identified by the witness and remain separate from the witness statement.
  18.4   Where a witness refers to an exhibit or exhibits, he should state 'I refer to the (*description of exhibit*) marked '…'".
  18.5   …
  18.6   Where a witness makes more than one witness statement to which there are exhibits, in the same proceedings, the numbering of the exhibits should run consecutively throughout and not start again with each witness statement.
  19.1   A witness statement should:
    (1)   be produced on durable quality A4 paper with a 3.5cm margin,

(2) be fully legible and should normally be typed on one side of the paper only,

(3) where possible, be bound securely in a manner which would not hamper filing, or otherwise each page should be endorsed with the case number and should bear the initials of the witness,

(4) have the pages numbered consecutively as a separate statement (or as one of several statements contained in a file),

(5) be divided into numbered paragraphs,

(6) have all numbers, including dates, expressed in figures, and

(7) give the reference to any document or documents mentioned either in the margin or in bold text in the body of the statement.

19.2 It is usually convenient for a witness statement to follow the chronological sequence of the events or matters dealt with, each paragraph of a witness statement should as far as possible be confined to a distinct portion of the subject.

Statement of Truth

20.1 A witness statement is the equivalent of the oral evidence which that witness would, if called, give in evidence; it must include a statement by the intended witness that he believes the facts in it are true.

20.2 To verify a witness statement the statement of truth is as follows:

'I believe that the facts stated in this witness statement are true'.

20.3 Attention is drawn to rule 32.14 which sets out the consequences of verifying a witness statement containing a false statement without an honest belief in its truth.

Alterations to witness statements

22.1 Any alteration to a witness statement must be initialled by the person making the statement or by the authorised person where appropriate (see paragraph 21).

22.2 A witness statement which contains an alteration that has not been initialled may be used in evidence only with the permission of the court.

Defects in witness statements and exhibits

25.1 Where …a witness statement, or …exhibit to …a witness statement does not comply with Part 32 or this practice direction in relation to its form, the court may refuse to admit it as evidence and may refuse to allow the costs arising from its preparation.

(B) EXCHANGE OF WITNESS STATEMENTS

[28.2]

CPR 32.4 – REQUIREMENT TO SERVE WITNESS STATEMENTS FOR USE AT TRIAL

(1) A witness statement is a written statement signed by a person which contains the evidence which that person would be allowed to give orally.

(2) The court will order a party to serve on the other parties any witness statement of the oral evidence which the party serving the statement intends to rely on in relation to any issues of fact to be decided at the trial.

(3) The court may give directions as to–

    (a)   the order in which witness statements are to be served; and

    (b)   whether or not the witness statements are to be filed.

(C)   HOW THE EVIDENCE OF WITNESSES IS TO BE GIVEN

[28.3]

CPR 32.2 – EVIDENCE OF WITNESSES – GENERAL RULE

(1)   The general rule is that any fact which needs to be proved by the evidence of witnesses is to be proved–

    (a)   at trial, by their oral evidence given in public; and

    (b)   at any other hearing, by their evidence in writing.

(2)   This is subject–

    (a)   to any provision to the contrary contained in these Rules or elsewhere; or

    (b)   to any order of the court.

(D)   USE OF WITNESS STATEMENTS AT TRIAL

[28.4]

CPR 32.5 – USE AT TRIAL OF WITNESS STATEMENTS WHICH HAVE
BEEN SERVED

(1)   If–

    (a)   a party has served a witness statement; and

    (b)   he wishes to rely at trial on the evidence of the witness who made the statement,

he must call the witness to give oral evidence unless the court orders otherwise or he puts the statement in as hearsay evidence.

(2)   Where a witness is called to give oral evidence under paragraph (1), his witness statement shall stand as his evidence in chief unless the court orders otherwise.

(3)   A witness giving oral evidence at trial may with the permission of the court–

    (a)   amplify his witness statement; and

    (b)   give evidence in relation to new matters which have arisen since the witness statement was served on the other parties.

(4)   The court will give permission under paragraph (3) only if it considers that there is good reason not to confine the evidence of the witness to the contents of his witness statement.

(5)   If a party who has served a witness statement does not–

    (a)   call the witness to give evidence at trial; or

    (b)   put the witness statement in as hearsay evidence,

any other party may put the witness statement in as hearsay evidence.

CPR 32.10 – PERMISSION REQUIRED TO RELY UPON WITNESS STATEMENT
SERVED LATE

If a witness statement or a witness summary for use at trial is not served in respect of an intended witness within the time specified by the court, then the witness may not be called to give oral evidence unless the court gives permission.

[28.5]   **Mealey Horgan plc v Horgan**

[1999] All ER (D) 1523, (1999) The Times, 6 July

The defendant had served witness statements two weeks late and applied for time for the exchange of witness statements to be extended and for permission to allow those witnesses to give oral evidence.

HELD: It would be unjust to exclude a party from adducing evidence save in extreme circumstances, for example, where there had been deliberate flouting of court orders or inexcusable delay. The claimant had received the statements six weeks before the trial date and could properly prepare for trial notwithstanding the delay. The claimant had urged the court to order the defendant to pay a substantial sum of money into court, either under CPR 3.1(5) or under CPR 3.1(3)(a). A payment into court might be appropriate where there was a history of repeated breaches of timetable, court orders or something in the conduct of the party that gave rise to the suspicion that it was not bona fide and the court thought that the other side should have protection. However, this was not such a case.

(E)   CROSS-EXAMINATION OF WITNESSES

[28.6]

CPR 32.7 – ORDER FOR CROSS-EXAMINATION AT A HEARING OTHER THAN THE TRIAL
(1)   Where, at a hearing other than the trial, evidence is given in writing, any party may apply to the court for permission to cross-examine the person giving the evidence.
(2)   If the court gives permission under paragraph (1) but the person in question does not attend as required by the order, his evidence may not be used unless the court gives permission.

CPR 32.11 – CROSS-EXAMINATION ON A WITNESS STATEMENT

Where a witness is called to give evidence at trial, he may be cross-examined on his witness statement whether or not the statement or any part of it was referred to during the witness's evidence in chief.

2.   WITNESS SUMMARIES

[28.7]

CPR 32.9 – WITNESS SUMMARIES
(1)   A party who–
   (a)   is required to serve a witness statement for use at trial; but
   (b)   is unable to obtain one, may apply, without notice, for permission to serve a witness summary instead.
(2)   A witness summary is a summary of–
   (a)   the evidence, if known, which would otherwise be included in a witness statement; or

(b)   if the evidence is not known, the matters about which the party serving the witness summary proposes to question the witness.

(3)   Unless the court orders otherwise, a witness summary must include the name and address of the intended witness.

(4)   Unless the court orders otherwise, a witness summary must be served within the period in which a witness statement would have had to be served.

(5)   Where a party serves a witness summary, so far as practicable rules 32.4 (requirement to serve witness statements for use at trial), 32.5(3) (amplifying witness statements), and 32.8 (form of witness statement) shall apply to the summary.

3.   WITNESS SUMMONSES

(A)   WHAT IS A WITNESS SUMMONS?

[28.8]

CPR 34.2 – WITNESS SUMMONSES

(1)   A witness summons is a document issued by the court requiring a witness to–

(a)   attend court to give evidence; or

(b)   produce documents to the court.

(2)   A witness summons must be in the relevant practice form.

(3)   There must be a separate witness summons for each witness.

(4)   A witness summons may require a witness to produce documents to the court either–

(a)   on the date fixed for a hearing; or

(b)   on such date as the court may direct.

(5)   The only documents that a summons under this rule can require a person to produce before a hearing are documents which that person could be required to produce at the hearing.

(B)   ISSUING

[28.9]

CPR 34.3 – ISSUE OF A WITNESS SUMMONS

(1)   A witness summons is issued on the date entered on the summons by the court.

(2)   A party must obtain permission from the court where he wishes to–

(a)   have a summons issued less than 7 days before the date of the trial;

(b)   have a summons issued for a witness to attend court to give evidence or to produce documents on any date except the date fixed for the trial; or

(c)   have a summons issued for a witness to attend court to give evidence or to produce documents at any hearing except the trial.

(3)   A witness summons must be issued by -

(a)   the court where the case is proceeding; or

(b)   the court where the hearing in question will be held.

(4)   The court may set aside or vary a witness summons issued under this rule.

(C)   TIME

[28.10]

CPR 34.5 – TIME FOR SERVING A WITNESS SUMMONS
(1)   The general rule is that a witness summons is binding if it is served at least 7 days before the date on which the witness is required to attend before the court or tribunal.
(2)   The court may direct that a witness summons shall be binding although it will be served less than 7 days before the date on which the witness is required to attend before the court or tribunal.
(3)   A witness summons which is–
  (a)   served in accordance with this rule; and
  (b)   requires the witness to attend court to give evidence,
is binding until the conclusion of the hearing at which the attendance of the witness is required.

(D)   SERVING

[28.11]

CPR 34.6 – WHO IS TO SERVE A WITNESS SUMMONS
(1)   A witness summons is to be served by the court unless the party on whose behalf it is issued indicates in writing, when he asks the court to issue the summons, that he wishes to serve it himself.
(2)   Where the court is to serve the witness summons, the party on whose behalf it is issued must deposit, in the court office, the money to be paid or offered to the witness under rule 34.7.

(E)   TRAVEL EXPENSES

[28.12]

CPR 34.7 – RIGHT OF WITNESS TO TRAVEL EXPENSES

At the time of service of a witness summons the witness must be offered or paid -
  (a)   a sum reasonably sufficient to cover his expenses in travelling to and from the court; and
  (b)   such sum by way of compensation for loss of time as may be specified in the relevant practice direction.

(F)   SETTING ASIDE A WITNESS SUMMONS

[28.13]   Harrison v Bloom Camillin
[1999] 45 LS Gaz R 32, (1999) The Independent, 28 June

The defendant served a witness summons on the claimant's father, who applied to have it set aside.

HELD: CPR 34.3(4) gives the court power to set aside or vary a witness summons, but no express guidance was given by the Civil Procedure Rules, and careful regard should be had to pre-CPR authorities, specifically *Re State of Norway's Application* [1987] 1 QB 433 and *Morgan v Morgan* [1977] 2 All ER 515, [1977] 2 WLR 712. The interests of a witness were to be taken into account but were second to the interests of the parties as litigants and the interests of justice. The witness summons was set aside as the defendant had been too general in the types of evidence sought, had acted with delay and the witness would be embarrassed by much of the evidence he was asked to give.

[28.14] South Tyneside BC v Wickes Building Supplies Ltd

[2004] EWHC 2428 (Comm)

[2004] All ER (D) 69 (Nov)

The claimant issued a number of witness summonses against non-parties. One of the documents sought by the summonses contained a confidentiality clause. The defendant applied to set the summonses aside.

HELD: The court had the power to set aside or vary a witness summons under CPR 34.3(4). However the Civil Procedure Rules gave no guidance and regard was therefore to be had to pre-CPR authorities and *Harrison v Bloom Camillin* (at para [28.13]). The position was as follows:

(1) A witness summons was designed to require production of specified documents at trial, and therefore it must specify the documents sought. It must not be used for speculative fishing expeditions.

(2) The production of the documents must be necessary for the fair disposal of the matter or to save costs. The court was permitted to take into account whether the same evidence could be obtained by other means.

(3) A witness summons would be set aside where the documents were not relevant to the proceedings. If the documents were relevant, nevertheless that would not be decisive as to whether the witness summons would be allowed.

(4) Confidential documents were not absolutely barred from production by means of a witness summons; but in the exercise of its discretion the court would have regard to the fact of confidentiality and to the fact that production might breach confidentiality. The claim that confidential documents were necessary for the fair disposal of proceedings might well be subject to close examination.

(5) The court was able to vary the terms of a witness summons but ordinarily it should not be asked to perform a redrafting exercise other than on the basis of a considered draft.

In the instant case, the witness summonses were set aside on the grounds that production of the documents was not necessary for the fair disposal of the arbitration (other evidence was available) and that the document was confidential.

[28.15] Brown v Bennett

(2000) The Times, 2 November

The claimant served a witness summons on his expert, whose trial fee he could not afford to pay, since legal aid funding had been withdrawn. The expert, unwilling to appear, applied to have the summons set aside.

HELD: As a general principle it was not right for a litigant to seek to avoid paying his expert by using a witness summons. This was subject to exceptions, but this case was not sufficiently exceptional to warrant it.

CHAPTER 29

Evidence and Admissibility

1.   THE COURT'S GENERAL POWER TO CONTROL EVIDENCE

[29.1]

CPR 32.1 – POWER OF COURT TO CONTROL EVIDENCE
   (1)   The court may control the evidence by giving directions as to–
      (a)   the issues on which it requires evidence;
      (b)   the nature of the evidence which it requires to decide those issues; and
      (c)   the way in which the evidence is to be placed before the court.
   (2)   The court may use its power under this rule to exclude evidence that would otherwise be admissible.
   (3)   The court may limit cross-examination.

POWER MUST BE EXERCISED IN ACCORDANCE WITH THE
OVERRIDING OBJECTIVE

[29.2]   **Grobbelaar v Sun Newspapers Ltd**

(1999) Times, August 12 , CA

HELD, ON APPEAL: Any trial judge has the power, under CPR 32.1, to exclude evidence 'that would otherwise be admissible'. This power must be exercised in accordance with the overriding objective to secure a just result.

[29.3]   **O'Brien v Chief Constable of South Wales Police**

[2003] EWCA Civ 1085

[2003] All ER (D) 381 (Jul)

HELD, ON APPEAL: There was no express limitation on the exercise by a trial judge of the power under CPR 32.1(2) to exclude admissible evidence. However it must be exercised in accordance with the overriding objective of dealing with cases justly.

[29.4]   **Post Office Counters Ltd v Mahida**

[2003] EWCA Civ 1583

[2003] All ER (D) 372 (Oct)

The claimant had destroyed evidence, it claimed routinely. The defendant, appealing against a decision based on secondary evidence about the content of the destroyed evidence, argued that relying on the secondary evidence was unfair and that the judge should have exercised his discretion under CPR 32.1(2) to exclude admissible evidence.

HELD, ON APPEAL: The secondary evidence was admissible, and although the judge at first instance had not been plainly wrong in his decision to admit that evidence, there had been substantial unfairness. The unfairness affected the weight to be given to the claimant's secondary evidence.
   Defendant's appeal allowed.

[29.5]   Secretary of State for Trade and Industry v Swan and Others
[2003] EWHC 1780 (Ch)

[2003] All ER (D) 372 (Jul), Ch

The defendant to proceedings to disqualify him as a director applied to strike out evidence made against him by way of affirmation, on the basis it contained matters which were irrelevant, expert evidence which failed to comply with CPR Pt 35 and failed to comply with the claimant's duty of fairness under s 6 of the Company Directors Disqualification Act 1986.

HELD, ON APPEAL: The evidence did contain irrelevant matters as the applicant argued, but it was not appropriate to strike out the entire affirmation, rather just those parts which were irrelevant.

[29.6]   Three Rivers District Council v Bank of England
[2005] CP Rep 46, CA

Per Rix LJ: CPR 32.1(3) provides 'The court may limit cross-examination'. In exercising that power, or declining to do so, the court is required to give effect to the overriding objective of dealing with cases justly ... [A case management decision is] peculiarly a matter for the judge's discretion. As such, it would only be disturbed upon appeal ... if it was outside the generous range allowed for such decisions ...

ISSUES OF ADMISSIBILITY SHOULD BE CONSIDERED AT AN EARLY STAGE

[29.7]   Woodford & Ackroyd (a firm) v Burgess
[1999] All ER (D) 31, [1999] Lloyd's Rep PN 231

A party issued an application seeking to challenge the admissibility of an expert's report served upon it. The judge hearing the application considered that the report was not properly to be considered an expert's report. On appeal, it was argued that the judge had no jurisdiction to make such an order, and that only the trial judge was permitted to rule on the question of admissibility.

HELD, ON APPEAL: It was desirable in the interests of economy and speed for issues of admissibility to be dealt with prior to trial, and the court should be permitted to exercise its discretion in such matters.

2.   NOTICES TO ADMIT

(A)   FACT

[29.8]

CPR 32.18 – NOTICE TO ADMIT FACTS
(1)   A party may serve notice on another party requiring him to admit the facts, or the part of the case of the serving party, specified in the notice.
(2)   A notice to admit facts must be served no later than 21 days before the trial.
(3)   Where the other party makes any admission in response to the notice, the admission may be used against him only–
   (a)   in the proceedings in which the notice to admit is served; and
   (b)   by the party who served the notice.
(4)   The court may allow a party to amend or withdraw any admission made by him on such terms as it thinks just.

(B)   DOCUMENTS

[29.9]

CPR 32.19 – NOTICE TO ADMIT OR PRODUCE DOCUMENTS
(1)   A party shall be deemed to admit the authenticity of a document disclosed to him under Part 31 (disclosure and inspection of documents) unless he serves notice that he wishes the document to be proved at trial.
(2)   A notice to prove a document must be served–
   (a)   by the latest date for serving witness statements; or
   (b)   within 7 days of disclosure of the document, whichever is later.

3.   SURVEILLANCE EVIDENCE

VIDEO/DVD FOOTAGE IS A 'DOCUMENT'

[29.10]   **Rall v Hume**
[2001] EWCA Civ 146
[2001] 3 All ER 248

At a case management conference, the district judge refused permission to the defendant to rely on video surveillance because the defendant had sought to adduce it too late. The defendant appealed.

HELD, ON APPEAL: The video footage obtained by the defendant's agents constituted a 'document' and therefore was subject to the normal rules of disclosure and inspection of documents set out in CPR Pt 31.

Once a decision had been taken to rely upon surveillance evidence, a party must raise the issue of the admissibility of the evidence with the judge managing the case at the first practicable opportunity.

Where surveillance evidence would undermine a claimant's case such that it might substantially reduce any award, then it was in the interests of justice to allow such evidence to be brought before the court and for the claimant and her medical experts to be subject to cross-examination upon it.

INFRINGEMENT OF HUMAN RIGHTS NOT DETERMINATIVE OF ADMISSIBILITY OF SURVEILLANCE EVIDENCE

[29.11]   **Jones v University of Warwick**

[2003] 3 All ER 760, [2003] 1 WLR 954, [2003] NLJR 230

The claimant had been injured whilst working for the defendant and alleged that she continued to suffer from her injuries. The defendant admitted liability but alleged that the claimant had recovered, submitting surveillance evidence which allegedly showed the claimant moving in a manner incompatible with her own evidence. The surveillance footage had been obtained by private investigators who had secretly filmed the claimant in her home whilst posing as market researchers. The claimant argued that the evidence should not be allowed to be admitted as to admit it would infringe her rights under the Human Rights Act 1998.

HELD, ON APPEAL: The defendant, by its agents, had committed trespass and infringed the claimant's Article 8 rights. However this infringement was only a relevant factor for the court to consider in exercising its discretion under CPR Pt 32. To not admit the video evidence would create an undesirable and artificial situation, and the defendant could be penalised in costs rather than be forced to proceed without the surveillance evidence being admitted.

4.   HEARSAY

(A)   MEANING OF HEARSAY

CIVIL EVIDENCE ACT 1995, S 1

[29.12]
1.   Admissibility of hearsay evidence
    (1)   In civil proceedings evidence shall not be excluded on the ground that it is hearsay.
    (2)   In this Act—
      (a)   'hearsay' means a statement made otherwise than by a person while giving oral evidence in the proceedings which is tendered as evidence of the matters stated; and
      (b)   references to hearsay include hearsay of whatever degree.
    (3)   Nothing in this Act affects the admissibility of evidence admissible apart from this section.
    (4)   The provisions of sections 2 to 6 (safeguards and supplementary provisions relating to hearsay evidence) do not apply in relation to hearsay evidence admissible apart from this section, notwithstanding that it may also be admissible by virtue of this section.

[29.13]

CPR 33.1 – INTRODUCTORY

In this Part–

(a)   'hearsay' means a statement made, otherwise than by a person while giving oral evidence in proceedings, which is tendered as evidence of the matters stated; and

(b)   references to hearsay include hearsay of whatever degree.

(B)   NOTICE REQUIRED TO RELY UPON HEARSAY EVIDENCE

CIVIL EVIDENCE ACT 1995, S 2

[29.14]
2.   Notice of proposal to adduce hearsay evidence

(1)   A party proposing to adduce hearsay evidence in civil proceedings shall, subject to the following provisions of this section, give to the other party or parties to the proceedings—

(a)   such notice (if any) of that fact, and

(b)   on request, such particulars of or relating to the evidence,

as is reasonable and practicable in the circumstances for the purpose of enabling him or them to deal with any matters arising from its being hearsay.

(2)   Provision may be made by rules of court—

(a)   specifying classes of proceedings or evidence in relation to which subsection (1) does not apply, and

(b)   as to the manner in which (including the time within which) the duties imposed by that subsection are to be complied with in the cases where it does apply.

(3)   Subsection (1) may also be excluded by agreement of the parties; and compliance with the duty to give notice may in any case be waived by the person to whom notice is required to be given.

(4)   A failure to comply with subsection (1), or with rules under subsection (2)(b), does not affect the admissibility of the evidence but may be taken into account by the court—

(a)   in considering the exercise of its powers with respect to the course of proceedings and costs, and

(b)   as a matter adversely affecting the weight to be given to the evidence in accordance with section 4.

[29.15]

CPR 33.2 – NOTICE OF INTENTION TO RELY ON HEARSAY EVIDENCE

(1)   Where a party intends to rely on hearsay evidence at trial and either–

(a)   that evidence is to be given by a witness giving oral evidence; or

(b)   that evidence is contained in a witness statement of a person who is not being called to give oral evidence;

that party complies with section 2(1)(a) of the Civil Evidence Act 1995 by serving a witness statement on the other parties in accordance with the court's order.

(2)   Where paragraph (1)(b) applies, the party intending to rely on the hearsay evidence must, when he serves the witness statement–

(a)   inform the other parties that the witness is not being called to give oral evidence; and

(b)   give the reason why the witness will not be called.

(3)   In all other cases where a party intends to rely on hearsay evidence at trial, that party complies with section 2(1)(a) of the Civil Evidence Act 1995 by serving a notice on the other parties which–

(a)   identifies the hearsay evidence;

  (b) states that the party serving the notice proposes to rely on the hearsay evidence at trial; and

  (c) gives the reason why the witness will not be called.

 (4) The party proposing to rely on the hearsay evidence must–

  (a) serve the notice no later than the latest date for serving witness statements; and

  (b) if the hearsay evidence is to be in a document, supply a copy to any party who requests him to do so.

[29.16]

CPR 33.3 – CIRCUMSTANCES IN WHICH NOTICE OF INTENTION TO RELY ON HEARSAY EVIDENCE IS NOT REQUIRED

Section 2(1) of the Civil Evidence Act 1995 (duty to give notice of intention to rely on hearsay evidence) does not apply–

 (a) to evidence at hearings other than trials;

 (aa) to an affidavit or witness statement which is to be used at trial but which does not contain hearsay evidence;

 (b) to a statement which a party to a probate action wishes to put in evidence and which is alleged to have been made by the person whose estate is the subject of the proceedings; or

 (c) where the requirement is excluded by a practice direction.

(C) CALLING A WITNESS FOR CROSS-EXAMINATION ON HEARSAY EVIDENCE

CIVIL EVIDENCE ACT 1995, S 3

[29.17]
3. Power to call witness for cross-examination on hearsay statement

Rules of court may provide that where a party to civil proceedings adduces hearsay evidence of a statement made by a person and does not call that person as a witness, any other party to the proceedings may, with the leave of the court, call that person as a witness and cross-examine him on the statement as if he had been called by the first-mentioned party and as if the hearsay statement were his evidence in chief.

[29.18]

CPR 33.4 – POWER TO CALL WITNESS FOR CROSS-EXAMINATION ON HEARSAY EVIDENCE

 (1) Where a party–

  (a) proposes to rely on hearsay evidence; and

  (b) does not propose to call the person who made the original statement to give oral evidence,

the court may, on the application of any other party, permit that party to call the maker of the statement to be cross-examined on the contents of the statement.

 (2) An application for permission to cross-examine under this rule must be made not more than 14 days after the day on which a notice of intention to rely on the hearsay evidence was served on the applicant.

[29.19]   Cottrell (on behalf of Lloyd's Syndicate 1173) v General Cologne Re UK Ltd

[2004] EWHC 2402 (Comm)

[2004] All ER (D) 384 (Oct)

During a trial concerned with a reinsurance contract, the defendant applied for an extension of time so that two short hearsay statements made by a former employee could be admitted into evidence. The claimants opposed the application on the basis they would suffer prejudice if the statements were to be admitted because the witness was not available for cross-examination.

HELD: To accept the statements into evidence would unfairly prejudice the claimants. The Civil Procedure Rules (CPR) required a party on whom a hearsay statement had been served, under CPR 33.4, to make an application for permission to cross-examine within 14 days. The claimants had not had an opportunity to make this application due to the timing of the notice. Further, it was found that the defendant had deliberately not contacted the hearsay witness in time. The court did not believe the hearsay evidence would, in any event, be helpful on the crucial points in the trial.

(D)   THE WEIGHT (IF ANY) TO BE GIVEN TO HEARSAY EVIDENCE

CIVIL EVIDENCE ACT 1995, S 4

[29.20]
4.   Considerations relevant to weighing of hearsay evidence
  (1)   In estimating the weight (if any) to be given to hearsay evidence in civil proceedings the court shall have regard to any circumstances from which any inference can reasonably be drawn as to the reliability or otherwise of the evidence.
  (2)   Regard may be had, in particular, to the following—
   (a)   whether it would have been reasonable and practicable for the party by whom the evidence was adduced to have produced the maker of the original statement as a witness;
   (b)   whether the original statement was made contemporaneously with the occurrence or existence of the matters stated;
   (c)   whether the evidence involves multiple hearsay;
   (d)   whether any person involved had any motive to conceal or misrepresent matters;
   (e)   whether the original statement was an edited account, or was made in collaboration with another or for a particular purpose;
   (f)   whether the circumstances in which the evidence is adduced as hearsay are such as to suggest an attempt to prevent proper evaluation of its weight.

(E)   CREDIBILITY OF HEARSAY EVIDENCE

CIVIL EVIDENCE ACT, S 5

[29.21]
5.   Competence and credibility
  (1)   Hearsay evidence shall not be admitted in civil proceedings if or to the extent that it is shown to consist of, or to be proved by means of, a statement made by a person who at the time he made the statement was not competent as a witness.

For this purpose 'not competent as a witness' means suffering from such mental or physical infirmity, or lack of understanding, as would render a person incompetent as a witness in civil proceedings; but a child shall be treated as competent as a witness if he satisfies the requirements of section 96(2)(a) and (b) of the Children Act 1989 (conditions for reception of unsworn evidence of child).

(2)   Where in civil proceedings hearsay evidence is adduced and the maker of the original statement, or of any statement relied upon to prove another statement, is not called as a witness—

(a)   evidence which if he had been so called would be admissible for the purpose of attacking or supporting his credibility as a witness is admissible for that purpose in the proceedings; and

(b)   evidence tending to prove that, whether before or after he made the statement, he made any other statement inconsistent with it is admissible for the purpose of showing that he had contradicted himself.

Provided that evidence may not be given of any matter of which, if he had been called as a witness and had denied that matter in cross-examination, evidence could not have been adduced by the cross-examining party.

[29.22]

CPR 33.5 – CREDIBILITY

(1)   Where a party–

(a)   proposes to rely on hearsay evidence; but

(b)   does not propose to call the person who made the original statement to give oral evidence; and

(c)   another party wishes to call evidence to attack the credibility of the person who made the statement,

the party who so wishes must give notice of his intention to the party who proposes to give the hearsay statement in evidence.

(2)   A party must give notice under paragraph (1) not more than 14 days after the day on which a hearsay notice relating to the hearsay evidence was served on him.

(F)   PREVIOUS STATEMENTS OF WITNESSES

CIVIL EVIDENCE ACT 1995, S 6

[29.23]
6.   Previous statements of witnesses

(1)   Subject as follows, the provisions of this Act as to hearsay evidence in civil proceedings apply equally (but with any necessary modifications) in relation to a previous statement made by a person called as a witness in the proceedings.

(2)   A party who has called or intends to call a person as a witness in civil proceedings may not in those proceedings adduce evidence of a previous statement made by that person, except—

(a)   with the leave of the court, or

(b)   for the purpose of rebutting a suggestion that his evidence has been fabricated.

This shall not be construed as preventing a witness statement (that is, a written statement of oral evidence which a party to the proceedings intends to lead) from being adopted by a witness in giving evidence or treated as his evidence.

(3)   Where in the case of civil proceedings section 3, 4 or 5 of the Criminal Procedure Act 1865 applies, which make provision as to—

(a)   how far a witness may be discredited by the party producing him,

(b)   the proof of contradictory statements made by a witness, and

(c)   cross-examination as to previous statements in writing,

this Act does not authorise the adducing of evidence of a previous inconsistent or contradictory statement otherwise than in accordance with those sections.

This is without prejudice to any provision made by rules of court under section 3 above (power to call witness for cross-examination on hearsay statement).

(4)   Nothing in this Act affects any of the rules of law as to the circumstances in which, where a person called as a witness in civil proceedings is cross-examined on a document used by him to refresh his memory, that document may be made evidence in the proceedings.

(5)   Nothing in this section shall be construed as preventing a statement of any description referred to above from being admissible by virtue of section 1 as evidence of the matters stated.

(G)   ADMISSIBILITY OF CERTAIN PUBLISHED WORKS, PUBLIC DOCUMENTS, RECORDS AND OTHER DOCUMENTS

CIVIL EVIDENCE ACT 1995, s 7

[29.24]
7.   Evidence formerly admissible at common law
(1)   The common law rule effectively preserved by section 9(1) and (2)(a) of the Civil Evidence Act 1968 (admissibility of admissions adverse to a party) is superseded by the provisions of this Act.

(2)   The common law rules effectively preserved by section 9(1) and (2)(b) to (d) of the Civil Evidence Act 1968, that is, any rule of law whereby in civil proceedings—

(a)   published works dealing with matters of a public nature (for example, histories, scientific works, dictionaries and maps) are admissible as evidence of facts of a public nature stated in them;

(b)   public documents (for example, public registers, and returns made under public authority with respect to matters of public interest) are admissible as evidence of facts stated in them; or

(c)   records (for example, the records of certain courts, treaties, Crown grants, pardons and commissions) are admissible as evidence of facts stated in them,

shall continue to have effect.

CIVIL EVIDENCE ACT 1995, s 9

[29.25]
9.   Proof of records of business or public authority
(1)   A document which is shown to form part of the records of a business or public authority may be received in evidence in civil proceedings without further proof.

(2)   A document shall be taken to form part of the records of a business or public authority if there is produced to the court a certificate to that effect signed by an officer of the business or authority to which the records belong.

For this purpose—

(a)   a document purporting to be a certificate signed by an officer of a business or public authority shall be deemed to have been duly given by such an officer and signed by him; and

(b)   a certificate shall be treated as signed by a person if it purports to bear a facsimile of his signature.

(3)   The absence of an entry in the records of a business or public authority may be proved in civil proceedings by affidavit of an officer of the business or authority to which the records belong.

(4)   In this section—

'records' means records in whatever form;

'business' includes any activity regularly carried on over a period of time, whether for profit or not, by any body (whether corporate or not) or by an individual;

'officer' includes any person occupying a responsible position in relation to the relevant activities of the business or public authority or in relation to its records; and

'public authority' includes any public or statutory undertaking, any government department and any person holding office under Her Majesty.

(5)   The court may, having regard to the circumstances of the case, direct that all or any of the above provisions of this section do not apply in relation to a particular document or record, or description of documents or records.

[29.26]

CPR 33.6 – USE OF PLANS, PHOTOGRAPHS AND MODELS AS EVIDENCE

(1)   This rule applies to evidence (such as a plan, photograph or model) which is not–

(a)   contained in a witness statement, affidavit or expert's report;

(b)   to be given orally at trial; or

(c)   evidence of which prior notice must be given under rule 33.2.

(2)   This rule includes documents which may be received in evidence without further proof under section 9 of the Civil Evidence Act 1995.

(3)   Unless the court orders otherwise the evidence shall not be receivable at a trial unless the party intending to put it in evidence has given notice to the other parties in accordance with this rule.

(4)   Where the party intends to use the evidence as evidence of any fact then, except where paragraph (6) applies, he must give notice not later than the latest date for serving witness statements.

(5)   He must give notice at least 21 days before the hearing at which he proposes to put in the evidence, if–

(a)   there are not to be witness statements; or

(b)   he intends to put in the evidence solely in order to disprove an allegation made in a witness statement.

(6)   Where the evidence forms part of expert evidence, he must give notice when the expert's report is served on the other party.

(7)   Where the evidence is being produced to the court for any reason other than as part of factual or expert evidence, he must give notice at least 21 days before the hearing at which he proposes to put in the evidence.

(8)   Where a party has given notice that he intends to put in the evidence, he must give every other party an opportunity to inspect it and to agree to its admission without further proof.

(H)   ADMISSIBILITY OF EVIDENCE OF CHARACTER

CIVIL EVIDENCE ACT 1995, s 7(3)

[29.27]
(3)   The common law rules effectively preserved by section 9(3) and (4) of the Civil Evidence Act 1968, that is, any rule of law whereby in civil proceedings—
  (a)   evidence of a person's reputation is admissible for the purpose of proving his good or bad character; or
  (b)   evidence of reputation or family tradition is admissible—
    (i)   for the purpose of proving or disproving pedigree or the existence of a marriage; or
    (ii)   for the purpose of proving or disproving the existence of any public or general right or of identifying any person or thing,
shall continue to have effect in so far as they authorise the court to treat such evidence as proving or disproving that matter.

Where any such rule applies, reputation or family tradition shall be treated for the purposes of this Act as a fact and not as a statement or multiplicity of statements about the matter in question.

(I)   PROOF OF STATEMENTS CONTAINED IN DOCUMENTS

CIVIL EVIDENCE ACT 1995, s 8

[29.28]
8   Proof of statements contained in documents
(1)   Where a statement contained in a document is admissible as evidence in civil proceedings, it may be proved—
  (a)   by the production of that document; or
  (b)   whether or not that document is still in existence, by the production of a copy of that document or of the material part of it, authenticated in such manner as the court may approve.
(2)   It is immaterial for this purpose how many removes there are between a copy and the original.

[29.29]   Orford v (1) Rasmi Electronics Ltd (2) Surendra

[2002] EWCA Civ 1762

[2002] All ER (D) 397 (Oct)

In defamation proceedings, related to separate personal injury proceedings, the claimant was served with a plan of his defendant employer's premises on the morning of a hearing. The plan had been in existence for over one year and had not been disclosed by the defendant. This meant that the claimant could not prepare evidence or conduct investigations to rebut the inferences made by the defendant based on the plan. The claimant applied to set aside a summary judgment previously granted and to admit fresh evidence.

HELD, ON APPEAL: The plan and its accuracy went to the heart of whether the defendant had an honest belief that the claimant's accident was staged. Producing the plan on the day of the hearing was a serious procedural unfairness. The application to admit fresh evidence was allowed and a re-trial in the county court was directed.

5. CONVICTIONS

ADMISSIBILITY IN CIVIL PROCEEDINGS

CIVIL EVIDENCE ACT 1968, S 11

[29.30]
11. Convictions as evidence in civil proceedings.
(1) In any civil proceedings the fact that a person had been convicted of an offence by or before any court in the United Kingdom or by a court-martial there or elsewhere shall (subject to subsection (3) below) be admissible in evidence for the purpose of proving, where to do so is relevant to any issue in those proceedings, that he committed that offence, whether he was so convicted upon a plea of guilty or otherwise and whether or not he is party to the civil proceedings; but no conviction other than a subsisting one shall be admissible in evidence by virtue of this section.
(2) In any civil proceedings in which by virtue of this section a person is proven to have been convicted of an offence by or before any court in the United Kingdom by a court-martial there or elsewhere—
   (a) he shall be taken to have committed that offence unless the contrary is proved; and
   (b) without prejudice to the reception of any other admissible evidence for the purpose of identifying the facts on which the conviction was based, the contents of any document which is admissible as evidence of the conviction, and the contents of the information, complaint, indictment or charge-sheet on which the person in question was convicted, shall be admissible in evidence for that purpose.
(3) Where in any civil proceedings the contents of any document are admissible in evidence by virtue of subsection (2) above, a copy of that document, or of the material part thereof, purporting to be certified or otherwise authenticated by or on behalf of the court or authority having custody of that document shall be admissible in evidence and shall be taken to be a true copy of that document or part unless the contrary is shown.

[29.31] **Wauchope v Mordecai**
[1970] 1 All ER 417, [1970] 1 WLR 317, CA

The claimant was injured when the defendant opened a car door and knocked him off his bicycle. The defendant admitted to the police that he had opened the car door. He was charged and convicted. The trial took place after the Civil Evidence Act 1968, s 11 had come into force. The judge was told of the conviction but said he would ignore it. He found for the defendant.

HELD, ON APPEAL: Section 11(1) of the 1968 Act made the conviction admissible as evidence to prove, where it was relevant, that the offence was committed. When the judge gave judgment he applied the standard of proof on the balance of probabilities. However, under s 11(2) the defendant was to be taken to have committed the offence unless the contrary was proved. It was for the defendant to prove he had not opened the car door. If the judge had had the 1968 Act in mind he must have found for the claimant.
   Appeal allowed.

[29.32] **Stupple v Royal Insurance Co Ltd**

[1971] 1 QB 50, [1970] 3 All ER 230, [1970] 3 WLR 217, CA

Per Lord Denning MR: 'The Act [Civil Evidence Act 1968] does not merely shift the evidential burden, as it is called. It shifts the *legal* burden of proof. ... Take a running down case where a [claimant] claims damages for negligent driving by the defendant. If the defendant had not been convicted, the legal burden is on the [claimant] throughout. But if the defendant has been convicted of careless driving the legal burden is shifted. It is on the defendant himself. At the end of the day, if the judge is left in doubt the defendant fails because the defendant has not discharged the legal burden which is on him. The burden is, no doubt, the civil burden: he must show, on the balance of probabilities, that he was not negligent.'

CHAPTER 30

Expert Evidence

1.   PROTOCOL FOR THE INSTRUCTION OF EXPERTS TO GIVE EVIDENCE IN CIVIL CLAIMS

(A)   INTRODUCTION

[30.1]   Any instruction issued to an expert after 5 September 2005 is governed by a code of practice introduced by the Civil Justice Council, the Protocol for the Instruction of Experts to give Evidence in Civil Claims.

(B)   TEXT OF THE PROTOCOL

[30.2]

1.   INTRODUCTION

Expert witnesses perform a vital role in civil litigation. It is essential that both those who instruct experts and experts themselves are given clear guidance as to what they are expected to do in civil proceedings. The purpose of this Protocol is to provide such guidance. It has been drafted by the Civil Justice Council and reflects the rules and practice directions current (in June 2005), replacing the Code of Guidance on Expert Evidence. The authors of the Protocol wish to acknowledge the valuable assistance they obtained by drawing on earlier documents produced by the Academy of Experts and the Expert Witness Institute, as well as suggestions made by the Clinical Dispute Forum. The Protocol has been approved by the Master of the Rolls.

2.   AIMS OF PROTOCOL
2.1   This Protocol offers guidance to experts and to those instructing them in the interpretation of and compliance with Part 35 of the Civil Procedure Rules (CPR 35) and its associated Practice Direction (PD 35) and to further the objectives of the Civil Procedure Rules in general. It is intended to assist in the interpretation of those provisions in the interests of good practice but it does not replace them. It sets out standards for the use of experts and the conduct of experts and those who instruct them. The existence of this Protocol does not remove the need for experts and those who instruct them to be familiar with CPR 35 and PD35.
2.2   Experts and those who instruct them should also bear in mind para 1.4 of the Practice Direction on Protocols which contains the following objectives, namely to:

(a) encourage the exchange of early and full information about the expert issues involved in a prospective legal claim;

(b) enable the parties to avoid or reduce the scope of litigation by agreeing the whole or part of an expert issue before commencement of proceedings; and

(c) support the efficient management of proceedings where litigation cannot be avoided.

3. APPLICATION

3.1   This Protocol applies to any steps taken for the purpose of civil proceedings by experts or those who instruct them on or after 5th September 2005.

3.2   It applies to all experts who are, or who may be, governed by CPR Part 35 and to those who instruct them. Experts are governed by Part 35 if they are or have been instructed to give or prepare evidence for the purpose of civil proceedings in a court in England and Wales (CPR 35.2).

3.3   Experts, and those instructing them, should be aware that some cases may be 'specialist proceedings' (CPR 49) where there are modifications to the Civil Procedure Rules. Proceedings may also be governed by other Protocols. Further, some courts have published their own Guides which supplement the Civil Procedure Rules for proceedings in those courts. They contain provisions affecting expert evidence. Expert witnesses and those instructing them should be familiar with them when they are relevant.

3.4   Courts may take into account any failure to comply with this Protocol when making orders in relation to costs, interest, time limits, the stay of proceedings and whether to order a party to pay a sum of money into court.

Limitation

3.5   If, as a result of complying with any part of this Protocol, claims would or might be time barred under any provision in the Limitation Act 1980, or any other legislation that imposes a time limit for the bringing an action, claimants may commence proceedings without complying with this Protocol. In such circumstances, claimants who commence proceedings without complying with all, or any part, of this Protocol must apply, giving notice to all other parties, to the court for directions as to the timetable and form of procedure to be adopted, at the same time as they request the court to issue proceedings. The court may consider whether to order a stay of the whole or part of the proceedings pending compliance with this Protocol and may make orders in relation to costs.

4. DUTIES OF EXPERTS

4.1   Experts always owe a duty to exercise reasonable skill and care to those instructing them, and to comply with any relevant professional code of ethics. However when they are instructed to give or prepare evidence for the purpose of civil proceedings in England and Wales they have an overriding duty to help the court on matters within their expertise (CPR 35.3). This duty overrides any obligation to the person instructing or paying them. Experts must not serve the exclusive interest of those who retain them.

4.2   Experts should be aware of the overriding objective that courts deal with cases justly. This includes dealing with cases proportionately, expeditiously and fairly (CPR 1.1). Experts are under an obligation to assist the court so as to enable them to deal with cases in accordance with the overriding objective. However the overriding objective does not impose on experts any duty to act as mediators between the parties or require them to trespass on the role of the court in deciding facts.

4.3   Experts should provide opinions which are independent, regardless of the pressures of litigation. In this context, a useful test of 'independence' is that the expert would express the same opinion if given the same instructions by an opposing party. Experts should not take it upon themselves to promote the point of view of the party instructing them or engage in the role of advocates.

4.4   Experts should confine their opinions to matters which are material to the disputes between the parties and provide opinions only in relation to matters which lie within their expertise. Experts should indicate without delay where particular questions or issues fall outside their expertise.

4.5   Experts should take into account all material facts before them at the time that they give their opinion. Their reports should set out those facts and any literature or any other material on which they have relied in forming their opinions. They should indicate if an opinion is provisional, or qualified, or where they consider that further information is required or if, for any other reason, they are not satisfied that an opinion can be expressed finally and without qualification.

4.6   Experts should inform those instructing them without delay of any change in their opinions on any material matter and the reason for it.

4.7   Experts should be aware that any failure by them to comply with the Civil Procedure Rules or court orders or any excessive delay for which they are responsible may result in the parties who instructed them being penalised in costs and even, in extreme cases, being debarred from placing the experts' evidence before the court. In *Phillips v Symes* [2005] 4 All ER 519 Peter Smith J held that courts may also make orders for costs (under section 51 of the Supreme Court Act 1981) directly against expert witnesses who by their evidence cause significant expense to be incurred, and do so in flagrant and reckless disregard of their duties to the Court.

5.   CONDUCT OF EXPERTS INSTRUCTED ONLY TO ADVISE

5.1   Part 35 only applies where experts are instructed to give opinions which are relied on for the purposes of court proceedings. Advice which the parties do not intend to adduce in litigation is likely to be confidential; the Protocol does not apply in these circumstances.

5.2   The same applies where, after the commencement of proceedings, experts are instructed only to advise (e.g. to comment upon a single joint expert's report) and not to give or prepare evidence for use in the proceedings.

5.3   However this Protocol does apply if experts who were formerly instructed only to advise are later instructed to give or prepare evidence for the purpose of civil proceedings.

6. THE NEED FOR EXPERTS

6.1 Those intending to instruct experts to give or prepare evidence for the purpose of civil proceedings should consider whether expert evidence is appropriate, taking account of the principles set out in CPR Parts 1 and 35, and in particular whether:

(a) it is relevant to a matter which is in dispute between the parties.
(b) it is reasonably required to resolve the proceedings (CPR 35.1);
(c) the expert has expertise relevant to the issue on which an opinion is sought;
(d) the expert has the experience, expertise and training appropriate to the value, complexity and importance of the case; and whether
(e) these objects can be achieved by the appointment of a single joint expert (see section 17 below).

6.2 Although the court's permission is not generally required to instruct an expert, the court's permission is required before experts can be called to give evidence or their evidence can be put in (CPR 35.4).

7. THE APPOINTMENT OF EXPERTS

7.1 Before experts are formally instructed or the court's permission to appoint named experts is sought, the following should be established:

(a) that they have the appropriate expertise and experience;
(b) that they are familiar with the general duties of an expert;
(c) that they can produce a report, deal with questions and have discussions with other experts within a reasonable time and at a cost proportionate to the matters in issue;
(d) a description of the work required;
(e) whether they are available to attend the trial, if attendance is required; and
(f) there is no potential conflict of interest.

7.2 Terms of appointment should be agreed at the outset and should normally include:

(a) the capacity in which the expert is to be appointed (e.g. party appointed expert, single joint expert or expert advisor);
(b) the services required of the expert (e.g. provision of expert's report, answering questions in writing, attendance at meetings and attendance at court);
(c) time for delivery of the report;
(d) the basis of the expert's charges (either daily or hourly rates and an estimate of the time likely to be required, or a total fee for the services);
(e) travelling expenses and disbursements;
(f) cancellation charges;
(g) any fees for attending court;
(h) time for making the payment; and
(i) whether fees are to be paid by a third party.
(j) if a party is publicly funded, whether or not the expert's charges will be subject to assessment by a costs officer.

7.3 As to the appointment of single joint experts, see section 17 below.

7.4 When necessary, arrangements should be made for dealing with questions to experts and discussions between experts, including any directions given by the court, and provision should be made for the cost of this work.

7.5   Experts should be informed regularly about deadlines for all matters concerning them. Those instructing experts should promptly send them copies of all court orders and directions which may affect the preparation of their reports or any other matters concerning their obligations.

Conditional and Contingency Fees

7.6   Payments contingent upon the nature of the expert evidence given in legal proceedings, or upon the outcome of a case, must not be offered or accepted. To do so would contravene experts' overriding duty to the court and compromise their duty of independence.

7.7   Agreement to delay payment of experts' fees until after the conclusion of cases is permissible as long as the amount of the fee does not depend on the outcome of the case.

8.   INSTRUCTIONS

8.1   Those instructing experts should ensure that they give clear instructions, including the following:

   (a)   basic information, such as names, addresses, telephone numbers, dates of birth and dates of incidents;
   (b)   the nature and extent of the expertise which is called for;
   (c)   the purpose of requesting the advice or report, a description of the matter(s) to be investigated, the principal known issues and the identity of all parties;
   (d)   the statement(s) of case (if any), those documents which form part of standard disclosure and witness statements which are relevant to the advice or report;
   (e)   where proceedings have not been started, whether proceedings are being contemplated and, if so, whether the expert is asked only for advice;
   (f)   an outline programme, consistent with good case management and the expert's availability, for the completion and delivery of each stage of the expert's work; and
   (g)   where proceedings have been started, the dates of any hearings (including any Case Management Conferences and/or Pre-Trial Reviews), the name of the court, the claim number and the track to which the claim has been allocated.

8.2   Experts who do not receive clear instructions should request clarification and may indicate that they are not prepared to act unless and until such clear instructions are received.

8.3   As to the instruction of single joint experts, see section 17 below.

9.   EXPERTS' ACCEPTANCE OF INSTRUCTIONS

9.1   Experts should confirm without delay whether or not they accept instructions. They should also inform those instructing them (whether on initial instruction or at any later stage) without delay if:

   (a)   instructions are not acceptable because, for example, they require work that falls outside their expertise, impose unrealistic deadlines, or are insufficiently clear;
   (b)   they consider that instructions are or have become insufficient to complete the work;

(c)   they become aware that they may not be able to fulfil any of the terms of appointment;

(d)   the instructions and/or work have, for any reason, placed them in conflict with their duties as an expert; or

(e)   they are not satisfied that they can comply with any orders that have been made.

9.2   Experts must neither express an opinion outside the scope of their field of expertise, nor accept any instructions to do so.

10.   WITHDRAWAL

10.1   Where experts' instructions remain incompatible with their duties, whether through incompleteness, a conflict between their duty to the court and their instructions, or for any other substantial and significant reason, they may consider withdrawing from the case. However, experts should not withdraw without first discussing the position fully with those who instruct them and considering carefully whether it would be more appropriate to make a written request for directions from the court. If experts do withdraw, they must give formal written notice to those instructing them.

11.   EXPERTS' RIGHT TO ASK COURT FOR DIRECTIONS

11.1   Experts may request directions from the court to assist them in carrying out their functions as experts. Experts should normally discuss such matters with those who instruct them before making any such request. Unless the court otherwise orders, any proposed request for directions should be copied to the party instructing the expert at least seven days before filing any request to the court, and to all other parties at least four days before filing it. (CPR 35.14).

11.2   Requests to the court for directions should be made by letter, containing:

(a)   the title of the claim;

(b)   the claim number of the case;

(c)   the name of the expert;

(d)   full details of why directions are sought; and

(e)   copies of any relevant documentation.

12.   POWER OF THE COURT TO DIRECT A PARTY TO PROVIDE INFORMATION

12.1   If experts consider that those instructing them have not provided information which they require, they may, after discussion with those instructing them and giving notice, write to the court to seek directions (CPR 35.14).

12.2   Experts and those who instruct them should also be aware of CPR 35.9. This provides that where one party has access to information which is not readily available to the other party, the court may direct the party who has access to the information to prepare, file and copy to the other party a document recording the information. If experts require such information which has not been disclosed, they should discuss the position with those instructing them without delay, so that a request for the information can be made, and, if not forthcoming, an application can be made to the court. Unless a document appears to be essential, experts should assess the cost and time involved in the production of a document and whether its provision would be proportionate in the context of the case.

13.   CONTENTS OF EXPERTS' REPORTS

13.1   The content and extent of experts' reports should be governed by the scope of their instructions and general obligations, the contents of CPR 35 and PD35 and their overriding duty to the court.

13.2   In preparing reports, experts should maintain professional objectivity and impartiality at all times.

13.3   PD 35, paragraph 2 provides that experts' reports should be addressed to the court and gives detailed directions about the form and content of such reports. All experts and those who instruct them should ensure that they are familiar with these requirements.

13.4   Model forms of Experts' Reports are available from bodies such as the Academy of Experts or the Expert Witness Institute.

13.5   Experts' reports must contain statements that they understand their duty to the court and have complied and will continue to comply with that duty (PD35 paragraph 2.2(9)). They must also be verified by a statement of truth. The form of the statement of truth is as follows: 'I confirm that insofar as the facts stated in my report are within my own knowledge I have made clear which they are and I believe them to be true, and that the opinions I have expressed represent my true and complete professional opinion.' This wording is mandatory and must not be modified.

Qualifications

13.6   The details of experts' qualifications to be given in reports should be commensurate with the nature and complexity of the case. It may be sufficient merely to state academic and professional qualifications. However, where highly specialised expertise is called for, experts should include the detail of particular training and/or experience that qualifies them to provide that highly specialised evidence.

Tests

13.7   Where tests of a scientific or technical nature have been carried out, experts should state:

(a)   the methodology used; and

(b)   by whom the tests were undertaken and under whose supervision, summarising their respective qualifications and experience.

Reliance on the work of others

13.8   Where experts rely in their reports on literature or other material and cite the opinions of others without having verified them, they must give details of those opinions relied on. It is likely to assist the court if the qualifications of the originator(s) are also stated.

Facts

13.9   When addressing questions of fact and opinion, experts should keep the two separate and discrete.

13.10   Experts must state those facts (whether assumed or otherwise) upon which their opinions are based. They must distinguish clearly between those facts which experts know to be true and those facts which they assume.

13.11   Where there are material facts in dispute experts should express separate opinions on each hypothesis put forward. They should not express a view in favour of one or other disputed version of the facts unless, as a result of particular expertise and experience, they consider one set of facts as being improbable or less probable, in which case they may express that view, and should give reasons for holding it.

Range of opinion

13.12   If the mandatory summary of the range of opinion is based on published sources, experts should explain those sources and, where appropriate, state the qualifications of the originator(s) of the opinions from which they differ, particularly if such opinions represent a well-established school of thought.

13.13   Where there is no available source for the range of opinion, experts may need to express opinions on what they believe to be the range which other experts would arrive at if asked. In those circumstances, experts should make it clear that the range that they summarise is based on their own judgement and explain the basis of that judgement.

Conclusions

13.14   A summary of conclusions is mandatory. The summary should be at the end of the report after all the reasoning. There may be cases, however, where the benefit to the court is heightened by placing a short summary at the beginning of the report whilst giving the full conclusions at the end. For example, it can assist with the comprehension of the analysis and with the absorption of the detailed facts if the court is told at the outset of the direction in which the report's logic will flow in cases involving highly complex matters which fall outside the general knowledge of the court.

Basis of report: material instructions

13.15   The mandatory statement of the substance of all material instructions should not be incomplete or otherwise tend to mislead. The imperative is transparency. The term 'instructions' includes all material which solicitors place in front of experts in order to gain advice. The omission from the statement of 'off-the-record' oral instructions is not permitted. Courts may allow cross-examination about the instructions if there are reasonable grounds to consider that the statement may be inaccurate or incomplete.

14.   AFTER RECEIPT OF EXPERTS' REPORTS

14.1   Following the receipt of experts' reports, those instructing them should advise the experts as soon as reasonably practicable whether, and if so when, the report will be disclosed to other parties; and, if so disclosed, the date of actual disclosure.

14.2   If experts' reports are to be relied upon, and if experts are to give oral evidence, those instructing them should give the experts the opportunity to consider and comment upon other reports within their area of expertise and which deal with relevant issues at the earliest opportunity.

14.3   Those instructing experts should keep experts informed of the progress of cases, including amendments to statements of case relevant to experts' opinion.

14.4   If those instructing experts become aware of material changes in circumstances or that relevant information within their control was not previously provided to experts, they should without delay instruct experts to review, and if necessary, update the contents of their reports.

15.   AMENDMENT OF REPORTS

15.1   It may become necessary for experts to amend their reports:
   (a)   as a result of an exchange of questions and answers;
   (b)   following agreements reached at meetings between experts; or
   (c)   where further evidence or documentation is disclosed.

15.2   Experts should not be asked to, and should not, amend, expand or alter any parts of reports in a manner which distorts their true opinion, but may be invited to amend or expand reports to ensure accuracy, internal consistency, completeness and relevance to the issues and clarity. Although experts should generally follow the recommendations of solicitors with regard to the form of reports, they should form their own independent views as to the opinions and contents expressed in their reports and exclude any suggestions which do not accord with their views.

15.3   Where experts change their opinion following a meeting of experts, a simple signed and dated addendum or memorandum to that effect is generally sufficient. In some cases, however, the benefit to the court of having an amended report may justify the cost of making the amendment.

15.4   Where experts significantly alter their opinion, as a result of new evidence or because evidence on which they relied has become unreliable, or for any other reason, they should amend their reports to reflect that fact. Amended reports should include reasons for amendments. In such circumstances those instructing experts should inform other parties as soon as possible of any change of opinion.

15.5   When experts intend to amend their reports, they should inform those instructing them without delay and give reasons. They should provide the amended version (or an addendum or memorandum) clearly marked as such as quickly as possible.

16.   WRITTEN QUESTIONS TO EXPERTS

16.1   The procedure for putting written questions to experts (CPR 35.6) is intended to facilitate the clarification of opinions and issues after experts' reports have been served. Experts have a duty to provide answers to questions properly put. Where they fail to do so, the court may impose sanctions against the party instructing the expert, and, if, there is continued non-compliance, debar a party from relying on the report. Experts should copy their answers to those instructing them.

16.2   Experts' answers to questions automatically become part of their reports. They are covered by the statement of truth and form part of the expert evidence.

16.3   Where experts believe that questions put are not properly directed to the clarification of the report, or are disproportionate, or have been asked out of time, they should discuss the questions with those instructing them and, if appropriate, those asking the questions. Attempts should be made to resolve such problems without the need for an application to the court for directions.

Written requests for directions in relation to questions

16.4   If those instructing experts do not apply to the court in respect of questions, but experts still believe that questions are improper or out of time, experts may file written requests with the court for directions to assist in carrying out their functions as experts (CPR 35.14). See Section 11 above.

17.   SINGLE JOINT EXPERTS

17.1   CPR 35 and PD35 deal extensively with the instruction and use of joint experts by the parties and the powers of the court to order their use (see CPR 35.7 and 35.8, PD35, paragraph 5).

17.2   The Civil Procedure Rules encourage the use of joint experts. Wherever possible a joint report should be obtained. Consideration should therefore be given by all parties to the appointment of single joint experts in all cases where a court might direct such an appointment. Single joint experts are the norm in cases allocated to the small claims track and the fast track.

17.3   Where, in the early stages of a dispute, examinations, investigations, tests, site inspections, experiments, preparation of photographs, plans or other similar preliminary expert tasks are necessary, consideration should be given to the instruction of a single joint expert, especially where such matters are not, at that stage, expected to be contentious as between the parties. The objective of such an appointment should be to agree or to narrow issues.

17.4   Experts who have previously advised a party (whether in the same case or otherwise) should only be proposed as single joint experts if other parties are given all relevant information about the previous involvement.

17.5   The appointment of a single joint expert does not prevent parties from instructing their own experts to advise (but the costs of such expert advisers may not be recoverable in the case).

Joint instructions

17.6   The parties should try to agree joint instructions to single joint experts, but, in default of agreement, each party may give instructions. In particular, all parties should try to agree what documents should be included with instructions and what assumptions single joint experts should make.

17.7   Where the parties fail to agree joint instructions, they should try to agree where the areas of disagreement lie and their instructions should make this clear. If separate instructions are given, they should be copied at the same time to the other instructing parties.

17.8   Where experts are instructed by two or more parties, the terms of appointment should, unless the court has directed otherwise, or the parties have agreed otherwise, include:

(a)   a statement that all the instructing parties are jointly and severally liable to pay the experts' fees and, accordingly, that experts' invoices should be sent simultaneously to all instructing parties or their solicitors (as appropriate); and

(b)   a statement as to whether any order has been made limiting the amount of experts' fees and expenses (CPR 35.8(4)(a)).

17.9   Where instructions have not been received by the expert from one or more of the instructing parties the expert should give notice (normally at least 7 days) of a deadline to all instructing parties for the receipt by the expert of such instructions. Unless the instructions are received within the deadline the expert may begin work. In the event that instructions are received after the deadline but before the signing off of the report the expert should consider whether it is practicable to comply with those instructions without adversely affecting the timetable set for delivery of the report and in such a manner as to comply with the proportionality principle. An expert who decides to issue a report without taking into account instructions received after the deadline should inform the parties who may apply to the court for directions. In either event the report must show clearly that the expert did not receive instructions within the deadline, or, as the case may be, at all.

Conduct of the single joint expert

17.10   Single joint experts should keep all instructing parties informed of any material steps that they may be taking by, for example, copying all correspondence to those instructing them.

17.11   Single joint experts are Part 35 experts and so have an overriding duty to the court. They are the parties' appointed experts and therefore owe an equal duty to all parties. They should maintain independence, impartiality and transparency at all times.

17.12   Single joint experts should not attend any meeting or conference which is not a joint one, unless all the parties have agreed in writing or the court has directed that such a meeting may be held and who is to pay the experts' fees for the meeting.

17.13   Single joint experts may request directions from the court – see Section 11 above.

17.14   Single joint experts should serve their reports simultaneously on all instructing parties. They should provide a single report even though they may have received instructions which contain areas of conflicting fact or allegation. If conflicting instructions lead to different opinions (for example, because the instructions require experts to make different assumptions of fact), reports may need to contain more than one set of opinions on any issue. It is for the court to determine the facts.

Cross-examination

17.15   Single joint experts do not normally give oral evidence at trial but if they do, all parties may cross-examine them. In general written questions (CPR 35.6) should be put to single joint experts before requests are made for them to attend court for the purpose of cross-examination.

18.   DISCUSSIONS BETWEEN EXPERTS

18.1   The court has powers to direct discussions between experts for the purposes set out in the Rules (CPR 35.12). Parties may also agree that discussions take place between their experts.

18.2   Where single joint experts have been instructed but parties have, with the permission of the court, instructed their own additional Part 35 experts, there may, if the court so orders or the parties agree, be discussions between the single joint experts and the additional Part 35 experts. Such discussions should be confined to those matters within the remit of the additional Part 35 experts or as ordered by the court.

18.3   The purpose of discussions between experts should be, wherever possible, to:

(a)   identify and discuss the expert issues in the proceedings;

(b)   reach agreed opinions on those issues, and, if that is not possible, to narrow the issues in the case;

(c)   identify those issues on which they agree and disagree and summarise their reasons for disagreement on any issue; and

(d)   identify what action, if any, may be taken to resolve any of the outstanding issues between the parties.

Arrangements for discussions between experts

18.4   Arrangements for discussions between experts should be proportionate to the value of cases. In small claims and fast-track cases there should not normally be meetings between experts. Where discussion is justified in such cases, telephone discussion or an exchange of letters should, in the interests of proportionality, usually suffice. In multi-track cases, discussion may be face to face, but the practicalities or the proportionality principle may require discussions to be by telephone or video conference.

18.5   The parties, their lawyers and experts should co-operate to produce the agenda for any discussion between experts, although primary responsibility for preparation of the agenda should normally lie with the parties' solicitors.

18.6   The agenda should indicate what matters have been agreed and summarise concisely those which are in issue. It is often helpful for it to include questions to be answered by the experts. If agreement cannot be reached promptly or a party is unrepresented, the court may give directions for the drawing up of the agenda. The agenda should be circulated to experts and those instructing them to allow sufficient time for the experts to prepare for the discussion.

18.7   Those instructing experts must not instruct experts to avoid reaching agreement (or to defer doing so) on any matter within the experts' competence. Experts are not permitted to accept such instructions.

18.8   The parties' lawyers may only be present at discussions between experts if all the parties agree or the court so orders. If lawyers do attend, they should not normally intervene except to answer questions put to them by the experts or to advise about the law.

18.9 The content of discussions between experts should not be referred to at trial unless the parties agree (CPR 35.12(4)). It is good practice for any such agreement to be in writing.

18.10 At the conclusion of any discussion between experts, a statement should be prepared setting out:

(a) a list of issues that have been agreed, including, in each instance, the basis of agreement;

(b) a list of issues that have not been agreed, including, in each instance, the basis of disagreement;

(c) a list of any further issues that have arisen that were not included in the original agenda for discussion;

(d) a record of further action, if any, to be taken or recommended, including as appropriate the holding of further discussions between experts.

18.11 The statement should be agreed and signed by all the parties to the discussion as soon as may be practicable.

18.12 Agreements between experts during discussions do not bind the parties unless the parties expressly agree to be bound by the agreement (CPR 35.12(5)). However, in view of the overriding objective, parties should give careful consideration before refusing to be bound by such an agreement and be able to explain their refusal should it become relevant to the issue of costs.

19. ATTENDANCE OF EXPERTS AT COURT

19.1 Experts instructed in cases have an obligation to attend court if called upon to do so and accordingly should ensure that those instructing them are always aware of their dates to be avoided and take all reasonable steps to be available.

19.2 Those instructing experts should:

(a) ascertain the availability of experts before trial dates are fixed;

(b) keep experts updated with timetables (including the dates and times experts are to attend) and the location of the court;

(c) give consideration, where appropriate, to experts giving evidence via a video-link.

(d) inform experts immediately if trial dates are vacated.

19.3 Experts should normally attend court without the need for the service of witness summonses, but on occasion they may be served to require attendance (CPR 34). The use of witness summonses does not affect the contractual or other obligations of the parties to pay experts' fees.

2. INSTRUCTING EXPERTS UNDER THE PERSONAL INJURY PRE-ACTION PROTOCOL

(A) TEXT OF THE PRE-ACTION PROTOCOL

[30.3]

NOTES OF GUIDANCE

Experts
2.14   The protocol encourages joint selection of, and access to, experts. The report produced is not a joint report for the purposes of CPR Part 35. Most frequently this will apply to the medical expert, but on occasions also to liability experts, e.g. engineers. The protocol promotes the practice of the claimant obtaining a medical report, disclosing it to the defendant who then asks questions and/or agrees it and does not obtain his own report. The Protocol provides for nomination of the expert by the claimant in personal injury claims because of the early stage of the proceedings and the particular nature of such claims. If proceedings have to be issued, a medical report must be attached to these proceedings. However, if necessary after proceedings have commenced and with the permission of the court, the parties may obtain further expert reports. It would be for the court to decide whether the costs of more than one expert's report should be recoverable.
2.15   Some solicitors choose to obtain medical reports through medical agencies, rather than directly from a specific doctor or hospital. The defendant's prior consent to the action should be sought and, if the defendant so requests, the agency should be asked to provide in advance the names of the doctor(s) whom they are considering instructing.

THE PROTOCOL

Experts
3.15   Before any party instructs an expert he should give the other party a list of the name(s) of one or more experts in the relevant speciality whom he considers are suitable to instruct.
3.16   Where a medical expert is to be instructed the claimant's solicitor will organise access to relevant medical records – see specimen letter of instruction at Annex C.
3.17   Within 14 days the other party may indicate an objection to one or more of the named experts. The first party should then instruct a mutually acceptable expert (which is not the same as a joint expert). It must be emphasised that if the Claimant nominates an expert in the original letter of claim, the defendant has 14 days to object to one or more of the named experts after expiration of the period of 21 days within which he has to reply to the letter of claim, as set out in paragraph 3.6.
3.18   If the second party objects to all the listed experts, the parties may then instruct experts of their own choice. It would be for the court to decide subsequently, if proceedings are issued, whether either party had acted unreasonably.

3.19   If the second party does not object to an expert nominated, he shall not be entitled to rely on his own expert evidence within that particular speciality unless:

- the first party agrees;
- the court so directs, or
- the first party's expert report has been amended and the first party is not prepared to disclose the original report.

3.20   Either party may send to an agreed expert written questions on the report, relevant to the issues, via the first party's solicitors. The expert should send answers to the questions separately and directly to each party.

3.21   The cost of a report from an agreed expert will usually be paid by the instructing first party: the costs of the expert replying to questions will usually be borne by the party which asks the questions.

Note—Annex C is not reproduced here – reference should be made to *The Civil Court Practice*, published by LexisNexis Butterworths.

(B)   STATUS OF EXPERTS NOMINATED UNDER THE PRE-ACTION PROTOCOL

[30.4]   Carlson v Townsend

[2001] EWCA Civ 511

[2001] 3 All ER 663, [2001] I WLR 2415, 62 BMLR 50

Prior to the issue of proceedings, the claimant gave the defendant a list of three orthopaedic surgeons, in accordance with the requirements of the Personal Injury Pre-action Protocol. The defendant objected to one of the named experts, whereupon the claimant instructed one of the remaining two. The expert produced a report, but the claimant refused to disclose the report. Instead, the claimant disclosed a report from another expert. Following the issue of proceedings, the defendant made an application to the court, and an order was made that the claimant must disclose the report of the first expert. The claimant successfully appealed the order, and the defendant appealed to the Court of Appeal.

HELD, ON APPEAL: The Pre-action Protocol encouraged but did not require the disclosure of medical reports obtained following the nomination procedure. An expert instructed following a nomination not objected to remained the expert of the nominating party, and the report was therefore privileged and need not be disclosed.

3.   INSTRUCTION OF EXPERTS AFTER PROCEEDINGS

(A)   THE EXPERT'S OVERRIDING DUTY TO THE COURT

[30.5]

CPR 35.3 – EXPERT'S OVERRIDING DUTY TO THE COURT

(1)   It is the duty of an expert to help the court on the matters within his expertise.

(2)   This duty overrides any obligation to the person from whom he has received instructions or by whom he is paid.

DUTIES AND RESPONSIBILITIES OF EXPERT WITNESSES

[30.6] **National Justice Cia Naviera SA v Prudential Assurance Co Ltd**
[1993] 2 Lloyd's Rep 68

Cresswell J summarised the duties and responsibilities of expert witnesses in civil cases as follows:
(1) Expert evidence presented to the court should be, and should be seen to be, the independent product of the expert uninfluenced as to form or content by the exigencies of litigation.
(2) Independent assistance should be provided to the court by way of objective unbiased opinion regarding matters within the expertise of the expert witness. An expert witness should never assume the role of advocate.
(3) Facts or assumptions upon which the opinion was based should be stated together with material facts which could detract from the concluded opinion.
(4) An expert witness should make it clear when a question or issue falls outside his expertise.
(5) If the opinion was not properly researched because it was considered that insufficient data was available then that had to be stated with an indication that the opinion was provisional. If the witness could not assert that the report contained the truth, the whole truth and nothing but the truth then that qualification should be stated on the report.
(6) If, after exchange of reports, an expert witness changed his mind on a material matter then the change of view should be communicated to the other side through legal representatives without delay and, when appropriate, to the court.
(7) Photographs, plans, survey reports and other documents referred to in the expert evidence had to be provided to the other side at the same time as the exchange of reports.

Note—Whilst this decision pre-dates the introduction of the Civil Procedure Rules (CPR), it nevertheless provides a useful summary of the duties of an expert. The second sentence of paragraph (5) above should now be read with reference to the expert's declaration as set out in CPR 35.10.

INDEPENDENCE

[30.7] **R (on the application of Factortame) v Secretary of State for Transport, the Environment and the Regions**
[2002] EWCA Civ 932
[2002] 4 All ER 97, [2002] 3 WLR 1104

HELD, ON APPEAL: A court will very rarely consent to an expert being instructed on a contingency fee basis. The expert would have an interest in the outcome of the case and the expert's independence would therefore be compromised.

[30.8] **Liverpool Roman Catholic Archdiocesan Trustees Inc v Goldberg (No 2)**
[2001] 4 All ER 950, [2001] 1 WLR 2337

The claimant issued proceedings against the defendant barrister in respect of the defendant's advice in relation to tax matters. The defendant instructed a barrister to give evidence as an expert. The claimant objected on the basis that the barrister had a close relationship with the defendant (they had known each other for 28 years, were good friends, and were members of the same chambers). The barrister had stated in his report: '… it is right to say that my personal sympathies are engaged to a greater degree than would probably be normal with an expert witness'.

HELD: Where it is demonstrated that there exists a relationship between an expert and the party instructing that expert which a reasonable man might think was capable of affecting the independence of the expert, then the evidence of the expert should not be admitted.

EXAMPLES OF THE COURTS DEALING WITH EXPERTS EXHIBITING INAPPROPRIATE BEHAVIOUR

[30.9]   Phillips v Symes

[2004] EWHC 2330 (Ch)

[2005] 4 All ER 519, [2005] 1 WLR 2043

Per Peter Smith J: It seems to me that in the administration of justice, especially, in the light of the clearly defined duties now enshrined in CPR 35 and the practice direction supplementing CPR 35, it would be quite wrong of the court to remove from itself the power to make a costs order in appropriate circumstances against an expert who, by his evidence, causes significant expense to be incurred, and does so in flagrant disregard of his duties to the court.

[30.10]   Hussein v William Hill Group

[2004] EWHC 208 (QB)

[2004] All ER (D) 296 (Feb)

Two medical experts, close friends of the claimant, were instructed by the claimant to prepare reports following an alleged assault. The trial judge found that the claimant had deliberately exaggerated his claim, and awarded only nominal damages of £50. He further found that the two experts had produced reports and given oral evidence to support the claimant in pursuing his exaggerated claim, and that the conduct of the experts should be reported to the General Medical Council.

(B)   RESTRICTING EXPERT EVIDENCE

[30.11]

CPR 35.1 – DUTY TO RESTRICT EXPERT EVIDENCE

Expert evidence shall be restricted to that which is reasonably required to resolve the proceedings.

[30.12]

CPR 35.4 – COURT'S POWER TO RESTRICT EXPERT EVIDENCE

35.4
(1)   No party may call an expert or put in evidence an expert's report without the court's permission.

(2)   When a party applies for permission under this rule he must identify–

    (a)   the field in which he wishes to rely on expert evidence; and

    (b)   where practicable the expert in that field on whose evidence he wishes to rely.

(3)   If permission is granted under this rule it shall be in relation only to the expert named or the field identified under paragraph (2).

(4)   The court may limit the amount of the expert's fees and expenses that the party who wishes to rely on the expert may recover from any other party.

ACCIDENT RECONSTRUCTION EVIDENCE IN STRAIGHTFORWARD
MOTOR CLAIMS

[30.13]   Liddell v Middleton

[1996] PIQR P36

The claimant was waiting in the centre of a road, intending to cross to the other side once the traffic allowed him to. As he crossed, he was struck by the defendant's vehicle. During the course of the trial, the judge heard evidence from four eye witnesses and from two experts in road traffic accidents. The judge found the defendant to blame, subject to a deduction of 25% to reflect the claimant's negligence. The defendant appealed.

HELD, ON APPEAL: The court substituted a finding of 50% contributory negligence, both parties were equally to blame.

Obiter, per Smith LJ: An expert is only qualified to give expert evidence on a relevant matter, if his knowledge and expertise relate to a matter which is outside the knowledge and experience of a layman ... In some cases expert evidence is both necessary and desirable in road traffic cases to assist the judge in reaching his primary findings of fact. Examples of such cases include those where there are no witnesses capable of describing what happened, and deductions may have to be made from such circumstantial evidence as there may be at the scene, or where deductions are to be drawn from the position of vehicles after the accident, marks on the road, or damage to the vehicles, as to the speed of a vehicle, or the relative positions of the parties in the moments leading up to the impact ... We do not have trial by expert in this country; we have trial by judge. In my judgment, the expert witnesses contributed nothing to the trial in this case except expense ... [In] road traffic accidents it is the exception rather than the rule that expert witnesses are required.

PROPORTIONALITY

[30.14]   Bandegani v Norwich Union Fire Insurance Society Ltd

(20 May 1999, unreported), CA

The claimant purchased a motor vehicle for £1,500 and insured it with the defendant. Another vehicle damaged the claimant's vehicle, causing sufficient damage that it was written off. The claimant claimed the sum of £1,500 from the defendant. The district judge considered that the claimant's own oral evidence of the purchase price was not sufficient to prove his claim and dismissed the claim. The circuit judge would not interfere with the district judge's findings.

HELD, ON APPEAL: In the absence of any other evidence, the district judge should have accepted the claimant's oral evidence.

Obiter, per Henry LJ: The case was conducted on the assumption that the question of the valuation of the car was a proper matter for the calling in person of expert evidence on both sides. I question that assumption on the grounds of proportionality.

[30.15]   S v Chesterfield and North Derbyshire Royal Hospital NHS Trust
[2003] EWCA Civ 1284
[2003] All ER (D) 448 (Jul), [2004] CP Rep 9

The claimant suffered cerebral palsy and issued proceedings against the defendant alleging clinical negligence. The allegations were directed against the conduct of two of the defendant's employees, who were both consultant obstetricians The master made an order that the expert evidence in the field of obstetrics be limited to one expert per party. The claimant applied for permission to instruct an additional obstetrician. Her solicitors argued that the claimant's sole expert would be confronted with the evidence of three consultant obstetricians, namely the two consultants against whom allegations had been made, and the defendant's permitted expert. The master refused the claimant's application because he considered that the evidence of the two consultants could be isolated from that of the medico-legal expert. The claimant appealed to the Court of Appeal.

HELD: As defined by CPR 35.1, the question to be asked was what expert evidence was reasonably required to resolve the issue. What was reasonably required was a fact sensitive issue, and should be considered in the context of the overriding objective. In this case, the defendant effectively had three experts who would be able to give evidence over a much wider spectrum of personal experience than could the claimant's single expert. The additional cost and extra time at trial of a second expert on behalf of the claimant was not disproportionate in a case of significant monetary value and importance, and the additional expert would be allowed.

APPROPRIATENESS

[30.16]   Coker v Barkland Cleaning Co
(6 December 1999, unreported), CA

The claimant was employed by the defendant as a cleaner. Whilst at work, he was bending down and was struck from behind by another employee who was driving a portable cleaner. The defendant denied liability, alleging that the machine was faulty. Both the claimant and the defendant instructed engineering experts, but the trial judge did not call upon their evidence. He held that the defendant was wholly liable for the accident. His findings in relation to the medical evidence were challenged on appeal.

HELD, ON APPEAL: The Court of Appeal upheld the judge's findings in relation to the medical evidence.

Per May LJ: Much energy and expense was incurred on each side with the engineering investigation, evidence and submissions ... A forthright look by both sides at the only real liability issue in this case shows and would have shown that if indeed [the claimant] was hit from behind by the cleaning machine there was no viable defence on liability ... The expense of the engineers and other expenses of dealing with the subject which they address would have been entirely avoided.

[30.17]   **Mwamda v East London Bus & Coach Co Ltd**
(6 February 2002, unreported)

The claimant was refused permission to rely upon a medical report prepared by a GP as the report had been obtained without the defendant's consent in breach of the personal injury pre-action protocol, and it failed to comply with CPR Pt 35 as the GP was not an expert in an 'appropriate discipline'. There was no indication of the GP's experience, and there had been a failure to set out the basis of the instructions on which the report was prepared.

[30.18]   **Prigmore v Welbourne**
[2003] EWHC 3259 (QB)
[2003] All ER (D) 301 (Nov)

The claimant issued proceedings in respect of the death of his wife in a road traffic accident caused by the defendant's motor vehicle. One of the dependants was the claimant's disabled daughter. An issue arose between the parties as to the appropriate multiplier and multiplicand to apply to the care claim. The district judge considered that this issue required the input of actuarial evidence, and granted permission to the parties to jointly instruct an actuary. The defendant appealed, arguing that there was no need for evidence from an actuary, and that actuarial evidence would simply make a complicated case more complicated.

HELD, ON APPEAL: Actuarial evidence was not required. The use of the Ogden Tables was sufficient for the purposes of the calculation.

[30.19]   **Heyward v Plymouth Hospital NHS Trust**
[2005] EWCA Civ 939
[2005] All ER (D) 212 (Jun)

The claimant issued proceedings in respect of a psychiatric injury which he alleged had been caused by his employer, the defendant. At the case management conference the parties advised the district judge that it was common ground that they should each have permission to instruct a psychiatrist. The district judge granted permission accordingly. However, he refused permission to the claimant to instruct an occupational psychologist in addition. The claimant appealed. It was argued on his behalf that whilst the psychiatrists could give evidence as to the causation of the injury, they could not give evidence as to the steps that the defendant should have taken to avoid causing the injury. The judge rejected the argument. The claimant appealed to the Court of Appeal.

HELD: The issues of causation to be determined were issues of fact – did the defendant's actions lead to the claimant's psychiatric injury? Accordingly, the district judge had been right to limit the expert evidence as he had.

PARTY DISSATISFIED WITH OWN REPORT – WHETHER PERMISSION TO RELY UPON SECOND EXPERT WILL BE GIVEN, AND IF SO, THE CONDITIONS LIKELY TO BE ATTACHED TO SUCH PERMISSION

[30.20]   Beck v Ministry of Defence

[2003] EWCA Civ 1043

[2003] All ER (D) 406 (Jun), [2005] 1 WLR 2206

The claimant issued proceedings against the defendant in respect of injuries he sustained during the course of receiving psychiatric treatment at the defendant's hospital. The court gave directions which included, *inter alia*, permission to each party to rely upon a psychiatric expert. The claimant was examined by the defendant's expert. He produced a report. Over time, the defendant lost confidence in the expert, and applied for permission to obtain a report from a second psychiatric expert. The district judge granted permission. The claimant appealed, arguing that a pre-condition of being permitted to instruct a new expert should be the disclosure of the original expert's report. The appeal was dismissed. The claimant appealed to the Court of Appeal.

HELD, ON APPEAL: The disclosure of the original report should be a pre-condition of the defendant being allowed to instruct a new expert. Neither the claimant nor the court should be left to wonder whether the real reason for the application was that the first report was favourable to the claimant.

[30.21]   Vasiliou v Hajigeorgiou

[2005] EWCA Civ 236

[2005] 3 All ER 17, [2005] 1 WLR 2195, (2005) Times, 22 March

The claimant issued proceedings in respect of the defendant's breach of a covenant in a lease of business premises where the claimant ran a restaurant. At the case management conference, the defendant contended that there were certain issues in relation to the value and the profits of the restaurant which could only be addressed by an expert, and identified a specific expert. The judge ordered that each party should have their own expert in the field of restaurant valuation and profitability. The order did not specify the name of the defendant's proposed expert. The defendant's expert attended the premises for the purposes of an inspection. Some time later, the defendant indicated that he would not be relying upon this expert, and intended to instruct an alternative expert, and requested permission from the claimant to have the second expert inspect the premises. The claimant refused, and the matter came before the court. The judge held that the defendant needed the court's permission to instruct an alternative expert, and that in accordance with *Beck v Ministry of Defence*, a pre-condition of that permission was that the defendant should disclose the first expert's report. The defendant appealed.

HELD, ON APPEAL: The order for directions did not identify the expert to be instructed by name, it only identified experts by reference to their field of expertise. Accordingly, the defendant did not require the permission of the court to instruct a second expert.

Obiter: If the court had been right to hold that permission was required, then the condition imposed by the judge – disclosure of the first report – was correct.

(C)   THE SINGLE JOINT EXPERT

[30.22]

CPR 35.7 – COURT'S POWER TO DIRECT THAT EVIDENCE IS TO BE GIVEN BY A SINGLE JOINT EXPERT

(1)   Where two or more parties wish to submit expert evidence on a particular issue, the court may direct that the evidence on that issue is to given by one expert only.

(2)   The parties wishing to submit the expert evidence are called 'the instructing parties'.

(3)   Where the instructing parties cannot agree who should be the expert, the court may–

  (a)   select the expert from a list prepared or identified by the instructing parties; or

  (b)   direct that the expert be selected in such other manner as the court may direct.

WHEN A SINGLE JOINT EXPERT IS APPROPRIATE, AND WHEN NOT

[30.23]   Peet v Mid Kent Healthcare NHS Trust
[2001] EWCA Civ 1703
[2002] 3 All ER 688, [2002] 1 WLR 210

Per Lord Woolf MR: Although the amount of a claim can be significantly influenced by non-medical evidence, in my view in the great majority of cases where there is the need for such non-medical evidence, that evidence should be given by a single expert rather than by experts called on behalf of the respective parties. This is not a matter of choice for the parties. In the absence of special circumstances I consider that the appropriate way that the power should be exercised is to require a single expert rather than an expert from each party.

Note—For full report, see para [30.30] below.

[30.24]   Watson v North Tyneside Metropolitan Borough Council
[2003] CLY 284

The claimant and the first defendant agreed to jointly instruct an orthopaedic surgeon to examine the claimant's injured wrist. The second defendant, who had not originally been involved in the claim, and was not involved in the joint instruction, objected to the resulting report. The second defendant argued that the value of the case, pleaded in the region of £120,000, was such that the appropriate expert to instruct was an upper limb expert.

HELD: The court had the power to make an order that expert evidence be provided by a single joint expert. The value of the claim was not the predominant factor to take into account when deciding whether a joint expert should be instructed. The more important question was whether the injury was such that it could provoke a range of professional opinion as to its nature and its implications.

[30.25] Smolen v Solon Co-operative Housing Services Ltd

[2003] EWCA Civ 1240

147 Sol Jo LB 1087

Directions were given in a claim in the Technology and Construction Court which included a direction for the joint instruction of an expert surveyor. It emerged that the expert recommended by the defendant and then appointed by both parties had in fact been instructed on many previous occasions by the defendant. The claimant applied to the trial judge to have the expert removed.

HELD: The claimant was entitled to feel doubts about the expert's impartiality and the court made an order removing the expert from the proceedings. However, the court did not find that the defendant had been at fault or had acted improperly in instructing the expert. The court therefore made an order that each party pay 50% of the expert's costs.

[30.26] Wright v Sullivan

[2005] EWCA Civ 656

[2005] All ER (D) 449 (May), [2006] PIQR 4, [2006] RTR 116

The claimant suffered a very severe concussive head injury resulting in brain injury when she was run down by the defendant's vehicle. Liability was compromised on a 70/30 basis in the claimant's favour. The defendant's insurer proposed that a clinical case manager should be instructed on a joint basis to examine the claimant and prepare a report. The claimant objected, primarily on the basis that a clinical case manager was an individual whose relationship with the claimant would be therapeutic, and who would not be called to give evidence in the capacity of an expert witness, but as a witness of fact. The judge refused to make an order that the case manager be appointed on a joint basis, and the defendant appealed.

HELD, ON APPEAL: It was not appropriate for a case manager to be appointed on a joint basis. The case manager owed a duty to the claimant alone and had to make decisions in the claimant's best interests. Any communications between the case manager and the medical experts would not be protected by litigation privilege. However, if in furtherance of the duty owed to the claimant, a case manager chose to attend a conference with counsel, then the case manager's contribution would be protected by privilege.

[30.27]

CPR 35.8 – INSTRUCTIONS TO A SINGLE JOINT EXPERT
  (1)   Where the court gives a direction under rule 35.7 for a single joint expert to be used, each instructing party may give instructions to the expert.
  (2)   When an instructing party gives instructions to the expert he must, at the same time, send a copy of the instructions to the other instructing parties.
  (3)   The court may give directions about–
    (a)   the payment of the expert's fees and expenses; and
    (b)   any inspection, examination or experiments which the expert wishes to carry out.
  (4)   The court may, before an expert is instructed–
    (a)   limit the amount that can be paid by way of fees and expenses to the expert; and

(b)   direct that the instructing parties pay that amount into court.

(5)   Unless the court otherwise directs, the instructing parties are jointly and severally liable for the payment of the expert's fees and expenses.

[30.28]   Yorke v Katra

[2003] EWCA Civ 867

[2003] All ER (D) 95 (Jun)

The claimant issued proceedings to recover the sum of £2,800 from the defendant in respect of building work that the claimant had performed. The claim was allocated to the small claims track, and proceedings were stayed so that a joint expert could be instructed to consider the quality of the building works. The district judge made an order that the defendant should sign a letter of joint instruction drafted by the claimant's solicitors. When the defendant made amendments to the letter before signing it, the district judge struck out the defence and counterclaim and made an order that the defendant pay the costs of the action. The defendant appealed to the circuit judge but the appeal was refused. The defendant then appealed to the Court of Appeal.

HELD, ON APPEAL: The district judge had failed to appreciate that CPR 35.8(1) provides that where the court directs that there is to be a joint expert, 'each instructing party may give instructions to the expert'. The court cannot impose one party's preferred version of the joint letter of instruction on the other.

SINGLE JOINT EXPERTS ATTENDING MEETINGS

[30.29]   Smith (a child by his Litigation Friend the Official Solicitor) v Stevens

(26 January 2001, unreported)

The claimant sought the attendance of a single joint expert at a conference with counsel without seeking the defendant's consent.

HELD: This did not accord with the overriding objective of the CPR. The court allowed the defendant's application to prevent the conference. Both parties were entitled to put written questions to the expert.

[30.30]   Peet v Mid Kent Healthcare NHS Trust

[2001] EWCA Civ 1703

[2002] 3 All ER 688, [2002] 1 WLR 210

The claimant, a child suing through his father and litigation friend, issued proceedings against the defendant health care trust in respect of personal injuries. Judgment was entered, and the master made an order for directions which provided that there be seven jointly instructed non-medical experts. A further order was made that there be no conference with the claimant in respect of any of the jointly instructed experts, unless the defendant gave consent. The claimant appealed.

HELD, ON APPEAL: The idea that one side should be permitted to test the views of an expert in conference in the absence of the other party was clearly wrong, and therefore a single joint expert should not attend any meeting or conference that was not a joint one without the written permission of all parties.

DISSATISFACTION WITH THE REPORT OF A SINGLE JOINT EXPERT

[30.31]   **Daniels v Walker**

[2000] All ER (D) 608, [2000] 1 WLR 1382, CA

The claimant sustained severe injuries in a road traffic accident caused by the negligence of the defendant. The parties agreed to jointly instruct an occupational therapist. The report included the cost of a care regime for the claimant. The defendant was not content with the figures in the report, and contended that they were in excess of figures in similar cases. The defendant sought permission to instruct his own expert. Permission was refused, and the defendant appealed.

HELD, ON APPEAL: Wherever possible, parties should seek to agree to jointly instruct an expert. In the event that a party is not satisfied with the report, and the reasons given are not fanciful, and the case is one which involves a substantial sum, then that party, subject to the discretion of the court, should be permitted to obtain their own report.

[30.32]   **Cosgrove v Pattison**

[2000] All ER (D) 2007, [2001] CPLR 177, [2001] CP Rep 68, CA

The parties were neighbours. In a boundary dispute a joint expert surveyor was appointed to report. Having prepared his report, both parties asked the expert questions. In the course of a telephone conversation with the expert, the defendant's solicitors formed the impression that the expert might be biased against the defendant. The defendant applied for permission to instruct his own expert. Permission was refused. On the following day, a report of *Daniels v Walker* appeared in The Times Law Reports. Permission to appeal was granted.

HELD, ON APPEAL: The appeal was allowed and the defendant was given permission to obtain his own expert report.

Per Neuberger LJ: In my judgment although it would be wrong to pretend that this is an exhaustive list, the factors to be taken into account when considering an application to permit a further expert to be called are these. First, the nature of the issue or issues; secondly, the number of issues between the parties; thirdly, the reason the new expert is wanted; fourthly; the amount at stake and, if it is not purely money, the nature of the issues at stake and their importance; fifthly, the effect of permitting one party to call further expert evidence on the conduct of the trial; sixthly, the delay, if any, in making the application; seventhly, any delay that the instructing and calling of the new expert will cause; eighthly, any other special features in the case; and finally ... the overall justice to the parties in the context of the litigation.

[30.33]   **Austin v Oxford City Council**

(17 April 2002, unreported), QBD

The claimant issued proceedings in respect of a lifting injury sustained in the course of her employment by the defendant. The nature of the orthopaedic injury was agreed by the parties' respective experts, save as to the causation of fibromyalgia. The parties then jointly instructed a consultant psychiatrist to resolve this issue. The expert's evidence was that it was highly unlikely that the claimant's symptoms of fibromyalgia were caused by the accident. The claimant applied to the court for permission to cross examine the psychiatrist, and the trial judge refused. The claimant appealed.

HELD, ON APPEAL: The decision in *Daniels v Walker* made it clear that the claimant ought to have made an application to obtain her own evidence from a consultant psychiatrist. However, in the absence of such an application, the court should not simply have held that the joint psychiatric report should stand as the agreed evidence, when it was obvious that the claimant did not rely upon it. The trial judge should have permitted the claimant to cross-examine the joint expert because that was the only way in which justice could have been done.

4. THE EXPERT'S REPORT

[30.34]

CPR 35.5 – GENERAL REQUIREMENT FOR EXPERT EVIDENCE TO BE GIVEN IN A WRITTEN REPORT
(1) Expert evidence is to be given in a written report unless the court directs otherwise.
(2) If a claim is on the fast track, the court will not direct an expert to attend a hearing unless it is necessary to do so in the interests of justice.

[30.35]

CPR 35.10 – CONTENTS OF REPORT
(1) An expert's report must comply with the requirements set out in the relevant practice direction.
(2) At the end of an expert's report there must be a statement that–
  (a) the expert understands his duty to the court; and
  (b) he has complied with that duty.
(3) The expert's report must state the substance of all material instructions, whether written or oral, on the basis of which the report was written.
(4) The instructions referred to in paragraph (3) shall not be privileged against disclosure but the court will not, in relation to those instructions–
  (a) order disclosure of any specific document; or
  (b) permit any questioning in court, other than by the party who instructed the expert,
unless it is satisfied that there are reasonable grounds to consider the statement of instructions given under paragraph (3) to be inaccurate or incomplete.

(A)   EXPERT'S REPORT MUST SET OUT THE 'SUBSTANCE OF ALL MATERIAL INSTRUCTIONS'

[30.36]   Morris v Bank of India

(15 November 2001, unreported)

Under CPR 35.10, an expert's report had to contain a statement setting out all material instructions relied upon and any report without such a statement was defective. In such circumstances the court had the power to order disclosure of the instructions.

[30.37]   Lucas v Barking, Havering and Redbridge Hospitals NHS Trust

[2003] EWCA Civ 1102

[2003] 4 All ER 720, [2004] 1 WLR 220

The claimant issued proceedings in respect of personal injuries suffered as a result of the alleged negligence of the defendant health authority. With his particulars of claim the defendant produced two experts' reports, both of which referred to a witness statement of the claimant, and one of which referred to a previous report of an expert. The defendant applied under CPR 31.14(2) for inspection of these documents. The claimant resisted the application, arguing that the documents requested were part of the instructions provided to the experts and therefore fell within the exception to CPR 31.14(2), namely CPR 35.10(4). The master made an order for disclosure of the documents, but granted permission to appeal. The matter went straight to the Court of Appeal.

HELD, ON APPEAL: CPR 35.10(4) requires that an expert should set out fully the substance of the material instructions upon which he has based his report. The material referred to was not privileged from inspection, but an order requiring that it be disclosed to the other party would only be made if there were reasonable grounds for considering that the expert's statement of instructions was inaccurate. CPR 35.10(4) was designed to protect a party who would otherwise have to waive privilege in respect of documents which had to be referred to by the expert when setting out 'the substance of all material instructions'. In the present case, there was no reason for supposing that the experts had provided an inaccurate summary of their material instructions, and so there would be no disclosure of the documents in question.

[30.38]   Jackson v Marley Davenport Ltd

[2004] EWCA Civ 1225

[2004] All ER (D) 56 (Sep), [2004] 1 WLR 2926

The claimant issued proceedings in respect of an injury sustained at work during the course of his employment with the defendant. Each party was given permission to obtain a report from an engineering expert. The claimant's expert prepared a report for the purposes of a conference with his instructing solicitors. Thereafter, he prepared a further report. It was this second report which was disclosed by the claimant's solicitors. A passage in the report suggested the existence of the original report, and the defendant's solicitors made an application for an order that the original report be disclosed. The district judge made such an order. The defendant successfully appealed. The claimant then appealed to the Court of Appeal.

HELD, ON APPEAL: If an expert prepared a report for the purposes of a conference with lawyers, then that report had been prepared in contemplation of litigation and attracted legal privilege. The CPR was not intended to override such privilege. The initial draft of an expert's report does not constitute a part of the 'substance of all material instructions'. Consequently, the court cannot make an order compelling disclosure of a report which a party chooses not to disclose.

5. QUESTIONS TO EXPERTS

[30.39]

CPR 35.6 – WRITTEN QUESTIONS TO EXPERTS
  (1)   A party may put to–
    (a)   an expert instructed by another party; or
    (b)   a single joint expert appointed under rule 35.7,
  written questions about his report.
  (2)   Written questions under paragraph (1)–
    (a)   may be put once only;
    (b)   must be put within 28 days of service of the expert's report; and
    (c)   must be for the purpose only of clarification of the report,
  unless in any case–
      (i)   the court gives permission; or
      (ii)   the other party agrees.
  (3)   An expert's answers to questions put in accordance with paragraph (1) shall be treated as part of the expert's report.
  (4)   Where–
    (a)   a party has put a written question to an expert instructed by another party in accordance with this rule; and
    (b)   the expert does not answer that question,
  the court may make one or both of the following orders in relation to the party who instructed the expert–
      (i)   that the party may not rely on the evidence of that expert; or
      (ii)   that the party may not recover the fees and expenses of that expert from any other party.

[30.40]   Mutch v Allen

[2001] EWCA Civ 76

[2001] All ER (D) 121 (Jan), [2001] PIQR 26

The claimant sustained serious injury in a road traffic accident whilst travelling as a passenger in a motor car driven by the defendant. The claimant was not wearing a seatbelt. The claimant relied upon a report from an orthopaedic surgeon. The defendant wrote to the expert, asking him to clarify his report under CPR 35.6 and comment upon whether the claimant's injuries would have been reduced or avoided had he been wearing a seatbelt. The claimant objected to the expert answering this question. At a case management conference, the district judge gave permission to the defendant to ask the question. The expert responded by stating in terms that the claimant's injuries would have been significantly reduced or avoided had he been wearing a seatbelt. The claimant argued that the defendant's question did not amount to clarification of the expert's original opinion, and therefore the expert's answer should not be given in evidence. The judge agreed. The defendant appealed to the Court of Appeal.

HELD, ON APPEAL: Irrespective of whether the question was 'for the purpose only of clarification' of the report, nevertheless the court would give permission to the defendant to ask the question. It was a question which would be put to the expert in cross-examination, whose answer could be relied upon by the defendant. It was also a question which would assist the implementation of the overriding objective and enable the matter to be resolved in the most cost effective and expeditious way.

6. DISCUSSIONS BETWEEN EXPERTS

[30.41]

CPR 35.12 – DISCUSSIONS BETWEEN EXPERTS
(1)   The court may, at any stage, direct a discussion between experts for the purpose of requiring the experts to–
　(a)   identify and discuss the expert issues in the proceedings; and
　(b)   where possible, reach an agreed opinion on those issues.
(2)   The court may specify the issues which the experts must discuss.
(3)   The court may direct that following a discussion between the experts they must prepare a statement for the court showing–
　(a)   those issues on which they agree; and
　(b)   those issues on which they disagree and a summary of their reasons for disagreeing.
(4)   The content of the discussion between the experts shall not be referred to at the trial unless the parties agree.
(5)   Where experts reach agreement on an issue during their discussions, the agreement shall not bind the parties unless the parties expressly agree to be bound by the agreement.

[30.42]   Hubbard v Lambeth, Southwark and Lewisham Health Authority
[2001] EWCA Civ 1455
[2001] All ER (D) 11 (Sep)

A without-prejudice meeting of experts should identify and narrow issues and was therefore appropriate, despite the reluctance of the claimant's expert to criticise the professional competence of a colleague at such a meeting.

(A)   EXPERT'S MEETINGS PRIVILEGED, RESULTING REPORT NOT PRIVILEGED

[30.43]   Stanton v Callaghan
[2000] QB 75, [1998] 4 All ER 961, [1999] 2 WLR 745

The claimant, a builder employed by the defendant, issued proceedings in respect of money allegedly due for work done. Each party instructed an expert, and an order was made requiring that the experts were to agree a joint statement setting out areas of agreement and disagreement. In compliance with the order, the experts met seventeen times and conducted a number of telephone conversations. They prepared what was termed an interim joint statement. The claimant objected to the defendant relying upon the joint statement, arguing that it was privileged.

HELD: The content of discussions between experts at meetings and on the telephone was privileged. However, once agreement is reached, privilege does not apply to the agreement. The joint statement of the experts setting out their agreement was not binding upon the parties – it merely set out the opinions of the experts themselves. Accordingly, if an expert changed his view in relation to a matter set out in a joint statement, then he had a duty to record that change of view.

7. THE WEIGHT TO BE GIVEN TO EXPERT EVIDENCE

[30.44] **McGill v Addy**

(28 May 1999, unreported), CA

The judge was entitled to prefer expert evidence over an eye witness account of an accident and to have found that the defendant motorcyclist had ample time to slow down and/or take alternative action to avoid an accident.

[30.45] **Coopers Payen Ltd v Southampton Container Terminal Ltd**

[2003] EWCA Civ 1223

[2003] All ER (D) 220 (Jul), [2004] 1 Lloyd's Rep 331

The defendant received a unitised load which had been sold to the first claimant by the second claimant. The load was placed on a mafi flat attached to a tug. The tug performed a u-turn on the quay side, and as it did so the unitised load fell off. The defendant called a lay witness whose evidence was that the tug was travelling at no more than 4.8 km per hour. The parties jointly instructed an expert, whose evidence was that the accident could only have occurred if the tug had been travelling at about 9.82 km per hour. The trial judge preferred the evidence of the lay witness on the basis that he was both credible and reliable, and held that the defendant had discharged its duty to the claimants. The claimants appealed.

HELD, ON APPEAL: The court had to balance all the evidence in the case. The single joint expert had identified only one possible cause of the accident. The judge should have judged the reliability of the lay witness evidence in this context. Instead, the judge had considered the lay witness evidence in isolation. Accordingly, whilst the Court of Appeal had not had the opportunity of hearing the witnesses give evidence, this was a case where the trial judge's assessment of the evidence had been plainly wrong. On the balance of probabilities, the tug had been travelling too quickly and the accident had been the result of that breach of duty.

[30.46] **Armstrong v First York**

[2005] EWCA Civ 277

[2005] All ER (D) 107 (Jan), [2005] 1 WLR 2751

In a road traffic accident case, the claimants gave evidence that the collision between their stationary motor car and the defendant's bus had caused them to be thrown forward and to the side, that they had immediately or shortly after the collision suffered symptoms of neck pain, and that they had visited both a hospital and their respective GPs. These visits were corroborated in the medical records.

An engineer was instructed as a joint expert. He found that the damage caused to the car was a scratch of approximately 200 microns, the equivalent of approximately two coats of paint. He concluded that the collision could not have caused any vehicle movement and that accordingly there could not have been any 'occupant displacement' sufficient to cause injury. The judge could find no identifiable error in his evidence.

The judge accepted that the conflicting evidence could only be reconciled if either the claimants were lying, or there was some error in the expert evidence. The judge found the claimants to be honest witnesses who, on the balance of probabilities, had proved their case. The defendant appealed.

HELD, ON APPEAL: There was no rule of law which required a judge to accept expert evidence on issues of fact. This was not a case where there was no evidence on one side to rebut the expert evidence. There was the evidence of the claimants. There was no principle of trial by expert in England and Wales. Trial was by judge, and the expert's role was to assist the court. Just because the engineer in this case said that there could not have been vehicle movement did not mean that there had been no vehicle movement. The claimants had said that there was, and the trial judge had found the claimants to be honest witnesses. The judge was fully entitled to weigh all the evidence as he had done, and the Court of Appeal would not interfere with his reasoning.

8.   ACCESS TO MEDICAL RECORDS

(A)   ACCESS TO MEDICAL RECORDS IN CASES WITH A VALUE OF LESS THAN £10,000

[30.47]   On 6 June 2006, the Law Society announced an agreement between the Law Society, the Association of British Insurers (ABI) and the Association of Personal Injury Lawyers(APIL):

'As part of a Cabinet Office initiative to reduce bureaucracy an agreement has been reached between the Law Society, APIL, the ABI and the health sector that, subject to the expert witnesses' view, there is a rebuttable presumption that no patient records will be requested for claims below £10,000.

This agreement was reached on the understanding that it takes the form of best practice guidance to try to reduce the bureaucracy involved in lower value claims.'

Note—Practitioners should think about how necessary patient records are to the particular case and whether they need to see them, since the purpose of this outcome measure is to try to reduce burdens on GPs and other health professionals. Practitioners should note it is not an absolute bar to seeking patient records and they can always be sought if the solicitor deems it necessary to do so. The outcome does not amend the Personal Injury Pre-action Protocol or the patient's right to see their own records.

(B)   DISPUTES AS TO RELEVANCE

[30.48]   **Hipwood v Gloucester Health Authority and Others**
[1995] ICR 999, [1995] 6 Med LR 187, 24 BMLR 27, [1995] PIQR P447

Per McCowan LJ: In principle it seems to me that it cannot properly be the legal and medical advisers [who resolve disputes as to disclosure of medical records]; it must be the court. The example has been debated in this case where general practitioner's records disclose that 20 years ago the [claimant] had a sexually transmitted disease, but that she recovered fully from it ... Faced with a claim of non-relevance the defendant's legal advisers would no doubt ask their medical advisers whether that particular entry had any relevance ... If told 'no' they might well accept that advice. If they chose not to they would be entitled to go to the court and say 'Please decide' ... That is how I for my part would envisage the matter being determined by the district judge or master.

(C)   PROCEDURE FOR OBTAINING RECORDS

[30.49]   **Bennett v Compass Group UK & Ireland Ltd**

[2002] EWCA Civ 642

[2002] All ER (D) 130 (Apr), [2002] ICR 1177

In the course of case management, the district judge made an order requiring that the claimant supply to the defendants a form of authority for the disclosure of the claimant's medical records. The claimant argued that the district judge did not have jurisdiction to make such an order. The matter was referred to the Court of Appeal.

HELD, ON APPEAL: The rules provided jurisdiction for an order in these terms to be made.

Per Clarke LJ: [S]uch an order should only be made in exceptional circumstances because in principle a patient should retain control over his or her own medical records ... [A] judge should think long and hard before making such an order because a defendant should only be allowed to see a claimant's medical records in carefully defined circumstances.

Per Chadwick LJ: The normal – and by far most satisfactory course – is for the medical records to be produced by the claimant's advisers for inspection and consideration by the defendant's experts. It should not be necessary for the defendant's advisers to approach the GP or the hospital directly. But I cannot say that there are not circumstances in which it may be necessary – in order to break through what appears to be a wall of unresponsive silence – for the court to make such an order.

Applications

1. GENERALLY

(A) HOW TO MAKE AN APPLICATION

[31.1]

CPR 23.1 – MEANING OF 'APPLICATION NOTICE' AND 'RESPONDENT'

In this Part–
'application notice' means a document in which the applicant states his intention to seek a court order; and
'respondent' means–
   (a)   the person against whom the order is sought; and
   (b)   such other person as the court may direct.

[31.2]

CPR 23.2 – WHERE TO MAKE AN APPLICATION
   (1)   The general rule is that an application must be made to the court where the claim was started.
   (2)   If a claim has been transferred to another court since it was started, an application must be made to the court to which the claim has been transferred.
   (3)   If the parties have been notified of a fixed date for the trial, an application must be made to the court where the trial is to take place.
   (4)   If an application is made before a claim has been started, it must be made to the court where it is likely that the claim to which the application relates will be started unless there is good reason to make the application to a different court.
   (5)   If an application is made after proceedings to enforce judgment have begun, it must be made to any court which is dealing with the enforcement of the judgment unless any rule or practice direction provides otherwise.

[31.3]

CPR 23.3 – APPLICATION NOTICE TO BE FILED
   (1)   The general rule is that an applicant must file an application notice.
   (2)   An applicant may make an application without filing an application notice if–
   (a)   this is permitted by a rule or practice direction; or
   (b)   the court dispenses with the requirement for an application notice.

[31.4]

CPR 23.5 – TIME WHEN AN APPLICATION IS MADE

Where an application must be made within a specified time, it is so made if the application notice is received by the court within that time.

[31.5]

CPR 23.6 – WHAT AN APPLICATION NOTICE MUST INCLUDE

An application notice must state–
    (a)   what order the applicant is seeking; and
    (b)   briefly, why the applicant is seeking the order.

(B)   NOTICE AND SERVICE OF AN APPLICATION

[31.6]

CPR 23.4 – NOTICE OF AN APPLICATION
    (1)   The general rule is that a copy of the application notice must be served on each respondent.
    (2)   An application may be made without serving a copy of the application notice if this is permitted by–
        (a)   a rule;
        (b)   a practice direction; or
        (c)   a court order.

[31.7]   **Connolly v Harrington**
(17 May 2002, unreported)

At a hearing of an application for summary judgment, the master allowed the defendant to make an oral application without notice, and assented to make an order that certain items on the defendant's schedule be submitted for detailed assessment. The claimant appealed.

HELD, ON APPEAL: A master has authority to dispense with written notice of an application under CPR 23.3(2)(b), and dispense with service under CPR 23.4(2)(c).

[31.8]

CPR 23.7 – SERVICE OF A COPY OF AN APPLICATION NOTICE
    (1)   A copy of the application notice–
        (a)   must be served as soon as practicable after it is filed; and
        (b)   except where another time limit is specified in these Rules or a practice direction, must in any event be served at least 3 days before the court is to deal with the application.
    (2)   If a copy of the application notice is to be served by the court, the applicant must, when he files the application notice, file a copy of any written evidence in support.
    (3)   When a copy of an application notice is served it must be accompanied by–
        (a)   a copy of any written evidence in support; and
        (b)   a copy of any draft order which the applicant has attached to his application.
    (4)   If–
        (a)   an application notice is served; but
        (b)   the period of notice is shorter than the period required by these Rules or a practice direction,

the court may direct that, in the circumstances of the case, sufficient notice has been given and hear the application.

(5)　This rule does not require written evidence–
(a)　to be filed if it has already been filed; or
(b)　to be served on a party on whom it has already been served.

(C)　WITHOUT NOTICE APPLICATIONS

[31.9]

CPR 23.8 – APPLICATIONS WHICH MAY BE DEALT WITH WITHOUT A HEARING

The court may deal with an application without a hearing if–
(a)　the parties agree as to the terms of the order sought;
(b)　the parties agree that the court should dispose of the application without a hearing, or
(c)　the court does not consider that a hearing would be appropriate.

[31.10]　Interoute Telecommunications v Fashion Gossip Ltd

(1999) Times, 10 November

HELD: It is the duty of counsel and solicitors on a without notice application to make a full note of the hearing where possible or at least to prepare a full note as soon as the hearing is over, and to provide a copy of that note to all parties affected.

[31.11]　Network Telecom (Europe) Ltd v Telephone Systems International Inc

[2003] EWHC 2890 (QB)

[2004] 1 All ER (Comm) 418, [2003] All ER (D) 350 (Oct)

HELD: On a without notice application, the duty of full and fair disclosure on the part of the applicant is not a duty which applies only at the time of the order, but is a continuing duty. Where facts arise after the date of the original order which are relevant, the applicant must return to court to obtain clarification whether the original order may stand.

[31.12]

CPR 23.9 – SERVICE OF APPLICATION WHERE APPLICATION MADE WITHOUT NOTICE
(1)　This rule applies where the court has disposed of an application which it permitted to be made without service of a copy of the application notice.
(2)　Where the court makes an order, whether granting or dismissing the application, a copy of the application notice and any evidence in support must, unless the court orders otherwise, be served with the order on any party or other person–
(a)　against whom the order was made; and
(b)　against whom the order was sought.

(3) The order must contain a statement of the right to make an application to set aside or vary the order under rule 23.10.

[31.13]

CPR 23.10 – APPLICATION TO SET ASIDE OR VARY ORDER MADE
WITHOUT NOTICE

(1) A person who was not served with a copy of the application notice before an order was made under rule 23.9, may apply to have the order set aside or varied.

(2) An application under this rule must be made within 7 days after the date on which the order was served on the person making the application.

[31.14] Sarayiah v Suren

[2004] EWHC 1981 (QB)

[2004] All ER (D) 62 (Sep)

The claimant failed to comply with CPR 23.9 by failing to inform the defendant of his right (under CPR 23.10) to apply to set aside an order made in a without notice application within seven days, and failing to provide copies of the application notice and evidence in support.

HELD: This was reason enough to allow the defendant to apply under CPR 23.10 outside the seven-day time limit, despite delay in bringing the application.

(D) FAILURE OF PARTY TO ATTEND APPLICATION

[31.15]

CPR 23.11 – POWER OF THE COURT TO PROCEED IN THE ABSENCE OF
A PARTY

(1) Where the applicant or any respondent fails to attend the hearing of an application, the court may proceed in his absence.

(2) Where–
  (a) the applicant or any respondent fails to attend the hearing of an application; and
  (b) the court makes an order at the hearing,
the court may, on application or of its own initiative, re-list the application.

[31.16] Riverpath Properties Ltd v Brammall

[2001] All ER (D) 281 (Mar), (2000) Times, 16 February

HELD: CPR 23.11(2) gave the court an unfettered discretion in relation to setting aside an order and ordering a re-hearing in respect of an order made in the absence of a party. However, the court would be unlikely to exercise this power where there was no real prospect of a different order being made than the order originally made. There might be circumstances in which it was more unjust to set aside the order than to refuse to do so, such as a situation in which the original order had been acted upon.

[31.17] **Fox v Graham Group Ltd**

(2001) Times, 3 August

A litigant in person did not attend his own application, at the last minute contacting the court and requesting an adjournment. The court was faced with a choice between causing unfairness to the respondent who had attended by adjourning, or causing unfairness to the applicant litigant in person by dismissing the application, even if it was considered that there was only a faint chance of success.

HELD: Where a litigant in person was requesting an adjournment for the first time, the court should be very careful before concluding that it would be appropriate to proceed without him or her – unless the court was satisfied that it ought to grant the applicant the relief sought on the basis of the papers before it, or that the application was bound to fail.

(E)   HEARINGS TO BE ON THE TELEPHONE
WHERE PRACTICABLE

[31.18]

Practice Direction – Pilot scheme for telephone hearings

This Practice Direction supplements Part 23

General
  1.1   This practice direction is made under rule 51.2. It provides for a pilot
        scheme ('the Telephone Hearings Pilot Scheme') to operate at the courts
        specified in the Appendix between the dates specified for each court in
        the Appendix. The purpose of the Telephone Hearings Pilot Scheme is to
        extend the scope of hearings which may be conducted by telephone.
  1.2   During the operation of the Telephone Hearings Pilot Scheme–
    (1)   paragraphs 6.1 to 6.3 of the practice direction supplementing Part 23
          do not apply to hearings conducted under the Telephone Hearings
          Pilot Scheme; but
    (2)   paragraphs 6.4 and 6.5 do apply where–
      (a)   the hearing is an allocation hearing, a listing hearing, a case
            management conference or a pre-trial review; or
      (b)   the court of its own initiative orders a telephone hearing,
            references in paragraph 6.5 to the applicant are to be read as
            references to the claimant or such other party as the court directs to
            arrange the telephone hearing; and
    (3)   paragraph 6.4 is modified so that it also applies to unrepresented
          parties.

Hearings to be conducted by telephone
  2.1   Subject to paragraph 2.2, the following hearings will be conducted by
        telephone unless the court otherwise orders–
    (1)   allocation hearings;
    (2)   listing hearings;
    (3)   interim applications, case management conferences or pre-trial
          reviews with a time estimate of no more than one hour; and
    (4)   any other application with the consent of the parties and the court's
          agreement.
  2.2   Paragraph 2.1 does not apply where–
    (1)   all the parties are unrepresented;

(2)   more than four parties may wish to make representations at the hearing (for this purpose where two or more parties are represented by the same person, they are to be treated as one party);

(3)   the hearing could result in the final determination of the whole or part of the proceedings.

2.3   An application for an order that a hearing under paragraph 2.1(1), (2) or (3) should not be conducted by telephone–

(1)   must be made at least 7 days before the hearing; and

(2)   may be made by letter,

and the court shall determine such application without requiring the attendance of the parties.

2.4   The claimant's legal representative (if any), or the legal representative of such other party as the court directs, shall be responsible for arranging the telephone hearing.

Documents

3.1   The legal representative responsible for arranging the telephone hearing must file and serve a case summary and draft order no later than 4 pm on the last working day before the hearing–

(1)   if the claim has been allocated to the multi-track; and

(2)   in any other case, if the court so directs.

3.2   Where a party seeks to rely on any other document at the hearing, he must file and serve the document no later than 4 pm on the last working day before the hearing.

Appendix

Newcastle Combined Court Centre	1 September 2003 – 1 October 2006
Bedford County Court	1 February 2004 – 1 October 2006
Luton County Court	1 February 2004 – 1 October 2006
Any county court specified on	1 April 2006 – 1 October 2006

Her Majesty's Court Service website at www.hmcourts-service.gov.uk as one in which telephone hearings are available

FROM HM COURTS SERVICES WEBSITE, AS AT 27 JUNE 2006

[31.19]

Telephone Hearings in County Courts

From 3 April 2006 a staged nation-wide rollout of the telephone-hearing scheme will commence. The pilot scheme has been running at Newcastle Combined Court Centre since September 2003 and at Luton and Bedford county courts since February 2004. The response from users of the pilot was very encouraging, and a subsequent consultation exercise of stakeholders met with overwhelmingly favourable responses to a proposal to extend the scheme nationally.

The nationwide rollout will be staged on a regional basis. This will enable telecommunications service providers to adapt their business to handle the increased demand for the service, whilst at the same time give individual courts time to prepare.

The timetable is as follows–

- North East Region: 3rd April 2006
- North West Region: 1st May 2006
- Wales and Chester Region: 1st June 2006
- South West Region: 3rd July 2006
- Midlands Region: 1st August 2006
- South East Region: 1st September 2006
- London Region: 2nd October 2006

There will also be a rolling programme with courts that cannot implement the scheme under the timetable, joining the scheme as they update their telecommunications infrastructure or when local conditions permit. A list of participating courts and Guidelines for Practitioners are available.

Once introduced in courts almost all allocation hearings, listing hearings, case management hearings and interim applications expected to last no more than one hour will be conducted by telephone conference. Any other application with the consent of all the parties and the agreement of the court will also be conducted by telephone.

VIDEO CONFERENCING

[31.20] **Pastouna v Black**

[2005] EWCA Civ 1389

[2005] All ER (D) 346 (Nov)

The claimant, who had the benefit of public funding in respect of her claim, together with her solicitor and counsel, attended the Court of Appeal in London from Liverpool.

Per Brooke LJ: [The appointment] could very easily have been conducted by video-conference between this court and Liverpool ... It is incumbent on those advising parties appearing before this, or any, court to take all the steps they can in accordance with CPR 1.1 and 1.3 to reduce the cost of the proceedings. This includes taking advantage of such costs-saving facilities as video-conferencing whenever they are available and it is appropriate to use them. In every case involving an application to the Court of Appeal which is likely to last half an hour or less, the court will expect the parties or their advisers to apply these criteria when they consider whether the use of VCF would be desirable.

(F)   EVIDENCE AT APPLICATIONS

[31.21]

CPR 32.6 – EVIDENCE IN PROCEEDINGS OTHER THAN AT TRIAL
(1)   Subject to paragraph (2), the general rule is that evidence at hearings other than the trial is to be by witness statement unless the court, a practice direction or any other enactment requires otherwise.
(2)   At hearings other than the trial, a party may, rely on the matters set out in–
    (a)   his statement of case; or
    (b)   his application notice, if the statement of case or application notice is verified by a statement of truth.

2.   REQUESTS FOR FURTHER INFORMATION

[31.22]

CPR 18.1 – Obtaining further information
  (1) The court may at any time order a party to–
    (a) clarify any matter which is in dispute in the proceedings; or
    (b) give additional information in relation to any such matter,
whether or not the matter is contained or referred to in a statement of case.
  (2) Paragraph (1) is subject to any rule of law to the contrary.
  (3) Where the court makes an order under paragraph (1), the party against whom it is made must–
    (a) file his response; and
    (b) serve it on the other parties,
within the time specified by the court.

[31.23]

CPR 18.2 – Restriction on the use of further information

The court may direct that information provided by a party to another party (whether given voluntarily or following an order made under rule 18.1) must not be used for any purpose except for that of the proceedings in which it is given.

3.   UNLESS ORDERS

[31.24]   Where a party has failed to comply with a rule, practice direction or court order, any sanction has immediate effect.
  Accordingly, a party has a choice as to how to deal with a sanction.
  The party can apply to the court within the time limit imposed by the rule, practice direction or order, for an extension of time to comply. The parties cannot simply agree an extension – an application to the court is required. The court must consider such an application in accordance with the overriding objective.
  Alternatively, the party can apply to the court for relief from the sanction following expiry of the time period. When asked to consider relief, the court is required to exercise discretion in accordance with the checklist set out in CPR 3.9.
  Unless orders should be taken seriously. In *RC Residuals Ltd v Linton Fuel Oils Ltd* (at para [19.61]), the claimant failed by a matter of minutes to serve evidence in accordance with an unless order. The judge debarred the claimant from relying upon the evidence. Whilst the order was overturned, it required a trip to the Court of Appeal.
  Reference should be made to Chapter 19, paras [19.54] and [19.62].

[31.25]   **Becker v Baileys Shaw and Gillet**
(4 November 1999, unreported), CA

An unless order was made requiring the claimant to provide full particulars of the loss which he claimed to have suffered as a result of the defendant's negligence. The claimant failed to comply. The judge held that the claimant was in deliberate breach of the unless order and had consistently failed to provide evidence.

HELD, ON APPEAL: The refusal of an extension of time for compliance with the unless order was, on the facts, plainly wrong. The Court of Appeal held that the judge was wrong in the decision he came to and had failed to have proper regard to the complexity of the task.

[31.26] **Britannia Zinc Ltd v Connect South West Ltd**
(27 March 2002, unreported)

Where a party has failed to comply with an unless order and seeks relief from sanctions on the basis that there has been substantial compliance with the order albeit late, the court should consider not only whether the order has been substantially complied with but whether previous orders have been substantially complied with. Substantial compliance was of particular importance in this case as there had not been substantial compliance in the past. The trial date was imminent, and the court had with some reluctance given the claimant a final opportunity to provide the defendant with documentation in support of a substantial claim for business interruption.

HELD: The information provided by the claimant out of time did not substantially comply with the order and the claim should not be reinstated.

4.   INTERIM REMEDIES

(A)   THE INTERIM REMEDIES RELEVANT TO MOTOR CLAIMS

[31.27]

CPR 25.1 – ORDERS FOR INTERIM REMEDIES
  (1)   The court may grant the following interim remedies–
     ...
    (c)   an order–
- for the detention, custody or preservation of relevant property;
- for the inspection of relevant property;
- for the taking of a sample of relevant property;
- for the carrying out of an experiment on or with relevant property;

     ...
    (k)   an order (referred to as an order for interim payment) under rule 25.6 for payment by a defendant on account of any damages, debt or other sum (except costs) which the court may hold the defendant liable to pay;

(B)   APPLYING FOR AN INTERIM REMEDY

[31.28]

CPR 25.2 – TIME WHEN AN ORDER FOR AN INTERIM REMEDY MAY
BE MADE
  (1)   An order for an interim remedy may be made at any time, including–

    (a)   before proceedings are started; and

    (b)   after judgment has been given.

(2)   However–

    (a)   paragraph (1) is subject to any rule, practice direction or other enactment which provides otherwise;

    (b)   the court may grant an interim remedy before a claim has been made only if–

        (i)   the matter is urgent; or

        (ii) it is otherwise desirable to do so in the interests of justice; and

    (c)   unless the court otherwise orders, a defendant may not apply for any of the orders listed in rule 25.1(1) before he has filed either an acknowledgment of service or a defence.

(3)   Where it grants an interim remedy before a claim has been commenced, the court should give directions requiring a claim to be commenced.

(4)   In particular, the court need not direct that a claim be commenced where the application is made under section 33 of the Supreme Court Act 1981 or section 52 of the County Courts Act 1984 (order for disclosure, inspection etc. before commencement of a claim).

[31.29]

CPR 25.3 – How to apply for an interim remedy

(1)   The court may grant an interim remedy on an application made without notice if it appears to the court that there are good reasons for not giving notice.

(2)   An application for an interim remedy must be supported by evidence, unless the court orders otherwise.

(3)   If the applicant makes an application without giving notice, the evidence in support of the application must state the reasons why notice has not been given.

(C)   INTERIM PAYMENTS

[31.30]

CPR 25.6 – Interim payments – General procedure

(1)   The claimant may not apply for an order for an interim payment before the end of the period for filing an acknowledgment of service applicable to the defendant against whom the application is made.

(2)   The claimant may make more than one application for an order for an interim payment.

(3)   A copy of an application notice for an order for an interim payment must–

    (a)   be served at least 14 days before the hearing of the application; and

    (b)   be supported by evidence.

(4)   If the respondent to an application for an order for an interim payment wishes to rely on written evidence at the hearing, he must–

    (a)   file the written evidence; and

    (b)   serve copies on every other party to the application,

at least 7 days before the hearing of the application.

(5)   If the applicant wishes to rely on written evidence in reply, he must–
  (a)   file the written evidence; and
  (b)   serve a copy on the respondent,
at least 3 days before the hearing of the application.
(6)   This rule does not require written evidence–
  (a)   to be filed if it has already been filed; or
  (b)   to be served on a party on whom it has already been served.
(7)   The court may order an interim payment in one sum or in instalments.

[31.31]

CPR 25.7 – INTERIM PAYMENTS – CONDITIONS TO BE SATISFIED AND
MATTERS TO BE TAKEN INTO ACCOUNT
(1)   The court may only make an order for an interim payment where any
of the following conditions are satisfied –
  (a)   the defendant against whom the order is sought has admitted
    liability to pay damages or some other sum of money to the
    claimant;
  (b)   the claimant has obtained judgment against that defendant for
    damages to be assessed or for a sum of money (other than costs) to
    be assessed;
  (c)   it is satisfied that, if the claim went to trial, the claimant would
    obtain judgment for a substantial amount of money (other than
    costs) against the defendant from whom he is seeking an order for
    an interim payment whether or not that defendant is the only
    defendant or one of a number of defendants to the claim;
  (d)   …
  (e)   in a claim in which there are two or more defendants and the order
    is sought against any one or more of those defendants, the
    following conditions are satisfied–
    (i)   the court is satisfied that, if the claim went to trial, the
      claimant would obtain judgment for a substantial amount of
      money (other than costs) against at least one of the defend-
      ants (but the court cannot determine which); and
    (ii)   all the defendants are either–
      (a)   a defendant that is insured in respect of the claim;
      (b)   a defendant whose liability will be met by an insurer
        under section 151 of the Road Traffic Act 1988 or an
        insurer acting under the Motor Insurers Bureau Agree-
        ment, or the Motor Insurers Bureau where it is acting
        itself; or
      (c)   a defendant that is a public body.
(4)   The court must not order an interim payment of more than a
reasonable proportion of the likely amount of the final judgment.
(5)   The court must take into account–
  (a)   contributory negligence; and
  (b)   any relevant set off or counterclaim.

[31.32]

CPR 25.8 – POWERS OF COURT WHERE IT HAS MADE AN ORDER FOR INTERIM PAYMENT

(1)   Where a defendant has been ordered to make an interim payment, or has in fact made an interim payment (whether voluntarily or under an order), the court may make an order to adjust the interim payment.

(2)   The court may in particular–

(a)   order all or part of the interim payment to be repaid;

(b)   vary or discharge the order for the interim payment;

(c)   order a defendant to reimburse, either wholly or partly, another defendant who has made an interim payment.

(3)   The court may make an order under paragraph (2)(c) only if–

(a)   the defendant to be reimbursed made the interim payment in relation to a claim in respect of which he has made a claim against the other defendant for a contribution, indemnity or other remedy; and

(b)   where the claim or part to which the interim payment relates has not been discontinued or disposed of, the circumstances are such that the court could make an order for interim payment under rule 25.7.

(4)   The court may make an order under this rule without an application by any party if it makes the order when it disposes of the claim or any part of it.

(5)   Where–

(a)   the defendant has made an interim payment; and

(b)   the amount of the interim payment is more than his total liability under the final judgment or order,

the court may award him interest on the overpaid amount from the date when he made the interim payment.

[31.33]   Turnbull v North Durham Community NHS Trust

[2006] 3 CL 44

The claimant sustained personal injuries in the course of his employment with the defendant as an ambulance driver. The defendant made an admission of liability and made a voluntary interim payment. The claimant issued proceedings just before the expiry of the primary limitation period. The proceedings were struck out on a procedural basis, and the defendant sought repayment of the interim payment. The district judge refused to exercise discretion under CPR 25.8(2)(a), and the defendant appealed.

HELD, ON APPEAL: The claimant's claim had been a valid claim, there had been an admission of liability, and the defendant had the benefit of the fact that the claimant's claim had been struck out. There was no automatic entitlement to repayment of the interim payment because there had been no final judgment. The court refused to overturn the district judge's exercise of discretion.

[31.34]

CPR 25.9 – RESTRICTION ON DISCLOSURE OF AN INTERIM PAYMENT

The fact that a defendant has made an interim payment, whether voluntarily or by court order, shall not be disclosed to the trial judge until all questions of liability and the amount of money to be awarded have been decided unless the defendant agrees.

[31.35]

Practice Direction to CPR 25 – Interim payments

This Practice Direction supplements CPR 25

General
  1.1   Rule 25.7 sets out the conditions to be satisfied and matters to be taken into account before the court will make an order for an interim payment.
  1.2   The permission of the court must be obtained before making a voluntary interim payment in respect of a claim by a child or patient.

Evidence
  2.1   An application for an interim payment of damages must be supported by evidence dealing with the following:
    (1)   the sum of money sought by way of interim payment,
    (2)   the items or matters in respect of which the interim payment is sought,
    (3)   the sum of money for which final judgment is likely to be given,
    (4)   the reasons for believing that the conditions set out in rule 25.7 are satisfied,
    (5)   any other relevant matters,
    (6)   in claims for personal injuries, details of special damages and past and future loss, and
    (7)   in a claim under the Fatal Accidents Act 1976, details of the person(s) on whose behalf the claim is made and the nature of the claim.
  2.2   Any documents in support of the application should be exhibited, including, in personal injuries claims, the medical report(s).
  2.3   If a respondent to an application for an interim payment wishes to rely on written evidence at the hearing he must comply with the provisions of rule 25.6(4).
  2.4   If the applicant wishes to rely on written evidence in reply he must comply with the provisions of rule 25.6(5).

Instalments
  3   Where an interim payment is to be paid in instalments the order should set out:
    (1)   the total amount of the payment,
    (2)   the amount of each instalment,
    (3)   the number of instalments and the date on which each is to be paid, and
    (4)   to whom the payment should be made.

Compensation recovery payments

4.1   Where in a claim for personal injuries there is an application for an interim payment of damages:

(1)   which is other than by consent,

(2)   which falls under the heads of damage set out in column 1 of Schedule 2 of the Social Security (Recovery of Benefits) Act 1997 in respect of recoverable benefits received by the claimant set out in column 2 of that Schedule, and

(3)   where the defendant is liable to pay recoverable benefits to the Secretary of State,

the defendant should obtain from the Secretary of State a certificate of recoverable benefits.

4.2   A copy of the certificate should be filed at the hearing of the application for an interim payment.

4.3   The order will set out the amount by which the payment to be made to the claimant has been reduced according to the Act and the Social Security (Recovery of Benefits) Regulations 1997.

4.4   The payment made to the claimant will be the net amount but the interim payment for the purposes of paragraph 5 below will be the gross amount.

Adjustment of final judgment figure

5.1   In this paragraph 'judgment' means:

(1)   any order to pay a sum of money,

(2)   a final award of damages,

(3)   an assessment of damages.

5.2   In a final judgment where an interim payment has previously been made which is less than the total amount awarded by the judge, the order should set out in a preamble:

(1)   the total amount awarded by the judge, and

(2)   the amounts and dates of the interim payment(s).

5.3   The total amount awarded by the judge should then be reduced by the total amount of any interim payments, and an order made for entry of judgment and payment of the balance.

5.4   In a final judgment where an interim payment has previously been made which is more than the total amount awarded by the judge, the order should set out in a preamble:

(1)   the total amount awarded by the judge, and

(2)   the amounts and dates of the interim payment(s).

5.5   An order should then be made for repayment, reimbursement, variation or discharge under rule 25.8(2) and for interest on an overpayment under rule 25.8(5).

OFFER AND ACCEPTANCE

[31.36]   Betts v Golden

(7 January 1999, unreported)

An interim payment was sent to the claimant for damage done to his vehicle by the defendant. The defendant's insurer failed to dispute or take issue with the terms on which the interim payment was accepted and therefore was deemed to have accepted them.

See also Current Law Monthly (April 1999).

MOTOR INSURERS' BUREAU

[31.37]   Sharp v Pereria
[1998] 4 All ER 145, [1999] 1 WLR 195, [1999] RTR 125, CA

The Motor Insurers' Bureau can be the subject of an order for an interim payment.

INTERIM PAYMENTS NOT SUITABLE WHERE FACTUAL ISSUES
ARE COMPLICATED

[31.38]   Ultraframe (UK) Ltd v Eurocell Building Plastics Ltd
[2005] EWHC 2111 (Ch)
[2006] All ER (D) 155 (Jan)

The claimant issued proceedings in respect of the infringement of certain patents by the defendant. There was a significant dispute between the parties as to the value of the claim. The claimant applied to the court for an interim payment.

HELD: Any interim payment should not exceed a reasonable proportion of the likely award. Where there was significant dispute between the parties, it was not appropriate for the court on an interim payment application to consider the dispute in detail. Instead, the court should determine what was the irreducible minimum value of the claim, and calculate the value of an appropriate interim payment in that context.

5.   SECURITY FOR COSTS

[31.39]

CPR 25.12 – SECURITY FOR COSTS
    (1)   A defendant to any claim may apply under this Section of this Part for security for his costs of the proceedings.
    (2)   An application for security for costs must be supported by written evidence.
    (3)   Where the court makes an order for security for costs, it will–
      (a)   determine the amount of security; and
      (b)   direct–
        (i)   the manner in which; and
        (ii)   the time within which
the security must be given.

[31.40]

CPR 25.13 – CONDITIONS TO BE SATISFIED
    (1)   The court may make an order for security for costs under rule 25.12 if–
      (a)   it is satisfied, having regard to the circumstances of the case, that it is just to make such an order; and
      (b)   (i)   one or more of the conditions in paragraph (2) applies; or
        (ii)   an enactment permits the court to require security for costs.

(2)   The conditions are–
   (a)   the claimant is–
      (i)   resident out of the jurisdiction; but
      (ii)   not resident in a Brussels Contracting State, a Lugano Contracting State or a Regulation State, as defined by section 1(3) of the Civil Jurisdiction and Judgments Act 1982
   (b)   the claimant is a company or other body (whether incorporated inside or outside Great Britain) and there is reason to believe that it will be unable to pay the defendant's costs if ordered to do so;
   (c)   the claimant has changed his address since the claim was commenced with a view to evading the consequences of the litigation;
   (d)   the claimant failed to give his address in the claim form, or gave an incorrect address in that form;
   (e)   the claimant is acting as a nominal claimant, other than as a representative claimant under Part 19, and there is reason to believe that he will be unable to pay the defendant's costs if ordered to do so;
   (f)   the claimant has taken steps in relation to his assets that would make it difficult to enforce an order for costs against him.

6.   AMENDING STATEMENTS OF CASE

(A)   WHEN PERMISSION FOR AN AMENDMENT IS REQUIRED

[31.41]

CPR 17.1 – AMENDMENTS TO STATEMENT OF CASE
(1)   A party may amend his statement of case at any time before it has been served on any other party.
(2)   If his statement of case has been served, a party may amend it only–
   (a)   with the written consent of all the other parties; or
   (b)   with the permission of the court.
(3)   If a statement of case has been served, an application to amend it by removing, adding or substituting a party must be made in accordance with rule 19.4.

[31.42]

CPR 17.2 – POWER OF COURT TO DISALLOW AMENDMENTS MADE WITHOUT PERMISSION
(1)   If a party has amended his statement of case where permission of the court was not required, the court may disallow the amendment.
(2)   A party may apply to the court for an order under paragraph (1) within 14 days of service of a copy of the amended statement of case on him.

[31.43]

CPR 17.3 – AMENDMENTS TO STATEMENTS OF CASE WITH THE PERMISSION OF THE COURT

(1) Where the court gives permission for a party to amend his statement of case, it may give directions as to–

    (a) amendments to be made to any other statement of case; and

    (b) service of any amended statement of case.

(2) The power of the court to give permission under this rule is subject to–

    (a) rule 19.1 (change of parties – general);

    (b) rule 19.4 (special provisions about adding or substituting parties after the end of a relevant limitation period); and

    (c) rule 17.4 (amendments of statement of case after the end of a relevant limitation period).

PRESUMPTION IN FAVOUR OF AMENDMENTS, SUBJECT TO THE OVERRIDING OBJECTIVE

[31.44] **Cobbold v Greenwich London Borough Council**

(9 August 1999, unreported), CA

HELD, ON APPEAL: 'Amendments in general ought to be allowed so that the real dispute between the parties can be adjudicated upon, provided that any prejudice to the other party or parties caused by the amendment can be compensated for in costs and the public interest in the administration of justice is not significantly harmed'.

[31.45] **Kuwait Airways Corpn v Iraqi Airways Corpn**

[2002] EWCA Civ 515

[2002] All ER (D) 444 (Mar)

The claimant applied to amend his particulars of claim to include claims which had been originally pursued but were later abandoned. At first instance the amendments were allowed. The defendant appealed on the basis the judge had no discretion to permit the amendments.

HELD: 'There is no rule of law that permission cannot be given to amend to include a claim for scheduled items which had earlier been abandoned'. The judge at first instance was not precluded from exercising his discretion to permit an amendment to put the unmentioned claims back into the proceedings.

    Appeal dismissed.

LIKELIHOOD OF AMENDMENTS BEING PERMITTED DEPENDENT UPON THE
STAGE AT WHICH PERMISSION IS SOUGHT

[31.46]   **Loutchansky v Times Newspaper Ltd**

[2002] EWHC 2726 (QB)

[2002] All ER (D) 159 (Dec)

The defendant sought permission to amend a defence in a libel action to add a plea
of justification after judgment had been given, but before the judgment had been
effected.

HELD: The court applied the principles laid down in *Ladd v Marshall* [1954] 3 All ER
745, [1954] 1 WLR 1489. 'A strong case was required before an application for
permission to amend at so late a stage would be allowed'. 'The object of the courts is
to decide the matters in controversy between the parties, so far as that can be done
without injustice to the other party. Amendment is not to be regarded as a matter of
grace or favour'. The court considered the question of lateness and whether the
evidence had a real prospect, as opposed to a fanciful prospect, of success and
whether admissible evidence would be adduced to prove the case. Permission to
allow the amendments was refused on the basis that the case did not have a real
prospect of success and there was insufficient admissible and apparently credible
evidence.

[31.47]   **Cook v News Group Newspapers Ltd**

[2002] EWHC 1070 (QB), QB

The defendant applied to make substantial re-re-amendments to the defence five
months before trial.

HELD: It was necessary to have regard to the overriding objective, the timeous
nature of the application, and to the consequences of late amendment in terms of
delay, cost and stress. 'Issues will not necessarily be permitted to be canvassed, in
particular if they are raised late in the day, merely because they are ... relevant'.

[31.48]   **Savings & Investment Bank Ltd (in liquidation) v Fincken**

[2003] EWCA Civ 1630

[2004] 1 All ER 1125, [2004] 1 WLR 667

The claimant applied to amend the particulars of claim shortly before trial to
include an admission said to have been made by the defendant at a without
prejudice meeting.

HELD, ON APPEAL: Whether an amendment has some prospect of success may be a
suitable test where the amendment was made early on in proceedings. However,
'the proper rule or guideline calls for a sliding scale: the later the amendment the
more it may require to commend it'. The amendments were refused.

[31.49]   **Kelly v Chief Constable of South Yorkshire Police**

[2001] EWCA Civ 1632

[2001] All ER (D) 377 (Oct)

The claimant alleged that, following her arrest, she sustained an injury to her knee
when she was travelling in the police car to the police station. At trial the claimant's

barrister attempted to advance an alternative case based on the defendant's evidence. An application made by the claimant to amend her case to plead in the alternative was dismissed.

HELD, ON APPEAL: The grounds for refusing permission to amend were insufficient to outweigh the justice of permitting the claimant to advance an alternative case based upon the defendant's evidence.

[31.50]   EDO MBM Technology Ltd v Campaign to Smash EDO

[2006] EWHC 598 (QB)

[2006] All ER (D) 338 (Mar)

The claimant brought proceedings against a number of defendants under the Protection from Harassment Act 1997. After issuing proceedings the claimant was granted an interim injunction on the basis the matter was progressed to trial quickly. The claimant then sought to amend his particulars of claim to include additional causes of action. The defendants' cross applied for an order that:
(1)   the claim be struck out for procedural failings; or
(2)   the claimant should lose the benefit of the interim injunction.

HELD: The mere fact that an issue could be said to arise from witness statements or documents does not lead to a general presumption in favour of granting permission to amend. If the proposed amendments would delay the trial then they needed to be carefully scrutinised to ascertain whether the point raised was important enough to warrant the trial being adjourned.

The court held there had been woeful neglect on the part of the claimant to focus on the need to prepare for a speedy trial. The claimant was deprived of the benefit of the interim injunction and ordered to pay the costs of the application to amend, although the amendments sought were permitted.

(B)   AMENDMENTS AND LIMITATION

[31.51]

CPR 17.4 – AMENDMENTS TO STATEMENTS OF CASE AFTER THE END OF A RELEVANT LIMITATION PERIOD
(1)   This rule applies where–
  (a)   a party applies to amend his statement of case in one of the ways mentioned in this rule; and
  (b)   a period of limitation has expired under–
    (i)   the Limitation Act 1980;
    (ii)   the Foreign Limitation Periods Act 1984; or
    (iii)   any other enactment which allows such an amendment, or under which such an amendment is allowed.
(2)   The court may allow an amendment whose effect will be to add or substitute a new claim, but only if the new claim arises out of the same facts or substantially the same facts as a claim in respect of which the party applying for permission has already claimed a remedy in the proceedings.
(3)   The court may allow an amendment to correct a mistake as to the name of a party, but only where the mistake was genuine and not one which would cause reasonable doubt as to the identity of the party in question.

(4)   The court may allow an amendment to alter the capacity in which a party claims if the new capacity is one which that party had when the proceedings started or has since acquired.

TEST TO BE APPLIED: AMENDMENTS MUST ARISE 'OUT OF THE SAME OR SUBSTANTIALLY THE SAME FACTS'

[31.52]   Royal Brompton Hospital NHS Trust v Hammond (No 2)
(1999) 69 Con LR 132

The ninth defendant applied for permission to amend the defence and counter-claim to allege acts or omissions by the thirteenth defendant (PMI). In response the claimant sought permission to re-amend the particulars of claim to raise corresponding allegations against PMI. PMI opposed the claimant's application on the grounds it would deprive it of a limitation defence.

HELD: The ninth defendant would be permitted to amend the defence and counterclaim and the claimant would be permitted to re-amend the particulars of claim. The amendments arose out of the same facts or substantially the same facts as the existing claims. The question as to whether a new claim arose out of substantially the same facts as an existing claim was a matter of impression.

[31.53]   Goode v Martin
[2001] EWCA Civ 1899
[2002] 1 All ER 620, [2002] 1 WLR 1828

Following service of an amended defence the claimant applied to serve an amended particulars of claim in response, based on the facts contained in the amended defence.
   The defendant objected on the basis the amended particulars of claim did not comply with CPR 17.4(2) as the amendments did not arise out of the same facts already claimed by the claimant but facts that had been put in issue by the defendant.

HELD: The amendment was permitted as there was no policy reason why the proposed amendment could not be added to the claim as no new facts were being introduced. A wide interpretation of CPR 17.4(2) was adopted to include the words in italics 'if the new claim arises out of the same facts or substantially the same facts as *are already in issue in* a claim …'.

[31.54]   Hemmingway v Smith Roddam (a firm)
[2003] EWCA Civ 1342
[2003] All ER (D) 123 (Sep)

The claimant applied to amend the particulars of claim. At first instance amendments relating substantially to the facts pleaded in the original particulars of claim were allowed. However, in respect of other amendments the judge held he had no jurisdiction under CPR 17.4 and, in any event, would not have exercised his discretion to allow them.

HELD, ON APPEAL: The test should be to look at the old pleadings to see what facts would have been in issue and litigated at trial if those pleadings had remained in their old form. In this case all of the new allegations arose out of substantially the same facts as those already in issue, as long as proper regard was had to facts pleaded in the defence. The amendments were allowed.

[31.55] Aldi Stores Ltd v Holmes Buildings plc
[2003] EWCA Civ 1882
[2003] All ER (D) 19 (Dec)

HELD, ON APPEAL: A claim for damages will be a new claim if the claimant seeks to justify it on a different factual basis from that originally pleaded, but it will not be a new claim if it does not involve the addition or substitution of an allegation of new facts constituting such a new cause of action. In this case, the amendment only added new heads of loss and not a new cause of action as there was no new duty or breach of duty alleged by the proposed amendments. The amendments were permitted.

[31.56] Hoechst UK Ltd v Inland Revenue Commissioners
[2004] EWHC 1002 (Ch)
[2004] STC 1486, [2003] All ER (D) 198 (Apr)

The claimant sought to amend its claim to include a claim for compensation for a timing disadvantage arising from the payment of advanced corporation tax following a dividend paid to it as an English subsidiary company by its German parent company. The application for relief was brought after expiry of the limitation period.

HELD: The claimant could only succeed if the amendment was one involving a new cause of action which arose out of substantially the same facts as the cause or causes of action already pleaded. Although the background to the cause of action was the same, it was not accepted that it arose out of the same facts as the cause of action pleaded and the court had no discretion to permit the amendment.

[31.57] Mersey Docks Property Holdings Ltd v Birse Construction Ltd and Others
[2004] EWHC 3264 (TCC)
[2004] All ER (D) 284 (Oct), 99 Con LR 122

The claimant applied for permission to amend the particulars of claim. The defendants objected on the basis the allegations amounted to new causes of action which were time barred. The defendants contended that CPR 17.4 must be construed according to its precise wording, ie that the amendments should only be permitted if the new claim arose out of the same facts as the claim in respect of which the party applying for permission had already claimed a remedy in the proceedings.

HELD: The court applied a wider construction of CPR 17.4, on the basis there were no policy considerations to prevent the claimant from relying on the facts in issue against the other defendants, as opposed to the narrower construction contended for by the defendants. 'The issue of discretion is of greatest importance particularly in relation to allowing draft amendments made on the basis that they arise out of claims made against other parties to the proceedings.'

[31.58]   **Carman v Cronos Group SA**

[2005] EWHC 2403 (Ch)

[2005] All ER (D) 90 (Nov)

The claimant's liquidator brought claims set out in a new particulars of claim. The court had to look at whether these new claims constituted a new cause of action for which the liquidator needed permission to amend to include them in the present proceedings.

HELD: Although the proposed re-amendments alleged facts which were not already pleaded it did not follow the new claim did not arise out of substantially the same facts as the claim already pleaded. The court was required to 'stand back from the mass of factual detail which was pleaded to view the new claim in that general context'.

> 'Although the proposed re-amendments inevitably allege facts not already pleaded nevertheless the allegations arise out of substantially the same facts as the existing claim … The fact that the new cause of action may give rise to relief in a different form than that sought by the claim as it stands does not mean that CPR 17.4(2) cannot be complied with'.

The amendment was permitted.

[31.59]   **Wood v Chief Constable of the West Midlands**

[2004] EWCA Civ 1638

[2004] All ER (D) 107 (Dec), [2005] EMLR 20

The claimant brought an action for libel against the defendant. The claimant was granted summary judgment on the defendant's plea of qualified privilege. At the trial, after the defendant had closed his case, the claimant applied for permission to re-amend his statement of case to add a claim for slander. The amendment was allowed. The defendant was given permission to appeal in respect of his plea of qualified privilege and the late amendment.

HELD: The basis for the claim for slander was a telephone conversation, the fact and content of which had been contained in a letter upon which the original claim for libel had been based. The evidence relating to the telephone conversation was dealt with at trial, through the oral evidence of one of the claimant's witnesses.

The criteria set out in CPR 17.4(2) had been met so the judge had a discretion to permit the amendment. The judge decided it was equitable to permit the late amendment and on appeal it was held that he had addressed all the relevant circumstances.

[31.60]   **Convergence Group plc v Chantrey Vellacott**

[2005] EWCA Civ 290

[2005] All ER (D) 271 (Mar)

The defendant applied to re-amend the defence and counterclaim to add further allegations of negligence. Some of the amendments were not permitted at first instance.

HELD, ON APPEAL: The amendments amounted to a new claim to which CPR 17.4(2) applied. In order to decide whether the new claim arose out of substantially the same facts as the claim already pleaded the court had to make a qualitative judgment. It did not follow that the new claim did not arise out of substantially the same facts as the claim already pleaded, simply because the proposed amendments made allegations of facts which were not pleaded.

'… whether the new facts arise out of substantially the same facts as that already pleaded is substantially a matter of impression, [but] the impression must nevertheless be derived from a reasoned assessment of the relevant factors; not least because, absent a reasoned assessment, it is not possible to know whether the judge took all relevant factors into account'.

The court concluded the new claim arose out substantially the same facts as the old claim and new amendments were permitted.

[31.61]   P&O Nedloyd BV v Arab Metals Co and Others

[2005] EWHC 1276 (Comm)

[2005] All ER (D) 237 (Jun), [2005] 1 WLR 3733, [2006] 1 Lloyd's Rep 111

A claimant applied to amend a claim form.

HELD: The new claims were time barred. In holding whether the new claims arose out of the same or substantially the same facts as the original claims the court held that application of CPR 17.4 must 'involve something going no further than minor differences likely to be the subject of inquiry, but not involving any major investigation and/or differences merely collateral to the main substance of the new claim'. In this case the facts underlying the new claims fell well outside the concept of 'substantially the same facts' and the court had no jurisdiction to permit the amendment.

PARTY MISNAMED OR SUBSTITUTION OF A NEW PARTY?

[31.62]   Gregson v Channel Four Television Corpn

[2000] All ER (D) 956, [2000] CP Rep 60

Shortly before the expiry of the limitation period the claimant commenced proceedings against Channel 4 Television Company Limited instead of Channel 4 Television Corporation. Service had been properly effected on the Corporation. The issue was whether this was a mistake to which CPR 17.4(3) applied, where the correct defendant had been misnamed, or whether CPR 19.5 applied, where the claimant had named the wrong party as the defendant, which could only be cured by the substitution of a new party.

HELD: The mistake was one to which CPR 17.4(3) applied. The correct and intended party was named in the claim form but there was a mistake as to the name. There was no requirement to substitute a new party. CPR 17.4(3) was not to be interpreted in so rigid a way that it would produce a result that was neither sensible or just.

ALTERING THE CAPACITY IN WHICH A PARTY CLAIMS

[31.63]   Haq v Singh and Another

[2001] EWCA Civ 957

[2001] All ER (D) 394 (May), [2001] I WLR 1594

The claimant was a discharged bankrupt and brought proceedings against the defendant as an individual. The defendant disputed the claim on the basis that the claimant's action vested in her trustee in bankruptcy. The trustee in bankruptcy subsequently assigned the cause of action to the claimant and she applied to amend her claim. In the first instance her application succeeded.

HELD, ON APPEAL: The meaning of capacity in CPR 17.4(4) was the legal competence or status to bring or defend a claim. An alteration in capacity was the alteration from a representative to a personal capacity or from a personal to a representative capacity. The assignment did not give rise to a change in the claimant's capacity so the order must be set aside.

7.   ADDITION AND SUBSTITUTION OF PARTIES

(A)   GENERALLY

[31.64]

CPR 19.1 – PARTIES – GENERAL

Any number of claimants or defendants may be joined as parties to a claim.

[31.65]

CPR 19.2 –CHANGE OF PARTIES – GENERAL
    (1)   This rule applies where a party is to be added or substituted except where the case falls within rule 19.5 (special provisions about changing parties after the end of a relevant limitation period.
    (2)   The court may order a person to be added as a new party if–
      (a)   it is desirable to add the new party so that the court can resolve all the matters in dispute in the proceedings; or
      (b)   there is an issue involving the new party and an existing party which is connected to the matters in dispute in the proceedings, and it is desirable to add the new party so that the court can resolve that issue.
    (3)   The court may order any person to cease to be a party if it is not desirable for that person to be a party to the proceedings.
    (4)   The court may order a new party to be substituted for an existing one if–
      (a)   the existing party's interest or liability has passed to the new party; and
      (b)   it is desirable to substitute the new party so that the court can resolve the matters in dispute in the proceedings.

(B) PROCEDURE

[31.66]

CPR 19.4 – PROCEDURE FOR ADDING AND SUBSTITUTING PARTIES
(1) The court's permission is required to remove, add or substitute a party, unless the claim form has not been served.
(2) An application for permission under paragraph (1) may be made by–
  (a) an existing party; or
  (b) a person who wishes to become a party.
(3) An application for an order under rule 19.2(4) (substitution of a new party where existing party's interest or liability has passed)–
  (a) may be made without notice; and
  (b) must be supported by evidence.
(4) Nobody may be added or substituted as a claimant unless–
  (a) he has given his consent in writing; and
  (b) that consent has been filed with the court.
(4A) The Commissioners for HM Revenue and Customs may be added as a party to proceedings only if they consent in writing.
(5) An order for the removal, addition or substitution of a party must be served on–
  (a) all parties to the proceedings; and
  (b) any other person affected by the order.
(6) When the court makes an order for the removal, addition or substitution of a party, it may give consequential directions about–
  (a) filing and serving the claim form on any new defendant;
  (b) serving relevant documents on the new party; and
  (c) the management of the proceedings.

[31.67]

CPR 19.5 – SPECIAL PROVISIONS ABOUT ADDING OR SUBSTITUTING PARTIES
AFTER THE END OF A RELEVANT LIMITATION PERIOD
(1) This rule applies to a change of parties after the end of a period of limitation under–
  (a) the Limitation Act 1980;
  (b) the Foreign Limitation Periods Act 1984; or
  (c) any other enactment which allows such a change, or under which such a change is allowed.
(2) The court may add or substitute a party only if–
  (a) the relevant limitation period was current when the proceedings were started; and
  (b) the addition or substitution is necessary.
(3) The addition or substitution of a party is necessary only if the court is satisfied that–
  (a) the new party is to be substituted for a party who was named in the claim form in mistake for the new party;
  (b) the claim cannot properly be carried on by or against the original party unless the new party is added or substituted as claimant or defendant; or
  (c) the original party has died or had a bankruptcy order made against him and his interest or liability has passed to the new party.

(4)   In addition, in a claim for personal injuries the court may add or substitute a party where it directs that–
  (a)   (i) section 11 (special time limit for claims for personal injuries); or
       (ii)   section 12 (special time limit for claims under fatal accidents legislation), of the Limitation Act 1980,
       shall not apply to the claim by or against the new party; or
  (b)   the issue of whether those sections apply shall be determined at trial.

[31.68]   Horne-Roberts v SmithKline Beecham plc

[2001] EWCA Civ 2006

[2001] All ER (D) 269 (Dec), [2002] 1 WLR 1662

The claimant issued proceedings under the Consumer Protection Act 1987 in respect of a vaccine administered to him, but brought proceedings against the wrong manufacturer. The identity of the correct manufacturer only became apparent after the 10-year limitation in respect of products claims had expired. The claimant applied to substitute the correct manufacturer as defendant. Section 35(3) of the Limitation Act 1980 requires that the court shall not allow any new claim by substituting a new party if that new claim is made after the expiry of the limitation period, unless s 33 of the 1980 Act applies, or the CPR permits.

HELD: CPR 19.5(3)(a) permits the substitution of a new party if the party named in the claim form was named 'in mistake'. The claimant had always intended to issue proceedings against the manufacturer of the vaccine. Accordingly, the substitution would be permitted.

CHAPTER 32

Offers and Payments into Court

1. GENERALLY

(A) INTRODUCTION

[32.1] The Civil Procedure Rules (CPR) introduced the concepts of the Part 36 offer and the Part 36 payment. These concepts were specifically designed to encourage parties to litigation to reach settlement without trial, and thereby reduce costs and court expenditure.

The encouragement to settle derives from the fact that, if offers are not accepted and then the offering party improves on the offer at trial, then the party making the offer may be entitled to awards of costs, penalty costs, and penalty interest on damages and/or costs.

In recent years, the courts have looked upon CPR Pt 36 as a useful tool for resolving cases more quickly, and a significant and important body of case law has built up.

(B) CPR 36.2 – PART 36 OFFERS AND PART 36 PAYMENTS – GENERAL PROVISIONS

[32.2]
(1) An offer made in accordance with the requirements of this Part is called–
    (a) if made by way of a payment into court, 'a Part 36 payment';
    (b) otherwise 'a Part 36 offer'.
(2) The party who makes an offer is the 'offeror'.
(3) The party to whom an offer is made is the 'offeree'.
(4) A Part 36 offer or a Part 36 payment–
    (a) may be made at any time after proceedings have started; and
    (b) may be made in appeal proceedings.
(5) A Part 36 offer or a Part 36 payment shall not have the consequences set out in this Part while the claim is being dealt with on the small claims track unless the court orders otherwise.

(C) CPR 36.5 – FORM AND CONTENT OF A PART 36 OFFER

[32.3]
(1) A Part 36 offer must be in writing.
(2) A Part 36 offer may relate to the whole claim or to part of it or to any issue that arises in it.
(3) A Part 36 offer must–
    (a) state whether it relates to the whole of the claim or to part of it or to an issue that arises in it and if so to which part or issue;

    (b)   state whether it takes into account any counterclaim; and

    (c)   if it is expressed not to be inclusive of interest, give the details relating to interest set out in rule 36.22(2).

(4)   A defendant may make a Part 36 offer limited to accepting liability up to a specified proportion.

(5)   A Part 36 offer may be made by reference to an interim payment.

(6)   A Part 36 offer made not less than 21 days before the start of the trial must–

    (a)   be expressed to remain open for acceptance for 21 days from the date it is made; and

    (b)   provide that after 21 days the offeree may only accept it if–

        (i)   the parties agree the liability for costs; or

        (ii)   the court gives permission.

(7)   A Part 36 offer made less than 21 days before the start of the trial must state that the offeree may only accept it if–

    (a)   the parties agree the liability for costs; or

    (b)   the court gives permission.

(8)   If a Part 36 offer is withdrawn it will not have the consequences set out in this Part.

[32.4]   **Hertsmere Primary Care Trust v Administrators of Balasubramani-um's Estate**

[2005] EWHC 320 (Ch)

[2005] 3 All ER 274, [2005] NLJR 743

The claimant brought proceedings against the estate of a deceased optician, who had falsely claimed fees in respect of eye tests. The claimant obtained a freezing order, and then an order for an account of payments made to the deceased. The claimant made an offer to settle its claim, expressed to be made under CPR Pt 36. The letter did not comply with CPR Pt 36 because it did not state that the offer was to remain open for 21 days, and thereafter could only be accepted if the parties agreed their liability for costs or if the court gave permission. The estate advised that the offer did not comply with the terms of CPR Pt 36 but did not elaborate further, despite being asked to do so. At trial, the claimant was awarded a sum in excess of the offer made, and sought an order for interest at 10% above base rate on the judgment sum, and indemnity costs.

   The court found that both parties were represented by lawyers, and that the error in the offer was obvious and purely a technicality, and accordingly the claimant should have the benefit of such an order. The estate appealed.

HELD, ON APPEAL: CPR 1.3 provides that the parties are required to help the court to further the overriding objective. CPR 1.4 provides that the court must further the overriding objective by actively managing cases and active case management includes encouraging the parties to cooperate with each other. Accordingly, the estate was obliged to give to the claimant the information requested, namely how the offer failed to comply with CPR 36. Its failure to do was reason for the court to make an order for penalty interest and indemnity costs.

(D)   CPR 36.6 – NOTICE OF A PART 36 PAYMENT

[32.5]

(1)   A Part 36 payment may relate to the whole claim or part of it or to an issue that arises in it.

(2)   A defendant who makes a Part 36 payment must file with the court a notice ('Part 36 payment notice') which–
    (a)   states the amount of the payment;
    (b)   states whether the payment relates to the whole claim or to part of it or to any issue that arises in it and if so to which part or issue;
    (c)   states whether it takes into account any counterclaim;
    (d)   if an interim payment has been made, states that the defendant has taken into account the interim payment; and
    (e)   if it is expressed not to be inclusive of interest, gives the details relating to interest set out in rule 36.22(2).
(3)   The offeror must–
    (a)   serve the Part 36 payment notice on the offeree; and
    (b)   file a certificate of service of the notice.

(E)   CPR 36.8 – TIME WHEN A PART 36 OFFER IS MADE AND ACCEPTED

[32.6]
(1)   A Part 36 offer is made when received by the offeree.
(2)   A Part 36 payment is made when written notice of the payment into court is served on the offeree.
(3)   An improvement to a Part 36 offer will be effective when its details are received by the offeree.
(4)   An increase in a Part 36 payment will be effective when notice of the increase is served on the offeree.
(5)   A Part 36 offer or Part 36 payment is accepted when notice of its acceptance is received by the offeror.

[32.7]   **Charles v NTL Group Ltd**
[2002] EWCA Civ 2004
[2002] All ER (D) 196 (Dec), [2003] CP Rep 44

The claimant issued proceedings in respect of an accident at work whilst in the employment of the defendant. The defendant made a CPR Part 36 offer which was sent by fax to ensure that it arrived more than 21 days before the trial. At the trial, the claimant failed to beat the offer. The claimant argued that the offer was not validly served because, whilst the solicitors' letterhead displayed a fax number, it was also made clear that they would not accept service by fax, and therefore the defendant had failed to comply with CPR Pt 6. Accordingly, the CPR Part 36 offer had only been received two days later when the hard copy of the fax arrived, and therefore had been received less than 21 days before trial. The trial judge agreed, and made an order for costs in favour of the claimant. The defendant appealed.

HELD, ON APPEAL: The distinction in language between CPR 36.8(1) and (3), and CPR 36.8(2) and (4), made it clear that a CPR Part 36 offer did not have to be served in accordance with CPR Pt 6 to be effective. Accordingly, a CPR Part 36 offer was effective once received by the offeree. The fact that the letterhead of the claimant's solicitors' notepaper made it clear that service by fax was not acceptable was irrelevant. However, because making a payment into court involved the court itself in the process, the rules of service did apply to the notice of payment in.

(F)   OFFER AND ACCEPTANCE

[32.8]   Conrad Ritblatt and Company v Jill Sanders AG

(24 April 2001, unreported)

The claimant property consultants issued proceedings against the defendant, alleging that they had been appointed by the defendant as sole agents to obtain suitable premises, and claiming 10% of the annual rent of the premises or £10,000 plus VAT and interest on a quantum meruit basis. The defendant made a CPR Part 36 payment into court of £12,807.80, which was stated to relate to the quantum meruit claim only. A covering letter stated that, in the defendant's view, the claimant could only accept the payment in provided the alternative claims were abandoned. The claimant accepted the payment in, but in their covering letter refused to accept that the alternative claims were thereby abandoned. The parties applied to the court.

HELD: A claimant could not accept a payment in made on one basis on a different basis. The notice of acceptance together with its covering letter did not amount to an acceptance, but constituted a counter offer, and therefore the notice of acceptance would be struck out. The payment into court had not been accepted.

(G)   TERMS WHICH CANNOT BE INCLUDED IN A CPR PART 36 OFFER

[32.9]   Mitchell v James

[2002] EWCA Civ 997

[2003] 2 All ER 1064, [2004] 1 WLR 158

The claimant made a CPR Part 36 offer in proceedings which provided that the claimant would settle the claim by way of a payment of £91,410, dismissal of the counterclaim, and by each party bearing its own costs. At trial, the claimant submitted that the judgment obtained was more advantageous than the CPR 36 Part offer and that accordingly he should be entitled to indemnity costs. The judge refused to make such an order and the claimant appealed.

HELD, ON APPEAL: The judgment obtained by the claimant in relation to monetary sums could not be said to be either more advantageous or less advantageous than the CPR 36 offer. Furthermore, the claimant could not rely upon the fact that the costs award was more advantageous than the CPR Part 36 offer because a term as to costs was not within the scope of a CPR Part 36 offer. Whilst that does not prevent a party making an offer which includes a term as to costs, it does prevent that offer amounting to a CPR Part 36 offer and having the benefit of sanctions as to interest and indemnity costs.

[32.10]   Ali Reza-Delta Transport Co Ltd v United Arab Shipping Co

[2003] EWCA Civ 811

[2003] 2 All ER (Comm) 276, [2003] 3 All ER 1297, [2004] 1 WLR 168, [2003] 2 Lloyd's Rep 455

The claimant made a CPR Part 36 offer to accept US $227,400 plus the costs of trial on an indemnity basis, but waiving any interest uplift on both damages and costs. On appeal, the Court of Appeal awarded the claimant US $227,400. The claimant applied for an order for costs.

HELD: Interest formed part of the defendant's liability, but the claimant's concession related to penalty interest, which did not. The position was analogous to an offer which included costs, which equally would not be taken into account when assessing whether or not a claimant had done better than a CPR Part 36 offer. Only the court was permitted to assess whether an award of penalty interest was appropriate, in accordance with CPR 36.21(1).

[32.11]   Perry Press (t/a Pereds) v Chipperfield

[2003] EWCA Civ 484

[2003] All ER (D) 374 (Mar)

In the course of proceedings, the defendant made an offer marked without prejudice save as to costs of £5,400 plus VAT in respect of the claim, withdrawal of the counterclaim, and a contribution towards the claimant's costs. The purported offer was made in the context of an invitation to mediate. At trial, both the claim and the counterclaim were dismissed. The trial judge made an order that there be no order as to costs. The defendant appealed.

HELD, ON APPEAL: The terms of the offer could not be said to be finalised and clear. The offer to make a 'contribution towards costs' was not defined or limited to a particular sum. It amounted to no more than an offer to enter into negotiations. The trial judge had quite properly taken the offer into account when exercising his discretion in relation to costs, in accordance with CPR 44.3(4)(c). Equally, he was perfectly entitled in his discretion to hold that the offer was not clear and therefore make no order as to costs.

(H)   IS THE OFFER A REALISTIC ATTEMPT TO SETTLE OR A TACTICAL STEP TO SECURE THE ADVANTAGES OF CPR PT 36

[32.12]   Huck v Robson

[2002] EWCA Civ 398

[2002] 3 All ER 263, [2003] 1 WLR 1340

The claimant issued proceedings in respect of a road traffic accident which occurred on a narrow country lane between her vehicle and a vehicle driven by the defendant. The defendant's insurer made an offer to settle the claim on a 50/50 basis. The claimant responded with a CPR Part 36 offer to settle liability on a 95/5 basis in her favour. At trial, the judge found that the accident had been caused entirely as a result of the defendant's negligence, and awarded judgment to the claimant. The claimant sought her costs on an indemnity basis. The judge refused, holding that the claimant's offer was meaningless and derisory. The claimant appealed.

HELD, ON APPEAL: Since CPR 36.21 applied, the court should make an order for indemnity costs unless it would be unjust to make such an order. In order for a CPR Part 36 offer to qualify for indemnity costs and/or penalty interest, it must represent a genuine and realistic attempt by the offeror to settle, as opposed to a tactical step merely designed to secure the benefit of CPR 36.21. Whether an offer was genuine and realistic or merely tactical was a matter for the court to consider in each individual case. In this case, the offer was a genuine attempt to resolve the case, and accordingly, there was no basis upon which the claimant should be denied the benefit of indemnity costs.

(I)   CLARIFICATION OF A CPR PART 36 OFFER

[32.13]

CPR 36.9 – CLARIFICATION OF A PART 36 OFFER
(1)   The offeree may, within 7 days of a Part 36 offer or payment being made, request the offeror to clarify the offer or payment notice.
(2)   If the offeror does not give the clarification requested under paragraph (1) within 7 days of receiving the request, the offeree may, unless the trial has started, apply for an order that he does so.
(3)   If the court makes an order under paragraph (2), it must specify the date when the Part 36 offer or Part 36 payment is to be treated as having been made.

PARTIES MUST GIVE FULL DISCLOSURE

[32.14]   **Ford v GKR Construction Ltd**
[2000] 1 All ER 802, [2000] 1 WLR 1397

Per Lord Woolf MR: 'Under the CPR it is possible for the parties to make offers to settle before litigation commences. As to the disclosure required in relation to that procedure, protocols in specific areas of litigation make express provision. Even where there is no express provision contained in a relevant protocol which applies to the particular litigation, the approach reflected in the protocols should be adopted by parties generally in the conduct of their litigation.

If the process of making Part 36 offers before the commencement of litigation is to work in the way which the CPR intends, the parties must be provided with the information which they require in order to assess whether to make an offer or whether to accept that offer …

… If a party has not enabled another party to properly assess whether or not to make an or offer, or whether or not to accept an offer which is made, because of non-disclosure to the other party of material matters, or if a party comes to a decision which is different from that which would have been reached if there had been proper disclosure, that is a material matter for a court to take into account in considering what orders it should make'.

WHAT CONSTITUTES 'CLARIFICATION'?

[32.15]   **Sharp v Europa Freight**
[2000] CLY 544

In the course of proceedings the defendant made a CPR Part 36 payment into court. Within seven days, the claimant wrote to the defendant to ask what proportion of the payment in related to general damages and what proportion amounted to special damage. The request was purported to be made pursuant to CPR 36.9. The defendant refused to provide the information requested, and the claimant issued an application for an order requiring the defendant to provide the information. The application was refused and the claimant appealed.

HELD, ON APPEAL: A request for clarification of a CPR Part 36 offer or payment required the party giving clarification to make clear the terms of the offer. It did not require the party to provide a breakdown the offer into its constituent heads.

[32.16] Jeffries v Fisher

[2001] CLY 618

The claimant applied for an order that the defendant clarify the CPR Part 36 payment into court by itemising each head of loss, on the grounds that the payment in had not been in the sum agreed between the parties. The court granted the application, *Sharp v Europa Freight Corp Ltd* (at para [32.15]) not followed.

[32.17] **Calderbank v Shields**

(5 July 2001, unreported), Preston CC

The defendant made a CPR Part 36 payment of £100,000. The claimant sought a breakdown of the offer stating that until it was received the offer was defective and had no costs consequences. The court made an order requiring that the defendant provide a breakdown of general damages, special damage and damages for disadvantage on the open labour market.

[32.18] Johnson v Deer

[2001] CLY 619, Liverpool CC

The claimant issued proceedings in respect of a road traffic accident. The defendant alleged contributory negligence and made a CPR Part 36 payment into court. The claimant requested clarification of the offer made, specifically a breakdown in respect of each head of loss claimed. The defendant refused to provide clarification, and the claimant issued an application. The judge dismissed the claimant's application on the grounds that the claimant was not entitled to the clarification that he sought. The claimant appealed.

HELD, ON APPEAL: The claimant was not entitled to use the provisions of CPR Pt 36 to interrogate the defendant and was not entitled to a precise breakdown of the constituent parts of the CPR Part 36 payment in. Nevertheless, in accordance with the overriding objective, the defendant would be ordered to specify either the approximate split between general damages and special damage, or the approximate deduction made for contributory negligence.

(J) OFFERS MADE BEFORE THE COMMENCEMENT OF PROCEEDINGS

[32.19]

CPR 36.10 – COURT TO TAKE INTO ACCOUNT OFFER MADE TO SETTLE BEFORE COMMENCEMENT OF PROCEEDINGS

(1) If a person makes an offer to settle before proceedings are begun which complies with the provisions of this rule, the court will take that offer into account when making any order as to costs.

(2) The offer must–

(a) be expressed to be open for at least 21 days after the date it was made;

(b) if made by a person who would be a defendant were proceedings commenced, include an offer to pay the costs of the offeree incurred up to the date 21 days after the date it was made; and

(c) otherwise comply with this Part.

(3)   Subject to paragraph (3A), if the offeror is a defendant to a money claim–
  (a)   he must make a Part 36 payment within 14 days of service of the claim form; and
  (b)   the amount of the payment must be not less than the sum offered before proceedings began.

(3A)   In a claim to which rule 36.2A applies, if the offeror is a defendant who wishes to offer to pay the whole or part of any damages in the form of a lump sum–
  (a)   he must make a Part 36 payment within 14 days of service of the claim form; and
  (b)   the amount of the payment must be not less than the lump sum offered before proceedings began.

(4)   An offeree may not, after proceedings have begun, accept–
  (a)   an offer made under paragraph (2); or
  (b)   a Part 36 payment made under paragraph (3) or (3A),
without the permission of the court.

(5)   An offer under this rule is made when it is received by the offeree.

DEFENDANT MUST MAKE A PAYMENT INTO COURT WITHIN 14 DAYS OF SERVICE OF THE CLAIM FORM

[32.20]   Edmonson v Premier Foods Ltd

[2003] CLY 354

The claimant issued proceedings in respect of an injury sustained during the course of her employment with the defendant. During the pre-action period, the defendant made a CPR Part 36 offer in the sum of £5,000. The offer was rejected and the claimant made a counter offer of £15,000. After proceedings were issued, and within 14 days, the defendant made a CPR Part 36 payment into court of £5,000. At the disposal hearing, the claimant failed to beat the payment into court and the claimant was ordered to pay the defendant's costs from 21 days after the original CPR Part 36 offer. The claimant appealed to the judge.

HELD, ON APPEAL: The costs order was not disproportionate, and was a proper exercise of the judge's discretion in accordance with CPR Pt 36 and CPR 44.3.

[32.21]   Walker Residential Ltd v Davis and Another

(9 December 2005, unreported)

The claimant alleged damage as a result of the defendant's misrepresentation. The defendant made a CPR Part 36 offer of £85,000. The offer was rejected and the claimant issued proceedings. The defendant paid the sum of £85,000 into court, but more than 14 days had elapsed since service of the claim form. The claimant accepted the payment in. The defendant applied for costs from the date of the pre-proceedings CPR Part 36 offer. The deputy master extended the 14-day time period provided for by CPR 36.10 by reference to CPR 3.1(2)(a) and made an order for costs in the defendant's favour. The claimant appealed.

HELD, ON APPEAL: The claimant was entitled to the costs up to the date of filing notice of acceptance. The defendant had not sought an extension of time prior to making the CPR Part 36 payment in, and the court did not have the power to retrospectively extend the time period when to do so would deprive the claimant of a mandatory costs order.

(K) TIME FOR ACCEPTANCE OF A CPR PART 36 OFFER OR PAYMENT

[32.22]

CPR 36.11 – TIME FOR ACCEPTANCE OF A DEFENDANT'S PART 36 OFFER OR PART 36 PAYMENT

(1) A claimant may accept a Part 36 offer or a Part 36 payment made not less than 21 days before the start of the trial without needing the court's permission if he gives the defendant written notice of acceptance not later than 21 days after the offer or payment was made.

(2) If–

    (a) a defendant's Part 36 offer or Part 36 payment is made less than 21 days before the start of the trial; or

    (b) the claimant does not accept it within the period specified in paragraph (1)–

        (i) if the parties agree the liability for costs, the claimant may accept the offer or payment without needing the permission of the court;

        (ii) if the parties do not agree the liability for costs the claimant may only accept the offer or payment with the permission of the court.

(3) Where the permission of the court is needed under paragraph (2) the court will, if it gives permission, make an order as to costs.

[32.23] Re Midland Linen Services Ltd
Chaudhry v Yap

[2004] EWHC 3380 (Ch)

[2004] All ER (D) 406 (Oct)

The claimant was a director and minority shareholder in Midland Linen Services Ltd. He was removed as a director and issued proceedings for unfair dismissal. The company made a CPR Part 36 offer to settle the claim in the sum of £80,000 less than 21 days before trial. The claimant indicated that he wanted to accept the offer. The company had no objection to acceptance of the offer, but did not agree that the claimant should be entitled to the costs of the action. Accordingly, application was made to the court to determine matters and exercise its discretion under CPR 36.11(3).

HELD: The court had a wide discretion. In exercising that discretion it should reach a conclusion which was fair and just in all the circumstances. The court should consider all the relevant circumstances, including the conduct of the parties.

[32.24]

CPR 36.12 – TIME FOR ACCEPTANCE OF A CLAIMANT'S PART 36 OFFER

(1) A defendant may accept a Part 36 offer made not less than 21 days before the start of the trial without needing the court's permission if he gives the claimant written notice of acceptance not later than 21 days after the offer was made.

(2) If–

    (a) a claimant's Part 36 offer is made less than 21 days before the start of the trial; or

    (b)   the defendant does not accept it within the period specified in paragraph (1) –

        (i)   if the parties agree the liability for costs, the defendant may accept the offer without needing the permission of the court;

        (ii)   if the parties do not agree the liability for costs the defendant may only accept the offer with the permission of the court.

(3)   Where the permission of the court is needed under paragraph (2) the court will, if it gives permission, make an order as to costs.

APPLICATION TO ACCEPT A CPR PART 36 OFFER OR PAYMENT OUT OF TIME

[32.25]   Uttley v Uttley

[2001] All ER (D) 240 (Jul), [2002] PIQR P123

HELD: When applying to accept a CPR Part 36 payment out of time, without costs penalty, the claimant must prove that it would be unjust not to apply the usual rule. In this case video surveillance evidence was disclosed late. It was accepted that such evidence was subject to the usual rules of disclosure and withholding it to ambush the claimant was not permissible. In this case the claimant's witness evidence had been delayed and the defendant was therefore entitled to withhold the video evidence for a reasonable period of time. In the absence of any reprehensible conduct on the part of the defendant's solicitors, the usual costs order should apply with the claimant paying the defendant's costs following expiry of the 21 day period.

[32.26]   Capital Bank plc v Stickland

[2004] EWCA Civ 1677

[2005] 2 All ER 544, [2005] 1 WLR 3914

The claimant bank alleged that the defendant was liable for interfering with the claimant's immediate right to possession of a vessel, of which the claimant was mortgagee. The claimant made a CPR Part 36 offer to settle but this was not accepted. On the morning of the trial, the defendant applied to the court for permission to accept the CPR Part 36 offer out of time. The judge refused, and the case proceeded. The claimant was awarded a sum in excess of the CPR Part 36 offer, and the judge made an order that the defendant should meet the claimant's costs from the date of the CPR Part 36 offer on an indemnity basis together with penalty interest. The defendant appealed.

HELD, ON APPEAL: The court had unfettered discretion to decide whether a CPR 36 offer could be accepted after the 21-day period had expired. In exercising discretion, the court was entitled to take all and any factors into account, in particular whether the claim was likely to succeed, the timeous nature of the application, and the parties' conduct throughout proceedings.

(L) CONSEQUENCES OF ACCEPTING A CPR PART 36 OFFER OR PAYMENT INTO COURT

[32.27]

CPR 36.13 – Costs consequences of acceptance of a defendant's Part 36 offer or Part 36 payment
(1) Where a Part 36 offer or a Part 36 payment is accepted without needing the permission of the court the claimant will be entitled to his costs of the proceedings up to the date of serving notice of acceptance.
(2) Where–
  (a) a Part 36 offer or a Part 36 payment relates to part only of the claim; and
  (b) at the time of serving notice of acceptance the claimant abandons the balance of the claim,
the claimant will be entitled to his costs of the proceedings up to the date of serving notice of acceptance, unless the court orders otherwise.
(3) The claimant's costs include any costs attributable to the defendant's counterclaim if the Part 36 offer or the Part 36 payment notice states that it takes into account the counterclaim.
(4) Costs under this rule will be payable on the standard basis if not agreed.

[32.28]

CPR 36.14 – Costs consequences of acceptance of a claimant's Part 36 offer

Where a claimant's Part 36 offer is accepted without needing the permission of the court the claimant will be entitled to his costs of the proceedings up to the date upon which the defendant serves notice of acceptance.

[32.29]

CPR 36.15 – The effect of acceptance of a Part 36 offer or a Part 36 payment
(1) If a Part 36 offer or Part 36 payment relates to the whole claim and is accepted, the claim will be stayed.
(2) In the case of acceptance of a Part 36 offer which relates to the whole claim–
  (a) the stay will be upon the terms of the offer; and
  (b) either party may apply to enforce those terms without the need for a new claim.
(3) If a Part 36 offer or a Part 36 payment which relates to part only of the claim is accepted–
  (a) the claim will be stayed as to that part; and
  (b) unless the parties have agreed costs, the liability for costs shall be decided by the court.
(4) If the approval of the court is required before a settlement can be binding, any stay which would otherwise arise on the acceptance of a Part 36 offer or a Part 36 payment will take effect only when that approval has been given.

(5)   Any stay arising under this rule will not affect the power of the court–
  (a)   to enforce the terms of a Part 36 offer;
  (b)   to deal with any question of costs (including interest on costs) relating to the proceedings;
  (c)   to order payment out of court of any sum paid into court.
(6)   Where–
  (a)   a Part 36 offer has been accepted; and
  (b)   a party alleges that–
      (i)   the other party has not honoured the terms of the offer; and
      (ii)   he is therefore entitled to a remedy for breach of contract,
      the party may claim the remedy by applying to the court without the need to start a new claim unless the court orders otherwise.

ACCEPTANCE OF A CPR OFFER OR PAYMENT WHICH RELATES TO ONLY PART OF THE CLAIM

[32.30]   **Clark Goldring & Page Ltd v ANC Ltd**
92(20) LSG 43
27 March 2001

The claimant issued proceedings against the defendant in respect of a claim for breach of contract and misrepresentation. In October 2000 the court made an order that the claimant provide security for costs of the claim up to trial. The claimant provided security by way of a legal expenses insurance policy (which provided for cover of £150,000), and a payment into court of £25,000.
  The defendant made a CPR Part 36 payment into court of £200,000 in respect of some, but not all of the issues. The claimant accepted the payment in. Upon acceptance, the cover provided by the legal expenses insurance policy ceased. Conscious that the only cover was the monies paid into court by the claimant for security, the defendant applied for an order that part of the £200,000 it had paid into court should be retained pending the trial. The claimant resisted the application, and argued that acceptance of the CPR Part 36 payment in gave it an automatic entitlement to substantial costs.

HELD: CPR 36.15(3) provides that if an offer which relates to only part of the claim is accepted, the claim will be stayed in relation to that part, and unless the parties agree otherwise, the court shall decide the liability for costs. Accordingly, the claimant had no automatic entitlement to costs, and the court was entitled to exercise its discretion as to the appropriate order to make. The court held that there was still a justification for security, and made an order that the claimant give further security in the additional sum of £30,000.

[32.31]

CPR 36.16 – PAYMENT OUT OF A SUM IN COURT ON THE ACCEPTANCE OF A PART 36 PAYMENT

Where a Part 36 payment is accepted the claimant obtains payment out of the sum in court by making a request for payment in the practice form.

[32.32]

CPR 36.17 – ACCEPTANCE OF A PART 36 OFFER OR A PART 36 PAYMENT
MADE BY ONE OR MORE, BUT NOT ALL, DEFENDANTS
(1)   This rule applies where the claimant wishes to accept a Part 36 offer
or a Part 36 payment made by one or more, but not all, of a number of
defendants.
(2)   If the defendants are sued jointly or in the alternative, the claimant
may accept the offer or payment without needing the permission of the
court in accordance with rule 36.11(1) if–
    (a)   he discontinues his claim against those defendants who have not
made the offer or payment; and
    (b)   those defendants give written consent to the acceptance of the
offer or payment.
(3)   If the claimant alleges that the defendants have a several liability to
him the claimant may–
    (a)   accept the offer or payment in accordance with rule 36.11(1); and
    (b)   continue with his claims against the other defendants if he is
entitled to do so.
(4)   In all other cases the claimant must apply to the court for–
    (a)   an order permitting a payment out to him of any sum in court; and
    (b)   such order as to costs as the court considers appropriate.

2.   CONSEQUENCES OF A CPR PART 36 OFFER OR PAYMENT

(A)   CLAIMANT FAILS TO DO BETTER THAN A DEFENDANT'S CPR PART 36 OFFER OR PAYMENT

[32.33]

CPR 36.20 – COSTS CONSEQUENCES WHERE CLAIMANT FAILS TO DO BETTER
THAN A PART 36 OFFER OR A PART 36 PAYMENT
(1)   This rule applies where at trial a claimant–
    (a)   fails to better a Part 36 payment;
    (b)   fails to obtain a judgment which is more advantageous than a
defendant's Part 36 offer or
    (c)   in a claim to which rule 36.2A applies, fails to obtain a judgment
which is more advantageous than the Part 36 offer made under
that rule.
(2)   Unless it considers it unjust to do so, the court will order the
claimant to pay any costs incurred by the defendant after the latest date on
which the payment or offer could have been accepted without needing the
permission of the court.

[32.34]   Burgess v British Steel plc
[2000] 05 LS Gaz R 33, 144 Sol Jo LB 58, [2000] PIQR 240

The claimant sustained serious orthopaedic and psychiatric injuries in a road traffic
accident. The defendants admitted liability. The claimant and the defendants each
commissioned psychiatric reports. The defendants' expert concluded that the
claimant was a malingerer. His report was disclosed in April 1998. The written
evidence was relied upon at trial, but the expert was not called to give evidence.

In August 1998 the defendants made a payment into court of £220,000. At trial, the claimant was only awarded £161,592.22, and the defendant applied for costs from 21 days after the date of the payment in. The trial judge made an order that there be no order for costs from that date, on the basis that the claimant was obliged to come to court to fight off the allegation made that he was a malingerer. The defendants appealed.

HELD, ON APPEAL: The fact that the defendants had made an allegation that the claimant was malingering was not reason to permit the trial judge to depart from the normal rule in relation to costs following a failure to better a payment into court.

[32.35]   Spilsbury v Martin International Holdings plc
[2002] CLY 375

The claimant, a child, issued proceedings against the defendant. The defendant made a CPR Part 36 payment into court in the sum of £2,250. Five days before trial, the defendant made a further payment into court, such that the monies in court totalled £2,500. At trial, the claimant was awarded the sum of £2,436. The defendant applied for an order that the claimant should pay the costs from the date of the second payment in. The judge agreed, firstly because he concluded that the claimant and his advisers had had sufficient time to consider the increased monies in court, and secondly because, with the benefit of legal expenses insurance, the claimant's damages would not be reduced by reason of a costs order made against him. The claimant appealed.

HELD, ON APPEAL: The usual order in relation to costs was that set out in CPR 36.20 and 36.11, and this case was not exceptional. The evidence upon which the defendant had based both the first and second payments in had been available for several months, and there was no reason why the defendant could not have made the second payment in much earlier. The judge's exercise of discretion was outside the reasonable parameters of judicial discretion.

DEFENDANT ENTITLED TO COSTS ON AN INDEMNITY BASIS

[32.36]   Excelsior Commercial & Industrial Holdings Ltd v Salisbury Hamer Aspden & Johnson
[2002] EWCA Civ 879
[2002] All ER (D) 39 (Jun)

The claimant failed to beat a CPR Part 36 payment into court of £100,000, and was awarded only nominal damages of £2. The defendants had together made the CPR Part 36 payment one day before the start of the trial. The claimant was ordered to pay the defendants' costs from the date of the CPR Part 36 payment, on an indemnity basis. The claimant appealed.

HELD: The appeal was dismissed. CPR 36.20, which applied to CPR Part 36 payments, was silent on the issue of indemnity costs, in contrast to CPR 36.21 which applied to claimant's offers. However, if there were circumstances which removed the case from the norm, then an order for indemnity costs was justified. The Court of Appeal refused to give guidance on when indemnity costs were justified but said that the circumstances were infinite.

(B)   CLAIMANT DOES BETTER THAN HIS PART 36 OFFER

[32.37]

CPR 36.21 – COSTS AND OTHER CONSEQUENCES WHERE CLAIMANT DOES
BETTER THAN HE PROPOSED IN HIS PART 36 OFFER
(1)   This rule applies where at trial–
    (a)   a defendant is held liable for more; or
    (b)   the judgment against a defendant is more advantageous to the
        claimant,
than the proposals contained in a claimant's Part 36 offer (including a
Part 36 offer made under rule 36.2A).
(2)   The court may order interest on the whole or part of any sum of
money (excluding interest) awarded to the claimant at a rate not exceeding
10% above base rate for some or all of the period starting with the latest
date on which the defendant could have accepted the offer without needing
the permission of the court.
(3)   The court may also order that the claimant is entitled to–
    (a)   his costs on the indemnity basis from the latest date when the
        defendant could have accepted the offer without needing the
        permission of the court; and
    (b)   interest on those costs at a rate not exceeding 10% above base rate.
(4)   Where this rule applies, the court will make the orders referred to in
paragraphs (2) and (3) unless it considers it unjust to do so.
(5)   In considering whether it would be unjust to make the orders
referred to in paragraphs (2) and (3) above, the court will take into account
all the circumstances of the case including–
    (a)   the terms of any Part 36 offer;
    (b)   the stage in the proceedings when any Part 36 offer or Part 36
        payment was made;
    (c)   the information available to the parties at the time when the
        Part 36 offer or Part 36 payment was made; and
    (d)   the conduct of the parties with regard to the giving or refusing to
        give information for the purposes of enabling the offer or payment
        into court to be made or evaluated.
(6)   Where the court awards interest under this rule and also awards
interest on the same sum and for the same period under any other power,
the total rate of interest may not exceed 10% above base rate.

[32.38]   **Gaynor v Blackpool Football Club Ltd**
(10 April 2002, unreported), Oldham CC

In the months preceding a trial in relation to the issue of liability, the claimant made
two CPR Part 36 offers to settle. The first offer stated that the claimant would
settle the issue of liability on the basis that there be judgment for the claimant with
damages to be assessed and costs. A second offer, made less than 21 days before
trial, stated that the claimant would settle the issue of liability on a 75/25 basis in
the claimant's favour. The trial judge gave judgment to the claimant, and made an
order that the defendant pay the claimant's costs, and that the claimant's costs
should be assessed on an indemnity basis from the date of the second CPR Part 36
offer. The claimant contended that the costs should be paid on an indemnity basis
from the date of the first offer.

HELD: The meaning of CPR 36.21 was plain, and accordingly the claimant had not achieved a judgment which was for more than or which was more advantageous than the first offer.

[32.39]   Read v Edmed

[2004] EWHC 3274 (QB)

[2005] All ER (D) 433 (Feb)

The claimant was injured when she was knocked off her bicycle by a car driven by the defendant. Liability was denied, and an order made for a split trial. The claimant made a CPR Part 36 offer to settle the issue of liability on a 50/50 basis. At the liability trial, the judge gave judgment to the claimant, subject to a 50% reduction for contributory negligence. The claimant sought an order for costs on an indemnity basis from 21 days after the date of the CPR 36 offer. The defendant contended that the claimant had not done better than her offer, she had only equalled it, and therefore should not have the benefit of an order for penalty costs.

HELD: The wording of CPR 36.21(1) was plain and could not be held to apply to a situation where the court's judgment exactly matched the offer made. Nevertheless, applying the spirit of the rules, per Bell J: 'as a matter of general principle, where in a relatively uncomplicated claim for damages for personal injury a claimant made a valid CPR 36 offer to settle an issue of liability at a given proportion of his or her claim, and the defendant refused that offer and the court gave judgment for precisely that proportion of the claim, the claimant should be entitled to the benefit of an award of indemnity costs from the time of the expiry of the offer and some interest on those costs just as he or she would if CPR r.36.21 had applied'.

[32.40]   Mamidoil-Jetoil Greek Petroleum Company SA v Okta Crude Oil Refinery AD

[2002] EWHC 2462 (Comm)

[2002] All ER (D) 102 (Dec), [2003] 1 Lloyd's Rep 42

The claimants obtained judgment in respect of breach of two contracts in the respective sums of US $8,418,323 and US $808,749. The claimants relied upon a CPR Part 36 offer in the sum of US $7m to argue that they should be entitled to their costs on an indemnity basis. The defendant argued that, in the circumstances of the case, this was inappropriate.

HELD: In deciding whether it was unjust to award a successful claimant indemnity costs and penalty interest, the court must take into account all the circumstances of the case. In the present case, the history of disclosure in the claim, together with other factors, had made it difficult for the defendant to gauge the proper value of the claim, and accordingly, the court held that it would be unjust to make an award of indemnity costs or penalty interest in favour of the claimant.

AWARD OF INTEREST ON DAMAGES OR COSTS UNDER CPR 36.21
NOT PUNITIVE

[32.41]   McPhilemy v Times Newspapers Ltd

[2001] EWCA Civ 933

[2001] 4 All ER 861, [2002] 1 WLR 934

The claimant issued proceedings against the defendant for libel. The claimant made a CPR Part 36 offer of £50,000. He was awarded £145,000 by the jury. The trial judge refused to make an order for interest on damages or indemnity costs. He considered that to do so would subvert the jury's award for damages, which in a libel case was designed to take account of everything down to the verdict and therefore implicitly included interest. Insofar as an award of indemnity costs was concerned, the trial judge considered that such an award carried a stigma and implied disapproval on the part of the court of the defendant's conduct. The claimant appealed.

HELD, ON APPEAL: CPR 36.21(3) set out the order which the court was expected to make in the event that a defendant failed to beat a claimant's CPR Part 36 offer, and was neither punitive nor did it indicate any measure of disapproval of the defendant's conduct. CPR 36.21(2) and (3) were designed to encourage the making of offers and the acceptance of offers.

CPR 36.21 ONLY APPLIES TO COSTS ORDERS MADE AFTER TRIAL

[32.42]   **Petrotrade Inc v Texaco Ltd**
[2001] 4 All ER 853, [2002] 1 WLR 947

The claimant agreed to supply gasoil to the defendant, who refused to pay the whole price on the ground that the gasoil did not comply with contractual specification. The claimant issued proceedings to recover the unpaid portion of the price. The claimant made a CPR 36 offer which was lower than the judgment eventually made in the claimant's favour on the claimant's application for summary judgment. However, the trial judge refused to award the claimant enhanced interest and costs on an indemnity basis. The claimant appealed to the Court of Appeal.

HELD, ON APPEAL: The provisions of CPR 36.21 only applied to costs orders made after trial, not after an application for summary judgment, and accordingly the claimant had no inherent right to an order for indemnity costs and/or interest on damages and/or costs. Whether such an order would be made in any event was a matter for the judge to consider in his discretion. The Court of Appeal indicated that had this matter been one upon which they were called upon to exercise discretion at first instance, then they would have made an order for indemnity costs and penalty interest, but in the present case, they could not interfere with the trial judge's exercise of discretion.

[32.43]   **Craig v Railtrack plc**
[2002] EWHC 168 (QB)
[2002] All ER (D) 212 (Feb)

The claimants issued proceedings in respect of injuries suffered in a train derailment. A split trial was ordered. The parties fully prepared for the hearing on liability. Six days before the liability trial, the issue of liability was conceded. The claimants relied upon CPR Part 36 offers made before the trial to recover their costs on an indemnity basis. The defendant argued that this was not appropriate because CPR 36.21(3) 'applies at trial'. Reliance was placed upon *Petrotrade v Texaco* (at para [32.42]).

HELD: Following *Petrotrade v Texaco*, the claimants were not entitled as of right to an order for indemnity costs. However, pursuant to CPR 44.3(1), the court did have the ability to exercise discretion to make such an order. The fact that it took the defendant five years to resolve the issue of liability was unreasonable, and provided sufficient grounds for an order for indemnity costs and penalty interest.

CLAIMANT ADVANCING ALTERNATIVE CASES, ONLY SUCCESSFUL ON ONE

[32.44]   Kastor Navigation Co Ltd and Others v AGF MAT and Others

[2003] EWHC 472 (Comm)

[2003] 1 All ER (Comm) 277, [2003] All ER (D) 245 (Mar)

The claimant issued proceedings for an indemnity from insurers in respect of the actual total loss of a vessel allegedly caused by fire. Pleadings were amended to introduce a claim against insurers in respect of the constructive loss of the vessel caused by fire, to cover the eventuality that the court found on the facts that the vessel had become a constructive loss before it sank. The claimant persisted with both arguments at trial, despite expert evidence that suggested that it was implausible that fire had caused the actual total loss of the vessel.

The claimant lost at trial on the basis of its primary argument, but won on the basis of the alternative argument. A CPR Part 36 offer had been made pre-litigation by the claimant on the basis of its primary argument on which it had lost at trial. The claimant applied for an order for costs on an indemnity basis.

HELD: The claimant had substantially increased the parties' costs and lengthened the case by persisting with its primary arguments when the evidence in support of those arguments was weak and without merit. The trial judge considered that it was appropriate to make different costs orders in respect of the different issues raised, to reflect the fact that costs had been incurred unnecessarily in relation to an argument without merit. An order was made that the defendant pay 15% of the claimant's costs, and that the claimant pay 85% of the defendant's costs.

CLAIMANT ADVANCING MORE THAN ONE CLAIM, ONLY SUCCESSFUL ON ONE

[32.45]   E Ivor Hughes Education Foundation v Leach

[2005] EWHC 1317 (Ch)

[2005] All ER (D) 127 (Jun)

The claimant charity brought proceedings against the defendant, a member of the board of governors, in respect of breach of fiduciary duty. The claimant's claim amounted to between £60,000 and £87,000. The defendant made a CPR Part 36 payment into court of £5,000 in respect of one head of claim. The claimant accepted the payment in, and conceded all remaining heads of claim. The claimant claimed the costs of the action, which amounted to £170,000.

HELD: The real winner of the case was the defendant. All the claimant's claims save one had been abandoned following acceptance of the payment into court, and the claimant had accepted a very small sum in respect of that claim. The court exercised its discretion pursuant to CPR 44.3 and made an order that the claimant should be entitled to costs in relation to the claim which was the subject of the payment into court, but that those costs should be restricted by reference to CPR Pt 27 (fixed costs in the small claims track). In relation to all other heads of loss, the claimant was ordered to pay the defendant's costs.

MULTIPLE DEFENDANTS – ASSESSING WHETHER THE CLAIMANT HAS DONE BETTER THAN HIS OFFER

[32.46] Humpheryes v Nedcon UK Ltd

[2004] EWHC 2558 (QB)

[2004] All ER (D) 152 (Nov)

The claimant wrote a letter of claim to the first defendant's insurer, who conceded liability on the part of the first defendant, subject to its right to allege contributory negligence. The claimant made a CPR Part 36 offer to settle in the sum of £311,490.15, and in support of that disclosed a report from a medical expert, an accountant's report, a calculation of special damage, and witness statements. The claimant indicated that if the first defendant required further time to consider the offer, then the first defendant should ask for an extension. The offer was rejected four days later. No counter offer was made, and no further information was sought. Proceedings were issued against the first defendant, who in turn issued CPR Pt 20 proceedings against Storage Engineering Services Ltd, following which the claimant was given permission to proceed against that company as second defendant. Neither defendant made any offers, and no money was paid into court.

Judgment was given to the claimant, and the judge held that both defendants were liable to the claimant in negligence and breach of statutory duty. The judge apportioned liability as to two thirds against the first defendant and as to one third against the second defendant. Damages were assessed in the total sum of £325,984.28 inclusive of interest. Deducting interest from the award to the date of the claimant's CPR Part 36 offer left a figure of £316,432.32. The claimant argued that he had bettered his CPR Part 36 offer and should therefore be entitled to penalty interest on damages, indemnity costs, and interest on those costs. The first defendant argued that it was only liable for two thirds of the judgment sum, and accordingly, the claimant had not bettered his CPR Part 36 offer.

HELD: The first defendant had confused liability with apportionment of damages. Both defendants were liable for the entirety of the judgment sum, and therefore liable to have the whole sum enforced against each of them. Accordingly, the claimant had beaten his CPR Part 36 offer and was *prima facie* entitled to penalty interest and indemnity costs.

(C)   DATE TO BE USED WHEN ASSESSING WHETHER AN OFFER HAS BEEN BETTERED

[32.47] Johnson v Gore Wood & Co (No 2)

[2003] EWCA Civ 1728

[2003] All ER (D) 58 (Dec), 147 Sol Jo LB 1427

HELD, ON APPEAL: The court should assess damages as at the date of the payment into court and not the date of trial. The claimant's argument that he had beaten the payment into court failed. Had the payment in been accepted when it was made, but for the accrual of interest between the date of the payment in and the date of trial, the claimant would have failed to beat the payment into court.

[32.48]   **Blackham v Entrepose UK**

[2004] EWCA Civ 1109

[2004] All ER (D) 478 (Jul), [2005] 1 Costs LR 68

The defendant paid £40,000 into court in accordance with CPR Pt 36. At trial, the claimant was awarded £40,854 including interest, and the court made an order for costs against the defendant on the basis that the payment into court had been beaten. The defendant appealed, on the basis that if interest was not included in the calculation, then the claimant had not beaten the payment into court:

HELD, ON APPEAL: The elements of damages and interest should be considered separately. Accordingly, the claimant had failed to beat the payment into court and the defendant should be awarded its costs.

3.   OFFERS NOT MADE IN ACCORDANCE WITH CPR PART 36

[32.49]

CPR 36.1 – MAKING OFFERS OTHER THAN IN ACCORDANCE WITH CPR 36
  (1)   …
  (2)   Nothing in this Part prevents a party making an offer to settle in whatever way he chooses, but if that offer is not made in accordance with this Part, it will only have the consequences specified in this Part if the court so orders.

(A)   RECTIFYING MISTAKES UNDER CPR 36.1(2)

[32.50]   **Neave v Neave**

[2003] EWCA Civ 325

[2003] All ER (D) 172 (Mar)

The defendant argued that the words 'this offer is open for 21 days from today' contained in an offer purported to have been made pursuant to CPR Pt 36 should be interpreted as meaning 21 days from the date of receipt of the offer, and that accordingly, the letter did not comply with CPR 36.5(6)(a) because it had been received less than 21 days before the trial.

HELD, ON APPEAL: The words were intended to comply with CPR 36.5(6)(a), and accordingly, the court had power to and would therefore rectify the mistake under CPR 36.1(2).

[32.51]

CPR 44.3(4) – COURT'S DISCRETION AND CIRCUMSTANCES TO BE TAKEN INTO ACCOUNT WHEN EXERCISING ITS DISCRETION AS TO COSTS
  (4)   In deciding what order (if any) to make about costs, the court must have regard to all the circumstances, including–
    …
    (c)   any payment into court or admissible offer to settle made by a party which is drawn to the court's attention (whether or not made in accordance with Part 36).

(B) COURT'S EXERCISE OF DISCRETION

[32.52] **Farag v Commissioner of Police for the Metropolis**

[2005] EWCA Civ 1814

[2006] All ER (D) 226 (Feb), 150 Sol Jo LB 91

The claimant was showing jewellery to passers-by on Frith Street in Soho when he was arrested by the police. He issued proceedings against the defendant for wrongful arrest, false imprisonment and four separate assaults. The defendant made an offer to settle of £3,001 in 1997, but withdrew the offer in May 2002. A jury dismissed all allegations against the defendant except one allegation of assault, and the claimant was awarded £1,465. The court awarded the claimant the costs of the action. The defendant appealed, arguing that, whilst the offer had been withdrawn, it was nevertheless an offer which should have been taken into account by the judge when exercising his discretion in relation to costs.

HELD, ON APPEAL: The decision of the Court of Appeal in *Trustees of Stokes Pension Fund v Western Power Distribution (South-West) plc* (see para [32.59]) decided in terms that the fact that an offer has been withdrawn does not deprive the offer of its effect. The trial judge had failed to take the offer into account, and accordingly his exercise of discretion would be set aside. The Court of Appeal ordered that there be no order as to the costs of the trial.

[32.53] **Rio Properties Inc v Gibson Dunn & Crutcher (a firm)**

[2005] EWCA Civ 534

[2005] All ER (D) 318 (Apr)

Per Arden LJ: In my judgment, CPR 36 should only be treated as applying to offers which fall within it; in other words, a judge should not regard himself as bound to award indemnity costs and interest in the same way that he would have been bound if the offer had fallen within CPR 36 ... [T]he question is one for the discretion of the judge. In exercising that discretion, I would accept that the judge should consider the public interest in encouraging parties to consider and evaluate offers to settle claims made against them and to accept them ... But it is a question for the discretion of the judge whether to award costs on a standard or an indemnity basis, and whether to award interest, or to make some other order to mark the fact that an offer should have been accepted.

4. A DEFENDANT'S OFFER REQUIRES A PAYMENT INTO COURT

(A) CPR 36.3 – A DEFENDANT'S OFFER TO SETTLE A MONEY CLAIM REQUIRES A PART 36 PAYMENT

[32.54]

(1) Subject to rules 36.2A(2), 36.5(5) and 36.23, an offer by a defendant to settle a money claim will not have the consequences set out in this Part unless it is made by way of a Part 36 payment.

(2) A Part 36 payment may only be made after proceedings have started.

(B)   POSSIBLE ORDERS WHERE THE DEFENDANT FAILS TO MAKE A PART 36 PAYMENT INTO COURT

[32.55]   **Amber v Stacey**

[2001] 2 All ER 88, [2001] 1 WLR 1225

The claimant carried out works to refurbish the defendant's butchers shop premises, and issued proceedings in respect of his outstanding invoice. The defendant wrote to the claimant, offering to settle the claim in the sum of £4,000 plus VAT and costs. The claimant rejected this offer. In the course of proceedings, the defendant paid £2,000 into court, and then a further £1,000, but never paid in a sum equal to the initial offer of £4,000 plus VAT. The claimant was ordered to pay the defendant's costs from the date of the second payment into court. The defendant argued that the claimant had failed to recover a sum greater than the initial offer of £4,000 plus VAT and that accordingly the claimant should pay the defendant's costs. The trial judge agreed and made an order accordingly. The claimant appealed.

HELD, ON APPEAL: The trial judge was permitted to consider the claimant's conduct and, having found it unreasonable, was then entitled to exercise his discretion when making an order in relation to costs. However, the defendant had no right to the benefits of CPR Pt 36 because the offer had not been paid into court, and it was wrong for the judge to treat the initial offer as tantamount to a payment into court. Nevertheless, the Court of Appeal held that the balance of justice required that the claimant should be ordered to pay a proportion of the defendant's costs, namely one half, for the period from the date of the initial offer to the date of the second payment into court.

[32.56]   **Hardy v Sutherland (t/a David Sutherland Architects)**

[2001] EWCA Civ 976

[2001] All ER (D) 117 (Jun)

The claimant engaged the first defendant as an architect in relation to building works, and thereafter contracted with a builder, the second defendant, to undertake the works. The claimant was not satisfied with the performance of the contract and issued proceedings. On 12 April 2000 the first defendant made a CPR Part 36 offer of £3,500 to settle the claim. This sum was eventually paid into court on 3 August 2000. Eventually the claim was compromised such that the first defendant paid to the claimant £3,000, and the second defendant paid £14,000. The issue of costs could not be resolved, and the matter came before the circuit judge who made an order that the first defendant pay 75% of the claimant's costs to 21 days after the date of the CPR Part 36 offer, and the claimant pay the first defendant's costs thereafter. The claimant appealed.

HELD, ON APPEAL: The trial judge's exercise of discretion failed to take into account the decision in *Amber v Stacey* (at para [32.55]) in that it gave insufficient recognition to the fact that an offer to settle does not have the same clarity or certainty as a payment into court. Accordingly, the Court of Appeal would substitute an order that the first defendant should recover only 50% of costs between the date of the CPR Part 36 offer and the date of the payment in.

[32.57] Southampton Container Terminals Ltd v Schiffahrts-Gesellschaft Hansa Australia MBH & Co (The Maersk Colombo)

[2001] EWCA Civ 717

[2001] All ER (D) 40 (May), [2001] 2 Lloyd's Rep 275

The defendant's container vessel, Maersk Colombo, entered the port of Southampton and whilst manoeuvring alongside the container terminal struck a crane causing it to fall over and collapse. Liability was admitted. The claim concerned the appropriate measure of damages, namely whether the measure should be the reinstatement cost of £2.4m, or the resale value of £665,000. The defendant made an offer to settle in the sum of £956,857, and advised that the offer would be drawn to the attention of the trial judge on the issue of costs. The offer referred to CPR Pt 36. The claimant responded by saying that in order to comply with CPR Pt 36, the defendant should pay the offer into court.

The trial judge held that the appropriate measure of damages was the resale value and awarded damages accordingly. The defendant's offer was drawn to the judge's attention. Having regard to CPR 44.3(4), in deciding what order (if any) to make about costs, the judge noted that he must have regard to all the circumstances including: '(c) any payment into court or admissible offer to settle made by a party which is drawn to the court's attention (whether or not in accordance with CPR 36)'. The judge made an order that the claimant pay the defendant's costs from 21 days after the date of the offer. The claimant appealed.

HELD, ON APPEAL: Offers should not be treated as the precise equivalent of payments into court. Nevertheless, CPR 36.1(2) gives the court a wide discretion to make an order under CPR 36.20 even when there has been no payment in. Whether an order should be made depended upon all the circumstances of the case. In the present case, the fact that there would have been a delay in obtaining the monies to pay in from the Swedish underwriters, that the offer was clearly one of substance, and that it would not have been accepted even if it had been paid in, were factors which the trial judge was entitled to take into account when exercising his discretion. The appeal was dismissed.

(C) PUBLIC BODIES AND DEFENDANTS 'GOOD FOR THE MONEY' NEED NOT MAKE A PAYMENT IN TO DERIVE THE BENEFITS OF PART 36

[32.58] Crouch v King's Healthcare NHS Trust

[2004] EWCA Civ 1332

[2005] 1 All ER 207, [2005] 1 WLR 2015

The claimant issued proceedings in respect of personal injury said to have been caused by the negligence of the defendant. The defendant made an offer to settle in the sum of £35,000 '... under the provisions of CPR 36 ...' which stated that there was no intention to pay the sum into court, because the defendant was a public body and the claimant should be in no doubt that the defendant would pay the amount of the offer if it was accepted. There was no CPR Part 36 payment into court. At trial, the claimant succeeded, but was only awarded damages of £29,000. The trial judge held that the defendant did not have the benefit of CPR Pt 36 because the monies had not been paid into court, and refused to exercise his discretion in favour of making a costs order for the benefit of the defendant. The defendant appealed.

HELD, ON APPEAL: It was not open to a defendant to decree unilaterally that it would not make a payment into court since CPR Pt 36 required that a defendant must make a payment into court in a money claim to have the benefit of CPR Pt 36. However, in the case of a defendant NHS trust, the form of offer was as sound as a payment in, and unless the offer was a sham or non-serious, a court should treat such an offer in the same way as a CPR Part 36 payment into court. The appeal was allowed, and the claimant was ordered to pay the defendant's cost from 21 days after the date of the letter.

[32.59]   **Trustees of Stokes Pension Fund v Western Power Distribution (South West) plc**

[2005] EWCA Civ 854

[2005] 3 All ER 775, [2005] 1 WLR 3595

In proceedings for trespass, the claimant rejected an offer of £27,000 made prior to the issue of proceedings. When proceedings were issued, the defendant did not pay the offer into court in accordance with CPR 36.10(3). Judgment was given to the claimant in the sum of £25,600. In dealing with the question of costs, the trial judge held that the defendant's offer afforded no protection because it had not been paid into court. There was no practical or good reason why the offer had not been paid into court. The judge awarded the claimant the costs of the action. The defendant appealed.

HELD, ON APPEAL: It was clear from CPR 36.3(1) that a defendant's offer should not have the automatic consequences specified unless that offer was paid into court. However, in exercising discretion under CPR 44.3(4)(c), such an offer should usually be treated as having the same effect as if it had been paid in, provided that:
  (1)   the offer was expressed in clear terms so that there was no doubt about what was being offered;
  (2)   it complied with the requirements of CPR 36.22(2);
  (3)   it was open for acceptance for at least 21 days;
  (4)   it was genuine, not a 'sham or non-serious'; and
  (5)   the defendant should be good for the money.
Those factors were satisfied in the present case, and the claimant was ordered to pay the defendant's costs after the expiry of 21 days from the date of the offer.

[32.60]   **Codent Ltd v Lyson Ltd**

[2005] EWCA Civ 1835

[2005] All ER (D) 138 (Dec)

The claimant issued proceedings against the defendant in respect of breach of contract. The defendant counterclaimed. In the course of proceedings, the defendant made a without prejudice save as to costs offer to pay £100,000, waive the counterclaim, and to meet the costs of the action. The offer was refused. The claimant was awarded a sum less than the offer to settle. When exercising discretion in relation to costs, the trial judge held that the defendant's offer was ineffective and that the defendant should have paid the offer into court. In the absence of a payment in, the claimant could not be certain that the defendant was good for the money. The trial judge therefore ordered the defendant to pay the claimant's costs of the action. The defendant appealed.

HELD, ON APPEAL: The defendant had made a clear offer to settle the claim, albeit that it had only been available for acceptance for a period of less than 21 days before the trial started. Applying *Trustees of Stokes Pension Fund v Western Power Distribution (South West) plc* (see para [32.59]), the Court of Appeal held that the offer should have been taken into account, even though it was not a CPR Part 36 offer, and made an order that the claimant should be entitled to 70% of its costs up to the date of trial, and that the defendant should be paid its costs thereafter.

(D)   WITHDRAWING OR REDUCING A CPR PART 36 OFFER OR PAYMENT

[32.61]

CPR 36.6(5)
(5)   A Part 36 payment may be withdrawn or reduced only with the permission of the court.

TEST TO BE APPLIED

[32.62]   **Marsh v Frenchay Healthcare NHS Trust**

(3 August 2001, unreported)

The claimant issued proceedings against the defendant NHS trust in respect of clinical negligence. The defendant made a CPR Part 36 payment into court on 17 November 2000. On 28 November 2000 the defendant obtained surveillance evidence which suggested that the claimant was not as disabled as he was claiming. On 4 December 2000, the claimant filed notice of acceptance. The defendant applied for a stay of proceedings, and to withdraw the whole or part of the monies paid into court.

HELD: The court should apply the overriding objective and deal with the application justly. The court heard from the medical experts and concluded that the evidence of the surveillance evidence was not such as to cast doubt upon the claimant's veracity. Accordingly, the defendant's application was dismissed.

[32.63]   **Flynn v Scougall**

[2004] EWCA Civ 873

[2004] 3 All ER 609, 148 Sol Jo LB 880

The claimant was a fire fighter who was injured when the fire engine in which he was a passenger was struck by the defendant's vehicle. Liability was admitted. The claimant's medical evidence was to the effect that the accident had accelerated the claimant's symptoms such that his retirement had been advanced by a period of five years. The defendant was given permission to obtain her own evidence. Six days before receipt of the expert's report, the defendant made a CPR Part 36 payment into court in the sum of £24,500. The report was received, and indicated that the acceleration period was no more than three months. The defendant issued an application to withdraw £14,500 of the monies paid into court. Following receipt of the defendant's application, and within 21 days of the date of the payment in, the claimant filed notice of acceptance of the sum of £24,500. The judge held that where a defendant issues an application for permission to reduce monies paid into court, an automatic stay is imposed which prevents the claimant from accepting the payment in. He further held that the content of the defendant's medical report constituted sufficient reason for the defendant's application to be granted. The claimant appealed to the Court of Appeal.

HELD, ON APPEAL: CPR 36.6(5) required that the defendant must seek the permission of the court to withdraw monies in court. CPR 36.11(1) allowed a claimant to accept a payment into court within 21 days, without the court's permission. The CPR does not provide for an automatic stay. Accordingly, it was for the court to decide whether the defendant should have permission to accept the payment in, in the knowledge that the claimant has accepted the monies in court. The claimant's acceptance was an important factor to take into account when considering whether the defendant should be granted permission to withdraw the monies. In the present case, the defendant had secured the advantage of a payment in whilst taking the risk that the medical evidence being awaited might be favourable and reduce the value of the claim. There had been no change in circumstances sufficient to demonstrate that the claimant should be deprived of his right to accept the monies. The appeal was therefore allowed.

[32.64]   Crouch v King's Healthcare NHS Trust

[2004] EWCA Civ 1332

[2005] 1 All ER 207, [2005] 1 WLR 2015, 148 Sol Jo LB 1245

Obiter: A CPR Part 36 offer can be withdrawn without the permission of the court. Accordingly, a defendant may prefer not to make a payment into court, since permission is required to withdraw monies from court.

5.   CONSEQUENCES OF NOT MAKING A CPR PART 36 OFFER OR PAYMENT IN

[32.65]   Painting v University of Oxford

[2005] EWCA Civ 161

[2005] All ER (D) 45 (Feb), [2005] PIQR 5

The claimant, whose pleaded claim exceeded £400,000, was found to have deliberately exaggerated her claim, and at trial was awarded only £23,331. The defendant had previously made a payment into court of £10,000. The trial judge held that, having beaten the payment into court, the claimant was entitled to an order that the costs of the action be paid by the defendant. The defendant appealed to the Court of Appeal.

HELD, ON APPEAL: The issue before the judge had essentially been whether the claimant had exaggerated her claim. The defendant had won that issue and should therefore be awarded costs from the date of the payment into court. In reaching its decision, the Court of Appeal took into account the fact that at no stage during the proceedings did the claimant make an offer or counter offer, nor did she make attempts to accept the payment into court. The Court of Appeal held that a claimant who had made no attempt to negotiate should expect the court to take that failure into account when determining costs.

[32.66]   Daniels v The Commissioner of Police for the Metropolis

[2005] EWCA Civ 1312

[2005] All ER (D) 225 (Oct)

The claimant, a serving police officer, was injured and issued proceedings against the defendant. The defendant denied negligence and alleged that the accident was caused or contributed to by the claimant's own negligence. At trial, the judge found for the defendant and dismissed the claimant's claim. The defendant applied for the costs of the action. The claimant argued that the defendant had rejected a CPR Part 36 offer to settle in the sum of £7,500, and two subsequent offers of £5,000 and £4,000. The defendant had made no offer and no payment into court. In those circumstances, the defendant had acted unreasonably and should be deprived of costs. The judge rejected the claimant's arguments. The claimant appealed to the Court of Appeal.

HELD, ON APPEAL: The mere fact that a successful defendant has refused to accept offers to settle is not of itself a reason for departing from the usual rule that the successful party should be awarded costs. A defendant that chooses to defend what is reasonably believed to be a claim without foundation should not be penalised.

6.   DEDUCTION OF BENEFITS

[32.67]

CPR 36.23 – DEDUCTION OF BENEFITS
(1)   This rule applies where a payment to a claimant following acceptance of a Part 36 offer or Part 36 payment into court would be a compensation payment as defined in section 1 of the Social Security (Recovery of Benefits) Act 1997.
(2)   A defendant to a money claim may make an offer to settle the claim which will have the consequences set out in this Part, without making a Part 36 payment if–
  (a)   at the time he makes the offer he has applied for, but not received, a certificate of recoverable benefit; and
  (b)   he makes a Part 36 payment not more than 7 days after he receives the certificate.
(3)   A Part 36 payment notice must state–
  (a)   the amount of gross compensation;
  (b)   the name and amount of any benefit by which that gross amount is reduced in accordance with section 8 and Schedule 2 to the 1997 Act; and
  (c)   that the sum paid in is the net amount after deduction of the amount of benefit.
(4)   For the purposes of rule 36.20(1)(a), a claimant fails to better a Part 36 payment if he fails to obtain judgment for more than the gross sum specified in the Part 36 payment notice.
(4A)   For the purposes of rule 36.20(1)(c), where the court is determining whether the claimant has failed to obtain a judgment which is more advantageous than the Part 36 offer made under rule 36.2A, the amount of any lump sum paid into court which it takes into account is to be the amount of the gross sum specified in the Part 36 payment notice.
(5)   Where–
  (a)   a Part 36 payment has been made; and
  (b)   application is made for the money remaining in court to be paid out,

the court may treat the money in court as being reduced by a sum equivalent to any further recoverable benefits paid to the claimant since the date of payment into court and may direct payment out accordingly.

(A)   GUIDANCE ON HOW TO DEDUCT BENEFITS

[32.68]   Williams v Devon County Council
[2003] EWCA Civ 365

[2003] All ER (D) 255 (Mar), [2003] PIQR Q68

The claimant issued proceedings in respect of an injury sustained during the course of her employment with the defendant. The defendant argued that there should be a deduction in respect of contributory negligence and that the claim for loss of earnings should be limited to a shorter period than the period over which the claimant had received earnings related benefits. The defendant made a CPR Part 36 payment into court of £25,669.91, which comprised £10,000 net and a sum equivalent to recoverable benefits of £15,669.91, the total sum set out in the certificate of recoverable benefits.

The court held that the defendant was primarily responsible for the accident, but that the claimant was one third to blame. The judge assessed damages at £34,587.58, and reduced these by one third to £23,058.39 to reflect the claimant's contributory negligence. He further held that the claimant had failed to do better than the CPR Part 36 payment in and awarded the costs from the date of the payment in to the defendant. The claimant appealed.

HELD, ON APPEAL: The Court of Appeal allowed the claimant's appeal in relation to contributory negligence, and awarded the claimant the full amount of £34,587.58, and therefore the CPR Part 36 payment had no relevance. However, the court then gave guidance in relation to the appropriate way to deal with recoverable benefits in a case where an award for damages was reduced for contributory negligence.

The first exercise is to reduce each head of damage awarded by the appropriate percentage deduction for contributory negligence. The second exercise is to reduce those heads of loss against which recoverable benefits can be deducted by a sum equivalent to the recoverable benefits shown on the certificate. If the value of recoverable benefits exceeds the value of the head of loss the defendant must still repay the entirety of the recoverable benefits. Damages for general damages are 'ring fenced'.

The consequence of this exercise in the present case meant that the claimant recovered £15,783.91 rather than the £10,000 paid into court, but that she failed to do better than the gross payment in of £25,669.91.

CPR 36.23(4) provides that 'a claimant fails to better a CPR 36 payment if he fails to obtain judgment for more than the gross sum specified in the CPR 36 payment notice'.

However, the Court of Appeal further held that the defendant had failed to comply with CPR 36.23(3)(b) which requires that the payment notice should state 'the name and amount of any benefit by which [the] gross amount is reduced in accordance with section 8 and Schedule 2 to the [Social Security (Recovery of Benefits) Act 1997]'. The defendant had argued that there should be a deduction in respect of contributory negligence and that the claim for loss of earnings should be limited to a shorter period than the period over which earnings related benefits had been awarded. Accordingly, the defendant should not have deducted all benefits, but only the appropriate proportion of benefits after reducing them in accordance with their arguments. Having failed to undertake this exercise, the notice of payment in was defective and ineffective.

7.   CPR PART 36 OFFERS NOT TO BE DISCLOSED TO TRIAL JUDGE

[32.69]

CPR 36.19 – RESTRICTION ON DISCLOSURE OF A PART 36 OFFER OR A PART 36 PAYMENT
(1)   A Part 36 offer will be treated as 'without prejudice except as to costs'.
(2)   The fact that a Part 36 payment has been made shall not be communicated to the trial judge until all questions of liability and the amount of money to be awarded have been decided.
(3)   Paragraph (2) does not apply–
   (a)   where the defence of tender before claim has been raised;
   (b)   where the proceedings have been stayed under rule 36.15 following acceptance of a Part 36 offer or Part 36 payment; or
   (c)   where–
      (i)   the issue of liability has been determined before any assessment of the money claimed; and
      (ii)   the fact that there has or has not been a Part 36 payment may be relevant to the question of the costs of the issue of liability.

[32.70]

CPR 52.12 – NON-DISCLOSURE OF PART 36 OFFERS AND PAYMENTS
(1)   The fact that a Part 36 offer or Part 36 payment has been made must not be disclosed to any judge of the appeal court who is to hear or determine–
   (a)   an application for permission to appeal; or
   (b)   an appeal,
until all questions (other than costs) have been determined.
(2)   Paragraph (1) does not apply if the Part 36 offer or Part 36 payment is relevant to the substance of the appeal.
(3)   Paragraph (1) does not prevent disclosure in any application in the appeal proceedings if disclosure of the fact that a Part 36 offer or Part 36 payment has been made is properly relevant to the matter to be decided.

(A)   CPR PART 36 OFFERS IN RELATION TO THE TRIAL OF A PRELIMINARY ISSUE

[32.71]   HSS Hire Services Group plc v BMB Builders Merchants Ltd
[2005] EWCA Civ 626
[2005] 3 All ER 486, [2005] 1 WLR 3158

HELD, ON APPEAL: If a CPR Part 36 offer or payment has been made in relation to the trial of a preliminary issue, the question of costs should be adjourned until the claim has been resolved, at which time the CPR Part 36 offer or payment can be brought to the attention of the court, so that the court can consider the issue of costs fully informed of all issues which might impinge upon the exercise of discretion.

(B)   TEST TO BE APPLIED IF OFFER DISCLOSED TO TRIAL JUDGE

[32.72]   **Garratt v Saxby**

[2004] EWCA Civ 341

[2004] All ER (D) 302 (Feb), [2004] 1 WLR 2152

The claimant, who was riding a bicycle, collided with the defendant's vehicle. Proceedings were issued. At first instance, the claim was dismissed. The claimant appealed. Amongst the papers presented to the judge on appeal was a transcript of the original judgment, which included a reference to a CPR Part 36 offer made by the defendant. The judge hearing the appeal said that she had read the papers but made no reference to the CPR Part 36 offer. Following the appeal, judgment was given against the defendant but subject to contributory negligence of 40%. The defendant appealed, arguing that the requirements of CPR 36.19(2) were mandatory.

HELD, ON APPEAL: The judge was unaware of the offer. However, even if she had been aware, that in itself was not sufficient to render the judgment given invalid. In these circumstances, the question a judge must ask himself is whether, having had sight of a CPR Part 36 offer, there could still be a fair trial. In the present case, which was a fast track case, there would have been delay and additional costs incurred, and accordingly, the correct exercise of discretion would have required that the judge proceeded with the appeal.

8.   CPR PART 36 OFFERS AND APPEALS

[32.73]   **Purdue v Devon Fire and Rescue Service**

[2002] EWCA Civ 1538

[2002] All ER (D) 125 (Oct)

The claimant was involved in a road traffic accident with the defendant's fire engine which occurred at a junction controlled by traffic lights. On 8 January 2001 the claimant made an offer under the terms of CPR Part 36 to settle the issue of liability on a 75/25 basis in favour of the claimant. The defendant rejected the offer. On 26 October 2001, the trial judge gave judgment to the claimant without deduction for contributory negligence. The defendant appealed. On 18 December 2001 the defendant made a CPR Part 36 offer to settle the issue of liability on a 60/40 basis in the claimant's favour.

HELD, ON APPEAL: The appropriate deduction for contributory negligence was 20%. The defendant's argument that the claimant's CPR Part 36 offer only applied to the original proceedings and not the appeal, and that accordingly only the defendant's CPR Part 36 offer should be considered, was rejected by the Court of Appeal. The court held that the consequence of a CPR Part 36 offer carried through to the eventual result, and if there was an appeal, through to the eventual result of the appeal. Accordingly, the claimant was awarded the costs of the action, including the appeal, on an indemnity basis.

[32.74] **Utaniko Ltd v P&O Nedlloyd BV**

[2003] EWCA Civ 174

[2003] All ER (D) 249 (Feb), [2003] 1 Lloyd's Rep 265n

In the course of proceedings the claimant made a CPR Part 36 offer to settle its claim on a 75/25 basis in its favour. At trial the claimant succeeded in full, and the claimant was awarded costs, on an indemnity basis from the date of the CPR Part 36 offer. The defendant appealed, but the appeal was rejected, and the claimant applied for the costs of the appeal to be paid on an indemnity basis.

HELD, ON APPEAL: The words 'at trial' in CPR 36.21(1) could legitimately be interpreted so that they referred either to a CPR Part 36 offer made more than 21 days before trial, or to a CPR Part 36 offer made more than 21 days before an appeal. They could not be interpreted as referring to both trial and appeal.

Per Brooke LJ: ... there is no hint that the rule makers ever considered that a claimant might make a portmanteau CPR 36 offer which would provide him with protection ... both at first instance and on a subsequent appeal. If he wants to protect himself as to the costs of an appeal, he must make a further offer in the appeal proceedings.

Note—Purdue v Devon Fire & Rescue (see para [32.73]) does not seem to have been cited in *P&O Nedlloyd*, and indeed does not seem to have been cited in any other of the cases in relation to this point.

[32.75] **KR v Bryn Alyn Community (Holdings) Ltd (in liq)**

[2003] EWCA Civ 85

[2003] QB 1441, [2004] 2 All ER 716, [2003] 3 WLR 107

The fourteen adult claimants in a consolidated action had all been in care as children in residential homes operated by the first defendant, and had been the subject of abuse at the hands of the first defendant's employees. The first defendant was in liquidation and the second defendant as insurers joined proceedings and ran the defence. Eight of the claimants made CPR Part 36 offers.

At trial, the judge held that the claims were statute barred but that discretion under s 33 of the Limitation Act 1980 should be exercised to allow the claims to proceed. He further held that liability was established. The trial judge then made awards of damages such that four of the eight who had made CPR Part 36 offers had beaten those offers. He awarded penalty interest on damages (CPR 36.21(2)), but did not make any order for indemnity costs or interest on costs (CPR 36.21(3)).

The second defendant put in an appeal ('the first appeal') in respect of the judge's findings in relation to limitation, and the claimants put in a respondents' notice in relation to the award of damages. The appeal was dismissed but the cross appeal was allowed. As a result, all claimants had their damages awards increased, so that a further three of the eight claimants found that they had beaten their CRP Part 36 offers.

In the meantime, the second defendant had put in a separate appeal notice ('the second appeal') in respect of the trial judge's ruling in respect of the four claimants who had been awarded penalty interest on damages, and in turn those claimant put in a respondents' notice in respect of the trial judge's ruling in respect of indemnity costs and interest. The issue then arose as to whether the further three claimants, who had only succeeded on their CPR Part 36 offers following the first appeal, should have the benefit of the Court of Appeal's ruling in the second appeal, even though they were not parties to the second appeal.

HELD: The further three claimants had succeeded in beating their CPR Part 36 offers following the appeal, and should be entitled to be made parties to the second appeal to have the benefit of any order made by the Court of Appeal under CPR 36.21(2) or CPR 36.21(3).

[32.76]   Hawley v Luminar Leisure plc

[2006] EWCA Civ 30

[2006] All ER (D) 12 (Feb)

The first defendant, who owned and operated a nightclub, contracted with the second defendant for the provision of security services, and in pursuance of that contract the second defendant supplied its employee, a doorman. The claimant sustained injury when he was punched in the face by the doorman outside the club. He issued proceedings against the first and second defendants, and the third defendant, the second defendant's insurers.

At trial, the judge held that the claimant was entitled to recover damages from the first defendant, as temporary employer of the doorman, but that the first defendant was not entitled to a contribution from the second defendant. The judge also held that the claimant's injury was covered by the policy of insurance issued by the third defendant, and that a default judgment entered against the second defendant should stand.

The first defendant appealed, and the third defendant cross-appealed. Both appeal and cross-appeal were listed to be heard on 16 and 17 November 2005. On 10 October 2005, the Court of Appeal delivered judgment in a different case which the first defendant considered might effect the outcome of the appeal. On 9 November 2005 the third defendant made a CPR Part 36 offer on the basis that the first and third defendants should each accept 50% of the claimant's claim. On 14 November 2005 the first defendant made a CPR Part 36 offer that liability should be divided on a one third/two thirds basis in their favour. The third defendant rejected the first defendant's offer, and withdrew its offer.

After the appeal was heard, judgment was reserved, and the first defendant wrote to accept the third defendant's CPR Part 36 offer of 50/50.

HELD, ON APPEAL: Following *P&O Nedlloyd BV* (at para [32.74]), the words 'at trial' in CPR 36.21 included 'on the hearing of an appeal'. CPR Pt 36 did not exclude the general law of contract so an unaccepted offer could be withdrawn. On the facts, the third defendant's offer was withdrawn and was not available for acceptance. Even if it had not been withdrawn, it carried an implied term that it could not be available for acceptance after the hearing ended and before judgment was handed down.

CHAPTER 33

Trial

1.   PRELIMINARY MATTERS

(A)   LISTING

[33.1]   **Matthews v Tarmac Bricks and Tiles Ltd**

[1999] All ER (D) 692, (1999) 54 BMLR 139, 143 Sol Jo LB 196, (1999) Times,
1 July, CA

Following the introduction of the Civil Procedure Rules (CPR) it was essential that
parties co-operate with each other and the court and fix cases for hearing as early
as possible if they wanted them to be heard in accordance with dates which met
their convenience.

Where agreement was not possible and the court had to fix a hearing date, the
parties had to ensure that all relevant material, including the reason for the
unavailability of witnesses on particular dates, was made available to the court.

Doctors who held themselves out as practising in the medico-legal field had to be prepared, so far as was practical, to arrange their affairs to meet the commitments of the court.

(B)   TRIAL TO BE IN PUBLIC

[33.2]

CPR 39.2 – GENERAL RULE – HEARINGS TO BE IN PUBLIC
    (1)   The general rule is that a hearing is to be in public.
    (2)   The requirement for a hearing to be in public does not require the court to make special arrangements for accommodating members of the public.
    (3)   A hearing, or any part of it, may be in private if–
        (a)   publicity would defeat the object of the hearing;
        (b)   it involves matters relating to national security;
        (c)   it involves confidential information (including information relating to personal financial matters) and publicity would damage that confidentiality;
        (d)   a private hearing is necessary to protect the interests of any child or patient;
        (e)   it is a hearing of an application made without notice and it would be unjust to any respondent for there to be a public hearing;
        (f)   it involves uncontentious matters arising in the administration of trusts or in the administration of a deceased person's estate; or
        (g)   the court considers this to be necessary, in the interests of justice.
    (4)   The court may order that the identity of any party or witness must not be disclosed if it considers non-disclosure necessary in order to protect the interests of that party or witness.

(C)   CONSEQUENCES OF FAILURE TO ATTEND TRIAL

[33.3]

CPR 39.3 – FAILURE TO ATTEND TRIAL
    (1)   The court may proceed with a trial in the absence of a party but -
        (a)   if no party attends the trial, it may strike out the whole of the proceedings;
        (b)   if the claimant does not attend, it may strike out his claim and any defence to counterclaim; and
        (c)   if a defendant does not attend, it may strike out his defence or counterclaim (or both).
    (2)   Where the court strikes out proceedings, or any part of them, under this rule, it may subsequently restore the proceedings, or that part.
    (3)   Where a party does not attend and the court gives judgment or makes an order against him, the party who failed to attend may apply for the judgment or order to be set aside.
    (4)   An application under paragraph (2) or paragraph (3) must be supported by evidence.
    (5)   Where an application is made under paragraph (2) or (3) by a party who failed to attend the trial, the court may grant the application only if the applicant–

(a)   acted promptly when he found out that the court had exercised its power to strike out or to enter judgment or make an order against him;

(b)   had a good reason for not attending the trial; and

(c)   has a reasonable prospect of success at the trial.

APPLICANT MUST SHOW A 'GOOD REASON' FOR FAILING TO ATTEND

[33.4]   **Southwark London Borough Council v Joseph**

(2000) Legal Action (March), CA

If an applicant fails to explain his or her non-attendance at trial, or there is no evidence in support of the reason for non-attendance, the application must fail.

APPLICANT MUST ESTABLISH THAT HE HAD A 'REASONABLE PROSPECT OF SUCCESS' AT TRIAL

[33.5]   **Regency Rolls Ltd v Carnall**

[2000] All ER (D) 1417 (Oct), CA

The claimant company and a director of the company issued proceedings against the defendant director to obtain an injunction and damages in respect of actions taken by the defendant in respect of the company's property. The defendant failed to attend the trial and judgment was entered for the claimants. The defendant applied pursuant to CPR 39.3 to set the judgment aside. The court held that the defendant had no reasonable prospect of success and refused to set the judgment aside. The defendant appealed.

HELD, ON APPEAL: There was no reasonable prospect of success and the appeal was refused. All three requirements of CPR 39.3(5) must be met, although on the facts of the present case, the defendant had failed to satisfy the court in relation to reasonable prospect of success. When seeking to establish whether the application had satisfied the requirement that it should be made promptly, the court should consider whether the applicant had acted with all reasonable speed in the circumstances.

[33.6]   **Barclays Bank plc v Ellis and Another**

[2001] CP Rep 50, (2000) Times, 24 October

The claimant bank brought proceedings in respect of the defendants' default on a loan. The defendants failed to attend court and judgment was entered for the claimant. The defendants attended court later the same day, having formed the impression that the trial was not due to start until midday as a result of misreading a letter from the claimant's solicitors. The defendants' application to set the judgment aside pursuant to CPR 39.3(5) was refused. They appealed.

HELD, ON APPEAL: The defendants could not satisfy the court that there was a reasonable prospect of defending the claim and the judge had been right not to allow the defendants' application.

[33.7]   **Boothe-Chambers v Dymond**

[2001] EWCA Civ 75

HELD, ON APPEAL: In considering whether to strike out a claim, it was correct for the judge to take into account whether there had been good reasons for the claimant failing to attend an earlier hearing at which his claim had been initially struck out, whether there was a reasonable prospect of success, and whether it was proper to grant an extension of time in any event. The judge had considered all of the circumstances in the case and there was no basis for holding that his discretion had been exercised incorrectly.

[33.8]   **Hackney London Borough Council v Driscoll**

[2003] EWCA Civ 1037

[2003] 4 All ER 1205, [2003] 1 WLR 2602

The local authority claimant sought to repossess a property when the defendant fell into arrears on the mortgage. Notice of the trial date was sent to the property which was the subject of the mortgage, but the defendant did not receive it because he had left. He did not attend the trial, and judgment was entered for the claimant. The defendant applied to have the order set aside, but his application was refused.

HELD, ON APPEAL: The defendant had been aware of the proceedings. He had failed to apply promptly and could not establish that he had reasonable prospects of success. His appeal was dismissed.

[33.9]   **Estate Acquisitions and Development Ltd v Wiltshire**

[2006] EWCA Civ 533

The defendant failed to attend trial and the trial judge gave judgment to the claimant. The defendant applied under CPR 39.3(3) to set aside the order but the circuit judge refused. The defendant appealed to the Court of Appeal.

HELD, ON APPEAL: The fact that the defendant had not made arrangements for correspondence to be forwarded from the deemed address for service to a current address was not sufficient to establish whether there had been a 'good reason' for the failure to attend. The court should apply the overriding objective when applying CPR 39.3(5)(b).

ATTENDANCE AT TRIAL THROUGH LEGAL REPRESENTATIVE

[33.10]   **Rouse v Freeman**

(2002) Times, 8 January

The claimant failed to attend trial, although he was represented by his lawyers. The court struck out the claimant's claim. The claimant appealed.

HELD: There were a great many occasions when the personal attendance of a party was irrelevant or unnecessary. The claimant had attended the trial through his legal representatives, and therefore the claim would be reinstated.

[33.11]

CPR 39.6 – REPRESENTATION AT TRIAL OF COMPANIES OR
OTHER CORPORATIONS

A company or other corporation may be represented at trial by an employee if–
(a)   the employee has been authorised by the company or corporation to
appear at trial on its behalf; and
(b)   the court gives permission.

[33.12]   Watson v Bluemoor Properties Ltd
[2002] EWCA Civ 1875
[2002] All ER (D) 117 (Dec)

The claimant purchased a plot of land owned by the defendant company which had
the benefit of planning permission for a house which was subject to a requirement
that an adjacent bungalow be demolished. A house was built on the land, but the
defendant failed to demolish the bungalow, and the claimant issued proceedings.
During the course of proceedings, the defendant company was represented by a
director of the company. By the time the case came to trial, the director had been
made bankrupt and was therefore disqualified from acting as a director of the
company. The judge held that the defendant was not represented and entered
judgment for the claimant. The defendant appealed.

HELD, ON APPEAL: The CPR introduced a greater measure of flexibility as to how
companies could choose to be represented. They no longer had to be represented
by directors, but could be represented by an authorised employee, subject to the
permission of the court. The court had entered judgment without taking into
account the provisions of CPR 39.3(5). On a proper analysis of the three
requirements of that rule, the judgment should be set aside.

2.   CONDUCT OF THE TRIAL

[33.13]

CPR 39.4 – TIMETABLE FOR TRIAL

When the court sets a timetable for a trial in accordance with rule 28.6 (fixing
or confirming the trial date and giving directions – fast track) or rule 29.8
(setting a trial timetable and fixing or confirming the trial date or week –
multi-track) it will do so in consultation with the parties.

[33.14]

CPR 39.5 – TRIAL BUNDLES
(1)   Unless the court orders otherwise, the claimant must file a trial
bundle containing documents required by–
(a)   a relevant practice direction; and
(b)   any court order.
(2)   The claimant must file the trial bundle not more than 7 days and not
less than 3 days before the start of the trial.

[33.15]

CPR 32.3 – Evidence by video link or other means

The court may allow a witness to give evidence through a video link or by other means.

3. THE ROLE OF THE JUDGE

(A) JUDGE MUST BALANCE THE EVIDENCE

[33.16] **Singh v Commissioner of Police for the Metropolis**
(25 March 1999, unreported), CA

The claimant was walking along the pavement when she was knocked down by a police car which was reversing into the station yard. The claimant stated that the police car reversed back at a fast speed and knocked her over. An independent witness supported her account. The defendant's case was that the police officer in the car had seen her and formed the impression that she was waiting for him to reverse into the yard and he had done so slowly using his mirrors.

HELD, ON APPEAL: The judge was entitled to prefer the evidence of the police officer as to how the accident occurred and it was not appropriate for the Court of Appeal to go behind the judge's findings which were based on the evidence he heard at the trial.

(B) JUDGE MUST GIVE REASONS

[33.17] **Dyson v Leeds County Council**
(22 November 1999, unreported), CA

Matter remitted to county court for re-hearing as the original trial judge had failed to give reasons for preferring the defendant's expert evidence to that of the claimant.

[33.18] **Mullan v Birmingham County Council**
(1999) Times, 29 July

Under the CPR it was permissible for a trial judge exercising his wide powers of case management, to entertain a submission of no case to answer at the close of the claimant's case, without requiring the defendant to elect not to call evidence in the event that his submission failed.

(C) SUFFICIENCY OF THE EVIDENCE

[33.19] **Lainton v P&N Construction**
(22 March 1999, unreported), CA

HELD, ON APPEAL: Where a trial judge had made primary findings of fact which were not supported by the evidence and which differed from the pleaded case it was in the interests of justice to order a retrial even though this was not sought by either party.

[33.20]   McRae v Chase International Express Ltd

[2003] EWCA Civ 505

[2003] All ER (D) 219 (Mar), [2004] PIQR 21

The claimant sustained injuries in a road traffic accident. At trial he recovered damages of £46,175.15 from the defendant. The defendant appealed to the Court of Appeal.

HELD, ON APPEAL, per Newman J: 'The lack of concern evident from the judgment in this case from the deputy district judge about the sufficiency and quality of the evidence and the apparent alacrity with which he felt able to make assumptions gives cause for concern ... There is a need for evidence and there is a need for analysis of such evidence; then the judge can make findings of fact by drawing inferences and doing the best he can, but on the evidence which is available. Approaching a matter with a broad brush does not mean an absence of material is acceptable'.

(D)   BIAS

[33.21]   Smith v Kvaerner Cementation Foundations Ltd

[2006] EWCA Civ 242

[2006] 3 All ER 593, [2006] All ER (D) 313 (Mar), [2006] NLJR 721

In a personal injury claim, the barristers representing each of the parties came from the same chambers as the judge hearing the case. Furthermore, the judge admitted a professional connection with the defendant in that he had previously represented the defendant in respect of certain commercial matters. Having been informed of these matters, the claimant nevertheless elected to allow the judge to conduct the trial. The claimant's claim was dismissed, and he appealed on the basis that the matters raised were such as to give the appearance of bias.

HELD, ON APPEAL: The mere fact that the barristers and the judge shared the same chambers did not give rise to the appearance of bias, even if the judge was the head of those chambers, given the independence and high professional standards of the Bar. Insofar as the judge's connections with the defendant were concerned, the claimant should have been advised of the implications of that and the implications of an adjournment so that another judge could hear the case. It was not appropriate for counsel to base advice on his own personal knowledge of the integrity of the judge. Accordingly, given the advice he received, the claimant did not give his waiver freely, and the appeal would be allowed.

Appeals

1.   PRELIMINARY MATTERS

(A)   GROUNDS OF APPEAL

[34.1]

CPR 52.11 – HEARING OF APPEALS
    (1)   Every appeal will be limited to a review of the decision of the lower court unless–
        (a)   a practice direction makes different provision for a particular category of appeal; or
        (b)   the court considers that in the circumstances of an individual appeal it would be in the interests of justice to hold a re-hearing.
    (2)   Unless it orders otherwise, the appeal court will not receive–
        (a)   oral evidence; or
        (b)   evidence which was not before the lower court.
    (3)   The appeal court will allow an appeal where the decision of the lower court was–
        (a)   wrong; or

(b) unjust because of a serious procedural or other irregularity in the proceedings in the lower court.

(4) The appeal court may draw any inference of fact which it considers justified on the evidence.

(5) At the hearing of the appeal a party may not rely on a matter not contained in his appeal notice unless the appeal court gives permission.

APPEAL LIMITED TO A REVIEW OF THE DECISION OF THE LOWER COURT

[34.2]   Leeson v Quinn

(28 February 2000, unreported)

HELD, ON APPEAL: The Court of Appeal will not interfere with findings of fact unless it can be demonstrated that there was not the evidence present before the trial judge which could support his findings of fact.

[34.3]   Bank of Ireland v Robertson and Others

(21 February 2003, unreported)   Lloyd J

Summary judgment was granted to the claimant when the defendant's application for a hearing date to be adjourned was heard in the defendant's absence. The defendant was acting in person.

HELD: The purpose of an appeal hearing was to review the lower court's decision, but CPR 52.11 permitted the court to hold a rehearing if it was in the interests of justice to do so. In the instant case, a rehearing was appropriate in the circumstances.

COURT WILL NOT RECEIVE EVIDENCE WHICH WAS NOT BEFORE THE
LOWER COURT

[34.4]   Ladd v Marshall

[1954] 3 All ER 745, [1954] 1 WLR 1489, 98 Sol Jo 870, CA

Per Denning LJ: In order to justify the reception of fresh evidence [on appeal] or a new trial, three conditions must be fulfilled: first, it must be shown that the evidence could not have been obtained with reasonable diligence for use at the trial; second, the evidence must be such that, if given, it would probably have an important influence on the result of the case, although it need not be decisive; third, the evidence must be such as is presumably to be believed, or in other words, it must be apparently credible, although it need not be incontrovertible.

[34.5]   House v Haughton Bros (Worcester) Ltd

[1967] 1 All ER 39, [1967] 1 WLR 148, 110 Sol Jo 891, CA

In the claimant's claim for damages for an injury received at work, an important issue was the number of scaffold boards available to him at the time of the accident. The judge accepted the evidence of the defendant's main witness that no further boards had been provided after the accident before the factory inspector's visit; and he dismissed the action. After the trial, three men tendered statements that additional boards had been delivered in the interval before the factory inspector's visit. These men had all been present at the trial and two had given evidence for the claimant but had not been asked any question on that issue.

HELD: The claimant was entitled to have a new trial. The requirement in *Ladd v Marshall* (at para [34.4]) – that the new evidence could not have been obtained with reasonable diligence for use at the trial – could be amplified by saying that where the situation was that although a witness was called at the trial and gave evidence on other matters but had not told solicitors what he was able to say on that issue, then if the solicitors were not shown to have been negligent or dilatory in the way in which they had interviewed him, the witness's evidence 'could not have been obtained with reasonable diligence'.

[34.6]   Singh v Singh

[2002] EWCA Civ 992

[2002] All ER (D) 263 (Jun)

The defendant attempted to raise fresh arguments on appeal that were not advanced at the trial.

HELD: The defendant sought to put forward a new case and whilst it was not that this could never be done, it was not clear what the first instance judge would have decided had such a new case been put to him. The total cost of putting the new issues before the first instance judge would probably exceed the sum in issue. It was unjust to allow the appeal points to be raised at this stage.

Appeal dismissed.

APPEAL COURT MAY DRAW INFERENCES OF FACT

[34.7]   Lincoln v Hayman

[1982] 2 All ER 819, [1982] 1 WLR 488, [1982] RTR 336, CA

Two lorries collided on a country lane too narrow for them to pass without one or both going on to the grass verge. Immediately after the accident police officers and a press photographer arrived; photographs were taken and a sketch plan made showing the positions of the vehicles and of certain wheel marks on the road and the grass verges. The accounts of the accident from the two drivers differed very widely.

HELD, ON APPEAL: Where, as here, the judge's reasoning was based on inferences from plans and photographs (and not from the demeanour of the witnesses) the Court of Appeal was in as good a position as the judge to draw its own inferences from the undisputed primary material. On appeal, the trial judge's finding against the defendant was altered to reflect contributory negligence of two thirds on the part of the claimant.

BASIS FOR ALLOWING AN APPEAL

[34.8]   Burdett v Dahill

(20 March 2002, unreported)

The defendant's application for summary judgment was refused. The defendant appealed.

HELD, ON APPEAL: A decision on summary judgment should only be interfered with by an appellate court if the judge was plainly wrong in coming to the decision he came to. The district judge in the court below had not been wrong to the required degree in reaching the decision that the claimant had a realistic prospect of success.

(B) ROUTES OF APPEAL

[34.9]

Practice Direction to CPR 52, paragraph 2A

Routes of appeal

2A.1 The court or judge to which an appeal is to be made (subject to obtaining any necessary permission) is set out in the tables below:

Table 1 addresses appeals in cases other than insolvency proceedings and [certain family] cases to which Table 3 applies;

Note—Table 2, which concerns insolvency proceedings, and Table 3, which concerns certain family cases, are not reproduced here.

Table 1

This is an edited version of the table which appears in the Practice Direction to CPR 52.

Court	Track or Nature of claim	Judge who made decision	Nature of decision under appeal	Appeal Court
County	Unallocated	District judge	Any	Circuit judge in county court
County	Small	District judge	Any	Circuit judge in county court
County	Fast	District judge	Any	Circuit judge in county court
County	CPR 8 (if not allocated to any track or if simply treated as allocated to the multi-track under CPR 8.9(c))	District judge	Final	Circuit judge in county court
County	Multi-track	District judge	Any decision other than a final decision	Circuit judge in county court
County	Multi-track	District judge	Final decision	Court of Appeal
County	Unallocated	Circuit judge	Any (except final decision in specialist proceedings; see below)	Single judge of the High Court
County	Small	Circuit judge	Any (except final decision in specialist proceedings; see below)	Single judge of the High Court
County	Fast	Circuit judge	Any (except final decision in specialist proceedings; see below)	Single judge of the High Court

Court	Track or Nature of claim	Judge who made decision	Nature of decision under appeal	Appeal Court
County	Multi-track	Circuit judge	Any decision other than a final decision	Single judge of the High Court
County	CPR 8 (if not allocated to any track or if simply treated as allocated to the multi-track under CPR 8.9(c))	Circuit judge	Final	Single judge of the High Court
County	Multi-track	Circuit judge	Final decision	Court of Appeal
High Court	Multi-track	Master or district judge sitting in a District Registry	Any decision other than a final decision	Single judge of the High Court
High Court	CPR 8 (if not allocated to any track or if simply treated as allocated to the multi-track under CPR 8.9(c))	Master or district judge sitting in a District Registry	Final	Single judge of the High Court
High Court	Multi-track	Master or district judge sitting in a District Registry	Final	Court of Appeal
High Court	Any	High Court judge	Any	Court of Appeal

Meaning of 'final decision'

2A.2   A 'final decision' is a decision of a court that would finally determine (subject to any possible appeal or detailed assessment of costs) the entire proceedings whichever way the court decided the issues before it. Decisions made on an application to strike-out or for summary judgment are not final decisions for the purpose of determining the appropriate route of appeal (Art. 1 Access to Justice Act 1999 (Destination of Appeals) Order 2000). Accordingly:
1.   a case management decision;
2.   the grant or refusal of interim relief;
3.   a summary judgment;
4.   a striking out,
are not final decisions for this purpose.

2A.3   A decision of a court is to be treated as a final decision for routes of appeal purposes where it:
   (1)   is made at the conclusion of part of a hearing or trial which has been split into parts; and

(2)   would, if it had been made at the conclusion of that hearing or trial, have been a final decision.

Accordingly, a judgment on liability at the end of a split trial is a 'final decision' for this purpose and the judgment at the conclusion of the assessment of damages following a judgment on liability is also a 'final decision' for this purpose.

2A.4   An order made:

(1)   on a summary or detailed assessment of costs; or

(2)   on an application to enforce a final decision,

is not a final decision and any appeal from such an order will follow the routes of appeal set out in the tables above.

(C)   PERMISSION

[34.10]

CPR 52.3 – PERMISSION

(1)   An appellant or respondent requires permission to appeal–

(a)   where the appeal is from a decision of a judge in a county court or the High Court […]; or

(b)   as provided by the relevant practice direction.

(2)   An application for permission to appeal may be made–

(a)   to the lower court at the hearing at which the decision to be appealed was made; or

(b)   to the appeal court in an appeal notice.

(3)   Where the lower court refuses an application for permission to appeal, a further application for permission to appeal may be made to the appeal court.

(4)   Where the appeal court, without a hearing, refuses permission to appeal, the person seeking permission may request the decision to be reconsidered at a hearing.

(5)   A request under paragraph (4) must be filed within 7 days after service of the notice that permission has been refused.

(6)   Permission to appeal may be given only where–

(a)   the court considers that the appeal would have a real prospect of success; or

(b)   there is some other compelling reason why the appeal should be heard.

(7)   An order giving permission may–

(a)   limit the issues to be heard; and

(b)   be made subject to conditions.

[34.11]

Practice Direction to CPR 52 – Permission to appeal (paragraphs 4.1–4.11)

Permission to appeal

4.1   Rule 52.3 sets out the circumstances when permission to appeal is required.

4.2   The permission of –

(1)   the Court of Appeal; or

(2)   where the lower court's rules allow, the lower court,

is required for all appeals to the Court of Appeal except as provided for by statute or rule 52.3.

4.3   Where the lower court is not required to give permission to appeal, it may give an indication of its opinion as to whether permission should be given.

4.3A
  (1)   This paragraph applies where a party applies for permission to appeal against a decision at the hearing at which the decision was made.
  (2)   Where this paragraph applies, the judge making the decision shall state
        –
      (a)   whether or not the judgment or order is final;
      (b)   whether an appeal lies from the judgment or order and, if so, to which appeal court;
      (c)   whether the court gives permission to appeal; and
      (d)   if not, the appropriate appeal court to which any further application for permission may be made.

4.3B   Where no application for permission to appeal has been made in accordance with rule 52.3(2)(a) but a party requests further time to make such an application, the court may adjourn the hearing to give that party the opportunity to do so.

Appeals from case management decisions

4.4   Case management decisions include decisions made under rule 3.1(2) and decisions about:
  (1)   disclosure;
  (2)   filing of witness statements or experts reports;
  (3)   directions about the timetable of the claim;
  (4)   adding a party to a claim;
  (5)   security for costs.

4.5   Where the application is for permission to appeal from a case management decision, the court dealing with the application may take into account whether:
  (1)   the issue is of sufficient significance to justify the costs of an appeal;
  (2)   the procedural consequences of an appeal (e.g. loss of trial date) outweigh the significance of the case management decision;
  (3)   it would be more convenient to determine the issue at or after trial.

Court to which permission to appeal application should be made

4.6   An application for permission should be made orally at the hearing at which the decision to be appealed against is made.

4.7   Where:
  (a)   no application for permission to appeal is made at the hearing; or
  (b)   the lower court refuses permission to appeal,
an application for permission to appeal may be made to the appeal court in accordance with rules 52.3(2) and (3).

4.8   There is no appeal from a decision of the appeal court to allow or refuse permission to appeal to that court (although where the appeal court, without a hearing, refuses permission to appeal, the person seeking permission may request that decision to be reconsidered at a hearing). See section 54(4) of the Access to Justice Act and rule 52.3(2), (3), (4) and (5).

Consideration of permission without a hearing

4.11 Applications for permission to appeal may be considered by the appeal court without a hearing.

[34.12] **Slot v Isaac**

[2002] EWCA Civ 481

[2002] All ER (D) 197 (Apr)

Where the High Court determines, on an application for permission to appeal, that it does not have jurisdiction, the application should be rejected. Such rejection is an administrative act and as such there is no requirement for the court to give reasons.

[34.13]

Practice Direction to CPR 52, paragraphs 4.12–4.14

4.12 If permission is granted without a hearing the parties will be notified of that decision and the procedure in paragraphs 6.1 to 6.6 will then apply.

4.13 If permission is refused without a hearing the parties will be notified of that decision with the reasons for it. The decision is subject to the appellant's right to have it reconsidered at an oral hearing. This may be before the same judge.

4.14 A request for the decision to be reconsidered at an oral hearing must be filed at the appeal court within 7 days after service of the notice that permission has been refused. A copy of the request must be served by the appellant on the respondent at the same time.

[34.14] **Hansen v Great Future International Ltd**

[2003] EWCA Civ 1646

HELD, ON APPEAL: Under the Practice Direction to CPR Pt 52, paragraph 4.14, a request for reconsideration of a refusal to appeal made by a single judge without a hearing must be filed within seven days. By analogy the time limit for reconsideration of a decision was the same. Although the court would have power to extend time in justifiable circumstances, the case in hand did not warrant this.

[34.15]

Practice Direction to CPR 52, paragraphs 4.14A–4.21

Permission hearing

4.14A
   (1) This paragraph applies where an appellant, who is represented, makes a request for a decision to be reconsidered at an oral hearing.
   (2) The appellant's advocate must, at least 4 days before the hearing, in a brief written statement –
      (a) inform the court and the respondent of the points which he proposes to raise at the hearing;
      (b) set out his reasons why permission should be granted notwithstanding the reasons given for the refusal of permission; and
      (c) confirm, where applicable, that the requirements of paragraph 4.17 have been complied with (appellant in receipt of services funded by the Legal Services Commission).

4.15   Notice of a permission hearing will be given to the respondent but he is not required to attend unless the court requests him to do so.

4.16   If the court requests the respondent's attendance at the permission hearing, the appellant must supply the respondent with a copy of the appeal bundle (see paragraph 5.6A) within 7 days of being notified of the request, or such other period as the court may direct. The costs of providing that bundle shall be borne by the appellant initially, but will form part of the costs of the permission application.

Appellants in receipt of services funded by the Legal Services Commission applying for permission to appeal

4.17   Where the appellant is in receipt of services funded by the Legal Services Commission (or legally aided) and permission to appeal has been refused by the appeal court without a hearing, the appellant must send a copy of the reasons the appeal court gave for refusing permission to the relevant office of the Legal Services Commission as soon as it has been received from the court. The court will require confirmation that this has been done if a hearing is requested to re-consider the question of permission.

Limited permission

4.18   Where a court under rule 52.3(7) gives permission to appeal on some issues only, it will –
   (1)   refuse permission on any remaining issues; or
   (2)   reserve the question of permission to appeal on any remaining issues to the court hearing the appeal.

4.19   If the court reserves the question of permission under paragraph 4.18(2), the appellant must, within 14 days after service of the court's order, inform the appeal court and the respondent in writing whether he intends to pursue the reserved issues. If the appellant does intend to pursue the reserved issues, the parties must include in any time estimate for the appeal hearing, their time estimate for the reserved issues.

4.20   If the appeal court refuses permission to appeal on the remaining issues without a hearing and the applicant wishes to have that decision reconsidered at an oral hearing, the time limit in rule 52.3(5) shall apply. Any application for an extension of this time limit should be made promptly. The court hearing the appeal on the issues for which permission has been granted will not normally grant, at the appeal hearing, an application to extend the time limit in rule 52.3(5) for the remaining issues.

4.21   If the appeal court refuses permission to appeal on remaining issues at or after an oral hearing, the application for permission to appeal on those issues cannot be renewed at the appeal hearing. See section 54(4) of the Access to Justice Act 1999.

2. THE APPELLANT

(A) THE APPELLANT'S NOTICE

[34.16]

CPR 52.4 – APPELLANT'S NOTICE
(1) Where the appellant seeks permission from the appeal court it must be requested in the appellant's notice.
(2) The appellant must file the appellant's notice at the appeal court within–
    (a) such period as may be directed by the lower court (which may be longer or shorter than the period referred to in sub-paragraph (b)); or
    (b) where the court makes no such direction, 21 days after the date of the decision of the lower court that the appellant wishes to appeal.
(3) Unless the appeal court orders otherwise, an appellant's notice must be served on each respondent–
    (a) as soon as practicable; and
    (b) in any event not later than 7 days,
after it is filed.

[34.17]

Practice Direction to CPR 52 – Filing and service of appellant's notice

5.19 Rule 52.4 sets out the procedure and time limits for filing and serving an appellant's notice. The appellant must file the appellant's notice at the appeal court within such period as may be directed by the lower court which should not normally exceed 28 days or, where the lower court directs no such period, within 21 days of the date of the decision that the appellant wishes to appeal.

5.20 Where the lower court judge announces his decision and reserves the reasons for his judgment or order until a later date, he should, in the exercise of powers under rule 52.4(2)(a), fix a period for filing the appellant's notice at the appeal court that takes this into account.

5.21
    (1) Except where the appeal court orders otherwise a sealed copy of the appellant's notice, including any skeleton arguments must be served on all respondents in accordance with the timetable prescribed by rule 52.4(3) except where this requirement is modified by paragraph 5.9(2) in which case the skeleton argument should be served as soon as it is filed.
    (2) The appellant must, as soon as practicable, file a certificate of service of the documents referred to in paragraph (1).

5.22 Unless the court otherwise directs a respondent need not take any action when served with an appellant's notice until such time as notification is given to him that permission to appeal has been given.

5.23   The court may dispense with the requirement for service of the notice on a respondent. Any application notice seeking an order under rule 6.9 to dispense with service should set out the reasons relied on and be verified by a statement of truth.

5.24
  (1) Where the appellant is applying for permission to appeal in his appellant's notice, he must serve on the respondents his appellant's notice and skeleton argument (but not the appeal bundle), unless the appeal court directs otherwise.
  (2) Where permission to appeal–
    (a) has been given by the lower court; or
    (b) is not required,
the appellant must serve the appeal bundle on the respondents with the appellant's notice.

[34.18]

Practice Direction to CPR 52 – Extension of time for filing appellant's notice

5.2   Where the time for filing an appellant's notice has expired, the appellant must–
  (a) file the appellant's notice; and
  (b) include in that appellant's notice an application for an extension of time.
The appellant's notice should state the reason for the delay and the steps taken prior to the application being made.

5.3   Where the appellant's notice includes an application for an extension of time and permission to appeal has been given or is not required the respondent has the right to be heard on that application. He must be served with a copy of the appeal bundle (see paragraph 5.6A). However, a respondent who unreasonably opposes an extension of time runs the risk of being ordered to pay the appellant's costs of that application.

5.4   If an extension of time is given following such an application the procedure at paragraphs 6.1 to 6.6 applies.

[34.19]   Simms v Oakes
[2002] EWCA Civ 08
[2002] All ER (D) 37 (Jan), CA

HELD, ON APPEAL: Where the Civil Appeals Office had no record of receiving a notice of appeal on time but there was evidence that it had been served on the other parties and evidence of it being sent to the Appeals Office, the just order was to declare that the appeal had been lodged on time.

[34.20]   Smith and Hutchinson v Brough
[2005] EWCA Civ 261

On 4 September 2001, judgment was given against the defendants in a boundary dispute. Between October 2001 and June 2002, the defendants sought to obtain new lay witness evidence in relation to the boundary. Thereafter, in April 2003 they obtained evidence from a surveyor. Between April 2003 and November 2004 the defendants were in discussion with the surveyor. On 6 December 2004, an application was made which sought, *inter alia*, an extension of time within which to apply for permission to appeal. It was submitted on behalf of the defendants that the court should have regard to the factors set out at CPR 3.9.

HELD: The defendants had wrongly conflated the need to obtain new evidence with the need to file a notice of appeal within the requisite time period. The delay in filing the application was 'unprecedented'. Furthermore, there was a public interest in the closure of litigation.

Per Brooke LJ: ... it is a fundamental principle of our common law that the outcome of litigation should be final ... the law exceptionally allows appeals out of time ... [in] ... rare and limited cases ... In interpreting CPR 3.9 in any case where an extension of time for appealing in excess of say two months has been sought, the court will bear in mind [these] matters ... in determining where the interests of the administration of justice truly lie.

(B)   DOCUMENTS TO BE FILED

[34.21]

Practice Direction to CPR 52 – Documents to be filed

Documents

5.6
- (1)   This paragraph applies to every case except where the appeal–
  - (a)   relates to a claim allocated to the small claims track; and
  - (b)   is being heard in a county court or the High Court.
- (2)   The appellant must file the following documents together with an appeal bundle (see paragraph 5.6A) with his appellant's notice–
  - (a)   two additional copies of the appellant's notice for the appeal court; and
  - (b)   one copy of the appellant's notice for each of the respondents;
  - (c)   one copy of his skeleton argument for each copy of the appellant's notice that is filed (see paragraph 5.9);
  - (d)   a sealed copy of the order being appealed;
  - (e)   a copy of any order giving or refusing permission to appeal, together with a copy of the judge's reasons for allowing or refusing permission to appeal;
  - (f)   any witness statements or affidavits in support of any application included in the appellant's notice.
  - (g)   a copy of the order allocating a case to a track (if any).

5.6A
- (1)   An appellant must include in his appeal bundle the following documents:
  - (a)   a sealed copy of the appellant's notice;
  - (b)   a sealed copy of the order being appealed;
  - (c)   a copy of any order giving or refusing permission to appeal, together with a copy of the judge's reasons for allowing or refusing permission to appeal;
  - (d)   any affidavit or witness statement filed in support of any application included in the appellant's notice;
  - (e)   a copy of his skeleton argument;

     (f)   a transcript or note of judgment (see paragraph 5.12), and in cases where permission to appeal was given by the lower court or is not required those parts of any transcript of evidence which are directly relevant to any question at issue on the appeal;

     (g)   the claim form and statements of case (where relevant to the subject of the appeal);

     (h)   any application notice (or case management documentation) relevant to the subject of the appeal;

     (i)   in cases where the decision appealed was itself made on appeal (e.g. from district judge to circuit judge), the first order, the reasons given and the appellant's notice used to appeal from that order;

     (j)   in the case of judicial review or a statutory appeal, the original decision which was the subject of the application to the lower court;

     (k)   in cases where the appeal is from a Tribunal, a copy of the Tribunal's reasons for the decision, a copy of the decision reviewed by the Tribunal and the reasons for the original decision and any document filed with the Tribunal setting out the grounds of appeal from that decision;

     (l)   any other documents which the appellant reasonably considers necessary to enable the appeal court to reach its decision on the hearing of the application or appeal; and

    (m) such other documents as the court may direct.

   (2)   All documents that are extraneous to the issues to be considered on the application or the appeal must be excluded. The appeal bundle may include affidavits, witness statements, summaries, experts' reports and exhibits but only where these are directly relevant to the subject matter of the appeal.

   (3)   Where the appellant is represented, the appeal bundle must contain a certificate signed by his solicitor, counsel or other representative to the effect that he has read and understood paragraph (2) above and that the composition of the appeal bundle complies with it.

5.7   Where it is not possible to file all the above documents, the appellant must indicate which documents have not yet been filed and the reasons why they are not currently available. The appellant must then provide a reasonable estimate of when the missing document or documents can be filed and file them as soon as reasonably practicable.

[34.22]

Practice Direction to CPR 52 – Skeleton arguments

Skeleton arguments

5.9

   (1)   The appellant's notice must, subject to (2) and (3) below, be accompanied by a skeleton argument. Alternatively the skeleton argument may be included in the appellant's notice. Where the skeleton argument is so included it will not form part of the notice for the purposes of rule 52.8.

   (2)   Where it is impracticable for the appellant's skeleton argument to accompany the appellant's notice it must be filed and served on all respondents within 14 days of filing the notice.

(3)   An appellant who is not represented need not file a skeleton argument but is encouraged to do so since this will be helpful to the court.

Content of skeleton arguments

5.10

(1)   A skeleton argument must contain a numbered list of the points which the party wishes to make. These should both define and confine the areas of controversy. Each point should be stated as concisely as the nature of the case allows.

(2)   A numbered point must be followed by a reference to any document on which the party wishes to rely.

(3)   A skeleton argument must state, in respect of each authority cited–
  (a)   the proposition of law that the authority demonstrates; and
  (b)   the parts of the authority (identified by page or paragraph references) that support the proposition.

(4)   If more than one authority is cited in support of a given proposition, the skeleton argument must briefly state the reason for taking that course.

(5)   The statement referred to in sub-paragraph (4) should not materially add to the length of the skeleton argument but should be sufficient to demonstrate, in the context of the argument–
  (a)   the relevance of the authority or authorities to that argument; and
  (b)   that the citation is necessary for a proper presentation of that argument.

(6)   The cost of preparing a skeleton argument which–
  (a)   does not comply with the requirements set out in this paragraph; or
  (b)   was not filed within the time limits provided by this Practice Direction (or any further time granted by the court),
will not be allowed on assessment except to the extent that the court otherwise directs.

5.11   The appellant should consider what other information the appeal court will need. This may include a list of persons who feature in the case or glossaries of technical terms. A chronology of relevant events will be necessary in most appeals.

[34.23]

Practice Direction to CPR 52 – Suitable record of judgment

5.12   Where the judgment to be appealed has been officially recorded by the court, an approved transcript of that record should accompany the appellant's notice. Photocopies will not be accepted for this purpose. However, where there is no officially recorded judgment, the following documents will be acceptable:

(1)   Where the judgment was made in writing a copy of that judgment endorsed with the judge's signature.

(2)   When judgment was not officially recorded or made in writing a note of the judgment (agreed between the appellant's and respondent's advocates) should be submitted for approval to the judge whose decision is being appealed …

(3)   When the appellant was unrepresented in the lower court it is the duty of any advocate for the respondent to make his/her note of judgment promptly available, free of charge to the appellant where there is no officially recorded judgment or if the court so directs. Where the appellant was represented in the lower court it is the duty of his/her

own former advocate to make his/her note available in these circumstances. The appellant should submit the note of judgment to the appeal court.

5.13   An appellant may not be able to obtain an official transcript or other suitable record of the lower court's decision within the time within which the appellant's notice must be filed. In such cases the appellant's notice must still be completed to the best of the appellant's ability on the basis of the documentation available. However it may be amended subsequently with the permission of the appeal court.

3.   THE RESPONDENT

(A)   THE RESPONDENT'S NOTICE

FILING AND SERVICE OF THE RESPONDENT'S NOTICE

[34.24]

CPR 52.5 – RESPONDENT'S NOTICE
  (1)   A respondent may file and serve a respondent's notice.
  (2)   A respondent who–
    (a)   is seeking permission to appeal from the appeal court; or
    (b)   wishes to ask the appeal court to uphold the order of the lower court for reasons different from or additional to those given by the lower court,
  must file a respondent's notice.
  (3)   Where the respondent seeks permission from the appeal court it must be requested in the respondent's notice.
  (4)   A respondent's notice must be filed within–
    (a)   such period as may be directed by the lower court; or
    (b)   where the court makes no such direction, 14 days after the date in paragraph (5).
  (5)   The date referred to in paragraph (4) is–
    (a)   the date the respondent is served with the appellant's notice where–
      (i)   permission to appeal was given by the lower court; or
      (ii)   permission to appeal is not required;
    (b)   the date the respondent is served with notification that the appeal court has given the appellant permission to appeal; or
    (c)   the date the respondent is served with notification that the application for permission to appeal and the appeal itself are to be heard together.
  (6)   Unless the appeal court orders otherwise a respondent's notice must be served on the appellant and any other respondent–
    (a)   as soon as practicable; and
    (b)   in any event not later than 7 days,
  after it is filed.

[34.25]

Practice Direction to CPR 52, paragraph 7

Respondent

7.1 A respondent who wishes to ask the appeal court to vary the order of the lower court in any way must appeal and permission will be required on the same basis as for an appellant.

7.2 A respondent who wishes only to request that the appeal court upholds the judgment or order of the lower court whether for the reasons given in the lower court or otherwise does not make an appeal and does not therefore require permission to appeal in accordance with rule 52.3(1).

7.3
- (1) A respondent who wishes to appeal or who wishes to ask the appeal court to uphold the order of the lower court for reasons different from or additional to those given by the lower court must file a respondent's notice.
- (2) If the respondent does not file a respondent's notice, he will not be entitled, except with the permission of the court, to rely on any reason not relied on in the lower court.

7.3A ...

Time limits

7.4 The time limits for filing a respondent's notice are set out in rule 52.5 (4) and (5).

7.5 Where an extension of time is required the extension must be requested in the respondent's notice and the reasons why the respondent failed to act within the specified time must be included.

(B) DOCUMENTS

[34.26]

Practice Direction to CPR 52 – Skeleton arguments

7.6 Except where paragraph 7.7A applies, the respondent must file a skeleton argument for the court in all cases where he proposes to address arguments to the court. The respondent's skeleton argument may be included within a respondent's notice. Where a skeleton argument is included within a respondent's notice it will not form part of the notice for the purposes of rule 52.8.

7.7
- (1) A respondent who–
  - (a) files a respondent's notice; but
  - (b) does not include his skeleton argument within that notice,
  must file and serve his skeleton argument within 14 days of filing the notice.
- (2) A respondent who does not file a respondent's notice but who files a skeleton argument must file and serve that skeleton argument at least 7 days before the appeal hearing.

7.7A
  (1)   Where the appeal relates to a claim allocated to the small claims track
        and is being heard in a county court or the High Court, the respondent
        may file a skeleton argument but is not required to do so.
  (2)   A respondent who is not represented need not file a skeleton
        argument but is encouraged to do so in order to assist the court.

7.7B   The respondent must–
  (1)   serve his skeleton argument on–
    (a)   the appellant; and
    (b)   any other respondent,
  at the same time as he files it at the court; and
  (2)   file a certificate of service.

Content of skeleton arguments

7.8   A respondent's skeleton argument must conform to the directions at
paragraphs 5.10 and 5.11 with any necessary modifications. It should, where
appropriate, answer the arguments set out in the appellant's skeleton argument.

Applications within respondent's notices

7.9   A respondent may include an application within a respondent's notice in
accordance with paragraph 5.5 above.

Filing respondent's notices and skeleton arguments

7.10
  (1)   The respondent must file the following documents with his respond-
        ent's notice in every case:
    (a)   two additional copies of the respondent's notice for the appeal court;
          and
    (b)   one copy each for the appellant and any other respondents.
  (2)   The respondent may file a skeleton argument with his respondent's
        notice and–
    (a)   where he does so he must file two copies; and
    (b)   where he does not do so he must comply with paragraph 7.7.

7.11   If the respondent wishes to rely on any documents which he reasonably
considers necessary to enable the appeal court to reach its decision on the appeal
in addition to those filed by the appellant, he must make every effort to agree
amendments to the appeal bundle with the appellant.

7.12
  (1)   If the representatives for the parties are unable to reach agreement, the
        respondent may prepare a supplemental bundle.
  (2)   If the respondent prepares a supplemental bundle he must file it,
        together with the requisite number of copies for the appeal court, at
        the appeal court–
    (a)   with the respondent's notice; or
    (b)   if a respondent's notice is not filed, within 21 days after he is served
          with the appeal bundle.

7.13   The respondent must serve–
  (1)   the respondent's notice;
  (2)   his skeleton argument (if any); and

(3)   the supplemental bundle (if any),
on–
   (a)   the appellant; and
   (b)   any other respondent,
at the same time as he files them at the court.

4.   PROCEDURE FOLLOWING THE GRANTING OF PERMISSION

[34.27]

(a) Practice Direction to CPR 52 – Procedure after permission is obtained

6.1   This paragraph sets out the procedure where:
  (1)   permission to appeal is given by the appeal court; or
  (2)   the appellant's notice is filed in the appeal court and–
    (a)   permission was given by the lower court; or
    (b)   permission is not required.

6.2   If the appeal court gives permission to appeal, the appeal bundle must be served on each of the respondents within 7 days of receiving the order giving permission to appeal.

6.3   The appeal court will send the parties–
  (1)   notification of–
    (a)   the date of the hearing or the period of time (the 'listing window') during which the appeal is likely to be heard; and
    (b)   in the Court of Appeal, the date by which the appeal will be heard (the 'hear by date');
  (2)   where permission is granted by the appeal court a copy of the order giving permission to appeal; and
  (3)   any other directions given by the court.

6.3A
  (1)   Where the appeal court grants permission to appeal, the appellant must add the following documents to the appeal bundle–
    (a)   the respondent's notice and skeleton argument (if any);
    (b)   those parts of the transcripts of evidence which are directly relevant to any question at issue on the appeal;
    (c)   the order granting permission to appeal and, where permission to appeal was granted at an oral hearing, the transcript (or note) of any judgment which was given; and
    (d)   any document which the appellant and respondent have agreed to add to the appeal bundle in accordance with paragraph 7.11.
  (2)   Where permission to appeal has been refused on a particular issue, the appellant must remove from the appeal bundle all documents that are relevant only to that issue.

5.   POWERS OF THE APPEAL COURT

[34.28]

(A)   CPR 52.6 – VARIATION OF TIME
(1)   An application to vary the time limit for filing an appeal notice must be made to the appeal court.
(2)   The parties may not agree to extend any date or time limit set by–
  (a)   these Rules;
  (b)   the relevant practice direction; or
  (c)   an order of the appeal court or the lower court.

[34.29]

(B)   CPR 52.7 – STAY

  Unless–
(a)   the appeal court or the lower court orders otherwise; or
(b)   the appeal is from the Immigration Appeal Tribunal,

an appeal shall not operate as a stay of any order or decision of the lower court.

[34.30]

(C)   CPR 52.8 – AMENDMENT OF APPEAL NOTICE

  An appeal notice may not be amended without the permission of the appeal court.

[34.31]

(D)   CPR 52.9 – STRIKING OUT APPEAL NOTICES AND SETTING ASIDE OR IMPOSING CONDITIONS ON PERMISSION TO APPEAL
(1)   The appeal court may–
  (a)   strike out the whole or part of an appeal notice;
  (b)   set aside permission to appeal in whole or in part;
  (c)   impose or vary conditions upon which an appeal may be brought.
(2)   The court will only exercise its powers under paragraph (1) where there is a compelling reason for doing so.
(3)   Where a party was present at the hearing at which permission was given he may not subsequently apply for an order that the court exercise its powers under sub-paragraphs (1)(b) or (1)(c).

[34.32]

(E)   CPR 52.10 – APPEAL COURT'S POWERS
(1)   In relation to an appeal the appeal court has all the powers of the lower court.

(2)   The appeal court has power to–

    (a)   affirm, set aside or vary any order or judgment made or given by the lower court;

    (b)   refer any claim or issue for determination by the lower court;

    (c)   order a new trial or hearing;

    (d)   make orders for the payment of interest;

    (e)   make a costs order.

(3)   In an appeal from a claim tried with a jury the Court of Appeal may, instead of ordering a new trial–

    (a)   make an order for damages; or

    (b)   vary an award of damages made by the jury.

(4)   The appeal court may exercise its powers in relation to the whole or part of an order of the lower court.

(5)   If the appeal court–

    (a)   refuses an application for permission to appeal;

    (b)   strikes out an appellant's notice; or

    (c)   dismisses an appeal,

and it considers that the application, the appellant's notice or the appeal is totally without merit, the provisions of paragraph (6) must be complied with.

(6)   Where paragraph (5) applies–

    (a)   the court's order must record the fact that it considers the application, the appellant's notice or the appeal to be totally without merit; and

    (b)   the court must at the same time consider whether it is appropriate to make a civil restraint order.

6.   APPEALS TO A COUNTY COURT JUDGE

[34.33]

(a)   Practice Direction to CPR 52, paragraph 8A

Appeals to a judge of a county court from a district judge

8A.1   The Designated Civil Judge in consultation with his Presiding Judges has responsibility for allocating appeals from decisions of district judges to circuit judges.

7.   APPEALS TO THE HIGH COURT

[34.34]

(a)   Practice Direction to CPR 52, paragraph 8

Application

8.1   This paragraph applies where an appeal lies to a High Court judge from the decision of a county court or a district judge of the High Court.

...

General provisions

8.10   Directions may be given for–
  (a)   an appeal to be heard at a hearing only centre; or
  (b)   an application in an appeal to be heard at any other venue,
instead of at the appeal centre managing the appeal.

8.11   Unless a direction has been made under 8.10, any application in the appeal must be made at the appeal centre where the appeal is being managed.

8.12   The appeal court may adopt all or any part of the procedure set out in paragraphs 6.4 to 6.6.

8.13   Where the lower court is a county court:
  (1)   subject to paragraph (1A), appeals and applications for permission to appeal will be heard by a High Court Judge or by a person authorised [...] to act as a judge of the High Court;
  (1A)   an appeal or application for permission to appeal from the decision of a Recorder in the county court may be heard by a Designated Civil Judge who is authorised [...] to act as a judge of the High Court; and
  (2)   other applications in the appeal may be heard and directions in the appeal may be given either by a High Court Judge or by any person authorised [...] to act as a judge of the High Court.

8.14   In the case of appeals from Masters or district judges of the High Court, appeals, applications for permission and any other applications in the appeal may be heard and directions in the appeal may be given by a High Court Judge or by any person authorised [...] to act as a judge of the High Court.

8.   THE COURT OF APPEAL

(A)   PERMISSION OF THE COURT OF APPEAL REQUIRED FOR SECOND APPEALS

[34.35]

CPR 52.13 – SECOND APPEALS TO THE COURT
  (1)   Permission is required from the Court of Appeal for any appeal to that court from a decision of a county court or the High Court which was itself made on appeal.
  (2)   The Court of Appeal will not give permission unless it considers that–
    (a)   the appeal would raise an important point of principle or practice; or
    (b)   there is some other compelling reason for the Court of Appeal to hear it.

(B) 'LEAPFROG' APPEALS

[34.36]

CPR 52.14 – ASSIGNMENT OF APPEALS TO THE COURT OF APPEAL
(1) Where the court from or to which an appeal is made or from which permission to appeal is sought ('the relevant court') considers that–
(a) an appeal which is to be heard by a county court or the High Court would raise an important point of principle or practice; or
(b) there is some other compelling reason for the Court of Appeal to hear it,
the relevant court may order the appeal to be transferred to the Court of Appeal.
(2) The Master of the Rolls or the Court of Appeal may remit an appeal to the court in which the original appeal was or would have been brought.

(C) MISCELLANEOUS MATTERS

[34.37]

Practice Direction to CPR 52 – Appeal questionnaire

Appeal Questionnaire in the Court of Appeal

6.4 The Court of Appeal will send an Appeal Questionnaire to the appellant when it notifies him of the hearing date.

6.5 The appellant must complete and file the Appeal Questionnaire within 14 days of the date of the letter of notification of the matters in paragraph 6.3. The Appeal Questionnaire must contain:
(1) if the appellant is legally represented, the advocate's time estimate for the hearing of the appeal;
(2) where a transcript of evidence is relevant to the appeal, confirmation as to what parts of a transcript of evidence have been ordered where this is not already in the bundle of documents;
(3) confirmation that copies of the appeal bundle are being prepared and will be held ready for the use of the Court of Appeal and an undertaking that they will be supplied to the court on request. For the purpose of these bundles photocopies of the transcripts will be accepted;
(4) confirmation that copies of the Appeal Questionnaire and the appeal bundle have been served on the respondents and the date of that service.

Time estimates

6.6 The time estimate included in an Appeal Questionnaire must be that of the advocate who will argue the appeal. It should exclude the time required by the court to give judgment. If the respondent disagrees with the time estimate, the respondent must inform the court within 7 days of receipt of the Appeal Questionnaire. In the absence of such notification the respondent will be deemed to have accepted the estimate proposed on behalf of the appellant.

[34.38]

Practice Direction to CPR 52, paragraph 15

Other special provisions regarding the Court of Appeal

Filing of Documents

15.1
   (1)   The documents relevant to proceedings in the Court of Appeal, Civil
           Division must be filed in the Civil Appeals Office Registry, Room E307,
           Royal Courts of Justice, Strand, London, WC2A 2LL.
   (2)   The Civil Appeals Office will not serve documents and where service is
           required by the CPR or this practice direction it must be effected by
           the parties.

15.1A
   (1)   A party may file by email–
      (a)   an appellant's notice;
      (b)   a respondent's notice;
      (c)   an application notice,
   in the Court of Appeal, Civil Division, using the email account specified in the
   'Guidelines for filing by Email' which appear on the Court of Appeal, Civil
   Division website at www.civilappeals.gov.uk.
   (2)   A party may only file a notice in accordance with paragraph (1) where
           he is permitted to do so by the 'Guidelines for filing by Email'.

Core Bundles

15.2   …

15.3   …

Preparation of bundles

15.4   …
   Note—The requirements in relation to appeal bundles in the Court of Appeal
are onerous. They are not set out here – reference should be made to *The Civil
Court Practice*, published by LexisNexis Butterworths.

Respondent to notify Civil Appeals Office whether he intends to file respondent's
notice

15.6   A respondent must, no later than 21 days after the date he is served with
notification that–
   (1)   permission to appeal has been granted; or
   (2)   the application for permission to appeal and the appeal are to be heard
           together,
inform the Civil Appeals Office and the appellant in writing whether–
      (a)   he proposes to file a respondent's notice appealing the order or
              seeking to uphold the order for reasons different from, or additional
              to, those given by the lower court; or
      (b)   he proposes to rely on the reasons given by the lower court for its
              decision.

Requests for directions

15.10   To ensure that all requests for directions are centrally monitored and
correctly allocated, all requests for directions or rulings (whether relating to listing

or any other matters) should be made to the Civil Appeals Office. Those seeking directions or rulings must not approach the supervising Lord Justice either directly, or via his or her clerk.

Papers for the appeal hearing

15.11B
    (1)   All the documents which are needed for the appeal hearing must be filed at least 7 days before the hearing. Where a document has not been filed 10 days before the hearing a reminder will be sent by the Civil Appeals Office.
    (2)   Any party who fails to comply with the provisions of paragraph (1) may be required to attend before the Presiding Lord Justice to seek permission to proceed with, or to oppose, the appeal.

9.   APPEALS TO THE HOUSE OF LORDS

[34.39]

(a)   Practice Direction to CPR 52, paragraphs 15.19–15.21

Application for leave to appeal

15.19   Where a party wishes to apply for leave to appeal to the House of Lords under section 1 of the Administration of Justice (Appeals) Act 1934 the court may deal with the application on the basis of written submissions.

15.20   A party must, in relation to his submission–
    (a)   fax a copy to the clerk to the presiding Lord Justice; and
    (b)   file four copies in the Civil Appeals Office,
no later than 12 noon on the working day before the judgment is handed down.

15.21   A copy of a submission must bear the Court of Appeal case reference, the date the judgment is to be handed down and the name of the presiding Lord Justice.

10.   DISPOSING OF APPLICATIONS OR APPEALS BY CONSENT

[34.40]

(a)   Practice Direction to CPR 52, paragraphs 12 and 13

Dismissal of applications or appeals by consent

12.1   These paragraphs do not apply where any party to the proceedings is a child or patient.

12.2   Where an appellant does not wish to pursue an application or an appeal, he may request the appeal court for an order that his application or appeal be dismissed. Such a request must contain a statement that the appellant is not a child or patient. If such a request is granted it will usually be on the basis that the appellant pays the costs of the application or appeal.

12.3   If the appellant wishes to have the application or appeal dismissed without costs, his request must be accompanied by a consent signed by the respondent or his legal representative stating that the respondent is not a child or patient and consents to the dismissal of the application or appeal without costs.

12.4 Where a settlement has been reached disposing of the application or appeal, the parties may make a joint request to the court stating that none of them is a child or patient, and asking that the application or appeal be dismissed by consent. If the request is granted the application or appeal will be dismissed.

Allowing unopposed appeals or applications on paper

13.1 The appeal court will not normally make an order allowing an appeal unless satisfied that the decision of the lower court was wrong, but the appeal court may set aside or vary the order of the lower court with consent and without determining the merits of the appeal, if it is satisfied that there are good and sufficient reasons for doing so. Where the appeal court is requested by all parties to allow an application or an appeal the court may consider the request on the papers. The request should state that none of the parties is a child or patient and set out the relevant history of the proceedings and the matters relied on as justifying the proposed order and be accompanied by a copy of the proposed order.

11. REOPENING APPEALS

[34.41]

(A) CPR 52.17 – REOPENING OF FINAL APPEALS
(1) The Court of Appeal or the High Court will not reopen a final determination of any appeal unless–
  (a) it is necessary to do so in order to avoid real injustice;
  (b) the circumstances are exceptional and make it appropriate to reopen the appeal; and
  (c) there is no alternative effective remedy.
(2) In paragraphs (1), (3), (4) and (6), 'appeal' includes an application for permission to appeal.
(3) This rule does not apply to appeals to a county court.
(4) Permission is needed to make an application under this rule to reopen a final determination of an appeal even in cases where under rule 52.3(1) permission was not needed for the original appeal.
(5) There is no right to an oral hearing of an application for permission unless, exceptionally, the judge so directs.
(6) The judge will not grant permission without directing the application to be served on the other party to the original appeal and giving him an opportunity to make representations.
(7) There is no right of appeal or review from the decision of the judge on the application for permission, which is final.
(8) The procedure for making an application for permission is set out in the practice direction.

THE APPELLANT MUST DEMONSTRATE A 'CORRUPTIVE PROCESS' OF INJUSTICE

[34.42]   **Re Uddin (a child) (serious injury: standard of proof)**

[2005] EWCA Civ 52

[2005] 3 All ER 550, [2005] I WLR 2398, [2005] I FCR 583, CA

The claimant was made the subject of a care order.

The claimant petitioned for permission to reopen an appeal, subject to the exceptional circumstances stipulated by CPR 52.17. The appellant sought to challenge the judgment on the basis of fresh evidence.

HELD, ON APPEAL: It was necessary for the appellant to demonstrate that the integrity of the earlier judgment had been critically undermined. The discovery of fresh evidence in order to justify the reopening of an appeal must demonstrate a 'corruptive process' of injustice to the appellant if the appeal was not reopened.

Appeal refused.

PART 4

QUANTUM
AND COSTS

CHAPTER 35

General Principles of Quantum

1.   FORESEEABILITY

(A)   INTRODUCTION

[35.1]   The present law of foreseeability derives from the decision in *Wagon Mound (No 1)* (or *Overseas Tank Ship (UK) Ltd v Morts Dock & Engineering Co Ltd*) (at para [35.2]). This modified the judgment in *Re Polemis* [1921] 3 KB 560 by establishing that if a defendant could have anticipated damage by fire resulting from his action then he would be liable for that damage. This view was confirmed by a series of later cases including *Hughes v Lord Advocate* [1963] 1 All ER 705 HL, the *Wagon Mound (No 2)* (at para [35.3]) and *Wieland v Cyril Lord Carpets Ltd* (at para [35.11]). Therefore a defendant will only be liable for harm if it is of a kind, type or class foreseeable by the reasonable man.

See also Lord Goff's judgment in *Cambridge Water Company v Eastern Counties Leather* [1994] 1 All ER 53 where he imported the test of foreseeability into actions under nuisance and *Rylands v Fletcher* (1868) LR 3 HL 330.

[35.2]   Overseas Tankship (UK) Ltd v Morts Dock and Engineering Co Ltd (The Wagon Mound)
[1961] AC 388, [1961] 1 All ER 404, [1961] 2 WLR 126, 105 Sol Jo 85, [1961] 1 Lloyd's Rep 1

The respondents were owners of a wharf which they used for their business of ship repairing. The appellants were charterers of a vessel which was discharging petroleum products and taking in furnace oil at another wharf about 600ft away. By carelessness of the appellants' servants a large quantity of furnace oil was allowed to spill into the water and spread over the surface, particularly along the foreshore near and under the respondents' wharf. Molten metal from welding operations on the respondents' wharf fell on some cotton waste or rag floating on debris beneath the wharf and set it alight. Flames from the cotton waste ignited the furnace oil on the water, as a result of which a conflagration developed which damaged the respondents' wharf. The appellants did not know and could not reasonably be expected to have known that the furnace oil was capable of being set on fire when spread on water. There was other damage directly caused by the oil but not caused by the fire, though the respondents had not claimed for it. The Supreme Court of New South Wales, following the decision in *Re Polemis* [1921] 3 KB 560, held that the appellants were liable for the fire damage.

HELD, ON APPEAL to the Privy Council: The respondents were not liable for the fire damage. The *Polemis* decision should no longer be regarded as good law. If a defendant is guilty of negligence he is liable only for those consequences of his act which were reasonably foreseeable. It is, no doubt, proper when considering tortious liability for negligence to analyse its elements and to say that the claimant must prove a duty owed him by the defendant, a breach of that duty by the defendant, and consequent damage. But there can be no liability without damage. It is not the act but the consequences on which tortious liability is founded. The test of liability for the consequences of a negligent act is the foreseeability of the damage which in fact happened.

[35.3]   Overseas Tankship (UK) Ltd v The Miller Steamship Co Pty, The Wagon Mound (No 2)
[1967] 1 AC 617, [1966] 2 All ER 709, [1966] 3 WLR 498, 110 Sol Jo 447, PC

As the result of the same fire as gave rise to the action and appeals in *Overseas Tankship (UK) Ltd v Morts Dock and Engineering Co Ltd* (at para [35.2]) a ship belonging to the Miller Steamship Co Pty was damaged. On trial of their action the judge found that:

(1) the officers of the *Wagon Mound* who allowed the oil to escape would regard furnace oil as very difficult to ignite on water;

(2) in their experience this had very rarely happened;

(3) they would have regarded it as a possibility which could become an actuality only in very exceptional circumstances.

He held that the damage was not reasonably foreseeable by them.

HELD, ON APPEAL to the Privy Council: A risk cannot be regarded as not reasonably foreseeable merely because it is remote. If a real risk exists but is one that could only happen in very exceptional circumstances the defendant is not justified in dismissing the risk from his mind and doing nothing about it in circumstances where action to eliminate it presents no difficulty, involves no disadvantage and requires no expense. A reasonable man would weigh the risk against the difficulty and expense of eliminating it. In the present case no question of balancing advantages and disadvantages arose: it was both the interest and duty of the appellant defendant's servants to stop the discharge of oil immediately. In *The Wagon Mound (No 1)* the Board were not concerned with degrees of foreseeability because the finding there was that the fire was not foreseeable at all. In the present case the findings of fact showed some risk of fire would have been present in the mind of a reasonable man in the shoes of the defendants' servants. The defendant was liable.

[35.4]   Vacwell Engineering Co Ltd v BDH Chemicals Ltd

[1971] 1 QB 88, [1969] 3 All ER 1681, [1969] 3 WLR 927, 113 Sol Jo 639   Rees J

The defendant supplied a quantity of boron tribromide, a substance which explodes in contact with water, to the claimant for industrial use in glass ampoules. It gave no warning of its explosive character. The claimant put a large number of the ampoules in water to remove the labels. Somehow an ampoule broke causing others to break and bringing about a vast explosion. The defendant could have foreseen that, in the ordinary course of handling, an ampoule might come into contact with water and cause a minor explosion, but a violent and damaging explosion of the size which actually occurred was not reasonably foreseeable.

HELD: Following *Smith v Leech Brain & Co* (at para [35.7]) an explosion and some damage to property being foreseeable it was immaterial that the magnitude of the former and the extent of the latter were not. The defendant was liable for the whole of the damage done.

Note—An appeal was settled before the end of the hearing on the basis that that part of Rees J's judgment dealing with remoteness of damages in negligence should not be challenged. See [1970] 3 All ER 533.

(B)   TYPE OF ACCIDENT

[35.5]   Bradford v Robinson Rentals Ltd

[1967] 1 All ER 267, [1967] 1 WLR 337, 111 Sol Jo 33   Rees J

In very cold weather on roads made difficult by ice and snow the claimant was required by his employer, the defendant, to take an old Austin van from Exeter to

Bedford, a distance of 240 miles, and bring back a new one. This was not his normal work. Neither vehicle had a heater. The claimant protested against having to do the journey in such weather but the defendant insisted. The journey took two days. Owing to the prolonged exposure to very low temperatures the claimant sustained injury to his health by 'frost bite' or cold injury. There was no evidence that before the claimant started the journey either the claimant himself or the defendant actually contemplated that the claimant might suffer from 'frost bite' if he were required to carry out the journey.

HELD: Any reasonable employer would know that if the claimant were required to carry out the journey he would be subjected to a real risk to his health from prolonged exposure to the exceptional cold—for example a common cold, or pneumonia or chilblains. The law does not require that liability for its consequences is attributed. *Salmond on Torts* (14th edn) p 719 conveniently states the principle to be followed since *The Wagon Mound* (or *Overseas Tankship (UK) Ltd v Morts Dock and Engineering Co Ltd*) (at para [35.2]): 'It is sufficient if the type, kind, degree or order of harm could have been foreseen in a general way. The question is, was the accident a variant of the perils originally brought about by the defendant's negligence?' In the present case the defendant knew that the claimant was being called upon to carry out an unusual task which would be likely to expose him for prolonged periods to extreme cold and considerable fatigue. By sending him on this journey it exposed him to a reasonably foreseeable risk of injury arising from such exposure. He sustained injury from it and was entitled to damages.

Note—See also *Malcolm v Broadhurst* [1970] 3 All ER 508.

[35.6]   **Jolley v Sutton London Borough Council**
[2000] 1 WLR 1082, [2000] 3 All ER 409, HL

An abandoned, dilapidated and dangerous boat was negligently left where children were likely to play on it. The claimant was one of two teenage boys who propped the boat up with a car jack to effect repairs. The boat collapsed on the claimant who was seriously injured. The trial judge found that the boat was a trap or allurement to children and the accident reasonably foreseeable. The Court of Appeal held that there was no liability because the accident which occurred was of a different kind to the accident which was foreseeable. The cause of the accident was not the rotten condition of the boat but the way in which the boys had propped it up. The claimant appealed.

HELD, ON APPEAL to the House of Lords: Appeal allowed. It was sufficient that there was a foreseeable risk of some kind of physical injury from meddling with the boat.

Note—See also *Crown River Cruises Ltd v Kimbolton Fireworks Ltd and London Fire and Civil Defence Authority* [1996] 2 Lloyd's Rep 533.

(C)   TYPE OF INJURY

Note—See also *Page v Smith* (at para [36.32]) where the House of Lords held that if the claimant was within the foreseeable range of the risk of physical injury, psychiatric damage was recoverable, even if such damage was itself unforeseeable and *Donachie v The Chief Constable of the Greater Manchester Police* (at para [35.34]).

[35.7]   **Smith v Leech Brain & Co Ltd**
[1962] 2 QB 405, [1961] 3 All ER 1159, [1962] 2 WLR 148, 106 Sol Jo 77   Lord Parker CJ

The claimant's husband received a burn on the lip in the course of his work due to the negligence of the defendant. The burn healed but later became ulcerated and cancerous. An operation was done to remove the cancer but secondary cancers developed and after further operations the claimant died about three years after sustaining the burn. In an action under the Fatal Accidents and Law Reform Acts the judge found that the burn was the promoting agency of the cancer in tissues which already had a pre-malignant condition as a result of the deceased's having worked in a gasworks. It was contended by the defendant that *The Wagon Mound* (or *Overseas Tankship (UK) Ltd v Morts Dock and Engineering Co Ltd*) (at para [35.2]) disentitled the claimant to recovery damages since the defendant could not reasonably have foreseen that the burn would cause cancer and that the deceased would die.

HELD: In *The Wagon Mound* the Privy Council did not have the 'thin skull' cases in mind. It has always been the law of this country that a tortfeasor takes his victim as he finds him: there is not a day goes by where some trial judge does not adopt that principle. If the Privy Council had any intention of making an inroad on that principle they would have said so. On the contrary a distinction was drawn in their advice between type of injury and extent of damage. The test was not whether the defendant could reasonably have foreseen that a burn would cause cancer and that the deceased would die: the question was whether the defendant could reasonably foresee the type of injury which he suffered, namely, the burn. The claimant was entitled to damages for her husband's death.

[35.8]   Warren v Scruttons Ltd

[1962] 1 Lloyd's Rep 497   Paull J

The claimant, a dockworker, was handling a wire rope when his finger was pricked by a projecting strand of wire. The wound became poisoned, causing a generalised poisoning of the system with a high temperature. Part of the injured finger had to be cut off and there was continuing tenderness. In his teens the claimant had suffered from ulceration of the right eye leaving some weakness of vision. The high temperature and poisoning of the system following the injury to the finger caused a further ulcer with some resulting deterioration of the vision. The medical evidence was that an eye which had once suffered ulceration may always get further ulcers if some condition of the body causes a high temperature. The defendant having been found liable for the injury to the finger, it was argued on its behalf that (on the principle of *The Wagon Mound* (or *Overseas Tankship (UK) Ltd v Morts Dock and Engineering Co Ltd*) (at para [35.2])) the eye condition was not a foreseeable result of the pricking of the finger and damages for the eye condition should not be awarded against them.

HELD: (Following *Smith v Leech Brain* (at para [35.7])), the defendant's argument was not right. You must look to the type of damage to see whether it was one which could reasonably be anticipated. The type of damage here was a pricked finger. Once it was found that that damage could have been reasonably anticipated then any consequence which resulted because the individual had some peculiarity was a consequence for which the tortfeasor was liable. Nevertheless, the fact that any febrile condition which the claimant suffered, eg a high temperature brought on by a very serious cold, would produce the same condition as the accident did must be taken into account in assessing damages. An award of £850 plus special damages of £41 was made.

[35.9]   **Burden v Watson**

1961 SLT (Notes) 67

The driver of a bus which collided with a motor cycle suffered a coronary thrombosis due to shock. It was contended on behalf of the motor cyclist that such an injury was not reasonably foreseeable.

HELD: Though the loss alleged to have been suffered must always be subject to the test of foreseeability, it need not be shown that the wrongdoer ought to have foreseen the precise type of physical injury suffered. The position might well be different if the loss sustained as a result of the accident was of a type which a reasonable man would not be expected to foresee, eg through being unable to keep an appointment or attend a meeting.

[35.10]   **Tremain v Pike**

[1969] 3 All ER 1303, [1969] 1 WLR 1556, 113 Sol Jo 182   Payne J

The claimant, a farm worker, contracted Weil's disease by handling materials contaminated by rat's urine. The disease was not a reasonably foreseeable result of rat infestation.

HELD: This was not a case like *Smith v Leech* (at para [35.7]) or *Bradford v Robinson Rentals Ltd* (at para [35.5]) in which the risk of injury from a burn or from extreme cold was foreseeable and in which it was only the degree of injury or the development of the sequelae which was not foreseeable. In the present case the risk of the initial infection was not foreseeable and was entirely different in kind from other possible injuries from rat infestation. The claimant was not entitled to succeed.

(D)   SECOND INCIDENT

[35.11]   **Wieland v Cyril Lord Carpets Ltd**

[1969] 3 All ER 1006   Eveleigh J

The claimant, a lady of 57 years of age was a passenger in a bus when she was thrown forward and sustained injury to her neck. She was treated at hospital where, two days later, she was fitted with a collar. On the same day whilst descending some stairs she fell and injured her ankles. The cause of her fall, the judge found, was that whilst wearing the collar she was unable properly to judge the position of the steps when wearing her bifocal lens spectacles. The defendant contended that the injury to the ankles was not due to its negligence; alternatively it was not foreseeable, relying on *The Wagon Mound* (or *Overseas Tankship (UK) Ltd v Morts Dock and Engineering Co Ltd*) (at para [35.2]).

HELD: (1) The fall and resultant injury was caused by the defendant's negligence. The claimant's ability to negotiate stairs had been impaired and this caused the fall. It had long been recognised that injury sustained in one accident may be the cause of a subsequent injury, eg the injury sustained by accident victims on the operating table. It is always a question for the court to decide on the facts whether the accident did cause the second injury; *Hogan v Bentinck Collieries* (at para [35.45]).

(2)   *The Wagon Mound* decided that damages can only be recovered if the injury complained of was an injury of a class or character foreseeable as a possible result of the negligence. 'The injury complained of' means

that personal injury, loss or damage which the law requires to constitute the tort of negligence. *The Wagon Mound* is not to be read as dealing with the extent of the injury or the degree to which it has affected the claimant, still less as requiring foreseeability of the manner in which that original injury has caused harm to the claimant. In determining liability for the possible consequences of the injury it is not necessary to show that each consequence was within the foreseeable extent or foreseeable scope of the original injury in the same way as the possibility of injury must be foreseen when determining whether or not the defendant's conduct gives a claim in negligence. The present case was concerned with the extent of the harm suffered by the claimant: the injury and damage suffered because of the second fall were attributable to the original negligence.

(3)   Another way of putting it is to say that it is foreseeable that one injury may affect a person's ability to cope with the vicissitudes of life and thereby be a cause of another injury. Foreseeability of this general nature will suffice.

Note—Applied in *Poole v Transbulk Services Ltd* (9 March 1998, unreported).

[35.12]   McKew v Holland and Hannen and Cubitts (Scotland) Ltd
[1969] 3 All ER 1621, 1970 SC 20, 1970 SLT 68, HL

On 14 February owing to the defender's negligence the pursuer sustained minor injuries to his left leg. On several occasions following the injury his left leg for a short time went numb and he lost control of it. On 5 March as he was about to descend a staircase he felt his leg give way again. To avoid a fall he jumped down the flight of stairs and sustained severe injury.

HELD: The defendant was not liable in damages for the second injury. The pursuer was acting unreasonably in choosing to descend the staircase without taking precautions against the possibility that his leg might give way. His unreasonable conduct was a *novus actus interveniens*.

Per Lord Reid: I do not think that foreseeability (of the defender) comes into this. A defender is not liable for a consequence of a kind which is not foreseeable. But it does not follow that he is liable for every consequence which a reasonable man could foresee ... It only leads to trouble if one tries to graft on to the concept of foreseeability some rule of law to the effect that a wrongdoer is not bound to foresee something which in fact he could readily foresee as quite likely to happen. For it is not at all unlikely or unforeseeable that an active man who has suffered such a disability will take some quite unreasonable risk. But if he does, he cannot hold the defender liable for the consequences.

Note—See also 'novus actus interveniens' at para [35.38].

(E)   CONTRACT AND TORT CONTRASTED

[35.13]   Koufos v C Czarnikow Ltd, The Heron II
[1969] 1 AC 350, [1967] 3 All ER 686, [1967] 3 WLR 1491, 111 Sol Jo 848, HL

The respondents chartered the appellant's ship to carry a cargo of sugar to Basrah. Owing to a deviation amounting to a breach of contract the ship arrived nine days later than anticipated. The price of sugar at Basrah fell during that period and the respondents obtained less for the cargo than if the ship had arrived on time. At the time the contract was made the appellant did not know what the respondents were going to do with the sugar but he knew there was a market in sugar at Basrah and could have assumed if he thought about it that the sugar would be sold there. The price might have gone up or down – there was an even chance of either happening.

HELD: The loss was not too remote and the appellant was liable for it.

Per Lord Reid: 'In cases [of contract] like *Hadley v Baxendale* (1854) 9 Exch 341 or the present case it is not enough that in fact the [claimant's] loss was directly caused by the defendant's breach of contract. It clearly was so caused in both. The crucial question is whether, on the information available to the defendant when the contract was made, he should, or a reasonable man in his position would, have realised that such a loss was sufficiently likely to result from the breach of contract to make it proper to hold, that the loss flowed naturally from the breach or that loss of that kind should have been within his contemplation. The modern rule in tort is quite different and it imposes a much wider liability. The defendant will be liable for any type of damage which is reasonably foreseeable as liable to happen even in the most unusual case, unless the risk is so small that a reasonable man would in the whole circumstances feel justified in neglecting it; and there is a good reason for the difference. In contrast, if one party wishes to protect himself against a risk which to the other party would appear unusual, he can direct the other party's attention to it before the contract is made … In tort, however, there is no opportunity for the injured party to protect himself in that way, and the tortfeasor cannot reasonably complain if he has to pay for some very unusual but nevertheless foreseeable damage which results from his wrongdoing.

[35.14]   Hargreaves Vehicle Distributors Ltd v Holbrook
[1970] RTR 380, CA

The defendant was acquiring a lorry by hire purchase and was using it as his only means of livelihood. It was badly damaged in an accident and was taken to the claimant's garage for repair on 4 April. An estimate was agreed with the defendant's insurers on 24 April but the claimant did not order essential parts until 17 May. It completed the work on 10 September but did not tell the defendant until 14 October. When he collected it he found the work had not been satisfactorily done. Meanwhile because of the delay he had been unable to keep up his payments to the hire-purchase company who in January repossessed itself of the vehicle and obtained judgment against the defendant for £418. The claimant sued for £10 excess under his insurance policy: the defendant counterclaimed in the amount of his loss.

HELD: The claimant knew it was a commercial vehicle and that when it was not available there would be loss of profit or other monetary loss to the defendant. It was under a contractual obligation to return the vehicle properly repaired within a reasonable time and the delay of at least two months was a breach of that duty. Whether or not it was aware of the precise circumstances of the hire purchase it was liable to the defendant for the amount of his loss.

Note—See also *Charnock v Liverpool Corpn* (at para [2.246]).

[35.15]   Batty v Metropolitan Realisation Ltd
[1978] QB 554, [1978] 2 All ER 445, [1978] 2 WLR 500, 112 Sol Jo 63, CA

The *ratio decidendi* of *Esso Petroleum Co Ltd v Mardon* [1976] QB 801, [1976] 2 All ER 5, [1976] 2 WLR 583, CA necessarily requires that the mere fact the claimant had obtained judgment for breach of contract does not preclude it from the entitlement which would have existed, apart from contract, to have judgment entered in its favour also in tort, assuming, eg that the claimant had established a breach by the defendant of a common law duty of care owed to the claimant.

[35.16]   Balfour Beatty Construction (Scotland) Ltd v Scottish Power plc
1994 SLT 807, HL

The defendant was an electricity supplier. It wrongly interrupted the power to a construction site whilst some concrete was being poured. The work had to stop. This caused the structure into which the concrete was being poured to become unstable. It was subsequently demolished and rebuilt at great expense. The claimant sought damages.

HELD, ON APPEAL to the House of Lords: The loss claimed was not within the reasonable contemplation of the defendant and was therefore too remote.

Per Lord Jauncey: It must always be a question of circumstances what one contracting party is presumed to know about the business activities of the other. No doubt the simpler the activity of the one, the more readily can it be inferred that the other would have reasonable knowledge thereof. However, when the activity of A involves complicated construction or manufacturing techniques, I see no reason why B who supplies a commodity that A intends to use in the course of those techniques should be assumed, merely because of the order for the commodity, to be aware of the details of all the techniques undertaken by A and the effect thereupon of any failure of or deficiency in that commodity.

[35.17]   Jackson v Royal Bank of Scotland
[2005] 2 All ER 71, [2005] 1 WLR 377

In a breach of contract claim, the House of Lords held that the claimant was entitled to an award of damages to put him in the same position as he would have been in had the breach not occurred. If no cut off point was stipulated in the contract, there was no arbitrary limit that could be set to the amount of damages once the test of remoteness had been satisfied. *Hadley v Baxendale* (1854) 156 ER 145 applied.

2.   CAUSATION OF DAMAGE

[35.18]   *Note*—The claimant must prove on the balance of probabilities that the particular negligent act caused the loss for which damages are claimed. The defendant will only be responsible for the loss that his negligent act has caused. In limited factual situations, the court may depart from that approach where the harm is 'indivisible' (see *Fairchild v Glenhaven Funeral Services Ltd* (at para [35.33]) and the subsequent case of *Barker v Saint Gobain Pipelines [2006] UKHL 20* (at para [35.37]) where the House of Lords held that because *Fairchild* imposed liability where a risk had been created but a causal link could not be proved on the balance of probability, it was fair that damages should also be apportioned on the basis of risk). The loss must be reasonably foreseeable and not too remote. An intervening act by someone other than the defendant may break the chain of causation (see para [35.38]) as will loss caused by the claimant's own unreasonable or voluntary behaviour.

(A)   DAMAGE TO CHATTELS

[35.19]   Liesbosch, Dredger v Edison SS
[1933] AC 449, 102 LJP 73, 149 LT 49, HL

While the dredger 'L' was lying moored alongside the breakwater at Patras Harbour, the steamship 'E' fouled the dredger's moorings and carried her out to sea, where she sank and was lost. The owners of the 'E' admitted sole liability for the loss. The 'L' had been bought in 1927 for £4,000 by her owners, who had spent a further £2,000 in bringing her to Patras. They were a syndicate of civil engineers. Under a contract with the Patras Harbour Commissioners they were engaged in construction work in the harbour, for which a dredger was necessary and for which they were using the 'L'. The contract provided for completion of the work within a specified time. The loss of the 'L' stopped the work and, being unable from want of funds to purchase any suitable dredger which was for sale, on 4 May 1929, they hired a dredger, the 'A' which was lying in harbour at Carlo Forte, Sardinia, to take the place of the 'L'. The 'A' was more expensive in working than the 'L' and required the attendance of a tug and two hopper barges. The 'L' was sunk on 26 November 1928. The 'A' got to work on the harbour on 17 June 1929.

HELD: The measure of damages was the value of the 'L' to her owners as a profit-earning dredger at the time and place of her loss; and that it should include:

(1)   a capital sum made up of: (a) the market price on 26 November 1928 of a dredger comparable to the 'L'; (b) the cost of adapting the new dredger and of transporting and insuring her from her moorings to Patras; and (c) compensation for disturbance and loss suffered by the owners of the 'L' in carrying out their contract during the period between 26 November 1928 and the date on which the substituted dredger could reasonably have been available for use at Patras, including in that loss such items as overhead charges and expenses of staff and equipment and the like thrown away, but neglecting any special loss or extra expenses due to the financial position of one or other of the parties;

(2)   interest upon the capital sum from 26 November 1928.

'If the appellants' financial embarrassment is to be regarded as a consequence of the respondents' tort, I think it is too remote; but I prefer to regard it as an independent cause, though its operative effect was conditioned by the loss of the dredger' (per Lord Wright).

Note—See Lord Hope in *Lagden v O'Connor* [2004] 1 AC 1067 (at para [35.83]) who held that 'it is not necessary for us to say that *The Liesbosch* was wrongly decided. But it is clear that the law has moved on, and that the correct test of remoteness today is whether the loss was reasonably foreseeable ... I would hold that this [impecuniosity] rule [in *The Liesbosch*] should now be departed from'.

[35.20]   Carslogie SS Co v Royal Norwegian Government
[1952] AC 292, [1952] 1 All ER 20, [1951] WN 609, [1951] 2 TLR 1099, 95 Sol Jo 801, HL

The elementary principle is that it is for the claimant in an action for damages to prove his case; to show affirmatively that damage under any particular head has resulted from the wrongful act of the defendant.

Note—See *Meah v McCreamer (No 2)* [1986] 1 All ER 943 (at para [36.19]).

[35.21]   Organic Research Chemicals Ltd v Ricketts

[1961] Times, 16 November, CA

The claimant had handed its car to the defendant to repair when it broke down. The car was towed to the defendant's garage. Attempts were made to restart it which caused further extensive damage to the engine. The first breakdown was due to a broken camshaft which would have cost £30 to replace. The extensive damage caused by the defendant's attempt to restart it made necessary the fitting of a re-conditioned engine at a cost of £61. The county court judge awarded the claimant the whole cost of the engine. On appeal the Court of Appeal reduced the award to £31 being the difference between the cost of the re-conditioned engine and the cost of replacing the camshaft. It was impossible to say that the claimant had suffered £61 damages, since the engine needed £30 spent on it before the damage was done. What it had suffered was the difference between the £61 for the re-conditioned engine and the £30 it would have had to pay anyhow. *The Bernina* (1886) 6 Asp MLC 65 and *The Munster* (1896) 12 TLR 264 were distinguishable on the grounds that the pre-existing damage to this car had rendered it completely immobile.

[35.22]   Performance Cars Ltd v Abraham

[1962] 1 QB 33, [1961] 3 All ER 413, [1961] 3 WLR 749, 105 Sol Jo 748, CA

The claimant's car was damaged in a collision with the defendant's car for which the defendant admitted he was to blame. The damage was such that the whole of the lower part of the claimant's car would need to be resprayed to put it right, at a cost of £75. A short time before this accident the claimant's car had been damaged in another collision and needed a re-spray of the whole of the lower part to put that damage right. The respray had not been done at the time of the second accident. A judgment had been obtained for £75 against the person responsible for the first accident but was unsatisfied. The claimant claimed it was entitled to £75 damages from the present defendant as one of two separate tortfeasors who must each be liable for the consequences of his own tortious act.

HELD: The defendant was not liable for the cost of the re-spray. The necessity for re-spraying was not the result of the defendant's wrongful act because the necessity already existed. The second collision had put no extra burden on the claimant in the matter of re-spraying, for the earlier collision had already imposed the burden of re-spraying on them. The rights of the claimant against the person who caused the first collision were not completely collateral and the quotation from *Mayne on Damages* referred to by Asquith LJ in *Shearman v Folland* (at para [36.153]) did not apply here. The principle to be applied was that adopted by the House of Lords in *Carslogie SS Co v Royal Norwegian Government* (at para [35.20]).

Note— Followed in *Steel v Joy* (at para [35.35]) where the claimant had two consecutive injuries. See also *Hodgson v General Electricity Co Ltd and Jobling v Associated Dairies Ltd* [1978] 2 Lloyd's Rep 210 (at para [35.53]).

[35.23]   Dodd Properties (Kent) Ltd v Canterbury City Council

[1980] 1 All ER 928, [1980] 1 WLR 433, 124 Sol Jo 84, 253 EG 1335, CA

A building owned by the claimant was damaged by building work next door carried out by the defendant, who eventually admitted liability to pay damages. The damage was done in 1968 and repairs could have been done in 1970 when they would have cost £11,375. For various reasons, including financial stringency (short of impecuniosity or financial embarrassment) the claimant had not done repairs at the time of the hearing in 1978. By then the cost of repairs had gone up to £30,000.

HELD: Though the general principle is that damages are to be assessed as at the date the damage occurs it is not a universal rule and is subject to many exceptions and qualifications. Where there is a material difference between the cost of repairs at the date of the wrongful act and the cost when the repairs can, having regard to all relevant circumstances, first reasonably be undertaken it is the latter time at which the cost of repairs should be taken in assessing damages. On the facts the claimant had good commercial reasons for not doing the repairs before the case was heard and were entitled to damages based on cost of repairs at £30,000. The decision in the *Liesbosch* case (at para [35.19] above) was not applicable: in that case the excess loss flowed directly from the lack of means and not from the tortious act.

Note—See also *London Congregational Union v Harriss and Harriss (a firm)* [1985] 1 All ER 335.

[35.24]   Perry v Sidney Phillips & Son (a firm)

[1982] 3 All ER 705, [1982] 1 WLR 1297, 126 Sol Jo 626, 263 EG 888, CA

The claimant bought a house on the strength of a report from the defendants that it was sound. In fact it suffered from a number of defects causing him anxiety and distress for which he claimed damages. It was pleaded for the defendants that he could have cut his losses by selling or having repairs done and that if lack of means prevented him from doing this, *Liesbosch, Dredger v Edison SS* (at para [35.19] above) was a bar to his recovering.

HELD: Per Kerr LJ: It was reasonable for the [claimant] not to do any repairs by the time of the trial, and those reasons went beyond his lack of means. In any event it seems to me that the authority of what Lord Wright said in the *Liesbosch* case is consistently being attenuated in more recent decisions of this court, in particular in *Dodd Properties v Canterbury CC* [1980] 1 All ER 928, [1980] 1 WLR 433, 124 Sol Jo 84, 253 EG 1335, CA … If it is reasonably foreseeable that the [claimant] may be unable to mitigate or remedy the consequences of the other party's breach as soon as he would have done if he had been provided with the necessary means to do so from the other party, then it seems to me that the principle of the *Liesbosch* case no longer applies in its full vigour.

[35.25]   Ramwade Ltd v WJ Emson & Co Ltd

[1987] RTR 72, [1986] LS Gaz R 2996, CA

The claimant's skip lorry was written off in an accident. The defendant, its insurance broker, had failed to arrange comprehensive insurance cover and the insurer correctly rejected the claim for the value of the lorry. The claimant obtained judgment against its broker for its losses flowing from the failure to obtain comprehensive cover. Damages were assessed to include amounts paid by the claimant to hire replacement vehicles. The defendant appealed against this award; the claimant conceded that a comprehensive policy would not have covered the cost of hiring replacement vehicles.

HELD: The appeal succeeded. It might seem superficially attractive to argue that the payment of hire charges was a foreseeable result of the broker's failure to arrange insurance, because of the resultant delay in payment, but correctly the foreseeable loss was the amount that the insurer would have paid. The hire charges were incurred either because the claimant could not afford to buy a substitute vehicle or because the damages were not paid at the proper time, so the claimant would be seeking to recover damages for non-payment of damages.

Note—In *London Congregational Union v Harriss and Harriss (a firm)* [1985] 1 All ER 335, Judge Newey assessed damages to reflect the cost of repairs when they could first reasonably have been undertaken.

This approach taken to the measure of damages was not questioned, although much of the judgment was the subject of a partially successful appeal.

[35.26] Mattocks v Mann

[1993] RTR 13, [1992] 31 LS Gaz R 34, CA

The claimant's two door Peugeot GTI was badly damaged in a road traffic accident for which the defendant admitted responsibility. The claimant needed a replacement vehicle and first hired a four-door saloon model for some 20 weeks exchanging it thereafter for a smaller two-door vehicle. The claimant claimed the full hire costs to the date when the defendant's insurance company provided money to pay for the repairs to her vehicle. The claimant argued that she was unable to meet these repair costs herself.

Assessing the damages the Master:

(1)   disallowed the extra cost of hiring the four-door saloon; but

(2)   allowed the claim for hire charges incurred for the period after the completion of the repairs to the claimant's vehicle to the time when the defendant released money to pay for the work. Both parties appealed.

HELD: (1) The Master applied the wrong test. It was not relevant that the claimant could have managed with the smaller vehicle hired after the saloon. The proper test was to look at whether or not the claimant had acted reasonably in hiring the saloon in the first place. There was nothing to indicate that the hiring of the saloon was unreasonable in the circumstances, particularly as it was still over £200 a week cheaper than if the claimant had hired a replacement Peugeot GTI.

(2)   The law of damages had moved on since the decision in *Liesbosch, Dredger v Edison SS* (at para [35.19]). The claimant's impecuniosity in this case could not be said to be the sole cause of the need to hire an alternative vehicle but:

'In these days when everybody looks to one or other of the insurers of vehicles involved in an accident, it is clearly contemplated that where the cost of repairs are of the substantial kind involved in this case, the source of payment of that cost will be the insurers. Looking here at the whole history of events, one cannot isolate the plaintiff's inability to meet the cost of those repairs and say that that brought an end to the period for which it was reasonable that the second defendant's insurers should be liable': per Beldam LJ.

The claimant was awarded her hire charge claim in full.

Note—See also hire of replacement vehicle at para [35.75].

(B)   PERSONAL INJURY

[35.27]   Cutler v Vauxhall Motors Ltd
[1971] 1 QB 418, [1970] 2 All ER 56, [1970] 2 WLR 961, 114 Sol Jo 247, CA

In November 1965 the claimant sustained a graze on the right ankle in an accident at work. It healed in a fortnight and he was not off work. In May 1966 he had pain in the right leg. He was found to have a varicose condition of both legs. An ulcer formed on the site of the original graze and because of this he was advised to have an immediate operation on both legs to cure the varicose condition. This was done in September 1966. The varicose condition was not the result of the accident but the ulcer was, and it was also the reason for having the operation done at once, though even if the accident had never occurred the operation would have been necessary by 1970 or 1971. The claimant lost wages amounting to £173 when the operation was done. The judge awarded him £10 for the graze but nothing for the discomfort of the operation or the resultant loss of wages.

HELD, ON APPEAL: The judge was right. The task of the court is to assess the totality of the damages to be awarded and to do so the court must have regard to future probabilities. There was no reasonable ground for supposing that if the accident had not happened the claimant would not have survived to 1970 or 1971 and then lose a sum at least equivalent to the £173. If the claimant were awarded £173 in this action the defendants would be recouping him for a loss which in all probability he would have had to bear even if the accident had not occurred.

[35.28]   McGhee v National Coal Board
[1973] 1 WLR 1, HL

The claimant was unable to prove whether the dermatitis he contracted had come from brick dust which adhered to his skin while he was working in the brick kilns or the dust which continued to adhere to his skin while he cycled home. Both risks had been created by the defendant employer. The only breach of duty was the defendant's failure to provide showers so that he could wash off the dust before cycling home.

HELD, ON APPEAL to the House of Lords: The claimant succeeded. It was sufficient for the defendant's breach of duty to have materially contributed to the risk of injury.

[35.29]   Kay's Tutor v Ayrshire and Arran Health Board
[1987] 2 All ER 417, 1987 SLT 577, HL

In November 1987, the appellant's son, Andrew, aged two years five months, contracted meningitis and was admitted to the defendant's hospital. While seriously ill, he was injected with a massive overdose of penicillin, causing temporary paralysis and convulsions. The mistake was immediately rectified and he recovered from the meningitis, but became severely deaf. The appellant sued the defendant in negligence on the grounds that the overdose of penicillin had caused the deafness.

HELD, ON APPEAL: There was no satisfactory evidence that an overdose of penicillin would have caused Andrew's deafness, or indeed that an overdose of penicillin had ever caused deafness. On the other hand, even when meningitis was treated correctly, deafness frequently occurred as an inevitable result. Accordingly, the appeal must be dismissed. In this case, there were two competing causes of injury:

the overdose, which was a tortious cause, and the result of the illness, which was not. The court could not presume that the tortious cause was responsible for the injury if this was not substantiated by the evidence.

[35.30]   Holtby v Brigham & Cowan (Hull) Ltd
[2000] 3 All ER 421, [2000] PIQR Q293, CA

The claimant was a marine fitter who suffered steadily deteriorating asbestosis while working for a series of negligent employers. The claimant sought damages from an employer with whom he had 12 years service and contended that he was entitled to recover all his losses from that employer as they had materially contributed to his condition.

HELD: As a general rule, the method of apportioning responsibility on a time exposure basis was the correct approach in law.

Per Smith LJ: [the claimant] will be entitled to succeed if he can prove that the defendant's tortious conduct made a material contribution to his disability. But strictly speaking, the defendant is liable only to the extent of that contribution. However, if the point is never raised or argued by the defendant, the claimant will succeed in full.

Note—See *Fairchild v Glenhaven* (at para [35.33]) where the injury is truly indivisible and *Barker v Saint Gobain Pipelines* (at para [35.37]).

[35.31]   Rahman v Arearose Ltd
[2001] QB 351, [2000] 3 WLR 1184, CA

The claimant was assaulted during the course of his employment and injured his eye. His employers were found negligent. The claimant subsequently underwent surgery to preserve his eye. The surgeon was negligent and the claimant suffered permanent loss of vision. The issue concerned the apportionment of damages between the two tortfeasors.

HELD: Per Laws LJ: '... the real question is, what is the damage for which the defendant under consideration should be held responsible. The nature of his duty ... is relevant. Causation, certainly, will be relevant – but it will fall to be viewed, and in truth can only be understood, in the light of the answer to the question, from what kind of harm was it the defendant's duty to guard the claimant.' It was sensible to conclude that whilst the surgeon had exclusively caused the blindness, that did not prevent the employers wrong from having an ongoing effect on the claimant's suffering. The judge's apportionment of 75% to the surgeon and 25% to the employer was not open to criticism. However, such an apportionment could not be applied to every head of damage since for example, the employer should be fully liable for the first three years loss of earnings.

The surgeon's negligence was not a 'novus actus interveniens' which broke the chain of causation. 'Every tortfeasor should only compensate the injured claimant in respect of that loss and damage for which he should justly be held responsible.'

[35.32]   Allen v British Rail Engineering Ltd
[2001] EWCA Civ 242

[2001] ICR 942, [2001] PIQR Q10

The claimant started working for the defendant in the late 1950s. He suffered from vibration white finger since 1968 as a result of using vibrating tools during the course of his employment. The court found that by 1973, the defendant should have had the requisite knowledge as to the risk. By 1976, the defendant should have taken steps to ameliorate the risk. The claimant left the defendant's employment in 1987 and moved to another job where he was exposed to vibrating tools which caused him further damage. The judge awarded the claimant £11,000 but deducted the following sums: £1,500 for the period prior to 1976; £1,500 for the period after 1987 and £4,000 being 50% of £8,000 for the period between 1976 and 1987. The issue on appeal concerned the 50% deduction – the judge made the deduction because during this time, a proportion of the harm was caused by unavoidable, non-negligent exposure.

HELD: The judge's findings were upheld. The claimant would establish liability if he could prove that the employer's tortious conduct made a material contribution to the claimant's damage. There may be cases where the evidence was such that two separate tortfeasors are found to have caused all the damage. The defendant's liability would be limited to the extent of his tortious contribution to the claimant's damage. The court must do the best it can on the evidence available to make any apportionment. The claimant should not be denied relief because he cannot accurately establish what proportion of his injury was attributable to the defendant's tortious conduct. The amount of evidence called to enable a judge to make an apportionment must be proportionate to the amount at stake.

[35.33]   **Fairchild v Glenhaven Funeral Services Ltd**
[2002] UKHL 22
[2003] 1 AC 32, [2002] 3 WLR 89, HL

This case concerned a claim brought by the widows where the deceased developed malignant mesothelioma following the inhalation of asbestos fibres during the course of their employment with various employers. The Court of Appeal held that the claimants had failed to prove on the balance of probabilities which period of exposure had caused or materially contributed to the cause of mesothelioma. The claimants appealed.

HELD, ON APPEAL to the House of Lords: Appeals allowed. Each defendant employer was liable in full for a claimant's damages but a defendant could seek a contribution against another employer who was liable for causing the disease. A court should be prepared to infer causation where:
  (i)   it was clear how an injury had occurred;
  (ii)   that a given defendant's breach of duty materially increased the risk of that injury;
  (iii) that a breach of duty by that person or a number of others in the same situation must have been responsible; and
  (iv)   that there was no means of showing which.

Note—See Lord Bingham's speech concerning the earlier decisions of *McGhee v National Coal Board* (at para [35.28]) and *Wilsher v Essex AHA* (at para [35.49]). In the latter case, a premature baby became blind in hospital. The blindness could have been caused by a number of factors – some of which were not the defendant's fault. The House of Lords held that the claimant had failed to prove his case. In *Fairchild*, Lord Bingham recognised that the court's approach was driven by policy considerations in cases where the harm suffered is truly indivisible. *Fairchild* has been modified by the House of Lords in *Barker v Saint Gobain Pipelines* (at para [35.37]).

[35.34] **Donachie v Chief Constable of Greater Manchester**

[2004] EWCA Civ 405

(2000) Times, 6 May, 148 Sol Jo LB 509, CA

The claimant police officer was required to fit a tagging device to a suspect's car. The claimant had to make nine trips to the car due to a faulty battery. This caused the claimant stress and aggravated his hypertension. He subsequently had a stroke. The judge found the defendant was negligent in failing to operate a safe system of work and held that the chain of causation between the breach of duty and the stroke was unbroken. The cardiologists' view was that the stress caused or materially contributed to the stroke. The claim however failed because the claimant had suffered no reasonably foreseeable injury. The claimant appealed and the defendant cross appealed on the causation finding.

HELD: Appeal allowed. Cross appeal dismissed. The general rule in personal injury claims remains the 'but for' test. The judge correctly applied this test when considering causation. On foreseeability, the Court of Appeal held that the claimant was a primary victim Physical injury was reasonably foreseeable. The judge was wrong to approach this issue on the basis that the relevant injury was psychiatric. *Page v Smith* [1996] AC 155 (at para [36.32]) applied.

[35.35] **Steel v Joy**

[2004] 4 All ER 920, [2004] 1 WLR 3002, CA

On 15 December 1996 the claimant was injured in an accident involving the first defendant. On 13 March 1999, he was injured in an accident involving the second defendant. The claimant bought proceedings against both defendants. The first accident accelerated the claimant's congenital spinal symptoms by seven to ten years; the second accident would have had the same effect as the first accident if it had not already occurred. The Recorder held that the second accident did not affect the long-term prognosis. The first defendant appealed.

HELD: The second defendant was not responsible for the consequences of the first injury even though but for the first accident the second one would have caused similar injury. The second defendant had not caused the damage because the claimant had already suffered it at the hands of the first defendant. *Performance Cars Ltd v Abraham* (at para [35.22]) followed. This was not a case of concurrent tortfeasors.

Note—See also *Chester v Afshar* [2004] UKHL 41, HL concerning the application of causation principles in a clinical negligence claim.

[35.36] **Clough v First Choice Holidays & Flights Ltd**

[2006] EWCA Civ 15

[2006] All ER (D) 165 (Jan), CA

The claimant, on holiday in Lanzarote and under the influence of alcohol, slipped from a wall that divided two swimming pools and broke his neck. The trial judge found that the defendant's failure to use non-slip paint on the wall was negligent but had not caused the accident. The claimant appealed contending he was not required to establish that the slip was caused by the absence of non-slip paint rather than his own careless movements, or lack of balance, or the degree of his inebriation. If the absence of non-slip paint had made a material contribution to the accident, the defendant should be liable. Material contribution the claimant contended applied to either damage (as in *Wilsher v Essex Health Authority* at para [35.49]) or in exceptional cases, risk of damage (as in *Fairchild v Glenhaven* at para [35.33]).

HELD: Appeal dismissed. The reasoning in *Fairchild v Glenhaven* did not undermine the principles relating to causation in cases concerning an individual, specific occasion of negligence. The distinction between material contribution to damage and material contribution to the risk of damage had no application to cases where the claimant's injuries arose from a single accident. The trial judge found that on the balance of probabilities, the accident would not have been avoided had non-slip paint been used on the surface of the wall. The increased risk caused by the non-slip paint had not caused or materially contributed to the accident.

[35.37]   Barker v Saint Gobain Pipelines

[2006] UKHL 20

[2006] 3 All ER 785, [2006] 2 WLR 1029, HL

The claimants had all successfully sued after contracting mesothelioma as a result of exposure to asbestos. They had not been able to identify the particular fibre which caused the mesothelioma, but had succeeded following the House of Lords ruling in *Fairchild v Glenhaven Funeral Services Ltd* (at para [35.33]). The defendant employers appealed on the basis that they should only have to pay a proportion of the damages commensurate to their contribution to the risk of injury. The critical issues were:

(1)   Whether a mesothelioma claimant who is known to have been exposed to asbestos, other than by a culpable employer, falls within the relaxed rule of causation in *Fairchild?*

(2)   Whether if the claim falls within *Fairchild*, damages should be calculated to reflect the employers' contribution to the risk of developing mesothelioma?

HELD, ON APPEAL to the House of Lords (Lord Rodger of Earlsferry dissenting): Because *Fairchild* imposed liability where a risk had been created but a causal link could not be proved on the balance of probability, it was fair that damages should also be apportioned on the basis of risk created. The claims were remitted for apportionment.

Per Lord Hoffmann: In my opinion the attribution of liability according to the relative degree of contribution to the chance of the disease being contracted would smooth the roughness of the justice which a rule of joint and several liability creates. The defendant was a wrongdoer, it is true, and should not be allowed to escape liability altogether, but he should not be liable for more than the damage which he caused and, since this is a case in which science can deal only in probabilities, the law should accept that position and attribute liability according to probabilities ... When liability is exceptionally imposed because you may have caused harm ... fairness suggests that if more than one person may have been responsible, liability should be divided according to the probability that one or other caused the harm.

Note—See the judgments for a discussion on causative principles in relation to the cases of *McGhee v National Coal Board* (at para [35.28]), *Wilsher v Essex AHA* (at para [35.49]) and *Gregg v Scott* (at para [35.50]).

Section 3 of the Compensation Act 2006 reverses the decision in *Barker*. It provides that in mesothelioma claims, the employee or his personal representatives will be able to obtain judgment for all the damages flowing from the illness (subject to any discount for contributory negligence) whether the exposure was tortious throughout or only for part of the period.

3.   NOVUS ACTUS INTERVENIENS

(A)   INTERVENING ACT

Note—The chain of causation between the defendant's wrongdoing and the claimant's damage may be broken if the immediate cause of the damage was the act of a third party.

[35.38]   Home Office v Dorset Yacht Co Ltd
[1970] AC 1004, [1970] 2 All ER 294, [1970] 2 WLR 1140, 114 Sol Jo 375, [1970] 1 Lloyd's Rep 453, HL

A party of borstal trainees were working on Brownsea Island under the supervision and control of three borstal officers employed by the appellants. During the night seven of the trainees escaped and went on board a yacht they found nearby. They set it in motion and collided with the respondent's yacht which was moored in the vicinity, causing damage.

HELD: The appellants were liable for the damage.

Per Lord Reid: The ground of liability is not responsibility for acts of the escaping trainees; it is liability for damage caused by the carelessness of these officers in the knowledge that their carelessness would probably result in the trainees causing damage of this kind. So the question is really one of remoteness of damage ... [and] to what extent the law regards the acts of another person as breaking the chain of causation between the defendants' carelessness and the damage of the [claimant] ... It has never been the law that the intervention of human action always prevents the ultimate damage from being regarded as having been caused by the original carelessness. The convenient phrase *novus actus interveniens* denotes those cases where such action is regarded as breaking the chain and preventing the damage from being held to be caused by the careless conduct. But every day there are cases where, although one of the connecting links is deliberate human action, the law has no difficulty in holding that the defendant's conduct caused the [claimant's] loss ... What then is the dividing line? ... The cases show that, where human action forms one of the links between the original wrongdoing of the defendant and the loss suffered by the [claimant], that action must at least have been something very likely to happen if it is not to be regarded as *novus actus interveniens* breaking the chain of causation. I do not think that a mere foreseeable possibility is or should be sufficient, for then the intervening human action can be more properly regarded as a new cause than as a consequence of the original wrongdoing. But if the intervening action was likely to happen I do not think it can matter whether that action was innocent or tortious or criminal.

Note—See also *Robinson v Post Office* (at para [35.46]) and *Lloyds Bank v Budd* (at para [8.3]).

[35.39]   West v Hughes of Beaconsfield Ltd
[1971] RTR 298   Mocatta J

In the hours of darkness the claimant, on a bicycle, wished to turn right from a busy road into a side road. When in the centre of the main road before turning he was struck from behind by a van and knocked over. He got up, picked up his bicycle, and was then hit and very severely injured by a car which was following the van. Neither driver saw him before the collisions though they were using headlights and there was nothing to prevent them from seeing him. The judge held both drivers to have been negligent. It was argued for the van driver that:

(1)   the car driver's negligence was a *novus actus*; alternatively

(2)   as the most serious injuries were caused by the car, the car owner should bear the major part of the responsibility.

HELD: (1) Although all the grave injuries were directly caused by the car there was not such a break in the chain of causation that the van driver could be held liable only for nominal damages. If a driver in a line of traffic on a busy road at night negligently knocks down a cyclist it is plainly foreseeable that the next following vehicle may injure the rider. The fact that the following driver could have avoided the cyclist if he had been keeping a proper look-out does not make his negligence a *novus actus*.

(2)   The negligence of each driver was causative of the claimant's injuries: as the van driver had a better opportunity of seeing the claimant than the car driver he should bear 55% of the responsibility and the car driver 45%.

[35.40]   Lamb v Camden London Borough Council

[1981] QB 625, [1981] 2 All ER 408, [1981] 2 WLR, 1038, 125 Sol Jo 356, CA

The claimant owned a house in a good neighbourhood. She let it to a tenant and went to America. Some months later the defendant council in doing work for renewal of a sewer damaged a water main. Water caused a subsidence of the house: it was not safe to live in and the tenant left. Repair work was not done until some years later. During the intervening period the house was locked up but squatters broke in and caused considerable damage to the interior. The council admitted liability for nuisance. The claimant claimed damages for the cost of repairs made necessary by the subsidence and in addition damages for the cost of making good the damage done by the squatters.

HELD: The defendants were not liable for the damage done by the squatters: it was too remote. Applying Lord Reid's test in *Home Office v Dorset Yacht Co* (at para [35.38]) the squatters' actions, though 'foreseeable', were not 'likely', the house being in a neighbourhood where squatting had not formerly occurred. But even Lord Reid's test may not be adequate where the fresh damage had been caused by the intervening act of a third party. A court may require a degree of likelihood amounting almost to inevitability before it fixes a defendant with responsibility for the act of a third party over whom he has and can have no control.

Note—Applied in *P Perl (Exporters) Ltd v Camden London Borough Council* [1984] QB 342, [1983] 3 All ER 161, [1983] 3 WLR 769, 127 Sol Jo 581, CA. See also *Ward v Cannock Chase District Council* [1986] Ch 546, [1985] 3 All ER 537.

[35.41]   Knightley v Johns

[1982] 1 All ER 851, [1982] 1 WLR 349, 126 Sol Jo 101, [1982] RTR 182, CA

Johns was driving his car through a tunnel having two carriageways when it overturned, blocking most of the northbound carriageway. The accident was admittedly due to his negligent driving. The driver of a following car reported the accident by telephone to the police control centre whence a message was transmitted by radio to the claimant, PC Knightley, a police officer on a motor cycle. He entered the tunnel, saw the situation, and then left it to radio further information to the control centre. On returning to the scene he found that Inspector Sommerville, the third defendant, had already arrived with other police officers. The Inspector said to him and another officer 'I have forgotten to close the tunnel; you go back and do it.' The two officers then rode south, in the opposite direction to the traffic stream. The claimant collided with an oncoming car near the entrance and was injured. There were in existence standing orders presumably known to the Inspector (who, though present at the trial, did not give evidence) specifying a procedure and precautions for dealing with accidents in the tunnel. They required, *inter alia*, the tunnel to be closed at the outset, for officers to go on foot only and for 'emergency vehicles' to be accompanied by an officer only when all traffic had been stopped. The trial judge held that the police officers were not negligent, that the whole sequence of events flowed from Johns's negligence, and that he was liable in damages to the claimant.

HELD, ON APPEAL: The decision was not right. The Inspector was negligent in not closing the tunnel and in ordering or allowing his subordinates to do a very dangerous thing contrary to standing orders. The question to be answered was whether his negligence was concurrent with the negligence of Johns or whether the acts and omissions of the claimant and the Inspector were new causes which broke the chain of causation. In considering the effects of carelessness the test is reasonable foreseeability; in this case, whether the whole sequence of events was a natural and probable consequence of Johns's negligence and a reasonably foresee-able result of it. Negligent conduct is more likely to break the chain of causation than conduct which is not; positive acts will more easily constitute new causes than inaction. The Inspector's negligence was not a concurrent cause running with Johns's negligence, but a new cause interrupting the effect of it. The judge's decision carried Johns's responsibility too far. The Inspector, not Johns, was liable in damages to the claimant.

Note—See also *Crown River Cruises Ltd v Kimbolton Fireworks Ltd* [1996] 2 Lloyd's Rep 533 where Potter J distinguished between intervening events that were the 'natural and probable consequence' of the original wrong and those that were not.

[35.42]   Smith v Littlewoods Organisation Ltd
[1987] 1 All ER 710, [1987] NLJ Rep 149, HL

Littlewoods purchased the Regal Cinema, Dunfermline to demolish it and build a supermarket. It was left empty and unattended from the end of the third week of June 1986; by the beginning of July there was obvious evidence that it was being regularly broken into and vandalised, but no one told Littlewoods or the police, nor were they told that a small fire had been stamped out. On 5 July 1986, after further acts of vandalism, a fire was deliberately started which razed the cinema and damaged adjoining buildings. The owners of these buildings claimed damages on the grounds of Littlewoods' negligence, contending that it was reasonably foreseeable that the cinema would be entered by vandals (or even just children) who would start fires which would spread to adjoining property.

HELD: The appellants could not recover damages from Littlewoods:
(1) On the information available to Littlewoods, these events were not reasonably foreseeable to it; it was under a general duty to take reasonable care to ensure that its premises were not a source of

danger to neighbours but the existence of any more specific duty to prevent this type of damage must depend on the circumstances – here no such specific duty was owed.

(2)   (Per Lord Mackay) where damage is the result of unpredictable human conduct ('every society will have a sprinkling of people who behave most abnormally'), what the reasonable man is bound to foresee is the highly likely result of any error of his own, not the merely possible. The more predictable the behaviour, the more foreseeable the result.

(3)   (Per Lord Goff) liability in negligence for damage deliberately caused by others could only exist in special circumstances, for example, where there is a special relationship (as between borstal officers and trainees in *Home Office v Dorset Yacht Co Ltd* (at para [35.38])), where a defendant negligently creates a source of damage (leaving a horse in a crowded street, as in *Haynes v Harwood* (at para [7.30])) or where (as in *Goldman v Hargrave* [1967] 1 AC 645, [1966] 2 All ER 989, [1966] 3 WLR 513, 110 Sol Jo 527, [1966] 2 Lloyd's Rep 65, PC) a defendant knows of a fire started by others on his premises, but fails to take reasonable steps to prevent it damaging adjoining property.

Note—For a detailed analysis of the judgments, see (1989) LQR 104 at 105.

[35.43]   Corr (**Administratrix of Corr Deceased**) v IBC Vehicles Ltd

[2006] EWCA Civ 331

[2006] 2 All ER 929, CA

Mr Corr was injured in a factory accident that caused post-traumatic stress disorder (PTSD) and depression requiring hospital admission. Six years after the accident Mr Corr committed suicide. Mrs Corr claimed damages under the Fatal Accidents Act 1976 against Mr Corr's employers who were responsible for the negligent accident. The trial judge dismissed the claim on the grounds that the death was not reasonably foreseeable and that Mr Corr's suicide broke the chain of causation.

HELD: The Court of Appeal (with Ward LJ dissenting) held that there was no break in the chain of causation and that there was no need for the claimant to show at the time of the accident that Mr Corr's suicide was reasonably foreseeable as a separate damage. It was adequate that the employers were responsible for the depression and the suicide flowed from that psychiatric injury. Mrs Corr could claim damages against the employer as a result of her husband's suicide.

(B)   NEGLIGENT TREATMENT

Note—See also *Rahman v Arearose Ltd* (at para [35.31]).

[35.44]   Rothwell v Caverswall Stone Co

[1944] 2 All ER 350, 171 LT 289, 113 LJKB 520, 61 TLR 17, CA

A workman met with an accident during employment on 23 March 1943, and suffered a fractured dislocation of his right shoulder. He was treated at the local hospital. His shoulder was not X-rayed and the injury was not correctly diagnosed. If it had been and been correctly treated, he would probably have completely recovered in six to eight weeks. Subsequently, when correctly diagnosed, it was too late for effective treatment and the arm was permanently stiff. On the hearing of an arbitration under the Workmen's Compensation Acts, the county court judge found the then existing incapacity was due to negligent medical treatment and was not the result of the accident.

HELD, ON APPEAL: The workman's condition was due to the negligent treatment and not the accident. No compensation was payable after the date on which he would have recovered if properly treated. The county court judge was bound by authority to come to the conclusion he did on the facts as found by him.

Per du Parcq LJ: In my opinion, the following propositions may be formulated upon the authorities as they stand: first, an existing incapacity 'results from' the original injury if it follows, and is caused by, that injury, and may properly be held so to result even if some supervening cause has aggravated the effects of the original injury and prolonged the period of incapacity. If, however, the existing incapacity ought fairly to be attributed to a new cause which has intervened and ought no longer to be attributed to the original injury, it may properly be held to result from the new cause and not from the original injury, even though, but for the original injury, there would have been no incapacity. Second, negligent or inefficient treatment by a doctor or other person may amount to a new cause and the circumstances may justify a finding of fact that the existing incapacity results from the new cause, and does not result from the original injury. This is so even if the negligence or inefficient treatment consists of an error of omission whereby the original incapacity is prolonged. In such a case, if the arbitrator is satisfied that the incapacity would have wholly ceased but for the omission, a finding of fact that the existing incapacity results from the new cause, and not from the injury will be justified. In stating these propositions I am far from seeking to lay down any new principles of construction. I have sought only to collect, by a process of induction, such general, and necessarily vague, rules as seen to emerge from the decided cases. Such rules do no more than indicate the bounds within which an arbitrator is free to decide – the province of fact. It is constantly being said, and must always be remembered, that the arbitrator is the sole judge of the facts.

Appeal dismissed.

[35.45]   Hogan v Bentinck West Hartley Collieries (Owners) Ltd
[1949] 1 All ER 588, [1949] WN 109, [1949] LJR 865, HL

If a surgeon, by lack of skill or failure in reasonable care, causes additional injury or aggravates an existing injury and so renders himself liable in damages, his intervention is a new cause and the additional injury or aggravation should be attributed to it and not to the original accident. On the other hand, an operation prudently advised and skilfully and carefully carried out should not be treated as a new cause, whatever its consequences may be.

[35.46]   Robinson v Post Office
[1974] 2 All ER 737, [1974] 1 WLR 1176, 117 Sol Jo 915, CA

The claimant, a post office employee, sustained a wound on his leg when he slipped on an oily rung whilst descending a tower wagon ladder. He visited his doctor who gave him an injection of anti-tetanus serum. A few days later the claimant developed symptoms due to an allergy to the serum and eventually suffered serious brain damage. The judge held the doctor was not negligent in administering the serum and that although he was negligent in failing to give a preliminary test dose it would have made no difference if he had. The post office admitted that the accident and injury to the claimant's leg was caused by negligence on its part but said it was not liable for the serious results of the injection because they were not reasonably foreseeable.

HELD: (1) The injection of serum by the doctor was not a *novus actus interveniens* which broke the chain of causation between the negligence of the post office and the claimant's disability caused by the injection. Conduct of the doctor falling short of negligence could not amount to a *novus actus* and such negligence as the judge found against him was of no effect in causing the disability.

    (2)   It was foreseeable both that the claimant might slip on an oily rung and sustain injury and that if he did he might well require medical treatment. The only unforeseeable result was the terrible extent of the injury caused by the claimant's allergy to the serum; in that respect the post office must take their victim as they found him. *Smith v Leech* (at para [35.7]) followed. If a wrongdoer ought reasonably to foresee that as a result of his wrongful act the victim may require medical treatment he is, subject to the principle of *novus actus interveniens*, liable for the consequences of the treatment applied although he could not reasonably foresee those consequences.

[35.47]   Emeh v Kensington and Chelsea and Westminster Area Health Authority

[1985] QB 1012, [1984] 3 All ER 1044, CA

Mrs Emeh underwent an abortion and sterilisation operation at the defendant hospital. Some eight months later she found herself 18–20 weeks pregnant. Mrs Emeh declined an abortion and when her baby was born she was found to be congenitally abnormal. It was held by the trial judge that the defendant had carried out the sterilisation operation negligently but the defendant sought to argue that, by refusing to undergo an abortion, the claimant had refused to take reasonable steps to minimise the damage and this constituted a *novus actus interveniens* which eclipsed the negligence of the surgeon. This argument was upheld by Park J. The claimant appealed.

HELD: The claimant's refusal to have an abortion did not break the chain of causation nor did it constitute a failure to mitigate her damages. Only in the most exceptional circumstances could the court declare it unreasonable for a woman to decline an abortion. In this case, there was no evidence to suggest there was any medical or psychiatric grounds for terminating this pregnancy.

[35.48]   Hotson v East Berkshire Health Authority

[1987] AC 750, [1987] 2 All ER 909, [1987] 3 WLR 232, 131 Sol Jo 975, HL

At the age of 13 the claimant fell 12ft from a tree and suffered an acute traumatic fracture of the left femoral epiphysis and damage to the blood vessels. His injury was not correctly diagnosed nor treated for five days and he suffered avascular necrosis which would result in disability of the hip joint and undoubtedly give rise to osteoarthritis. The judge held that even if there had been no delay, there was a 75% chance that avascular necrosis would have occurred so he awarded £11,500 damages for the loss of the 25% chance of a full recovery. The defendant's appeal was dismissed by the Court of Appeal; it appealed to the House of Lords.

HELD, ON APPEAL to the House of Lords: The appeal would be granted. The claimant had to prove on the balance of probabilities that the delay was a material contributory cause of the avascular necrosis before quantification of the claim could be considered. He had not done so. If he had, the defendant would not have been entitled to a discount from the full damages to reflect the chance that the necrosis might well have developed anyway given prompt treatment.

Lord McKay quoted Lord Diplock in *Mallet v McMonagle* (at para [37.41]): 'In determining what did happen in the past a court decides on the balance of probabilities. Anything that is more probable than not it treats as certain.'

Note—See also *Ricci Burns Ltd v Toole* [1989] 3 All ER 478, [1989] 1 WLR 993, CA.

[35.49] Wilsher v Essex Area Health Authority

[1988] AC 1074, [1988] 1 All ER 871, HL

The claimant was born prematurely and was placed in a special baby care unit at a hospital managed by the defendants. The claimant needed oxygen but a catheter was wrongly inserted into an umbilical vein as opposed to an artery and the claimant was given too much oxygen. He developed retrolental fibroplasia which resulted in blindness. Medical science could not establish whether the likely cause of the condition was the excessive oxygen or one or more of four other possible agents. The claimant claimed damages from the defendant health authority for negligent medical treatment. At first instance, the judge held that the defendants were liable because they had failed to prove that the claimant's condition had not been caused by the doctor's negligence. The Court of Appeal dismissed the defendants' appeal.

HELD, ON APPEAL to the House of Lords: Appeal allowed. The burden of proof of causation rested on the claimant. Where a number of different agents could have caused the condition, including the administration of excess oxygen, its occurrence provided no evidence and raised no presumption that it was excess oxygen rather than one of the other agents which caused or contributed to the condition. Since there was a conflict of medical evidence as to whether the excess oxygen caused or contributed to the claimant's condition and the judge had failed to make relevant findings of fact on this, the issue of causation was remitted to a different judge to try.

[35.49A] Webb v Barclays Bank plc

[2001] EWCA Civ 1141

[2002] PIQR P8, CA

The claimant injured her leg in a fall at her employer's premises. She subsequently received negligent medical advice that she should have the leg amputated. There was evidence from six independent consultants who all said that they would not have advised an amputation. One issue concerned whether the hospital's negligence broke the chain of causation.

HELD: The medical advice was not grossly negligent. The chain of causation was not broken and the employer remained responsible for its share of the damages. The chain would only be broken where the medical treatment was of such a degree of negligence as to be an entirely inappropriate response to the injury.

[35.50] Gregg v Scott

[2005] 2 AC 176, [2005] 4 All ER 812, [2005] 2 WLR 268, HL

The defendant, Dr Scott, negligently diagnosed as benign a lump under the claimant's left arm. It was in fact cancerous. The misdiagnosis delayed the claimant's treatment by nine months and his condition deteriorated. This deterioration reduced his prospects of disease-free survival for ten years from 42% when he first consulted Dr Scott, to 25% at the date of the trial. The judge found that if treated promptly, the claimant's initial treatment would probably have achieved remission without an immediate need for high dose chemotherapy. It would also have initially prevented the cancer from spreading to the left pectoral region. The judge dismissed the claim because the delay had not deprived the claimant of the prospect of a cure. At the time of the misdiagnosis, the claimant had a less than 50% chance of surviving more than ten years anyway. A split Court of Appeal dismissed the claimant's appeal. The claimant appealed to the House of Lords contending that firstly, the delay in diagnosis and treatment had caused physical injury as the cancer had spread and the losses he had suffered were consequential on that physical damage. Secondly, the claimant argued that apart from any other injury, the reduction in his chances of survival was itself a compensatable head of damage.

HELD, ON APPEAL to the House of Lords (Lord Nicholls and Lord Hope dissenting): Appeal dismissed. The claimant had not shown on the balance of probabilities that the delay in commencing his treatment that was attributable to the defendant's negligence had affected the course of his illness or his prospects of survival, which had never been as good as even. The claimant had to establish causation on the balance of probabilities. Liability for the loss of a chance of a more favourable outcome should not be applied to personal injuries. Otherwise, as Baroness Hale held, would not every claimant be able to argue that that he had, say, a 30% chance of proving his case and therefore should be entitled to 30% of the damages? Such a development would play havoc with the rules on proof. Lord Hoffmann expressly restricted the *Fairchild v Glenhaven Funeral Services Ltd* (at para [35.33]) decision to cases where there was a causation difficulty in connecting the breach of duty to the eventual outcome.

Note—The dissenting judgments held that the claimant was entitled to be compensated for the significant reduction in his prospects of a successful outcome which the defendant's negligence caused (a 'diminution in prospects' claim). What had to be valued was what the claimant had lost, and the principle on which that loss had to be calculated was the same, irrespective of whether the prospects were better or less than 50%.

See also *Bright v Barnsley DH NHS Trust* [2005] Lloyd's Rep Med 449 where the court held that for the purposes of establishing causation in civil claims, each step of factual and medical causation must be decided in its own right.

(C)   SUBSEQUENT INJURY/DISEASE

[35.51]   Baker v Willoughby

[1970] AC 467, [1969] 3 All ER 1528, [1970] 2 WLR 50, 114 Sol Jo 15, HL

In September 1964 the claimant's left leg was fractured in a road accident caused by the defendant's negligent driving. In a shooting accident in November 1967 the same leg was injured so badly that it had to be amputated. His action for damages for the first injury was heard in February 1968. The judge held that the claimant's prospective loss from the defendant's negligence should not be reduced by the fact of the subsequent amputation and awarded damages which included an amount for the prospect of loss of earnings and pain and suffering which the claimant would have suffered after 1967 if the amputation had never occurred.

The Court of Appeal said this was wrong. The court must have regard to events which had occurred since the date of the accident and must be guided by those events in so far as they had made certain what would otherwise be uncertain. The award should be restricted to the period up to the shooting incident.

HELD, ON APPEAL to the House of Lords: The judge's award was restored. Lord Reid said it was not correct that the second injury had submerged or obliterated the effect of the first. A man was not compensated for the physical injury but for the loss he suffered as a result of it. The claimant's losses were his inability to lead a full life and earn as much as he used to earn or could have earned if there had been no accident. The second injury did not diminish any of those. Whether injuries received before trial reduced the damages depended on the nature and result of those injuries. If the later injury either reduced the disabilities from the injury for which the defendant was liable or shortened the period during which they would be suffered by the claimant the defendant would have to pay less damages. But if the later injuries merely became a concurrent cause of the disabilities caused by the first injury they could not diminish the damages. So far as pain and suffering were concerned if the result of the amputation was that the claimant suffered no more pain he could not claim for pain he would never suffer, but the judge's award for pain (as distinct from loss of earnings) subsequent to the amputation was probably only a small part of the award and no deduction from the award should be made for this.

[35.52] Hodgson v General Electricity Co Ltd

[1978] 2 Lloyd's Rep 210   Latey J

The claimant sustained very serious injuries to his left hand in an accident at work in September 1971. In 1974 liability was agreed at 70%. In mid-1976 a serious heart condition developed making the claimant unfit for any work in the future. But for the heart condition his employers would have been able to find him suitable light work. Trial was reached in July 1978. He claimed on the basis of the speeches in *Baker v Willoughby* (at para [35.51]) that he was entitled to compensation for the difference between his pre-accident earnings and the earnings he would have received in such light work during the remainder of his expectation of life. It was accepted that there was no causal connection between the injury to his hand and the heart disease.

HELD: In *Baker's* case the second injury was tortious; in this case not. If what was said in *Baker's* case was meant also to apply to cases where the second injury was non-tortious it was *obiter* and not binding. There was no reason in logic or justice why the defendants should compensate the claimant for a consequence for which they were not to blame, namely, loss of earnings due to heart disease which came upon him unconnected with anything the defendants did. An award of damages is not the imposition of a fine or penalty but is made to compensate the victim for consequences of the wrongful act of the defendants and nothing else. The defendants were not liable for loss of earnings from mid-1976 onwards.

[35.53] Jobling v Associated Dairies Ltd

[1982] AC 794, [1981] 2 All ER 752, [1981] 3 WLR 155, 125 Sol Jo 481, HL

In January 1973 the appellant claimant slipped and fell at work in circumstances imposing liability for damages in tort on the respondents, his employers. The accident caused injury to his back which kept him off work for a time and on his resuming work his earning capacity was 50% less than before the accident. In 1976 he became totally disabled by myelopathy a disease not brought on by the accident. At the trial of the action in 1979 the judge, following Lord Reid's views in *Baker v*

Willoughby (at para [35.51]) awarded the claimant damages for loss of earnings for a period after 1976, considering himself 'bound to leave out of account the disability caused to the [claimant] by the myelopathy in assessing the damages resulting from the 1973 incident'. The Court of Appeal reversed the finding.

HELD, ON APPEAL to the House of Lords: Appeal dismissed. The appellant was not entitled to damages for loss of earnings after he became disabled by myelopathy. Where the victim of a tort is overtaken before trial by a wholly unconnected and disabling illness the decision in *Baker v Willoughby* does not apply. No consideration of policy warrant placing liability for loss of earnings on the respondents after the emergence of myelopathy; the onset or emergence of illness is one of the vicissitudes of life relevant to the assessment of damages. Whether the decision in *Baker's* case was correct on its facts (ie as a case of two successive tortious injuries) must be left open, but Lord Reid's *ratio decidendi* in that case could not be accepted. Per Lord Edmund-Davies: 'I can formulate no convincing juristic or logical principles supportive of the decision of this House in *Baker v Willoughby*.'

Note—See also *Rahman v Arearose Ltd* (at para [35.31]).

4.   ECONOMIC LOSS

[35.54]   *Note*—Mere economic loss unaccompanied by damage to the claimant's person or property is irrecoverable in an action for negligence.

(A)   NEGLIGENT CONDUCT

[35.55]   Weller & Co v Foot and Mouth Disease Research Institute
[1966] 1 QB 569, [1965] 3 All ER 560, [1965] 3 WLR 1082, 109 Sol Jo 702, [1965] 2 Lloyd's Rep 414

The defendant allowed foot and mouth virus to escape into the atmosphere. As a result the Minister of Agriculture ordered the Guildford and Farnham cattle markets to be closed: the claimant was an auctioneer there and lost business by reason of the closure.

HELD: The claimant could not recover damages from the defendant. A great volume of authority both before and after *Donoghue v Stevenson* [1932] AC 562 was to the effect that a claimant suing in negligence for damages suffered as a result of an act or omission of the defendant could not recover if the act or omission did not directly injure, or at least threaten directly to injure, the claimant's person or property but merely caused consequential loss, as, for example, by upsetting his business relations with a third party who was the direct victim of the act or omission. A duty of care which arose from a direct injury to person or property was owed only to those whose person or property might foreseeably be injured by a failure to take care. If the claimant could show that the duty was owed to him, he could recover both direct and consequential loss which was reasonably foreseeable and there was no reason for saying that proof of direct loss was an essential part of the claim. The claimant had, however, to show he was within the scope of the defendant's duty to take care. In the present case the duty to take care to avoid an escape of virus was owed to the owners of cattle which might be infected by the virus. The claimant was not an owner of cattle and had no proprietary interest in anything that might conceivably be damaged by the virus if it escaped.

Note—See also *Lee Cooper v CH Jenkins & Sons Ltd* [1967] 2 QB 1, [1965] 1 All ER 280, [1965] 3 WLR 753, 109 Sol Jo 794, [1964] 1 Lloyd's Rep 300.

[35.56]   British Celanese Ltd v AH Hunt (Capacitors) Ltd

[1969] 2 All ER 1252, [1969] 1 WLR 959, 113 Sol Jo 368   Lawton J

The claimant and the defendant both occupied premises on an industrial estate about 150 yards apart, supplied with electricity from a sub-station about 100 yards from the claimant's premises. Metal foil strips were blown by the wind from the defendant's premises on to busbars at the sub-station and caused a breakdown in the electricity supply to the claimant's factory. Material solidified in their machines which had to be cleaned. It claimed damages for loss of production and profit. Metal foil strips had been blown into the sub-station on a previous occasion and the electricity board had warned the defendant that it could cause a failure of electricity supply to premises on the estate.

HELD: The damages claimed were not too remote. The solidifying of material in the machines was damage to property and the loss claimed for was not merely economic. Unlike the claimant in *Weller & Co v Foot and Mouth Disease Research Institute* (at para [35.55]) the present claimant was a direct victim of the negligence alleged. In the present case, too, the defendant owed the claimant a duty of care because it foresaw or ought to have foreseen that the interruption of power supplies would injure the claimant's property.

[35.57]   SCM (UK) Ltd v WJ Whittall & Son Ltd

[1971] 1 QB 337, [1970] 3 All ER 245, [1970] 3 WLR 694, 114 Sol Jo 706, CA

The defendant was digging a trench in a road adjoining a number of factories of which the claimant's was one. In the course of the work the defendant damaged an electric cable, causing a power failure in the claimant's factory. Molten material solidified in the machines causing physical damage to the claimant's materials and tools. It claimed damages, confining the claim to the physical damage and to economic loss directly consequential on that physical damage.

HELD: The claimant was entitled to recover. The defendant owed it a duty of care not to damage the cable because it knew that if it damaged it the current would be cut off and damage would be suffered by the factory owners. It was immaterial that the factory was not liable to be directly injured. A man may owe a duty of care to those whom he foresees may be indirectly injured as well as to those whom he foresees may be directly affected. But (per Lord Denning) when the claimant has suffered no damage to his person or property, but has only sustained economic loss, the law does not usually permit him to recover that loss; this is not because no duty of care is owed to him but because it is too remote to be a head of damage. *Weller & Co v Foot and Mouth Disease Research Institute* (at para [35.55]) depends on remoteness, not duty of care; similarly *Electrochrome v Welsh Plastics* [1968] 2 All ER 205.

Per Winn LJ: There is no liability (except in the special case of negligently uttered false statements) for unintentional negligent infliction of any form of economic loss which is not consequential on foreseeable physical injury or damage to property. *British Celanese Ltd v Hunt* (at para [35.56]) approved.

[35.58]   **Spartan Steel and Alloys Ltd v Martin & Co (Contractors) Ltd**
[1973] QB 27, [1972] 3 All ER 557, [1972] 3 WLR 502, 116 Sol Jo 648, CA

The claimant's factory was supplied with electricity by a direct cable from the power station. The defendants was doing work in a road about a quarter-mile from the factory and negligently damaged the cable causing the power supply to the factory to be cut off for 14 hours. As a result the claimant suffered loss from:
- (1)   damage to metal in an electric furnace;
- (2)   loss of profit on that melt of metal;
- (3)   loss of profit on metal which they would have subsequently melted during the period the power was off.

HELD: The claimant was entitled to damages under heads (1) and (2) but not head (3). The loss under head (3) was economic loss independent of the physical damage to the metal in the furnace when the power failed.

Note—Applied in *Greater Nottingham Cooperative Society v Cementation Piling & Foundations Ltd* [1989] QB 71, [1988] 3 WLR 396, CA. See also *Muirhead v Industrial Tank Specialities* (at para [4.16]).

[35.59]   **Junior Books Ltd v Veitchi Co Ltd**
[1983] 1 AC 520, [1982] 3 All ER 201, [1982] 3 WLR 477, HL

The claimant alleged that the flooring laid by the defendants was defective and sought the cost of replacing the floor. The damages included economic loss.

HELD, ON APPEAL to the House of Lords: (Brandon LJ dissenting) the relationship of the parties was very close. The defendants were specialists and knew that economic loss would result if flooring defects had to be remedied. Liability for economic loss was allowed when it was linked to physical damage. A duty was owed and there was no reason to limit its scope in view of the proximity of the parties. 'There was no physical damage or risk of it' (per Brandon LJ).

Note—See the comments in *Muirhead v Industrial Tank Specialities* (at para [4.16]).

[35.60]   **Simaan General Contracting Co v Pilkington Glass Ltd (No 2)**
[1988] QB 758, [1988] 1 All ER 791, [1988] 2 WLR 761, 132 Sol Jo 463, CA

The claimant was main contractor for the construction of the Al-Oteiba Building in Abu Dhabi, which was to be walled in green glass. It subcontracted the installation of the glass to another company who bought it from Pilkingtons. Simaan sued the defendant in negligence, alleging that Pilkington, as the specified suppliers of the glass units, owed it a duty to take reasonable care to avoid defects in the units which (it was assumed for the purposes of a preliminary issue) had caused the claimant economic loss. Did it? The defendant appealed against the judge's finding that it did.

HELD, ON APPEAL: It did not. There was no special relationship between the claimant and defendant – the claimant had merely instructed its subcontractor to buy the units from Pilkington because it was contractually obliged to do so and Pilkington had assumed no direct responsibility to the claimant for the units.

[35.61]   **Smith v Smith**
(4 November 1997, unreported), Rawtenstall County Court

The claimant owned a taxi which he rented to a friend at nights for £100 per week. The defendant negligently collided with the taxi whilst it was being driven by the friend. The friend was injured and was unable to continue renting the taxi from the claimant. The claimant included in his claim the loss of income from renting the taxi to his friend.

HELD: (Per DJ Pickup) this loss was pure economic loss and was irrecoverable. The defendant did not owe a duty of care to prevent such loss being suffered by the claimant. *Spartan Steel & Alloys Ltd v Martin & Co (Contractors) Ltd* (at para [35.58]) followed.

(B)   PHYSICAL DAMAGE TO PROPERTY

[35.62]   D & F Estates Ltd v Church Comrs for England and Wales
[1989] AC 177, [1988] 2 All ER 992, [1988] 3 WLR 368, HL

The claimant owned a flat in Gloucester Square, London. It was built between 1963 and 1965. Wates Ltd was the main contractor. The plaster work was incorrectly applied by its subcontractors: in 1980 the plaster was found to be loose and some fell. The claimant sued Wates for damages for negligence to cover the cost of replacing the plaster and some consequential losses.

HELD: The cost of repairing the plaster incurred by the claimant was pure economic loss, not recoverable in tort. There is no right of action in tort for the cost of rectifying a negligently caused defect where that defect has not caused personal injury or physical damage to other property. Damages for personal injury and for damage to extraneous property remain recoverable under the conventional *Donoghue v Stevenson* [1932] AC 562 principles.

[35.63]   Greater Nottingham Co-operative Society v Cementation Piling and Foundations Ltd
[1989] QB 71, [1988] 2 All ER 971, [1988] 3 WLR 396, 132 Sol Jo 754, CA

The claimant employed contractors to execute extension works at their premises in Lumley Road, Skegness. Cementation was the piling contractor but entered into a direct collateral agreement with the claimant, covering standards of design, workmanship and materials. A Cementation employee negligently operated the piling equipment and caused damage to the Windsor Restaurant next door. This had two effects:
  (1)   the claimant had to compensate the restaurant owners for damage to their property; and
  (2)   the building contract was delayed, causing the claimant economic loss. The claimant claimed against Cementation, in negligence, under both heads and was successful before an official referee.

HELD, ON APPEAL: That the claimant's economic loss, although a reasonably foreseeable consequence of Cementation's negligence, was pecuniary loss unconnected with any damage to the claimant's own property. Moreover, the collateral agreement between the claimant and Cementation illustrated the lack of any assumption (voluntary or otherwise) by Cementation of any responsibility for economic loss and thus that no duty in tort should be imposed. (*Spartan Steel and Alloys Ltd v Martin* (at para [35.58]), *Junior Books Ltd v Veitchi Co Ltd* (at para [35.59]) and *Muirhead v Industrial Tanks Specialities Ltd* (at para [4.16])) distinguished).

[35.64]   Murphy v Brentwood District Council

[1991] 1 AC 398, [1990] 2 All ER 908, HL

The claimant purchased a house built on an infilled site. The house had been built on a concrete raft foundation. The plans for this foundation had been approved by the defendant council following discussions with consulting engineers. Some 11 years after the purchase the claimant noticed cracks in his house caused by the failure of the foundations. The claimant sold his house subject to the defect for £35,000 less than its market value in sound condition and sued the council. The claimant claimed that he and his family had suffered an imminent risk to health and safety due to the fact that the soil pipes had broken and there was a risk of further breakages. The judge found for the claimant and this was upheld on appeal. The council appealed to the House of Lords.

HELD: The claimant's claim failed. The defects were defects within the structure of the property and had not caused either damage to other property or physical injury. Thus the claimant's loss was purely economic and not recoverable. The council owed no duty of care to the claimant when it approved the plans for the foundations for his house.

> 'I see no reason to doubt that the principle of *Donoghue v Stevenson* [1932] AC 562 does indeed apply so as to place the builder of premises under a duty to take reasonable care to avoid injury through defects in the premises to the person or property of those whom he should have in contemplation as likely to suffer such injury if care is not taken': per Lord Keith.

(C)   SPECIAL RELATIONSHIP

[35.65]   Caparo Industries plc v Dickman

[1990] 2 AC 605, [1990] 1 All ER 568, HL

The claimants both held shares in Fidelity plc. The defendant was the company's auditors. The claimants relied on the defendant's accounts to purchase further shares in Fidelity plc and eventually mount a successful take over bid for the company. The claimants alleged that the accounts were misleading and inaccurate in that they showed a pre-tax profit whereas they should have recorded a loss. The claimants claimed that had they been aware of the proper figures they would not have purchased the further shares and made the take over bid. The court was asked to decide whether the auditors owed a duty of care to the claimants.

HELD, ON APPEAL to the House of Lords: The defendant auditors owed no duty of care to shareholders in the company or to members of the public in respect of the accuracy of the accounts. The accounts were prepared for the shareholders of the company to assist them in controlling and managing that company, not to promote the interests of potential investors. The House of Lords applied a three-stage test for determining a duty of care: foreseeability of damage, proximity, and whether it was just and reasonable to that the law should impose a duty of care.

> '… the necessary relationship between the maker of a statement or giver of advice (the adviser) and the recipient who acts in reliance on it (the advisee) may typically be held to exist where (1) the advice is required for a purpose, whether particularly specified or generally described, which is made known, either actually or inferentially to the adviser at the time when the advice is

given, (2) the adviser knows, either actually or inferentially, that his advice will be communicated to the advisee, either specifically or as a member of an ascertainable class, in order that it should be used by the advisee for that purpose, (3) it is known, either actually or inferentially, that the advice so communicated is likely to be acted on by the advisee for that purpose without independent inquiry and (4) it is so acted on by the advisee to his detriment': per Lord Oliver.

Note—See also *Hedley Burn & Co Ltd v Heller & Partners Ltd* [1964] AC 465, [1963] 2 All ER 575, [1963] 3 WLR 101, HL.

[35.66]   Smith v Eric S Bush (a firm)
[1990] 1 AC 831, [1989] 2 All ER 514, HL

Mrs Smith purchased a house with the assistance of a building society mortgage. The building society instructed a building surveyor from the defendant firm to value the property for which Mrs Smith paid a fee of £36.89. The report stated that the house did not require any essential repairs. Mrs Smith did not obtain her own independent surveyors report but purchased the house in reliance upon the defendant's findings. Unfortunately two chimney breasts had been removed but the chimney breast in the loft and the chimneys had not been supported. Eighteen months after purchase the bricks from the chimneys collapsed and caused damage.

The question to be asked was did the defendant owe a duty of care to the claimant? The defendant sought to rely upon a clause excluding liability.

HELD: The defendant valuer did owe a duty of care to the claimant. The valuer assumed a responsibility to both the building society and the claimant by agreeing to carry out the valuation for mortgage purposes. He knew that the valuation fee had been paid by the claimant and he knew that the valuation would probably be relied upon by the claimant in order to decide whether or not she would purchase the property. The claimant, who had paid the fee, was entitled to rely upon the professional skill and advice given by the defendant valuer.

The disclaimer of liability was subject to the test of reasonableness as defined by s 11(3) of the Unfair Contract Terms Act 1977. The defendant valuer had been paid for his services. It was common knowledge that 90% of purchasers relied on the mortgage valuation to purchase their property and did not commission their own survey. Many purchasers could not afford a second valuation. It was therefore inevitable that a great many purchasers would rely upon the mortgage valuation commissioned by the building society. Furthermore, the defendant valuer knew that failure on his part to exercise reasonable care and skill would be disastrous to the purchaser. Therefore the disclaimer was not effective to exclude liability for the negligence of the valuer.

[35.67]   Henderson v Merrett Syndicates Ltd
[1995] 2 AC 145, [1994] 3 All ER 506, [1994] 2 Lloyd's Rep 468, HL

The claimants were Lloyd's names and members of various syndicates managed by the defendant underwriting agents. The claimants alleged that the defendant had been negligent in the management and conduct of the claimants' syndicates. For limitation purposes the claimants wished to establish that the defendant owed them a duty of care in tort in addition to any contractual duties that the defendant may have owed. The claimants were successful at first instance and in the Court of Appeal. The defendant appealed to the House of Lords.

HELD: A duty of care was owed by the managing agents at Lloyd's to a name who is a member of a syndicate under management of the agents.

Per Lord Goff of Chieveley: The managing agents have accepted the names as members of a syndicate under their management. They obviously hold themselves out as possessing a special expertise to advise the names on the suitability of risks to be underwritten; and on the circumstances in which, and the extent to which, reinsurance should be taken out and claims should be settled. The names, as the managing agents well knew, placed implicit reliance on that expertise, in that they gave authority to the managing agents to bind them to contracts of insurance and reinsurance and to the settlement of claims. I can see no escape from the conclusion that, in the circumstances, *prima facie* a duty of care is owed in tort by the managing agents to such names. To me, it does not matter if one proceeds by way of analogy from the categories of relationship already recognised as falling within the principle in *Hedley Burn & Co Ltd v Heller & Partners Ltd* [1964] AC 465, [1963] 2 All ER 575, [1963] 3 WLR 101, HL or by a straight application of the principle stated in the *Hedley Byrne* case itself. On either basis the conclusion is, in my opinion, clear. Furthermore since the duty rests on the principle in *Hedley Byrne*, no problem arises from the fact that the loss suffered by the names is pure economic loss.'

In addition it was held that the existence of a tortious duty of care could arise irrespective of the contractual relationship between the parties. Therefore, unless the contract between the parties precluded him from doing so, a claimant who had available to him concurrent remedies in contract and tort was entitled to choose that remedy which appeared to him to be the most advantageous.

Note—See also *Spring v Guardian Assurance plc* (at para [4.10]) and *Lennon v Metropolitan Police Commissioner* [2004] EWCA Civ 130, [2004] 2 All ER 266.

5.   MITIGATION

(A)   THE RULE

[35.68]

The burden is on the defendant to show that the claimant failed to take reasonable steps to mitigate his damages. See *Geest plc v Monica Lansiquot* (at para [35.91]) and *Garnac Grain Co v Faure & HMF Fairclough Ltd* [1968] AC 1130n, [1967] 2 All ER 353, HL.

(B)   VALUE OF REPAIRS

[35.69]   **Pomphrey v James A Cuthbertson**
1951 SC 147, 1951 SLT 191, Ct of Sess

The pursuer:
   (1)   the cost of a vehicle which he had bought to replace his damaged car;
   (2)   the cost of adapting it to his purposes; and
   (3)   hire charges until replacement; less the scrap value of his damaged car.

HELD: This was the wrong basis; the correct basis being either the cost of repair plus hire charges, or the market value of the damaged car immediately before the accident, plus hire charges until replaced, less its scrap value.

[35.70]   The Pacific Concord

[1961] I All ER 106, [1961] I WLR 873, 105 Sol Jo 492, [1960] 2 Lloyd's Rep 270

The claimants' vessel was damaged in a collision with the defendants' vessel for which the defendants admitted liability. The repairs (for which there was no urgency) were carried out at London where repair charges were about 50% more than at Newcastle where the claimants could have had them done if they had taken reasonable precautions to give adequate notice to stem a dry dock. Moreover by having the repairs done before the cancellation of a charter party instead of after it they lost £2,319 profit on the charter.

HELD: The claimants' duty was to make such arrangements for the repair of the damage as a prudent uninsured owner would make for himself. It was an unreasonable decision to have the repairs done when and where the claimants had them done: they were not entitled to recover from the defendants the additional expense by having them done at London, nor the loss of profit on the charter party. *Dunkirk Colliery Co v Lever* (1878) 9 Ch D 20, 26 WR 481, CA applied.

[35.71]   O'Grady v Westminster Scaffolding Ltd

[1962] 2 Lloyd's Rep 238   Edmund Davies J

The claimant claimed for the loss and expense he had sustained by the negligence of the defendants in damaging his car on 13 July 1960. The car was a 1937 MG which he had bought in 1947 for £475. It had been maintained by him in exceptionally good condition at considerable expense: in the year before the accident the claimant had spent over £300 on a new engine and coachwork. It was doubtful whether a car of the same type in similar condition could be found on the open market. The claimant had the car repaired at a price of £253 and claimed this sum plus hire charges of £207 for cars hired whilst the repairs were being carried out. The defendant contended that the pre-accident value of the car was about £180 and the salvage value £35 to £40 and that the claimant had acted unreasonably in having the car repaired.

HELD: The pre-accident market value of chattels affords a guide to the measure of compensation when, and only when, a similar chattel can be obtained in the open market. The claimant acted reasonably in having the car repaired and in hiring other cars whilst the repairs were being done.

[35.72]   Harbutts Plasticine Ltd v Wayne Tank and Pump Co Ltd

[1970] I QB 447, [1970] I All ER 225, [1970] 2 WLR 198, 114 Sol Jo 29, CA

Per Widgery LJ: The distinction between those cases in which the measure of damages is the cost of repair of the damaged article and those in which it is the diminution in value of the article is not clearly defined ... Each case turns on its own facts, it being remembered, first, that the purpose of the award of damages is to restore the [claimant] to his position before the loss occurred, and second, that the [claimant] must act reasonably to mitigate his loss. If the article damaged is a motor car of popular make, the [claimant] cannot charge the defendant with the cost of repair when it is cheaper to buy a similar car on the market. On the other hand if no substitute for the damaged article is available and no reasonable alternative can be provided, the [claimant] should be entitled to the cost of repair.

[35.73]   Payton v Brooks

[1974] RTR 169, [1974] 1 Lloyd's Rep 241, CA

The claimant's car, only four weeks old, was damaged by the defendant. He claimed from her not only the cost of repairs but also the sum of £100 being the estimated loss of market value of the car, even after repair, due to its being a repaired car. The judge awarded only the cost of repairs, finding on the evidence that no diminution in market value had been established by the claimant.

HELD, ON APPEAL: The judge's finding of fact must be accepted, but *obiter*, if the judge had found that the diminution in value had been established the claimant would have been entitled to an award. The normal measure of damages is the cost of repair but if, despite good repairs, a reduced market value can be proved, compensation for the reduction can be awarded to the claimant, the value of his property as a saleable asset having been reduced.

(C)   LOSS OF PROFIT CLAIMS

[35.74]   Bellingham v Dhillon

[1973] QB 304, [1973] 1 All ER 20, [1972] 3 WLR 730, 116 Sol Jo 566   Forbes J

The claimant was a driving school proprietor. In 1967 he was negotiating to install an electronic simulator to teach driving but because of injuries he had sustained in an accident for which the defendant was responsible the negotiations broke down. A simulator would have cost him £1,824 a year for five years and then £71 per year. In 1971 he was able to, and did, buy one outright secondhand from a company in liquidation. But for this purchase his net loss of profit on simulator teaching would be £2,774; if the defendant was entitled to take the purchase of the secondhand simulator into account the loss was nil. It was argued for the claimant that sums which came to him as a result of the tortious act and would not have come to him but for the tort were not to be taken into account.

HELD: The claimant had a duty to mitigate his damage by buying equipment just as much when that damage arose in tort as if it had arisen in contract. Applying the principles set out by Lord Haldane in *British Westinghouse v Underground Electric Railways Co* [1912] AC 673, 81 LJKB 1132, 107 LT 325, HL the damages were to be arrived at by subtracting the profits the business earned after the wrong had been suffered from the profits the business would have earned on the hypothesis that the defendant's wrong had not reduced them, looking at the whole of the facts and ascertaining the result. On this basis no loss arose on the simulator venture.

(D)   HIRE OF REPLACEMENT VEHICLE

Note—Mitigation arguments in respect of hire will concern need, period and/or rate.

[35.75]   Macrae v Swindells

[1954] 2 All ER 260, [1954] 1 WLR 597, 98 Sol Jo 233   Barry J

A garage negligently or by breach of contract damaged a customer's car which was with the garage for repairs. The garage lent the customer another car until it was properly repaired. The customer's servant negligently drove the lent car and it was destroyed in an accident. The garage obtained judgment against the customer for the value of the lent car. No other car was offered by the garage and the customer hired another car till he received his car back and sued the garage for the amount of the hire charges incurred.

HELD: The hire was the result of the negligence or breach of contract of the garage and not the result of the negligence of the customer's servant; the reason the lent car ceased to be available was irrelevant.

[35.76] Watson-Norie Ltd v Shaw
[1967] 1 Lloyd's Rep 515, 111 Sol Jo 117, CA

The claimant company's Jensen car, used by the managing director was damaged by the defendant's negligence. The company hired a Rover and later a Jaguar car for seven weeks at £40 per week whilst it was being repaired, these cars being of equivalent value and prestige to a Jensen. The defendant objected that the amount was unreasonable and the claimant had failed to mitigate its damage. There was evidence that a Triumph Herald could be hired at £17 10s per week or a Ford Zephyr at £25 per week. The county court judge thought it was not reasonable to expect the claimant to use the Triumph but that the Ford would have been suitable. He considered the claimant had been casual in hiring a replacement, not having made inquiries to find out if a suitable car could be obtained more cheaply. He awarded only £25 per week loss of use.

HELD, on the claimant's appeal: There was material before the judge that a reasonable substitute could be hired for £25 per week and he was entitled to reach the conclusion he did. Where as here it was necessary to hire a car for only a short period it was not necessarily right that the defendants had to pay the cost of hiring a car equal in value and prestige to the damaged car.

[35.77] Martindale v Duncan
[1973] 2 All ER 355, [1973] 1 WLR 574, 117 Sol Jo 168, CA

On 27 November the claimant's taxi was damaged. He obtained an estimate of the cost of repair on 1 December and claimed the estimated amount from the defendant. He did not instruct the repairers to carry out the repairs, not being able to afford them and believing he had to allow the defendant's insurers to inspect the vehicle and also to get permission from his own insurers. It was not until 26 January that the defendant's insurers wrote agreeing the cost of repairs after an engineers' inspection. The claimant then instructed the repairers and the repairs were completed by 25 February. Meanwhile the claimant had hired a replacement vehicle for ten weeks, starting a month after the accident. The defendant contested payment of the hire charges on the ground that the repairs should have been put in hand immediately after the accident.

HELD: It was not a case like *Liesbosch, Dredger v Edison SS* (at para [35.19]). The claimant was seeking to recover his damages from the defendant's insurers and, if that went wrong, to recover from his own insurers. Until he had authorisation to do the work he could not be certain of being in a good position vis-à-vis the insurance company.

[35.78] HL Motorworks (Willesden) Ltd v Alwahbi
[1977] RTR 276, CA

The claimant was a motor repairer. When giving a test run to a customer's car, a Rolls Royce, it was damaged by the defendant's negligence and was off the road 11 days for repairs. The owner hired another Rolls Royce for those 11 days at a cost of £467.55, which the claimant paid. In a claim against the defendant for reimbursement the judge held that it was unnecessary for so great an expense to be incurred and awarded only £160 as being sufficient for hiring a suitable car.

HELD: He should have awarded the whole amount. The owner of the car was entitled to have another Rolls Royce during the 11 days he had been deprived of his own. He was the claimant's customer and it might have been damaging to the relationship to try to cut down the amount of his claim. *Watson Norie Ltd v Shaw* (at para [35.76]) was quite a different case.

[35.79]   Daily Office Cleaning Contractors v Shefford
[1977] RTR 361   Stabb J

The claimant company supplied its directors with so-called 'prestige' cars for use in their work. One of these, an American-made Rambler car, was damaged in a collision by the defendant's negligent driving. The claimant sent its car to their usual garage by whom it was sent to coachwork repairers who applied to the main suppliers for the necessary parts. Meanwhile the claimant obtained from the garage on hire a Jaguar XJ6 at £75 per week, a concessionary price: the normal price was £100 per week. Because of long delays in obtaining necessary parts repairs were not completed until 25 weeks had elapsed. The claimant claimed 25 weeks' hire at £75 per week. The defendant contended that to hire a Jaguar XJ6 for so long was unreasonable in that a medium-sized car would have sufficed.

HELD: A claimant had only to act reasonably when dealing with a situation he finds himself in as a result of the act of a tortfeasor. There was no call for the claimant to shop around to hire a car at a lesser sum from someone with whom it did not normally deal, especially as the Jaguar was supplied at a concessionary rate. Although the repairs took a long time the claimant had pressed the repairers to hasten completion and it would be wrong to blame the claimant for the American Motor Corporation's delay in delivery.

[35.80]   Giles v Thompson, Devlin v Baslington
[1994] 1 AC 142, [1993] 3 All ER 321, HL

The claimant's vehicles were damaged in road traffic accidents for which the defendants were entirely to blame. The claimant hired alternative vehicles until its own vehicles were repaired. The claimant entered into an arrangement with hire car companies whereby the claimant agreed that proceedings for the recovery of these charges could be brought in their names. The claimant was not obliged to make any payments to the hire car company. The defendant argued that the arrangement was champertous, against public policy and, in any event, the claimant had not suffered any loss. The cases were appealed to the House of Lords.

HELD: The law of champerty (which has its origins in medieval times) was designed to prevent the 'wanton and officious intermeddling' in other peoples disputes. There was nothing to indicate that any of the actions of the hire companies had been champertous nor were the arrangements contrary to public policy.

The terms of the arrangements between the claimant and the hire companies were such that the claimant remained liable throughout for the hire charges and therefore had suffered a recoverable loss.

Per curiam: 'The need for a replacement car is not self-proving ... there remains ample scope for the defendant in an individual case to displace the inference that might otherwise arise': per Lord Mustill.

Note—See also *Mattocks v Mann* (at para [35.26]).

[35.81] **Dimond v Lovell**

[2002] 1 AC 384, [2000] 2 All ER 897, [2000] 2 WLR 1121, HL

The defendant ran into the rear of the claimant's vehicle. The claimant's vehicle was damaged but drivable. During the time that the claimant's vehicle was in the garage the claimant hired a replacement vehicle from a car hire company called First Automotive Ltd. The charge was £30 per day for the eight days during which the claimant's vehicle was off the road together with a £5 collision damage waiver and £15 delivery charge. The total charge including VAT was £346.63.

The defendant accepted liability but refused to pay for the hire of the replacement car for the following reasons—

(a) the agreement between the claimant and First Automotive Ltd was a 'regulated agreement' within the terms of the Consumer Credit Act 1974. As such the agreement fell foul of the Consumer Credit Act Regulations and was unenforceable. Therefore the claimant had not suffered any loss because she could not be required to pay for the hired vehicle;

(b) the claimant had failed to mitigate her loss as the sum claimed for the eight-day period of hire was excessive.

HELD, ON APPEAL to the House of Lords: The agreement between the claimant and First Automotive Ltd did provide credit and was therefore subject to the provisions of the Consumer Credit Act 1974. Given the prescribed terms were absent from the agreement, the agreement was improperly executed and 'irredeemably unenforceable' (per Lord Hoffmann) against the claimant.

The claimant had had the car for free. She was also not entitled to damages. The House of Lords was not prepared to accept that she can sue as trustee in respect of the hire company's charges. This would be contrary to the Consumer Credit Act 1974.

A claimant who hires a car from a credit hire company cannot fail to mitigate his loss. The majority of the House of Lords held that the claimant was not entitled to recover the full credit hire rate because that rate incorporated additional benefits which were not recoverable as a matter of law. In the view of Lords Hoffmann and Browne-Wilkinson, the net loss would ordinarily be the spot hire rate. Lord Hobhouse preferred to describe it as 'making a commercial apportionment between the cost of hiring a car and the cost of other benefits described included in the scheme'.

Comment: Where there is a contractual liability on a hirer to pay hire charges, there is a recoverable loss. Credit hire companies will be able to continue to make their agreements exempt from the Consumer Credit Act 1974 if they include a clause that requires that the hire should in any event be paid (if at all) within 12 months.

[35.82] **Clark v Ardington Electrical Services**

[2002] EWCA Civ 510

[2002] 3 WLR 762

The Court Appeal gave judgment in four 'Helphire' litigation test cases and one other concerning credit hire schemes and repair services to innocent drivers of road traffic accidents. The Court of Appeal upheld the decision of HHJ Charles Harris QC that the Helphire agreement should be regarded as an exempt agreement and did not fall within the ambit of s 15 of the Consumer Credit Act 1974. The court further considered that the claimant was entitled to recover 100% of the repair costs, even where an agreement is reached by Helphire to reduce the actual costs paid to the garage.

If there were any delays in carrying out those repairs which are not attributable to the claimant, the defendant will be able to bring the garage into proceedings if they are the cause of the delays. It was further held that it is for the defendant to establish that the claimant had failed to mitigate their loss as the claimant is not required to shop around for the best deals.

[35.83]   Lagden v O'Connor

[2003] UKHL 64

[2004] 1 AC 1067, HL

The claimant was unemployed and in poor health. He could not afford to hire a replacement car and entered into an agreement with Helphire, a credit hire company. The judge held that the claimant had no option but to use the credit hire company and allowed the charges in full. The Court of Appeal upheld the decision. The defendant appealed contending that following *Dimond v Lovell* (at para [35.81]) the claimant was not entitled to the full costs which included additional benefits but only the spot hire rate of hiring.

HELD, ON APPEAL to the House of Lords: Appeal dismissed (Lord Scott and Lord Walker dissenting). It was foreseeable that the claimant would need another car whilst his was being repaired. Due to his circumstances, the claimant had no choice but to use the services of a credit hire company and accept the additional benefits. Had he been able to afford to pay the cost of hire up front, the claimant would not have been entitled to recover those additional costs. The defendant must take his victim as he finds him.

Dimond v Lovell distinguished as the impecunious motorist was not directly in issue in that case.

(E)   LOSS OF EARNINGS

[35.84]   Luker v Chapman

(1970) 114 Sol Jo 788   Browne J

The claimant's injuries, caused by the defendant's negligent driving, were such that he was unable to continue his pre-accident job as a telephone engineer. His employers offered him clerical work but he refused it, deciding instead to train as a teacher. He claimed his loss of earnings during the period of his training.

HELD: Though the claimant was showing courage in undertaking this training he was under a duty to mitigate his damage and should have accepted the clerical job. The defendant could not be held liable for that loss.

Note—See also *Rowden v Clarke Chapman & Co* [1967] 3 All ER 608n where the court held that the claimant had acted reasonably in retraining and securing a job at reduced earnings.

[35.85]   Samuels v Benning

[2002] EWCA Civ 858, CA

The claimant was seriously injured in a road traffic accident. Having lost his job, the claimant enrolled on a degree course rather than retraining. The judge concluded that the claimant should have chosen a more appropriate and less ambitious course for someone who had only undertaken manual work. As he had had ample time to retrain, the judge rejected his claim for future loss of earnings. The claimant appealed.

HELD: There was force in the defendant's contention that the claimant had failed to mitigate his loss and seek appropriate new employment. The claimant had taken no steps to equip himself for paid work. However, the court should also appreciate that the claimant was the innocent party and was injured in the accident. The objective evidence was that his injuries had significantly disadvantaged him on the labour market and would still be there however much he mitigated his loss. The claimant was awarded a lump sum of £35,000 to reflect this disadvantage.

Note—See para [36.69] for further cases on *Smith v Manchester* awards.

[35.86]   Morris v Richards

[2003] EWCA Civ 232

[2004] PIQR Q3, CA

The claimant was injured in a road traffic accident in 1996. As a result, she was eventually forced to give up her job as a radiographer. She found a new better paid job as a marketing manager but resigned after seven months in November 2000. The trial judge awarded loss of earnings from the date of her resignation until the trial in October 2001. The defendant appealed the loss of earnings following her resignation.

HELD: Appeal dismissed. The correct approach in these cases was to start from the position that the claimant was not to blame for her injuries and that she lost her original job because of the claimant's tortious act. The judge had been entitled to find that the claimant was not suited to the job of marketing manager and that she had not acted unreasonably in resigning.

Note—See also *Froggatt v LEP International* [2002] EWCA Civ 600, [2002] All ER (D) 108 (Apr), CA.

[35.87]   Butler v Thompson

[2005] EWCA Civ 864

[2005] All ER (D) 164 (Jul), CA

The claimant was injured in a road traffic accident. The Recorder found that she had had to give up teaching and that her part-time earnings of £2,018 a year did not represent a failure to mitigate her loss. Although the claimant agreed that she could work extra hours, there was 'no obligation to work harder than is reasonable'. The defendant contended she could earn £7,000 a year or more and appealed.

HELD: The Recorder should have asked whether it was reasonable to expect the claimant's earning capacity to be greater than her earnings. The claimant had a residual earning capacity of £3,500 a year and the award should be recalculated.

(F)   REFUSAL TO UNDERGO OPERATION/TREATMENT

[35.88]   McAuley v London Transport Executive
[1957] 2 Lloyd's Rep 500, CA

It cannot be laid down as a general rule that a claimant can disregard the advice given by a doctor examining him, even though the doctor examining him is doing so on behalf of the defendant. The question is one of fact in each particular case. Was the advice, and were the prospects of success of the proposed operation or treatment, clearly put to the claimant, so that he, as a reasonable man, would appreciate that he was being advised that this treatment or operation would put him right? If the evidence shows that, the claimant, as a reasonable person, ought either to accept that advice, or else go to his own doctor and ask for his advice.

[35.89]   Morgan v T Wallis Ltd
[1974] 1 Lloyd's Rep 165, QBD

Per Browne J: The [claimant] in the present case is not in the slightest degree a malingerer and is a completely honest man who genuinely holds the beliefs about which he has told us in evidence. But in deciding whether the defendants have proved that he had unreasonably refused to have the investigation and operation in question here, it seems to me clear from the authorities to which I have referred [*Steele v Robert George & Co* ([1942] AC 497, [1942] 1 All ER 447), *Marcroft v Scruttons Ltd* ([1954] 1 Lloyd's Rep 395, CA)] that I must apply an objective test, in this sense, would a reasonable man, in all the circumstances, receiving the advice the [claimant] did receive, have refused the operation? I think this question must be considered as at the times when his decision was made and on the basis of the advice he then received. If the [claimant] preferred and prefers to go on as he is rather than have the operation [for removal of a prolapsed intervertebral disc] no one can blame him. But the question I have to consider is not, 'Is the [claimant] to blame for refusing the operation?' but 'Is it fair and reasonable to make the defendants pay for his refusal?'

[35.90]   Selvanayagam v University of West Indies
[1983] 1 All ER 824, [1983] 1 WLR 585, 127 Sol Jo 288, PC

The appellant sustained injury to his neck in an accident. There was evidence from a specialist who had treated him that surgical therapy which he had recommended would have reduced his disability and enabled him to resume his professional work. However, the specialist said in evidence that as the appellant was diabetic and knew of the risks of infection it was for him to decide whether to have the operation or not. The judge accepted the appellant's decision not to have the operation as reasonable and awarded damages accordingly.

HELD, ON APPEAL to the Privy Council: The judge was entitled so to decide. The rule that a claimant who rejects a medical recommendation of surgery must show that he acted reasonably is based on the principle that a claimant is under a duty to act reasonably so as to mitigate his damage. The question is one of fact: whether in all the circumstances, including particularly the medical advice received, the claimant acted reasonably in refusing surgery; the burden of reasonableness was on him.

Note—This decision was disapproved in *Geest plc v Lansiquot* (at para [35.91]).

[35.91]   Geest plc v Lansiquot

[2002] UKPC 48

[2003] 1 All ER 383, PC

The claimant was injured at work. Her damages were reduced because she failed to undergo recommended surgery. Relying on the decision of *Selvanayagam v University of the West Indies* (at para [35.90]), the court held that it was for the claimant to prove that her refusal had not been unreasonable.

HELD, ON APPEAL to the Privy Council: The burden of proof fell upon the defendant. *Selvanayagam* disapproved.

[35.92]   Edmonds v Lloyds TSB Bank PLC

[2004] EWCA Civ 1526

[2004] All ER (D) 329 (Oct), CA

The claimant tripped over some boxes during the course of her employment. She suffered a soft tissue injury to her coccyx and had not worked since the accident. The defendant contended that she had failed to mitigate her loss by refusing to have three injections that may have allowed her to recover and return to work. The claimant said that she was anxious about the injections and that her GP had advised her that they were unlikely to be successful. Her medical expert did not guarantee that the injections would work and respected her decision. The judge found that it was unreasonable for the claimant to have refused the injections because there was a 50% chance that the injections would offer her significant improvement. He limited her claim for damages. The claimant appealed.

HELD: Appeal allowed. The claimant has a duty to take reasonable steps to mitigate her loss. It is for the defendant to prove that the claimant has failed to do so. The question as to whether or not the claimant has mitigated her loss is a question of fact for the judge to decide. In this case, the judge failed to properly consider all the evidence before him and give proper weight to the claimant's reasons for refusing to have the injections.

6.   MALINGERING

[35.93]   Stojalowski v Imperial Smelting Corpn (NSC) Ltd

(1976) 121 Sol Jo 118, CA

The defendant was the claimant's employer from whom he claimed damages for injury sustained at work. The employer alleged he was malingering. There was a conflict of medical evidence. The judge accepted the written evidence of a hospital registrar in deciding the claimant was a malingerer.

HELD, ON APPEAL: The judge was wrong to treat the registrar's written evidence as proof of his views. An allegation of malingering was a charge of fraud and any positive evidence from the defendant should be put to the witness. Damages increased from £4,000 to £37,328.

[35.94]   Joyce v Yeomans

[1981] 2 All ER 21, [1981] 1 WLR 549, 125 Sol Jo 34, CA

It is not correct that where expert (ie medical) witnesses are concerned the trial judge has no significant advantage over an appellate court in forming a correct judgment between conflicting views: *Stojalowski v Imperial Smelting Corpn (NSC) Ltd* (at para [35.93]) was not intended to go as far as that. Even when dealing with expert witnesses, a trial judge has an advantage over an appellate court in assessing the value, the reliability and impressiveness of the evidence given by experts called on either side.

Note—This case also appears at para [36.10].

[35.95]   Khan v Armaguard Ltd
[1994] 3 All ER 545, [1994] I WLR 1204, (1994) Times, 4 March, CA

The defendant obtained video evidence which it claimed demonstrated that the claimant was deliberately malingering. The defendant made an application to the district judge pursuant to RSC Ord 38 r 5 for an order that there be pre-trial non-disclosure of the video evidence. The defendant relied upon the judgment in *McGuinness v Kellogg Co of Great Britain Ltd* ([1988] 2 All ER 902, [1988] I WLR 913), arguing that non-disclosure was in the interests of justice between the parties when it was the defendant's intention to uncover the claimant's deceit. The district judge refused to make the order and the defendant appealed.

HELD: Three changes had occurred in the conduct of personal injury actions since the decision in the *McGuinness* case. There were now provisions for the pre-trial exchange of witness statements, discovery in personal injury accidents was automatic and the 'cards on the table' approach to this sort of litigation had continued to develop. The interests of the parties would be best served by an early settlement of the claimant's action and this would be facilitated by the pre trial disclosure of the video evidence. It would only be in the most exceptional circumstances that an order for non-disclosure pursuant to RSC Ord 38 r 5 would be justified.

Note—A video is a 'document' for the purposes of CPR 31.4 and is subject to the normal rules of disclosure. It may well be subject to legal professional privilege but a party seeking to rely on video evidence must disclose it as soon as it comes within his control (CPR 31.11). See however *Uttley v Uttley* [2002] PIQR P123 where the court held that the defendant had not acted unreasonably by delaying disclosure of the video evidence. It was appropriate to await up to date medical evidence and a witness statement which post dated the video evidence. See also *Libby-Mills v Commissioner of Police of the Metropolis* [1995] PIQR P324, CA concerning the principle of openness and disclosure of video evidence.

See *Jones v University of Warwick* [2003] 1 WLR 954, CA at para [29.11] for the adverse cost consequences where there was misconduct by the defendant in obtaining surveillance evidence.

See also *Painting v University of Oxford* [2005] PIQR Q5, CA, at para [38.180] (also at para [32.65]) concerning exaggeration, conduct and costs; *Hussein v William Hill Group* [2004] EWHC 208 (QB), [2004] All ER (D) 296 (Feb) where the claimant was found to have deliberately exaggerated his claim and was awarded only nominal damages and *Burch v Ainscough Crane Hire Ltd* (13 April 2006, unreported) where the claimant was found to have forged letters to boost his loss of earnings claim.

[35.96]   Blyth Valley Borough Council v Henderson
[1996] PIQR P64

As soon as the defendant's solicitors became aware of allegations of malingering, they were under a duty to bring a case to trial as quickly as possible. In this case, the claimant issued proceedings in February 1996 relating to an alleged accident at work in February 1989. The defendant's application to strike out should succeed where by December 1992 the case had still not been set down for trial and the defendant could show prejudice.

7. APPEALS ON AMOUNT

(A) THE RULE

[35.97] **Greenfield v London and North Eastern Rly Co**
[1945] KB 89, [1944] 2 All ER 438, 171 LT 337, 61 TLR 44, CA   MacKinnon LJ

The principle on which the Court of Appeal reviews the assessment of damages, whether too high or too low, is not because the Court of Appeal might have given rather more or rather less, but only:

(1)   if the judge has omitted some relevant consideration or admitted some irrelevant consideration, or

(2)   if the amount is so excessive, or insufficient, as to be plainly unreasonable.

[35.98] **Pickett v British Rail Engineering Ltd**
[1980] AC 136, [1979[1 All ER 779, HL

Per Lord Wilberforce: It is important that judges' assessments should not be disturbed unless such error can be shown, or unless the amount is so grossly excessive or insufficient as to lead to the conclusion that some such error must have taken place.

[35.99] **Witten v Robson**
(1989) Independent, 2 June, CA

The plaintiff was awarded £50,000 for pain and suffering and loss of amenities. The defendant appealed on the ground that it was excessive.

HELD: Per Parker LJ: A proper approach of the Court of Appeal in this type of case was to ask whether the award was so grossly excessive as to lead it to the conclusion that some error of principle, albeit undemonstrable must have taken place in the judgment, or in a wholly erroneous estimate of the damage suffered (*Pickett v British Rail Engineering Ltd* at para [35.98] approved).

The figure of £50,000 was a high one although not sufficiently high to justify interference from the Court of Appeal.

(B) COURT OF APPEAL EXAMINING INJURY

[35.100] **Ellis v Sayers Confectioners Ltd**
(1963) 61 LGR 299, CA

The Court of Appeal was invited by counsel to see the appellant's injured leg. The Court declined. Whilst there is no definite rule it is, on the whole, not desirable for the Court of Appeal to see the claimant.

[35.101] **Stevens v William Nash Ltd**
[1966] 3 All ER 156, [1966] 1 WLR 1550, 110 Sol Jo 710, CA

The claimant's right arm was seriously injured in an accident resulting in permanent weakness and loss of movement both in the arm and in the hand and fingers. At the hearing of his appeal against the amount of an award of damages the Court of Appeal was invited by counsel to see the claimant's arm. The court rejected the invitation.

Per Winn LJ: In general it is probably not wise for this court to embark on examinations of the physical conditions of appellants – though there may be some cases which call for it. There may be a suggestion of malingering; a man might be tempted to refrain from exerting quite so much movement as he really is capable of. Cases of scarring or shortening are in a different category since they are objective.

Note—See *Matthews v Flora* (1989) Times, 20 March where the Court of Appeal said that it was helpful for them to observe seriously scarred claimants.

(C)   NEW OR MISTAKEN EVIDENCE

Note—CPR 52.11(2) provides that the appeal court will not receive fresh evidence (oral or written) unless it orders otherwise.

[35.102]   Beaton v Naylors of Plymouth
(1965) 109 Sol Jo 632, CA

The claimant gave evidence on the hearing of his action for damages for personal injuries that he had not been able to work since the accident. On that basis his special damages were agreed at £848. The judge awarded him £1,500 general damages in addition. Subsequent to the trial the defendants obtained evidence to show that the claimant had done quite a lot of work between the accident and the trial.

The Court of Appeal ordered a new trial. The tests to be applied were:
(1)   that the new evidence could not reasonably have been available at the trial;
(2)   that it was apparently credible; and
(3)   that it would have had an important influence on the judge. All these tests were satisfied.

[35.103]   Jenkins v Richard Thomas and Baldwins Ltd
[1966] 2 All ER 15, [1966] 1 WLR 476, 110 Sol Jo 111, [1966] 1 Lloyd's Rep 473, CA

The claimant was employed by the defendants as a pitman, earning £19 10s per week. He received an eye injury which prevented him from doing the work of a pitman and he was employed instead as a labourer at £11 per week. At the trial of his action for damages the defendants said he could be trained to work as a grinder and in that job would earn £17 per week. The judge awarded £3,040 damages of which £1,040 was in respect of future loss at £2 10s per week. After the trial the claimant started working as a grinder but showed no aptitude for it and continued to earn only £11 per week. He appealed against the award. The Court of Appeal allowed fresh evidence to be called including that of two eye surgeons, the claimant and a fellow employee.

HELD: The appeal should be allowed. It was only in very special circumstances that the court would hear fresh evidence but here the expectation on which the judge has assessed damages had been entirely falsified by events: the claimant had been told he would get £17 per week and only got £11. The general rule in actions of this type is that damages have to be assessed once and for all at the trial. It must not be thought that whenever the assessment of the claimant's future earnings turns out to be wrong one or other of the parties can appeal for damages to be increased or reduced. In the present case an exceptional circumstance was that the assessment was based on what the defendants had genuinely but mistakenly said at the trial.

[35.104]   Day v Harland and Wolff Ltd
[1967] 1 Lloyd's Rep 301, CA

At the trial of an action in which the claimant alleged he injured his wrist by falling over a pile of dunnage, judgment was given in his favour for £1,055. Some days later the defendant received a message that the injury had not been caused in the way alleged but in a fight on the evening of the same day. The defendant's solicitors then obtained statements from a publican and two other men to show that the claimant had been injured in a fight at a public house. They applied for a new trial.

HELD: There must be a new trial. The evidence could not have been obtained by reasonable diligence for use at the trial and if given it would have been likely to have had an important influence on the result.

[35.105]   Murphy v Stone-Wallwork Ltd
[1969] 2 All ER 949, [1969] 1 WLR 1023, 113 Sol Jo 546, HL

The claimant, aged 54, was injured at work on 17 March 1965. Both the judge at first instance and the Court of Appeal made their awards on the footing that the rest of his working life would probably be spent in the employment of the defendants. Within a fortnight of the Court of Appeal's award the defendants dismissed him from their employment. He appealed within time to the House of Lords.

HELD: The House had a discretion to take evidence of something which had occurred after the date of the decision from which the appeal was brought and which had altered the effect of the order of that court, especially when as here the appeal was launched within the time allowed. The defendants, though acting in good faith, had falsified the basis of the judgment of the Court of Appeal and it was right that the House should admit the new evidence to enable the damages to be adjusted to the new situation. It was a power which a court should exercise sparingly: *Curwen v James* [1963] 2 All ER 619 was rightly decided but *Jenkins v Richard Thomas & Baldwins* (at para [35.103]) might call for reconsideration, since in that case it was not the defendants who had caused the change of circumstances.

[35.106]   Power v Standard Triumph Motor Co Ltd
(1970) Times, 10 December, CA

The claimant sustained a head injury at work which, he said, had changed his whole personality. His life had become a misery, he had lost all sense of taste and smell and could not walk properly. He was awarded £17,648 damages. The defendant appealed and applied to adduce fresh evidence relating to matters both before and after trial which would show that so far from being a cripple the claimant could walk up ladders, paint his house, move paving stones and chase vandals.

HELD: The court clearly had power to admit such evidence under RSC Ord 59. Applying *Ladd v Marshall* (at para [34.4]) the evidence was apparently credible, could have a material influence on the case, and the defendant's solicitors had acted reasonably. Further if the fresh evidence were true the claimant had perpetrated a gross fraud and the court should not allow it to succeed. New trial ordered.

[35.107]   Mulholland v Mitchell

[1971] AC 666, [1971] 1 All ER 307, [1971] 2 WLR 93, 115 Sol Jo 15, HL

At the trial of an action the judge assessed damages for very serious personal injury on the basis that it would be possible for the claimant to be looked after at home or alternatively at a nursing home where the charges would be at the rate of £903 a year. The claimant appealed and applied for leave to adduce fresh evidence that after the trial it had been found impossible to look after him at home, and that he would have to go to a special nursing home where the charges were £1,827 a year.

HELD: RSC Ord 59, r 10(2) gave the Court of Appeal 'power to receive further evidence on questions of fact … but … no such further evidence (other than evidence as to matters which have occurred after the date of trial or hearing) shall be admitted except on special grounds'. It is generally undesirable to admit fresh evidence on appeal because there ought to be finality in litigation. The question is largely a matter of degree. Fresh evidence ought not to be admitted when it bears on matters falling within the field or area of uncertainty in which the judge's estimate had previously been made. It may be admitted if some basic assumptions common to both sides have been clearly falsified by subsequent events (particularly if this has happened by the act of the defendant) or when to refuse it would affront common sense or a sense of justice. The situation in the present case was sufficiently exceptional that it could not be said the Court of Appeal had wrongly exercised its discretion in giving leave.

[35.108]   McCann v Sheppard

[1973] 2 All ER 881, [1973] 1 WLR 540, 117 Sol Jo 323, CA

Because of great pain from his injuries, McCann needed a pain-killing drug, palfrium. By the date of the trial of his action for damages in June 1972 he had become reliant on the drug. He was awarded general damages for pain, suffering and loss of amenities, for loss of future earnings and special damage. The defendants lodged notice of appeal in July 1972. On 18 October McCann was convicted in the magistrates' court of procuring drugs by deception. On 22 October 1972, he was found dead from an overdose of drugs. The hearing of the defendant's appeal was begun on 28 February 1973.

HELD, by the Court of Appeal: (1) Evidence of McCann's death should be admitted. Where notice of appeal has been served within the time prescribed by the rules and an event has taken place at a time reasonably proximate to the date of the trial which falsifies the facts on which judgment proceeded the Court of Appeal should not rehear the matter on the basis of the fiction that the event has not taken place.

(2)   Damages for future loss of earnings must consequently be reduced from 15 years to 20 weeks.

[35.109]   Riyad Bank v Ahli United Bank (UK) plc

[2005] EWCA Civ 1419 (Comm)

[2005] All ER (D) 299 (Nov)

The Court of Appeal considered an application to adduce fresh evidence. Applying *Ladd v Marshall* [1954] 3 All ER 745, [1954] 1 WLR 1489, the court tested the fresh evidence by reference to the pre-CPR principles:

(1)   that the evidence could not have been obtained with reasonable diligence for use at the trial;

(2)   the evidence must be such that if given it would probably have an important influence on the result of the case, though it need not be decisive;

(3)   the evidence must be such as is presumably to be believed; it must be apparently credible though it need not be incontrovertible.

Note—See also Lord Phillips, MR, in *Hamilton v Al Fayed* (2000) Times, 13 October.

Quantification of Damages

1. INTRODUCTION

[36.1] **H West & Son Ltd v Shephard**

[1964] AC 326, [1963] 2 All ER 625, [1963] 2 WLR 1359, 107 Sol Jo 454, HL

The damages which are to be awarded for a tort are those which 'so far as money can compensate, will give the injured party reparation for the wrongful act and for all the natural and direct consequences of the wrongful act' (*Admiralty Comrs v Susquehanna (Owners), The Susquehanna* [1926] AC 655). The words 'so far as money can compensate' point to the impossibility of equating money with human suffering or personal deprivations. A money award can be calculated so as to make good a financial loss. Money may be awarded so that something tangible may be procured to replace something else of like nature which has been destroyed or lost. But money cannot renew a physical frame that has been battered and shattered. All that judges and courts can do is to award sums which must be regarded as giving reasonable compensation. In the process there must be the endeavour to secure some uniformity in the general method of approach. By common assent awards must be reasonable and must be assessed with moderation. Furthermore, it is eminently desirable that so far as possible comparable injuries should be compensated by comparable awards: per Lord Morris of Borth-y-Gest.

The practice of the courts hitherto has been to treat bodily injury as a deprivation which in itself entitles a claimant to substantial damages according to its gravity. In *Phillips v London & South Western Rly Co* (1879) 5 QBD 78, Cockburn CJ, in enumerating the heads of damage which the jury must take into account and in respect of which a claimant is entitled to compensation said:

'These are the bodily injury sustained; the pain undergone: the effect on the health of the sufferer according to its degree and its probable duration as likely to be temporary or permanent; the expenses incidental to attempts to effect a cure or to lessen the amount of the injury; the pecuniary loss ...'

In *Rose v Ford* [1937] AC 826, [1937] 3 All ER 359, HL Lord Roche said: 'I regard impaired health and vitality not merely as a cause of pain and suffering but as a loss of a good thing in itself.' If a claimant has lost a leg, the court approaches the matter on the basis that he had suffered a serious physical deprivation no matter what his condition or temperament or state of mind may be. That deprivation may also create future economic loss which is added to the assessment. Past and prospective pain and discomfort increase the assessment. If there is loss of amenity apart from the obvious and normal loss inherent in the deprivation of the limb—if, for instance, the claimant's main interest in life was some sport or hobby from which he will in future be debarred, that too increases the assessment. If there is a particular injury to the nervous system, that also increases the assessment. So too with other personal and subjective matters that fall to be decided in the light of common sense in particular cases. These considerations are not dealt with as separate items but are taken into account by the court in fixing one inclusive sum for general damages: per Lord Pearce.

Note—Salmon LJ said in his dissenting judgment that he found the majority view in the Court of Appeal difficult to understand. In his view, it was necessary to assess the value of each head of loss to arrive at the true loss.

[36.2]   George v Pinnock

[1973] 1 All ER 926, [1973] 1 WLR 118, 117 Sol Jo 73, CA

Per Sachs LJ: Whatever may have been the differing judicial views up to a few years ago and indeed up to 1970 as to whether a judge should simply award a global sum or whether he should state in his judgment what are the main components in that figure, the modern practice ... is to adopt the second course ... The [claimant] and defendant alike are entitled to know what is the sum assessed for each relevant head of damage and thus be able on appeal to challenge any error in the assessments ... It is of course always open to a respondent to do something which was not done here; that is, to give a cross-notice [of appeal] that even if one head as awarded by the judge is held to be demonstrably too low, some other head is demonstrably too high and thus seek to produce what is sometimes called a swings and roundabouts position. In other circumstances it seems to me that a court should normally be slow to deal with an appeal on such a basis.

Note—The Court of Appeal considered *George v Pinnock* (at para [36.2]) in the case of *Pritchard v JH Cobden Ltd* (at para [36.15]).

[36.3]   Fletcher v Autocar and Transporters Ltd

[1968] 2 QB 322, [1968] 1 All ER 726, [1968] 2 WLR 743, 112 Sol Jo 96, CA

The claimant, a quantity surveyor aged 56, was seriously injured in a motor accident. Head injuries had so seriously affected his mental capacity that he had little thought or feeling, was incapable of looking after himself and would never be able to work again. He was partly paralysed. He was dependent on his wife for everyday care but in three years or so would have to go into an institution for the rest of his life. His expectation of life was not reduced and was about 16 years. Before the accident he had been leading a very full and active life. He had an income from his profession of £4,000 a year, tax paid, and spent all of it. He had no savings and would have continued at work at least to the age of 69. At trial the judge assessed the following main heads of damage:
(1) special damage £10,000;
(2) future loss of earnings after allowing for tax and calculating the loss actuarily as a lump sum, £32,000;

(3)   additional expense (i e expense he would not have incurred but for the accident) in the future comprising the cost of being looked after by his wife for the next three years and then for the rest of his life at an institution, less a saving on food and laundry at home, £14,000;

(4)   pain and suffering and loss of amenities £10,000.

He added them up and awarded £66,000 damages.

HELD, ON APPEAL: The judge had awarded too much. He was wrong to take each item separately and then just add them up at the end. There is a risk of overlapping if the items are just added up. The claimant had spent his income on the pleasures of living and on recreations such as golf, fishing and shooting without saving anything. It was fair to compensate him for the loss of these but not unless account was taken of the fact that he had to pay for them. He should not therefore have been given his full loss of earnings. Another way of looking at it was to say that he should not be given both the cost of his keep at the institution and also his full salary, for that would mean that he would be saving full salary and spending nothing. Award reduced to £51,000.

[36.4]   Harris v Harris

[1973] I Lloyd's Rep 445, CA

The claimant was 14 when injured in a road accident. The main damage was to her brain: though she had been able after the accident to complete her education and pass GCE examinations she would not be able to take up a career nor do ordinary domestic tasks, such as cooking. She would probably never marry. She was of good middle-class background and might, but for the injuries, have become a solicitor or civil servant. The judge awarded her £20,000 for pain and suffering and loss of amenities including loss of marriage prospects; £22,500 for loss of future earnings (15 years at £1,500 p.a.); and £15,974 for the cost of a housekeeper when she would need a place to live of her own.

HELD, on the defendant's appeal: (1) The award of £20,000 for loss of amenities for life was justified.

(2)   £22,500 for loss of future earnings was too much. She might have married and not have been able to earn so much; damages for loss of marriage prospects were already compensated for in the first item; in any event she might not have earned for any great length of time.

(3)   On the third item there was doubt whether she would in fact set up in a flat of her own; having regard to the uncertain prospect and the amounts awarded for the other items the right figure for cost of future support was £6,000. It was very important where a judge was following the modern practice of sub-dividing the claim under various headings to avoid overlapping. There was here a serious overlap between the allowance made for loss of claimant's prospects of marriage on the one hand and loss of future earnings and the additional cost of domestic assistance on the other.

[36.5]   Lim Poh Choo v Camden and Islington Area Health Authority

[1980] AC 174, [1979] 2 All ER 910, [1979] 3 WLR 44, HL

The claimant, after a minor surgical operation, suffered a cardiac arrest caused by the negligence of an employee of the defendants. Extensive and irremedial brain damage resulted leaving her only intermittently conscious, totally dependent on others and not able to appreciate what had happened to her. She was 36 years of age at the time of the incident; her life expectation was unaffected. The judge at first instance awarded £254,765. The defendant's appeals to the Court of Appeal and the House of Lords were dismissed but with small variations after hearing further evidence. On matters of principle—

HELD: (1) The sheer size of the total award was not a reason for reducing it. The burden on the public through insurance premiums or taxes or the availability of National Health Service care were matters for a legislator, not a judge.

(2) The award of general damages for pain and suffering and loss of amenities at £20,000 was not too large, either on the ground that the claimant was unaware of what had happened to her or that she was not suffering any pain. *Wise v Kaye* [1962] 1 QB 638, [1962] 1 All ER 257, [1962] 2 WLR 96, 106 Sol Jo 14, CA and *H West & Son Ltd v Shephard* (at para [36.1]) were rightly decided. Those cases drew a distinction between damages for pain and suffering and damages for loss of amenities. The latter are awarded for the fact of deprivation whether the claimant is aware of it or not.

(3) It is right to award damages for actual and future loss of earnings, even in a catastrophic case, but care should be taken to avoid duplication or overlap with other heads of damage. Two reductions fall to be made, (a) the expenses of earning the income which has been lost and (b) from damages for the cost of caring for the claimant, the living expenses she would have incurred had she not been injured (*Shearman v Folland* (at para [36.153])).

(4) Damages for cost of future care are recoverable but must be assessed on the basis that capital as well as income is to be used in meeting the cost. In the present case a multiplier of 12 applied to the annual cost of the claimant's care from date of judgment in the House of Lords would be fair.

(5) Only in exceptional cases, where justice can be shown to require it, will the risk of future inflation be brought into account in assessing damages for future loss. It would be unrealistic to refuse to take inflation into account at all, but the better course in the great majority of cases is to disregard it. The victims of tort who receive a lump sum award are entitled to no better protection against inflation than others who have to rely on capital for their future support.

Note—In *Re Crowther & Nicholson Ltd* ((1981) 125 Sol Jo 529, (1981) Times, 10 June) the directors claimed compensation for the balance of their service agreements, which provided for the company to pay inflation-proofed salaries, received annually. The judge said that in *Lim Poh Choo v Camden and Islington Area Health Authority* Lord Scarman had said the correct approach was to assess damages without regard to future inflation, but in that case the claimant had no contractual right to protection against inflation. In the present case the service agreements did provide protection and this must be taken into account in assessing compensation.

See also *Housecroft v Burnett* [1986] 1 All ER 332 for a full discussion of catastrophic injury claims and the correct approach to damages.

Lim Poh Choo v Camden and Islington Area Health Authority also appears at para [36.5] concerning loss of earnings.

2. WHO CAN RECOVER?

[36.6] There is no general principle of English law which entitles a person to recover damages against someone who has caused physical injury to a third person. Thus, for example, a partner cannot recover damages against a person who has caused him financial loss, however direct, by negligently injuring his partner. Section 2 of the Administration of Justice Act 1982 abolished the two common law exceptions to this principle and reads as follows:

[36.7]
2.   Abolition of actions for loss of services etc
No person shall be liable in tort under the law of England and Wales or the law of Northern Ireland—
(a)   to a husband on the ground only of his having deprived him of the services or society of his wife;
(b)   to a parent (or person standing in the place of a parent) on the ground only of his having deprived him of the services of a child; or
(c)   on the ground only—
   (i)   of having deprived another of the services of his menial servant;
   (ii)   of having deprived another of the services of his female servant by raping or seducing her; or
   (iii)   of enticement of a servant or harbouring a servant.

Note—In claims for gratuitous care, the award is made to the claimant on the basis that the claimant will make a payment to the person who has provided that care. See para [36.79].

3.   DAMAGES FOR PAIN, SUFFERING AND LOSS OF AMENITY

[36.8]   *Note*—Damages for for non-pecuniary loss, or general damages, are awarded to a claimant for the pain, suffering and loss of amenity caused by a physical or mental injury.

[36.9]   Heil v Rankin
[2001] QB 272, [2000] 3 All ER 138, [2000] 2 WLR 1173

The Law Commission Report No 257 issued in April 1999 recommended that damages for non-pecuniary loss in cases of serious injuries should be increased. The Commission recommended that the increase should be a factor of at least 1.5 (ie 50%) but no more than 2 (ie 100%). The report defined 'serious injury' as being an injury in respect of which an award for pain, suffering and loss of amenity would be worth more than £2,000.

Against the background of this report the Court of Appeal gave judgment in this case which was a consolidation of eight appeals of the level of damages of pain, suffering and loss of amenity (also known as 'general damages').

HELD: There was no increase where general damages of the existing guidelines would be £10,000 or less.

The increase will be applied to general damages between £10,000 and £150,000 ranging from a nil increase at £10,000 to one-third of the increase at £150,000.

The increase would be minimal for claims under £25,000.

General damages will continue to increase in line with inflation.

Note—Below is a table setting out the changes of awards between £10,000 to £150,000 as a consequence of this decision.

Ready Reckoner

Old Award	New Award	Increase	%
£10,000	£10,000	£0	0.0%
£20,000	£20,500	£500	2.5%
£30,000	£32,500	£2,500	6.7%
£40,000	£44,000	£4,000	10.0%
£50,000	£56,000	£6,000	12.0%
£60,000	£68,000	£8,000	13.3%
£70,000	£80,000	£10,000	14.3%
£80,000	£92,500	£12,500	15.6%
£90,000	£107,000	£17,000	18.9%
£100,000	£121,000	£21,000	21.0%
£110,000	£137,500	£27,500	25.0%
£120,000	£152,500	£32,500	27.1%
£130,000	£167,000	£37,000	28.5%
£140,000	£183,000	£43,000	30.7%
£150,000	£200,000	£50,000	33.3%

These figures are intended to provide an approximate and practical guide to the consequences of the Court of Appeal's decision. They have been extrapolated from the actual awards made by the court and individual decisions may differ slightly. The table should be used as a 'ready reckoner' only. The Judicial Studies Board Guidelines incorporate the effects of the above decision. Please see the Judicial Studies Board *Guidelines for the Assessment of General Damages in Personal Injury Cases*, 8th edn (2006).

(A)   EPILEPSY

[36.10]   Joyce v Yeomans
[1981] 2 All ER 21, [1981] 1 WLR 549, 125 Sol Jo 34, CA

The claimant, a boy of ten, was hit by a car, sustaining a head injury, ruptured spleen and a fractured clavicle. Some months later he showed symptoms of epilepsy and during three years had four or five grand mal attacks. The judge accepted a doctor's opinion that the boy would have developed epilepsy by the time he was 14 even without the injuries but that they had caused the epilepsy to appear earlier and to be more disabling. The claimant had done poorly at school and had been unable to pass any 'O' level examinations. The judge awarded £7,500 inclusive of loss of future earning capacity which he did not assess separately.

HELD, ON APPEAL: The injuries and epilepsy in themselves justified an award of £6,000, which left too little for loss of earning capacity. It was not appropriate to use the multiplier/multiplicand method to calculate this loss because there were so many imponderables but a proper figure in the circumstances would be £7,500, making a total of £13,500 but with interest on the £6,000 only.

Note—This case now has to be considered in the light of the ability of the courts to award provisional damages (see para [36.219]).

[36.11]   **Re Hancock**

(12 January 1998, unreported), CICB (London)

The claimant, aged 20, sustained serious head injuries following an assault. He developed grand mal epilepsy which was uncontrolled for three and a half years and which forced him to give up his job. He ran the permanent risk of having epileptic seizures and required life-long medication. The claimant was able, however, to undertake a morning only therapeutic job with a charity. His other injuries included migraines, partial loss of vision in his right eye and depression. Twelve years after the assault, he was awarded general damages of £55,000.

[36.12]   **Re Conway**

[2001] 6 QR 5

The claimant, aged 31, sustained a compound depressed fracture to his head following an attack with a hammer. He developed post-traumatic grand mal epilepsy and initially suffered one epileptic attack per week. This lessened to one every three to six weeks before settling at three per year. The claimant required daily medication. He also suffered from headaches around three days a week, had impaired memory and a tendency to moody behaviour and irritability. The condition was permanent and no improvement in any of his symptoms was likely. He was unlikely to work again.

The Criminal Injuries Compensation Appeal Panel awarded £70,000 for general damages.

[36.13]   **C (a child) v Walters**

[2003] 4 QR 15

The claimant, a child of 11 months, fell from a highchair and struck his head on a tiled floor. He suffered a linear fracture across the left parietal bone. After some swelling and tenderness which persisted for 6 weeks after the accident, he returned to normal. 13 months after the accident, it was advised that the claimant had a 1.6 percent risk of suffering epilepsy in the future and that risk would persist for a period of 5 years after the accident. The risk to the general population is about 0.5 percent.

The agreed and approved award for general damages was £3,500.

Note—Awards for provisional damages are often considered in epilepsy cases where the claimant faces a chance or risk of developing the condition or a deterioration in his condition. See para [36.224].

(B)   PERSONALITY CHANGE

[36.14]   **Jones v Jones**

[1985] QB 704, [1984] 3 All ER 1003, CA

The claimant was very seriously injured in a road accident, so much that he suffered a personality change and his affairs were administered by the Court of Protection. He was awarded a total of £177,500 damages. At the time of the accident he had a wife and one child with another expected. As a result of his injuries the marriage broke down; his wife divorced him and lived separately with the two children. It was conceded that the breakdown of the marriage and separation or divorce were reasonably foreseeable by the defendant. The judge at first instance in the light of this concession held there was no reason in principle for refusing to award damages for the extra expense to the claimant in maintaining his wife and children in a separate establishment but said at the time of the trial that the claimant had not proved any additional loss and expense. After the trial the claimant's wife in matrimonial proceedings obtained an order for periodical payments at £2,445 a year and for a lump sum of £25,000 which had been spent on a house for the wife.

HELD: As it was conceded that the particular type of loss was reasonably foreseeable the only issue was quantum (*McLoughlin v O'Brian* (at para [36.23])). In respect of the periodical payments for maintenance there were so many imponderables it was not proved that such payments were greater than the claimant would have had to spend if his wife and family had continued to live with him. But the lump sum payment would not have been necessary if they had continued to live together. On the other hand if she had remained with him he may (or even the Court of Protection on his behalf may) have thought it right to make her a gift for giving up her life to care for him. £10,000 ought to be deducted in respect of this: there should accordingly be an award of a further £15,000 damages additional to the amount awarded in the court below.

[36.15]   Pritchard v JH Cobden Ltd
[1988] Fam 22, [1988] 1 All ER 300, [1987] 2 WLR 627, [1987] 2 FLR 30, CA

In 1976 the claimant, aged 30, suffered serious brain damage as a result of a motor accident. He was married with a six-and-a-half-year-old daughter; seven months later his wife gave birth to twins. His injuries meant that he was unemployable; he had suffered a complete change of personality and the marriage did not survive. The defendants did not dispute that the marriage breakdown was a result of the injuries. The judge awarded £53,000 to cover the financial loss arising as a result of the divorce (taking into account the need for separate dwellings, the costs of the divorce and the ancillary relief proceedings). The defendants appealed.

HELD: Appeal allowed. Although the marriage breakdown was caused by the injuries the resultant financial arrangements were a redistribution of the financial assets of the couple, including any damages awarded to the claimant for his personal injuries. Any orders under the Matrimonial Causes Act 1973 were therefore not losses to the claimant over and above the damages payable and had to be wholly disregarded when calculating compensation. It would also be contrary to public policy and open to abuse to take considerations relevant to matrimonial proceedings into account in personal injury litigation. Damages reduced by the sum of £53,000.

[36.16]   Simmons v British Steel plc
[2004] UKHL 20
[2004] ICR 585, 2004 SC (HL) 94, 2004 SLT 595, 2004 SCLR 920, HL

In 1996, the pursuer was injured at work when he fell from a table and struck his head against a metal stanchion. The accident caused an exacerbation of a pre-existing skin condition and he developed a change in personality resulting in a severe depressive illness. At first instance, the Lord Ordinary found that the pursuer had become angry after the accident and that it was his anger that had led to the exacerbation of his skin condition and the depressive illness. He did not believe that there was a sufficient causal connection between the accident and these conditions to justify an award of damages. The anger had been caused by the defendant's treatment following the accident and not the accident itself. The Inner House reversed the Lord Ordinary because it took a different view of the case on the facts.

HELD, ON APPEAL to the House of Lords: The pursuer was entitled to recover damages. Causation was established because the accident made a material contribution to the pursuer's anger.

(C)   CRIMINAL ACTS

[36.17]   Meah v McCreamer
[1985] 1 All ER 367, [1985] NLJ Rep 80   Woolf J

The claimant sustained a close-head injury to the left frontal lobe of the brain in a road accident. Some years before the accident he had shown a pattern of violent behaviour but no serious crime: he had a number of convictions for offences of dishonesty. After the accident he had become violently and sexually aggressive and was, by the time of trial, serving two life sentences for crimes of rape and wounding. There was medical evidence that the frontal lobe injury sustained in the accident had removed the inhibitions formerly restraining his aggressiveness. His condition was untreatable and he had to be kept in prison for the protection of society.

HELD: *Jones v Jones* (at para [36.14]) had shown that awards could be made in head injury cases that at first sight seemed surprising. The claimant had shown that, on a balance of probabilities, but for the accident he would not have committed the crimes for which he was now in prison. He was entitled to damages for the resulting imprisonment but they were reduced to take account of his previous criminal tendencies which probably would have resulted in imprisonment, in any event. The right figure in general damages was £60,000 to be reduced by 25% for contributory negligence.

[36.18]   W v Meah and D v Meah
[1986] 1 All ER 935, [1986] NLJ Rep 165, QBD

Two victims that Meah attacked as a result of his injuries referred to in *Meah v McCreamer (No 1)* (at para [36.17]) brought actions against him claiming damages for personal injury and aggravated damages for rape, assault and battery and wounding in one case and assault and battery in another. The sums awarded were assessed on the basis of conventional personal injury actions although a moderate award was nominally included for aggravated damages to take into account the circumstances.

See also *Meah v McCreamer (No 2)* (at para [36.19]) for questions of remoteness of damages for criminal acts, and *Smith v Littlewoods Organisation Ltd* (at para [35.42]).
   Note—See also the case of *Stubbings v Webb* (at para [18.18]).

[36.19]   Meah v McCreamer (No 2)
[1986] 1 All ER 943, [1986] NLJ Rep 235, QBD

Following the judgment in *Meah v McCreamer* (at para [36.17]) two victims of Meah's sexual attacks sued him in damages and were awarded substantial sums, in each case. Meah in the present action sued McCreamer and his insurers to recover the amounts awarded to the two victims.

HELD: The damages were too remote to be recoverable from McCreamer. The claimant was seeking to recover, not in respect of his own injuries or damage, but in respect of damage he caused to third parties. Although in deciding what is or is not foreseeable the question is not a pure matter of policy, there is a proper role for the court to play: the right approach is to deal with the matter in a 'robust' manner. On that basis the loss was not recoverable, either from the driver of the car or that driver's insurers. On the question of the liability of the insurers the same approach should be applied as in *Gray v Barr* [1971] 2 QB 554, [1971] 2 All ER 949, [171] 2 WLR 1334, 115 Sol Jo 364, [1971] 2 Lloyd's Rep 1, CA.

Note—See also exemplary and aggravated damages at para [36.131].

(D)   PSYCHIATRIC ILLNESS

[36.20]   *Note*—A cause of action in negligence for damages for psychiatric illness has the same constituents as any other personal injury claim:
(1)   a duty to the claimant to take reasonable care;
(2)   a careless act amounting to a breach of that duty;
(3)   causation of some identifiable physical or psychiatric injury that was reasonably foreseeable. Failing to foresee the extent of the damage is immaterial.

The early nervous shock cases following *Hay (or Bourhill) v Young* [1943] AC 92, [1942] 2 All ER 396, HL determined liability for shock on the basis of foreseeability of the consequence of the defendant's negligence. The question as to which claimants can recover damages for psychiatric illness has proved a difficult one. The law is considered and has evolved in the following cases.

For claims involving stress at work, see *Sutherland v Hatton* [2002] EWCA Civ 76 [2002] 2 All ER 1, CA and *Barber v Somerset County Council* [2004] 2 All ER 385, HL. There are no special control mechanisms applying to claims for psychiatric (or physical) illness or injury arising from the stress of doing the work the employee is required to do. The ordinary principles of employer's liability apply. The threshold question is whether this kind of harm to this particular employee was reasonably foreseeable: this has two components: (a) an injury to health (as distinct from occupational stress) which (b) is attributable to stress at work (as distinct from other factors). In *Hatton*, the Court of Appeal listed the factors that are likely to be relevant in answering the threshold question. In summary, the onus is upon an employee to alert his or her employer that he or she is suffering from work related stress absent any actual knowledge in the employer that the employee is so suffering.

[36.21]   **Dooley v Cammell Laird & Co Ltd**
[1951] 1 Lloyd's Rep 271   Donovan J

A crane driver was lowering a sling when the rope broke and the load fell, and out of sight of the claimant dislodged some scaffolding which crashed into the hold where the claimant knew fellow workmen were at work. The claimant was thereby put into a state of apprehension and acute anxiety and suffered severe nervous shock.

The defendant contended it owed no duty except in the case of impact upon the claimant, his wife or child, or reasonable fear of such impact.

HELD: There is no duty unless physical injury to the person or his relations or friends is reasonably to be expected, or unless shock was reasonably to be expected to him as a result of defendant's negligence. The fear that fellow workmen may have been injured was not baseless or extravagant and was a consequence reasonably to have been foreseen as likely to cause a nervous shock, which fear was not unreasonable in the circumstances and was not too remote. The claimant was awarded damages.

Note—It is arguable that the claimant in this case would now be regarded as a primary victim (see [para [36.32] below). See also *Robertson v Forth Road Bridge Joint Board* 1996 SLT 263 where the claimant failed.

[36.22] Chadwick v British Transport Commission

[1967] 2 All ER 945, [1967] 1 WLR 912, 111 Sol Jo 562 Waller J

The claimant, a window cleaner aged 41, was at home when a serious railway accident occurred about 200 yards away. He did not see it, but went to help. He spent several hours at the scene helping passengers who had serious and horrifying injuries. Afterwards he fell into a condition of depression and nervousness that was eventually diagnosed as an anxiety neurosis caused by his experiences at the scene of the disaster. He claimed damages against the defendant who admitted the railway accident was its fault but denied liability for the claimant's condition.

HELD: (1) Shock, other than caused by fear for oneself or children, may be the subject of a claim for damages.
    (2)   It was reasonably foreseeable by the defendants that if trains collided and people were killed some persons who were physically unhurt might suffer from shock.
    (3)   The defendant owed a duty of care to the claimant because it could have foreseen that, if passengers were injured by its negligence, somebody might try and rescue the passengers and suffer injury in the process.
    (4)   The fact that the risk run by the rescuer was not precisely that run by the passengers did not deprive the claimant of his remedy; it was sufficient that shock was foreseeable and that rescue was foreseeable.
Judgment for the claimant.

Note—See the comments of Lord Steyn in *White v Chief Constable of South Yorkshire Police* at para [36.34] where the right of a rescuer to claim damages was restricted further.

[36.23] McLoughlin v O'Brian

[1983] 1 AC 410, [1982] 2 All ER 298, [1982] 2 WLR 982, 126 Sol Jo 347, [1982] RTR 209, HL

The claimant's husband and three of her children, George aged 17, Kathleen, 7 and Gillian, 3 were in a car which collided with a lorry. The claimant was not present: she was at home two miles away. She was told of the accident by a witness who said he thought George was dying. He drove her to hospital where she was told by her second son (who was not in the car) that Gillian was dead. She saw Kathleen crying and her face cut. She heard George shouting and screaming. She saw her husband, head in hands, covered in mud and oil. As a result she suffered severe shock, organic depression and change of personality, with numerous symptoms of a physiological character. She claimed damages against the defendant lorry drivers and owners responsible for the collision. The judge dismissed her claim on the ground that injury by shock was not reasonably foreseeable in the circumstances. The Court of Appeal dismissed her appeal: the Lord Justices held that injury by shock was reasonably foreseeable but that public policy required a limit to be placed on the extent of the duty of care in such cases: it should be limited to those on or near the highway at or near the time of the accident.

HELD, ON APPEAL, to the House of Lords: The claimant was entitled to succeed. When injury from shock was reasonably foreseeable to the claimant the duty of care was not to be limited merely by considerations of public policy. A cause of action for injury by shock had developed through a series of cases:

(1)   without the need for injury to oneself;

(2)   by injury or fear of it to a near relative (*Hambrook v Stokes Bros* [1925] 1 KB 141, 94 LJKB 435, 41 TLR 125, CA, *Boardman v Sanderson* [1964] 1 WLR 1317, 105 Sol Jo 152, CA);

(3)   by coming upon the immediate aftermath (*Boardman's* case);

(4)   coming upon the scene as a rescuer (*Chadwick v British Transport Commission* (at para [36.22]).

If the process of logical progression was followed it was hard to see why this claimant should not succeed. Her claim may be upon the margin of what the process of logical progression will allow, but the facts being strong and exceptional her case ought to be assimilated to those which have passed the test. There was no requirement of public policy that the damage to a claimant should be on or adjacent to the highway. A defendant's duty of care must depend on reasonable foreseeability and be adjudicated only upon a case-by-case basis.

Note—Lord Wilberforce allowed the appeal but noted in his judgment that a stricter test should be introduced in these cases. This included examining the degree of proximity in time and space to the accident and the relationship between the claimant and injured or deceased person. See para [36.28] below.

See also *Videan v British Transport Commission* (at para [7.42]).

[36.24]   Galt v British Railways Board

(1983) 133 NLJ 870

The claimant, driving a train at 65mph in conditions of restricted visibility, suddenly saw two men on the track about 30 yards away. He could not stop and thought (mistakenly as it turned out) they had been killed. He suffered nervous shock bringing on a myocardial infarction, to which he was predisposed by a pre-existing symptomless condition.

HELD: He was entitled to damages, no speed limit having been in force. The injury was reasonably foreseeable and the defendant, his employer, owed him a duty to take reasonable care not to expose him to injury from nervous shock. It was liable for the further damage caused by the pre-existing disease, applying *The Wagon Mound* (or *Overseas Tankship (UK) Ltd v Morts Dock and Engineering Co Ltd*) (at para [35.2]) and *Jason v Batten (1930) Ltd* [1969] 1 Lloyd's Rep 281.

Note—See *Hunter v British Coal Corpn* [1999] QB 140 (at para [36.35]).

[36.25]   Whitmore v Euroways Express Coaches Ltd

(1984) Times, 4 May

The claimant was with her husband in a coach which overturned causing her husband serious injuries. She suffered shock by witnessing him in his injured condition. It was argued by the defendant that she could not recover damages for the shock without adducing medical or psychiatric evidence.

HELD: The claimant was claiming for shock in its everyday meaning, not in a medical or psychiatric sense. It was 'ordinary shock' not susceptible of further definition but it was a concept which everyone understood. Damages could be awarded for it without departing from the law that damages for worry, strain and distress, occasioned by the continuing effects of the injury to a spouse, were not recoverable. The right figure in the present case was £2,000, bearing in mind that the shock had continued while her husband remained in hospital in France and for some weeks afterwards.

[36.26]   Brice v Brown

[1984] I All ER 997, 134 NLJ 204   Stuart-Smith J

The claimant, 42 years old at the time of the accident, sustained relatively trivial physical injuries in a road accident. She was a passenger in a hire car with her daughter aged 12, who sustained alarming facial injuries causing the claimant both fear and panic. Dating from childhood the claimant had a personality disorder which had caused turbulent spells in her married life but it was on the whole well controlled and for a year or so before the accident her home life had been reasonably happy. After the accident and throughout the time to date of trial her behaviour had become wild and disorderly. There were spells when she left home for days or weeks and lived rough; there were several attempts at suicide. At the time of trial she lived in the same house as her husband and family but her conduct was bizarre and she was severely deranged. She was unfit to give evidence. The defendant argued that before the claimant could succeed she needed to prove first that she sustained a psychiatric illness and second that that illness was reasonably foreseeable by the defendant.

HELD: 'Nervous shock' is a convenient phrase to describe mental injury or psychiatric injury to distinguish it from grief and sorrow or from physical or organic injury. The circumstances of the accident had caused or materially contributed to the claimant's nervous shock, which was a reasonably foreseeable consequence of the tortfeasor's breach of his duty of care. For this purpose, the claimant is assumed to be a person of normal disposition − not for example the pursuer in *Hay (or Bourhill)v Young* [1943] AC 92, [1942] 2 All ER 396 HL or a person who faints at the sight of a road accident. On establishing these first points, the claimant is entitled to compensation for nervous shock and for its direct consequences whether or not they were initially reasonably to be foreseen. There is no reason why mental injury should be in a different category to physical: see *Smith v Leech* (at para [35.7]). The fact that the tortfeasor could not foresee the precise name the psychiatrists were to put on the claimant's condition or the precise mental or psychological process that led to that result is immaterial. She was entitled to succeed.

[36.27]   Attia v British Gas plc

[1988] QB 304, [1987] 3 All ER 455, CA

The defendant was engaged to install central heating. The claimant returning home during the afternoon of the installation found smoke coming from the loft of her house. She called the Fire Brigade who took over four hours to control the fire, by which time the house and contents were extensively damaged. The claimant sued for nervous shock resulting in a psychiatric or mental illness. The defendant argued that such a reaction was not reasonably foreseeable, and that if it was reasonably foreseeable damages could only in any event be awarded as a matter of law and public policy for injury or death, or fear of such, to a person closely related to the claimant.

HELD, ON APPEAL: There was no principle that the claimant should not recover damages for nervous shock as a result of seeing her house destroyed by fire if this amounted to psychiatric damage or illness and not merely normal grief, sorrow, or emotional distress. Psychiatric damage had, in all the circumstances of the case, to be reasonably foreseeable.

[36.28]   **Alcock v Chief Constable of the South Yorkshire Police**
[1992] 1 AC 310, [1991] 4 All ER 907

Shortly before the commencement of a football match at the Hillsborough Stadium the police responsible for crowd control permitted too many spectators into a part of the ground already full. As a result 95 spectators were crushed to death and over 400 injured. The disaster was broadcast live on television. None of the depicted scenes showed the suffering or dying of recognisable individuals.

Sixteen relatives, and in one case the fiancee of a person who was in the area, brought actions against the defendant claiming damages for nervous shock, causing psychiatric illness. In the case of 13 of the claimants their relatives and friends were killed. In two other cases relatives and friends were injured and in the case of one claimant the relative escaped unhurt.

The defendant admitted liability and negligence but denied it owed a duty of care to the claimants. Assuming each claimant had suffered nervous shock the question of whether the claimants were entitled to damages was tried as a preliminary issue. Hidden J ([1991] 1 All ER 353) found for 10 of the 16 claimants and against 6. The defendant appealed and the six unsuccessful claimants cross-appealed. The Court of Appeal ([1991] 3 All ER 88) allowed the defendant's appeal and dismissed the cross appeals holding that none of the claimants could recover. Ten of the claimants appealed to the House of Lords.

HELD: There are three elements inherent in any claim for shock. The elements to be considered are: (1) the class of persons whose claims should be recognised; (2) the proximity of such persons to the accident in time and space; and (3) the means by which the shock has been caused.

(1)   The duty of care could in particular circumstances extend to an innocent bystander if, for example, a petrol tanker careered into a school session and burst into flames. 'I would not be prepared to rule out a potential claim by a passer by so shocked by the scene as to suffer psychiatric illness': per Lord Ackner.

The claims by those in close family relationships referred to by Wilberforce LJ in *McLoughlin v O'Brian* (at para [36.23]) arise from a rebuttable presumption that the intimacy of the relationship should reasonably be contemplated by a defendant. As for more remote relatives Nolan LJ stated: 'For my part, I would accept at once that no general definition is possible. But I see no difficulty in principle in requiring a defendant to contemplate that the person physically injured or threatened by his negligence may have relatives or friends whose love for him is like that of a normal parent or spouse, and who in consequence may similarly be closely and directly affected by nervous shock ... The identification of the particular individual who comes within the category, like that of parent and spouses themselves could only be carried out ex poste facto, and would depend upon evidence of the "relationship" in a broad sense which gave rise to the love and affection'.

(2) 'The proximity to the accident must be close both in time and space. Direct and immediate sight or hearing of the accident is not required ... shock can arise through sight or hearing of its immediate aftermath': per Lord Ackner.

   Following Wilberforce LJ in *McLoughlin* the claimants in the present case were not in sufficient proximity in time and space to the accident or its immediate aftermath.

(3) The claimants must suffer nervous shock through seeing or hearing the accident or its immediate aftermath. In the present case the defendant was entitled to suspect that whilst the scenes would be distressing they would not show pictures of suffering by a recognisable individual. 'Although the television pictures certainly gave rise to feelings of deepest anxiety and distress, in the circumstances of this case the simultaneous television broadcasts of what occurred cannot be equated with the 'sight or hearing of the event or its immediate aftermath'. Accordingly shock sustained by reason of these broadcasts cannot find a claim': per Lord Ackner. Lord Ackner did recognise that in certain circumstances the simultaneous broadcast of a disaster could satisfy the necessary requirements.

The appeals were dismissed.

Note—The decisions in *Hevican v Ruane* [1991] 3 All ER 65 and in *Ravenscott v Rederiaktiebolaget Transatlantic* [1991] 3 All ER 73 were specifically doubted by Lord Keith and Lord Oliver. In his judgment, Lord Oliver distinguished between those claimants who were involved in the accident as a participant and those who were 'no more than a passive and unwilling witness of injury caused to others'.

[36.29] Hicks v Chief Constable of the South Yorkshire Police
[1992] 2 All ER 65, HL

The two Hicks sisters were killed as a result of overcrowding at the Hillsborough Football Stadium. The administrators of the sisters' estates brought a claim against the defendant for damages to compensate for pre-death suffering. The sisters suffered from trauma asphyxia caused by the crushing. The judge at first instance accepted medical evidence to the affect that in cases of death by traumatic asphyxia the victim would lose consciousness within a matter of seconds from the crushing of the chest and would die within minutes thereafter. The claimant's claims were dismissed by the judge and the Court of Appeal and the claimant then appealed to the House of Lords.

HELD, ON APPEAL to the House of Lords: The decisions of the preceding courts were upheld. There was no indication that either of the sisters had suffered injuries other than those that had caused the asphyxia and death and, as the unconsciousness and death occurred in such a short space of time, in reality the asphyxia was part of the death itself. 'It is perfectly clear law that fear by itself, on whatever degree, is a normal human emotion for which no damages can be awarded': per Lord Bridge of Harwich.

Note—In *Reilly v Merseyside RHA* [1995] 6 Med LR 246 the Court of Appeal applied *Hicks v Chief Constable of South Yorkshire* and held that apprehension, fear, discomfort and shortness of breath were not compensatable. See also *Inez Brown v David Robinson and Sentry Service Co* (at para [37.94]).

[36.30]   Nicholls v Rushton

(1992) Times, 19 June, CA

The claimant was involved in a road traffic accident with the defendant. The defendant admitted liability. The claimant obtained judgment for £1,151.76 of which £175 was awarded for 'severe shock and shaking up'. The defendant appealed this part of the award.

HELD: It was conceded that no damages for a nervous reaction could be awarded for an illness unless it resulted from some physical trauma. The claimant had suffered no physical trauma nor any recognised psychiatric condition and so she could not recover damages under this head.

Per Parker LJ: Unless there is a physical injury, there can be no award of damages for mental suffering, fear, anxiety under this head.

Note—See also *Page v Smith* (at para [36.32]) where it was held that in order for a claimant to succeed as a secondary victim in a claim for nervous shock, he had to show that the psychiatric injury was foreseeable in a person of normal fortitude.

[36.31]   McFarlane v E E Caledonia Ltd

[1994] 2 All ER 1, [1994] 1 Lloyd's Rep 16, [1993] NLJR 1367, CA

The claimant was employed on the Piper Alpha Oil Rig in the North Sea which exploded and burst into flames causing the deaths of 164 men. The claimant was staying on a support vessel some 500m from the rig. The support vessel took some part in the rescue operation as a result of which the closest the claimant came to the burning oil rig was 100m. The claimant suffered psychiatric illness arising out of his experiences and claimed damages against the operators of the rig. The question before the court was whether the rig operators owed the claimant a duty of care. The judge at first instance held that they did. The defendant appealed.

HELD: The claimant's claim failed. The judge considered correctly that the existence of a duty of care depended upon the test of foreseeability of harm and the proximity of relationship between the claimant and defendant. However the judge did not go far enough for this test is an objective one, i e it is a foreseeability of the reasonable man in the position of the defendants that is material.

The support vessel was never in a position of danger. No one on it sustained any physical injury and there was no evidence that anyone other than the claimant suffered psychiatric injury. The circumstances of the claimant's movements suggested, and the Court of Appeal accepted, that the claimant was not genuinely in fear of his own safety. The claimant was not a rescuer having taken no active part in the rescue operation himself. Thus:

'In my judgment it cannot be said that the defendants ought reasonably to have foreseen that the claimant or other non essential personnel on board (the support vessel) would suffer such injury': per Stuart Smith LJ.

Furthermore there had to be a sufficiently close tie of love and affection between the claimant and the victims to satisfy the test of proximity as confirmed in the Alcock decision above.

'In my judgment both as a matter of principle and policy the court should not extend the duty to those who are mere bystanders or witnesses of horrific events unless there is a sufficient degree of proximity, which requires both nearest in time and place and a close relationship of love and affection between [claimant] and victim': per Stuart Smith LJ.

[36.32]   Page v Smith

[1996] AC 155, [1995] 2 All ER 736, [1995] RTR 210, HL

Mr Smith, the defendant, was travelling in the opposite direction to the claimant and turned across the claimant's path causing a collision. The claimant suffered no physical injury. However the claimant was a long-term sufferer of myalgic encephalomyelitis (ME). The claimant alleged that as a result of this accident the ME had become chronic and permanent and he could never work again.

The claimant was successful at first instance and failed in the Court of Appeal. The claimant appealed to the House of Lords.

HELD, ON APPEAL: The claimant succeeded on a majority of three to two. He was within the range of foreseeable injury and was therefore a primary victim. The leading judgment was given by Lord Lloyd whose conclusions were:

(1)   In cases involving nervous shock it is essential to distinguish between the primary victim and the secondary victims.

(2)   In claims by secondary victims the law insists on certain control mechanisms in order, as a matter of policy, to limit the number of potential claimants. Thus the defendant will not be liable unless psychiatric injury is foreseeable in a person of normal fortitude. These control mechanisms have no place where the claimant is the primary victim.

(3)   In claims by secondary victims it may be legitimate to use hindsight in order to be able to apply the test of reasonable foreseeability. Hindsight, however, has no part to play where the claimant is the primary victim.

(4)   Subject to the above qualifications, the approach in all cases should be the same, namely, whether the defendant can reasonably foresee that his conduct will expose the claimant to the risk of personal injury, whether physical or psychiatric. If the answer is yes, then the duty of care is established even though physical injury does not, in fact, occur. There is no justification for regarding physical and psychiatric injury as different 'kinds of damage'.

(5)   A defendant who is under a duty of care to the claimant, whether as a primary or secondary victim, is not liable for damages for nervous shock unless the shock resulted in some recognised psychiatric illness. It is no answer that the claimant was disposed to psychiatric injury nor is it relevant that the illness takes a rare form or is of unusual severity. The defendant must take his victim as he finds him.

The case was returned to the Court of Appeal to consider causation.

Note—See also *Donachie v The Chief Constable of the Greater Manchester Police* [2004] EWCA 405, CA (at para [35.34]).

[36.33]   Vernon v Bosley (No 2)

[1997] 1 All ER 614

The claimant's young daughters were killed in a road traffic accident where a car crashed down a bank into a fast flowing river. The claimant arrived on the scene shortly after the accident and watched rescue attempts not knowing whether the children were alive or dead. The defendant admitted that she owed the claimant a duty of care and conceded that the experience suffered by the claimant might cause psychiatric damage to a person of normal fortitude. The claimant alleged that he had suffered a very severe degree of nervous shock which subsequently developed into a severe post-traumatic type of neurosis complicated by a severe grief reaction.

HELD: The claimant had had a vulnerable personality prior to the accident but the claimant's mental illness had become an inexplicable mixture of psychiatric disorder and personality disorder. Though not the sole cause of the claimant's subsequent deterioration, the accident was the initial cause and the judge held that the claimant was entitled to recover damages. The defendant appealed.

HELD, ON APPEAL: The Court of Appeal dismissed the appeal. The majority decision can be summarised as follows:

(1)   A successful claimant is required to establish, *inter alia*, that he suffered injury from nervous shock. The types of '*recognisable psychiatric illness*' constituting nervous shock should not be confined in any way. If a claimant proves that he has suffered from pathological grief disorder which may be a recognisable psychiatric illness as well as all the other necessary features of success as defined by Lord Oliver in *Alcock v Chief Constable of South Yorkshire Police* (at para [36.28]) he is entitled to succeed.

(2)   A claimant claiming damages for mental injury as a secondary victim, having witnessed an accident in which the primary victim was killed, is only entitled to recover damages if he proves that his mental illness was caused or contributed to by the traumatic experience of witnessing the accident as distinct from grief and bereavement. If symptoms of mental illness are exclusively referable to grief and bereavement and are not at least partly referable to the traumatic experience of witnessing the accident, then the claim must fail. Damages should not be discounted to exclude the consequence of bereavement and damages are not limited to compensation for that part of the mental illness which can be ascribed to the traumatic experience of witnessing the accident.

(3)   In considering whether the claimant has suffered mental illness, regard is to be had in the first instance to the factual evidence of lay witness rather than to the different interpretations advanced by the expert witnesses of the facts established. Given that the claimant's experience was a very distressing one which might have caused psychiatric injury to a person of normal fortitude and given that the claimant had a vulnerable personality and had suffered a mental illness after but not before the accident, it was sufficient to establish at least a prima facie case that his mental illness was caused by the traumatic experience of witnessing the accident.

[36.34]   White v Chief Constable of South Yorkshire

[1999] 2 AC 455, [1999] 1 All ER 1, [1998] 3 WLR 1509, HL

Following the Hillsborough Football Stadium disaster in which 95 spectators died and hundreds were injured due to overcrowding, 52 serving police officers commenced proceedings against the Chief Constable for damages for psychiatric illness. They claimed that they had suffered post-traumatic stress disorder as a result of their involvement in the aftermath. The Chief Constable admitted that the police's negligence had caused the overcrowding and conceded liability to those police officers who had entered the pens to help with the removal of spectators who were being crushed. Liability was however disputed in respect of those police officers who were on duty in other parts of the stadium and six claimants (four by the time the matter reached the House of Lords) were selected for trial on the issue of liability. At first instance, the claims were dismissed. The Court of Appeal allowed the appeals.

HELD, ON APPEAL, to the House of Lords: The police officers were not entitled to compensation as employees or rescuers. They were not 'primary' victims but were merely 'secondary' victims, because, they had never been at any foreseeable risk of injury. There was no extension of the Chief Constable's duty to protect police officers from psychiatric injury where there had been no breach of their duty to protect the officers from physical injury. If such a duty was created, it would have far reaching consequences for other professions such as doctors and hospital workers who were exposed to grievous injuries and suffering. Secondary victims must satisfy the three control mechanisms laid down in *Alcock v Chief Constable of South Yorkshire* at [para [36.28]).

Lord Steyn held that 'in order to contain the concept of rescuer in reasonable bounds for the purposes of recovery of compensation for pure psychiatric harm, the claimant must at least satisfy the threshold requirement that he objectively exposed himself to danger or reasonably believed that he was so doing'. Lord Griffiths said that a claimant would not qualify as a rescuer if the assistance given was trivial or peripheral.

Note—Lord Goff said in his dissenting judgment that the decision in *Page v Smith* (at para [36.32]) represented a 'remarkable departure' from generally accepted principles in that it 'dethroned foreseeability of psychiatric injury from its central position as the unifying feature of this branch of the law'.

See also *Hatton v Sutherland* [2002] EWCA Civ 76, [2002] 2 All ER 1, [2002] PIQR P21 concerning the control mechanisms for workplace stress.

[36.35]   Hunter v British Coal Corpn

[1999] QB 140, [1998] 2 All ER 97, [1998] 3 WLR 685, CA

The claimant drove an underground vehicle into a hydrant causing it to leak water. He and a fellow employee were unable to turn off the hydrant. As the claimant went to look for a hose, the hydrant exploded killing his colleague. The claimant did not witness the accident but suffered shock at hearing of the death about 15 minutes later. He felt responsible and developed a depressive illness. His employer was found to be negligent and in breach of statutory duty for failing to maintain the roadway along which the claimant had driven. The claimant's claim for psychiatric injury failed at first instance as the claimant was not found to be a primary or secondary victim under the test laid down in *Alcock v Chief Constable of South Yorkshire* (at para [36.28]). The claimant appealed.

HELD: The appealed was dismissed and the claim failed. The necessary physical and temporal proximity to the accident had not been established. His abnormal reaction to the event was not reasonably foreseeable and he was not to be treated as a secondary victim.

[36.36]   Galli-Atkinson v Seghal

[2003] EWCA Civ 697

[2003] Lloyd's Rep Med 285, [2003] All ER (D) 341 (Mar), CA

A 16-year-old girl, was killed when the defendant's car mounted the pavement and struck her as she walked along the pavement. About an hour later, her mother, the claimant, arrived on the scene and was informed for the first time that her daughter had been involved in an accident and was dead. The claimant became hysterical and collapsed. She visited the mortuary an hour later where she held her daughter and saw her disfigured body. At first instance, the claim failed because the visit to the mortuary was not part of the aftermath of the accident and the claimant could not recover damages for the shock of being told that her daughter was dead.

HELD: The claimant was entitled to recover damages for her psychiatric injury since it was sustained as a result of shock in reaction to what she was told at the accident scene and her visit to the mortuary. This constituted a single event and its immediate aftermath because the events retained sufficient proximity to the accident. The case of *Alcock v Chief Constable of South Yorkshire* (at para [36.28] was distinguished).

Note—See also *Walters v North Glamorgan NHS Trust* [2002] EWCA Civ 1792, [2003] PIQR P16.

[36.37]   Duddin v Home Office
[2004] EWCA Civ 181, CA

A prison officer made inappropriate comments to a prisoner's wife. The prisoner (claimant) brought a claim in negligence and misfeasance in public office. He claimed that he had suffered psychiatric damage. The judge dismissed the claim in its entirety.

HELD, ON APPEAL: The claim failed because the claimant had not established that psychiatric damage was reasonably foreseeable from the conversation between the prison officer and his wife. The claimant was a secondary victim. To impose a duty of care, the claimant must satisfy the requirements of foreseeability and proximate relationship. It must also be fair, just and reasonable to impose a duty. The claimant had failed to show that he had a direct perception of the incident which had caused a sudden and violent shock to his own nervous system.

[36.38]   Grieves v FT Everard & Sons Ltd
[2006] EWCA Civ 27, CA

The defendant negligently exposed the claimants to asbestos dust. The claimants developed pleural plaques. The Court of Appeal held by a majority of 2:1 in the test litigation that there can be no compensation for asymptomatic pleural plaques which are accompanied by the usual risks of future asbestos related disease and feelings of worry. There can also be no compensation for claimants exposed to asbestos who in the absence of physical injury develop a recognised psychiatric condition as a result of worry about the consequences for the future.

One of the eight claimants had developed depression as a result of knowledge that he had asymptomatic pleural plaques and claimed that irrespective of the Court of Appeal's findings on pleural plaques he had a free standing claim for recognised psychiatric injury which was a foreseeable consequence of the breach of duty and recoverable in accordance with the principles in *Page v Smith* (at para [36.32]). The Court of Appeal held that the principles in *Page* did not apply and following decisions in the US Supreme Court found a defendant who exposed an employee to asbestos in breach of duty but with no physical manifestation of disease could not be liable for free standing psychiatric injury caused by fear of future disease.

The Court of Appeal also held that such a claim could not be made in the alternative and well established route where employees can recover damages for psychiatric injury caused as a result of stress at work in accordance with principles laid down in *Barber v Somerset County Council* [2002] 2 All ER 1. One of those principles is that the injury is a foreseeable consequence of breach. In this appeal however, the medical evidence for the claimant failed to address the issue of whether psychiatric injury from exposure to asbestos and knowledge of pleural plaques and the risk of future disease was a foreseeable consequence in an employer of normal mental fortitude. As such the claim failed.

Note—The case is being appealed to the House of Lords.

[36.39]   French v Chief Constable of Sussex Police
[2006] EWCA Civ 312, CA

Five police officers participated in an armed raid that resulted in a fatal shooting. The shooting was not witnessed by these five officers. Disciplinary and criminal charges were initiated against the officers which they claimed caused them stress and psychiatric damage. The officers brought a claim for negligence against the Chief Constable alleging systemic shortcomings in training with the type of operations that led to the fatal shooting. The claims for psychiatric damage were supported by medical evidence. The claim was struck out at first instance on the basis that the allegations had no reasonable prospect of success. The police officers had not witnessed the shootings and were not secondary victims. They had also not established that their employers were on notice that they were vulnerable to stress. The claimants appealed.

HELD: Appeals dismissed. It was not reasonably foreseeable that corporate failings would cause the officers psychiatric injury by reason of the disciplinary and criminal proceedings. Police officers who witness shootings cannot claim as secondary victims and therefore the officers in this claim, who were more remotely affected, could not succeed.

Lord Phillips CJ referred to the case of *Rothwell v Chemical & Insulating Co Ltd* [2006] EWCA Civ 27 which was heard with the *Grieves v FT Everard & Sons Ltd* case at (para [36.38] above). In that test litigation, the Court of Appeal considered the development of liability for psychiatric injury. Lord Phillips CJ summarised it as follows:

'(i) There is a duty to exercise reasonable care not to cause psychiatric injury by putting the claimant in fear for his or her physical safety – *Dulieu v White* [1901] 2 KB 669.

(ii) A defendant who breaches his duty of care not to endanger the physical safety of a claimant will be liable if the breach causes not physical injury but psychiatric injury, even if it was not reasonably foreseeable that psychiatric injury alone might result – *Page v Smith* [1996] 1 AC 155 [at para [36.32]].

(iii) There is no general duty to exercise reasonable care not to cause psychiatric injury as a result of causing the death or injury of someone (the 'primary victim') which is witnessed by the claimant ('secondary victim') – *Alcock v Chief Constable of Yorkshire Police* [1992] 2 AC 310 [at para [36.28]].

(iv) Proposition (iii) applies equally where the claimant is employed by the defendant –*White v Chief Constable of South Yorkshire* [1999] 2 AC 455 [at para [36.34]].

(v) As an exception to proposition (iii) there is a duty of care not to cause psychiatric injury to a claimant as a result of causing the death or injury of someone loved by the claimant in circumstances where the claimant sees or hears the accident or its aftermath – *McLoughlin v O'Brian* [at para [36.23]].

Turning to the duties owed by an employer to an employee, an employer is usually entitled to expect that an employee will be capable of withstanding the stresses inherent in his or her employment. Where, however, an employer knows or ought to know that these stresses are putting a particular employee at risk of psychiatric injury, the employer will come under a duty to take reasonable steps to protect the employee against that risk – see *Barber v Somerset CC* [2002] 2 All ER 1.'

(E) INCONVENIENCE, DISTRESS AND DISCOMFORT

[36.40]   *Note*—The following cases generally arise from breach of contract.

[36.41]   Hobbs v London and South Western Rly Co
(1875) LR 10 QB 111, 44 LJQB 49, 32 LT 252

The claimant and his family were put on the wrong train and so found themselves at Esher late at night instead of at Hampton Court, as a consequence of which they had to suffer the inconvenience of walking home in the rain.

HELD: Damages were recoverable; they could have hired a carriage had one been available and charged the cost as special damage.

[36.42]   Stedman v Swans Tours
(1951) 95 Sol Jo 727, (1951) Times, 6 November, CA

The claimant contracted with travel agents for transport for a party of six and a fortnight's accommodation at a first-class hotel with superior rooms with a sea view. The rooms were very inferior and had no sea view. The party were unable to obtain accommodation elsewhere. Romer J awarded £13 15s 0d special damages but no general damages.

HELD, ON APPEAL: General damages could be recovered for appreciable inconvenience and discomfort caused by breach of contract assessed at £50 by the Court of Appeal. *Bailey v Bullock* [1950] 2 All ER 1167 followed.

[36.43]   Jackson v Horizon Holidays Ltd
[1975] 3 All ER 92, [1975] 1 WLR 1468, 119 Sol Jo 759, CA

The claimant booked a holiday with the defendant for himself, his wife and their three-year-old twin sons in Ceylon for a month at a cost of £1,450. For the first fortnight they were housed in a hotel which did not fulfil the description given in the defendants' brochure. The judge awarded £1,100 damages for:
(1)   the difference in value between what the claimant got and what he bargained for;
(2)   compensation for distress and disappointment.

HELD, ON APPEAL: The award should stand. The claimant was making a contract for the benefit of the whole family. He could recover damages for the discomfort, vexation and upset which the whole family suffered.

Note—In *Woodar Investment Development Ltd v Wimpey Construction (UK) Ltd* ([1980] 1 All ER 571, [1980] 1 WLR 277, 124 Sol Jo 184, HL) Lord Wilberforce referred to *Jackson v Horizon Holidays* (at para [36.43]) and said

> 'I am not prepared to dissent from the actual decision in that case. It may be supported either as a broad decision on the measure of damages or possibly as an example of a type of contract, examples of which are persons contracting for family holidays, ordering meals in restaurants for a party, hiring a taxi for a group, calling for special treatment ... [but] I cannot agree with the basis on which Lord Denning MR put his decision in that case.'

[36.44]   Jarvis v Swans Tours Ltd

[1973] QB 233, [1973] 1 All ER 71, [1972] 3 WLR 954, 116 Sol Jo 822, CA

The claimant booked a skiing holiday in Switzerland on the strength of the description in the defendants' catalogue promising a house party each week, a wide variety of ski runs, hire of skis, sticks and boots and other facilities. On the second week of the holiday he was the only person in the hotel, the skiing was disappointing and there was no satisfactory equipment available. The county court judge awarded as damages only one-half of the cost of the holiday.

HELD, ON APPEAL: This was not the right measure of damages. If the contracting party in a contract for a holiday breaks his contract damages can be given for the disappointment, the distress, the upset and frustration caused by the breach. The damages should be increased to £125.

[36.45]   Ichard v Frangoulis

[1977] 2 All ER 461, [1977] 1 WLR 556, 121 Sol Jo 287   Peter Pain J

The claimant and defendant were injured when their cars collided on a road in Yugoslavia where both were on holiday. The defendant after hospital treatment continued to Athens where he spent his holiday, though his enjoyment was spoiled by his injuries. The claimant conceded he was to blame for the collision.

HELD: On the defendant's counterclaim, the loss of enjoyment was a factor to be taken into account in assessing damages in a claim in tort as it is in contract (eg *Jarvis v Swans Tours* (at para [36.44]) and *Jackson v Horizon Holidays* (at para [36.43])) provided the damages were foreseeable by the negligent party. Where as here the accident took place in a holiday area much frequented by tourists it was obviously foreseeable.

[36.46]   Hayes v James & Charles Dodd

[1990] 2 All ER 815, [1988] EGCS 107, [1988] 138 NLJ Rep 259, CA

The claimant purchased a commercial property relying on his solicitor's representation that there was a right of way. There was not and the claimant's business venture failed. The claimant successfully brought a claim against his solicitor for breach of contract. Among other heads of damage, he was awarded £1,500 for the anguish and vexation he suffered.

HELD, ON APPEAL: An award of damages for anguish and vexation is not recoverable in a case concerning a purely commercial contract. Such awards should be limited in contractual claims to those where the object of the contract is 'comfort or pleasure or the relief of discomfort'.

[36.47]   Firsteel Cold Rolled Products v Anaco Precision Pressings Ltd
(1994) Times, 21 November

English law does not, as a general rule and as a matter of policy, award damages for breach of contract in respect of inconvenience, stress and difficulty caused by a breach of contract.

There are two well recognised exceptions to this rule: holiday cases and claims in connection with physical inconvenience and discomfort caused as a result of negligent advice in connection with the advance of property.

[36.48]   Alexander v Rolls Royce Motor Cars Ltd
[1996] RTR 95, CA

The claimant purchased a second hand Corniche Rolls Royce motor car from the defendants in 1983. Shortly after the purchase the claimant complained of knocking noises in the engine and various minor mechanical and cosmetic defects. The Rolls Royce was then involved in an accident and a respray was required. The claimant was unhappy with the quality of the respray. The mechanical defects continued and a new engine was required.

The claimant attempted to sell the Rolls Royce but without success and gave evidence to the effect that 'he thought he had bought perfection. Realising he had a car with so many suspected problems detracted from his pleasure in owning it.'

The judge held that the Rolls Royce was not of merchantable quality and awarded the claimant damages for this and other remedial requirements. The judge did not award the claimant damages for:
(1)   disappointment, loss of enjoyment and distress, and
(2)   loss of use.
The claimant appealed on the points.

HELD, ON APPEAL: (1) The general rule is that damages for distress, inconvenience or loss of enjoyment are not recoverable for breach of ordinary commercial contract but only when the contract is one for the provision of pleasure, freedom from harassment or relaxation. The claimant's counsel argued that the contract for the repair of a motor car was within this exceptional class of case for it was akin to the kind of contract to provide a relaxing holiday as was the subject of the claim in *Jarvis v Swan Tours Ltd* (at para [36.44]) or to provide freedom from worry and anxiety, as in *Heywood v Wellers* [1976] QB 446, CA. This argument was not accepted by the Court of Appeal. A breach of contract to repair a motor car, even one so prestigious as a Rolls Royce, does not give rise to a liability for damages for distress and inconvenience and loss of enjoyment for the use of the car.
(2)   The claimant did not use the Rolls Royce for his ordinary day-to-day travel. There was no evidence of any inconvenience caused to the claimant.

Note—See also the case summary for this case at para [36.144].

[36.49]   Taylor v Browne
[1995] CLY 1842   Cook HHJ

The claimant claimed damages following a road traffic accident. Liability was resolved in the claimant's favour. In addition to the cost of repairs, the claimant claimed for £100 by way of general damages for the general inconvenience in dealing with administrative matters arising out of the accident, including making telephone calls, writing letters and attending upon insurers, and repairers.

HELD: A claim for inconvenience can only relate to the loss of use of the vehicle and cannot be extended to cover the aggravation inevitably involved in litigation. The judge refused to make any award under this heading.

[36.50]   **O'Brien-King v Phillips**
(15 April 1996, unreported)

The defendant damaged the claimant's motor car. There was an issue as to whether general damages could be claimed for inconvenience.

HELD: It was necessary to distinguish between the inconvenience and aggravation of dealing with the litigation process (correspondence and attending solicitors) and other matters. The former was a matter of costs and not damages. Damages were recoverable for the latter which included using public transport and loss of earnings for time taken to obtain repair estimates.

Note—Taylor v Browne (at para [36.49]) was distinguished.

(F)   MULTIPLE INJURIES

[36.51]   **Dureau v Evans**
[1996] PIQR Q18, (1996) 146 NLJ 1280, CA

The claimant sustained multiple injuries in a road traffic accident. The Court of Appeal considered the assessment of damages in multiple injury cases and Kennedy LJ gave the following guidance:

'To a limited extent, in a case where there are multiple injuries, the figures in the Judicial Studies Board table can help but I accept [the] criticism of them that, where one has a multiplicity of injuries, it is necessary to take an overall view. The off-setting process may mean it is not possible to derive a great deal of benefit from that particular source. One then looks to see if anything can be gained from looking at a comparable award, if one is to be found, in another case. Even that may not prove to be a particularly fruitful source of inquiry. It may be necessary, if it be possible, to select what may be the most serious head of injury to see if a comparable award can be found relating to that and, if so, build on it to allow for the other heads of injury which have been sustained by the claimant in the instant case'.

4.   LOSS OF CONGENIAL EMPLOYMENT

[36.52]   **Hale v London Underground Ltd**
[1993] PIQR Q30

The claimant was a fireman and aged 39 at the date of the accident. He had to give up being an active fireman when he was injured attending the King's Cross underground station fire in 1987. The job had provided him with great satisfaction. He did not enjoy his subsequent job as a fire prevention officer as much. By the date of trial, he was 44.

HELD: It is well recognised that loss of congenial employment is a separate head of damage. The claimant was awarded £5,000. The court took into account the claimant's age and the fact that the claimant may in the future find a job that provided greater satisfaction.

[36.53]   Langford v Hebran

[2001] EWCA Civ 361

[2001] PIQR Q13

The claimant was aged 27 when he was injured in a road traffic accident. Since leaving school he had been unemployed for significant periods but had commenced work as a trainee bricklayer a few months before the accident. The claimant had also become the world light-middleweight amateur kick boxer champion and turned professional a few months before the accident. The accident prevented him from continuing his career as a professional kick boxer.

HELD: At first instance, the claimant was awarded £7,500 for loss of congenial employment. The case was appealed to the Court of Appeal on loss of earnings.

Note—This case also appears para [36.61] concerning loss of earnings.

[36.54]   Willbye v Gibbons

[2003] EWCA Civ 372

[2003] All ER (D) 275 (Mar), [2004] PIQR P15, (2003) 147 SJLB 388, CA

The claimant was aged 12 when, as a pedestrian, she was struck by a car. She sustained serious injuries including a head injury. At first instance, she was awarded £15,000 for loss of congenial employment.

HELD, ON APPEAL: The award for loss of congenial employment would be reduced to £5,000. It is important to keep this head of damages in proportion. Awards here rarely exceed £5,000. The claimant was being compensated for being unable to pursue a career she thought she would have enjoyed. Although she had never embarked upon a career, she probably had the ability to obtain the required qualifications. As such, this was really an award for a particular disappointment.

[36.55]   Stepton v Wolseley

(17 January 2005, unreported)

The claimant, aged 20 at the date of the road traffic accident, sustained serious and permanently disabling injuries. At the time of the accident, he had just begun a career in hairdressing and had hoped to become a hairdressing lecturer. Following the accident, he retrained to become a receptionist.

HELD: The claimant was awarded £3,000 for loss of congenial employment.

[36.56]   Watson v Gray

(1999) CL August 1999

The claimant was a professional footballer aged 25 at the date of injury. He sustained a serious fracture to his leg as a result of a negligent tackle by an opponent. The fracture was surgically repaired but he was left in plaster and having treatment for a period of eight months. He made a good functional recovery from his physical injuries but suffered from anger and depression. Experts agreed that he had lost the pace and sharpness of a top striker.

HELD: The claimant's career had been blighted and he had been deprived of the opportunity to play at the top level of football. He was likely to end his career in the lower divisions at a greatly reduced income and had a low residual earning capacity outside the game. The claimant was awarded £25,000 in general damages to include enhanced loss of amenity to a professional footballer together with loss of congenial employment as a result of his likely early retirement from the game.

5.   LOSS OF EARNINGS AND THE MULTIPLIER

(A)   THE CASES

[36.57]   Wells v Wells
Page v Sheerness Steel Co plc, Thomas v Brighton Health Authority
[1999] 1 AC 345, [1998] 3 All ER 481, HL

Three seriously injured claimants argued that the court should not adopt the conventional approach of awarding a multiplier consistent with the return of 4% or 5% per annum on the capital sum. Instead the claimants argued that the multiplier should be calculated on the basis that damages were invested in low risk, index linked Government stocks (ILGS) which would fix the multiplier at an equivalent 3% return per annum. As a consequence the multiplier and therefore the damages award would be significantly higher.

The claimants relied upon two propositions:
(1)   the award must be fixed on the assumption that the claimant is entitled to invest taking the minimum risk;
(2)   the test is not whether it would be prudent to invest in equities but whether to invest in ILGS would achieve the necessary object with the greatest precision.

HELD, ON APPEAL to the Court of Appeal: The court held that existing guidelines were still valid and was not persuaded that the case had been made out that the courts of their own motion should adopt ILGS in their place. Consequently a discount rate of 4.5% would continue to apply.

HELD, ON APPEAL to the House of Lords: The decision of the Court of Appeal was reversed. The court held that when assessing damages for anticipated future losses and expenses in personal injury cases a court should fix the award by assuming that the claimant will invest the damages in ILGS. While the court accepted that this approach would result in a heavier burden on the defendant and the insurance industry that did not in itself make it unfair as the claimant, who was not in a position to take risks and wished to protect himself against inflation, would be prudent to invest in ILGS. It was desirable that there should be a consistent rate applying across the board which would have the benefit of avoiding the necessity of expert evidence on rates at a trial, and also by using the ILGS, savings would be made by obviating the need for a claimant to seek annual investment advice regarding damages.

The House of Lords therefore ruled that when assessing the discount rate to be applied, the figure of 3% should be used rather than the 4.5% determined in the judgment of the Court of Appeal.

Furthermore, where there was an agreed life expectancy the full multiplier taken from the Ogden tables should be used and while the House of Lords' decision does not entirely rule out additional discounts when calculating loss of future earnings, it significantly limits judges' powers to do so.

Note—See *Lim Poh Choo v Camden and Islington Area Health Authority* (at para [36.5]).

[36.58]   **Blamire v South Cumbria Health Authority**

[1993] PIQR Q1, CA

When assessing loss of earnings where there are a number of imponderables, the judge is entitled to reject the multiplier/multiplicand approach and make a global award.

Note—This approach was followed by the Court of Appeal in *Goldborough v Thompson and Crowther* [1996] PIQR Q86 and *Chase International Express v McCrae* [2003] EWCA Civ 505, [2004] PIQR P21.

[36.59]   **Kent v British Railways Board**

[1995] PIQR Q42, CA

The claimant and her husband ran a tea shop and bed and breakfast business in Dorset. There were no formal contracts, partnership deeds or other documents between them. The business was ran as a joint venture although for taxation purposes the husband was assessed on 60% of the profit share and the plaintiff, the remaining 40%. The claimant was injured in a road traffic accident and the business profits suffered as a consequence. The claimant claimed for 100% of the loss of profits both past and future on the basis that the business was a team effort and it would be artificial to try and separate out the parts played individually by the claimant and her husband. The Master agreed and the defendant appealed.

HELD, ON APPEAL: The husband had no claim in law against the defendant. By allowing the claimant to recover 100% of the loss of profits the Master had, in effect, given the claimant's husband a right of recovery against the defendant which could not be correct. Therefore the claimant could not recover the full amount of the loss of profit.

   It was an equal partnership between husband and wife who were entitled to a 50% share of the profits. The court had to look at the reality of the situation. The presumption in s 24 of the Partnership Act 1890 that partners shared equally in the profits of the business was not rebutted by the 40/60 split arrangement with the Inland Revenue. The correct apportionment was 50/50.

Note—See also *Ward v Newalls* [1998] PIQR Q41 and *Neal v Jones* [2002] EWCA Civ 1731, [2002] All ER (D) 10 (Nov) where the Court of Appeal re-affirmed this approach.

[36.60]   **Doyle v Wallace**

[1998] PIQR Q146, CA

The claimant, aged 19, was injured in a road traffic accident and sustained moderately severe brain damage. The claimant submitted that but for the accident, she would have become a drama teacher rather than a clerical worker. The judge quantified loss of earnings on the basis that there was a 50% chance that the claimant would have become a teacher. The defendant appealed and contended that any earnings from teaching should not be taken into account because it was not probable that the claimant would have qualified as, and become, a drama teacher.

HELD: The judge had correctly applied a percentage to reflect the claimant's chance of becoming a teacher. Otton LJ held that there is a key distinction between a claimant having to prove on the balance of probabilities that a particular result would come about and a claimant needing to prove only that a chance of achieving that particular result had been lost.

[36.61]   **Langford v Hebran**

[2001] PIQR Q13, CA

The claimant, aged 27, injured his neck and shoulder in a road traffic accident. At the time of the accident, the claimant had just started work as a trainee bricklayer following lengthy periods of unemployment. He was also the World light-middleweight kick boxer champion and had turned professional a few months before the accident. He had fought and won one professional fight. The claimant's injuries prevented him from resuming training and hindered his career plans. The claimant obtained evidence from a forensic accountant and presented his future loss of earnings claim on the basis of four scenarios. His basic claim was that he would achieve kick boxing earnings and work part time as a bricklayer. Once his kick boxing career ended, he would become a full time bricklayer until age 60. The other scenarios assumed a more successful kick boxing career. Applying the approach in *Doyle v Wallace* (at para [36.60]), the judge used his basic claim as a starting point and added a percentage to reflect the loss chance of achieving each of those alternatives. The defendant contended that this approach was wrong as there were a number of possibilities and appealed.

HELD: Appeal dismissed. The evidence supported the four scenarios and the judge's approach was correct, although he had overestimated the claimant's percentage chance of success to some extent. A broad-brush approach would have produced an unfair result.

[36.62]   **Royal Victoria Infirmary and Associated Hospitals NHS Trust v B (a child)**

[2002] EWCA Civ 348

[2002] PIQR Q10, CA

The claimant claimed damages for severe cerebral palsy caused by the defendant's negligence. The only issue before the trial judge was the multiplier to be applied to the agreed cost of care. He decided upon the claimant's expected life expectancy, took a discount of 3% and applied Ogden Table 38 (multipliers for pecuniary loss for term certain). The hospital authority (appellant) contended that the judge should not have decided how long the claimant was expected to live but 'the average number of remaining years of life of a cohort of individuals with (her) age and condition' by reference to statistical evidence.

HELD: Appeal dismissed. The judge followed the approach in *Wells v Wells* (at para [36.57]). He was entitled to determine the issue of life expectancy on all the evidence available. Statistical evidence alone was not sufficient in such a case. 'It would be wrong to allow a statistician, or an actuary, to do more than inform the opinions of the medical witnesses and the decision of the court, on what is essentially a medical, or clinical, issue' per Sir Anthony Evans at paragraph 39 of his judgment.

[36.63]   **Herring v Ministry of Defence**

[2004] 1 All ER 44, CA

The claimant suffered serious spinal injuries in a parachuting accident. Prior to the accident, the claimant was a qualified sports coach and lifeguard in a leisure centre. He was also a Special Air Service physical training instructor and member of the Territorial Army. His long-term ambition was to join the police force. The judge assessed the future loss of earnings claim on the basis that he would have joined the police force and discounted the multiplier by 25% to account for uncertainty.

The claimant's view was that the discount was far too high. He appealed and submitted that it was not appropriate to calculate future loss of earnings upon a loss of chance basis.

HELD: Appeal allowed. Per Potter LJ: 'the cases in which the percentage loss of chance approach has been adopted appear to me to be those where the chance to be assessed has been the chance that the career of the claimant will take a particular course leading to significantly higher overall earnings than those which it is otherwise reasonable to take as the baseline for the calculation'. Distinguishing *Doyle v Wallace* (at para [36.60]) and *Langford v Hebran* (at para [36.61]), Potter LJ continued 'in a case where the career model adopted by the judge has been chosen because it is itself the appropriate baseline and/or is one of a number of alternatives likely to give more or less similar results, then it is neither necessary nor appropriate to adopt the percentage chance approach in respect of the possibility that the particular career identified will not be followed after all. That seems to me to be the position in this case.' The discount of 25% was reduced to 10%.

Note—The approach in *Herring* was applied in *Dixon v Were* [2004] EWHC 2273, [2004] All ER (D) 356 (Oct).

[36.64]   Brown v Ministry of Defence

[2006] EWCA Civ 546

[2006] All ER (D) 133 (May), CA

The claimant, aged 24, sustained a serious ankle injury during basic military training. She was unable to complete her training and was discharged. She came from an army family and had intended to join the army from a young age. After a series of temporary jobs, the claimant trained as a physiotherapist. The defendant admitted liability for the accident. At first instance, the trial judge awarded the claimant damages for the loss of the full pension entitlement she would have received had she left the army after 22 years' service with the rank of Staff Sergeant. The defendant appealed contending that the judge should not have adopted the balance of probabilities test but instead assessed the chance of a future event happening. The claimant cross-appealed against the decision to make no award for disadvantage on the labour market.

HELD: Appeal allowed. The judge should have assessed the chances of the event occurring. The claimant's chances of obtaining the right to a pension after 22 years was 30%. The Court of Appeal also allowed a cross-appeal by the claimant and made a limited award (approximately four months loss of earnings) for disadvantage on the labour market. There was sufficient evidence to support a finding that there was a more than insignificant risk that the claimant would develop osteoarthritis in her injured ankle which could force her to give up her job as a physiotherapist.

Note—See also *Evans v Tarmac Central Ltd* (at para [36.71]).

(B)   DAMAGES ACT 1996, S 1

[36.65]
1.   **Assumed rate of return on investment of damages**
    (1)   In determining the return to be expected from the investment of a sum awarded as damages for future pecuniary loss in an action for personal injury, the

Court shall, subject to and in accordance with the Rules of Court made for the purposes of this section, take into account such rate of return (if any) as may from time to time be prescribed by an Order made by the Lord Chancellor.

(2)   Subsection (1) above should not however prevent the Court taking a different rate of return into account if any party to the proceedings shows that it is more appropriate in the case in question.

(3)   An Order under subsection (1) above may prescribe different rates of return for different classes of case.

(4)   Before making an Order under subsection (1) above the Lord Chancellor shall consult the Government Actuary and the Treasurer; and any Order under that sub-section shall be made by statutory instrument subject to annulment in pursuance of a resolution of either House or Parliament.

(5)   ...

Note—The discount rate set by the Lord Chancellor is currently 2.5%. In *Cooke v United Bristol Healthcare NHS Trust* [2004] 1 All ER 797, the claimants attempted to show that the cost of their future care would increase at a substantially greater rate than general inflation and that this constituted exceptional circumstances entitling the court to depart from the rate set under the Damages Act pursuant to s 2(1) of that Act. The Court of Appeal rejected their argument and held that to seek an increase on that basis was an illegitimate attempt to subvert the discount rate set by the Lord Chancellor. See also *Warriner v Warriner* [2003] 3 All ER 447 and *Page v Plymouth Hospitals NHS Trust* (at para [36.100]).

[36.66]   *Note*—The Ogden Actuarial Tables issued by the Government Actuaries Department are admissible in evidence for the purpose of assessing, in an action for personal injury, the sum to be awarded as general damages for future pecuniary loss: Civil Evidence Act 1995, s 10(1).

6.   LOSS OF EARNING CAPACITY

Note—Loss of earning capacity is a general damage but included in this section for ease of reference.

(A)   ADULT

[36.67]   Smith v Manchester Corpn
(1974) 17 KIR 1, CA

The claimant, aged 51, sustained a serious injury to her right elbow in May 1971. She was off work for 14 months. She was then able to resume her work without a drop in earnings and would be able to continue indefinitely, though she was left with severe restriction of movements in the elbow and shoulder which would be permanent. As a result she would be at considerable disability in the competitive labour market should she lose her job, though her employer, the defendant, undertook to continue to employ her so far as it could. The judge awarded £2,000 general damages for pain and disability but only £300 for future financial loss.

HELD, ON APPEAL: The award for future financial loss should be increased to £1,000. An award for loss of future earnings is usually compounded of two elements:

(1)   actual continuing loss multiplied by the appropriate number of years' purchase; and

(2)   the weakening of the claimant's competitive position in the open labour market; if the claimant loses her present employment what are her chances of obtaining comparable employment in the open labour

market? If there is a real risk that a claimant will lose his or her present employment it calls for real compensation.

Note—See also *Mitchell v Liverpool Area Health Authority* (1985) Times, 17 June, CA.

[36.68]   Clarke v Rotax Aircraft Equipment Ltd
[1975] 3 All ER 794, [1975] 1 WLR 1570, 119 Sol Jo 679, CA

The claimant contracted dermatitis of the hands as a result of his work with the defendant. After two attacks he had to take work away from the irritant substance, resulting in a loss of £9 a week in wages. In addition to special damage the judge awarded £2,700 for future loss (being £9 per week for six years) and £1,250 for loss of earning capacity.

HELD: (1) It was essential to avoid overlap of the awards for loss of future earnings and for loss of earning capacity. If the claimant lost his present lower-paid job he would probably be able to find another at similar wages. In these circumstances £1,250 was too much; a nominal award of £250 was adequate.

(2)   No interest should be added to the award for loss of earning capacity.

Note—See also *Nicholls v National Coal Board* [1976] ICR 266, CA.

[36.69]   Moeliker v Reyrolle & Co Ltd
[1977] 1 All ER 9, [1977] 1 WLR 132, 120 Sol Jo 165, CA

In an action for damages for injuries to his left hand sustained at work the claimant claimed an award for loss of earning capacity as in *Smith v Manchester Corpn* (at para [36.67]). He was a skilled man, valued by his employer for whom he had worked for 30 years. He had resumed his pre-accident work after the accident and his employer had no intention of ending his employment. If he ever lost his job he would be at a disadvantage in getting an equally well-paid job because of the permanent injuries to his left index finger and thumb. The judge awarded £750 for loss of earning capacity.

HELD: The award was sufficient. *Smith v Manchester Corpn* laid down no new principle of law. An award for loss of earning capacity had been made in *Ashcroft v Curtin* [1971] 3 All ER 1208, [1971] 1 WLR 1731, CA three years before *Smith's* case. This head of damage usually arises where a claimant is, at the date of trial, in employment but there is a risk of his losing that employment at some time in the future and then because of his injury may be at a disadvantage in getting equally well paid work. It was not correct that whenever a claimant establishes a claim under this head the damages must be considerable. Whether and what to award should be considered in two stages:

(1)   Is there a 'substantial' or 'real' risk that a claimant will lose his present job before the end of his working life?

(2)   If there is (but not otherwise) the court must assess and quantify the present value of the risk of financial damage which the claimant will suffer if the risk materialises. A judge must look at all the relevant factors and do the best he can.

Note—In *Page v Enfield & Haringey Area Health Authority* (1986) Times, 7 November the Court of Appeal held that when assessing damages for loss of earning capacity or handicap on the labour market it was not permissible to make a conventional award or to apply any formula, tariff, or marker following previously decided cases. No assistance could be derived, save in the most general sense, from the levels of awards made in other cases as each case was unique.

[36.70] **Cook v Consolidated Fisheries Ltd**

[1977] ICR 635, CA

Following an accident at work in February the claimant resumed his pre-accident work in June but gave it up in December partly because he found the heavy work difficult because of the injury. He decided to become a lorry driver though he was not actually working at the date of the trial. There was persisting disability which might affect his working ability within 10 to 15 years. The judge awarded £3,000 general damages but only £500 for loss of future earning capacity as a total of £3,500 seemed about right.

HELD, ON APPEAL: Loss of future earning capacity should be assessed separately without reference to what was being awarded for general damages. The award of £500 should be increased to £1,500. An award for loss of earning capacity is possible even if the claimant is not actually in employment at the time of trial.

Note—See also: *Robson v Liverpool City Council* [1993] PIQR Q78, CA where the claimant was awarded £2,500 by way of *Smith v Manchester* damages for the loss of vision in one eye and *Samuels v Benning* (at para [35.85]).

[36.71] **Evans v Tarmac Central Ltd**

[2005] EWCA Civ 1820

[2005] All ER (D) 172 (Dec), CA

The claimant was diagnosed with a disc herniation causing permanent damage following heavy lifting at work. The medical evidence showed that the claimant had a pre-existing back problem. At the quantum trial, the judge used a multiplier of 14.72 and awarded £30,000 *Smith v Manchester* damages. The claimant earned £17,750 net per annum. The defendant contended on appeal that the multiplier should be reduced to reflect the pre-existing back problem and a *Smith* award was not appropriate as the claimant had not proved that he was at substantial risk of finding himself on the labour market.

HELD: Appeal allowed. The more than fanciful chance that the claimant may have suffered from a disc herniation in any event was not reflected in the Ogden Tables. The multiplier should be reduced to 11 to reflect this special risk. The absence of positive evidence that the claimant might lose his job did not defeat the *Smith* claim. There was evidence of the claimant's permanent disability. However, the *Smith* award was too high. The judge had estimated the risk where there was no evidence and the court leant against such speculation. The judges asked the questions formulated by Browne LJ in *Moeliker v Reyrolle & Co Ltd* (at para [36.69]) and reduced the award to £10,000.

Note—See also *Forey v London Buses* [1992] 1 PIQR 48 and *Brown v Ministry of Defence* (at para [36.64]).

(B)   CHILD

[36.72] **Cronin v Redbridge London Borough Council**

(1987) Times, 20 May, CA

The claimant was aged 12 when, during a metal work lesson at school, a fragment of perspex flew into her right eye causing the loss of all useful vision in that eye. Virtually no evidence was called about her future earning capacity save that she had a vague feeling that she would have liked to be an air hostess. Peter Pain J allowed £10,000; the defendant appealed.

HELD, ON APPEAL: Awarding damages to a child still at school for future handicap on the labour market involved much speculation and unsatisfactory guesswork. The claimant was an average student and her academic progress had not been hindered to any significant degree. If there was a deterioration she could return to court under s 32A of the Supreme Court Act 1981 (provisional damages). The judge had been excessively generous and a modest sum only was appropriate. The award was reduced to £4,000.

[36.73]   Mitchell v Liverpool Area Health Authority (Teaching)
(1985) Times, 17 June, CA

The claimant was barely one month old when, as a result of the defendant's negligence, he suffered damage to the circulation of his right arm necessitating amputation at the elbow level. The judge made no award for loss of earning capacity; to look into so remote a future without having any real guidance 'is inevitably to indulge in such speculation that it would be unfair to the defendants to find that they are liable for an additional sum'. The claimant appealed.

HELD: The appeal succeeded; although the court had to allow a heavy discount for the acceleration of the award (the claimant was now only two years old) and a further discount because of the large choice of occupations open to the claimant. In all the circumstances it was held that the appropriate award was £5,000. Per Purchas LJ: 'The [claimant] had suffered a substantial disability. It might be that he would find well-paid employment but it was impossible to disregard entirely the risk that he would not do so.'

Note—See also *Warren v Northern General Hospital Trust* [2000] 1 WLR 1404, CA. The court applied a discount in line with the Odgen Tables to assess a child's future loss of earnings.

7.   LOSS OF PROSPECTIVE EARNINGS

[36.74]   Pickett v British Rail Engineering Ltd
[1980] AC 136, [1979] 1 All ER 774, [1978] 3 WLR 955, 122 Sol Jo 778, HL

The claimant, aged 51, was found to be suffering from mesothelioma caused by the defendant's admitted negligence. His expectation of life was reduced to one year. He claimed damages for loss of expectation of life. The Court of Appeal following *Oliver v Ashman* [1962] 2 QB 210, [1961] 3 All ER 323, [1961] 3 WLR 669, 105 Sol Jo 608, CA held that damages for loss of earnings during the 'lost years' were not recoverable.

HELD, ON APPEAL to the House of Lords: *Oliver v Ashman* was wrongly decided. It had been based on a dictum of Lord Simon in *Benham v Gambling* [1941] AC 157: 'No regard must be had to financial losses and gains during the period of which the victim has been deprived.' But in *Benham's* case no claim for loss of earnings had been made and Lord Simon could not be taken to intend that his words should apply to a case where there was such a claim. Though damages for loss of earnings during the 'lost years' should be assessed with moderation, they must not be fixed at a conventional figure because, being damages for pecuniary loss, they can be measured in money. In assessing those damages the claimant's own living expenses which the claimant would have expended during the lost years should be deducted but whether he had dependants or not or whether he would have looked after them is immaterial.

Case remitted for damages to be assessed.

[36.75] Connolly v Camden and Islington Area Health Authority

[1981] 3 All ER 250 Comyn J

When only a few days old the infant claimant (four and three-quarters years at the date of trial) suffered serious brain damage when being anaesthetised for a surgical operation. He was left with extensive mental and physical disabilities. His expectation of life, as found by the judge on the evidence, was shortened to 27½ years. Damages were claimed for loss of earnings during the 'lost years'.

HELD: The claimant qualified for a 'lost years' payment but the assessment was nil. From *Pickett v British Rail Engineering Ltd* (at para [36.74]) and *Gammell v Wilson* (at para [37.57]) it was clear that a young or middle-aged man could rightly expect an award for the financial benefit of the years' earnings which he had lost even though it involved a great deal of guesswork, but those cases show that a child is in a different position. No hard and fast rule can be laid down but a child qualifies under this head of damage dependent on the ability to prove the potential loss. As Lord Scarman said in *Gammell's* case the lost years of earning capacity will ordinarily be so distant that no estimate is possible, though there may be exceptions, eg that of a child television star. Other possible examples are the son of a father who owns a prosperous business or the son of a farmer who is able to leave the estate to his son. But in the present case on the evidence, though there is a claim, the assessment is nil.

[36.76] Croke v Wiseman

[1981] 3 All ER 852, [1982] I WLR 71, CA

The infant claimant when 21 months old suffered a cardiac arrest due to negligence of the defendant. He survived but with severe loss of brain function, paralysis of all four limbs and blindness. His expectation of life was limited to 40 years. Damages were claimed for (*inter alia*) loss of future earnings during life and during the 'lost years' of life expectation.

HELD: Though it is a task of great difficulty to assess an appropriate sum for a young child it has been frequently done, eg in the thalidomide cases. Taking a figure of £5,000 per annum for estimated future loss and a maximum working life of 22 years (ie from 18 to 40) the actuarial figure for the multiplier is 8.876. But this makes no allowance for the receipt of a capital sum at least 11 years before earnings would begin nor for the possibility that the child would never have become an earner. The multiplier should be reduced to five years making a total of £25,000 for future loss of earnings. As for earnings during the lost years there are compelling reasons as in *Pickett v British Rail Engineering Ltd* (at para [36.74]) for awarding a sum of money to a living claimant of mature years which would have been available to spend on his dependants, but in the case of a child there are no dependants and, if the injuries are catastrophic, there never will be any. In such a case the court should refuse to speculate. No sum should be awarded for the lost years.

[36.77]   **Cassel v Riverside Health Authority**

[1992] PIQR Q168, CA

The claimant was born on 3 September 1982. Shortly before his birth he was severely asphyxiated. As a result he suffered cerebral palsy causing grave and irreparable brain damage. He needed care and would never work. The claimant was aged 8 at the date of trial and had a life expectancy to 65.

In assessing the appropriate multiplicand the trial judge stated: 'I start from what I hope is an uncontroversial proposition, mainly that heredity and environment each play a part in a person's make up and development' (per Rose J).

The judge was referring to the professional history of the family. Both the claimant's family were very high-level professional achievers. On this basis the judge estimated a multiplicand of £35,000 with a multiplier of 10. The multiplicand and multiplier were upheld on appeal.

[36.78]   **Phipps v Brooks Dry Cleaning Services Ltd**

[1996] PIQR Q100, CA

The claimant was exposed to asbestos dust during his employment with the defendant company. The claimant developed mesothelioma which was diagnosed in October 1994. The claimant's life expectancy was drastically reduced.

The claimant claimed damages for loss of earnings he would have received during the remainder of his expected working life less a reduction for his living expenses. The claimant claimed the living expenses should be assessed at no more than a third on the basis that this would be consistent with such a claim had it been brought under the Fatal Accidents Act 1976.

Secondly, the claimant claimed for the value of his DIY services for the lost years on the basis of a multiplier and multiplicand assessment.

HELD: (1) The Court of Appeal decision in *Harris v Empress Motors Ltd* (at para [37.28]) could not be distinguished. It was held in this case that common expenses should be divided equally between those involved. Therefore if the primary victim lived with his wife or partner alone the expenses should be divided in half.

(2)   The value of the DIY services was a loss of amenity to be taken into account in general damages to a modest extent and not on a multiplier/multiplicand basis.

The defendant's appeal to the Court of Appeal failed on these two points.

8.   CARE AND NURSING

(A)   GRATUITOUS CARE

[36.79]   **Cunningham v Harrison**

[1973] QB 942, [1973] 3 All ER 463, [1973] 3 WLR 97, 117 Sol Jo 547, CA

The claimant's neck was broken in a motor accident, paralysing him for life in all four limbs and his body. He was entirely dependent on others for dressing, bath, evacuation of bowels and feeding. His wife did everything for him for two years, then committed suicide. Trial of his action for damages came three days afterwards. Because of a difficult personality the claimant was considered unsuitable to enter a home and would have to live and be looked after in his own home.

HELD, ON APPEAL: Had the claimant's wife continued to look after him the value of her nursing services could have been claimed by the claimant without his having to make an agreement with her to pay her for them. On recovering such damages he would hold them on trust for her and pay them over to her; the judge's award for the cost of future nursing was too high. There should be moderation in all things, even in a claim for personal injuries. It was not right that the defendant should have to pay extra because of the claimant's difficult personality. Moreover it would be difficult to find people to look after him at home all the time and he would sometimes have to use other and state-provided facilities, eg under the Chronically Sick and Disabled Persons Act 1970.

[36.80]   Donnelly v Joyce

[1974] QB 454, [1973] 3 All ER 475, [1973] 3 WLR 514, 117 Sol Jo 488, CA

The claimant, aged six, received injury to his leg in a road accident. After his discharge from hospital his mother gave up her work for six months to look after him. The judge awarded the claimant £147 in respect of her loss of earnings. On appeal the defendant argued that the time was not claimable by the claimant but that his mother might have recovered it had she been a party to the action.

HELD, ON APPEAL: The loss of the mother's wages was rightly claimed by and awarded to the claimant. It was his own loss – the existence of the need for nursing services of his mother, valued for the purposes of damages as the proper and reasonable cost of supplying those needs. It would not have been possible to recover loss of income as well as the value of the care provided. It does not matter, so far as concerns the defendant, how or by whom the services have been provided nor whether the claimant has a legal liability to repay the provider. Nor is the existence of a moral obligation a material factor, nor an agreement between the injured person and the provider of the services to pay for them. *Roach v Yates* [1938] 1 KB 256 was authority for holding that the claimant was entitled to recover damages referable to the past and future financial value of voluntary services rendered to a claimant by others. *Liffen v Watson* (at para [36.97]) embodied the same principle. Contrary to the defendant's 'concession' the claimant's mother would not have been entitled to recover the loss herself had she been a party.

Note—See *Housecroft v Burnett* [1986] 1 All ER 332, CA where this reasoning was reiterated. The test has been established as 'what is it reasonable for this claimant to pay those who have cared for him as a reward for what they have done?'. The conventional way that this is assessed is to calculate the number of hours spent by the voluntary carer, multiply this by the commercial rate for care and then deduct a percentage to reflect the fact that tax and NI is not payable on those damages (25–33%). However the court can also make a lump sum award to reflect the additional need for care and to allow the claimant to provide some monetary acknowledgement to show appreciation for what the carer has done.

[36.81]   Mills v British Rail Engineering Ltd

[1992] PIQR Q130, CA

Compensation for gratuitous care was limited to voluntary help which was 'well beyond the ordinary call of duty' or beyond what a wife would ordinarily have done for her husband'.

Note—See *Giambrone v Sunworld Holidays Ltd* (at para [36.84]).

[36.82]   Hunt v Severs

[1994] 2 AC 350, [1994] 2 All ER 385, [1994] 2 WLR 602, 138 Sol Jo LB 104, HL

The claimant was a pillion passenger on a motorcycle driven by the defendant. An accident occurred as a result of which the claimant suffered serious injury. The defendant admitted liability. The defendant regularly visited the claimant during her stay in hospital and provided care for her thereafter when she returned home. The claimant and defendant later got married. The claimant was awarded £77,000 for the cost of past and future care provided by the defendant. The defendant appealed this part of the award on the basis that he was rendering these services voluntarily and was not obliged to compensate the claimant by paying damages as well. On appeal, it was held that there was no double recovery for it was accepted that the claimant's need for services represented a loss for which she was entitled to be compensated for by the tortfeasor. The defendant appealed to the House of Lords.

HELD, ON APPEAL to the House of Lords: The defendant's appeal was upheld. The purpose of an award in respect of voluntary care was compensation for the voluntary carer. In this case, the defendant had gratuitously rendered these services to the claimant. There was no ground in public policy, or otherwise, for requiring the tortfeasor to pay to the claimant a sum of money in respect of the services which the claimant then had to repay to him. Therefore, the award of damages was reduced by the amount awarded for services rendered.

Note—If the commercial cost of care exceeds the loss of earnings figure significantly the court may make an additional award to reflect this: *Bell v Gateshead Area Health Authority* (22 October 1996, unreported), per Alliott J.

[36.83]   **Havenhand v Jeffrey**

(24 February 1997, unreported), CA

The claimant, aged 84, was injured in a road traffic accident. Her claim for care included time spent by her family attending her in hospital. The court distinguished between time spent socialising and time spent assisting the claimant with nursing care and other services which the hospital did not provide. Only the latter was recoverable.

[36.84]   **Giambrone v Sunworld Holidays Ltd**

[2004] 2 All ER 891, CA

This group action concerned gastro-enteritis and other similar illnesses suffered by several hundred holidaymakers who had stayed at one resort in Majorca. The appeal related to a finding by the trial judge, in the claimants favour, in six of the lead cases, that an award could be made for the value of care which they received after they returned home. Five of these cases involved parental care of children and in the remaining one the adult claimant sought the worth of extra care provided by his wife. All the sums involved were relatively modest. The defendant argued that this was not a very serious case and the care did not go distinctly beyond that which was part of the ordinary regime of family life.

HELD: The mothers had provided additional care. An award of £50.00 per day was made to indicate that the value of such care was very modest. The test for recoverability is whether a claimant's illness or injury is sufficiently serious to give rise to a need for care and attendance significantly over and above that which would be given anyway in the ordinary course of family life. The right to claim is not confined to very serious cases. In the child cases parental input was described as nursing, attendance and child minding. There was a combination of love, support and care which the trial judge could not separate out. The court drew no distinction between these categories. They were 'part and parcel of the same need – to look after the child during his/her illness'. In future cases, Brooke LJ considered that any award for gratuitous care in excess of £50 à week for a similar complaint should be reserved for more serious cases.

(B)   DISCOUNT FOR NON-COMMERCIAL CARE

[36.85]   *Note*—In *Evans v Pontypridd Roofing* [2002] PIQR 5 the Court of Appeal suggested that 'the court should avoid putting first instance judges into too restrictive a straight jacket ... the circumstances of each claim vary enormously and what is appropriate and just in one case is not so in another'. The court will not be pressed into making a conventional percentage discount for gratuitous care. A 25% discount to the commercial rate was applied in *Evans* and the case of *Fairhurst v St Helens Health Authority* [1995] PIQR Q1. In *Nash v Southmead Health Authority* [1993] PIQR Q156, the court applied a discount of 33%. However, each case turns on its own particular facts. The case of *Hogg v Doyle* (6 March 1991, unreported) concerned care claimed by the claimant's wife, who was a qualified nurse. The court awarded 50% more than the normal commercial rate on the basis that the quality of care provided was equivalent to two full-time nurses. *Newman v Folkes* [2002] PIQR Q2 featured a claimant who was 'obsessive, violent and needed round the clock care'. The court allowed the full commercial rate because only the wife was able to provide adequate care for the claimant.

(C)   PROFESSIONAL/PAID CARE

[36.86]   *Note*—In serious injury cases some element of care will normally be provided either by the NHS, the local authority or a combination of both. This care may be topped up with additional private care if the claimant has sufficient private means. The burden of proof is on the defendant to prove that any existing or alternative arrangement is better for the claimant. If this evidence is not obtained the claimant will succeed in a claim for a full private regime: *Eagle v Chambers* (at para [36.210]).

[36.87]   **Rialas v Mitchell**

(1984) 128 Sol Jo 704, (1984) Times, 17 July, CA

The claimant aged six suffered severe brain damage in a road accident resulting in spastic quadriplegia. He could not speak or feed himself and had to be looked after day and night. Figures for heads of damage if the claimant was to be cared for at home were agreed – the cost of a suitable house, future nursing care etc. Evidence was adduced by the defendant that private institutions had homes where the claimant could be cared for at substantially less, and that it was unreasonable to compensate him at more than the lower cost.

HELD: Before the accident the claimant had been a healthy uninjured child of six living with his parents. He was then in hospital for a year and returned home where he had been looked after for four years. The court was being asked to say that the claimant should live in an institution because it would cost less. That was not the true alternative. Once it had been decided by the judge that it was reasonable for the claimant to remain at home there was no acceptable reason for saying the defendant should not pay the reasonable cost of caring for him there.

(D)   OFFSET OF STATUTORY FUNDING

(I)   NHS CARE

[36.88]   The Secretary of State is responsible for arranging and funding a range of services to meet the needs of people who require continuing physical or mental health care. The obligation to provide these services is contained in ss 1 and 2 of the National Health Service Act 1977. Under s 23 the Secretary of State may arrange for such services to be provided by third parties, e g private nursing homes. Provision of services under the NHS is mainly free. Medical prescriptions, dental treatment and spectacles are examples of services for which charges may be made.

Section 2(4) of the Law Reform (Personal Injuries) Act 1948 established that it is not open to a defendant to object to the reasonableness of a claim for private care on the basis that the care is available on the NHS. A claimant is entitled to make a claim for the cost of private nursing care. But the defendant can still object to that claim if, on the balance of probabilities, it is proved that the claimant will in fact use NHS care services and not private facilities (*Woodrup v Nicol* [1993] PIQR Q104) or that the resources needed are not in fact available outside the NHS (*Lim Poh Choo v Camden and Islington Area Health Authority* (at para [36.5]). These situations are only likely to be established in the more serious claims for personal injuries.

Section 150 of the Health and Social Care (Community Health and Standards) Act 2003 provides for direct recoupment of payment for NHS services against tortfeasors but this provision is not yet in force save as regards the power to make regulations under this section.

(II) LOCAL AUTHORITY

[36.89] There is an obligation upon a local authority to provide residential accommodation under s 21 of the National Assistance Act 1948 to a claimant aged 18 or over who by reason of illness or disability is in need of care and attention which is not otherwise available to him. The authority must first assess the needs and then assess whether it can recoup or charge for the services. The obligation to assess arises irrespective of the individual's resources – see *R v Berkshire CC ex parte P* (1998) I CCL Rep 141 and *R v Bristol CC ex parte Penfold* (1997–98) 1 CCL Rep 315 – (unlawful for an authority to take resources into account when deciding whether or not to carry out a community care assessment).

The cost of any care provided by the local authority may be capable of being offset against the cost of a private regime. Local authorities have the right of recovery under s 17 of the Health and Social Services and Social Security Adjudications Act 1983 subject to the person's means. Section 53 of the Health and Social Care Act 2001 provides that in determining whether or not care and attention are otherwise available to a person (the test in s 21(1)(a) of the National Assistance Act 1948), a local authority shall disregard so much of the person's resources as may be specified in regulations. The regulations provide that capital shall be calculated as set out in the National Assistance (Assessment of Resources) Regulations 1992, SI 1992/2977 and that capital under the capital limit of £20,500 (see reg 20 of the 1992 Assessment Regulations) shall be disregarded.

In most circumstances where a personal injury payment is paid into a personal injury trust or the payment is administered by the court, the payment will be disregarded. Stanley Burnton J in *Bell v Todd* [2002] Lloyds' Rep Med 12 at 18 held that *R v Sefton MBC ex parte Help the Aged* [1997] 4 All ER 532 remained good law and that income which would fall to be disregarded under the recoupment regime should also be ignored in taking into account an individual's need for care and attention under s 21(1)(a) of the National Assistance Act 1948.

(III) RECOUPMENT

Section 21 of the National Assistance Act 1948: Accommodation

[36.90] Personal injury payments cannot be taken into account as income for the purpose of calculating recoupment: Schedule 3 of the National Assistance (Assessment of Resources) Regulations 1992, SI 1992/2977 provides that a relevant payment should be disregarded in the calculation of income other than earnings. 'Relevant payment' is defined to include a payment from a trust whose funds are derived from a payment made in consequence of any personal injury to the resident; or a payment under an annuity purchased pursuant to any agreement or court order to make payments to the resident or in consequence of any personal injury to the resident; or a payment received by virtue of any agreement or court order to make payments to the resident in consequence of any personal injury to the resident.

Periodic payments are to be treated as income and not capital (and are thus to be disregarded in calculating recoupment) for these purposes (reg 16(5)).

Payments from a personal injury trust are to be disregarded in calculating capital for the purpose of recoupment – para 10 of Sch 4 to the 1992 Regulations and para 12 of Sch 10 to the Income Support (General) Regulations 1987, SI 1987/1967. The income derived from these are categorised as income, but should then probably be disregarded as income received by virtue of an agreement or court order to make payments in consequence of any personal injury (this appears to overcome the difficulty identified in both *Bell v Todd* (29 June 2001, unreported) and *Ryan v Liverpool HA* [2002] Lloyd's Rep Med 23 whereby the income derived from a fund administered by the Court of Protection was to be disregarded in assessing income for the purposes of recoupment but the income derived from a personal injury trust was not to be so disregarded).

Compensation for personal injuries which is administered by the court is to be disregarded in calculating capital for the purpose of recoupment – parag 19 of Sch 4 to the 1992 Regulations and para 44(a) of Sch 10 to the Income Support (General) Regulations 1987.

The capital value of an annuity falls to be disregarded under para 9 of Sch 4 to the 1992 Assessment Regulations referencing para 11 of Sch 10 to the Income Support (General) Regulations 1987. Payments under an annuity are income – see reg 16(2) of the 1992 Assessment Regulations. Stanley Burnton J in *Bell v Todd* held that they were not income derived from capital (within the meaning of reg 22(4) of the 1992 Assessment Regulations) and that they were to be treated as income and not capital. However, as income, they fall to be disregarded as being a relevant payment in Sch 3 to the 1992 Assessment Regulations.

Regulation 25 of the 1992 Assessment Regulations makes it clear that an individual is entitled to place moneys derived from a personal injury claim into a trust and that it thereby falls to be disregarded under the recoupment provisions (ie it is not treated as notional capital under the recoupment provisions).

The policy of the restricted provisions as to disregarding capital derived from personal injury claims was explained by Stanley Burnton J in *Bell v Todd* as being to encourage seriously injured personal injury claimants to place the settlement proceeds in trust.

The only circumstances where a personal injury payment falls to be taken into account for the purpose of recoupment and/or the assessment of need for section 21 accommodation or services is where the claimant chooses not to place the sum in a personal injury trust and it is therefore taken into account as capital for the purposes of assessing the right to charge for the services provided.

Section 29 of the National Assistance Act 1948: Services

[36.91]   Section 17 of the Health and Social Services and Social Security Adjudications Act 1983 provides that local authorities have the power to charge such sum as it considers reasonable for the services provided under s 29 of the National Assistance Act 1948, save that a person may satisfy the local authority that his means are insufficient to pay for the service in which case the authority shall not require him to pay more than is reasonably practicable in the circumstances.

(IV) TOP-UP PAYMENTS

[36.92]   Section 54 of the Health and Social Care Act 2001 provides that individuals can in certain circumstances make additional payments to secure more expensive accommodation by the authority. The relevant regulation is the National Assistance (Residential Accommodation) (Additional Payments and Assessment of Resources) (Amendment) (England) Regulations 2001, SI 2001/3441. This provides that in certain defined circumstances additional top-up payments can be made either by the resident (out of capital or income disregarded for the purpose of recoupment provisions) or by third parties.

The National Assistance Act 1948 (Choice of Accommodation) Directions 1992 as amended by the National Assistance Act 1948 (Choice of Accommodation) (Amendment) Directions 2001 provides that where an authority has decided that section 21 accommodation should be provided it shall be provided at the place of the individuals choice provided that:

(1)   the preferred accommodation appears to the authority to be suitable; and

(2)   the cost of making arrangements for him at his preferred accommodation is not more than they would usually expect to pay having regard to his assessed needs; and

(3)   the preferred accommodation is available and can be provided subject to the authority's usual terms and conditions.

The guidance in the Directions also provide that if a resident requests more expensive accommodation then, provided that there is a third party willing and able to pay the difference between the cost the authority would usually expect to pay and the actual cost of the accommodation, then the authority must arrange for care in that accommodation.

The Court of Appeal in *Sowden v Lodge* (at para [36.93]) held that the issue of top-up payments required very careful consideration by a judge and must be raised and fully investigated in written schedules and counter-schedules prior to the hearing of the claim. It is for the defendant to assert that local authority care will meet the reasonable needs of the claimant, either without or with top-up, and then for the claimant to meet that case if she so chooses. Moreover, the interrelationship between top up payments/care regimes and the care regime being provided by the local authority may well be such that the whole scheme is deemed not to be workable.

[36.93]   Sowden v Lodge

[2004] EWCA Civ 1370

[2005] 1 All ER 581, CA

Louise Sowden suffered a catastrophic head injury when she was 13 years old. Settlement was reached on the basis of 50% contributory negligence. She required assistance or supervision with all aspects of personal care. She was capable of only very limited understanding or communication. Since 1998 she had been a resident at a residential home in Mirfield known as Rooftops. She would have to move from there when aged 25, but the Holly Bank Trust had expressed a willingness to house her in a bungalow it was proposing to buy on the condition that Doncaster MCBN fund the placement.

The issue was whether damages should be assessed on the basis of the cost of a private arrangement for care and accommodation or on the cost of a residential arrangement. The defendant accepted that if the finding was for a residential arrangement then the appropriate sum would need to be topped up by further provision for care and attendance.

The legal question identified by the Court of Appeal was 'the effect upon the liability of tortfeasors in personal injury cases of the duty upon local authorities under s 21 of the National Assistance Act 1948'.

It was agreed before the Court of Appeal that:

(1)   A judge is entitled to hold on appropriate evidence that the statutory provision for care and accommodation meet the claimant's reasonable requirements. In such circumstances the tortfeasor may not be required to pay for care and accommodation.

(2)   Statutory provision for care and accommodation augmented by payments on behalf of the tortfeasor for further care may, on appropriate evidence, meet the reasonable requirements of a claimant.

(3)   If the local authority provides care and accommodation under s 21 of the National Assistance Act 1948 it cannot recover its costs from the claimants' damages. This is because the income would be from capital administered by the court and would be treated as capital and disregarded under the National Assistance (Assessment of Resources) Regulations 1992, SI 1992/2977.

(4)   The effect of the regulatory scheme was that personal injury trusts and compensation for personal injuries which is administered by the court, are to be disregarded for the purposes of recoupment, and for the purposes of determining whether or not there is an obligation to provide section 21 accommodation and services. Thus, the cost of providing local authority accommodation or care under s 21 could not be recovered out of the damages awarded.

HELD: Per Pill LJ:

(1)   That the test to be applied is not whether treatment is reasonable but whether the treatment (or care) chosen and claim for is reasonable (taken from *Rialas v Mitchell* (at para [36.87]). Pill LJ rejected the test of

best interests applied by the judge on the basis that 'In this context, paternalism does not replace the right of a claimant, or those with responsibility for a claimant, making a reasonable choice'.

(2) The situation is different where there are serious doubts about the evidence as to the claimant's wishes.

(3) Where there is doubt as to the claimant's wishes, it is necessary for the judge to assess the nature and extent of the claimant's needs. The difference between best interests and reasonableness is considerably reduced. Here, the judge was entitled to treat what he assessed to be in the claimant's best interests with what was a reasonable requirement in all the circumstances. The judge's criticism that Louise Sowden reasonably required residential accommodation was not perverse.

(4) The approach then is to compare what a claimant reasonably requires with what a local authority are likely to provide in the discharge of their duty under s 21 of the National Assistance Act 1948.

(5) If the local authority provision falls significantly short of the reasonable requirements then the tortfeasor must pay, subject to the argument that the local authority provision can meet the claimant's reasonable requirements if topped up.

(6) If the statutory provision meets the claimant's reasonable requirements then the tortfeasor does not have to pay for a different regime.

(7) In making the comparison the court may have regard to the power to compel the local authority to perform its duties.

(8) The Court of Appeal sent the case back for consideration as to the augmentation of the statutory scheme, and to give the claimant the opportunity to argue that that was not a practicable solution in the circumstances, and whether it is likely to be implemented. Pill LJ emphasised that: 'Having decided what is and what is not practicable, the judge should re-visit his conclusion as to whether, in the circumstances as found, a local authority based residential arrangement still meets the common law test'.

(9) Pill LJ found that the damages should be assessed without regard for the fact of the agreed reduction for contributory negligence, which should then be taken into account at the end of the assessment exercise. The reduction for contributory negligence could not be relied upon as an argument in support of the contention that the claimant would not in any event be able to afford private care for the rest of her life and would not in fact avail herself to this.

Note—The Court of Appeal heard the appeals of *Sowden v Lodge* and *Crookdake v Drury* (at para [36.94]) together.

[36.94] Crookdake v Drury

[2004] EWCA Civ 1370

[2005] 1 All ER 581, CA

Philip Crookdake was a 36-year-old husband and father who sustained an extremely serious head injury and had profound cognitive and intellectual deficits. He had a problem with verbal and physical aggression. The judge agreed with the local authority's assessment that he required 24-hour care in his own home. The evidence was that Mrs Crookdake could not live with her husband but that she intended to continue to visit him. There was no evidence as to what the local authority would in fact provide under s 21 of the National Assistance Act 1948 and there was no expert assessment of how proposed additional provision would be applied.

When considering the differences between the local authority accommodation and the privately funded care regime, it was noted that only in a private regime would suitable accommodation be available for Mrs Crookdake during her visits and that the location would be convenient. The judge found 'it cannot in my judgment be said that there is no material difference between the provision that the local authority is obliged to make and the assessment of his requirements for the purpose of quantification of his claim for damages'.

The defendant's case was that if the local authority provision did not meet the reasonable requirements of the claimant the defendant could be required to pay an additional sum to augment the care provided by the local authority.

HELD: 'If top up care was privately provided, it would not be open to a local authority to argue that in some way diminished their obligations under section 21 of the National Assistance Act 1948. This was because the care was by definition additional to the section 21 provision and was funded by damages which were to be disregarded for the purposes of sections 21 and 22 of the National Assistance Act 1948' (per Pill LJ).

The judge had been entitled to find that the local authority provision would not meet the reasonable requirements of the claimant. He emphasised the lack of any evidential basis for the top-up offer made by the defendant, and the lack of any evidence from the defendant as to the nature or extent of local authority provision which would be available. Whatever is proposed should be particularised and costed in the schedule (or counter schedule) of damages. Pill LJ expressly found that 'while claimants, and those advising them, must be expected to co-operate with local authorities discharging their statutory duties, they claim in the action that to which they believe the claimant is entitled and there is no legal burden on them to disprove that statutory provision will be adequate. It may of course be prudent to call evidence, as in any situation where a judgment upon the facts is to be made, as to why statutory funding is inadequate'.

Note—The approach in *Sowden* (at para [36.93]) and *Crookdale* was rejected at first instance in *Tinsley v Sarkar* [2005] EWHC 192, [2006] PIQR Q1, QBD in relation to aftercare services under s 117 of the Mental Health Act 1983. That decision is subject to appeal.

[36.95] Islington London Borough Council v University College London Hospital NHS Trust

[2005] EWCA Civ 596, CA

The claimant local authority sought to recover the cost of it providing residential accommodation to a third party who was injured by the defendant's clinical negligence. The case was based on the fact that the defendant had escaped liability to compensate for the care costs because they were provided by the local authority under s 21 of the National Assistance Act 1948 and that the injured patient could not recover such costs because she could not make payment for them to the local authority. The claim was one of pure economic loss. The trial judge held that the care costs incurred by the local authority were a matter of speculation and not foreseeable. As such, the prerequisite for a duty of care was not satisfied. There was no relationship of proximity between the parties. The fact that local authorities must bear the care costs even where there was a negligent tortfeasor who caused the need for care was the result of a deliberate stance taken by Parliament and there was thus no lacuna in the law. It was 'an abuse of language' to call this a gross injustice calling for a remedy. The local authority appealed.

HELD: Appeal dismissed. It was reasonably foreseeable that that the third party would suffer injury as a result of the defendant's negligence requiring care at the public's expense. The judge had set too high a standard in determining foreseeability. The issue of proximity was closely related to whether it was just, fair and reasonable to impose a duty of care on the defendant. Both parties were public authorities. Parliament should resolve funding issues as they are a matter of policy. It would not be fair, just and reasonable to impose a duty of care on the defendant trust.

[36.96]   Freeman v Lockett
[2006] EWHC 102 (QB), QB

The court was asked to consider whether the local authority or insurance company should fund care and accommodation for the injured claimant. Tomlinson J declined to make any deduction from an award of damages to reflect the possible continued availability to the claimant of local authority funding in the form of direct payments. He held that the defendant's insurers had failed to offer an indemnity in case the claimant's local authority funding failed or was withdrawn.

Note—See also *Crofton v NHSLA* [2006] Lloyds Rep Med 168 where HHJ Reid took a contrary view to that of Tomlinson J In *Freeman*.

   In *Walton v Calderdale Healthcare NHS Trust* (at para [36.242]), the claimant proved his reasonable care needs by means of agreed expert reports. Silber J held that the defendant had failed to establish that a local authority could wholly or partially satisfy those reasonable needs.

9.   OTHER FUTURE LOSSES

(A)   BOARD AND LODGING

[36.97]   Liffen v Watson
[1940] 1 KB 556, [1940] 2 All ER 213, 109 LJKB 367, 162 LT 398, 56 TLR 442, 84 Sol Jo 368, CA

The claimant before an accident, was a domestic servant receiving a weekly wage of £1 plus board and lodging, which was claimed at 25s. It was for the court to assess the value of the board and lodging, but the loss of the board and lodgings was damage along with the loss of earnings. The fact that her father provided board and lodgings without receiving payment did not alter the fact that she sustained this loss in kind.

   Per Goddard LJ: The right to recover does not depend upon whether or not she made a contract with somebody else to give her board and lodging. She has lost it with the cash wages because she lost her work. It does not matter in the least whether she is taken in by her father or whether she is taken in by a friend. She might say to a friend, "I cannot make a contract to pay you, but if I get damages I shall pay you something for board and lodging". These considerations are immaterial. The only consideration is what has she lost. She has lost the value of the board and lodging, just the same as she has lost her wages.

Note—See also *Shearman v Folland* (at para [36.153]) and *Lim Poh Choo v Camden and Islington AHA* (at para [36.5]).

(B)   ACCOMMODATION COSTS

[36.98]   **Roberts v Johnstone**
[1989] QB 878, [1988] 3 WLR 1247, CA

Before the claimant's birth her mother had been given a transfusion of an incorrect blood type. This led to the claimant contracting haemolytic disease and as a result suffering permanent and serious brain damage. A total award of £334,769.88 was made, including an award for the cost of a suitable bungalow (less the value of property sold) and the cost of conversion of that accommodation (less the value of some improvements) at a total of £28,800. The claimant appealed to the Court of Appeal seeking, *inter alia*, an increase in those damages.

HELD: The claimant was not entitled to the capital cost of the new home (approving *George v Pinnock* (at para [36.2])) but was entitled to the additional annual cost of purchasing the new property taken at 2% of the difference between the sale price of the old property and the purchase price of the new, after any appropriate deductions, plus the net conversion costs after deduction of that part of the conversion costs which added to the recoverable capital value of the house on resale. The additional annual cost was to be multiplied – here a multiplier of 16 was adopted. The sum of £50,204 was substituted for the award of £28,800.

Note—The actual interest rate to be applied is the discount rate, set by Lord Chancellor, which is currently 2.5%.

(C)   DIY AND HOUSEKEEPING

[36.99]   **Daly v General Steam Navigation Co Ltd, The Dragon**
[1980] 3 All ER 696, [1981] 1 WLR 120, 125 Sol Jo 100, [1980] 2 Lloyd's Rep 415, CA

The claimant, seriously injured by the defendant's negligence, claimed damages for, *inter alia*, her inability to do the heavier kind of housework in her home. She was 34 years of age at the time of the injuries, married and lived with her husband and two children. She was not gainfully occupied before the accident nor did she employ any domestic help. Her incapacity would last for the rest of her life. Trial was reached seven years after the accident. The judge held that:
  (1)   the partial loss of housekeeping capacity should be treated as a separate head of damage and not merely an element in the general damages for loss of amenities;
  (2)   such damages should be assessed by reference to the cost of employing someone else to do the work, even for the period before trial when no one was employed and the claimant's husband acted in part as a substitute housekeeper himself;
  (3)   they should be calculated on a basis of ten hours per week at an average of 90p per hour before date of trial and eight hours per week at £1.40 per hour for the future at a multiplier of 15 years: total £11,427.

HELD: The award was varied. In respect of the award for future partial loss of housekeeping capacity in the figure of £8,736, the judge was right in assessing it at the estimated cost of employing some third person to come in and do that which the claimant was unable to do. It was not requisite that the claimant should satisfy the court that she had a firm intention in any event that such a person should be employed. It was immaterial whether the claimant, having received those damages, should choose to alleviate her housekeeping burden by employing someone to do it, or to spend the damages on luxuries she would otherwise be unable to afford. In respect of the award of £2,691 for loss of housekeeping capacity up to the date of trial, however, it was wrong to assess it by reference to the cost of employing domestic help which she had not in fact employed but which had been furnished by her husband and daughter. The judge ought instead to have asked himself to what extent the difficulties which the claimant had had to contend with in performing her household duties ought to have increased the award for pain and suffering. The judge's award of £8,000 for pain and suffering should be increased to £9,761. The award for special damages should be increased by £930, the amount of the husband's loss of earnings.

Note—See also *Phipps v Brooks Dry Cleaning Services* (at para [36.78]).

(D)   COST OF INVESTMENT AND MANAGEMENT ADVICE

[36.100]   **Page v Plymouth Hospitals NHS Trust**

[2004] EWHC 1154 (QB)

[2004] 3 All ER 367, [2004] PIQR Q6, QB

The High Court decided that a claimant was not entitled to claim for the cost of investment and management advice as a separate head of loss. Davies J giving judgment in this case expressed concern that the claim for the cost of this advice was an indirect attack on the Lord Chancellor's prescribed discount rate. Specifically Davies J dealt with the claimant's arguments as follows:

(1)   As the Lord Chancellor had set the 2.5% discount rate slightly above the actual rate of return for ILGS at the time there was an acceptance that some of the award would have to be invested elsewhere to achieve that 2.5% return. Therefore investment advice was required in order to achieve that additional return. This argument was rejected. There was nothing to indicate that the Lord Chancellor intended claimants to invest in a mixed portfolio to achieve a rate of return equivalent to the discount rate.

(2)   The claimants argued that the down turn in the market meant that achieving 2.5% would not be possible without investment advice. This argument was rejected on the basis that the whole point of the Lord Chancellor prescribing the discount rate was to achieve certainty. A discount rate could not be altered to reflect ever-changing market conditions.

(3)   The claimants argued that the Lord Chancellor had not taken into account investment charges when setting the discount rate. The court rejected this argument referring to the wide-ranging discussions conducted by the Lord Chancellor's department recorded in the various consultation papers.

(4)   The claimants argued that there was nothing to indicate that courts would find it difficult to deal with the issue of investment advice on a case-by-case basis. The court rejected this argument. Davies J added that if investment charges were incurred then they were within the 'territory' of the discount rate.

Note—The Court of Appeal approved this reasoning in *Eagle v Chambers* (at para [36.210]) where the claimant was subject to the Court of Protection.

10.   BETTERMENT

[36.101]   Moss v Christchurch RDC
[1925] 2 KB 750, 95 LJKB 81

A cottage was set on fire as the result of the negligence of the defendant. The fabric was seriously damaged and a quantity of the household effects destroyed. The Official Referee assessed the damage sustained by the owner and tenant as the cost of replacement in each case. The defendant appealed contending the damages were limited to the value of the property at the time it was destroyed.

HELD: The measure of damages is not the cost of replacement but is the value to the owner of the property at the time it was destroyed. The true measure of damage is the difference between the money value of the interest before the damage and the money value of the interest after the damage.

[36.102]   Uctkos v Mazzetta
[1956] 1 Lloyd's Rep 209   Ormerod J

An Admiral's barge constructed in America was sold after the war in 1947 by the Admiralty for £600. The owner did work on it and it was moored in the Thames at Isleworth and used for visits at weekends. A painter and decorator known to the owner visited it as a purely social arrangement, and helped to recondition the ship presumably in the hope that he would be allowed some use of it. By his negligence on 2 May 1952 the ship was destroyed. The owner claimed £5,000 as the cost of purchasing another ship or replacing it. The ship was quite an unusual type and was irreplaceable. Evidence was given by an agent for the disposal of craft by the Admiralty after the war of the sale of four other ships of a comparatively similar design and construction and performance, that the value of the ship was about £750.

HELD: The owner was not entitled to damages on the basis of the replacement of his ship, but to the reasonable cost of another craft that reasonably met his needs and in reasonably the same condition. Judgment for £800 plus £108 for fittings.

Note—See also *O'Grady v Westminster Scaffolding Ltd* (at para [35.71]).

[36.103]   Hollebone v Midhurst and Fernhurst Builders Ltd
[1968] 1 Lloyd's Rep 38   Norman Richards Esq QC, Official Referee

The claimant's house was damaged by fire caused by the negligence of the second defendant. The cost of making good the damage was £18,991. The difference in value between the pre-fire value and the value after the fire was £14,850. It was urged on behalf of the defendants that the right measure of damage was the difference in value ie £14,850, not the cost of making good.

HELD: On the authorities there was no firm rule that the diminution in value is the correct measure of damage. In *The Susquehanna* [1926] AC 655 Lord Dunedin said no rigid rule or rules apply and one must consider all the relevant circumstances. These must depend on such matters as the interest which the injured party had in what is damaged, the purpose for which it is used and whether its life is likely to be short or long. In the present case where the property was of a nature that comparable properties were few and far between the cost of repair was the correct measure of damage as providing fair and proper restitution for the damage sustained. The question remained whether an allowance should be made for 'betterment' on the basis of substitution of new material for old. If an allowance of new for old must always be made this may well prevent a claimant from being fairly compensated. It was conceded that the old rafters and floors would have lasted out the life of the house so there could be no betterment for those. In the case of new electrical wiring it had deferred the need for this for 15 to 20 years and there was some benefit to the claimants in this. But it was not a case in which it would be fair to deduct it from the cost of repair.

Note—See also *Almond v Leeds Western HA* [1990] 1 Med LR 370 (QBD) in the context of a personal injury claim where the claimant converted a new property.

[36.104]   Hole & Son Ltd v Harrisons

[1973] 1 Lloyd's Rep 345, QBD

The defendant's lorry crashed into a row of three ancient cottages owned by the claimant company, causing damage. Two of the cottages were occupied as an office and store by the claimants; the third was occupied by a statutory tenant at a rent of 15s per week and was so badly damaged that she had to move elsewhere, losing her tenancy. The claimant claimed the estimated cost of reinstating all the damaged cottages at a cost of £4,079. At the trial it appeared that the claimant, even before the accident, had intended to demolish the cottages and build new premises in place of them; the departure of the tenant had now enabled it to do this, for which it had obtained planning permission.

HELD: A claim for damage to property was either for cost of reinstatement or diminution in value. The evidence showed that the claimant had no intention of reinstating; the departure of the statutory tenant had increased the value rather than diminished it. The only damages the claimant was entitled to was the cost of a temporary repair already done and an agreed sum for loss of rent.

[36.105]   CR Taylor (Wholesale) Ltd v Hepworths Ltd

[1977] 2 All ER 784, [1977] 1 WLR 659, 121 Sol Jo 15, 242 EG 631   May J

The claimants owned property consisting of a billiard hall and three shops. The billiard hall had been out of use as such for 30 years and two of the shops were unlet. The claimants had not tried for some time to let or sell; the site was regarded as ripe for redevelopment. By negligence of a servant of the defendant the property caught fire and was damaged. The claimant claimed damages assessed at the amount which it would cost to reinstate the premises, though they were never rebuilt.

HELD: The two basic principles were that:
   (1)   damages awarded against a tortfeasor shall be such as will, so far as money can, put the claimant in the same position as he would have been had the tort not occurred, but
   (2)   the damages to be awarded are to be reasonable as between the claimant on the one hand and the defendant on the other.
The claimants had been holding on to the property merely for its development value which lay in the site itself, not the buildings. It would be totally unrealistic as well as unreasonable as between the claimant and the defendant to award the

notional cost of reinstating the premises. The measure of damages was the diminution in the value of the property assessed at £2,500 but as it would have cost the claimant more than that to clear the site for redevelopment it was entitled to nothing in respect of that head of damage.

[36.106]   Bacon v Cooper (Metals) Ltd
[1982] 1 All ER 397   Cantley J

In the course of the claimant's business as a scrap metal dealer he used a large and expensive machine, called a fragmentiser, for the purpose of reducing scrap metal to fragments. He purchased a consignment of metal from the defendant which, in breach of the contract of sale, contained a large lump of steel. The rotor of the machine was broken by it and had to be replaced by a new one, costing £41,000. No secondhand rotors were available. A rotor lasted seven years; at the time of the damage the claimant's rotor had been in use three and a quarter years. The defendant contended that the claimant ought to give credit for three and a quarter years' use, reducing the claim to £22,232.

HELD: Not so. Each case should depend on its own facts. There was no certainty that the claimant would have needed to buy a new rotor at the end of another three and a quarter years if there had been no damage. After that time the fragmentiser may be out of date or the claimant may be using a different process or have died or retired from business. It would be wrong to charge the defendant for the whole cost if the damaged rotor had, say, only three months of the seven years to run, but that was not the case. The claimant was entitled to recover the whole cost of the replacement rotor.

Note—Applied in *Dominion Mosaics & Tile Co v Trafalgar Trucking Co* [1990] 2 All ER 246, CA. See however *The Baltic Surveyor* (at para [36.108]).

[36.107]   Farmer Giles Ltd v Wessex Water Authority
[1988] 42 EG 127, QBD

The claimant owned land and a dilapidated mill by a river. The defendant, the water authority and its contractors, negligently caused the collapse of part of the mill during river improvement work. The claimant claimed the cost of rebuilding the mill; the water authority accepted liability in contract and tort, and the contractors only in tort. They disputed quantum, arguing that the proper measure of damage should be the reduction in value of the mill. The court found that the mill would cost up to £155,000 to rebuild, but that the sale value of the rebuilt building would be then only about £63,000. The market value of the mill at the time it was damaged was £10,000. Refurbishment of the mill before damage would have cost £30,000 and made the building worth £40,000. The site value was £1,000.

HELD: The sum of £34,100 should be awarded. The measure of damages, whether in contract or in tort, should put the claimant in the same position as it would have been if it had not suffered the wrong in question. The court could either award damages for the cost of reinstatement, or in respect of the diminution in value but where, as in this case, the cost of rebuilding the structure was unreasonable in proportion to the value of the building, the appropriate measure of damage was the value of the original structure if it had been refurbished, less the estimated cost of such refurbishment and the site value.

[36.108]   **Voaden v Champion (The Baltic Surveyor and the Timbuktu)**

[2002] EWCA Civ 89

[2002] 1 Lloyd's Rep 623

CA

A pontoon with a useful life of eight years was sunk. The new replacement cost was £60,000 but it had a likely lifespan of 30 years. The judge awarded £16,000 which equated to 8/30 of £60,000. The Court of Appeal upheld the decision.

11.   LOSS OF USE

[36.109]   *Note*—See also the hire of a replacement vehicle at para [36.113].

[36.110]   **The Mediana**

[1900] AC 113, 69 LJP 35, 82 LT 95

The owner of a chattel who is wrongfully deprived of its use may recover substantial damages for the deprivation, though he may have incurred no out of pocket expenses consequent thereon.

'Nominal damages' is a technical phrase, which means that you have negatived anything like real damage, but that you are affirming by your nominal damages that there is an infraction of a legal right, which, though it gives you no right to any real damages at all, yet gives you a right to the verdict or judgment because your legal right has been infringed. But the term 'nominal damages' does not mean small damages: per Lord Halsbury LC.

Note—See also *The Hebridean Coast* [1961] AC 545, [1961] 1 All ER 82, 105 Sol Jo 37, [1960] 2 Lloyd's Rep 423, HL.

[36.111]   **Dixons (Scholar Green) Ltd v Cooper**

[1970] RTR 222, 114 Sol Jo 319, CA

The claimant claimed £589 for loss of use of its 9-ton lorry. This figure comprised £1,189 average deficiency in turnover for 11 weeks during which it was off the road for repair less sums for wear and tear, running costs and wages plus further sums for depreciation etc. The defendant though admitting liability contested the figures. The judge said it was for the claimant to establish its financial loss and it had failed to do so to his satisfaction: he accordingly awarded nominal damages of £2.

HELD, ON APPEAL: This could not be right. This was a valuable vehicle in constant demand and it had been off the road 11 weeks. There were difficulties in arriving at an exact figure but having heard the claimant's evidence (the defendant called none) it was the duty of the judge to make the best he could out of the evidence and choose a figure which was a reasonable estimate of the damage suffered by the claimant. The amount awarded, on examination of the figures, should be £450.

[36.112]   **McAll v Brooks**

[1984] RTR 99, CA

The claimant had a comprehensive insurance policy in respect of his car membership of a scheme whereby for a payment of £5 per annum he would be entitled to the use of a car if his own car was damaged and out of use. In an accident for which the defendant was wholly to blame the claimant's car was damaged and, as arranged, he was supplied by the brokers with a car for three weeks. A reasonable hire charge for such a car was £328. In proceedings against the defendant in which he claimed the amount of the excess and £328 as the measure of damages for loss of use, the county court judge awarded £50 for the excess but held that he was not entitled to the £328 because:

(1)   he had not lost it;

(2)   the £5 scheme was insurance business and therefore illegal under the Insurance Companies Act 1974 and there was no right of subrogation;

(3)   the claimant's contract under the scheme was tainted with illegality.

HELD, ON APPEAL: The claimant was entitled to recover the sum of £328. It had been accepted that the claimant had needed a car when his own was off the road and that £328 was a reasonable hire charge. Following *Donnelly v Joyce* (at para [36.80]) the claimant's need of a car had to be paid for by the wrongdoer and £328 was to cover that need. If the scheme was tainted with illegality and the claimant had been a knowing party to that illegality he could not recover, but this was not the case. If there was any taint of illegality on the part of the brokers it was not the concern of the claimant. The court was not concerned to consider what the claimant was going to do with his money or whether he owed any legal or moral obligation to the brokers or any other third party.

Note—Applied in *Ramskill v Pepper* (25 September 1998, unreported).

[36.113]   Birmingham Corpn v Sowsbery

[1970] RTR 84, (1969) 113 Sol Jo 877   Geoffrey Lane J

The claimant's omnibus was out of use for 69 days for repairs following a collision. It claimed as special damages the cost of maintaining a spare fleet omnibus for 69 days at £4 11s per day.

HELD: (1) If the claimant had hired a replacement vehicle it could have claimed the cost of hire as special damages but as a non-profit making body not needing to hire another vehicle different consideration applied and the claim was one for general not special damage. The maintenance of a stand-by fleet was reasonable and necessary and the whole fleet including the stand-bys must be taken as being in operation at any one time. The claimant had been deprived of the use of a valuable chattel during the relevant period and was entitled to substantial (ie not nominal) general damages for the loss of use.

(2)   There were two possible methods of arriving at a proper figure to compensate the claimants:

(a)   the cost of maintaining and operating the damaged vehicle (excluding running charges) on the assumption that this figure must represent approximately the value of the vehicle to the operators where the concern is non-profit making, or

(b)   interest on capital value of the vehicle and depreciation, as in *The Hebridean Coast* [1961] AC 545, [1961] 1 All ER 82, 105 Sol Jo 37, [1960] 2 Lloyd's Rep 423, HL.

If the latter method were used a proper rate of interest to take would be 7% on the value of the bus at the material time plus a sum for depreciation. But this method suffers from possible variations in capital value and interest rates. It is important that there should be as much consistency as possible between awards of general damages. In the present case where £4 11s per day was agreed as an accurate estimate of the standing charges of such a vehicle run by a reasonably efficient organisation the first method of assessment was a proper solution of the problem.

Judgment for £313 19s being 60 days at £4 11s per day.

Note—This approach was followed in *London General Transport Services Ltd v Sunlight Services* (30 November 2005, unreported), Romford County Court. The claimant, whose bus was damaged in a collision, claimed damages for loss of use whilst the bus was being repaired. The judge held that where an operator operates a fleet of buses, it is not the bus itself that generates the revenue but the operation of the fleet as a whole. The claimant recovered £100 a day for loss of use on this basis.

[36.114]   Alexander v Rolls Royce Ltd
[1996] RTR 95, CA

The claimant's unsatisfactory Rolls Royce was damaged and he was unable to drive it. No damages were awarded for loss of use because the claimant disliked driving the Rolls Royce and had two other cars.

Note—See case summary at para [36.48].

[36.115]   East London Bus & Coach Co Ltd v Nijjar
(22 November 2000, unreported)

The claimant claimed damages for loss of use of a public service vehicle for one day when his double decker bus was damaged following a road traffic accident. Adopting the approach taken in *Birmingham Corpn v Sowsbery* (at para [36.113]), the claimant sought both the direct and indirect costs of operating the vehicle. The defendant contended that indirect costs could only be claimed by non-profit making public transport corporations and that any damages should be calculated as loss of net profit.

HELD: The correct measure of damages for the loss of use in this case was loss of net profit. *Sowsbery* distinguished.

[36.116]   Quinn v O'Donavan
(30 June 2003, unreported)

The claimant sought damages for loss of use following a road traffic accident. Fifteen months after the accident, the defendant's insurers admitted liability and sent the claimant a cheque representing the write off value of the vehicle. During the 62-week period without her vehicle, the claimant advised the defendant that her claim for loss of use was continuing and that she was particularly inconvenienced because she had a disabled son and ill husband.

HELD: The claimant was awarded £500 for travelling expenses which took into account a deduction for the running costs of the motor vehicle which she would have used but for the accident. Loss of use awarded at £70 per week for the 62-week period plus an additional two week period during which she would have to deposit the cheque and find an alternative vehicle.

Note—See also *Mattocks v Mann* [1993] RTR 13, CA.

[36.117]   **Mullins v Phillips**

(18 April 2005, unreported)

The claimant's vehicle was damaged in a road traffic accident. The claimant was not provided with a hire care until three days after the accident. He claimed loss of use during that period.

HELD: The appropriate rate for loss of use of a motor vehicle was now £15 per day.

12.   MISCELLANEOUS SPECIAL DAMAGES

(A)   LOSS OF NO CLAIMS BONUS

[36.118]   **Ironfield v Eastern Gas Board**

[1964] 1 All ER 544n, [1964] 1 WLR 1125, 108 Sol Jo 691   Streatfield J

The claimant was driving his father-in-law's car when it collided with the defendant's lorry due to the defendant's negligence. He was injured and the car was damaged. In a claim for damages for his personal injuries he included a claim for £10 excess insurance and £15 for loss of no-claims bonus.

HELD: (1) The loss of the 'no-claims bonus' was a real loss sustained by the assured, the father-in-law, and formed part of the damage which resulted from the accident. He should be put in the same position as if he had not made a claim under the policy at all.
  (2)   Though they were items of loss suffered by the father-in-law and not the claimant, there was no reason why they should not be dealt with in this action and awarded to the claimant on his undertaking to pay them over to his father-in-law.

[36.119]   **Baker v Courage**

[1989] CLY 2057

The claimant and defendant were involved in a motor accident. The defendant was primarily liable but the claimant was found 15% contributory negligent. The claimant claimed damages for the loss of the no-claims bonus.

HELD: To retain her no-claims bonus the claimant had to show to her insurance company that the defendant was 100% to blame for the accident. The claimant was 15% to blame and therefore the no claims bonus was lost in any event and so the claimant's claim against the defendants for the recovery of this no claims bonus failed.

(B)   LOSS OF PREMIUM

[36.120]   **Patel v London Transport Executive**

[1981] RTR 29, CA

Only a week or so after the claimant had paid £222.75 for a year's full comprehensive insurance, his car was damaged beyond repair by negligence of the defendants. He claimed under his policy and his insurers paid him the total loss value of the car. It was a term of the policy that on settlement of a claim on a total loss basis all benefits of the insurance would terminate as from the date of the accident without return of premium. The claimant claimed from the defendant £218.47 being the balance of the year's premium from the date of the accident. It was acknowledged by the defendant that the term of the policy was a usual one.

HELD: The claimant was entitled to succeed. He had acted reasonably in claiming under his policy instead of incurring the greater delay and expense of claiming for his loss directly against the defendants. The claim on the policy was foreseeable by the defendants; therefore the loss following from that claim was foreseeable. The case was analogous with *Ironfield v Eastern Gas Board* (at para [36.118]) which was rightly decided.

(C)   LOSS OF ROAD FUND TAX

[36.121]   Sandhu v Roberts
[1989] CLY 1291

In addition to the recovery of the pre-accident value of her vehicle, storage and towing charges, the claimant was entitled to damages in respect of the unrecovered road fund tax. This was a foreseeable loss.

[36.122]   Ajibade v Leech
[1994] CLY 1505, Reading County Court   District Judge Keogh

The claimant claimed £55 for loss of car tax. The judge held that the car tax should have been reclaimed and the claimant should have mitigated her loss in this respect.

13.   DAMAGES FOR REDUCED MARRIAGE PROSPECTS

Note—For cases where an injured unmarried female claimant has sustained a diminution in marriage prospects see the following cases.

[36.123]   Moriarty v McCarthy
[1978] 2 All ER 213, [1978] 1 WLR 155, 121 Sol Jo 745   O'Connor J

In October 1973 the claimant sustained spinal injuries which resulted in complete loss of the power to move or feel from the waist down, with no control of bladder and bowel and no sexual sensation; she would be confined to a wheelchair for the rest of her life. She was then 20 years of age, 24 at the date of assessment for damages, living with her mother and sisters in the Republic of Ireland. Despite some training for sedentary work she had not shown herself capable of any gainful employment.

HELD: Her damages should be assessed under the following heads:
  (1)   Future loss of earnings at a net figure of £1,820 per annum, applying a multiplier of 11 years = £20,000. The multiplier of 11 was taken instead of the 15 years' purchase which would be applicable in the case of a man of the same age so as to allow for the likelihood that the claimant would have married and ceased work at least for a number of years.
  (2)   General damages £27,500 plus £7,500 to compensate her for the lost opportunity of marriage and the support of the husband = £35,000.

(3) Resident domestic help from someone who would live in, a service that would probably be done many years by her mother, £1,000 per annum at 15 years' purchase = £15,000.
(4) The cost of converting or adapting (not buying) an existing house in Ireland, say £8,000.
(5) The cost of adapting a suitable car, but not buying one, £70.
(6) The cost of future medical expenses in Ireland, £2,500.
(7) Telephone on a 15-year multiplier, £820.
(8) Agreed special damage, £9,896. The sum of £511 per annum which she was receiving from the Irish State should not be deducted: it was completely non-contributory and a wrongdoer should not have the benefit of it.

[36.124]   Hughes v McKeown

[1985] 3 All ER 284, [1985] 1 WLR 963   Leonard J

At four and a half years of age in 1973 the claimant was struck by the defendant's car and badly injured. Both her prospects of marriage and future earnings were diminished. The case came to trial in December 1984.

HELD: In *Moriarty v McCarthy* (at para [36.123]) O'Connor J applying the decision in *Harris v Harris* (at para [36.4]) had reduced the multiplier in respect of future earnings but had added a sum equal to that by which the future earnings award had been reduced to compensate for lost marriage prospects. In *Carrick v Camden London Borough Council* (25 July 1979, unreported) he had adopted an approach from *Martin v Scott* (unreported) which was to consider the claimant's economic loss. The simplest method of assessing such loss was to use the multiplier applicable to a man and disregard the intervention of marriage altogether. The claimant's net annual loss of earnings was £2,812 and the appropriate multiplier, disregarding the possibility of the claimant marrying and having children was 17. This figure should be reduced to 14 to take into account the difficulty she would have in the current economic climate in getting employment.

Note—See *Housecroft v Burnett* [1986] 1 All ER 332 where the Court of Appeal considered the relationship between loss of marriage prospects and future loss of earnings.

14.   INCOME TAX

See also *British Transport Commission v Gourley* (at para [36.141]).

[36.125]   Diamond v Campbell-Jones

[1961] Ch 22, [1960] 1 All ER 583, [1960] 2 WLR 586, 104 Sol Jo 249, [1960] TR 131, 53 R & IT 502   Buckley J

In a case in which a dealer in real property claimed damages for breach of a contract for sale of a house which he intended to convert, it was held that he was entitled to a sum equal to the amount of the profit which he would be likely to have made. The damages he recovered were liable to attract tax as part of the profits or gains of his business: *British Transport Commission v Gourley* (at para [36.141]) was distinguished on the grounds that in that case it was conceded that no part of the sum awarded as damages would be subject to tax.

[36.126]   **London and Thames Haven Oil Wharves Ltd v Attwooll**

[1967] Ch 772, [1967] 2 All ER 124, [1967] 2 WLR 743, 110 Sol Jo 979, CA

A jetty was damaged as a result of negligent navigation of a ship. It was out of use for 380 days as a result. The jetty owners recovered damages of which £21,000 was in respect of use of the jetty. They were assessed to tax on the £21,000 under case I of Schedule D.

HELD, ON APPEAL: They were rightly assessed. If the damages a trader receives from another person pursuant to a legal right (whether in contract or tort) includes a sum to compensate him for losing money, which, if it had been received would have been credited to the amount of profits arising in any year from the trade carried on by him the compensation is to be treated in the same way for tax purposes as that sum of money would have been had it not been lost. The £21,000 was compensation for the loss of amounts the company would have received from customers for use of the jetty less the expenses they would have incurred in earning those sums during the 380 days. Such amounts would have been credited to profits and the £21,000 was to be treated for income tax purposes in the same way.

Note—Applied in *Raja's Commercial College v Gian Singh & Co Ltd* [1977] AC 312, [1976] 2 All ER 801, [1976] 3 WLR 58, 120 Sol Jo 404, PC.

(A)   DAMAGES IN FOREIGN CURRENCY

[36.127]   *Note*—It was formerly the rule that a claim in damages must be made in sterling and the judgment given in sterling. In *Miliangos v George Frank (Textiles) Ltd* [1976] AC 443, [1975] 3 All ER 801 the House of Lords departed from this rule to the extent of holding that in an action for the recovery of money due under a contract (eg the price of goods sold) the court has power to give judgment for payment of the money in a foreign currency. The question whether the same rule should apply to claims for damages for breach of contract or for tort was expressly left open. In an action of tort the question came before the House of Lords in the following case.

[36.128]   **The Despina R**

[1979] AC 685, [1979] 1 Lloyd's Rep 1, HL

After a collision in which two ships were damaged the owners of one of them incurred expenses of temporary and permanent repairs and other services which had to be paid for in various foreign currencies. All payments were made from a US dollar account in New York; all the expenses incurred in the foreign currencies other than US dollars were met by transferring US dollars from that account. The Court of Appeal, in an action claiming the amount of the expenses from the owners of the negligent vessel, held that the *Miliangos v George Frank (Textiles) Ltd* [1976] AC 443, [1975] 3 All ER 801 entitled the court to abrogate the former rule and give the money judgment in currency other than sterling.

HELD, ON APPEAL to the House of Lords: An English court had the power to give judgment or make an award in foreign currency. Applying the normal principles in tort of *restitutio in integrum* and reasonable foreseeability of damage, the award should be made in the 'claimant's currency', namely, the currency in which the loss was effectively felt by him, having regard to the currency in which he generally operated with which he had the closest connection.

[36.129] **Hoffman v Sofaer**

[1982] 1 WLR 1350, 126 Sol Jo 611   Talbot J

The claimant was an American citizen who was injured by negligent medical treatment when on a visit to England. Damages for pain and suffering were assessed at £19,000. The remainder of the damages comprising special damage and future loss related mainly to loss of earnings and future loss as president of a company in the USA, where he lived.

HELD (applying *The Despina R* (at para [36.128])): The question was: with what currency was the claimant's loss closely linked? All the losses in effect for which damages had been awarded other than for pain and suffering were closely linked with the currency of his country, namely, dollars. To meet his losses he would have to pay in dollars: the judgment would be in US dollars with the exception of the £19,000.

[36.130] **The Texaco Melbourne**

[1994] 1 Lloyd's Rep 473, HL

The claim was for breach of contract. There was no agreed currency between the parties in which damages should be paid. It was held that damages could be paid in a different currency if the original currency had depreciated to such an extent as to make the payment of damages in that currency insufficient compensation to the claimant.

15. EXEMPLARY AND AGGRAVATED DAMAGES

[36.131] **Kuddus v Chief Constable of Leicestershire**

[2001] UKHL 29

[2002] 2 AC 122, [2001] 3 All ER 193, [2001] 2 WLR 1789, HL

The case concerned misfeasance in public office where a police officer had forged a signature on a written statement which withdrew a complaint of theft.

HELD, ON APPEAL: The claim for exemplary damages succeeded. It did not matter that such damages may not have been awarded for this cause of action before 1964. For the court to have a discretion to award exemplary damages in tort, the claimant must either satisfy one of the two factual tests set out by Lord Devlin in *Rookes v Barnard* [1964] 1 All ER 367, HL, or the award of exemplary damages in the circumstances of the case must be expressly authorised by statute.

The two factual categories are firstly oppressive, arbitrary or unconstitutional actions by servants of the Government, and secondly conduct (by the defendant) calculated to make a profit for himself which may well exceed the compensation payable to the claimant.

Exemplary damages are not available in claims of vicarious liability.

Note—Lord Scott commented upon Lord Devlin's second category (profit exceeds the compensation payable to the victim) and noted that it had been largely overtaken by developments in the common law. Restitutionary damages are available in many tort and breach of contract actions where the profit made by a wrongdoer can be extracted from him without the need to rely on exemplary damages. See *Attorney-General v Blake* [2001] 1 AC 268, 278–280.

[36.132]   **Richardson v Howie**

[2004] EWCA Civ 1127

[2005] PIQR Q3, CA

The claimant brought a claim for damages for assault and battery against her boyfriend following a spiteful attack with a bottle. At first instance, the judge awarded the claimant £5,000 for aggravated damages and £5,000 in respect of the assault. The defendant appealed on the basis that the award was too high and such an award was wrong in principle.

HELD: Appeal allowed. Aggravated damages are only to be awarded in exceptional cases. The claimant was entitled to be compensated for injury to feelings following the assault but this was to be reflected in the award for general damages. The award was reduced to £4,500 to cover the scarring, injured feelings and other matters.

Note—See also *W v Meah* (at para [36.18]), *Appleton v Garrett* [1996] PIQR P1 where awards for aggravated damages were made.

[36.133]   **Watkins v Home Office and Others**

[2006] UKHL 17

[2006] 2 All ER 353, HL

The claimant was a prisoner serving a life sentence and engaged in several legal proceedings. Under the Prison Rules 1999, he was entitled to confidentiality with regards to correspondence with his legal advisers and the courts. In contravention of these Rules, various prison officers read the claimant's mail. He issued proceedings against the Home Office and the individual prison officers, claiming damages for misfeasance in public office. At first instance, it was held that the majority of the prison officers who had interfered with his correspondence had not done so in bad faith. However, three of the officers had acted in bad faith, albeit these claims were dismissed on the ground that misfeasance in public office was not a tort actionable without proof of damage, with the claimant being unable to prove financial loss or physical or mental injury. The claimant successfully appealed to the Court of Appeal on the grounds that his right under the rules was constitutional and, as such, there could be a cause of action in misfeasance in public office for infringement of that right without the need to prove damage.

HELD, ON APPEAL to the House of Lords: (1) The Lords overturned the Court of Appeal's decision. The appeal judges had been wrong to assert that the claimant's right to protection of the confidentiality of his legal correspondence could be described as constitutional.

(2)   There was no right to damages where misfeasance in public office had caused no material damage to the victim. The lack of remedy in tort did not leave the claimant without legal remedy as he could have brought a claim under ss 6, 7 and 8 of the Human Rights Act 1998.

(3)   While exemplary damages could in principle be awarded where it was felt that a compensatory award was insufficient to mark the court's disapproval of proven misfeasance in public office, exemplary damages could not be awarded where there was no material damage for which to compensate the victim.

16. DEDUCTIONS FROM DAMAGES

[36.134]   Note—To avoid double recovery, compensation payments to claimants should be discounted to reflect all benefits that accrue to them as a result of their injuries (see *Hodgson v Trapp* (at para [36.145]). The rule is subject to exceptions where there are charitable payments, insurance payments and social security benefits. See also offset of statutory funding concerning care and nursing (at para [36.88]). In fatal cases, see para [37.81].

(A)   CHARITABLE OR VOLUNTARY PAYMENTS

[36.135]   *Note*—The claimant is not required to give credit for charitable or voluntary payments. The House of Lords held in *Parry v Cleaver* (at para [36.148]) that it would be 'contrary to public policy, that the sufferer should have his damages reduced so that he would gain nothing from the benevolence of his friends or relations or of the public at large, and that the only gainer would be the wrongdoer'. The court will however consider the circumstances and source of such payments.

[36.136]   **Redpath v Belfast and County Down Rly**
[1947] NI 167

A distress fund supported by voluntary contributions from the public was established to assist passengers injured in a railway accident. In an action by a passenger against the railway company claiming damages for negligence, the railway company applied to interrogate the claimant as to the amount received by him from the fund.

HELD: The interrogatories were irrelevant. The claimant's damages were not to be reduced because the claimant had received without legal right monies voluntarily subscribed by third parties.

[36.137]   **Dennis v London Passenger Transport Board**
[1948] 1 All ER 779, 92 Sol Jo 350   Denning J

An injured claimant received no wages during disability but the Minister of Pensions and his employer, the London County Council (LCC), paid him approximately the amount of the wages in pension and sick pay. The Minister, without contending there was a legal obligation to refund, said the claimant would be expected to refund out of the damages if recovered and the LCC told the claimant the same. The claimant undertook to repay if he recovered damages.

HELD: The claimant was under a moral obligation to repay. A wrongdoer is not to be allowed to reduce damages because other persons have made up the wages. The claimant had lost his wages, and *prima facie* he should be paid them by the wrongdoer. They had been made up to him by other people who expect to be repaid and should be included as damages, subject to the direction that the amounts should be repaid. *Allen v Waters & Co* [1935] 1 KB 200 followed.

[36.138]   **Berriello v Felixstowe Dock & Rly Co**
[1989] 1 WLR 695, CA

The claimant was an Italian seaman injured at an English port. He received monies from the Italian State Seamen's Fund on account of future loss of earnings on terms that these monies would be refunded to the extent that damages for loss of earnings were recovered from the defendant. It was held at first instance that the monies should be deducted from the claimant's damages. The claimant appealed.

HELD: Since the sums received by the claimant were refundable, they could not be deducted from the settlement figure. There would be no double recovery since repayment had to be made to the Italian State Seamen's Fund.

Note—See also para [36.163].

[36.139]   Gaca v Pirelli General plc
[2004] EWCA Civ 373
[2004] 3 All ER 348, CA

The claimant was seriously injured at work. The defendant employer terminated the claimant's employment on the grounds of ill health and paid the claimant an ill health gratuity. The claimant also received monies under the employer's permanent health insurance policy for temporary total disablement. The employer admitted liability for the accident. The issue on appeal was whether these sums should be deducted from the claimant's damages.

HELD, ON APPEAL: The ill health gratuity payment and insurance payments should be deducted from the damages. The benevolence exception applies where payments have been made to claimants out of sympathy by third parties. The position is different where the payment is made by the tortfeasor who should not have to compensate the claimant twice for the same loss. Unless the tortfeasor specifically states that the payment is a gift which is not to be deducted from the damages, it falls to be deducted.

There was no evidence to show that the claimant paid or contributed to the cost of the insurance policy. As such, those payments should also be deducted.

Note—See also *Williams v BOC Gases Ltd* [2000] PIQR Q253 where the Court of Appeal held that a charitable payment made by the tortfeasor (the employer) is to be treated as an advance against damages and should be deducted. See para [36.140] below for cases on permanent health insurance.

(B)   PERMANENT HEALTH INSURANCE

[36.140]   Hussain v New Taplow Paper Mills Ltd
[1988] AC 514, [1988] 1 All ER 541, [1988] 2 WLR 266, [1988] ICR 259, HL

The claimant was injured at work resulting in the amputation of his left arm below the elbow. He was unable to work but the defendant continued to employ him. Shortly before the hearing the defendant offered him a job as a weighbridge attendant at reduced wages. His contract of employment entitled him to receive full earnings for 13 weeks and then 50% of lost earnings or the difference between present earnings and earnings before incapacity. The payments were financed out of a permanent health insurance scheme which the defendant paid for; the claimant's earnings would not have been higher in the absence of such a scheme so he was not contributing to the scheme himself. The judge did not take into account this long-term sickness payment when calculating future losses because it was the benefit of insurance. The defendant appealed successfully to the Court of Appeal and the claimant appealed to the House of Lords.

HELD, ON APPEAL to the House of Lords: Appeal dismissed. The sums were payable under the contract of employment to the employee as a partial substitute for loss of earnings. The employee did not contribute to the cost; the fact that the employer had insured itself against its liability under the contract of employment was irrelevant. The payments should be deducted from the future loss claim.

Note—See also *Parry v Cleaver* (at para [36.148]), *Hodgson v Trapp* (at para [36.145]) and *Gaca v Pirelli General plc* (at para [36.139]).

(C) INCOME TAX

(I) GOURLEY'S CASE

[36.141]   **British Transport Commission v Gourley**

[1956] AC 185, [1955] 3 All ER 796, [1956] 2 WLR 41, 100 Sol Jo 12, [1955] 2 Lloyd's Rep 475, HL

The claimant was 65 years of age and was a partner in a firm of civil engineers. He was totally disabled for some time and after returning to work his earning capacity was reduced. Pearce J awarded £47,720 being £9,000 for pain and suffering, £1,000 out of pocket expenses, £15,220 for actual loss of earnings before the end of 1953 and £22,500 for estimated future loss of earnings. The two latter sums (ie £37,720) did not take income tax or surtax into account. If tax had been, the award would have been £6,695, being £4,945 instead of £15,220 and £1,750 instead of £22,000. The parties agreed that one or other of the two sums fixed by the judge should be awarded.

Per Earl Jowitt: It was agreed by counsel on both sides – and I think rightly agreed – that the respondent [claimant] would incur no tax liability in respect of the award of £37,720 or alternatively £6,695. The broad principle is an award of such sum of money as will put the injured person in the same position as he would have been if he had not sustained the injuries. The principle of *restitutio in integrum* affords little guidance for pain and suffering and impairment but affords some guidance in assessing financial loss and was referred to by Lord Wright (*Liesbosch, Dredger v Edison SS* [1933] AC 449, 102 LJP 73, 149 LT 49, HL [at para [35.19]]) as 'the dominant rule of law'. There is no distinction between cases under PAYE where tax is deducted before payment, and cases where tax is paid after the money is received. It is fallacious to consider the problem as though a benefit was being conferred on a wrongdoer. The problem is rather for what damages he is liable. He is liable for such damages as, by reason of his wrongdoing, the [claimant] has sustained. The tax element is not too remote and no sensible person regards his gross earnings as equivalent to his available income. In determining what the respondent has really lost, the judge ought to have considered his tax liability. The assessment of tax liability need not be elaborate, but an estimate formed on broad lines, even rough and ready.

Appeal allowed.

[36.142]   **Hartley v Sandholme Iron Co Ltd**

[1975] QB 600, [1974] 3 All ER 475, [1974] 3 WLR 445, 118 Sol Jo 702   Nield J

The claimant was off work for 19 weeks as a result of injury and claimed loss of earnings for that period calculated on the weekly pre-accident wage after deduction of income tax on a PAYE basis. Afterwards he received a tax rebate of £18.70 due to his not having earned wages during the 19 weeks off work.

HELD: Applying the principles of *British Transport Commission v Gourley* (at para [36.141]), his claimed loss should be reduced by the amount of the tax rebate. The saving of tax to the claimant was not too remote but stemmed directly from the consequences of the accident; it was not *res inter alios acta* (acts of others, or transactions between others) nor completely collateral, and the amount of the saving was not a matter of speculation but was accurately quantified.

[36.143] Duller v South East Lincs Engineers
[1981] CLY 585, QBD

The claimant claimed damages for severe personal injuries sustained in an accident. Before the accident in addition to his full time job he had worked as a part-time barman, but had not disclosed his earnings from the part-time job for income tax purposes.

HELD: He was entitled to be compensated for the loss of the part-time earnings. They did not come from any criminal origin but came lawfully into his hands. His unlawful conduct came later and was only with the Inland Revenue, not with the earnings. He did not base his claim on any unlawful act of his and it was not defeated by being tainted with illegality, but deductions must be made in respect of income tax. *Burns v Edman* (at para [37.49]) distinguished.

Note—See also *Newman v Folkes and Dunlop Tyres Ltd* [2002] PIQR Q2, QBD where the *Duller* case was followed (at para [36.143]); *Hunter v Butler* (at para [37.50]) where the court took a different view; *Hewison v Meridan Shipping* [2002] EWCA Civ 1821 where the claimant was employed as a crane operator and seriously injured at work. Liability for the accident was admitted. The defendant argued it would be contrary to public policy to award the claimant damages for future loss of earnings because he had deceived his employer by repeatedly failing to disclose that he had epilepsy. The Court of Appeal held that the claimant had obtained a pecuniary advantage by deception and could not recover loss of earnings.

[36.144] Thomas v Wignall
[1987] QB 1098, [1987] 1 All ER 1185, [1987] 2 WLR 930, CA

At sixteen and a half the claimant (during a routine operation for the removal of her tonsils) suffered severe permanent brain damage leaving her unaware of what had happened. She needed constant care and attention. At the hearing the claimant was 27 years old. The judge awarded, *inter alia*, £435,000 for future care. He had considered the appropriate multiplier to be 14 but in view of the size of the award, increased this to 15 to make allowance for the higher incidence of taxation on the investment income. The defendant appealed arguing that the appropriate multiplier in any event was 13 and that to increase the multiplier as an allowance for the high incidence of tax was wrong in law.

HELD, ON APPEAL, (Lloyd LJ dissenting): High rates of income tax were a fact of life. The larger the income, the greater percentage that would be paid in tax. It would be wrong to impose inflexible rigidity and disallow some adjustment to the multiplier to reflect the increased incidence of tax on the income element of the compensation. The original award of 14 was within the range of possible awards and although the adjustment was generous it was not excessive.

Appeal dismissed.

Note—But see *Hodgson v Trapp* (at para [36.145]).

[36.145]   Hodgson v Trapp

[1989] AC 807, [1988] 3 All ER 870, [1988] 3 WLR 1281, [1989] 2 LS Gaz R 36, HL

At 33 the claimant, a wife, mother and woman of many talents and interests suffered catastrophic injuries in a road accident. As a result she became wholly dependent on others and would always remain so. The judge calculated the multiplicand for loss of earnings and chose a multiplier of 11. He then increased this to 12 to take into account the higher tax rates payable on investment income, applying *Thomas v Wignall* (at para [36.144]). He adopted the same approach to nursing care and attendance raising the basic multiplier for that head of damage from 13 to 14. The defendant appealed not on the basis that high tax rates might allow for a multiplier at a higher end of the conventional scale but on the basis that having decided on a multiplier the making of a specific addition to take tax into account as a separate feature was incorrect in law.

HELD, ON APPEAL to the House of Lords: Appeal allowed. It was a falsity to assume that higher rates of taxation would not be reduced. Just as inflation is an imponderable and not to be taken into account (see *Cookson v Knowles* at para [37.31]), so (save in exceptional circumstances) income tax should not be used to raise the multiplier for future losses as a separate item.

The dissenting view of Lloyd LJ in *Thomas v Wignall* [1987] 1 All ER 1185 was correct. Per Lord Oliver: 'The incidence of taxation in the future should ordinarily be assumed to be satisfactorily taken care of in the conventional assumptions of an interest rate applicable to a stable currency and the selection of a multiplier appropriate to that rate'.

Note—See Lord Bridge's judgment concerning the assessment of damages and deductions for which the claimant should give credit.

[36.146]   **Tessel Meike Merel van Oudenhoven v Griffin Inns Ltd**

(12 March 1999, unreported), RCJ   Wright J

The claimant was a civil engineering student in Holland with a very bright career ahead of her; she was also likely to graduate in the top 5% of her class. During a trip to London she was injured in a pub when a blackboard fell on her skull, knocking her unconscious and leaving her with both psychological and physical injuries.

She graduated a year later than anticipated but with a distinction. She entered into employment in 1993 with a company that she considered to be lower than those she had planned to apply to before the accident occurred. She had to leave the employment in 1996 as it was causing her to become exhausted and distressed.

It was held that her physical injuries would improve in the future but whilst her intelligence had been preserved, her physiological injuries were such that her cognitive functioning had been disturbed and she was operating at a far less effective level. She could not undertake the same type of employment as she had initially anticipated.

HELD: For loss of earnings a comparator was looked at, being a fellow student of the claimant who had followed a similar career path to that which had been anticipated for the claimant. This loss was established at £197,371.05, but was reduced by 25% on the basis that there was the risk that the claimant would not have achieved all that she set out to achieve and the comparator had achieved a lot more than would normally be anticipated for a 27 year old.

The same comparator was used for future loss of earnings however, the multiplier had to be increased from 21.03 to 28.52 given that higher taxes would be in place in Holland, with up to 60% tax being in place for investments. An initial figure of £1,615,599 was looked at for the multiplicand but was reduced significantly, initially by the same 25% as for past loss of earnings. It was also believed that the claimant would be able to obtain employment with a higher salary than the national average, so a total of 40% was deducted from the initial figure.

(D)   PENSION

[36.147]   *Note*—Pension payments are ignored in the assessment of damages for loss of earnings, but after retirement age they are taken into account in the assessment of damages for loss of pension rights (including any proportion of a pension lump sum which is attributable to the period after retirement age). The rule is the same whether or not the provider of the pension is the tortfeasor.

[36.148]   Parry v Cleaver
[1970] AC 1, [1969] 1 All ER 555, [1969] 2 WLR 821, HL

The claimant, a policeman, had to leave the police force because of injury caused by the defendant's negligence. He was then aged 36. But for the injury he would not have retired from the force until he was 48 and would then have been entitled as of right to a pension of £10 per week for life. On leaving the force at 36 he became entitled as of right to a pension of £3 per week for life. He had contributed to the fund during his service by payments which were compulsory. The trial judge, following *Judd v Hammersmith Borough Council* [1960] 1 All ER 607, [1960] 1 WLR 328, 104 Sol Jo 270 held that in assessing damages the pension should be ignored during the period up to age 48, when the claimant would have left the force, but should be taken into account thereafter.

HELD, by the Court of Appeal: This was not correct. The general rule is that the injured party should give credit for all sums which he received in diminution of his loss save for exceptional cases such as insurance benefits. The case was indistinguishable from *Browning v War Office* [1963] 1 QB 750, and the pension must be taken into account for the whole period.

The decision of the Court of Appeal was reversed by the House of Lords who by a majority of three to two restored the decision of the trial judge.

Lord Reid drew attention to the two types of payments which are disregarded in assessing damages—benevolent gifts (*Redpath v Belfast and County Down Railway* (at para [36.136])) and monies coming to the claimant under a contract of insurance (*Bradburn v Great Western Rly Co* (1874) LR 10 Exch 1, 44 LJ Ex 9, 31 LT 464). There was no reason to regard these types of receipt as anomalous. In the case of benevolent payments it would be revolting to a man's sense of justice that the sufferer should have his damages reduced so that he would gain nothing from the benevolence of his friends and relatives. In the case of insurance monies they are not taken into account because the claimant has bought them, and it would be unjust and unreasonable to hold that the benefit from the money he had prudently spent on premiums should ensure to the benefit of the tortfeasor. Why should it make any difference that he insured by arrangement with his employer rather than with an insurance company? If it did not, then a contributory pension, which is a form of insurance, should not be taken into account either. There is no relevant difference between a pension, for which payments are made into a fund to meet future contingencies, and other forms of insurance. The reason the pension was to be taken into account after age 48 was that in the later period it was a comparison of like with like. In the period before age 48 the claimant was receiving something different in kind from what he had lost, namely, wages. *Browning v War Office* was wrongly decided.

Note—See *Cantwell v CICB* [2001] UKHL 36, HL concerning the application of *Parry v Cleaver* when assessing compensation under the Criminal Injuries Compensation Scheme in Scotland.

[36.149]   Dews v National Coal Board

[1988] AC 1, [1987] 2 All ER 545, [1987] 3 WLR 38, [1987] ICR 602, HL

The claimant was a miner who was required by his contract of employment to belong to and contribute to a compulsory pension scheme. As a result of an accident at work he was absent on sick leave for 31 weeks. Towards the end of that period he received no pay and so paid no pension contributions. His pension entitlement was not affected. He claimed loss of earnings including the contributions he would have made if he had been earning.

HELD, ON APPEAL to the House of Lords: This claim failed; if the claimant had not been injured he would not have received his pension contributions as they would have been paid directly into the scheme. As his pension entitlement was not affected, to award him the contributions would have enriched him rather than compensated him. He was not entitled to them as damages for loss of earnings.

Per Lord Griffiths: The fundamental principle of English law is that damages for personal injury are compensatory and intended, so far as possible, to put the [claimant] in the same financial position as if the accident had never happened.

[36.150]   Smoker v London Fire and Defence Authority, Wood v British Coal Corpn

[1991] 2 AC 502, [1991] 2 All ER 449, HL

Both claimants were injured at work and brought proceedings against their employers for damages. The claimants claimed, *inter alia*, loss of earnings and the defendant argued that the loss of earnings claimed should be reduced by the amount of ill health pension the claimants had received as a result of suffering the injury.

Mr Smoker had become a member of a firemans' pension scheme from the time that he joined the service and contributed 10.75% of his wages to the scheme. His employer contributed twice that much. Mr Wood was a member of the Mine Workers' Pension Scheme and contributed 5.4% of his pay and his employers contributed the same amount.

At first instance, it was held that Mr Smoker's pension would not be deducted and the defendant appealed direct to the House of Lords. Mr Wood's pension was deducted in full at first instance, a decision that was overturned in the Court of Appeal. The defendant appealed to the House of Lords.

HELD, ON APPEAL to the House of Lords: Both claimants had purchased their pensions by way of the contributions they had made to them and, in the words of Lord Reed in *Parry v Cleaver* (at para [36.148]) these pensions were 'the fruit, through insurance, of all the money which was set aside in the past in respect of his past work'. Therefore the amounts of the ill health pension were not to be deducted from the claimants' damages. It made no difference that the defendants were in the triple position of being employer, tortfeasor and insurer.

Note—See also *Hopkins v Norcros plc* [1994] ICR 11, [1994] IRLR 18, CA where it was held that monies received by way of a pension arising out of a termination of employment were not to be set off against the damages which an employee was entitled to due to the fact that the termination of his contract of employment was wrongful.

[36.151]   **Longden v British Coal Corpn**
[1998] AC 653, [1997] 3 WLR 1336, HL

The claimant an injured employee, received an incapacity pension in the form of early periodical payments in a lump sum. The defendant employer argued that it was entitled to deduct these payments from the claimant's overall claim for pension loss on the basis that without such a deduction, the claimant would benefit from double compensation. The defendant's argument was rejected at the first instance and the defendant appealed to the Court of Appeal where it was held that the defendant was not entitled to deduct the periodical payments and lump sum from the overall pension loss claim on the basis that the claimant had contributed to the scheme and that the incapacity pension was not to be treated as insurance.

HELD, ON APPEAL: The defendant appealed to the House of Lords. The appeal was allowed in part. The incapacity and disability pensions were exceptions to the general rule and the payments made to the claimant during the period prior to normal retirement age could not be taken into consideration as a deduction as against loss of earnings claim. However the lump sum received by him on resignation under the scheme should be apportioned as between the periods before and after the normal expected retirement date and the amount referable to the period after this notional retirement age could be set against his claim.

(E)   REDUNDANCY PAYMENTS

[36.152]   **Colledge v Bass Mitchells & Butlers**
[1988] 1 All ER 536, [1988] ICR 125, CA

The claimant was injured at work. As a result of his injuries, he was made redundant and received £9,000 by way of a redundancy payment. The trial judge did not deduct this sum from the claim for past loss of earnings. The defendant appealed.

HELD: The redundancy payment fell to be deducted. It would not be deducted if the claimant would have been made redundant regardless of the accident.

Note—See also *Parry v Cleaver* (at para [36.148]) and *Wilson v National Coal Board* 1981 SLT 67.

(F)   LIVING EXPENSES

[36.153]   **Shearman v Folland**
[1950] 2 KB 43, [1950] 1 All ER 976, 66 TLR 853, 94 Sol Jo 336, CA

The claimant, a lady aged 67, was healthy, active and young for her years. One of her legs was amputated at the thigh and the other was permanently unstable and in practice largely useless. She was unable to walk more than 150 yards and that was only on a perfectly even surface. The claimant was also unable without assistance to go up and down stairs or to get into or out of a bath or motor car. The special damages included a claim of £12 12s per week for nursing home fees. Before the accident she resided in hotels in London and paid £7 7s per week for board and lodging. Slade J deducted all or most of the £7 7s 0d from the £12 12s and drastically cut down the claim of £12 12s per week on the ground that it was unreasonable and exorbitant.

HELD, ON APPEAL: The £7 7s could not be set off. The precise style in which she would probably or might have lived was a collateral matter. 'Matter completely collateral and merely *res inter alios acta* (acts of others, or transactions between others), cannot be used in mitigation of damages', *Mayne on Damages*. The expenses of a millionaire accustomed to live at a palatial hotel would far exceed the charges of a nursing home. Could a wrongdoer say in such a case that he was entitled to go scot free? A court would not pursue beyond a certain limit what would have been the position if no accident had occurred. Ordinarily a householder or lodger has fixed expenses or charges which continue. Those parts which do not (eg, food) may be difficult to disengage from the total. *Contra* a claim for extra nourishments by implication concedes that the claimant is giving credit for the food for which he would have to pay apart from the accident. No such claim to set off had previously been advanced, let alone succeeded. The defendant is entitled to set off living expenses of some amount, and if evidence had been adduced to show what proportion of the £12 12s had been attributable to living expenses, it would have been open to the judge to make a deduction in respect of that.

Note—The House of Lords approved this approach in *Lim Poh Choo v Camden & Islington Area Health Authority* (see para [36.5]). Where the claimant will be permanently hospitalised, living expenses which would not be incurred and expenses in earning a living can be deducted.

[36.154]   **Independent Assessor v O'Brien and Others**
[2004] EWCA Civ 1035, CA

The respondents were imprisoned following a miscarriage of justice and sought compensation. The Court of Appeal upheld an offset of 25% from an award for loss of earnings to take account of the living expenses that would have been incurred had the respondents not been in prison.

(G)   SECTION 5 OF THE ADMINISTRATION OF JUSTICE ACT 1982

[36.155]   In claims based on causes of action accruing on or after 1 January 1983 maintenance of a claimant at public expense is to be taken into account in assessing damages. The Administration of Justice Act 1982, s 5 reads:

'5. Maintenance at public expense to be taken into account in assessment of damages

In an action under the law of England and Wales or the law of Northern Ireland for damages for personal injuries (including any such action arising out of a contract) any saving to the injured person which is attributable to his maintenance wholly or partly at public expense in a hospital, nursing home or other institution shall be set off against any income lost by him as a result of his injuries.'

17.   SOCIAL SECURITY BENEFITS

(A)   THE PRINCIPLE

[36.156]   The recovery of benefits is governed by the Social Security (Recovery of Benefits) Act 1997. The main provisions of the scheme are that an injured person should not be compensated twice in respect of the same accident, injury or disease. The tax payer should not subsidise a liable third party in their obligation to fully compensate the injured person. The Act applies to all compensation payments made on or after 6 October 1997. The defendant (or compensator) is required to investigate, before damages are paid, whether the claimant has received any recoverable benefits over the same period of time as that to which the damages relate. If appropriate, recoverable benefits can be offset against particular heads of damages.

Recoupment is limited to 'the relevant period' which is five years from the date of the accident/injury or the period between the accident/injury and the final compensation payment, whichever is the shorter.

Where there is more than one compensator, the sum to be paid by the compensators shall not exceed the total amount of the recoverable benefits.

(B)   SOCIAL SECURITY (RECOVERY OF BENEFITS) ACT 1997 ('THE 1997 ACT')

[36.157]
6.   Liability of person paying compensation
(1)   A person who makes a compensation payment in any case is liable to pay to the Secretary of State an amount equal to the total amount of the recoverable benefits.
(2)   The liability referred to in subsection (1) arises immediately before the compensation payment or, if there is more than one, the first of them is made.
...

[36.158]
8.   Reduction of compensation payment
(1)   This section applies in a case where, in relation to any head of compensation listed in column 1 of Schedule 2—
  (a)   any of the compensation payment is attributable to that head, and
  (b)   any recoverable benefit is shown against that head in column 2 of the Schedule.
(2)   In such a case, any claim of a person to receive the compensation payment is to be treated for all purposes as discharged if—
  (a)   he is paid the amount (if any) of the compensation payment calculated in accordance with this section, and
  (b)   if the amount of the compensation payment so calculated is nil, he is given a statement saying so by the person who (apart from this section) would have paid the gross amount of the compensation payment.
(3)   For each head of compensation listed in column 1 of the Schedule for which paragraphs (a) and (b) of subsection (1) are met, so much of the gross amount of the compensation payment as is attributable to that head is to be reduced (to nil, if necessary) by deducting the amount of the recoverable benefit or, as the case may be, the aggregate amount of the recoverable benefits shown against it.
(4)   Subsection (3) is to have effect as if a requirement to reduce a payment by deducting an amount which exceeds that payment were a requirement to reduce that payment to nil.
(5)   The amount of the compensation payment calculated in accordance with this section is—
  (a)   the gross amount of the compensation payment,
less
  (b)   the sum of the reductions made under subsection (3), (and, accordingly, the amount may be nil).
...

[36.159]
10.   Review
(1)   The Secretary of State may review any certificate of recoverable benefits if he is satisfied—
  (a)   that it was issued in ignorance of, or was based on a mistake as to, a material fact, or
  (b)   that a mistake (whether in computation or otherwise) has occurred in its preparation.
...
(2)   On a review under this section the Secretary of State may either—
  (a)   confirm the certificate, or
  (b)   (subject to subsection (3)) issue a fresh certificate containing such variations as he considers appropriate, or
  (c)   revoke the certificate.
(3)   The Secretary of State may not vary the certificate so as to increase the total amount of the recoverable benefits unless it appears to him that the variation is required as a result of the person who applied for the certificate supplying him with incorrect or insufficient information.

[36.160]
11.   Appeal
(1)   An appeal against a certificate of recoverable benefits may be made on the ground-
  (a)   that any amount, rate or period specified in the certificate is incorrect, or
  (b)   that listed benefits which have been, or are likely to be, paid otherwise than in respect of the accident, injury or disease in question have been brought into account, or
  (c)   that listed benefits which have not been, and are not likely to be, paid to the injured person during the relevant period have been brought into account, or
  (d)   that the payment on the basis of which the certificate was issued is not a payment within section 1(1)(a).
(2)   An appeal under this section may be made by—
  (a)   the person who applied for the certificate of recoverable benefits, or
...
  (b)   (in a case where the amount of the compensation payment has been calculated under section 8) the injured person or other person to whom the payment is made.
(3)   No appeal may be made under this section until—
  (a)   the claim giving rise to the compensation payment has been finally disposed of, and
  (b)   the liability under section 6 has been discharged.
...
(5)   Regulations may make provision—
  (a)   as to the manner in which, and the time within which, appeals under this section may be made,
  (b)   as to the procedure to be followed where such an appeal is made, and
  (c)   for the purpose of enabling any such appeal to be treated as an application for review under section 10.
...

[36.161]

Schedule 2
Calculation of compensation payment

(1)	(2)
Head of compensation	*Benefit*
1. Compensation for earnings lost during the relevant period	...
	Disability pension payable under section 103 of the 1992 Act
	Incapacity benefit
	Income support
	Invalidity pension and allowance
	Jobseeker's allowance
	Reduced earnings allowance
	Severe disablement allowance
	Sickness benefit
	Statutory sick pay
	Unemployability supplement
	Unemployment benefit
2. Compensation for cost of care incurred during the relevant period	Attendance allowance
	Care component of disability living allowance
	Disablement pension increase payable under section 104 or 105 of the 1992 Act
3. Compensation for loss of mobility during the relevant period	Mobility allowance
	Mobility component of disability living allowance

Note—References to incapacity benefit, invalidity pension and allowance, severe disablement allowance, sickness benefit and unemployment benefit also include any income support paid with each of those benefits on the same instrument of payment or paid concurrently with each of those benefits by means of an instrument for benefit payment.

For the purpose of this Note, income support includes personal expenses addition, special transitional additions and transitional addition as defined in the Income Support (Transitional) Regulations 1987, SI 1987/1969.

Any reference to statutory sick pay includes only 80% of payments made between 6 April 1991 and 5 April 1994, and does not include payments made on or after 6 April 1994.

In this Schedule 'the 1992 Act' means the Social Security Contributions and Benefits Act 1992.

(C)   DAMAGES NOT INCLUDED/EXEMPT PAYMENTS

[36.162]   No benefits are deducted from compensation for pain and suffering, loss of amenity or other heads of loss not listed in Sch 2 of the 1997 Act (at para [36.161] above).

Part 1 of Sch 1 to the 1997 Act and reg 2 of the Social Security (Recovery of Benefits) Regulations 1997, SI 1997/3030 list payments that are exempted from the provisions of the 1997 Act. The main exemptions are Fatal Accident Act claims (Law Reform Act payments are not exempt), redundancy payments, contractual sick pay from an employer and costs.

(D)   BENEFITS NOT LISTED IN THE 1997 ACT

[36.163]   *Note*—Section 17 of the 1997 Act provides 'in assessing damages in respect of any accident, injury or disease, the amount of any listed benefits paid or likely to be paid is to be disregarded'. Listed benefits are at para [36.161] above. Benefits which are not listed (such as housing and council tax benefits) but which have been received as a result of the accident may be taken into account. See *Clenshaw v Tanner* [2002] All ER (D) 203 (Jan), CA where housing benefit received by the claimant between the date of the accident and the date of trial was deducted in full from his claim for loss of earnings. At first instance, Silber J held that 'the housing benefit in this case covers loss of earnings and so is deductible. If this were not the case, the claimant would be in a position of being substantially better off, as he would receive both compensation for loss of income and, as a result of the housing benefits, reduced level of expenditure to which the income would have been put, and that would mean that the claimant would be compensated twice'. See also *Hodgson v Trapp* (at para [36.145]), *Rand v East Dorset Health Authority* (2000) unreported and *Berriello v Felixstowe Dock & Railway Co* (at para [36.138]).

Compensation under the Pneumoconiosis (Workers Compensation) Act 1979 is deducted in full from an award of damages: *Ballantine v Newalls Insulation Co Ltd* [2001] ICR 25.

(E)   CONTRIBUTORY NEGLIGENCE

[36.164]   There is no provision to reduce recoupment to take into account contributory negligence.

(F)   INTEREST AND BENEFITS

[36.165]   John Wadey v Surrey County Council
[1999] 2 All ER 334, [1999] 1 WLR 1614, HL

This was primarily a case of statutory interpretation of s 17 of the Social Security (Recovery of Benefits) Act 1997. At first instance the county court decided that in assessing the interest on special damage, which was significant in this case, benefits should be deducted from the figure of special damages before the calculation of interest.

On appeal however to the Court of Appeal it was decided that this was wrong as it was provided under s 17 of the 1997 Act that '*in assessing damages in respect of any accident, injury or disease, the amount of any listed benefits paid or likely to be paid is to be disregarded*'. It was stated that the 1997 Act was not meant as a piecemeal amendment but was designed by Parliament to be an entirely new scheme and that the omission of a provision similar to s 103 of the Social Security Administration Act 1992 cannot have been simply accidental. The court therefore determined that simply because the disregarding of benefits for the purpose of calculation of special damage interest would create a windfall to a claimant was not a matter of concern for the court.

HELD, ON APPEAL to the House of Lords: The decision of the Court of Appeal was upheld.

Per Lord Millett: On this analysis the statutory scheme does not depart from the traditional approach of the common law. The listed benefits are disregarded in the assessment of damages because they are refundable by or at the expense of the claimant and accordingly do not diminish his loss. The damages carry interest before as well as after judgment in the normal way. The link between the amount of the judgment and the amount recoverable under the judgment is not broken since the claimant's obligation to apply the damages in repayment of benefit is discharged by the tortfeasor. The claimant's apparent double recovery of interest is due to the fact that the Secretary of State is content to be repaid without interest but this is a matter between the Secretary of State who paid the benefits and the claimant who received them and enures for the benefit of the claimant.

[36.166]   Griffiths v British Coal Corpn
[2001] 1 WLR 1493, CA

The claimant contended that benefits could only be set off against the compensation payment made 'in consequence of any accident, injury and disease'. It was the claimant's case that payment of interest was not 'in consequence' of an accident, injury or disease.

HELD: 'In a case in which the claimant has received benefit which exceeds the amount recovered as compensation, that excess should be set-off against the combined total of damages and interest up to the level of total benefit paid' (per Lord Phillips MR).

Note—This case also decided that benefits can be offset against gratuitous care but gardening, decorating, DIY, car maintenance and window cleaning did not fall within the meaning of care and therefore statutory benefits cannot be offset against awards for these services.

(G)   PAYMENT INTO COURT

[36.167]   Hilton International v Smith
(5 October 2000, unreported)

The defendant paid the gross sum of £46,124 into court. Of this sum, £40,124 was withheld under the 1997 Act. The claimant accepted the payment in. £6,000 was paid out of court to the claimant and £40,124 was paid by the defendant to the Secretary of State. Both parties then appealed the certificate and a fresh nil certificate was issued. The defendant was reimbursed the sum of £40,124, which the claimant demanded.

HELD: The defendant had told the claimant that the gross payment in was £46,124 without reservation of any kind. The claimant was therefore entitled to the sum of

£40,124. The defendant should have identified the gross compensation payment as nil (or such lesser sum for which they were appealing the certificate) or served a Calderbank letter making it clear that their intention was to appeal the certificate and retain any benefits that were subsequently reimbursed.

[36.168]   Williams v Devon County Council

[2003] EWCA Civ 365

CA

The defendant paid a sum into court and withheld a global sum representing a range of recoverable benefits. There was a finding of contributory negligence and a dispute as to whether the claimant had beaten the payment into court. The Court of Appeal held that the Part 36 payment had been wrongly calculated because the amount of recoverable benefits had not been reduced in accordance with s 8 of the 1997 Act (see para [36.158] above). Under CPR 36.23(3)(b), the payment in notice is required to state the name and amount of any benefit by which the gross payment in was reduced in accordance with the 1997 Act. Had this exercise been carried out, general damages would have been correctly ring fenced and the claimant would have been able to make a properly informed decision on whether or not to accept the payment.

Note—See also *Bruce v Genesis Fast Food* [2003] EWHC 788.

(H)   CHALLENGING THE RECOVERABILITY OF BENEFITS

(I)   REVIEW OF CERTIFICATE

[36.169]   *Note*—The certificate of recoverable benefit may be reviewed at any time before the final Compensation Recovery Unit (CRU) liability is discharged on the application of the compensator, the claimant or their respective representatives. This is dealt with under s 10 of the 1997 Act. The certificate will be reviewed if:
(1)   the certificate was issued in ignorance of, or based on a mistake as to a material fact; or
(2)   a mistake was made in its preparation; or
(3)   the certificate was incorrect or insufficient information was supplied to the Secretary of State by the person who applied for the certificate and in consequence the amount of benefits specified in the certificate was less than it would have been had the information supplied been correct or sufficient; or
(4)   a ground for appeal is satisfied under s 11 of the 1997 Act.
Following review, the Department for Work and Pensions will either confirm that the certificate is correct or revoke the certificate and issue a fresh one. The total on the certificate may not be increased unless the person applying for the review had supplied incorrect or insufficient information.

(II)   APPEAL OF CERTIFICATE

[36.170]   Under s 11 of the 1997 Act, appeals may be brought against CRU certificates on any of the following grounds:
(1)   any amount, rate or period specified in the certificate is wrong;
(2)   the certificate shows benefits which were not paid as a direct result of the accident, injury or disease;
(3)   listed benefits listed which have not been, and are not likely to be, paid to the injured person during the relevant period have been brought into account;

(4)   the compensation payment was not made in consequence of any accident, injury or disease.

There is no appeal to a tribunal against the provisions for offsetting of benefits against heads of special damage. Such disputes must be resolved through the courts and, where cases are settled, appropriate provisions must be included in consent orders for resolution of the issues.

(III)   PROCEDURE

[36.171]   A compensator or injured person may appeal the certificate within one month of full payment of recoverable benefits. Late appeals may only be accepted with permission of the chairperson of the appeal service. There is a cut off date of 13 months for late appeals. The CRU must refer an appeal to the Appeals Service to arrange for an Appeals Tribunal hearing. The tribunal may decide that the amount on the certificate is correct or that the amount may be either increased or decreased. A refund will be issue where the amount is reduced. Appeals lie from a tribunal to a Social Security Commissioner on a point of law.

The burden of proving that benefit would not have been paid in the absence of the relevant injury or disease, or should not have been paid, rests on the person challenging the decision: R(CR) 3/03.

Note—The relevant legislation concerning recoverability and procedure is contained in the Social Security (Recovery of Benefits) Act 1997, the Social Security (Recovery of Benefits Regulations) 1997, SI 1997/3030 and the Social Security and Child Support (Decisions and Appeals) Regulations 1999, SI 1999/991. Decisions of the Social Security Commissioners are published, some of which may be accessed at: www.osscsc.gov.uk/decisions/decisions.htm.

The Department for Work and Pensions Form Z2 provides guidance on appeal.

(IV)   CASE LAW

[36.172]   **Hassall v Secretary of State for Social Security**
Pether v Secretary of State for Social Security
[1995] 3 All ER 909, [1995] 1 WLR 812, CA

Mr Hassall was an unemployed claimant. Prior to his accident he had been in receipt of unemployment benefit. Following his accident Mr Hassall continued to claim benefit but the basis upon which his benefits were paid changed. Now the benefits were paid as a consequence of his accident, not his unemployment. It was accepted that Mr Hassall would have remained unemployed irrespective of the accident.

The claimant accepted settlement of £25,000 for general damages. Upon settlement the Secretary of State demanded recoupment of £7,500 representing the benefits paid to Mr Hassall between the date of the accident and the date of settlement. The claimant challenged this recoupment to the Court of Appeal.

HELD, ON APPEAL: The benefit was clearly paid as a direct consequence of the accident. The position Mr Hassall found himself in was unfair but that unfairness stemmed not from the operation of Part IV of the Social Security Administration Act 1992 but from the failure of the claimant's solicitors in the original action to include a claim for the loss on non-recoupable benefits. The mere fact that there is a change in the basis on which a claimant is receiving benefit before and after an accident, or that a claimant would have received a different benefit even had the accident not occurred does not render benefit irrecoverable.

Note—This was a decision of the Court of Appeal relating to the old Act. The jurisdiction of the appeals service has been considered further in the cases below.

[36.173] McClelland v William Rodgers & Bodel Distributors Ltd
(C6/99 CRS)

A certificate of recoverable benefit showed income support received since the accident as a repayable benefit. The claimant had been in receipt of income support prior to the accident. There was no claim for loss of earnings and the medical evidence suggested a full recovery within 18 months of the accident. The insurer applied for a review and subsequently appealed the certificate. The tribunal found that they could not interfere with the decision of the earlier social security appeals tribunal which had allowed the claimant's income support to continue on the basis of inability to work. The matter was referred to the Northern Ireland Court of Appeal.

HELD: There is no public policy reason why the tribunal should not come to a different decision from the social security appeals tribunal. The tribunal is not bound to follow the decision of any court in a compensation claim although this is a relevant factor. A decision about recoupment of benefits does not mean that a prior award of benefits was necessarily wrong.

[36.174] Secretary of State for Social Security v Oldham MBC and Others
(CCR/6524/1999)

The claimant injured his back following a fall. He was paid £33,904 in benefits throughout the 5-year 'relevant period' for statutory sick pay, invalidity benefit, incapacity benefit, disablement pension and mobility allowance. The compensator settled the claim and appealed the certificate on the grounds that the medical evidence indicated that the claimant's disability due to the accident was limited to 12 months. The medical appeal tribunal agreed that the claimant's ongoing incapacity was due to an unrelated disc hernia and reassessed the benefits at £4,289. The Secretary of State appealed. This was one of four lead cases heard at a special tribunal of the Social Security Commissioners on 15 May 2001. The cases were heard together because they all raised the question whether, on an appeal under s 11 of the 1997 Act, a tribunal is entitled to reach a decision that implies that benefit was wrongly awarded to a victim of the relevant accident, injury or disease.

HELD: It could not have been the intention of Parliament to require compensators to reimburse the Secretary of State for benefits mistakenly paid. That would be unjust. In deciding whether payments were made 'otherwise than in respect of the accident, injury or disease in question' a tribunal is entitled to reach a conclusion that is inconsistent with the award of benefits. Such a decision does not actually affect the award of benefits but it is plainly open to the Secretary of State to consider, in the light of it, whether an award should be revised.

[36.175]

General principles established from decisions of Social Security Commissioners concerning benefits paid otherwise than in respect of the accident are as follows:

(1)   If a claimant is rendered permanently incapable of work by an accident and then suffers from a an unrelated illness which would have rendered him incapable of work even if the accident had not occurred, the claimant is still to be regarded as incapable of work in consequence of the accident. For benefits to be recoverable, the injury or disease need not be the sole (or even the main) cause of the claimant's incapacity. However, it must be 'an effective cause' of the payment of benefit: CCR/5336/95; CCR/4307/2000.

(2)   Separate causes of the payment of benefit (whether pre-dating or post-dating the relevant accident, and whether arising naturally or as a result of another incident) must necessitate the payment of benefit irrespective of the effects of the accident if the benefit is to be irrecoverable: CCR/3482/2000; R(CR) 2/04.

(3)   If the claimant receives different benefits but some are not paid in respect of the relevant injury or disease, those benefits will not be recoverable: R(CR) 3/03.

(4)   If neither the accident nor the other factors would have caused the payment of benefit of themselves but cause the benefit to be paid in combination, the benefit is recoverable: CCR 2231/2003.

(5)   Benefits are paid 'in respect of' an accident if they are paid as a result of the symptoms resulting from an operation undergone by the claimant in response to the relevant accident: CCR 2046/2002.

(6)   Benefits are paid 'in respect of' an accident if they are paid as a result of psychiatric illness following medical negligence: R(CR)4/03.

(7)   A negligent act may break the causal link between the accident and the payment of benefit: CCR/4037/2000.

(8)   Benefits were not paid 'in respect of' the accident if they should never have been paid at all: R(CR) 1/02.

(9)   If the claimant received benefit at a higher rate than he or she should have done, an appeal can be made against recovery of the excess: R(CR) 1/03.

18.   RECOVERY OF NHS CHARGES

(A)   THE PRINCIPLE

[36.176]   The Road Traffic (NHS Charges) Act 1999 provides a scheme for the recovery of charges in connection with the treatment of road traffic casualties by the National Health Service. An insurer making a compensation payment is liable to pay NHS charges if:

(a)   there has been an injury or death as a result of a road traffic accident;

(b)   a compensation payment is made in respect of that injury or death;

(c)   the traffic casualty has received treatment at a NHS hospital in respect of their injuries.

'Compensation payment' means a payment made by an authorised insurer, the MIB under their agreements or a vehicle owner who has made a deposit or provided security under the RTA provisions.

The scheme covers treatment received in NHS hospitals in England, Scotland and Wales. The Act came into force on 5 April 1999 but the charges apply retrospectively to NHS treatment in respect of accidents which occurred on or after 2 July 1997.

(B)   CHARGES

[36.177]   The revised charges recoverable for NHS treatment are as follows—

Date of accident	Out-patient treatment (£)	In-patient treatment (£ per day)	In-patient maximum (£)
Before 2.7.97	295	435	3,000
On or after 2.7.97	354	435	10,000
On or after 1.1.03	440	541	30,000
On or after 1.4.03	452	556	33,000
On or after 1.4.04	473	582	34,800
On or after 1.4.05	483	593	35,500
On or after 1.4.06	505	620	37,100

NHS charges cannot be offset against any compensation awarded.

Note—The Department of Health plan to expand the scheme for recovery of NHS costs to all cases where personal injury compensation is paid.

(C)   EMERGENCY TREATMENT FEES

[36.178]   Emergency treatment fees are allowed under the Road Traffic Act 1988 but can no longer be claimed by NHS hospitals.

With effect from 5 April 1999 emergency treatment fees can only be claimed by GPs in NHS non-profit making hospitals (ie charitable hospitals).

(D)   MOTOR INSURERS' BUREAU (MIB)

[36.179]

These new charges only apply to MIB claims for accidents occurring on or after 5 April 1999.

(E)   FATALITIES

[36.180]   Any compensation payments made under the Fatal Accidents Act 1976 in respect of deceased road traffic victims will be subject to NHS charges (not benefit recovery). These claims must be notified to the Department for Work and Pensions.

(F)   REVISED PROCEDURES

[36.181]   The CRU1 contains a section on hospital details which must be used by all claim compensators. Since June 2004, all NHS charges certificates issued are valid for the life of the claim. The start date of the certificate is the date of the accident.

(G)   PAYMENT OF NHS CHARGES

[36.182]   Payment must be made in full, taking no account of contributory fault within 14 days of making a compensation payment if a valid certificate is held or 14 days of receiving the certificate.

(H)   EXEMPT PAYMENTS

[36.183]   The inclusion of the words 'by an authorised insurer' in s 1(3)(a) of the Road Traffic (NHS Charges) Act 1999 mean that the NHS charges costs recovery scheme is not invoked where the whole compensation payment is made by the insured party, rather than the insurer, because the payment in settlement of the primary claim falls below the threshold of the excess on the insured's policy. The insurers must prove that a particular case falls into this category and provide a copy of the insurance policy or schedule, a description of the excess level in operation and how it operates and evidence that the compensation payment in settlement of the personal injury claim has been made by a third party and not the insurer.

Those excepted from the requirement to hold compulsory third party insurance do not have to pay NHS charges. The charges will be applicable if the body chooses to purchase insurance.

(I)   APPEALS

[36.184]   An appeal may only be made once final compensation has been paid and full payment of the charges set out in the certificate has been made.

There are three grounds of appeal—

(1)   amount specified on the certificate is incorrect;

(2)   amount on the certificate is not in respect of NHS treatment received at a health service hospital, by their casualty department, for injury;

(2)   no compensation payment for the purposes of triggering NHS recoupment exists.

An appeal must be made within three months of the date on which the compensator makes full payment of the NHS charges.

19.   INTEREST

(A)   THE RULE

[36.185]   *Note*—The reason for awarding interest is because the claimant has been kept out of his money. The court's power to award simple interest on damages is contained in the Supreme Court Act 1981, s 35A and the County Courts Act 1984, s 69. The amount of interest awarded is discretionary. CPR 36.21(2) provides that higher rates of interest may be awarded where the claimant beats an effective Part 36 offer at trial (see para [36.204]).

(I) PERSONAL INJURY CASES

Supreme Court Act 1981, s 35A

[36.186]
35A. Power of High Court to award interest on debts and damages
(1)   Subject to rules of court, in proceedings (whenever instituted) before the High Court for the recovery of a debt or damages there may be included in any sum for which judgment is given simple interest, at such rate as the court thinks fit or as rules of court may provide, on all or any part of the debt or damages in respect of which judgment is given, or payment is made before judgment, for all or any part of the period between the date when the cause of action arose and—
    (a)   in the case of any sum paid before judgment, the date of the payment; and
    (b)   in the case of the sum for which judgment is given, the date of the judgment.
(2)   In relation to a judgment given for damages for personal injuries or death which exceed £200 subsection (1) shall have effect—
    (a)   with the substitution of 'shall be included' for 'may be included'; and
    (b)   with the addition of 'unless the court is satisfied that there are special reasons to the contrary' after 'given', where first occurring.
(3)   Subject to rules of court, where—
    (a)   there are proceedings (whenever instituted) before the High Court for the recovery of a debt; and
    (b)   the defendant pays the whole debt to the claimant (otherwise than in pursuance of a judgment in the proceedings),
the defendant shall be liable to pay the claimant simple interest at such rate as the court thinks fit or as rules of court may provide on all or any part of the debt for all or any part of the period between the date when the cause of action arose and the date of the payment.
(4)   Interest in respect of a debt shall not be awarded under this section for a period during which, for whatever reason, interest on the debt already runs.
(5)   Without prejudice to the generality of section 84, rules of court may provide for a rate of interest by reference to the rate specified in the Judgments Act 1838, section 17 as that section has effect from time to time or by reference to a rate for which any other enactment provides.
(6)   Interest under this section may be calculated at different rates in respect of different periods.
(7)   In this section 'claimant' means the person seeking the debt or damages and 'defendant' means the person from whom the claimant seeks the debt or damages and 'personal injuries' includes any disease and any impairment of a person's physical or mental condition.
(8)   [Bills of Exchange.]

The County Courts Act 1984, s 69 is in similar terms (as is subsection (8) of that section) but not including subsection (5) above.

County Courts Act 1984

[36.187]
69. Power to award interest on debts and damages

(8) In determining whether the amount of any debt or damages exceeds that prescribed by or under any enactment, no account shall be taken of any interest payable by virtue of this section except where express provision to the contrary is made by or under that or any other enactment.

[36.188] Jefford v Gee

[1970] 2 QB 130, [1970] 1 All ER 1202, [1970] 2 WLR 702, 114 Sol Jo 206, CA

The claimant sustained severe injuries by accident on 30 November 1966. At trial on 16 June 1969 the judge awarded special damages (mainly loss of earnings) at £2,131 and general damages at £3,500. On an application for interest under the Law Reform (Miscellaneous Provisions) Act 1934 he allowed no interest on the special damages but awarded 6½% on the general damages from the date of the accident to date of trial.

HELD, ON APPEAL: The principle of the Law Reform (Miscellaneous Provisions) Act 1934 (which is unaltered by the 1969 Act) is that interest should be awarded to a claimant for being kept out of money which ought to have been paid to him. In detail the principles to be applied in a case of personal injury are as follows:

(1) *Special damages* should be dealt with on broad lines. Medical expenses and damage to clothing etc are too small to warrant special calculation. Interest on loss of earnings in principle should be calculated on each week's loss from that week to date of trial but that would mean too much detail. In ordinary cases it would be fair to award interest on the total sum of special damages at half the rate allowed on the other damages.

(2) *Loss of future earnings*: no interest should be awarded.

(3) *Pain and suffering and loss of amenities*: interest should run from the date of service of the writ to the date of trial.

(4) *Fatal Accidents Acts and Law Reform damages*: interest should be awarded from date of service of the writ.

(5) *Rate of interest* should be the rate payable on money in court placed in a short-term investment account. This rate is fixed from time to time by rules made by the Lord Chancellor. Since 1 March 1970 it has been 7%, but over a period which included lower rates a mean or average of the rate obtainable should be taken: in the present case it should be 6%.

(6) *Tax*: the courts should not concern themselves with deduction of tax but merely award a gross sum of interest. The judgment should state the rate of interest and the period for which it is awarded.

(7) *County courts*: the same principles apply.

(8) *Exceptional cases* (eg where a party has been guilty of gross delay) may require the court to depart from the proposals above either in the rate of interest or the period for which it is allowed.

In the present case interest on special damage awarded at 3% from date of accident, on general damages of £2,500 for pain and suffering at 6% from date of service of the writ, on £1,000 general damages for future loss of earnings no interest.

Note—Income tax is not payable on interest awarded on damages for personal injuries (see s 329 of the Income and Corporation Taxes Act 1988).

On making payments into court, interest calculated up to date of payments in should be included if appropriate.

In *Cookson v Knowles* [1977] QB 913, [1977] 2 All ER 820, [1977] 3 WLR 279, 121 Sol Jo 461) Lord Denning in the Court of Appeal said the guideline in *Jefford v Gee* should be changed because of inflation and that no interest should be awarded on the lump sum for pain and suffering and loss of amenities. 'The courts invariably assess the lump sum on the scale for figures current at the date of trial, which is much higher than the figure current at the date of the injury or at the date of the writ. The claimant thus stands to gain by the delay in bringing the case to trial. He ought not to gain still more by having interest from the date of service of the writ.' This dictum was disapproved by the House of Lords in *Pickett v British Rail Engineering* (at para [36.74]). Lord Scarman said it was wrong for two reasons:

(1)   It was a fallacy to say that because the award at trial was greater than it would have been if assessed at the date of service of the writ therefore it was of greater monetary value; the cash awarded was more but its purchasing power was the same or even less.

(2)   The Administration of Justice Act 1969, s 22 made the award of interest mandatory in the absence of special reasons why no interest should be given. Inflation was general to society and was not a special reason.

However, the Court of Appeal has considered the matter again in the following case (at para [36.189]).

[36.189]   Chadwick v Parsons

[1971] 2 Lloyd's Rep 49, (1971) 115 Sol Jo 127, Mars-Jones J; affd [1971] 2 Lloyd's Rep 322, CA

In *Jefford v Gee* (at para [36.188]) the Court of Appeal did contemplate that interest might be awarded from a date earlier than the service of the writ, namely, the date of the letter before action. It may well be that in exceptional cases it would be right for the court to award interest on general damages from a date even earlier than that; for example, in cases where the claimant has not issued proceedings at an earlier date because he has been suffering under some disability, or where the defendant has fraudulently concealed the facts upon which a cause of action might be based.

[36.190]   Slater v Hughes

[1971] 3 All ER 1287, [1971] 1 WLR 1438, 115 Sol Jo 428, CA

The claimant was injured on 23 April 1966. On 7 December 1966 she served a writ on the defendant Hughes who on 29 April 1968 served a third-party notice on Jones. On 31 March 1969 the claimant joined Jones as a defendant. At the trial liability was found against the defendants in the proportions 40% to Hughes 60% to Jones. The judge awarded interest on the general damages against both defendants from the date of service of the writ on Hughes. Jones appealed against the award of interest against him from 7 December 1966, as he had no notice of the proceedings until 29 April 1968 when he was served with the third-party notice.

HELD: The principle as established in *Jefford v Gee* (at para [36.188]) was that interest should be paid to a claimant from the time when the defendant ought to have paid it. It followed that a party ought not to be treated as liable to pay interest until that party received notice of the claim. Interest should be payable by Jones only from 29 April 1968.

[36.191]   Birkett v Hayes

[1982] 2 All ER 710, [1982] 1 WLR 816, 126 Sol Jo 399, CA

The claimant sustained very serious injury in a road accident on 23 February 1975. She issued a writ for damages on 10 May 1976. On 19 January 1981 the judge assessed her damages for pain and suffering and loss of amenities at £30,000. He added £16,000 interest for the period from service of the writ at the rates available on the short-term investment account (STI), reducing the total award by 25% because of her failure to wear a seat belt. The defendant appealed against the amount of interest awarded.

HELD: To award the full rate of interest at the high rates of the STI account on the whole of the award was wrong for the following reasons:
  (1)   the damages were assessed on the value of money at the date of the award, not the date of proceedings;
  (2)   interest on damages was tax free;
  (3)   there may be good reasons for delay in bringing the action on for trial and the defendant should not be penalised by the rate of interest chosen.
Though *Pickett v British Rail Engineering* (at para [36.74]) decided that to award no interest was wrong it was for the court to award it 'at such rate as it thinks fit' (Law Reform (Miscellaneous Provisions) Act 1934) so as to arrive at a final figure which will be fair to both parties. The appropriate rate here was 2%.

[36.192]   Wright v British Railways Board

[1983] 2 AC 773, [1983] 2 All ER 698, [1983] 3 WLR 211, 127 Sol Jo 478, HL

In an action for damages for personal injuries the judge awarded general damages for pain suffering and loss of amenity in the sum of £15,000. In awarding interest on these damages he felt himself bound to follow the guideline in *Birkett v Hayes* (at para [36.191]) and awarded interest at the rate of 2% per annum from the date of service of the writ to the date of judgment.

HELD, ON APPEAL to the House of Lords: Under the 'leap-frog' procedure (Administration of Justice Act 1969, s 13) there were no grounds for holding the guideline of 2% wrong during a period when inflation was proceeding at a very rapid rate. That guideline should continue to be followed for the time being.

[36.193]   Prokop v Department of Health and Social Security

(5 July 1983, unreported), CA

The claimant was injured following accidents at work in 1977. All the special damages had accrued by the end of 1979. The trial judge awarded interest on special damages at the full rate from January 1980.

HELD: The Court of Appeal allowed interest at the full rate. The half rate guidance in *Jefford v Gee* (at para [36.188]) is only applicable to cases where the special damages comprise more or less regular periodical losses which continue to accrue over a period of time.

[36.194]   Dexter v Courtaulds

[1984] 1 All ER 70, [1984] 1 WLR 372, 128 Sol Jo 81, CA

The claimant was awarded damages for personal injury he sustained on 22 August 1977. Trial of his action was not reached until May 1982. His damages included sums for loss of wages for four months in 1977 and six weeks in 1978. Interest on these sums was awarded at only half rate from the date of the accident following the method in *Jefford v Gee* (at para [36.188]). On appeal it was argued on his behalf that as the whole amount of his loss of wages was ascertained as long ago as 1978 he should have interest at the full rate on the loss calculated from the end of each period.

HELD, dismissing the appeal: This was a straightforward case of personal injuries and the *Jefford v Gee* method of awarding half interest on the wage loss from the date of the accident to date of trial was the right one. There may be special circumstances in which the *Jefford v Gee* method would not be fair but this was not such a case. In the case of a high-earning self-employed man for example, off work for three or four months, whose action does not reach trial for four or five years, or where he has paid for an expensive operation out of his own pocket it may be fair to award interest at the full rate but in the generality of cases *Jefford v Gee* should not be departed from. In special cases the claimant claiming full interest should set out the special facts in the claim, so as to enable the defendant to make an appropriate calculation of interest for a payment into court.

Note—The Court of Appeal was not referred to the in the case of *Prokop v Department of Health and Social Security* (at para [36.193] above).

[36.195]   **Thomas v Bunn, Wilson v Graham and Lea v British Aerospace plc**
[1991] 1 AC 362, [1991] 1 All ER 193, HL

The House of Lords was asked to decide the question whether interest on damages awarded pursuant to s 17 of the Judgments Act 1838 should run from the date of the order or judgment on liability (the liability judgment) or from the date when damages were agreed or assessed and final judgment entered for that figure (the damages judgment).

The argument had arisen out of the decision in *Hunt v R N Douglas (Roofing) Ltd* ([1990] 1 AC 398, [1988] 3 All ER 823) which established the principle that interest on awards of costs ran from the date upon which judgment was pronounced and not from the date upon which the taxation of costs was completed thereafter.

HELD: 'I accordingly take the view that the judgment referred to in s 17 of the 1838 Act does not relate to an interlocutory or interim order or judgment establishing any of the defendant's liability. The judgment contemplated by that section is the judgment which quantifies the defendant's liability, the judgment which has been referred to in the course of these appeals as the 'damages judgment' (per Lord Ackner).

[36.196]   **Bristow v Judd**
[1993] PIQR Q117, CA

Interim payments are taken into account when calculating interest on the damages awarded. In this case, the interim payments exceeded the past losses. Until an interim payment is made, the claimant is entitled to claim interest on the full amount payable at half the special account rate. Thereafter, the claimant would be entitled to interest at half the special account rate on the amount of special damages outstanding or such damages that subsequently accrue. Interim payments should first be set off against past losses. Any remaining payments should be set off against general damages.

[36.197] **L (a patient) v Chief Constable of Staffordshire**
[2000] PIQR Q349, CA

The claimant contended that the rate of interest on general damages should be higher than 2% because in *Wells v Wells* [1999] I AC 345, [1998] 3 All ER 481, the discount rate had been set at three per cent for calculating multipliers for future losses and expenses.

HELD: Appeal dismissed. Interest on general damages did not serve the same purpose as the discount rate for multipliers. The former compensated the claimant for being kept out of his money; the latter was part of an actuarial calculation of future loss. There is no compelling case for increasing the rate of interest on general damages above 2%.

(B)   INTEREST ON DAMAGES

[36.198]   *Note*—The Law Reform (Miscellaneous Provisions) Act 1934, s 3 empowers the court to award interest on damages for which judgment is given. This section has been superseded as from 1 April 1983, so far as it applied to the High Court and County Courts, by the Supreme Court Act 1981, s 35A and the County Courts Act 1959, s 97A (now the County Courts Act 1984, s 69) respectively. See para [36.186] and [36.187]. Section 3 of the 1934 Act (including the subsections added by the Administration of Justice Act 1969, s 22) remains in force in respect of other courts of record, e g the Court of Appeal. Except in cases where judgment is given for damages for personal injuries or death exceeding £200, the award of interest is not mandatory but is at the discretion of the court.

[36.199]   **Harbutt's Plasticine v Wayne Tank and Pump Co Ltd**
[1970] I QB 447, [1970] I All ER 225, [1970] 2 WLR 198, 114 Sol Jo 29, CA

The claimant's factory was burned down on 6 February 1963. On 8 November 1968 the defendant was held liable and judgment given against it for £146,581 damages. The claimant applied for interest under the Law Reform (Miscellaneous Provisions) Act 1934. It had received various payments from time to time before trial totalling £143,658 from its insurers who would not be reimbursed. The judge said that in exercising his power to award interest he could not ignore the fact that the claimant had not been kept out of all its money until that date but had had its loss reduced by periodical payments from its insurer. He awarded three years' interest on the whole sum at an agreed rate of 6%.

HELD, ON APPEAL: The judge had applied the right principle but had done so rather unscientifically. The basis of the award of interest is that the defendant has kept the claimant out of his money, but this reasoning does not apply when he had in fact been indemnified by an insurance company. The judge should award interest from the date when the defendant should have paid the money but only on the balance remaining after payment had been received from the insurers.

[36.200]   **Cousins & Co Ltd v D and C Carriers Ltd**
[1971] 2 QB 230, [1971] I All ER 55, [1971] 2 WLR 85, 114 Sol Jo 882, [1970] 2 Lloyd's Rep 397, CA

In an action for damages for loss of goods a claim was made for interest. The Master awarded interest from the date when the claimant would have been paid if the goods had not been lost until the date when its insurer paid it in full the amount of its loss. The claimant appealed. The defendant argued that the point was decided beyond argument by *Harbutt's Plasticine v Wayne Tank and Pump Co Ltd* (at para [36.199]).

HELD: *Harbutt's* case was decided on the basis (not argued) that the interest would be retained by the claimant and not handed over together with the damages to the insurer. In the present case the question had been raised whether interest awarded for the period after the claimant had been indemnified by its insurer could be retained by the claimant or could be claimed by the insurer by subrogation. On the authorities and in particular Brett LJ's wide statement of principle in *Castellain v Preston* [1883] 11 QBD 380, 52 LJQB 366, 49 LT 29, 31 WR 557, CA, any recovery of interest after the date of payment under the policy could be claimed by the insurer. It followed that interest should not be limited to the period up to the date of indemnity.

[36.201]   Vehicle and General Insurance Co Ltd v Christie
[1976] 1 All ER 747, QBD

The claimant claimed from the defendant insurance broker, money received for insurance premiums. After proceedings were started by writ which included a claim for interest the parties agreed in March 1975, that the amounts of premiums due was £314.30. The claimant asked for interest on the agreed amount. The defendant refused arguing that interest was not payable unless there was a judgment. It paid £314.30 into court. The claimant took the action to trial in October 1975.

HELD: The claimant was entitled to interest and should have the costs of the whole action before and after payment in. Lord Denning had said in *Jefford v Gee* (at para [36.188]) that a claimant who thought the amount paid into court was enough would tell the defendant he was disposed to go to trial to collect the interest. He would not have said this if he thought the claimant must necessarily pay all the costs after payment in. The court had discretion as regards costs and where, as here, the parties had come to court on the issue of interest, the amount in court not being in dispute, justice required the discretion to be exercised in the claimant's favour.

Note—See also *Wentworth v Wiltshire County Council* [1993] QB 654, [1993] 2 All ER 256. The issue of interest was dealt with *per curiam*. In this case the claimant was awarded damages for loss of profit, damages for bank interest incurred on his increased overdraft together with interest on both these awards. As the award for interest on the loss of profit claim compensated the claimant for delayed payment of these lost profits and his need to borrow money from the bank in the meantime a further award for damages representing the bank interest amounted to double recovery. Furthermore, the award of interest on the award for bank interest amounted to an award of interest on interest which was contrary to s 35A (1) of the Supreme Court Act 1981 which provides that only simple interest may be awarded.

[36.202]   Metal Box Ltd v Currys Ltd
[1988] 1 All ER 341, [1988] 1 WLR 175, 132 Sol Jo 51, [1987] LS Gaz R 3657, QBD

A fire occurred on or about 1 March 1977 destroying stock worth £456,562 belonging to three claimants. Letters before action were sent on behalf of two of the claimants by loss adjusters in April of 1977 and writs were finally issued in those actions in June of 1981. Agreement on quantum was reached in April 1982 and judgment finally given in May 1986, nine years and two months after the fire. The third claimants issued their writ in February 1983, and served it in February

1984. The defendants argued firstly that interest should not be paid because the stock was not income producing until removed from storage and sold so the loss was the value of the goods alone; secondly, that because these were subrogated actions therefore, in reality, interest was of benefit not to the claimants but only to their insurers; thirdly, there had been unjustifiable delay in prosecuting the claim so that interest, if payable, should be for just four years at the most (the period from service of the writ to judgment was four years seven months in the first two cases and two years three months in the third); and fourthly, that the rate of interest should not be at the commercial rate as this was not a commercial dispute in the strict sense but a dispute between insurers.

HELD: Firstly, there was no authority to say that those who were kept out of the value of a chattel as a result of another's tort were not entitled to interest on that value; secondly, it was plain that in subrogated claims insurers were entitled to reimbursement and interest on the judgment sum; thirdly, there had been unjustifiable delay and the appropriate period for interest in the first two cases was the compromise of seven years but in the third case interest was only payable for the two years and three months from service of the writ; fourthly, the appropriate rate of interest was the commercial rate of 1% over Bank Base Rate.

(C)   PLEADING INTEREST

[36.203]   *Note*—A claim for interest must be specifically pleaded: CPR 16.4(1)(b).

(D)   INTEREST AND PAYMENTS INTO COURT/ PART 36 OFFERS

[36.204]   CPR 36.22 provides:
(1)   Unless–
   (a)   a claimant's Part 36 offer which offers to accept a sum of money; or
   (b)   a Part 36 payment notice,
indicates to the contrary, any such offer or payment will be treated as inclusive of all interest until the last date on which it could be accepted without needing the permission of the court.
(2)   Where a claimant's Part 36 offer or Part 36 payment notice is expressed not to be inclusive of interest, the offer or notice must state –
   (a)   whether interest is offered; and
   (b)   if so, the amount offered, the rate or rates offered and the period or periods for which it is offered.

Note—CPR PD 36.7 provides that unless agreed otherwise, interest accruing up to the date of the acceptance will be paid to the offeror and interest accruing as from the date of acceptance until payment out will be paid to the offeree.

A party accepting money in court and entitled under rules to costs is entitled to interest on costs under s 17 of the Judgments Act 1838, and s 74 of the County Courts Act 1984.

[36.205]   CPR 36.21 provides that the court may order interest at a rate not exceeding 10% above the base rate where the claimant does better than he proposed in his Part 36 offer.

Note—See *Various v Bryn Alyn Community (Holdings) Ltd (In Liquidation)* [2003] EWCA Civ 383, [2003] PIQR P30 where the claimant was awarded 8% cent above base rate pursuant to CPR 36.21(2) from the last day on which the defendant could have accepted the claimants' offer to the date of judgment.

(E)   INTEREST ON INCREASED DAMAGES ON APPEAL

[36.206]   Cook v JL Kier & Co Ltd
[1970] 2 All ER 513, [1970] 1 WLR 774, 114 Sol Jo 207, CA

After being awarded £9,589 damages the claimant appealed. The appeal was reached nearly a year later when the Court of Appeal raised the award to £15,045. The claimant asked for interest on the difference since the original judgment.

HELD: Interest should be awarded on the amount by which the award was increased at 5% but credit was to be given against it for 4% which would automatically be running from the date of the judgment under the Judgments Act 1838.

[36.207]   AC International v Healthcare Productions
[1995] CLY 3892, Hitchin County Court   District Judge Coward

The claimant and defendant were involved in a road traffic accident. The defendant was liable. The cost of repairs to the claimant's vehicle was settled by way of a 'knock-for-knock' agreement between the two insurers. The defendant's insurer paid over to the claimant £1,566.31 in settlement of the uninsured losses.

The defendant refused to pay interest on the uninsured losses on the basis that the matter had settled prior to the issue of proceedings. The claimant refused to accept the payment and returned the cheque to the defendant's insurers and issued proceedings, in effect solely for the interest.

The claimant applied for summary judgment for £1,566.31 plus interest and costs.

HELD: Summary judgment was granted in respect of the uninsured losses but the claimant was only entitled to interest on damages once proceedings had been properly issued. As a payment was made prior to the commencement of proceedings the claimant is not entitled to any interest. The claimant should have accepted the offer and settled when it was made and was unreasonable in rejecting the defendant's insurer cheque. The claimant was not awarded costs.

(F)   ADJOURNMENT AND DELAY

[36.208]   May v A G Bassett & Sons Ltd
(1970) 114 Sol Jo 269   Paull J

The claimant's action for damages under the Fatal Accidents Acts was due to be tried on 7 July 1969 but she asked for an adjournment to which the defendant agreed. She died on 6 September. Her administrator was substituted and the action was heard on 20 March 1970. The defendant opposed an award of interest after 7 July 1969 on the ground that the case would have been heard then but for the claimant's request for the adjournment.

HELD: Award of interest was in the discretion of the judge. The deciding factor here was that the defendant had had the advantage of keeping the money during the period of the adjournment and had drawn interest on it. The claimant should have interest to actual date of trial. There was no principle that interest should cease to be paid because of an adjournment.

[36.209]   Read v Harries

[1993] PIQR Q25

The claim took seven years to come to trial. The claimant was responsible for delays of over three years. During this time, she had failed to provide her solicitors with sufficient information to prepare her claim. The court allowed interest for four of the seven years only. Interest is not recoverable in full if it is established that there has been a gross and unjustifiable delay in prosecuting the claim and bringing the action to trial.

[36.210]   Eagle v Chambers

[2004] EWCA Civ 1033

[2005] 1 All ER 136, [2004] 1 WLR 3081, [2005] PIQR Q2, CA

The claimant was seriously injured in a road traffic accident in June 1989. Quantum was not tried until December 2003. At first instance, the judge took the view that the case should have been tried by the end of 1996 and that seven years of delay was inexcusable. The claimant was kept out of her money by her own advisors who had failed to progress the case. The judge refused to award interest for those seven years. The claimant sought to reduce that period from seven to two years.

HELD: The logic of the judge's ruling was impeccable. His decision was upheld and the appeal dismissed.

Note—See also *Jefford v Gee* (at para [36.188]) and *Nash v Southmead Health Authority* [1993] PIQR Q156.

(G)   RATE OF INTEREST

[36.211]   The rate of interest on general damages for pain, suffering and loss of amenities is at 2% per annum (see *L (a patient) v Chief Constable of Staffordshire* (at para [36.197])).

The rate of interest on special damages is paid at the Special Investment Account Rate which varies from time to time. The Special Investment Account Rate has been 6% since 1 February 2002.

Note—See *Prokop v Department of Health and Social Security* (at para [36.193]), *Jefford v Gee* (at para [36.188]) and *Dexter v Courtaulds* Ltd (at para [36.194]) concerning the application of the full and half rate of the Special Investment Account award.

(H)   INCOME TAX AND INTEREST

[36.212]   Section 751 of the Income Tax (Trading and Other Income) Act 2005 provides that:
(1)   No liability to income tax arises in respect of interest on damages for personal injury or death if—
    (a)   it is included in a sum awarded by a court,
    (b)   it does not relate to the period between the making and satisfaction of the award, and
    (c)   in the case of an award by a court in a country outside the United Kingdom, it is exempt from any charge to tax in that place.
(2)   No liability to income tax arises in respect of interest if—

(a) it is included in a payment in satisfaction of a cause of action (including a payment into court), and

(b) it would fall within subsection (1) if it were included in a sum awarded by a court in respect of a cause of action.

Note—The 2005 Act repealed the Income and Corporation Taxes Act 1988, s 329 and has effect for the 2005–06 tax year and subsequent tax years.

Personal injury includes disease and impairment of a person's physical or mental condition.

20. INFANT DAMAGES

[36.213] *Note*—Where a claim is made by or on behalf of a child, CPR 21.10(1) provides that the approval of the court is required for a binding settlement to be reached – see para [20.2]. The claimant's solicitor will often instruct counsel to provide a written opinion on quantum where court approval is sought.

[36.214] **Gold v Essex County Council**

[1942] 2 KB 293, [1942] 2 All ER 237, 112 LJKB 1, 167 LT 166, 58 TLR 357, 86 Sol Jo 295, CA

Tucker J awarded £125 to an infant aged five, taking into account that the amount would be considerably increased when the time came for it to be handed over. The CA said this was wrong. It held that it ought not to have been taken into account, and awarded £300.

(A) INJURIES TO UNBORN CHILDREN

[36.215] *Note*—The Congenital Disabilities (Civil Liability) Act 1976 which came into force on 22 July 1976, provides for children born with a disability to have a remedy in damages in circumstances specified in the Act where the disability can be proved to result from a wrongful act committed by any person. The sections likely to be relevant to motor claims are the following:

[36.216]
1.   Civil liability to child born disabled
(1)   If a child is born disabled as the result of such an occurrence before its birth as is mentioned in subsection (2) below, and a person (other than the child's own mother) is under this section answerable to the child in respect of the occurrence, the child's disabilities are to be regarded as damage resulting from the wrongful act of that person and actionable accordingly at the suit of the child.
(2)   An occurrence to which this section applies is one which—
(a) affected either parent of the child in his or her ability to have a normal, healthy child; or
(b) affected the mother during her pregnancy, or affected her or the child in the course of its birth, so that the child is born with disabilities which would not otherwise have been present.
(3)   Subject to the following subsections, a person (here referred to as 'the defendant') is answerable to the child if he was liable in tort to the parent or would, if sued in due time, have been so; and it is no answer that there could not have been such liability because the parent suffered no actionable injury, if there was a breach of legal duty which, accompanied by injury, would have given rise to the liability.
(4)   In the case of an occurrence preceding the time of conception, the defendant is not answerable to the child if at that time either or both of the parents knew the risk of their child being born disabled (that is to say, the particular risk created by

the occurrence); but should it be the child's father who is the defendant, this subsection does not apply if he knew of the risk and the mother did not.
...
(6)   Liability to the child under this section may be treated as having been excluded or limited by contract made with the parent affected, to the same extent and subject to the same restrictions as liability in the parent's own case; and a contract term which could have been set up by the defendant in an action by the parent, so as to exclude or limit his liability to him or her, operates in the defendant's favour to the same, but no greater, extent in an action under this section by the child.

(7)   If in the child's action under this section it is shown that the parent affected shared the responsibility for the child being born disabled, the damages are to be reduced to such extent as the court thinks just and equitable having regard to the extent of the parent's responsibility.

[36.217]
2.   Liability of woman driving when pregnant

A woman driving a motor vehicle when she knows (or ought reasonably to know) herself to be pregnant is to be regarded as being under the same duty to take care for the safety of her unborn child as the law imposes on her with respect to the safety of other people; and if in consequence of her breach of that duty her child is born with disabilities which would not otherwise have been present, those disabilities are to be regarded as damage resulting from her wrongful act and actionable accordingly at the suit of the child.

[36.218]
4.   Interpretation and other supplementary provisions

(1)   References in this Act to a child being born disabled or with disabilities are to its being born with any deformity, disease or abnormality, including predisposition (whether or not susceptible of immediate prognosis) to physical or mental defect in the future.

(2)   In this Act—
   (a)   'born' means born alive (the moment of a child's birth being when it first has a life separate from its mother), and 'birth' has a corresponding meaning; and
   (b)   'motor vehicle' means a mechanically propelled vehicle intended or adapted for use on roads.

(3)   Liability to a child under section 1 or 2 of this Act is to be regarded—
   (a)   as respects all its incidents and any matters arising or to arise out of it; and
   (b)   subject to any contrary context or intention, for the purpose of construing references in enactments and documents to personal or bodily injuries and cognate matters,

as liability for personal injuries sustained by the child immediately after its birth.

(4)   No damages shall be recoverable ... in respect of any loss of expectation of life ... unless ... the child lives for at least 48 hours.

(5)   This Act applies in respect of births after (but not before) its passing, and in respect of any such birth it replaces any law in force before its passing, whereby a person could be liable to a child in respect of disabilities with which it might be born; but in section 1(3) of this Act the expression 'liable in tort' does not include any reference to liability by virtue of this Act, or to liability by virtue of any such law.'

The Act binds the Crown and extends to Northern Ireland but not to Scotland.

21.   PROVISIONAL DAMAGES

(A)   THE STATUTORY FRAMEWORK

(I)   SUPREME COURT ACT 1981, S 32A; COUNTY COURTS ACT 1984, S 51

[36.219]   Provisional damages are awarded in an action for damages for personal injury where there is proved or admitted to be a chance that at some definite or indefinite time in the future the injured person will, as a result of the act or omission which gave rise to the cause of action, develop some serious disease or suffer some serious deterioration in his physical or mental condition. CPR 41.2 provides the framework for such damages.

[36.220]
CPR 41.2   Order for an award of provisional damages
(1)   The court may make an order for an award of provisional damages if—
  (a)   the particulars of claim include a claim for provisional damages; and
  (b)   the court is satisfied that SCA s 32A or CCA s 51 applies.
...
(2)   An order for an award of provisional damages—
  (a)   must specify the disease or type of deterioration in respect of which an application may be made at a future date;
  (b)   must specify the period within which such an application may be made; and
  (c)   may be made in respect of more than one disease or type of deterioration and may, in respect of each disease or type of deterioration, specify a different period within which a subsequent application may be made.
(3)   The claimant may make more than one application to extend the period specified under paragraph (2)(b) or (2)(c).

[36.221]
CPR 41.3   Application for further damages
(1)   The claimant may not make an application for further damages after the end of the period specified under CPR 41.2(2), or such period as extended by the court.
(2)   Only one application for further damages may be made in respect of each disease or type of deterioration specified in the award of provisional damages.
...

[36.222]   *Note*—Note the following criteria for provisional damages awards:
(1)   applies only to personal injury claims;
(2)   applies only if a claim for provisional damages is made (it is the claimant's choice);
(3)   the future disease or deterioration must be to the claimant's physical or mental condition. This could even include an injury suffered in a second accident resulting from the injury suffered in the accident for which the defendant is responsible;
(4)   the future disease or deterioration must be 'serious';

(5)   there must be a 'chance' that the future deterioration 'will' be suffered;
(6)   the power to award provisional damages is discretionary.

(II)   DAMAGES ACT 1996

[36.223]
3.   Provisional damages and fatal accident claims
(1)   This section applies to where a person is awarded provisional damages and subsequently dies as a result of the act or omission which gave rise to the cause of action for which the damages were awarded.
(2)   The award of the provisional damages shall not operate as a bar to an action in respect of that person's death under the Fatal Accidents Act 1976.
(3)   Such part (if any) of—
   (a)   the provisional damages; and
   (b)   any further damages awarded to the person in question before his death, as was intended to compensate him for pecuniary loss in a period which in the event falls after his death shall be taken into account in assessing the amount of any loss of support suffered by the person or persons for whose benefit the action under the Fatal Accidents Act 1976 is brought.
(4)   No award of further damages made in respect of that person after his death shall include any amount for loss of income in respect of any period after his death.

Note—See Chapter 37 concerning damages in fatal cases.

(B)   TYPES OF CLAIM WHERE PROVISIONAL DAMAGES ARE TYPICALLY CONSIDERED

[36.224]   *Post-traumatic neurosis.* Where there is a delayed reaction to a psychologically shocking event.
Epilepsy. See, for example, *O'Kennedy v Harris* (9 July 1990, unreported). The risk of epilepsy immediately after the injury was 1.5%. At the date of trial, some 4½ years later, it was 0.25%. Ten years after the accident the risk would be 0.015%. The defendant argued that the risk was so low as not to constitute a 'chance'. The court held that since the consequences of the development of epilepsy could be serious and far-reaching, this percentage sufficed to constitute a 'chance', particularly as the period could be limited to 10 years from the date of the accident.
Meningitis. From a head injury.
Osteoarthritis. See *Allott v CEGB* (19 December 1988, unreported) (a pleural plaques claim which should now be read in the light of *Grieves v FT Everard & Sons Ltd* (at para [36.38]) where the judge said 'I am not very enthusiastic, save in the clearest case – of which there are a number, and of course it is for that reason that provisional damages were introduced – in assessing provisional damages, because judges are experienced in assessing damages in which they have to quantify a risk. If provisional damages were to be generally awarded in cases where there is some orthopaedic injury and a possibility of traumatic arthritis supervening, then there would be an award of provisional damages in almost every case, which (in my view) would be absurd'.
See also *Willson v Ministry of Defence* (at para [36.228]). Compare *Robertson v British Bakeries Ltd* 1991 SLT 434 (a Scottish case). A 44-year-old man suffered a fracture dislocation of his ankle. There remained the future likelihood of osteoarthritis as a result of the injury. The court held that there was a

risk of a serious deterioration in his physical condition and the onset of post-traumatic osteoarthritis was a recognisable threshold for an award of provisional damages.

Provisional damages are not suitable for cases where the prognosis is merely uncertain, for example the claimant has suffered multiple injuries which are only slowly resolving.

(C)   COSTS

[36.225]   The defendant can protect his position on costs by making either or both of:

(a)   a payment into court, on the basis that the court will exercise its discretion to reject the application for provisional damages and instead make a final award;

(b)   a tender offer, on the basis that the court will make a provisional damages award.

[36.226]

CPR 36.7   Offer to settle a claim for provisional damages

(1)   A defendant may make a Part 36 payment in respect of a claim which includes a claim for provisional damages.

(2)   Where he does so, the Part 36 payment notice must specify whether or not the defendant is offering to agree to the making of an award of provisional damages.

(3)   Where the defendant is offering to agree to the making of an award of provisional damages the payment notice must also state—

(a)   that the sum paid into court is in satisfaction of the claim for damages on the assumption that the injured person will not develop the disease or suffer the type of deterioration specified in the notice;

(b)   that the offer is subject to the condition that the claimant must make any claim for further damages within a limited period; and

(c)   what that period is.

[36.227]   If a claimant accepts a 'final' payment into court, he thereby abandons his claim for provisional damages. If he accepts a tender offer, the court must make an award for provisional damages. Clearly acceptance of a 'final' payment into court means that a tender offer cannot be accepted and vice versa.

Generally, the position will be as follows. If a 'final' payment into court is made and the court awards provisional damages, the claimant will be entitled to his costs. If the court rejects provisional damages, but makes a final award in excess of the payment into court, the claimant will be entitled to his costs. If the court rejects a provisional damages award, and makes a final award lower than the amount of the payment into court, the claimant will be ordered to pay the defendant's costs from the date of payment in. If the court makes a provisional damages award but makes an order for provisional damages of an amount less than the tender offer, the claimant will pay the defendant's costs from the date of the offer. However, the court has a wide discretion as to costs and therefore these principles are subject to that discretion and to the circumstances of each case. See Chapter 38 concerning costs.

(D)   THE CASES

[36.228]   Willson v Ministry of Defence
[1991] 1 All ER 638, [1991] ICR 595

The claimant suffered an injury to his left foot at work. He sued his employers seeking provisional damages on the basis that:
- (a)   he would remain prone to further injury as a result of the weakened ankle;
- (b)   the ankle would deteriorate over time as it suffered from degeneration and
- (c)   there was a risk that at some time in the future the claimant would not be able to continue with his chosen alternative employment.

Under the Supreme Court Act 1981, s 32A the court is empowered to make an award of provisional damages where, *inter alia*, there is shown to be: 'a chance that at some time ... in the future' the claimant would 'suffer some serious deterioration in his physical condition' as a result of the defendant's negligence.

HELD: A 'chance' has to be something measurable rather than fanciful. However slim the chances of events numbered (a)–(c) above occurring they were measurable within the meaning of the section.

'Serious deterioration' within the meaning of s 32A of the 1981 Act meant a clear and severable risk rather than any continuing deterioration. Furthermore, it had to be deterioration that was more than ordinary deterioration. Each case depends on its own facts. On the facts of this case, the risk of arthritis developing and that arthritis necessitating surgery did not constitute 'serious deterioration'. The risk of further injury from a fall and the risk of losing alternative employment was speculative and not a risk that could be equated with 'serious degeneration'.

Note—See also *Hurditch v Sheffield Health Authority* [1989] 2 All ER 869 where an agreement between solicitors was construed by the court as an acceptance of an order for provisional damages under RSC Ord 37, r 9.

[36.229]   *Note*—Section 3 of the Damages Act 1996 provides that where a person is awarded provisional damages and subsequently dies as a result of the act or omission which gave rise to the cause of action for which the damages were awarded, the award of provisional damages shall not operate as a bar to an action under the Fatal Accidents Act 1976.

[36.230]   Curi v Colina
(1998) Times, 14 October, CA

The claimant had been injured in a road traffic accident. As a result of the injury it was agreed between the medical experts that her condition would significantly deteriorate within five to seven years. At the time of the trial the claimant was able to work in well-remunerated employment but it was not known whether or not the expected deterioration would prevent her from continuing with this work. The claimant sought an award for provisional damages. The trial judge refused to make an award under this head and the claimant appealed.

HELD, ON APPEAL: An award for provisional damages was appropriate where there was a proved or admitted chance that at some time in the future the injured claimant would develop some serious disease or suffer from serious deterioration in either a mental or physical condition. It must also be the case that:
- (1)   Damages could not be awarded at the trial date for the chance that the disease or deterioration would occur.

(2) Additional damages could be awarded at a future date when and if the disease or deterioration envisaged manifested itself.

The deterioration must be a possibility and not a probability as in this case it would be *possible* to deal with the future complication at trial rather than making a provisional damages award. Furthermore, the chance had to be more than fanciable but less than probable and must be measurable and the disease or deterioration must be such that an award of damages to include or have factored in an amount for '*chance*' would not be adequate to compensate the claimant.

The trial judge had correctly not exercised his discretion to make a provisional damages award and the claimant's appeal on this ground failed.

22. PERIODICAL PAYMENTS

(A) RULE

[36.231] Section 100 of the Courts Act 2003 states:
(1) For section 2 of the Damages Act 1996 (periodical payments by consent) substitute—
2. Periodical payments
(1) A court awarding damages for future pecuniary loss in respect of personal injury—
    (a) may order that damages are wholly or partly to take the form of periodical payments, and:
    (b) shall consider whether to make that order.
(2) A court awarding other damages in respect of personal injury may, if the parties consent, order that damages are wholly or partly to take the form of periodical payments.
(3) A court may not make an order for periodical payments unless satisfied that the continuity of payment under the order is reasonably secure.
Section 2(5)(d) of the 2003 Act states that an order for periodical payments may include provision enabling a party to apply for a variation of provision. Section 2B deals with variation of orders and settlements.

Section 4 of the Damages Act 1996 (as amended by the Courts Act 2003) deals with enhanced protection for periodical payments.

Section 6 of the Damages Act (as amended by the Courts Act 2003) provides that if periodical payments are not paid by way of an annuity but paid by a government department by way of agreement or order then the Crown will guarantee those payments.

(B) BACKGROUND

[36.232] The compensation of future losses by periodical payments as opposed to payment of a lump sum is intended to:
(1) avoid over or under-compensation;
(2) reduce the time and costs involved in argument on life expectancy and obtaining financial advice;
(3) transfer risk from claimants to defendants.
While structured settlements involve the 'top down' view of investing a particular lump sum to obtain regular payments, the 'bottom up' view of periodical payments takes as the starting point the amount of the regular payments.

(C) POWER TO ORDER PERIODICAL PAYMENTS

[36.233] Section 2 of the Damages Act 1996, as amended by s 100 of the Courts Act 2003, gives the court power to order the defendant to make periodical payments in respect of future pecuniary loss. This power came into effect on 1 April 2005 and applies to all claims not finalised before that date.

The power to order periodical payments without the consent of the parties is limited to the award for future pecuniary loss although it is open to the court to make an order for periodical payments on other heads of damage (eg damages for pain, suffering and loss of amenity, or for past loss of earnings) with the consent of the parties.

The courts must consider the use of periodical payments in all claims involving future pecuniary loss, including claims under the Fatal Accidents Act 1976 and the Law Reform (Miscellaneous) Provisions Act 1934.

(D) FACTORS TO BE CONSIDERED

[36.234] The factors to be taken into account by the court when considering whether to order periodical payments are set out in CPR 41 and the associated Practice Direction.

The primary consideration is whether the continuity of any such payments will be reasonably secure. Certain sources are automatically deemed to provide reasonable security pursuant to s 2(4) of the Damages Act 1996 as amended. These include certain classes of liability insurer, government and health service bodies.

Criteria for the security of alternative methods of funding are set out at CPR 41.9(2) and the Practice Direction. If an alternative method of funding is approved by the court, this must be specified in the periodical payments order.

The court will also consider:
(1) what award best meets the claimant's needs;
(2) the amount of the payments, including any reduction for contributory negligence;
(3) the claimant's preference and the reasons for that preference;
(4) the defendant's preference and the reasons for that preference.

(E) INDEXATION

[36.235] Unless otherwise ordered, periodical payments are linked to the retail prices index.

(F) TAXATION

[36.236] Periodical payments to the injured claimant or under the Fatal Accidents Act 1976 are exempt from income tax. If payments continue after the claimant's death, there may be income tax payable depending on the method by which the payments are funded.

(G) ASSIGNMENT

[36.237] Under s 2(6) of the Damages Act 1996 as amended, the claimant may not assign the right to receive periodical payments, or use the right as security for a loan without the permission of the court. The factors for the court to consider on such an application are set out in CPR PD 41.

(H)   PART 36

[36.238]   CPR 36 was amended by the Civil Procedure (Amendment No. 3) Rules 2004 to take offers of periodical payments into account. The lump sum element of any offer should be paid into court, and the details of the periodical payment element set out in accordance with CPR 36.2A(5).

(I)   CONSENT ORDERS

[36.239]   Where a settlement including periodical payments is embodied in a consent order, that order must set out details of the agreement in compliance with CPR 41.8.

(J)   VARIATION

[36.240]   Section 2B of the Damages Act 1996 as amended also gives the Lord Chancellor power to allow the court in certain circumstances to vary an order for periodical payments. That power has been implemented by the Damages (Variation of Periodical Payments) Order 2005 and applies to proceedings issued on or after 1 April 2005.

The courts may now make an order for periodical payments where the claimants can apply for variation on the development of a disease or deterioration related to the act or admission giving rise to liability. The periodical payments may also be varied if there is a significant improvement in condition. The disease, deterioration or improvement must be specified in the original order for periodical payments, and the court may also limit the time for making any application to vary.

Before making a variable order, the court must consider the defendant's suitability to meet varied periodical payments.

The parties must preserve various documents in case an application to vary is made. The types of document required are set out at Art 8 of the 2005 Order.

Evidence in support of an application to vary must be provided in accordance with Art 10 of the 2005 Order, and notice of the application must be given to the defendant and its insurers or defence society (if known).

Further provision for the conduct of such applications is given in Arts 10, 11 and 12 of the 2005 Order.

The power to order variable periodical payments does not alter the power to make an order for provisional damages.

(K)   CASES

[36.241]   **Godbold v Mahmood**
[2005] EWHC 1002 (QB)
[2005] All ER (D) 251 (Apr), QB

The claimant sustained head and orthopaedic injuries in a road traffic accident. He suffered from epilepsy as a result of the head injury. Liability was not in issue. Loss of earnings and care were in dispute, as was life expectancy. Neither party indicated periodical payments were their preferred method of settlement.

HELD: The award for future loss of earnings was to be paid as a lump sum. The future care claim was to be met by retail price index (RPI)-linked periodical payments for life commencing at £50,000 per annum and rising to £61,000 per annum after four years. Periodical payments would be fairer in view of the dispute over life expectancy.

[36.242]   **Walton v Calderdale Healthcare NHS Trust**

[2005] EWHC 1053 (QB)

[2005] All ER (D) 370 (May), QB

The claimant suffered cerebral palsy as a result of perinatal asphyxia. Liability was not in dispute. Quantum was agreed, save for the future care of the claimant from age 19 onwards.

HELD: The future care claim should be paid by way of periodical payments of £50,548 per annum RPI-linked. There would be no reduction for local authority contribution to care costs because the defendant had not discharged the burden of proof in that such contribution would be forthcoming. The claimant preferred periodical payments on the basis of independent financial advice and because of a long life expectancy. The defendant had not opposed an order for periodical payments.

[36.243]   **Thacker v Steeples (1) Motor Insurers' Bureau (2)**

(16 May 2005, unreported)

The claimant sustained brain injury in a motorcycle accident. He became tetraplegic and required 24-hour care. Liability was agreed at 85:15 in the claimant's favour.

Settlement terms agreed by the parties and approved by the court were for a lump sum of £1.3million plus RPI-linked periodical payments of £236,424 per annum for life. The claimant undertook to seek NHS or local authority funding and account to the Motor Insurers' Bureau (MIB) for any such funding.

HELD: The continuity of periodical payments funded by the MIB was reasonably secure although the MIB was not automatically deemed secure by s 2(4) of the Damages Act 1996.

[36.244]   **Daniels v Edge (1) Motor Insurers' Bureau (2)**

(3 June 2005, unreported)

The claimant suffered brain and orthopaedic injuries in a road traffic accident. There was a dispute on contributory negligence and whether the claimant's wife would continue to care for him.

The parties agreed and the court approved a lump sum of £450,000 plus periodical payments of £25,000 per annum increasing to £45,000 per annum after six years and five months.

[36.245]   **Barringer v Ashford & St Peter's Hospitals NHS Trust**

(19 July 2005, unreported)

The claimant suffered cerebral palsy as a result of acute hypoxia during birth. Liability was not in dispute. A lump sum of £1.8 million had been agreed in respect of pain, suffering and loss of amenity, past special damages and some future losses. Life expectancy was disputed.

HELD: In addition to the agreed lump sum, the claimant would receive periodical payments for life commencing at £58,750 per annum to age 12, increasing to £65,000 per annum until he ceased education, and finally increasing to £153,00 per annum.

[36.246]   Dann v Breckman

(15 July 2005, unreported)

The claimant suffered brain injury in a road traffic accident. Liability was agreed at 80:20 in the claimant's favour.

A settlement agreed between the parties and approved by the court consisted of a lump sum of £300,000 for pain, suffering and loss of amenity, past losses and future loss of earnings and pension, plus periodical payments for life of £12,500 per annum RPI-linked. In addition there was a provisional damages order in respect of epilepsy.

[36.247]   Reynolds v Buckingham Hospitals NHS Trust

(3 October 2005, unreported)

The claimant suffered cerebral palsy due to hypoxic brain damage during birth. Breach of duty was disputed. Causation was admitted. The claimant required continuing care from a resident carer.

The parties agreed a lump sum settlement of £1 million reflecting litigation risks. The parties considered, and the court agreed, that periodical payments were not appropriate partly because of the dispute on liability.

[36.248]   Flora v Wakom (Heathrow) Ltd

[2006] EWCA Civ 1103

[2006] NLJR 1289, CA

The claimant had an accident at work and brought a personal injury claim including continuing care. In the statement of case, the claimant sought periodical payments linked to indices other than the RPI. The defendant applied to strike out that part of the statement of case.

HELD: The Court of Appeal held that the court did have the power, pursuant to the Damages Act 1996, s 2(9) to depart from the ordinary position, making periodical payments subject to the RPI as per s 2(8) of the 1996 Act, when the court considered it fair and just in all circumstances. There is no need to show exceptional circumstances. Brooke LJ distinguished between a lump sum and periodical payment award.

[36.249]   YM v Gloucestershire Hospitals NHS Foundation Trust
Kanu v Kings College Hospital Trust

[2006] EWHC 820 (QB)

[2006] All ER (D) 187 (Apr)

The parties sought approval of settlements including periodical payments. The question of whether periodical payments would be secure arose because the first defendants were already or were applying for Foundation Trust status.

HELD: The particular arrangements and form of order provided reasonable security because of the agreements reached between the NHS Trusts, the NHSLA (National Health Service Litigation Authority) and the Secretary of State. A model form of order was provided for future use.

CHAPTER 37

Damages in Fatal Cases

1. BACKGROUND

[37.1]   The Fatal Accidents Act 1976 allows a claim for the benefit of the deceased's dependants and those entitled to an award of bereavement damages. The Law Reform (Miscellaneous Provisions) Act 1934 allows a claim for the benefit of the deceased's estate.

Before 1 January 1983, fatal accident claims were regulated by the provisions of the Fatal Accidents Act 1976. The Administration of Justice Act 1982 then brought into effect a number of important changes to both that Act (which itself consolidated the Fatal Accidents Acts 1846 to 1959) and the Law Reform (Miscellaneous Provisions) Act 1934.

The Fatal Accidents Act 1976 abolished the old common law rule that the death of a person gave no cause of action to others either for mental suffering or material loss. Section 1 gives to a 'dependant' a right of action and an entitlement to recover damages in place of the deceased person provided that the person themselves would have been entitled to pursue an action but for their death.

Similarly, the rule that the wrong done to the deceased himself died with him (*actio personalis moritur cum persona*) was largely overcome by the Law Reform (Miscellaneous Provisions) Act 1934.

The Administration of Justice Act 1982 not only introduced the new ss 1 to 4 of the Fatal Accidents Act 1976, set out below, but also largely overruled the case law which enabled actions to be brought under the Law Reform (Miscellaneous Provisions) Act 1934 for loss of expectation of life and loss of earnings during the 'lost years'. Additionally, damages for loss of income for any period after death can no longer be claimed pursuant to s 4 of the Administration of Justice Act 1982, substituting s 1(2)(a) of the Law Reform (Miscellaneous Provisions) Act 1934.

The new s 1A of the Fatal Accidents Act 1976 extends the category of 'dependants' and introduces a bereavement award (£10,000 for causes of action accruing after 1 April 2002) for a limited class of claimants. The requirement of s 4 of the Act to ignore 'benefits' accruing to the estate as a result of the death has required interpretation and some of the more important cases are discussed below.

Note—See the Law Commission report 'Claims for Wrongful Death' (LC263, 2 November 1999).

(A)   FATAL ACCIDENTS ACT 1976

Fatal Accidents Act 1976, ss 1–4 (as substituted by the *Administration of Justice Act 1982, s 3*)

[37.2]
1.   Right of action for wrongful act causing death
(1)   If death is caused by any wrongful act, neglect or default which is such as would (if death had not ensued) have entitled the person injured to maintain an action and recover damages in respect thereof, the person who would have been liable if death had not ensued shall be liable to an action for damages, notwithstanding the death of the person injured.
(2)   Subject to section 1A(2) below, every such action shall be for the benefit of the dependants of the person ('the deceased') whose death has been so caused.
(3)   In this Act 'dependant' means—
　(a)　the wife or husband or former wife or husband of the deceased;
　(aa)　the civil partner or former civil partner of the deceased;
　(b)　any person who —
　　(i)　was living with the deceased in the same household immediately before the date of the death, and
　　(ii)　had been living with the deceased in the same household for at least two years before that date; and
　　(iii)　was living during the whole of that period as the husband or wife or civil partner of the deceased;
　(c)　any parent or other ascendant of the deceased;
　(d)　any person who was treated by the deceased as his parent;

(e) any child or other descendant of the deceased;

(f) any person (not being a child of the deceased) who, in the case of any marriage to which the deceased was at any time a party, was treated by the deceased as a child of the family in relation to that marriage;

(fa) any person (not being a child of the deceased) who, in the case of any civil partnership in which the deceased was at any time a civil party, was treated by the deceased as a child of the family in relation to that civil partnership;

(g) any person who is, or is the issue of, a brother, sister, uncle or aunt of the deceased.

(4) The reference to the former wife or husband of the deceased in subsection (3)(a) above includes a reference to a person whose marriage to the deceased has been annulled or declared void as well as a person whose marriage to the deceased has been dissolved.

(4A) The reference to the former civil partner of the deceased in subsection (3)(aa) above includes a reference to a person whose civil partnership with the deceased has been annulled as well as a person whose civil partnership with the deceased has been dissolved.

(5) In deducing any relationship for the purposes of subsection (3) above —

(a) any relationship by marriage or civil partnership shall be treated as a relationship by consanguinity, any relationship of the half blood as a relationship of the whole blood, and the stepchild of any person as his child, and

(b) an illegitimate person shall be treated as the legitimate child of his mother and reputed father.

(6) Any reference in this Act to injury includes any disease and any impairment of a person's physical or mental condition.

Note—The Civil Partnership Act 2004 extends the provisions of the Fatal Accidents Act 1976 to include same sex civil partners so that they can claim compensation in the same way as a spouse. The term 'stepchild' at s 1(5)(a) includes relationships arising under the 2004 Act. The 2004 act came into force on 5 December 2005.

See *Kotke v Saffarani* [2005] EWCA Civ 221, [2005] 1 FCR 642 where the Court of Appeal approved the dismissal of a dependency claim on the basis that the dependant had not lived with the deceased for the requisite two years under s 1(3)(b) of the 2004 Act. However, the court recognised that a person may be a member of the household notwithstanding that they have a second house to which they depart temporarily.

[37.3]
1A. Bereavement

(1) An action under this Act may consist of or include a claim for damages for bereavement.

(2) A claim for damages for bereavement shall only be for the benefit—

(a) of the wife or husband or civil partner of the deceased; and

(b) where the deceased was a minor who was never married or a civil partner—

(i) of his parents, if he was legitimate; and

(ii) of his mother, if he was illegitimate.

(3) Subject to subsection (5) below, the sum to be awarded as damages under this section shall be [£10,000].

Note—£3,500 for causes of action between 1 January 1983 and 31 March 1991; £7,500 between 1 April 1991 and 31 March 2002.

(4) Where there is a claim for damages under this section for the benefit of both the parents of the deceased, the sum awarded shall be divided equally between them (subject to any deduction falling to be made in respect of costs not recovered from the defendant).

Note—See para [37.11].

(5)   The Lord Chancellor may by order made by statutory instrument, subject to annulment in pursuance of a resolution of either House of Parliament, amend this section by varying the sum for the time being specified in subsection (3) above.

[37.4]
2.   Persons entitled to bring the action

(1)   The action shall be brought by and in the name of the executor or administrator of the deceased.

(2)   If—

(a)   there is no executor or administrator of the deceased, or

(b)   no action is brought within six months after the death by and in the name of an executor or administrator of the deceased,

the action may be brought by and in the name of all or any of the persons for whose benefit an executor or administrator could have brought it.

(3)   Not more than one action shall lie for and in respect of the same subject matter of complaint.

(4)   The claimant in the action shall be required to deliver to the defendant or his solicitor full particulars of the persons for whom and on whose behalf the action is brought and of the nature of the claim in respect of which damages are sought to be recovered.

[37.5]
3.   Assessment of damages

(1)   In the action such damages, other than damages for bereavement, may be awarded as are proportioned to the injury resulting from the death to the dependants respectively.

(2)   After deducting the costs not recovered from the defendant any amount recovered otherwise than as damages for bereavement shall be divided among the dependants in such shares as may be directed.

(3)   In an action under this Act where there fall to be assessed damages payable to a widow in respect of the death of her husband there shall not be taken into account the re-marriage of the widow or her prospects of re-marriage.

(4)   In an action under this Act where there fall to be assessed damages payable to a person who is a dependant by virtue of section 1(3)(b) above in respect of the death of the person with whom the dependant was living as husband or wife or civil partner there shall be taken into account (together with any other matter that appears to the court to be relevant to the action) the fact that the dependant had no enforceable right to financial support by the deceased as a result of their living together.

(5)   If the dependants have incurred funeral expenses in respect of the deceased, damages may be awarded in respect of those expenses.

(6)   Money paid into court in satisfaction of a cause of action under this Act may be in one sum without specifying any person's share.

[37.6]
4.   Assessment of damages: disregard of benefit

In assessing damages in respect of a person's death in an action under this Act, benefits which have accrued or will or may accrue to any person from his estate or otherwise as a result of his death shall be disregarded.

2.   WHO HAS THE RIGHT OF ACTION?

(A)   LIABILITY TO THE DECEASED

[37.7]   If the deceased settled his own claim during his lifetime then no cause of action accrues to dependants. In *McCann v Sheppard* (at para [35.108]) the question was raised whether in the events which happened in that case, the claimant's widow could have a cause of action under the Fatal Accidents Acts. Lord Denning and James LJ were of the opinion that the wording of s 1 of the Act ' would appear to put an insuperable obstacle in the path of such proceedings'.

[37.8]   Read v Great Eastern Rly Co

(1868) LR 3 QB 555, 9 B & S 714, 37 LJQB 278, 18 LT 822, 33 JP 199, 16 WR 1040

Declaration by claimant as widow of D under Lord Campbell's Act 1846, and Fatal Accidents Act 1864, against a railway company for negligence whereby D, a passenger, was injured, of which injuries he died. Plea, that in the lifetime of D, defendants paid him, and he accepted, a sum of money in full satisfaction and discharge of all the claims and causes of action he had against defendants. Demurrer, on the ground that the accord and satisfaction with D was no accord and satisfaction of the claim arising from his death.

HELD: The cause of action was the defendant's negligence, which had been satisfied in deceased's lifetime, and the death of D did not create a fresh cause of action. Nor will there be an award of damages when the deceased obtained Judgment in his lifetime (*Murray v Shuter* [1972] 1 Lloyd's Rep 6, CA).

The Limitation Act 1980, s 12 provides that no action lies under the Fatal Accidents Act where the injured person could no longer maintain an action but otherwise an action is to be brought under the Fatal Accidents Act within three years of the date of death or date of knowledge of the person for whose benefit the action is brought, whichever is the later. Section 33 of the Limitation Act 1980 entitles the court to exercise its discretion in certain circumstances.

Although the common law has allowed a defendant to pursue a defence of *volenti* (*Morris v Murray* [1991] 2 QB 6, [1990] 3 All ER 801 and *Pitts v Hunt* [1990] 3 All ER 344) in road traffic cases such a plea is prevented by virtue of s 149 of the Road Traffic Act 1988 (formerly s 148 of the Road Traffic Act 1972).

(B)   AN INDIVIDUAL RIGHT

[37.9]   The Fatal Accidents Act 1976 gives a remedy to an individual and the mere fact one dependant of the deceased is precluded from bringing an action has no effect on any other dependant.

[37.10]   Dodds v Dodds

[1978] QB 543, [1978] 2 All ER 539, [1978] 2 WLR 434, 121 Sol Jo 619   Balcombe J

The administrators of the estate of the deceased claimed damages under the Fatal Accidents Act 1846 on behalf of his son as a dependant. The defendant was the child's mother, the deceased's wife whose negligent driving was the cause of his death. It was conceded that she, though also dependent on the deceased, had no claim. The question was raised whether her negligence affected the claim of the child, the other dependant.

HELD: The negligence of one dependant does not affect the rights of other dependants. The remedy under the Fatal Accidents Act 1846 was given to individuals, not to the dependants as a group.

[37.11]   **Ryan v Ryan**

(17 September 2004, unreported), Birmingham CC

The claimant's 9-year-old son was killed in a car driven by his father, the defendant. The defendant admitted liability for the accident but opposed the mother's bereavement award of £7,500 on the basis that she was only entitled to half the award because the other 'dependant' parent was the tortfeasor.

HELD: The claimant was entitled to the full statutory sum of £7,500 because she had brought the claim for her benefit only. If the defendant (father) had brought a claim for an award, it would have been struck out as he was the tortfeasor. The case of *Cooper v Williams* (at [para 37.12]) provided helpful guidance as it held that a dependant could bring an action for her own benefit and did not have to claim on behalf of other dependants, so long as those dependants knew about the claim and could be joined if they so wished.

Note—The judge found that the case of *Navei v Navei* (1995) CL 1827, where in similar circumstances the judge awarded only half the bereavement award, was wrongly decided.

(C)   ONE ACTION ONLY

[37.12]   **Cooper v Williams**

[1963] 2 QB 567, [1963] 2 All ER 282, [1963] 2 WLR 913, 107 Sol Jo 194, CA

In a road accident on 4 December 1959 caused by the negligence of the defendants a man was killed. He left two dependants: (1) his widow; and (2) an illegitimate daughter aged 10. They instructed separate solicitors to deal with their respective claims under the Fatal Accidents Acts. On 1 March 1960 the daughter by her next friend issued a writ, having reached agreement with the defendants on the amount of damages to be paid to her, subject to the approval of the court. On 18 May an application to approve the settlement was granted by the District Registrar who made an order by consent staying the proceedings except for such steps as may be necessary to enforce the order. The widow's solicitors had been notified by the daughter's solicitors of the application and the Registrar and the defendants also knew of the widow's existence. By virtue of s 3 of the Fatal Accidents Act 1846 'not more than one action shall lie for and in respect of the same subject-matter of complaint'. In July 1961 the widow issued proceedings claiming damages under the Fatal Accidents Acts, but these were met by the defence that only one action was possible and that the daughter's action had barred any further claim. The widow then applied to intervene in the daughter's action and to have the stay set aside.

HELD: A stay of proceedings is not equivalent to a discontinuance or to a judgment. It can be and may be removed if proper grounds are shown. In the circumstances it would lead to a breach of natural justice to allow the consent order to stand and the court could and should set aside the order of the district registrar, remove the stay and allow the widow to intervene in the daughter's action.

[37.13]   **Cachia v Faluyi**

[2001] EWCA Civ 998

[2002] 1 All ER 192, [2001] 1 WLR 1966, [2001] CP Rep 102, [2002] PIQR P39, [2001] 29 LS Gaz R 39, 145 Sol Jo LB 167

On 6 October 1988, M's wife was hit by a car driven by the defendant. She died 12 days later. On 16 October 1991, just within the three-year limitation period, solicitors for M issued a writ claiming damages on behalf of the estate and M's four dependent children under the Fatal Accidents Act 1976. The writ was never served. On 18 April 1997 M instructed new solicitors who issued a new writ on 10 June 1997 and served it ten days later, within the primary limitation period for three of the dependent children. M applied for a declaration that the three youngest children had a right to bring the claim despite the earlier writ. F applied to strike the claim out. Harris J held that s 2(3) of the Fatal Accidents Act 1976,'... not more than one action shall lie for and in respect of the same subject-matter of complaint ...' meant that the 1997 action could not be brought as the 1991 action had been allowed to die. M appealed raising the Human Rights Act 1998.

HELD: Under the Human Rights Act 1998 primary legislation had to be interpreted in a way which was compatible with the European Convention on Human Rights. The European Convention allowed restrictions on the right of access to a court only when the restriction did not impair the essence of the right to access, had a legitimate aim and the means used had to be reasonably proportionate to the aims sought. It was possible to interpret the word 'action' in s 2(3) of the 1976 Act to mean served process so as to give effect to the child dependant's rights under the Convention. Since the 1991 writ had not been served s 2(3) did not prevent the bringing of the 1997 action.

(D) ADOPTED CHILDREN

[37.14] By virtue of the Adoption Act 1976, s 39(2) which provides that 'an adopted child shall be treated in law as if he were not the child of any person other than the adopters or adopter' (adoption is defined by s 38 of the 1976 Act), a right of action accrues to an adopted child as a dependant. When assessing the dependency, account needs to be taken of the adoptive parents' financial standing.

[37.15] Watson (administrators of) v Willmott
[1991] 1 QB 140, [1991] 1 All ER 473

The mother of Thomas Watson, the infant claimant, was killed in a car accident on 9 June 1985. His father committed suicide four months later. Thomas was subsequently adopted by his maternal uncle and his wife who brought proceedings on behalf of Thomas and the estate of his father for damages. The claimant's counsel contended that the cause of the action accrued at the time of the parents death and that the adoption should be ignored in entirety. The defendant argued that the young child's dependency on his parents was extinguished at the date of his adoption, as the Children Act 1975 required him to be treated as if born to the adoptive parents.

Garland J adopting the claimant's alternative submission held that the correct approach was to calculate the infant's pecuniary dependency on his natural father and then deduct the dependency on his adoptive father. He further held that the adoptive mother's services had replaced those of the natural mother and that no loss had followed under that head of the claim as from the date of adoption.

Note—Contrast this case with the others under s 4 of the Fatal Accidents Act 1976 and the requirement to ignore benefits resulting from death.

(E) CHILD EN VENTRE SA MERE

[37.16] An unborn child at the date of death is entitled to claim damages. See also *Lindley v Sharp* (at para [37.18]).

[37.17] The George and Richard
(1871) LR 3 A & E 466, 24 LT 717, 20 WR 245, 1 Asp MLC 50

In a suit for limitation of liability, instituted on behalf of the owners of a brig (lost in a collision), an appearance was entered on behalf of a child of one of the drowned men *en ventre sa mere*. The court reserved leave to the child, *en ventre*, if born within due time, to prefer its claim for damages sustained by the death of its father.

(F) ILLEGITIMATE CHILD DEPENDANT

[37.18] Lindley v Sharp
(1973) 4 Fam Law 90, CA

The claimant, an illegitimate child born on 18 December 1970, sued by his mother as next friend for fatal accident damages for the death of the father, killed in a road accident on 12 August 1970. Paternity was accepted. The deceased was 17 at the time of his death and had not had any steady employment. The judge put a figure of £4 per week on dependency and considered five years' purchase enough.

HELD, ON APPEAL: The question was what would the financial benefit to the claimant have been had the father not been killed? Would he have married the mother? Once paternity was established the mother would have been entitled to mainte-nance whether or not they had married. Five years' purchase was not enough; nine years should have been awarded at £208 a year = £1,872.

[37.19] Manley v Erith Haulage Co Ltd
(10 September 2001, unreported), QBD

On 14 May 1997 the first claimant's husband was killed when a lorry driven by an employee of the defendant collided with his bicycle. An action was brought on behalf of the first claimant and her three children. The deceased was not the fourth claimant's natural father. The fourth claimant lived with the deceased and his family for six months of the year and with his natural father for the remaining six months. For the purposes of the approved out of court settlement the fourth dependant was treated as a child of the family.

3. DAMAGES RECOVERABLE

(A) BEREAVEMENT

[37.20] Section 1A of the Fatal Accidents Act 1976 (see para [37.3]) introduces a new concept of damages for bereavement which, for causes of actions accruing on or after the 1 April 2002, is a fixed award of £10,000. The claimant is entitled to interest on bereavement damages from the date of death to the date of trial or settlement of the action. This head of damage is intended only to benefit those within the statutory definition, namely the deceased's spouse or civil partner and parents (if legitimate or the mother if illegitimate). The Law Commission's report 'Claims for Wrongful Death' (LC263, 2 November 1999) recommended that this be extended to cover children and siblings.

[37.21]   Doleman v Deakin

(1990) Times, 30 January, CA

The fact the injury resulting in death occurred before the deceased had attained the age of 18, did not entitle the parents to recover damages for bereavement if the actual death occurred when he was of majority and unmarried.

[37.22]   Hicks v Chief Constable of South Yorkshire Police

[1992] 2 All ER 65, 8 BMLR 70, HL

Sarah and Victoria Hicks died from asphyxia when they were crushed in the crowd at the Hillsborough Football Stadium. At the time Victoria was aged 15 and the estate was entitled to the bereavement award of £7,500 (Administration of Justice Act 1982). However, the parents' claim for damages for personal injury had been rejected by the trial judge on the basis that the medical evidence given at trial suggested that death was virtually instantaneous.

The House of Lords, dismissing the parents' appeal, commented that damages for negligence were compensatory and not punitive, and whilst fear of death was an understandable emotion, it did not in itself sound in damages so far as the estate of the deceased was concerned.

Note—See *Wheatley v Cunningham* (at para [37.44]) which illustrates the courts' differing approach where the claimant survived the ordeal.

[37.23]   Martin v Grey

(13 May 1998, unreported), QBD

The deceased was killed in a road traffic accident. Her death occurred between decree nisi and absolute. Her husband was entitled to benefit from a bereavement award. He would not have done so had the accident occurred after pronouncement of the decree absolute.

(B)   DEPENDENCY

(I)   GENERALLY

[37.24]   Malyon v Plummer

[1964] 1 QB 330, [1963] 2 All ER 344, [1963] 2 WLR 1213, 107 Sol Jo 270, CA

It has been established, first, that the pecuniary loss to the persons for whose benefit the action is brought is the only damage recoverable, and, secondly, that the pecuniary loss recoverable is limited to the loss of a benefit in money or money's-worth which, if the deceased had survived, would have accrued to a person within the defined relationship to the deceased and would have arisen from that relationship and not otherwise.

The pecuniary loss which the court has to assess is a loss which will be sustained in the future. This involves making an estimate of the benefit in money's worth arising out of the relationship. Because in most cases the most reliable guide as to what would happen in the future if the deceased had lived is what did in fact happen in the past when he was alive, the common and convenient way of making the first estimate where the deceased at the time of his death was the breadwinner of the family is:

(a)   to ascertain what annual benefit in money or money's worth in fact accrued to the person for whom the action is brought from the deceased and arising out of the relationship before the death of the deceased;

(b)   to assess the extent (if any) to which that benefit would be likely to have increased or diminished in value in the future if the deceased had lived;

(c)   to assess the number of years for which that benefit would have been likely to have continued if the deceased had not been killed by the tortious act of the defendant; and

(d)   to apply to the annual benefit, assessed under (a) and (b) and generally called 'the dependency', the appropriate multiplier derived from (c), allowance being made for the present receipt of a capital sum in respect of annual losses which would be sustained in the future.

But the fact that it is convenient to have recourse to the past for guidance as to what would have been likely to happen in a hypothetical future which, owing to the death of the deceased, will never occur, must not blind one to the fact that one is estimating a loss which will be sustained in the future: per Diplock LJ.

Note—See below for deductibility of 'benefits'.

[37.25]   O'Loughlin v Cape Distribution Ltd

[2001] EWCA Civ 178

[2001] PIQR Q8, CA

On 13 May 1995 the claimant's husband died from mesothelioma caused by exposure to asbestos while employed by the defendant. In 1989 the deceased had started a property development business. By 1994 this was the family's sole income. At trial Forbes J awarded damages for loss of dependency on the deceased's flair, experience and business acumen. The award was based on the cost of professional investment advice. The defendant appealed arguing that dependency should have been calculated on the usual basis of determining the likely financial situation if the deceased had lived and subtracting the actual consequences of his death. In that case arguments as to benefits to the dependant resulting from the death could have been brought.

HELD, ON APPEAL: There was no prescribed method for determining non-bereavement damages. The court should use whatever material appears best to fit the facts of the particular case in order to determine the extent of that loss. Where a court is invited to adopt an unusual or unconventional approach the judge should ensure that the conventional approach would not be fairer and stand back from the figure reached and examine whether it fairly reflected the practical realities of the case. The trial judge was entitled to take the approach he did. The judge's approach reflected the views of a reasonable jury seeking to achieve a fair balance between the interests of both sides on the facts of the case.

[37.26]   ATH v MS

[2002] EWCA Civ 792

(2002) 31 LS Gaz R 33, [2002] NLJR 969, CA

The claimants' mother died in a road traffic accident on 22 November 1996. The deceased had four children from a marriage to P, which had ended in divorce. Since

1994 the deceased and her children had received no support from P who was in prison serving four years for attempting to murder the deceased. Following the death, two of the dependent children were cared for by P. At trial HHJ Hutton rejected the defendant's argument that there should be no award for dependency on services and financial support of the mother as P and his wife were unlikely to provide these. He also rejected the defendant's argument that P could not be compensated for discharging his parental obligations. The judge reasoned that:

(a) under the Fatal Accidents Act 1976 the award was made to dependants, not carers;

(b) if the mother had not died P would have provided no services to the dependants so none of the award would be held on trust for P; and

(c) the services and financial support provided by P following the accident were a benefit resulting from the accident and should be disregarded under s 4 of the 1976 Act.

The defendant appealed the findings as to entitlement to dependency, the multiplicand, the deceased's career prospects, the multiplier, the evaluation of the services and services only a mother can provide.

HELD, ON APPEAL: Where children have been cared for solely by their deceased mother and her new partner up until the mother's death and where there was unlikely to have been any future involvement by the father but for the accident, subsequent support provided by the father and his new partner following the accident is a benefit which has accrued as a result of the death and, pursuant to s 4 of the 1976 Act, must be disregarded, both in the assessment of loss and in the calculation of damages. Such damages are intended to reimburse the carer for past and future services and should be held on trust. If the terms of the trust appear unlikely to be fulfilled, the damages should be paid into an account and dealt with as directed by the court.

When calculating the multiplicand, the evidence may justify a departure from the normal approach of ⅔ of the net joint income less the net income of the survivor. However as the children were never likely to have been maintained solely by their deceased mother's income, the multiplicand was reduced from 75% to 60% of her net earnings.

The Court of Appeal would not interfere with the judge's findings on the deceased's prospects of promotion in the absence of contradictory evidence. The judge was wrong to find the dependency would extend beyond the age of 21 given the real possibility that the claimants might not proceed to tertiary education. When calculating the multiplier, the trial judge was wrong to depart from the approach adopted by the House of Lords in *Cookson v Knowles* (at para [37.31]) and *Graham v Dodds* (at para [37.32]). The reasoning of Nelson J in *White v ESAB Group (UK) Ltd* (at para [37.33]) was approved.

The trial judge was entitled to reject the expert evidence of both parties when evaluating the deceased's services but the award of £50,000 was outside the bracket and accordingly reduced to £37,500. The awards for the special services only a mother can provide were outside the normal bracket and therefore reduced from £5,000 and £7,000 to £3,500 and £4,500 respectively.

[37.27] There is now a general tendency to value the dependency by deducting a percentage from the deceased's net income to represent the sums he would have spent on himself.

[37.28]   **Harris v Empress Motors Ltd**

[1983] 3 All ER 561, [1984] I WLR 212, 127 Sol Jo 647, CA

In the course of time the courts have worked out a simple solution to the problem of calculating the net dependency under the Fatal Accidents Acts in cases where the dependants are the wife and children. In times past the calculation called for a tedious inquiry into how much housekeeping money was paid to the wife, who paid how much for the children's shoes etc. This has all been swept away and the modern practice is to deduct a percentage from the net income figure to represent what the deceased would have spent exclusively on himself. The percentages have become conventional in the sense that they are used unless there is striking evidence to make the conventional figure inappropriate because there is no departure from the principle that each case must be decided on its own facts. Where the family unit was husband and wife the conventional figure is 33% and the rationale of this is that broadly speaking the net income was spent as to one-third for the benefit of each and one-third for their joint benefit. Clothing is an example of several benefit, rent an example of joint benefit. No deduction is made in respect of the joint portion because one cannot buy or drive half a motor car. Part of the net income may be spent for the benefit of neither husband nor wife. If the facts are, for example, that out of a net income of £8,000 per annum the deceased was paying £2,000 to a charity, the percentage would be applied to £6,000 and not £8,000. Where there are children the deduction falls to 25%, as was the agreed figure in the *Harris* case: per O'Connor LJ.

Note—See also *Dodds v Dodds* (at para [37.10]) and *Coward v Comex Diving Ltd* (at para [37.37]).

[37.29]   **(1) Farmer (2) Rose (Executors of the Estate of A L Farmer) v (1) Rolls Royce Industrial Power (India) Ltd (2) NEI Clarke Chapman Ltd (3) Babcock International Ltd (4) Mitsui Babcock Energy Ltd**

(26 February 2003, unreported), QBD

The deceased died in 1999 aged 47 from asbestos-induced mesothelioma. The defendants admitted liability and agreed an apportionment between them. The deceased was a successful businessman having sold his interest in his business for over £15 million in 1998. The issues before the court concerned the assessment of damages and in particular, the dependency claims arising from his death. The defendants contended that conventional percentages should be applied to the dependency of 75% (with children) and 67% (without children). The claimant, relying on a detailed analysis by a forensic accountant, submitted a figure of 85%. The purpose of the reduction being to exclude sums which the deceased spent exclusively on himself or on non-dependants.

HELD: The appropriate percentage is a matter of fact. Eighty-five per cent was a reasonable percentage rate of dependency on earnings and capital throughout the period of dependency because this was a high-income family and there were significant savings which benefited the dependants.

(II)   MULTIPLIER AND MULTIPLICAND

[37.30]   Gavin v Wilmot Breeden Ltd

[1973] 3 All ER 935, [1973] 1 WLR 1117, 117 Sol Jo 681, [1973] 2 Lloyd's Rep 501, CA

The claimant and her husband, both aged 19, were married in 1971. A child was born in November; in December, three months after the marriage, the husband was killed. During the three months or so since the marriage they had lived with his parents, paying £6 for accommodation. The husband had been earning £30 per week of which they had put aside £10 per week in a bank account in her name alone. On an appeal against an award of £16,848 made by the judge using an agreed multiplier of 18, the defendant complained that the judge had made no reduction for the £10 weekly savings in determining the widow's dependency at £18 per week.

HELD: If the £10 per week had been spent instead of saved, the standard of living of both spouses would have gone up. Some part of the £10 per week, whether saved or spent, should be regarded as likely to have been spent eventually for the benefit of the husband himself. To that extent the loss was not the widow's. The dependency should be reduced by £3 per week to £15.

[37.31]   Cookson v Knowles

[1979] AC 556, [1978] 2 All ER 604, [1978] 2 WLR 978, 122 Sol Jo 386, [1978] 2 Lloyd's Rep 315, HL

The claimant's husband, aged 49, was killed in a motor accident on 14 December 1973. He was a woodworker earning £1,820 a year. His wife, aged 45, earned £900 a year as a school cleaner but £300 of this was attributable to the help her husband gave her with certain jobs. Without her husband's help she was unable to do the job and gave it up. At the date of the trial, 27 May 1976, her husband's earnings would, but for his death, have been £2,318 a year and hers £1,056 a year. There were three children aged 16, 13 and 12 at the time of their father's death. The Court of Appeal assessed the damages in two parts: the actual pecuniary loss to date of trial and the future pecuniary loss from the date of the trial onwards. Although the widow could not do her former work she still had an earning capacity which should be taken into account. After allowing for this and adding a notional sum of £200 for services rendered by the husband at home dependency was £1,614 a year at the date of death and £1,980 at date of trial. Actual pecuniary loss to date of trial was thus £4,492 plus interest at 4½% (ie half rate) for 2½ years = £4,997 for the first part. A multiplier of 11 less 2½ (number of years from death to date of trial) = 8½ × £1,980 = £16,830 for the second part with no interest. The total award for Fatal Accidents Act damages was £21,827.

HELD, ON APPEAL to the House of Lords: The method adopted by the Court of Appeal was correct:
(1)   In a normal fatal accidents case the damages should be split into two parts, (a) the pecuniary loss which it is estimated the dependants have already sustained from the date of death up to the date of trial, and (b) the pecuniary loss which it is estimated they will sustain from the trial onwards.
(2)   The pre-trial loss is the total of the amounts assumed to have been lost by the claimant for each week between the date of death and the trial, though as a matter of practical convenience it is usual to take the median rate of wages as the basis for the multiplicand.

(3)   Interest on the pre-trial loss should be awarded at half the short term interest rates current during that period.

(4)   For calculating future loss the figure for dependency to be multiplied by a number of years' purchase is to be calculated as at the date of trial.

(5)   The multiplier will be related primarily to the deceased's age and hence to the probable length of his working life at date of death. The figure selected as appropriate is to be reduced by the number of years between the date of death and trial — in this case reducing 11 to 8½.

(6)   No increase in the award should be made to make allowance for inflation. Though the theory that investment in equities would give protection against inflation has been exploded, the high interest rates available from fixed interest securities will give protection to persons not subject to a high rate of income tax when the courts continue to use about the same multiplicand and multiplier as formerly.

(7)   No interest should be awarded on post-trial loss. (8) (Per Lord Salmon): 'In my view it is impossible to lay down any principles of law which will govern the assessment of damages for all time. We can only lay down broad guidelines for assessing damages … where economic factors remain similar to those prevailing.'

Note—See also *Pidduck v Eastern Scottish Omnibuses Ltd* at para [37.83].

[37.32]   Graham v Dodds

[1983] 2 All ER 953, [1983] 1 WLR 808, 147 JP 746, HL

The claimant claimed damages under the Fatal Accidents (Northern Ireland) Order 1977, SI 1977/1251 (NI 18) for the death of her husband at the age of 41 in a road accident. The judge suggested to the jury a figure of £14,400 for loss of dependency up to date of trial and that a reasonable multiplier for calculating future loss might be 11 to 14 years. He also suggested a figure of £4,800 as a figure for the annual loss of dependency after the date of trial. The jury awarded £103,000.

HELD, ON APPEAL to the House of Lords: The award implied an excessively high multiplier in the case of a man 41 years old at the date of death. The gross multiplier should be calculated as from the date of death, not trial. It would be wrong to award a sum for loss up to date of trial and then apply a multiplier for the future as if the deceased had survived to trial. The number of years between death and trial should be deducted from the overall figure for the multiplier before applying it to the estimated future loss of dependency per annum. New trial ordered.

[37.33]   White v ESAB Group (UK) Ltd

[2002] All ER (D) 02 (Jan)

The claimant pursued damages under the Law Reform (Miscellaneous) Provisions Act 1934 and the Fatal Accidents Act 1976 as a result of her husband dying from mesothelioma caused by exposure to asbestos in the course of his employment with the defendant. The issue was whether the multiplier used in assessing future dependency under the 1976 Act should be determined as at the date of death or at the date of trial.

HELD: The Law Commission recommendation that the multiplier ought to be calculated at the date of trial was correct but the court was bound by authority to follow the date of death calculation rule set out in *Cookson v Knowles* (at para [37.31]) and *Graham v Dodds* (at para [37.32]). These decisions were not expressly or implicitly overruled by the decision of the House of Lords in *Wells v Wells* (at para [36.57]).

Note—The claimant submitted that calculating the multiplier from the date of death resulted in under-compensation because the actuarial tables used were adjusted to discount for early receipt. No such early receipt had taken place in respect of pre-trial losses. Despite criticism of this approach, the Court of Appeal followed *White v ESAB Group Ltd* in *H v S* (see para [37.89]).

(III)   WIFE'S INCOME

[37.34]   Whilst a wife's private income is not relevant to assessment of dependency, her earned income is and should be deducted unless the widow only goes out to work after the death.

[37.35]   **Shiels v Cruickshank**
[1953] 1 All ER 874, [1953] 1 WLR 533, 97 Sol Jo 208, HL

The deceased had a salary of £20,000 per annum, of which £17,000 ceased on his death. The widow had a considerable private income.

HELD: The widow's private means could not be taken into account in the assessment of damages.

Note—The House of Lords followed this approach in *Taylor v O'Connor* [1971] AC 115, [1970] 1 All ER 365, [1970] 2 WLR 472, HL.

[37.36]   **Davies v Whiteways Cyder Co Ltd**
[1975] QB 262, [1974] 3 All ER 168, [1974] 3 WLR 597, 118 Sol Jo 792, [1974] 2 Lloyd's Rep 556, [1974] STC 411   O'Connor J

The first claimant's husband, a successful businessman, had over the years made various dispositions of his money for her benefit and that of their son. He was killed in a road accident by negligence of the defendant's driver before the period of seven years had elapsed; as a result nearly £40,000 was brought back for estate duty and £17,000 duty was paid.

HELD: In the claim by the widow and son under the Fatal Accidents Acts, the sum of £17,000 (less £500 to cover the small chance of the deceased's not surviving the remainder of the seven years had the accident not happened) was recoverable from the defendants as damages for the death. It was:
  (1)   a financial loss which the claimants had suffered and would suffer as a result of death, and
  (2)   arose from the relationship of husband and father, and was accordingly within the words of s 2 of the 1846 Act.

[37.37]   **Coward v Comex Houlder Diving Ltd**
(18 July 1988, unreported), CA

Mr Coward worked as a self-employed diver. His wife was a midwife. On 5 November 1983 he died as a result of an accident caused by the defendant's negligence. Much evidence was given about the state of the diving industry and Mr Coward's future prospects within it. The Court of Appeal also considered the effect of the widow's earnings on the multiplicand.

HELD: (1) Following *Higgs v Drinkwater* (at para [37.39]), the court refused to assess the claimant's dependency at 75% despite her evidence that she would have started a family but for the death of her husband. The dependency was assessed at two thirds of the joint net earnings. The court would look at the particular facts of the case. The guidance in *Harris v Empress Motors* (see para [37.25]) may not be appropriate where the claimant herself had a reasonable income. It would be unrealistic to ignore the claimant's continuing earnings. They should be offset against the two thirds of the joint net earnings.

(2)   Whilst the court had discretion to admit new evidence on appeal, in this instance evidence as to Parliament's intention to change to the tax rules was not something which the court would concern itself with, not least of all because there should be finality in litigation. The calculations made at trial and before the announcement of the tax changes would stand.

Note—See also *Crabtree (Administratrix of the Estate of Crabtree) v Wilson* [1993] PIQR Q24 where the Court of Appeal considered *Comex* and held that the widow's earnings were to be taken into account.

(IV)   FUTURE FINANCIAL PROSPECTS

[37.38]   Where there is likely to be a change in the parties' circumstances the court will adjust the multiplicand to take this into account.

[37.39]   Higgs v Drinkwater
[1956] CA Transcript 129A

The husband was 25 years old earning £550 a year as a maintenance assessor with nylon spinners. The wife was aged 33 earning about £800 a year as a lecturer with the local authority. The parties had only been married a year during which they were both working and building up a home, getting furniture and so forth. The widow hoped not to continue her work indefinitely but in a year or two to start a family. At that stage she would have become more dependent on her husband. Approximately £150 to £200 of the husband's earnings was being spent yearly for the wife's advantage.

HELD: The figure of loss of earnings to be taken into account was the £150 to £200, and there was to be added his loss of prospects of promotion and the increased benefit from that to her. The contributory pension scheme would ensure to her benefit as well as to his.

[37.40]   Malone v Rowan
[1984] 3 All ER 402   Russell J

The claimant's husband was killed in a road accident. She was at the time 25 years old and he 27. Her earnings were about £60 per week and his £76 which by the date of trial would have risen to £102. At the date of death the claimant's dependency was 55% of the deceased's earnings. The claimant said in evidence that she had wanted to start a family and would then have given up her job. Her dependency would then have increased (as the judge found) to two-thirds of the deceased's earnings. The judge accepted that she would have become pregnant in the very near future and would have given up her job to look after the children.

HELD: The material facts were indistinguishable from those of *Higgs v Drinkwater* (at para [37.39]). In that case Denning LJ, said it was not right to increase the figure for pecuniary loss because of the possibility of the claimant having a family. 'She had not suffered any financial loss on that account ... We can only award damages for financial loss and she has suffered none through not having a family. On the contrary, she had kept at work earning [her] salary'. The judge reluctantly held that judgment was binding in the present case and the fraction for dependency as at the date of death could not be altered.

[37.41]   Mallett v McMonagle

[1970] AC 166, [1969] 2 All ER 178, [1969] 2 WLR 767, 113 Sol Jo 207, HL

The claimant claimed damages under the Fatal Accidents Acts for herself and her three children aged six, four and two. Her husband was aged 25 at his death in 1964. She was 24. He worked as a machine operator earning a net wage of £12 per week and had for six weeks before his death supplemented his earnings by working as a vocalist in a dance band earning £6 to £10 per week. He gave the claimant about £10 per week from his wages and about £3 10s per week from his earnings with the band. The claimant spent about £3 10s per week on his food leaving a net dependency of about £10 per week. His employers closed down in January 1967, but evidence was given by a man who said he would have employed the deceased as an asphalter at £22 10s per week though this would have called for long hours and much travelling. A jury awarded £21,500 damages.

HELD, ON APPEAL to the House of Lords: The award was so excessive that there must be a new trial. The amount awarded, wisely invested, could without resorting to capital produce an income double the rate of dependency at the time of death. This would not necessarily be wrong in the case of a young man with clear prospects of rising high on the ladder of financial prosperity but this was not such a case; there was no evidence that the deceased was likely to rise high on any ladder to success.

[37.42]   Hodgson v Trapp

[1989] AC 807, [1988] 3 All ER 870, [1988] 3 WLR 1281, [1989] 2 LS Gaz R 36, HL

Note—See summary at para [36.145].

(V)   MARRIAGE BREAKDOWN

[37.43]   Davies v Taylor

[1974] AC 207, [1972] 3 All ER 836, [1972] 3 WLR 801, 116 Sol Jo 864, HL

The claimant and her husband were married in 1955. From December 1966 to February 1968, unknown to her husband she had an adulterous association with a man she met at work. In May 1968 she gave up her job and on the 9 July she left her husband saying she no longer had any feeling for him. She went to live with her parents. Her husband very much wanted her to return to him and begged her to do so. On 31 July he went to her and asked her to return but she told him of her adulterous affair. On 2 August he instructed solicitors to begin divorce proceedings. On 14 August he met the claimant by chance, in the street, told her he had consulted a solicitor but again asked her to return to him; she refused, saying she wanted time to think. Later on the same day he was killed in a motor accident. At the trial of the claimant's claim for damages under the Fatal Accidents Acts the judge said that on the question of dependency the test he had to apply was whether the claimant had discharged the onus of proving that it was more probable than not that there would have been a reconciliation between her and her husband. He said he was not satisfied there was likely to be a reconciliation and that accordingly the claimant had not proved any dependency.

HELD, ON APPEAL to the House of Lords: The judge had applied the wrong test. In this case it had to be decided whether there was a reasonable expectation of a reconciliation, not whether a reconciliation was more likely than not. If, although there was a reasonable expectation, the chance of the reconciliation happening was slight then the damages would be such as would reflect that degree of probability. The claimant's damages would be scaled down as the possibility became progressively more remote. But a mere speculative or fanciful possibility of a reconciliation was not sufficient. On the evidence the judge had rightly decided that there was no likelihood of a reconciliation and the claimant's claim failed. *Taff Vale Rly Co v Jenkins* (at para [37.60]) applied.

[37.44]   Wheatley v Cunningham

[1992] PIQR Q100

Paul Wheatley died on the 21 January 1989, six days after a road traffic accident involving the defendant and his wife Jane in whose car he was a passenger. Jane had discovered the day before the accident that she was pregnant, but she subsequently miscarried. She suffered minimal physical injuries in the accident.

HELD: Tudor Evans J awarded general damages of £10,000 to reflect the psychiatric problems she had encountered after the accident and the 'terrifying circumstances in which the accident occurred on the issue of nervous shock'. The judge dismissed the statistics on divorce (given as 40% of all marriages failing) as speculative.

Note—See *Owen v Martin* (at para [37.45]) where the court took cognizance of those statistics.

[37.45]   Owen v Martin

[1992] PIQR Q151, CA

The claimant widow had twice committed adultery which, in the court's view, tended to suggest that she had little respect for the institution of marriage. The Court of Appeal, taking judicial notice of the statistics of divorce (one in three marriages ending in a decree), reduced the multiplier from 15 to 11 on the basis that the marriage may not have lasted the duration of the joint lives of the claimant and the deceased. Section 3(3) of the Fatal Accidents Act 1976 did not prevent the court from so doing, though it could not take into account the prospect of marriage or actual re-marriage of the widow.

[37.46]   Dalziel and Dalziel v Donald

(4 December 2000, unreported)

On 8 April 1996 the deceased, husband of the first claimant and father to the second, died in a road traffic accident. The deceased had been a soldier since 1988. In December 1995 he was demoted from lance corporal to sapper as a result of disciplinary issues due to his financial problems and was put on a three-month discharge warning. At the time of the accident the deceased was having a long-term affair with S, the pillion passenger on his motorcycle. The motorcycle was defective, uninsured, untaxed and had false plates. The defendant argued that:

(a)   the deceased's recent disciplinary problems put into question his future in the army, and that this should be reflected in the multiplier;

(b)   that the deceased's 'double life' with S meant that he spent less than would be usual on his family, and

(c)   the long-term affair meant that the deceased's marriage was unlikely to have lasted.

HELD: The deceased's affair was unlikely to last as S made clear that had she known he was married she would have ended it. The deceased would have remained in the army and there was a substantial chance that he would have been promoted. The deceased's double-life could not have continued indefinitely and the conventional 75% dependency figure should be adopted. The deceased's income meant that the first claimant would have needed to work, though only on a part-time basis as her first priority was her daughter. A multiplier of 11 was assessed to take into account the chance that the marriage would have failed. No pension dependency was awarded as it was sheer speculation whether, had the deceased lived, there would have been any such dependency.

(VI)   OTHER FACTORS AFFECTING DEPENDENCY

[37.47]   Williamson v John I Thorneycroft & Co
[1940] 2 KB 658, [1940] 4 All ER 61, 110 LJKB 82, CA

An action brought by a widow under the Fatal Accidents and Law Reform Acts. She died before trial. The trial judge ignored the death of the widow before trial.

HELD, by the Court of Appeal: While the damages had to be assessed at the date of the husband's death, the court was entitled to inform its mind of subsequent events throwing light upon the realities of the case, such as the fact that one dependant had only a short tenure of life before her dependence was brought to an end, and that, therefore, only a comparatively small sum ought to have been allowed to the widow under the Fatal Accidents Acts.

[37.48]   Cox v Hockenhull
1999 15 June, CA

At the time of the accident the claimant and his wife were 58 and the claimant was the full-time carer of his disabled wife. They were both fully dependent on state benefits. The claimant was in effect employed by the state to care for his severely disabled wife. The claimant's wife died due to an accident caused by the defendant's negligence.

The claimant claimed for loss of financial dependency. He argued that as a result of his wife's death he no longer received the disability benefits paid to both him and his wife. The claimant was also unlikely to be able to get any other form of gainful employment.

HELD, ON APPEAL: With regards to the Invalid Care Allowance which was paid direct to the claimant, it was held that this sum cannot make up part of the dependency as if the disabled person had been anyone other than his wife, this would not give rise to a compensatable loss. The fact that the relationship of marriage existed was incidental.

The Disability Living Allowance was paid direct to the claimant's wife as the disabled person. This was to be regarded as a source of the claimant's dependency.

It was held that the appropriate apportionment figure should be one half. The judge at first instance had taken two thirds of the relevant income as constituting the dependency. This was too high.

The loss of services figure was held to be £7,500. The claimant's wife was clearly severely disabled and this was not a case where it was possible to quantify the loss of services on the basis of employing a housekeeper or even home help for part of the time.

[37.49]   Burns v Edman

[1970] 2 QB 541, [1970] 1 All ER 886, [1970] 2 WLR 1005, 114 Sol Jo
356   Crichton J

The claimant sued for damages for herself and her four children under the Fatal
Accidents Acts for the death of her husband. He had had no record of honest
employment and no capital assets; he had two convictions for felony. He used to
give the claimant £20 every Friday. The inference was that such support as he gave
came from the proceeds of crime.

HELD: The claimant was not entitled to damages. What each dependant was in effect
saying was 'I have been deprived of my share of other people's goods brought to
me by the deceased dishonestly', and in so far as that was the 'injury' within s 2 of
the Acts it was a *turpi causa* and therefore no action in respect of it could be
maintained.

Note—See *Newman v Folkes* at para [37.51].

[37.50]   Hunter v Butler

[1996] RTR 396, CA

A dependency claim could not be based on undeclared earnings. The deceased had
enjoyed earnings from a part-time job for many years prior to his death but those
sums had not been declared to the Department of Social Security from whom he
continued to receive benefits at the full rate. His widow's claim would therefore fail.

[37.51]   Newman v Folkes

[2002] EWCA Civ 591

[2002] All ER (D) 47 (May), CA

The claimant was seriously injured in a car accident. When assessing damages, the
court had difficultly in ascertaining the claimant's pre-accident earnings because he
had never paid tax and national insurance or kept proper accounts. At first instance,
Garland J. held that this failure did not prevent the claimant from advancing a claim
for loss of earnings although an adjustment would have to be made to take account
of the tax and national insurance that he should have paid. The defendant appealed
against the amount awarded for loss of earnings but did not contend that the
earnings claim should have been disallowed. The Court of Appeal unanimously found
that the claim for loss of earnings 'was little short of scandalous' but said that it was
correct in their view that there had been no appeal against Garland J's finding that
this did not debar the claimant from seeking this loss.

(C)   FUNERAL AND OTHER EXPENSES

[37.52]   *Note*—Section 1(2)(c) of the Law Reform (Miscellaneous Provisions)
Act 1934 allows the deceased's estate to claim funeral expenses. If the expenses are
incurred by a dependant of the deceased rather than by the estate, the dependant may
claim the expenses as part of the fatal accident claim by s 3(5) of the Fatal Accidents
Act. Funeral expenses are not defined in either Act.

[37.53]   Schneider v Eisovitch

[1960] 2 QB 430, [1960] 1 All ER 169

The Court of Appeal held that where services were provided to someone as a result of a tortious action, then reasonable expenses were recoverable as an item of special damage. It was irrelevant that those services were provided on a voluntary basis, if the individual to whom help was given agreed to repay those costs, if awarded. Thus the expenses incurred by the claimant's brother-in-law and his wife in travelling to France to collect the claimant after a road traffic accident were properly included by the claimant in her claim and were recoverable against the tortfeasor.

Note—See also *St George v Turner* (10 May 2002, unreported).

[37.54]   Hart v Griffith-Jones
[1948] 2 All ER 729   Streatfield J

Funeral expenses of a girl aged four included embalming the body.

HELD: Not unreasonable and allowed as part of the funeral expenses. By amendment as an afterthought, a claim for £225 was added for a monument over the grave. Citing *Goldstein v Salvation Army Assurance Society* [1917] 2 KB 291, 86 LJKB 793, 117 LT 63 (per Rowlatt J, that a tombstone was not allowed as a funeral expense for estate duty), the allowance under the Assurance Companies Act 1909, of a stone or tablet on the grave as a reasonable and proper expense in an insurance for funeral expenses including the erection of a tombstone, and the construction of 'funeral expenses' under that Act was irrelevant. The claim for £225 was wholly unreasonable and was disallowed.

[37.55]   The costs of attending an inquest are not damages resulting from the death and were disallowed by Hilbery J in *Gryce v Tuke* at Winchester Assizes on 1 March 1940. However see *Schneider v Eisovitch* [1960] 2 QB 430, [1960] 1 All ER 169, [1960] 2 WLR 169, 104 Sol Jo 89 (at para [37.53]), for travelling expenses.

[37.56]   Stanton v Ewart F Youlden Ltd
[1960] 1 All ER 429, [1960] 1 WLR 543, 104 Sol Jo 368

A claim for funeral expenses included a sum of £194 15s comprising £155 for a marble memorial erected over the grave six months after the death, synagogue fees £34 10s and £5 5s extra letters on the memorial. The claim also included £5 paid to the minister for attending the funeral, £8 for two additional limousine cars at the funeral, and £5 for removing the body to the house (£18 in all).

HELD: (1) The claimant was entitled as executor to recover reasonable expenditure on a gravestone for his wife's grave, and, in the circumstances, an amount of £40 would be included in the damages in respect of the stone.
(2)   The payments, amounting to £18 as specified would also be included as funeral expenses in the damages recoverable by the claimant.

[37.57]   Gammell v Wilson
[1982] AC 27, [1981] 1 All ER 578, [1981] 2 WLR 248, 125 Sol Jo 116, HL

The claimant father sought to recover the cost of a gravestone as part of his deceased son's funeral expenses. Reviewing the case law, the trial judge distilled the principle that 'there is a distinction between a headstone finishing off, describing and marking a grave, which is part of the funeral expense, and a memorial, which is not'. He found that the gravestone was a recoverable funeral expense. The Court of Appeal refused to interfere with the award.

Note—The trial judge referred to the case of *Hart v Griffith-Jones* (at para [37.54]) and noted that the decision there was largely based on the trial judge's distaste for the expensive tombstone which was really an 'after-thought'. He consequently preferred the reasoning in *Stanton v Ewart F Youlden Ltd* (at para [37.56]).

[37.58]   Harding v Scott-Moncrieff

[2004] EWHC 1733 (QB)

[2004] All ER (D) 429 (Jul), QBD

Funeral expenses did not include the expenses of a memorial service, solicitors' fees, accountants' fees and a valuer's report.

(D)   CHILD KILLED – PARENT'S CLAIM

[37.59]   There is little recent authority, but as a general principle damages may be awarded where there is actual financial support being given by a child to his parents or where there is reasonable probability of future pecuniary advantage.

[37.60]   Taff Vale Rly Co v Jenkins

[1913] AC 1, 82 LJKB 49, 107 LT 564, 29 TLR 19, 57 Sol Jo 27, HL

It is not a condition precedent to the maintenance of an action under the Fatal Accidents Act 1846, that the deceased should have been actually earning money or money's worth or contributing to the support of claimant at or before the date of the death, provided that claimant had a reasonable expectation of pecuniary benefit from the continuance of the life. An action was brought by a father under the Fatal Accidents Act 1846, for damages for the loss of a daughter, aged 16, who was killed by the negligence of defendants and it was proved that at the date of her death the deceased, who lived with her parents, was nearing the completion of her apprenticeship as a dressmaker and was likely in the near future to earn a remuneration which might quickly have become substantial.

HELD: There was evidence of damage upon which the jury could reasonably act.

[37.61]   Barnett v Cohen

[1921] 2 KB 461, 90 LJKB 1307, 125 LT 733, 37 TLR 629   McCardie J

In an action under the Fatal Accidents Act 1846, it is not sufficient for a claimant to prove that he has lost, by the death of deceased, a mere speculative possibility of pecuniary benefit. In order to succeed it is necessary for him to show that he has lost a reasonable probability of pecuniary advantage.

The deceased child was four years of age. The boy was subject to all the risks of illness, disease, accident and death. His education and upkeep would have been a substantial burden to the claimant for many years if he had lived. He might or might not have turned out a useful young man. He would not have earned anything until about 16 years of age. He might never have aided his father at all. He might have proved a mere expense. The court could not adequately speculate one way or the other in any event. He would scarcely have been expected to contribute to his father's income, for the claimant even then possessed £1,000 a year by his business and may have increased it further, nor could the son have been expected to do any domestic service. The whole matter was beset with doubts, contingencies and uncertainties.

HELD: Upon the facts the claimant had not proved damage either actual or prospective. His claim was pressed to extinction by the weight of multiplied contingencies. The action therefore failed.

[37.62]   Buckland v Guildford Gas Light and Coke Co

[1949] 1 KB 410, [1948] 2 All ER 1086, 93 Sol Jo 41   Morris J

The deceased was a bright intelligent girl aged 13 who was competent to look after a younger child aged eight. She assisted her parents in the home and it was anticipated that her gifts would later have enabled her to contribute financially as well as by services to the household, subject to the changes and chances that might have affected her and her parents.

   An award for £500 was made under the Fatal Accidents Act.

[37.63]   Dolbey v Goodwin

[1955] 2 All ER 166, [1955] 1 WLR 553, 99 Sol Jo 335, CA

The claimant sought damages under the Fatal Accidents Act following the death of her son, aged 29. At the time of his death, the son was living with his mother and contributing to her support. The defendant appealed against the amount awarded on the ground that it was excessive.

HELD: The Court of Appeal reduced the sum awarded. The trial judge had approached the case as if the son was the husband instead of the son of the mother. The son would probably have married and contributed less to his mother in the future. Unlike a spouse, the son was not under any legal obligation to support his mother.

[37.64]   Wathen v Vernon

[1970] RTR 471, CA

The claimant's son aged 17 was killed by the negligence of the defendant. He was an apprentice at an engineering works who was paying for his upkeep only £3 per week to his parents out of a wage of £6 10s but who would have probably earned upwards of £19 per week at 21 and £26 per week at 25. The claimant, his father, was aged 56: he had suffered a stroke some years earlier and though he had returned to work there was a possibility of a recurrence which would disable him. He had a wife and three other children, two of them grown up. He claimed damages under the Fatal Accidents and Law Reform Acts. The judge, though accepting that the dead boy was a good son who would have helped his parents if there was a recurrence of the claimant's illness, held that the deceased would probably have married within about five years and that the possibility of the claimant's illness recurring within that time was not sufficiently high to justify an award under the Fatal Accidents Acts.

HELD, on the claimant's appeal: *Taff Vale Rly Co v Jenkins* (at para [37.60]) and *Buckland v Guildford Gas Light & Coke Co* (at para [37.62]) were authorities for saying that the court was entitled in proper circumstances to give damages for loss of support where no support had ever been given. Though the chances against the recurrence of the claimant's illness within five years were six to one it was right to make some award to cover the possibility. The award under the Fatal Accidents Act should be one of £500 for the deceased's mother, not the claimant.

Per Widgery LJ: If we had to decide it on the assumption that the father's health was normal ... I would not be able to assent that a case had been made out.

(E)   PARENTS KILLED – CHILD'S CLAIM

[37.65]   Eifert v Holt's Transport Co Ltd
[1951] 2 All ER 655n, 95 Sol Jo 561, CA

The deceased was an electrical engineer aged 28 earning £659 per annum with excellent prospects. His widow was aged 23 and child aged one year. The court made an award of £6,400 under the Fatal Accidents Acts and £350 under the Law Reform Acts.

After hearing counsel for the widow, Barry J apportioned £2,000 to the widow and £4,400 to the child. The defendant appealed and contended the award to the child was excessive and therefore the amount of the total award should be reduced.

HELD: If the total was proper, the defendant should not be concerned with the apportionment between widow and child.

[37.66]   Kassam v Kampala Aerated Water Co Ltd
[1965] 2 All ER 875, [1965] I WLR 668, 109 Sol Jo 291, PC

In an action in Uganda for Fatal Accidents Acts damages the claimants were eight children, aged 3 to 23, of the deceased, a shopkeeper aged about 45. Their mother was also killed in the accident. The judge of first instance awarded £6,000 but did not apportion the sum among the claimants. The Court of Appeal for Eastern Africa reduced the award to £1,795, holding that only four of the children were dependent. The deceased's total annual expenditure on the family had been £572; the court took four-ninths of this (for the four children) and multiplied by 11¼ representing the average dependency in years of these four. The court made deductions to allow for the advantage of having a capital sum and for the estimated value of the acceleration of the children's interests in their father's estate.

The Privy Council considered the award too low. 'Pure arithmetic does not always lead to a just result where there are so many imponderables. The aim in assessing damages in a case such as the present is to estimate the loss of reasonable expectation of pecuniary benefit. This must in most cases be a matter of speculation and may be conjecture. The more usual method of assessing damages is that adopted by the trial judge of estimating the total dependency as a lump sum and thereafter apportioning it among the various dependants. Another method may be to assess each dependency separately. But if the method of assessing the support for each dependant separately leads to a result which is so out of line with what would be a reasonable estimate of the loss of each individual dependant this suggests that some stop in the calculation must be erroneous.' On the evidence there were eight dependants, not four. But the original award of £6,000 was too high because the judge had taken 15 years as the period of dependency, ignoring the fact that not all the children would have been dependant so long. A figure of £3,500 would fairly represent the total loss of dependency among the eight dependants.

[37.67]   Dodds v Dodds
[1978] QB 543, [1978] 2 All ER 539, [1978] 2 WLR 434, 121 Sol Jo
619   Balcombe J

The defendant was driving a car with her husband as a passenger when there was an accident in which he was killed and for which she was wholly to blame. It was conceded that she could make no claim for herself under the Fatal Accidents Acts; the only other dependant was her son, aged eight and a half. The deceased, aged 29 at death and earning £3,000 a year, could reasonably have expected rapid promotion and increases in his earnings had he lived and might by the date of trial have had take-home pay of £4,720 a year. The defendant had trained as a typist after her husband's death and her take-home pay at the time of the trial was £2,080.

HELD: (1) The way to assess the child's loss was to divide up the family expenditure into four columns – items benefiting the father exclusively, items benefiting the mother exclusively, items which benefited the child exclusively and finally those which benefited the whole family (ie rent or mortgage instalments, rates, repairs and decoration of the family house, heating and lighting, telephone, TV, garden, house insurance etc). The sum of columns three and four was the child's dependency.

    (2)   As at the date of trial the child's estimated dependency was £2,750 a year and the combined family income would have been £6,800 a year. Of this the father's contribution would have been £4,720 so that the child's loss of the benefit of his father's income was £1,908 a year.

    (3)   The multiplier should not be reduced by the number of years which had elapsed from death to trial – the judgment in *Cookson v Knowles* (at para [37.31]) must be taken to have been given *per incuriam* on this point – and the multiplier at the date of trial, the child being then 12½, was 5.

    (4)   The pecuniary loss from the death to trial, calculated at £7,628, should be added.

The total award under Fatal Accidents Acts was £17,168.

(F) DAMAGES FOR LOSS OF SERVICES

[37.68] Dependants can claim for the services that the deceased would have provided if the deceased had not died. These may include DIY, gardening and nursing care provided to a sick member of the family. Where the deceased was a parent and non-wage earner, a claim may be made by dependants for the services which they reasonably expected to receive had that parent not died. Such services can be quantified by reference to the commercial cost of employing a nanny or housekeeper or the loss of earnings incurred by a family member who has given up work to look after the children. The courts usually adopt the multiplier/multiplicand approach to calculate the loss. A lump sum (or reduced multiplicand) may be appropriate where there is insufficient evidence to determine the level of services that the deceased would have provided.

(1) WIFE

[37.69] **Berry v Humm & Co**
[1915] 1 KB 627, 84 LJKB 918, 31 TLR 198

The claimant, a workman earning 38s a week, sued the defendants to recover damages for the death of his wife, who was knocked down by a motor taxicab belonging to defendants and instantly killed. The wife had performed the ordinary household duties of a woman in her position, and in consequence of her death the claimant had to employ a housekeeper and to incur extra expenses of management by the housekeeper instead of his deceased wife. The jury assessed the claimant's damages at £50.

HELD: Under Lord Campbell's Act 1846, the damages recoverable in such an action are not limited to the value of money loss, or the money value of things lost, but include the monetary loss incurred by replacing services rendered gratuitously by the deceased where there was a reasonable prospect of their being rendered freely in the future but for the death, and, therefore, the claimant was entitled to recover the damages assessed by the jury.

[37.70]   Burgess v Florence Nightingale Hospital for Gentlewomen

[1955] 1 QB 349, [1955] 1 All ER 511, [1955] 2 WLR 533, 99 Sol Jo 170   Devlin J

The deceased became a dancing partner of the claimant for amateur purposes in 1942. In July 1948, they started dancing professionally. In 1951 she was divorced by her husband. In September 1952, she married the claimant. After the beginning of 1953 they were nearing the peak of professional status. In January 1953, she entered the defendant's hospital and her death resulted from negligent treatment.

The gross income of the claimant, who was 38 years of age, was between £1,000 and £1,250 with prospects of increase by £400 or £500. The deceased was 36. The claimant was unable to obtain a suitable dancing partner and his estimated income was reduced to £600 per annum. The parties had lived in a flat and the deceased had performed the household duties. After her death the claimant had to employ a woman at 25s per week and to have his meals outside. The deceased had contributed towards the household expenses. The rent was £9 13s monthly and there were expenses for gas and electricity. She had also contributed to the school fees of the child of her previous marriage and had spent money on her clothes. The school fees had been reduced by half and the claimant paid them. The wife had paid at least £1 weekly to her widowed mother who was 66 years of age.

The joint ability to earn an income greatly exceeded the ability of either of them individually. The joint earnings were shared and so were the living expenses. The loss to the claimant of his wife as a dancing partner was assessed at £2,500. The other assessments were £1,000 for the loss as wife (services); £1,000 for loss of wife's contribution; £350 for loss by child of wife's payment and prospective assistance; £300 for loss of wife's payment to her mother.

HELD: As to loss of £2,500 as a dancing partner, it is necessary to read some limitations into the rather wide and general wording of the 1846 Act. The loss would fall within the mere wording but the decisions showed that if, eg a servant lost his employment by the death of his employer or of a departmental manager; or a junior partner lost business by the death of a senior partner; there would be no claim under the Act. It makes no difference that the junior partner was a son. The loss would be *qua* junior partner, not *qua* son. The benefit here was as partner and not as wife. The husband and wife relationship was regarded as incidental and superimposed upon their professional partnership. The £2,500 was therefore not recoverable.

Contributions to household expenses: contributions 50 or 100 years ago, where the husband paid all the joint living expenses, and money earnings of the wife were a kind of pin money, do not apply to modern life. The parties were earning equally and contributing equally. No case of mutual dependence of that sort has been cited but there was no difficulty in principle. Where the living expenses are less than twice the expense of each living separately, the benefit which each confers on the other comes within the Fatal Accidents Acts.

[37.71] **Morris v H Rigby (Road Haulage) Ltd**

(1966) 110 Sol Jo 834, CA

The husband, a medical officer earning £2,820 a year, claimed damages under the Fatal Accidents Acts for the death of his wife. He had five children aged two to fifteen years. He arranged for his wife's sister to come to take care of them and do the domestic duties his wife had done, paying her a gross wage of £20 per week. The judge awarded £8,000.

HELD, ON APPEAL: The award was not too high. The claimant was entitled to the reasonable cost of replacing his wife's services: *Berry v Humm & Co* (at para [37.69]). He had acted reasonably in employing his wife's sister at £20 per week.

[37.72] **Hurt v Murphy**

[1971] RTR 186   Talbot J

The claimant was aged 45, his wife 42. On her death he was left with five children aged from 22 to nine. She had fulfilled all the normal tasks of housewife and mother and also earned £3 pw in part-time work. The claimant's house was a council house with only two bedrooms. He had insufficient money to buy a house.

HELD: It would not be proper that the defendant should have to pay for a house big enough to enable the claimant to employ a resident housekeeper. Damages should be based on the cost of a daily help. The hours of domestic help needed would reduce as the children grew older. On a multiplier of nine, the award was £4,118.

[37.73] **Thomas v Kwik Save Stores**

(2000) Times, 27 June, CA

On 29 September the claimant's wife slipped and fell while shopping at the defendant's supermarket. On 21 October 1995, as a result of her injuries, she collapsed and died from a pulmonary embolism. At the time of the accident the claimant had a long history of joint pain caused by osteoarthritis and degenerative changes together with osteoporosis. She also had diabetes, high blood pressure, an excess of fat in her blood, a family history of heart and blood vessel problems as well as signs of mild myocardial fibrosis and moderate atherosclerosis in the cardiovascular system. The deceased's condition would have got worse. She was in receipt of disability living allowance and there was evidence that she spent 20–25 hours a week on household tasks. The judge awarded £50,000 to the claimant for the loss of his wife's services. The defendant appealed, arguing that the judge had failed to take into account the deceased's disabilities and the progressive nature of her condition and that the award effectively constituted an annual figure of £5,000.

HELD: In this case it would be wholly inappropriate to use the multiplier/ multiplicand method of calculating dependency. The services carried out by the deceased were less than would be carried out by a full-time housekeeper. The award of £50,000 valued services at about a quarter to one-third of the value of a full-time housekeeper, which was too high. An appropriate award would be £20,000. General damages were reduced from £5,000 to £2,500.

(II) MOTHER

[37.74]   **Regan v Williamson**

[1976] 2 All ER 241, [1976] I WLR 305, 120 Sol Jo 217   Watkins J

At the time of her death the claimant's wife was 37 years of age. There were four children of the marriage, all boys, aged 13, 10, 7 and 2. The claimant had, after her death, engaged a relative to come in daily, except weekends, to provide meals and look after the boys when he was out at work; he paid her £16 per week and it cost him a further £6.50 per week for her food, journeys to and from home and national insurance stamp. The claimant estimated that his wife had cost him £10 per week to clothe and feed. The defendant contended that the claimant could have found cheaper alternative help.

HELD: Precedent would suggest that the overall figure of dependency for calculation of the claimant's damages under the Fatal Accidents Acts was £22.50 less £10 per week but this would work an injustice. In valuing the loss of the services of a wife and mother the word 'services' in earlier cases had been too narrowly construed. It should include an acknowledgment that she does not work to set hours nor to rule. She may well during those hours give the children instruction on essential matters or on such things as homework. The figure for dependency should be raised from £12.50 to £20 per week and a further £1.50 per week added for her financial contribution to the home had she eventually gone out to work again. The multiplier should be 11 years. Further, it was reasonable for the father to employ the relative to look after the family and pay her the sums of money he did.

[37.75]   **Bailey v Barking and Havering Area Health Authority**

(1978) Times, 22 July

The claimant claimed damages under the Fatal Accidents Acts for the death of his wife. Before her death he was employed as a hospital porter but after her death he gave up work and stayed at home to look after his three daughters. He claimed that damages should be assessed on the basis that he had lost a housekeeper; the wages of a housekeeper were more than the wages of a hospital porter.

HELD: Approaching the matter as a juryman would, it was repugnant that a claimant should make a profit out of the situation. Common sense indicated that a husband should be compensated for his actual loss. That was the measure of the damages.

[37.76]   **Mehmet v Perry**

[1977] 2 All ER 529, QBD

The claimant's wife was killed in September 1973 by the negligence of the defendants. There were five children of the marriage aged, at her death, 14, 11, 7, 6 and 3. The two youngest suffered from a serious hereditary blood disease requiring regular medication and frequent visits to hospital. Because of this the claimant gave up work after his wife's death and devoted himself full time to the care of the family. Between September 1973 and trial in October 1976 his net average loss of earnings was £1,500 a year. His future net loss would be at the rate of £2,000 a year. By the date of trial he had received a total of £4,197 supplementary benefit.

HELD: (1) In the particular circumstances, including the illness of the youngest children it was reasonable for the claimant to have given up work rather than employ a housekeeper and the proper measure of the loss of the general housekeeping services which his wife had undertaken was his net loss of earnings.

(2)   For loss of the personal attention of their mother the children were entitled to an additional award (following *Regan v Williamson* (at para [37.74])) but within modest limits because their father was acting as a full-time housekeeper.

(3)   The claimant was entitled to damages for the loss of his wife's services to himself but the sum should be quite small because he was now rendering services to the family unit as a whole as full-time house-keeper and damages were being assessed under (1) by reference to those services.

(4)   The amount received in supplementary benefit should be deducted from the total. Award for loss of housekeeping services £1,500 x 3 years plus £2,000 x 5 years; £1,500 for children for loss of their mother's care and attention; £3,000 for the claimant's loss of his wife's care and attention divided as to £1,000 for the first 8 years and £2,000 thereafter. After deduction of supplementary benefit, the total award was £14,800.

[37.77]   Spittle v Bunney

[1988] 3 All ER 1031, [1988] 1 WLR 847, [1988] Fam Law 433, CA

At the time of her mother's death Kate Hall was aged 3. Kate was also injured in the same accident and proceedings were brought by her maternal aunt for the benefit of the estate and for Kate herself. The natural father was not a beneficiary of the estate and indeed had left the child to the care of the aunt almost immediately following the death of her mother with whom he had lived prior to the accident. The judge awarded damages for personal injury and for loss of the mother's services. He reduced the award of interest on those damages owing to the unjustifiable delay in prosecuting the action. The defendant appealed on quantum.

HELD, ON APPEAL: (1) It was agreed that an acceptable approach to quantification of the loss suffered by a minor as a result of the mother's death was to look at the costs of hiring a notional nanny. Ultimately the test was a jury one and the judge should stand back and look at the matter as would a jury. In this case the jury would have realised that the child's dependency on a nanny decreased with age and would therefore have reduced the multiplicand in the later years so as to arrive at a lower overall figure.

(2)   The guidelines on rates of interest were well established by the courts and these should be departed from only where there were special reasons particular to the case. In this instance there was nothing to prevent deduction of interest at the full short-term investment rate rather than at a lesser rate where the claimant's advisers had been guilty of an unjustifiable delay in prosecuting the action.

Note—See also *Corbett v Havering and Barking Health Authority* (at para [37.79]) and *Bordin & Anor v St Mary's NHS Trust* (at para [37.80]) where the gross cost of hiring a nanny commercially was reduced by 35%.

[37.78]   Cresswell v Eaton

[1991] 1 All ER 484, [1991] 1 WLR 1113

The three children of the deceased were initially cared for by their grandmother and on her death, by their aunt. The aunt reluctantly left full time employment to care for the children (and her own two) and she sought to recover her lost earnings. Simon Brown J awarded her that loss on the basis that it had been entirely reasonable for her to leave employment, though discounted it by 15% to reflect the fact that the natural mother had been in part-time employment at the date of her death and therefore had provided part-time care. The discount also reflected the diminishing needs of the children with age and the loss of the special qualitative factor of maternal care (see *Regan v Williamson* (at para [37.70])).

Note—The position would be somewhat different if the carer had not lost any income, in which event the notional nanny/housekeeper approach would probably have been followed. See *Spittle v Bunney* (at para [37.77]).

[37.79]   Corbett v Barking, Havering and Brentwood Health Authority

[1991] 2 QB 408, [1991] 1 All ER 498

The mother of an infant claimant died two weeks after giving birth as a result of the negligence of the defendant. The trial of the action took place 11½ years after her death. There was no dispute on liability and the hearing was for the assessment of damages. The court was asked to consider the appropriate multiplier, the multiplicand and to assess interest.

HELD, ON APPEAL: The court would not interfere with the judge's calculation of the multiplicand which had been based on the adjusted net cost of a nanny (following *Spittle v Bunney* (at para [37.77])) and discounted by 50% once the infant attended school at the age of six. Although the starting point was to take the wages of a notional nanny, the assessment of the loss was effectively a jury question and the judge was entitled to stand back and assess the appropriateness of the figures.

By a majority the court held that although the judge was right to calculate the multiplier from the date of the mother's death, he should have adjusted the unexpired portion to take into account that the infant claimant may have gone on to tertiary education and to reflect the fact that the delay in bringing the action to trial had resulted in a multiplier of only six month's future loss even though the child was now only aged 11½.

The judge was entitled to reduce the amount of interest recovered to reflect the delays of prosecuting the action.

[37.80]   Bordin and Another v St Mary's NHS Trust

[2000] Lloyd's Rep Med 287

On 14 May 1995 the deceased, wife of the first claimant and mother to the second, died in the defendant's hospital. The first claimant failed to attend the assessment of damages hearing. The question in issue was whether the second claimant should receive an award for the actual care he had received since his mother's death or the care that she would have provided had she lived. The defendant argued that a broad-brush approach, such as in *Stanley v Saddique* (at para [37.84]) should be applied. A second question was whether carer's travel expenses could be recovered.

HELD: On the wording of the Fatal Accidents Act 1976 it was appropriate to ask what expenses had been incurred to replace the mother's services. It was not appropriate to use a broad-brush approach artificially or arbitrarily and this approach had been used in *Stanley v Saddique* for specific reasons. Travelling expenses could be recovered as they were incurred as part of a necessary replacement of the deceased's services. Gratuitous care provided by the first claimant to the second claimant could be recovered notwithstanding the first claimant's absence from the hearing and the consequent failure of his own claim. These damages are those to which the second claimant is entitled.

4. DEDUCTIONS

(A) BENEFITS TO BE DISREGARDED (SECTION 4)

[37.81]   Both pecuniary and non-pecuniary benefits are to be ignored when assessing the level of dependency. But see Chapter 36 (para [36.162]) concerning social security benefits.

[37.82]   Hay v Hughes
[1975] QB 790, [1975] 1 All ER 257, [1975] 2 WLR 34, 118 Sol Jo 883, [1975] 1 Lloyd's Rep 12, CA

Mr and Mrs Hay, aged 29 and 24, were killed in a road accident. Their children, aged four and a half and two and a half, were then taken by their maternal grandmother, Mrs Toone, into her own home and cared for by her. She did so without thought of being paid and intended to continue to bring them up. Mr Hay was a welder at the time of his death who would, at the date of trial, have been earning £40 per week. Mrs Hay did not work. In assessing damages for the children under the Fatal Accidents Acts the judge adopted a figure of £1,000 per annum as the amount by which they were worse off by the loss of their father and £1,000 per annum by the loss of their mother. The latter figure was based on the assumed cost of providing the housekeeper or nanny. He took a multiplier of 8 and, after deducting £2,500 representing the value of the parents' estates, awarded £16,400 damages. On appeal it was argued for the defendant:

(1)   as the deceased's mother's services had not been replaced, no award for the pecuniary loss of those services should be made;

(2)   the services rendered by Mrs Toone in looking after the children for nothing were 'benefits resulting from the death' and should be taken into account.

HELD: The award was right. On point (1) (above) the fact that a widower decided to manage for himself after the death of his wife would not disentitle him to sue for and recover damages for the pecuniary loss he had nevertheless sustained. Similarly the fact that the orphaned children had not incurred the expense of a housekeeper did not destroy or diminish their right to be compensated. On point (2) it is not possible to discover from the decided cases any established principle to determine whether the benefits conferred by Mrs Toone on the children should be taken into account or not. It was a jury question to which the judge addressed himself and decided in a way which seemed fair, namely, that Mrs Toone's care conferred no benefit which should be taken into account. The principle that the assessed loss of a claimant should be reduced by any pecuniary advantage coming to him by reason of the death has been so seriously eroded by legislation that in the light of history the court should hesitate to extend the principle to classes of benefit not directly covered by binding authority.

[37.83]   Pidduck v Eastern Scottish Omnibuses Ltd

[1989] 2 All ER 261, [1989] I WLR 317, 132 Sol Jo 1593, CA

Upon the death of her husband, two years after retiring from the bank, the claimant received a widow's allowance and a lump sum (payable in the event of death within five years of retiring). The defendant argued at trial that these sums should be deducted from her dependency claim as they were simply extensions of the pension paid to the deceased prior to his death. The claimant contended that they were 'benefits' and were to be ignored in assessing a loss by virtue of s 4 of the Fatal Accidents Act 1976.

HELD: The allowances and the lump sum were benefits and were therefore to be ignored in any calculation of her dependency claim by virtue of s 4, even though this in effect meant that the claimant enjoyed the widow's allowance.

Note—See *Stanley v Saddique* (at para [37.84]).

[37.84]   Stanley v Saddique

[1992] QB 1, [1991] I All ER 529, CA

The infant claimant was brought up by his father and the woman his father married following the death of his natural mother in a road traffic accident when he was aged one. The child enjoyed a stable family life, probably rather more so than had his mother lived. The judge awarded damages having heard evidence about the cost of professional care assistance, though he reduced the overall sum to reflect the decreasing reliance of the child on help and having found that the mother was likely to have returned to part-time employment in any event.

The defendant appealed:

(1)   on the basis that the court was entitled to take into account the care and support provided by the stepmother which was not a benefit to be disregarded by virtue of s 4 of the Fatal Accidents Act 1976;

(2)   that in any event the mother was unreliable, the court having heard that she left her first three children to live with the claimant's father and that even if she had lived she may not have provided services to the child to the age of 18.

HELD, ON APPEAL: The Court of Appeal accepted the defendant's second contention and using the jury approach it took into account the natural mother's limitations and reduced the award accordingly. The multiplier/multiplicand approach was inappropriate because there was a 'lack of steady prospects of support'. However, it was not attracted by the first argument for s 4 was drafted widely enough to require the court to disregard any benefit which may have accrued to the child from the deceased's estate 'or otherwise as a result of the death', both of a pecuniary and non-pecuniary nature.

[37.85]   Hayden v Hayden

[1992] 4 All ER 681, [1992] I WLR 986

Danielle Hayden's mother was killed in a road traffic accident caused as a result of her father's negligent driving. Danielle, suing by her maternal grandmother, recovered damages for the loss of her mother's services, despite the fact that they were largely replaced by her father, the tortfeasor. The judge awarded £20,000 under s 3(1) of the Fatal Accidents Act 1976. The father appealed and his daughter cross-appealed.

HELD, ON APPEAL: The services provided by the father were not benefits within s 4 of the 1976 Act, for they did not accrue as a result of the mother's death (the father simply continuing to discharge his parental responsibilities) and the daughter's cross appeal would be dismissed. The child was entitled to be compensated for the loss she had suffered by the deprivation of her mother's services, at least to the extent to which they had not been replaced by the father. The judge's award was not unreasonable and the Court of Appeal would not interfere.

Per Sir David Croom-Johnson: Valuing a minor's loss by reference to the cost of employing a notional nanny was inappropriate where it was evident from the facts that a nanny would not have been employed and as quantification of damages was ultimately a jury question, where a tortfeasor had made good the [claimant's] loss, he did not need special protection.

Note—McCowan LJ dissenting held that the services provided by the father should be disregarded. See also *R v CICB* (at para [37.87]).

[37.86]   Wood v Bentall Simplex Ltd
[1992] PIQR P332, CA

The dependants inherited a farm following the death of a farmer. Section 4 of the Fatal Accidents Act 1976 (as amended by the Administration of Justice Act 1982) prevented the court from taking into account any benefits accruing to the claimants from the estate irrespective of the source of those benefits. Even if the loss could be compensated for by using another part of the deceased's estate, this was to be ignored. Therefore the deceased's share of the assets of a farming partnership which passed to the widow and the parties children were to be ignored when assessing the loss to the dependants. There would however have been no loss to the dependants if they had inherited a capital asset from which the deceased provided them with an income. In this case, only a small proportion of the deceased's income was derived from the capital asset. The majority came from his labour which was lost following his death.

[37.87]   R v Criminal Injuries Compensation Board, ex parte K (Minors)
[1999] QB 1131, QBD

The deceased mother was murdered by her husband. The panel of the Criminal Injuries Compensation Board (CICB) considered themselves bound by the decision in *Hayden v Hayden* (at para [37.85]) and held that the dependants had suffered no loss of services because those provided by their uncle and aunt were at least as good as those provided by their mother before her death. The Official Solicitor sought guidance as to the correct approach.

HELD: The CICB should follow s 4(1) of the Fatal Accidents Act 1976 and *Stanley v Saddique* (at para [37.84]) and disregard the services provided by the uncle and aunt. *Hayden v Hayden* (at para [37.85]) was distinguished on the basis that the father there was the tortfeasor. He expanded the scope of his parental duties because no one else was available to care for the child.

[37.88]   L (a child) v Barry May Haulage
[2001] All ER (D) 264 (Jul)

The claimant's mother died in a road traffic accident on 11 October 1997. After the accident the claimant went to live with his father. The father had separated from the claimant's mother four years earlier and had provided no financial support. The mother and father were never married. The father was named as guardian in the mother's will. The defendant argued that the claimant had suffered no loss of services as the father now provided these. Furthermore, these services should not be disregarded under the Fatal Accidents Act 1976, s 4 as they did not result from the mother's death.

HELD: But for the accident it is unlikely that the father would have provided any financial support and, in view of his own position, may not have been able to. The claimant had therefore suffered a true loss. Loss of services from the mother was recoverable until the claimant reached 21. Two-thirds dependency was used to the age of 18 and one-half until 21.

[37.89]   H v S

[2002] 3 WLR 1179, CA

The dependants' divorced mother was killed in a road traffic accident. She supported her four children, three of whom were minors, without any financial support from their father. Following the accident, the youngest two children were cared for by their father and his new wife, their stepmother.

HELD, ON APPEAL: The services provided to the children by their father and stepmother following the accident was a benefit which had accrued as a result of the death. As such, those services had to be disregarded. 'However, such damages can only be awarded on the basis that they are used to reimburse the voluntary carer for the services already rendered, and are available to pay for such services in the future.' They are held on trust for the carer.

[37.90]   Roerig v Valiant Trawlers Ltd

[2002] EWCA Civ 21

[2002] 1 All ER 961, [2002] 1 WLR 2304, CA

A Dutchman was killed on an English registered trawler owned by the defendant, an English company. The defendant contended that Dutch law should apply to the claim and that under Dutch law, benefits paid to the deceased's dependants were deductible from any compensation. The claimant dependants lived in Holland and had brought the claim under the Fatal Accidents Act 1976.

HELD: Dutch law did not apply to the claim. The English court was required to implement the provisions of the Fatal Accidents Act 1976, including s.4 by which benefits were to be disregarded in calculating compensation.

[37.91]   McIntyre v Harland & Wolff plc

[2006] EWCA Civ 287

[2006] All ER (D) 406 (Mar), [2006] ICR 1222, [2006] 15 LS Gaz R 23, CA

The deceased's employers contributed to a provident fund scheme which paid out at the termination of the deceased's employment and when the deceased retired from work. The wife brought a dependency claim and sought payment in respect of the retirement clause. The deceased's employers argued that she was not entitled to it because the deceased had already benefited, whilst he was alive, from the payment at the end of his employment with them. In addition the widow had already benefited from that payment and had suffered no loss.

HELD: Damages must put the widow in the same position as she would have been in had the tort not occurred. But for the tort, the deceased would have retired.

Therefore the widow was entitled to the retirement payment as she had lost out on it due to the premature death of her husband. Under s 4 of the Fatal Accidents Act 1976, the payment on termination had to be disregarded.

5. REMARRIAGE

[37.92] *Note*—Both a widower and widow's remarriage and remarriage prospects are to be ignored. The non-deductibility of pecuniary and non-pecuniary benefits pursuant to s 4 of the Fatal Accidents Act 1976 has put widowers on a par with widows whose re-marriage is to be ignored by virtue of s 3(3) of the Fatal Accidents Act 1976.

[37.93]   **Thompson v Price**
[1973] QB 838, [1973] 2 All ER 846, [1973] 2 WLR 1037

As s 4(1) of the Fatal Accident Acts applies to damages 'payable to a widow' the proportion of damages allotted to a child is to be assessed, where the widow had remarried, having regard to that fact.

The deceased died at the age of 24 years. His widow was 22 and child 18 months. His widow remarried two or three months later, the second husband being in as good a financial position as the deceased would have been. The dependency of the widow was assessed at £9 per week with a multiplier of 17 years having regard to ages of deceased and widow. The child was entitled to two years three months at £3 per week (£337.50) rounded up to £500 to allow for his receiving perhaps less from his stepfather than he would from his own father and having to compete with children of second marriage.

Note—A dependant may argue that the income and/or services provided by the stepfather is a benefit which falls to be disregarded. See *Stanley v Saddique* (at para [37.84]).

6. LAW REFORM ACT CLAIMS

(A)   LAW REFORM (MISCELLANEOUS PROVISIONS) ACT 1934, S 1

[37.94]
1.   **Effect of death on certain causes of action**
   (1)   Subject to the provisions of this section, on the death of any person after the commencement of this Act all causes of action subsisting against or vested in him shall survive against, or, as the case may be, for the benefit of, his estate. Provided that this subsection shall not apply to causes of action for defamation.
   (1A)   The right of a person to claim under section 1A of the Fatal Accidents Act 1976 (bereavement) shall not survive for the benefit of his estate on his death.
   (2)   Where a cause of action survives as aforesaid for the benefit of the estate of a deceased person, the damages recoverable for the benefit of the estate of that person—
      (a)   shall not include—
         (i)   any exemplary damages:
         (ii)   any damages for loss of income in respect of any period after that person's death;
      (b)   [...]
      (c)   where the death of that person has been caused by the act or omission which gives rise to the cause of action, shall be calculated without

reference to any loss or gain to his estate consequent on his death, except that a sum in respect of funeral expenses may be included.

(4)   Where damage has been suffered by reason of any act or omission in respect of which a cause of action would have subsisted against any person if that person had not died before or at the same time as the damage was suffered, there shall be deemed, for the purpose of this Act, to have been subsisting against him before his death such cause of action in respect of that act or omission as would have subsisted if he had died after the damage was suffered.

(5)   The rights conferred by this Act for the benefit of the estates of deceased persons shall be in addition to and not in derogation of any rights conferred on the dependants of deceased persons by the Fatal Accidents Acts ...

Note—It will be seen that, taken with the Administration of Justice Act 1982, s 1(1)(a) these changes abolish the right of an estate, first established in *Rose v Ford* [1937] AC 826, HL to recover damages for loss of expectation of life where personal injury has resulted in death. Subsection 2(a)(ii) also renders obsolete cases such as *Kandalla v British Airways* [1981] QB 158, [1980] 1 All ER 341 and *Gammell v Wilson* (at para [37.57]) where damages were awarded for loss of earnings during the years lost by the death.

They do not, of course, affect the right of the estate to recover damages for the injury, pain and suffering inflicted on the deceased and suffered by him between the moment of injury and death; e g the award of £2,000 in *Andrews v Freeborough* (at para [11.2]) or the awards of £20 and £2 in *Rose v Ford* itself. In *Inez Brown v David Robinson and Sentry Service Co* [2004] UKPC 56, the court held that damages for pain, suffering and loss of amenity between the accident and death must be proportionate to the length of time between the accident and death.

In *Gammell v Wilson* it was held, in the House of Lords, that s 1(2)(c) of the 1934 Act was not intended to deprive the estate of the right to recover damages in respect of losses when the right to recover damages was already vested in the deceased immediately before his death.

CHAPTER 38

Costs

1. AFTER THE EVENT (ATE) INSURANCE PREMIUMS

[38.1] Section 29 of the Access to Justice Act 1999 (AJA 1999) states:

'Where in any proceedings a costs order is made in favour of any party who has taken out an insurance policy against the risk of incurring a liability in those proceedings, the costs payable to him may, subject in the case of court proceedings to rules of court, include costs in respect of the premium of the policy.'

[38.2] Callery v Gray
[2002] UKHL 28

[2002] 3 All ER 417, [2002] 1 WLR 2000; affirming [2001] 3 All ER 833, [2001] 4 All ER 1, [2001] 1 WLR 2112, [2001] 1 WLR 2142, HL

The claimant sustained minor injuries when a passenger in a car which was struck side-on by a vehicle driven by the defendant. On the day the letter of claim was sent, the claimant took out an ATE insurance policy with a premium of £367.50, inclusive of insurance premium tax (IPT). The policy covered the opponent's costs and own disbursements up to £100,000. The defendant admitted liability two weeks after the claim was made and the claim settled for £1,500 prior to the issue of proceedings. At the detailed assessment hearing the premium was allowed.

The House of Lords declined to interfere with the decision of the Court of Appeal which therefore stands.

HELD, ON APPEAL: (1) There was jurisdiction under s 29 of AJA 1999 to include in an award of costs an ATE premium paid in respect of a claim settled before proceedings were issued.
- (2) It was reasonable for a claimant to take out ATE cover when he first consulted his solicitor and before it was known whether the defendant was contesting the claim.
- (3) The cover for own disbursements fell within the description 'insurance against the risk of liability' in s 29.
- (4) The amount of the premium was not manifestly disproportionate to the risk and was therefore reasonable.

[38.3] Tilby v Perfect Pizza Ltd
[2002] All ER (D) 72 (Mar)

The claimant sustained a whiplash injury when a vehicle driven by the defendant's employee collided with the rear of her vehicle. Two weeks after the letter of claim the claimant took out an ATE policy with a premium of £367.50 including IPT. The policy covered the opponent's costs and own disbursements and the premium was payable at the conclusion of the case. The claim settled for £2,000 prior to the issue of proceedings.

HELD: (1) ATE insurance was a developing area and there was currently no requirement to pay the premium at the inception of the policy.
- (2) For the purposes of the Consumer Credit Act 1974 (CCA 1974), payment of the premium was not deferred unless it was deferred beyond the conclusion of the case for a significant period.
- (3) The case was not concluded until the conclusion of the costs proceedings.

(4) In the circumstances, the ATE policy was not a credit agreement and not caught by CCA 1974.

[38.4] Re Claims Direct Test Cases

[2003] EWCA Civ 136

[2003] 4 All ER 508

Under the Claims Direct scheme, the claimant agreed to pay a 'premium' of £1,312.50 (£1,250 plus £62.50 IPT) for an insurance policy. The policy provided cover up to £50,000 for both sides' costs and the amount of the premium, plus interest. The premium was broken down as follows:
(1) Underwriters – £202.50 (£140 plus £62.50 IPT);
(2) Commission – £110;
(3) MLSS insurance services – £775;
(4) MLSS retention fund – £225.

HELD, ON APPEAL: (1) The cost of funding litigation was not recoverable between the parties.
(2) Section 29 of AJA 1999 permitted the recovery of payment for insurance against the risk of liability for costs but not collateral benefits.
(3) A reasonable and proportionate premium recoverable under s 29 was £621.13 (underwriters – £451.55, commission – £110, insurance services – £30 plus £29.58 IPT).

[38.5] Pirie v Ayling

SCCO 18 February 2003

The claimant was injured in a road traffic accident. Following the issue of proceedings, the claimant accepted the defendant's Part 36 payment in the sum of £13,000. The claimant's costs included an ATE premium of £2,600, 20% of the damages.

HELD: (1) The agreement for the insurance premium to be 20% of any damages was not champertous because there was no danger of the insurer being tempted to interfere in the litigation for personal gain. Further, there was no opportunity for the insurer to act otherwise than as the risk bearer.
(2) The premium was however unreasonable for a simple road accident case and £367.50 including IPT was allowed.

[38.6] Sarwar v Alam

[2003] All ER (D) 162 (Sep)

The claimant was injured in a relatively minor road traffic accident which settled for £2,250. The issue of the enforceability of the claimant's conditional fee agreement reached the Court of Appeal where the claimant was successful (see para [38.37]). The claimant then served a bill of costs which included an ATE premium for the Court of Appeal hearing in the sum of £62,500.

HELD: (1) Although the claimant's solicitors paid the whole premium out of their own funds, the claimant remained liable for the premium and accordingly there was no breach of the indemnity principle.
(2) Solicitors were not to be condemned for financing their potentially impecunious client's litigation therefore there was nothing improper in the solicitors paying the premium.

(3)   The solicitors attempted unsuccessfully to obtain an alternative quotation in a very risky case where the claimant had failed before the district judge and the circuit judge. In the circumstances, the whole premium was recoverable.

[38.7]   Sharratt v London Central Bus Co Ltd sub nom The Accident Group Test Cases

[2004] EWCA Civ 575

[2004] 3 All ER 325

Under The Accident Group (TAG) Scheme which was very similar to that operated by Claims Direct, the claimant agreed to pay a 'premium' of £800 or £950 for an insurance policy. The premium was broken down as follows:

	2000	*2001*
Underwriters	£320	£300
TAG	£480	£650

In addition, a fee of £310 plus VAT was paid to Accident Investigation Ltd (AIL) to investigate the claim.

HELD, ON APPEAL: (1) The 'Loss Experience Adjustment Premium' was paid by TAG to further its business and had nothing to do with the claimant therefore did not fall within s 29 of AJA 1999.

(2)   Although it was doubtful whether the cost of insurance services provided by TAG to the underwriters was a proper addition to the premium, in the absence of proper evidence, the senior costs judge had no alternative but to accept the £30 attributed to similar services in the *Claims Direct Test Cases* (see para [38.4]) and there was no basis to interfere with his conclusion.

(3)   A reasonable and proportionate premium recoverable under s 29 was £525 to include sums paid to underwriters and commission.

(4)   The AIL fee was a referral fee not properly payable by the solicitors. Therefore it was not chargeable to the claimant and not recoverable from the defendant.

[38.8]   Wooldridge (by Edward William Wooldridge her litigation friend) v Hayes and Vulcan Motors Ltd

[2005] EWHC 90007 (costs)

The claimant suffered severe head injuries in a road accident and the court approved a settlement exceeding £600,000. The claim was initially funded by a before the event (BTE) insurance policy however when the claimant's solicitors' costs exceeded the limit of indemnity of £50,000, an ATE policy was taken out with a premium of £7,469 plus £373.45 IPT.

HELD: (1) Applying *Callery v Gray (No 2)*, the cost of insuring against the risk of being unable to recover the premium as a consequence of losing fell within s 29 of AJA 1999 (see para [38.2]).

(2)   The basic premium calculated at 10% of the limit of indemnity (£60,000) was reasonable. The defendant's general search of The.Judge-.co.uk to find alternative ATE policies could not be relied upon because the range of premiums were indicative only and varied depending on a number of factors. In the absence of reliable evidence that comparable

insurance was available at cheaper cost, the costs judge drew upon the report he prepared in *Callery v Gray*. In addition, it was relevant that the ATE insurance was taken out long after proceedings had commenced and consequently if there was a claim on the policy, the insurer was likely to have to pay the maximum limit of indemnity.

(3)   The cost of the option to increase the limit of indemnity calculated at 10% of the basic premium was reasonable. Although liability had been admitted before the insurance was taken out, there was a real risk of incurring a liability for costs in excess of the original limit of indemnity.

(4)   In the circumstances, the premium was allowed in the amounts claimed.

[38.9]   Royal and Sun Alliance (RSA) Pursuit Test Cases

[2005] All ER (D) 88 (Aug)

First Assist provided an ATE insurance policy underwritten by Royal and Sun Alliance (RSA). The policy was aimed at claims involving greater risk and each was individually assessed and the premium calculated accordingly. The issues fell into two categories, the first related to the enforceability of the policy and the second to the reasonableness of the premium.

HELD: (1) The method by which the premium was calculated, namely a percentage of the costs of the claimant's solicitors, was clear from the policy. It was not necessary for the amount of the premium to be agreed at the time the policy was taken out. Therefore, the contract of insurance was not void for uncertainty.

(2)   The insurance arrangement between the claimants, the insurer and/or the solicitors was not unlawful on the grounds of champerty because there was no agreement for the insurer to share in the proceeds of the litigation, ie the damages.

(3)   It was difficult for a solicitor to estimate its own costs and those of its opponent therefore, given the unreliability of such inaccurate estimates, a calculation of the premium based on them was inherently flawed.

(4)   The claimants acted reasonably in not taking out ATE insurance earlier.

(5)   The claimants acted reasonably in taking out the RSA policy, except for Mr Baker, because his premium was disproportionate to the maximum level of damages obtainable (£5,000).

(6)   Only a reasonable and proportionate premium was recoverable by each claimant. The correct approach was to use the actual costs involved by the parties and then apply the policy formula in order to calculate the recoverable premium.

For the amounts allowed in each of the test cases, see the table at para [38.13].

[38.10]   Tyndall v Battersea Dogs Home

SCCO 16 September 2005

This was a fast-track claim following an accident on a roundabout. The defendant denied liability and did not accept the claimant's Part 36 offer of £2,672. The claimant subsequently took out an ATE insurance policy with Europ Assistance and issued proceedings. At trial the claimant was awarded damages of £3,345.63. The ATE premium was staged as follows:

(1)   £367.50 inclusive of IPT up to the issue of proceedings – stage 1;

(2)   £787.50 inclusive of IPT up to 45 days before trial – stage 2;

(3)   £1,890.00 inclusive of IPT if the case continued after 45 days before trial – stage 3.

HELD: (1) The defendant had failed to show that there was any alternative ATE policy available to the claimant having regard to the fact that liability was denied and proceedings were inevitable.
(2)   The decision in the case of *Baker v Euromark* (one of the *RSA Pursuit Test Cases*, at para [38.9]) and the premiums allowed in the *Claims Direct* (at para [38.4]) and *The Accident Group* (at para [38.7]) cases were not helpful because in those cases, proceedings were not inevitable.
(3)   The choice of the Europ Assistance policy was reasonable.
(4)   The adverse costs risk was £3,905.25 based on actual figures taken from the parties' costs schedules for trial. In addition, the risk of losing was 40% because success depended upon the trial judge accepting the claimant's evidence. In the circumstances, the premium was within a reasonable bracket and recoverable in full.
(5)   A policy with staged premiums had considerable advantages over single premium policies. In particular, it gave the defendant an incentive to settle the claim early and reduce the premium.

[38.11]   Richards v Davis

[2005] EWHC 90014 (costs)

The claimant was injured in a head on collision and his claim for damages was settled for the sum of £1,600. The claim was funded by the TAG Scheme and included an ATE premium of £997.50. However, the claimant had BTE insurance with DAS.

HELD: The claimant's solicitors failed to consider the appropriateness of the DAS policy therefore it was unreasonable to have taken out the TAG policy and the ATE premium was not recoverable.

[38.12]   Able UK Ltd v Reliance Security Services Ltd

SCCO 29 March 2006

This case arose out of a contractual dispute. During a telephone conversation between the claimant's solicitor and the loss adjuster appointed on behalf of the defendant, it became clear that the claim was going to be strongly defended. Subsequently, the claimant took out an ATE insurance policy which covered both sides' costs and provided a limit of indemnity of £200,000. The premium was £60,000 plus IPT of £3,000. The claim was later concluded by the defendant being ordered to pay damages of £285,000 and costs on the standard basis. At the detailed assessment hearing, the sole issue for the costs judge was the reasonableness and proportionality of the ATE premium. The defendant contended the claimant should have obtained quotations from other insurers and had provided the insurer with insufficient information to properly assess the prospects of success which the claimant's solicitor had assessed at 70%.

HELD: (1) It was reasonable for the claimant to accept a premium based on 30% of the cover with 70% prospects of success.
(2)   The total costs would have been higher if the claimant had entered into a conditional fee agreement and purchased insurance which only covered the opponent's costs and own disbursements.
(3)   The level and extent of the cover provided was reasonable.
4)   The claimant's solicitor had considerable experience of ATE policies and took into account the alternative options that were available.
(5)   The defendant did not ask any of the insurers it approached for a

specific quotation therefore the defendant had not provided any evidence that a suitable alternative quotation would have been available. The claimant made a reasonable choice and it would have been disproportionate to incur the costs of obtaining alternative quotations.

(6) In the circumstances, the ATE premium of £63,000 including IPT was reasonable and proportionate.

[38.13]

Table of ATE premium awards

Case	ATE insurer	Date of policy	Stage of conclusion of claim	Policy cover	Limit of indemnity	Damages	Premium claimed	Premium allowed
Callery v Gray	Temple Legal Pro-tection Ltd	4 May 2000	Pre-issue	Opponent's costs and own dis-bursements	£100,000	£1,500	£367.50	£367.50
Tilby v Perfect Pizza Ltd	Temple Legal Protection Ltd	1 June 2000	Pre-issue	Opponent's costs and own dis-bursements	£100,000	£2,000	£367.50	£367.50
Claims Direct Test Cases	Litigation Protection Ltd	Various after August 1999	Pre and post-issue	Both sides' costs	£50,000	Various	£1,312.50	£621.13
Pirie v Ayling	London & Edinburgh Insurance Co Ltd	27 March 2001	Post-issue	Opponent's costs and own dis-bursements	£10,000	£13,000	£2,600	£367.50
Sarwar v Alam	Lloyds	18 July 2001	Post issue	Opponent's costs and own dis-bursements	£125,000	£2,250	£62,500	£62,500
The Accident Group Test Cases	Lloyds and NIG	Various in 2000 and 2001	Various	Opponent's costs and own dis-bursements	Unknown	Various	£800 or £950	£525
Wool-dridge v Hayes	Greystoke Legal Services	2 Septem-ber 2002	Post-issue	Opponent's costs and own dis-bursements	£67,100	>£600,000	£7,842.45	£7,842.45
RSA Pursuit Test Cases:								
(1) *Baker v Adden-brookes Hospital*	Royal and Sun Alliance	20 Septem-ber 2002	Post-issue	Opponent's costs and own dis-bursements	£18,500	£400,000	£54,787.37	£13,695
(2) *Baker v Euro-mark*	Royal and Sun Alliance	16 October 2002	Post-issue	Opponent's costs and own dis-bursements	£2,000	£1,250	£8,962	£787.50

Case	ATE insurer	Date of policy	Stage of conclusion of claim	Policy cover	Limit of indemnity	Damages	Premium claimed	Premium allowed
(3) *Clarke v James*	Royal and Sun Alliance	29 August 2002	Post-issue	Opponent's costs and own disbursements	£7,000	£20,000	£32,392.38	£11,666
(4) *Sandiford v Price's Patent Candles*	Royal and Sun Alliance	23 August 2002	Post-issue	Opponent's costs and own disbursements	£10,000	£44,000	£16,986	£16,986
(5) *Farr v Kerslake*	Royal and Sun Alliance	23 January 2003	Post-issue	Opponent's costs and own disbursements	Unknown	£250,000	£161,047.69	£41,708
Tyndall v Battersea Dogs Home	Europ Assistance	10 December 2003	Trial	Opponent's costs and own disbursements	£25,000	£3,345.63	£1,890	£1,890
Richards v Davis	NIG	Unknown	Post-issue	Opponent's costs and own disbursements	Unknown	£1,600	£997.50	£0
Able UK Ltd v Reliance Security Services Ltd	Greystoke	23 June 2003	Post-issue	Both sides' costs	£200,000	£285,000	£63,000	£63,000

2.   CONDITIONAL FEE AGREEMENTS (CFAS)

(A) FORMALITY REQUIREMENTS

[38.14]   Section 58 of the Courts and Legal Services Act 1990, as amended:
'(1)   A conditional fee agreement which satisfies all of the conditions applicable to it by virtue of this section shall not be unenforceable by reason only of its being a conditional fee agreement; but ... any other conditional fee agreement shall be unenforceable.
(2)   ...
(3)   The following conditions are applicable to every conditional fee agreement–
 (a) It must be in writing;
 (b) It must not relate to proceedings which cannot be the subject of an enforceable conditional fee agreement; and
 (c) It must comply with such requirements (if any) as may be prescribed by the Lord Chancellor.
(4)   The following further conditions are applicable to a conditional fee agreement which provides for a success fee ...
 (a) ...
 (b) It must state the percentage by which the amount of the fees which would be payable if it were not a conditional fee agreement is to be increased;

(c)   That percentage must not exceed the percentage specified in relation to the description of proceedings to which the agreement
relates by order made by the Lord Chancellor.'

[38.15]   Hollins v Russell

[2003] EWCA Civ 718

[2003] 4 All ER 590, [2003] 1 WLR 2487, [2003] 28 LS Gaz R 30, [2003] NLJR
920, (2003) Times, 10 June, 147 Sol Jo LB 662, [2003] All ER (D) 311 (May)

The Conditional Fee Agreements Regulations 2000, SI 2000/692 (CFA Regulations 2000) were made under s 58(3)(c) of the Courts and Legal Services Act 1990
and came into force on 1 April 2000. After this date, defendants increasingly
challenged the enforceability of claimants' CFAs by demanding disclosure of the
CFA and alleging one or more breaches of the Regulations.

The Court of Appeal therefore brought together six appeals to consider three
issues:

(1)   The circumstances in which a court should put a receiving party in
detailed assessment proceedings to its election, so that it must choose
whether to disclose its CFA to the paying party or to endeavour to
prove its claim by other means.

(2)   The proper construction of the words 'satisfies all of the conditions
applicable to it' in s 58(1) of the 1990 Act and whether any costs or
disbursements are recoverable from a paying party in the event of non
compliance with the CFA Regulations 2000.

(3)   Whether, on the particular facts of the six appeals, the requirements of
regs 2, 3 and 4 of the CFA Regulations 2000 were not complied with.

HELD, ON APPEAL: (1) To ensure greater transparency and enable the paying party to
see whether or not the CFA Regulations 2000 were complied with, a costs judge
should normally exercise his discretion so as to require the receiving party to
produce a copy of the CFA to the paying party, subject to the receiving party's right
to elect to prove the CFA by other evidence. Any privileged material may be
redacted before disclosure of the CFA. In the absence of full argument, the court
was unwilling to express a view whether or not a CFA was privileged. Ordinarily,
the attendance notes of the claimant's solicitors showing compliance with reg 4
should not be disclosed unless the paying party could show there was a genuine
issue as to whether there was compliance.

(2)   In order to decide whether or not the CFA satisfied all of the
conditions applicable to it by virtue of s 58 of the 1990 Act, costs
judges should ask themselves: 'Has the particular departure from a
regulation pursuant to s 58(3)(c) of the 1990 Act or a requirement in
s 58, either on its own or in conjunction with any other such departure
in this case, had a materially adverse effect either upon the protection
afforded to the client or upon the proper administration of justice?' If
the answer is 'yes', the conditions have not been satisfied. If the answer
is 'no', the departure is immaterial and the conditions have been
satisfied.

(3)   If the CFA was unenforceable, the ATE premium and paid disbursements were still recoverable from the paying party (cf *Richards v Davis*
at para [38.48], where the ATE premium was not recoverable because
the claimant had the benefit of BTE insurance).

The decisions in the individual appeals were as follows (at paras [38.17]–[38.27]).

[38.16] Regulation 2(1)(d) of the CFA Regulations 2000 states:

'A CFA must specify the amounts which are payable in all the circumstances and cases specified or the method to be used to calculate them
and, in particular, whether the amounts are limited by reference to the
damages which may be recovered on behalf of the client'.

[38.17] Hollins v Russell

[2003] EWCA Civ 718

[2003] 4 All ER 590, [2003] 1 WLR 2487, [2003] 28 LS Gaz R 30, [2003] NLJR
920, (2003) Times, 10 June, 147 Sol Jo LB 662, [2003] All ER (D) 311 (May)

The Law Society's April 2000 model CFA was used which contained the following
provision:

'If you win your claim, you pay our basic charges, our disbursements and a
success fee. The amount of *the success fee* is not based on or limited by
reference to the damages.' (emphasis added)

HELD, ON APPEAL: (1) The ordinary meaning of 'specify' is to state explicitly
therefore there was a departure from the regulation because the CFA should have
said that basic charges, disbursements and the success fee were not limited by
reference to the damages.
(2)   The CFA read as a whole was sufficiently clear and the failure to specify
      did not affect the protection given to the claimant or the administration
      of justice to any material degree. The result would have been different if
      the CFA would not have been reasonably comprehensible to a lay
      person.

[38.18] Tichband v Hurdman

[2003] EWCA Civ 718

[2003] 4 All ER 590, [2003] 1 WLR 2487, [2003] 28 LS Gaz R 30, [2003] NLJR
920, (2003) Times, 10 June, 147 Sol Jo LB 662, [2003] All ER (D) 311 (May)

The CFA made no reference to the question whether any element of the amounts
payable were limited by reference to the damages recovered.

HELD, ON APPEAL: (1) There was a departure from reg 2(1)(d) of the CFA
Regulations 2000.
(2)   The CFA read as a whole was in plain language and perfectly clear
      therefore the claimant could have been in no doubt about its effect. The
      requirements of s 58(1) of the Courts and Legal Services Act 1990
      were satisfied.

[38.19] Regulation 3(1)(b) of the CFA Regulations 2000 states:

'A CFA which provides for a success fee must specify how much of the
percentage increase, if any, relates to the cost to the legal representative of
the postponement of the payment of his fees and expenses.'

[38.20]   **Tichband v Hurdman**

[2003] EWCA Civ 718

[2003] 4 All ER 590, [2003] 1 WLR 2487, [2003] 28 LS Gaz R 30, [2003] NLJR 920, (2003) Times, 10 June, 147 Sol Jo LB 662, [2003] All ER (D) 311 (May)

The postponement element of the success fee had to be specified because CPR 44.3B(1)(a) provided this part could not be recovered from the paying party. The CFA clearly specified that none of the success fee was attributable to postponement however the risk assessment provided that 5% was attributable to postponement.

HELD, ON APPEAL: The CFA prevailed over the risk assessment and therefore the CFA complied with the reg 3(1)(b) of the CFA Regulations 2000.

[38.21]   Regulation 4(2)(c) of the CFA Regulations 2000 states:

'Before a CFA is made the legal representative must inform the client whether the legal representative considers that the client's risk of incurring liability for costs in respect of the proceedings to which the agreement relates is insured against under an existing contract of insurance.'

[38.22]   **Pratt v Bull**

[2003] EWCA Civ 718

[2003] 4 All ER 590, [2003] 1 WLR 2487, [2003] 28 LS Gaz R 30, [2003] NLJR 920, (2003) Times, 10 June, 147 Sol Jo LB 662, [2003] All ER (D) 311 (May)

The 80-year-old claimant was severely injured when struck by the defendant's vehicle while using a pedestrian crossing. Initial instructions were given by relatives while the claimant was in intensive care. When she had recovered a month later, a CFA was made when the solicitor visited her in hospital.

HELD, ON APPEAL: (1) It was ridiculous to expect a solicitor dealing with a seriously ill old woman in hospital to delay making a CFA while her home insurance policy was found and checked to see if BTE insurance was available.

(2)   It was sufficient to satisfy s 58 of the Courts and Legal Services Act 1990 that the solicitor had discussed it with her and formed a view on the funding options.

[38.23]   Regulation 4(2)(e)(ii) of the CFA Regulations 2000 states:

'Before CFA is made the legal representative must inform the client whether the legal representative considers that any particular method or methods of financing any or all of those costs is appropriate and, if he considers that a contract of insurance is appropriate or recommends a particular such contract ... whether he has an interest in doing so.'

[38.24]   **Dunn v Ward**

[2003] EWCA Civ 718

[2003] 4 All ER 590, [2003] 1 WLR 2487, [2003] 28 LS Gaz R 30, [2003] NLJR 920, (2003) Times, 10 June, 147 Sol Jo LB 662, [2003] All ER (D) 311 (May)

The CFA did not state that the solicitor had no interest in recommending a particular insurance contract.

HELD, ON APPEAL: The word 'whether' in the regulation meant 'if' not 'whether or not'. Therefore it was not necessary for a solicitor to state if he had no interest, only if he had an interest.

[38.25]   Regulation 4(5) of the CFA Regulations 2000 states:

'Information required to be given under paragraph (1) about the matters in paragraph (2)(a) to (d) must be given orally (whether or not it is also given in writing), but information required to be so given about the matters in paragraph (2)(e) and the explanation required by paragraph (3) must be given both orally and in writing.'

[38.26]   Dunn v Ward

[2003] EWCA Civ 718

[2003] 4 All ER 590, [2003] I WLR 2487, [2003] 28 LS Gaz R 30, [2003] NLJR 920, (2003) Times, 10 June, 147 Sol Jo LB 662, [2003] All ER (D) 311 (May)

The claimant's solicitor orally explained the effects of a CFA then posted to the claimant the Law Society's July 2000 model CFA and the Law Society Conditions. The claimant signed the CFA and the statement confirming her solicitor had given the verbal explanation.

HELD, ON APPEAL: (1) There was no reason in principle why the CFA should not be or contain an explanation of its own terms and effect and there was nothing in the Courts and Legal Services Act 1990 Act or the CFA Regulations 2000 which excluded this possibility.
(2)   Although there was no breach of reg 4(5) of the 2000 Regulations, it was preferable to have a free-standing explanatory letter which may cross-refer to the Law Society Conditions.

[38.27]   Sharratt v London Central Bus Co Ltd sub nom The Accident Group Test Cases

[2003] EWCA Civ 718

[2003] 4 All ER 590, [2003] I WLR 2487, [2003] 28 LS Gaz R 30, [2003] NLJR 920, (2003) Times, 10 June, 147 Sol Jo LB 662, [2003] All ER (D) 311 (May)

Under the TAG Scheme, a TAG representative visited the claimant at home by appointment to explain the CFA and complete a document called 'The fact find and oral explanation sheet'. During the visit the claimant signed the CFA.

HELD, ON APPEAL: The legal representative's duties under reg 4 of the CFA Regulations 2000 could be delegated to someone who was not a qualified solicitor or a Fellow of the Institute of Legal Executives. This included a duly authorised agent such as TAG and its representatives provided that in so doing the solicitor was not abandoning the supervisory responsibilities required by the Solicitors' Practice Rules.

[38.28]   Farrelly v Denmark

(24 June 2003, unreported), Penzance County Court

The CFA between the solicitor and claimant was in the form of the Law Society model agreement which imposed upon the claimant obligations to cooperate and provide instructions. If the claimant did not fulfil his obligations the solicitors had the right to end the CFA and claim charges and disbursements.

HELD: The claimant's failure to respond to correspondence was a breach of the CFA and the solicitor was entitled to terminate the CFA and claim fees.

[38.29]   Myler v Williams

[2003] EWHC 1587 (QB)

[2003] All ER (D) 364 (Jun), [2003] 4 Costs LR 566

The CFA did not specify a method to be used to calculate the hourly rates and there was no precise formula for calculating the success fee.

HELD, ON APPEAL: (1) The failure to specify a method of calculating the hourly rates was a breach of reg 2(1)(d) of the CFA Regulations 2000 however the breach did not render the CFA unenforceable because it had not had a materially adverse effect on the protection afforded to the client or on the proper administration of justice. *Hollins v Russell* applied.

(2)   Although there was no precise formula for calculating the success fee, there was a method of calculation and accordingly there was no breach of reg 2(1)(d) of the CFA Regulations 2000.

[38.30]   Ghannouchi v Houni Ltd

(2004) 148 Sol Jo LB 508, SC

The CFA between the solicitors and claimant was the Law Society's model agreement dated July 2000. The defendants contended the CFA failed to comply with:

(1)   regulation 3(2)(c) of the CFA Regulations 2000 as its effect was that the solicitors were only entitled to recover the costs agreed between the parties and they could not recover any remaining element of the bills they had rendered to the claimant; and

(2)   regulation 4(3) and (5) of the CFA Regulations 2000 as the explanation it provided in relation to resolution of the claim by detailed assessment or agreement was unclear.

HELD: (1) The sole reference in regulation 3(2)(c) to 'percentage increase' is to the party liable to pay base costs to which the success fee is to be added. The CFA did not comply with regulation 3(2)(c).

(2)   The CFA did not make clear to the claimant that he did not have to pay the shortfall in base costs as well as the shortfall on the success fee where there had been an agreement on costs. The CFA did not comply with regulation 4(3) and (5).

(3)   The CFA read as a whole was clear and accordingly there was no materially adverse effect upon the protection afforded to the client or upon the proper administration of justice.

(4)   The validity of a CFA must be judged at the date of the detailed assessment (cf *Richards v Davis* at para [38.48]).

[38.31]   Spencer v Wood t/a Gordon Tyres (a firm)

[2004] EWCA Civ 352

(2004) 148 Sol Jo LB 356

The CFA between the claimant and his solicitors did not specify what proportion of the 75% success fee, if any, related to the postponement of the solicitors' fees and expenses. The risk assessment provided, 'Deferment of costs until conclusion of case – 50%'.

HELD, ON APPEAL: (1) There was a breach of reg 3(1)(b) of the CFA Regulations 2000 because it was unclear how the postponement charge was reflected in the success fee of 75%.

(2)   The breach had a materially adverse effect upon the protection afforded to the claimant because he did not know which part of the 75% success fee was not recoverable from the defendant, therefore the CFA was unenforceable.

[38.32]   **Garrett v Halton Borough Council**

[2006] EWCA Civ 1017

(2006) Times, 25 July, CA

The claimant's solicitors were a member of the Ashley Ainsworth panel and recommended to the claimant that she use the ATE policy offered by Ashley Ainsworth. The CFA stated the solicitors had no interest in making that recommendation. In the points of dispute the defendant asserted there was an interest because the solicitors were obliged to recommend the Ashley Ainsworth policy as a condition of panel membership. The assertion was never denied. The circuit judge held:

(1)   The failure to answer the assertion in the points of dispute gave rise to an inference that it was true. The deputy district judge was therefore entitled to find the solicitors had an interest and the failure to inform the claimant was a breach of reg 4(2)(e)(ii) of the CFA Regulations 2000.

(2)   The question of whether the breach was material and therefore whether the CFA was enforceable, had to be determined as at the day the CFA was made, not with the benefit of hindsight (cf *Ghannouchi v Houni Ltd* at para [38.30]). The focus of the test in *Hollins v Russell* was on whether the client had, in the result, suffered loss. The breach was material and the claimant could have relied on it successfully against the solicitors in order properly to give effect to s 58 of the Courts and Legal Services Act 1990 and reg 4(2)(e)(ii) of the CFA Regulations 2000.

The CFA was therefore unenforceable.

HELD, ON APPEAL: (1) The enforceability of a CFA must be determined (or determinable) at its commencement.

(2)   The materiality of a breach does not require consideration of the actual prejudice to the claimant caused by the breach.

(3)   The word 'interest' in reg 4(2)(e)(ii) included membership of a panel of a claims management company.

(4)   The obligation in reg 4(2)(e)(ii) is not to inform the client whether the solicitor believes that he has an interest in recommending a particular insurance contract; it is to inform the client whether he has an interest in doing so in fact.

(5)   The solicitors did have a financial interest in recommending the policy to the claimant because failure to recommend the policy would have led to termination of panel membership and loss of a substantial amount of work.

(6)   There was insufficient disclosure of the interest by the solicitors because they did not disclose to the claimant that they had a financial interest in remaining on the panel which would be lost if the claimant

did not accept their recommendation that she enter into the policy. In the circumstances, there was a material breach of reg 4(2)(e)(ii) and the CFA was unenforceable.

[38.33] **Gaynor v Central West London Buses Ltd t/a First Transforming Travel**

[2006] EWCA Civ 1120

(2006) Times, 25 August, CA

The claimant issued proceedings for damages arising out of a road traffic accident which occurred in November 2002. Subsequently the claim was settled and the terms of settlement included a provision that the defendant would pay the claimant's costs, to be decided by detailed assessment if not agreed. The parties were unable to agree costs and within the detailed assessment proceedings, the defendant argued the retainer agreement between the claimant and her solicitors evidenced in a letter dated 20 November 2002 was an unenforceable CFA. The costs judge found there was no intention by the claimant to enter into a CFA and therefore held the retainer letter did not amount to a CFA. The circuit judge held:

(1)   The claimant and her solicitors did not intend to enter into a CFA. However, the terms of the retainer letter, 'If your claim is disputed by your opponent and you decide not to pursue your claim then we will not make a charge for the work we have done to date' created a CFA because the fees of the solicitors were payable only in certain circumstances.

(2)   An intention to enter into a CFA was not a necessary element of the agreement.

(3)   As Brooke LJ made clear in *Hollins v Russell* (at para [38.15]), only CFAs that complied with s 58 of the Courts and Legal Services Act 1990 were enforceable.

(4)   In the circumstances, the CFA between the claimant and her solicitors was unenforceable.

HELD, ON APPEAL: (1) The object of s 58 of the 1990 Act and the CFA Regulations 2000 was to provide protection to clients. The need for protection assumed that the solicitor was to provide litigation services and therefore, if no such services were provided, the client had no need of protection.

(2)   The work done by the solicitors before the claimant decided whether or not to pursue her claim (advising the claimant about the merits of her claim and writing a letter of claim) was not litigation services.

(3)   In the circumstances, the retainer letter was not, and did not evidence, a CFA.

[38.34] **Jones v Caradon Catnic Ltd**

[2005] EWCA Civ 1821, CA

The solicitors' risk assessment recorded a success fee of 120% and this led to a 120% success fee being claimed in the bill of costs. Although the solicitors conceded it should be limited to 100%, the district judge found the solicitors intended there to be a 120% success fee.

HELD, ON APPEAL: (1) There was a clear breach of s 58(4)(c) of the Courts and Legal Services Act 1990 and Art 4 of the Conditional Fee Agreements Order 2000 (which prescribes a maximum success fee of 100%).

(2)   Under the terms of the agreement (in this case a collective CFA) the claimant was never going to be liable for a success fee of more than 100% therefore this was not a case where consumer protection or client protection was relevant. To determine whether or not the breach was material, the administration of justice had to be considered. The breach was more serious compared with the trivial breaches in *Hollins v Russell* and *Tichband v Hurdman*, therefore the CFA was unenforceable.

[38.35]   Sharratt and Others v London Central Bus Co Ltd and Others
[2005] EWHC 3018 (QB)
[2005] All ER (D) 344 (Dec), QB

This case was one of the appeals heard by the Court of Appeal in *Hollins v Russell* (at para [38.15]). Following the decision of the Court of Appeal, the claimant served a bill of costs totalling £485,791.58 which included £450,691.75 claimed as agency charges of Rowe Cohen Solicitors who were retained by the claimant's solicitors under a CFA. The defendants contended they had no liability for the agency charges because the claimant had no liability to pay them beyond those recovered from the defendants or at all. The costs judge decided the defendants' liability for the agency charges under the indemnity principle was nil. The claimant appealed.

HELD, ON APPEAL: (1) The court will, if it properly can, avoid a construction of an agreement which involves a breach of the indemnity principle because of the unfairness such a conclusion leads to.

(2)   Costs Practice Direction 4.16(6) confirmed that there was no privity of contract between a claimant and a solicitor-agent and the client was not directly liable to the solicitor-agent for his fees. The fees of the solicitor-agent were treated as the fees of the solicitor-principal as if he carried out the work himself.

(3)   Rowe Cohen were appointed as the agents of the claimant's solicitors and all work done by Rowe Cohen was as agent not principal, notwithstanding the reference to acting as principal in the CFA.

(4)   There was no reason in principle why a solicitor-principal could not enter into a CFA with a solicitor-agent.

(5)   The effect of the CFA was to limit the liability of the claimant's solicitors for the charges of and disbursements incurred by Rowe Cohen, not to exclude liability. The liability was limited to costs awarded against and recovered from the defendants.

(6)   The CFA between the claimant and his solicitors provided that the claimant was liable for the costs of a solicitor-agent therefore the claimant was liable for the charges and disbursements payable to Rowe Cohen by his solicitors which were recoverable from the defendants under the indemnity principle.

(7)   The CFA between a solicitor-principal and a solicitor-agent did not vary the terms of the CFA between the claimant and the solicitor-principal which could only be varied with the claimant's agreement.

(B)   ALTERNATIVE METHODS OF FUNDING

[38.36]   Regulation 4 of the CFA Regulations 2000 provides:
   '(1)   Before a conditional fee agreement is made the legal representative must–

    (a) inform the client about the following matters …

(2)   Those matters are–

    …

    (c) Whether the legal representative considers that the client's risk of incurring liability for costs in respect of the proceedings to which the agreement relates is insured against under an existing contract of insurance.

    (d) Whether other methods of financing those costs are available, and, if so, how they apply to the client and the proceedings in question …'

See para [38.92] for the application of reg 4 to claims subject to fixed recoverable costs under CPR Pt 45 where the road traffic accident occurred on or after 6 October 2003.

[38.37]   **Sarwar v Alam**

[2001] EWCA Civ 1401

[2001] 4 All ER 541, [2002] 1 WLR 125, CA

The claimant was injured when he was a passenger in a vehicle driven by the defendant. The claimant told his solicitors he was not aware of any legal expenses insurance available to him so he entered into a CFA (which predated 1 April 2000 and therefore did not have to comply with the CFA Regulations 2000) and took out ATE insurance. The claim was settled for £2,250 prior to the issue of proceedings. During the costs only proceedings the defendant's insurers disclosed for the first time that the defendant's motor insurance policy had the benefit of BTE legal expenses insurance with DAS Legal Expenses Insurance Company Ltd which might have covered the claim. The BTE policy covered both sides' costs up to £50,000.

HELD, ON APPEAL: (1) If a claimant possesses pre-existing BTE cover which appears to be satisfactory for a straightforward claim not exceeding £5,000, then the claimant should be referred to the BTE insurer. The costs are more likely to be proportionate to the value of the claim since there will be no success fee or ATE premium and the cost of the BTE premium is not recoverable.

   (2)   Proper practice dictates that a solicitor should normally ask the claimant to bring to the first interview any motor policy, household policy and stand-alone BTE policy belonging to the claimant and/or any spouse or partner living in the same household for inspection by the solicitor. At the interview the solicitor should ask the claimant whether anybody else may fund his claim for example his employer or trade union.

   (3)   If the claimant was a passenger, the solicitor should ask the claimant to obtain a copy of the driver's policy, if reasonably practicable. If the BTE policy requires the driver's consent, the solicitor should tell the claimant to obtain consent before making a claim to the BTE insurer.

   (4)   If, in the future, credit card companies publish the BTE cover they provide, the claimant should also be asked to bring to the first interview any credit cards belonging to him and/or any spouse or partner living in the same household.

   (5)   If there is a reasonable possibility of the passenger blaming the driver or vice versa, it is not incumbent on the passenger to use the driver's

BTE cover if the passenger is denied the solicitor of his choice. The position might be different if the claim was handled by a transparently independent organisation.

(6)   As soon as the solicitor is satisfied that no appropriate BTE cover is available, there is no reason why the claimant should not enter into a CFA and take out ATE insurance. If, however, the inquiry about BTE cover cannot be satisfactorily resolved at the first interview, the claimant should not enter into a CFA or take out ATE insurance until such further enquiries into the availability of BTE cover as are reasonable and proportionate to the value of the claim have been concluded.

(7)   In the circumstances, the BTE policy did not provide the claimant with appropriate cover because the defendant's insurer through its chosen representative retained full conduct and control of the claim.

[38.38]   Jackson v Tierney

(1 November 2002, unreported), Liverpool County Court

The claimant was injured in a road traffic accident and entered into a CFA with his solicitors dated 25 October 2000. On 1 November 2000 the claimant took out an ATE policy with a premium of £530.80. The claimant however had pre-existing insurance cover therefore his solicitors did not pursue a claim for the success fee and ATE premium. The district judge did not allow base costs after the date of the CFA and the claimant appealed.

HELD, ON APPEAL: (1) The requirement of 'consideration' in reg 4(2) of the CFA Regulations 2000 is a requirement which must be satisfied before the CFA can be enforced.

(2)   In order to comply with the requirement, the solicitor must examine the claimant's insurance policies. It is not sufficient to merely ask the claimant to consider the availability of pre-existing insurance and rely upon the response if the claimant is uneducated about insurance.

(3)   If a solicitor departs from the procedure set out in *Sarwar v Alam* (at para [38.37]) he does so at his peril.

(4)   In the circumstances, there was no proper consideration by the legal representative of other policies which might provide BTE insurance and the district judge's decision was correct.

[38.39]   Culshaw v Goodliffe

(24 November 2003, unreported), Liverpool County Court

The claimant informed her solicitors that she had no legal expenses insurance but the solicitors did not examine any of her insurance policies. In fact the claimant did have BTE insurance.

HELD, ON APPEAL: (1) The decision in *Jackson v Tierney* survived *Hollins v Russell* (at para [38.15]) and the word 'considers' in reg 4(2)(c) of the CFA Regulations 2000 required more than the solicitors asking the claimant a question about pre-existing insurance and getting an answer, where there is no reasonable explanation of the claimant realising they have BTE insurance. The solicitors had breached the regulations by not examining any of the claimant's insurance policies.

(2)   Although the BTE policy was not available for consideration, the court

was entitled to take cognizance of the general thrust of BTE policies from the BTE policy in *Sarwar v Alam* (at para [38.37]) and general knowledge.

(3)   The claimant was disadvantaged by having a CFA as opposed to BTE insurance in a number of respects including the Part 36 position, change of solicitor, termination of the agreement and potential shortfall on detailed assessment. The breach was material having regard to the test in *Hollins v Russell* because the claimant was unable to make an informed choice about the funding options available to her. The CFA was therefore unenforceable.

[38.40]   Chappell v De Bora's of Exeter (a firm)
(29 January 2004, unreported), Exeter County Court

The claimant, who lived near Exeter, had BTE insurance with DAS. Her chosen solicitors in Exeter were not on the DAS panel so she entered into a CFA with the solicitors and took out an ATE policy. The defendant alleged contributory negligence which the claimant did not admit. The claim was settled in the sum of £31,156.

HELD, ON APPEAL: It was reasonable in a case of this kind for the claimant to instruct the solicitors of her choice in Exeter rather than the nearest DAS panel solicitor in Salisbury or Bristol.

[38.41]   Bowen and 10 Others v Bridgend County Borough Council
SCCO 25 March 2004

All of the claimants instructed the same firm of solicitors in Liverpool to represent them in their housing disrepair claims. The claimants entered into a CFA, took out ATE insurance and applied for a disbursement funding loan.

HELD: (1) The solicitors had failed to comply with reg 4(2)(c) of the CFA Regulations 2000 by wrongly placing on the claimants the responsibility for considering the availability of existing insurance.

(2)   The solicitors had also failed to comply with reg 4(2)(d) of the CFA Regulations 2000 by not properly considering the availability of legal aid. All of the claimants should have been told to seek legal aid.

(3)   The failure to comply with reg 4(2)(c) did not by itself have a materially adverse effect upon the protection afforded to the claimants because the possibility they already had BTE cover was minimal.

(4)   The failure to comply with reg 4(2)(d) did have a materially adverse effect upon the protection afforded to the claimants because they had been exposed to unreasonably high and disproportionate expenses not covered by the ATE insurance in particular, the interest at 13.9% per annum payable under the loan agreement.

(5)   The failure to comply with regulations 4(2)(c) or 4(2)(d) had a materially adverse effect upon the proper administration of justice because it caused the litigation to be unnecessarily expensive and some of the costs claimed were improper in particular, profit costs claimed by way of backdating.

(6)   In the circumstances, the CFAs were unenforceable and the defendant's maximum liability was for paid disbursements and any costs of assessment allowed.

(7)   The ATE premium was not recoverable because no reasonable claimant properly advised would have chosen this method of funding in preference to legal aid.

[38.42]   **Samonini v London General Transport Services Ltd**

[2005] EWHC 90001 (costs)

[2006] All ER (D) 84 (Mar), [2006] NLJR 457

The claimant was injured in a rear end collision. His claim was funded by a CFA and an ATE policy with a premium of £798 including IPT. In addition to the premium, the claimant agreed to pay a management fee of £233.83 and an accident investigation fee of £410.08. The claimant recovered damages of £1,814 and was therefore required to repay a loan which he took out to cover these expenses together with interest at 10% per month (APR 13.6%). In fact, as it turned out, he did not have BTE insurance.

HELD: (1) The claimant was required to pay an ATE premium of £798 in a very straightforward, low value claim which on its face was disproportionate. Therefore it was appropriate to go behind the solicitor's signature on the bill.
 (2)   The solicitor did not carry out his own enquiries about pre-existing insurance and instead relied on the enquiries made by Accident Advice Helpline (AAH). On the evidence it was not possible to decide whether the duties of the legal representative under reg 4 of the CFA Regulations 2000 had been properly delegated to AAH. Even if they had, the enquiries made by AAH were insufficient to comply with the Regulations. In particular, the claimant was only asked about his motor policy. Accordingly, there was a breach of reg 4(2)(c).
 (3)   The breach had a materially adverse effect upon the protection afforded to the claimant because he had entered into a CFA, loan agreement and ATE policy. In addition, the breach had a materially adverse effect upon the proper administration of justice because it had led to costly satellite litigation. Further, 'if solicitors are permitted to skimp on proper investigation of LEI [legal expenses insurance] the administration of justice will be badly served since there will be no improvement in the way in which solicitors conduct proceedings of this type, added to which the client will have been badly served.'
 (4)   In the circumstances, the CFA was unenforceable.

[38.43]   **Campbell v MGN Ltd**

[2005] UKHL 61

[2005] 4 All ER 793, [2005] 1 WLR 3394

See also at para [38.226].

The claimant sued the defendant for breach of confidence and her award of £3,500 was restored following her successful appeal to the House of Lords. The claimant funded her appeal to the House of Lords pursuant to a CFA and her costs of the appeal amounted to £594,470. The defendant contended it should not be liable for any success fee because the claimant could have afforded to fund her own costs, as she did at the trial and in the Court of Appeal.

HELD: A solicitor does not have to inquire into the claimant's means before entering into a CFA and it is irrelevant whether or not the claimant had the means to pay. A means test would be impractical and Parliament intended CFAs to be available to everyone.

[38.44]   Hughes v London Borough of Newham

SCCO 28 July 2005

Each claimant brought housing disrepair proceedings against the defendant, their landlord, funded by a CFA and ATE insurance. The claimants took out a loan of £2,000 each to fund disbursements.

HELD: (1) By failing to properly inform the claimants of the availability of legal aid, the solicitors had breached reg 4(2)(d) of the CFA Regulations 2000.

(2)   The breach had a materially adverse effect upon the protection afforded to the claimants because they were unable to make an informed choice about the available funding options. The breach had led to the claimants entering into a funding arrangement under which they had incurred substantial irrecoverable costs including the ATE premium and interest on the loan. The CFAs were therefore unenforceable.

(3)   The failure to give proper advice about the availability of legal aid meant it was not reasonable for the defendant to pay the ATE premiums.

[38.45]   Myatt and Others v National Coal Board

[2006] EWCA Civ 1017

[2006] All ER (D) 239 (Jul), (2006) Times, 25 July, CA

The four claimants suffered noise induced hearing loss as a result of their employment with the defendant. They entered into CFAs and took out ATE insurance costing £1,522.50 each. The claims settled for £3,000, £3,500, £3,000 and £4,375. The costs judge held:

(1)   The claimants' solicitors had not complied with reg 4(2)(c) of the CFA Regulations 2000 in asking the claimants whether they had any credit cards, insurance policies or trade union membership to fund a claim for noise induced hearing loss against the defendant because this meant the unsophisticated claimants were being asked to interpret what could well have been complex documents. The solicitors should have asked whether they, or any spouse or partner living in the same household, had any credit cards, insurance or trade union membership, without more. Although it may not have been necessary to visit the claimants at home, the solicitors should have asked the claimants to send the policies or copies to them for inspection.

(2)   The non-compliance with the regulation was material because it led to the claimants taking out ATE premiums which were disproportionate to the value of the claims.

The CFAs were therefore unenforceable.

HELD ON APPEAL: (1) There was no logical necessity to apply the test in *Sarwar v Alam* (at para [38.37]) to reg 4(2)(c). *Sarwar* did not propound a rigid test and the overriding principle was that the claimant and his solicitor should act reasonably.

(2)   The regulation 4(2)(c) duty did not require solicitors slavishly to follow the detailed guidance in *Sarwar*. In particular, the statement that a solicitor should normally invite a client to bring to the first interview

any relevant policy should be treated with considerable caution. It had no application in high volume, low value litigation conducted by solicitors on referral by claims management companies.

(3) The factors relevant to the steps that a solicitor should reasonably take to discharge the obligation under reg 4(2)(c) included the nature of the client, the circumstances in which the solicitor is instructed, the nature of the claim, the cost of the ATE premium and whether the claim is referred to solicitors on a panel.

(4) A solicitor is not required in every case to ask the client to send him insurance policies or a trade union membership document. In some circumstances it is reasonable for the solicitor to rely on what he is told by the client about the availability of legal expenses insurance.

(5) Defendants should not embark on fishing expeditions and the court should not require further disclosure unless there is a genuine issue as to whether there has been compliance with reg 4.

(6) The costs judge was right to find that the solicitors should not have asked the claimants to decide whether they had BTE which would cover their risk as to costs in respect of their claims. Therefore, there was a breach of reg 4(2)(c).

(7) Although none of the claimants had BTE which would cover their claim, this was irrelevant to the materiality of the breach. In the circumstances, the breach was material and the CFAs were unenforceable.

[38.46] **Howarth v Britton Merlin Ltd**

SCCO 27 September 2005

The claimant was injured at work and his original solicitors obtained legal aid for the claim against his employer. Subsequently, proceedings were commenced against the wrong defendant and the claimant instructed new solicitors to whom the legal aid certificate was transferred. The action against the wrong defendant was discontinued and the new solicitors applied for the legal aid certificate to be discharged. The fresh action against the employer was funded by a CFA and the new solicitors did not inform the claimant that legal aid was available. On the first day of trial, the employer agreed to pay damages of £87,000 and costs. At the detailed assessment hearing, the costs judge rejected the claimant's argument that legal aid was not available for the second action. The CFA was therefore unenforceable because the solicitors had failed to advise the claimant that legal aid was available in breach of reg 4(2)(d) of the CFA Regulations 2000 and the breach had a materially adverse effect upon the protection afforded to the claimant. In addition, the ATE premium was not recoverable. The claimant appealed.

HELD, ON APPEAL: (1) The costs judge was right to find that legal aid was available for the second action and therefore there was a breach of reg 4(2)(d).

(2) The CFA was more disadvantageous than legal aid because under the CFA, the claimant was liable for disbursements, interest on a disbursement loan, the postponement element of the success fee and any base costs and ATE premium not recovered from the defendant. The freedom from legal aid bureaucracy, if it existed, benefited the solicitor not the claimant and the costs protection provided by the ATE cover was not better than that provided by a legal aid certificate.

(3) Although at the time the ATE cover was purchased no other form of

protection was available, the costs judge was not wrong to decide that the responsibility for that misfortune fell upon the claimant rather than the defendant.

(4)   In the circumstances, the solicitors' charges were not recoverable and the claimant was only entitled to recover paid disbursements, excluding the ATE premium.

[38.47]   Newby-Grossett and Newby-Grossett (by their mother and litigation friend) v Arriva London South

SCCO 8 November 2005

The child claimants were passengers in a car driven by their mother which was struck from behind by a bus driven by one of the defendant's employees. The claimants entered into CFAs and subsequently their claims were settled and the settlements approved by the court. Their mother pursued her own claim funded by the legal expenses insurance attached to her motor policy. The defendant contended the CFAs were unenforceable because the mother's legal expenses insurance covered the children's claims and should have been used.

HELD: (1) Although the claimants' solicitors' file appeared to show that all necessary enquiries about alternative funding had been undertaken, the evidence obtained by the defendant showed that the claimants had the benefit of their mother's legal expenses insurance. In the circumstances, the solicitors had made inadequate enquiries about BTE insurance and were therefore in breach of reg 4(2)(c) of the CFA Regulations 2000.

(2)   The breach had a materially adverse effect upon the proper administration of justice.

(3)   The CFAs were therefore unenforceable and the claimants were not entitled to recover any costs.

[38.48]   Richards v Davis

[2005] EWHC 90014 (costs)

See also at para [38.11].

The claimant was injured in a head on collision and his claim for damages was settled in the sum of £1,600. The claim was brought under The Accident Group (TAG) Scheme funded by a CFA and ATE insurance costing £997.50. In fact, the claimant had BTE insurance with DAS as part of his motor policy.

HELD: (1) The defendant's liability insurer, Churchill, was not a party to the TAG test cases (see para [38.7]) or mediation. Therefore it was not an abuse of process for the defendant to raise the issue of compliance with reg 4 of the CFA Regulations 2000.

(2)   Neither the TAG representative nor the claimant's solicitors complied with reg 4(2)(c) of the CFA Regulations 2000 by failing to request and inspect the claimant's motor policy.

(3)   There was also a breach of reg 4(2)(d) and (e) because of the complete failure to consider any alternative funding, other than the TAG scheme.

(4)   The breaches had a materially adverse effect upon the protection afforded to the claimant because he would lose a significant proportion of his damages as a result. In addition, the breaches had a materially adverse effect upon the proper administration of justice because the costs were unnecessarily inflated by the excessive ATE premium. The CFA was therefore unenforceable.

(5)   The validity of a CFA must be judged at the date of the CFA as otherwise it would vary from being enforceable to unenforceable as time goes by. (Cf *Ghannouchi v Houni Ltd* at para [38.30]).

[38.49]   **Hussein and Others v Leeds City Council**
SCCO 16 December 2005

Eleven housing disrepair claims were funded by CFAs which provided for a 100% success fee and were supported by ATE insurance. All of the claims settled before trial and the damages ranged from £600–£2,000. Following settlement, the cases were transferred to the Supreme Court Costs Office for detailed assessment and the costs judge had to decide whether or not the solicitors had complied with reg 4(2)(d) and (e) of the CFA Regulations 2000.

HELD: (1) The solicitors had failed to comply with reg 4(2)(d) of the CFA Regulations 2000 because the claimants were not provided with sufficient information about legal aid to be able to choose whether or not to apply for it. It was not sufficient to merely mention the existence of legal aid and the main advantages and disadvantages of each method of funding had to be explained.

(2)   The departure from reg 4(2)(d) did not have a materially adverse effect upon the proper administration of justice.

(3)   In order to determine whether or not the departure from the regulation had a materially adverse effect upon the protection afforded to the claimants, the proper test was whether the claimants acted reasonably in entering into CFAs rather than obtaining legal aid.

(4)   The materiality of a departure from a regulation had to be determined at the time the CFAs were entered into, not with the benefit of hindsight. The court was however entitled to discount hypothetical risks.

(5)   It was the long standing practice of the claimants' solicitors not to claim from clients any costs not recovered from the defendant, therefore the risk of the claimants paying increased hourly rates, the postponement element of the success fee and disbursements was hypothetical and to be discounted.

(6)   The cost of obtaining ATE insurance however remained the claimants' liability and amounted to a substantial disadvantage. The court could not take into account the amount of damages recovered and the solicitors' later agreement not to make a deduction from damages, because to do so would employ hindsight.

(7)   In the circumstances, there was a material departure from reg 4(2)(d) unless any claimant would not have sought legal aid and could justify the decision not to do so.

(8)   The CFAs were unenforceable for the eight claimants who would have qualified for legal aid with nil contribution. The CFAs were enforceable for the three claimants who would have qualified for legal aid subject to a contribution because they would have chosen a CFA rather than payment of a contribution to legal aid and the consequent effect upon their living standards.

(9)   CFAs were available to any litigant who reasonably chose to protect his finances (see *Campbell v MGN Ltd* at para [38.43]).

Note—Master O'Hare commented (*obiter*) that if the CFAs had not been subject to the CFA Regulations 2000, he would have only disallowed the success fee and insurance premium on the basis that they were unreasonable expenses.

[38.50] **Harmieson v Northumbrian Water Ltd**

(I March 2006, unreported), Newcastle-Upon-Tyne County Court

The claimant was injured when he twisted his ankle in an uncovered manhole. Two days before trial his claim was settled in the sum of £10,000. The defendant believed the claimant was a trade union member, however, the claim was funded by a CFA which the district judge decided was unenforceable.

HELD, ON APPEAL: (I) The defendant had raised a genuine issue about compliance with reg 4 of the CFA Regulations 2000 therefore the claimant had the burden of proving the indemnity principle had been observed. The claimant's solicitors chose to produce file notes to the court and there was no procedural error in the district judge considering them.

(2)   The word 'consider' in reg 4(2)(c) of the CFA Regulations 2000 meant more than the Oxford English Dictionary definition of 'to think over, take note of'. It was therefore insufficient for the solicitor to merely rely on the claimant's statement that he did not have trade union cover without exploring whether or not he did have such cover. Accordingly, there was a clear breach of reg 4(2)(c), (d) and (e).

(3)   It was for the claimant to show that Union funding was not available or was not more favourable than the CFA and he had failed to adduce such evidence. There was a materially adverse effect upon the proper administration of justice because the claimant's solicitors made only a superficial attempt to see if other funding was available and failed in a genuine way to engage with their duty under reg 4.

[38.51] **Brierley v Prescott**

SCCO 31 March 2006

See also at para [38.55].

The claimant was driving a taxi when he was involved in a head on collision with a hire car driven by the defendant on 7 January 2000. The owner of the taxi had the benefit of an uninsured loss recovery service provided by 'Cabcare' who instructed a firm of solicitors to pursue the claims of the taxi owner and the claimant. The Cabcare policy did not cover the cost of proceedings therefore when it became apparent that the claimant's claim would not be settled before the expiry of the limitation period, the solicitors entered into a CFA with the claimant dated 13 November 2002. Following the issue of proceedings, the claimant's claim was settled in the sum of £101,085.48 and the defendant agreed to pay costs, to be decided by detailed assessment if not agreed. The parties were unable to agree costs and one of the issues to be decided at the detailed assessment hearing was whether the claimant's solicitors had failed to comply with reg 4 of the CFA Regulations 2000. Although the issue had not been raised by the defendant in his points of dispute, the deputy district judge saw reference to the enquiries made about BTE insurance when reading the correspondence files of the claimant's solicitors. The claimant was given the opportunity to file evidence and his solicitor provided a witness statement setting out the enquiries he had made about BTE insurance before entering into the CFA. The solicitor had obtained a motor policy from the claimant and was told by the broker that the claimant had BTE legal expenses insurance. The solicitor had then written to the insurer however the insurer denied it was the legal expenses insurer for the claimant's motor policy.

The defendant contended there was a breach of reg 4 because the claimant was not asked to provide copies of all policies which might have contained BTE legal expenses cover.

HELD: (1) The guidance relating to the checks for pre-existing legal expenses insurance began with *Sarwar v Alam* (at para [38.37]) and was next considered in *Hollins v Russell* (at para [38.15]).

(2)   The solicitor had fallen short of proper modern practice by asking the claimant to check if he had BTE insurance and to provide details if he thought he had cover. However, the solicitor could not be criticised because its letter to the claimant dated 7 November 2002 pre-dated *Hollins v Russell* and a number of other decisions on reg 4.

(3)   The telephone attendance note dated 13 November 2002 should be taken at face value and therefore it was accepted that there was a discussion between the solicitor and the claimant about BTE insurance.

(4)   In the circumstances, the solicitor did consider whether the claimant had BTE insurance and therefore there was no breach of Regulation 4. Given the response from the legal expenses insurer, it was difficult to see how the solicitor could have progressed matters before the limitation period expired.

(5)   If there was a breach, it did not have a materially adverse effect upon the protection afforded to the claimant because the claim had not been notified to the possible BTE insurer in time and there was no evidence of any other means of funding the claim. In addition, there was no adverse effect upon the proper administration of justice because the ATE premium and success fee were proportionate and if the BTE insurer had accepted the claim, there would have been no funding for disbursements.

(6)   In the circumstances, the base profit costs, success fee and ATE premium were recoverable.

(C)   ASSIGNMENT OF CFAS

[38.52]   **Jenkins v Young Brothers Transport Ltd**

[2006] EWHC 151 (QB)

[2006] 2 All ER 798, [2006] NLJR 421, QB

The claimant entered into a CFA with a firm of solicitors, Girlings on 7 August 2000. On 13 August 2002 the CFA was assigned by Girlings to a second firm of solicitors, T G Baynes and subsequently on 1 April 2003 by T G Baynes to a third firm of solicitors, Thomson Snell & Passmore. The reason for the assignments was the solicitor with conduct of the claim moved from Girlings to T G Baynes and then to Thomson Snell & Passmore and the claimant had trust and confidence in her. The issues for the court to decide were whether a CFA could be lawfully assigned and the consequences if not.

HELD, ON APPEAL: (1) The general rule was that the benefit of a contract could be assigned but the burden could not without the consent of all three parties involved in the assignment. There was however an exception to the general rule where the burden had been made a condition of the benefit.

(2)   When considering benefit and burden it was necessary to look at the original CFA between the claimant and Girlings. The benefit to Girlings

was being paid but this was conditional upon Girlings discharging its burden of ensuring the claimant succeeded. Therefore the CFA was validly assigned by the agreements dated 13 August 2000 and 1 April 2003.

Note—It was unnecessary for the court to reach a conclusion whether a CFA could be validly assigned in circumstances where the claimant did not have trust and confidence in the solicitor with conduct of the case.

(D)   BACKDATING OF CFAS

[38.53]   King v Telegraph Group Ltd
SCCO 2 December 2005

The CFA between the claimant and his solicitors was dated 11 September 2002 but provided:

'Basic charges
These are for work done by us from the date you first consulted us concerning your case, namely 22 August 2002 until this agreement ends ...'.

HELD: (1) As between the solicitors and the claimant, the CFA could be backdated such that there was a valid retainer before the date the CFA was signed. The claimant was therefore entitled to recover base costs from 22 August 2002 to 11 September 2002.
  (2)   It was wrong and contrary to public policy to allow the solicitors to recover a success fee prior to the signing of the CFA. In particular, there was no duty to give notice of funding until the CFA had been signed and until the defendant had notice of the success fee, it could affect how the litigation was conducted.

[38.54]   Holmes v Alfred McAlpine Homes (Yorkshire) Ltd
[2006] EWHC 110 (QB)
[2006] All ER (D) 68 (Feb), QB

The CFA between the claimant and his solicitors was dated 15 July 2000 but was not signed by the claimant's wife on his behalf until 25 August 2000.
  The CFA provided:

'Basic charges
These are for work done from now until this agreement ends.'

HELD, ON APPEAL: (1) The backdating of the CFA required an explanation to the claimant. A properly drafted CFA would have borne the date on which it was signed but provided for its application to work done from a prior date agreed by the claimant and the solicitors. The CFA was therefore misleading and the backdating had not been properly explained to the claimant. In the circumstances, there was a breach of reg 4(2)(a) and 4(3) of the CFA Regulations 2000.
  (2)   The breach did not have a materially adverse effect upon the protection afforded to the claimant. The natural meaning of 'now' is the time when the agreement is entered into therefore the CFA did not apply to work done before 25 August 2000.
  (3)   In the absence of impropriety, the backdating did not have a materially

adverse effect upon the proper administration of justice. The backdating of documents was however wrong and liable to mislead third parties.

(E)   RECTIFICATION OF CFAS

[38.55]   Brierley v Prescott

SCCO 31 March 2006

See also at para [38.51] where the facts of this case are fully set out.

The CFA dated 13 November 2002 between the claimant and his solicitors provided that it covered, 'Your claim against Hertz UK Limited Car Hire for damages for personal injury suffered on 7 January 2000'. Subsequently, the claimant issued proceedings against the hire company, Hertz (UK) Limited and it was wrongly pleaded that Mr Prescott was driving the vehicle as servant or agent of Hertz. When the error was pointed out, Mr Prescott was substituted as defendant. Following settlement of the claim, the defendant in his points of dispute contended the claimant had not won against Hertz (UK) Limited therefore the claimant was not liable to pay any costs under the CFA. In an attempt to rectify the situation, on 18 May 2005 the claimant and his solicitors entered into a second CFA which bore the same date as the first but provided, 'Your claim against Hertz UK Limited Car Hire and Mr Jeffrey Prescott for damages for personal injury suffered on 7 January 2000'.

HELD: (1) Whether or not the claimant was liable to pay costs under the first CFA was simply a matter of construction of the agreement.
   (2)   At the time the first CFA was entered into, the claim was being handled by Hertz (UK) Limited and the defendant had no involvement other than to lend his name to the title of the proceedings. It was open to the claimant and his solicitors not to name the opponent in the CFA and therefore the erroneous addition of Hertz was an unnecessary detail.
   (3)   In the circumstances, the words used in the first CFA meant, 'the claim for damages arising out of the accident and which was being handled by Hertz' and therefore included the proceedings against the defendant. The intention of the parties to the CFA was obvious and there was only ever one 'claim'.
   (4)   The claimant was therefore liable to pay costs under the first CFA.
   (5)   The second CFA was no more than an attempt to rectify the first CFA. Although a CFA could be retrospective, an agreement to vary a CFA made after the conclusion of proceedings, would be unenforceable as contrary to public policy and a material breach of the CFA Regulations 2000.

[38.56]   Oyston v Royal Bank of Scotland plc

SCCO 16 May 2006

The claimant entered into a CFA with his solicitors dated 2 July 2002 which provided, 'Success Fee – this is 100% of our base fees. In addition you will pay £50,000 provided you recover damages in excess of £1 million'. Subsequently, the claimant issued proceedings against the defendant for the sum of £4,705,216.00 plus interest but obtained judgment for £258,373.00 plus interest of £144,543.37, a total of £402,916.37. Following judgment, the claimant and his solicitors attempted to rectify the CFA by entering into a deed of variation on 16 August 2005 which removed all reference to the payment of £50,000 which appeared at various points in the original CFA. The defendant contended that the CFA was unenforceable because it did not comply with s 58 of the Courts and Legal Services Act 1990, was not made valid by the deed of variation and the offending words could not be severed.

HELD: (1) The CFA dated 2 July 2002 was in clear breach of s 58(4) of the Courts and Legal Services Act 1990 because it provided for a success fee in excess of 100% to apply in certain circumstances. The fact that those circumstances did not later arise was irrelevant.

(2)   The deed of variation was ineffective to rectify the situation as against the defendant. By the date of the deed, the issues between the parties had been resolved and following the decision of the Privy Council in *Kellar v Carib West Ltd* [2004] UKPC 40, a deed of variation could not be used to impose a greater burden on the defendant than existed before judgment. The fact that the claimant was in agreement was of no assistance.

(3)   The decision of the Court of Appeal in *Jones v Caradon Catnic Ltd* (at para [38.34]) made it clear that a breach of s 58(4) of the 1990 Act brought about a materially adverse effect upon the proper administration of justice. As stated in *Richards v Davis* (at para [38.48]), the validity of a CFA must be judged at the date of the CFA.

(4)   It would be contrary to public policy to permit severance. As Brooke LJ stated in *Spencer v Wood* (at para [38.31]), '... Parliament decided that unless a CFA satisfied all the conditions applicable to it by virtue of section 58(1) it would not be exempt from the general rules as to the unenforceability of CFAs at common law. In my judgment, we have to interpret the statute as we find it.'

(5)   To permit either the deed of variation or severance would have the effect of enabling virtually all defective CFAs to be rectified and this would not accord either with the CFA statutory framework or public policy. In the circumstances, the CFA was unenforceable.

Note—Senior costs judge Hurst commented that the question of the effect of a deed of variation entered into before judgment had not been argued and therefore he expressed no view about it.

[38.57]   Brennan v Associated Asphalt Ltd

SCCO 18 May 2006

The claimant was injured when she fell while crossing a road which the defendant had left in a poor state of repair. The claimant entered into a CFA with her solicitors on 19 September 2001 which provided for a success fee of 50%. On 20 January 2004, her claim was settled for £4,000 plus costs prior to the issue of proceedings. Subsequently, the CFA was disclosed and the defendant informed the claimant's solicitors that it was defective because it did not specify the postponement element of the success fee. The claimant and her solicitors then entered into a deed of rectification on 22 November 2004 which provided the CFA should be construed such that the postponement element was 0%. At the hearing of a preliminary issue in detailed assessment proceedings, the defendant contended the CFA was in breach of reg 3(1)(b) of the CFA Regulations 2000 because it did not specify how much of the success fee related to the irrecoverable postponement element. The claimant did not seek to rely on the deed of rectification in order to retrieve the situation, only to confirm the state of mind of the parties to the CFA at the time it was entered into.

HELD: (1) Regulation 3(1)(b) was perfectly clear and the CFA must specify how much of the success fee related to the cost of postponement. The words 'if any' did not mean that if the postponement element was nil there was no need to mention it because the claimant had to be in no doubt about the position. In the circumstances, there was a breach of reg 3(1)(b).

    (2)   The breach did not have a materially adverse effect upon the protection afforded to the claimant for the reasons given by the Court of Appeal in *Hollins v Russell* (at para [38.15]) that the solicitors would not be able to recover the postponement element from the claimant.

    (3)   The breach did not have a materially adverse effect upon the proper administration of justice and no assistance could be derived from the decision in *Garrett v Halton Borough Council Liverpool County Court* (at para [38.32]) relied on by the defendant.

    (4)   In the circumstances, the CFA was enforceable.

Note—Senior costs judge, Hurst, commented that because of the basis upon which he reached his decision, there was no need for him to come to a concluded view about the deed of rectification. He did however indicate during the course of argument that the deed was open to severe criticism and may not have been effective, so far as the defendant was concerned, because of the decision of the Privy Council in *Kellar v Carib West Ltd* [2004] UKPC 40. (See *Oyston v The Royal Bank of Scotland plc* SCCO 16 May 2006 (at para [38.56]) for a detailed consideration of the decision in *Kellar* by senior costs judge Hurst).

(F)   SUCCESS FEES IN ROAD TRAFFIC ACCIDENTS OCCURRING BEFORE 6 OCTOBER 2003

For success fees where the road traffic accident occurred on or after 6 October 2003, see para [38.102].

[38.58]   Callery v Gray

[2001] EWCA Civ 1117

[2001] 3 All ER 833

The claimant sustained minor injuries when a passenger in a car which was struck side on by a vehicle driven by the defendant. The claimant entered into a CFA with his solicitors at the outset and before it was known whether the defendant was contesting the claim. The CFA provided for a success fee of 60%. The defendant admitted liability two weeks after the claim was made and the claim settled for £1,500 prior to the issue of proceedings. The claimant sought to recover a success fee of 40% conceding that 20% related to postponement of fees and therefore was not recoverable pursuant to CPR 44.3B(1)(a).

HELD, ON APPEAL: (1) It will normally be reasonable for the claimant to enter into a CFA when he first instructs his solicitors.

    (2)   Where a CFA is agreed at the outset in a modest and straightforward road traffic accident claim, 20% is the maximum success fee recoverable from the defendant.

    (3)   It is open to a solicitor and claimant to agree a 'two-stage' success fee, for example, 100% from the outset but reduced to 5% if the claim

settles before the end of the pre-action protocol period. In the future, once the claims data necessary to determine a reasonable two-stage success fee becomes available, 'consideration will need to be given to the question whether, where fees are agreed at the outset, the requirement to act reasonably mandates the agreement of a two-stage success fee'. (But see *Ku v Liverpool City Council* at para [38.62]).

[38.59] **Halloran v Delaney**

[2002] EWCA Civ 1258

[2003] 1 All ER 775

The claimant was injured in a road traffic accident on 22 May 2000 and two days later entered into a CFA with the solicitors instructed to act for him. The CFA provided for a success fee of 40% of which 10% related to the cost of postponement of payment of the solicitors' fees. The claim settled for £1,500 without the need for substantive proceedings. Following the issue of costs only proceedings, the parties agreed the amount of the success fee and all that remained in dispute was the costs of the costs only proceedings.

HELD, ON APPEAL: (1) The CFA covered the costs only proceedings because the claim was not concluded until the costs had been finally assessed. The district judge was not wrong to allow a 20% success fee for the costs only proceedings because of the uncertainties at the time the CFA was made including the recoverability of ATE insurance premiums.
   (2)   Since the second judgment of the Court of Appeal in *Callery v Gray* on 31 July 2001 (at para [38.58]), the uncertainties had been removed so it was appropriate to reassess the appropriate success fee in straightforward claims settled without proceedings. For all CFAs entered into on or after 1 August 2001, a success fee of 5% should be allowed, including the costs of the costs only proceedings.

[38.60] **Mason v Whapplington**

(8 October 2002, unreported), Sheffield County Court

The claimant, a driver, was involved in a rear end shunt and entered into a CFA with his solicitors. The CFA provided for a success fee of 100% subject to a cap of 10% of the damages. Liability was accepted within four days of the letter of claim and eight months later the claim settled for £5,067.79. The parties were unable to agree the success fee.

HELD: (1) Applying *Callery v Gray*, a 100% success fee was not appropriate.
   (2)   Significant weight should not be given to the 10% cap which served no useful purpose where the claimant was likely to succeed. (3) Assessing the risks at the time the CFA was entered into and not using the benefit of hindsight, a success fee of 40% was reasonable. Using the 20% success fee allowed in *Callery v Gray* (at para [38.58]) as a starting point, it was then necessary to take into account other factors including acting for a driver and the solicitors had agreed to pay the defendant's costs and the claimant's disbursements if the claimant was unsuccessful.

[38.61] **Atack v Lee and Grechan**
Ellerton v Harris

[2004] EWCA Civ 1712

[2005] 1 WLR 2643

These two appeals were heard together because they both concerned the appropriate level of success fee in a personal injury claim arising out of a road traffic accident.

In *Atack*, the claimant was riding his motorcycle when he was injured as a result of an incident involving a lorry on a roundabout. The defendants denied liability based upon the evidence of an off-duty policeman who blamed the claimant. Subsequently on 22 March 2001, the claimant entered into a CFA with a 100% success fee. The defendants maintained their denial of liability and at trial the first defendant was held 100% to blame. The following day the claim settled for £30,000. At the detailed assessment hearing the deputy district judge allowed a 50% success fee.

HELD: (1) The reasonableness of the success fee had to be assessed taking into account what the solicitors knew or ought to have known at the time the CFA was entered into. In particular, based on the locus report, the solicitors knew the lorry was in the wrong lane and not signalling and the independent witness could not have seen anything but the last few seconds before the accident.
   (2)   The solicitors' risk assessment was of no value at all so the deputy district judge was right not to take it into account.
   (3)   In the circumstances, the 50% success fee allowed by the deputy district judge was within the range reasonably available to him.

In *Ellerton*, the claimant was injured when a vehicle reversed into her as she was walking in a supermarket car park. The claimant entered into a CFA on 22 September 2000 with a 60% success fee then sent a letter of claim. The defendant accepted liability four months later. Following the issue of proceedings, the defendant served a defence again admitting liability. The claim settled five weeks later for £15,378.79. At the detailed assessment hearing the district judge allowed a 30% success fee.

HELD, ON APPEAL: (1) The guidance given in *Callery v Gray* (at para [38.58]) could be applied by analogy to this case even though it was a multi-track claim.
   (2)   The uncertainty about the identity of the driver could have been resolved by the solicitor telephoning the police prior to entering into the CFA. The only significant risk related to the claimant not beating a payment into court in which case the solicitor would not be paid base costs or a success fee. This risk justified a success fee of 20%.
   (3)   In future, it would be legitimate for parties to refer to the report by Paul Fenn and Neil Rickman, 'Calculating Reasonable Success Fees for RTA Claims' dated October 2003 in relation to success fees in RTAs occurring before 6 October 2003. It was not however appropriate to adopt the fixed recoverable success fees provided by CPR Pt 45 when assessing the reasonableness of a success fee in such cases.

[38.62]   U (a child) v Liverpool City Council
[2005] EWCA Civ 475
[2005] 1 WLR 2657

The claimant entered into a CFA with her solicitors that provided for a single-stage success fee of 100%.

HELD, ON APPEAL: (1) The court did not have the power to impose a two-stage success fee where a single-stage success fee had been agreed. In so far as paragraph 11.8(2) of the Costs Practice Direction said otherwise, it was wrong.

(2)   The single-stage success fee covered the whole of the claim including the detailed assessment proceedings.

(3)   Costs judges should allow higher success fees in claims that do not settle at an early stage if the claimant and solicitor have agreed a two-stage success fee.

[38.63]   Haines v Sarner

SCCO 27 April 2005

The claimant was knocked off his bicycle by a vehicle driven by the defendant and sustained severe brain injuries. By consent, judgment was entered in favour of the claimant for 70% of his claim on 8 October 2003. Subsequently on 24 November 2003, the claimant entered into a new CFA when his solicitor changed firms. The new CFA provided for a success fee of 60%.

HELD: (1) By the time the new CFA was entered into the issue of liability had been resolved including the issues referred to in the solicitor's risk assessment such as causation, extent of the claimant's injuries and exaggeration.

(2)   The claim for damages had been finally decided in the claimant's favour and therefore the solicitors was never at risk of not being paid. The only relevant risk related to the claimant failing to beat a Part 36 offer or payment into court but even then the solicitor would still be entitled to its base costs. Only the success fee was at risk. Therefore the recoverable success fee had to be less than the 20% allowed in *Ellerton v Harris* (at para [38.61]) where the solicitor was at risk of not being paid base costs and a success fee if the claimant did not beat a payment into court.

(3)   The defendant was not liable for the risk of the bankruptcy of the claimant or the defendant's insurers, which in essence related to the postponement of payment of the solicitor's charges.

(4)   The recoverable success fee was 5%.

[38.64]   Burton and Haynes v Kingsley and Harper

[2005] EWHC 1034 (QB)

[2005] All ER (D) 378 (May), QB

The claimants were passengers in a vehicle being driven by the first defendant. The second defendant was driving his vehicle in the same direction. The first defendant's vehicle suddenly left the road and overturned. Both claimants were seriously injured. Less than four weeks after the accident, each claimant entered into a CFA with a success fee of 100%. On the day of the liability trial, the parties agreed terms of settlement and an order was made providing for judgment against the first defendant and dismissal of the claims against the second defendant. The claimants sought to recover the success fee of 100%.

HELD: (1) At the time the CFAs were entered into, the solicitors had made reasonable initial enquiries which included speaking to the police. Although the solicitors had correctly assessed the claimants had a strong case, there was still a significant element of risk and in particular there remained the possibility that no one was to blame or the claimants would be unable to establish who was to blame.

(2)   The prospects of success were higher than 50/50 and a reasonable success fee was in the bracket 33% to 50%. The claimants were allowed 50%.

(G)   SUCCESS FEES FOR COSTS DRAFTSMEN

[38.65]   **Cannon v Mid Essex Hospital Services NHS Trust**
SCCO 23 March 2005

In this costs appeal, the defendant argued that the fees of the claimant's costs draftsman should have been charged as a disbursement and not part of the solicitors' profit costs and therefore a success fee was not payable on the costs draftsman's fees.

HELD, ON APPEAL: (1) The decisions in *Smith Graham v Lord Chancellor* [1999] 2 Costs LR 55 and *Stringer v Copley* (at para [38.165]) supported the contention that the costs draftsman was to be treated as if he was formally employed by the solicitors and therefore the work done by him was correctly included as part of the solicitors' charges.
   (2)   In the circumstances, the costs draftsman's fee did attract a success fee.

[38.66]   **Guy v Castle Morpeth Borough Council**
(12 January 2006, unreported), Newcastle Upon Tyne County Court

The claimant suffered injuries in a tripping accident and her claim for damages was settled by negotiation. The parties were unable to agree costs and the issue for the court to decide was whether the success fee provided for by the claimant's CFA extended to the costs of the claimant's law costs draftsman. At the detailed assessment hearing, the district judge determined the costs draftsman's costs were a disbursement and therefore did not attract a success fee.

HELD, ON APPEAL: (1) The issue turned on the proper construction of the CFA which incorporated The Law Society Conditions.
   (2)   The solicitors' basic charges included, 'the cost of advocacy and any other work by us or by any solicitor agent on our behalf …' and disbursements included, 'payments we make on your behalf such as court fees, experts' fees, (etc.).' Therefore the CFA drew a distinction between basic charges and disbursements.
   (3)   The words 'solicitor agent' did not cover non-solicitors.
   (4)   In the circumstances, the district judge's decision was correct.

[38.67]   **Crane v Canons Leisure Centre**
SCCO 1 March 2006

The claimant was injured at work and his trade union instructed solicitors on his behalf. His claim was settled for £1,500 plus costs prior to the issue of proceedings. Subsequently, the claimant's solicitors instructed an independent firm of costs draftsmen to recover their costs however the parties could not reach agreement and the claimant issued costs only proceedings. At the detailed assessment hearing, the costs officer allowed a success fee upon the costs draftsmen's fees. The defendant appealed on the grounds that the costs draftsmen's fees were a disbursement, not part of the profit costs of the solicitors and therefore did not attract a success fee.

HELD, ON APPEAL: (1) The fundamental question was whether the agreement between the claimant and his solicitors permitted the costs draftsmen's fees to be treated as part of the solicitors' profit costs to which a success fee could be added.
   (2)   It did not follow from Costs Practice Direction section 4.16(6) that the

fees of a costs draftsman or costs negotiator should be treated as part of the instructing solicitors' profit costs.

(3) The costs draftsmen were not instructed as solicitor-agents and their fees fell within the definition of disbursements in the agreement between the claimant and the solicitors.

(4) The costs officer was therefore wrong to allow a success fee on the costs draftsmen's fees.

[38.68]

Table of success fee awards

Case	Date of CFA	Stage of claim when CFA entered into	Damages	Success fee claimed	Success fee allowed
Callery v Gray	28 April 2000	Prior to letter of claim	£1,500.00	40%	20%
Halloran v Delaney	24 May 2000	Prior to letter of claim	£1,500.00	30%	20%
Mason v Whapplington	Unknown	Prior to letter of claim	£5,067.79	100%	40%
Atack v Lee & Grechan	22 March 2001	After denial of liability	£30,000.00	100%	50%
Ellerton v Harris	22 September 2000	Prior to letter of claim	£15,378.79	60%	20%
Haines v Sarner	24 November 2003	After judgment in favour of the claimant	£425,000.00	60%	5%
Burton & Haynes v Kingsley & Harper	9 September 2001	Prior to letter of claim	Unknown, but catastrophic injuries	100%	50%

3. COSTS CAPPING

[38.69] Griffiths v Solutia UK Ltd

[2001] EWCA Civ 736

[2001] All ER (D) 196 (Apr)

The claimants recovered damages of £90,000 and their solicitors' bill of costs amounted to £210,000. The issue for the court was the reasonableness of the solicitors' hourly rate. However, Mance LJ took the opportunity to remark:

'The present litigation was conducted under the old rules preceding the Woolf reforms. It is to be hoped that subsequent to the Woolf reforms Judges conducting cases will make full use of their powers under the Practice

Direction about costs, section 6 ... to obtain estimates of costs and to exercise their powers in respect of costs and case management to keep costs within the bounds of the proportionate in accordance with the overriding objective. That the amount of costs should play an important part, both in the court's orders about costs and in its orders about case management, is indicated expressly in paragraph 6.1 of that Practice Direction ...'

[38.70]   AB and Others v Leeds Teaching Hospitals NHS Trust
[2004] EWHC 644 (QB), QB

This case represented the first instance of a costs capping order in the High Court. It concerned group litigation arising out of the retention by hospitals of organs of deceased children and adults. The defendant applied for an order to cap the claimants' costs both retrospectively and prospectively.

HELD: (1) The court had power to make a costs capping order pursuant to s 51 of the Supreme Court Act 1981 (as amended) and various parts of the Civil Procedure Rules including in particular the general powers of case management in CPR 3.1(2)(m) and 44.3. In addition, the provision for estimates of costs in Costs Practice Direction section 6 was consistent with such a power.
    (2)   The costs capping order had to be proportionate to the amount at stake and the complexity of the issues.
    (3)   The costs cap applied retrospectively and prospectively to solicitors' costs, counsel's fees, experts' fees and other disbursements.

[38.71]   France v McVeigh
(26 June 2003, unreported), Doncaster County Court

The claimant was injured in a road traffic accident and the value of the claim was between £5,000 and £15,000. The claim was funded by a CFA and the claimant estimated base costs of £9,000 to the conclusion of the case. The defendant applied to cap the claimant's base costs.

HELD: This was a routine case and there was no genuine reason to cap the claimant's costs. In particular, there was no evidence the costs would escalate. It was however disproportionate to spend £2,500 on a costs capping application in a fast track claim.

[38.72]   Various Ledward Claimants v Kent & Medway Health Authority and East Kent Hospitals NHS Trust
[2003] EWHC 2551 (QB)
[2003] All ER (D) 12 (Nov), QB

This case concerned group litigation arising out of alleged rape and sexual assault by a consultant gynaecologist. The parties agreed there should be a retrospective costs capping order but did not agree the amount of the cap. The trial was to commence in two months.

HELD: (1) It was unfortunate that the costs capping application had not been made earlier before unnecessary and unreasonable costs were incurred.
    (2)   The cap applied to the solicitors' costs and counsels' fees of both parties. It was surprising that the parties agreed not to cap experts' fees.

[38.73]   **Smart v East Cheshire NHS Trust**

[2003] EWHC 2806 (QB)

(2003) 80 BMLR 175, QB

This was a clinical negligence case arising out of the claimant's treatment at a hospital managed by the defendant.

HELD: (1) The court had power to make a costs capping order in litigation involving a single claimant. In such a case however, a costs cap should not be imposed unless there was evidence of a real and substantial risk that costs would be disproportionately or unreasonably incurred which could not be managed by conventional case management and detailed assessment.

(2)   This was not a case where a costs cap should be made because the claimant's solicitors were experienced in clinical negligence therefore there was no real risk of disproportionate or unreasonably incurred costs.

[38.74]   **King v Telegraph Group Ltd**

[2004] EWCA Civ 613

[2004] All ER (D) 242 (May), [2005] 1 WLR 2282

The claimant's defamation action against the defendant was funded by a CFA but he did not take out ATE insurance. The defendant applied for a conditional order for security for costs on the grounds that the claim was unlikely to succeed and any costs order against the claimant was likely to be difficult to enforce. The judge refused the application. Having dismissed the defendant's appeal, Brooke LJ took the opportunity to remark on the court's powers to control costs. In his judgment, the court had the power to make a costs capping order under s 51 of the Supreme Courts Act 1981 and CPR 3.1(2)(m) and this should be the court's first response when a defendant raised concern about the claimant's costs. 'The service of an over-heavy estimate of costs with the response to the allocation questionnaire may well trigger off the need for such a step to be taken in future.'

[38.75]   **Sheppard v Essex Strategic Health Authority**

(13 May 2005, unreported), QBD

This was an appeal against a costs capping order in an action brought by twins injured at birth.

HELD, ON APPEAL: Although the claimants were represented by very experienced solicitors who would not knowingly incur costs unnecessarily, there was a risk that costs might escalate unreasonably unless a costs capping order was made. The amount of the cap was to be assessed by a costs judge.

Note—The judge was assisted in reaching her conclusion by the direction of Brooke LJ in *King v Telegraph Group* (at para [38.74]).

[38.76]   **The claimants set out in schedule 1 to the order of the Senior Master dated 17 January 2005 v TUI UK Ltd**

SCCO 11 August 2005

A group litigation order provided that the claimants' costs be capped with the amount to be determined by a costs judge.

HELD: (1) A costs capping order was not retrospective unless specifically provided for in the order. In *AB and Others v Leeds Teaching Hospitals NHS Trust* (at para

[38.70]) the costs capping order was retrospective by agreement of the parties. There was no such agreement in this case.

(2) The cap applied to the solicitors' fees and other disbursements but the parties had liberty to apply to vary the cap in the event of an unforeseen factor arising in the future.

[38.77] Henry v British Broadcasting Corpn

[2005] EWHC 2503 (QB)

[2006] 1 All ER 154, [2005] NLJR 1780, QB

The claimant's defamation action was funded by a CFA and ATE insurance. The defendant applied for a costs capping order one week before trial.

HELD: (1) The ATE policy was not privileged and should be disclosed to enable the defendant to consider the amount of cover and the existence of material exclusions and then decide whether to apply for a costs capping order.

(2) Costs capping orders should invariably operate prospectively and not retrospectively.

(3) The application was made far too late and the making of a costs capping order so close to trial would penalise the claimant. In addition, the amount of a costs cap should not be determined by a judge sitting alone. Such an exercise was more suitable for a costs judge or a judge sitting with a costs judge.

[38.78] Knight (known as Bowvayne) v Beyond Properties Pty Ltd

[2006] EWHC 1242 (Ch)

[2006] All ER (D) 400 (May), [2006] NLJR 989

The claimant's passing off action against the defendants was funded by a CFA which provided for a success fee of 100% but he did not take out ATE insurance cover. In his allocation questionnaire, the claimant estimated costs to date of £48,000 and costs to trial of £200,000. The defendants applied for a costs-capping order to prospectively limit their liability for costs in the event that the claimant was successful.

HELD: (1) The remarks of Brooke LJ in *King v Telegraph Group Ltd* (at para [38.74]) were uttered in the particular context of a defamation action and he was not laying down principles applicable to all litigation. Gage J's indication in *Smart v East Cheshire NHS Trust* (at para [38.73]) that costs should be capped if the normal post-trial assessment of costs would or might not achieve justice, was an important guideline. Costs judges could be expected to filter out extravagant costs.

(2) A CFA with no ATE cover was not, by itself, sufficient to justify a costs cap. It was necessary to establish on evidence that there was a real risk of excessive expenditure that could not be controlled by case management or detailed assessment.

(3) Although there was a risk of extravagant costs expenditure on documents and witnesses, this could be satisfactorily dealt with on a detailed assessment and should be left to the costs judge. In the circumstances, a costs-capping order was not appropriate.

(4) The trial judge might consider giving guidance or directions as to particular costs.

4. DETAILED ASSESSMENT PROCEEDINGS

(A) DELAY

[38.79] **McGuigan v Tarmac Ltd**

(3 February 2003, unreported), Central London County Court

The defendant commenced detailed assessment proceedings but subsequently failed to request a hearing date within the three months provided by CPR 47.14. A hearing date was eventually requested over two years after commencement of the assessment proceedings and the delay was due to an oversight. The defendant conceded its claim for interest. However, the district judge additionally reduced the costs by 60% pursuant to CPR 44.14.

HELD, ON APPEAL: (1) Under CPR 47.14, the only sanction for delay was that interest be disallowed. However, this was subject to CPR 44.14 which provided a wider range of sanctions for breach of a rule. CPR 44.14 was not triggered by mere delay, only by delay sufficient to amount to misconduct.
   (2)   Although the district judge was right to disallow costs given the length of the delay, a 60% reduction was outside the available ambit of discretion, given the absence of good evidence of prejudice to the claimant.
   (3)   A 25% reduction was substituted and the concession on interest was accepted as inevitable.

[38.80] **Less and Others v Benedict**

[2005] EWHC 1643 (Ch)

[2005] All ER (D) 355 (Jul)

The claimants alleged delay on the part of the defendant following the commencement of detailed assessment proceedings. The Master disallowed interest for a period of 3½ years but refused to impose any other sanction.

HELD, ON APPEAL: (1) There was no violation of the claimants' rights under Art 6 of the European Convention on Human Rights because they could have made an application under CPR Pt 47 to bring the defendant's delay to the attention of the court.
   (2)   There was no abuse of process because a fair hearing was still possible. It was the receiving party's papers that were important on an assessment, not the paying party's, therefore it was the receiving party which was likely to lose out by delay. The defendant was not wholly responsible for the delay because the claimants did not avail themselves of the remedy of an application under CPR Pt 47.
   (3)   CPR 44.14 was intended to cover breaches going beyond mere non-compliance with a time limit under CPR Pt 47. Therefore it would only be in an exceptional case that mere delay resulted in costs being disallowed. The Master was right to only disallow interest.

[38.81] **Haji-Ioannou and Others v Frangos and Others**

[2006] EWHC 279 (Ch)

[2006] All ER (D) 375 (Feb)

The defendants commenced detailed assessment proceedings five years out of time. The costs judge refused to disallow a proportion of the defendants' costs which were assessed in the sum of approximately £328,000.

HELD, ON APPEAL: (1) Delay sufficient to amount to misconduct was not required in order to trigger CPR 44.14.

    (2)   In exercising the discretion to disallow costs conferred by CPR 44.14, the court could not ignore the defendants' concession as to interest which resulted in a very substantial disadvantage given the amount of the assessed costs. The costs judge was right not to disallow any part of the defendants' costs.

(B)   DISCLOSURE

[38.82]   Dickinson (t/a John Dickinson Equipment Finance) v Rushmer (t/a FJ Associates)

[2001] All ER (D) 369 (Dec), [2002] 1 Costs LR 128

In detailed assessment proceedings, the defendant served points of dispute which included a request for the claimant to disclose a copy of his solicitor's client care letter and evidence of payment of the solicitors' bills. At the hearing of the preliminary issue as to whether there was a breach of the indemnity principle, the claimant's solicitor produced various documents to the costs judge which the defendant was not allowed to see. The costs judge found the indemnity principle had not been breached.

HELD, ON APPEAL: (1) The calculation showing what the claimant had paid and the client care letter were not privileged and should have been disclosed to the defendant.

    (2)   Paragraph 40.14 of the Costs Practice Direction was not relevant because the costs judge did not direct the production of documents to the court rather the claimant volunteered them.

    (3)   The defendants had raised a genuine issue about the claimant's liability for costs and the procedure adopted by the costs judge was unfair. The costs judge should have adopted the procedure in *Pamplin v Express Newspapers Ltd* [1985] 1 WLR 689 and put the claimant to election whether he wished to waive privilege in the solicitor's bills of costs delivered to him or to assert privilege and prove the documents in another way. The preliminary issue would have to be remitted for a rehearing unless the claimant was willing to disclose the documents.

[38.83]   South Coast Shipping Co Ltd v Havant Borough Council

(21 December 2001, unreported), Chancery Division

At the hearing of the preliminary issue as to whether there was a breach of the indemnity principle, the claimant produced privileged documents to the costs judge which were not shown to the defendant. The costs judge found there had been no breach of the indemnity principle.

HELD, ON APPEAL: (1) It was assumed that the solicitors' bills to the claimant and the claimant's cheques paying them were privileged. This was however arguably wrong, at least in so far as the cheques were concerned.

    (2)   Once the costs judge decided to rely upon the bills he should have

asked the defendant if they had any objection. If the defendant had objected, the claimant should have been put to the election either to waive privilege or prove the documents by other means. Nevertheless, based upon the material before the costs judge, his decision was correct.

[38.84]   McCreery v Massey Plastic Fabrications Ltd

(23 January 2003, unreported), Queen's Bench Division Manchester District Registry

In detailed assessment proceedings, the defendant sought disclosure of the claimant's CFA and the related risk assessment.

HELD: (1) The CFA was not a privileged document because it was not entered into for the purpose of giving advice. The CFA should therefore be disclosed and inspection of it permitted.
 (2)   The risk assessment was not a privileged document and inspection of it was necessary to confirm the success fee.
 (3)   Subject to the right to claim privilege, other documents which substantiate the claim for costs should be disclosed and inspection permitted.

[38.85]   Hollins v Russell

[2003] EWCA Civ 718

[2003] 4 All ER 590, [2003] 1 WLR 2487

This case is more fully set out at para [38.15].

HELD, ON APPEAL (on the issue of disclosure of a CFA in detailed assessment proceedings): (1) The receiving party should either disclose the CFA to the paying party or prove the CFA by other evidence.
 (2)   Any privileged material may be redacted before disclosure.
 (3)   Ordinarily, attendance notes should not be disclosed unless a genuine issue is raised about compliance with the CFA Regulations 2000.

Note—In the absence of full argument, the Court of Appeal was unwilling to express a view whether or not a CFA was privileged. The court did not comment in detail on the judgment in *McCreery v Massey Plastic Fabrications Ltd* (at para [38.84]) but noted the district judge's decision relating to disclosure of CFAs and risk assessments went beyond the practice laid down by the Court of Appeal.

[38.86]   NG Bailey & Co Ltd v Amec Design & Management Ltd

SCCO 6 October 2003

The costs judge in this case disagreed with the decision in *McCreery v Massey Plastic Fabrications Ltd* (at para [38.84])in relation to general documents which support the claim for costs and refused to order disclosure. It was for the Court of Appeal to move the law forward in the way suggested in *McCreery*, not a costs judge.

[38.87]   Owen v Biffa Waste Services Ltd

SCCO 22 April 2004

Each claimant entered into a CFA and in most if not all cases the CFA bore a date in 2001. The defendant alleged the dates were false and sought:
 (1)   disclosure of correspondence and attendance notes relating to the execution of each CFA;

(2)   further information relating to the signing of each CFA.

HELD: (1) In the first instance, it was appropriate to order the claimants to prepare, for the court only, a list of all the correspondence and attendance notes which the defendant sought disclosure of and at the same time produce those documents for inspection by the court. The defendant could decide whether or not to pursue the application for disclosure at a later interim hearing, having firstly seen the claimants' witness statements.

(2)   The defendant was entitled to the further information requested to be supplied with the witness statements.

5.   ESTIMATES OF COSTS

[38.88]   **Leigh v Michelin Tyre plc**

[2003] EWCA Civ 1766

[2004] 2 All ER 175, [2004] 1 WLR 846

The claimant's estimate of costs in his allocation questionnaire recorded profit costs to date at £3,000 plus VAT and overall profit costs at £6,000 plus VAT. Following settlement of the claim, the claimant's bill of costs totalled £21,741.28 comprising £14,482.80 in respect of profit costs. The district judge made no deduction to reflect the wholly inadequate estimate.

HELD, ON APPEAL: (1) The purpose of requiring accurate costs estimates pursuant to section 6 of the Costs Practice Direction is to keep the parties informed about their potential liability for costs and to control the costs of litigation by case management. A costs estimate may be taken into account when assessing costs in the following circumstances:

(a)   if there is a substantial difference between the estimate and the costs claimed and the receiving party fails to provide a satisfactory explanation, the court may conclude the costs claimed are unreasonable;

(b)   if the paying party shows it relied on the estimate;

(c)   if the court would have made different case management directions had a realistic estimate been given.

(2)   It was not however appropriate to hold a party to their estimate as a penalty for providing an inadequate estimate as this amounted to a costs cap.

(3)   The costs judge should decide how to take the costs estimate into account before going on to assess the receiving party's costs.

[38.89]   **Burns (Executor of the estate of Leslie Burns deceased) and Adcock (Common law widow and Executrix of the estate of Leslie Burns deceased) v Novartis Grimsby Ltd and Tioxide Group**

SCCO 16 February 2004

The claimants' estimate of costs in their allocation questionnaire recorded costs to date at £17,500 and overall costs at £35,000. Following trial, the claimants' bill of costs totalled £99,215.52.

HELD: Applying the guidance in *Leigh v Michelin Tyre plc* (at para [38.88]), the substantial difference between the estimate and the costs claimed called for an explanation. The reason for the difference was that the case changed after the estimate was given. The claim became very difficult and complex as a result of the decision and subsequent appeals in *Fairchild v Glenhaven Funeral Services Ltd* [2002] UKHL 22 and more work was necessary than had been anticipated. In the circumstances, the claimants' costs should not be limited to their estimate nor was it appropriate to take the estimate into account in the assessment of costs.

From 1 October 2005, section 6 of the Costs Practice Direction was amended and now provides:

'6.5A(1) If there is a difference of 20% or more between the base costs claimed by a receiving party on detailed assessment and the costs shown in an estimate of costs filed by that party, the receiving party must provide a statement of the reasons for the difference with his bill of costs.

(2) If a paying party—
   (a) claims that he reasonably relied on an estimate of costs filed by a receiving party; or
   (b) wishes to rely upon the costs shown in the estimate in order to dispute the reasonableness or proportionality of the costs claimed,
   the paying party must serve a statement setting out his case in this regard in his points of dispute.

6.6(1) On an assessment of the costs of a party, the court may have regard to any estimate previously filed by that party, or by any other party in the same proceedings. Such an estimate may be taken into account as a factor, among others, when assessing the reasonableness and proportionality of any costs claimed.

(2) In particular, where—
   (a) there is a difference of 20% or more between the base costs claimed by a receiving party and the costs shown in an estimate of costs filed by that party; and
   (b) it appears to the court that—
      (i) the receiving party has not provided a satisfactory explanation for that difference; or
      (ii) the paying party reasonably relied on the estimate of costs,
   the court may regard the difference between the costs claimed and the costs shown in the estimate as evidence that the costs claimed are unreasonable or disproportionate.'

[38.90] Garbutt and Another v Edwards and Another

[2005] EWCA Civ 1206

[2006] 1 All ER 553

The issue which arose in this case was whether a paying party can rely on a failure by the solicitor for the receiving party to give his client an estimate of costs in order to discharge or reduce the paying party's liability to the receiving party.

HELD, ON APPEAL: (1) The court assumes the certificate of accuracy in a bill of costs has been properly given by the receiving party's solicitor and there must be good reason to go behind it.

(2) An estimate of costs was required only by the Solicitors' Costs Information and Client Care Code 1999 made pursuant to rule 15 of the Solicitors' Practice Rules which themselves were made pursuant to s 31 of the Solicitors' Act 1974. The purpose of the Code was to protect the interests of the client, not to relieve a paying party of their obligation to pay costs.

(3)   The failure to give an estimate of costs as required by the Code did not render the retainer between the solicitor and client unlawful and unenforceable.

(4)   If the paying party has real grounds to show the costs would have been lower had an estimate been given, the costs judge should follow the procedure in *Pamplin v Express Newspapers Ltd* [1985] 1 WLR 689 and put the receiving party to its election to either disclose the estimate or otherwise prove it was given.

(5)   The costs judge conducting a party and party assessment of costs may take into account the failure by a solicitor to give an estimate of costs to the receiving party but a specific reduction or tariff was not appropriate and this situation was different from that in *Leigh v Michelin Tyre plc* (at para [38.88]) which concerned an estimate given to the other party.

(6)   If there is a substantial difference between an estimate given but not updated and the costs claimed, in the absence of a satisfactory explanation, the court may conclude the costs claimed are unreasonable.

[38.91]   Henry v British Broadcasting Corpn

[2005] EWHC 2503 (QB)

[2006] 1 All ER 154, [2005] NLJR 1780, QB

The claimant's allocation questionnaire contained an estimate of costs to trial in the sum of £360,000 excluding VAT, success fee and ATE premium. One month before trial, the claimant served a revised estimate in the sum of £694,000.

HELD: Both parties should keep each other informed with up to date estimates of costs. If a party delays, the other party should make a prompt application to the court pursuant to paragraph 6 of the Costs Practice Direction for an order that an estimate be provided.

6.   FIXED RECOVERABLE COSTS

(A)   FIXED RECOVERABLE BASE COSTS AND DISBURSEMENTS IN ROAD TRAFFIC ACCIDENTS OCCURRING ON OR AFTER 6 OCTOBER 2003

[38.92]

Part II of CPR Pt 45 provides that only specified fixed costs are recoverable, other than in exceptional circumstances, in relation to disputes arising out of road traffic accidents occurring on or after 6 October 2003 which are settled prior to the issue of proceedings for an amount of agreed damages not exceeding £10,000.

'45.9(1)Subject to paragraphs (2) and (3), the amount of fixed recoverable costs is the total of–
    (a) £800;
    (b) 20% of the damages agreed up to £5,000; and
    (c) 15% of the damages agreed between £5,000 and £10,000.
(2)   Where the claimant–

(a) lives or works in an area set out in the relevant practice direction; and

(b) instructs a solicitor or firm of solicitors who practise in that area, the fixed recoverable costs shall include, in addition to the costs specified in paragraph (1), an amount equal to 12.5% of the costs allowable under that paragraph.

(3) Where appropriate, value added tax (VAT) may be recovered in addition to the amount of fixed recoverable costs and any reference in the section to fixed recoverable costs is a reference to those costs net of any such VAT.'

Note—For the purposes of rule 45.9(2), the area is London.

'45.10(1) The court–

(a) may allow a claim for a disbursement of a type mentioned in paragraph (2); but

(b) must not allow a claim for any other type of disbursement.

(2) The disbursement referred to in paragraph (1) are–

(a) the cost of obtaining–
   (i) medical records;
   (ii) a medical report;
   (iii) a police report;
   (iv) an engineer's report; or
   (v) a search of the records of the DVLA;

(b) the amount of an insurance premium;

(c) where they are necessarily incurred by reason of one or more of the claimants being a child or patient as defined in Part 21–
   (i) fees payable for instructing counsel; or
   (ii) court fees payable on an application to the court;

(d) any other disbursement that has arisen due to a particular feature of the dispute.'

[38.93] Cook v Graham

(12 October 2004, unreported), Liverpool County Court

The claim fell within the fixed recoverable costs scheme. The defendant refused to pay costs due on the claimant's insurance policy excess and the outlay of the claimant's insurer on the grounds that these items were not in dispute.

HELD: The balance of the costs was payable because the heads of loss were included in the claim by the claimant's solicitors.

[38.94] Swatton v Smithurst

(3 February 2005, unreported), Oxford County Court

Following a road traffic accident, the damage to the claimant's vehicle and hire charges was dealt with directly between insurers. The claimant's personal injury claim was conducted by a solicitor and settled for £1,850.

HELD, ON APPEAL: The expression 'total value of agreed damages' in CPR 45.7(2)(c) meant those aspects of the claim conducted by the solicitor. The solicitor should not be paid for the work carried out by the insurers.

[38.95] Earle v Centrica plc

(22 July 2005, unreported), Ipswich County Court

On 5 February 2004 the claimant was injured in a road traffic accident. His claim settled for £3,850 prior to the issue of proceedings. The defendant disputed liability to pay the fees of the medical experts and agency.

HELD: (1) The cases of *Stringer v Copley* (at para [38.165]) and *Claims Direct Test Cases (Tranche 2* issues (at para [38.166]) concerned the fees of medical agencies when assessing costs on a standard basis. Here the court was concerned with the fixed recoverable costs scheme.

(2)   To allow recovery of the medical agency's fees would carry the risk of solicitors attempting to circumvent the restrictions on their profit costs by delegating work to third parties who could claim as disbursements that which the solicitor would normally perform.

(3)   The claimant was therefore only entitled to recover the GP records fee of £50 and the medical expert's fee of £285.

(4)   Had the claimant disclosed the medical agency's agreement sooner, proceedings would not have been necessary. In the circumstances, the claimant was not entitled to either interest or the costs of the proceedings.

[38.96]   Thorpe v McClean

(8 November 2005, unreported), Rawtenstall County Court

The claimant was injured in a road traffic accident involving a rear end collision and brought a straightforward claim for damages. The defendant made an early admission of liability and shortly after disclosure of medical records, made an offer of £1,500. The claimant rejected the offer, made no counter-offer and issued proceedings. A few weeks after issue, the claimant made an offer of £1,900 but accepted the defendant's counter-offer of £1,812. The claimant sought costs of £4,422.11 and the defendant contended proceedings had been issued prematurely therefore the cost should be limited to those recoverable under the fixed recoverable costs regime.

HELD: (1) The claimant's conduct was unreasonable. In particular, he had failed, without good reason, to make an offer before the issue of proceedings.

(2)   The claimant's costs were to be limited to those recoverable under the predictable costs scheme and the claimant was to pay the defendant's costs of the hearing.

(3)   Permission to appeal refused.

[38.97]   Binch v Freedman

(6 December 2005, unreported), Stoke-on-Trent County Court

The claimant was injured in a road traffic accident on 15 December 2004 and her solicitors sent a letter of claim on 21 December 2004. The defendant's insurer conceded liability on 31 December 2004 and requested details of the claim. On 25 January 2005 the defendant offered £1,000 which was rejected on 17 February 2005. Subsequently on 22 June 2005 the claimant served her medical report and requested a reasonable offer of settlement within 21 days otherwise proceedings would be issued. On 8 July 2005 the defendant offered £2,750, however, the claimant's solicitors did not receive the letter and on 1 August 2005 gave notice of the issue of proceedings. The defendant did not respond and judgment in default was entered on 19 September 2005. On 27 October 2005, the defendant made a payment into court of £2,750. Subsequently, the claimant wished to accept the payment into court out of time but the parties were unable to agree liability for costs so the claimant made an application.

HELD: (1) The claimant was not justified in issuing proceedings and should have made further enquiries of the defendant following service of the medical report.

    (2)   The proceedings were issued prematurely without attempting to negotiate.

    (3)   Had the claimant's solicitors contacted the defendant's insurer, a settlement would have been reached without the need for proceedings and the fixed recoverable costs regime would have applied.

    (4)   In the circumstances, the defendant was to pay the claimant's costs limited to such costs as would have been recoverable under the fixed recoverable costs regime.

    (5)   The defendant was not entitled to his costs because of his own inactivity following receipt of the letter dated 1 August 2005.

[38.98]   Robinson v Doselle

(19 December 2005, unreported), Milton Keynes County Court

On 15 March 2004, the claimant was a passenger on a bus struck by a lorry driven by the defendant. Her personal injury claim settled for £3,250 and fell within Part II of CPR Pt 45. The claim was funded by a CFA however the claimant had the benefit of BTE legal expenses insurance, provided as an extension of the bus operator's motor policy. The defendant therefore disputed the claimant's entitlement to costs.

HELD: (1) The failure by the claimant's solicitor to make enquiries of the bus operator was a breach of reg 4(2)(c) of the CFA Regulations 2000. The breach was material because it led to the claimant proceeding without ATE insurance and therefore being potentially liable for disbursements which she would not have been if the BTE cover had been used. The CFA was accordingly unenforceable.

    (2)   Part II of CPR Pt 45 did not disapply the indemnity principle therefore the fixed costs were only recoverable if the claimant had a liability to pay her solicitors.

[38.99]   Nelson v Blessed

(January 2006, unreported), Plymouth County Court

The claimant was a passenger in a car and sustained orthopaedic and psychological injuries. His claim settled for less than £10,000 prior to the issue of proceedings and was therefore subject to the fixed recoverable costs scheme. The claimant made an application under CPR 45.12 for costs exceeding fixed recoverable costs on the grounds of exceptional circumstances. In particular, the claimant relied upon the fact that another passenger who was a good friend of his had died and orthopaedic and psychological reports were required.

HELD: (1) Many cases which came before the court involved tragic deaths and required orthopaedic and psychological expert evidence.

    (2)   The fact that a good friend of the claimant died in the accident did not make the case exceptional.

    (3)   The defendant's conduct had not led to an exceptional amount of additional work being required.

    (4)   In the circumstances, the application was refused and the claimant's costs were to be limited to those recoverable under the predictable costs scheme.

(5)   The claimant was to pay the defendant's costs of the application.

[38.100]   Nizami v Butt

[2005] EWHC 159 (QB)

[2006] 2 All ER 140, [2006] NLJR 272, QB

On 30 December 2003, the claimant was a passenger in a car struck from behind by a vehicle driven by the defendant. His personal injury claim settled for £1,675.05 and fell within Part II of CPR Pt 45. The claim was funded by a CFA. The costs judge decided that the entitlement to fixed recoverable costs did not depend on the existence of a valid and enforceable CFA.

HELD, ON APPEAL: (1) Section 51(2) of the Supreme Court Act 1981, as amended, conferred the power to make Rules of Court which provided for the recovery of costs which would otherwise be precluded by the Indemnity Principle.

(2)   The Indemnity Principle had no application to Part II of CPR Pt 45 because the intention underlying the fixed recoverable costs regime was to provide for fixed levels of remuneration without the need for further recourse to the court.

(3)   In cases falling under Part II of CPR Pt 45, the receiving party did not have to demonstrate a valid retainer between solicitor and client.

[38.101]   Woollard and Woollard v Fowler

(24 May 2006, unreported), Weston Super Mare County Court

On 20 October 2003, the second claimant was injured when hit from the rear by a vehicle driven by the defendant. Medical evidence was commissioned by Mobile Doctors Ltd and the claim settled for £4,000. The issue for the district judge to decide was whether the second claimant could recover the full amount charged by a medical reporting agency for providing a solicitor with a medical report and medical records as a disbursement under Part II of CPR Pt 45. The district judge found that:

(1)   The cases of *Claims Direct Test Cases Tranche 2* (at para [38.166]) and *Stringer v Copley* (at para [38.165]) were distinguishable because the costs in those proceedings were not subject to the fixed recoverable costs regime in Part II of CPR Pt 45.

(2)   CPR 45.10(2)(a) did not permit work done by an agency to be recovered as a disbursement. *Moss v Campbell* [2005] rejected.

(3)   The second claimant was therefore only entitled to recover the actual fees charged by the medical expert, GP and hospital.

The second claimant appealed.

HELD, ON APPEAL: (1) The judgment in *Nizami v Butt* (at para [38.100]) gave a helpful insight into the court's approach in cases subject to predictable costs under Part II of CPR Pt 45.

(2)   The word 'obtaining' in CPR 45.10(2)(a) was not superfluous because the Rules Committee was well aware of the use of medical agencies to obtain medical records and reports.

(3)   The test on all assessments was one of reasonableness and proportionality but there was no reason why an agency should not be used to obtain an engineer's report if it was reasonable and proportionate to do so.

(4)   The payment to Mobile Doctors Limited was not a disbursement but

should be treated as a disbursement made on behalf of the claimant and therefore recoverable on her behalf.

(5)   The fees paid to medical agencies should not be treated differently under the predictable costs regime because until a case was settled, it was not known whether or not the predictable costs regime would apply.

(6)   If the defendant's arguments were correct, there would be uncertainty in relation to medical agency fees until the last moment, settlement would be impeded and costs increased.

(7)   In the circumstances, the fees of the medical agency were recoverable.

(B)   FIXED RECOVERABLE SUCCESS FEES IN ROAD TRAFFIC ACCIDENTS OCCURRING ON OR AFTER 6 OCTOBER 2003

[38.102]   Part II of CPR Pt 45 provides for fixed recoverable success fees for solicitors and counsel where a dispute arises from a road traffic accident which occurred on or after 6 October 2003.

CPR 45.16 provides:

'Subject to rule 45.18, the percentage increase which is to be allowed in relation to solicitors' fee is–

(a)   100% where the claim concludes at trial; or

(b)   12.5% where -

  (i)   the claimant concludes before a trial has commenced; or

  (ii)   the dispute is settled before a claim is issued.'

CPR 45.17 provides for fixed recoverable counsel's success fees the amount of which depends upon:

(1)   the stage at which the claim is concluded; and

(2)   the track to which the claim is allocated.

CPR 45.18 provides that a party may apply for an alternative success fee if the damages exceed £500,000 or would have done if there had been no contributory negligence.

CPR 45.19 provides for the applicant to pay the costs of the application for and assessment of the alternative success fee if the alternative success fee is assessed as no greater than 20% and no less than 7.5%.

7.   HOURLY RATES

[38.103]   Truscott v Truscott
Wraith v Sheffield Forgemasters Ltd
[1998] 1 All ER 82, [1998] 1 WLR 132

These two appeals concerned the issue whether a paying party's liability for costs should be restricted to what a reasonably competent solicitor practising in the area of the court (or in the area where the receiving party lived) might have been expected to charge, or whether the receiving party should be entitled to recover the costs claimed by the solicitor who was in fact instructed.

In Truscott, the defendant instructed London solicitors having become dissatisfied with his solicitors in East Grinstead.

In Wraith, the claimant lived in Sheffield but his trade union instructed London solicitors.

HELD, ON APPEAL: (1) In deciding whether or not it was reasonable to instruct a particular solicitor, the court should have regard to:
- (a)   the importance of the matter to the receiving party;
- (b)   the legal and factual complexities, in so far as the receiving party might reasonably be expected to understand them;
- (c)   the location of the receiving party's home, place of work and the court in which the proceedings were commenced;
- (d)   possibly well-founded dissatisfaction with a previous solicitor;
- (e)   a recommendation to consult the new solicitor;
- (f)   the location of the new solicitor;
- (g)   knowledge of the likely fees of the solicitor compared with those of other solicitors who might reasonably have been considered.
- (2)   In Truscott the choice of London solicitors was reasonable. In Wraith, it was not reasonable to instruct London solicitors because the case had no connection with London and did not require expertise only found there.

[38.104]   Mann v Powergen plc

(9 February 1999, unreported), Plymouth County Court

The claimant lived in Plymouth but his union instructed solicitors in Richmond to represent him in his claim for damages following exposure to asbestos in Plymouth.

HELD: (1) Following *Truscott v Truscott; Wraith v Sheffield Forgemasters Ltd* (at para [38.103]), it was not reasonable to instruct Richmond solicitors.
- (2)   The case was not complex, there were competent local solicitors and witnesses of fact were likely to come from the Plymouth area. Accordingly, Plymouth rates were allowed.

[38.105]   Sullivan v Co-operative Insurance Society Ltd

[1999] 2 Costs LR 158

The claimant lived in Manchester and through his union instructed London solicitors.

HELD, ON APPEAL: (1) 'The fact that a case has no obvious connection with London is a relevant factor, the more so if the case does not require expertise only to be found there.'
- (2)   Although the case was very important to the claimant it was an asbestosis case without unusual complication and there were competent solicitors in Manchester.
- (3)   Following *Truscott v Truscott; Wraith v Sheffield Forgemasters Ltd* (at para [38.103]), it was not reasonable to instruct London solicitors.

[38.106]   MacDougall v Boote Edgar Esterkin

[2000] EWHC 9015

The claimants and their solicitors met to discuss costs and following the meeting, the solicitors wrote to the claimants confirming an agreement to pay £300 per hour for all work. Subsequently, the claimants disputed this has been agreed, however, the costs judge found in favour of the solicitors. The claimants appealed.

HELD, ON APPEAL: (1) For consent to be implied, the claimants' approval had to be informed. The solicitors had to satisfy the court that the approval was secured following a full and fair exposition of the factors relevant to it so that the lay claimants could be reasonably bound by it.

(2) Based upon an analysis of the attendance notes of the meeting and the oral evidence of the claimants and the solicitors, consent had not been informed. In particular, the solicitors had not explained the relationship between party and party and solicitor/client costs and the approach of the costs judge or specified what they were going to seek by way of party and party charging rate.

(3) In the circumstances, the court had to fix a reasonable hourly charging rate.

[38.107] **Griffiths v Solutia UK Ltd**

[2001] EWCA Civ 736

[2001] All ER (D) 196 (Apr)

The claimants were a group of 165 residents living in the vicinity of the defendant's chemical works in North Wales and instructed London solicitors to pursue their claims following a gas leak.

HELD, ON APPEAL: (1) It was not unreasonable to instruct the London solicitors who had acted previously in similar claims and who therefore knew the facts and had done a significant amount of background work which did not need to be repeated.

(2) Unfortunately, the appeal did not raise the real concern whether or not it was reasonable to have instructed London solicitors for the previous claims.

[38.108] **Patterson v Cape Darlington**

(May 2001, unreported), QBD

The claimant lived and worked in Liverpool and suffered from an asbestos-related disease as a result of his employment with the defendants. His union advised him to instruct London solicitors.

HELD, ON APPEAL: It was reasonable to instruct London solicitors recommended to the claimant.

[38.109] **Carpenter v Mid-Kent Healthcare Trust**

(1 August 2001, unreported), Mayors & City of London County Court

The claimant lived in Kent where the accident occurred but her union instructed London solicitors.

HELD, ON APPEAL: The claimant's choice of London solicitors was objectively reasonable given where she lived and the solicitors' expertise. *Truscott v Truscott; Wraith v Sheffield Forgemasters Ltd* (at para [38.103]) distinguished.

[38.110] **Bensusan v Freedman**

[2001] All ER (D) 212 (Oct), SC

The claimant lived in Tunbridge Wells, Kent and instructed solicitors in Nantwich, Cheshire. Following settlement of her dental negligence claim for £2,000, costs only proceedings were issued in Crewe County Court for the convenience of the claimant's solicitors.

HELD: (I) It was not reasonable to instruct the distant, specialist solicitor because the claim was straightforward. However, the Nantwich hourly rate was lower than the Tunbridge Wells rate, therefore it was appropriate to allow the rate for the area where the work was done.
  (2) The claim should have been conducted by a grade 2 fee earner, therefore £110 per hour was recoverable as opposed to the £180 per hour claimed.

[38.111]   Ryan v Tretol Group Ltd
SCCO 20 December 2001

The claimant initially instructed Nottingham solicitors to pursue his asbestos-related claim but later changed to London solicitors when the proceedings were well advanced.

HELD: (I) It was not reasonable to instruct London solicitors when other local solicitors could have handled the case.
  (2) There was no evidence why the claimant had lost confidence in the Nottingham solicitors, *Truscott v Truscott; Wraith v Sheffield Forgemasters Ltd* (at para [38.103]) distinguished.
  (3) Nottingham rates therefore applied.

[38.112]   Walbrook Properties Ltd v Severn Trent Waters Ltd
SCCO 5 February 2002

Following a discontinuance against the third defendant, the claimant disputed its liability to pay the hourly rates of the city solicitors instructed by the defendants. The costs judge agreed the case had no real connection with London and although it was of such a size and complexity that a team of fee earners was required, there were several such firms in Birmingham, one of whom worked for the first defendants.

HELD, ON APPEAL: The costs judge's decision to allow Birmingham rates was not wrong taking into account all the circumstances.

[38.113]   Gill v South East Kent and London Bus Co Ltd
(6 November 2002, unreported), Croydon County Court

The claimant contended that the defendant's representative with conduct of the case, a paralegal of 18 years' personal injury experience, was a Grade C fee earner for the purposes of the SCCO Guide to the Summary Assessment of Costs.

HELD: (I) Applying the SCCO Guide, the defendant's representative was very clearly a Grade C fee earner.
  (2) *Obiter*: the rate to be applied under the SCCO Guide should be the rate for the court in which the litigation proceeded, rather than the rate for where the work was done.

[38.114]   Higgs v Camden and Islington Health Authority
[2003] EWHC 15 (QB)
[2003] All ER (D) 76 (Jan), 72 BMLR 95, QB

The claimant's clinical negligence claim settled for £3.8 million three days before trial. The partner with conduct of the case claimed an hourly rate of £300. At the detailed assessment hearing, the costs judge tested the reasonableness of the hourly rate by carrying out a pre-CPR 'A plus B' calculation, ie taking the hourly expense rate and adding the percentage uplift to reflect care and conduct. In allowing the rate claimed, the costs judge took into account this was a difficult and complex claim conducted by a specialist in the field of clinical negligence.

HELD, ON APPEAL: (1) The SCCO Guide was of limited assistance in a demanding and sensitive case and the Guide recognised hourly rates exceeding the guideline figures may well be justified.
(2)   Although the Civil Procedure Rules commended the use of a single charging rate, the costs judge was not wrong to use the A plus B method in order to gauge the reasonableness of the hourly rate claimed.
(3)   £300 per hour was a high figure but not wrong in the circumstances of the case.

[38.115]   Colpitts v Harris
SCCO 22 July 2003

The claimant, aged 9, sustained a severe brain injury in a road traffic accident. The claim settled in the sum of £3.15 million the day before trial.

HELD: An hourly rate of £300 was reasonable having regard to the seriousness of the injuries. *Higgs v Camden and Islington Health Authority* (at para [38.114]) referred to.

[38.116]   Jemma Trust Co Ltd v Liptrott and Forrester (as executors of Sir Geoffrey Alan Hulton Bt deceased) and Another
[2003] EWCA Civ 1476
[2004] 1 All ER 510, [2004] 1 WLR 646

Although the subject matter of this appeal was non-contentious probate costs, the judgment of the Court of Appeal concerned the issue of how the value element should be rewarded, which is fundamental to contentious costs.

HELD, ON APPEAL: (1) In the quantification of solicitors' costs, the value element was still relevant and important.
(2)   The prescribed factors known as the 'seven pillars of wisdom' and set out at CPR 44.5(3) had to be applied by the court when deciding whether costs were proportionately and reasonable incurred.

[38.117]   Mattel Inc and Others v RSW Group plc
[2004] EWHC 1610 (Ch)
[2004] All ER (D) 58 (Jul)

The claimants instructed City of London solicitors to commence proceedings against the defendant, a company based in Manchester.

HELD, ON APPEAL: It was reasonable to instruct City of London solicitors who were the claimants' normal solicitors and who had knowledge of the claimants' strategy. It was far from obvious that the instruction of Manchester solicitors would have resulted in any significant savings.

[38.118]   Ross v Stonewood Securities Ltd
[2004] EWHC 2235 (Ch)

[2004] All ER (D) 72 (Oct)

The claimant's solicitor claimed a rate for a Grade 1 fee earner of £280 per hour, inclusive of 175% uplift. This implied an expense rate of £102. The charging rate for Inner Birmingham was £158. The costs judge allowed an uplift of 85% on the expense rate of £102, rounded up to £190 per hour.

HELD, ON APPEAL: (1) *Higgs v Camden and Islington Health Authority* (at para [38.114]) was a decision on its own facts and did not establish any general rule about the appropriate level of charging rates, even in specialised cases.
- (2)   An appropriate comparator was the claimant's previous solicitors who claimed a rate of £150 per hour.
- (3)   There was no cogent reason for the uplift of 175%.
- (4)   The rate allowed was above the guideline rate and the costs judge's decision was not wrong.

[38.119]   Holland and Holland v PKF (a firm) and Others
SCCO 11 October 2004

The claimants lived in Stone, Staffordshire and instructed solicitors in London to represent them in their professional negligence claim against the defendants.

HELD: (1) The claimants acted reasonably in instructing London solicitors and were not obliged to instruct local solicitors, in particular because of the predicament the defendants had placed them in and the strength of the opposition they would face.
- (2)   Allowing a single (average) hourly rate for each fee earner was more practicable than different hourly rates for each year which would involve the expense of re-drawing the bill.

[38.120]   Gazley v Wade and News Group Newspapers Ltd
[2004] EWHC 2675 (QB)

[2004] All ER (D) 291 (Nov), QB

The claimant lived in Great Yarmouth and in the first instance, consulted a local firm of solicitors who advised him to accept the defendants' offer of £10,000. The claimant was dissatisfied with this advice and instructed new solicitors in London who secured a settlement of £50,000.

HELD, ON APPEAL: (1) Applying the test in *Truscott v Truscott; Wraith v Sheffield Forgemasters Ltd* (at para [38.103]), this was not 'a Norfolk case' and the defendants were based in London. Nevertheless, any competent litigation solicitor can instruct specialist counsel.
- (2)   The overriding objective of ensuring parties were on an equal footing was relevant in judging the reasonableness of instructing specialist solicitors.
- (3)   The costs judge was not wrong to conclude it was unreasonable to instruct London solicitors, particularly given that liability was not in issue.

[38.121] **Paturel v Marble Arch Services Ltd**

[2005] EWHC 1055 (QB)

[2005] All ER (D) 401 (May)

At the detailed assessment hearing in this case, the Deputy Master allowed £200 per hour applicable to a grade B fee earner in Central London for the work done by the defendant's solicitor. The solicitor was admitted on 2 April 2002 and therefore did not have over four years' post-qualification experience. However, he had 15 years' litigation experience.

HELD, ON APPEAL: (1) The experience of the representative was relevant and was often as valuable as a professional qualification.

(2) The SCCO guidelines were not binding and litigation experience should be taken into account in determining the appropriate grade of fee earner and hourly rate.

(3) The Deputy Master was not wrong to allow the rate applicable to a Grade B fee earner.

[38.122] **King v Telegraph Group Ltd**

SCCO 2 December 2005

See also at para [38.53].

The claimant instructed City of London solicitors to pursue his defamation claim. The solicitors claimed the following hourly rates:

Grade A	£375
Grade B	£265
Grade D	£150
Costs draftsman	£150

HELD: (1) 'City rates for city solicitors are recoverable where the city solicitor is undertaking city work, which is normally heavy commercial or corporate work ... A city firm which undertakes work, which could be competently handled by a number of Central London solicitors, is asking unreasonably and disproportionately if it seeks to charge city rates'.

(2) Under the CFA, the claimant would, in reality, never have to pay and therefore had no real interest in the hourly rates charged.

(3) Rates allowed and conceded on detailed assessments in previous cases were of historical interest but did assist in arriving at appropriate rates.

(4) The claimant could not apply market forces to control his solicitors' fees and the best evidence about central London solicitors' fees was the rates charged by the defendant's solicitors.

(5) The following rates were allowed:

Grade A	£325
Grade B	£210
Grade D	£105
Costs draftsman	£125

[38.123]   Campbell v MGN Ltd
8 March 2006
HL

See also at para [38.43] where the facts and procedural history of this case are set out.

Following conclusion of the substantive proceedings, the Judicial Taxing Officers of the House of Lords (one of which was the senior costs judge, Master Hurst) heard argument concerning the following hourly rates claimed by the claimant's specialist West End solicitors:

Grade A   £500
Grade B/C   £230–£240
Grade D   £105–£120

The defendant put forward the 2005 SCCO guideline rates for central London which the claimant submitted were inappropriate for specialist solicitors in a high profile case.

HELD: (1) The court was not a regulator of the amount of the solicitors' charges to the claimant or concerned to influence any market. Its function was to assess the rates which were reasonable and proportionate for the defendant to pay.
   (2)   While the claimant's solicitors might be able to command significantly higher rates from their clients than other solicitors, the rates claimed were not payable by the defendant.
   (3)   The following rates were recoverable from the defendant:

Grade A   £375
Grade B/C   £200
Grade D   £105–£115

[38.124]   Cox and Carter v MGN Ltd and Others
[2006] EWHC 1235 (QB)
[2006] All ER (D) 396 (May), QB

See also at para [38.227].

The claimants instructed London solicitors to pursue their claims for invasion of privacy and breach of confidence. The solicitors claimed hourly rates ranging from £400 to £450. The costs judge allowed a range of £300 to £315 and the claimants appealed.

HELD, ON APPEAL: (1) The claimants' solicitors had failed to produce evidence to demonstrate why their expenses were higher than those of the average firms in the same geographical area and without such evidence there was no justification for increased hourly rates.
   (2)   The decision of the senior costs judge, Master Hurst in King v Telegraph Group Ltd SCCO 2 December 2005 (at para [38.225]) provided valuable guidance.
   (3)   The SCCO guideline hourly rates were published to assist with summary assessments and the court had a discretion to allow rates in excess of the guidelines from time to time in appropriate cases. The court should not follow the guidelines slavishly.

(4)   An element for care and conduct was built into the guideline rates although the precise percentage was not ascertainable.

(5)   No weight was to be attached to the evidence of comparator rates provided by the claimants' solicitors as it would require further investigation to evaluate properly.

(6)   The entitlement to claim for periodic increases in hourly rates was essentially a matter of construing the contractual obligations as between the claimants and their solicitors. The increases were required to be agreed with the claimants and that involved a need for their informed approval.

(7)   In the circumstances, there was no justification for interfering with the decision of the costs judge.

8.   INDEMNITY COSTS UNDER CPR PT 44

For indemnity costs under CPR Pt 36, see Chapter 32.

[38.125]   Petrotrade Inc v Texaco Ltd
[2001] 4 All ER 853

This appeal was the Court of Appeal's first opportunity to consider the approach to be adopted by the court where a defendant was ordered to pay a sum in excess of a claimant's Part 36 offer (see at para [32.42]).

Lord Woolf, Master of the Rolls as he then was, remarked that an order for indemnity costs was compensatory, not penal. Although proportionality did not have to be considered, the receiving party was restricted to recovering only the amount of costs incurred.

[38.126]   Reid Minty (a firm) v Taylor
[2001] EWCA Civ 1723

[2002] 2 All ER 150, [2002] 1 WLR 2800

At trial, the defendant was successful but the trial judge refused to make an indemnity costs order in his favour.

HELD, ON APPEAL: (1) The court had a wide discretion under CPR 44.3 and it was not correct that indemnity costs were only awarded if there had been moral lack of probity or conduct deserving moral condemnation by the paying party.

(2)   The unreasonable conduct of litigation could give rise to an award of costs on an indemnity basis in favour of either party.

[38.127]   Kiam v MGN Ltd (No 2)
[2002] EWCA Civ 66

[2002] 2 All ER 242

The successful claimant applied for the costs of the appeal on an indemnity basis.

HELD, ON APPEAL: (1) Simon Brown LJ agreed with the differently constituted Court of Appeal in *Reid Minty (a firm) v Taylor* (at para [38.126]) that conduct can be so unreasonable as to justify an order for indemnity costs. However, such conduct needed to be unreasonable to a high degree and not merely wrong or misguided in hindsight.

(2)   An indemnity costs order under CPR Pt 44 (unlike one made under CPR Pt 36) did carry some stigma and was penal in nature.

(3)   It would be rare for the refusal of an offer of settlement to lead to an order for indemnity costs under CPR Pt 44.

[38.128]   Craig v Railtrack plc (in Railway Administration)

[2002] EWHC 168 (QB)

[2002] All ER (D) 212 (Feb), QB

The claimants were a group of post office workers injured as a result of a collision between two trains on 8 March 1996. Following the issue of proceedings, the defendants conceded liability and consented to judgment on 6 March 2001, 6 days before trial. Settlement of the claims of the most seriously injured did not take place until after the assessment of damages hearing had commenced on 28 January 2002.

HELD: (1) It was not unreasonable for the defendants to proceed to the assessment of damages hearing once liability was conceded however, five years was far too long to resolve liability and amounted to highly unreasonable conduct.

(2)   The claimants were entitled to their costs of the issue of liability on an indemnity basis from 1 October 1999 by which date the defendants had been served with proceedings and had ample opportunity to assess liability.

[38.129]   ABCI v Banque Franco-Tunisienne

[2002] EWHC 567 (Comm)

The defendants applied for an order for costs on an indemnity basis on the grounds that the claimant constantly changed his case and produced wholly unacceptable volumes of documents.

HELD: Each ground warranted an order for indemnity costs.

[38.130]   Phoenix Finance Ltd v Federation International de l'Automobile and Others

[2002] EWHC 1028 (Ch)

The claimant joined the second and third defendants into proceedings without sending them a letter of claim or other form of advance warning of their involvement in the litigation. The claimant was subsequently unsuccessful.

HELD: An order for indemnity costs against the claimant was appropriate because a letter before action was as important under the Civil Procedure Rules as it was under the previous rules.

[38.131]   Excelsior Commercial & Industrial Holdings Ltd v Salisbury Hamer Aspden & Johnson (a firm)

[2002] EWCA Civ 879

[2002] All ER (D) 39 (Jun), CA

At trial the claimant recovered damages of £2 against one defendant and failed entirely against the other. The defendants had made a joint payment into court of £100,000 six weeks before trial.

HELD, ON APPEAL: (1) CPR Pt 44 was of general application and continued to be applicable in relation to case to which CPR Pt 36 applied.

(2)   There was an infinite variety of situations which justified an order for indemnity costs and therefore it would be dangerous to attempt to give guidance as to when such an order should or should not be made.

(3)   The trial judge was entitled to order indemnity costs to reflect that the claimant pursued a speculative claim to trial.

[38.132]   Naskaris v ANS plc

[2002] EWHC 1782 (Ch)

The claimants discontinued four days before trial and the defendants sought an order for indemnity costs.

HELD: An order for indemnity costs was appropriate to reflect the claimants' unreasonable attempts to adjourn the trial and failure to cooperate with the defendants' solicitors regarding trial preparation.

[38.133]   Brawley v Marczynski (No 2)

[2002] EWCA Civ 1453

[2002] 4 All ER 1067, CA

The claimant was legally aided and obtained an order for indemnity costs against the defendants to reflect the defendants' refusal to supply documents.

HELD, ON APPEAL: (1) The defendants' conduct justified an order for indemnity costs.
(2)   An order for indemnity costs was usually made where the court disapproved of a party's conduct in the litigation however such an order may be made where there was little or no stigma attached to the manner in which the litigation was conducted.
(3)   An order for indemnity costs could be made in favour of a legally aided claimant.

[38.134]   P Simms v The Law Society

[2005] EWCA Civ 849

[2005] All ER (D) 131 (Jul)

This case concerned intervention and disciplinary proceedings brought by The Law Society against Mr Simms. The Law Society obtained summary judgment and an order for indemnity costs. The Law Society's costs were estimated at over £1 million for all proceedings.

HELD, ON APPEAL: (1) An order for indemnity costs was not appropriate in this case. Mr Simms had little time to respond to the intervention and the consequences were potentially drastic therefore his defence was justified.
(2)   The Law Society undertook a large volume of work which had produced the estimated costs. The effect of an order for indemnity costs was to displace the issue of proportionality which was expressly provided for on the standard basis and this had to be taken into account because it would limit the scope of the arguments in the assessment of costs.
(3)   An order for standard basis costs was substituted.

[38.135]   Zissis v Lukomski and Carter

[2006] EWCA Civ 341

[2006] All ER (D) 63 (Apr), CA

In this case the first defendant attempted to compromise the claim at a very early stage but the claimant insisted on proceeding. The claim was subsequently dismissed and the claimant was ordered to pay the first defendant's costs on an indemnity basis. The claimant appealed.

HELD, ON APPEAL: (1) It was now established that there must be some element of a party's conduct of the litigation which deserved a mark of disapproval before an order for indemnity costs should be made (see *Kiam v MGN (No 2)* at para [38.127]).

    (2)   The claimant was entitled to take the view that she should bring proceedings against the first defendant and she acted throughout on professional advice.

    (3)   In the circumstances, the claimant's conduct did not merit indemnity costs.

[38.136]   **Three Rivers District Council and Bank of Credit and Commerce International SA (in liquidation) v The Governor and Company of The Bank of England**

[2006] EWHC 816 (Comm)

[2006] All ER (D) 175 (Apr)

This case arose out of the liquidation of the Bank of Credit and Commerce International SA. The claimant's liquidators pursued the defendant for 12 years alleging dishonesty by the defendant's officers. On day 256 of the trial, the claimant discontinued its claim and the defendant sought an order that the claimant pay its costs on an indemnity basis.

HELD: (1) The pursuit of hopeless allegations of dishonesty took the case out of the norm and accordingly the court had jurisdiction to make an order for indemnity costs.

    (2)   The defendant was entitled to indemnity costs to reflect the substantial costs to which it was put in order to defend the hopeless allegations.

    (3)   The trial judge should express his views for the benefit of the costs judge and if necessary, sit with him to assist on the assessment of costs.

9.   INTERIM PAYMENTS ON ACCOUNT OF COSTS

[38.137]   **Mars UK Ltd v Teknowledge Ltd (No 2)**

[2000] FSR 138, [1999] 2 Costs LR 44

Following trial, the claimant applied for an interim payment on account of costs pursuant to CPR 44.3(8). The claimant's costs totalled £550,000.

HELD: (1) As a matter of principle, the successful party should normally receive an interim payment on account of costs in an amount less than the likely assessed costs.

    (2)   The claimant was to recover two-thirds of its assessed costs. The likely assessed costs were estimated at £200,000 therefore the claimant was likely to be awarded approximately £133,000.

    (3)   The appropriate interim payment was £80,000, being approximately two-thirds of the likely award.

[38.138]   **Dyson Ltd v Hoover Ltd**

[2003] EWHC 624 (Ch)

[2003] 2 All ER 1042, [2004] 1 WLR 1264

Following settlement, the successful claimant applied for an interim payment on account of costs pursuant to CPR 44.3(8) in the sum of £1,472,000, being 60% of its total costs.

HELD: (1) Different considerations applied where there was no trial because the court did not have the benefit of hearing the evidence. Therefore in this situation, there was no presumption that an interim payment should be ordered.
  (2)   The court should consider the application on its merits and the receiving party must justify the application.
  (3)   An interim payment was not appropriate because there was insufficient material before the court to make a reasonable assessment and the costs judge would be better placed to do so.

10.   INQUESTS

[38.139]   **Stewart and Howard v The Medway NHS Trust**

SCCO 6 April 2004

In this clinical negligence case, the claimants' bill of costs included the costs of preparing for and attending an inquest. The issue for the court to decide was whether such costs were recoverable from the defendant in the civil proceedings.

HELD: (1) The costs of an inquest could be of and incidental to the civil action.
  (2)   The claimants attended the Inquest for the purpose of facilitating the negligence claim.

[38.140]   **King (Administratrix of the estate of Robert Gadd, deceased) v Milton Keynes General NHS Trust**

SCCO 13 May 2004

The claimant's solicitor attended an Inquest and participated fully, asking questions of the witnesses and making submissions as to the law. Following settlement of the clinical negligence claim, over 90% of the costs in the claimant's bill related to the attendance at the Inquest.

HELD: (1) If the costs of attending the inquest were incidental to the subsequent civil claim, they were recoverable provided they were reasonably incurred, reasonable in amount and proportionate.
  (2)   The court must look at the purpose of attending and in this case it was to obtain evidence for the subsequent civil claim. Therefore the costs of attending to take notes and question the witnesses were recoverable.
  (3)   However, the costs of work done to persuade the coroner to reach a particular verdict and the cost of adducing the evidence of a doctor were not recoverable.

11.   INTEREST ON COSTS UNDER CPR PT 44

For interest on costs under CPR Pt 36, see Chapter 32.

[38.141] **Powell (by her father and litigation friend Leslie John Powell) v Herefordshire Health Authority**

[2002] EWCA Civ 1786

[2003] 3 All ER 253

The claimant sustained severe brain damage soon after her birth on 26 June 1986. Proceedings were issued in June 1989 and in April 1994, liability was admitted and judgment entered by consent for damages to be assessed and costs. In June 2001, the court approved a settlement of £2,175,000 and ordered the defendant to pay the claimant's costs. The costs judge ordered that the date from which interest on costs ran was the date when the original judgment was entered in 1994.

HELD, ON APPEAL: (1) The costs judge based his decision upon s 17 of the Judgments Act 1938 and CPR 40.8(1) and therefore wrongly believed he had no power to order that interest run from any date other than the date that judgment was given.

(2) Unfortunately, neither party drew the costs judge's attention to CPR 44.3(6)(g) which provided that interest on costs may run from or until a certain date, including a date before judgment.

(3) The decision of the costs judge could not stand but it was not necessary to exercise the discretion afresh because the parties had agreed terms relating to interest on costs in the light of CPR 44.3(6)(g).

[38.142] **Bim Kemi AB V Blackburn Chemicals Ltd**

[2003] EWCA Civ 889

At first instance, the claimant was successful and the defendant was ordered to pay the costs of the trial which were subsequently assessed and paid. On appeal to the Court of Appeal, the defendant was largely successful.

HELD, ON APPEAL: (1) The claimant was to pay the defendant's costs of the detailed assessment proceedings below and interest on those costs at 1% over base rate.

(2) The claimant was to repay the costs already paid by the defendant pursuant to the order of the trial judge with interest at the judgment rate from the date of the order of the Court of Appeal. In addition, the claimant was to pay interest on those costs at 1% above base rate from the date of payment by the defendant up to the date of the order of the Court of Appeal.

(3) The claimant was to pay 75% of the defendant's costs of the trial and the appeal with interest at the judgment rate from the date of the order of the trial judge. In addition, the claimant was to pay interest on those costs at 1% above base rate from the date of each solicitors' invoice up to the date of the order of the trial judge.

[38.143] **Douglas v Hello! Ltd**

[2004] EWHC 63 (Ch)

[2004] All ER (D) 202 (Jan)

Following the trials at which the claimants were largely successful, the parties were unable to agree terms as to costs including interest on costs.

HELD: (1) The appropriate dates, when measuring the extent to which a party has been out of pocket, were the dates on which the solicitors' invoices were actually paid, not the dates of the invoices.

(2) Such interest should stop when interest on costs is replaced by judgement interest.

(3)   The appropriate rate was 1½% over base rate. *Bim Kemi AB v Blackburn Chemicals Ltd* (at para [38.142]) considered.

12.   LIMITATION – LIMITATION ACT 1980, S 24

[38.144]   **Chohan v Times Newspapers Ltd**

[2001] EWCA Civ 964

[2001] All ER (D) 243 (Jun), [2001] 1 WLR 1859

In 1993, the claimant obtained three costs orders against the defendant, such costs to be assessed if not agreed. After assessment, the costs certificate was issued on 8 November 1994. The defendant failed to pay the assessed costs so the claimant issued a bankruptcy petition on 18 February 2000. The issue for the court to decide was whether the petition to enforce the costs was statute barred.

HELD, ON APPEAL: (1) Section 24 of the Limitation Act 1980 prohibited an action being brought on a judgment, after six years from the date when the judgment became enforceable.
(2)   The word 'enforceable' must mean enforceable in a practical way and there was nothing to enforce until the amount of costs was certified in 1994.
(3)   In the circumstances, the petition was not statute barred.

13.   LITIGANTS IN PERSON

[38.145]   **Stockinger v Highdorn Co Ltd and Others**

(5 April 2001, unreported), QBD

The claimant was a solicitor and represented himself in his successful claim against the defendants.

HELD, ON APPEAL: (1) CPR 48.6(2) provided that the costs allowed to a litigant in person must not exceed two-thirds of the amount which would have been allowed if the litigant in person had been legally represented. A reasonable rate for a notional solicitor employed at a medium-sized firm outside of the City of London was £150 up to 1998, therefore the claimant was entitled to £100 per hour.
(2)   Work done by the claimant which would not have been undertaken by a legal representative on the claimant's behalf was not recoverable.
(3)   The time spent by two paralegals employed by the claimant was recoverable at £25 per hour.
(4)   The uplift for care and conduct was already included in the hourly rate allowed and therefore there could be no further claim for uplift.

[38.146]   **R (on the application of Wulfsohn) v Legal Services Commission**

[2002] EWCA Civ 250

The claimant represented himself in judicial review proceedings and was successful. The judge only allowed the claimant costs of £120 for photocopying and a train journey.

HELD, ON APPEAL: (1) In principle, a litigant in person was entitled to compensation for his time, subject to a cap of two-thirds of what a legal representative would have been allowed.

(2)   The claimant was to be compensated for his time spent on research in the sum of £10,000, being two-thirds of the estimated costs if the work had been done by a solicitor.

(3)   The claimant was additionally entitled to photocopying, postage and travel in the sum of £460.

[38.147] Joseph v Boyd & Hutchinson

[2003] EWHC 413 (Ch)

[2003] All ER (D) 227 (Mar)

The claimant was a solicitor who commenced proceedings against the driver of a motor vehicle following a collision. Subsequently the claimant instructed the defendant firm of solicitors to conduct the litigation on her behalf. The defendant successfully recovered damages and costs from the driver but looked to the claimant for payment of costs not recovered. The claimant sought an assessment of the defendant's bill and represented herself at the detailed assessment hearing. Subsequently the claimant instructed counsel for further hearings.

HELD, ON APPEAL: (1) It was clear from CPR 48.6(6) that a solicitor who acted for herself was a litigant in person.

(2)   The effect of paragraph 52.5 of the Costs Practice Direction (CPD) however created a distinction between a solicitor who acted as a litigant in person and one who acted for herself in her firm name. The former was treated as a litigant in person but the latter was not.

(3)   For the purposes of CPD paragraph 52.5, 'solicitor' means practising solicitor.

(4)   The claimant was therefore a litigant in person under CPR 48.6(6).

[38.148]   Sisu Capital Fund Ltd and Others v Tucker & Spratt and Others

[2005] EWHC 2321 (Ch)

[2006] 1 All ER 167

Following the handing down of judgment, the parties requested the trial judge to decide a point of principle which would arise in the detailed assessment proceedings. A substantial amount of time was spent by the defendant liquidators and their colleagues in dealing with the proceedings and the issue for the judge to decide was whether their remuneration was recoverable as costs from the claimant. The work undertaken included a variety of tasks, some requiring special expertise and others which, if undertaken by a litigant who instructed a solicitor, would not be recoverable from the paying party.

HELD: (1) CPR 48.6 and CPR Pt 48 PD 52.5 drew no distinction between a litigant who was a professional other than a solicitor and an ordinary litigant in person.

(2)   A non-solicitor professional was able to recover, as a litigant in person, the cost of any independent expert advice but not the cost of general assistance in the conduct of litigation. A litigant in person, even if a professional, could not recover his time spent other than on matters within his own professional expertise and requiring the attention of an expert.

(3)   The Civil Procedure Rules had not changed the meaning of 'costs'.

(4)   In the circumstances, only the time spent by the defendants and their colleagues on truly expert matters were recoverable.

[38.149]   Agassi v Robinson

[2005] EWCA Civ 1507

[2006] 1 All ER 900

The claimant was a well-known professional tennis player resident in the USA. A differently constituted Court of Appeal decided he was not liable to pay income tax in respect of payments connected with his activities in the UK as a sportsman. The question of costs was adjourned because issues of considerable importance to the legal profession were raised by the defendant who disputed the claimant's entitlement to the costs he had incurred in retaining the services of Messrs Tenon Media. The court was assisted by the senior costs judge sitting as an assessor.

Mr Mills of Tenon was an expert in tax law and as a member of the Chartered Institute of Taxation, licensed to instruct counsel under the Bar's 'Licensed Access' scheme. The claimant had instructed Tenon for many years and considered it was more efficient to use them rather than a firm of solicitors.

HELD: (1) Tenon did not have the right to conduct litigation within the meaning of s 28 of the Courts and Legal Services Act 1990.
(2)   Under the 1990 Act, there was no reason why a party should not be a litigant in person for the purposes of conducting litigation, even if rights of audience on his behalf were exercised by an authorised advocate. Accordingly, the claimant was a litigant in person within the meaning of CPR 48.6.
(3)   The correct meaning of 'act as a solicitor' was, as stated by Potter J in *Piper Double Glazing Ltd v D C Contracts* [1994] 1 WLR 777 and approved in *R (Factortame Ltd and Others) v Secretary of State for Transport, Local Government and Regions (No 8)* [2003] QB 381, limited to the doing of acts which only a solicitor may perform.
(4)   The costs recoverable by a litigant in person were determined by CPR 48.6. If the expenditure was for work which a legal representative would normally have done himself, it was not a disbursement within the language of CPR 48.6(3)(a)(ii). A distinction had always been made between disbursements made and work done by a legal representative. Work delegated by a legal representative to a third party was not to be regarded as a disbursement and formed part of the legal representative's costs.
(5)   In the circumstances, the claimant was not entitled to recover as a disbursement work done by Tenon which would normally have been done by a solicitor, for example, providing general assistance to counsel in the conduct of the appeals.
(6)   The provision by Tenon of specialist ancillary assistance might be recoverable as a disbursement as this was work which would normally be done by an expert, not a solicitor. However, it would be wrong to express a view because this was not argued by the parties.
(7)   None of the work undertaken by Tenon was legal services within the meaning of CPR 48.6(3)(b).

14.   MEDIATION

[38.150]   **Dunnett v Railtrack plc**

[2002] EWCA Civ 303

[2002] 2 All ER 850, [2002] 1 WLR 2434

The claimant was unsuccessful at trial and applied for permission to appeal. When granting permission, the Court of Appeal suggested alternative dispute resolution but the defendant refused. The defendant subsequently won the appeal.

HELD, ON APPEAL: (1) Although the defendant succeeded, there would be no order for costs because of the defendant's refusal to participate in alternative dispute resolution.

(2)   Brooke LJ remarked that the case would draw the attention of lawyers to the duty to further the overriding objective and the possibility that if a party turned down alternative dispute resolution suggested by the court, the refusal may give rise to adverse costs consequences.

[38.151]   **Hurst v Leeming**

[2002] EWHC 1051 (Ch)

[2002] All ER (D) 135 (May)

The claimant's action against his former counsel for negligence was dismissed on the grounds it had no realistic prospects of success. Both before and after the commencement of proceedings, the defendant refused mediation because he considered the claim lacked any merit and there was no real prospect of a successful outcome to the mediation.

HELD: (1) The defendant's refusal to mediate was reasonable because, objectively viewed, the mediation had no realistic prospect of success given the character and attitude of the claimant.

(2)   The defendant was therefore entitled to his costs of the action (but see *Halsey v Milton Keynes General NHS Trust* at para [38.159]).

[38.152]   **Société Internationale de Telecommunications Aeronautiques SC (SITA) v Wyatt Co (UK) Ltd and others (Maxwell Batley (a firm), Pt 20 Defendant)**

[2002] EWHC 2401 (Ch)

[2002] All ER (D) 189 (Nov)

The claimants were unsuccessful in their claim against the defendant. On three occasions before trial the defendant declined to participate in a mediation.

HELD: (1) The defendant's refusals to mediate were reasonable and accordingly they were entitled to costs.

(2)   The first two requests to mediate were made at too short notice. The defendant had not long been served with proceedings and there were vast quantities of documents to study. In addition, the claimants were attempting to put unreasonable pressure upon the defendant to contribute to a claim by other parties against the claimants.

(3)   The third request to mediate was too close to the start of the trial for a mediation to be realistic.

[38.153] **Leicester Circuits Ltd v Coates Brothers plc**

[2003] EWCA Civ 333

[2003] All ER (D) 331 (Apr)

In this case, a mediation had been agreed to take place shortly before trial but the defendant withdrew from the mediation two days before. At trial the claimant was successful, however, the defendant won on appeal. The claimant argued the defendant's withdrawal form the mediation was unjustified.

HELD, ON APPEAL: (1) The mediation had a realistic prospect of success and should have been proceeded with.
- (2) The defendant was entitled to costs in the proceedings below up to the time the mediation was agreed but no costs thereafter. Accordingly, each party had to bear their own trial costs.
- (3) The defendant was entitled to the costs of the appeal.

[38.154] **Royal Bank of Canada v Secretary of State for Defence**

[2003] EWHC 1841 (Ch)

The defendant was largely successful and sought an order that the claimant pay his costs. On a number of occasions the claimant expressed a willingness to mediate but the defendant refused.

HELD: (1) The defendant's refusal was surprising in the light of the Lord Chancellor's Department's pledge committing government departments to alternative dispute resolution (ADR) if the other party agreed.
- (2) Although the dispute involved a question of law, it was still suitable for ADR.
- (3) The mediation may well have succeeded and therefore no order for costs was appropriate (but see *Halsey v Milton Keynes General NHS Trust* at para [38.159]).

[38.155] **Corenso (UK) Ltd v The Burnden Group plc**

[2003] EWHC 1805 (QB), QB

The claim was settled by the claimant accepting the defendant's payment into court made less than 21 days before trial, but the parties were unable to agree the liability for costs. The defendant argued the claimant should be deprived of costs because of its failure to respond to the defendant's offers of mediation.

HELD: (1) A party could discharge its obligations to consider ADR without necessarily being prepared to enter into mediation, which was one form of ADR. There could be other forms of ADR more suited to the case.
- (2) The claimant was not at fault for not entering into mediation particularly as the defendant failed to pass on a list of potential mediators. There were attempts at negotiation and only at a late stage did the defendant make concerted efforts to move forward with mediation.
- (3) The claimant was therefore entitled to its costs.

[38.156]   **Virani Ltd v Manuel Revert y Cia SA**

[2003] EWCA Civ 1651

[2003] All ER (D) 324 (Jul), [2004] 2 Lloyd's Rep 14

This was the first reported case where a successful party obtained a costs sanction against an unsuccessful party for their refusal to mediate.

The defendant was unsuccessful at trial and applied for permission to appeal. When granting permission, the single Lord Justice directed the defendant to the Court of Appeal Mediation Scheme. Subsequently the defendant lost its appeal.

HELD, ON APPEAL: (1) The claimant was prepared to mediate despite the strength of its case.

(2)   The defendant was to pay the claimant's costs on an indemnity basis.

[38.157]   **Valentine v Allen**

[2003] EWCA Civ 915

[2003] All ER (D) 79 (Jul)

The claimant was unsuccessful at trial and on appeal but contended the defendants' costs should be disallowed or reduced because they unreasonably refused to mediate before trial. The defendants produced extensive correspondence to show their real efforts to settle by making reasonable offers and proposing a roundtable meeting.

HELD, ON APPEAL: Distinguishing *Dunnett v Railtrack* [2002] 2 All ER 850, the defendants' refusal to mediate was not unreasonable and therefore they were entitled to their costs.

[38.158]   **Shirayama Shokusan Co Ltd v Danovo Ltd**

[2003] EWHC 3006 (Ch)

[2003] All ER (D) 114 (Dec)

The defendant proposed mediation of the various disputes but the claimants refused on the grounds that the defendant's allegations of dishonesty were such that a mediation had no prospect of success. The defendants therefore sought an order that the parties mediate their disputes.

HELD: (1) The court had jurisdiction to order ADR pursuant to the overriding objective in CPR Pt 1, notwithstanding that one party objected.

(2)   It was appropriate to order mediation particularly as the parties were in a long-term financial relationship and had a shared interest in the success of the premises which were the subject of the dispute. (Cf *Halsey v Milton Keynes General NHS Trust* at para [38.159]).

[38.159]   **Halsey v Milton Keynes General NHS Trust**
Steel v Joy and Halliday

[2004] EWCA Civ 576

[2004] All ER (D) 125 (May), [2004] 4 All ER 920, [2004] 1 WLR 3002

These two appeals raised a question of general importance: 'when should the court impose a costs sanction against a successful litigant on the grounds that he has refused to take part in an alternative dispute resolution (ADR)?'

In *Halsey*, the claim was dismissed and the judge awarded the defendant its costs. The defendant had refused a number of invitations by the claimant to mediate.

In *Steel*, the judge awarded the successful second defendant his costs against the first defendant. The second defendant had refused a number of invitations by the first defendant to mediate.

HELD, ON APPEAL: (1) The court did not have jurisdiction to order parties to mediate against their will as this would be an unacceptable violation of their right of access to the court under Art 6 of the European Convention on Human Rights. The court's role was to robustly encourage ADR.

(2)   The burden was on the unsuccessful party to show why there should be a departure from the general rule that the unsuccessful party pays the costs of the successful party. Therefore it must be shown that the successful party acted unreasonably in refusing to agree to ADR.

(3)   There was no presumption in favour of mediation and regard must be had to all the circumstances of the case. The factors relevant to the question whether a party had unreasonably refused ADR included:

(a)   *the nature of the dispute* – most, but not all, cases were suitable for ADR. Those that were not suitable included cases involving points of law where a binding precedent would be useful, fraud or commercially disreputable conduct or the court is required to determine issues essential to the future trading relations of the parties;

(b)   *the merits of the case* – if a party reasonably believes he has a watertight case this may well be sufficient justification for a refusal to mediate. If the belief is unreasonable, this is not justification for refusing mediation;

(c)   *other settlement methods have been attempted* – previous settlement offers are potentially relevant but are no more than an aspect of factor (f);

(d)   *the costs of the mediation would be disproportionately high* – this is particularly important where the sums at stake are comparatively small.

(e)   *delay* – this may be relevant if mediation is suggested late and may delay the trial;

(f)   *whether the mediation had a reasonable prospect of success* – a party adopting a position of intransigence was a proper basis for concluding a mediation had no reasonable prospect of success such that the other party's refusal to mediate was reasonable. A successful party cannot however rely on his own intransigence. The approach adopted by Lightman J in *Hurst v Leeming* (at para [38.151]) was too narrow.

(4)   If the court has encouraged ADR, this is another factor to take into account. The stronger the encouragement the easier it will be for the unsuccessful party to show the successful party's refusal was unreasonable.

(5)   An order for the parties to consider ADR and justify why the case was not suitable for ADR should be routinely made in general personal injury litigation.

(6)   The judge in *Royal Bank of Canada v Secretary of State for Defence* (at para [38.154]) was wrong to attach significant weight to the Lord Chancellor's Department's ADR pledge which was no more than an undertaking to consider ADR and use it in all suitable cases.

The decisions in the individual appeals were as follows:

Halsey v Milton Keynes General NHS Trust
The defendant's refusal to mediate was not unreasonable because it reasonably believed it had a strong case and the costs of a mediation would be disproportionately high compared to the value of the claim.

Steel v Joy and Halliday
The second defendant's refusal to mediate was not unreasonable because the court had to resolve a question of law and therefore the case was not suitable for ADR. In addition, the second defendant reasonably believed the claim against him had no merit. Further, the costs of the mediation would have been excessive in comparison with the costs of the trial and the offer of mediation came late after substantial costs had already been incurred.

[38.160]   Burchell v Bullard and Others

[2005] EWCA Civ 358

[2005] All ER (D) 62 (Apr)

This case arose out of a building dispute. The claimant suggested mediation prior to the issue of proceedings but the defendants refused on the grounds that the issues were complex and as such mediation was not appropriate. At trial, the claimant was successful on his claim and the defendants were successful on their counterclaim. The claimant was granted permission to appeal the award of costs and invited the defendants to use the Court of Appeal Mediation Scheme but the defendants responded this was neither necessary nor appropriate.

HELD, ON APPEAL: (1) Applying the guidance in *Halsey v Milton Keynes General NHS Trust* (at para [38.159]), the dispute was well suited to ADR and the defendants behaved unreasonably in believing their case was so watertight they need not engage in attempts to settle. It was plain nonsense to say the dispute was too complex for mediation. In addition, the costs of ADR would have been insignificant compared to the costs of the litigation. Further, the claimant was honest and prepared to admit where he was wrong therefore mediation would have had a reasonable prospect of success.

   (2)   Nevertheless, a costs sanction was not appropriate because the offer of mediation was made prior to the decision in *Dunnett v Railtrack plc* (at para [38.150]).

[38.161]   Wethered Estate Ltd v Davis and Others

[2005] EWHC 1903 (Ch)

[2005] All ER (D) 336 (Jul)

Prior to the issue of proceedings, the defendants proposed mediation on a number of occasions but the claimant did not agree at that stage on the basis that if mediation was to succeed, it was necessary for the parties to fully understand the nature of the other party's case and this should be set out within court proceedings. Following the issue of proceedings, the defendants repeated the invitation to mediate and the claimant repeated the need to fully understand each party's case. The defendants then served a defence and again proposed mediation but the claimant still required clarification of the issues. Eventually a mediation took place but was unsuccessful and the claimant substantially succeeded at trial.

HELD: (1) Applying the guidance in *Halsey v Milton Keynes General NHS Trust* (at para [38.159]) and *Burchell v Bullard* (at para [38.160]), the claimant's conduct in delaying mediation was not unreasonable. In particular, there were questions of construction of an agreement against a disputed factual matrix and it was not foreseeable that the evidence would take so long to complete. Most significantly, the nature of the dispute was unclear and required explanation.

(2)   Mediation was an entirely without prejudice process and therefore the court could not admit evidence about what occurred in the mediation unless the parties waived privilege.

(3)   In the circumstances, the claimant's costs were not to be reduced because of the mediation issue.

[38.162]   Daniels v The Commissioner of Police for the Metropolis

[2005] EWCA Civ 1312

[2005] All ER (D) 225 (Oct)

The claimant was a police officer who was injured when she was thrown from a horse. The defendant refused to contemplate any form of negotiations, rejected three offers of settlement made by the claimant and confirmed he would be defending the claim to trial. At trial the defendant was successful and the claimant was ordered to pay costs.

HELD, ON APPEAL: (1) It was difficult to envisage circumstances in which it would ever be right to deprive a successful defendant of his costs solely because he refused to accept an offer by the claimant.

(2)   Although mediation was not proposed, the general approach in *Halsey v Milton Keynes General NHS Trust* (at para [38.159]) should be adopted and it was not unreasonable to refuse to accept the claimant's offer or negotiate.

(3)   The defendant reasonably considered the claim was unfounded and was entitled to insist on a trial even though the costs were disproportionate to the value of the claim.

[38.163]   Hall and Another v Pertemps

[2005] EWHC 3110 (Ch)

[2005] All ER (D) 15 (Nov)

Following the issue of proceedings, the action was stayed for the purposes of settlement discussions and mediation. A two-day mediation was unsuccessful and eight months later, the defendants began a satellite action against the claimants alleging they had, in breach of the mediation agreement, stated to third parties that threats had been made at or shortly after the mediation. The issue for the court to decide was whether regard should be had to the threats when considering the appropriate order for costs.

HELD: (1) The Court of Appeal in *Reed Executive plc and Another v Reed Business Information Ltd and Others* [2004] EWCA Civ 887 agreed the assumption made in *Halsey v Milton Keynes General NHS Trust* (at para [38.159]) that what happens in a mediation is protected by the without prejudice rule was correct and the parties may mutually agree to waive that protection.

(2)   Ordinarily, allegations of threats made in a mediation were covered by without prejudice protection. In the satellite litigation however, the factual issue of what happened in the mediation was raised in the statements of case and this amounted to a mutual waiver by both parties of the without prejudice protection.

[38.164]   **Hickman v Blake Lapthorn and Fisher**

[2006] EWHC 12 (QB)

[2006] All ER (D) 67 (Jan), QB

The claimant sued his former solicitors and counsel for negligence in advising him to settle his personal injury claim at an undervalue. At trial, the claimant succeeded against both defendants. The first defendant submitted the second defendant should pay all of the claimant's costs by reason of the second defendant's refusal to negotiate or mediate.

HELD: (1) Applying the guidance in *Halsey v Milton Keynes General NHS Trust* (at para [38.159]), the second defendant's refusal to negotiate or mediate was not unreasonable because he reasonably estimated the strength of the claimant's case and it was legitimate not to agree to pay more than he thought the claim was worth as otherwise the threat of a costs sanction could be used to extract more than the claim was worth.

(2) The claimant's valuation of the claim was three times that of the second defendant.

15.   MEDICAL AGENCIES

[38.165]   **Stringer v Copley**

(17 May 2002, unreported), Kingston upon Thames County Court

This case involved an appeal by the claimant against a detailed assessment of her costs in relation to proceedings arising out of a road traffic accident in which she was injured. The claimant had obtained two medical reports, both through medical agencies.

HELD, ON APPEAL: (1) There was no principle precluding the fees of a medical agency being recovered provided the charges did not exceed the reasonable and proportionate costs of the work if it had been done by the solicitors.

(2) It was important that the invoices of the medical agency distinguished between the medical fee and its own charges. The charges should be sufficiently particularised for the court to be satisfied they did not exceed the reasonable and proportionate cost of the solicitors doing the work.

(3) The fees of a medical agency could also be treated as though the work had been done by the solicitors and charged accordingly because paragraph 4.16(6) of the Costs Practice Direction provided, 'Agency charges as between a principal solicitor and his agent will be dealt with on the principle that such charges, where appropriate, form part of the principal solicitor's charges.'

[38.166]   **Claims Direct Test Cases Tranche 2**

[2003] EWHC 9005

Under the Claims Direct Scheme, Mobile Doctors Limited (MDL) charged a fee for obtaining a medical report on behalf of the claimant. One of the issues for the court to decide was whether the fee was recoverable from the defendant.

HELD: (1) MDL carried out work which would otherwise be done by the claimant's solicitors and to the extent that such work was carried out at the same or a lower cost than the solicitors, it was recoverable. The judgment of Judge Cook in *Stringer v Copley* (at para [38.165]) was trite costs law.

(2)   There was no principle precluding the recoverability of the fees of a medical agency provided the charges did not exceed the reasonable and proportionate costs of the work if it had been done by the solicitors.

(3)   The administration element of any fee was not recoverable because it was not costs of the action and not necessary when considering the question of proportionality.

(4)   Judge Cook was correct when he stated that it was important for the invoices of the medical agency to distinguish between the medical fee and its own charges to enable the court to be satisfied the charges did not exceed the reasonable and proportionate costs of the solicitors doing the work.

(5)   The fees of the medical agency should be treated as a disbursement and not part of the solicitors' costs.

16.   MISCONDUCT

[38.167]

CPR 44.3 provides:

'(4)   In decided what order (if any) to make about costs, the court must have regard to all the circumstances, including:

(a)   the conduct of the parties;

(b)   whether a party has succeeded on part of his case, even if he has not been wholly successful; and

(c)   any payment into court or admissible offer made by a party which is drawn to the court's attention.

(5)   The conduct of the parties includes:

(a)   conduct before, as well as during, the proceedings;

(b)   whether it was reasonable for a party to raise, pursue or contest a particular allegation or issue;

(c)   the manner in which a party has pursued or defended his case or particular allegation or issue; and

(d)   whether a claimant who has succeeded in his claim, in whole or in part, exaggerated his claim.'

Note—For cases involving partial success as opposed to misconduct, see para [38.193]–[38.216] onwards.

[38.168]   Ford v GKR Construction
[2000] 1 All ER 802, [2000] 1 WLR 1397

The claimant sustained personal injuries in a road traffic accident. The defendants admitted liability. However, the parties were unable to agree damages. The assessment of damages hearing was adjourned after two days of evidence and during the adjournment the defendants obtained video surveillance evidence of the claimant which was favourable to their case. The videos were disclosed prior to the resumed hearing. The trial judge found the claimant was not deliberately lying about her disability but awarded her damages substantially below what would have been awarded if the video evidence had not been available. The defendants were ordered to pay the claimant's costs of the action because although the award was less than the defendants' payment into court, the video evidence had been obtained late.

HELD, ON APPEAL: (1) If a defendant contends the claimant is a malingerer, fabricating evidence or exaggerating his symptoms, the claimant should have a reasonable opportunity to deal with such allegations.

(2)   There was no good reason why the video evidence could not have been obtained sooner and in the absence of a finding of dishonesty, the judge's exercise of discretion in relation to costs was not wrong.

[38.169]   **Hawker v British Steel plc**

(2 November 1999, unreported), Cardiff County Court

The claimant was injured in an accident at work and served an inflated schedule of special damages totalling £376,000. At trial, the claimant's evidence was discredited and he was criticised for creating documents to support his claim for special damages.

HELD: Although the claimant was successful against the first defendant, he should only recover 50% of his costs because of his misconduct.

[38.170]   **Molloy v Shell UK Ltd**

[2001] EWCA Civ 1272

[2001] All ER (D) 79 (Jul)

The claimant was injured in an accident at work and served a schedule of loss claiming over £300,000 for past and future loss of earnings. Shortly before trial, the defendant discovered the claimant had returned to work 14 months after the accident and had worked regularly since then. At trial the claimant was awarded £18,897 which was less than the defendant's payment into court. Despite the claimant's gross and deliberate exaggeration of his claim, the defendant was awarded only 75% of its costs after the date of the payment into court.

HELD, ON APPEAL: (1) The judge should have considered all of the claimant's conduct, not just that after the payment into court.

(2)   The claimant's conduct was 'nothing short of a cynical and dishonest abuse of the court's process'.

(3)   The defendant was entitled to all of its costs after the date of the payment into court.

(4)   It was questionable whether the court should have entertained the case at all, save to order the dishonest claimant to pay the defendant's costs.

[38.171]   **Frost v James Finlay Bank Ltd**

(3 October 2001, unreported), Chancery Division

The claimant was successful in her claim but the defendant contended she should pay its costs because the evidence at trial differed substantially from earlier written evidence and the size of the claim had been greatly exaggerated.

HELD: The claimant was entitled to 60% of her costs to reflect her exaggeration of the claim.

[38.172]   **Booth v Britannia Hotels Ltd**

[2002] EWCA Civ 579

[2002] All ER (D) 422 (Mar)

The claimant injured her left hand in an accident at work and after a two-day trial, obtained judgment on the issue of liability with damages to be assessed. Subsequently, the defendant obtained video surveillance evidence of the claimant which showed a full range of movement in the left hand. Two months before the assessment of damages hearing the claimant served a schedule of loss claiming £617,000. The defendant disclosed the video evidence five weeks before the hearing. One week before the hearing, the claim was settled by the claimant accepting the defendant's payment into court in the sum of £2,500 made two years before and the defendant agreed to pay the claimant's costs. The claimant's bill of costs exceeded £96,000 and the defendant contended the claimant should only recover costs required to prove a £2,500 claim.

HELD, ON APPEAL: (1) This case was to be distinguished from *Ford v GKR Construction* (at para [38.168]) because here the inference was that the claimant deliberately exaggerated her claim.
   (2)   Even though the video evidence was disclosed relatively late, the defendants should not have to pay the costs incurred by the claimant in pursuit of her exaggerated claim.
   (3)   The case was to be remitted to the district judge for a reassessment of the claimant's costs.

[38.173]   **Devine v Franklin**

[2002] EWHC 1846 (QB), QB

The claimant alleged he was injured in a road traffic accident and the defendant alleged the claim was fraudulent. At trial, the judge found the claimant sustained only a minor injury to his leg and shin and awarded £500 for pain, suffering and loss of amenity. The claimant was awarded costs of approximately £7,000.

HELD, ON APPEAL: (1) The claimant had exaggerated his symptoms therefore he was only entitled to the costs which he would have been entitled if there had been no exaggeration.
   (2)   In the circumstances, the claimant was limited to costs recoverable on the small claims track plus an additional £1,000 to reflect the defendant's conduct.

[38.174]   **Znaidi v Znaidi**

(24 September 2002, unreported), Central London County Court

The claimant alleged he sustained a brain injury as a result of a road traffic accident. The defendant arranged for the claimant to be examined by a neuropsychologist but at the interview, the claimant failed to cooperate and performed as if he was mentally retarded. Following settlement of the claim, the defendant sought an order that the claimant pay the costs of the examination.

HELD: The claimant was to pay the costs of the defendant's expert pursuant to CPR 44.3 on the grounds he had deliberately underachieved on the neuropsychological tests.

[38.175]   Hall v Rover Financial Services (GB) Ltd (t/a Land Rover Financial Services)

[2002] EWCA Civ 1514

[2002] All ER (D) 129 (Oct), (2002) Times, 8 November

The claimant was successful but the judge refused to award her costs. She appealed on the grounds the judge was wrong to rely on misconduct which was extraneous to the proceedings.

HELD, ON APPEAL: For a successful claimant to be deprived of costs, the misconduct must be in relation to the litigation, not extraneous to it.

[38.176]   Smith v Havering Hospitals NHS Trust

SCCO 30 May 2003

The claimant suffered personal injuries during the birth of her child and issued proceedings because limitation was about to expire. After issue, the claimant served a letter of claim. Subsequently proceedings were served and the claim settled for £30,000. The defendant sought an order disallowing all or part of the claimant's costs on the grounds that the claimant's non-compliance with the pre-action protocol for the resolution of clinical disputes amounted to misconduct.

HELD: (1) The claimant's solicitors had ample opportunity to serve a letter of claim prior to the issue of proceedings therefore there was a breach of the pre-action protocol.
(2)   There was however no misconduct justifying a costs sanction because the claimant gave the defendant extensions of time to serve its defence.

[38.177]   Johnson v Gore Wood & Co

[2004] EWCA Civ 14

[2004] All ER (D) 248 (Jan), (2004) Times, 17 February

In this case, the claim for damages exceeded £4.3million but at trial, the claimant was awarded approximately £170,000, less than the defendant's payment into court. The claimant was ordered to pay the defendant's costs from the date of the payment into court.

HELD, ON APPEAL: (1) It was unjust to order the claimant to pay all of the defendant's costs after the date of the payment into court having regard to the way the defendant conducted the trial. In particular, the defendant had contested every issue and aggressively cross-examined the claimant's witnesses.
(2)   The claimant should pay 50% of the defendant's costs from the last date for acceptance of the payment into court.

[38.178]   Aaron v Shelton

[2004] EWHC 1162 (QB)

[2004] 3 All ER 561, [2004] NLJR 853, QB

In this case, the issue for the court to decide was whether or not the paying party could rely upon the conduct of the receiving party as a reason to reduce the costs payable when the conduct might have been raised at the time the costs order was made.

During the trial, the claimant consented to a dismissal of his action and agreed to pay the defendant's costs. In his points of dispute to the defendant's bill of costs, the claimant raised the defendant's conduct at trial as a reason for disallowing costs. In reply, the defendant contended the claimant should have raised the issue of conduct with the trial judge when costs fell to be considered and it was now too late to do so.

HELD, ON APPEAL: (1) Conduct must be raised by a party before the judge making the costs order where it is appropriate to do so for example, the trial judge following a trial. If a party fails to do so, he cannot then raise conduct on the assessment of costs.

(2)   The judge may deal with the issue or direct that it be considered by the costs judge on assessment.

(3)   In the case of a costs order made by consent, the paying party can seek to include a provision in the consent order which deals with the issue of conduct or which refers the issue to the costs judge for determination.

(4)   It was an abuse of process to raise an issue before the costs judge which should have been raised before the judge making the costs order.

Note—The Court of Appeal in *Gray v Going Places Leisure Travel Ltd* [2005] EWCA Civ 189, [2005] All ER (D) 94 (Feb) agreed with the analysis in *Aaron v Shelton*.

[38.179]   **Gil v Baygreen Properties Ltd (in liquidation)**

[2004] EWHC 2029 (Ch)

[2004] All ER (D) 108 (Aug)

The claimant was successful in her claim but the defendants objected to payment of her costs on a number of grounds, including fabrication of evidence.

HELD: (1) The appropriate order was for the defendants to pay the claimant's costs less after assessment, the sum of £20,000, to reflect the fabrication of documents.

(2)   The court had power to make such an order pursuant to CPR 44.3(1) and (2).

[38.180]   **Painting v University of Oxford**

[2005] EWCA Civ 161

[2005] All ER (D) 45 (Feb)

The claimant was injured in an accident at work and commenced proceedings against the defendant. Subsequently the parties agreed an 80/20 apportionment of liability in favour of the claimant. The defendant then obtained video surveillance evidence and was granted permission to withdraw all but £10,000 of a previous payment into court. At the assessment of damages hearing, the claimant maintained she had suffered a long-term debilitating back injury which prevented her from working again and claimed damages of £400,000, net of the agreed 20% reduction for contributory negligence. The trial judge found the claimant had deliberating misled the jointly instructed medical expert, exaggerated her injuries and effectively recovered 3½ years after the accident. The claimant was awarded damages of £25,331.78 and the defendant was ordered to pay her costs.

HELD, ON APPEAL: (1) The defendant was the real winner in the litigation. The two-day hearing was very largely concerned with the issue of exaggeration and the claimant lost that issue.

(2) There was a strong likelihood the claim would have settled in the absence of exaggeration and the claimant failed to negotiate.

(3) Beating a payment into court was not conclusive because it was necessary to have regard to all the circumstances of the case.

(4) The appropriate order was for the defendant to pay the claimant's costs up to the date when the court granted the defendant permission to reduce the money in court and for the claimant to pay the defendant's costs thereafter.

[38.181] **E Ivor Hughes Education Foundation v Leach**

[2005] EWHC 1317 (Ch)

[2005] All ER (D) 127 (Jun)

The claimant made very substantial claims against the defendant totalling £610,545.28. One month before trial, the defendant made a payment into court in the sum of £5,000 in respect of part of the claim. One week before trial, the claimant accepted the payment into court and abandoned the entirety of the rest of the claims. The claimant's costs were approximately £170,000 and the defendant's costs were approximately £140,000. The claimant sought an order for payment of its costs of the action but the defendant objected, relying in particular upon *Devine v Franklin* (at para [38.173]) to argue his liability for costs should be limited by reference to the damages recovered.

HELD: (1) The claimant seriously exaggerated its claims and the defendant was entitled to his costs of the abandoned claims.

(2) The defendant was also the real winner in relation to the part of the claim not abandoned which had also been exaggerated. Following *Devine v Franklin*, it was appropriate for the claimant to recover no more costs than it would have recovered if it had brought a £5,000 claim.

[38.182] **Jackson v Ministry of Defence**

[2006] EWCA Civ 46

[2006] All ER (D) 14 (Jan)

The claimant was injured in an accident at work and originally claimed more than £1 million including future loss of earnings of over £400,000 and adapted accommodation of more than £250,000. The defendant made a payment into court of £150,000 and subsequently no settlement was reached at a joint settlement meeting ordered by the court. The claimant abandoned substantial parts of his claim and his final, pre-trial schedule of loss claimed approximately £240,000. At trial, the claimant gave evidence about his disability which went beyond the agreed medical evidence and he was awarded damages of £155,000. The trial judge ordered the defendant to pay 75% of the claimant's costs to reflect that the claimant had exaggerated his disability and only just beaten the payment into court.

HELD, ON APPEAL: (1) The case of *Painting v University of Oxford* (at para [38.180]) was an exceptional case where the claimant persisted in a claim for £400,000 and was awarded £25,000.

(2) Here the trial judge took into account who was the overall winner and made an appropriate reduction to reflect that.

(3) The judge's 25% reduction also took into account that the defendant had incurred costs in defending the exaggerated claim.

(4)   Although another judge might have made a larger reduction, there was no basis for interfering with the judge's decision which was well within his wide discretion.

17.   MULTIPLE DEFENDANTS

[38.183]   **Alpha Chauffeurs Ltd v Citygate Dealerships Ltd (t/a HR Owen) and Lombard North Central plc**

[2003] EWCA Civ 207

[2003] All ER (D) 301 (Feb)

The claimant commenced proceedings against the defendants who both denied liability. In addition, the second defendant served notice upon the first defendant seeking indemnity against the claims. At trial, the claimant succeeded against both defendants and the second defendant was successful in its claim against the first defendant. The orders as to costs made by the judge were as follows:

(1)   No order for costs as between the claimant and the first defendant up to the date of the payment into court, the claimant to pay the first defendant's costs thereafter.

(2)   Second defendant to pay 80% of the claimant's costs of the action to include the claimant's costs of its claim against the first defendant and 80% of the costs payable by the claimant to the first defendant.

(3)   First defendant to pay the second defendant's costs of its claim for indemnity.

HELD, ON APPEAL: (1) Application of the general rule that the unsuccessful party pays the successful party's costs, led to the conclusion that the costs of the litigation should be paid by the first defendant. That was not the effect of the costs orders made by the judge.

(2)   To give effect to the general rule from which there was no reason to depart, paragraphs (2) and (3) of the judge's order as to costs was set aside and substituted with the following:

(2) Second defendant to pay: (i) 80% of the claimant's costs of the action; and (ii) the claimant's costs of the second defendant's counter-claim.

(3) First defendant to pay the second defendant's costs of the action and of the claim for indemnity (such costs to include the costs payable by the second defendant to the claimant under sub-paragraph (i) of paragraph 2 but not those payable under sub-paragraph (ii) of that paragraph or the second defendant's own costs of its counterclaim.)

[38.184]   **Irvine v Commissioner of Police for the Metropolis, Carillion plc and Town and Country Flooring Ltd**

[2005] EWCA Civ 129

[2005] All ER (D) 46 (Feb)

The claimant, a police officer, was injured at a police station when he tripped and fell on a carpeted staircase. The claimant commenced proceedings against the following defendants:

(1)   first defendant – the claimant's employer;

(2)   second defendant – the manager of the first defendant's property services;

(3)   third defendant – a sub-contractor instructed by the second defendant to repair the stair carpet.

At trial, the claimant succeeded on breach of statutory duty against the first defendant but failed in his claims for negligence against all three defendants. The judge decided not to make a Bullock or Sanderson order and ordered the claimant to pay the costs of the second and third defendants.

HELD, ON APPEAL: (1) The jurisdiction to make a Bullock or Sanderson order had survived the introduction of the Civil Procedure Rules but the exercise of discretion to make such an order had to be guided by CPR Pt 1 and CPR 44.3.

(2)   Ordinarily, a Bullock or Sanderson order was made where a claimant sued more than one defendant in the alternative and succeeds against only one, but there was power to make such an order even when the claims were not in the alternative.

(3)   An important consideration was the reasonableness of the claimant's conduct in suing a defendant against whom he did not succeed. The fact that one defendant blamed another did not make the action against the other reasonable.

(4)   In this case, it was not reasonable to sue the second defendant for a number of reasons, including in particular that the second defendant was never sued in the alternative and no proper case was ever put forward against it.

(5)   It was also unreasonable to sue the third defendant particularly because the claimant had no cogent evidence to prove the repair was defective or negligently done.

(6)   In the circumstances the judge's decision was correct.

[38.185]   Arkin v Borchard Lines Ltd and Others

[2005] EWCA Civ 655

[2005] 3 All ER 613

The claimant commenced proceedings against four defendants and subsequently the first defendant brought claims against three Part 20 defendants. At trial, the judge gave judgment in favour of the defendants and Part 20 defendants and ordered the first defendant to pay 90% of one of the Part 20 defendant's costs and 80% of each of the other two.

HELD, ON APPEAL: (1) Ordinarily, the court considered the costs in the main action separately from the costs in the Part 20 proceedings but the rule was not inviolable.

(2)   The normal rule was that a successful Part 20 defendant was entitled to an order for costs against the unsuccessful Part 20 claimant and should not be deprived of such an order merely because the claimant in the main action was impecunious.

(3)   In this case the interests of justice required a different order to be made particularly because the judge indicated he could not properly try the case without evidence from one of the Part 20 defendant's which had not cooperated prior to being joined.

(4)   The appropriate order was for the defendants and Part 20 defendants to bear their own costs both in the main action and in the Part 20 proceedings, save the costs of experts should be shared equally between the defendants and Part 20 defendants.

[38.186]   **Rackham v Sandy, Etheridge and Hardman**

[2005] EWHC 1354 (QB)

[2005] All ER (D) 326 (Jun), QB

At trial the claimant succeeded against the first defendant but failed against the second and third defendants. The parties were unable to agree liability for costs.

HELD: (1) The first defendant was to pay two-thirds of the claimant's costs.
  (2)   The claimant was to pay to each of the second and third defendants one quarter of the total defendants' costs.
  (3)   The claimant's decision to sue the second and third defendant's was unreasonable therefore it would not be just to order the first defendant to pay the costs payable by the claimant to the second and third defendants.

18.   NOTICE OF FUNDING

[38.187]   **Hardcastle and Hardcastle v Leeds and Holbeck Building Society**

(16 October 2002, unreported), Leeds District Registry

The claimants initially attempted to resolve their dispute with the defendant themselves but consulted solicitors for advice when the defendant made an offer of settlement. Subsequently, on 20 October 2000, the claimants entered into a conditional fee agreement with the solicitors which provided for a 100% success fee but did not notify the defendant at that stage. The parties were unable to negotiate a settlement of the claim and proceedings were issued on 5 October 2001 at which time the claimants gave notice of funding to the defendant. The claim was later settled for £32,500 and the defendant agreed to pay the claimants' costs. One of the issues for the district judge at the detailed assessment hearing was whether or not the claimants should be deprived of their success fee between 20 October 2000 and 5 October 2001.

HELD: (1) The Costs Practice Direction recommended that notice of funding be given prior to the issue of proceedings. However, paragraph 19.2(5) made clear there was no obligation to do so until proceedings were commenced.
  (2)   In the context of the rules relating to costs, the word 'proceedings' referred to the issuing of the court process by claim form.
  (3)   The court was nevertheless entitled to consider disallowing all or part of the success fee for failing to give notice prior to the issue of proceedings if the paying party could show prejudice.
  (4)   There was no evidence the defendant's stance would have been different had it known of the CFA sooner therefore it was not fair or appropriate to disallow or reduce the success fee between October 2000 and October 2001 (but cf *Bainbridge v MAF Pipelines Ltd* at para [38.189]).

[38.188]   **Wilkins v Plymouth Community Services NHS Trust**

(1 November 2002, unreported), Plymouth County Court

The claimant issued personal injury proceedings on 23 January 2002 but failed to give notice of the CFA and insurance policy taken out in February 2001. Subsequently the claimant realised the error in July 2002, served notice of funding and made an application for relief from sanctions pursuant to CPR 3.9. The district judge refused the application and the claimant appealed.

HELD, ON APPEAL: (1) The district judge had failed to consider all of the factors in CPR 3.9 as required by *Woodhouse v Consignia* [2002] 2 All ER 737, [2002] 1 WLR 2558.
   (2)   The defendant had not suffered any prejudice and the modest mistake of the claimant's solicitor should not deprive the claimant of her entitlement to the success fee.
   (3)   Relief was granted for the whole period of default.

[38.189]   Bainbridge v MAF Pipelines Ltd

(19 March 2004, unreported), Teesside County Court

In this case, the claimant's personal injury claim settled prior to the issue of proceedings. The defendant challenged the recoverability of the claimant's success fee and insurance premium on the grounds the claimant failed to give notice of funding prior to settlement of the claim. The claimant therefore issued costs only proceedings in order to recover the additional liabilities.

HELD: (1) Under the personal injury pre-action protocol, the claimant should have informed the defendant of the funding arrangement at the outset, and in this context, the word 'should' meant 'must'.
   (2)   The requirement to notify the defendant of a funding arrangement was not triggered only by the issue of a claim form. The dealings between the parties leading up to the settlement of the claim fell within the term 'proceedings' in this context, following the comments of Brooke LJ in *Crosbie v Munroe* [2003] 2 All ER 856.
   (3)   The claimant delayed without good reason in making an application for relief from sanctions under CPR 3.9 therefore it was not appropriate to grant relief.
   (4)   In the circumstances, the defendant was not liable for the success fee or insurance premium (but cf *Hardcastle and Hardcastle v Leeds and Holbeck Building Society* at para [38.187]).

[38.190]   Metcalfe v Clipston

SCCO 6 April 2004

The claimant entered into a CFA on 10 January 2001 and his claim settled prior to the issue of proceedings. The claimant's bill of costs included a 100% success fee and the defendant disputed his entitlement to it on the grounds the claimant had failed to give notice of funding. The claimant therefore issued costs only proceedings on 4 June 2003 to recover the success fee, served notice of funding on 13 January 2004 and issued an application on 20 January 2004 for relief from sanctions pursuant to CPR 3.9.

HELD: (1) There was no absolute requirement to give notice of a funding arrangement until proceedings were issued.
   (2)   Notification should be given prior to the issue of proceedings and in this context the word, 'should' meant 'ought to' which was not the same as 'has to' or 'must'.
   (3)   The word, 'proceedings' meant the issue of court process and not prospective proceedings.
   (4)   In the circumstances, the claimant was not precluded from recovering a

success fee prior to the issue of the costs only proceedings (but cf *Bainbridge v MAF Pipelines Ltd* at para [38.189]).

[38.191] **Trustees of Wasps Football Club v Lambert Smith Hampton Group Ltd**

[2004] EWHC 1503 (Comm)

[2004] All ER (D) 113 (Jul)

The claimants entered into a CFA which provided for a success fee of 100% and notified the defendant of the CFA by letter. When proceedings were subsequently issued, the claimant did not serve form N251 notice of funding. The claimant made a prompt application for relief from sanctions when the defendant raised the failure to serve the notice.

HELD: (1) The claimants were in breach of paragraph 19.2(5) of the Costs Practice Direction for failing to serve notice of funding with the claim form.
   (2)   The defendant knew from the outset that the claim was funded by a CFA with a success fee and therefore there was no prejudice to the defendant.
   (3)   The claimants were entitled to relief from sanctions pursuant to CPR 3.9 and were not to be deprived of the success fee.

[38.192] **Connor v Birmingham City Council**

(16 March 2005, unreported), Birmingham County Court

The claimant entered into a CFA which provided for a success fee and took out ATE insurance. In correspondence before the claim was issued, the defendant was notified of the funding arrangement. Subsequently, the claimant issued proceedings and served notice of funding in form N251. However, the form did not disclose the funding arrangement. The defendant raised the failure to serve a proper notice of funding in its points of dispute but the claimant did not apply for relief from sanctions until the detailed assessment hearing. The district judge refused to allow recovery of the success fee and the claimant appealed.

HELD, ON APPEAL: (1) The case of *Trustees of Wasps Football Club v Lambert Smith Hampton Group Ltd* (at para [38.191]) was distinguishable because there the claimant had made a formal application under CPR 3.9 in advance of the hearing.
   (2)   Prejudice was not the determinative factor and it was incumbent on the claimant to comply strictly with the requirement to serve a proper notice of funding when the proceedings were issued.
   (3)   The district judge's decision was within the generous ambit for which reasonable disagreement was possible.

19.   PARTIAL SUCCESS

CPR 44.3(4) and (5) is set out at para [38.167]).

For cases involving misconduct as opposed to partial success, see paras [38.168]–[38.182].

[38.193] **AEI Redifussion Music Ltd v Phonographic Performance Ltd**
[1999] 2 All ER 1507, [1999] 1 WLR 1507

In this costs appeal, Lord Woolf MR took the opportunity to review the general rule that 'costs follow the event' and observed the Civil Procedure Rules required courts to be more ready to make separate orders which reflected the outcome of different issues. A party could be deprived of his costs of an issue on which he had failed, even if he had not acted unreasonably or improperly.

Lord Woolf remarked, 'It is now clear that a too robust application of the "follow the event principle" encourages litigants to increase the costs of litigation, since it discourages litigants from being selective as to the points they take. If you recover all your costs as long as you win, you are encouraged to leave no stone unturned in your effort to do so.'

[38.194]
Liverpool City Council v Rosemary Chavasse Ltd and Walton Group plc
(18 August 1999, unreported), Chancery Division

At trial, the claimant was successful on three issues and unsuccessful on two issues. The claimant contended the defendants should pay all of its costs and the defendants contended there should be no order for costs.

HELD: (1) The claimant was the overall winner and if only the relative success of the parties on the issues was considered, the claimant was entitled to 75% of its costs.
   (2)   It was however necessary to take into account the claimant's conduct, in particular its failure to set out the entirety of its case prior to the issue of proceedings and properly consider its position until the last minute. This had resulted in additional costs and deprived the defendants of a reasonable opportunity to consider the issues.
   (3)   In the circumstances, the right order was for the defendants to pay 50% of the claimant's costs.

[38.195] **Shirley v Caswell**
[2002] 2 Costs LR 1, [2000] Lloyd's Rep PN 955

The claimants sued their former barrister for losses incurred as a result of the defendant's negligent advice. At trial, the claimants succeeded on one of three issues and recovered damages of £156,000 which was subsequently less than the £2.7 million claimed. The Judge ordered the defendant to pay 60% of the claimants' costs and the claimants to pay 40% of the defendant's costs.

HELD, ON APPEAL: (1) The judge was entitled to order the claimants to pay 40% of the defendant's costs so that the defendant was reimbursed costs incurred in relation to issues that the claimants abandoned before trial or did not succeed on at trial.
   (2)   The judge was wrong not to order the defendant to pay 100% of the claimants' costs because the costs of abandoned issues ought to be disallowed by the costs judge and therefore should not be taken into account when making the costs order otherwise there was a risk of the claimants being doubly penalised.

[38.196]   **Carver v Hammersmith & Queen Charlotte's Health Authority**

(31 July 2000, unreported), QBD

At trial the claimant succeeded on the issue of liability and sought an order that the defendant pay her costs. The defendant contended the claimant was not entitled to all of her costs because she abandoned allegations of negligence and delayed in the prosecution of her claim.

HELD: (1) The claimant had failed to abandon allegations which could not be sensibly pursued as early as she should have done and had seriously delayed in the prosecution of her claim. As a consequence, the defendant incurred unnecessary costs.

(2)   The appropriate order was for the defendant to pay a proportion of the claimant's costs and prior to hearing full argument, 85% of the claimant's costs was indicated.

[38.197]   **Winter v Winter and Winter**

(10 November 2000, unreported), Court of Appeal

At trial the judge gave judgment in favour of the claimant and ordered the defendants to pay the claimant's costs.

HELD, ON APPEAL: (1) The claimant had abandoned a significant issue and this should have been reflected in the costs order.

(2)   The costs order was varied to provide that the claimant should pay the defendant's costs of the abandoned issue.

[38.198]   **Antonelli v Kandler**

(29 November 2000, unreported), Chancery Division

At trial the claim against the defendant was dismissed and the defendant sought an order that the claimant pay his costs.

HELD: (1) In a case involving a number of issues on which the winning party did not succeed, a number of factors had to be considered. Firstly, the reasonableness of the winning party in taking a point which he lost. Secondly, the manner in which the point was taken. Thirdly, the reasonableness of the point. Fourthly, the additional costs taken up by the point. Fifthly, the extra time taken in court over the point. Sixthly, the extent to which the point was inter-related with other points upon which the successful party won.

(2)   The defendant had failed on two issues but they were reasonably arguable. If they had not been taken however, the evidence and arguments would have been significantly reduced.

(3)   The claimant was to pay 75% of the defendant's costs.

[38.199]   **Stocznia Gdanska SA v Latvian Shipping Co**

[2001] LTL May 25

At trial, the claimant was successful against the first and second defendants but unsuccessful against the other defendants.

HELD: (1) It was clear from CPR 44.3(4)(b) that the reasonableness of raising, pursuing or contesting an allegation or issue was not necessarily relevant and was quite distinct from the conduct of the parties. Such a construction would encourage litigants to be selective about the points to take and therefore reduce the costs of litigation.

(2)   The claimant had abandoned one issue and failed on another and therefore should pay the first defendant's costs of those issues.

(3)   The appropriate course was to apply percentages to the overall recovery rather than attempt to unravel the costs of issues during the assessment of costs. Much of the evidence would have been needed for the one issue upon which the claimant succeeded and in the circumstances, the first defendant was to pay 38% of the claimant's costs.

(4)   The second defendant was to pay 20% of the claimant's costs.

[38.200]   **Hardy v Sutherland and King**

[2001] EWCA Civ 976

[2001] All ER (D) 117 (Jun)

In proceedings arising out of a building dispute, the first and second defendant agreed to pay the claimant £3,000 and £14,000 respectively. The parties were unable to agree costs and following argument, the Recorder ordered the defendants to pay 75% of the claimant's costs. The claimant appealed on the grounds that the Recorder was wrong not to award her 100% of her costs.

HELD, ON APPEAL: (1) The proportion of costs which a claimant recovered was always a matter for the judge's discretion.

(2)   There were no grounds for interfering with the judge's exercise of discretion in this case.

[38.201]   **Firle Investments Ltd v Datapoint International Ltd**

[2001] EWCA Civ 1106

[2001] All ER (D) 258 (Jun), [2001] NPC 106

At trial the claimant recovered damages of £53,695.25 and the trial judge awarded the claimant 33.3% of its costs up to the date of the defendant's second payment into court and 15% thereafter.

HELD, ON APPEAL: (1) An appellate court would not interfere with the decision of the judge relating to costs unless the judge was plainly wrong.

(2)   An important consideration was whether a party's unreasonable conduct prevented the other party from making a properly informed decision about their prospects in the litigation.

(3)   Although the claim was for £385,000, the claimant succeeded by a substantial amount and this was not a case where there were clear separate issues. The claimant was therefore entitled to 100% of its costs up to the date of the second payment into court.

(4)   The claimant's actions lengthened the trial unnecessarily and accordingly it was entitled to 70% of its costs after the date of the second payment into court.

[38.202]   **Summit Property Ltd v Pitmans (a firm)**
[2001] EWCA Civ 2020
[2001] All ER (D) 270 (Nov)

At trial the judge gave judgment for the defendant and ordered the claimant to pay 30% of the defendant's costs and the defendant to pay 65% of the claimant's costs. The trial judge made the costs order because the defendant failed on the main issue, breach of duty, even though they succeeded on causation and quantum. By far the greater part of the trial had been taken up by the issue of breach of duty.

HELD, ON APPEAL: (1) It was not necessary for a party to have acted unreasonably or improperly before he could be required to pay the costs of an issue on which he had failed. That was the substance of what Woolf MR said in *AEI Rediffusion Music Ltd v Phonographic Performance Ltd* (at para [38.193]).
   (2)   In the special circumstances of the case, there was no error of principle and even though other judges would not necessarily have reached the same view, the decision of the judge was not wrong.

[38.203]   **Professional Information Technology Consultants Ltd v Jones**
[2001] EWCA Civ 2103
[2001] All ER (D) 90 (Dec)

The day before trial the claimant applied to amend the particulars of claim to fundamentally change its case. Permission to amend was granted and subsequently at trial the claimant recovered damages of £12,143.95. The trial judge ordered the defendant to pay two-thirds of the claimant's costs because the claim would have failed without the amendments which should have been made sooner.

HELD, ON APPEAL: (1) The correct starting point was that the claimant had won and should get its costs but taking into account all relevant factors, the judge was entitled to award the claimant a proportion of its costs.
   (2)   The principle in *Beoco v Alfa Laval Co* [1995] QB 137 that where a claimant makes a late amendment which substantially alters the case the defendant is entitled to costs up to the date of the amendment, was not the only way of reflecting a fundamental amendment. It was therefore open to the judge to make the order that he did.

[38.204]   **Darougar v Belcher t/a Park Street Garage**
[2002] EWCA Civ 1262
[2002] All ER (D) 395 (Jul)

Immediately prior to the start of the trial the claimant was claiming damages of £21,800 and the defendant was counterclaiming £8,577 as the balance of monies due. On the first day of the trial the case was settled on the basis that there would be judgment for the defendant in the sum of £5,000. In effect, the claimant had abandoned his claim. The parties were unable to agree costs and the judge ordered the defendant to pay all of the claimant's costs up to the date the defendant returned the claimant's vehicle and one-third thereafter.

HELD, ON APPEAL: (1) The claim abandoned by the claimant was the largest amount claimed by either party and led to a material increase in the costs of both parties. The judge was therefore wrong not to take this into account when making the costs order.

(2) The proper result in the circumstances was for the claimant to pay 50% of the defendant's costs after the date the vehicle was returned.

(3) If the judge's order had been allowed to stand, this would have failed to recognise that the defendant was the overall winner in respect of the issues which remained after the return of the vehicle.

[38.205]   **Budgen v Andrew Gardner Partnership**

[2002] EWCA Civ 1125

[2002] All ER (D) 528 (Jul)

The claimant pursued a claim in excess of £1million but at trial was awarded damages of £328,970 and the defendant was ordered to pay 75% of the claimant's costs. The reason for the costs order was that the claimant had failed on one issue, the claim for loss of earnings, that should not have been pursued and which had taken up a substantial part of the trial. The defendant appealed on the grounds that the judge should have ordered the claimant to pay the costs of the lost issue rather than making a percentage order.

HELD, ON APPEAL: (1) Judges should be prepared to make costs orders which reflected the overall outcome of proceedings and the loss of particular issues.

(2) If the winning party pursued an issue he should not have done, this should be reflected in the costs order as a sanction to deter such conduct in future and to relieve the losing party of part of his liability for costs.

(3) The judge was entitled to make a percentage costs order rather than an issue based costs order because this was more practicable than the costs judge having to master the issue in detail and then analyse what work was or was not attributable to the issue.

(4) The court did not have a transcript of the trial therefore did not know what proportion of the trial costs were attributable to the issue. In addition, the court did not know the judge's view of the extent to which the issue had increased the overall costs of the action. In the circumstances, the court would not interfere with the judge's discretion even though the 25% reduction appeared too low.

Mance LJ (dissenting): 'I would allow this appeal to the extent of increasing the deduction to be made from the claimant's otherwise recoverable costs of the action from 25% to 50%'.

[38.206]   **AL Barnes Ltd v Time Talk (UK) Ltd**

[2003] EWCA Civ 402

[2003] All ER (D) 391 (Mar)

In this appeal, one of the issues for the Court of Appeal to consider was the order made by the trial judge that the claimant should pay 50% of the defendant's costs. This was despite the fact that the claimant had recovered a monetary amount on its claim which was greater than the defendant on its counterclaim.

Longmore LJ remarked, 'In what may generally be called commercial litigation … the disputes are ultimately about money. In deciding who is the successful party the most important thing is to identify the party who is to pay money to the other. That is the surest indication of success and failure'.

HELD, ON APPEAL: (1) The claimant was the successful party.

(2)   Most of the time in court was spent on an issue on which the claimant failed.

(3)   The appropriate order was for the defendant to pay 25% of the claimant's costs on the claim and counterclaim.

[38.207]   Islam v Ali

[2003] EWCA Civ 612

[2003] All ER (D) 384 (Mar)

The claimant pursued a claim for £156,000 and at trial recovered £12,746.41. The trial judge ordered the defendant to pay the claimant's costs and the defendant appealed on the grounds that the claimant had recovered a relatively small amount compared to the sum claimed.

HELD, ON APPEAL: (1) A trial judge had a wide discretion in respect of costs and the Court of Appeal should only interfere with the judge's exercise of it if he had 'exceeded the generous ambit within which reasonable disagreement is possible': per Brooke LJ in *Tanfern v Cameron-MacDonald (practice note)* [2000] 2 All ER 801, [2000] 1 WLR 1311, or '... erred in principle in his approach, or has left out of account, or taken into account, some feature that he should, or should not, have considered, or that [the exercise of] his discretion is wholly wrong because the court is forced to the conclusion that he has not balanced the various factors fairly in the scale': per Sir Murray Stuart Smith in *Adamson v Halifax plc* [2003] 4 All ER 423, [2003] 1 WLR 60.

(2)   The reality of the case was that the defendant was the winner because she faced a claim substantially greater than the amount awarded and the claimant had failed on the main issues.

(3)   The proper order should be no order as to costs.

[38.208]   BCT Software Solutions Ltd v C Brewer & Sons Ltd

[2003] EWCA Civ 939

[2003] All ER (D) 196 (Jul)

One month before trial the claimant radically amended its claim such that the main part of the case was abandoned and the issues were narrowed to four specific claims. Shortly after the trial began, the parties compromised the action on detailed terms set out in a schedule to a Tomlin order but were unable to agree costs. The trial judge ordered the claimant to pay 85% of the defendant's costs before the amendment and 62.5% of the defendant's costs after the amendment. The basis of the judge's decision was that the claimant had lost on three out of four issues and under the settlement recovered a small sum compared with the original claim.

HELD, ON APPEAL: (1) In the absence of manifest injustice, an appellate court should not interfere with a judge's discretion which had been exercised with the agreement of the parties following settlement of the claim, rather than at the conclusion of a trial.

(2)   The judge was right to make a percentage costs order rather than an issue based costs order.

(3)   No order as to costs was attractive in cases where it was difficult to ascertain who was the winner and who was the loser but there was no convention that such an order should be made wherever the court was asked to decide costs following settlement of the claim.

(4)   The judge had not erred in principle and the court would not interfere with his decision.

[38.209]   **Fleming v Chief Constable of the Sussex Police Force**

[2004] EWCA Civ 643

[2004] All ER (D) 25 (May)

Following a bitterly fought trial, the claimant was awarded £5,025. The trial judge ordered no order for costs upon one issue which was part of the original claim but later struck out by consent prior to trial, otherwise the defendant was to pay the claimant's costs.

HELD, ON APPEAL: (1) The judge should not have taken into account the effect upon the parties' means of the incidence of an order or costs.

(2)   The claimant had succeeded on two out of three issues and the pleading of the unsuccessful issue did not add to the substance or the background of the issues which had to be explored at trial. There was therefore no discrete identifiable issue which, if omitted, would have reduced the length of the trial significantly.

(3)   In the circumstances, there was no good reason to displace the general rule that costs should follow the event and the judge was not wrong in not making a percentage costs order.

[38.210]   **Clarke v Devon County Council**

[2005] EWCA Civ 266

[2005] 1 FCR 752, [2005] All ER (D) 285 (Mar)

The claimant brought proceedings against the defendant alleging negligence by at least five of its employees and claimed special damages of approximately £217,000. At trial the judge found the defendant was only liable in respect of the negligence of one employee and the claimant was awarded £10,000 general damages and £25,000 special damages for loss of earnings. The trial judge ordered the defendant to pay all of the claimant's costs despite the fact that:

(1)   allegations of negligence against four other employees of the defendant were either abandoned or failed at trial;

(2)   a claim for psychiatric damage for a major depressive disorder failed;

(3)   a claim for failure to diagnose dyspraxia was dropped at the beginning of the trial;

(4)   the claimant had only limited success on the quantum of damage.

When granting permission to appeal May LJ indicated that attempts should be made to compromise the appeal having regard to the disproportionate costs, but attempts at mediation failed.

HELD, ON APPEAL: (1) Claimants should carefully consider which individuals it was reasonable to allege were negligent.

(2)   The claimant was unsuccessful on a number of discrete issues and the judge was wrong not to reflect this in the costs order.

(3)   The court had to take into account that many of the witnesses would have been called to give evidence even if the claim had been limited to the one issue on which the claimant succeeded and the trial would not have been significantly shorter if the other allegations had not been made.

(4)   The appropriate order was for the defendant to pay 70% of the claimant's costs.

[38.211]   Burchell v Bullard and Bullard

[2005] EWCA Civ 358

[2005] All ER (D) 62 (Apr)

See also at para [38.160].

This case arose out of a building dispute. The claim against the defendants was for the sum of £18,318.45 and the defendants counterclaimed for £100,815.34. At trial, the claimant was awarded £18,327.04 and the defendants were awarded £14,373.15. The trial judge ordered the defendants to pay the claimant's costs of the claim and the claimant to pay the defendants' costs of the counterclaim.

HELD, ON APPEAL: (1) The judge fell into error by resorting to costs following the event and failing to consider what alternatives were available to him. The frequently most desirable option was to order a proportion of a party's costs to be paid.
  (2)   In commercial litigation the unsuccessful party was the one who wrote the cheque at the end of the case and here that was the defendants. Therefore the starting point was that the claimant was entitled to the costs of the claim and counterclaim.
  (3)   The claimant had not exaggerated his claim but the defendants had exaggerated their counterclaim and conducted the litigation more unreasonably. The defendants also lost many more issues than they won.
  (4)   The claimant was not to recover all of his costs however because a large part of the trial was taken up with the counterclaim on which the defendants had some success.
  (5)   The appropriate order was for the defendants to pay 60% of the claimant's costs of the claim and counterclaim.

[38.212]   Allison v Brighton & Hove City Council

[2005] EWCA Civ 548

[2005] All ER (D) 324 (Apr)

The claimant initially sought damages in the region of £90,000 but by the close of submissions at trial, the claim had been reduced to £47,000. The trial judge awarded the claimant £3,172.41 and rejected all other claims. The defendant was ordered to pay 25% of the claimant's costs up to the last date for acceptance of the payment into court of £7,500 and thereafter the claimant was to pay the defendant's costs. The claimant appealed that part of the order which related to the claimant's costs up to the last date for acceptance of the payment into court.

HELD, ON APPEAL: (1) Since the introduction of the Civil Procedure Rules, percentage costs orders were more common.
  (2)   Some judges may have been more generous to the claimant but it could not be said that the judge's decision was wrong.

[38.213]   Alli v Luton & Dunstable NHS Trust

[2005] EWCA Civ 551

[2005] All ER (D) 377 (Apr)

The claimant fell as she was descending a staircase in darkness. At trial, the factual basis of the claimant's case changed when she was cross-examined however there was no application to adjourn in order to amend her statement of case so the judge proceeded to give judgment in favour of the claimant. The trial judge decided to make no order for costs because the claimant's late change had misled the defendants and affected their approach to the claim.

HELD, ON APPEAL: (1) The main issue was whether or not the defendants were liable either at common law or under the Workplace (Health, Safety and Welfare) Regulations 1992, SI 1992/3004 and that remained the claimant's case throughout. Accordingly, the judge's conclusions were not affected by the change in the claimant's case.

    (2)   The judge was wrong to depart from the normal rule that costs follow the event and the defendant should pay the claimant's costs.

[38.214]   **Thompson t/a ACT Construction v Mackie and Mackie**

[2005] EWCA Civ 1336

[2005] All ER (D) 280 (Oct)

The claim against the defendants was for £35,890.67 and the defendants counter-claimed for £21,250. After a four-day trial, the claimant was successful on the claim and the defendants were only partially successful on the counterclaim. Judgment was given for the claimant for £19,389.68. The judge ordered the defendants to pay 80% of the claimant's costs of the claim and the claimant to pay all of the defendants' costs of the counterclaim. The judge deducted 20% from the claimant's costs of the claim because he called two additional witnesses to give oral evidence, however, this did not have any significant effect on the length of the trial. When granting the claimant permission to appeal, Longmore LJ gave directions that mediation be attempted however the defendants failed to respond.

HELD, ON APPEAL: (1) The claimant had succeeded to the extent of 61% of his claim while the defendants had only succeeded to the extent of 25% of the counterclaim.

    (2)   The principle stated by Longmore LJ in *AL Barnes Ltd v Time Talk (UK) Ltd* (at para [38.206]) that in a dispute about money the unsuccessful party is the one who is to pay money to the other, applied in this case.

    (3)   The claimant was not entitled to all of his costs because of the time taken for the additional evidence and to reflect the fact that he did not succeed on all issues. The claimant had however recovered a substantial proportion of his claim.

    (4)   The appropriate order was for the defendants to pay 75% of the claimant's costs of the claim and counterclaim.

[38.215]   **Hickman v Blake Lapthorn and Fisher**

[2006] EWHC 12 (QB)

[2006] All ER (D) 67 (Jan), QB

See also at para [38.164].

The claimant sued his former solicitors and counsel for negligence in advising him to settle his personal injury claim at an undervalue. At trial, the claimant was successful against both defendants and awarded the sum of £130,000. The claimant sought an order that the defendants pay all of his costs save 50% of the costs of obtaining reports from an occupational physician. The second defendant submitted the defendants should be liable for no more than 80% of the claimant's costs on the grounds that the claimant had failed on a number of distinct issues and in particular, the claimant sought an award in excess of £600,000 for future care and case management but recovered approximately £35,000.

HELD: (1) The trial was not sufficiently lengthened by the issues upon which the claimant had failed to merit reflection in the order for costs.

(2)   It was reasonable for the claimant to pursue his largely unsuccessful care claim which was not exaggerated however, the claimant should pay the costs of the defendants' care reports and the costs of the claimant's care reports should not be payable by the defendants. A special order in respect of the care costs incurred at trial was not appropriate.

(3)   The claimant was not to recover from the defendants 75% of the costs of the reports of the occupational physician, the court having refused permission to rely on such evidence although some use was made at trial of the documentary material collected by the expert.

[38.216]   Promar International Ltd v Clarke

[2006] EWCA Civ 332

[2006] All ER (D) 35 (Apr)

The claimant issued proceedings against the defendant seeking an injunction and substantial damages of £132,921. At the start of the trial, the defendant offered to give an undertaking to the court which the claimant accepted and abandoned its claim for damages. The trial judge was reluctant to rule on the issue of costs so adjourned for the parties to negotiate. No agreement could be reached by the parties so the judge agreed to determine the issue of costs. The judge was unable to say which party would probably have won but concluded the defendant was primarily responsible for the dispute continuing until trial in not making an offer earlier. The defendant was ordered to pay 75% of the claimant's costs. Subsequently the defendant's counsel discovered the Court of Appeal's decision in *BCT Software Solutions Ltd v C Brewer and Sons Ltd* (at para [38.208]) and sent a copy to the judge who ordered a fresh hearing. The judge heard further argument from the parties, concluded his previous approach was probably wrong in the light of the *BCT* case and decided the appropriate order was no order as to costs.

HELD, ON APPEAL: (1) The judge was correct to take into account the guidance given by the Court of Appeal in the *BCT* case as it was an authority of general applicability to settled cases where the Judge was asked to rule on costs.

(2)   In *Venture Finance plc v Mead and Another* [2005] EWCA Civ 325, Chadwick LJ said a judge was not obliged to make an order for costs where all substantive issues had been agreed. There were dangers in doing so, as illustrated in the *BCT* case, where it was impossible to say that one party have obviously won and the other party had obviously lost.

(3)   As stated by Mummery LJ in the *BCT* case, the Court of Appeal would not interfere with the judge's decision unless it was manifestly unjust because the judge had been invited by the parties to rule on costs when he was not in a position to do so properly and should not have done at all.

(4)   The judge's decision in this case was not manifestly unjust. In particular, he was correct to find there was no winner and no loser because the claimant had obtained an undertaking but abandoned a substantial claim for damages.

(5)   This case reinforced the warnings given in the *BCT* and *Venture Finance*

cases 'of the dangers of trial judges being persuaded to decide issues of costs when all issues, save costs, have been settled, or resolved without the necessity for a judgment.'

20.   PRE-ACTION PROTOCOL COSTS

[38.217]   **McGlinn v Waltham Contractors Ltd and Others**

[2005] EWHC 1419 (TCC)

[2005] 3 All ER 1126, TCC

The claimant alleged the defendants were liable for the defective building work carried out at his property. The claimant complied with the Pre-Action Protocol for Construction and Engineering Disputes which led to an unsuccessful mediation. The claimant subsequently issued proceedings and the claims made in the particulars of claim were, in part, different to the claims made at the commencement of the pre-action protocol. At the first case management conference, the second defendant sought an interim payment of £20,000 for the costs thrown away at the pre-action protocol stage in considering and responding to the two claims which the claimant had abandoned.

HELD: (1) As a matter of construction of s 51 of the Supreme Court Act 1981 and by reference to *In re Gibson's Settlement Trusts* [1981] Ch 179 and *Callery v Gray* (at para [38.58]), the costs incurred in complying with a pre-action protocol may be recoverable as costs 'incidental to' any subsequent proceedings.

   (2)   Save in exceptional circumstances such as unreasonable conduct, costs incurred by a defendant at the pre-action protocol stage in dealing with issues which were subsequently dropped when proceedings were commenced, were not costs 'incidental to' the proceedings and therefore were not recoverable under s 51. It would be wrong in principle to penalise a claimant for narrowing issues in compliance with the protocol.

   (3)   The second defendant's costs were not therefore recoverable as a matter of principle but even if they were, discretion would have been exercised in the claimant's favour because it would be contrary to the purpose of the protocol to penalise the claimant for abandoning two claims at the commencement of proceedings.

21.   PROPORTIONALITY

[38.218]   **Jefferson v National Freight Carriers plc**

[2001] 2 Costs LR 313

The claimant injured his back at work and at trial was awarded damages of £2,275.24. The claimant's schedule of costs totalled £6,905.49 and the trial judge summarily assessed the costs at £3,500. The judge considered the costs claimed were disproportionate to the damages awarded.

HELD, ON APPEAL: (1) The claimant's schedule of costs was clearly disproportionate and proportionality was a very important feature of the assessment of costs on the standard basis, particularly in fast track claims.

(2)   Claimants must conduct modest litigation in as economic a manner as possible.

(3)   Lord Woolf CJ endorsed the following comments of Judge Alton in *Stevens v Watts* (22 June 2000, unreported), Birmingham County Court: 'In modern litigation, with the emphasis on proportionality, it is necessary for parties to make an assessment at the outset of the likely value of the claim and its importance and complexity, and then to plan in advance the necessary work, the appropriate level of person to carry out the work, the overall time which would be necessary and appropriate to spend on the various stages in bringing the action to trial, and the likely overall cost. While it was not unusual for costs to exceed the amount in issue, it was, in the context of modest litigation such as the present case, one reason for seeking to curb the amount of work done, and the cost by reference to the need for proportionality.'

(4)   The costs allowed by the judge were within the range of acceptable awards and therefore the court would not interfere with his decision.

[38.219] Griffiths and Others v Solutia UK Ltd

[2001] EWCA Civ 736

[2001] All ER (D) 196 (Apr)

See also at para [38.107].

The claimants were a group of 165 residents living in the vicinity of the defendant's chemical works in North Wales and instructed London solicitors to pursue their claims following a gas leak. The claimants recovered damages of £90,000 and their solicitors' bill of costs amounted to £210,000. The issue for the Court of Appeal was the reasonableness of the solicitors' hourly rate. However, Mance LJ took the opportunity to remark, 'The present litigation was conducted under the old rules preceding the Woolf reforms. It is to be hoped that subsequent to the Woolf reforms judges conducting cases will make full use of their powers under the Practice Direction about costs, section 6 ... to obtain estimates of costs and to exercise their powers in respect of costs and case management to keep costs within the bounds of the proportionate in accordance with the overriding objective. That the amount of costs should play an important part, both in the court's orders about costs and in its orders about case management, is indicated expressly in paragraph 6.1 of that Practice Direction ...'.

[38.220] SCT Finance Ltd v Bolton

[2002] EWCA Civ 56

[2003] 3 All ER 434

At trial the claimant was awarded the sum of £351 and the defendant's counterclaim was dismissed. The trial judge ordered the defendant to pay the claimant's costs on the standard basis but subject to an overall ceiling of £15,000. The claimant appealed against the cap placed on recoverable costs because its estimate of costs was £51,000.

HELD, ON APPEAL: (1) The judge had imposed the ceiling because the costs were disproportionate to the amounts at stake and the defendant was not a man of means.

(2)   The judge had ample discretion to impose a ceiling on costs however he erred in the exercise of his discretion because he had already

ordered costs to be paid on the standard basis. Therefore, only proportionate costs could be recovered in any event within the assessment proceedings.

(3)   The appropriate order was to set aside the provision which imposed the ceiling.

[38.221]   Lownds v Home Office

[2002] EWCA Civ 365

[2002] 4 All ER 775

This appeal raised issues of principle which had a direct bearing on the policy that litigation should be conducted in a proportionate manner and, where possible, at a proportionate cost. Given the importance of the issues, the Court of Appeal sat with Master Hurst, the senior costs judge, as assessor.

   The claimant issued proceedings and following service of the defence in which liability was denied, the claimant made a Part 36 offer to settle of £5,000. The claim was settled by negotiation five months later in the sum of £3,000 and the defendant agreed to pay the claimant's costs. The bill of costs served by the claimant amounted to £19,405.38 and at the detailed assessment hearing the district judge allowed costs of £16,784.53. May LJ granted the defendant permission to make a second appeal to the Court of Appeal because the case raised important points of principle including whether costs may or should be reduced if they are disproportionate to the amount claimed or recovered in the action.

HELD, ON APPEAL: (1) Lord Woolf CJ gave the judgment of the court and repeated the approach of Judge Alton which was approved in *Jefferson v National Freight Carriers Ltd* (at para [38.218]).

(2)   Necessity was the key to how judges in assessing costs should give effect to the requirement of proportionality. If the costs were necessarily incurred then proportionality did not prevent recovery of all the costs either on an item-by-item approach or on a global approach.

(3)   A two-stage approach was required, a global approach and an item by item approach. The global approach would indicate whether the total sum claimed was disproportionate having regard to CPR 44.5(3).

(4)   If the total costs were not disproportionate, each item should be reasonably incurred and reasonable in amount.

(5)   If the total costs were disproportionate, each item should be necessarily incurred and reasonable in amount and no greater sum could be recovered than that which would have been recoverable item by item if the litigation had been conducted proportionately.

(6)   In a case where proportionality was likely to be an issue, the costs judge must make a preliminary judgment at the start of the detailed assessment hearing. Once a decision has been made, the costs judge will be able to consider the costs, item by item, applying the appropriate test.

(7)   A sensible standard of necessity must be adopted which makes allowances for the different judgments which practitioners can come to as to what is required and the benefit of hindsight must be avoided however, the threshold requirement for necessity was higher than that of reasonableness.

(8)   The conduct of the paying part was highly relevant to what was necessary.

(9)   Where a claimant recovered significantly less than claimed, the proportionality of the claimant's costs should be determined having regard to the sum that it was reasonable for him to believe that he might recover at the time he made his claim.

[38.222]   Giambrone and Others v JMC Holidays Ltd (formerly Sunworld Holiday Ltd)

[2003] 1 All ER 982, QBD

Following the decision of the Court of Appeal in *Lownds v Home Office* (at para [38.221]), the defendant argued the claimant's costs were disproportionate at the hearing of a preliminary issue in advance of the detailed assessment hearing. The claimant's costs exceeded £1million and the costs judge determined there was disproportionality.

HELD, ON APPEAL: (1) If a costs judge has ruled the bill of costs is not disproportionate, he is not precluded from deciding that an item is disproportionate having regard to the matters in issue. The costs judge should consider whether an item was proportionate and reasonable in amount.
(2)   The effect of the judgement in Lownds was that if the costs judge has ruled the costs are disproportionate, the receiving party must show each item has been proportionately and by a sensible standard necessarily incurred and proportionate and reasonable in amount.
(3)   The preliminary judgment of proportionality determines the manner of the detailed assessment, not the final sum payable to the receiving party. If a costs judge is unable to say whether the costs as a whole are disproportionate, he will be obliged to carry out a detailed assessment applying the dual test of sensible necessity and reasonableness of amount for each item.
(4)   An experienced costs judge, if provided with skeleton arguments, should be able to determine proportionality within an hour and without having to consider voluminous material.
(5)   VAT should be excluded when considering proportionality because it had no bearing on the steps taken in the litigation or the costs of them.
(6)   The decision of the costs judge was not wrong.

[38.223]   Lloyds TSB Bank plc v Lampert and Lampert

[2003] EWHC 249 (Ch)

[2003] All ER (D) 270 (Feb), [2003] 2 Costs LR 286

At trial the claimant was awarded the sum of £32,500 and the trial judge ordered the second defendant to pay the claimant's costs. The bill of costs served by the claimant for the substantive proceedings amounted to £62,197.61 and at the detailed assessment hearing the claimant was allowed £48,845.00. The claimant then submitted a claim for £40,145.50 for the costs of the assessment proceedings which was reduced to £32,181.44 by the judge. In summary, the claimant had recovered the sum of £32,500 in the substantive proceedings and costs of approximately £81,000. The second defendant appealed the costs decisions.

HELD, ON APPEAL: (1) The judge had failed to apply the *Lownds* test to the issue of proportionality because the case was not cited to him, nevertheless this was a procedural irregularity of a serious nature.

(2)   The matter was to be referred back to the judge for a rehearing for him to apply the *Lownds* test.

(3)   The second defendant should pay the costs of the appeal for failing to draw the *Lownds* case to the attention of the judge.

[38.224]   Hesp v Willemse

(9 March 2005, unreported), QBD

The claimant was injured in a road traffic accident and claimed damages of approximately £500,000. At trial he was awarded damages of £212,620. The Court of Appeal reduced the award for future loss of earnings from £110,00 to £50,000 therefore the total damages were reduced to £152,620. The claimant then served a bill of costs of £231,450. At the detailed assessment hearing, the costs judge agreed with the defendant that the costs were disproportionate to the issues. Applying the dual test of necessity and reasonableness, the costs judge decided the instruction of leading counsel was not necessary and reasonable and disallowed the brief fee of £12,500.

HELD, ON APPEAL: (1) The costs judge's decision had not exceeded the generous ambit within which a reasonable disagreement was possible.

(2)   This was never going to be a substantial case and could have been conducted by a senior junior.

(3)   Following his decision on proportionality, the costs judge was correct to disallow leading counsel's brief fee.

[38.225]   King v Telegraph Group Ltd

SCCO 2 December 2005

See also at para [38.53].

The claimant instructed City of London solicitors to pursue his defamation claim which was settled in the sum of £60,000 and the defendant agreed to pay costs on the standard basis. The claimant's base costs amounted to £317,523 plus success fees of £294,903 (a total of £612,427) which the defendant argued was disproportionate.

HELD: (1) The Costs Practice Direction clearly envisaged that the court would assess the base costs and any additional liability separately however both must be proportionate. Conclusive support for this was to be found in *Campbell v MGN Ltd (No 2)* (at para [38.226]).

(2)   Even if the total of the base costs and additional liabilities was disproportionate, this was not a factor to take into account when considering whether or not the base costs were disproportionate.

(3)   The claimant's costs on a global view were disproportionate having regard to all the circumstances and in particular the potential level of recovery of £130,000 and ignoring the success fee.

(4)   On way of testing the proportionality of costs was to ask whether a private paying client of adequate means would have been prepared to pay that level of costs in order to achieve success. It was inconceivable that such a person would have proceeded with the claim if told it would cost £317,523 to recover damages of £130,000.

(5)   The test of necessity would have to be applied throughout on an item-by-item basis and in particular have to reflect a great deal more delegation to assistant solicitor level and restriction to one counsel.

[38.226]   **Campbell v MGN Ltd**

(8 March 2006, unreported), HL

See also at para [38.123].

Following conclusion of the substantive proceedings, the Judicial Taxing Officers of the House of Lords (one of which was the senior costs judge, Master Hurst) heard argument concerning the proportionality of the claimant's costs. The base costs, excluding VAT and any additional liability were £170,439.82 for a one-day hearing before the House of Lords. The claimant's solicitors had spent a total of 372 hours and the defendant contended there was insufficient delegation of the work.

HELD: (1) The principle of proportionality and the approach in *Lownds v The Home Office* (at para [38.221]) applied to costs assessments in the House of Lords.
   (2)   The base costs were disproportionate and therefore the test of necessity was to be applied in the assessment.

[38.227]   **Cox and Carter v MGN Ltd and Others**

[2006] EWHC 1235 (QB)

[2006] All ER (D) 396 (May), QB

See also at para [38.124].

The claimants brought proceedings alleging an invasion of privacy and breach of confidence in respect of photographs taken of them on honeymoon. Their claims were initially funded privately but later they entered into a CFA prior to service of defences. The claims were eventually settled for £50,000 and the defendants agreed to pay costs. At a hearing of preliminary issues in the detailed assessment proceedings, the costs judge concluded the base costs of £142,728 were not disproportionate. The defendants appealed.

HELD, ON APPEAL: (1) The amount of financial compensation provided a useful starting point however, this was a case in which other remedies assumed greater significance.
   (2)   The conclusion of the costs judge in applying the *Lownds* stage-one test was well within the range of reasonable options open to him, he did not misdirect himself as to the law and his decision was entirely correctly.

22.   SUMMARY ASSESSMENT

[38.228]   **R v Cardiff County Council, ex parte Brown**

[1999] EWHC 379 (Admin)

The respondent successfully resisted an application for judicial review and sought a summary assessment of its costs at the conclusion of the hearing. The applicant requested the court to order a detailed assessment of costs on the grounds that there was an issue about the rate charged for work done by the respondent's solicitors.

HELD: (1) There should be a summary assessment of costs unless there was a good reason not to for example, where the paying party showed substantial grounds for disputing the sum claimed.

(2)   The issue raised by the applicant involved a possible breach of the indemnity principle and should be decided at a detailed assessment hearing.

[38.229]   Crossley v North Western Road Car Co Ltd

(18 June 1999, unreported), Sheffield County Court

The claimant brought proceedings for damages for the personal injuries and financial losses sustained in a road traffic accident. The defendant's application for the claim to be transferred to the small claims track was unsuccessful because the judge found he could not be sure the claim for personal injuries would attract damages of less than £1,000. The defendant resisted the claimant's application for the costs of the hearing on the grounds that the claimant's statement of costs had been faxed the day before the hearing and therefore the defendant had not been given 24 hours' notice. The district judge disallowed the claimant's costs because no reason was provided for the failure to serve on time. The claimant appealed.

HELD, ON APPEAL: (1) The court had a discretion to allow costs where a statement was submitted out of time.
(2)   The claimant served the statement one hour and nine minutes late. By contrast, the defendant served its statement three days before the hearing.
(3)   The Civil Procedure Rules had to be complied with and the judge was right to disallow the claimant's costs in circumstances where no reason was given for the failure to comply.

[38.230]   Wright v Manchester City Council

(14 December 1999, unreported), Altrincham County Court

At the conclusion of a fast track trial, the trial judge found in favour of the defendant on the issue of liability. The claimant sought no order for costs on the grounds that the defendant had not served a statement of costs before the start of the trail. The trial judge decided that a summary assessment was appropriate and there would be no order for costs because of the defendant's failure to serve a statement of costs in time. The defendant appealed.

HELD, ON APPEAL: (1) The defendant had failed to serve a statement of costs at least 24 hours before the start of the trial in breach of the Costs Practice Direction.
(2)   The trial judge had a discretion on costs and his decision could not be interfered with.

[38.231]   Macdonald v Taree Holdings Ltd

(7 December 2000, unreported), Chancery Division

The claimant's application to set aside a statutory demand served by the defendant was successful and he sought a summary assessment of his costs at the conclusion of the hearing. The defendant objected on the grounds that the claimant's statement of costs was only faxed on the day of the hearing. The district judge found there was no reasonable excuse for failing to serve the statement at least 24 hours before the hearing and accordingly made no orders for costs. The claimant appealed.

HELD, ON APPEAL: (1) Where a statement of costs was not served more than 24 hours before a hearing, the court should take that into account but the decision should be proportionate.

(2)   In the case of mere failure to comply without more, if there was no prejudice to the other party, the court should summarily assess the costs and it would not be right to deprive a party of all his costs.

(3)   If there was prejudice, the court had three options. Firstly, grant a brief adjournment for the paying party to consider the statement of costs then proceed to a summary assessment. Secondly, order the costs to be decided by detailed assessment. Thirdly, order the parties to submit written submissions and for the court to then carry out a summary assessment without a further hearing.

(4)   If there was a failure to comply plus an aggravating factor, it may be right to deprive a party of all or a significant proportion of his costs. Examples of aggravating factors included deliberate or repeated failure to comply.

(5)   The district judge was wrong not to allow the claimant's costs because there was a mere failure to comply with no aggravating factors. The appropriate order was for the defendant to pay the claimant's costs of the appeal and of the proceedings below, both to be summarily assessed by the Appeal Court. In this case it would be wrong to order a detailed assessment of the costs below as this would involve further expense and delay in circumstances where the costs claimed below were £5,200 plus VAT.

[38.232]   Edwards (administrator of the estate of Erica Louise Edwards) v Devon & Cornwall Constabulary

[2001] EWCA Civ 388

[2001] All ER (D) 143 (Mar)

The claimant's wife was injured in a collision with a police car but her subsequent death was unconnected to the accident. The claimant took over his wife's proceedings against the defendant and by the date of the trial, the only outstanding issue was the care received by the deceased following the accident. The judge heard arguments on both sides very late in the day, reached a conclusion and after a short adjournment for the parties to agree calculations, awarded the claimant £1,132.08 having deducted the counterclaim. The trial judge then summarily assessed the claimant's costs in the sum of £2,500 inclusive of VAT. The claimant appealed on the grounds that the judge should not have carried out a summary assessment or alternatively, he should have conducted it properly by hearing full argument and not reaching an arbitrary conclusion.

HELD, ON APPEAL: (1) A summary assessment was appropriate because the hearing was short, the amount of money involved was small and the claimant's costs were simple and straight forward.

(2)   The judge failed to give the claimant an adequate opportunity to address him on costs and this led to the substantial injustice of the claimant's solicitors' costs being reduced unfairly.

(3)   It would be disproportionate to order a detailed assessment so the Appeal Court would carry out a summary assessment if the parties were unable to agree the costs.

[38.233]   **1–800 Flowers Inc v Phonenames Ltd**

[2001] EWCA Civ 721

[2001] All ER (D) 218 (May)

Following an appeal lasting one day, the judge decided to carry out a summary assessment of costs. The defendant claimed costs of £38,000 which the judge assessed at £10,000 as being appropriate for a one day case in the High Court. The defendant appealed to the Court of Appeal on the grounds that the judge should have ordered a detailed assessment of costs or alternatively should not have selected the arbitrary figure of £10,000 without reference to the actual costs incurred as set out in the statement of costs.

HELD, ON APPEAL: (1) The judge erred in principle by applying his own tariff to the case without carrying out a detailed analysis of the costs set out in the statement.

(2)   It was the essence of a summary assessment of costs that the court should focus on the detailed breakdown of costs actually incurred as shown in the statement. The court may have reference to costs allowed in comparable cases and reduce the sum assessed still further if it appears unreasonable or disproportionate.

(3)   Summary assessment was not to be used as a vehicle to introduce a scale of judicial tariffs for different categories of cases.

(4)   The appropriate order was to direct a detailed assessment of the defendant's costs.

[38.234]   **Thompson v Anderson**

SCCO 9 December 2003

The substantive proceedings in this case were concluded by the claimant serving Notice of Discontinuance. The costs appeal concerned the success fees allowed by the costs officer at the detailed assessment hearing on costs which had previously been summarily assessed. The claimant submitted the summary assessment included additional liabilities therefore the defendant was not entitled to further success fees. The defendant submitted only base costs which had been summarily assessed leaving the success fees to be assessed at the detailed assessment hearing.

HELD, ON APPEAL: (1) The proceedings were concluded by service of the Notice of Discontinuance therefore it was open to the court to make one of the three orders permitted by CPR 44.3(A)(2)(a) to (c).

(2)   The claimant was correct that the court had decided to summarily assess both the base costs and additionally liabilities rather than either summarily assess the base costs and refer the additional liabilities for detailed assessment or refer all the costs to detailed assessment.

(3)   The defendant should have made plain to the court at the time the orders were made that he intended to claim additional liabilities and had he done so, it would have been clear that only the base costs were to be summarily assessed and the additional liabilities were to be referred to the costs officer for detailed assessment.

[38.235]   McLinden v Redbond

[2006] EWHC 234 (Ch)

[2006] All ER (D) 320 (Feb)

The claimant served a statutory demand upon the defendant for the balance of a debt in the sum of £470. The defendant's application to set aside the statutory demand was dismissed and he was ordered to pay £1,000 towards the claimant's costs. The claimant appealed the order for costs.

HELD, ON APPEAL: (1) The judge did not base his summary assessment of the claimant's costs on the detailed breakdown shown in his statement of costs totalling £5,236.39 and was therefore wrong in law.

(2)   A summary assessment of costs to be paid on the standard basis required the application of the two-stage approach to proportionality as in *Lownds v The Home Office* (at para [38.221]).

(3)   It would be disproportionate to order a detailed assessment of the costs below therefore the claimant's costs were summarily assessed in the sum of £2,863.75.

23.   THIRD PARTY FUNDING OF LITIGATION

[38.236]

Section 51 of the Supreme Court Act 1981 provides:

'(1)   ... subject to the provisions of this or any other enactment and to rules of court, the costs of and incidental to all proceedings in ...

(a)   the Civil Division of the Court of Appeal;

(b)   the High Court, and

(c)   any county court

shall be in the discretion of the court ...

(3)   ... the court shall have full power to determine by whom and to what extent the costs are to be paid.'

(A)   LEGAL EXPENSES INSURERS

[38.237]   Murphy v Young & Co's Brewery plc and Sun Alliance and London Insurance

[1997] 1 All ER 518, [1997] 1 WLR 1591

The claimants were unsuccessful and unable to pay costs, however, they had legal expenses insurance with cover up to £25,000. The defendant's costs were £42,806 so an order for costs was sought against the legal expenses insurer. The trial judge refused to make the order and the defendant appealed.

HELD, ON APPEAL: (1) The mere fact of funding did not give rise to a liability for costs.

(2)   The insurer had no interest in the litigation and did not commence it or interfere in it.

(3)   The contractual limit of cover having been reached, the insurer had no obligation to pay more.

(B)   LIABILITY INSURERS

[38.238]   TGA Chapman Ltd and Benson Turner Ltd v Christopher and Sun Alliance and London Insurance plc

[1998] 2 All ER 873, [1998] 1 WLR 12

The claimants obtained judgment against the first defendant in the sum of £1,129,212 and were awarded costs. The first defendant was without means but had insurance cover with the second defendant up to £1million inclusive of costs. The claimants applied for an order under s 51 of the Supreme Court Act 1981 that their costs be paid by the insurer. At first instance, the judge granted the application and the insurer appealed.

HELD, ON APPEAL: (1) The insurer had conduct of the litigation and defended the claim exclusively for its own interests.
  (2)   The claim would not have been defended but for the insurer's own interests in avoiding or reducing its liability to the claimants.
  (3)   In the circumstances, it was right for the insurer to pay the claimants' costs.

[38.239]   Gloucestershire HA v MA Torpy & Partners Ltd (No 2)

[1999] Lloyd's Rep IR 203

The claimant obtained judgment against the defendant in the sum of £7million. Following judgment, the defendant informed the claimant that its insurance cover was limited to £4million. The defendant's insurer had conduct of the litigation and vigorously defended the claim. The claimant sought an order that the insurer pay its costs.

HELD: (1) An order for costs under s 51 of the Supreme Court Act 1981 against a non-party was only made in exceptional circumstances.
  (2)   The insurer had control of the litigation, however, the defence had not been conducted only for the insurer's interests.
  (3)   There was therefore no reason to make a costs order against the insurer.

(C)   PURE FUNDERS

[38.240]   Hamilton v Fayed and Others

[2002] EWCA Civ 665

[2002] 3 All ER 641

The claimant lost his action and was ordered to pay the defendants' costs which were assessed in the sum of £1,467,576. Only £277,576 was paid and the claimant was bankrupt so the defendants sought an order that their costs be paid by a number of individuals who made charitable contributions to the claimant's costs. The judge rejected the section 51 application and the defendants appealed.

HELD, ON APPEAL: (1) The law should give priority to a funded party gaining access to justice over an unfunded party recovering his costs if successful. The pure funding of litigation was in the public interest provided the purpose was to enable a party to bring a genuine case. If pure funders were made liable for costs, funds would dry up and prevent access to justice.

    (2)   The funders acted through sympathy for the claimant, not malice towards the defendants and had no control over the litigation. They had no interest in the litigation other than the hope of getting their contribution back.

[38.241]   Gulf Azov Shipping Co Ltd and Others v Chief Humphrey Irikefe Idisi and Others

[2004] EWCA Civ 292

[2004] All ER (D) 284 (Mar)

The claimants obtained judgment against the defendants for substantial damages and costs, the majority of which were not paid so the claimants sought an order that their costs be paid by a third party who funded the defence and intervened in the conduct of it.

HELD, ON APPEAL: (1) The provision of funds by the third party to assist the defendants discharge their liability for interim costs orders did not justify an order for costs against the third party.

    (2)   The third party was not to be criticised for encouraging a witness to give evidence on behalf of the defendants.

    (3)   There was no evidence the third party had colluded with the defendants to deceive the court.

    (4)   The third party had no personal interest in the outcome of the litigation.

(D)   PROFESSIONAL FUNDERS

[38.242]   R (Factortame) Ltd v Transport Secretary (No 8)

[2002] EWCA Civ 932

[2002] 4 All ER 97

In this case the claimants were successful and were awarded costs. The defendant challenged the recoverability of fees paid by the claimants to a firm of accountants, Grant Thornton. The claimants had agreed to pay Grant Thornton 8% of the final settlement and in return Grant Thornton provided litigation services. The defendant contended the agreement was champertous and unenforceable.

HELD, ON APPEAL: (1) Grant Thornton did not influence the conduct of the litigation and the 8% recovery was fair remuneration for its services.

    (2)   The agreement was necessary for the claimants to secure access to justice and the introduction of conditional fee agreements was evidence of a change in public policy to payment of fees being contingent upon success.

[38.243]   Philips Electronics NV v Aventi Ltd

[2003] EWHC 2589

A third party paid some of the defendant's costs of defending an action brought by the claimant and the action was defended because of the funding provided. Subsequently the funding was withdrawn and the defendant went into liquidation. The claimant applied for an order that its costs be paid by the third party funder.

HELD: (1) The third party had a commercial interest in the outcome of the litigation and the funding was causative of the defence of the action. The defendant could not afford to defend the action and would not have done so but for the funding.

(2)   The third party should pay the claimant's costs.

[38.244]   **Arkin v Borchard Lines Ltd and Others**

[2005] EWCA Civ 655

[2005] 3 All ER 613, [2005] 1 WLR 3055

See also at para [38.185].

The claimant was a man without means and was only able to pursue his claim because of financial support in excess of £1.3million provided by a professional funder, Managers and Processors of Claims Ltd ('MPC'). If the claim had succeeded, MPC would have received a percentage of the recovery but in the event the claim failed and the defendants sought an order for costs against MPC.

HELD, ON APPEAL: (1) Costs should normally follow the event and it would be unjust for a funder who purchased a stake in the litigation to be protected from all liability for costs.

(2)   MPC had funded expert evidence and such funding would not be provided if there was a risk of paying all of the defendants' costs.

(3)   The just and practicable solution was to make the professional funder liable to the extent of the funding provided. Therefore MPC was to pay £1.3million by way of contribution to the defendants' costs.

(4)   This approach was not appropriate however where the agreement to provide funding was champertous and a funder who entered into such an agreement was likely to be liable for all of the successful party's costs.

(E)   DIRECTORS

[38.245]   **Bournemouth & Boscombe Athletic Football Club Ltd v Lloyds TSB Bank plc**

[2004] EWCA Civ 935

[2004] All ER (D) 323 (Jun)

The claimant's action against the defendant was unsuccessful and the defendant sought an order that its costs be paid by a director of the claimant who conducted the litigation.

HELD, ON APPEAL: (1) The director caused the claimant to bring proceedings at a time when it was insolvent.

(2)   A person who causes a hopeless case to be brought on behalf of an insolvent client must face the financial consequences of their conduct.

(3)   In the circumstances, the director was to pay the defendant's costs.

[38.246]   **Dymocks Franchise Systems (NSW) Pty Ltd v Todd and Others**

[2004] UKPC 39

[2005] 4 All ER 195, [2004] 1 WLR 2807

The claimant was successful against the defendants and awarded costs. As the defendants were unable to pay, the claimant sought an order that its costs be paid by a company beneficially owned by one of the defendant's family.

HELD: (1) The company funded the defendants' appeals and stood to benefit financially if the defendants succeeded.
    (2)   The company was to pay the claimant's costs.

[38.247]   **Goodwood Recoveries Ltd v Breen**

[2005] EWCA Civ 414

[2006] 2 All ER 533

In this case, the trial judge made a costs order against a director and shareholder of the claimant following the claimant's unsuccessful action against the defendant.

HELD, ON APPEAL: (1) Where a non-party director was the 'real party' and controlled and/or funded the litigation for his own benefit, justice often demanded he be liable for costs.
    (2)   The litigation would not have taken place but for the director's involvement and his involvement caused costs to be incurred.
    (3)   Lack of good faith was not a pre-condition to the making of an order for costs against a non-party.
    (4)   In the circumstances, the costs order was justified.

[38.248]   **Petromec Inc v Petroleo Brasileiro SA Petrobras and Another**

[2006] EWCA Civ 1038

[2006] All ER (D) 260 (Jul), CA

The claimants were successful against the defendant and applied for their costs to be paid by non-parties including an individual with interests in the defendant. The judge held:
    (1)   The individual exercised complete control over the litigation and had control of the defendant's affairs.
    (2)   The funds for the litigation all came from sources under the individual's control and were made available at his direction.
    (3)   The individual had a financial interest in the outcome of the litigation.
    (4)   In the circumstances, an order for costs was appropriate.

HELD, ON APPEAL: (1) The judge was unassailably correct in his factual conclusions and there were compelling reasons to order the non-party to pay costs.
    (2)   It was not a pre-requisite for the exercise of the court's jurisdiction under s 51 of the Supreme Court Act 1981 that the individual funded the litigation himself. It was enough to establish jurisdiction that the individual effectively controlled the proceedings and sought to derive potential benefit from them.
    (3)   The exercise of the jurisdiction to order a non-party to pay the costs of the proceedings should not be over-complicated by reference to authority.

[38.249]   BE Studios Ltd v Smith & Williamson Ltd

[2005] EWHC 2730 (Ch)

[2006] 2 All ER 811

In this case, the claim was dismissed and the defendant applied for an order that its costs be paid by a director of the claimant.

HELD: (1) The director authorised the commencement of speculative proceedings, controlled the litigation and gave instructions to the claimant's solicitors.
- (2)   Without the director's funding there would have been no litigation and accordingly no defence costs.
- (3)   It was not necessary to show impropriety before a costs order could be made against a director who funded and controlled litigation.
- (4)   The director was a loan creditor of the claimant and therefore stood to benefit financially if the claims succeeded.
- (5)   An order for costs against the director was appropriate.

Index